Critical White Studies

Critical White Studies

LOOKING BEHIND THE MIRROR

Edited by Richard Delgado and Jean Stefancic

TEMPLE UNIVERSITY PRESS PHILADELPHIA

Temple University Press, Philadelphia 19122
Copyright © 1997 by Temple University
All rights reserved
Published 1997

Printed in the United States of America

♾ The paper used in this publication meets the requirements of the American
National Standard for Information Sciences—Permanence of Paper for Printed
Library Materials, ANSI Z39.48–1984

Text design by Erin Kirk New

Library of Congress Cataloging-in-Publication Data

Critical white studies : looking behind the mirror / edited by Richard
    Delgado and Jean Stefancic.
        p.   cm.
    Includes bibliographical references and index.
    ISBN 1-56639-531-3 (cloth : alk. paper). — ISBN 1-56639-532-1
(paper : alk. paper)
    1. United States—Race relations. 2. Whites—United States—Race
identity. 3. Whites—United States—Attitudes. I. Delgado,
Richard. II. Stefancic, Jean.
E184.A1C75   1997
305.8'00973—dc21   96-46408

"Mirror, mirror, on the wall,

who is the fairest of them all?"

THE BROTHERS GRIMM, "SNOW-WHITE"

Contents

Acknowledgments   xv

Introduction   xvii

PART I   How Whites See Themselves   1

1   The End of the Great White Male
John R. Graham   3

2   White Racial Formation: Into the Twenty-First Century
Charles A. Gallagher   6

3   The Skin We're In
Christopher Wills   12

4   The Way of the WASP
Richard Brookhiser   16

5   Hiring Quotas for White Males Only
Eric Foner   24

6   Innocence and Affirmative Action
Thomas Ross   27

7   Doing the White Male Kvetch (A Pale Imitation of a Rag)
Calvin Trillin   33

8   Growing Up *White* in America?
Bonnie Kae Grover   34

9   Growing Up (What) in America?
Jerald N. Marrs   36

10   White Images of Black Slaves (Is What We See in Others
Sometimes a Reflection of What We Find in Ourselves?)
George Fredrickson   38

Synopses of Other Important Works   46

From the Editors: Issues and Comments   46

Suggested Readings   47

PART II   How Whites See Others   49

11   The White Race Is Shrinking: Perceptions of Race
      in Canada and Some Speculations on the Political Economy
      of Race Classification
      Doug Daniels   51

12   Ignoble Savages
      Dinesh D'Souza   55

13   Darkness Made Visible: Law, Metaphor, and the Racial Self
      D. Marvin Jones   66

14   Playing in the Dark: Whiteness and the Literary Imagination
      Toni Morrison   79

15   Transparently White Subjective Decisionmaking: Fashioning
      a Legal Remedy
      Barbara J. Flagg   85

16   The Rhetorical Tapestry of Race
      Thomas Ross   89

17   Imposition
      Richard Delgado and Jean Stefancic   98

18   Racial Reflections: Dialogues in the Direction of Liberation
      Derrick A. Bell, Tracy Higgins, and Sung-Hee Suh, Editors   106

19   The Tower of Babel
      Eleanor Marie Brown   112

20   The Quest for Freedom in the Post-*Brown* South:
      Desegregation and White Self-Interest
      Davison M. Douglas   117

21   "Soulmaning": Using Race for Political and Economic Gain
      Luther Wright, Jr.   125

22   Dysconscious Racism: Ideology, Identity, and Miseducation
      Joyce E. King   128

      Synopses of Other Important Works   133

      From the Editors: Issues and Comments   134

      Suggested Readings   135

PART III   Whiteness: History's Role   137

23   Race and Manifest Destiny: The Origins of American Racial
      Anglo-Saxonism
      Reginald Horsman   139

24   The Invention of Race: Rereading *White Over Black*
      James Campbell and James Oakes   145

25 "Only the Law Would Rule between Us": Antimiscegenation,
    the Moral Economy of Dependency, and the Debate over Rights
    after the Civil War
        Emily Field Van Tassel   152

26 The Antidemocratic Power of Whiteness
        Kathleen Neal Cleaver   157

27 Who's Black, Who's White, and Who Cares
        Luther Wright, Jr.   164

28 Images of the Outsider in American Law and Culture
        Richard Delgado and Jean Stefancic   170

29 Back to the Future with *The Bell Curve:* Jim Crow, Slavery, and G
        Jacqueline Jones   179

30 The Genetic Tie
        Dorothy E. Roberts   186

    Synopses of Other Important Works   190

    From the Editors: Issues and Comments   192

    Suggested Readings   192

PART IV   Whiteness: Law's Role   193

31 White Law and Lawyers: The Case of Surrogate Motherhood
        Peter Halewood   195

32 Social Science and Segregation before *Brown*
        Herbert Hovenkamp   199

33 Mexican-Americans and Whiteness
        George A. Martinez   210

34 Race and the Core Curriculum in Legal Education
        Frances Lee Ansley   214

35 The Transparency Phenomenon, Race-Neutral Decisionmaking,
    and Discriminatory Intent
        Barbara J. Flagg   220

36 Toward a Black Legal Scholarship: Race and Original
    Understandings
        Jerome McCristal Culp, Jr.   227

37 Identity Notes, Part One: Playing in the Light
        Adrienne D. Davis   231

38 The Constitutional Ghetto
        Robert L. Hayman, Jr., and Nancy Levit   239

    Synopses of Other Important Works   248

    From the Editors: Issues and Comments   248

    Suggested Readings   249

PART V **Whiteness: Culture's Role**   251

39   Do You Know This Man?
     Daniel Zalewski   253

40   The Curse of Ham
     D. Marvin Jones   255

41   Los Olvidados: On the Making of Invisible People
     Juan F. Perea   258

42   White Innocence, Black Abstraction
     Thomas Ross   263

43   Race and the Dominant Gaze: Narratives of Law and
     Inequality in Popular Film
     Margaret M. Russell   267

44   Residential Segregation and White Privilege
     Martha R. Mahoney   273

45   Mules, Madonnas, Babies, Bathwater: Racial Imagery and
     Stereotypes
     Linda L. Ammons   276

46   The Other Pleasures: The Narrative Function of Race in
     the Cinema
     Anna Everett   280

     Synopses of Other Important Works   285

     From the Editors: Issues and Comments   288

     Suggested Readings   288

PART VI **White Privilege**   289

47   White Privilege and Male Privilege: A Personal Account
     of Coming to See Correspondences through Work in
     Women's Studies
     Peggy McIntosh   291

48   From Practice to Theory, or What Is a White Woman Anyway?
     Catharine A. MacKinnon   300

49   Racial Construction and Women as Differentiated Actors
     Martha R. Mahoney   305

50   The GI Bill: Whites Only Need Apply
     Karen Brodkin Sacks   310

51   Making Systems of Privilege Visible
     Stephanie M. Wildman with Adrienne D. Davis   314

52   Race and Racial Classifications
     Luther Wright, Jr.   320

53   Reflections on Whiteness: The Case of Latinos(as)
     Stephanie M. Wildman   323

54   Stirring the Ashes: Race, Class, and the Future of Civil
      Rights Scholarship
      Frances Lee Ansley   327

55   The Social Construction of Whiteness
      Martha R. Mahoney   330

      Synopses of Other Important Works   334

      From the Editors: Issues and Comments   334

      Suggested Readings   335

PART VII   The Ladder of Whiteness   337

56   The Mind of the South
      W. J. Cash   339

57   Old Poison in New Bottles: The Deep Roots of Modern Nativism
      Joe R. Feagin   348

58   The First Word in Whiteness: Early Twentieth-Century European
      Immigration
      David Roediger   354

59   Life on the Color Line
      Gregory Williams   357

60   Others, and the WASP World They Aspired To
      Richard Brookhiser   360

61   Beyond the Melting Pot
      Nathan Glazer and Daniel Patrick Moynihan   368

62   The Economic Payoff of Attending an Ivy-League Institution
      Philip J. Cook and Robert H. Frank   378

63   Useful Knowledge
      Mary Cappello   381

64   Stupid Rich Bastards
      Laurel Johnson Black   387

65   How Did Jews Become White Folks?
      Karen Brodkin Sacks   395

66   How White People Became White
      James R. Barrett and David Roediger   402

67   Paths to Belonging: The Constitution and Cultural Identity
      Kenneth L. Karst   407

68   Is the Radical Critique of Merit Anti-Semitic?
      Daniel A. Farber and Suzanna Sherry   414

      Synopses of Other Important Works   420

      From the Editors: Issues and Comments   421

      Suggested Readings   421

PART VIII   The Color Line: Multiracial People
                 and "Passing for White"   423

          69   Passing for White, Passing for Black
                 Adrian Piper   425

          70   Black Like Me
                 John Howard Griffin   432

          71   The Michael Jackson Pill: Equality, Race, and Culture
                 Jerome McCristal Culp, Jr.   438

          72   Did the First Justice Harlan Have a Black Brother?
                 James W. Gordon   444

          73   Learning How to Be Niggers
                 Gregory Williams   458

          74   What Does a White Woman Look Like? Racing and Erasing
                 in Law
                 Katherine M. Franke   467

          75   La Güera
                 Cherríe Moraga   471

          76   Notes of a White Black Woman
                 Judy Scales-Trent   475

          77   Our Next Race Question: The Uneasiness between Blacks
                 and Latinos
                 Jorge Klor de Alva, Earl Shorris, and Cornel West   482

          78   A Review of Life on the Color Line
                 Martha Chamallas and Peter M. Shane   493

          79   What Is Race, Anyway?
                 Tod Olson   499

                 Synopses of Other Important Works   501

                 From the Editors: Issues and Comments   502

                 Suggested Readings   503

PART IX   Biology and Pseudoscience   505

          80   The Misleading Abstractions of Social Scientists
                 Jerome Kagan   507

          81   Caste, Crime, and Precocity
                 Andrew Hacker   510

          82   Embodiment and Perspective: Can White Men Jump?
                 Peter Halewood   512

          83   Bell Curve Liberals: How the Left Betrayed IQ
                 Adrian Wooldridge   515

          84   Brave New Right
                 Michael Lind   519

85   Race and Parentage
     Dorothy E. Roberts   523

86   The Sources of *The Bell Curve*
     Jeffrey Rosen and Charles Lane   528

87   Hearts of Darkness
     John B. Judis   530

88   Thank You, Doctors Murray and Herrnstein (Or, Who's
     Afraid of Critical Race Theory?)
     Derrick A. Bell   534

89   Dangerous Undertones of the New Nativism
     Daniel Kanstroom   538

     Synopses of Other Important Works   542

     From the Editors: Issues and Comments   542

     Suggested Readings   543

PART X   White Consciousness, White Power   545

90   The Rise of Private Militia: A First and Second Amendment
     Analysis of the Right to Organize and the Right to Train
     Joelle E. Polesky   547

91   The Changing Faces of White Supremacy
     Loretta J. Ross and Mary Ann Mauney   552

92   Hatelines: Week of Sunday, April 7, 1996
     Compiled by the Center for Democratic Renewal   558

93   Blue by Day and White by [K]night
     Robin Barnes   561

94   The Race Question and Its Solution
     James Armstrong, Jr.   566

95   The American Neo-Nazi Movement Today
     Elinor Langer   573

96   Talking about Race with America's Klansmen
     Raphael S. Ezekiel   586

97   Antidiscrimination Law and Transparency: Barriers to Equality?
     Barbara J. Flagg   589

98   White Supremacy (And What We Should Do about It)
     Frances Lee Ansley   592

99   White Superiority in America: Its Legal Legacy, Its Economic
     Costs
     Derrick A. Bell   596

     Synopses of Other Important Works   601

     From the Editors: Issues and Comments   604

     Suggested Readings   604

PART XI What Then Shall We Do? A Role for Whites 605

100 Treason to Whiteness Is Loyalty to Humanity
An Interview with Noel Ignatiev of Race Traitor *Magazine* 607

101 How to Be a Race Traitor: Six Ways to Fight Being White
Noel Ignatiev 613

102 Rodrigo's Eleventh Chronicle: Empathy and False Empathy
Richard Delgado 614

103 Obscuring the Importance of Race: The Implications of Making
Comparisons between Racism and Sexism (or Other Isms)
Trina Grillo and Stephanie M. Wildman 619

104 White Men Can Jump: But Must Try a Little Harder
Peter Halewood 627

105 "Was Blind, but Now I See": White Race Consciousness and the
Requirement of Discriminatory Intent
Barbara J. Flagg 629

106 White Women, Race Matters: The Social Construction of
Whiteness
Ruth Frankenberg 632

107 Resisting Racisms, Eliminating Exclusions: South Africa and
the United States
David Theo Goldberg 635

108 Dysconscious Racism: The Cultural Politics of Critiquing
Ideology and Identity
Joyce E. King 640

109 What Should White Women Do?
Martha R. Mahoney 642

110 Confronting Racelessness
Eleanor Marie Brown 644

111 A Civil Rights Agenda for the Year 2000: Confessions of
an Identity Politician
Frances Lee Ansley 646

112 What We Believe
The Editors of Race Traitor *Magazine* 653

113 Segregation, Whiteness, and Transformation
Martha R. Mahoney 654

114 White Out
Roger Wilkins 658

From the Editors: Issues and Comments 664

Suggested Readings 664

About the Contributors 665

Index 671

Acknowledgments

We are grateful for the assistance of the many authors and publishers who contributed their ideas and genius to make this book possible. Blaine Lozano Milne performed research, editing, and production feats far beyond the call of duty. Gabriel Carter, Lance Oehrlein, Kim Quinn, and Linda Ramirez carried out editing and computer searching with intelligence and dispatch. Linda Spiegler, Cynthia Carter, Marge Brunner, and Kay Wilkie prepared the manuscript with precision and care. Frank Austin copyedited it with surpassing skill. We acknowledge the support of an IMPART grant from the University of Colorado and a summer research grant from the University of Colorado School of Law. Finally, we thank our editor, Doris Braendel, for her continued support and inspiration.

Introduction

Are you white? (Or, do you have a friend who is?) If so, how do you know? Is race real—or is it constructed, an "as-if" concept, something we all agree to bestow on each other? Is it a relational concept, existing only in binary fashion (e.g., black/white), so that if all the people on a tropical island, say, looked pretty much the same, there would be no race or races? Modern-day scientists tell us that whites and blacks have more genes in common than the ones that distinguish them—the variability between the average white and the average black, in genetic makeup and physical appearance, is less than the variability within each group. What then, does it mean to be white—or of any other race, for that matter?

This book, a sequel to *Critical Race Theory: The Cutting Edge* (Temple University Press, 1995), examines these and related questions, putting whiteness under the lens. It presents the best of an emerging body of scholarship that analyzes what it means to be white, as well as a number of classic works dealing with the white race and its legacy. You will read about upward (and downward) mobility of white and near-white immigrant groups. (The Irish, for example, were at first not considered white, but given a status similar to that of Negroes.) You will also learn about white privilege, the invisible bundle of expectations and courtesies that go along with membership in the dominant race. You will encounter an astonishing argument that law plays a large part in defining who is white, and even in changing the physical features of the American population.

You will read about the experience of Judy Scales-Trent, a light-skinned black woman who identifies with the black race but is treated in most daily encounters as a white person, and of a white-looking law school dean who was raised first as a white, then as a black. You will read a deliciously satirical description by Calvin Trillin of racial complainers and "wannabes" who *kvetch* because others of different hue seem to be getting all the advantages in life. You will encounter the rich, textured analysis of Supreme Court—and public—rhetoric of Thomas Ross, a white Southern writer who shows how such narratives and "stories" as *innocence* and *advantage-taking* help us understand the relations between blacks and whites in this country. You will learn about the race-conscious (and the racist) mind, as seen by writers of vastly different persuasions, such as Dinesh D'Souza on the right and Raphael S. Ezekiel on the left. You will come across the "one drop" rule, according to which anyone with any trace of black heritage is considered black. Why is there no "one drop" rule for whites, and what does this say about the reality (or lack of it) of race as a concept? What does it say about power?

Nobel laureate Toni Morrison tells how whites and blacks systematically misperceive each other. Luther Wright, Jr., asks how we should see multiracial people—those with a black mother and a white father, for example. David Roediger and Noel Ignatiev argue that whiteness has no useful meaning (and sometimes a bad one) and should be abolished. Other writers argue that white consciousness, even white power, is not to be deplored, any more than is consciousness raising and solidarity among women and blacks.

Can we get beyond race, and would that be a good idea? A number of our authors imply that it would. One, James W. Gordon, argues that close friendships and even intermarriage may be the way. He suggests that John Marshall Harlan, associate justice of the Supreme

Court and author of the famous dissent in *Plessy v. Ferguson*, may have had a black brother, and that their close relationship while growing up in the antebellum South may have influenced the young justice-to-be to become the passionate race reformer he was in later life.

What have science and pseudoscience had to say about race and racial hierarchy? Debates about the supposed superiority of a particular race, prominent in earlier periods of our history, are now being revived. How has the authority of science shaped social and legal attitudes toward whites and nonwhites? Contributors to this book who are both lawyers and social scientists address these questions. Others examine how cultural imagery, language, children's tales (e.g., "Snow White"), songs, and even classical literature construct whiteness and blackness so that they are not neutral descriptors but concepts freighted with meaning, value, and status.

Is white power dangerous? Any more so than, say, black power? Can one take pride in one's whiteness (blackness, etc.) without becoming a narrow nationalist who puts down members of other races? The reader will find these and other issues treated in the eleven parts of this book. Each part is preceded by a brief introduction and is followed by questions and issues for discussion and by a suggested reading list. We were not able to include a small number of significant authors who have written about race and whiteness. In such cases, we have paraphrased their thoughts and have indicated where the original works may be found.

Critical race theory emerged in the late 1970s with the work of Derrick Bell, Alan Freeman, and others. For the most part progressive scholars committed to racial and social transformation, critical race theorists found themselves discontented with standard liberal approaches to racial justice. Seeing the gains of the civil rights era of the 1960s slip away, they believed that new, more searching theories were necessary to understand the phenomena of race and racism. Drawing on critical sociology, neo-Marxism, postmodern philosophy, and shrewd observation, they set out to develop a more hard-headed assessment of our society's racial predicament and ways of dealing with it. Critical race theory, itself the child of critical legal studies (a leftist movement in the law that arose in the 1970s), has in turn spawned two additional movements, critical race feminism and critical white studies. Other parallel movements, such as gay-legal narratives and Latino critical studies, are just now springing up.

What all these approaches have in common is an effort to get beyond received wisdoms and ask basic questions about race, power, and society. It is in the belief that all people can move toward a more decent, humane society by exposing ourselves to the best minds writing about vexing issues of race and by thinking about them critically that we offer this book. If you are white, we hope you will, in the words of our title, look behind the mirror. If you are nonwhite, we hope this book will help you understand what it means to be white in a society whose majority is of that color—and to begin to understand where and how you figure in.

Boulder, Colorado

Part I

How Whites See Themselves

If any theme is characteristic of contemporary thought in the social sciences and in cultural studies, it is "perspectivalism"—the idea that one's viewpoint matters. Indeed, every chapter in this book can be seen as an effort to analyze, defend, criticize, celebrate, or examine one perspective or another about race and whiteness. Some even question, not how, but *do* whites see themselves? Upon looking into and beyond the mirror, whites have found their whiteness both opaque and transparent. Most whites have not thought much about their race. Few, upon being asked to identify themselves by attributes, would name whiteness among their primary characteristics.

Part I offers a variety of ways whites, and some nonwhites, see the white race, ranging from biological and social-construction theory, to economic determinism and advantage and disadvantage, to innocence (feigned or real). Later parts deal with how whites see other races (Part II), how earlier periods saw whites and whiteness (Part III), the role of language and color imagery (Part V), and white consciousness and white power (Part X). As the reader will soon notice, these sections overlap thematically to some extent. The reason is simple: Race seems to be, to a large extent, relational. Whiteness, acknowledged or not, has been a norm against which other races are judged. One cannot get clear about whiteness without also gaining a sense of what it means to be nonwhite—and vice versa.

The examinations of whiteness presented in this book may open a way for whites to talk about race and racial problems acceptably and nondefensively.

1

The End of the Great White Male

JOHN R. GRAHAM

After more than two centuries of running the nation,
American white men are being threatened with loss of power.

Five centuries ago, the foundations of the world were shaken. So-called immutable truths toppled forever as man was replaced by the sun as the center of our universe. Equally wrenching is the current shattering of white males' world view, in which they long have seen themselves as the central characters on society's stage. All around are the effects of a revolution that is both painfully distressing and totally confusing to what well may become known as the last of the great white males.

As the turmoil continues, white males are the inevitable scapegoats—and their difficulties only are beginning. The illustrations are everywhere. Even though rumblings have been heard for more than a decade now, the Earth really shook when the national United Way organization was disrupted in 1992. The white male who built and ran the powerful agency for two decades was knocked out of his seat of power and replaced by an Asian woman. To focus on the fact that she is Asian and female is to miss the point. She happens to know the current rules of the game: You don't turn the business into a private sandbox. Limos and other self-serving luxuries aren't part of the bargain today, a lesson that has been lost on white males, many of whom continue to believe that they possess a divine right to the perks of power.

The cracks in the Earth's surface widened as the quakes have come fast and furious with the deposing of great white males throughout Fortune 500 firms. The great white males feel threatened and somewhat confused about why it is happening. Until now, the great white male had considered it no one's business what he takes out of the company, the way he conducts business, how much he is paid, or even how he treats his subordinates, particularly women.

Throughout the last several hundred years, the great white male has lived by the strict code of the old-boy network. The dismissal of corporate leaders symbolizes the replacement of the old-boy network by quite a different code of behavior—competence. Who you know is giving way to what you know, a sure sign that Americans finally have entered the information age full tilt.

Several other threats plague the great white male. One of them is sheer numbers. The Huns once again are invading, but this time they come masked as Hispanics, Asians, and, yes, women. Even though Americans are told in a dozen ways that Hispanics are the fastest growing segment of U.S. society, the great white male mentality can not accept change, just as many refused to acknowledge that the sun was the cen-

USA Today, November 26, 1993. Originally published in *USA Today*. Reprinted by permission.

ter of our universe. Meanwhile, sheer energy, drive, and education soon will give Asians the upper hand in American business. Although they may be today's small merchants, they will emerge as tomorrow's leaders in manufacturing, education, and finance. The great white male is no match for the Asian drive and work ethic. At one point, the *Wall Street Journal* noted that American business is not running as fast as it did in the past. The great white males are having a difficult time keeping up with the emerging minorities.

The major threat to the great white male, however, clearly is women. He honestly believes there is a conspiracy afoot and that females are the enemy, working feverishly to take control of everything. Like most other conspiracy theories, the conclusion does not reflect the facts. What actually is happening is totally different, since the great white male is doing everything possible to hand over the jobs and to transfer the power of business and politics to women. The number of females elected to the U.S. Senate and House in 1992 affirms the direction.

The most intense drama in the world of politics was presented on TV for everyone to see. This watershed event was the 1991 Clarence Thomas Supreme Court confirmation hearings that were brought to the public's attention by the Senate, the last bastion of the great white male. No single subject drives the great white male into an irrational frenzy faster than Anita Hill. The debate continues long after Thomas has taken his seat on the Court. The attempts to discredit Hill and resurrect Thomas' reputation continue unabated. More than a desire to arrive at the facts, it would appear that this may well be the last effort to help the American male become whole again.

Why was it that the great white males of the Senate Judiciary Committee found it so easy to sympathize with Thomas? Or, to state it more accurately, why did they find it so hard to side with Hill? Had they found her truthful, they would be presiding over their own demise. Many women seem to understand easily what white males have difficulty grasping. When it was over and all the votes had been tallied, Thomas lost (even though he was confirmed as a Supreme Court justice) and Hill won.

It is no accident that hundreds of women have burst upon the political scene following the confirmation hearings. Nor is it a quirk of fate that the great white males in the halls of Congress are dropping like flies. The number who chose to retire at the end of 1992 was the highest in history. Although they expressed disdain for politics as the main reason for leaving office on their own, they saw that *their* world had changed.

It is fascinating that the great white male always expects to be taken care of by his co-conspirators—the other great white males. While growing up, every boy learned the first lesson of manhood: "Take care of your friends and they will take care of you." Later, going to college, it was given a socially acceptable description of "male bonding."

In many important ways, women are different from the great white males of the past. Women seem to harbor the strange notion that hard work, knowledge, competence, and persistence are the proper ingredients for success. On the other hand, the traditional great white male scoffs at such nonsense. "Who you know is all that counts," he repeats confidently. The lairs of maledom down through the decades—everywhere from the poker party to the private club—attest to belief in the proposition.

The corollary is that the great white male harbors the illusion that, once he rises to the top, he has a right to all the goodies he can get and that he has to answer to no one. It really doesn't make any difference how the goodies are obtained. Wasn't that the lesson men learned when they were elected to the House of Representatives—to the victors belong the spoils? This applied even to accepting cash bribes or propositioning a woman in the office—or elsewhere.

Those who are threatening the great white male—women, Hispanics, and Asians—hold a totally different view of the world, as different from that of the great white male as the change which occurred 500 years ago. The code of competence holds that the farther one rises, the greater the responsibility—a truly remarkable idea! Where you park your car or the location of your office in reference to the power brokers is inconsequential in terms of defining your worth, status, or importance when it comes to the business of business or the business of politics. In effect, American society finally may be arriving at the point where it's what you know, not who you know, that counts.

Extinction Ahead?

What about the future? Will the great white male become extinct? Will he no longer be seated in the offices of the corporation, at the head of the table? Will he be only a memory in the halls of political power? What about the U.S. presidency? These questions are far more pertinent than even in the recent past. It is no accident so many jokes about Hillary Clinton are making the rounds today. One way or another, they all point in one direction and make one point as they portray "The President of the United States and Mr. Clinton." However, Americans shouldn't be surprised that the stories bring only uncomfortable laughter. Something happened when Bill and Hillary moved to 1600 Pennsylvania Ave. that is very different from the days of Ronnie and Nancy or Babs and George.

Many are having difficulty accepting that Hillary Clinton is comfortable with herself, a situation that makes great white males (and others) uneasy. The critics were quick to complain that she wasn't elected to office when her husband appointed her to head the powerful commission on health care. Yet few thought it unseemly that a James Baker or Sherman Adams should exert such inordinate influence without benefit of election. Why is Hillary Clinton so different?—simply because she is a woman who has dared to enter the male lair.

What about the future of the great white male? Whether he is destined for a final resting place in the museums of the land remains to be seen. There will be pitiful efforts to restore his feathers, to prop up his prowess and power. Nevertheless, the great white male's day has passed, along with his unlimited, unilateral power and influence. Even as noble a figure as Lee Iacocca is in danger of finding himself sadly irrelevant, somehow out of step with the times. From now on, the great white male will be one of many. He no longer will be able to say, "It's lonely at the top." Whether it takes another 500 years for the next total upheaval in the intellectual history of society remains to be seen. In the meantime, it will be interesting to watch how the great white males take to their changing circumstances.

2

White Racial Formation: Into the Twenty-First Century

CHARLES A. GALLAGHER

[The author, a sociologist, interviewed white and non-white students at "Urban University." The following passage, excerpted from the concluding chapter of an upcoming book, summarizes his research findings. Ed.]

Whiteness is in a state of change. One only need browse book stands or news racks for examples of how the idea of whiteness is being interpreted, defined, reinterpreted, and contested by popular writers and journalists. Whites perceive themselves, according to one account, as being part of a distinctly different, colorblind, sympathetic generation that has learned to look beyond "the color of the skin" to "the beauty within."[1]

Whereas some whites see a common humanity with their nonwhite counterparts, others see whiteness as a liability. A white sergeant with the Los Angeles County Sheriff's Office announced creation of the Association of White Male Peace Officers, with the goal of defending the rights of white officers who are "distinctly averse to the proposal that, as a class, we be punished or penalized for any real or purported transgressions of our forbears."[2] This "class" of white men seeks the same types of legal protection afforded to other groups organized around their race or gender. Samuel Francis, an editorial writer for the *Washington Times* and advisor to Patrick Buchanan's presidential campaign, declared that "whites must reassert our identity and our solidarity . . . in explicitly racial terms through the articulation of racial consciousness as whites."[3] Francis believes whites have ignored or disregarded their racial identity and must (re)unite as whites to stop the influx of nonwhite immigrants. It is no wonder many whites feel confused and overwhelmed about who they are racially and how they fit into American race relations.

The meaning of whiteness is not to be found in any single one of the preceding descriptions of how whites imagine themselves or come to understand their racial identity. The contemporary meaning is an amalgamation of these white narratives. Whites can be defined as naïve because they attach little meaning to their race, humane in their desire to reach out to nonwhites, defensive as self-defined victims, and reactionary in their calls for a return to white solidarity.

It is not surprising, then, that my respondents would generate similar disparate (and at times schizophrenic) renderings when asked what meaning they attach to their race. As in the anecdotes above, the extent to which whiteness was a salient form of identity for my respondents varied greatly, ranging from the naïve, to the reactionary, to the situational. Some described their sense of whiteness as being partially veiled, becoming visible and salient only when they felt they were a racial minority. This momentary minority status and the anxiety often associated with this experience colored how respondents saw themselves and their relationship to other racial groups. For other respondents, whiteness had been made explicitly visible at some earlier point in their lives. Their understanding of the concept was often no more than a list of what they were not, why they should not feel guilty about being white, or why their race was now being held against them. The extent to which a sense of whiteness was just emerging for some and had already evolved as an overt identity for others obscures an obvious and important finding: If whiteness was ever invisible for these respondents, it no longer is.

What, however, have we learned about the social, political, and cultural construction of whiteness? How is the construction of whiteness linked sociologically to the structural elements that shape those meanings? Respondents may "know they are white," but what does that mean and what are its political and social consequences? A number of patterns emerged in my data, each of which delineates a particular facet of how white racial identity is constructed and made salient. These patterns point to one clear and significant finding: Whiteness is in the midst of fundamental transformation. White identity is not only a reaction to the entrance of historically marginalized racial and ethnic groups into the political arena and the ensuing struggle over social resources. The construction of whiteness is based, at least among the respondents in my study, on a perception of current and future material deprivation and the need to delineate white culture in a nondemonized fashion. The majority of whites in this study have come to understand themselves and their interests as white. Many of my respondents now think about themselves as whites, not as ethnics; they see themselves as individuals who are members of a racial category with its own particular set of interests. They have attached new meanings to being white and have used those meanings as the basis for forging an identity centered around race. They have, to borrow Michael Omi and Howard Winant's term, gone through the process of racialization. The factors shaping white racialization include the decline of ethnicity, the rise of identity politics, the perception that whiteness is a social and economic liability, and the precepts of neoconservative racial politics. While I do not suggest whiteness is constructed in a uniform, linear fashion, I do believe that white racialization has emerged at this particular moment due to a confluence of these trends. I see them as being linked in the following ways.

The Ethnic Vacuum

A lack of ethnic identity among my respondents has created an emptiness that is being filled by an identity centered on race. Almost fifty years ago, W. Lloyd Warner observed: "The future of American ethnic groups seems to be limited; it is likely that they will quickly be absorbed. When this happens one of the great epochs of American history will end, and another, that of race, will begin."[4] My interviews and survey data bear out Warner's prediction. For the majority of the white respondents in my study, little is left in the way of ethnic solidarity, ethnic identity, or even symbolic nostalgia for the ethnic traditions of their older kin. When asked to define themselves in ethnic or racial terms (or both), the majority of students labeled themselves as white or Caucasian, ignoring such labels as Italian-American. Like most whites their age, these students have undergone such extensive generational assimilation and convergence of cultural experiences that only a few chose to describe themselves as "plain old American," "mutt," or "nothing." The young whites I interviewed were so removed from the immigrant experience that even the small minority who defined themselves in ethnic terms acknowledged that their ethnicity was in name only. As one remarked, he thought of his mixed Polish heritage only when he ate kielbasa at Christmas. Ethnicity is a subjective series of choices (or, as Mary Waters writes, an "option") in constructing an identity, but the majority of white students I interviewed and surveyed came from families where very little in the way of "ethnic options" existed because the symbolic ethnic practices had all but died out.

Young whites selectively resurrect their ethnicity through "immigrant tales" mainly when they feel white privilege is being contested, even though their perceived ethnic history does not necessarily concern a specific nation but rather a generalized idea of a European origin. This common, yet fuzzy, connection to the "old country" provides the historical backdrop and cultural space for the construction of white identity, or "a yearning for a usable past."[5] As the importance of ethnicity wanes in the lives of young whites, the immigration experience of older (or dead) kin becomes a mythologized narrative providing a historical common denominator of passage, victimization, and assimilation. As white students often tell it, blacks can point to the middle passage and slavery; Japanese and Chinese can speak of internment and forced labor, respectively; and whites have the immigrant experience. In a sense, past group victimization or hardship is part of the American experience; young whites, when confronted by real or perceived charges of racism, can point to the mistreatment of their older relatives when they were newly arrived immigrants in the United States.

Although whites did experience prejudice and discrimination when they arrived in the United States, it is unlikely that their descendants encounter anything remotely similar today. Unlike the case of the white ethnic revival movement of the 1960s and 1970s, it is now impossible to mobilize young whites politically based on their ethnicity; an ethnic identity no longer exists, as it did for their parents or grandparents.

The markers of ethnic identity have all but disappeared. A "subjective belief in common descent" did not exist for the majority of my respondents. These students could not speak, nor had they been exposed to, a "mother tongue." They did not feel obligated to marry or date people from similar ethnic backgrounds. Nor did they derive a "sense of honor" from being part of an ethnic group or draw on their heritage to become "a carrier of 'interests,' economic or political, which the members of an ethnic group lay claim to or defend."[6] The generation of older whites who were part of the "ethnic revival" and who used their ethnicity as the basis for group claims has been displaced by one that feels increasingly comfortable using their racial identity as the sole carrier of their interests.

Race matters for my respondents because it is racial, not ethnic, identity that is bound up in popular culture and the political order. As David Roediger sees it, "*Among whites, racial identity (whiteness) and ethnic identity are distinct.*"[7] I would argue, on the contrary, that for many respondents there is no distinction because ethnic identity has all but vanished. After generations of assimilation, only whiteness is left as an identity with any real social or political import. The decline of ethnicity among later-generation whites has created an identity vacuum, one that has been at least partially replaced by an identity grounded in race.

White Identity Politics

The second influence on white racialization is how identity politics has raised white consciousness. The generation of whites I studied, born around 1975, grew up with a brand of racial politics and media exposure that are unique. This generation is the first to witness the full social, political, and cultural effects of identity politics. As Herbert Blumer puts it, "To characterize another racial group is, by opposition, to define one's own."[8] The political and cultural mobilization of racially defined minorities has forced many of my white respondents to think about who they are racially in relation to other racial groups.

The racially charged and politically conservative environment of the late 1980s and 1990s has reinterpreted whiteness as a liability. The cultural mythology that has become today's commonsense understanding of race relations is a definition of society that is color blind. The ascendancy of color blindness as the dominant mode of race thinking and the emergence of liberal individualism as a source of white entitlement and racial backlash was a central finding in my work. It is, I believe, a view that is not specific to the student population at Urban University. Stanley Fish sums up how color blindness has been twisted politically to maintain white privilege. "When the goal was to make discrimination illegal," he argues, color blind meant lifting barriers to full citizenship, but the term now means blind to the effects of prejudice on people because of their color.[9]

The social movements that challenged the racial status quo unfolded over twenty-five years. The first "revolution" my respondents witnessed, however, was President Reagan's attack on civil rights legislation in the name of democracy and fair play. They grew up hearing that the United States was a color-blind nation, saw the rise of a black and Asian middle class, and were told stories about a federal government that "blocks opportunities for white workers."[10] Whites of this generation "have no knowledge of the disciplined, systematic, and collective *group* activity that has structured white identities in American society."[11]

Racial Politics: The Right and White Victimization

The belief that whites were subject to racial discrimination (reverse discrimination) appeared as a dominant theme throughout my research. One example of this belief was the perception that a racial double standard exists on campus. In the majority of my interviews and focus groups, white students felt that race-based organizations at Urban University were a form of reverse discrimination. Twenty-nine of 119 campus organizations used race as their primary organizing principle. Mainly cultural and political, these groups encourage an affirmation of racial identity and provide a safe, supportive space for students of color to develop social and professional networks. The latent effect of these organizations, however, is that they transform and contribute to redefining the meaning of racial identity for whites on campus. When they are excluded, white students get a taste of what it is like to be reduced to a racial category. They are generally unnerved by this experience and quickly slip into reactionary, defensive posturing. The resentment, anger, and frustration white students express because they are excluded provide the foundation for a white identity based on the belief that whites are now under siege. Student groups like the Black Pre-Law Society or the Korean Cultural Club were sanctioned by the university, but, as was said many times in my interviews, if whites tried to establish an organization and it had "white" in the title a major controversy would ensue and the group and its members would be labeled racist. Nor could white respondents retreat into an Italian-American House or a Hibernians Club, because there was no basis for solidarity around an ethnic identity.

If a loss of ethnic identity has created a void among many of my respondents, and if identity politics has made whiteness a visible racial category, then the perception that being white is now a social liability has most certainly raised white consciousness. The social cost of whiteness arose whenever issues of affirmative action on and off campus were discussed. The majority of white students felt that contemporary affirmative action measures were unfair because issues of overt racism, discrimination, and equal opportunity had been addressed by their parents' generation in the 1960s. A majority of white students argued that the United States is a meritocracy where nonwhites have every advantage whites do (and in some cases more because of affirmative action). Most of my respondents want to believe the United States is an egalitarian, "color-blind" society because to think otherwise would raise the irritating issue of white privilege. The working- and middle-class young people I interviewed do not see themselves as privileged or benefiting from their skin color. It becomes difficult for working-class college students to think about white privilege when they are accumulating college debt, forced to live with their parents, working twenty-five hours a week on top of their studies, and are concerned that Starbucks or the Gap may be their future employer.

A fundamental transformation of how young whites define and understand themselves racially is taking place. The white students I interviewed believe that the American class system is fair and equitable: Anyone who delays gratification, works hard, and follows the rules will succeed regardless of color. Black television stars, the media's treatment of the black middle class, and stereotypes of Asians as model minorities have provided young whites with countless nonwhite success stories. For many of them, the "leveled playing field" argument has rendered affirmative action policies a form of reverse discrimination and a source of resentment. White students who believe social equality has been achieved are able to assert a racial identity and not regard themselves as racist—they are merely affirming their identity in ways similar to the language and actions of other racially defined groups. On the individual level, the racism most prevalent among the respondents was not the cultural stereotypes some white students used to counter charges of white privilege but the racist projections many made about how blacks perceive whites.

In large part, white identity is a reaction to the entry of historically marginalized racial and ethnic groups into the political arena and the ensuing struggle over social resources. But it is not only that. Whiteness as an explicit cultural product may be taking on a life of its own, developing its own racial logic and essence as it is molded by the political right. The rhetoric of neoconservatives serves to legitimate the benefits that accrue to whites based on skin color. Starting with the false premise of social equality and equal opportunity, neoconservatives can speak of America's Western roots and traditions in racial terms but not appear racist. This ostensibly nonracist "white" space that is being carved out of our cultural landscape allows whites to be presented like any other racial contender in the struggle over political and cultural resources and self-definition.

Notes

1. Benjamin Demott, The Trouble with Friendship: Why Americans Can't Think Straight about Race (New York: Atlantic Monthly Press, 1995), p. 45.

2. *Police Officer Starts Group to Defend White Men*, NEW YORK TIMES, November 19, 1995, §
1, at 36.

3. NEW YORK TIMES, February 23, 1995, at A23.

4. Quoted in MICHAEL BANTON, RACIAL AND ETHNIC COMPETITION (London: Cambridge University Press, 1983), p. 64.

5. Bob Blauner, *Talking Past Each Other: Black and White Languages of Race*, in RACE AND ETHNIC CONFLICT, edited by Howard J. Ehrlich and Fred L. Pincus (Boulder, Colo.: Westview Press, 1994), p. 27.

6. Richard Alba suggests that these beliefs are the fundamental benchmark of what it means to be part of an ethnic group. See ETHNIC IDENTITY: THE TRANSFORMATION OF WHITE AMERICA (New Haven, Conn.: Yale University Press), p. 313.

7. DAVID ROEDIGER, TOWARDS THE ABOLITION OF WHITENESS (New York: Verso Press, 1994), p. 182.

8. Herbert Blumer, *Race Prejudice as a Sense of Group Position*, 1:1 PAC. SOC. REV. 4.

9. Stanley Fish, *How the Right Hijacked the Magic Words*, NEW YORK TIMES, August 13, 1995, § 4, at 15.

10. Frederick R. Lynch, *Race Unconsciousness and the White Male*, 29:2 SOCIETY 31. Lynch is quoting the pollster Stanley Greenberg.

11. George Lipsitz, *The Possessive Investment in Whiteness: Racialized Social Democracy and the "White" Problem in American Studies*, 47:3 AMERICAN QUARTERLY 369 (September 1995).

3

The Skin We're In

CHRISTOPHER WILLS

Melanin is in the news these days. There's a pseudoscientific idea floating around that says that if you have lots of melanin—the pigment that colors your skin and hair and the irises of your eyes—you will be smart and exquisitely attuned to life's rhythms and have a warm, outgoing personality. In short, you will be nicer and more talented than people with less melanin—that is, white people.

Proponents of this idea, such as Leonard Jeffries, chairman of the Department of Black Studies at the City College of New York, have based their conclusions on the single scientific fact that melanin is found not only in the skin but also in the brain, and they have used the compound's presence there to imbue it with magical properties. Their "melanist" approach has gone beyond promulgation in a few pamphlets and backroom debates; it is now being taught at a number of high schools and colleges in the United States, usually as part of an effort to correct a Eurocentric view of the world. Not surprisingly, such programs have generated a great deal of criticism in the mainstream, white-dominated press—which the melanists claim is an expression of racism. Why, they counter, hasn't an equal amount of disapproval been directed against the pronouncements of white biological superiority?

Two wrongs do not make a right. As a reaction and antidote to white racism, melanism is understandable. But from a scientific standpoint it is just wrong. There's no evidence for melanist claims of black superiority, just as there's no evidence for the pseudoscientific claims of white superiority that have been made for centuries. That's not to say that melanin isn't a fit subject for scientific inquiry. What research has shown us is that the real story of melanin is much more interesting, and tells us more about ourselves, than any magical hokum trotted out to support divisions between the races.

We are visually oriented animals, and the color of a stranger's skin, if different from our own, is often the characteristic we notice first. Of all the superficial differences that divide us—the shape of our nose, the texture of our hair, and so on—none seems to mesmerize us as much as skin color. As psychologists have shown, among blacks in this country the darkest-skinned children in a group or family are often treated less well than other children by their teachers, their peers, and even their parents and thus suffer repeated blows to their self-esteem. Obviously, differences in skin color matter greatly to society—but is there any physical basis for all the prejudice and psychological damage?

Today geneticists like myself would say no. We have known for decades that variation in skin color is caused by rather small genetic differences, and it seems *highly* unlikely that these differences have anything to do with intelligence, personality, or ability. Sadly,

DISCOVER 77 November 1994. Copyright © 1994 The Walt Disney Co. Reprinted with permission of *Discover Magazine*.

though, genetics itself has not always been free of racism. The models that early geneticists used to explain the inheritance of skin color actually had a segregationist bias, reflecting the pervasive prejudice of their time. The white American eugenicist Charles Benedict Davenport set the tone in 1913 with an investigation into the genetics of "Negro-white crosses." As racist as most of his contemporaries, Davenport assumed that blacks were inferior to whites. He did, however, correctly deduce that there were distinct genes that control skin color. But he thought only two genes were involved and that each of them came in two forms, or alleles: a "white" allele and a "black" allele. How dark you were depended on how many black alleles you inherited from your mother and father.

Davenport assumed that the black and white alleles were as clearly different from each other as he thought the black and white races were different. We now know that this is not correct and that the differences between the alleles are small. But Davenport was right in his conclusion that a rather small number of genes make substantial contributions to skin color—more than two, but fewer than half a dozen. And skin color is inherited independently of other characteristics used to differentiate between races. Among the grandchildren of interracial marriages, he saw, there were often individuals with light skin and tightly kinked hair, and others with dark skin and straight hair. Skin color and hair texture were thus not indissolubly wedded.

Davenport knew nothing about how genes work and so had no notion of how his black alleles caused pigment to form. Only recently have studies at the molecular level shown how slight the allelic differences between races really are, and how few the steps that separate all of us from being as dark as the Bougainville Islanders of the South Pacific or as pale as Swedes.

The mechanics of pigment formation are surpassingly subtle. Melanocytes, the cells that form the pigment melanin, are closely related to nerve cells. Both types of cell arise in a part of the early embryo, but while nerve cells mostly stay put to form the core of the nervous system, melanocytes migrate along with other cells to give rise to the skin.

We now know that in mice more than 50 different genes influence how melanin forms and when and where it's deposited. So it's likely that a similar number of genes will turn up in humans as well, although perhaps only half a dozen will be shown to have really substantial effects. The pigments they produce, though they're all lumped together under the melanin label, can actually be black, brown, yellow, or red. They all have a common starting point in tyrosine, an amino acid made in large amounts in the melanocytes and converted by the enzyme tyrosinase into a compound called dopaquinone. Dopaquinone follows two different routes, one leading to black and brown pigments, and the other to red and yellow pigments.

The master enzyme in all this is tyrosinase. If the gene for this enzyme is defective, the result is a person with albinism, someone who makes no melanin at all. But the most remarkable discovery made by molecular biologists has been that most of us, regardless of skin color, have quite enough tyrosinase in our melanocytes to make us very black. In those of us with light skin, something is preventing the enzyme from functioning at full capacity—and that seems to be a combination of two genetic mechanisms: a switch that causes the cell to make most of the tyrosinase in an inactive form, and a tendency to make a lot of inhibitors of the enzyme. In the body, the effects of either or both of these mechanisms can be modified by such environmental factors as exposure to ultraviolet light. People with albinism are highly sensitive to ultraviolet, which can easily damage skin and eyes, but most of us, regardless of which alleles we have for skin color, can protect ourselves by darkening our skin through tanning.

So it turns out that what separates blacks and whites is not different numbers of clearly different black and white alleles, but rather a collection of tiny genetic differences in the way the genes possessed by all of us are regulated—how much tyrosinase is made in an active form, how much and how many of the various tyrosinase inhibitors are made, and so on. Mutations with dramatic effect do contribute to color variation in the human population—for example, people with albinism don't make functional tyrosinase. Other mutations that lighten or darken skin color occasionally happen. Children with piebaldism, for instance, are born with a white forelock and colorless patches on their forehead and trunk. Another example is melasma, a skin condition that sometimes runs in families. A child with this condition is born with large patches of darker-than-normal pigmentation, which spread as the child grows older. In the late 1970s an even more unusual condition was described, in Mexico: a child was born with light skin that turned a deep, uniform black by the age of 21 months.

Such mutations are probably the tip of the iceberg. Richard King, a molecular geneticist who has examined color variation in mice, suspects that much milder mutations must also happen in humans but that they tend to go unnoticed because they fall within the range of normal pigmentation. He is convinced that we are not exempt from the mutation-and-selection process that has repeatedly resulted in lighter and darker strains of animals over the course of evolution.

In animals, melanin comes and goes at the dictates of evolutionary pressures. It is reasonable to assume that we humans have this molecule not because it makes us smarter but primarily because it helps us survive a variety of environmental conditions. Clearly melanin protects us from the ravages of ultraviolet light. Some of the most darkly pigmented people in the world, natives of the North Solomon Islands, almost never get basal cell carcinoma or melanoma, and if they do have melanomas, these tumors arise on the light-skinned soles of their feet. Caucasians living in Hawaii, on the other hand, have the highest documented skin cancer rate in the United States.

While the protective effect of having a lot of melanin is clear, it is less clear why many groups of humans living far from the equator have lost much of their pigment. One popular theory is that exposure of our skin cells to ultraviolet light is necessary for the formation of a precursor of vitamin D, which in turn is required for proper bone formation. Thus, the theory goes, people who live at high latitudes, where people are forced to keep their skin covered during much of the year, can still make enough of this precursor if they have little ultraviolet-blocking pigmentation in their skin. Conversely, the large quantities of pigment in the skins of people in the tropics should prevent them from producing too *much* vitamin D, which can be as harmful as too little and can cause inappropriate calcium deposits in tissues.

In evolutionary terms it makes sense that most of us have all the machinery in place to make us black or white or anything in between. Darker and lighter "races" of animals are quite common, and probably arose as a response to the dangers of predation. Over a span of hundreds of millions of years our remote animal ancestors had to change color repeatedly, for a great variety of reasons ranging from protective camouflage to sexual attractiveness. Much of this must have taken place long before they had acquired enough brains to be prejudiced about it.

Even in *Homo sapiens* there are many examples of groups that have evolved toward a lighter or darker skin color than that of their close relatives. The Negritos of the islands of Luzon and Mindanao in the Philippines, for instance, superficially resemble other dark-skinned groups in Africa and Australia. Yet their overall genetic affinities turn out to be far stronger to the lighter-skinned Asian peoples who surround them. This suggests that the

Negritos' ancestors may once have been lighter and that they independently evolved features that are somewhat reminiscent of black Africans, or that the Asian peoples surrounding them were also once much darker and evolved toward lighter skin—or possibly both. Another example is the Ainu of northern Japan, who have light skin but overall are very similar genetically to the darker-skinned groups that surround them. The evolution of skin color is not a onetime event; it has occurred repeatedly during the history of our species.

What about neuromelanin, that other melanin, found in our brains, that melanists have made so much of? More skin melanin, they imply, must mean more brain melanin—which is, in some undefined fashion, good. As we have seen, melanocytes and nerve cells *do* have a common origin in the fetus, and indeed it's likely that nerve cells once evolved from primitive melanocytes. But this evolutionary connection does not mean that the pigment of the skin is connected with the function of the brain. People with albinism, who have no melanin in their skin, hair, or eyes, have normal amounts of melanin in their brain cells. Even though the ultimate source of both types of melanin is tyrosine, the processing pathways leading to neuromelanin are quite different from those leading to skin melanin. Finally, while neuromelanin is highly visible in brain tissues, it is only one of thousands of compounds unique to the brain and is unlikely to be freighted with mystic significance. As for the real significance of brain melanin, the jury is still out—we have no idea what it does. We do know that a lot of it is found in the *substantia nigra* (the "black substance"), a darkly colored structure buried deep in the brain that makes dopamine.

Still, melanin may confer some benefits we have yet to learn about. Intriguingly, there are hints that people with lots of skin melanin are less prone to hearing damage than the more lightly pigmented. As it turns out, melanin of the skin variety is found in certain cells of the inner ear. But whether it is melanin or something else that confers the protection is unknown.

Clearly melanin is a handy and fascinating compound, with an intriguing evolutionary history. But because its effects are so visible in our skin, it has for centuries been made to bear an utterly undeserved burden of sociological and political significance. There are far more genetic differences among the people who make up these arbitrary constructs we call races than there are differences between races. It is time to move away from simplistic efforts to explain all our differences in terms of just one molecule and to pay attention to the tens of thousands of other molecules that make up our wondrously complex cells—and selves.

4

The Way of the WASP

RICHARD BROOKHISER

When Benjamin Franklin decided to improve his own character, he drew up the list of virtues which so annoyed D. H. Lawrence [*Studies in Classic American Literature*, chapter 2. Ed.]. Originally there were twelve. "But a Quaker friend having kindly informed me that I was generally thought proud . . . of which he convinced me by mentioning several instances; I determined endeavoring to cure myself, if I could, of this vice or folly among the rest, and I added *Humility to* my list"—along with an explanatory note: "Imitate Jesus and Socrates."[1]

Virtues, which we hope to acquire, may be listed. Character, which is what we are, is more complex. The basic WASP character can be broken down into six traits, which may be arranged in the following mandala. Traits form pairs and connections across the pattern, as well as between neighbors.

Conscience

Antisensuality   Industry

Use   Success

Civic-mindedness

Let us take the traits in order, starting at noon.

Conscience. Conscience is the great legacy of P [Protestantism. Ed.]. It is the way WASPs regulate their inner life and monitor their behavior. You let your conscience be your guide. It guides by offering a clear vision of the way you should go. The way may be spelled out in law or scripture, but conscience is the window through which each man comes to see it. All WASPs, not just Quakers, believe in the inner light.

Sight is the sense of conscience. George Fox in his perplexity heard a voice, and so did the born-again Englishman John Newton.

Amazing Grace! How sweet the *sound* . . .

Yet after the first rearranging experience, sight and insight take over the management of life.

I once was lost but now am found,
Was blind but now I *see.*

This was the WASP's point of contact with the Enlightenment and its self-evident (evident = completely seen) truths. This was also what Emerson, that subtle renegade, appropriated for his own project. "Standing on bare ground—my head bathed by the blithe air and uplifted into infinite space . . . I become a transparent eyeball; I am nothing; I see all . . .[2]

The way that conscience sees must be plain, or else what good is it for guidance? The way that can be seen is not the way, said Lao Tzu, but the way that cannot be seen is not the way of the WASP. Paradox and ambiguity are distractions, if not worse. The path is straight as well as plain. Byways lead to waste and confusion, if not actual Hell.

The punishment for ignoring the guidance of conscience is administered by conscience itself, in the form of guilt. Guilt, like conscience, is a private matter, inward and individual. No amount of external opprobrium can increase or enlarge it. It is a very different thing from shame. Shame is embarrassment before someone else—parents, friends, community. It is publicly displayed by the blush. Guilt is a pang. If it shows itself to the world, as in the mark that appears finally on the Reverend Arthur Dimmesdale's breast, it is only after long internal gnawing and a conscious act of self-exposure by the guilty party. Shame, being a public transaction, is a two-way street. It may be induced by peers or betters. The conviction of guilt is always *in camera*.

Wherever societies are small, tight, and stable, approaching the condition of oyster beds or coral reefs—peasant societies the world over—shame is the preferred method of discipline. WASPs believe in guilt, which travels anywhere.

This is why conscience is the most effective monitor of behavior ever devised. It doesn't quit when the oracles fall silent or when the cops go off duty. In societies ruled by conscience, people stop for red lights at three o'clock in the morning. In societies with less alert monitors, people drive on the sidewalk.

Conscience is the source of whatever freedoms WASP society enjoys. Since all consciences have an equally clear view of truth, who could presume to meddle with any man's? But conscience also limits freedom, which becomes the freedom to do what you know you should do. "Confirm thy soul in self-control, / Thy liberty in [moral] law."

Industry. One of the things conscience directs you to do is work. Idle hands do the Devil's. "The hours have wings," wrote John Milton, "and fly up to the Author of Time with reports on how we have used them"—a sentiment I first read not for some English major's project, but as a little boy in an advice column by Billy Graham that ran in the innermost pages of the local paper. I usually didn't read Graham, but this struck me as a bull's-eye. What could be more obvious?

Busy-ness suggests business, which suggests in turn Max Weber's proposition that Protestantism, especially in its Calvinist forms, is the engine of work in the Western world. Sociologists have recently found that the economic gap between white Protestants and white Catholics in this country has vanished, which means, however, not that Catholicism has suddenly become hospitable to work, but that American Catholics have Americanized (Protestantized) themselves. John Cuddihy, in his elegant encapsulation of Weber, hints that Protestant industry is a kind of nervous ritual, almost a reaction formation: "To rid themselves of this intolerable uncertainty"—predestination—Calvinists "reassured themselves by creating capitalism."[3] Whatever the dynamic, you must be doing things. Contemplation—the mystic's way, or the hermit's—is not an option.

Industry devalues all forms of prestige that rest on other criteria. So much for aristocracy. George Bush, graduating from college, went to Texas rather than Brown Brothers, Harriman, to make his nut (though he would use money raised through friends and relatives back east). One of Herbert Hoover's cousins once asked their grandmother if it was true that they were related to John Wesley, and got the following response: "What matter if we descended from the highest unless we are something ourselves? Get busy."[4]

Success. The reward of industry is success, which WASPs admire extravagantly. In theological terms, success is the outward and visible sign of grace—Cuddihy's "reassurance." By your works you know yourself. It is ironic, of course, that a religious impulse that began with a rejection of the doctrine of salvation by works should end in a glorification of the results of work. But the mere fact that WASPs distrust paradoxes does not mean they are immune to them.

An obvious measure of success is cash. Yet there are times when the only success that has been achieved is internal—when an effort or an exertion that has been good for nothing else has been good for you. The maxim that is commonly, but wrongly, attributed to Vince Lombardi—"Winning isn't everything, it's the only thing"—is a case of getting it not quite right. The climactic football game in *Stover at Yale* is a defeat; the heroes don't even manage to score. What Dink Stover learns from the experience is to take his lumps without complaining. Which leads him to later triumphs, of course.

What Lombardi actually said was that "winning isn't everything; wanting to win is." Is this any better? Success follows industry, yet the motivational spark between the two is problematic. James Madison, in one of the most famous Federalist papers, put ambition at the center of the constitutional system. But he handled the subject with the care—and distaste—of a lab technician preparing inoculations. "Ambition," he wrote, "must be made to counteract ambition. It may be a reflection on human nature," he went on, "that such devices should be necessary to control the abuses of government. But what is government itself but the greatest of all reflections on human nature?"[5] Only our depravity forces us to consider such depraved subjects. This was the aspect of WASPhood, facsimile and authentic, which the young Norman Podhoretz found hardest to bear: "the hunger for worldly success was regarded as low, ignoble, ugly . . . something to be ashamed of and guilty about. My own conversion to such values" marked "the first lap in the long, blind journey I was making."[6]

The English who stayed home are also suspicious of ambition, but the social origin of their leeriness is rather different—an emulation of the attitudes of an aristocracy, which does not yearn to win because it has, by definition of birth, won already. Hoover's grandmother would have been appalled. What the WASP wants is to follow the work conscience lays out. Success, public or personal, will come in the nature of things. But that is the operation of providential or natural laws. The credit is Providence's, or Nature's.

Industry and success together explain why America, whose original colonial economy—tobacco and pelts—was strictly Third World, a page out of Lenin, became, in three centuries, the largest economy on the globe. Economists make the point continually, but it has to be stated again, because people forget it continually: America didn't get rich because it had "natural resources." Plenty of places on earth have them in equal or greater measure. Americans did well for themselves because of their moral resources—the obligations of industry and the respect they accorded success.

Civic-mindedness. WASPs pay lip service, and often even service, to the good of society as a whole. All other social facts—honor, family, group—take a back seat.

Consider the rarity in WASP America of duels, feuds, and secret societies, all expressions of loyalties to subcivic ideals. Alexander Hamilton died in a duel, but he opposed the practice, and religious opposition stamped it out in the early nineteenth century. Feuds occur only in the boondocks. The Masons, after provoking the first third party in American history, the Anti-Masonic Party, became like Ralph Kramden's Racoon Lodge. Skull and Bones, Dink Stover's secret college society—and George Bush's—justified itself by its social usefulness.

WASP defenders of capitalism also make their case in civic terms. The rising tide lifts all boats. *Atlas Shrugged*, a bald sermon on love of self, sells thousands of copies to teenage girls every year. But Ayn Rand's pitch—like Lombardi's—is slightly off. Among WASPs, free enterprise preens itself on what it does for everybody, not just for supermen. Without civic-mindedness, the successful would have no sense of social responsibility. They often have little enough. But thanks to civic-mindedness—the operation of conscience in social relations—they have some. Even Social Darwinism in its most naked form, which enjoyed a vogue at the end of the nineteenth century, promised, by casting aside the unfit, to benefit society as a whole in the long run.

Special interests have been the demons of American political rhetoric from the days of the Populists until now. Madison called them factions—parts, less than the whole, mobilized for advantage or gain. Realistically, he knew they would emerge. But he devised a system to blunt their effectiveness, which he expected the country to possess sufficient civic virtue to maintain. In politics, the charge of representing special interests, if true, is indefensible. The only recourse is to accuse the accuser of defending worse ones.

WASPs have long been fascinated with tales of groups that are hierarchical, secret, self-interested (in short, criminal): Jesuits, the Mafia, Bloods and Crips. It is a fascination with the foreign. Equally popular are tales of the loner—the vigilante, the private eye, the gunslinger—who, when society reneges on its responsibilities, takes the law into his own hands. Pretty clearly, these are daydreams of people who do not often do likewise.

Civic society exercises discipline not so much by the force of law—people may not break the law very often; if the laws are plain, why should they?—as by conformity. The relentless conformism of WASP life seems to negate the primacy of conscience, and many books have become cocktail chatter by plying the apparent contradictions: inner-direction vs. other-direction, Consciousness I vs. Consciousness II. The contradictions vanish with a little thought. Even if conscience is our guide, only a handful of eccentrics—half geniuses, half lunatic—are ever able to live completely from their own resources at all times. A normal man requires the additional support of some authority in many of the occasions of his life. What will the authority be? the past? the gods? the police? Or the example of his peers, each one of whom, after all, bears a conscience akin to his own? WASPs, when they must obey, choose to obey each other. They are encouraged in conformity by the additional fact that since the insights of conscience are plain, men's consciences will tend naturally to follow a similar course.

The pressure of conformity, finally, ensures that crackpots—who may be prophets—must pass the test of time. Conformity's enemies accuse it of muzzling invention, of keeping Miltons mute and inglorious. But it also inhibits charlatans and maniacs. Genuine contributions to the common weal, WASPs believe, will always make their way.

Use. We have encountered use, or usefulness, before in other points of the pattern—the usefulness of work, the usefulness of capitalism. But it is important enough to be given a portion to itself. For nothing is ever good, the WASP believes, simply and of itself. It must be good for something.

A good use of something is the fulfillment of its proper task. WASPs like to think of themselves as handy: with wrenches and committees, assembly lines and constitutions. They like getting the job done, and they enjoy contemplating "last things, fruits, consequences, facts."[7] Inefficiency is the practical equivalent of ambiguity—a kind of sin. H. G. Wells, in one of his novels, shows the secretary of the Massachusetts Society for the Study of Contemporary Thought reacting to the contrary habits of an English country house. "The point that strikes me most about all this is that that barn isn't a barn any longer, and that this farmyard isn't a farmyard. There isn't any wheat or chaff or anything of that sort in the barn, and there never will be again: there's just a pianola and a dancing floor, and if a cow came into this farmyard, everybody in the place would be shooing it out again."[8]

Use affects the WASP's attitude to time. The self-improving Franklin, believing that "the precept of *Order* requir[ed] that *every part of my business should have its allotted time,*" devised the following plan for his day.

The Morning	5	Rise, wash, and address
Question. What good shall I do this day?	6	*Powerful Goodness!* Contrive
	7	day's business, and take the resolution of the day; prosecute the present study, and breakfast.
	8	
	9	
		Work
	10	
	11	
Noon	12	Read, or overlook my accounts,
	1	and dine.
	2	
	3	
		Work
	4	
	5	
Evening	6	Put things in their places.
Question. What good have I	7	Supper. Music or diversion,
done today?	8	or conversation. Examination
	9	of the day.
	10	
	11	
	12	
Night	1	Sleep
	2	
	3	
	4	

("I found myself," he added ruefully, "incorrigible with respect to order.")[9] Time is the tyrant of daily life; it must be obeyed, and more than obeyed. To arrive anywhere only on time is to arrive late.

Use also molds the WASP's view of time past. Despite the Bicentennial Tall Ships, colonial Williamsburg, and a hundred other restorations, authentic and fake, the WASP's attitude to his own history is nostalgic, wistful, curious—but not intimate. (The Civil War may be the lone exception.) To his European prehistory he has even less connection. History washed overboard into the Atlantic. In Dublin, a speaker can draw a crowd in mid-week, in business hours, by talking about Wolfe Tone. As recently as seventy years ago, Michael Dukakis's cousins were trying to undo the fall of Constantinople. These events might have happened yesterday. In men's minds, they're still happening today. The WASP mind asks irritably, What good does it do me, now? "The only history worth a tinker's dam," wrote Henry Ford, "is the history we make today."[10] Important history flunks the test of time, but so do grudges and festering hatreds.

Antisensuality. Every other point of the pattern is some positive thing or quality. Here we resort to the negative. What is negated is any keen attachment to pleasures that operate through the senses. No single positive term quite covers all cases. The suggestion of vigilant guardedness makes the negative doubly appropriate.

We should not exaggerate. The WASP is not a crazed oppressor of the body, no anchorite, no saddhu. Sports of all kinds have always been important to him. WASPs race horses and cars, and blast away at birds; they invented baseball, basketball, and football, and took up polo (those who could afford it) with enthusiasm. Yet sports are always, inescapably, good for you. They build your muscles and your character. ("How did your *team* do, dear?") They may yield spiritual gratifications like success, but not sensual ones. The body is to be exercised, not pleased.

So it goes, through everything men enjoy. Consider the plainness of WASP food. Not that most non-WASP Americans have anything to boast about in this regard. An immigrant pool drawn largely from Ireland, Germany, and Eastern Europe was not calculated to improve the national cuisine. (Just what America needed—five hundred kinds of starch.) One of the mysteries of American life is how the injection of millions of Italians could have failed utterly to raise the general level. It is the same with drink as with food. WASPs drink to get drunk. The only alternative to drunkenness is temperance. The care the French, Italians, and Germans take over wine, or even the English over beer and ale, is incomprehensible to them.

WASPs break the Seventh Commandment as often as anybody else. But mistresses, as an established aristocratic or *haut-bourgeois* institution, are as rare as spice racks. Transgressors show indecent disrespect for the opinion of mankind. The best posthumous defense Richard Harding Davis could make for his friend Stanford White, who had been murdered by a former lover's husband, was that the dead man got a lot of exercise outside the bedroom. "Described as a voluptuary, his greatest pleasure was to stand all day waist deep in the rapids of a Canadian river and fight it out with a salmon."[11] The ground has shifted on sex, but old habits die hard. What was forbidden becomes compulsory. The real subject of *The Joy of Sex*, as its National Lampoon parodists realized, was *The Job of Sex*.

The arts too are a job. WASPs are great consumers of culture even if, as we shall see, they are burdened and ambivalent producers of it. But the pleasure they take is inevitably alloyed with self-improvement—among the sincere, that is. Among the insincere, the pleasure comes from the joys of status. To be on "speaking terms" with "fine things," observed Santayana, "was a part of social respectability, like those candlesticks, probably candleless, sometimes displayed as a seemly ornament in a room blazing with electric light."[12]

Antisensuality serves the practical function of limiting the enjoyment of success, at least of unearned success. Plantation owners did not live austerely, and neither did robber barons. But they could all claim to have done something, even if it was only assembling a trust. For WASPs, all rewards exist on sufferance; rewards that are simply inherited excite suspicion. "A great fortune had been entrusted to him," one of Trollope's characters says of the Duke of Omnium, "and he knew that it was his duty to spend it. He did spend it, and all the world looked up to him."[13] Not the WASP world. Antisensuality threatens the lazy rich with a bad conscience. And so we come back to noon.

WASPs have no monopoly on any one of these traits: Chinese work hard; Jews know something about guilt. But the combination of all of them, and the way they temper and modify each other—success depending on industry; use giving industry its tasks; civic-mindedness placing obligations on success, and antisensuality setting limits to the enjoyment of it; conscience watching over everything—is uniquely WASP. The way of the WASP was shaped by the same forces that shaped him. English notions of liberty and society molded his notions of civic-mindedness. WASP Protestantism generated WASP ideas about work, success, and sensuality. Both helped establish the primacy of conscience, with Protestantism playing the larger role. Any change in the shaping forces, or in any of the traits themselves, would change the WASP's character.

The way of the WASP can lead in a number of different directions and take a variety of social forms. WASPs can be, and have been, imperialists and America firsters, followers of Social Darwinism and of prairie socialism. For more than eighty years, the country they built was half slave and half free. Yet certain social structures, some good, most monstrous—fascism, communism, the caste system—are out of bounds. Everything that is within bounds will be done in the characteristic behavioral style.

The way of the WASP can also lead to frustrations. Millions of WASPs have committed every imaginable un-WASPy act, from coming to the theater after the curtain goes up to coveting other men's wives. This is disobedience, not deviance. All thieves support the institution of property; they are simply original in their way of acquiring it. The way of the WASP may be shaken by revolt or weakened by defection, but, like any other way, it withstands ordinary failure.

Two other forms of disobedience, or at least relaxation, are humor and fun (as in *good, clean*). Bergson thought laughs were human barks, a means of warning and social control, a conservative force. But they are also an outlet, an underside. WASP humor, like all humor, conceals many a tiny rebellion. In its occasional savagery there is revolt against as well as expression of conscience's grip. Fun, meanwhile, operates as a distraction. It fools the radar of conscience and allows the WASP to enjoy activities—music, for instance—without confronting the potentially serious counterclaims they make against his way. Fun is the Stealth technology of the psyche.

But the most important thing the way of the WASP has led to is American peace and prosperity. It explains why we are richer than Russia, though we have fewer natural resources; calmer than Lebanon, though we have more sects; freer and more just than either. It also explains why so many Russians and Lebanese, and people of numerous other societies, have come here.

Notes

1. Benjamin Franklin, *The Autobiography and Other Writings* (New York: Bantam Books, 1982), pp. 84, 77.

2. Ralph Waldo Emerson, *The Portable Emerson* (New York: Viking Penguin, 1981), p. 11.

3. John Murray Cuddihy, *No Offense* (New York: Seabury Press, 1978), p. 17.

4. George Nash, *The Life of Herbert Hoover* (New York: W. W. Norton, 1983), vol. I, p. 3.

5. *The Federalist Papers* (New York: New American Library, 1961), p. 322.

6. Norman Podhoretz, *Making It* (New York: Random House, 1967), p. 55.

7. William James, *Pragmatism*, quoted in Will Durant, *The Story of Philosophy* (New York: Time Inc., 1962), p. 476.

8. H. G. Wells, *Mr. Britling Sees It Through* (New York: Macmillan, 1916), p. 33.

9. Franklin, pp. 81–82.

10. Quoted in John Lukacs, *Outgrowing Democracy* (Garden City, N.Y.: Doubleday, 1984), p. 37.

11. Quoted in Stephen Garmey, *Gramercy Park* (New York: Routledge Books, 1984), p. 131.

12. George Santayana, *Character and Opinion in the United States* (New York: Charles Scribner's Sons, 1920), p. 6.

13. Anthony Trollope, *Phineas Redux* (New York: Oxford University Press, 1983), p. 269.

5

Hiring Quotas for White Males Only

ERIC FONER

Thirty-two years ago, I graduated from Columbia College. My class of 700 was all-male and virtually all-white. Most of us were young men of ability, yet had we been forced to compete for admission with women and racial minorities, fewer than half of us would have been at Columbia. None of us, to my knowledge, suffered debilitating self-doubt because we were the beneficiaries of affirmative action—that is, favored treatment on the basis of our race and gender.

Affirmative action has emerged as the latest "wedge issue" of American politics. The recent abrogation of California affirmative action programs by Governor Pete Wilson, and the Clinton Administration's halting efforts to re-evaluate federal policy, suggest the issue is now coming to a head. As a historian, I find the current debate dismaying not only because of the crass effort to set Americans against one another for partisan advantage but also because the entire discussion lacks a sense of history.

Opponents of affirmative action, for example, have tried to wrap themselves in the mantle of the civil rights movement, seizing upon the 1963 speech in which Martin Luther King Jr. looked forward to the time when his children would be judged not by the "color of their skin" but by the "content of their character." Rarely mentioned is that King came to be a strong supporter of affirmative action.

In his last book, *Where Do We Go From Here?*, a brooding meditation on America's long history of racism, King acknowledged that "special treatment" for blacks seemed to conflict with the ideal of opportunity based on individual merit. But, he continued, "a society that has done something special *against* the Negro for hundreds of years must now do something special *for* him."

Our country, King realized, has never operated on a colorblind basis. From the beginning of the Republic, membership in American society was defined in racial terms. The first naturalization law, enacted in 1790, restricted citizenship for those emigrating from abroad to "free white persons." Free blacks, even in the North, were barred from juries, public schools, government employment and the militia and regular army. Not until after the Civil War were blacks deemed worthy to be American citizens, while Asians were barred from naturalization until the 1940s.

White immigrants certainly faced discrimination. But they had access to the political power, jobs and residential neighborhoods denied to blacks. In the nineteenth century, the

THE NATION 924 June 26, 1995. Reprinted with permission from *The Nation* magazine. Copyright © by The Nation Company, L.P.

men among them enjoyed the right to vote even before they were naturalized. Until well into this century, however, the vast majority of black Americans were excluded from the suffrage except for a period immediately after the Civil War. White men, native and immigrant, could find well-paid craft and industrial jobs, while employers and unions limited nonwhites (and women) to unskilled and menial employment. The "American standard of living" was an entitlement of white men alone.

There is no point in dwelling morbidly on past injustices. But this record of unequal treatment cannot be dismissed as "vague or ancient wrongs" with no bearing on the present, as Republican strategist William Kristol recently claimed. Slavery may be gone and legal segregation dismantled, but the effects of past discrimination live on in seniority systems that preserve intact the results of a racially segmented job market, a black unemployment rate double that of whites, and pervasive housing segregation.

Past racism is embedded in the two-tier, racially divided system of social insurance still on the books today. Because key Congressional committees in the 1930s were controlled by Southerners with all-white electorates, they did not allow the supposedly universal entitlement of Social Security to cover the largest categories of black workers—agricultural laborers and domestics. Social Security excluded 80 percent of employed black women, who were forced to depend for a safety net on the much less generous "welfare" system.

The notion that affirmative action stigmatizes its recipients reflects not just belief in advancement according to individual merit but the older idea that the "normal" American is white. There are firemen and black firemen, construction workers and black construction workers: Nonwhites (and women) who obtain such jobs are still widely viewed as interlopers, depriving white men of positions or promotions to which they are historically entitled.

I have yet to meet the white male in whom special favoritism (getting a job, for example, through relatives or an old boys' network, or because of racial discrimination by a union or employer) fostered doubt about his own abilities. In a society where belief in black inferiority is still widespread (witness the success of *The Bell Curve*), many whites and some blacks may question the abilities of beneficiaries of affirmative action. But this social "cost" hardly counterbalances the enormous social benefits affirmative action has produced.

Nonwhites (and even more so, white women) have made deep inroads into the lower middle class and into professions once reserved for white males. Columbia College now admits women and minority students. Would these and other opportunities have opened as widely and as quickly without the pressure of affirmative action programs? American history suggests they would not.

It is certainly true, as critics charge, that affirmative action's benefits have not spread to the poorest members of the black community. The children of Harlem, regrettably, are not in a position to take advantage of the spots Columbia has opened to blacks. But rather than simply ratifying the advantages of already affluent blacks, who traditionally advanced by servicing the segregated black community, affirmative action has helped to create a *new* black middle class, resting on professional and managerial positions within white society.

This new class is much more vulnerable than its white counterpart to the shifting fortunes of the economy and politics. Far more middle-class blacks than whites depend on public employment—positions now threatened by the downsizing of federal, state and municipal governments. That other actions are needed to address the problems of the "underclass" hardly negates the proven value of affirmative action in expanding black access to the middle class and skilled working class.

There is no harm in rethinking the ways affirmative action is effectuated—in re-examining, for example, the expansion to numerous other groups of a program originally intended to deal with the legacy of slavery and segregation. In principle, there may well be merit in redefining disadvantage to include poor whites. The present cry for affirmative action based on class rather than race, however, seems as much an evasion as a serious effort to rethink public policy. Efforts to uplift the poor, while indispensable in a just society, are neither a substitute for nor incompatible with programs that address the legacy of the race-based discrimination to which blacks have historically been subjected. Without a robust class politics, moreover, class policies are unlikely to get very far. The present Congress may well dismantle affirmative action, but it hardly seems sympathetic to broad "color-blind" programs to assist the poor.

At a time of deindustrialization and stagnant real wages, many whites have come to blame affirmative action for declining economic prospects. Let us not delude ourselves, however, into thinking that eliminating affirmative action will produce a society in which rewards are based on merit. Despite our rhetoric, equal opportunity has never been the American way. For nearly all our history, affirmative action has been a prerogative of white men.

6

Innocence and Affirmative Action

THOMAS ROSS

When we create arguments, when we act as rhetoricians, we reveal our-selves by the words and ideas we choose to employ. Verbal structures that are used widely and persistently are especially worth examination. Arguments made with repeated, almost formulaic, sets of words suggest a second argument flowing beneath the apparent argument. Beneath the apparently abstract language and the syllogistic form of these arguments, we may discover the deeper currents that explain, at least in part, why we seem so attached to these verbal structures.

In particular, the rhetoric of *innocence* persists as an important tool in discussions of race. It is hard to know how rhetoric works. We do know, however, that both judges and academicians often use the rhetoric of innocence. Those who use the rhetoric presumably find it persuasive or at least useful. What then could be the sources and nature of its apparent power?

Innocence

"Innocence" is connected to the powerful cultural forces and ideas of religion, good and evil, and sex. "Innocence" is defined typically as "freedom from guilt or sin" or, in the sexual sense, as "chastity." The idea of innocent victims, particularly when coupled with the specter of those who victimize them, is a pervasive and potent story in our culture.

The centrality of the conception of "innocence" to the Christian religion is obvious. Christ is the paradigmatic "innocent victim." Mary is the perfect embodiment of innocence as chaste. Although the concept of "original sin" complicates the notion of innocence in Christian theology, the striving toward innocence and the veneration of those who come closest to achieving it and thereby suffer are important ideas in modern Christian practice. "Blessed are those who are persecuted for righteousness' sake, for theirs is the kingdom of heaven."[1]

The idea of innocence also is connected to the myths and symbols of evil. For example, Paul Ricoeur in *The Symbolism of Evil* demonstrates the cultural significance of the "dread of the impure" and the terror of "defilement."[2] The contrasting state for "impure," or the state to which the rites of purification might return us, is "innocence," freedom from guilt or sin. Ricoeur's thesis spans the modern and classical cultures. He makes clear the persistence and power of the symbolism of evil and its always present contrast, the state of innocence.

What is central within the modern culture surely will be reflected in its literature. And

43 VAND. L. REV. 297 (1990). Originally published in the *Vanderbilt Law Review*. Reprinted by permission.

in literature the innocent victim is everywhere. In *Innocent Victims: Poetic Injustice in Shakespearean Tragedy*, R. S. White argued "that Shakespeare was constantly and uniquely concerned with the fate of the innocent victim." White observed, "In every tragedy by Shakespeare, alongside the tragic protagonist who is proclaimed by himself and others as a suffering centre, stands, sometimes silently, the figure of pathos who is a lamb of goodness: Lavinia, Ophelia, Desdemona, Cordelia, the children."[3] Shakespeare was not alone in the use of women and children drawn as innocent victims. In the work of Dickens, Hugo, Melville, and others, the suffering innocent is a central character.

The innocent victim is part of sexual practice and mythology. The recurring myth of the "demon lover" and its innocent victim is one example.[4] Moreover, we are preoccupied with innocence in the female partner as part of the mythological background of rape and prostitution and in our prerequisites in the chosen marriage partner.[5]

The idea of the innocent victim always conjures the one who takes away her innocence and who thereby himself becomes both the "defiler" and the "defiled." In literature and in life the innocent victim is used as a means of conjuring the notion of defilement. In fact, it is impossible to make sense of the significance of either the "innocent victim" or the "defiler" without imagining the other. Each conception is given real significance by its implicit contrast with the other. Thus, the invocation of innocence is also the invocation of sin, guilt, and defilement.

Race and Innocence

The rhetoric of innocence in affirmative action discourse uses one of the most powerful symbols of our culture, that of innocence and its always present opposite, the defiled taker. When the white person is called the innocent victim of affirmative action, the rhetorician is invoking not just the idea of innocence but also that of the not innocent, the defiled taker. The defiled taker is given a particular name in one of two ways. First, merely invoking the "innocent white victim" triggers at some level its rhetorically natural opposite, the "defiled black taker." This implicit personification is made explicit by the second part of the rhetoric, the questioning of the "actual victim" status of the black person who benefits from the affirmative action plan. The contrast is between the innocent white victim and the undeserving black taker. The cultural significance of the ideas of innocence and defilement thus gives the rhetoric of innocence a special sort of power.

The rhetoric of innocence draws its power not only from the cultural significance of its basic terms but also from its connection with "unconscious racism." As Professor Charles Lawrence puts it:

> Americans share a common historical and cultural heritage in which racism has played and still plays a dominant role. Because of this shared experience, we also inevitably share many ideas, attitudes, and beliefs that attach significance to an individual's race and induce negative feelings and opinions about nonwhites. To the extent that this cultural belief system has influenced all of us, we are all racists. At the same time, most of us are unaware of our racism. We do not recognize the ways in which our cultural experience has influenced our beliefs about race or the occasions on which those beliefs affect our actions. In other words, a large part of the behavior that produces racial discrimination is influenced by unconscious racial motivation.[6]

We are each, in this sense of the word, racists.

Lawrence's thesis is disturbing especially to the liberal who can think of a no more offensive label than that of "racist." Moreover, the white intellectual, whether politically liberal or conservative, typically expresses only disgust for the words and behavior of the supremacists and neo-Nazis he connects with the label "racist." The dominant public ideology has become nonracist. Use of racial epithets, expressions of genetic superiority, and avowal of formal segregation are not part of the mainstream of public discourse. These ways of speaking, which were part of the public discourse several decades ago, are deemed by most today as irrational utterances emanating from the few remaining pockets of racism.

Notwithstanding that the public ideology has become nonracist, the culture continues to teach racism. Racial stereotypes pervade our media and language, both reflecting and influencing the complex set of individual and collective choices that make our schools, our neighborhoods, our work places, and our lives racially segregated.[7]

Racism today paradoxically is both "irrational and normal." Racism is at once inconsistent with the dominant public ideology and is embraced by each of us, albeit at the unconscious level. This paradox of irrationality and normalcy is part of the reason for racism's unconscious nature. When our culture teaches us to be racist and our ideology teaches us that racism is evil, we respond by excluding the forbidden lesson from consciousness.

The repression of our racism is a crucial piece of the rhetoric of innocence. First, we sensibly can claim the mantle of innocence only by denying the charge of racism. As white persons and nonracists, we are innocent; we have done no harm to those people and do not deserve to suffer for the sins of the other, not innocent white people who were racists. If we accept unconscious racism, this self-conception unravels. Second, the black beneficiaries of affirmative action can be denied "actual victim" status only so long as racists are thought of as either historical figures or aberrational and isolated characters in contemporary culture. By thinking of racists in this way we deny the efficacy of racism today, relegating the ugly term primarily to the past. Thus, by repressing our unconscious racism we make coherent our self-conception of innocence and make sensible the question of the actual victimization of blacks.

The existence of unconscious racism undermines the rhetoric of innocence. The "innocent white victim" is no longer quite so innocent. Furthermore, the idea of unconscious racism belies the "victim" part of the characterization. The victim is one who suffers an undeserved loss. If the white person who is disadvantaged by an affirmative action plan is also a racist, albeit at an unconscious level, the question of desert becomes more complicated.

The implications of unconscious racism for the societal distribution of burdens and benefits also undermine the "innocent" status of the white man. As blacks are burdened in a myriad of ways because of the persistence of unconscious racism, the white man thereby is benefited. On a racially integrated law faculty, for example, a black law professor must overcome widespread assumptions of inferiority held by students and colleagues, while white colleagues enjoy the benefit of the positive presumption and of the contrast with their black colleague.[8]

Undoubtedly, the historical manifestations of racism have worked to the advantage of whites. Just as slavery provided the resources to make possible the genteel life of the plantation owner and his white family in early nineteenth century Virginia, more than a century later the state system of public school segregation diverted the State's resources to me and not to my black peers in Virginia. The lesson of unconscious racism, however, is that the obvious advantages of state-sponsored racism are not the only ones skewing the societal balance sheet. Even after abolition of state racism, the cultural teachings persist and unconscious racism continues to operate to the disadvantage of blacks and the advantage of whites today—in job interviews, in social encounters, in courtrooms and conference rooms, and on the streets. In our culture whites are necessarily advantaged, because blacks are presumed at the unconscious level by most as lazy, dumb, and criminally prone. Because the white person is advantaged by assumptions that consequently hurt blacks, the rhetorical appeal of affirmative action's unfairness to the "innocent white victim" is undermined.

Moreover, the "actual victim" status of the black person who benefits from affirmative action is much harder to question once unconscious racism is acknowledged. Because racial discrimination is part of the cultural structure, each person of color is subject to it, everywhere and at all times. Recognition of unconscious racism makes odd the question whether this person is an "actual victim."

The white rhetorician often seeks to acknowledge and, at the same time, to blunt the power of unconscious racism by declaring that "societal discrimination" is an insufficient predicate for affirmative action. "Societal discrimination" never is defined with any precision, but it suggests an ephemeral, abstract kind of discrimination, committed by no one and against no one in particular, a kind of amorphous inconvenience for persons of color. By this term the white rhetorician at once can acknowledge the idea of unconscious racism but, by giving it a different name, give it a different and trivial connotation.

The rhetoric of innocence coupled with the idea of "societal discrimination" thus obscures unconscious racism and keeps rhetorically alive the innocence of the white person and the question of actual victimization of the black person. Unconscious racism meets that rhetoric on its own terms. Once one accepts some version of the idea of unconscious racism, the rhetoric of innocence is weakened, if not defeated.

The rhetoric of innocence and unconscious racism connect in yet another way. Through the lens of unconscious racism the rhetoric can be seen to embody racism. Professor Lawrence described the two types of beliefs about the out-group held by racists:

> [S]tudies have found that racists hold two types of stereotyped beliefs: They believe the out-group is dirty, lazy, oversexed, and without control of their instincts (a typical accusation against blacks), or they believe the out-group is pushy, ambitious, conniving, and in control of business, money, and industry (a typical accusation against Jews).[9]

The stereotype of lazy and oversexed is abundant in our culture's characterization of the black person. As William Brink and Louis Harris put it, "The stereotyped beliefs about Negroes are firmly rooted in less-privileged, less-well-educated white society: the beliefs that Negroes smell different, have looser morals, are lazy, and laugh a lot."[10] Angus Campbell stated:

> When asked directly whether they believe the disadvantaged status of urban Negroes to be the result of discrimination or to be "something about Negroes themselves," a majority choose the latter explanation. . . . Most commonly the "something" they have in mind is what they take to be the Negro's lack of ambition, laziness, failure to take advantage of his opportunities.[11]

In a recent article, Wyn Craig Wade recounted the twentieth-century revival of the Klan and the release of *The Birth of a Nation*, a 1915 movie which had as its centerpiece the suicide of an "innocent" white girl forced to choose between the physical touch of a black man and death.[12]

The stereotypical depiction of blacks has been a persistent feature of American literature. In 1937 Sterling Brown, a black poet and literary theorist, published a compelling analysis of the depiction of blacks in American literature. Brown found the stereotypical depiction the norm and expressed his analysis: "Whether the Negro was human was one of the problems that racked the brains of the cultured Old South. The finally begrudged admission that perhaps he was, has remained largely nominal in letters as in life. Complete, complex humanity has been denied to him."[13]

The two parts of the rhetoric of innocence connect to and trigger at some level the stereotypical racist beliefs about blacks. The assertion of the innocent white victim draws power from the implicit contrast with the "defiled taker"—the black person who undeservedly reaps the advantages of affirmative action. The use of the idea of innocence, and its opposite, defilement, coalesces with the unconscious racist belief that the black person is not innocent in a sexual sense, that the black person is sexually defiled by promiscuity.[14] The "over-sexed" black person of the racist stereotype becomes the perfect implicit, and unconsciously embraced, contrast to the innocent white person.

A similar analysis applies to the second part of the rhetoric of innocence. The question whether the black person is an actual victim implies that he or she does not deserve what the black person gets. This question draws power from the stereotypical racist belief that the black person is lazy. The lazy black seeks and takes the unearned advantages of affirmative action.

In this fashion, the white rhetorician is constantly but unconsciously drawing on the stereotypical racist beliefs. Nor is the white audience consciously embracing those beliefs when they experience the rhetoric of innocence in affirmative action discourse. Both the rhetoricians and their audience are likely to reject the stereotypes at the conscious level. Moreover, they would be offended at the very suggestion that they might hold such beliefs. The great lesson of Professor Lawrence's work is that the beliefs are still there, even in the white liberal. This is so because the teacher is our culture; any person who is part of the culture has been taught the lesson of racism. While most of us have struggled to unlearn the lesson and have succeeded at the conscious level, none of us can slough off altogether the lesson at the unconscious level.

Examination of the rhetoric of innocence may teach us that "innocence" is a powerful and very dangerous idea which simply does not belong in the affirmative action debate. Real and good people certainly will suffer as a result of the use of affirmative action. Yet, we will be much further along in our efforts to deal with that painful fact if we put aside the loaded conception of innocence. The choice for us is not whether we shall make innocent people suffer or not; it is how do we get to a world where good people, white and of color, no longer suffer because of the accidental circumstances of their race. We cannot get from here to there if we refuse to examine the words we use and deny the unconscious racism that surrounds those words.

Notes

1. Matthew 5:10 (New King James).
2. P. RICOEUR, THE SYMBOLISM OF EVIL 25 (1969).
3. R. WHITE, INNOCENT VICTIMS: POETIC INJUSTICE IN SHAKESPEAREAN TRAGEDY 5–6 (1986).
4. *See generally* T. REED, DEMON-LOVERS AND THEIR VICTIMS IN BRITISH FICTION (1988).
5. *See* H. LIPS & N. COLWILL, THE PSYCHOLOGY OF SEX DIFFERENCES 112–13 (1978). During the early times of Christianity, a woman thought to have become pregnant by a man other than her husband was humiliated publicly by a priest. Her hair was untied and her dress torn, and she was made to drink a potion consisting of holy water, dust, and ink. "If she suffers no physical damage from that

terrifying psychological ordeal, her innocence is presumed to have protected her." W. Phipps, Genesis and Gender: Biblical Myths of Sexuality and Their Cultural Impact 71 (1989).

6. Charles Lawrence, *The Id, the Ego, and Equal Protection: Reckoning with Unconscious Racism,* 39 Stan. L. Rev. 317, 322 (1987).

7. A process known as the tipping phenomenon occurs when white families abandon a neighborhood after the black percentage of the population exceeds a certain amount, usually between 30 and 50% black. Bruce Ackerman, *Integration for Subsidized Housing and the Question of Racial Occupancy Controls,* 26 Stan. L. Rev. 245, 251 (1974); *see also* Reynolds Farley, *Residential Segregation and Its Implication for School Integration,* 39 Law & Contemp. Probs. 164 (1975). In 1970 a study of 109 cities was conducted to determine the degree of racial integration. In every one of those cities, at least 60% of either the white or the black population would have had to shift their places of residence to achieve complete residential integration. In all but three of those cities, the figure was increased to at least 70%. *Id.* at 165. "Where neighborhoods are highly segregated, schools tend also to be highly segregated." *Id.* at 187. In some Northern districts where the courts and the HEW [U.S. Department of Health, Education, and Welfare] had not integrated schools, school segregation was even higher than would be expected based on residential segregation levels. *Id.*

8. *See* Randall Kennedy, *Racial Critiques of Legal Academia,* 102 Harv. L. Rev. 1745 (1989); *see also* Derrick A. Bell, *Strangers in Academic Paradise: Law Teachers of Color in Still White Law Schools,* 20 U.S.F. L. Rev. 385 (1986); Andrew Haines, *Minority Law Professors and the Myth of Sisyphus: Consciousness and Praxis Within the Special Teaching Challenge in American Law Schools,* 10 Nat'l Black L.J. 247 (1988). Interestingly, this point is used by the white rhetoricians to make an argument against affirmative action. The "stigma" of affirmative action on blacks is offered as a reason for precluding hiring preferences for blacks. What rarely is mentioned is that the stigma already is present through unconscious racism. We are all taught that blacks are lazy and dumb. We do not need affirmative action to embrace an idea that is everywhere in our culture and long predates the very idea of affirmative action. There is no doubt, however, that many whites use the phenomenon of affirmative action as a way of explaining this piece of unconscious racism. And of course the white rhetorician can distort the meaning and purpose of affirmative action to fit the stereotypes of unconscious racism and thereby feed the racism.

9. Lawrence, *supra* at 333 (footnotes omitted).

10. W. Brink & L. Harris, Black & White 137 (1976).

11. A. Campbell, White Attitudes Toward Black People 14 (1971).

12. W. Wade, The Fiery Cross: The Ku Klux Klan in America 119–39 (1987).

13. S. Brown, The Negro in American Fiction 2–3 (1937). The depiction in American literature of the humanness of blacks has been expressed most powerfully by this century's black poets, playwrights, and novelists. *See* N. Tischler, Black Masks: Negro Characters in Modern Southern Fiction 26–27 (1969). The stereotypical depiction of blacks also has been a persistent feature of American art. A recent art exhibition, *Facing History: The Black Image in American Art 1710–1940,* is devoted to this particular instance of stereotyping. *See Two Centuries of Stereotypes,* Time, Jan. 29, 1990, at 82–83; *Black Images of American History,* N.Y. Times, Jan. 18, 1990, at 17, col. 1. *See generally* 4 H. Honour, The Image of the Black in Western Art, pts. 1 & 2 (1976).

14. *See* J. Kovel, White Racism 67–79 (1970). The miscegenation laws finally ruled unconstitutional in *Loving v. Virginia,* 388 U.S. 1 (1967), are a testament to the connection between racism and sex.

7

Doing the White Male Kvetch
(A Pale Imitation of a Rag)

CALVIN TRILLIN

You're not allowed to give the wife a smack.
And people get their jobs because they're black.
Reverse discrimination's just not right.
We earned our jobs, by God, by being white.

(Chorus)
You put your right wing out.
You pop a can of brew.
You jiggle—just a bit,
Not like those black guys do.
You settle on the couch,
And then you yawn and stretch.
You're doin' paleface jive.
It's called the white male kvetch.

The Brady bill is flat unfair to shooters.
A guy these days can't even mention hooters—
A word the femiNazis now forbid.
You're also not allowed to smack your kid.

(Repeat chorus)

The welfare queens with Cadillacs eat steaks.
It's true: these colored folks get all the breaks.
They've got a right to sing the blues? Our rights
Should sure include the right to whine the whites.

(Repeat chorus, to distraction)

8

Growing Up *White* in America?

BONNIE KAE GROVER

Growing up *white* in America. How do you do that? I mean, lots of folks grow up Italian in America, lots more grow up capitalist in America, and legions of us have grown up middle class, working class, poor, or even rich in America. But *white*?

White is transparent. That's the point of being the dominant race. Sure, the whiteness is there, but you never think of it. If you're white, you never *have* to think of it. Sometimes when folks make a point of thinking of it, some (not all) of them run the risk of being either sappy in the eyes of other whites or of being dangerous to nonwhites. And if white folks remind each other about being white, too often the reminder is about threats by outsiders—nonwhites—who steal white entitlements like good jobs, a fine education, nice neighborhoods, and the good life.

And now, in an instant, it comes to me—the burr I've been feeling since I started getting a nasty itch from this idea. It's this—Is "white culture" really *white* culture? Or is it just American culture, nothing more, and the white folks who think it's white culture have just moved in like they've discovered it, like the white Europeans decided they'd discovered America and just moved in and took it over like they were entitled to it, never mind that five hundred nations already lived and worshipped in America, or the Land between the Great Waters, they just moved in and said they had God on their side and the Indians weren't much anyway but a few of them could work for them sometimes if they behaved themselves, and the rest were lined up for disposal.

Maybe I'm uncomfortable extolling white culture especially if it replaces other folks' culture, like prayer in the schools and boarding schools for Indian children and English Only and the Ku Klux Klan. It seems to me that too much of white culture is built on stamping out culture that isn't white, or culture that isn't white enough, or even culture that just doesn't happen to be the correct brand or shade of white.

No, I'm not ashamed of being white. But I sure am ashamed of what being white can mean to some folks who *are* proud of being white. And I'm ashamed of what it can mean to be white when that whiteness can so easily be used to hurt people who aren't white. I definitely *am* ashamed of that part of whiteness. Because in America, whiteness means being dominant, and it stands to reason that if somebody's dominant, somebody else is down. It's delightful to be able to mindlessly enjoy "white" culture. But is it really white? Or did white folks just apply the Discovery Doctrine like the white Europeans did when they took over this continent? And did somebody else or at least their culture get stamped out in the bargain one more time?

If one is going to get all sentimental over being white, be careful. With your white privilege, there ought to be one or two white responsibilities. Like, take the cleats off. They're in your genes. I realize it's tough having to be responsible about your whiteness. But blacks and Indians and Asians have to handle their own racial and ethnic selves with some level of awareness whites are not used to, even when they're celebrating who they are. When they celebrate ethnicity, they still have to be aware of themselves in the context of a larger society that is just not like them, and it won't hurt to become aware of ourselves in the context of all people, not just white ones. Whiteness is only one possible part—your part—of the greater wonder of being alive in this world. Make that awareness part of your celebration.

And make a point of seeing what you can find in your family's heritage and traditions that goes beyond the color of your skin. How did your parents meet? How did your grandparents meet? Anybody in your family come to America in steerage? Or chains?

9

Growing Up (What) in America?

JERALD N. MARRS

I'm Mr. Green Christmas, I'm Mr. Sun,
I'm Mr. Heat Blister, I'm Mr. Hundred-and-one,
They call me Heat Miser, Whatever I touch,
Starts to melt in my clutch, I'm too much.
  Mr. Heat Miser
  "The Year Without a Santa Claus" (1974)

Do you recognize these lyrics? Can you hum them to yourself and include the next verse about Mr. Cold Miser? Are these words part of your culture?

These are the words that first triggered a realization in my life. A realization that no matter how hard I try, I can't stop being white. I can't undo my *culture*. And I have tried hard to do just that. But what does this mean? What does this make me?

I grew up white. Born in Utah, raised in New Mexico and Colorado. Graduated from a white/middle-class high school near Denver, and then went out into the world to discover life. In the process I moved to California, joined the air force, went to six colleges, and finally graduated from Berkeley with a degree in anthropology. The years after my graduation from high school were spent learning about and exploring other cultures.

I studied the Salmon Indians of the Northwest, the Nuer of Africa, the Ecstatics of Morocco. I became a Vietnamese linguist for the U.S. Air Force, and was immersed in their culture while I learned the language at the Defense Language Institute. I was transferred to Japan, where I refused to live on base because it seemed ludicrous to isolate myself when I could experience the country itself. While there, I married my wife, a Chinese-American woman I'd met while working in California.

I studied different religions, including the Taoist, Buddhist, and Baptist, and took another look at my own religion, Episcopalian.

I did all this in a quest to discover who I was and who I wanted to be. I was looking for a culture, a set of ideals and beliefs, something to cling to in a world where I was positive it was bad to be "white." Then, I returned to Colorado to attend law school in Boulder. And suddenly I was once again immersed in white America. While living in white America, I realized something: I am white; I cannot change it; in fact, I kind of enjoy it.

This realization began to set in during my first Christmas back in Colorado, while I was in my first year of law school. My wife and I had some friends over for dinner. He is a

Latino from Venezuela, she a blue-eyed blond from Wisconsin. We began discussing the Christmas specials that were coming on, and one of my favorites flashed back. The song hit me and I started singing:

I'm Mr. Green Christmas, I'm Mr. Sun,
I'm Mr. Heat Blister, I'm Mr. Hundred-and-one.

My wife and my friend from Venezuela just stared at me, but my friend from Wisconsin joined in. We had something in common from our past, and, as I later realized, we shared a culture.

I had never been able to see—or really consider—the culture of whites because I was always a part of it. A cultural analogy I've heard used in anthropology holds that when you are standing in a line trying to analyze it, it's very hard to do because you're a part of the line. When you step out of the line, however, you can look back in on it and see the dynamics that are affecting and shaping the actions of the people that are in the line. I hadn't realized it, but because I had looked so hard at other cultures (lines) for the past nine years, I had stepped out of *my* white American line. Therefore, when I found myself back in the line it came as a big shock: I suddenly realized I was white.

Here I was, white. I was standing in this line looking out at all the other lines around me. I have something in common with those who are in line with me. I may be standing in the express, cash-only, nine-item line, yet I'm able to see the people standing next to me in the twelve-item, check-okay line of which I am not a part. And of course, in this cultural supermarket once you're in line you're stuck. There is nowhere else to go. Likewise, the folks in the other line are stuck. We are all in line looking at the other lines around us, but we are not able truly to understand the other lines because we can never be a part of them.

I have tried to get in the other lines. I have gotten my cart and filled it with different languages, foods, ideas, beliefs, and so on. But I have never been able to figure out why the carts in this line have these certain foods. I can imitate, but never understand, the cultural forces that drive people in other lines to fill their carts with the items they do. Likewise, I can never understand what mental images and urges are conjured up by the items in the carts. Granted, I've gotten fairly good at predicting what may be in some of the carts, but I have never been able to *feel why* the items are there.

But this is not such a bad thing. I think the mysteries that surround the carts in the other lines are what make other cultures so intriguing. If I could understand the other lines, what would be the point of studying them?

Underlying all this is the simple realization that we are all standing in a line, filling our carts with all our cultural goodies and paying for them by the culturally appropriate means. But this doesn't mean that any one line is more important or dominant than any other line. What it means is that every line is full of mysteries, pleasures, and the occasional hemorrhoidal cure. But to judge one line based on another is ludicrous. What we need to realize is that the line we are in is special, but no more so than any other. I realized I was standing in a particular line when I started singing my little song. What makes you realize you are standing in line? Is it an old Bogart movie, a familiar story, a nursery rhyme? Stop. Look at and listen to your line. What does it tell you? Who are you?

Now, look at the other lines. Aren't they just as amazing as yours?

10

White Images of Black Slaves (Is What We See in Others Sometimes a Reflection of What We Find in Ourselves?)

GEORGE FREDRICKSON

In his provocative study of American slavery, Stanley Elkins provides a vivid description of the black slave as he was usually represented in antebellum southern lore:

> Sambo, the typical plantation slave, was docile but irresponsible, loyal but lazy, humble but chronically given to lying and stealing; his behavior was full of infantile silliness and his talk inflated with childish exaggeration. His relationship with his master was one of utter dependence and childlike attachment: it was indeed this childlike quality that was the very key to his being. Although the merest hint of Sambo's "manhood" might fill the Southern breast with scorn "the child in his place" could be both exasperating and loveable.[1]

No one has seriously denied that this image existed. But Elkins provoked a massive controversy, first by arguing that such a conception of the slave personality was a uniquely North American phenomenon—that Sambo would have been inconceivable in other New World slave societies—and second by advancing the bold hypothesis that Sambo was not a "mere stereotype" but an image that accurately reflected a dominant personality type among southern slaves. To sustain the second proposition, Elkins introduced his provocative concentration camp analogy to demonstrate the possibility of adult infantilization in "closed systems" where inmates or slaves were subjected to the absolute authority of guards or masters.[2]

Criticism of the Elkins thesis has proceeded along several lines, but it has been, primarily, devoted to establishing that Sambo was in fact a "mere stereotype," that actual slave behavior and psychology did not conform to the image. Some of this criticism was beside the point; for Elkins did not argue, as some of his critics seemed to suggest, that all slaves were Sambos, only that the Sambo type was a frequent and logical outcome of the plantation regime. Some of this criticism was patently ideological and ahistorical: since Sambo could not be a source of pride to blacks in the 1960s, he could not have existed in the 1850s. But the controversy helped provoke an intensive examination of plantation society, patterns of slave behavior, and black self-images as revealed in the narratives and autobiographies of exslaves.[3] The result of all this scholarship has been to suggest that there *were* real Sambos, but that they constituted a distinct minority among a variety of plantation types. As alternatives to Sambo, John Blassingame discovered "Jack" and "Nat." "Jack," he writes, "worked faithfully as long as he was well treated. Sometimes sullen and uncooperative, he generally refused to be driven beyond the place he set for himself. . . . Although often proud, stubborn, and conscious of the wrongs he suffered, Jack tried to repress his anger. His patience was, however, not unlimited."[4] "Nat," of course, was Nat Turner, the out-and-out rebel and source of recurring fears among whites that their slaves might rise up at any time and cut their throats. Other historians have suggested that slaves, like inmates of some modern "total institutions," were adept at role playing and could shift from one pattern of behavior to another depending on which strategy would yield the greatest personal satisfaction.[5]

All the interpretations that stress the variability of the slave personality are premised on a conception of the plantation that would make it sufficiently *unlike* a concentration camp to provide the slaves with considerable room to maneuver, to develop their own cultural standards and sense of justice, and hence to assert themselves in various ways incompatible with the Sambo image.[6]

The image is, after all, a "mere stereotype," based like most stereotypes on a kernel of truth but, in its totality and coerciveness, a distortion of reality. But stereotypes themselves are important historical phenomena. If they tell us little that is reliable about the objects of such conceptions, they may reveal a great deal about those who hold them. And they *can* be used for comparative study. If different slave societies did indeed project differing public conceptions of the nature and character of their slaves, this might tell us something about the varying ways that social, cultural, or ideological circumstances could shape what Eugene Genovese calls "the world the slaveholders made."[7]

It has also been argued that Sambo was not a uniquely North American stereotype but has existed in all slave societies. "On close inspection," Genovese has written, "the Sambo personality has been neither more nor less than the slavish personality; wherever slavery has existed Sambo has also." He then goes on to quote David Brion Davis in support of his contention. "Throughout history," according to Davis, it has been said that slaves, although occasionally as loyal and faithful as good dogs, were for the most part lazy, irresponsible, cunning, rebellious, untrustworthy, and sexually promiscuous."[8] If Genovese and Davis are correct, the Sambo image is of no use for comparative analysis; it is simply a universal epiphenomenon of the master-slave situation.

This argument is persuasive if one includes, as Davis does, enough "slavish" characteristics in the image. But look at the way contradictory elements are treated in his formulation: "Occasionally" slaves are seen as "loyal and faithful," but "for the most part," they are "rebellious" and "untrustworthy." Then recall Elkins's stress on "docility" and "utter dependence" as characteristics of the Sambo type. For Elkins the emphasis would appear to be reversed: North American slaves "for the most part" were seen as "docile and loyal" and only occasionally regarded as "rebellious." If "childishness" in some very general sense is universally attributed to slaves, one might still want to distinguish between the docile child and the rebellious child. And in the Americas the rebellious child often ceased to be a child at all and became for anxious whites a bloodthirsty savage who could be controlled only by brute force. What was truly universal about the black slave stereotype was its inherently dichotomous or contradictory nature. This essential duality is particularly well described in Philip Curtin's account of planter ambivalence in Jamaica: "The attitude of the master toward the slave," he writes, ". . . was a combination of fear on the one hand, leading to the picture of the slave as the lazy savage and murdering brute, and a desire to justify the institution on the other, leading to the picture of the happy Negro, harmless but fitted only for his life of hard work."[9] The latter "picture" is instantly recognizable as Sambo, or "Quashee" as he was called in British West Indies, but the former is something quite different. As Curtin makes clear, situational factors and ideological pressures tended to dictate which of the two images—"the happy Negro" or the dangerous savage—would be at the forefront of the slaveholder's consciousness.

Comparative historians of American slavery should be on the lookout, therefore, not for absolute differences in slave stereotypes, but for differences in emphasis. If a slave society stresses one side of the universal polarity in a peculiarly insistent way, this stress might provide a clue to some of the special circumstances surrounding slavery in that society.

In his review of black literary stereotypes in two cultures, Carl Degler has concluded in effect that the Sambo image has been much less pervasive in Brazil than in the United States: "In the literature of Brazil . . . , the person of color appears in all garbs and stations. He is the faithful as well as the rebellious slave; he is the irresponsible *moleque* and the highly educated urban sophisticate; the person of color appears also as the carnal beast and self-sacrificing mother. Such a wide range cannot be duplicated in North American literature."[10] If we limit our attention more precisely to the image of the Negro as slave in nineteenth-century American literature, we find that in the overwhelming majority of cases the black is represented precisely as described by Elkins as the "happy Negro" or "Sambo."[11]

But the Sambo of plantation romances or minstrel shows does not exhaust the white American conception of the black slave. Here, as elsewhere, the stereotype was an unstable compound of opposites. As Blassingame has shown, whites were forced to acknowledge Nat as well as Sambo. According to Ronald Takaki, southern whites wanted to believe that the slave was a Sambo or "happy child," but feared that he might under some circumstances turn into a murderous savage.[12] Elsewhere, I myself have discussed the role of the savage side of the stereotype in antebellum southern racial ideology. Apologists for slavery who stressed racist conceptions of the black character as justifying the institution usually made it clear that loyalty and docility were not inevitable African characteristics, but rather an artificial creation of absolute white dominance and control. Weaken the bonds of servitude, they frequently argued, and the black slave would revert to type as a bloodthirsty brute.[13] Approaching the question from a different angle, Winthrop Jordan has suggested that "the happy Negro" image was a relatively late development in white racial imagery. "Nothing would have surprised [Americans of the revolutionary era] more," he contends, "than to learn that later generations spoke knowingly of the contented slave. . . . " Since black slaves, like all human beings, were thought to "crave liberty," revolt was to be expected. It was the natural result of an "appetite for freedom," "nonetheless real for being unwelcome."[14]

When all this has been said, however, it remains true that Sambo was the predominant white southern image of the securely enslaved Negro, at least in the period from 1830 to 1860, and that it was exceptional for a slave society to stress this side of child-savage duality so insistently. What remains to be explored is the role that the stereotype played and what light, if any, its career sheds on the special nature or situation of North American slavery during this period.

Perhaps the best way to begin such an exploration is to draw directly on the work of social psychologists concerned with racial and ethnic stereotypes in our own times. According to Gordon Allport, a stereotype is an "exaggerated belief associated with a category. Its function is to justify (rationalize) our conduct in relation to that category." It is the rationalizing role of a stereotype that allows it to be, in some cases, "inherently contradictory." "The fact that prejudiced people so readily subscribe to self-contradictory stereotypes is one proof that genuine group traits are not the point at issue. The point at issue is rather that a dislike requires justification, and that any justification that fits the immediate conversational circumstances will do."[15] As Earl Raab and Seymour Martin Lipset point out, however, a stereotype is not the same as a prejudiced attitude. It is a mistake to see a one-to-one correlation between hostility against a group and stereotypical conception of its members: for "it is possible for an individual to have the stereotype without the hostility, or the hostility without the stereotype."[16] Also, the same stereotype can be applied to two different groups without reflecting the same attitudes. If a stereotype is not an accurate index of feeling, neither is it a sure guide to behavior. Depending on the immediate situation or "frame of reference," an individual holding a stereotyped conception of the members of another group may act in ways that are inconsistent with his beliefs, without necessarily changing the beliefs themselves.[17]

A widely held and publicly sanctioned stereotype, such as Sambo, can therefore be seen as a social and ideological "norm," reflecting what Herbert Blumer has called a "sense of group position."[18] It legitimizes the status of one group relative to another, but becomes the vehicle for overt and active hostility only when the subordinate group is seen as getting out of "its place." It seems compatible with these conceptions to suggest that a shift in the emphasis given to various and sometimes contradictory elements in the stereotype would reflect changing perceptions of the threat posed by the subordinate or minority group. Hence both the emotive and cognitive content of the stereotype would vary over time and from place to place in response to historical circumstances. The only thing that a historian might want to add to this body of theory is a greater recognition of the extent to which the evolution of this dominant group's cultural values might require an adjustment of the traits assigned to a subordinate group.

On the most obvious level, the Sambo stereotype was a direct rationalization of slavery. If slaves could be regarded as contented and naturally servile, their enslavement could more easily be justified. It follows from this elemental perception that the Sambo image would tend to be especially prominent when a slaveholding group found itself the object of sustained and uncompromising criticism and hence had a particularly strong need to defend or justify its labor system. Such was obviously the case in the American South after the rise of militant northern abolitionism in the 1830s.

The stereotype, however, would not predetermine how masters interacted with individual slaves on their plantations. It was in fact a matter of practical necessity for slaveholders to recognize a variety of types. In a slave inventory of 1849, for example, one of course finds the "good Negro," but also such others as the "runaway no account," the "good hand but tricky," the "African king no account," the "bad Negro," the "very bad woman, great temper," and the "mischief maker, all talk."[19] The official stereotype could exert only a very limited effect on day-to-day plantation attitudes and practices. A recalcitrant or disobedient slave would normally be treated with greater hostility than if he or she were simply a wayward child and might in fact be brutally beaten or sold to a trader. On the other hand, a slave who was not only loyal but skilled and resourceful in caring for the master's interests was likely to be treated with greater *respect* than the stereotype would permit. Furthermore, even when they were talking of blacks in general and not of individual slaves, planters were quite capable of contradicting themselves to "fit the immediate conversational situation." James S. Buckingham, an English traveler of the 1830s, noted that when masters "spoke of coercion employed toward the negroes, and endeavored to justify the necessity of it, they [the slaves] were represented as [an] 'indolent worthless and ungrateful race' . . . and so ungrateful for favors received that the better they were treated the worse they behaved." But when it was suggested that their characters might be improved, it was argued that "they were perfectly contented with their condition, and on the whole a much better race without education than with, as they were now faithful, kind-hearted and attached to their masters, whereas education would destroy all their natural virtues, and make them as vicious as the lower orders in other countries."[20]

It should be recalled that the massive campaign of southern opinion-makers to promote the image of the happy and docile slave, and to repress any contrary conceptions, was only just beginning in the 1830s. By the end of the antebellum period, planters were likely to be somewhat more consistent, at least when confronting inquisitive travelers. Contradictions remained, but they were more often between theory and practice than in the discourse itself. In 1861, for example, another British traveler—the journalist William Howard Russell—could give the following account of planter attitudes toward slave rebelliousness: "No planter hereabouts has any dread of his slaves, but I have seen, within the short time I have been in this part of the world, several dreadful accounts of murder and violence, in which masters suffered at the hands of their slaves. There is something suspicious in the never-ending statement that 'we are not afraid of our slaves.' The curfew and night patrol in the streets, the prisons and watchhouses, and the police regulations, prove that strict supervision, at all events, is needed and necessary."[21] When directly questioned on their elaborate security measures, late antebellum slaveholders were likely to point to the danger of Yankee abolitionists, meddling with their slaves and putting alien ideas into their simple heads rather than to any innate intractability that would conflict with the Sambo image.

It would simplify matters too much, however, to account for the heavy stress on slave docility and loyalty in the period 1830–1860 solely in terms of a polemical counterattack against the northern antislavery movement. First, a group stereotype, or a special variation of a group stereotype, usually has some factual grounding, although what the facts really mean may be distorted or misinterpreted. To support their image of the slave, southerners could point, first of all, to the absence of any large-scale revolts after the Nat Turner uprising of 1831. But the explanation provided—the natural docility of the black slave—ignored the growing pattern of repression and the inherent difficulty of successful slave resistance in a society where a majority of the total population were free whites. Second, there was the changing character of the slave population. The official closing of the external slave trade in 1808 meant that by the 1830s most North American slaves had been born and raised in the United States. Evidence from other New World slave societies suggests that creole slaves were less likely to be openly rebellious than those brought directly from Africa.[22] The preponderance of creole slaves also allowed for some softening of the earlier image of the African savage, although, as we have seen, the nightmare of the rampaging brute continued to trouble the sleep of anxious slaveholders and was openly invoked by proslavery advocates to dramatize the alleged horrors of emancipation. Finally, most historians of slavery now agree that the antebellum period saw a general improvement in the material conditions of southern slaves, as reflected most dramatically in an average life expectancy that by 1850 compared favorably with that of many free white populations in the nineteenth century. These advances were limited to what E. P. Thompson has called "standard of life" as opposed to "way of life" and were accompanied by parallel efforts to restrict manumission and to repress the growth of a semiautonomous black culture and community; but they could give plausibility to the claim that slaves *ought* to be contented with their lot because they were physically well-off in comparison with slave or other dependent groups elsewhere in the world.[23]

Since this was the great age of Anglo-American humanitarianism, it was particularly important for southerners to be able to claim with some degree of conviction that they were fulfilling their humane obligation toward the inherently weak and childlike by taking good care of their slaves. That a childlike Sambo figure would be an object of special humanitarianism or sentimental concern—in much the same way that orphans, idiots, or even dumb animals were by the mid–nineteenth century—did create some problems for proslavery adherents. Abolitionists could use a similar slave stereotype and land telling blows by pointing to well-documented examples of the cruel usage and sexual exploitation of these allegedly simple and harmless creatures.[24] But if Sambo gave an opening for the abolitionists to touch on some sore points, it did not do so in a way that called into question the South's commitment to slavery itself. If Sambo did not revert to savagery when emancipated, if indeed he simply remained a helpless dependent, then it could be argued that he would die out because of his inability to support himself without a master. Many of those who contended that slavery was "a positive good," admitted at least privately that there were abuses in the South's particular form of slavery; and there was in fact a reform movement of sorts to make some humanitarian adjustment in the slave codes, such as prohibiting the breakup of families and removing barriers to religious education.[25] But these concerns and initiatives did not call slavery itself into question; the institution must be retained, so the oft-repeated reasoning went, because blacks were not ready for freedom and hence their liberation would be an act of cruelty.

It seems safe to conclude, therefore, that the Sambo stereotype arose in the first instance from a process of rationalization, but there was a supporting framework of circumstantial evidence and current cultural values that could make it seem genuinely persuasive. The stereotype did not rule out inconsistencies and did not predetermine day-to-day behavior. Stereotypes do not in fact function in that way. But its existence as a social and ideological norm does reflect the peculiar character of antebellum southern slavery. Nowhere else did a prosperous and expansive slavocracy come under such sustained and unqualified attack from antislavery forces and feel such pressure to develop self-justifying images and ideologies. Nowhere else did the same combination of factors—advanced creolization of the slave population, generally effective slave control, and improvement in the material conditions of slaves—lend such circumstantial support to the image of "the happy Negro."

Yet there is another side to the question that has to be confronted. As the work of Herbert Blumer has suggested, a relatively benign group stereotype is likely to be recast or reinterpreted when a dominant group perceives a genuine and immediate threat to its "sense of position." In such circumstances active racial hostility comes to the fore.[26] There is reason to believe that the other side of the child-savage duality—the Negrophobic image of the black savage turned loose on white society—actually inspired the more militant assertions of southern nationalism and secessionism. As Steven Channing's study of secession in South Carolina makes clear, John Brown's raid of 1859 and the election of Lincoln in 1860 were viewed in parts of the lower South as opening salvos in an open northern war against "the group position" of southern whites. The reaction to these provocations tended to arouse the deeply seated racial fears that the Sambo image had helped to repress. The resulting panic or "crisis of fear" provided the spark for an active bid for southern independence.[27] This seemingly paradoxical development makes sense if we recall that Sambo was the image of the black slave and not of the Negro under all circumstances. If Sambo was more prevalent as a slave stereotype in the southern United States than elsewhere, so also was the image of the freedman as a savage brute. When the fear of emancipation reached panic proportions, the savage side of the dual black image tended to re-emerge with dramatic suddenness. The key to understanding the larger history of white supremacist imagery in the United States, both during slavery and afterwards, is this sharp and recurring contrast between "the good Negro" *in his place* and the vicious black *out of it*.[28]

Notes

1. Stanley M. Elkins, *Slavery: A Problem in American Institutional and Intellectual Life*, 2nd ed. (Chicago, 1968), 82.

2. Ibid., 81–139.

3. John W. Blassingame, *The Slave Community: Plantation Life in the Antebellum South* (New York, 1972); George M. Fredrickson and Christopher Lasch, "Resistance to Slavery," *Civil War History* 13 (December 1967): 315–29; Eugene D. Genovese, *Roll, Jordan, Roll: The World the Slaves Made* (New York, 1974); Leslie H. Owens, *This Species of Property: Slave Life and Culture in the Old South* (New York, 1976); George P. Rawick, *The American Slaves: A Composite Autobiography*, 19 vols. (Westport, Conn., 1972), vol. 1.

4. Blassingame, *The Slave Community*, 133–34.

5. See Fredrickson and Lasch, "Resistance to Slavery."

6. Ann J. Lane, *The Debate Over Slavery: Stanley Elkins and His Critics* (Urbana, Ill., 1971).

7. Eugene D. Genovese, *The World the Slaveholders Made: Two Essays in Interpretation* (New York, 1969).

8. Eugene D. Genovese, *In Red and Black: Marxian Explorations of Southern and Afro-American History* (New York, 1971), 77–78; David Brion Davis, *The Problem of Slavery in Western Culture* (Ithaca, N.Y., 1966), 59–60.

9. Philip D. Curtin, *Two Jamaicas: The Role of Ideas in a Tropical Colony, 1830–1865* (Cambridge, 1955), 40.

10. Carl N. Degler, *Neither Black nor White: Slavery and Race Relations in Brazil and the United States* (New York, 1971), 13.

11. John H. Nelson, *The Negro Character in American Literature* (Lawrence, Kans., 1926); William R. Taylor, *Cavalier and Yankee: The Old South and American National Character* (New York, 1961), 299–313.

12. Ronald Takaki, "The Black Child-Savage in Antebellum American," in G.B. Nash and R. Weiss, eds., *The Great Fear: Race in the Mind of America* (New York, 1970), 39.

13. George M. Fredrickson, *The Black Image in the White Mind: The Debate on Afro-American Character and Destiny, 1817–1914* (Middletown, Conn., 1987), 52–55.

14. Winthrop D. Jordan, *White Over Black: American Attitudes Toward the Negro, 1550–1812* (Chapel Hill, N.C., 1968), 388–89.

15. Gordon W. Allport, *The Nature of Prejudice*, abridged ed. (Garden City, N.Y., 1968), 187, 190, 191.

16. Earl Raab and Seymour Martin Lipset, "The Prejudicial Society," in Earl Raab, ed., *American Race Relations Today: Studies of the Problems Beyond Desegregation* (Garden City, N.Y., 1962), 30.

17. Ibid., 30–34.

18. Herbert Blumer, "Race Prejudice as a Sense of Group Position," *Pacific Sociological Review* 1

(Spring 1958): 307; William J. Wilson, *Power, Racism and Privilege: Race Relations in Theoretical and Sociohistorical Perspectives* (New York, 1973), 36–37.

19. Willie Lee Rose, *A Documentary History of Slavery in North Amercia* (New York, 1976), 338–43.

20. Quoted in Owens, *This Species of Property*, 215.

21. W. H. Russell, *My Diary North and South* (Boston, 1863), 131–32.

22. Degler, *Neither Black nor White*, 52–60.

23. Robert W. Fogel and Stanley L. Engerman, *Time on the Cross: The Economics of American Negro Slavery* (Boston, 1974), vol. 1, 125–26; Genovese, *Roll, Jordon, Roll*, 53–68; E. P. Thompson, *The Making of the English Working Class* (New York, 1963), 211.

24. Taylor, *Cavalier and Yankee*, 304–11.

25. Genovese, *In Red and Black*, 49–66, 69–70.

26. Blumer, "Race Prejudice as a Sense of Group Position"; Wilson, *Power, Racism and Privilege*, 35–37.

27. Steven A. Channing, *Crisis of Fear: Secession in South Carolina* (New York, 1970).

28. See Fredrickson, *Black Image in the White Mind*.

Synopses of Other Important Works

Whiteness as Property: Cheryl Harris

In a long, groundbreaking law review article (106 *Harvard Law Review* 1707), Chicago-Kent law professor Cheryl Harris investigates the relationship between race and property. "Whiteness as Property," published in 1993, examines how whiteness, which began as a form of racial identity, evolved into a property interest for those who were able to bring themselves under its definition. Professor Harris shows how the origins of whiteness as a property interest lie in systems of domination by whites of colored peoples, principally Native Americans and blacks. Then, over time, whiteness became a sort of asset, like a ranch or money in the bank. Whiteness and property have a common quality or premise, namely, the right to exclude. These features enabled white identity to become the basis of a system of privilege that allocates social benefits, one that in turn became legitimated in law as a kind of status property.

The law never repudiated this property-like quality of whiteness, but merely transformed it in cases like *Plessy* and *Brown*. Moreover, recent affirmative action cases mask the privileging of whiteness in the guise of enshrining the current situation as a neutral baseline. Professor Harris argues that focusing on distortions created by the implicit equation of property and whiteness helps us understand civil rights progress and regression. It also helps us understand what is at stake when we categorize by race. Finally, it opens alternative perspectives on the affirmative action debate.

From the Editors: Issues and Comments

If you are white, how do *you* see your own race? Since you are reading this book, presumably you have an interest in what it means to be white. What is your concept of whiteness: A race? An ethnic group? An interest group? If you are white, do you identify more as white, or as a member of a subgroup, such as Italian, Jewish, or Teutonic? Which one of the many views of whiteness set out in this part comes closest to yours? If you are nonwhite (e.g., black or Chicano), how do *you* see whiteness? Do you think most white people see themselves that way?

Do you agree with Cheryl Harris that whiteness is a kind of property, or asset, that has almost a monetary worth? Suppose that one day you, a white person, receive a phone call from a representative of the government advising you that a terrible mistake had been made: You were supposed to have been born black. It will now be necessary to rectify that mistake—a painless operation will be performed, at no expense to you, that will transform you into an African-American. The government is prepared, however, to compensate you for its mistake. How much would you want? Professor Andrew Hacker reports that he has asked this very question of his classes over the years and that the answers given have remained stable—one million dollars a year. (See Andrew Hacker, *Two Nations*, cited in full in the selected readings for Part I.)

Suggested Readings

Aleinikoff, T. Alexander, *A Case for Race-Consciousness*, 91 COLUM. L. REV. 1060 (1991).

Appiah, Anthony, *The Conservation of "Race,"* 23 BLACK AM. LIT. F. 36 (1989).

Bonnett, Alastair, *"White Studies": The Problems and Projects of a New Research Agenda*, 13 THEORY, CULTURE AND SOCIETY 145 (1996).

Citron, Abraham, THE "RIGHTNESS OF WHITENESS": THE WORLD OF THE WHITE CHILD IN A SEGREGATED SOCIETY (1971).

Delgado, Richard, *The Imperial Scholar: Reflections on a Review of Civil Rights Literature*, 132 U. PA. L. REV. 561 (1984).

Dudziak, Mary L., *Desegregation as a Cold War Imperative*, 41 STAN. L. REV. 61 (1988).

Fredrickson, George, WHITE SUPREMACY: A COMPARATIVE STUDY IN AMERICAN AND SOUTH AFRICAN HISTORY (1981).

Hacker, Andrew, TWO NATIONS: BLACK AND WHITE, SEPARATE, HOSTILE, UNEQUAL (1992).

IMPACTS OF RACISM ON WHITE AMERICANS (B. Bowser and R. Hunt, eds., 1981).

Stowe, David W., *Uncolored People: The Rise of Whiteness Studies*, LINGUA FRANCA, Sept./Oct. 1996: 68–77.

Warren, Donald I., *White Americans as a Minority*, TELOS, Summer 1995: 127.

Part II

How Whites See Others

Can one see, or even understand the idea of, another race without juxtaposing it immediately against oneself and one's own group? That is, is race inevitably an oppositional concept, so that one can only think of another group in contradistinction to one's own? And need that oppositionality be hostile or adverse, as opposed to friendly? The selections in this part suggest that in this country, at least, the white majority has generally seen members of other races, for want of a better term, as one-down. In few quarters has race seemed not to matter, much less not exist. Several authors assert that racial fairness and equality are either impossible—because of what is embedded in our culture or language—or only achieved through great effort. Some argue that difference is never neutral, but contrived—created and maintained for the advantage of the more powerful majority. Some consider race consciousness a predisposing condition for the disease of racism. One argues that racial differentiation is rational and that it is allied with the scientific impulse.

Is it possible, if one is white, to see persons of other racial groups without the blinders of race and racial categorization? Would this entail having no race at all, and is that possible in our world?

11

The White Race Is Shrinking: Perceptions of Race in Canada and Some Speculations on the Political Economy of Race Classification

DOUG DANIELS

For many years I have been teaching a sociology class on 'Minorities and Ethnic Group Relations' at the University of Regina, Canada, where the ethnic make-up of the student body is quite unremarkable. As on so many campuses in North America, our student body is almost exclusively 'white' in the sense that most come from British and East European families. We have a smattering of students from abroad (mainly Hong Kong) and a very few Canadian Indian and Metis students. In addition, our population is inundated with the usual US television programs, magazines, and university texts, so our perceptions of race are very much influenced by the culture of 'middle America.'

In the early 1970s I found unexpected resistance whenever I would attempt to make a critique of pseudo-scientific race classification. I found that the students were quite a bit more stingy than I in the number of nationalities that they considered 'white.' Let me give two examples. When my lectures were dealing with the problems of perception of skin colour, like the well-known phenomenon in Brazil where 'money whitens' people's perceptions of race and class, I also got into the problem of borderline cases. Why, I asked, should we have ideal types only for black and white 'races' (negroid and caucasoid) when in-between areas like Turkey and Morocco could just as well serve as a light brown ideal type?

To my surprise, some of the students countered that the Turks, whatever else they might be, were certainly not white. I was taken aback by the certitude—even the vehemence—of the assertion. The next fall, when I was discussing the 1973 CIA coup against the Allende government in Chile, I pointed out that Chile had had a long history of stability in government that surpassed many European countries. One of my students interjected that he had no idea that Chileans were 'white' people! I was flabbergasted by this whole train of thought. So I decided to find out what was going on and devised the following, rather informal, questionnaire. It is a list of countries and/or nationalities, and I introduced it something like this:

'I'm going to read you a list of names of different nationalities. I want you to tell me whether you think they are "white" people or not. Don't stop and think about it—I don't

4 ERS 352 (July 1981). Originally published in *Ethnic and Racial Studies*. Reprinted by permission of Routledge, a division of Routledge, Chapman & Hall Ltd.

want your scientific opinion but just what we absorb from our popular culture. Just pretend you're on a psychologist's couch doing word associations and answer as quickly as possible.'

In the past eight years the results have been consistent in a way that is scientifically pleasing but politically puzzling.

Here is the list, together with the normal results:

'Who is white?'

List of nationalities

Swedes	Yes
Congolese	No
Canadians	Yes
Icelanders	Yes
Spaniards	Slow yes, or some nos
Belgians	Yes
Dutch	Yes
Turks	No (very rare yes)
Germans	Yes
Algerians	No
English	Yes
Welsh	Yes
Cubans	No
Danes	Yes
Israelis	Yes (an occasional no)
Chileans	No (very few 'yes' replies)
Ugandans	No
Scots	Yes
Americans	Yes
Japanese	No (a very occasional yes)
Swiss	Yes
Portuguese	hesitation, half of class unsure, most of remainder say 'no'
Poles	Yes
Russians	Yes
Mexicans	90% no, 10% yes
Arabs	No
Argentinians	80% no, 20% yes
Finns	Yes
Bulgarians	30% yes, 70% don't know
Norwegians	Yes
Italians	hesitation, 50% yes, 50% no
Chinese	No
Moroccans	80% no, 20% yes
Egyptians	60% no, 20% yes, rest undecided
Iranians	No (100%)
Greeks	Yes (after some hesitation)
Vietnamese	No
Québecois	Laughter
Ukrainians	(Laughter) Yes

The only variability that I could detect in the results was that classes that were politically more liberal tended to be more 'generous' with the white appellation. Other than that I was taken aback to find virtually identical results every time I gave the test.

So apparently the 'white race' is shrinking from my memory of what it was supposed to be. Spain and Portugal, the protectors of Christian civilization against the Moorish infidels, and the missionaries of Latin America, are no longer really 'white.' Fallen too, or at least sullied, are the great cradles of Western civilization, Greece and Italy. Iran, despite being the home of Blumenbach's famous 'Caucasoid,' and despite all Shah Pahlavi's prattle about Iran's Aryan ancestry and the 'Great White Throne,' is definitely out! So are the Arabs— all of them—though Israel gets the nod. One might guess that the perception of Israel is affected by the infusion of European immigration, but that doesn't seem to help Argentina much, the most 'European' of countries in South America. Chile and Cuba are out, and multi-racial situations like the USA and Canada are resolved in favour of the dominant ('white') population. An exotic, socialist country like Bulgaria often draws a blank. And finally the occasional student will call the Japanese 'white' and most classes start chuckling when I ask their opinion on Québecois, the 'white niggers of North America,' or Ukrainians, the arrivistes of the Canadian prairie's cycle of immigration and upward mobility.

So how does this all boil down? To me it is abundantly clear that melanin content—strict biological skin colour—has very little to do with the verdict on the great mass of light brown, in-between people who reside around the Mediterranean and from the Rio Grande to Tierra del Fuego. To be labelled a 'white' nation it is at least as important to be a member of NATO or another pro-Western alliance, politically stable, wealthy and industrialized. Anti-Western, poor, politically unstable (especially revolutionary) and non-industrial countries tend to be excluded from the white race of the 1980s. However one may quibble with the 'tightness of my experimental design,' the pattern is unmistakable.

So if the popular perception of who belongs to the white race is shrinking along with Western imperialism, perhaps we can posit some other hypotheses. In the late nineteenth and early twentieth centuries it is my impression that one reads a lot more about the 'British Race,' the German, French, Italian and other *national* 'races,' than one hears about the 'white race' as a whole. Is it too mechanical to suggest that the white race as a popular concept did not fully develop until after World War I and the consolidation of European imperialism under Britain, then the USA? Perhaps one can trace the history of the 'Aryans' from Gobineau's multinational European aristocracy, through the nationalisms of Vachers de LaPouge, H. S. Chamberlain and Hitler as a reflection of the growth and decline of the nation-state in capitalist development? This perspective on the political economy of race classification suggests that future racialists will have to have very fertile imaginations indeed. For if, as I am implying, whiteness or master race membership has been virtually synonymous with ruling class membership, then the new international class structure of the 'silicon age' will present the racist demagogue with far more complex paradoxes than the one Hitler solved, for example, by giving the Japanese status as honorary Aryans.

If future racist demagogues choose to go the exclusionist route that our quiz seems to indicate is already underway, then they must follow Hitler's scheme of paring down all candidates for whiteness to a select few 'pure' Aryans. This would result in a narrowing of political and military support by excluding important minorities in the imperial centres, such as blacks in the USA. Because such an exclusionist policy has built-in barriers to growth, future racists will more likely have to make some of the political compromises that Hitler was forced to, as when he declared the Japanese to be 'honorary Aryans.' Judging by some recent American movies, one might predict that pro-imperialist American blacks will be so promoted. The recent cinema hits like *The Deerhunter* and *Apocalypse Now* portray American whites and blacks as heroes united against the subhuman mongoloids.

For a new racism to meet the class realities of late empire it will have to include in the master race many people who are not now being thought of as white—people like the Marcoses of the Philippines, the Gandhis of India, the Houphouët-Boignys of Africa and the Pinochets of Chile. Perhaps future racists would be better off jumping back to Gobineau's tack. His post-feudal assertion that the crowned heads of all the countries of Europe were Aryan could be updated so that the modern master race would include the ruling classes of all the countries in the Western orbit. Remember that racists never have put a fine point on the science of the matter, so such stratagems may not be as far-fetched as they seem.

Consider that although the nineteenth-century racist theorist H. S. Chamberlain saw the bourgeois democratic revolution in France as a rising of the 'long suffering Germanic peoples,' almost every other racist portrays revolutions of all types as attempts by the inferior races to gain power. Socialism is seen by them as a plot by inferior races to mongrelize the superior. Racist theorists have thus used the ideology and class background of people to lighten or darken their perceived 'race' to a degree far beyond the limits of common sense, and have been doing this for centuries. So there is no reason for us to assume that racists need be any less extravagant in the future about such fantasies as an international master race. The force that will stifle the racists' imagination is the incredulity of an ever more sophisticated world population that has seen the fruits of racism.

12

Ignoble Savages

DINESH D'SOUZA

The Embarrassment of Primitivism

For the Europeans who first voyaged abroad, much of the rest of the world came as a shock for which they were poorly prepared. Early modern accounts, such as Richard Hakluyt's sixteenth century *Principal Navigations* or Samuel Purchas's seventeenth century *Purchas His Pilgrimage* and *Hakluytus Posthumus*, convey the stupefaction of the Europeans who encountered distant and unfamiliar peoples. Europeans who were even then making a transition into the modern era found themselves genuinely amazed and horrified at other cultures which appeared virtually static, confined from time immemorial in the nomadic or the agrarian stage. The consequence was that many Europeans viewed the nonwhite peoples of Africa, the Americas, and elsewhere as savages and barbarians, "beyond the pale of civilization," to borrow Metternich's phrase.

Significantly, it was the Portuguese who arrived on the shores of black Africa and not black Africans who voyaged to Europe. The Portuguese had the three-mast ship, the compass, the quadrant, the astrolabe, navigation charts, and a comparatively good knowledge of winds, currents, stars, and latitudes. The Portuguese knew, as did educated Europeans of the time, that the earth was not flat. When the Portuguese sailed abroad in the second half of the fifteenth century, they left an emerging modern European civilization which had almost a hundred universities; which had several hundred printing presses and some fifteen thousand book titles in circulation; which had cannons and body armor and gunpowder; which used modern business methods such as checks, bills of exchange, insurance, and double-entry bookkeeping; which had mechanical clocks and precision instruments; which had harnessed the power of wind and water to grind grain, crush ore, mash pulp for paper, saw lumber and marble, and pump water; which had built Gothic cathedrals. This technical head start would soon produce a very large gap between Europe and the rest of the world. The enormous European lead is suggested by just a few European inventions and technological advances of the period, a list which could be vastly multiplied: the microscope (1590), the telescope (1608), the barometer (1643), the pendulum clock (1656), the thermometer (1714), the spinning jenny (1770), the steam engine (1781), vaccination (1796), the electric battery (1800).

Essentially what happened, partly by historical accident, is that between the sixteenth and the nineteenth centuries, the most advanced civilization in the world crashed into the shores of sub-Saharan Africa and the Americas, two regions which were, by European standards, incomparably primitive. In many of the tribes of southern Africa and the Americas, the natives had no numbers that went beyond one or two. The Europeans, increasingly skeptical and rationalistic in their outlook, became disdainful of cultures that insisted upon patterning behavior on the miraculousness of everyday life: one could converse with rocks, daily events were controlled by ancestral spirits, dancing and shouting made it rain, diseases could be cured by wearing masks, women could give birth to animals, and so on.

Southern Africa and the Americas were not the most primitive cultures in the world. Indeed between the sixth and the fifteenth centuries, Africa saw the rise of the kingdoms of Ghana, Mali, and Songhai, which were large, rich in gold, and politically integrated. Foreigners frequently visited the trading centers of Benin and Kanem-Bornu. Undoubtedly it was a black African people who constructed the great monuments, including an ancient temple, in Zimbabwe. Parts of southern Africa enjoyed the benefits of Muslim literacy and learning. Ethiopia retained an ancient Christian civilization. In the Americas, the Maya, Inca, and Aztec civilizations were impressive for their sophisticated knowledge of the seasons and stars, an advanced calendar, elaborate techniques of weaving and ornamentation, and architectural brilliance that amazed the Spanish. Africa and the Americas were undoubtedly more developed than some of the monsoon forests of southeast Asia, some of the steppe and forest zones of northern Eurasia, and the islands off the coast of India and Australia, such as Tasmania and the Andaman and Nicobar islands, which were still in the paleolithic stage when Europeans arrived there in the eighteenth and nineteenth centuries.

According to Robert Hughes in *The Fatal Shore*, before the Europeans arrived the aborigines of the Australias "had not invented the bow and arrow." Some tribes "had no conception of agriculture—they neither sowed nor reaped." The Iora people never washed themselves, but "spent their lives coated with a mixture of rancid fish oil, animal grease, sand, dust and sweat." The aborigines had "no property, no money . . . no farming, no houses, clothes, pottery, or metal. . . . They had no idea of stock-raising. They saved nothing, lived entirely in the present." One common form of courtship was for a man to "fix on some female of a tribe at enmity with his own . . . stupefy her with blows on her head, back, neck . . . then drag her streaming with blood . . . till he reaches his tribe."[1] Anthropologist Robert Edgerton gives an equally riveting account of Tasmania. Men hunted with wooden spears and by hurling rocks at the heads of animals. Women too foraged for food, typically prying shellfish off rocks, digging up roots, or clubbing possums and seals to death. Tasmanians traveled virtually naked except for kangaroo skins slung over their shoulders. "In all the entire Tasmanian inventory of manufactured goods came to no more than two dozen items." Amazingly, Edgerton points out, Tasmanians could not take advantage of the ocean surrounding their island, because although they once learned how to fish, they forgot or gave up the practice. Thus many Tasmanians perished of starvation despite the availability of a plentiful food source all around them. Nor did they know how to build boats or rafts in order to communicate with other islands. Tasmanian medicine consisted mainly of "slashing the patient with deep cuts until the victim was covered with blood." Edgerton proclaims much of Tasmanian culture "frankly maladaptive."[2]

What the Australian and Tasmanian examples illustrate is the extreme civilizational disadvantage imposed by relative isolation. Apart from the availability of natural resources, the main reason for the relative underdevelopment of Africa, the Americas, and many other parts of the world, compared with China, India, Europe, and the Arab world, seems to be geographical separation. Civilization is largely a product of cultural interaction and shared knowledge. Yet the Americas were cut off from the rest of the world by the Atlantic and Pacific oceans. Black Africa is largely partitioned from North Africa by the Sahara desert. It is true that camels could be used to cross the desert with great difficulty, but the camel is not native to southern Africa. Camels only came into general use for desert journeys around the fourth century A.D. The Arabs were the first to use dromedaries imported from Asia for large-scale caravans across the Sahara. Similarly American Indians did not enjoy the advantages either of the horse or cattle until the Spanish brought them from Europe; consequently, native tribes were compelled to use inefficient modes of transportation, such as llamas and domesticated dogs. "Other cultures could pick up things from traders and missionaries and foreign visitors," remarks historian Philip Curtin. "The sub-Saharan Africans, like some of the Indian tribes, had to invent everything for themselves."

Three of the crucial instruments for a society to rise above the meager subsistence level are the wheel, the plow, and writing. One of the decisive human inventions for improving the efficiency of labor, the wheel is one of the oldest of civilizational resources. Every advanced civilization depended on it, and its invention is usually credited to ancient Mesopotamia, where there is evidence of its use before 3500 B.C. But more than 5000 years later, the wheel was unknown in virtually all of black Africa, and also in pre-Columbian America, although strangely enough the wheel did exist in Mexico, where it was only used as a toy. An essential instrument for the human transition from hunter-gatherer society to some form of settled agriculture, the plow was first used in ancient Sumeria around 3500 B.C. Virtually no community in the Americas nor black Africa knew about the plow until Europeans introduced it in the modern era. Every generation builds upon the knowledge of its ancestors largely because of the invention of writing, which is a mechanism for storing and accumulating knowledge, without which societies are forced to rely on the foibles of memory. "The lack of writing," African philosopher Kwasi Wiredu observes with characteristic understatement, "is a definite handicap in the preservation and enhancement of a philosophical tradition."[3] Also first encountered in Sumeria around 3500 B.C., writing became the foundation for learning in both the East and the West. But with the exception of Mayan hieroglyphics, writing was unknown in the Americas, even to the relatively advanced Aztecs; the Incas frequently communicated through the use of knotted threads. In black Africa, literacy was confined to small enclaves: Islamic outposts such as Timbuktu, the Christian culture in Ethiopia.

The Collapse of Environmentalism

Alexis de Tocqueville remarks that the historical results are usually beneficial when a civilizationally inferior power overwhelms a culturally superior power by force. The reason is that the barbaric victors can then acknowledge their cultural deficiencies, and learn from the society they have subdued.[4] For example, when the Romans supplanted the Greeks as the primary force in southern Europe, Romans acknowledged Greek cultural superiority, as suggested by the Roman poet Horace: "Captive Greece enslaved her fierce captor." Similarly the primitive hordes from northern Europe who sacked Rome over time embraced the Christian faith and acquired, however partially, the essentials of Greco-Roman civilization. The Mongol swordsmen who overran China, India, Europe, and the Middle East inevitably encountered superior cultures and assimilated into them.

By contrast, the Europeans of the modern era were both the more advanced civilization and the conquering power, which resulted, as Tocqueville warned, in uninhibited arrogance on the part of the victors and the total degradation of the vanquished. Europeans from ancient times were familiar with themes of civilizational superiority, and had generally attributed them to climate—the theory we have called environmentalism. Racism developed when the environmental explanation was found by many Europeans to be untenable. Neither skin color nor lack of scientific and intellectual achievement could be plausibly blamed on the soil or the sun. Thus atmospheric theories fell into disrepute.

Along with the Arabs, many Europeans had argued that blackness derives from the sun's heat. The eminent naturalist Comte de Buffon insisted at the end of the eighteenth century that Africans were blackened by the sun, and then passed on blackness as a hereditary feature to their descendants. Buffon predicted that if Negroes were brought to cold countries, over a few generations their skin would lighten.[5] It did not take very long for Europeans to realize the error of that assumption. Europeans also noted, with some chagrin, that the darkest people in Africa were the Wolof living near Cape Verde, not the Africans nearest the Equator. It came as a further surprise that Negro children born in Europe did not come out white. Nor did whites who lived and worked in the West Indies and other tropical zones turn black. When the English and French in America went north, where the climate was cooler, they were confident that they would find Indians with lighter skin; again, this expectation was proven wrong. Many Europeans who followed the path of Columbus to the Americas also believed that the primitive condition of the native Indians was largely the result of their living close to the line of the Equator. As Englishmen and Frenchmen moved northward, many of them expected to see Indian civilization improve in temperate and cooler climates. This turned out not to be the case. Indeed, in some respects, the pattern was reversed. The most advanced Indian civilization was centered in the relatively hot environs of Mexico City; as the French moved north into what is now Canada, they found nothing of comparable sophistication.

It is important to recognize that Europeans were entirely convinced, based on the Bible, that all humans were simultaneously created by God and had inhabited the earth for the same amount of time. How to explain why one people had palaces and cathedrals and technology to explore the seas and the heavens, while other peoples rowed about in canoes and shot blowdarts at each other? Europeans found it difficult to give an explanation for why, over the same period, one society seemed to have accomplished so much and other societies so little. Europeans have also had a long tradition of regarding noble and base qualities to be hereditary. This was part of the justification for a hereditary monarchy and aristocracy. In much of European literature we see suggestions that physical form is revealing, if not determinative, of qualities of character and intelligence. "Let me have men about me that are fat," Julius Caesar says. "Yond' Cassius has a lean and hungry look . . . such men are dangerous." Finally, long before Darwin there is a European anthropomorphic habit of linking human beings and animals, and devising intermediaries such as mermaids and centaurs believed to share human and animal attributes. For all these reasons, it was not difficult for many Europeans to biologize their perceptions of the civilizational inferiority of other cultures. Philip Curtin writes:

> Europeans could now see and measure their superiority—in factory production, agricultural yields, or the cost of transportation by railway or steamship. While superiority feelings had once rested on little more than religious arrogance and ordinary xenophobia, they could now

be buttressed by demonstrable superiority in power and knowledge. . . . Culture prejudice slid off easily toward color prejudice.[6]

Many Europeans began to assert, with increasing frequency and confidence, that the attributes of race, color, and human achievement are intrinsic. Some people are simply superior to others by nature. And since race and color appear to be hereditary, and since Europeans could not help noticing that they were white and the people they considered barbarian were dark-skinned, they concluded that there must be some relationship between physical attributes or race and civilizational achievement. Moreover, they came increasingly to believe that these racial inequities must be dictated by nature or history or even by God. Thus it was that European racism came into the world.

Who Is the Fairest One of All?

Although European convictions of intrinsic superiority are perhaps understandable in this context, there remains an interesting puzzle: both American Indians and Africans were viewed by Europeans as hopelessly primitive, but Europeans only singled out one group, Africans, for dehumanization. A clue to the different way Europeans perceived the two groups is provided by their names. The term "Indian" is a geographical term, reflecting the mistaken belief of Columbus that he had arrived in the Indies. The term "Negro" is racial, and refers to the color black. Why, then, did Europeans distinguish between Indians and blacks, regarding the former as backward but the latter as not really human?

Certainly Europeans condescended to American Indians, who were routinely described as savages. There is a good deal of bestial imagery in Spanish and later French and English accounts of Indians, who are likened to jungle animals in their primitivism and brutality. Indians too were enslaved in the Americas. At the same time, however, European hostility is frequently complemented by genuine admiration. The Indian may be a savage but he is a "noble savage."[7] In many ways, the Indians looked like Europeans and reminded them of their own ancestral past. Some argued that the Indians were the descendants of the Lost Tribes of Israel. When the Europeans vanquished the Indian, they drowned their spoils of conquest with tears of contrition. Even if partly insincere, these homages to the greatness of a disappearing people are entirely absent from European discussion of black Africa. George Fredrickson writes in *White Supremacy* that owing to differences in stature and appearance, the so-called Hottentots "struck Europeans as so outlandish that there was some doubt whether they were fully human."[8]

Taken as a whole, the record suggests that in the minds of Europeans the Indian was dehumanized, but he was not animalized, he was not considered part of the world of beasts. All of this is in stark contrast with the collective European perception of black Africa that would coalesce between the sixteenth and the nineteenth centuries. This contrast dates back to the debates at the University of Salamanca in the sixteenth century over the question of whether Indians had souls and natural rights; the church and the Spanish court concluded that they did. It never occurred to anyone to debate seriously these matters in connection with black Africans. Indeed the basic humanity and natural rights of Negroes did not become an issue in Europe until two centuries later. Despite the inferiorization of both black Africans and American Indians on account of large civilizational gaps between them and Europeans, the white man saw Indians as original human beings, innocent of Christianity but capable of being instructed, savage in customs but worthy of being civilized. This same white man increasingly saw black Africans as degraded beneath the standards of humanity, corrupt in religion to the point of being in league with the devil, incorrigibly barbarian to the point where slavery seemed appropriate to their natures.

Puzzling over the reasons for these anomalies, scholars such as David Brion Davis and Winthrop Jordan have conducted detailed research into European attitudes. From this work, three explanations emerge, one overlooked largely because it is so obvious, two of them acknowledged by these authors. The obvious explanation is natural environment, the perennial recourse of the ancients to account for human differences. Europeans saw the Americas and Africa very differently: as a result, they grew favorably disposed to the former, and increasingly hostile to the latter. Columbus encountered the Indians first in the Bahamas and then on other Caribbean islands, some of the most beautiful parts of the world. His natural reaction, echoed by many subsequent voyagers, was that he was in the garden of Eden.[9] Many Europeans were captivated by the Americas, which they saw as a land largely uninhabited, a land flowing with milk and honey, a land of long beaches, ideal climate, abundant fruits, and singing birds. As Daniel Defoe's *Robinson Crusoe* suggests, the conflict between the desire to settle the continent, combined with a haunting fear of corrupting its natural beauty, impressed itself powerfully on the European mind. Increasingly, Europeans thought about settlement; to many, it sounded like paradise, a prospect for which it was worth leaving Europe. By contrast, Africa was virtually uninhabitable to Europeans, whose primary interest in it was confined to gold and slaves. Their constitutions could not endure the insects and disease, to which black Africans had developed immunities. The climate was for the most part intolerably hot, they considered the continent already inhabited, and they feared the hazards of impenetrable forest, powerful warrior clans, snakes and wild animals. Europeans had no interest whatsoever in venturing deep into Africa, let alone living there. To many, it sounded like hell.

A second critical reason for European differentiation between blacks and Indians is the white man's association of African primitivism with the negative connotations of the color black. This point has been widely misunderstood. In contemporary racial debates, many are fond of pointing out the linguistic implications of the term "black." The *Oxford English Dictionary* definition describes blackness as "deeply stained with dirt, soiled, dirty, foul, malignant, deadly, baneful, disastrous, sinister, iniquitous, atrocious, horrible, and wicked." This definition, however, is given before the sixteenth century, when Europeans had virtually no exposure to black Africa at all.[10] Winthrop Jordan and other scholars have shown that contrary to the conventional wisdom, which views racism as engraved in the English language, the European association of black with darkness and evil long precedes any application to black Africans. All the familiar English metaphors—black sheep in the family, a black mark against one's name, black as the color of death, to blackball or blackmail—evolved independently of racism. So did the religious symbolism of white as the color of angels, and black as the color of the devil.[11] We see a hint of this in Shakespeare, where Iago warns Desdemona's father about Othello: Desdemona is being "covered with a Barbary horse," indeed, "an old black ram is tupping your white ewe."

Europeans, however, are not uniquely disposed to attach benign significance to their own skin color. Extensive research by historians and anthropologists has shown that the color symbolism of white and black is universal. Many scholars suspect that it originates in the basic distinction between darkness and light.[12] We can therefore reappraise black imagery as used by the ancient Greeks and Romans, and medieval Christians and Muslims. By itself, such imagery does not prove racism at all. But Jordan suggests that, combined with the perception of black Africans as extremely primitive, the term "black" begins to be associated with civilizational backwardness in a way that it never was in the premodern world. In the European mind, Africa truly becomes what Joseph Conrad termed the "heart of darkness."

A third and final reason which inspired the distinction between black Africans and American Indians derives from an historical coincidence. It turns out that Englishmen discovered black Africans as a group in the same place and at the same time that they discovered an animal they had never encountered before: the chimpanzee or two-legged ape, which they called an orang-outan.[13] Many writers bent on scientific classification and journalistic speculation found it irresistible to make a linkage between the two, assuming that two-legged apes were the product of sexual intercourse between the monkey and the African. In the middle of the seventeenth century, reports about chimpanzees and orang-outans circulated in Europe and America. During the 1690s, Edward Tyson, an anatomist from the Royal Society of London, argued that there were astonishing similarities in the muscle and skeleton structure between apes and human beings. He dissected a chimpanzee, which he mistook for a "pygmy." Amazed at the human qualities of this unique creature, Tyson maintained that the so-called pygmy occupied an intermediate position between beasts and men on the Great Chain of Being.[14] Tyson was no scandal-mongering journalist; he was a reputable scientist. As Audrey Smedley points out, in some ways his theories foreshadowed the "missing link" debates of evolutionary biologists two centuries later.[15]

Many European travelers placed these accounts of black Africans in the context of lascivious discussions of sexuality. Undoubtedly African sexual mores shocked Europeans throughout the seventeenth and eighteenth centuries. Moreover, information from black Africa continued to be scarce, and travel accounts undoubtedly italicized perceived differences for the purpose of titillating the folks back home. Subsequent research has shown that African sexual customs were not laissez-faire, although they seemed so to many Europeans, who viewed blacks as furnaces of libidinal passion. Thus although many African tribes outlawed adultery, it was customary in some of them for a man to show hospitality by offering his wife or daughter for the night. To the European mind, these kinds of accounts conveyed debauchery pure and simple. Black sexuality was regarded as purely animalistic, and no report seemed too farfetched to win adherents, or at least to inspire lurid fascination. To make matters worse, some African tribes espoused a mythology which traced their own origins to the union of women with animals. Scholars like Jordan and Davis cite numerous travel reports which confirm early European perceptions of black Africans. Traveling the circumference of the African coast in the seventeenth century, Richard Jobson reported on "the enormous size of the virile member among the Negroes." Jobson invokes this observation as "infallible proof" that blacks are descended from Noah's son, cursed in his loins for uncovering his father's nakedness.[16] Another fantastic but influential account of blacks came not from Africa but from a traveler in Jamaica, Edward Long, in 1774. Playing on the morbid fascination of his European readers, Long narrated spellbinding accounts of iniquitous huts, to which African apes carried black women. Long took into account the possible skepticism of some in his audience in his conclusion, "Ludicrous as the opinion may seem, I do not think that an orang-outan husband would be any dishonour to a Hottentot female."[17]

If black Africans were debased by these perverse links, monkeys gained by being elevated to the level of men. Indeed the very term "orang-outan" derives from the Malay word meaning "man of the woods."[18] The scientist Buffon had reported that chimpanzees could be taught to eat dinner with a knife and fork. Lord Monboddo, a firm believer in men with tails, was a kind of champion of the rights of animals; orang-outans, he insisted, were entirely rational beings who happened to live in a primitive state of nature, untainted by civilization. Edward Long himself insisted that apes came in different varieties, and the more intelligent among them could learn to speak a little and to "perform a variety of menial domestic service," just like blacks.[19]

The Nature of Superiority

Far from being ignorant and fearful, the early European racists were the most learned and adventurous men of the age, and their views developed as a rational and increasingly scientific attempt to make sense of the diverse world that was for the first time being encountered as a whole. Environmentalism, which the ancient Greeks and many others used to explain human differences, was intellectually discredited along with much of the other cosmology and biology of the ancients. We see evidence of racism, complete with rejection of environmentalism, in the greatest thinkers of the Enlightenment. Hume, Voltaire, Montesquieu, Kant, and Hegel were among the many who entertained racist views, although these did not make up the main part of their philosophy.

David Hume, in his famous description of barbarism in Africa and around the world, examines the possibility that black inferiority is not inherited but imposed by slavery. Hume dismisses that explanation on the grounds that the descendants of slaves and "low people" all over Europe have proved that they can rise above their ancestral histories and achieve literary, mathematical, and scientific distinction, whereas the backwardness of black Africans seems to him comprehensive and apparently ineradicable. "In Jamaica," Hume writes, "they talk of one Negro as a man of parts and learning, but it is likely he is admired for very slender accomplishments, like a parrot, who speaks a few words plainly."[20] Similarly Immanuel Kant is skeptical that black inferiority is the sole product of unfortunate circumstance. "Among the whites," he observes, "people constantly rise up from the lowest rabble and acquire esteem through their superior gifts."[21]

But for the classic expression of European racism we must turn to the French diplomat and scholar Joseph Arthur de Gobineau, who is today unknown or considered the embodiment of wickedness, but who was a friend and respected correspondent of Tocqueville and in some respects one of the most learned exponents of the *Zeitgeist* of the nineteenth century. Nowhere is the racist worldview more comprehensively stated than in Gobineau's *The Inequality of Human Races*, published in 1853. When Gobineau sent his book to Tocqueville, he received only mild dissent about the soundness of his theories, although Tocqueville strongly protested their demoralizing effect.[22] But such warnings could hardly be expected to deter Gobineau, a deep pessimist, who feared that currents of race-mixing and democratic ideas of equality were diluting Teutonic blood and destroying the greatness of the Aryan aristocracy.[23] Gobineau was also an acquaintance of Josiah Nott, an apologist for slavery who publicized Gobineau's views in the American South, and of the philosopher Friedrich Nietzsche and the composer Richard Wagner, both of whom shared Gobineau's love of aristocracy of birth and his hatred of equality. Gobineau was an elitist and an eccentric, but his racism made him a man of his time, elevated to high posts and widely admired. Even the *Encyclopaedia Britannica* echoed his views.[24] Moreover, his influence would prove lasting: in the twentieth century, Gobineau was one of Adolf Hitler's favorite authors and his works were popular textbooks in the schools of Nazi Germany.

Gobineau drew on the discoveries made by Orientalists such as William Jones that there was a common Aryan source for Indo-European languages such as Sanskrit, Persian, Greek, Latin, and German. Gobineau argued that the highest aspirations of humanity were embodied in these Aryans, a single white family of Germanic peoples who had infused European and even Asian culture with its brilliance and vigor.[25] He writes that the existence of advanced and backward races—the former who live by codes of civility, ingenuity, and technological comfort, the latter who live by laws of force at a subsistence level—proves that some races are naturally superior to others. This superiority, Gobineau stresses, applies to races as groups, not to individuals. Considering the environmental account of human differences, Gobineau sarcastically writes, "The humidity of a marsh, I suppose, will produce a civilization which would inevitably have been stifled by the dryness of the Sahara." Gobineau quickly proceeds to rebut such a notion.

> In spite of wind and rain, cold and heat, sterility and fruitfulness, the world has seen barbarism and civilization flourishing everywhere on the same soil. The brutish fellah is tanned by the same sun as scorched the powerful priest of Memphis; the learned professor of Berlin lectures under the same inclement sky that once beheld the wretched existence of the Finnish savage.

If environmentalism is true, Gobineau asks, why have some groups endowed with rich natural resources nevertheless failed to produce a comparable civilization to that of Europe? "So the brain of a Huron Indian contains in an undeveloped form an intellect which is absolutely the same as that of the Englishman or the Frenchman!" he explodes. "Why, then, in the course of the ages, has he not invented printing or steam power?" Gobineau suggests that "nowhere is the soil more fertile, the climate milder, than in certain parts of America. There is an abundance of great rivers, the gulfs, the bays, the harbours, are large, deep, magnificent, and innumerable. Precious metals can be dug out almost at the surface of the ground." And the same is true for large parts of Africa. So where, Gobineau asks, is the American Indian or African version of Caesar, Newton, Charlemagne, and Homer?

> We often hear of Negroes who have learned music, who are clerks in banking houses, and who know how to read, write, count, dance, and speak like white men. People are astonished at this, and conclude that the Negro is capable of everything! I will not wait for the friends of equality to show me such and such passages in books written by missionaries or sea captains, who declare that some Wolof is a fine carpenter, some Hottentot a good servant, that some Kaffir dances and plays the violin, that some Bambara knows arithmetic. . . . Let us leave these puerilities, and compare together not men but groups.

The equality of the races could be expected to produce a rough civilizational equality among cultures, Gobineau writes. "Early in the world's history, they would have gladdened the face of the earth with a crowd of civilizations, all flourishing at the same time." Gobineau argues that the historical record refutes such political expectations. In fact, he contends, it is whites who have developed modern civilization, while other people have proved at best adept imitators. Civilization, Gobineau argues, depends not on mere mimicry. "No one has a real part in any civilization until he is able to make progress by himself, without direction from others." In rhetoric that is bound to offend contemporary ears, Gobineau defies his readers to cite one example of a black civilization satisfying these criteria, or even one truly great scientific invention accomplished solely by a black African. "I will wait long for the work to be finished," he says, "I merely ask that it may be begun. But it has never been begun; it has never even been attempted."[26]

In the twentieth century, many of these racist ideas would come under ferocious assault, both on intellectual and moral grounds. Eventually the antiracist view would prevail, and racism would be redefined to suit the politics of a new age. But it is important to recover the origin of racism, because it teaches us that racism had a beginning both in space and in time. Whatever its later career, racism began as part of a rational project to understand human differences. Racism originated as an assertion of Western cultural superiority that was eventually proclaimed to be intrinsic. From the ancient world we get a glimpse of societies that respected nature rather than seeking to subdue and conquer it; that were aware of physical differences but attached no importance to them—perhaps a model for a better society than the one we have now. In any event, there is no historical warrant for the extreme pessimism which holds that racism has always existed and will always exist. Painful though we may find it to read what people in earlier centuries had to say about others, it remains profoundly consoling to know that racism had a beginning, because then it becomes possible to envision its end.

Notes

1. Robert Hughes, *The Fatal Shore*, Collins Harvill, London, 1987, pp. 12–15, 273.

2. Robert Edgerton, *Sick Societies: Challenging the Myth of Primitive Harmony*, Free Press, New York, 1992, pp. 47–50.

3. Kwasi Wiredu, "African Philosophical Tradition: A Case Study of the Akan," *The Philosophical Forum* 24, Nos. 1–3, 1992–1993, p. 36.

4. "But when the side that has the physical force has intellectual superiority too, it is rare for the conquered to become civilized; they either withdraw or are destroyed. For this reason one can say that, generally speaking, savages go forth in arms to seek enlightenment but do not accept it as a gift." Alexis de Tocqueville, *Democracy in America*, edited by J. P. Mayer, Harper & Row, New York, 1988, pp. 330–31.

5. George Louis Leclerc Buffon, *Natural History*, translated by William Smellie, London, 3rd edition, 1791, III, pp. 201–4.

6. Philip D. Curtin, *Imperialism*, Harper & Row, New York, 1971, p. xv.

7. David Brion Davis, *The Problem of Slavery in Western Culture*, Oxford University Press, New York, 1988, p. 168.

8. George Fredrickson, *White Supremacy: A Comparative Study in American and South African History*, Oxford University Press, New York, 1981, p. 39.

9. Christopher Columbus, *The Four Voyages*, J. M. Cohen, trans., Penguin Books, New York, 1969, p. 221.

10. Winthrop Jordan, *White Over Black: American Attitudes Toward the Negro, 1550–1812*, University of North Carolina Press, Chapel Hill, 1968, p. 7. See also Joel Kovel, *White Racism: A Psychohistory*, Columbia University Press, New York, 1984, p. 62.

11. Jordan, *White Over Black*, p. 7. See also Gary Nash and Richard Weiss, *The Great Fear: Race in the Mind of America*, Holt, Rinehart and Winston, New York, 1970, p. 11; Barry Schwartz, ed., *White Racism*, Laurel Leaf Books, New York, 1978, p. 6.

12. "It is surely more than a coincidence that in Africa and Asia as well as Europe, black is associated with unpleasantness, disaster or evil." Carl N. Degler, *Neither Black Nor White: Slavery and Race Relations in Brazil and the United States*, Macmillan, New York, 1971, p. 211. "Recent research has shown a pancultural preference for light over dark, presumably derived from the worldwide fear of the night together with the association of daylight with fear reduction and need satisfaction."

Thomas Pettigrew, George Fredrickson, Dale Knobel, Nathan Glazer, and Reed Veda, *Prejudice*, Harvard University Press, Cambridge, 1982, p. 15. See also Harry Levin, *The Power of Blackness*, Ohio University Press, Athens, 1980; David Brion Davis, *Slavery and Human Progress*, Oxford University Press, New York, 1984, p. 38; Kathy Russell, Midge Wilson, and Ronald Hall, *The Color Complex*, Harcourt Brace Jovanovich, New York, 1992, p. 37.

13. See Jordan, *White Over Black*, esp. p. 29.

14. Edward Tyson, *Orang-Outang, Sive Homo Sylvestris: Or the Anatomy of a Pygmie Compared with That of a Monkey, an Ape, and a Man*, Thomas Bennet and Daniel Brown, London, 1699.

15. Audrey Smedley, *Race in North America*, Westview Press, Boulder, Colo., 1993, p. 162.

16. Cited by Davis, *The Problem of Slavery in Western Culture*, pp. 452–53; Jordan, *White Over Black*, p. 34.

17. Edward Long, *The History of Jamaica*, London, 1774. Cited by Davis, *The Problem of Slavery in Western Culture*, pp. 455, 462–63. See also Winthrop Jordan, *The White Man's Burden*, Oxford University Press, New York, 1974, pp. 197–98.

18. *Compact Edition of the Oxford English Dictionary*, Oxford University Press, New York, 1971, p. 2002.

19. Jordan, *The White Man's Burden*, pp. 106, 197.

20. "Not to mention our colonies, there are Negro slaves dispersed all over Europe, of which none ever discovered any symptoms of ingenuity; though low people, without education, will start up amongst us, and distinguish themselves in every profession." David Hume, "Of National Characters," in David Hume, *Essays Moral, Political and Literary*, edited by T. H. Green and T. H. Grose, Longmans, Green and Co., London, 1875, Vol. 1, p. 252.

21. Immanuel Kant, *Observations on the Feeling of the Beautiful and Sublime*, translated by John Goldthwait, University of California Press, Berkeley, 1960, pp. 111–13.

22. "If only your doctrine . . . could serve mankind better! What purpose does it serve to persuade lesser peoples living in abject conditions of barbarism or slavery that, such being their racial status, they can do nothing to better themselves, to change their habits, or to ameliorate their status?" Tocqueville also termed Gobineau's theories "probably quite false" and "certainly very pernicious." Alexis de Tocqueville, *The European Revolution and Correspondence with Gobineau*, edited by John Lukacs, Greenwood Press, Westport, Conn., 1959, pp. 286–88.

23. Michael Biddiss, introduction to Joseph Arthur Gobineau, *Selected Political Writings*, Harper & Row, New York, 1970.

24. "No full-blooded Negro has ever been distinguished as a man of science, a poet or an artist, and the fundamental equality claimed for him is belied by the whole history of the race." *Encyclopaedia Britannica*, 9th edition, London, 1884, Vol. 17, p. 318.

25. See, e.g., Leon Poliakov, *The Aryan Myth: A History of Racist and Nationalist Ideas in Europe*, Basic Books, New York, 1971.

26. Arthur de Gobineau, *The Inequality of Human Races*, translated by Adrian Collins, Howard Fertig, New York, 1967, pp. 27, 37–38, 54, 74–75, 154, 168, 180.

13

Darkness Made Visible: Law, Metaphor, and the Racial Self

D. MARVIN JONES

Then it dawned upon me with a certain suddenness that I was different from the others; or like, mayhap, in heart and life and longing, but shut out from their world by a vast veil. . . . The shades of the prison-house closed round us all: walls strait and stubborn to the whitest, but relentlessly narrow, tall and unscalable to sons of night who must plod darkly on in resignation, or beat unavailing palms against stone, or steadily, half hopelessly, watch the streak of blue above.[1]

In August 1862, Abraham Lincoln called a number of "Negro" leaders to the White House. Laboring under harsh racial assumptions, which conflicted with the moral eloquence to come at Gettysburg, Lincoln told his assembled audience, "You and we are different races. . . . This physical difference is a great disadvantage to us both, as I think your race suffer very greatly, many of them by living among us, while ours suffer from your presence."[2] With these prefatory remarks, Lincoln proceeded to try to persuade his audience of the merits of his plan: To emancipate slaves and expatriate them to a colony in Central America.

For Lincoln, race signified a natural and immovable wall between communities, a wall of difference. Homogeneity, by contrast, is the basic stuff of the social bond. By invoking the notion of race, and invoking it in a strong essentialist sense,[3] Lincoln rhetorically posited that blacks and whites lacked any basic human bond upon which they could form one society. Race reverberated as a metaphor of kinship, denying that there was the requisite brotherhood between blacks and whites, and denying that blacks and whites could co-exist on the same social plane.[4]

Historically, this world view was most explicitly expressed in institutional structures such as de jure and de facto segregation. This bleak nineteenth century world view remains in our current constitutional jurisprudence. The idea of race as a natural, objective demarcation of difference between groups is the lens through which courts continue to view claims by blacks. Thus, in *City of Richmond v. J. A. Croson Co.*,[5] Justice O'Connor criticizes as fundamentally illogical the means-ends connection of a set-aside program requiring thirty percent participation by "minorities." O'Connor explains:

[T]he 30% quota cannot be said to be narrowly tailored to any goal, except perhaps outright racial balancing. It rests upon the "completely unrealistic" assumption that minorities will choose a particular trade in lockstep proportion to their representation in the local population.[6]

82 GEO. L.J. 437 (1993). Originally published in the *Georgetown Law Journal*. Reprinted by permission.

On the surface, this opinion represents hostility toward using groups, rather than the individual, as the unit of social inquiry, a relentlessly particularizing perspective that denies both the problem of caste and the relevance or reality of societal discrimination. Moreover, it is a denial that group disparities between the socioeconomic situations of blacks and whites are legally meaningful. The source of this denial of meaning is a conception of race as difference. O'Connor seems to say: "Blacks and whites are *different* races. . . . Why assume they would have similar interests or display statistically similar occupational patterns?"

But race, for all its rhetorical power, is an incoherent fiction. "The truth is," as Anthony Appiah notes, "there are no races."[7] Racial categories are neither objective nor natural, but ideological and constructed. In these terms race is not so much a category but a practice: *people are raced.* Yet conventional legal theory understands race as something that is already "there," freestanding.[8] As we shall see, this conventional account ultimately collides with its own lurking objectivism. From President Lincoln to Justice O'Connor, from classical to modern American law, this specious perspective has imposed false horizons on our values and discourse. This figure of race seeks to draw its line of difference in the dialogue about democracy and equality between those who fit within and those who fit without. So long as this trope of difference remains as the dark glass through which we view the world, it will distort our vision and conceptions of law, justice, and ourselves.

Law Through the Eye/I of the Other: Racial Identity as a Lens

Race is a mask that grins and lies.[9] Its assumptions distort our images of ourselves and close off our vision of the world. Like the doll-wood mask of African ritual, its cramped confines become the limits of our vision. The black mask envelops us in a sealed hemisphere where we may observe only the darkness of the mask's own interiority. The white mask becomes a lens through which the eye/I may visualize itself at the center of the universe, hermetically sealed. The mask—black or white—becomes a screen between self and other.[10] The two masks represent a singular phenomenon—the radical falsification of the self. The mask of race does not merely divide between self and other; it divides internally. We become two people, inhabiting radically different worlds. One of us is a child of the enlightenment: an autonomous, individual actor with discrete tastes and values. Our other person is an undifferentiated part of a whole.[11] We live as a fragmented entity, with two faces, two lives, and two identities: one individual, one racial.[12]

The white minstrels of the nineteenth century wore a mask when they painted themselves with black greasepaint symbolic of racial identity. This racial identification prompted the acting out of fantasies, referring equally to the caricatures of blacks they sought to represent and to the inner conflict about their own powerlessness in the changing industrial order. This process of racial identification and the acting out of internal instability occurred as parody in the minstrel shows and continues as an unconscious drama in contemporary American law. By accepting the posts inscribed with the historical narrative of black and white to which we have been tied, we engage in the psychological equivalent of the putting on of greasepaint. The categories of racial identity become the mask that stands between the judge or jury and the black subject.

This problematic of racial identity accounts for a number of cases that the conventional problematic of racism does not. The conventional problematic of "racism" conceives of the difficulty as a problem of ethos—in the moral sphere.[13] The problematic of race locates it as a problem of world view, structured by historical narratives that transform our picture of experience. Racism understands the problem in terms of moral opposites: in good/bad and like/dislike distinctions. It understands the problem as a cognitive difficulty flowing from positional status in which notions of inside versus outside and center versus periphery structure both empathy and perception.

Race inscribes its meaning through the ordinary rituals of adjudication. Historically, race was an idea whose significance was worked out on the bodies of blacks, particularly black slaves. Uncannily, the significance of race is particularly apparent today in cases in which black men have been brutalized or killed. In our modern context, the body remains the medium in which the significance of race is most dramatically seen in law. I trace this to a cognitive problem—an almost systematic distortion of thinking and perception that is not random, but follows the general pattern of historical narrative. It is as though the judge or jury is looking at the record through a filter constituted by the symbols, concepts, and imagery of race. Rather than reconstruct what happened and search for truth within the welter of statements and circumstances presented in the legal record, their search is conducted among the ruins of our racial mythology. It is as if, when race is involved, we substitute the notion of an essentialistic model of truth as internal to race itself for a notion of truth as empirical. A few examples will illuminate this point.

A Dark Night of the Soul

When a white man faces a black man, especially if the black man is helpless, terrible things are often revealed.[14]

At 12:47 A.M., California Highway Patrol (CHP) officers are in pursuit of a white Hyundai for failing to yield. The driver is Rodney Glenn King—a black, unemployed construction worker—who will later say he fled from police because he felt the traffic infraction would interfere with his parole. After several units of the Los Angeles Police Department (LAPD) take up chase, Rodney King's vehicle is finally stopped in full view of the Mountainback apartment complex. There, he finds himself surrounded by over twenty armed LAPD officers, several of whom proceed to "beat him half to death" while he is lying defenseless on the ground. King is hit between fifty-three and fifty-six times by officers wielding their batons. The bones holding his eye in its right socket are broken, and he suffers broken bones at the base of his skull. In addition to clubbing him wildly, one officer stomps on his head.[15]

At first sight, the story of King's midnight beating sounds a familiar note. Brutality against blacks by police officers in urban areas is generally not exposed to the light of day. It generally occurs in darkness: in neighborhoods and settings where the only witness is the victim or his peers, who are also victims of socioeconomic disadvantage. Within the shadow of race and class and attendant matters such as criminal records, a black person becomes invisible. Miraculously, King found visibility through a black and white videotape that shows, in grisly detail, King—prone and unarmed—being beaten by at least three officers. King offers no resistance while ten or more officers stand around. After the beating, the following transmissions occur over police computers:

From [Officers Laurence] Powell and [Tim] Wind to Foot Patrol Officers: *"Oops."*
From Foot Patrol Officers to Powell and Wind: *"Oops, what?"*

Powell and Wind to Foot Patrol Officers: *"I haven't beaten anyone this bad in a long time."*
From Sergeant Stacey Koon to Watch Commander: *"U [Unit] just had a big-time use of force. Tased [electrically shocked] and beat the subject of a CHP pursuit big time."*
From Watch Commander to Sergeant Stacey Koon: *"Oh well . . . I'm sure the lizard didn't deserve it."*[16]

At the hospital, Officer Powell jokes with King: "Don't you remember the hardball game? We hit quite a few home runs."[17] And before the King incident, Powell referred to a previous police encounter with blacks in which he (Powell) was involved as something straight out of *Gorillas in the Mist.*[18]

Thus far, all this fits neatly within the simple, conventional notion of racism, a problem of "sick minds." Perhaps. However, what happens at trial, I suggest, is more complex. Officers Tim Wind, Laurence Powell, Stacey Koon, and Theodore Briseno were charged, among other things, with assault with a deadly weapon. They were tried before a jury of ten whites, one Asian, and one nonblack Hispanic.

At trial, there was no claim that the officers acted in self-defense, no claim that King was armed, and no denial of participation. The video tape and all of the computer messages containing racial slurs referring to gorillas in the mist and lizards were played and entered as exhibits in the record.[19]

The officers told a story dramatically different from what appeared on the film. They began by claiming that the video did not film the entire event. They said that King, in a desperate attempt to escape the California Highway Patrol, had caused a traffic accident and that when he finally was blocked and made to stop, he got out of the car and shook his behind at the police officers.[20] The officers also characterized the scene on the tape in a way to suggest a struggle. They claimed that King refused to be handcuffed, acted oblivious to blows and tasing, charged into police officers, and swung his arms in a wild and hostile manner. They also argued that their blows were "jabs." Officer Briseno, who was observed by witnesses and was captured by the film stomping King's head, testified he was only trying to get King to stay down. The police told a story of embattled police handling an unruly suspect with statements from a defense witness that King was in a "trance-like" state, and that he was on PCP.[21]

The story of the police was contradicted—in some instances by the film itself and in other instances by eyewitnesses, including police officers:

King caused accident during chase.	CHP officer Melanie Singer said no.
King was on PCP.	Dr. Mancia, who treated King, said no.
King charged into over 20 armed policemen.	Eyewitnesses consistently said no.
King swung his arms wildly and in hostile manner.	According to *L.A. Times* reporter who saw tape, King moves his arms "feebly."

The question before the jury was simply whether the force used to subdue Rodney King, the fifty-plus baton blows (many to the head), the stomping on King's neck, the tasing while he was unarmed (most of it while he was prone on the ground), was reasonable. The jury, however, found none of the officers guilty. Three of the policemen were acquitted outright and the jury hung on the others.

For the jury to find that the force used was reasonable, the jury had to see something different from what the witnesses saw at Mountainback, different from what the reporters who viewed the film saw, different from what I saw. One juror, for example, said that he saw clearly that some of the blows did not connect. I submit that what they saw, at a deep cognitive level, was race. The story told by Sergeant Koon—of a black man who was in a trance, immune to electric shock, unfazed by blows, who kept fighting, charging unarmed into a crowd of LAPD officers—was the old story of blacks as beasts or animals. The initial corollary is that black men like Rodney King are particularly dangerous because they are semi-animals, dramatically less controlled, less rational, and less predictable than white men. Moreover, the scene of the beating—across the street from a place where drugs are sold—is, in a real sense, a jungle (albeit an urban version). This, at a cognitive level, argues for a different way of looking at things.

A second corollary, which is evident within the historical narratives about blacks as Others, is the idea of the black man as anticitizen, as the archetypal threat to law and order. Rodney King, by failing to yield, causes car accidents and endangers life instead of submitting to arrests. In this anticitizen narrative white police officers are faced with an alien "black" consciousness that does not partake of the notions of responsibility accepted by whites. Rodney King, who is perceived by all of the interpretive communities as a representation of urban blacks, became the embodiment of alien "black consciousness": the anticitizen. This image is sharpened by his status as an unemployed and uneducated parolee.

Ironically, the concept of citizenship figures prominently in another story, the "story" people of color hold concerning the Fourteenth Amendment: The Fourteenth Amendment represented a promise of "full citizenship." This promise was made during the Reconstruction Era and remade within the framework of the panoply of state and federal laws that were passed over the last thirty years guaranteeing equal treatment of blacks—the "second reconstruction." The unconscious image of black identity as anticitizenship became the counterstory to the narrative about equal citizenship that minorities and many others would have liked to tell. This same image of black identity worked as a distorting prism, powerfully filtering how the jury saw the film.

The jury simply revised what they "saw" to fit the narrative they already knew, a story that resonates deep within our social history. None of the racial slurs, none of the contradictions in the testimony, and none of the graphic brutality of the video really mattered to the jurors. It was the race story that mattered. The jury merely chose the essentialist knowledge of the story over the lived experience-as-knowledge of the film: This phenomenon has been referred to as a function of the "mythic mentality."

In the mythic mentality,

> the nuances of significance and value which knowledge creates in its concept of the object, which enable it to distinguish different spheres of objects and to draw a line between the world of truth and the world of appearance, are utterly lacking. . . . Instead of the dialectical movement of thought, in which every given particular is linked with other particulars in a series and thus ultimately subordinated to a general *law* and process, we have here a mere subjection to the impression itself and its momentary "presence."[22]

The will to knowledge, like a rushing river, is drawn down through the primitivism of racial symbols, from the experientialist conceptions of truth down a more ancient path. We leave a surface legal world of rationality and empiricism, and descend to a subterranean world of racial essentialism and mythic models of knowledge. From this perspective, the filmed experience cannot penetrate the darkness. How could the film help us to know what happens in the ghetto anyway? Like Africa, the ghetto is a place beyond the experience of whites and, hence, a place of darkness. Who knows what happened? King's blackness blended with both the blackness of the setting and the black and white of the video to become a screen upon which the image of race and racial fears could be projected.

The source of the projection would seem to be the racial self: the jurors identified with the white policemen who were "like them." An admission of racial barbarism on the part of the officers would be an admission of their own racial barbarism and, as such, self-negating. Like Joseph Conrad's Kurtz,[23] the jury flees from "the horror" into the primitive narrative fantasies of the colonial regime.

The Manichean World

Nightmare
That's what I am
America's Nightmare
I am what you made me
The hate and evil that you gave me. . . .[24]

According to the Transit Authority Police, "[a] middle-aged man with a silver-colored pistol strode into a subway car rolling through lower Manhattan yesterday and shot four young men he had apparently singled out from among the passengers."[25] In this second story, life imitated film: the shootings by Bernhard Goetz—a thirty-nine year old, straitlaced white man—appeared to parallel the ritualized violence of the protagonist in *Death Wish*,[26] who walked the streets hunting for "criminals" to execute. Witnesses and police on the scene testified that Goetz pursued the men from car to car and shot each of the four "methodically"—shooting two of his victims in the back. Goetz would later confess that he calmly drew a pistol from his belt and shot at each of the four teenagers. As Goetz himself stated, he shot them while they were running away: "[T]hey trapped themselves. The two from left to right, they had nowhere to go. . . . The two on my left, they tried to run through the crowd and of course they had nowhere to run, because the crowd would stop them and I . . . got 'em. . . ." When he discovered that the fourth man, cowering on a bench, was not bleeding, he said, "You seem to be alright, here's another." In his confession, Goetz stated, "I know this sounds horrible, but my intention was to murder them, to hurt them, to make them suffer as much as possible." This gratuitous gunplay against four unarmed teenagers was referred to the morning after as "one of the worst crimes of the year." Yet, immediately after the shootings, the gunman clearly perceived himself as a hero. He helped frightened women off the floor and held a conversation with the conductor before jumping from the train and fleeing "in the dark tunnel."[27]

Goetz was later indicted and tried for attempted murder and assault. He pleaded self-defense. Legally, if the facts were as initially described by the transit police, by the witnesses on the scene, and by Bernhard Goetz himself in his confession, his defense should fail. As Police Commissioner Benjamin Ward stated: "You don't shoot two people running away from you and say it's self-defense."[28]

However clear and grotesquely culpable the actual events appeared, they were later shrouded in the minds of the jury in ambiguity and shadow. As fleshed out by the "evidence" and the opening and closing statements of the defense attorneys, the four youths got up and went over to Goetz to ask for five dollars. Three of the victims had large screwdrivers in their jacket pockets, but Goetz couldn't have known that. The victims all had criminal records, but Goetz could not have known that either. Goetz confessed that the shooting was not linked to anything they said. Rather, he based the "threat" on two things: that they were standing there and that they had "shiny" eyes.[29] The image the defense literally conjured up for the jury—less from the spotty and inconsistent record than from courtroom theatrics and lawyer oratory—was of four black men standing around Goetz, menacing him with their presence and "looks," thus prompting him to draw his revolver and shoot them out of fear.

Much was made to hinge upon whether the youths actually stood around Goetz. Although standing around conveys no objective threat, there was the notion that one with street sense would recognize a potential threat when certain types of kids gather around in certain ways. There is much in this particular flight into "common sense": this arbitrary and subjective reasoning represented the collapse of legal reasoning or legal sense into a sense of fear and the substitution of racial assumptions or fantasies for traditional factual determinations (i.e., Was there a threat? Was there a use of force?). For example, asserting that the youths were standing and "menacing" would require an explanation of how the bullets ended up in the backs of two of the teenagers. Aside from the self-contradictory and transparently speculative ruminations of "experts" paid by the defense, there was literally no evidence whatsoever to explain the position of the bullets. The only uncontroversial evidence that explains why two of the victims were shot in the back was Goetz's own statement: "[M]y intention was to murder them."[30]

Thus, how to get from the physical evidence (from the explicit, detailed confession) to a finding that Goetz was innocent of attempted murder and assault was less a matter of what happened and more a matter of who was involved. Logic and reason were overshadowed by the invocation of historical narratives of race. The story of actual events, as told by the physical evidence and by Goetz himself, was transformed by the Manichean[31] allegory of an inner story of racial symbols that appeared within the surface narrative of evidence and facts.

In this narrative, middle class people are cast as innocent victims who work hard and are preyed upon by shiftless, *dirty* criminals who come out of the alleys and dim recesses of the urban sprawl. Meanwhile, the legal system designed to protect middle class people has become so corrupted with liberalism—sympathizing with blacks and other minorities—that the system no longer works. To New Yorkers and other American urban dwellers, the legal system has become part of the darkness.

Implicit in the story is a familiar representation: the criminals are stereotyped as black and the innocent victims are stereotyped as white. The criminal is not merely black, he is the African Other constructed by the early European travelers: he is uncivilized and part beast. This African Other was explicitly invoked when Slotnick, Goetz's lead defense counsel, called the black victims "savages."[32] The imagery of a moral Great Chain of Being was also mobilized when Slotnick alternatively referred to the victims as "predators" and as a "wolf pack."[33] The moral of the story is that it is natural for whites to subdue savages who threaten social order.

Goetz was cast not merely as someone acting in self-defense, but also as the vanguard of the forces of light who comes to enforce rough justice upon the untamed, dark hordes. Through the economy of Manichean allegory, all individuality vanishes, allowing a transference of the anger (felt by Goetz and white society) to black society, as represented by four anonymous, faceless black youths. In this projection of negative personhood, Cabey, Canty, Ramseur, and Allen cease to be victims or youths or even criminals. They are quite simply black and, as such, proper targets for shooting.

The process at work here is neither the individual desire for domination or aversion, nor a problematic of ethos or morality. That would be far too simple. Rather, it is a process of a collective unconscious perception: a paradigm of cognition. The metaphor of race as embedded in historical narrative becomes a lens that polarizes and colors how we see the social world. This contemporary narrative revises and reinscribes the historical narrative. Its truths are the "truths" of racial myths: truths that do not vary over time or social contexts. The revised historical narrative transforms the experienced facts of a particular case into an invocation of racial essence, racial identity, and racial fear. Racial fear becomes the cognitively distorting medium in which Goetz's confession is silenced, in which physical evidence dissolves, and in which some of our aspiration for community disappears.

The Rebirth of Bigger Thomas

She was dead and he had killed her.
He was a murderer, a *Negro* murderer, a *black* murderer. . . .[34]
We are here in the realm of fiction, with which it is said the law has always been connected.[35]

The *Boston Globe* reported the story: "A Reading man and his pregnant wife were shot in Roxbury last night by a gunman who forced his way into their car after the couple left Brigham and Women's Hospital." The suburban couple had come into the inner city to attend childbirth classes. Carol Stuart was shot in the head and her husband, Charles, in the abdomen by a gunman who fled with Carol's purse and about one hundred dollars in jewelry. Although Carol died shortly after the incident, her seven month old fetus was delivered by cesarean section. Officers at the highest levels of the police department participated in the telling of the story. The Deputy Superintendent offered an explanation as to why the shooting occurred: "The gunman who robbed the couple apparently thought the driver was a police officer, perhaps because he saw a cellular phone in the car. . . ." Before he shot the Stuarts, the Deputy Superintendent alleged that the gunman said, "I think you're five-o," a slang term for police.[36]

In the story, the police go on to describe Charles Stuart as ignoring pain, making a desperate call for help for his wife and himself on his cellular phone. Charles reportedly blacked out, but the phone line remained open. The story of heroic intervention continued with the police dispatcher resourcefully ordering cars to take turns turning on their sirens. The couple's location is triangulated by matching sounds heard through the phone with the actual location of police cars. The murderer, who fired a thirty-eight caliber round into Carol Stuart's head, was described as a black man with a raspy voice dressed in a jogging suit.

The story combined elements of melodrama and fevered racial vision: it portrayed white heroes as the personification of innocence and a black villain as the personification of evil.[37] The police and newspapers painted a picture of a suburban white couple mercilessly gunned down when they entered the inner city for the most blameless of purposes. The narrative continued with both Charles and the police painted in bright colors as heroes, overcoming odds to snatch the lives of Charles and his young son from the jaws of death.

The story told first by Charles Stuart, then adopted almost simultaneously by the staid *Boston Globe* and the normally skeptical Boston police, is a story about indiscriminate violence in the city; it is a story about dark men in rumpled jogging clothes who come out of the fog to invade cars, abduct families, shoot helpless pregnant women, and then fade back into the fog. The story brimmed over with archetypal images of urban "savages" threatening the "innocent." The then-Mayor of Boston, Raymond Flynn, injected into the story: "I demand that the Boston Police department continue to be extremely aggressive in cracking down on people who are using guns and killing *innocent* people. It's intolerable. We will use every lawful tool to support our police officers in cracking down on gun-wielding criminals."[38] Notice how, again, the innocents are white and the savage, real or imagined, is black.

The "crackdown" that actually occurred following the incident featured indiscriminate stops and, in some instances, strip searches of scores of black men whose only crime was being young and black. During the manhunt for the killer, a minister reported watching as "officers lined 15 black teen-agers against a wall and made them empty their pockets and drop their pants and undershorts. 'After about 15 minutes there were 15 bare bottoms displayed on the street.'" The searches were not limited to gang members or even to particular places; black men were searched in frontyards, in pizza shops, on their way to work. Soon thereafter, two black teenagers overheard a relative of a black man named Bennett jokingly say he believed Mr. Bennett had committed the killing. They were repeatedly picked up and threatened with twenty years in prison unless they signed an affidavit implicating Bennett.[39]

In their zeal to find the black killer, the police failed to learn that a thirty-eight caliber revolver had been stolen from the fur store where Charles Stuart worked, or that Charles had recently taken out large amounts of insurance on his wife. Charles eventually killed himself by jumping into the Mystic River. His brother confessed that he and Charles had murdered Carol. In the end, the black man with the raspy voice who stepped out of the fog to penetrate the lives of suburban whites was imaginary. If Ellison is correct that a living black exists as an invisible man,[40] as a reified abstraction to whites who refuse to see the actual "person," then the phantom of the Stuart case was the invisible man's twin. The raspy-voiced man was a mirage, but one no less illusory than the image the jurors had of Rodney King, the image Goetz had of the Bronx teenagers he attempted to kill, or the image the police had of the black youths they searched and violated.

But I think there is something more precise than unexamined racial assumptions that would explain why only the usual suspects were rounded up, why the most obvious suspect was never questioned, why the most elementary police work was not done, and why the black robber in the jogging suit was *seen* to be so real. There is operating in this story something that is internal to the racial stereotype, something that is all-encompassing in its cognitive effect. It is our set of basic assumptions about self and other that have become intertwined in the problematic of the racial self. The omissions of the Boston police were less a problem of negligent overlooking than of outward looking. Race, the great signifier, draws a circle around the signified. It is a figure of inside/outside distinctions. Inside the circle, individuals are presumed to be good, decent, normal, and white. Outside the circle is the realm of criminals, deviants, and savages. The circle of race traces the dividing line of innocence and guilt along the dividing line between self and other, which is cognitively a difference between the within and the without. For the police to look at Charles would have required them to look within the circle, to look within *themselves* in a sense. More than that, to recognize Charles as "the savage" raises questions about the coherence of the circle altogether.

In each case, there is an opposition in which whites confront real or imagined blacks as "blacks"; that is, as blacks asserting themselves such that whites are physically threatened (Stuart), their manhood is threatened (King), or their sense of well-being is threatened by cultural alterity (Goetz). This confrontation leads to a moment of what I call "racial recognition." It takes the white observer to a mental plane at which logic and reason occur along an essentialist axis.

In adjudication, whites insist upon an interpretation of the facts that does violence to notions of equality and truth as lived experience. The illogical (seemingly impossible) results are entirely logical within the mythic zone of race. The idea of race is not to frame truth from past events, but to convert events into their own mythical structure with cognitive and cosmological distortions as the result. What emerges from cases like *People v. Powell*, the *Goetz* case, and the *Stuart* case is not justice or truth, but a picture of race as a practice and as a source of signification that still mediates between us and the world as it is.

Notes

1. W.E.B. DuBois, The Souls of Black Folk 8 (John E. Wideman ed., 1990) (1903).
2. Abraham Lincoln, Collected Works 371 (Roy Basler ed., 1953).
3. By essentialist, I refer to the notion that there is some unchanging, immanent nature in things. See Garth L. Hallett, Language and Truth 7 (1988). From an essentialist perspective, race is an immutable essence and "exists" independently of what individuals might think about it.
4. This framework provided the organizing logic for Southern opposition to the Civil Rights Acts of the Reconstruction Era. Thus, in opposing the Civil Rights Act of 1871, Joshua Hill argued:

> I must confess, sir, that I cannot see the magnitude of this subject. I object to this great Government descending to the business of regulating the hotels and common taverns of this country, and the street railroads, stage-coaches, and everything of that sort. It looks to me to be a petty business for the government of the United States.

Cong. Globe, 42d Cong., 2d Sess. 242 (1871).
And he further explained: "What he may term a right may be the right of any man that pleases to come into my parlor and to be my guest. That is not the right of any colored man upon earth, nor of any white man, unless it is agreeable to me." *Id.*

5. 488 U.S. 469 (1992).
6. 488 U.S. at 507.
7. "The truth is there are no races. . . . Talk of 'race' is particularly distressing for those of us who take culture seriously. For, where race works . . . it does so only at the price of biologizing what *is* culture, or ideology." Anthony Appiah, *The Uncompleted Argument*, in Race, Writing, and Difference 21, 35–36 (Henry Louis Gates, Jr. ed., 1985); *see also* Peter Figueroa, Education and the Social Construction of "Race" 9–10 (1991) ("'Physical and cultural differences do not of themselves create groups or categories.' Race and ethnicity are not natural or fixed categories. 'It is only when physical and cultural differences are given cultural significance . . . that social forms result.'" (quoting M. Banton, Racial and Ethnic Competition 105 (1983)); Ashley Montagu, Statement on Race 10 (Oxford University Press, 3d ed. 1972) ("For all practical social purposes 'race' is not so much a biological phenomenon as a social myth.").
8. *See* Gordon W. Allport, The Nature of Prejudice 3–15 (1958).
9. We wear the mask that grins and lies,
   It hides our cheeks and shades our eyes,
   This debt we pay to human guile,
   With torn and bleeding hearts we smile;
   And mouth with myriad subtleties.

Fenton Johnson, *We Wear the Mask*, in American Negro Poetry 14 (1963).

10. Racial identity mediates between the legal interpreter and the subject. Through this filter, there appears to be an inside and an outside, an us and a them. Whites perceive themselves in the inside, which is to say at the center—as an us. Blacks are outside, decentered—a them. Thus, the problem of blacks may be understood as one of positional inferiority.

11. Racial thinking is not some foreign cultural artifact somehow embedded in an "autonomous" individual subjectivity, but rather represents, at a deep level, one dimension of our subjectivity. The self that constructs and projects racial identity onto others must itself be constituted by, and defined in terms of, race. The individual awareness and the cultural framework are mutually entailed. Charles Lambi explains:

> For myself, earth-bound and fettered to the scene of my activities, I confess that I do feel the differences of mankind, national and individual. . . . I am, in plainer words, a bundle of prejudices—made up of likings and dislikings—the veriest thrall to sympathies, apathies, and antipathies.

ALLPORT, *supra* at 3 (quoting Charles Lambi).

12. For blacks, the self is fragmented between a subjective self (individual identity) and an objective or racial self. This line tracks the division between a self that is within society and within the language, and a self that is negated by society and language and is alienated from it.

13. For a classic expression of this conception, *see* MARTIN LUTHER KING, JR., WHY WE CAN'T WAIT 28 (1964) (speaking of racial problems as moral and spiritual problems); *cf.* ANTHONY APPIAH, IN MY FATHER'S HOUSE (1992) (speaking of racialism or the problem of race as implicit in the claim of racism).

14. JAMES BALDWIN, THE PRICE OF THE TICKET 355 (1985).

15. Tracy Wood & Sheryl Stolberg, *Patrol Car Log in Beating Released*, L.A. TIMES, Mar. 19, 1991, at A1.

16. Richard A. Serrano, *Officers Are Heard Laughing on Tapes*, L.A. TIMES, Mar. 12, 1992, at B1.

17. Michael Miller, *Police Told King He Was Used as a Baseball*, REUTERS, Mar. 13, 1992, *available in* LEXIS, News library.

18. Richard A. Serrano & Tracy Wilkinson, *All Four in King Beating Acquitted*, L.A. TIMES, Apr. 30, 1992, at A1.

19. Lois Timnick, *Judge Will Allow Race Evidence in King Case*, L.A. TIMES, June 11, 1992, at B1.

20. Richard A. Serrano, *CHP Officer Describes Chase, Beating of King*, L.A. TIMES, Mar. 7, 1992, at A1. The struggle between King and the police takes place on a field of pain and violence and a field of symbolic expression. That is, the violence against King is intended as a particular representation of something more specific than white supremacy. It seems to stand for something like white manhood. If King was a threat to the police officers, I suggest he became a threat at the point at which white maleness is constructed, a juncture at which race and sex intersect. Under this view, King's shaking his behind at the police officers was qualitatively the same as shaking his penis at them. As it is traditionally constructed, maleness is concerned with domination and power, and depends on hierarchy for coherence. The notion of white maleness depends for its coherence not only upon domination vis-à-vis women, but also vis-à-vis blacks. King's wagging of his body represented a negation of that hierarchy and, therefore, his beating was no doubt designed to represent a restoration of the "proper order."

21. Richard A. Serrano & Leslie Berger, *Koon Quizzed on Accuracy of Report on King Beating*, L.A. TIMES, Mar. 21, 1992, at A1.

22. 2 ERNST CASSIRER, PHILOSOPHY OF SYMBOLIC FORMS 35 (Ralph Manheim trans., 1955).

23. Kurtz is a figure who resides at the "inner station" in the "Congo." Alone in this "dark" place Kurtz dies muttering about "the horror." JOSEPH CONRAD, *Heart of Darkness*, in TALES OF LAND AND SEA 33 (1953). According to the orthodox interpretation, Kurtz represents the deterioration of the mind from solitude and isolation. However, the imagery speaks, even if only unconsciously, of fan-

tasies of Africa not merely as a land of dark people, but as a place of darkness that is the moral antithesis of Europe. This demonizing of Africa and Africans is a projection of the evil of colonialism itself.

24. 2 PAC, *Words of Wisdom*, on 2 APOCALYPSE NOW (Interscope Records 1991).

25. Robert D. McFadden, *A Gunman Wounds Four on IRT Train then Escapes*, N.Y. TIMES, Dec. 23, 1984, at A1.

26. *See generally* DEATH WISH (Paramount Pictures 1974); DEATH WISH II (Paramount Pictures 1982). In the original film, Charles Bronson plays an architect who becomes a self-appointed executioner of criminals after his wife is murdered and his daughter raped by New York muggers. Interestingly, the muggers who rape Bronson's daughter are cast as blacks. Bronson, who portrays in his role the growing racially adumbrated rage that would produce a Bernhard Goetz, described his role in these films not as brutal but as heroic—that of a gardener ridding his garden of snakes.

27. McFadden, *supra*; David E. Sanger, *Callers Support Subway Gunman*, N.Y. TIMES, Dec. 25, 1984, at A1; Alan Finder & Albert Scardino, *Goetz Checked, Then Fired Another Round*, N.Y. TIMES, Mar. 3, 1985, § 4, at E6; *You Have to Think in a Cold-Blooded Way*, N.Y. TIMES, Apr. 30, 1987, at B6; Dennis Hevesi, *Goetz Confronts Victims in Court Suit Hearing*, N.Y. TIMES, Sept. 27, 1990, at B2.

28. Joyce Purnick, *Ward Declares Goetz Didn't Shoot in Self-Defense*, N.Y. TIMES, Feb. 22, 1985, at A1.

29. Goetz explained:

I looked at his face, and, you know, his eyes were shiny. . . . [T]hey wanted to play with me . . . like a cat plays with a mouse before, you know, it's horrible. . . . [I]t's the confrontation, that was the threat right there. It was seeing his smile and his eyes lit up and the presence of the other four. . . .

You Have to Think in a Cold-Blooded Way, supra at B6 (quoting Bernhard Goetz).

30. *Id.*

31. Manicheanism is a syncretistic religious dualism that originated in Persia and was widely adhered to in the Roman empire during the third and fourth centuries A.D. It teaches that a cosmic conflict exists between a good realm of light and an evil realm of darkness. *See* WEBSTER'S THIRD NEW INTERNATIONAL DICTIONARY 1375 (Phillip Babcock ed., 1971).

32. Kirk Johnson, *Everybody Is Edgy as Goetz Trial Opens*, N.Y. TIMES, May 3, 1987, § 4, at 6.

33. Margot Hornblower, *Jury Exonerates Goetz in Four Subway Shootings; New Yorker Convicted of Weapon Possession*, WASH. POST, June 17, 1987, at A1.

34. RICHARD WRIGHT, NATIVE SON 75 (1940) (emphasis added).

35. H.L.A. HART, THE CONCEPT OF LAW 11 (1961).

36. Peter S. Canellos & Irene Sege, *Couple Shot After Leaving Hospital; Baby Delivered*, BOSTON GLOBE, Oct. 24, 1989, Metro Sec., at 1.

37. The black man who supposedly murdered the pregnant Carol Stuart and shot her apparently loving husband is characterized as the extreme instance of a depraved black criminal. He bears an uncanny resemblance to Bigger Thomas, a figure created by Richard Wright in the classic *Native Son*. *See generally* WRIGHT, *supra*. Bigger is a fearful, and in a deep sense innocent, black man who in a moment of fear of being caught in a white woman's bedroom "accidentally" smothers her. He is portrayed and hunted as a sadistic murderer, a negro murderer, a *black* murderer, becoming the incarnation of racial fears. So is the black man with the raspy voice equally an incarnation of the same fear, not a real person, but a figure who expresses, and allows for the expression of, shared anxiety.

38. Canellos & Sege, *supra* (emphasis added).

39. Fox Butterfield, *Massachusetts Says Police in Boston Illegally Stopped Black Youths*, N.Y. TIMES, Dec. 20, 1990, at B16.

40. Ellison wrote:

I am an invisible man. No, I am not a spook like those who haunted Edgar Allan Poe. . . . I am a man of substance, of flesh and bone, fiber and liquids—and I might even be said to possess a mind. I am invisible, understand, simply because people refuse to see me. Like the bodiless heads you see sometimes in circus sideshows, it is as though I have been surrounded by mirrors of hard distorting glass. When they approach me they see only my surroundings, themselves, or figments of their imagination. . . .

RALPH ELLISON, INVISIBLE MAN 3 (1980) (1952).

14

Playing in the Dark: Whiteness and the Literary Imagination

TONI MORRISON

At the end of *The Narrative of Arthur Gordon Pym,* Edgar Allan Poe describes the last two days of an extraordinary journey:

> *"March 21st*—A sullen darkness now hovered above us—but from out the milky depths of the ocean a luminous glare arose, and stole up along the bulwarks of the boat. We were nearly overwhelmed by the white ashy shower which settled upon us and upon the canoe, but melted into the water as it fell. . . .
>
> *"March 22d*—The darkness had materially increased, relieved only by the glare of the water thrown back from the white curtain before us. Many gigantic and pallidly white birds flew continuously now from beyond the veil, and their scream was the eternal *Tekeli-li!* as they retreated from our vision. Hereupon Nu-Nu stirred in the bottom of the boat; but upon touching him, we found his spirit departed. And now we rushed into the embraces of the cataract, where a chasm threw itself open to receive us. But there arose in our pathway a shrouded human figure, very far larger in its proportions than any dweller among men. And the hue of the skin of the figure was of the perfect whiteness of the snow."

They have been floating, Pym and Peters and the native, Nu-Nu, on a warm, milk-white sea under a "white ashy shower." The black man dies, and the boat rushes on through the white curtain behind which a white giant rises up. After that, there is nothing. There is no more narrative. Instead there is a scholarly note, explanation, and an anxious, piled-up "conclusion." The latter states that it was *whiteness* that terrified the natives and killed Nu-Nu. The following inscription was carved into the walls of the chasms the travelers passed through: "I have graven it in within the hills, and my vengeance upon the dust within the rock."

No early American writer is more important to the concept of American Africanism than Poe. And no image is more telling than the one just described: the visualized but somehow closed and unknowable white form that rises from the mists at the end of the journey—or, at any rate, at the end of the narration proper. The images of the white curtain and the "shrouded human figure" with skin "the perfect whiteness of the snow" both occur after the narrative has encountered blackness. The first white image seems related to the expiration and erasure of the serviceable and serving black figure, Nu-Nu. Both are figurations of impenetrable whiteness that surface in American literature whenever an Africanist presence is engaged. These closed white images are found frequently, but not always, at the end of the narrative. They appear so often and in such particular circumstances that they give pause. They clamor, it seems, for an attention that would yield the meaning that lies in their positioning, their repetition, and their strong suggestion of paralysis and incoherence; of impasse and non-sequitur.

These images of impenetrable whiteness need contextualizing to explain their extraordinary power, pattern, and consistency. Because they appear almost always in conjunction with representations of black or Africanist people who are dead, impotent, or under complete control, these images of blinding whiteness seem to function as both antidote for and meditation on the shadow that is companion to this whiteness—a dark and abiding presence that moves the hearts and texts of American literature with fear and longing. This haunting, a darkness from which our early literature seemed unable to extricate itself, suggests the complex and contradictory situation in which American writers found themselves during the formative years of the nation's literature.

Young America distinguished itself by, and understood itself to be, pressing toward a future of freedom, a kind of human dignity believed unprecedented in the world. A whole tradition of "universal" yearnings collapsed into that well-fondled phrase, "the American Dream." Although this immigrant dream deserves the exhaustive scrutiny it has received in the scholarly disciplines and the arts, it is just as important to know what these people were rushing from as it is to know what they were hastening to. If the New World fed dreams, what was the Old World reality that whetted the appetite for them? And how did that reality caress and grip the shaping of a new one?

The flight from the Old World to the New is generally seen to be a flight from oppression and limitation to freedom and possibility. Although, in fact, the escape was sometimes an escape from license—from a society perceived to be unacceptably permissive, ungodly, and undisciplined—for those fleeing for reasons other than religious ones, constraint and limitation impelled the journey. All the Old World offered these immigrants was poverty, prison, social ostracism, and, not infrequently, death. There was of course a clerical, scholarly group of immigrants who came seeking the adventure possible in founding a colony for, rather than against, one or another mother country or fatherland. And of course there were the merchants, who came for the cash.

Whatever the reasons, the attraction was of the "clean slate" variety, a once-in-a-lifetime opportunity not only to be born again but to be born again in new clothes, as it were. The new setting would provide new raiments of self. This second chance could even benefit from the mistakes of the first. The New World offered the vision of a limitless future, made more gleaming by the constraint, dissatisfaction, and turmoil left behind. It was a promise genuinely promising. With luck and endurance one could discover freedom; find a way to make God's law manifest; or end up rich as a prince. The desire for freedom is preceded by oppression; a yearning for God's law is born of the detestation of human license and corruption; the glamor of riches is in thrall to poverty, hunger, and debt.

There was very much more in the late seventeenth and eighteenth centuries to make the trip worth the risk. The habit of genuflection would be replaced by the thrill of command. Power—control of one's own destiny—would replace the powerlessness felt before the gates of class, caste, and cunning persecution. One could move from discipline and punishment to disciplining and punishing; from social ostracism to social rank. One could be released from a useless, binding, repulsive past into a kind of history-lessness, a blank page waiting to be inscribed. Much was to be written there: noble impulses were made into law and appropriated for a national tradition; base ones, learned and elaborated in the rejected and rejecting homeland, were also made into law and appropriated for tradition.

The body of literature produced by the young nation is one way it inscribed its transactions with these fears, forces, and hopes. And it is difficult to read the literature of young America without being struck by how antithetical it is to our modern rendition of the American Dream. How pronounced in it is the absence of that term's elusive mixture of hope, realism, materialism, and promise. For a people who made much of their "newness"—their potential, freedom, and innocence—it is striking how dour, how troubled, how frightened and haunted our early and founding literature truly is.

We have words and labels for this haunting—"gothic," "romantic, "sermonic," "Puritan"—whose sources are to be found in the literature of the world these immigrants left. But the strong affinity between the nineteenth-century American psyche and gothic romance has rightly been much remarked. Why should a young country repelled by Europe's moral and social disorder, swooning in a fit of desire and rejection, devote its talents to reproducing in its own literature the typology of diabolism it wanted to leave behind? An answer to that seems fairly obvious: one way to benefit from the lessons of earlier mistakes and past misfortune is to record them so as to prevent their repetition through exposure and inoculation.

Romance was the form in which this uniquely American prophylaxis could be played out. Long after the movement in Europe, romance remained the cherished expression of young America. What was there in American romanticism that made it so attractive to Americans as a battle plain on which to fight, engage, and imagine their demons?

It has been suggested that romance is an evasion of history (and thus perhaps attractive to a people trying to evade the recent past). But I am more persuaded by arguments that find in it the head-on encounter with very real, pressing historical forces and the contradictions inherent in them as they came to be experienced by writers. Romance, an exploration of anxiety imported from the shadows of European culture, made possible the sometimes safe and other times risky embrace of quite specific, understandably human, fears: Americans' fear of being outcast, of failings of powerlessness; their fear of boundarylessness, of Nature unbridled and crouched for attack; their fear of the absence of so-called civilization; their fear of loneliness, of aggression both external and internal. In short, the terror of human freedom—the thing they coveted most of all. Romance offered writers not less but more; not a narrow a-historical canvas but a wide historical one; not escape but entanglement. For young America it had everything: nature as subject matter, a system of symbolism, a thematics of the search for self-valorization and validation—above all, the opportunity to conquer fear imaginatively and to quiet deep insecurities. It offered platforms for moralizing and fabulation, and for the imaginative entertainment of violence, sublime incredibility, and terror—and terror's most significant, overweening ingredient: darkness, with all the connotative value it awakened.

There is no romance free of what Herman Melville called "the power of blackness," especially not in a country in which there was a resident population, already black, upon which the imagination could play; through which historical, moral, metaphysical, and social fears, problems, and dichotomies could be articulated. The slave population, it could be and was assumed, offered itself up as surrogate selves for meditation on problems of human freedom, its lure and its elusiveness. This black population was available for meditations on terror—the terror of European outcasts, their dread of failure, powerlessness, Nature without limits, natal loneliness, internal aggression, evil, sin, greed. In other words, this slave population was understood to have offered itself up for reflections on human freedom in terms other than the abstractions of human potential and the rights of man.

The ways in which artists—and the society that bred them—transferred internal conflicts to a "blank darkness," to conveniently bound and violently silenced black bodies, is a major theme in American literature. The rights of man, for example, an organizing principle upon which the nation was founded, was inevitably yoked to Africanism. Its history, its origin is permanently allied with another seductive concept: the hierarchy of race. As the sociologist Orlando Patterson has noted, we should not be surprised that the Enlightenment could accommodate slavery; we should be surprised if it had not. The concept of freedom did not emerge in a vacuum. Nothing highlighted freedom—if it did not in fact create it—like slavery.

Black slavery enriched the country's creative possibilities. For in that construction of blackness *and* enslavement could be found not only the not-free but also, with the dramatic polarity created by skin color, the projection of the not-me. The result was a playground for the imagination. What rose up out of collective needs to allay internal fears and to rationalize external exploitation was an American Africanism—a fabricated brew of darkness, otherness, alarm, and desire that is uniquely American. (There also exists, of course, a European Africanism with a counterpart in colonial literature.)

What I wish to examine is how the image of reined-in, bound, suppressed, and repressed darkness became objectified in American literature as an Africanist persona. I want to show how the duties of that persona—duties of exorcism and reification and mirroring—are on demand and on display throughout much of the literature of the country and helped to form the distinguishing characteristics of a proto-American literature.

Earlier I said that cultural identities are formed and informed by a nation's literature, and that what seemed to be on the "mind" of the literature of the United States was the self-conscious but highly problematic construction of the American as a new white man. Emerson's call for that new man in "The American Scholar" indicates the deliberateness of the construction, the conscious necessity for establishing difference. But the writers who responded to this call, accepting or rejecting it, did not look solely to Europe to establish a reference for difference. There was a very theatrical difference underfoot. Writers were able to celebrate or deplore an identity already existing or rapidly taking a form that was elaborated through racial difference. That difference provided a huge payout of sign, symbol, and agency in the process of organizing, separating, and consolidating identity along culturally valuable lines of interest.

Bernard Bailyn has provided us with an extraordinary investigation of European settlers in the act of becoming Americans. I want to quote a rather long passage from his *Voyagers to the West* because it underscores the salient aspects of the American character I have been describing:

> "William Dunbar, seen through his letters and diary, appears to be more fictional than real—a creature of William Faulkner's imagination, a more cultivated Colonel Sutpen but no less mysterious. He too, like that strange character in *Absalom! Absalom!*, was a man in his early twenties who appeared suddenly in the Mississippi wilderness to stake out a claim to a large parcel of land, then disappeared to the Caribbean, to return leading a battalion of 'wild' slaves with whose labor alone he built an estate where before there had been nothing but trees and uncultivated soil. But he was more complex than Sutpen, if no less driving in his early ambitions, no less a progenitor of a notable southern family, and no less a part of a violent biracial world whose tensions could lead in strange directions. For this wilderness planter was a scientist, who would later correspond with Jefferson on science and exploration, a Mississippi planter whose contributions to the American Philosophical Society (to which Jefferson proposed him for membership) included linguistics, archaeology, hydrostatics, astronomy, and climatology, and whose geographical explorations were reported in widely known publications. Like Sutpen an exotic figure in the plantation world

of early Mississippi—known as 'Sir' William just as Sutpen was known as 'Colonel'—he too imported into that raw, half-savage world the niceties of European culture: not chandeliers and costly rugs, but books, surveyor's equipment of the finest kind, and the latest instruments of science.

"Dunbar was a Scot by birth, the youngest son of Sir Archibald Dunbar of Morayshire. He was educated first by tutors at home, then at the university in Aberdeen, where his interest in mathematics, astronomy, and belles-lettres took mature shape. What happened to him after his return home and later in London, where he circulated with young intellectuals, what propelled, or led, him out of the metropolis on the first leg of his long voyage west is not known. But whatever his motivation may have been, in April 1771, aged only twenty-two, Dunbar appeared in Philadelphia. . . .

"Ever eager for gentility, this well-educated product of the Scottish enlightenment and of London's sophistication—this bookish young *litterateur* and scientist who, only five years earlier, had been corresponding about scientific problems—about 'Dean Swifts beatitudes,' about the 'virtuous and happy life,' and about the Lord's commandment that mankind should 'love one another'—was yet strangely insensitive to the suffering of those who served him. In July 1776 he recorded not the independence of the American colonies from Britain, but the suppression of an alleged conspiracy for freedom by slaves on his own plantation. . . .

"Dunbar, the young *erudit*, the Scottish scientist and man of letters, was no sadist. His plantation regime was, by the standards of the time, mild; he clothed and fed his slaves decently, and frequently relented in his more severe punishments. But 4,000 miles from the sources of culture, alone on the far periphery of British civilization where physical survival was a daily struggle, where ruthless exploitation was a way of life, and where disorder, violence, and human degradation were commonplace, he had triumphed by successful adaptation. Endlessly enterprising and resourceful, his finer sensibilities dulled by the abrasions of frontier life, and feeling within himself a sense of authority and autonomy he had not known before, a force that flowed from his absolute control over the lives of others, he emerged a distinctive new man, a borderland gentleman, a man of property in a raw, half-savage world."[1]

Let me call attention to some elements of this portrait, some pairings and interdependencies that are marked in the story of William Dunbar. First is the historical connection between the Enlightenment and the institution of slavery—the rights of man and his enslavement. Second, we have the relationship between Dunbar's education and his New World enterprise. The education he had was exceptionally cultivated: it included the latest thought on theology and science, an effort perhaps to make them mutually accountable, to make one support the other. He is not only a "product of the Scottish enlightenment" but a London intellectual as well. He read Jonathan Swift, discussed the Christian commandment to love one another, and is described as "strangely" insensitive to the suffering of his slaves. On July 12, 1776, he records with astonishment and hurt surprise a slave rebellion on his plantation: "Judge my surprise. . . . Of what avail is kindness & good usage when rewarded by such ingratitude." "Constantly bewildered," Bailyn goes on, "by his slaves' behavior. . . [Dunbar] recovered two runaways and 'condemned them to receive 500 lashes each at five different times, and to carry a chain & log fixt to the ancle.'"

I take this to be a succinct portrait of the process by which the American as new, white, and male was constituted. It is a formation with at least four desirable consequences, all of which are referred to in Bailyn's summation of Dunbar's character and located in how Dunbar felt "within himself." Let me repeat: "a sense of authority and autonomy he had not known before, a force that flowed from his absolute control over the lives of others, he emerged a distinctive new man, a borderland gentleman, a man of property in a raw, half-savage world." A power, a sense of freedom, he had not known before. But what had he known before? Fine education, London sophistication, theological and scientific thought. None of these, one gathers, could provide him with the authority and autonomy that Mississippi planter life did. Also this sense is understood to be a force that flows, already present and ready to spill as a result of his "absolute control over the lives of others." This force is not a willed domination, a thought-out, calculated choice, but rather a kind of natural resource, a Niagara Falls waiting to drench Dunbar as soon as he is in a position to assume absolute control. Once he has moved into that position, he is resurrected as a new man, a distinctive man—a different man. And whatever his social status in London, in the New World he is a gentleman. More gentle, more man. The site of his transformation is within rawness: he is backgrounded by savagery.

I want to suggest that these concerns—autonomy, authority, newness and difference, absolute power—not only become the major themes and presumptions of American literature, but that each one is made possible by, shaped by, activated by a complex awareness and employment of a constituted Africanism. It was this Africanism, deployed as rawness and savagery, that provided the staging ground and arena for the elaboration of the quintessential American identity.

Note

1. Bernard Bailyn, *Voyagers to the West: A Passage in the Peopling of America on the Eve of the Revolution* (New York: Alfred A. Knopf, 1986), pp. 488–492.

15

Transparently White Subjective Decisionmaking: Fashioning a Legal Remedy

BARBARA J. FLAGG

Goodson, Badwin & Indiff is a major accounting firm employing more than five hundred persons nationwide. Among its twenty black accountants is Yvonne Taylor, who at the time this story begins was thirty-one years old and poised to become the first black regional supervisor in the firm's history. Yvonne attended Princeton University and received an M.B.A. from the Kellogg Graduate School of Management at Northwestern University. While employed at Goodson, she was highly successful in attracting new clients, especially from the black business community. In all other respects her performance at the firm was regarded as exemplary.

Yvonne always was comfortable conforming to the norms of the corporate culture at Goodson, and in fact had been comfortable with "white" norms since childhood. Her manner of speech, dress, and hairstyle, as well as many of her attitudes and beliefs, fell well within the bounds of whites' cultural expectations. However, Yvonne may have adapted to the corporate culture *too* well. It is common practice at Goodson to be less than absolutely precise in keeping records of one's billable hours. Instead, accountants generally estimate time spent on clients' accounts at the end of each day, and tend to err on the side of over- rather than underbilling. On the rare occasions this practice is discussed, it is explained in terms of the firm's prestige in the business community; the idea is that clients should consider themselves fortunate to be associated with Goodson at all. Like other young accountants, Yvonne at first attempted to keep meticulous records, but she soon realized others were surpassing her in billable hours without spending more time actually at work. Consequently, and consistent with her general pattern of conforming to prevailing norms, she gradually adopted the less precise method.

Under Goodson's promotion procedure, the decision whether to promote an accountant to regional supervisor rests on senior partners' evaluations of the candidate's accounting knowledge and skills and, to a lesser extent, on assessments of her interpersonal skills solicited from clients and from peers in the office. The reports on Yvonne's accounting skills were uniformly excellent. Comments from some peers had overtones of distance and mild distrust suggesting that they were somewhat uncomfortable with Yvonne as a black

From "Fashioning a Title VII Remedy for Transparently White Subjective Decisionmaking," 104 YALE L.J. 2009 (1995). Originally published in the *Yale Law Journal*. Reprinted by permission of The Yale Law Journal Company and Fred B. Rothman & Company.

woman, but these comments fell far below the level necessary to raise serious doubts about her interpersonal skills. However, several of Yvonne's clients took the occasion to register complaints about possible overbilling. The firm launched an extensive investigation and eventually reached the conclusion that Yvonne had been careless in her recordkeeping and that therefore she should not be promoted. As a practical matter, this episode ended Yvonne's prospects for advancement at Goodson; the firm has an informal policy of not reconsidering an individual once she has been passed over for promotion.

Yvonne has a younger sister who, sometime during college, legally changed her name from Deborah Taylor to Keisha Akbar. As her decision to change her name suggests, Keisha places an emphasis on her African heritage that Yvonne does not,[1] and she has adopted speech and grooming patterns consistent with that cultural perspective.[2] Keisha majored in biology at Howard University, and after graduation went to work as the only black scientist at a small research firm dedicated to identifying and developing environmentally safe agricultural products for commercial uses. Like Yvonne, Keisha excelled at the technical aspects of her work, but she brought to it a much less assimilationist personal style. At first, her cultural differences had little impact on her job performance. This changed, however, when the once-small firm began to grow rapidly and reorganization into research divisions became necessary. For the most part, the firm planned to elevate each of the original members of the research team to positions as department heads, but Keisha was not asked to head a department because the individuals responsible for making that decision felt that she lacked the personal qualities of a successful manager. They saw Keisha as just too different from the researchers she would supervise to be able to communicate effectively with them. The firm articulated this reasoning by asserting a need for a department head who shared the perspectives and values of the employees under her direction. When Keisha raised the possibility that her perceived differences might be race-dependent, the decisionmakers replied that they would apply the same conformity-related criteria to white candidates for the position of department head.

Thus, in spite of the diametrically different cultural styles adopted by Yvonne and Keisha, their stories have the same ending: Each encountered the glass ceiling at a relatively early stage of what should have been a very successful career.[3] A case can be made that both were disadvantaged because of race. Yvonne would argue that there is no nonracial element of her performance or her personal characteristics that could account for the way her recordkeeping practices were singled out for special scrutiny, and therefore that race is left as the most plausible explanation of the different treatment she received. Even if the basis for the special treatment was unconscious, this is a relatively easily understood form of discrimination: Yvonne's contention would be that she was treated differently from similarly situated others because of her race.

Keisha, on the other hand, arguably was given the same treatment that would have been afforded anyone who was perceived as unable or unwilling to fit smoothly into the corporate culture. Nevertheless, it can be argued that she too was disadvantaged because of her race, in that the personal characteristics that disqualified her from a management position intersect seamlessly with her self-definition as a black woman. I previously have characterized this form of discrimination as an outgrowth of the transparency phenomenon:

> White people externalize race. For most whites, most of the time, to think or speak about race is to think or speak about people of color, or perhaps, at times, to reflect on oneself (or other whites) in relation to people of color. But we tend not to think of ourselves or our racial cohort as racially distinctive. Whites' "consciousness" of whiteness is predominantly *unconsciousness*

of whiteness. We perceive and interact with other whites as individuals who have no significant racial characteristics. In the same vein, the white person is unlikely to see or describe himself in racial terms, perhaps in part because his white peers do not regard him as racially distinctive. Whiteness is a transparent quality when whites interact with whites in the absence of people of color. Whiteness attains opacity, becomes apparent to the white mind, only in relation to, and contrast with, the "color" of nonwhites.[4]

Just as whites tend to regard whiteness as racelessness, the transparency phenomenon also affects whites' decisionmaking; behaviors and characteristics associated with whites take on the same aura of race neutrality. Thus, white people frequently interpret norms adopted by a dominantly white culture as racially neutral, and so fail to recognize the ways in which those norms may be in fact covertly race-specific. Keisha would argue that she was not promoted because her personal style was found wanting when measured against a norm that was in fact transparently "white."

The manner in which both Yvonne and Keisha were treated violates the norm of colorblindness—the principle that race should not be taken into account in assessing the individual. In Yvonne's case, the claimed violation should be obvious; arguably she was treated differently from others solely because she is black. With regard to Keisha, the violation of the colorblindness norm takes the form of applying unconsciously white, and in that sense race-specific, criteria of decision. Thus, laws and policies designed to implement the colorblindness principle ought equally to disapprove the outcomes in both sisters' cases.

Because these race-specific acts occurred in employment settings, both Yvonne and Keisha would turn to Title VII for legal relief. However, even though Title VII provides a cause of action for adverse employment decisions taken "because of" race, Keisha and Yvonne would find themselves in quite different positions under existing judicial interpretations of that statute. Yvonne would have a relatively easy time framing a disparate treatment claim (though that is not to say that she necessarily would prevail), but as a practical matter Keisha would have difficulty because the form of discrimination she encountered cannot easily be addressed under either the disparate treatment or the current disparate impact model.[5]

Keisha's case raises the question whether transparently white decisionmaking falls within the category of race-specific employment practices proscribed by Title VII. I have argued elsewhere that government has a special obligation not to participate in the maintenance of white supremacy. However, the question whether private employers have a similar obligation raises a different constellation of issues concerning role and responsibility. Thus, an examination of the fundamental policy regarding race discrimination embodied in Title VII is a necessary prerequisite to any proposal that would require judicial recognition of a new or amended approach to Title VII liability. I contend that judicial acceptance of a revised model of liability would be wholly consistent with current congressional policy regarding Title VII, as evidenced in the amendments to the statute adopted in the Civil Rights Act of 1991. Exploring transparency may tell us something about what race discrimination doctrine might become, and examining doctrinal possibilities may tell us something about who we want and choose to be.

Notes

1. This is not to suggest that Yvonne denies her African heritage, but only that she interprets it differently; she sees being black as congruent with many of the norms of the dominant culture.

2. To elaborate, Keisha often wears clothing that features African styles and materials, frequently braids her hair or wears it in a natural style, and at times speaks to other black employees in the dialect linguists designate "Black English," though she always uses "Standard English" when speaking with whites.

3. For a discussion of the many difficulties faced by blacks in the corporate world, see GEORGE DAVIS & GLEGG WATSON, BLACK LIFE IN CORPORATE AMERICA: SWIMMING IN THE MAINSTREAM (1982).

4. Barbara J. Flagg, *"Was Blind, But Now I See": White Race Consciousness and the Requirement of Discriminatory Intent*, 91 MICH. L. REV. 953, 970 (1993).

5. In brief, the disparate treatment model requires proof that one has been treated differently from similarly situated coworkers. In contrast, the disparate impact approach targets racially neutral employment practices.

16

The Rhetorical Tapestry of Race

THOMAS ROSS

For many, the rhetoric supporting the institution of slavery was constructed simply. Once one got past establishing the nonhuman nature of blacks, the rest was easy. If whites had any moral obligation in the matter, it was to use blacks to further the interests of society, a society from which the black was excluded. The horrific conditions of slave existence became the tokens of charity and benevolence to the black brute. This particular rhetoric took various forms but always avoided any real conflict in values and principles by placing blacks outside the community of humans.

The rhetoric of the nineteenth-century Supreme Court Justices seems at first glance to be not at all like this form of virulent racism. Yet their rhetoric often worked in much the same manner, not explicitly denying, but obscuring the humanness of blacks as part of a rhetoric dressed up in abstractions, syllogisms, and legal vernacular. The abstract principles of individual freedom and human equality, ideas that were at the core of Revolutionary and constitutional discourse, ostensibly conflicted with the reality of slavery, and later in the century, the reality of de jure ["by law." Ed.] segregation and oppression of blacks. This conflict was the cracked surface of reality which demanded the smoothing veneer of legal rhetoric. Those judges who denied themselves the rhetorical move of explicitly placing blacks outside the human community needed more sophisticated arguments. They had to construct a more subtle rhetorical artifice, yet one that embodied its own version of racism.

The best of the rhetoricians constructed exquisitely horrific rhetorical structures to justify choices that society has since discredited. Woven through the Supreme Court's opinions in *Dred Scott*, the *Civil Rights Cases*, and *Plessy*,[1] the themes of white innocence and black abstraction made the subjugation of blacks intellectually coherent. This rhetoric did not create the conditions of subjugation. The rhetoric, however, did dress up the choices which were, at the least, not choices to mitigate that subjugation. In this sense, the rhetoric was a symptom of the disease of racism that gripped the legal culture, and the larger culture, of nineteenth-century America.

Dred Scott and Taney's Narrative of Subjugation

Chief Justice Taney's opinion in *Dred Scott* stained the Court's history and virtually ruined the historical standing of its author. Nonetheless, it is a remarkable and revealing rhetorical structure.

32 WM. & MARY L. REV. 1 (1990). Originally published in the *William and Mary Law Review*. Reprinted by permission.

Taney's opinion was infamous in his time mostly for its declaration that Congress lacked the power to prohibit slavery in the Territories, thus declaring the Missouri Compromise unconstitutional. The opinion is infamous in our time for its assertion that blacks were not citizens of the United States.[2] To establish the latter assertion, Taney's central rhetorical structure was the narrative of subjugation. He told the story of the subjugation of blacks through colonial times and into the constitutional period. Linking this narrative with an original intent interpretive theory, he concluded that because the drafters of the Constitution could not have imagined blacks as citizens, he was bound by their intentions on the matter.

Taney's narrative is remarkable in various ways. Black abstraction was a central theme of nineteenth-century jurisprudence, the rhetoricians typically portraying the black outside of any real and rich social context. Yet Taney placed the black in a social context and purported to tell the black person's story.

Taney's narrative of subjugation is a departure from black abstraction, but in form only and, in all important respects, is simply another way of arriving at the rhetorical end of black abstraction. The essential purpose of black abstraction is to deny, or obscure, the humanness of blacks. Taney got to that end by narrative, not abstraction.

Taney achieved his narrative end because of the inescapable logic of certain choices he made. He chose not simply what to tell out of the rich set of possibilities; he also chose to place his narrative in a particular place and time and then, from within that place and time, he chose what pieces of that story to tell. Taney did not choose to place any portion of his narrative in Africa, where the black person was part of a real and rich culture. Taney chose not to tell the story of seventeenth-century colonial life with its relative tolerance for blacks. Moreover, he found virtually no place for the story of free blacks living in the constitutional period.[3]

Taney's narrative of subjugation was neither lie nor fiction. Blacks were subjugated in the various ways he chronicled. He constructed his narrative, however, for a rhetorical end, demonstrating that the rhetoric of black abstraction, like any rhetoric, can be put aside whenever the same rhetorical ends can be achieved otherwise. Taney's narrative, coupled with his interpretive theory, achieved perfectly the rhetorical ends of white innocence and black abstraction. [See Chapter 6. Ed.] He argued that the narrative demonstrated the pervasive subjugation of blacks preceding the constitutional era. Thus, the Founding Fathers never could have intended that this subjugated race would be citizens with the same constitutional status as white persons. Under his theory, these intentions concluded the matter.

> The question before us is, whether the class of persons described in the plea in abatement compose a portion of this people, and are constituent members of this sovereignty? We think they are not, and that they are not included, and were not intended to be included, under the word "citizens" in the Constitution. . . . On the contrary, they were at that time considered as a subordinate and inferior class of beings, who had been subjugated by the dominant race, and, whether emancipated or not, yet remained subject to their authority, and had no rights or privileges but such as those who held the power and the Government might choose to grant them.
>
> It is not the province of the court to decide upon the justice or injustice, the policy or impolicy, of these laws. The decision of that question belonged to the political or law-making power; to those who formed the sovereignty and framed the Constitution. The duty of the court is, to interpret the instrument they have framed, with the best lights we can obtain on the subject, and to administer it as we find it, according to its true intent and meaning when it was adopted.[4]

Thus, the constructed narrative and the interpretive theory formed a complete rhetorical edifice. Blacks simply were not citizens. The rhetoric made this appalling conclusion coherent.

Taney's narrative reduced blacks to an inferior, if not subhuman, status, not just in history but in the moment. By using the story to justify the conclusion that blacks could not be citizens, Taney reinforced the "less than human" legal status of blacks in his own time.

Taney's use of the original intent theory in this case also is connected with the theme of white innocence. Although the original intent interpretive theory is not unique to the *Dred Scott* case, its use did permit Taney to shun responsibility for his choice. Depending on the extent of Taney's racism, he may have felt little need to evade personal responsibility for his choice. Nonetheless, his originalism theory permitted him to pretend that he was not saying blacks ought not be deemed citizens. He was saying that the Constitution, properly interpreted, did not include them. Whether conscious or not, Taney's theory is an example of the white man taking the position of nonculpability for the circumstances of the black person.

Generally, Taney's opinion suggested a naturalness to the subjugation of the blacks. In his rhetorical world, blacks were unidimensional characters, always subjugated. This portrayal suggested that the subjugation was a product of their natural difference as opposed to the brute force of the white master race, which mitigated the dissonance between the reality of subjugation and the principles of freedom and equality.

The *Civil Rights Cases* and the "Special Favorites"

The Reconstruction Amendments[5] negated the formal rhetoric of Taney's opinion in *Dred Scott*. Legal rhetoric could not explicitly deny blacks the status of citizen. Moreover, any originalism interpretive argument had to accommodate a new set of "Founding Fathers" who created their piece of the Constitution at an importantly different moment in our history.

The scope of the Reconstruction Amendments has been, from their beginning, controversial. In the *Civil Rights Cases*, the Court held that the first and second sections of the Civil Rights Act of 1875, Congress's effort to provide some source of statutory protection for the southern blacks in the waning days of Reconstruction, were unconstitutional.[6] Justice Bradley, writing for the majority, concluded that neither the thirteenth nor the fourteenth amendment gave Congress the power to enact a law that prohibited racial discrimination in public accommodations and conveyances. Bradley's opinion relied on the concept of "state action" to limit the authority that the fourteenth amendment granted to Congress. The statute, he argued, regulated private action, which the fourteenth amendment did not reach. The thirteenth amendment did not authorize the federal statute because racial segregation in public facilities was not deemed a "badge" of slavery.

Bradley's opinion contained perhaps the most outrageous example of black abstraction in the nineteenth-century rhetoric:

> When a man has emerged from slavery, and by the aid of beneficent legislation has shaken off the inseparable concomitants of that state, there must be some stage in the progress of his elevation when he takes the rank of a mere citizen, and ceases to be the special favorite of the laws, and when his rights as a citizen, or a man, are to be protected in the ordinary modes by which other men's rights are protected.[7]

Bradley's assertion is coherent, but only in the abstract. The special treatment that the statute accorded blacks was the product of the reality of pervasive oppression of blacks by whites. The purpose of the federal statute struck down was to create the possibility of some continued federal presence and power in the South to protect blacks as Reconstruction came to a close and the federal government began what became ultimately an abandonment of the southern blacks.[8] Thus, the statutes especially protected black citizens. Whites were not especially favored precisely because they were the oppressors.

Harlan, in dissent, responded to the "special favorites" argument:

> It is, I submit, scarcely just to say that the colored race has been the special favorite of the laws. . . . What the nation, through Congress, has sought to accomplish in reference to that race is . . . to secure and protect rights belonging to them as freemen and citizens; nothing more. . . . The one underlying purpose of congressional legislation has been to enable the black race to take the rank of mere citizens.[9]

Harlan's opinion, unlike Bradley's, reflected some sense of the actual social context in which the statute would have operated. [See Chapter 72 for more on Justice Harlan and his unique—for its time—insight. Ed.]

Bradley's opinion also has an abstract quality in its assertion that only the random acts of individuals victimized blacks and that victimized blacks could get redress in the state courts.

> The wrongful act of an individual, unsupported by any [state] authority, is simply a private wrong, or a crime of that individual; an invasion of the rights of the injured party, it is true, whether they affect his person, his property, or his reputation; but if not sanctioned in some way by the State, or not done under State authority, his rights remain in full force, and may presumably be vindicated by resort to the laws of the State for redress.[10]

Bradley's suggestion was disconnected from the reality of social context. The wrongs for which blacks might have sought redress were rapidly becoming the official state policy. Redress in the state courts was a fanciful illusion—except on the rhetorical field of abstraction.

By keeping his rhetoric above the field of play and in the strata of abstract assertions, Bradley made assertions that were laughable in their real and operating environment. He was able to smooth over the dissonance in the Court's exercise of its power to void a statute designed to address the real and pervasive oppression of blacks. In Bradley's rhetorical world, the Civil War and the Reconstruction Amendments ended all forms of state-sanctioned racial oppression. All that was left were the random acts of individual law-breakers, which the state courts, of course, would effectively redress.

Plessy and the Self-Imposed Stigma

In *Plessy v. Ferguson*,[11] the Court reviewed a Louisiana statute that segregated railroad passengers by race, a statute that exemplified the proliferating new "Black Codes" which established de jure segregation throughout the South in the late nineteenth century. Justice Brown held the statute constitutional. That the segregation law posed no thirteenth amendment problem was "too clear for argument." He reduced the fourteenth amendment conflict to the question whether the statute was a "reasonable regulation," a question that implied the extension of "a large discretion" to the legislature. Brown found the statute to be reasonable in its connection with "established usages, customs, and traditions of the people, and with a view to the promotion of their comfort, and the preservation of the public peace and good order."[12]

The only problem with the reasonableness of the law was that the law was grounded in racism. The "traditions" were those of racism; the "comfort" was that experienced by whites who were legally protected from the physical proximity of blacks; and the threat to "public peace" was the specter of whites reacting violently to the efforts of blacks to take a place of social equality. Both the law itself and the reasons for the law that Brown advanced were expressions of the pervasive and virulent racism that gripped this country in the latter nineteenth century.

Nonetheless, the legal rhetoric of Brown's opinion made the choice somehow intellectually coherent. Brown built his opinion on the assertion that segregation by law does not degrade or stigmatize the black person. "Laws permitting, and even requiring, [racial segregation] in places where they are liable to be brought into contact do not necessarily imply the inferiority of either race to the other. . . ."[13] Moreover, Brown asserted that any sense of stigma felt by a black person would be self-imposed:

> We consider the underlying fallacy of plaintiff's argument to consist in the assumption that the enforced separation of the two races stamps the colored race with a badge of inferiority. If this be so, it is not by reason of anything found in the act, but solely because the colored race chooses to put that construction upon it.[14]

Yet, the purpose and effect of the racial segregation laws throughout our legal history has always been to express the racial inferiority of blacks. These laws were a product of, and an expression of, racism. When a black person subject to laws commanding racial segregation in railroad cars felt a sense of stigma, she had not misunderstood the message, she had not revealed some idiosyncratic sensitivity; rather, she had heard and received the message sent by those responsible for the law.

Only in some abstract conception of the society could one say, with a straight face, that these segregation laws were not premised on racism and did not express a message of racial inferiority. Only in this abstract conception could the argument of equal treatment under the law have any real power. Any attempt to imagine the motivation for the passage of these laws and the effect the laws would have on black citizens unravels Brown's argument.

At several points Brown did leave the rhetorical field of black abstraction and demonstrate the reality of racism, specifically through the expression of his own racism, which was part of the public and widely shared ideology of his time. Brown argued that if a state legislature dominated by blacks passed a racial segregation law like the one challenged in *Plessy*, whites would not assume it was an expression of the inferiority of whites. Brown stepped out of the realm of abstraction and made a sensible comment on the society in which he lived. Brown lived in a society which was so racist that the very notion of a white man thinking himself inferior to a black man would have been considered lunatic.

Brown revealed again his sense of the real society within which these laws operated in his conclusion, referring to the inherent problem in the implementation of a racial segregation law; that is, the problem of defining a "white" person. Brown noted that a statutorily specified blood ratio typically resolved this definitional problem. The state statutes on this subject differed. In some states, "the predominance of white blood must only be in the proportion of three fourths." In other states, "any visible admixture of black blood stamp[ed] the person as belonging to the colored race."[15] The laws were patently racist. The conception of "tainted black blood" is obvious when the spectrum of white ranges from "only . . . three fourths" white blood to the absence of any "visible admixture."

Brown's self-imposed-stigma argument thus permitted whites to evade responsibility for any degradation felt by blacks. Moreover, the racism expressed explicitly and implicitly throughout the opinion gave a naturalness and logic to the de jure segregation which, in turn, let whites off the hook. Blacks were different and inferior. Thus, the segregation of blacks was natural and not an act of oppression.

The Contemporary Rhetoric of Race

We have our own cracked surface of tragic reality. Prior to *Brown v. Board of Education*,[16] our tragedy was the continuing presence of de jure segregation and all that it entailed. Post-*Brown*, the tragedy is different but nonetheless powerful. Black people constitute a disproportionate percentage of the poor. Segregation has shifted from de jure to de facto. The efforts to use constitutional principles and federal courts to desegregate our society have not worked and our courts seem to be withdrawing from the struggle.

As we walk away from the contemporary reality of economic deprivation and segregation of blacks, we run into a conflict. In a society committed to racial equality, where racism is no longer part of the official ideology, how are we to account for the separation and apparent subjugation of black citizens? Even as the Court retreats from the effort to bring about change, the conflict seems even more pressing. Still, we go on as though economic deprivation and segregation of blacks somehow makes sense.

Our ability to make intellectually coherent and tolerable this apparent conflict is largely a product of a rhetoric much like the legal rhetoric of the nineteenth century. Like the earlier rhetoric, our version helps smooth over the apparent inconsistency between our realities and our principles. Our rhetoric also expresses our version of the themes of white innocence and black abstraction.

At one time, we might have supposed that we would need not confront such a conflict in the late twentieth century. That time was the moment of *Brown v. Board of Education*. *Brown* changed much and held the promise of more. Yet, one can see in *Brown* both the promise and the specter of what was to come by discerning both the change and the continuity in the rhetoric of race.

Brown v. Board of Education was a moment of transition. It dramatically changed constitutional law. It set off a firestorm of controversy about the institutional role of the Court. In important ways, nothing could ever be the same after *Brown*.

The case was also a moment of transition in the legal language and rhetoric of race. The advocates for racial segregation brought to the Court a rhetoric that advanced the following propositions: (i) segregation did not harm blacks (if anything, blacks were its beneficiaries); (ii) whites had no reason to apologize or feel ashamed; and (iii) the felt need of whites for segregation ought to be respected and, if integration were to come, it must be done with careful attention to the potential harm to whites.

The legal champions of segregation brought their versions of white innocence and black abstraction to the debate. The Attorney General of Virginia, J. Lindsay Almond, argued:

> They are asking you to disturb the unfolding evolutionary process of education where from the
> dark days of the depraved institution of slavery, with the help and the sympathy and the love

and the respect of the white people of the South, the colored man has risen under that educational process to a place of eminence and respect throughout this nation. It has served him well.[17]

The segregationists also were adamant in their denial of any racist motives. The lawyer for North Carolina spoke of the mysterious nonracist phenomenon, "race consciousness":

[E]verybody in North Carolina—practically everybody in North Carolina—is either Anglo-Saxon or Negro. As a result of that, we have more consciousness of race in North Carolina than is to be found in some of the border and northern states. That race consciousness is not race prejudice. It is not race hatred. It is not intolerance. It is a deeply ingrained awareness of a birthright held in trust for posterity.[18]

The star of the segregationist advocates, John W. Davis, expressed the themes of the absence of racism and the absence of any harm to the blacks:

You say that [segregation is a product of] racism. Well, it is not racism. Recognize that for sixty centuries and more humanity has been discussing questions of race and race tension, not racism. Say that we make special provisions for the aboriginal Indian population of this country; it is not racism. Say that 29 states have miscegenation statutes now in force which they believe are of beneficial protection to both races. Disraeli said, "No man will treat with indifference the principle of race. It is the key of history."

. . . Let me say this for the State of South Carolina. . . . It is confident of its good faith and intention to produce equality for all of its children of whatever race or color. It is convinced that the happiness, the progress and the welfare of these children is best promoted in segregated schools, and it thinks it a thousand pities that by this controversy there should be urged the return to an experiment which gives no more promise of success today than when it was written into their Constitution during what I call the tragic era.[19]

This rhetoric expressed a form of white innocence and black abstraction. The segregationists insisted on the absence of racism as a motive. Blacks were not harmed. The only victims on the horizon were whites who might be compelled to give up a way of life without good reason. Only an abstract depiction of the context could advance this benign picture. To say that racism was absent from the explanation for the segregation laws made no sense once one considered the laws in any real social and historical context. To assert that segregation did not harm blacks seemed ludicrous when one imagined the history of separate but unequal education. The entire rhetorical structure tumbled with the embrace of even so simple an imagining as the feelings and circumstances of black children being bussed many miles across Texas to the black school, passing along the way the schools for white children.

The most eloquent response to the segregationist rhetoric was that of Thurgood Marshall.

They can't take race out of this case.

. . . [T]he only way that this Court can decide this case in opposition to our position is that there must be some reason which gives the state the right to make a classification . . . and we submit the only way to arrive at this decision is to find that for some reason Negroes are inferior to all other human beings. . . . The only [explanation] is an inherent determination that the people who were formerly in slavery, regardless of anything else, shall be kept as near that stage as is possible; and now is the time, we submit, that this Court should make it clear that that is not what our Constitution stands for.[20]

Marshall insisted that segregation was by its nature an expression of racial inferiority and a product of racist motives. He denied the innocence of the white segregationist and argued the palpable harm to the stigmatized black person.

The Court decided the *Brown* case in two stages: first, the declaration of the unconstitutionality of segregated public schools in the *Brown I* opinion; and, second, the adoption of the "with all deliberate speed" remedy in the *Brown II* opinion. The other important feature of the rhetoric of *Brown I* was the Court's treatment of the rhetorical theme of white innocence. On this issue, the *Brown I* opinion offered a howling silence. The Court spoke not at all of the racist motives for segregation. This silence thus left standing the segregationists' insistence on white innocence. This silence is important to understand the history of the rhetoric of race. The point is not that the Court erred in failing to reject explicitly the formal assumption of white innocence. The cost of an explicit charge of racist motives would have been at least the loss of unanimity in the *Brown* decision. The important observation is that the price of unanimity was, in effect, the preservation of the rhetoric of white innocence. In this sense, *Brown I* was both a moment of transition and a moment of continuity in our rhetoric of race. Black abstraction was rejected; white innocence was left intact.

We cannot know what would have been different had the Court explicitly rejected white innocence. We can see, however, the significance of the choice not to do so in the Court's choice of remedy in *Brown II*. Having concluded that segregated schools violated the constitutional rights of black families, the Court had to decide what to do about it. Thurgood Marshall's position was simple and powerful. He granted no basis for delay. Having found that segregated schools violated the constitutional rights of black families, the Court had the duty to put the machinery of desegregation immediately into effect.

In *Brown II*, the Court rejected Marshall's analysis and adopted the "with all deliberate speed" remedy. Again, there were powerful pragmatic arguments for the delay in implementation. Yet, whether right or wrong, the implicit backdrop of white innocence made the delay in implementation intellectually and socially tolerable. Had the Court in *Brown I* spoken of the racism that motivated the segregation laws, the delay in *Brown II* would have been more difficult to justify. To permit some period of time for families to adjust to a new way of life is one thing; to permit racists a period of continued expression of their racism out of fear of their resistance and lawlessness is another.

Nonetheless, *Brown* could have been understood in its time as a moment of transition in both the law and rhetoric of race. As with all periods of important transition, society must give up some things and yet, at the same time, hold on to some of the past. White innocence as a rhetorical theme might have been a piece of the past, kept in *Brown* but soon to fade away.

Notes

1. Plessy v. Ferguson, 163 U.S. 537 (1896); The Civil Rights Cases, 109 U.S. 3 (1883); Dred Scott v. Sandford, 60 U.S. 393 (1856).

2. "The effect of Taney's statement [that the Negro had no rights that the white man was bound to respect] was to place Negroes of the 1780s—even free Negroes—on the same level, legally, as domestic animals. As 'historical narrative,' it was a gross perversion of the facts." D. FEHRENBACHER, THE DRED SCOTT CASE 349 (1978).

3. "No one of that race had ever migrated to the United States voluntarily; all of them had been brought here as articles of merchandise. The number that had been emancipated at that time were but few in comparison with those held in slavery; and they were identified in the public mind with

the race to which they belonged, and regarded as a part of the slave population rather than the free." *Dred Scott*, 60 U.S. at 411.

4. *Id.* at 404–05.

5. U.S. Const. amends. XIII & XIV.

6. The Civil Rights Cases, 109 U.S. 3 (1883).

7. *Id.* at 25.

8. "[B]lacks in the Redeemers' New South found themselves enmeshed in a seamless web of oppression, whose interwoven economic, political, and social strands all reinforced one another. In illiteracy, malnutrition, inadequate housing, and a host of other burdens, blacks paid the highest price for the end of Reconstruction and the stagnation of the Southern economy." E. FONER, RECONSTRUCTION 598 (1988).

9. *The Civil Rights Cases*, 109 U.S. at 61 (Harlan, J., dissenting).

10. *Id.* at 17.

11. 163 U.S. 537 (1896).

12. *Id.* at 537, 542, 556.

13. *Id.* at 544. The brief for the segregationist position also expressed the formal equality of the statute:

> [A]ny passenger insisting on going into a coach or compartment to which, by race, he does not belong, shall be liable to be punished according to its provisions. Should a *white* passenger insist on going into a coach or compartment to which by race he does not belong, he would thereby render himself liable to punishment according to this law. There is, therefore, no distinction or unjust discrimination in this respect *on account of color* (emphasis added).

Brief on Behalf of Defendant in Error at 14–15, Plessy v. Ferguson, 163 U.S. 537 (1896), *reprinted in* 13 LANDMARK BRIEFS AND ARGUMENTS OF THE SUPREME COURT OF THE UNITED STATES 95–96 (1975) (Brief of M.J. Cunningham, Attorney General of Louisiana).

14. *Plessy*, 163 U.S. at 551.

15. *Id.* at 552.

16. 347 U.S. 483 (1954).

17. Transcript of Oral Argument at 11, Davis v. County School Bd. of Prince Edward County, 347 U.S. 483 (1954), *reprinted in* 49A LANDMARK BRIEFS, *supra* at 512 (Argument of J. Lindsay Almond on Behalf of Appellees).

18. Transcript of Oral Argument at 13–14, Brown v. Board of Educ., 347 U.S. 483 (1954), *reprinted in* 49A LANDMARK BRIEFS, *supra* at 1227–28.

19. Transcript of Oral Argument at 43, 44, Brown v. Board of Educ., 347 U.S. 483 (1954), *reprinted in* 49A LANDMARK BRIEFS, *supra* at 491, 492 (Argument of John W. Davis on Behalf of Appellees).

20. Transcript of Oral Argument at 21–22, Brown v. Board of Educ., 347 U.S. 483 (1954), *reprinted in* 49A LANDMARK BRIEFS, *supra* at 522–23 (Rebuttal Argument of Thurgood Marshall on Behalf of Appellants).

17

Imposition

RICHARD DELGADO AND JEAN STEFANCIC

Society generally deploys terms of *imposition* at key moments in the history of a reform effort, such as blacks' struggle for equal opportunity, or women's campaign for reproductive rights. Before reaching that point, society tolerates or even supports the new movement. We march, link arms, and sing with the newcomers, identifying with their struggle. At some point, however, reaction sets in. We decide the group has gone far enough. At first, justice seemed to be on their side. But now we see them as imposing, taking the offensive, asking for concessions they do not deserve. Now they are the aggressors, and we the victims.

At precisely this point in a reform's history, we begin to deploy what we call "imposition language"—language of encroachment. We decide the group is asking for "special" status. We find their demands excessive, tiresome, or frightening. The imposition narrative delegitimizes the reform movement, portraying it as unprincipled. But by a neat switch, it also enables us to feel comfortable about withdrawing our support; the imposition paints us as morally entitled to oppose the movement and bring it to a halt.

Words That Impugn the Outsider Personally

Sometimes society deems an individual guilty of imposing by virtue of who he or she is—that is, simply by being a Jew, woman, Chinese, or black engaged in some ordinary activity of life. These examples were somewhat more common early in our history than they are now. But they have not entirely died out; one hears overtones of the essentialist approach even today, fifty years after we abandoned the pseudoscientific theories of human differences that gave rise to it.

Certain social commentators have no inhibition against using imposition language. For example, Linda Chavez, writing in the *New Republic*, seems to ridicule in the title of her article, *Just Say Latino*, Hispanic groups who insist on calling themselves "Latino." How tiresome—yet another new name, yet another imposition on our good natures! Her article also describes the call for affirmative action programs for Hispanics in Washington, D.C., as amounting to quotas, and the group's troubles as its own fault for refusing to legalize and assimilate into the culture as previous immigrants have done. There is little to indicate that Chavez wrote as she did to exhort Hispanic Americans to do better. She de-

35 Wm. & Mary L. Rev. 1025 (1994). Originally published in the *William and Mary Law Review*. Reprinted by permission.

scribes their traits in fatalistic terms, as though they are inborn and unlikely to change.[1] The English-only movement supplies further examples of inherent imposition. Supporters speak of immigrants who wish to maintain their culture with an irritation that verges on revulsion. They are unpatriotic and unfit to reside here, their presence (in their unreformed foreign language speaking condition) calculated only to precipitate "white flight."[2] Certain Latino and Asian groups' insistence on speaking their own language with each other merits special scorn.

In an ironic twist, Asians who succeed can also draw unfavorable attention. Recently, a United States Representative met with leaders of two Asian groups to make amends for what he was forced to admit were "poorly chosen words" related to Asian American students who win scholarships. Speaking to the Maryland congressional delegation, Republican congressman Roscoe G. Bartlett noted that of recently awarded scholarly prizes, "half went to those with Oriental names, a sixth . . . to Indian names, and the rest to what we would consider normal Americans." Bartlett later explained that he meant "normal" only in the sense of average, that he did not mean to offend anyone, and that the news media had taken liberties[3]—thereby completing a nearly perfect triple-trope. The Asian schoolchildren overstepped by being here in the first place—note the use of the slightly derogatory term "Oriental." Next, the Asian students had the effrontery to apply themselves at school, thereby imposing on the prerogative of the native-born to take things easy and still get good grades—witness the use of the word "normal" to imply that the Asian children were strange. Finally, the media overstepped by reporting the congressman's remarks, thereby invading his prerogative to put the foreigners in their place without drawing attention.

Words That Impugn the Outsider's Motives

Imposition language also can cast reformers or an outsider group in a negative light because of their supposed bad motives or unstated agenda. The outsider is not looking for social justice, but spoiling for a fight, with a chip on his shoulder. For example, detractors criticized Representative Maxine Waters for her role in the wake of the Los Angeles disturbances in 1992 following the verdict in the first trial of police officers accused of beating Rodney King. Waters had spoken to reporters about the causes of the riots, namely, black poverty and the unresponsiveness of the city's bureaucracy. Her accusers charged her with cynically exploiting the tragedy and attempting to thrust herself into a limelight she had not deserved or won.[4] Another writer, in an article on the English-only movement, described activists working with immigrants and bilingual teachers as disrespectful of the majority culture, seemingly only because they were respectful of the immigrants' culture.[5]

Words That Find Imposition in Particular Forms of Behavior

In a third variant, the speaker does not impeach reformers or their motives, but rather their actions. These accusations tend to be less harsh than the first kind. Nevertheless, they hold that the reformer is doing something wrong—either demanding something that by its very nature constitutes imposition, or going about things the wrong way, e.g., by try-ing to vault to the head of the line.

Conservative writers see many forms of behavior and advocacy as encroachment. For ex-ample, some advocates of immigration restraints charge that illegal aliens sneak into the United States, insinuate themselves into our midst, hide, and remain without asking per-mission.[6] The introjection language, language of overstepping, is both literal and unmis-takable.

Imposition Through Effects or Implications

A final approach portrays a reform movement as threatening en-croachment through its effects or symbolic impact. Popular writers have wielded the "drawing the line" or "where will it all stop?" arguments with frequency and fervor. Dinesh D'Souza, for example, both in his book *Illiberal Education* and elsewhere, warns that giving in to the demands of campus radicals eventually could spell the end of the university as we know it. He depicts minority students' demands for meeting places, theme houses, and special dormitories as steps toward Balkanization of the campus and the politicization of university life. For D'Souza this first wave of requests was not so much dangerous in itself as for what it portended: a university in which knowledge is not unitary, but shifting and contestable, a community that contains not one voice but many.[7]

Shelby Steele also draws attention to the ramifications of multiculturalism, but adds a new element—the dangers that the movement holds for blacks. According to Steele, African American college students who seek special courses, professors, and departments will end up marginalizing themselves, and will fail to acquire the types of knowledge and competence that really matter. Everyone will regard their degrees as second rate, while the rest of the university will feel it has discharged its obligation to the newcomers. Steele warns of a kind of self-imposition in which black leaders demand changes the rest of the black community does not want or need.[8]

The Narrative's Efficacy and Attraction

The narrative of imposition appears at predictable periods in history, namely, when reform has gained momentum and appears poised to produce changes that make us uneasy. When so deployed, it seems to have real bite. What accounts for its per-sistence and power?

Our research disclosed a veritable landscape of imposition types, corresponding to a se-ries of basic, almost innate, subnarratives, ranging from "who are you, anyway?" to "no-body talks about me anymore." Perhaps the most basic subnarrative of all is that of the bully. Everyone recalls childhood games and activities in which one of the opponents did not play fair—relied on force, broke the rules, or insisted on special treatment. In adult life, things are almost never so simple. Most reformers are not seeking to break the rules but to change the game entirely. We still carry images, however, from these early experiences and apply them to situations where they may or may not fit.

Baselines and Tipping Points—"The Way Things Are"

Recently a columnist complained that all the recent books seemed to be about women. In actuality, the writer was referring to a small group of books, mostly written by women, and dealing with such issues as child care, divorce reform, spousal battery, and menopause.[9]

In any literal sense, the reviewer was wildly inaccurate. Every year tens of thousands of books are published, a considerable majority of them dealing with subjects such as war, sports, mechanics, and power politics predominantly of interest to men. To the reviewer, however, these did not seem like men's books, but just books. The current distribution, in other words, seemed fair and equal; the small group of new books about women unbalanced the publishing world. With minority hiring, according to Derrick Bell, much the same happens.[10] We think this perception is common. The reformer seems to be seeking special treatment, asking for a departure from a situation we have come to regard as neutral and fair. We fail to notice how the current situation itself reflects a particular distribution of power and authority, arrived at long ago. But we do notice changes and proposals for change. These stand out starkly, seem like departures, and require justification.

The Rule and the Exception—"What's So Special About You?"

In a related mechanism, we view outsiders as seeking an exemption from universal rules that all of us must obey. For example, in *Employment Division v. Smith*,[11] the Supreme Court portrayed a small group of Indians in Oregon as requesting to be excused from a uniform criminal law. Demands associated with multiculturalism often trigger the same response—why should we excuse the new writers and curricula from the same test of time we apply to Shakespeare, Milton, and Mark Twain?

Our preference for rules over ad hoc treatment gives this argument some initial plausibility. The difficulty is that there are rules and *rules*. For example, one could argue in the *Smith* case that the applicable rule is toleration for diverse cultures. Then, Oregon's law would be seen as an exception, as an imposition on the Indians. Everything thus depends on the choice of rule that one declares central: the criminal prohibition, according to which taking mild drugs is illegal, or the principle of tolerance, according to which Oregon was overstepping, imposing on the Indians who were merely trying to practice their religion.

Justice Brown's opinion in *Plessy v. Ferguson* found blacks guilty of imposing on other travellers by demanding to sit in the same railroad cars as whites.[12] Viewed in that light, the Negroes were imposing on the whites' customary rule—separate but equal. Of course, if one declared that the relevant norm was the contrary one, the one that the Supreme Court adopted in *Brown v. Board of Education*[13]—namely, that citizens are entitled to public services regardless of color—then the railroad imposed on the blacks.

"If You Give Them an Inch . . ."

Many deployments of the imposition figure rest on a fear of the floodgates. Because the first request strikes us as extreme, the possibility of others raises real fears. Giving in could set a precedent, start us down a path at the end of which is a world we might not even recognize. This in turn taps a related narrative—fear of the unfamiliar, fear of loss of control.

Fear of Loss of Control—"I Know What They Really Want"

All of us derive part of our self-definition from the wider society. Thus, on some level we understand that radical changes in our surroundings could change us as persons. Changes in our city government, the curriculum or teachers in our children's schools, or the composition of our neighborhood could require us to adjust, to become different. In time our very identities might change—a prospect that of course discomfits. Anyone who makes this fear seem plausible commands our instant attention.

The Reformer as Ingrate—"After All We Have Done for Them"

Part of our identity is an image of ourselves as a tolerant and generous society. Reformers, however, suggest that we have not lived up to our national ideals—that all men are not brothers, all immigrants are not welcome, and so on. This assertion cannot be true; the reformer must be wrong for even having raised the idea. The impositionist trope neatly enables us to accomplish both objectives. We get to reaffirm that society is as we think, and that the outsider has transgressed by suggesting the contrary.

The Usual and the Aberrant—"They're Standing the World on Its Head"

Most of us believe that the United States is a relatively fair, just society, one that offers opportunities to all. We prefer to think of racism, sexism, and homophobia as exceptions, occasional mistakes that with diligence can be reduced, if not eliminated entirely. Reformers, however, often seem to be saying the opposite—that injustice is the norm and fairness the exception. This view seems to us to turn the world on its head, to insist that night is day, and day night.

Evasion of Responsibility, the Role of Denial—"It's Not My Fault"

Avoidance of blame and responsibility are universal human tendencies. No one likes to believe that he or she may be responsible for serious continuing injustice. Yet the outsider seems to be saying just that. Declaring him misguided or an opportunist eliminates any need for soul-searching or admission of error.

The Ordinary and the Extraordinary—"I Have Problems Too"

The reformer's plea demands attention and possibly reallocation of resources. But everyone has problems. What about mine? If we can characterize the outsider group's complaints as unexceptional and ordinary, any urgency in addressing them of course dissipates. One may even discover that one's own problems are more interesting, more gripping, more subtle than those of the outsider group. The outsider group is imposing, monopolizing attention that we deserve as well.

The Metaphor's Seeming Legitimacy: Its Manifest Content and Why It Rings True

A final question which we must address concerns the metaphor's manifest righteousness. A narrative might be powerful, but unattractive on its face for some reason—for example, white supremacy, or the idea that men should be women's protectors. In short, a rhetorical device must appear right and true, must enable the speaker to use it and still maintain his or her self-image as a moral actor.

The imposition narrative performs these tasks admirably. First, we typically apply it only to a group that bears a preexisting stigma. When such a group mobilizes to make demands on us, it is easy to attach a further element to its stereotype: now, in addition to being shiftless, hapless, immoral, and so forth, it is overstepping and pushy. The new element seems to stand in a logical relation to the ones we have already assigned it. The attachment causes few qualms; indeed, it seems self-evidently correct. The group's demanding nature in itself verifies the accusation and shows that what we think of them is true.

Characterizing the outsider group as imposing also justifies our rejection of their claim. We seize the moral high ground. They are the ones metaphorically throwing the first blow. As victims, we are entitled not only to deny their demands, but to tell the world how unfair and unprincipled they are. Many writers who employ imposition language do so with a kind of relish and zeal. They expect no rebuttal, for none is possible. Indeed, the background against which they deliver their message assures them that the rest of us will nod assent. Of course, that group is overstepping. That is what they do.

Underlying many uses of the imposition metaphor is nonreflexivity, the quite natural tendency to believe that one's own way of seeing and doing things is natural and universal. The nonreflexive person—which includes most of us on many occasions—on hearing his or her most settled beliefs impugned by an outsider immediately thinks that the outsider must be wrong. By a kind of backward reasoning we conclude that because the individual is questioning what we believe, he or she must be wrong and probably operating from base motives as well.

At early stages of most reform movements, the culture responds generously. We are curious, interested in the new things the reformers are saying. We invite them to our homes, read their books, discuss their theories and ideas. Behaving in this fashion reaffirms our self-image as an open, sharing people. Little seems to be at stake; indeed, our lives appear to be enriched—there is a new piquancy at parties, some welcome variety to talk in the faculty lounge. Later, the reality of what the reformers are asking for starts to sink in. Our attitudes change. We begin to wonder whether the reformers actually can be asking for that. We question the reformers' factual predicate or description of the world as containing much injustice. We ask is there not another possible account? Could not the lack of blacks in the construction industry be due to some reason other than discrimination? We question the necessity or plausibility of their story. Or, we shrink from the substance of their demands, retreating into proceduralism. We profess not to understand their claim, or ask questions demanding greater specificity: Where would you draw the line? We wonder about implications and floodgates. If we heeded your request, what other things would we have to do? What would you be asking for next?

We also question the remedy the reformers request. In our view, racism or other injustices are aberrations, hence any remedy would naturally have to be short-lived and bounded. But this group's proposed reform appears to go on forever—how can that be? We express concern, ask for clarification, pretend not fully to understand what the outsiders are demanding. Each of these replies is a kind of shrinking from substance, an instance of canon-fear, a fear of the earth shifting, of what might happen if it turns out that structural change in fact is in order.

At later stages we put procedure behind us. We tell the reformer, "all right, we will reach the merits of your claim. We understand full well what you are saying, its implications, whom it will affect, who has standing. And, we find your claim illegitimate, unprincipled, and wrong." In the last decade or so, we seem to have reached such a decisive end point with blacks. The imposition narratives we apply to them have lost the tentative, nibbling-at-the-edges quality we apply to groups that have merely begun to tax our patience. We now apply to them, practically alone, the most scathing forms of rejection—rejection on the merits, rejection that finds their claims, their very presence as persons, imposition-in-itself.

The Special Situation of American Blacks

Throughout most of its history, the United States' formal values—its central federal ones—have been higher, more inclusive, more aspirational, more nonracist and nonsexist, than the private ones, the ones we act on during moments of intimacy, when among friends, in our club, in a neighborhood bar or cafe. On these other occasions, many Americans feel freer to tell a racist joke, or exclude a black from a small gathering. More Americans feel entitled to select a white tenant than an equally qualified black for an in-law apartment in their own home than would vote to permit similar behavior on the part of a governmental housing authority. In recognition of this, most grass roots civil rights efforts have focused on formal, central structures—law, federal government, large institutions— because these are the ones most receptive to change, the ones whose formal values are the more egalitarian national ones. At these levels, it is possible to remind one's target of the values to which our society formally is committed, and hope that the structure will change.

Significantly, one would *not* employ that strategy in a society where the opposite situation prevails, the former South Africa for example, where the national values until recently were less egalitarian than the private ones. In that other kind of place, one is best off seeking succor from a private individual. If one is black and ill, out of money, or has a car breakdown during a long road trip, one is far more likely to find kindness at the hands of a private citizen, not a government agency or the police. Until recently, much the same was true in the American South.

We believe that the United States is in the process of changing imperceptibly, so that it is becoming more like South Africa. Today, for the first time in half a century, large groups of people behave according to a lower standard than do individuals or small cities. By the same token, the national government and Supreme Court are becoming less receptive to minority concerns than their state or local counterparts. There is, thus, a type of double axis. In all times and ages minority reformers face resistance, pretended incomprehension, and hostility at predictable points. And, at certain points in history, society is especially resistant to reform of any sort, because its formal values are beginning to move in another direction. With resistance of both types, imposition language serves as a prime mediating mechanism, portraying the reformer as extreme and irresponsible, portraying localism, love, and sympathy as out of order, wrong, subordinate to universalistic meritocratic, neutralist rules that assure the ascendancy of managerial whites. Imposition language reminds all concerned that the center holds power and authority, dictates rules, controls results—and under those rules the reformer is out of line, is imposing, is wrong. How dare he?

Notes

1. Linda Chavez, *Just Say Latino*, New Republic, Mar. 22, 1993, at 18; ("Given these realities"—the group's illegality, rapid growth rate, and poor education—an affirmative action program to redress Hispanic underemployment in D.C. "is a little absurd."); *id.*

2. *See, e.g.,* Juan Perea, *Demography and Distrust: An Essay on American Languages, Cultural Pluralism, and Official English,* 77 Minn. L. Rev. 269 (1992) (analyzing antibilingualism rhetoric); Abigail M. Thernstrom, *Bilingual Miseducation,* Commentary, Feb. 1990, at 44 (asserting that bilingualism entrenches difference and weakens consensus); *Bilingualism,* Economist, May 22, 1993, at 32 (implying that the backers of the bicultural movement are unpatriotic and that an influx of non–English speaking immigrants will cause whites to leave).

3. *Ways and Means,* Chron. Higher Educ., Mar. 17, 1993, at A23.

4. Midge Decter, *How the Rioters Won,* Commentary, July 1992, at 17, 18–19 (implying that Waters basked in the limelight and posed as an expert and commenting that "never again would she have . . . quite so good a time").

5. James Traub, *Back to Basic: P.C. v. English,* New Republic, Feb. 8, 1993, at 18.

6. *See, e.g.,* Peter Brimelow, *Time to Rethink Immigration?,* Nat'l Rev., June 22, 1992, at 30 (commenting on the adverse history of immigration in the United States and the need to change the country's image as an immigrant nation); *The Immigrants,* New Republic, Apr. 19, 1993, at 7 (discussing the latest wave of Arab immigrants and their supposed connection with the World Trade Center bombing).

7. Dinesh D'Souza, Illiberal Education: The Politics of Race and Sex on Campus 46–51, 55–68, 82–93, 112–15, 157–67, 184–90, 230–42 (1991).

8. Shelby Steele, The Content of Our Character 21–35, 90, 111–25, 127–48, 173 (1990).

9. *See* Jack Kisling, *No . . . Uh . . . Men Need Apply,* Denver Post, May 4, 1993, at 9B.

10. *See* Derrick Bell, And We Are Not Saved: The Elusive Quest for Racial Justice, at 142–44, 152–53 (1987) (commenting on the "tipping point" phenomenon in university faculty hiring).

11. 494 U.S. 872 (1990).

12. *Plessy,* 163 U.S. 537 at 538–51 (1896).

13. 347 U.S. 483 (1954).

18

Racial Reflections: Dialogues in the Direction of Liberation

DERRICK A. BELL, TRACY HIGGINS, AND
SUNG-HEE SUH, EDITORS

How can we explain the willingness of so many white Americans to sacrifice their interests in social reform to insure that blacks they deem "undeserving" do not gain? What precisely are they trying to protect in this land where equality is a concept while ownership of property is a basic measure of worth?

Over time, beliefs in white dominance, reinforced by policies subordinating black interests to those of whites, have led to an unrecognized, but no less viable, property right in whiteness. In challenging the legality of racial segregation in the late nineteenth century, the plaintiff in *Plessy v. Ferguson* recognized, and the Court acknowledged, a property right in being white: an entitlement to those advantages gained over blacks by virtue of a white identity.[1] Although there is no such overt recognition in contemporary racial decisions, the application of the strict scrutiny standard of review—once reserved for the most invidious forms of racism—to affirmative action programs reflects a concern for "innocent whites" and implicitly recognizes what the *Plessy* Court was willing to acknowledge openly.

Viewing racial discrimination as a phenomenon based on property rights, students explored why whites so often oppose social reforms that work to their advantage while perpetuating racial barriers that disadvantage them.

Examining the Property of Rights in Whiteness
WILHELMINA WRIGHT

The practice of American racism is based on two principles: the sanctity of property and the belief in the hierarchy of races. The first principle is firmly protected by the words and action of the Constitution; the second is proscribed by the words of the instrument, but not by its effect. History shows that when these two principles are juxtaposed (which happens constantly) property rights are given absolute priority.

American liberalism, embodied in the Constitution, was designed to protect life, liberty, and property. The polity was given the rights to these three things, and the state was given the power only to act to protect these rights. Slavery, the Black Codes, and Jim Crow laws could only exist under a constitutional regime when justified by the belief that the lives and liberty of members of the black race were worth less than the property of the white race. Few persons today would use that conception to justify their position against affirmative action, yet it remains a primary motivation for their actions. Modern America has publicly rejected advocacy of racial supremacy, that is, the argument that the life, liberty, and property of whites are worth more than those of blacks. What we face today, however, is equally damaging and little discussed: that property is worth more than life or liberty. That whites own the vast majority of what Americans define as property does not usually enter this argument, and it therefore appears nonracist.

The failure of today's racial discourse lies in its belief that property is neutral, that the deed to a suburban home is "property," while the opportunity to move out of a slum is not. The fungibility of property can be no better exemplified than it is by slavery. That our Constitution once recognized one person's very life and liberty as another's property should teach us the danger of letting property determine liberty rather than looking to liberty to define property.

Defining the Property Right in "Whiteness"
TRACY HIGGINS

The notion of a property right in "whiteness" seems to thwart the progress of civil rights for blacks in at least two ways. Within the political sphere, if an interest in "whiteness" is culturally defined and recognized even implicitly, the interests of blacks become separated from those of whites. This separation of interests allows blacks to become a "bargaining chip" among different white economic groups. In addition, the separation (and subordination) of black interest functions to soothe lower class white dissatisfaction with its own position and prevents the mobilization of both black and white economically exploited groups; within the judicial system, the implicit recognition of a property right in whiteness has led to frustration when relief for black plaintiffs would mean undermining this property right. For example, *Washington v. Davis*[2] protected this property right in whiteness by severely limiting the possibility of relief for victims of all types of discrimination. Other decisions, such as *Wygant*[3] and *Bakke*,[4] established limitations on affirmative action, again preserving a property right in whiteness. *Milliken v. Bradley*,[5] by protecting "neighborhood schools," in effect protected white neighborhoods' right to white schools.

The theory of a property right in whiteness initially emerged as a means of understanding and explaining at least in part the racial oppression that has existed in this country throughout its history. Ultimately, however, the idea of a property right in whiteness may offer not only a critique of existing conditions and strategies but also a hope for a new one. Whites must recognize that they are paying too much for their rights in whiteness. A critical analysis of this property right reveals it is also used as a tool for class oppression, the costs of which are borne by blacks and whites alike.

Whites With Nothing but Whiteness
YVETTE GLASGOW

I did not realize how much poor whites were willing to sacrifice to hold on to their property right in whiteness until I worked on my first pro bono case last summer, a child custody matter. The woman had been a foster child, a victim of child molestation, rape, and husband abuse. The child she sought to regain custody of was fathered by one of her foster fathers. In addition, she was mildly retarded, unemployed, homeless, and deaf. I witnessed poor whites' belief in a property right in whiteness through this woman who was living an absolute nightmare. On two occasions I watched while this woman with so little held on to the last vestiges of perceived superiority.

First, efforts to move her out of a Salvation Army Shelter failed when she refused to move to any complex where black people lived. I told the interpreter to ask her to explain. Frank in her reply, she told her interpreter to tell me she was a white woman, and that it was not safe for her to live alone among black men. She stressed that she was not "raised" this way. I was angry at this woman, who could hardly characterize her childhood experience of being shuttled from foster home to foster home as being "raised" in a particular way. My anger subsided when I realized that her only sense of self-esteem came from her belief that she was better than black people. I felt sorry for her, because she could not hear the sarcastic voices of rejection and scorn each time I called predominantly white apartment complexes to inquire about their policy of accepting welfare recipients.

The second incident was one in which she was accused of sexual misconduct with a twelve-year-old boy in the homeless shelter. She denied the allegations, but not in the manner that I expected. She was not alarmed that someone would accuse her of molesting a child. Only the embarrassment of being accused of sleeping with a black man seemed to bother her. She emphatically signed that the story could not be true, because he was black. Perhaps she forgot that I was black, or perhaps she did not care. The interpreter apologized for what was momentarily a very tense situation. I was not angry at the close of our conference; I only felt sorry for this woman, who did not realize that she was one of society's most pitiful victims.

"Whiteness" Rights Exercised by People of Color
LISA CASTANON

In the words of Professor C. Vann Woodward, Jim Crow laws were intended to "bolster the creed of white supremacy in the bosom of a white man working for a black man's wages."[6] The concept of a property right in whiteness illustrates that racism offers poor whites the illusion of superiority while maintaining the reality for rich whites. As a class stabilizer, racism maintains the status quo of economic exploitation of both black and white victims. Yet the white victims' perverse clinging to racial exclusiveness only serves to divert attention away from economic reform, thereby preventing the potentially powerful coalition they could form with blacks.

The concept of a property right in whiteness thus highlights white racial solidarity over class-based interests. There are two sides to this property right in whiteness—for poor whites, it may mean forgoing economic improvement for white exclusivity; for minorities, on the other hand, it may mean gaining economic improvement at the expense of racial solidarity. Crudely speaking, the poor white may say, "If I can't have the wealth, at least I have the right color," while the rich non-white may say, "If I can't have the right color, at least I have the wealth." This is *not* to say that we all have the desire suddenly to turn white. A friend told me that as a child she would sometimes wrap a towel around her head and imagine herself with "long flowing blonde hair." We're older now. We no longer dream of white physical characteristics but instead of white privilege and success.

Recognizing the many-sided aspect of this so-called property right in whiteness, we have to ask ourselves, "How much do we consciously see a property right in whiteness?" All of us to some extent are trying to obtain that which is encompassed in the concept of whiteness. It may be too easy only to evaluate the impact that a property right in whiteness has in poor whites. It may be more difficult but in the end more beneficial to recognize its influence in our own lives.

The Acid Test of Black Dominance
MITCHELL CHESTER

Several years ago I was aggressively pursuing an administrative appointment within the public sector of an urban, mostly minority district. In the course of one year, eight positions became open. I was selected as a finalist for three of them. Each position was filled by a staff member from within the district (which I was not) and the majority of those chosen were minority group members.

I knew that my qualifications, skills, and abilities were impeccable. I attributed my lack of success to characteristics beyond my control: my white, male status and being from outside the system. At moments during that year I harbored feelings of resentment, which were bolstered by internalized putdowns of individuals who had succeeded in their job pursuit. My reactions did not target a race in general, but were focused on individual members of minority groups. I checked those thoughts quickly, for they were not pretty nor constructive. They did, however, both frighten me and lead me to reexamine my feelings about minority advancement and self-help. Perhaps my feelings of resentment were simply defensive reflexes for justifying my experiences. Had I been in control of the advancement of those who come from the ranks of the oppressed, I am sure that any personal resentment would not have surfaced. I would have been able to balance such promotions in a manner that served my own self-interest.

In the end, I confirmed my belief in affirmative action and minority advancement. But I had to face serious questions about self-help and just how much minority advancement can be tolerated before the "fleeting thoughts" overwhelm the rational intellect. Denying minorities access to the control of their advancement decimates the chances of large-scale, substantive progress.

Searching for the Innocent, White Victim
VADA BERGER

The truly disturbing aspect of *Bakke* and similar cases is the focus on the sacrifice of the "innocent" white victim. I have yet to meet any innocent whites. I do not mean that all whites are consciously experiencing or acting on racial animus. Rather, every day of our lives we whites benefit from white privilege. This means we are enjoying benefits that are not fairly ours, that we have not worked for and often do not need, at another's expense.

The assumption in the *Bakke* case is that all of the whites at the medical school at the University of California at Davis attend the school because they deserve to and they work hard. Why do the whites deserve to attend the school? They deserve to attend because they scored higher on a racially biased test, one of their parents is an alumnus of the school, one of their ancestors provided large donations to the school, they attended a suburban high school where they received individualized attention, and/or they attended a college with an outstanding reputation.

Of course, whites can claim that it is not their fault that they are blessed with these attributes and that they as individuals did nothing to promote the benefits bestowed upon them. However, these people miss the point. They are not viewed merely as individuals, they are viewed by their status as whites. Every accomplishment they would like to claim as their own is tainted by having been gained through their whiteness. Therefore, the truly questionable group in any medical school setting, the ones who should operate in a "cloud of suspected incompetency," are the white students.

Equal Opportunity Employer
ERIC RICHARDS

A third-year law student, I recently completed a hectic schedule of fall interviewing with law firms, government agencies, and others, seeking post-graduate employment. Typical of one of my interviews was a visit to a highly regarded New York law firm of about 260 lawyers which proudly adjusted its recruiting pitch to appeal to me as a black student. "We are one of the most progressive firms in the country," I was assured by one of the older partners, "certainly one of the first in this city to hire blacks, women, and Jewish attorneys." He confidently continued, "You need not worry about being a minority lawyer in our firm. We are and have always been a meritocracy. You will advance or not advance here solely on the basis of your own merit."

If the appeal to meritocracy was meant to impress me as a minority, it failed to do so. Despite the partner's assurances, I did worry. The firm's own statistics revealed that, while it hired a small number of minority associates each year, all would be gone long before they were considered for partnership. Yet the firm still insisted that it was a meritocracy, where factors other than merit, and certainly not race or sex, supposedly have no bearing on an individual's ability to advance. Even a conservative foe of affirmative action might concede that the firm's complete lack of minority partners suggested that firm may be indifferent to individual merit, but not race or sex, in advancing lawyers towards partnership.

The Chronicle of the Race Change Gun
MICHAEL LINFIELD

Can *Plessy*'s nineteenth century sophism survive twentieth century science-fiction technology?

A new weapon is developed. When fired at a person, it transforms that person's color and racial characteristics. Other than race-related physical appearances, the person is unchanged. A Caucasian is "zapped" by the gun and instantly becomes a black man. Angered, insulted, and deprived of personal identity, the white man sues his assailant, claiming a drastic curtailment of his economic potential because he no longer is a member of the society's dominant group and because he must live his life as a member of the group occupying the lowest rung of the societal ladder. He may be disowned by wife and family. He would claim that as an involuntarily black man, he can expect harsher treatment from the criminal justice system; conversely, if murdered, his assailant would likely receive a lesser penalty than if he had remained white. Expecting that any white jury would be sympathetic to his claims, he claims damages for lost earnings, pain and suffering for his lost status, as well as punitive damages.

Suppose a black man is "zapped" by the gun and is transformed into a white? On what grounds might he sue for damages? His economic potential has improved and he can expect his lifetime earnings to soar dramatically. But what of his pride in being black and part of the black community, and his role in the black struggle against racism? The loss of personal identity and cultural pride is a serious loss, but is it one that a typical white jury will likely understand or be willing to compensate? Would either the late nineteenth century Court that decided *Plessy v. Ferguson* or its late twentieth century counterpart understand the basis for the black's claim for a pain and suffering award and for punitive damages?

Notes

1. Justice Brown, for the Court, wrote:

   It is claimed by the plaintiff in error that, in any mixed community, the reputation of belonging to the dominant race, in this instance the white race, is "property", in the same sense that a right of action, or of inheritance, is property. Conceding this to be so, for the purposes of this case, we are unable to see how this statute deprives him of, or in any way affects his right to, such property. If he be a white man and assigned to a colored coach, he may have his action for damages against the company for being deprived of his so called property. Upon the other hand, if he be a colored man and be so assigned, he has been deprived of no property, since he is not lawfully entitled to the reputation of being a white man.

   163 U.S. 537, 549 (1896).
2. 426 U.S. 229 (1976) (equal protection claims cannot be sustained solely on proof that challenged policies adversely affect blacks more than whites).
3. *Wygant v. Jackson Bd. of Educ.*, 476 U.S. 267 (1986).
4. *Regents of the Univ. of Cal. v. Bakke*, 438 U.S. 265 (1978).
5. 418 U.S. 717 (1974).
6. Derrick Bell, Race, Racism and American Law 29 (2d ed. 1980).

19

The Tower of Babel

ELEANOR MARIE BROWN

Social scientists have identified a number of features that characterize contemporary white attitudes toward blacks. First, traditional stereotypes and blatant discrimination are no longer common. Most whites, regardless of their political orientation, reject these traditional forms of discrimination. This is particularly true of white liberals who condition their behavior toward blacks on beliefs that strongly condemn traditional discrimination. Second, whites use ostensibly nonracial factors to justify any behavior that may have a disproportionate impact on blacks or could be perceived as being racist. Third, whites harbor attitudes of ambivalence toward blacks resulting in extreme positive or negative reactions. These attitudes are amplified by individualistic notions of opportunity that cause whites to explain disproportionate black disadvantage by individual black shortcomings rather than larger societal failures.

Attitudinal surveys by social scientists almost unanimously show marked improvements in white perceptions of African-Americans and other minorities, and the commitment of whites to using the law to prohibit racial discrimination. The most recent report of the National Research Council (NRC)[1] concludes that white commitment to legal enforcement of integrationist principles has been steadily increasing.[2] Northern whites are more likely to hold egalitarian views, but Southerners have also become increasingly egalitarian.

For example, in one of the early national surveys on school integration in 1942, only 2% of Southerners and 40% of Northerners supported integrated schools. In 1970, the numbers had increased to 45% and 83%, respectively, and in the late 1980s the percentages were even higher. Since the late 1950s, the number of whites willing to vote for a black candidate has increased from 37% to 81%, while those willing to have a black neighbor swelled from 56% to 86%. Some social scientists were so impressed by the improved racial attitudes that they described these results as a "liberal leap."[3]

Yet even as white commitment to de jure racial equality has increased, the NRC report shows "substantially less support for policies intended to implement principles of racial equality." The report notes that "whites are more accepting of equal treatment with regard to the public domains of life than private domains of life, and they are especially accepting of relations involving transitory forms of contact."[4]

For example, although white support for desegregated schools increased by 22% between 1964 and 1978, support for federal interventionist policies to implement these principles decreased by 17%. Similar disparities between theoretical support and actual implementation policies exist with respect to integration of neighborhoods, job opportunities,

Reprinted by permission of The Yale Law Journal Company and Fred B. Rothman & Company from *The Yale Law Journal,* vol. 105, pages 513–547.

and access to public accommodations. These paradoxical trends generally remained consistent through the late 1980s. Moreover, whites are more likely to support egalitarian principles if blacks remain in the minority. Enthusiasm for sending white children to hypothetical integrated schools generally decreases as the percentage of black children in the schools increases.[5]

The surveys reviewed in the NRC report focus on whites' self-perceptions. As attitudinal surveys, they decline to study whites' actual practices. However, in response to some sociologists' assessment of a "liberal leap," others highlight the distinction between idealism and reality, noting that when sociologists survey what whites actually do as compared to what they say they will do, stark disparities emerge.[6]

John McConahay and his colleagues have concluded that many of the traditional tests used to survey prejudice are influenced by white subjects' perceptions of socially desirable responses.[7] Harold Sigall and Richard Page have found that white subjects who feel that they are being psychologically monitored for truthfulness are less egalitarian in their responses than whites who do not believe that they are being monitored.[8] These sociologists agree that white Americans are not only less egalitarian than they appear, but also less egalitarian than they perceive themselves to be. They are proponents of what has been termed the "ambivalence theory" of racial attitudes.[9] Such studies have led an increasing number of researchers to acknowledge the complexity of racial attitudes in the post–civil rights movement period. Samuel Gaertner and John Dovidio explain that "the fundamental nature of white America's current attitudes toward blacks is complex and conflicted. . . . The attitudes of many whites toward blacks and other minorities are neither uniformly negative nor totally favorable, but rather are ambivalent."[10]

To explain this ambivalence, Gaertner and Dovidio have developed a theoretical model known as "aversive racism." The individuals they define as aversive racists typically claim to abhor prejudice and discrimination but sometimes exaggerate their positive behavior to confirm their nondiscriminatory perceptions of themselves. When they display negative feelings about African-Americans, this is done in "subtle, rationalizable ways." The "aversive racism" model holds that there is a veneer of acceptance of racial equality among many whites (as indicated by stated belief) without internalization (as indicated by behavior).

The aversive racism model predicts that aversive racists will be particularly cognizant of acting appropriately in interracial contexts. It further suggests that a subject's concern about external perceptions that she is not racist serves as a monitor on behavior toward blacks. Given these predictions, the researchers anticipate clearer instances of discrimination when the "normative structure within the situation is weak, ambiguous, or conflicting." On the other hand, when the normative structure is "clear and unambiguous," charges of racism will be more difficult to deny, and behavior should be more strictly nonracist.

Based on this theoretical framework, the researchers devised a number of protocols that presented white subjects with situations varying from "weak, ambiguous, or conflicting" norms to "clear and unambiguous" norms. They then studied white responses to African-Americans in these situations. The protocols they devised tested the willingness of liberal whites to be outwardly helpful toward blacks.

In one experiment, the researchers focused on whites who belonged to a political party that was widely perceived to be liberal. Their behavior was contrasted with whites who belonged to a party that was perceived to be conservative. Wrong-number phone calls were made to the subjects' houses; these phone calls soon transformed into requests for assistance. The caller indicated that she was attempting to call a garage from the highway since her car had broken down. She had run out of coins and asked for the subject's help in contacting the garage. If the subject hung up after the explanation or declined to help, the response recorded was "not helping." A "premature hang-up" indicated that the subject disconnected prior to hearing the motorist's predicament.

The researchers found that those who identified themselves as liberal were significantly more helpful to blacks than nonliberals were.[11] However, a paradox appeared. Liberals hung up prematurely on blacks significantly more than they did on whites. Black male callers were particularly susceptible to this treatment by liberals.[12]

Some of the subjects who identified themselves as liberals and some who declined this identification were polled about what they anticipated they would do if they received such a phone call. Across the board, they insisted that they would be helpful without regard to the person's race. The results of the experiment fit well with the predictions of the "aversive racism" paradigm. When it was clear that a person was in need, liberals helped blacks and whites almost equally. In these instances, the normative structure was unambiguous: According to widespread norms of social responsibility, we should help people in difficult situations. Before the motorist's needs were clear, however, when all that was known was that the caller had reached a wrong number, liberals hung up disproportionately on blacks, and particularly black males. In this situation, it was easier for a liberal's suppressed feelings toward blacks to emerge.

The study discussed above focused on whites' perceptions of black people. However, as James Kleugel and Eliot Smith emphasized in *Whites' Beliefs about Blacks' Opportunity*, such studies do not address the racial issues that preoccupy the increasingly sophisticated white minds of the post–civil rights movement period. Kleugel and Smith conclude that "in general, the literature on whites' racial attitudes has focused on conventional racial prejudice, to the neglect of studying beliefs about blacks' opportunity."[13]

Kleugel and Smith identified a representative sample of the white adult population. They randomly chose their subjects from within the sample and interviewed them by telephone. The researchers posed a series of questions to assess whites' beliefs about institutional barriers to blacks' opportunities. Although approximately 75% of the whites surveyed believed that some type of discrimination still existed, 73% maintained that the opportunities available to blacks were equal to or even greater than those available to the average American. Moreover, nearly a third of the whites surveyed thought that chances for blacks to get ahead were better than those for the average American. Finally, among whites surveyed, the majority was convinced that reverse discrimination was a widespread problem (53%).

Kleugel and Smith's study proposes an explanation for the unidimensional character of recent changes in whites' racial attitudes. For most whites, the race problem reduces simply to racial tolerance and ensuring equality of rights. The average white American assumes that the opportunities available to her are equally available to other Americans. The prominence of egalitarian notions in mainstream discourse reinforces these views. Given this premise, it is rational to assume that another's place on the ladder of social success is directly related to that individual's willingness to take advantage of her opportunities.[14]

These theories share a finding of what I would characterize as "schizophrenia." The actions of white subjects in particular circumstances seem contradictory in light of what they believe in principle and how they perceive themselves. This implicitly discriminatory behavior occurs even as opinion surveys indicate increasing friendliness to integration and a decreasing tendency to assign negative stereotypes to African-Americans.

It is striking that social science researchers, despite the different behaviors they observe, consistently resist labeling this behavior as conventionally racist. This reluctance occurs even as they bring a heavy dose of skepticism to their white subjects' perception of themselves. These social scientists reject "the widespread existence of genuinely pro-black, favorable components of whites' racial attitudes that are independent of egalitarian values. Sympathy without additional feelings of friendship or respect does not in their view represent a truly positive racial attitude."[15] Yet, even these skeptics reject the notion that whites who pay lip service to racial equality while shirking substantive results are knowing participants in racial discrimination.

This is not to deny naïvely that old-fashioned racism has disappeared. Such racism, however, plays a minor role in white attitudes in the post–civil rights movement era. Nor do these observations suggest an unwillingness in the social science community to recognize the reality of continued racial subordination, even as researchers argue that these behaviors defy conventional categorization.

Cornel West makes a parallel argument in his account of how race is constructed in mainstream public discourse. He too senses a societal "schizophrenia," a large-scale societal analogue to what sociologists observe in individuals: equivocation between one of two extremes, fluctuating between the "Scylla of environmental determinism and the Charybdis of a blaming-the-victims perspective."[16] There is no sense of a coherent middle. One sentiment maintains that government can play a positive role in the elevation of depressed living conditions, but is unwilling to criticize behavior in the African-American community. Another focuses on the work ethic and moral behavior of poor blacks, with little discussion of an economic framework for improvement of their conditions. One camp focuses on the *structural* to the exclusion of the *behavioral*;[17] the other focuses on the *behavioral* to the exclusion of the *structural*. Egalitarianism or individualism? Oppressed or lazy? This larger societal ambivalence can only work to exacerbate the tensions in whites, leading to an amplification of the divergence between egalitarian instincts and self-perception, on the one hand, and actual behaviors, on the other hand.

Labeling contemporary white behavior as conventionally racist undermines our ability to confront these attitudes in their present manifestation. The challenge for critical race theory is to reflect this "schizophrenia," as it exists both in the minds and attitudes of modern-day white individuals and on a societal level.

Notes

1. NATIONAL RESEARCH COUNCIL, A COMMON DESTINY: BLACKS AND AMERICAN SOCIETY (Gerald D. Jaynes & Robin M. Williams, Jr., eds., (1989)) [hereinafter COMMON DESTINY]. This report is widely acknowledged as the most comprehensive statistical compilation of race opinion surveys. It has documented nearly five decades of surveys, starting in 1940 and ending in 1986. The next comprehensive report will be published at the end of this decade.

2. *See* Paul B. Sheatsley, *White Attitudes Toward the Negro*, 95 DAEDALUS 217, 217–18 (1966); Andrew M. Greeley & Paul B. Sheatsley, *Attitudes Toward Racial Integration*, SCI. AM., Dec. 1971, at 13, 13; Herbert H. Hyman & Paul B. Sheatsley, *Attitudes Toward Desegregation*, SCI. AM., July

1964, at 16, 16–23; Herbert H. Hyman & Paul B. Sheatsley, *Attitudes Toward Desegregation*, Sci. Am., Dec. 1956, at 35, 35–39; D. Garth Taylor et al., *Attitudes Toward Racial Integration*, Sci. Am., June 1978, at 42, 42–49. The data used to support these conclusions have been based primarily on information collected by the National Opinion Research Center between 1940 and 1978 and the National Advisory Committee on Civil Disorders.

3. Taylor et al., *supra* at 42–50.

4. Common Destiny, *supra* at 117.

5. *Id.* at 117, 121, 126, 127. Whites express less egalitarian sentiments when asked what they personally would do to ensure equality as compared to what they think the law should do. When the questions move from the legal to the personal, the distinctions become especially stark. Large percentages of whites oppose discrimination in housing, but they are decidedly less enthusiastic about living in neighborhoods that make proactive efforts to recruit black families. *Id.* at 124–27.

6. *See, e.g.*, Samuel L. Gaertner & John F. Dovidio, *The Aversive Form of Racism*, in Prejudice, Discrimination, and Racism 61 (John F. Dovidio & Samuel L. Gaertner eds., 1986); Irwin Katz et al., *Racial Ambivalence, Value Duality, and Behavior*, in Prejudice, Discrimination, and Racism, *supra*, at 35, 42–44.

7. John B. McConahay et al., *Has Racism Declined in America?: It Depends on Who Is Asking and What Is Asked*, 25 J. Conflict Resol. 563 (1981).

8. Harold Sigall & Richard Page, *Current Stereotypes: A Little Fading, A Little Faking*, 18 J. Pers. & Soc. Psychol. 247, 250–54 (1971).

9. *See* Katz et al., *supra* at 35.

10. Gaertner & Dovidio, *supra* at 61.

11. Nonliberals aided blacks and whites in 65% and 92% of calls, respectively. For those who identified themselves as liberals, the disparity was far less striking; they helped blacks and whites in 75% and 85% of calls, respectively. *Id.* at 69. Gaertner and Dovidio indicate that callers were "clearly identifiable from their dialects" as being black or white. *Id.* at 68.

12. Twenty-eight percent of liberal respondents prematurely ended a call from a black man. Only 10% hung up prematurely on a white man. *Id.*

13. James R. Kleugel and Eliot R. Smith, *Whites' Belief about Blacks' Opportunity*, 47 Am. Soc. Rev. 518–29 (1982).

14. *Id.* at 519–23.

15. Gaertner & Dovidio, *supra* at 62.

16. *See* Cornel West, Race Matters 57 (1993).

17. *Id.* at 11–14.

20

The Quest for Freedom in the Post-*Brown* South: Desegregation and White Self-Interest

DAVISON M. DOUGLAS

In their response to the civil rights movement of the 1960s, moderate southern communities differed from their recalcitrant counterparts in at least one significant aspect. These communities understood that white self-interest demanded a certain degree of accommodation to integration demands. Thus, in many moderate southern cities, white elites, especially business leaders, played critical roles in facilitating limited racial integration as a means of preserving a strong business environment. At the same time, this need to appear racially moderate provided the black community with an important opportunity to challenge racial segregation that activists successfully exploited in many southern communities.

The desegregation experience in Charlotte, North Carolina, confirms, in large measure, the conclusions of those who have noted the correlation between the success of desegregation initiatives and a community understanding that economic goals were more important than adherence to traditional racial patterns. Previous studies of the desegregation experiences in individual southern communities have suggested that those communities that desegregated schools and public accommodations relatively early were influenced by the support of a white business class that favored such action. In Charlotte, for example, each time the city engaged in early desegregation, the city's black community had threatened racial disruption through either litigation or public protest. Fearing the negative impact of racial strife on the city's strong economic climate, Charlotte's white business elite, closely allied with the city's elected officials, took action to fend off black protest by engaging in voluntary but token integration in advance of most other southern cities. What distinguished Charlotte and its moderate counterparts like Atlanta and Dallas from more obstreperous southern communities like Birmingham and New Orleans was not so much a philosophical embrace of racial integration but rather a calculated understanding that controlled desegregation could serve broader economic interests.

Compare Charlotte with Greensboro, North Carolina, for example. Like Charlotte, Greensboro (another moderate Southern city) captured national attention in 1957 when it joined Charlotte as one of the first southern cities to integrate its schools voluntarily without a court order. Moreover, both Charlotte and Greensboro are medium-sized cities located in the urban Piedmont section of a state that studiously avoided open defiance of the *Brown* decision. Yet despite the presence in Greensboro of a better educated and more politically

70 Chi-Kent L. Rev. 689 (1994). Originally published in the *Chicago-Kent Law Review*. Reprinted by permission.

active black community that pressed its racial demands more aggressively than its counter-part in Charlotte, racial desegregation generally came sooner and with less conflict in Char-lotte, particularly public accommodations desegregation. The difference between Charlotte and Greensboro is largely due to the differing response of the white business and political elite—especially the mayor—to racial demands. Charlotte's white elite, under the direction of Mayor Stanford Brookshire, was considerably more active in resolving racial conflict and far more willing to expend its moral and political capital to those ends than was the white elite in Greensboro. The experience in other moderate southern cities confirms the positive correlation between an active white elite and the speed with which desegregation took place.

At the heart of Charlotte's acquiescence in limited desegregation in the late 1950s and early 1960s lies its white business elite's desire to retain control over the city's carefully nurtured public image. When black activists mounted a serious threat to that image through threat of litigation or public demonstrations, the city quickly negotiated limited integration. The Char-lotte School Board chose to engage in the voluntary integration of its schools in 1957 because it understood that allowing four black children to attend a white school—in a school system with over 50,000 students—could prevent judicial control over the school system and pupil mixing of an even greater magnitude. Similarly, in 1962, the city's school board adopted a pupil assignment plan based in part on geography because it understood that without such a plan the system was vulnerable to legal challenge with uncertain results. In 1963, the city's business leaders capitulated quickly to black leaders' demands for integrated public accom-modations, recognizing that to do otherwise could lead to widespread demonstrations that would paint an unflattering portrait of the city's race relations. By controlling the pace of in-tegration in each of these instances, integration remained token and minimally intrusive, while the white business elite retained control over the city's economic and public life.

By the same token, the black community in Charlotte, as in other southern communi-ties, understood that the white elite's need to preserve a favorable public image provided an opportunity to challenge the racial status quo. The black community exploited that op-portunity by embracing two effective strategies: judicial action and public demonstrations.[1] Local black activists understood that the city's white leaders feared the intervention of ex-ternal judicial authority, and that the city would compromise on race issues to avoid this risk. Indeed, the courts, as they grew more receptive to the interests of black litigants dur-ing the early 1960s, provided an effective external authority that black activists could and did exploit. Similarly, the city's black activists understood that racial demonstrations ex-posed the city—and its image—to the whims of negative public opinion. Aware that Char-lotte's business elite feared their city becoming another Little Rock or Birmingham, black activists skillfully used demonstrations and the threat of demonstrations in the early 1960s to force various forms of integration. Hence, the ability of the city's black community to challenge white control through both litigation and demonstrations proved highly effec-tive during much of the post-*Brown* era.

By the late 1960s, Charlotte operated one of the most thoroughly integrated urban school systems in the United States pursuant to a pupil assignment plan that had received the blessing of the federal courts.[2] Thus, when confronted with additional integration de-mands in 1969 and 1970 that required extensive school busing to overcome residential seg-regation, the white business and political elite of Charlotte proved unresponsive. For the first time, the city's white elite ceded control over the pace of integration to an outside agency: the federal courts. This shift took place for two reasons: first, a significant portion of the city's white leaders remained convinced that the busing demands of the local federal judge were illegitimate and would be so demonstrated through the appellate process; second, massive urban school integration presented demands of an entirely different magnitude than did the desegregation of public accommodations or the admission of a few black children to white schools.

Although eventually many of the city's business leaders came to accept the reality of school busing, their silence during the height of the busing controversy created a vacuum of authority and ultimately allowed other community groups and interests to gain legitimacy and political power. As a result, during the 1970s, Charlotte experienced a transformation in the city's political power structure, with a redistribution of power away from the white business class in the direction of community and neighborhood groups throughout the city. Thus, the integration demands of the late 1960s and early 1970s not only transformed the racial climate of Charlotte, they also transformed the distribution of political power in the city.

By 1960, Charlotte had demonstrated that it was prepared to engage in token racial integration to avoid judicial intervention and to preserve control over the pace of desegregation. No litigation challenging racial discrimination in Charlotte would succeed until 1969. In the context of the late 1950s, a handful of black children in white schools was all that was required to prevent litigation and to forge a reputation for racial moderation. By 1959, even though only one black child attended a desegregated school in the entire city, Charlotte was perceived throughout the country as a model of racial moderation and enjoyed the fruits of that reputation through the attraction of new business to the city. Token integration had permitted the city's leaders to retain careful control over the process of integration by taking the issue away from the courts. Communities that failed to do likewise, such as New Orleans and Newport News, Virginia, found themselves on the losing end of litigation that demanded far more extensive integration than Charlotte voluntarily embraced.[3]

Charlotte Confronts the Civil Rights Movement

During the late 1950s and early 1960s, the dynamics of racial protest in America changed, as black leaders increasingly turned to direct action as an alternative to litigation to challenge racial discrimination. Civil rights leaders in Charlotte embraced this new strategy. During the 1950s, the city's black community, led by the NAACP, had used petitions and an occasional lawsuit to encourage greater desegregation; during the early 1960s, however, the city's black leadership supplemented this litigation strategy with public demonstrations as a means of pressuring the white community to yield to additional desegregation demands. To a certain extent, this shift from petitions and litigation to public demonstrations reflected a diffusion of leadership in the black community away from the NAACP and toward other community groups.

Charlotte's white business leaders responded to this new pressure by drawing on the city's experience with token school desegregation in the 1950s: voluntary but token integration could fend off unwanted public demonstrations, control the pace of desegregation, and preserve the city's progressive national image as a good place to live and do business. By 1963, Charlotte had once again received national acclaim for its integration efforts, this time for its restaurants and hotels.

Since the 1940s, African Americans had conducted a handful of racial demonstrations in Charlotte. In the 1940s, a group of black protesters, led by a reporter from the *Pittsburgh Courier*, picketed the Charlotte Post Office to challenge the postal service's discriminatory employment practices. Similarly, in 1953, several black men sat down at the Dogwood Room at the Charlotte airport and demanded service; as a result, the restaurant began operating on a nondiscriminatory basis. Neither of these incidents, however, led to a sustained use of public demonstrations to challenge patterns of racial segregation in Charlotte.

The first sustained demonstration challenging racial segregation in Charlotte began on February 9, 1960, when Charles Jones, a theological student at Johnson C. Smith University, led a group of over one hundred students in a sit-in protest at several downtown Charlotte lunch counters that refused service to black customers. The Charlotte sit-ins came on the heels of similar protests that had begun in Greensboro a few days earlier and which spread throughout the state and the South during February 1960. These protests helped change the dynamics of racial change in the American South. In the wake of the protests, black southerners began to challenge the racial status quo more aggressively.

Jones would prove himself to be a savvy leader. Though only twenty-two years old, Jones, the son of a Presbyterian minister father and an English professor mother, had considerable worldly experience. As a regional officer of the National Student Association, Jones traveled to the Vienna Youth Festival during the summer of 1959, where he extolled the benefits of American democracy to students from around the world. In early February 1960, Jones testified before the House Committee on Un-American Activities to counter an appearance by Paul Robeson, Jr. While driving home from Washington following his congressional appearance, Jones heard a radio report describing the Greensboro sit-ins, which had begun just a few days earlier. Moved by the courage of the Greensboro students, Jones decided to initiate similar action in Charlotte. Jones, who was vice-president of the Smith student council, announced at a council meeting his plan to conduct a sit-in the following day. The next morning, over two hundred Smith students joined him, sitting down and demanding service at the lunch counters in eight Charlotte stores. Each of these stores permitted black customers to take food away from the lunch counters to eat elsewhere but denied them the opportunity to sit down and eat in the store. In the following days and weeks, the number of protesting students steadily increased.

The students enjoyed considerable support in the African-American community. Black professionals and business leaders organized a caravan of Cadillacs to transport the students from the Smith campus to the downtown stores. Black women who worked as domestics in the homes of prominent white families overheard conversations at work concerning the sit-ins and reported them to Jones. Many African Americans wore old clothes at Easter church services in April 1960 as a show of support. The students also enjoyed some support from the white community. The *Charlotte Observer* backed the students in its editorial pages and helped apply pressure on the recalcitrant storeowners by publicizing the results of a survey that indicated that most Charlotteans would patronize a store that operated an integrated lunch counter. Many white shoppers canceled their credit cards at stores targeted by the protesters. In March, the Mecklenburg Christian Ministers Association unanimously resolved for an end to racial discrimination in the city and county.

Jones carefully distanced his group of demonstrators from national civil rights organizations such as the Congress of Racial Equality, which had identified with the sit-in movement in other cities. Anxious to defuse the typical white view that racial unrest was the result of "outside agitators," Jones emphasized that all his group wanted was to "sit down and eat" when they were tired.[4]

Mayor James Smith and Chamber of Commerce president Stanford Brookshire met in February 1960 to discuss the potential impact of the protests on Charlotte's image and business climate. Smith was entering his last year as mayor; Brookshire would take his place in the mayor's office in 1961, a position he would hold until 1969. During those eight years, Brookshire would emerge as one of the central figures in Charlotte's desegregation efforts. Prior to entering public life, Brookshire said very little about issues of racial discrimination and did not enjoy significant black support in his first election bid. During the course of his tenure as mayor, however, Brookshire would become increasingly outspoken about the evils of racial discrimination, characterizing it as both immoral and bad for business. On several occasions, Brookshire would request the city and his fellow business owners to hire more black workers. Indeed, Brookshire was one of the first Charlotte business leaders to favor non-discriminatory hiring at the Chamber of Commerce board meetings in the 1950s. To Brookshire, expanding job opportunities made good economic sense; in his view, many of Charlotte's black citizens were an "economic liability" to the city and increased employment would enable them to make a stronger contribution to the economic health of the community.

Brookshire and Mayor Smith agreed on the need for the mayor's office to take a prominent role in the resolution of the sit-ins. Within several weeks, Smith announced the establishment of a bi-racial community organization, known as the Mayor's Committee on Friendly Relations, devoted to improving race relations. Both Smith and Brookshire perceived significant advantages to be gained from taking preemptive action to control the demonstrations. Brookshire in particular relied quite heavily on this bi-racial committee during his tenure as mayor to resolve racial disputes out of the public eye. Public demonstrations, Brookshire believed, "set up tensions and create ill-will which . . . retard progress."[5] Negotiating racial conflict in private committee meetings permitted the city's white leadership to retain tight control over the pace of integration without any significant damage to the city's carefully nurtured moderate image.

The Mayor's Committee managed to secure a hiatus in the sit-ins while it attempted to negotiate a settlement with the merchants. In June, when the negotiations bore no fruit, the students resumed their protests, coupled with a boycott of the entire downtown business area that won broad support among black customers. A threatened July 4 demonstration proved decisive. The owners of the targeted businesses requested a meeting with the Mayor's Committee that resulted in a settlement providing for integrated lunch counters. On July 9, black students were served at seven Charlotte lunch counters for the first time; by agreement, the local newspapers did not report the desegregation until after the fact to avoid conflict. Charlotte thereby became one of the first southern communities to integrate its lunch counters.

The sit-ins during the spring of 1960 unleashed several years of direct action protest throughout the South, a supplement to much of the litigation-orientation of earlier civil rights activity. In some measure, the courts' weak enforcement of *Brown* signaled that direct action would be required to force racial change. The NAACP would continue its desegregation litigation with increasing success, but with the sit-ins of the spring of 1960 the dynamics of racial protest in the American South had shifted. In cities like Charlotte, which were acutely aware of their national image on racial issues and the economic consequences of a reputation for poor race relations, demonstrations would be highly successful at forcing city leaders to take action.

During August 1961, public demonstrations erupted over a separate issue: school segregation. In April of that year, the Charlotte-Mecklenburg School Board had decided to convert a white high school, Harding, into an all-black junior high school, renaming it Irwin Avenue Junior High School. As part of the conversion, the Board transferred all of the white students and faculty at Harding High School to a newly constructed building and then moved over 800 African-American students and teachers from Northwest Junior High School to Irwin Avenue. The new Harding High School was slated to operate as an all-white school whereas Irwin Avenue would educate only black students. Although traditionally a white school, old Harding High School, located near the downtown area of the city, was the closest school to a number of black residential areas. Over the years, a number of nearby black students had sought transfers to the white school. Although the School Board denied most of these requests, pressure to desegregate Harding High School increased in light of its proximity to black neighborhoods.

The School Board's actions engendered protest in both the black and white communities. About 150 white parents, who lived in neighborhoods close to Harding, petitioned the School Board to make Harding available to both white and black children at the junior high level, although requiring black children to pass an entrance examination before being admitted. The unexpected white push for a neighborhood desegregated school was motivated largely by economic considerations. The decision to change Harding from a white to a black school caused a drop in property values in white neighborhoods near the school; white residents believed that it was better to have a neighborhood desegregated school than a neighborhood black school.

At the same time, a group of black parents, calling themselves the Westside Parents Council, under the leadership of Dr. Reginald Hawkins, a local dentist and Presbyterian minister, complained that the white students from old Harding were being provided a new school, leaving the black students with an old school. They asked the School Board to operate old Harding High School as an integrated facility.

During the early 1960s, Hawkins emerged as the leading black activist in Charlotte. Born in Beaufort, North Carolina, Hawkins had been educated at Johnson C. Smith University, where he quarterbacked the football team, and at Howard University's dental school. Hawkins' years at Howard were particularly significant, as he was exposed to a community that took seriously the need to challenge the discriminatory treatment of African Americans. Hawkins spent the early 1950s in the army, during which time he developed an awareness of the potential of organized religion to influence the political development of black Americans. One of Hawkins' army colleagues, a Jewish psychologist, spent much time explaining to Hawkins the significance of religion in the political and social development of the Jewish people. Upon leaving the army in 1953, Hawkins returned to Charlotte to open a dental practice and to enroll in the theological seminary at Johnson C. Smith. Upon completing his theological degree, Hawkins did not enter the fulltime pastorate—choosing instead to maintain his dental practice—but did begin a long history of close work with the United Presbyterian Church around issues of racial discrimination.

In 1959, Hawkins organized his own political group—the Mecklenburg Organization on Political Affairs (MOPA). Consistent with the actions of black activists in many other southern communities, Hawkins did not affiliate his new organization with any national civil rights organization. Although MOPA initially focused its attention on increasing black voter registration, in the early 1960s the organization began to challenge various aspects of racial segregation in the city—particularly in the schools and hospitals—through public demonstrations. At the same time, Hawkins established close contacts with both the administration of Governor Terry Sanford in Raleigh and the Kennedy Administration in Washington, which enabled him to supplement his public demonstrations against segregation with governmental pressure. In time, Hawkins would alienate much of the city's white power structure. Moreover, many blacks, while respecting Hawkins' courage to take on the white establishment, kept their distance from Hawkins because of his outspoken nature. Unquestionably, however, Hawkins' confrontational actions profoundly influenced the pace of racial desegregation in Charlotte.

During the summer of 1961, Hawkins argued that the School Board, in converting Harding High School from a white to a black school and providing a new school for the Harding white students, was simply continuing its practice of closing certain white schools that were under pressure to admit neighboring black students and replacing those closed schools with newly constructed ones in distant white neighborhoods. Hawkins had a legitimate point. Earlier, the Board had closed a white high school and junior high school that had desegregated in 1957 and that were located near a significant black population and built in their stead new schools in white neighborhoods. At the elementary school level, the Board converted three schools from white to black in response to changing neighborhoods. Hawkins complained at the time: "[W]hen a neighborhood begins to desegregate and its Negro residents become eligible under the Pupil Assignment Act to apply for admission to an all-white school, the school is abandoned, moved somewhere else, to suburbia."[6]

To publicize his complaints, Hawkins organized a student boycott of the newly named Irwin Avenue Junior High School. When the school opened on the morning of August 30, 1961, picketers greeted the arriving African-American students, urging them to return to their previous school. Hawkins marched at the head of the line, carrying a sign that read "Desegregate on a Geographical Basis." The boycott won broad support; approximately 500 of the 800 students assigned to Irwin returned to their old school and attempted to enroll. When they were denied admission, a number simply stayed home.

Hawkins understood that to be successful he needed to gain the attention of the city's white business leaders. Charlotte was scheduled to host the North Carolina World Trade Fair in October 1961 and Hawkins announced plans to use the Fair to publicize the city's discriminatory practices. Hawkins told a newspaper reporter that he planned to write letters to President John Kennedy and the presidents of Mexico and Finland, each of whom might attend the Trade Fair, explaining his protest and telling them that all was "not fair in Charlotte." Hawkins conceded that the city's white business leadership had warned him against causing the city "embarrassment during the Trade Fair," but he made it clear that he would ignore those warnings: "[W]hat do they know of embarrassment? We have been embarrassed all our lives."[7]

Confronted with the ugly specter of an ongoing school boycott and potential disruption and embarrassment in connection with the Trade Fair, school board chair David Harris agreed to meet with Hawkins. At the same time, Brookshire's committee passed a resolution urging an end to the boycott and authorizing the appointment of a permanent subcommittee on education to assist with racial problems in the public schools. In the meantime, the School Board announced plans to build a new junior high school that would operate on an integrated basis. Following these actions, Hawkins called off the boycott.

Notes

1. On a few occasions, the black community also successfully employed a third source of external authority to challenge the racial status quo: the Kennedy Administration. The ability of the black community to access the power of the Kennedy Administration contributed to the successful desegregation of the city's hospitals.

Many scholars have debated the comparative efficacy of litigation and direct action as a means for securing racial change. The experience of Charlotte teaches that both methods of challenging segregation were effective and often worked in tandem with one another.

2. *Swann v. Charlotte-Mecklenburg Bd. of Educ.,* 369 F.2d 29 (4th Cir. 1966) (en banc).

3. *Adkins v. School Bd. of Newport News,* 148 F. Supp. 430, 446 (E.D. Va.), *aff'd,* 246 F.2d 325 (4th Cir.), *cert. denied,* 355 U.S. 855 (1957); *Bush v. Orleans Parish Sch. Bd.,* 138 F. Supp. 337, 341 (E.D. La. 1956), *aff'd,* 242 F.2d 156 (5th Cir.), *cert. denied,* 354 U.S. 921 (1957).

4. Telephone Interview with Charles Jones. Jones would later identify with national civil rights efforts, however, becoming a leader in the Student Non-Violent Coordinating Committee.

5. Stanford Brookshire, Unpublished Address (1961) (transcript available with the Stanford Brookshire Papers, Box 26–4, Special Collections, Atkins Library, University of North Carolina at Charlotte).

6. *School Unit Told it is Evading Desegregation Opportunities,* CHARLOTTE OBSERVER, Apr. 19, 1961, at 1A.

7. *Hawkins Heaps Abuse on School Officials,* CHARLOTTE OBSERVER, Sept. 4, 1961, at 1C.

21

"Soulmaning": Using Race for Political and Economic Gain

LUTHER WRIGHT, JR.

Philip and Paul Malone, twin brothers from Boston, applied to be fire-fighters in 1975, but were not hired because of low civil service test scores. The brothers reapplied in 1977, changing their racial classifications from "white" to "black."[1] Due to a court mandate requiring Boston to hire more minority firefighters and police,[2] the Malones were hired in 1978, even though their test scores remained the same. Had the Malones listed their race as white in 1977, they most likely would have been denied employment a second time. In 1988, ten years after being hired, the Malone brothers' racial classifications were questioned by a Boston Fire Commissioner when the twins applied for promotions. The commissioner, who knew the twins personally, was puzzled that they listed their race as black. After a state hearing, Philip and Paul Malone were fired for committing "racial fraud."[3]

Hispanic and black organizations in Boston criticized the city government for allowing the Malones to work for ten years before questioning their racial identity. These organizations called for a full investigation of the Malones' case and for prompt investigation of other allegations of racial fraud. One Boston official claimed that as many as sixty other firefighters had engaged in racial fraud, but other officials estimated that the actual number was closer to ten. Shortly after the Malones' hearing, eleven Boston firefighters classifying themselves as Hispanic were investigated; two resigned.[4]

In the mid-1980s, allegations of racial fraud also surfaced in the political arena. In 1984, Stockton, California, City Councilman Mark Stebbins survived a recall election organized by a black councilman he had defeated.[5] Stebbins, described as a man with a "broad nose, light complexion, blue eyes and curly brown hair . . . worn in a short Afro style," had run as a black candidate in the city council election. While the birth certificates of Stebbins's parents and grandparents listed their race as white, and Stebbins acknowledged that his siblings were white, he contended that he was black. At the time of the election, Stebbins's council district was forty-six percent Latino and thirty-seven percent black. Accused of lying about his race to get votes, Stebbins argued that he first believed he was black when he was growing up and other children referred to him as "niggerhead." Stebbins also hinted he believed he had a black ancestor who had passed as white. Despite this somewhat tenuous assertion, many of the black leaders in the community accepted him as black, apparently to gain more minority influence on the council.[6]

American society has long differentiated among individuals on the basis of race. Paul

48 Vand L. Rev. 513 (1995). Originally published in the *Vanderbilt Law Review*. Reprinted by permission.

Finkelman recently noted, "the word 'race' defies precise definition in American Law."[7] No physical attribute or collection of physical attributes adequately defines "race." This lack of a precise definition led to accusations of racial fraud in the Malones and Stebbins cases. The make-shift definition of race used during the Malones' hearing encompassed appearance, self-identification of the family in the community, and ancestry. In the Stebbins election, California voters and leaders created a definition of race premised on physical features and personal self-identification, but paid absolutely no attention to Stebbins's obviously white ancestry. Finkelman argues, and the Malones and Stebbins cases support the assertion, that the American definition of race is much like Justice Potter Stewart's definition of obscenity—"I know it when I see it."[8] The problem with race, as with pornography, is that people "see it" differently.

From slavery to the present, some blacks have passed for white. In recent years, incidents of whites claiming to be black have become more and more frequent. I use the term "soulmaning"[9] to describe whites passing for black to gain employment, education, and political opportunities. The Malones and Stebbins incidents illustrate soulmaning. [See Chapter 43, below. Ed.]

While the case of Mark Stebbins may seem unbelievable, his case is probably more common. The "Black Pride" movement of the 1960s encouraged people to take pride in and embrace their fractional black heritage. Mark Stebbins may have been one of these individuals, but that seems highly unlikely. The political benefit that he received by identifying himself as black in a district composed of thirty-seven percent blacks and eighty-three percent minorities is a classic example of soulmaning. Running as a white candidate against a black incumbent would have resulted in defeat if the voters voted along racial lines. It is not unreasonable to argue that Stebbins declared himself black in order to win.

Regardless of his motivations, blacks in the district were willing to embrace Stebbins because of the much needed black political power he could generate as a black council member. In a society so heavily reliant on race, it is advantageous for all minority groups to accept those who self-identify with the group. Consequently, minority groups may welcome those who are soulmaning when it is beneficial to the group. However, when the benefit is only incurred by the individual, the attitude is usually more hostile.

The case of the Malone twins demonstrates soulmaning in employment. The Malones were found guilty of committing racial fraud to obtain work. The Malones apparently believed that there was some benefit to be gained by classifying themselves as blacks. Soulmaning in obtaining work did not elicit the open-armed response that Stebbins received in the political arena. As Massachusetts Department of Personnel administrator David Hayley pointed out at the time of the Malone incident, the reaction of minorities in that instance was much different. Hayley argued that because the Malones denied two minorities the opportunity to serve as Boston firefighters, no one would ever know what those two minority firefighters might have accomplished. The Malones took advantage of a hiring policy designed to remedy past and present discrimination. In this remedial context, a standardless definition of race allows racial fraud to continue with no remedy for past discrimination. The reality of affirmative action, calls for diversity, and even political campaigns may make soulmaning a recurring phenomenon. Failure to develop intelligent rules in this arena could lead to strained racial tensions and the blatant abuse of policies designed to bring about social justice.

Notes

1. Peggy Hernandez, *Firemen Who Claimed to be Black Lose Appeal*, Boston Globe 13 (July 26, 1989).

2. For a history of the court mandate to hire minorities in the Boston firefighting and police departments, see *Boston Chapter NAACP v. Beecher*, 679 F.2d 965 (5th Cir. 1982).

3. Peggy Hernandez and John Ellement, *Two Fight Firing Over Disputed Claim That They are Black*, Boston Globe 29 (Sept. 29, 1988). Id. Affirming the decision of the State Department of Personnel Administration, Justice Wilkins of the State Supreme Judicial Court asserted that the Malones "had a powerful incentive to seize on any means to enhance their chances of appointment as firefighters." Id. The term "racial fraud" is used to characterize situations in which individuals racially misclassify themselves in order to obtain some tangible benefit. In the black community, "racial fraud" has been called "passing" (i.e., blacks misclassifying themselves as white). See Gunnar Myrdal, *An American Dilemma: The Negro Problem and Modern Democracy* 683–86 (Harper, 1944).

4. Hernandez and Ellement, *supra* at 29, 32; Hernandez, *supra* at 14.

5. *City Council Member Survives Recall Vote*, Wash. Post A6 (May 15, 1984).

6. United Press Int'l, *Black or White? Race Becomes Political Issue* (April 19, 1984). Stebbins claimed that the fact that Latinos outnumbered blacks in the district meant that lying about his race would not have been very beneficial. Id. Interestingly enough, Stebbins won 39% of the vote in a district that was only 17% white. Id. If groups in the district had voted along strict racial lines, a white candidate would have had no chance to be elected.

7. Paul Finkelman, *The Color of Law*, 87 Nw. U. L. Rev. 937, 937 n.3 (1993) (book review).

8. See *Jacobellis v. Ohio*, 378 U.S. 184, 197 (1964) (Stewart, J., concurring); Finkelman, 87 Nw. U. L. Rev. at 937 n.3 (cited in note 24). This standardless conception of race is particularly troubling since race, unlike hard-core pornography, has broad significance in American society.

9. *Soul Man* was a 1986 movie starring C. Thomas Howe, Rae Dawn Chong, and James Earl Jones. In the movie, Howe plays Mark Watson, a wealthy California student who is admitted to Harvard Law School, but whose father refuses to pay the tuition. Unable to qualify for student aid and loans because of his father's wealthy status, Watson takes tanning pills and puts on make-up to make himself appear black, so that he can win a minority scholarship for which no minority has applied.

22

Dysconscious Racism: Ideology, Identity, and Miseducation

JOYCE E. KING

[The author, a professor of teacher education when this was written, describes her experience of racism in the classroom. Ed.]

"Dysconscious racism" is a form of racism that tacitly accepts dominant white norms and privileges. It is not the *absence* of consciousness but an *impaired* consciousness or distorted way of thinking about race as compared to, for example, critical consciousness. Uncritical ways of thinking about racial inequity accept certain culturally sanctioned assumptions, myths, and beliefs that justify the social and economic advantages white people have as a result of subordinating others. Anything that calls this ideology of racial privilege into question inevitably challenges the self-identity of white people who have internalized these ideological justifications. The reactions of my students to information I have presented about societal inequity have led me to coin the term "dysconscious racism" to describe one form that racism takes in this post–civil rights era.

Most of the students begin my teacher education courses with limited knowledge and distorted understanding of societal inequity. Not only are they often unaware of their own ideological perspectives, most are also unaware of how their own subjective identities reflect an uncritical identification with the existing social order. Moreover, they have difficulty explaining "liberal" and "conservative" standpoints on contemporary social and educational issues, and are even less familiar with "radical" perspectives. My students' explanations of persistent racial inequity consistently lack evidence of any ethical judgment regarding racial (and class/gender) stratification; yet, these same students maintain that they personally deplore racial prejudice and discrimination. This suggests that the ability to imagine a society reorganized without racial privilege requires a fundamental shift in the way white people think about their status, their self-identities, and their conceptions of black people.

For example, when I broach the subject of racial inequity with my students, they often complain that they are "tired of being made to feel guilty" because they are white. The following entries from the classroom journals of two undergraduate students in an education course typify this reaction:

> With some class discussions, readings, and other media, there have been times that I feel guilty
> for being white which really infuriates me because no one should feel guilty for the color of

their skin or ethnic background. Perhaps my feelings are actually a discomfort for the fact that others have been discriminated against all of their life because of their color and I have not.

How can I be thankful that I am not a victim of discrimination? I should be ashamed. Then I become confused. Why shouldn't I be thankful that I have escaped such pain?

That students often express such feelings of guilt and hostility suggests they accept certain unexamined assumptions, unasked questions, and unquestioned cultural myths regarding both the social order and their place in it. The discussion that follows will show how dysconscious racism, manifested in student explanations of societal inequity and linked to their conceptions of black people, devalues the cultural diversity of the black experience and limits what teachers can do to promote equity.

The Findings

Since the fall academic quarter 1986 I have given the student teachers in my course statistical comparisons such as those compiled in 1987 by Marian Wright Edelman's Children's Defense Fund regarding black and white children's life chances (e.g., "Compared to white children, black children are twice as likely to die in the first year of life."). I then ask each student to write a brief explanation of how these racial inequities came about by answering the question: "How did our society get to be this way?" An earlier study comparing student responses to this question in the fall 1986 and spring 1987 quarters identifies three ways students explain this inequity: As the result of slavery (Category I), the denial or lack of equal opportunity for African Americans (Category II), or part of the framework of a society in which racism and discrimination are normative (Category III). I use these same categories to compare student responses collected in this present study. The responses presented below are representative of 22 essay responses collected from students in 1986 and 35 responses collected in 1988.

Category I explanations begin and end with slavery. Their focus is either on describing African Americans as "victims of their original (slave) status," or they assert that black/white inequality is the continuing result of inequity which began during slavery. In either case, historical determinism is a key feature; African Americans are perceived as ex-slaves, and the "disabilities of slavery" are believed to have been passed down intergenerationally. As two students wrote:

I feel it dates back to the time of slavery when the blacks were not permitted to work or really have a life of their own. They were not given the luxury or opportunity to be educated and *each generation passed this disability on* [italics added].

I think that this harkens back to the origin of the American black population as slaves. Whereas other immigrant groups started on a low rung of our economic (and social class) ladder and had space and opportunity to move up, blacks did not. They were perceived as somehow less than people. This view may have been passed down and even on to black youth . . .

It is worth noting that the "fixed and universal beliefs" Europeans and white Americans held about black inferiority/white superiority during the epoch of the Atlantic slave trade, beliefs that made the enslavement of Africans seem justified and lawful, are not the focus of this kind of explanation. The historical continuum of cause and effect evident in Category I explanations excludes any consideration of the cultural rationality behind such attitudes; that is, they do not explain *why* white people held these beliefs.

Category II explanations emphasize the denial of equal opportunity to black people (e.g., less education, lack of jobs, low wages, poor health care). Although students espousing Category II arguments may explain discrimination as the result of prejudice or racist attitudes (e.g., "Whites believe blacks are inferior"), they do not necessarily causally link it to the historical fact of slavery or to the former status of black people as slaves. Rather, the persistently unequal status of African Americans is seen as an *effect* of poverty and systemic discrimination. Consider these two responses from 1986 and 1988:

> ... Blacks have been treated as second class citizens. Caucasians tend to maintain the belief that black people are inferior ... *for this reason* [italics added] blacks receive less education and education that is of inferior quality. ... less pay than most other persons doing the same job; (and) live in inferior substandard housing, etc.

> Because of segregation—overt and covert—blacks in America have had less access historically to education and jobs, which has led to a poverty cycle for many. *The effects described are due to poverty* [italics added], lack of education and lack of opportunity.

In addition, some Category I and Category II explanations identify negative psychological or cultural characteristics of African Americans as effects of slavery, prejudice, racism, or discrimination. One such assertion is that black people have no motivation or incentive to "move up" or climb the socioeconomic ladder. The following are examples of Category II explanations:

> Blacks were brought to the U.S. by whites. They were/are thought to be of a "lower race" by large parts of the society. ... society has impressed these beliefs/ideas onto blacks. (Therefore) blacks probably have lower self-esteem and when you have lower self-esteem, it is harder to move up in the world. ... Blacks group together and stay together. Very few move up ... partly because society put them there.

> Past history is at the base of the racial problems evident in today's society. Blacks have been persecuted and oppressed for years ... Discrimination is still a problem which results in lack of motivation, self-esteem and hence a lessened "desire" to escape the hardships with which they are faced.

In 1986 my students' responses were almost evenly divided between Category I and Category II (10 and 11 responses, respectively, with one Category III response). In 1988 all 35 responses were divided between Category I (11) and Category II (24) responses, or 32% and 68%, respectively. Thus, the majority of students in both years explained racial inequality as a historically inevitable consequence of slavery or as a result of prejudice and discrimination. Their explanations fail to recognize structural inequity built into the social order or to link racial inequity to other forms of exploitation. In addition, these explanations, which give considerable attention to black people's negative characteristics, fail to account for white people's beliefs and attitudes that have long justified societal oppression and inequity in the form of racial slavery or discrimination.

Discussion

An obvious feature of Category I explanations is the devaluation of the African American cultural heritage, a heritage which certainly encompasses more than the debilitating experience of slavery. Moreover, the integrity and adaptive resilience of the culture of enslaved African Americans is ignored and implicitly devalued. Indeed, Category

I explanations reflect a conservative assimilationist ideology that blames contemporary racial inequity on the presumed cultural deficits of African Americans. Less obvious is the way the historical continuum of these explanations, beginning as they do with the effects of slavery on African Americans, fails to consider the specific cultural mode of rationality that justified slavery as acceptable and lawful. Also excluded from these explanations as possible contributing factors are the particular advantages white people gained from the institution of racial slavery.

Category II explanations devalue diversity by not recognizing how opportunity is tied to an individual's willingness to assimilate mainstream norms and values. These explanations also fail to call into question the basic structural inequity of the social order; instead, the cultural mythology of the American Dream, most specifically the myth of equal opportunity, is tacitly accepted (i.e., with the right opportunity, African Americans can climb out of poverty and "make it" like everyone else). This approach ignores the widening gap between the haves and the have nots, the downward mobility of growing numbers of whites (particularly women with children), and other social realities of contemporary capitalism. While not altogether inaccurate, these explanations are nevertheless *partial* precisely because they fail to make appropriate connections between race, gender, and class inequity.

How do Category I and Category II explanations exemplify dysconscious racism? Both types defend white privilege. For example, Category I explanations rationalize racial inequity by attributing it to the effects of slavery on African Americans while ignoring the economic advantages it gave whites. A second rationalization, embraced by many of my students, conceives of equal opportunity, not as equal access to jobs, health care, education, etc., but rather as a sort of "legal liberty" which leaves the structural basis of the racial status quo intact. In effect, by failing to connect a more just opportunity system for blacks with fewer white-skin advantages for whites, these explanations, in actuality, affirm the racial status quo.

The existing social order cannot easily provide for unlimited (or equal) opportunity for black people while maintaining racial privileges for whites. Thus, elimination of the societal hierarchy is inevitable if the social order is to be reorganized; but before this can occur, structural inequity must be recognized as such and actively struggled against. This, however, is not what most of my students have in mind when they refer to "equal opportunity."

Category I and Category II explanations rationalize the existing social order in yet a third way by omitting any ethical judgment against the privileges white people have gained as a result of subordinating black people (and others). These explanations thus reveal a dysconscious racism which, although it bears little resemblance to the violent bigotry and overt white supremacist ideologies of previous eras, still takes for granted a system of racial privilege and societal stratification that favors whites. Few of my students even think of disputing this system or see it as disputable.

Category III explanations, on the other hand, do not defend this system. They are more comprehensive, and thus more accurate, because they make the appropriate connections between racism and other forms of inequity. They locate the origins of racial inequity in a society in which racial victimization is *normative*, identifying and criticizing racist ideology and societal structures without placing the responsibility for changing the situation solely on African Americans or exaggerating the role of white prejudice. I have received only one Category III response from a student at the beginning of my courses, the following:

[Racial inequity] is primarily the result of the economic system. . . . racism served the purposes of ruling groups; e.g., in the Reconstruction era . . . poor whites were pitted against blacks—a pool of cheap exploitable labor is desired by capitalists and this ties in with the identifiable differences of races.

Why is it that more students do not think this way? I suggest that their thinking is impaired by dysconscious racism. My point is not that my students are racist; rather, their uncritical and limited ways of thinking must be identified, understood, and brought to awareness. Dysconscious racism must be brought to the forefront if we want students to consider seriously the need for fundamental change in society and in education. [See Chapter 108 for further analysis of this subject by Dr. Joyce King. Ed.]

Synopses of Other Important Works

The Racial Mind: Raphael S. Ezekiel and Martin Luther King, Jr.

In addition to the authors represented in this part, two other distinguished commentators, Raphael S. Ezekiel and Martin Luther King, Jr., have addressed the white mind-set. In his book *The Racist Mind* (1995), Ezekiel, a professor at the University of Michigan, reports on his studies of and interviews with American neo-Nazis and Klansmen. He begins with a query: "Who am I? How do I fit in the world?" This is a question that "[w]e ask . . . of ourselves, each of us, including the Klansmen and the Nazi. For these people, the answer is race: 'I am a member of the white race. My people built this civilization. . . .'" Ezekiel goes on to address that prideful mind-set. After examining white supremacist literature, attending meetings, and talking with members of Klan and Nazi groups, Ezekiel offers some tentative explanations for the far-right worldview. A common feature is essentialism, the idea that race identifies a single, defining quality and that the white race is superior to others. Most Americans subscribe to this belief to one degree or another; white supremacists hold it to an extreme extent. Neo-Nazis and Klan members also consider race as a "biologically meaningful description of reality." For that reason it is a sensible and fundamental way to categorize our fellow human beings. This idea, too, is held by most Americans, if only to a slightly lesser extent.

Supremacists also see the world in terms of power and legitimate authority. In our society, one sees that white people hold most positions of power. Klansmen infer that this is because whites (and men) are superior in nature and that this superiority grants them the power of command. As our economy worsens and immigration increases, Ezekiel predicts, these beliefs will only gain greater currency, both among more moderate Americans and among the extreme right. The author cites statistics from groups like the Center for Democratic Renewal and the Southern Poverty Law Center holding that the militant white racist movement counts between 23,000 and 25,000 members; had 150,000 sympathizers who buy movement literature, send money, or attend rallies; and includes another 450,000 people who do not buy the literature but read it. He describes the militant movement as a "loose confederation of small groups," whose "[c]oordination comes from the constant circuit riding of the leaders." Membership is fluid, joiners cycling in and out of organizations. To his surprise, Professor Ezekiel discovered that economic fears were not central for the white supremacists he talked with; rather, "the agreement on basic ideas is the glue that holds the movement together. . . . The white racist movement is about an idea." The contents of that idea include white specialness, the biological fixedness of race, and the special place of power in human relations, race being an aspect of deservingness to wield this power.

Martin Luther King, Jr., in a collection entitled *Where Do We Go from Here? Chaos or Community?* (1967) highlights a different dimension of white supremacist thought and ideology. While Professor Ezekiel concentrates on their most recent manifestations, the Nobel laureate and civil rights leader draws attention to their origin in early elite colonial circles. King remarks:

> Generally, we think of white supremacist views as having their origins with the unlettered, un-derprivileged, poor-class whites. But the social obstetricians who presided at the birth of racist views in our country were from the aristocracy: rich merchants, influential clergymen, men of medical science, historians and political scientists from some of the leading universities of the nation. With such a distinguished company . . . what was there to inspire poor, illiterate, un-skilled white farmers to think otherwise?

Early in our history, then, the doctrine of white supremacy was incorporated into textbooks, sermons, and other cultural expressions, becoming over time part of the country's cultural structure. The Supreme Court ratified it in the *Dred Scott* decision, which held that black peo-ple had no rights that whites were bound to respect. King points out that practically "all of the Founding Fathers . . . , even those who rose to the heights of the Presidency, those whom we cherish as our authentic heroes, were so enmeshed in the ethos of slavery and white supremacy that not one . . . emerged with a clear, unambiguous stand on Negro rights." King points out that George Washington was a slaveholder who only allowed Negroes to enter the Continen-tal Army because the British were attempting to recruit them to His Majesty's cause; that Jef-ferson, in *Notes on the State of Virginia*, portrayed the Negro as greatly inferior to the white in intellect and morals (although better at picking out tunes on the "bajar"); and that even Lin-coln was perplexed over what to do about blacks and wrote that the only answer might be to send them back to Africa or to the West Indies or some other isolated location.

From the Editors: Issues and Comments

Is the white race endangered? Beleaguered? In disfavor? "Imposed upon," as Delgado and Stefancic put it? Is this sense of imposition or beleaguerment real or imagined? Do whites sometimes feign sympathy for the struggles of nonwhite groups in order to get government off their backs, as Davison Douglas reports in his study of Southern desegregation? Some whites subscribe to *color blindness,* the notion that the best way to think about other races is not at all. But does not one need to notice another per-son's race before deciding not to notice it—that is, as the foundation for resolving to treat that other exactly as you would if he or she were like you? Are all, some, or many whites racist, in the sense of Ezekiel's *Racist Mind?* How many embrace the dismal metaphor of which Marvin Jones writes? Is it burdensome for whites to have to take account of each new ethnic group that comes forward demanding recognition or to learn the new politi-cally correct term of the month? And what do you make of Dinesh D'Souza's call for an "end of racism"? Is it possible? Feasible? Would it entail first getting rid of race? Or becoming even more conscious of it and our own participation (complicity?) in the various myths that sustain it? Is whiteness "transparent" to most whites, as Barbara Flagg says, so that they do not even notice their own preconceptions and practices?

Suggested Readings

ANATOMY OF RACISM (David T. Goldberg, ed. 1990).

Ball, Milner S., *Stories of Origin and Constitutional Possibilities*, 87 MICH. L. REV. 1855 (1989).

Bell, Derrick A., Jr., *After We're Gone: Prudent Speculations on America in a Post-Racial Epoch*, 34 ST. LOUIS U. L.J. 393 (1990).

Bell, Derrick A., Jr., AND WE ARE NOT SAVED: THE ELUSIVE QUEST FOR RACIAL JUSTICE (1987).

Bell, Derrick A., Jr., FACES AT THE BOTTOM OF THE WELL (1992).

Carter, Stephen L., *When Victims Happen to Be Black*, 97 YALE L.J. 420 (1988).

Delgado, Richard, *Rodrigo's Eighth Chronicle: Black Crime, White Fears: On the Social Construction of Threat*, 80 VA. L. REV. 503 (1994).

Forbes, Jack, *The Manipulation of Race, Caste, and Identity: Classifying AfroAmerican, Native American, and Red-Black People*, 17 J. ETHNIC STUD. 1 (1990).

FROM DIFFERENT SHORES: PERSPECTIVES ON RACE AND ETHNICITY IN AMERICA (Ron Takaki, ed., 1987).

Hacker, Andrew, TWO NATIONS: BLACK AND WHITE, SEPARATE, HOSTILE, UNEQUAL (1992).

Hunsberger, Bruce, *Racial Awareness and Preference of White and Indian Canadian Children*, 10 CANAD. J. BEHAV. SCI. 176 (1978).

Johnson, Sheri Lynn, *Racial Imagery in Criminal Cases*, 67 TUL. L. REV. 1739 (1993).

Jordan, Winthrop, WHITE OVER BLACK: AMERICAN ATTITUDES TOWARD THE NEGRO, 1550–1812 (1968).

Kovel, Joel, WHITE RACISM: A PSYCHOHISTORY (1970).

Lawrence, Charles R., III, *The Id, the Ego, and Equal Protection: Reckoning with Unconscious Racism*, 39 STAN. L. REV. 317 (1987).

Lott, Eric, LOVE AND THEFT: BLACKFACE MINSTRELSY AND THE AMERICAN WORKING CLASS (1993).

Mailer, Norman, THE WHITE NEGRO (1957).

Matsuda, Mari J., *Voices of America: Accent, Antidiscrimination Law, and a Jurisprudence for the Last Reconstruction*, 100 YALE L.J. 1329 (1991).

Williams, Patricia J., THE ALCHEMY OF RACE AND RIGHTS (1991).

Williams, Robert A., Jr., *The Algebra of Federal Indian Law*, 1986 WIS. L. REV. 219.

Part III

Whiteness: History's Role

Our current attitudes toward race and our own racial selves did not spring up out of a vacuum. Rather, they have long cultural antecedents. In this part, several writers, most of them well-known in law or social science, reveal how contemporary understandings about race originated. Some show how whiteness-as-superior began during periods of turmoil, competition, or religious self-scrutiny. Others argue that the idea of the white race began with a justificatory purpose—to rationalize exploitation of weaker groups. Several point out earlier excesses of white consciousness and glorification similar to those we see taking place today. And one author argues, essentially, that racial classifications are often malign, scientifically inexact, and useless, and might as well be jettisoned.

23

Race and Manifest Destiny: The Origins of American Racial Anglo-Saxonism

REGINALD HORSMAN

By 1850 American expansion was viewed in the United States less as a victory for the principles of free democratic republicanism than as evidence of the innate superiority of the American Anglo-Saxon branch of the Caucasian race. In the middle of the nineteenth century a sense of racial destiny permeated discussions of American progress and of future American world destiny. Many think of rampant doctrines of Caucasian, Aryan, or Anglo-Saxon destiny as typical of the late years of the nineteenth century, but they flourished in the United States in the era of the Mexican War.

The contrast in expansionist rhetoric between 1800 and 1850 is striking. The debates and speeches of the early nineteenth century reveal a pervasive sense of the future destiny of the United States, but they do not have the jarring note of rampant racialism that permeates the debates of mid-century. By 1850 the emphasis was on the American Anglo-Saxons as a separate, innately superior people who were destined to bring good government, commercial prosperity, and Christianity to the American continents and to the world. This was a superior race, and inferior races were doomed to subordinate status or extinction. This new racial arrogance did not pass unnoticed at the time. A minority frequently asked why the American Anglo-Saxons could so easily read God's intentions for mankind, and some, unkindly but accurately, pointed out that there was no "Anglo-Saxon race"; England clearly contained a mixture of peoples, and the white population of the United States was even less homogeneous. The religious orthodox had the additional problem of reconciling the idea of a superior separate race with the biblical notion of one human species descended in just a few thousand years from Adam and Eve through Noah. But the logical inconsistencies and contradictions were ignored. Even the critics of the new assumptions of peculiar racial destiny acknowledged that the idea had caught the political and popular imagination, and even the opponents of a vigorously expansionist foreign policy cast their arguments in racial terms.

The origins of this American rejection of other peoples have to be sought both in Europe and the United States. In one respect the new assumptions stemmed logically from a whole trend toward racialist thinking in Western thought in the first half of the nineteenth century. The ideas of superior and inferior races that permeated American thinking about continental and world mission also often permeated the thinking of the English and of western Europeans in general by the mid-nineteenth century. When Gobineau published his work on the inequality of the human races in 1854, he was summarizing and amplifying more than half a century of ideas on race rather than inaugurating a new era. It is impossible to understand why the United States viewed its international role racially by 1850 without understanding why the European nations had also come to think of themselves in racial as well as political terms.

But the United States had a history that gave a particularly fervent and unique quality to the arguments of special racial destiny and accentuated the rate at which a racial explanation of world power was accepted. Since the seventeenth century the idea of the Americans as a "chosen people" had permeated first Puritan and then American thought. It is not uncommon for a people to think of themselves as chosen, but it is much rarer for a people to be given apparent abundant empirical proof of God's choice. God's intentions were first revealed in the survival and prosperity of the tiny colonies, elaborated by the miracle of a successful revolution against the might of Great Britain, and confirmed by a growth that amazed the world in the sixty years after that conflict. When religious fervor assumed a less central role in America, it was succeeded by the political fervor of a successful revolution.

If the continent had been empty and colonized only by white Europeans, the remarkable success of the United States would have still made it a rich breeding ground for the new racial thought of the nineteenth century; but it was neither empty nor exclusively white. In the first half of the nineteenth century many in the United States were anxious to justify the enslavement of the blacks and the expulsion and possible extermination of the Indians. The American intellectual community did not merely absorb European ideas, it also fed European racial appetites with scientific theories stemming from the supposed knowledge and observation of blacks and Indians. In this era the popular periodicals, press, and many American politicians eagerly sought scientific proof for racial distinctions and for the prevailing American and world order; the intellectual community provided the evidence they needed.

The success of the Puritan settlement, the triumph of republicanism in the Revolution, the extensive material prosperity, the rapid territorial growth, and the presence of blacks and Indians all gave a special quality to the manner in which the United States received and developed the racial thought of western Europe. Yet American racial thought was also peculiarly English. As English colonials, the new Americans fell heir to a long Anglo-Saxon-Teutonic tradition. In the seventeenth and eighteenth centuries, long before a specifically racialist Anglo-Saxon concept emerged, the Americans shared with the English a belief in the political and individual freedoms of the Anglo-Saxon period. Americans of the Revolutionary generation believed they were helping to recreate freedoms enjoyed in England more than seven hundred years before.

The term "Anglo-Saxon" has had a long history of misuse. In reality there was never a specific Anglo-Saxon people in England. A number of tribes from northern Germany began to settle in England in large numbers in the fifth century; they were not an homogeneous group of "Anglo-Saxons," and they did not completely replace the Celtic tribes already living in England. Later the Viking invasions resulted in the settlement of other groups from northern Europe, and the Normans were added to the mix by the Conquest. When in the nineteenth century the English began writing "Anglo-Saxon" in a racial sense, they used it to describe the people living within the bounds of England, but, at times, they also used it to describe a vague brotherhood of English-speaking peoples throughout the British Isles and the world.

In the United States in the nineteenth century the term "Anglo-Saxon" became even less precise. It was often used by the 1840s to describe the white people of the United States in contrast to blacks, Indians, Mexicans, Spaniards, or Asiatics, although it was frequently acknowledged that the United States already contained a variety of European strains. Yet even those who liked to talk of a distinct "American" race, composed of the best Caucasian strains, drew heavily on the arguments developed to elevate the Anglo-Saxons. It was repeatedly emphasized that it was the descendants of Anglo-Saxons who had successfully settled the eastern seaboard and established free government by means of a revolution. An Irishman might be described as a lazy, ragged, dirty Celt when he landed in New York, but if his children settled in California they might well be praised as part of the vanguard of the energetic Anglo-Saxon people poised for the plunge into Asia.

The process by which long-held beliefs in the superiority of early Anglo-Saxon political institutions became a belief in the innate superiority of the Anglo-Saxon branch of the Caucasian race was directly linked to the new scientific interest in racial classification. But in a more general sense it involved the whole surging Romantic interest in uniqueness, in language, and in national and racial origins. Both directly from Germany and by transmission through England, the Americans were inspired to link their Anglo-Saxon past to its more distant Teutonic or Aryan roots. Even in colonial America the ancient idea of the westward movement of civilization had brought dreams of a great new empire on the North American continent, but as German philologists linked language to race and wrote of tribes spreading westward from central Asia following the path of the sun, the Americans were able to see new meaning in their drive to the Pacific and Asia. They could and did conceive of themselves as the most vital and energetic of those Aryan peoples who had spilled westward, "revitalized" the Roman Empire, spread throughout Europe to England, and crossed the Atlantic in their relentless westward drive. Americans had long believed they were a chosen people, but by the mid-nineteenth century they also believed that they were a chosen people with an impeccable ancestry.

By 1850 a pattern was emerging. From their own successful past as Puritan colonists, Revolutionary patriots, conquerors of a wilderness, and creators of an immense material prosperity, the Americans had evidence plain before them that they were a chosen people; from the English they had learned that the Anglo-Saxons had always been peculiarly gifted in the arts of government; from the scientists and ethnologists they were learning that they were of a distinct Caucasian race, innately endowed with abilities that placed them above other races; from the philologists, often through literary sources, they were learning that they were the descendants of those Aryans who followed the sun to carry civilization to the whole world.

The new ideas fell on fertile ground in the 1830s and 1840s. In a time of rapid growth and change, with its accompanying insecurities and dislocations, many Americans found comfort in the strength and status of a distinguished racial heritage. The new racial ideology could be used to force new immigrants to conform to the prevailing political, economic, and social system, and it could also be used to justify the sufferings or deaths of blacks, Indians, or Mexicans. Feelings of guilt could be assuaged by assumptions of historical and scientific inevitability.

In the 1840s and 1850s there were obviously specific reasons why particular Americans desired Texas, Oregon, California, Cuba, Canada, and large parts of Mexico and Central America, and why many urged the commercial penetration of Asia. Agrarian and commercial desires and the search for national and personal wealth and security were at the heart of mid-nineteenth-century expansion, but the racial ideology that accompanied and permeated these drives helped determine the nature of America's specific relationships with other peoples encountered in the surge to world power. By the 1850s it was generally believed in the United States that a superior American race was destined to shape the destiny of much of the world. It was also believed that in their outward thrust Americans were encountering a variety of inferior races incapable of sharing in America's republican system and doomed to permanent subordination or extinction.

In the three quarters of a century after the American Revolution, Americans rethought their relationships with other peoples of the world. By the 1850s two ideas were firmly engrained in American thinking: that the peoples of large parts of the world were incapable of creating efficient, democratic, and prosperous governments; and that American and world economic growth, the triumph of Western Christian civilization, and a stable world order could be achieved by American commercial penetration of supposedly backward areas.

It is not difficult to find the seeds of this rejection of non-American, non-Anglo-Saxon peoples in the eighteenth century at the time of the greatest optimism concerning the ameliorating effects of American republicanism. The prevailing eighteenth-century intellectual belief in an innate general human capacity for progress had never convinced whites in close proximity to large numbers of black slaves, or frontiersmen clashing with Indians, that those they dominated or destroyed were fully their equals. At that time the possibility of the United States inspiring republican progress across Latin America and large areas of the globe undoubtedly seemed more likely because the peoples who were to be involved in this transformation were largely unknown and distant, and because they appeared to have no basic interests which clashed with those of the United States. The peoples of Mexico, Central America, and the Caribbean could still be viewed benignly in the late eighteenth century, for the United States had seemingly limitless horizons of opportunity stretching westward across the Mississippi Valley. The latent racialism which permeated southern plantation society or the western frontiers could be ignored when talking or writing of transformations that were to occur among distant peoples. Even in the 1850s, when the racialism was no longer latent, the peoples of the distant Pacific were often written or talked of in the vague language of regeneration and redemption because, in the immediate future, it seemed impossible that the United States would have to work out specific relationships with such peoples.

Yet while there were potential problems with eighteenth-century attitudes, the change from the time of the Revolution to the mid-nineteenth century is still striking. At the time of the Revolution America's leaders sincerely believed that they could teach the peoples of the rest of the world to govern themselves in happiness and prosperity; they did not believe that the majority of other peoples were unteachable or expendable. The doubts that already existed about the innate capacity of America's black slaves were not allowed to overshadow the belief that ultimately most of the peoples of the world could be taught to share in the republican system of the new nation. America's leaders were able to envision an expansion across the North American continent that would quickly transform the lives of America's Indians for the better and would, by enhancing the power and prosperity of the United States, demonstrate to the world that the Americans had found in their federal republicanism a way to ensure the happiness as well as the security of their citizens. The incipient racialism which frequently shaped the acts of southern slaveowners or western frontiersmen had no coherent body of thought to justify and enlarge it. The Americans of the Revolutionary generation were ethnocentric, and in their attitudes to other peoples it is possible to perceive a nascent racialism, but their dominant mood in approaching other peoples of the world was optimistic. They thought of them as fellow human beings, not as members of inferior races. Even in considering black slaves they readily conceded the possibility of some transformation, some solution, that would end the dilemma of slavery. In the dawn of republicanism, when hope was high, everything seemed possible.

The remarkable outward thrust, economic growth, and rise to power of the United States in the seventy-five years after 1783 not only turned optimism into arrogance but also brought obvious conflicts of interest with other peoples. At the heart of the American and western European consignment of other races to an inferior, lesser human status was the need to justify exploitation and destruction. This need was particularly pressing in countries that prided themselves on their democratic ideals. The rhetoric of freedom could not countenance the mistreatment, exploitation, or destruction of equals. It took only a few years for it to become obvious that the creation of a new American republican government would neither make the Indians happy to yield their lands for the benefit of world civilization nor in some magic manner cause slavery and the slaves to disappear. Governmental dreams of an Indian policy based on Enlightenment ideals were in disarray by 1815 and shattered by 1830. It was easier to blame Indian incapacity for this failure than to condemn the American desire for lands and profit. It was similarly convenient for Southerners to deny the innate potential of blacks when they realized fully that continuing slavery suited them much better than abolishing it. By the 1830s pro-Indian and antislavery spokesmen were drawn almost exclusively from areas in which there were few blacks and fewer Indians. It was much easier to take a high moral tone in Boston than in Nashville or Mobile. When basic interests were involved, intellectuals thought hard to discover why blacks should be enslaved or Indians dispossessed.

America's racial theorists in these years have to be considered as an integral part of the society in which they lived. They cannot simply be discussed as part of an intellectual tradition that stretched from the rethinking of attitudes toward human beings in the sixteenth and seventeenth centuries through the Enlightenment and into the nineteenth century. Their prejudices helped shape their research, and their research helped give society the justifications it needed for its actions. They obviously drew heavily on a transatlantic intellectual tradition, but they also drew on American experience with blacks and Indians and European experience with their colonial peoples to explain the apparent wide discrepancies between the achievements of different races. Scientific discussions of race were hopelessly confused in the first half of the nineteenth century. Race, culture, language, nationality were jumbled together in even the most respected works. Physical scientists bolstered their theories of racial differentiation with cultural observations and apparent historical evidence. In effect, by mid-century, America's racial theorists were explaining the enslavement of blacks, the disappearance of Indians, and the defeat of the Mexicans in a manner that reflected no discredit on the people of the United States.

Scientific theories of superior and inferior races were eagerly grasped by an American society undergoing complex changes. As Jacksonian America brought at least a much greater expectation, if not always the reality, of social mobility, and as the old order began to crumble, the elaborate racial hierarchies provided a new certainty and created a new aristocracy, an aristocracy of race. There was no logic in the way this new superior race was defined. By the late 1840s most Americans either thought of themselves as the descendants of English immigrants, speaking English, bound together by a common culture and a talent for government, or they thought of themselves as a superior, distant "American" race, drawn from the very best of the stocks of western and northern Europe. The former argument was clearly in the ascendancy, but there were indications by the early 1850s that the idea of the Americans as a distinct race might challenge the Anglo-Saxon theorists. This potential challenge never developed, mainly because of the increasing fear of mass immigration by non-Teutonic peoples.

A professed dislike of the English aristocratic government and a commercial rivalry with Great Britain were not enough to drive the American political and cultural establishment into a fervent kinship with the rapidly increasing immigrant masses. Even those who had been attracted by the idea of a superior "American" race balked at the idea of the creation of a "mongrel" America with traits drawn from a mass of new immigrants. The established basis of society might be changing, but it was still possible to cling to the continuity of a special heritage that stretched back across the Atlantic to England and then across the North Sea to Germany. Immigrants could not be made to change their own racial heritage, but they could be forced to conform to prevailing standards in language and culture and could be absorbed as quickly as possible within the main Anglo-Saxon tradition. In the later years of the century, as the new immigration threatened to become overwhelming, many argued that the entrance of the new stocks should be checked before the American Anglo-Saxon race was polluted by the presence of inferior strains.

The acceptance of "Anglo-Saxon" as the prevailing type in America in the latter part of the century was made easier by continuing confusion over race, language, culture, and nationality. Many who were not of exclusively English origin had already found it easy to slip into the prevailing Anglo-Saxon rhetoric and beliefs, and Theodore Roosevelt was to see his heritage and name as no obstacle in defending a full-scale Anglo-Saxon interpretation of American and world history. The American Anglo-Saxonists reached new heights of confidence in the last years of the nineteenth century.

Many Americans continued to reject a formal imperial system as well as the admission of inferior peoples into the union, but practically all were able to support American world trade and the economic penetration of distant lands. The transformation of other areas by American enterprise was repeatedly defended as a moral as well as a commercial good; it was the means by which the superior Anglo-Saxon race could bring Christian civilization and progress to the world as well as infinite prosperity to the United States. Without taking on the dangerous burdens of a formal empire, the United States could obtain the markets and raw materials its ever-expanding economy needed. American and world economic growth, the triumph of Western Christian civilization, and a stable world order could be achieved by American economic penetration of underdeveloped areas. And as Anglo-Saxons sought out the most distant corners of the globe, they could ultimately replace a variety of inferior races. The Anglo-Saxonism of the last half of the century was no benign expansionism, though it used the rhetoric of redemption, for it assumed that one race was destined to lead, others to serve—one race to flourish, many to die. The world was to be transformed not by the strength of better ideas but by the power of a superior race.

24

The Invention of Race:
Rereading *White Over Black*

JAMES CAMPBELL AND JAMES OAKES

When Winthrop Jordan's *White Over Black* was published in 1968, big reviews came out right away, followed by big prizes. Everyone noticed; everyone raved. Yet for all its monumental proportions, the book cast a curiously slender historiographical shadow. Jordan's work did not become the centerpiece of a long and fruitful scholarly debate. It sits on our shelves, the proverbial book we read in graduate school. It was Jordan's singular misfortune to produce a history of racial attitudes at the same time that Americans were beginning to look beyond racism to the political and economic sources of social inequality. The "real" issue was class, not race.

Reception of *White Over Black* was also influenced by the famous Handlin-Degler debate about the origins of slavery and racism in America. In a pathbreaking essay of 1950, Oscar and Mary Handlin argued that Africans in seventeenth-century Virginia were not initially singled out for enslavement, but were treated pretty much like English indentured servants. It was only under the pressures of the New World environment that Africans came eventually to be associated with the condition of slavery. And it was this association which led, over time, to the development of a historically specific ideology of black inferiority. Several years later Carl Degler challenged the Handlins' thesis. Citing evidence of European and very early American contempt for Africans, Degler argued that blacks were subjected to uniquely discriminatory treatment right from the start. Economics may have given rise to slavery and racism may have developed only later but prejudice against blacks was nevertheless crucial in the decision to enslave Africans. Indeed, he frequently suggested that prejudice has been so widespread in human history as to be nearly universal. Unfortunately, the subtleties of the Handlin-Degler debate quickly gave way to a crude dichotomy that caricatured both positions and forever shaped the way *White Over Black* was read. By 1968 many readers approached Winthrop Jordan's book looking for a definitive answer to the question: Did slavery cause racism or did racism cause slavery?

But Jordan had rejected these alternatives, offering an interpretation of the origins of racism that was distinct from the Handlins' and even more depressing than Degler's. Unlike either the Handlins or Degler, Jordan argued that white prejudice did not crystallize into racism in the seventeenth century but in the late eighteenth century, and not as a simple byproduct of slavery but in response to the specter of emancipation. Indeed, of *White Over Black*'s nearly six hundred pages, five hundred cover the years after 1700. Jordan's

21 REVIEWS IN AMERICAN HISTORY 172 (March 1993). Copyright © 1993 by the Johns Hopkins University Press. Reprinted by permission.

discussion of the American Revolution begins about halfway through the book, which means that 50 percent of his text is devoted to the last half of the eighteenth century.

Jordan's emphasis on the radical transformation of the late 1700s is only one of the ways that *White Over Black* resonates with more recent scholarship. Rereading the book a quarter century after publication, what stands out is not its obsolescence but its prescience. Historians are fascinated by the social and cultural "construction" of reality, the complex processes that produce the "common-sense" categories of everyday life. In this setting, *White Over Black* commands our attention as the definitive history of the long and agonizing process by which Americans invented the idea of race. As do today's "New Atlantic" historians, Jordan recognized that the American colonies were embedded in a wider economic and intellectual world, that events in London and Paris and Port-au-Prince reverberated through Boston and Charleston. Jordan understood that building an American nation involved "imagining" a community, and that this process entailed exclusion as well as inclusion. In surprising ways the quintessential book of the 1960s reads like a primer for the 1990s.

The best way to appreciate this is by carefully reconstructing the book's complex argument, beginning with the opening chapters on Elizabethan England and seventeenth-century America. Notwithstanding Jordan's strong emphasis on the late eighteenth century, his first hundred pages deserve special attention. They are among the most tightly argued and establish several of Jordan's most persistent themes.

Chapter 1, "First Impressions," examines the explosion of commentary that attended England's first sustained "face-to-face" encounter with sub-Saharan Africans in the sixteenth century. Four things struck the English with peculiar force. First, they described Africans as *black*—"an exaggerated term" freighted with negative connotations—inaugurating a long tradition of speculation on the causes of skin color. Second, but far more impressive to the English at the outset, Africans appeared to be "heathens." Unlike Catholics or Muslims, they seemed to have no religion. Third, Africans appeared to be devoid of civilization, to be "savage," an attribute they shared with Native Americans, though observers drew different conclusions in the two cases. Finally, Africans struck the English as peculiarly lewd and libidinous, almost bestial, an ancient association that acquired new saliency in the sixteenth century.

Each of these impressions was critically ambiguous; none led automatically to the enslavement of Africans by Englishmen. The encounter with "black" people spurred the development of cultural relativism as much as prejudice. The same Protestants who were appalled by heathenism tended also to be moved by the spirit of Christian universalism. Englishmen generally considered savagery a cultural curiosity produced by the environment; not until the eighteenth century did they invoke it as a justification for enslavement. Even skin color was often seen as a consequence of climate and subject to change. In short, Elizabethan attitudes toward African blacks did not constitute racism and cannot explain the origins of slavery in North America. They certainly did not add up to a vision of innate, ineradicable inferiority, rooted in the body, which forms the core of Jordan's conception of racism.

Yet many readers took "First Impressions" as proof that English colonists were racist from the outset. Barbara J. Fields, the book's most severe critic, read *White Over Black* that way, accusing Jordan of treating racism as a transhistorical phenomenon, embedded in the white psyche, rather than as an ideological construction masking underlying class relations. Fields's criticism hinges on a misreading of the central argument of *White Over*

Black. Jordan is scrupulous in insisting that the issue in the first chapter is not race or racism but a conception of difference, registered along a variety of axes, only one of which was skin color. Seventeenth-century perceptions of Africans, however derogatory, were still too inchoate, too ambiguous about the sources and meaning of perceived differences, to provide a firm justification for enslaving blacks.

For Jordan, English prejudices are interesting primarily for what they reveal about the English. The important question is why the English suddenly took so much interest in exploring the differences between themselves and Africans. Having passed through a Protestant reformation and a Puritan revolution, pious Englishmen were inclined to fall into fits of intense self-scrutiny. They were also obsessed with social order as they confronted the first dramatic stirrings of capitalist development.

In this "charged atmosphere" the English looked at Africans as "social mirrors" and "were especially inclined to discover attributes in savages which they found first but could not speak of in themselves" (p. 40). In the lexicon of today's anthropologists, Africans became the "other," a negative reference for Englishmen struggling to reconstruct their own sense of identity. This was even more true in America, where the English colonists confronted a wilderness which simultaneously evoked the dream of freedom and the specter of complete social breakdown. By selectively isolating a host of physical and cultural differences between Africans, Native Americans, and themselves, the English were able to "triangulate" their own position thereby recovering the sense of order and control they so desperately craved.

Thus for Jordan the white encounter with blacks always was a psychological as well as a social transaction; it engaged not only conscious interests but unconscious fears and obsessions. Jordan's emphasis on the unconscious and irrational is most evident in his investigation of the enduring linkages between racial prejudice and sexual insecurity. He suggests that the colonists' feverish discussion of black sexual potency provided a way of externalizing their own buried anxieties about sexual license, figuratively chaining "the blackness within." This preoccupation with the white psyche has irked a number of Jordan's critics, who maintain that it obviates class distinctions and leads to a consensus vision of American history. Yet nothing in Jordan's formulation precludes class analysis, or the possibility that prejudice could be used instrumentally to advance or obscure class interests.

Ultimately, Jordan locates the origins of slavery not in the white psyche but in the material interests of English colonizers. In a chapter entitled "Unthinking Decision," Jordan carefully distinguishes two questions often conflated by historians: What caused slavery? and Why were some groups enslaved rather than others? To the first question, Jordan's unambiguous answer is: economics, or more specifically, the labor shortage. This premise leads Jordan into an examination of the English class structure of the late sixteenth and early seventeenth centuries. At that time, the English knew of three very different forms of labor: wage labor, indentured servitude, and slavery. Each had a distinct history with its own prospects for success or failure in America. Given the availability of land, few settlers would voluntarily sell their labor for wages. So very early on, the English turned to indentured service, a relatively new form that grew out of the apprenticeship system. A response to the social turmoil of the sixteenth century, indentured servitude combined feudal elements of coercion with a recognition of certain basic rights for all Englishmen. As such, indentured service was very different from slavery.

While the practice of slavery had long since died out in Britain, the concept endured in

English law and to a lesser extent in English imaginations. Jordan pieces together contemporary understandings of what it meant to be enslaved. Unlike the medieval villein, the slave's loss of freedom was total. And unlike indentured servitude, slavery was perpetual, usually hereditary. Slavery, Jordan writes, "was somehow akin to a loss of humanity," the loss being symbolized in the belief that slaves were captives of war whose physical lives had been spared in return for the loss of social life. Unlike the indenture system or wage labor, slaves were "others," which in the seventeenth century generally meant non-Christians.

All of which raises the second question: Why were some groups enslaved and others not? English settlers were well aware that the Spanish and Portuguese were enslaving Africans on both sides of the Atlantic, that fellow Englishmen were doing the same thing in the West Indies, and that the Dutch were constructing a robust trade in Africans. Equally important, English impressions of Africans dovetailed neatly with their concept of the slave: Africans were captives, apparently devoid of civilization and religion, and resoundingly un-English. By the same logic Native Americans were vulnerable to enslavement, and many were enslaved, though certain practical difficulties—the relative ease of escape, appalling morbidity, and the ever-present threat of retaliation—kept their numbers relatively small. The English were also accustomed to treating the Scottish, Welsh, and Irish differentially, often barbarically, but powerful inhibitions weighed against enslaving fellow Christians. Thus indentured servants were often brutalized, degraded, and subjected at times to harsher treatment than slaves, but they were never stripped of all their freedom. Thus Jordan's cryptic title—"Unthinking Decision"—may be partly explained by his sense that the English "choice" of Africans was overdetermined. They were vulnerable, available, and they fit colonists' "rough" ideas about slavery quite well.

But the decision was "unthinking" in another sense as well. In the specific conditions of seventeenth-century America, it was easy for whites to enslave Africans without resorting to racial arguments. Probably the most striking feature of the documentary record is the virtual absence of any attempt by seventeenth-century Virginians to justify slavery. This absence underscores Jordan's claim that a coherent ideology of racism did not exist when the English began enslaving Africans in North America. Indeed only in the early eighteenth century—after mass enslavement had begun and after social and economic conditions had given rise to slavery in every colony—did skin color replace religion as the chief distinction the English made between themselves and their African slaves. Difference of color, Jordan concludes, was not a reason for enslaving Africans; it was the rationale for it, after the fact.

White Over Black next examines the process by which this rationale was elaborated during the first half of the eighteenth century. The material realities of slavery propelled this development. Slave population was reaching significant proportions in northern cities as well as southern colonies. Controlling the slaves on a day-to-day basis was proving difficult. Slave rebellion became a very real concern. Colonists also confronted a dramatic increase in the population of Christian Africans, further undermining the distinction between heathen and Christian that initially served as a rationale for the specific enslavement of Africans. Also, what was the place of free blacks? What about the children of "mixed" couples? All of these issues forced whites to think about blacks more systematically than they ever had.

As they did so whites drew on two secular traditions, the Great Chain of Being and the Linnaean system of biological classification. Although the former was ancient and hierarchical and the latter modern and horizontal, both were influenced by the eighteenth-century zeal for scientific categorization. Together these trends led to "the naturalization of man," the elevation of the ancient science of anatomy into something entirely new: the use of the human body as a basis for distinguishing between different groups of people. Precisely which physical differences mattered was, as Jordan points out, a highly selective affair. Thus blacks were placed beside apes in biological classifications, even though factors such as bodily hair (and even skin color) might just as well have placed whites in that position.

Jordan is careful to distinguish this preoccupation with physical distinctions from racism. But even in 1750, more than a century removed from Elizabethan England, with African slavery long since established, American colonists could not have instituted recognizably modern forms of racial segregation, in part because "until the latter part of the eighteenth century . . . there was no explicit racist doctrine in existence which could have served as rationale for separate water pumps" (p. 131). However, the building blocks for what would later become racism were being gathered.

The critical shift to racism began with the American Revolution. It was no small coincidence that the slave economy faltered as America declared its independence. The implications for the place of blacks in the new nation were immense. During the American Revolution the principle of human equality leaped beyond its traditional religious boundaries and became a secular ideal in American political culture. Environmentalism became the accepted form of explaining human differences, while everywhere in revolutionary America the basic sameness of all humans was emphasized. It was in these years that Americans became conscious of "prejudice." Antislavery and humanitarian ideas sprouted rapidly in the soil of a moribund slave economy. Many of the harshest features of the slave codes were eliminated. Every northern state instituted some plan of emancipation. A wave of manumissions swept the upper South. In Delaware and certain parts of Maryland and Virginia the free black population increased tenfold, outstripping the population of slaves.

The last quarter of the eighteenth century witnessed a remarkable crystallization of racial thought. It is difficult to unravel this process because the discussion of "race" took place in many registers and was often embedded in larger debates about hierarchy, national identity, and the endowments of nature. Jordan frames the issue in terms of "self-scrutiny," suggesting that white Americans were forced, by declaring themselves free and independent, to account for those in their midst who were neither. Whatever the sources, the result was an explosion of speculation about African Americans (and to a lesser extent Native Americans), most of it couched in the deceptively transparent language of natural science. By the early 1800s the ideological building blocks that had been gathering for centuries had been assembled into the coherent conviction that blacks were innately inferior to whites, and that the two "races" could never live together as equals. Here, at last, was "racism."

What of postrevolutionary America? The rapid rise of the cotton economy in the 1790s, after slavery had been abolished or languished elsewhere, effectively created a momentous sectional division at the very moment that America was defining itself as a nation. The decline of revolutionary antislavery organizations, Jordan writes, "dovetails with the timing of economic changes in the South and the development of American nationhood" (p. 342). Political and social turmoil spawned the impulse to restrict liberal egalitarianism. Conservatives reacted sharply to the political upheavals of the 1780s and the French Revolution. The racial dimension of such fears, long smoldering below the surface, burst into flames with the outbreak of slave revolution in Haiti. The slave rebellion in Virginia in 1800 struck even closer to home.

Although Jordan sees revolutionary ideology as overwhelmingly libertarian, he is also sensitive to its internal contradictions. The inability of most antislavery advocates to consider the place of emancipated blacks was yet another indication of the "limits of antislavery" in the Age of Revolution. Nowhere were these internal limits more evident than in the environmentalist critique of slavery. Antislavery scholars such as Samuel Stanhope Smith and Benjamin Rush insisted that African Americans were capable of improvement, that their degraded condition was a reflection not of innate inferiority but of a stultifying environment. Yet in making this argument both Smith and Rush accepted "whiteness"— both physical and cultural—as the norm. And both partook of the era's naturalistic temper, blithely assuming that the effects of the environment could be read in the body. Thus Smith not only argued that African Americans' mental and moral faculties were improving through exposure to the American environment, but insisted that this improvement was registered physically in both sharpening of countenance and lightening of skin. Similar premises underlay Rush's notorious suggestion that blackness was a tropical disease akin to leprosy which would, when cured, leave blacks white. Such concessions fatally weakened environmentalism's antislavery thrust. It was only a matter of time before proponents of black inferiority began proffering their own environmental explanations, arguing, for example, that long exposure to luxuriant tropical climes had rendered blacks constitutionally indolent, mentally torpid, and thus unfit for freedom.

Widespread fear and loathing of free blacks was a crucial component in the development of racist ideology. It was the prospect of emancipation, after all, that provoked Jefferson's appalling outburst in the *Notes on the State of Virginia*. Indeed, one of the central ironies of *White Over Black*, and of the period itself, is that the enlarged population of free people of color was one of the proximate causes of postrevolutionary racism. "In retrospect," Jordan writes, "it is easy to see that [the existence of free blacks] constituted an invitation to development of a new rationale which would tell white men who they were and where they stood in the community—the rationale of racial superiority" (p. 134).

Soon, a familiar pattern of segregation emerged: black testimony was increasingly restricted from American courtrooms; black schools were separated from white; blacks were consigned to the galleries of white churches. Radical environmentalism was dead. Even the most ardent opponents of slavery argued that emancipation had to be accompanied by the removal of blacks from the United States. "What American intellectuals did in the post-Revolutionary decades was, in effect, to claim America as a white man's country" (p. xiii). This claim was based on a critical premise that blacks were not simply inferior to whites, but that they were inherently inferior and would therefore never be equal.

By Jordan's account it took hundreds of years to reach that conclusion. It follows, then, that Jordan cannot believe that racism caused slavery; the very opposite of what his book is often said to argue. He does not even argue that slavery caused racism—at least not in the straightforward way the phrase seems to imply. Jordan does not see racial attitudes as independent entities; they exist only in wider historical contexts that give them meaning and change over time. He does not see "race" as a transhistorical category; he does not see racism as an "ultimate reality." Indeed, what is most striking about *White Over Black*, a quarter-century after its publication, is how easily it fits among the more recent attempts to demonstrate the historically or culturally constructed nature of powerful social categories.

We live in an age when public commentators respond to seemingly intractable social problems by denying the existence of "the social" as a meaningful category of analysis.

Crime, unemployment, homelessness, are commonly reduced to individual failures of character or, more ominously, to genetic predisposition. Distinguished sociologists casually interpret statistical correlations as evidence that blacks have inherited their lower IQ scores or that they commit violent crimes because they are born with extra Y chromosomes. That no geneticist has ever located a gene for either "intelligence" or "aggression" suggests the continued power of racial ideology in the interpretation of statistical data. To appreciate the point, turn the tables: imagine a scholarly search for a gene that predisposes prosperous white men to embezzle funds from savings and loans, violate SEC restrictions against insider trading, cheat on their tax returns, and pad their expense accounts—all on the basis of strong statistical correlations between white-collar crimes and white skin. If such racialist leaps of logic are palpably absurd when the subjects are white men, it must be asked why the absurdity is less striking when comparable arguments are made about African Americans. To answer that question, there is no better place to begin than Winthrop Jordan's masterpiece.

25

"Only the Law Would Rule between Us": Antimiscegenation, the Moral Economy of Dependency, and the Debate over Rights after the Civil War

EMILY FIELD VAN TASSEL

Gender and race were closely connected in the ideology of the white South; they were mutually defining. Consider legal prohibitions on interracial marriage, for example. At the core of the early debate were several closely linked questions about what kind of contract marriage was, its social and legal meaning in the shambles of the slave system, and, finally, what the limits of the right to marry, or to choose one's associates, might be in a world where the meaning and content of "rights" remained to be decided.

Another question, from the perspective of whites, was how manhood would be defined and its attributes protected from dilution or negation by black men. From the perspective of blacks, the question of access to manhood was equally pressing from the other direction. Rights—civil, political, and social—were the locus of this battle, with contract, suffrage, and public accommodations at the center of each category. The fear of interracial marriage, and the social equality it was made to represent, was used to forestall access by blacks to a whole range of public rights and privileges, because such access, according to its opponents, would ultimately lead to interracial marriage.

Antebellum defenses of slavery, in conjunction with slave management literature, laid out much of what Southern whites came to believe was a hierarchical structure of rights that had a concept of dependent rights and reciprocal duties. This belief was especially true in the context of the regulation of marriage and the marriage contract. Southern judges were faced with the difficulty of explaining and justifying a paternalist social and labor system through the use of legal language that Northern jurists had devised for supporting an individualistic, free labor society. In fitting their legal doctrines with Northern precedents in market settings, "slave owners found it difficult to explain paternalism in the [Northern] language of individualism."[1] But slave owners had another language at their disposal, one that was familiar to Northerners: the language of domesticity and dependence. The Southern version of domesticity provided Southern slaveholders with a nationally understood lexicon for articulating a patriarchal vision of rights-in-servitude that they characterized and defended as "dependent rights."[2] Slaveholders' assertions that slaves possessed certain moral claims against their masters, which slaveholders expressed as the rights of

70 CHI-KENT L. REV. 873 (1995). Originally published in the *Chicago-Kent Law Review*. Reprinted by permission.

slaves and the duties of masters, functioned ideologically as a "moral economy" of dependency and slavery. Dependency was the defining factor in a patriarchal social system which encompassed all household relationships.

According to this model of social life, the filial household was not only the basis of society, but the only place where weakness and dependence could be granted what were commonly referred to as "rights" and what was claimed to be actual, although not formal, equality in the allocation of these "rights." Through the "slavery-as-a-positive-good" argument, planters sought to justify and explain—in a very real sense, to create and re-create—their social system. Part of this endeavor was an appeal to at least two distinct categories of rights, categories that would later be broken down even more. On the one hand they claimed constitutional, political "rights as trumps" for themselves; on the other, they averred the existence of dependent, economic rights, or rights as *the fulfillment of needs* rather than as *entitlements,* for their households.[3] Rights language in the hands of white slaveholders, given the context of other language about servitude and hierarchy, clearly had a meaning quite different from the dominant liberal one, which focused on individualism, autonomy, and the institutional vindication of those values for white males. But underneath that dominant meaning another strata of rights-talk existed that was applied to people, such as women, children, idiots, and lunatics, who were denied access to liberal political rights: those who in the language of the law were defined as dependent. Although needs were explicitly equated with rights in reference to dependents, when placed next to the lexicon of legal rights for which there existed legal remedies, the language of dependent rights more accurately reflected a concept of reciprocal duties. It was this language that slaveholders appropriated in their defense. And, it was this set of ideas that would underpin and influence Southern whites' attempts to shape the post-war meaning and limits of fundamental Constitutional rights, privileges, and immunities for former slaves, and to cabin them off from other categories of rights.

Most nineteenth-century Americans, North and South, probably believed that all household relationships either were or should be governed by notions of the rights and duties of dependency. But these notions reached their fullest articulation in the antebellum South under pressure to defend slavery as a moral organization of society. In the slave management literature that proliferated in the middle years of the nineteenth century, the phrase "rights of slaves" was synonymous with "duties of masters." By the 1850s, the well-developed proslavery understanding of rights paid no lip service to a classical liberal notion of natural individual rights. Instead, slavery's defenders explicitly harkened back to an older understanding that found the bases of social order in reciprocal relationships of duty and obligation reposing in the family or household.

The argument had a distinctly moral and explicitly Christian tone, as it was based on scriptural interpretations of biblical patriarchy and slavery. Without institutional state guaranteed remedies, these "slaves' rights" were "dependent rights" in more than one sense of the term. Their recognition or enforcement relied entirely on the predilections of the slaveholder, or the intervention of some civil-rights-bearing individual (i.e., a white male) on behalf of the slave. Thus, to the extent that these "entitlements" can be understood as rights in a modern sense, they must be understood, not so much as "rights of dependents," but precisely as "dependent rights."

Dependent rights were familiar to all nineteenth-century Americans through the popular ideal of domesticity, which mandated a duty of support that free men owed their dependent wives and children. Thus, when Virginia's George Fitzhugh claimed for slaves an equality, though not an identity, of rights with their masters, he was appealing to a discourse of reciprocal duties in families that existed underneath America's Revolutionary discourse of Constitutional rights. According to Fitzhugh, "The dependent exercise, because of their dependence, as much control over their superiors, in most things, as those superiors exercise over them. Thus, and thus only, can conditions be equalized. This constitutes practical equality of rights, enforced not by human, but by divine law."[4] The model for such a system of dependent rights owed more to the patriarchy of Filmer than to Lockean contract or Jeffersonian republicanism. Rights were personal and, like rights for married women, depended on the proper feelings of the "lord and master." Rights were to be vindicated by the operation of natural law or the "law of the father" within the interdependent "family," with the father's power supported implicitly by the state through the legal system.

In the 1850s, E. N. Elliott explained the content of dependent rights:

> The master, as the head of the system, has a right to the obedience and labor of the slave, but the slave has also his mutual rights in the master; the right of protection, the right of counsel and guidance, the right of subsistence, the right of care and attention in sickness and old age. He has also a right in his master as the sole arbiter in all his wrongs and difficulties, and as a merciful judge and dispenser of law to award the penalty of his misdeeds.[5]

In the 1830s, Harriet Martineau provided a more succinct explanation of slaveholders' understanding of rights for slaves: "Sufficient subsistence in return for labor."[6] This prescription has a familiar ring: "support for labor" echoes through family law, which of course was paired with master and servant in the law of domestic relations throughout the nineteenth century.

Among the most significant of the rights that slaveholders claimed for their slaves were rights to subsistence, housing, and clothing, or economic, as opposed to political, rights. White Southerners found it morally comfortable to defend slavery as a system of labor in part because they lived in a world that, rhetoric of egalitarianism to the contrary, saw dependency as a necessary part of a rational society. Dependency was most often contained within a household and was defined as a relationship to the head of the household. Dependent statuses were arranged in a hierarchy under the rule of the husband/father/master. Wives occupied the step under husband, descending in order to children, wage laborers, indentured servants and apprentices, down finally to slaves (who whites did not differentiate, legally or otherwise, by family status).

In response to abolitionist attacks on slavery, Southern elites defended their "peculiar institution" by assailing the free labor system of the North and Europe, under which, slaveholders argued, work was wrongly separated from worker and job from home, in a manner that would lead to the ultimate destruction of society. The lack of control over the total lives of workers that freedom of contract and domestic privacy required was anathema to southern sociology both before and after the war. The Black Codes of the immediate post-war South are eloquent testament to the centrality of total labor control in the mind of the White South.[7]

Unlike the free labor system, slavery linked the economic and domestic spheres in one location—the household. In return for the unquestioning obedience thought necessary for social order, domestic slavery offered "cradle to grave" security for workers in a household economy. To defenders of slavery, a paramount danger of free labor was its supposed destruction of the organic bonds of dependency. As Senator James Henry Hammond thundered to the North in his famous "mudsill speech" of 1858:

[I]n short, your whole hireling class of manual laborers and "operatives," as you call them, are essentially slaves. The difference between us is, that our slaves are hired for life and well compensated. There is no starvation, no begging, no want of employment among our people, and not too much employment either. Yours are hired by the day, not cared for, and scantily compensated. . . . [8]

For nearly all of the 250 years of slavery in America, one constant was the prohibition on sexual relations between whites and blacks. Begun as a religious ban on relations between Christians and pagans, it soon became racialized, grounded in ideas about color. Ira Berlin has pointed out the haphazard regulation of free blacks during the colonial period, noting the inconsistencies, ambiguities, and incomplete nature of white thought as represented in the Black Codes. But, he further notes that "only on the sensitive question of interracial sexual relations did whites throughout the South reach a firm consensus: no black, free or slave, could legally sleep with a white."[9] Why should this have been?

Antimiscegenation rules, long a small part of Southern slave and caste law (applying to free people as well as slaves), were revived after the war, given new, independent emphasis, and put in service as a symbol of white resistance to "social equality" with former slaves. Miscegenation restrictions, while on one level directed towards control of sexuality and maintenance of racial boundaries, were on another used to redefine white households as racially impregnable institutions, most particularly in terms of regulations of marriage.

White Georgians who had been imbued with the racial/patriarchal rationale for slavery in the years of sectional animosity leading up to the Civil War found adjusting to the new world of wage labor and free contract as severe a shock as the pre-war polemics against free society might have foretold. One woman, writing of her family's generations-old heritage of slaveholding and of her father's boyhood training for mastery, suggested that perhaps those who never had actually become masters clung tighter to ideals of patriarchy than their fathers: "it would seem it [mastery] left a special stamp on men who lived this life. But more particularly in a special way it stamped their sons, who were reared to expect it and then saw it snatched away."[10]

In emancipating the slaves, the North had raised the specter of social equality through black claims of place within the very families to which whites had long asserted to Northerners that they rightfully belonged.[11] Once the relationship between whites and blacks was no longer based on a legal structure of inferiority and servitude, however, and white power could no longer be taken for granted, the cozy familial justification for slavery in an ostensibly free nation became dangerous for those suddenly facing the possibility that both whites and blacks might believe that familialism could be exercised on an egalitarian rather than a dependent basis. No longer could white planters rely on the law and system of slavery to maintain social relations of dominance and distance within the spatial and emotional confines of a household.

The "deep conviction of superiority" that planters held regarding slaves had maintained a hierarchial social structure in the face of levels of intimacy that went far beyond mere proximity. But in the absence of its legal support, this sense of superiority alone was clearly not sufficient for planters facing a free labor force of independently minded people; particularly since these people, to the surprise of many planters, did not seem disposed to acquiesce to planter superiority. Proximity, and even intimacy, had not been troublesome (other than in a moral sense) when the law of slavery made "social equality" a concept not easily contemplated. Several Southern states had no antimiscegenation statutes on the books prior to the Civil War. But without racial slavery to define boundaries, white Southerners seemed truly panicked by the possibility that "white supremacy" was a figment of the slaveholding imagination, insupportable without new caste barriers enthroned in law. Congressional debates from 1866 through 1875 are replete with references to fears of legalized racial intermarriage as the ultimate symbol of "social equality."

Notes

1. MARK TUSHNET, THE AMERICAN LAW OF SLAVERY, 1810–1860: CONSIDERATIONS OF HUMANITY AND INTEREST 36 (1981).

2. The concept of dependent rights was not unique to Southern slaveholders, but the need to defend their way of life led them to create one of the most explicit and sustained defenses of the concept.

3. *See* Hendrik Hartog, *Constitution of Aspiration, The Rights That Belong to Us All*, 74 J. AM. HIST. 1013, 1020–21 (1987); DREW G. FAUST, A SACRED CIRCLE: THE DILEMMA OF THE INTELLECTUAL IN THE OLD SOUTH, 1840–1860, at 120 (1977). *See also* THOMAS R. R. COBB, AN HISTORICAL SKETCH OF SLAVERY, FROM THE EARLIEST PERIODS, at ccxl (Philadelphia, T. & J. Johnson & Co., 1858).

4. GEORGE FITZHUGH, CANNIBALS ALL! OR SLAVES WITHOUT MASTERS 204–05 (C. Vann Woodward ed., 1960). *See also* EUGENE GENOVESE, ROLL, JORDAN, ROLL: THE WORLD THE SLAVES MADE 75–86 (1976) (revealing the themes of duty and burden). For various slaveholders' equation of rights with duties, see ADVICE AMONG MASTERS: THE IDEAL IN SLAVE MANAGEMENT IN THE OLD SOUTH 43, 46–47 (James O. Breeden ed., 1980).

5. E. N. ELLIOTT, AN INTRODUCTION TO COTTON IS KING AND PRO-SLAVERY ARGUMENTS, *reprinted in* GENOVESE, ROLL, JORDAN, ROLL, *supra* at 76. These "rights" almost perfectly parallel the appurtenances of patriarchy listed by Cobb.

6. GENOVESE, ROLL, JORDAN, ROLL, *supra* at 78.

7. ERIC FONER, RECONSTRUCTION: AMERICA'S UNFINISHED REVOLUTION, 1863–1877, at 199–201 (1988).

8. Senator James Henry Hammond, Speech in the Senate (Mar. 4, 1858), in CONG. GLOBE, 35th Cong., 1st Sess., App. 71 (1858).

9. IRA BERLIN, SLAVES WITHOUT MASTERS: THE FREE NEGRO IN THE ANTEBELLUM SOUTH 8 (1976).

10. KATHARINE DU PRE LUMPKIN, THE MAKING OF A SOUTHERNER 41–44 (1946).

11. White Southerners did not corner the market on "social equality" fears. *See* DAVID H. FOWLER, NORTHERN ATTITUDES TOWARDS INTERRACIAL MARRIAGE: LEGISLATION AND PUBLIC OPINION IN THE MIDDLE ATLANTIC AND THE STATES OF THE OLD NORTHWEST, 1780–1930, at 147–221 (1987) (Northern debates over bans on racial intermarriage during the height of the slavery controversy). It seems, however, that white Southerners took their fears far more seriously. *Id.* at 216–17.

26

The Antidemocratic Power of Whiteness

KATHLEEN NEAL CLEAVER

Like the formally neutral concept of "civil rights," "race" usually makes one think of blacks. To link the idea of race with the social construct of whiteness is uncommon. As a rule, white Americans no longer see race in relation to their own identity, and genuinely believe that racism poses a problem for "others." A widespread failure to acknowledge that whiteness conveys internal meanings at the same time it fulfills anti-black functions helps frustrate programs that seek to eliminate racism's pernicious legacy.[1] Thus, *The Wages of Whiteness*, a sophisticated analysis of the significance of racism in the formation of the nineteenth-century white working class, offers a welcome addition to the emerging literature interrogating whiteness.

Labor historian David R. Roediger draws upon recent scholarship in social history, such as the study of gender roles, industrial discipline, and popular republicanism, in examining the specific ways that beliefs in white racial superiority became part of the consciousness of working men. Going beyond the obvious results in order to understand the motives of their choices, Roediger does not focus on the material benefits of "white skin privilege." Instead, he looks at the agency of working men themselves in constructing the meaning of whiteness. Understanding this process is crucial, because Roediger shares African-American scholar W.E.B. Du Bois's conclusion concerning the deepest injury that white supremacy caused. Du Bois wrote that though "the consequences of [racist] thought were bad enough for colored people the world over," they were "even worse when one considers what this attitude did to the [white] worker. . . . He began to want, not comfort for all men but power over other men. . . . He did not love humanity and he hated niggers."[2] This passionate devotion to white supremacy partially explains the failure of the post–Civil War Reconstruction and the collapse of its legal framework for black freedom.

Indebted to the dialectical study of race and class that W.E.B. Du Bois pioneered,[3] Roediger adopted Du Bois's formulation that the status and privileges conferred on the basis of whiteness provided compensation for exploitive and alienating class relationships, that even when white workers were paid a lowly wage, they were "compensated in part by a . . . public and psychological wage."[4] Du Bois concluded that nineteenth-century workers prized whiteness to such an extent that instead of joining with black workers with whom they shared common interests, they adopted a white supremacist vision that approved of capitalism and "ruined democracy."[5] White supremacy served as the unifying theme of the militant resistance that defeated Confederates mounted against the revolution that ended the political and legal structure of slavery. The triumph of white supremacy helped destroy

70 CHI-KENT L. REV. 1375 (1995). Originally published in the *Chicago-Kent Law Review*. Reprinted by permission.

the legal transformation of the entire political system that Reconstruction initiated and eviscerated the laws of freedom that would have extended democracy to freed slaves.

Until the 1860s, the United States was not only an expanding but also a slaveholding nation. In the republican vision of a nation composed of small independent producers, suspicion ran deep both against the ranks of the powerful and the powerless. One rarely sung verse of *"The Star-Spangled Banner"* that Francis Scott Key based on the British military's use of mercenaries and freed slaves to burn down the White House during the War of 1812 says:

> No refuge could save the
> hireling and the slave
> From the terror of flight or
> the gloom of the grave.[6]

Back when this verse was written in 1814, "hireling" was a term of disgrace. Those gradations of dependency that whites experienced during the eighteenth century, such as apprenticeship, impressment, indentured servitude, farm tenancy, and convict labor, Roediger argues, prevented the drawing of hard distinctions between an "idealized white worker and a pitied or scorned servile black worker." Many eighteenth-century whites worked as servants, the same term used with the modifier "perpetual" or "negro" to describe blacks.[7] Racial attitudes during the eighteenth century were more contradictory and promiscuous than they later became given the galling varieties of "unfreedom" whites experienced as well as the popular denunciation of "slavery" which flourished in anti-British rhetoric of the revolutionary era. From 1800 to 1860, the gradual transition into an economy in which wage labor became widespread, and the class of "hireling" expanded dramatically, produced problems for republican ideology. Dependency on wages, however, was not merely compared unfavorably with the ideal form of labor but it also faced comparison with the genuine slave.[8]

Roediger explains the setting in which the consciousness of a working class was developing in this way:

> On the one hand, the specter of chattel slavery—present historically in no other nation during the years of significant working class formation—made for a remarkable awareness of the dangers of dependency and a strong suspicion of paternalism. On the other hand, hard thought about "the hireling and the slave" could make the position of the hireling comparatively attractive. The white hireling had the possibility of social mobility the Black slave did not. The white hireling was usually a political freeman, and the slave, and with very few exceptions, the free Black, were not. The comparison could lead to sweeping critiques of wage labor as "white slavery," but it could also reassure wage workers that they belonged to the ranks of "free white labor." . . .[9]

Roediger argues that the particular constellation of social developments and attitudes that connected "white" with worker did not fully come together before the nineteenth century. Not until the 1860s did the process that reduced nearly one-half of the nonslave labor force to dependence upon wages and subjected them to new forms of capitalist discipline reach its completion.[10] Also by the 1860s those republican notions of political and economic independence that had inflamed the nation's imagination during the Revolutionary era were waning. America's newly industrializing commercial empire in formation was something unprecedented. As new types of production and social relations emerged during the raucous transition to capitalism, the political rhetoric of the day wrestled to define the new working conditions variously called "wage slavery," "white slavery," or "free white labor."

Central to the nineteenth-century worker's devotion to whiteness was his assertion of maleness, with its perils and yearnings, and his uncertain claim to republican citizenship in the world of men.[11] Roediger's examination of the way laborers cherished the term "freeman" is illuminating. "In an urban society in which work and home became more radically separated and masculinity underwent extensive redefinition, its masculine ending may have had special appeal." The word held the double meaning of economic and political independence. And in the antebellum era, "Blackness," Roediger explains, "almost perfectly predicted lack of the attributes of a freeman." This surprises no one, but what Roediger's study clarifies is how important it is that blacks were perceived as "*anticitizens*, as 'enemies rather than members of the social compact.'" Thus, along with agitation to expand male suffrage to include all freemen went efforts to bar free blacks from exercising the franchise or to make the legal definition of freeman congruent with white adult males.[12]

The increasing use of the words "help" or "hired man" or "hired hand" to replace "servant" developed early in the nineteenth century. The decline in the willingness of white domestic workers to be called servants Roediger attributes to the egalitarian notions current in post-revolutionary America plus the obnoxious association between "servant" and the work slaves performed. Roediger found that virtually all the evidence from the nineteenth-century sources shows that the new usages were initiated by the workers, not, as some historians have claimed, by their employers. The new terminology for household and farm laborers was the worker's means of asserting claims to greater dignity and freedom than the term "servant" permitted, given the link between servility, slavery, and blacks.[13]

Widespread repudiation of the term *master*, for which the Dutch word *boss* was substituted, was another innovation. Webster's 1829 dictionary did not yet include *boss*. And in 1837, James Fenimore Cooper bristled at the popular usage of "boss," complaining that "'the laboring classes of whites' moved by a desire not to be connected with 'negro slaves' had dispensed with the term *master*. . . . [But] they have resorted to the use of the word *boss*, which has precisely the same meaning in Dutch!"[14] Tracing the transformation of slang terms into racist slurs more explicitly demonstrates the changing consciousness. As late as 1840, the connotation of "coon" was that of a country bumpkin or city slicker. Later in the century, the blackface minstrel character Zip Coon came to personify the stereotypical irresponsible, dandified free Northern black, and by the end of the nineteenth century the "coon song" craze reached such intensity that Zip's songs sold millions of copies of sheet music.[15] The popularity of minstrel songs and blackface entertainment provided urban wage earners with a sentimental, rowdy, but safe form of rebellion. Explaining the phenomenal appeal after the Civil War of the "coon songs," Roediger cites the work of scholars who found that this appeal lay in the songs' projection onto emancipated blacks of those values and actions that aroused both fascination and fear among working class whites.

The elaborate cultural disguise of "blacking up" emphasized that those on stage performing were in reality white and that whiteness mattered. All whites could participate in the central joke of the minstrel show, despite their own ethnic and religious diversity. The masking process holds the key to the genius of these shows, for it allowed the performer to both display and then reject the natural self in the way he could so convincingly take on and then take off blackness. It also offered the working masses an illusory opportunity to retain the joys of preindustrial culture amidst the discipline and repression associated with industrialization, social mobility, and respectability.[16] These shows addressed the broadest tensions produced by the creation of the first American working class, and their uninhibited wildness gave the men in the audience a representation of psychological perversity that was the antithesis of the qualities associated with capitalist acquisitiveness.[17]

The late-nineteenth-century neologism *miscegenation,* coined by the combination of the Latin words *miscere* ('to mix') and *genus* ('race'), also illustrated the way changes in language mirrored the growing racist consciousness. Introduced in an 1863 pamphlet, the term was created by Democrats who sought to smear their Republican opponents, insinuating that pro-Republican abolitionists would bring about race mixing. The new word soon replaced the older term "amalgamation" in the virulent political rhetoric denouncing the impending "mongrelization" of the United States.[18]

In *The Wages of Whiteness,* Roediger paraphrases the concept of *herrenvolk* democracy that sociologist Pierre L. van den Berghe applied to the ideology of nations such as the United States and South Africa that were democratic for the master race but tyrannical towards subordinated racial groups,[19] into "*herrenvolk* republicanism." "We should perhaps speak of a *herrenvolk* republicanism, which read African-Americans out of the ranks of the producers and then proved more able to concentrate its fire downward onto the dependent and Black than upward against the rich and powerful."[20] The main strength of such an ideology was that *herrenvolk* republicanism reassured whites who constantly feared downward mobility that no matter what else they lost, they could never lose their whiteness. Since this nineteenth-century republicanism placed mainly negative demands on the state, it easily degenerated from its lofty hatred of slavery into a clear disdain for slaves, and then free Blacks, and then into mere racial pettiness.[21]

The later half of the nineteenth century, when recently emancipated slaves lost all the political gains that the Civil War amendments and the Civil Rights Acts[22] had won, fully brought the *herrenvolk* republic into being. The official withdrawal of Federal troops from the defeated Confederacy in 1877 represented the final abandonment of most post-war Reconstruction reforms and guaranteed the resurgence of Southern Democrats. Once restored to power, these resentful Southern politicians used the legislatures, the courts, and Ku Klux Klan terrorism to impose vicious regimes of paternalism, peonage, and segregation on freed blacks. Popular commitment to white supremacy was so entrenched by the time of Emancipation that even fundamental alteration in the political position of blacks did not remove the ingrained perception of inferiority. "But if Northern white workers developed new attitudes toward people of color only slowly and contradictorily," Roediger writes, "emancipation made for much more consistent and dramatic changes in how such workers conceived of *themselves.*" The role assigned to blacks in the white worker's view of the world became more complex. "Whiteness" could no longer "be an unambiguous source of self-satisfaction. . . . No longer could the supposedly servile, lazy, natural and sensual African-American serve as so clear a counterpoint to white labor and so convenient a repository for values that white workers longed for and despised."[23]

The Irish immigrants' fierce appropriation of whiteness provides a classic study. Early in the nineteenth century, it was an open question among the native born white Protestants whether these Celtic immigrants belonged to the white race. Vilified, segregated, excluded, and castigated, the "paddy" was believed to be an inferior race. "Bestial," "simian," "savage," and "wild" were descriptions repeatedly applied to the Irish immigrant, who was ridiculed as a "nigger" turned inside out. The connections drawn between blacks and Irish did not always favor the Irish.[24] The imperative driving Irish workers to define themselves as whites, despite their hatred of the British and distaste for their American descendants, was that "public and psychological wage" that whiteness promised to desperate immigrants in an industrializing society that held them in contempt.

The millions of Irish forced to come to America during the Great Famine between 1845 and 1855 helped seal the later marriage between the Democratic Party and the Irish Catholics, who brought in thousands upon thousands of largely urban voters, and used their political strength to buy acceptance as "white." In part, the Irish immigrant's anguish over the divorce from the rhythms of nature and the land were covered over by attacking preindustrial behaviors as "black," and the more frantically they sought to distance themselves from blacks, the more apparent became the mixture of fascination with their repulsion. The attacks by pro-slavery Democrats could not match the monomaniacal focus on race in the political appeals by and to Irish immigrants. Any advocacy of natural rights for blacks or abolition of slavery they attacked as "political amalgamation," and Irish politicians attacked the failure to keep free blacks out of "white" jobs as the "amalgamation of labor."[25]

The analysis Roediger develops starts from a position black scholars and writers have long articulated: the race problem is a white problem.[26] The traditional theoretical approach to labor history will simply perpetuate an oversimplified view of race which sees whiteness as natural, until it recognizes how workers participated in the creation of their own racial identity.[27]

For Marxist historians, class remains the privileged category of analysis even when scholars acknowledge the deformations of race, for to them economic class seems to have greater objective validity and therefore more political importance. Roediger is critical of this preference. "[W]hiteness," in the broadest strokes, "was a way in which white workers responded to a fear of dependency on wage labor and to the necessities of capitalist work discipline."[28] The most pressing task that social and cultural historians face "is not to draw precise lines separating race and class but to draw lines connecting race and class."[29] The study of class must be reconceptualized, he argues, to recognize how race operates to create class consciousness.

Roediger's analysis of the meaning of whiteness to the worker's self concept will have lasting significance if its insights bring clarity to the remarkable power of racism to sustain itself. The structural economic crisis now disrupting our society is the most severe this nation has seen in a century. If whiteness in the nineteenth century offered a way for the newly forming working class to express fears of dependency and anguish over the imposition of capitalist discipline, is it predictable that the fears and agonies modern day workers face may also seek expression in resurgent white male superiority? Whatever connection exists between the racially charged political rhetoric of recent campaigns and the disturbing fragmentation and decline facing the industrial worker, the abiding significance attached to whiteness is clear and stark.

Notes

1. The intense public controversy that has accompanied legally enacted programs to diminish preferences formerly accorded to whites—such as affirmative action, civil rights laws barring racial discrimination in employment, programs that promote diversity in professional-school admissions, and the redrawing of the boundaries of electoral districts to conform to Voting Rights Act

provisions—all testify to the recalcitrant nature of this problem, quaintly attributed to "white backlash."

2. DAVID R. ROEDIGER, THE WAGES OF WHITENESS 6 (1991) (citing W.E.B. DU BOIS, THE WORLD AND AFRICA: AN INQUIRY INTO THE PART WHICH AFRICA HAS PLAYED IN WORLD HISTORY 18–21 (1965)).

3. W.E.B. DU BOIS, BLACK RECONSTRUCTION IN AMERICA 1860–1880 (1935).

4. ROEDIGER, *supra* at 12 (quoting DU BOIS, *supra* note 3, at 700–01).

5. ROEDIGER, *supra* at 13 (quoting DU BOIS, *supra* note 3, at 700).

6. *Id.* at 44.

7. *Id.* at 25.

8. *Id.* at 45–46.

9. *Id.* at 46–47.

10. *Id.* at 20.

11. *Id.* at 11.

12. *Id.* at 55–58.

13. *Id.* at 48–49.

14. *Id.* at 54.

15. *Id.* at 98.

16. *Id.* at 116–18.

17. *Id.* at 118, 127.

18. *Id.* at 155–56.

19. Written in the 1960s, van den Berghe's explanation of the evolution of such regimes is based on the changes that followed the undermining of a paternalistic system of race and ethnic relations. He wrote:

> In the political sphere aristocratic, colonial, or white settler regimes became transformed into "representative" governments with wider participation in the polity, though in South Africa and until recently in the United States the democratic process was still restricted to the dominant racial caste. However, even these *Herrenvolk* democracies are clearly different from the colonial government or the planter slave-owning oligarchy which preceded them, if only because they were legitimized in terms of an ideology that could be effectively used to challenge the racial status quo. Thus these *Herrenvolk* democracies contained the ideological seeds of their own destruction, providing the educated elite within the oppressed groups and the progressive minority of the dominant group with a set of values to deny legitimacy to the established order.

PIERRE L. VAN DEN BERGHE, RACE AND RACISM 126 (2d ed. 1978).

20. ROEDIGER, *supra* at 59–60.

21. *Id.* at 60.

22. The Thirteenth Amendment abolished slavery throughout the United States and authorized Congress to pass appropriate legislation to enforce its provisions. The Civil Rights Act of 1866 was the first designed to protect the newly granted legal rights of emancipated blacks. The Fourteenth Amendment, ratified in 1868, was enacted to eliminate questions regarding the constitutionality of the 1866 Civil Rights Act. The Enforcement Act of 1870 and the Ku Klux Klan Act of 1871 were subsequently enacted to give federal courts the authority to intervene in the vigilante actions of Southern mobs who used terrorism to intimidate the enfranchised freed slaves and subject them again to white control. Following the enactment of the Fifteenth Amendment, which was ratified in 1870, Congress passed the Civil Rights Act of 1875.

The United States Supreme Court held that Act unconstitutional in *The Civil Rights Cases,* 109 U.S. 3 (1883), paving the way for the decision in *Plessy v. Ferguson,* 163 U.S. 537 (1896), which found no bar in the Fourteenth Amendment to race discrimination under the principle of "separate but equal."

23. ROEDIGER, *supra* at 175.

24. *Id.* at 133.

25. *Id.* at 150, 154.

26. *See, e.g.,* RALPH ELLISON, *Beating that Boy,* in SHADOW AND ACT 99–100 (1964); DU BOIS, *supra* note 2, at ch. 2; JAMES BALDWIN, THE PRICE OF THE TICKET 87–89, 251, 666 (1985).

27. ROEDIGER, *supra* at 6–10.

28. *Id.* at 13.

29. *Id.* at 11.

27

Who's Black, Who's White, and Who Cares

LUTHER WRIGHT, JR.

Strict racial classification rules were at the very core of maintaining the institution of slavery and the system of white dominance. One problem with the existence of indentured servants and slaves in a free society was the ease with which slaves or servants could escape if they were not distinguishable from free citizens. By linking slavery to race, slave escape became much more difficult, particularly once all blacks were presumed to be slaves. Suddenly, racial classification became of critical importance in American society—it could be the difference between freedom and slavery and later, the difference between privilege and disenfranchisement. As more people began to claim the benefits of whiteness, the racial classifications became more strict.

Analysis of this period in American history leads to the conclusion that the need for the adoption of rules defining race grew out of two phenomena: (1) the decision to deny blacks and Indians the same treatment as whites under the law; and (2) the birth of children who had only one white parent or who had ancestors who were not white. The presence of both of these factors in American society created the significance of racial classifications.[1]

Early Statutory Attempts to Define Race

Virginia was the first state in the Union to offer a statutory definition of race.[2] However, the first statute, written in 1662, only purported to determine the legal status of children born to negro women by Englishmen. The Virginia rule declared that the status of a child's mother determined the status of the child, breaking away from the English rule of determining inheritance status from the paternal line, and resolving the status of most mixed race children by declaring them black, like their mothers.[3] Because the early Virginia statute would have allowed the child of a black man (even if a slave) and a white or Indian woman to assume the free status of its mother, it is not surprising that such children and their parents were banished from the colony.

Later statutory definitions of race embraced different criteria. Early statutes in Virginia and Arkansas used a physical appearance approach, defining negroes as those who had "a visible and distinct admixture of African blood." Later, other states defining race would adopt one-fourth, one-sixteenth, and one-thirty-second rules which declared that people

48 VAND. L. REV. 513 (1995). Originally published in the *Vanderbilt Law Review*. Reprinted by permission.

with these fractional quantities of black ancestry were black under the law. The majority of states classified people who were at least one-eighth black as negro. Formula-based definitions of race, known as "hypodescent rules,"[4] were the law of the land for many years and are still relied upon in some instances today. As the likelihood that more biracial people could be classified as white under existing laws increased, the laws became more restrictive, often progressing from one-fourth to one-eighth to one-sixteenth to one-thirty-second, and finally culminating in the one-drop rule. By 1910, almost all southern states had adopted the "one-drop rule."[5] Under this rule, individuals with any African or black blood in their veins were black under the law.

Although some individuals had as much as ninety-three percent or more white ancestry, they would be considered black under the laws of many states. This illustrates the early statutory favoritism for white racial purity and a belief that at some point in history there were pure white, black, and Indian races. Individuals were often considered tainted with black or Indian blood at a remote generational level, denying them the right to be classified white. Early statutes permitted courts to delve deep into an individual's genealogy to show that a great-great-great-grandparent, or an even more remote ancestor, was black. The primary flaw with the more restrictive racial definitions was their enforceability. To the extent that racial perceptions turned on appearance, it was highly unlikely that individuals with "one drop" of African blood would be readily distinguishable from so-called pure white persons.

Early Attempts by Courts to Interpret Race Statutes

The Slavery Era

One of the most often cited early cases on the issue of racial definition is *Hudgins v. Wrights*.[6] In *Hudgins*, three generations of slave women sued for their freedom arguing that they were the descendants of a free female ancestor. Faced with the women's apparent mixture of Indian and black ancestry, the court was forced to decide the burden of proof in freedom suits. The Virginia Supreme Court created a set of legal presumptions tied to the appearance of a person seeking freedom. These presumptions were laid out in Judge Roane's concurring opinion: Negroes had the burden of proving that they were free; whites and Indians were presumed free unless their accusers could prove their slave status. The more difficult question, as noted by Judge Tucker in the majority opinion, concerned where to place the burden when presumptions based on appearances were weakened because races had been intermingled. [See Chapter 37 for additional discussion of this case. Ed.]

In *Gregory v. Baugh*[7] the court was confronted with a biracial slave seeking freedom. His maternal grandmother had the appearance of an Indian but, according to the court, was too dark to be a full-blooded member of that race. The critical issue was whether the plaintiff's dark color came from his maternal or paternal line. In attempting to establish the legal status of the plaintiff as a slave or a free man, the court permitted the introduction of hearsay [A legal term for an out-of-court assertion used to prove the matter asserted. Because of its unreliability, hearsay is generally not admitted under the rules of evidence. Ed.] and general reputation testimony to prove the freedom of the plaintiff's ancestors as far back as his great-grandparents' generation. The *Baugh* court imposed upon the mixed-race plaintiff the additional burden of proving the status of his maternal ancestors.

As noted in *Baugh*, the racial appearance of a party seeking freedom could trigger early American legal presumptions and special rules. While this appearance standard probably allowed many free blacks to be enslaved, it also undoubtedly allowed some enslaved blacks who looked white to be set free. Even during the era when race was linked to slavery, courts relied on appearance to enforce racial classifications. As the phenomenon of passing clearly indicates, however, appearance was not a reliable method of enforcement.

The "Separate but Equal" Era

In the landmark case of *Plessy v. Ferguson*,[8] Homer Plessy attacked the "separate but equal" doctrine under which the United States operated dual social systems; one for blacks, and one for whites. Arrested when he attempted to board a coach reserved for whites only, Plessy challenged as unconstitutional a Louisiana law which required racial segregation in the state's railway system. Among other issues, Plessy claimed to be seven-eighths white. According to his plea, "the mixture of African blood was not discernible." Plessy's argument challenged Louisiana's racial classification system, but the argument was summarily dismissed. The Supreme Court's refusal to address the issue of racial classification is indicative of the racial policy of the time: avoidance. Early courts seemed unwilling to concede that such racial rules were too difficult to enforce.

By the turn of the century, the free status of blacks and the growing difficulty in distinguishing them from whites sharpened the nation's need to define race.[9] It was during this period that states began to establish more restrictive definitions of race. During this period courts began speaking more forthrightly about racial classification. In *State v. Treadway*,[10] the court laid out the sub-classification of "colored" in very specific terms. The court's categories of griffe, octoroon, quadroon, and mulatto betray a society so concerned with racial purity that it began to define distinct categories by which to delineate the degree of "taint." In some instances, a person's racial category could mean the difference in what rights the person could claim.[11]

According to the court's classifications, a "mulatto was the child of one black and one white person." The person too black to be a mulatto and too pale in color to be a negro was a griffe, the child of a mulatto and a negro. The quadroon, the child of a white and a mulatto, was thought to be "distinctively whiter than the mulatto." The octoroon, the child of a white and a quadroon, was thought to be "whiter" than the fair-skinned quadroon. The court in *Treadway* asserted that there was not much difficulty in distinguishing among these different shades of blackness. When the last hypodescent statute was struck down in 1983, the kind of categorization evidenced in *Treadway* was finally removed.

During this period the need to define race became extremely important. The doctrine of "separate but equal" replaced the class definitions that slavery had once provided. As racial classification grew in importance, so did incidents of "passing."[12] The passing phenomenon illustrates the extent to which physical characteristics provided an unreliable standard of racial classification. With apparent ease, many people who were black under the racial statutes fooled the white citizenry into believing they were white.

That passing was so common during the "separate but equal" era leads to but one conclusion: There were great societal benefits, even after slavery, to being classified as a white person.[13] Race often determined where one lived, worked, attended school, and who one could marry. With a premium on racial purity, the courts and society relied primarily on distinctions in physical appearance to enforce restrictive racial statutes, even though physical appearance was often unreliable.[14] To admit that there were some blacks who could pass for white would mean that the ideal of a pure "white" race was not ascertainable. No court wanted to admit that some blacks looked white. The pre– and post–Civil War treatment of race displays a fruitless attempt to establish a system of white racial dominance premised on the concept of a discernible, pure white race.[15]

Limits Placed Upon Individuals Because of Race

Slavery was not the only legal and social disability associated with race before the Civil War. A host of other legal and social disadvantages were associated with it. Indentured servants who were black were punished more severely for running away than whites. White indentured servants were generally sentenced to extended terms of indenture, while blacks were usually sentenced to a life of servitude. In 1705, Virginia made it a crime for blacks and Indians to hold public office. In the South, blacks could not testify in court, which allowed whites to perpetrate crimes upon blacks as long as no other whites witnessed them. In Virginia, any white marrying a non-white was banished from the colony within three months. Such statutes forbidding marriage between the races, known as antimiscegenation laws, remained the law of most southern states for many years after slavery.[16]

Restrictions on freedom of movement also turned on race. By 1860, every southern state prohibited the immigration of free blacks. Rhode Island prohibited free blacks from being out after nine o'clock at night without a lawful excuse. Laws in Pennsylvania prohibited blacks from congregating in groups larger than four. Blacks were not free to come and go as they pleased, to run for office, or to associate amongst themselves. One's racial classification determined, to a large extent, the quality of life one could lead.

Notes

1. See Bijan Gilanshah, *Multiracial Minorities: Erasing the Color Line,* 12 L. and Ineq. 183, 190 (1993). See also D. Marvin Jones, *Darkness Made Visible: Law, Metaphor, and the Racial Self,* 82 Geo. L. J. 437, 470 (1993).

2. The first statute read in relevant part:

Whereas some doubts have arisen whether children got by an Englishman upon a negro woman should be slave or free. Be it therefore enacted and declared by this present grand assembly, that all children borne in this country shall be held bond or free only according to the condition of the mother. . . .

Act XII, 2 Laws of Va. 170 (Hening 1823) (enacted Dec. 1662).

3. Finkelman, *The Crime of Color,* 67 Tulane L. Rev. at 2063, 2071 (1993). Professor Finkelman suggests that this result was largely due to the frequent incidents of black slave women bearing children by their white slave masters and infrequent incidents of white women bearing children by black male slaves. Finkelman argues that the law purposely condoned enslaving the mulatto child because of the slave master's economic benefit. In effect, a slave master eager to increase the number of slaves

he owned could impregnate as many of his female slaves as possible because all of his children would also become slaves.

4. Id. at 2081–86, 2109–10. "Hypodescent" is the term used by anthropologist Marvin Harris to describe the American system of racial classification in which the subordinate classification is assigned to the offspring if there is one "superordinate" and one "subordinate" parent. Under this system, the child of a black parent and a white parent is black. Cheryl Harris, *Whiteness as Property*, 106 Harv. L. Rev. 1707, 1738 n.137 (1993) (citing Marvin Harris, *Patterns of Race in the Americas* 37, 56 (Walker, 1964)).

5. See Pauli Murray, *States' Laws on Race and Color* (Woman's Division of Christian Service, 1950). In the years preceding *Brown v. Board of Education*, 347 U.S. 483 (1954), a number of states had adopted the one-drop rule, under which an individual with any African or black ancestry was classified as black. These states included Tennessee, Arkansas, Texas, and Alabama. A number of other states used similar definitions for specific purposes like marriage or school attendance, but did not adopt a general rule. Louisiana enforced a one-drop rule in the post-*Brown* era until 1970.

6. 11 Va. 134 (1806).

7. 25 Va. 611 (1827).

8. 163 U.S. 537 (1896).

9. See Ray Stannard Baker, *Following the Color Line* 151 (Harper & Row, 1964). Baker writes:

I have seen blue-eyed Negroes and golden-haired Negroes; one Negro girl I met had an abundance of soft, straight red hair. I have seen Negroes I could not easily distinguish from the Jewish or French types; . . . And I have met several people, passing everywhere for white, who, I knew, had Negro blood.

Id.

10. 126 La. 300, 52 S. 500, 508 (1910):

We do not think there could be any serious denial of the fact that in Louisiana the words "mulatto," "quadroon," and "octoroon" are of as definite meaning as the word "man or child;" and that, among educated people at least, they are well and widely known. . . . Nor can there be, we think, any serious denial of the fact that in Louisiana, and indeed, throughout the United States (except on the Pacific slope), the word "colored," when applied to race has the definite and well-known meaning of a person having Negro blood in his veins.

11. For example, in some limited instances, mulattoes, quadroons, and octoroons would be allowed to testify, but their credibility would still be at issue. See Finkelman, 67 Tulane L. Rev. at 2089–92.

12. See Gunnar Myrdal, *An American Dilemma* at 683–86 (1944). "For all practical purposes, 'passing' means that a Negro becomes a white man. . . . This can be accomplished only by the deception of the white people with whom the passer comes to associate and by a conspiracy of silence on the part of other Negroes who might know about it."

13. Id. at 683 (stating that passing, becoming a white man, means moving from the lower to the higher caste). Passing was almost always linked to enhanced employment opportunities. It was common, particularly among black females, who often passed to get jobs as stenographers and social workers and the like. Blacks who passed "professionally" most often interacted socially as a black. Id. at 685.

14. Since the major premise for passing was looking white, whites were presumably fooled by individuals who appeared to be white. Consequently this system of racial classifications based on physical appearance could only work when people who looked white, but were black according to the race statutes, identified themselves as being black. This probably never happened when these individuals attempted to pass. For an interesting discussion of presumptions and physical appearance, see generally John Griffin, *Black Like Me* (Houghton Mifflin, 1961) (describing the experiences of a white man who altered his appearance to experience life as a black man).

15. Anthropologists estimate that the average American white has 5% black ancestry and the average American black has 25% white racial background. See Chris Ballentine, Note, *"Who Is a Negro?" Revisited: Determining Individual Racial Status for Purposes of Affirmative Action*, 35 U. Fla. L. Rev. 683, 688 n.40 (1983). The goal of white racial purity also explains the tough laws on interracial marriage that existed until 1967.

16. Robert J. Sickels, *Race, Marriage, and the Law* 64 (U. New Mexico, 1972). The last antimiscegenation laws were invalidated in 1967 in Alabama, Arkansas, Delaware, Florida, Georgia, Kentucky, Louisiana, Mississippi, Tennessee, Texas, Virginia, and West Virginia when the Supreme Court ruled the laws unconstitutional in *Loving v. Virginia*, 388 U.S. 1 (1967).

28

Images of the Outsider in American Law and Culture

RICHARD DELGADO AND JEAN STEFANCIC

Several museums have featured displays of racial memorabilia from the past.[1] Each of these collections depicts a shocking parade of Sambos, mammies, coons, uncles—bestial or happy-go-lucky, watermelon-eating African-Americans. They show advertising logos and household commodities in the shape of blacks with grotesquely exaggerated facial features. They include minstrel shows and film clips depicting blacks as so incompetent, shuffling, and dim-witted that it is hard to see how they survived to adulthood. Other images depict primitive, terrifying, larger-than-life black men in threatening garb and postures, often with apparent designs on white women.

Seeing these haunting images today, one is tempted to ask: "How could their authors—cartoonists, writers, film-makers, and graphic designers—individuals of higher than average education, create such appalling images? And why did no one protest?" The collections mentioned focus on African-Americans, but the two of us, motivated by curiosity, examined the history of ethnic depiction for each of the four main minority subgroups of color—Mexicans, African-Americans, Asians, and Native Americans—in the United States.[2]

African-Americans

Early in our history, slave traders rounded up African villagers and transported them to the New World in chains. En route, many died; those who survived were sold and forced to work in the fields and houses of a colonial nation bent on economic development and expansion. Slave codes regulated behavior, deterring rebellion and forbidding intermarriage. They also prohibited Southern blacks from learning to read and write, denying them access to the world of print then replete with arguments about "the rights of man." The dominant image of blacks in the popular theater and literature of the late eighteenth century was that of the docile and contented slave—childlike, lazy, illiterate, and dependent on the protection and care of a white master. The first appearance of Sambo, a "comic Negro" stereotype, occurred in 1781 in a play called *The Divorce*. This black male character, portrayed by a white in blackface, danced, sang, spoke nonsense, and acted the buffoon. The black man's potential as a sexual and economic competitor was minimized by portraying him as an object of laughter.

Blackface minstrelsy found a new popularity in the 1830s when Thomas D. Rice created Jim Crow, modeled on an elderly crippled black slave who shuffle-danced and sang. It is thought that Rice even borrowed the old man's shabby clothes for a more authentic stage performance. Rice's performance of Jump Jim Crow won him immediate success in the United States and England. By the 1840s minstrel shows were standard fare in American music halls. In these shows, whites in blackface created and disseminated stereotypes of African-Americans as inept urban dandies or happy child-like slaves.[3] Probably more whites—at least in the North—received their understanding of African-American culture from minstrel shows than from first hand acquaintance with blacks.

Because laws forbade slaves to learn to read or write, slave culture was primarily oral. Thus, it is highly significant that former slaves such as Frederick Douglass and William Wells Brown published accounts of captivity, life on plantations, and escapes to freedom.[4] These early slave narratives, published in the North and circulated among abolitionist societies, presented counterimages to the prevailing myths of the dominant culture. The abolitionist movement reached its apogee with the publication of Harriet Beecher Stowe's *Uncle Tom's Cabin*. Though Stowe was successful in presenting the slave master as villain, her portrayal of Uncle Tom changed the stereotype of the black slave only a little: Previously he had been docile, content, or comic, while in her depiction he became gentle, long-suffering, and imbued with Christian piety.

After the Civil War, the black image bifurcated. The "good slave" image continued, but was soon joined by an ominous "shadow" figure. The Uncle Tom character became romanticized, a black mouthpiece espousing an apologia for the beliefs of the old genteel white Confederacy. Though never overtly sexual, his masculine form re-emerged as the avuncular storyteller Uncle Remus, as well as various other "uncles." His feminine form evolved into a "mammy" figure—cook, washerwoman, nanny, and all-round domestic servant—responsible for the comfort of the Southern white household. With no life of her own, imbued with practical wisdom, she took an intense interest in the welfare and well-being of the white family she cared for.

During the tumultuous Reconstruction period, the sexuality denied to uncles and mammies found a crude outlet in a new stereotype of the recently freed male Negro as brutish and bestial. The Ku Klux Klan justified their reign of terror as necessary to control newly freed blacks whom they believed ready to force sex on any white woman they might encounter. This stereotype was offered to justify the widespread lynching that took 2,500 black lives between 1885 and 1900.[5]

The myth of the out of control ambitious black was fueled by currents prevalent in the marketplace of Western thought during the late nineteenth century: 1) the growth of American imperialism; 2) the absorption of "inferior races"; 3) the white man's burden mentality—the white South bearing the burden in the U.S.; 4) the manifest destiny belief of the Anglo-Saxons; and 5) the new social science theory concerning genetic inferiority.[6] Many of these ideas found expression in the powerful, crass, and influential writings of Thomas Dixon. His work represented an effort to satisfy his two goals in life: making money and converting people to racism. He believed that whites, both Northern and Southern, were duty bound to protect the Anglo-Saxon heritage, particularly white women, who were destined to produce a superior race. In 1905, Dixon wrote *The Clansman*, a tale of two families, one Northern and one Southern, united through marriage. It proved a sensation, particularly in the South. Ten years later, film-maker D.W. Griffith used the plots of this and another of Dixon's novels for his epic three-hour film, *The Birth of a Nation*.

The film transformed Dixon's novels into vivid visual images, featuring uncles, mammies, buffoons, an interfering mulatto mistress, and a chase scene in which a black man with animal-like traits pursues a young white woman until she leaps to her death from a pedestal-like perch at the edge of a cliff. The film played to audiences throughout the country. New white immigrants from Eastern and Southern Europe saw the film in numerous movie houses in poor neighborhoods, where it played for almost a year. In the South it played for fifteen years. A special screening was held at the White House for Dixon's former classmate President Woodrow Wilson, his guests, and the entire Supreme Court. Wilson later described the film as "like writing history with lightning."[7] Blacks could do little to confront the overwhelming popularity of *The Birth of a Nation*. The NAACP, by then established with its own newspaper, mobilized opposition. But the film's momentum was unstoppable. Film critics, many of them liberal, though decrying its racism, praised the film for its technical and artistic merits.

In contrast, efforts to present the story of Reconstruction from a black point of view were unsuccessful. Novelist Albion Tourgee, a white superior court judge and activist, used black characters who spoke in their own voices to show the freed man as a person who worked hard and attempted to succeed, but was victimized by the Ku Klux Klan. Tourgee believed the answer to racism lay in portraying blacks as normal. His novel, *Bricks Without Straw*, attracted a devoted but small audience; the South's treatment of blacks no longer interested many Northerners, and few Southerners were willing to listen. Black writers suffered a similar fate. While Charles Chesnutt, author of *The Conjure Woman*, was included in a list of "the foremost storytellers of the time," his publisher refused to release his next novel because the previous two about racial themes had been commercially unsuccessful.

Although blacks had gained formal legal equality, the Supreme Court, in 1896, upheld segregation in *Plessy v. Ferguson*.[8] Lynchings continued; racist stereotypes prevailed. Blacks had little access to the press or the film industry and could do little to change the racism that both industries propagated. Nevertheless, blacks joined the army in droves during World War I. Segregation in the ranks was rigidly enforced, however, and many blacks returned angry and disheartened. After the war, unrest in the country led to at least twenty-five urban race riots, many in the previously peaceful North. Repressive images immediately increased and prevailed for a little over a decade. Then, as the disruption abated, a few writers, such as Eugene O'Neill and Sinclair Lewis, portrayed blacks and their plight sympathetically. Black writers and artists in New York created the Harlem Renaissance. Blacks' image metamorphosed yet again. Whites, excited and enthusiastic over this new artistic rapprochement with blacks, quickly praised them and their work for elements of the exoticism and primitivism popularized by Gauguin. Echoing early images of good-natured, happy-go-lucky blacks, white society began to regard African-Americans as musically talented, rhythmical, passionate, and entertaining. Although these developments heralded a somewhat more positive image of blacks, nevertheless the new images retained elements of condescension and previous stereotypes. The majority-race critics, intellectuals, and artists who were entranced by the Renaissance may have intended no harm, yet they perpetuated views of African-Americans as the exotic other.[9]

With World War II, black soldiers and workers were needed for the war effort; the more virulent forms of racism were held in abeyance. However, when the war ended and the soldiers returned, racial hostilities again sharpened. Having experienced a relatively racism-free environment during the war, black workers and soldiers were not prepared to return to lives of menial work and subservience to whites. For many, expectations of improvement were fed by war propaganda depicting the U.S. as fighting for freedom. Activism sprang up; the Civil Rights movement began, and once again the dominant image of blacks took on new forms: the cocky, street-smart black who knows his rights; the unreasonable, opportunistic community leader and militant; the safe, comforting, cardigan-wearing ("nice") black of TV sitcoms; and the Black Bomber of superstud films, all mutations of, and permutations of, old familiar forms.

Native Americans

When the colonists arrived in Virginia and Massachusetts in the seventeenth century, they brought with them images of the Indian created in England and Europe. Early explorers described native peoples of the "new world" as innocent, ingenuous, friendly, and naked.[10] At first, relations between the two groups were cordial. Later, however, more settlers arrived, bringing with them English concepts of property—land transfer, titles, deeds—that were foreign to Indian thought. Indians who did not cooperate with the settlers' plans were forced off their lands; eventually hostilities broke out,[11] resulting in a conflict that lasted over two centuries.

Early writings about Native Americans reflected two romanticized images—"the Indian princess," incarnated most notably in Pocahantas, and "the man Friday," found in *Robinson Crusoe*, earlier as the troublesome servant Caliban,[12] later as the faithful loyal Chingachgook,[13] and in the twentieth century the buffoon and sidekick Tonto. The first instance of the "captivity narrative" appeared in Massachusetts in 1682 with Mary Rowlandson's *Captivity and Restoration*.[14] Early fiction portrayed Indians as looters, burners, and killers—but not rapists, because New Englanders knew that Indians rarely committed rape. But the erotic elements of Rowlandson's story, although mild and subordinated to her religious message, made it the prototype for later captivity tales that emphasized sexual aggression directed toward Simon-pure captives.

Other writers followed suit without Rowlandson's delicacy, portraying Indians as animal-like and sub-human, a characterization whose roots go back to Paracelsus (1493–1541), who proposed that Indians were not among "the sons of Adam." Shakespeare explored this theme when he wrote *The Tempest* and created a servant for Prospero—Caliban—whose name was an anagram of the newly coined word "cannibal." Cotton Mather and other Puritan writers called Indians wolves, lions, sorcerers, and demons possessed by Satan. By the nineteenth century, Indians had become variously savage, barbarous, or half-civilized. In early movies restless natives and jungle beasts were practically interchangeable. No wonder, then, that Indians were removed, with little protest from the dominant society, to reservations, just as wild and rare beasts were confined to animal reserves.

Later movies of the "cowboys and Indians" genre built on these images when they featured war dances, exotic dress, drunkenness, surprise attacks, scalping, raiding, raping, tomahawks, tomtoms, and torture.[15] D.W. Griffith, creator of *The Birth of a Nation*, incorporated these elements in *The Battle at Elderbush Gulch* (1913). In that movie, a white woman, trapped in a cabin surrounded by Indians, awaits her fate, not knowing whether the Indian attackers will kill her or whether one of her white defenders will shoot her before letting the Indians take her alive. By 1911, portrayal of Indians in film had become so demeaning that representatives of four western tribes protested to President William Howard Taft and to Congress.[16] But little change occurred until World War II, when Hollywood transferred the enemy role to the Japanese and Germans. Many of these early Indian movies are still shown on television, feeding the psyches of new generations of Americans with the familiar stereotypes.

Shortly after the end of the war, Hollywood released *Broken Arrow* (1950), the first movie ever to feature an Indian as hero—Cochise of the Apaches. Other "noble savage" films reversed the stereotype in the opposite direction, portraying Native Americans with exaggerated nobleness—a striking parallel to the treatment adulating whites gave black writers during the Harlem Renaissance. In 1969, N. Scott Momaday, a Kiowa-Cherokee writer, won the Pulitzer Prize for his novel *House Made of Dawn*. In 1972, PBS ran a BBC production of *The Last of the Mohicans*. In each of these cases, much of the audience was struck by the intelligence of the Native American voice—a far cry from the earlier steady diet of chiefs saying "ugh," braves shrieking war whoops, and Tonto saying "me gettum." It was not always so. Thomas Jefferson wished Congress could speak half as well as orators of Indian nations. William Penn praised the Lenni Lenapi language of the Delaware for its subtlety. Yet, speech of the Indians—as well as that of African-Americans, Mexicans, and Asians—has been mangled, blunted and rendered inarticulate by whites who then became entitled to speak for them. Like the other groups of color, Native Americans have been disempowered by the very element which, they are told, will save them.[17]

Asian-Americans

In the middle years of the nineteenth century, Chinese were welcomed into the land for their labor: They were needed to operate the mines, build railroads, and carry out other physical tasks necessary to the country's development. The industrious immigrants soon, however, began to surpass white American workers. They opened small businesses, succeeded in making profitable mines that others had abandoned. Not surprisingly, Chinese became the scapegoats for the 1870s Depression. Unionists and writers exaggerated negative traits thought associated with them—opium smoking, gambling—and succeeded in having anti-Chinese legislation enacted. By 1882 public sentiment had been mobilized sufficiently so that Congress was able to pass an Exclusion Act, which reduced the number of Chinese in the U.S. from 105,000 in 1880 to 65,000 in 1908.

During this period, Japan's international position was on the rise, yet U.S. writers and politicians depicted all Asians as inferior, unassimilable, willing to work inhuman hours at low wages, and loyal to foreign despots. When Japan defeated first China and then Russia, it began to replace China as the "yellow peril." By 1924, all Asians were barred, an exclusion the Supreme Court had upheld for the Chinese in 1889. During a period of increasing tensions between the two countries, the film industry portrayed Japanese and other Asians in unremittingly negative terms. As with African-Americans and Native Americans, Asian men were depicted as cunning, savage, and as potential rapists interested in defiling white women. (In sharp contrast, white male actors were seen as having legitimate access to Asian women.)

As U.S. militancy grew, films began to devalue Asian—principally Japanese—life. Not even *they* valued life, the narratives of the day said. Why should we value theirs? During earlier periods, when racism against Asians was relatively quiescent, writers and film-makers employed the stock character of the Charlie Chan—the hapless, pidgin-talking Asian, in many respects the functional equivalent of the Sambo or uncle. But as anti-Japanese sentiment increased, we began depicting even domestic Asians as foul and tricky.

W.R. Hearst sponsored *Patria,* an anti-Asian film serial that began in 1919 and continued for several years, depicting Asians as a Yellow Menace. At one point, Woodrow Wilson became disturbed by the virulence of Hearst's production and wrote asking him to soften it. Hearst responded by changing the series so that it became dominantly anti-Mexican. In the period immediately preceding and following World War II, anti-Japanese images continued to proliferate. A stock character was the master Oriental criminal, often played by Anglo actors in make-up. By this time, films and novels were distinguishing between Chinese (who were good), and Japanese (who were bad). After Pearl Harbor, intense anti-Japanese propaganda resulted in federal action to intern 110,000 Japanese-Americans, many of whom had lived in the United States all their lives. Many lost farms, houses, and other property. It later came to light that much of the evidence of likely sabotage and fifth column activities had been fabricated.[18]

Following World War II, depictions of blacks and Indians were upgraded to some extent, but those of Asians only a little. Many of James Bond's villains, for example, have been Asian. In recent days, Japan has once again become a serious economic rival of the United States, producing automobiles, computers, and other products at a price and quality American industry has proven unable to match. Predictably, a further wave of anti-Asian sentiment and stereotyping is re-emerging.

Mexican-Americans

Images of Mexican-Americans ("Chicanos") fall into three or four well-delineated stereotypes—the greaser; the conniving, treacherous *bandido;* the happy-go-lucky shiftless lover of song, food, and dance; and the tragic, silent, "Spanish" tall, dark, and handsome type of romantic fiction—which change according to society's needs. As with blacks, Asians, and Indians, most Americans have relatively few interpersonal contacts with Mexican-Americans; therefore, these images become the individual's only reality. When such a person meets an actual Mexican-American, he or she tends to place the other in one of the ready-made categories. Stereotyping thus denies members of both groups the opportunity to interact with each other on anything like a complex, nuanced human level.

During and just after the conquest, when the U.S. was seizing and then settling large tracts of Mexican territory in the Southwest, "Western" or "conquest" fiction depicted Anglos bravely displacing shifty, brutal, and treacherous Mexicans. After the war ended and control of the Southwest passed to American hands, a subtle shift occurred. Anglos living and settling in the new regions were portrayed as Protestant, independent, thrifty, industrious, mechanically resourceful, and interested in progress; Mexicans, as traditional, sedate, lacking in mechanical resourcefulness and ambition. Writers both on and off the scene created the same images of indolent, pious Mexicans—ignoring the two centuries of enterprising farmers and ranchers who withstood or negotiated with Apaches and Comanches and built a sturdy society with irrigation, land tenure, and mining codes.

In the late conquest period, depiction of this group bifurcated. Majority-race writers created two images of the Mexican: the "good" (loyal) Mexican peon or sidekick, and the "bad" fighter/greaser Mexican who did not know his place. The first was faithful and domestic; the second, treacherous and evil. As with other groups, the second ("bad") image had sexual overtones: the greaser coveted Anglo women and would seduce or rape them if given the opportunity. Children's books of this time, like the best-selling Buffalo Bill series, were full of Mexican stereotypes used to reinforce moral messages to the young: They are like this, we like that. The series ended in 1912.

The first thirty years of this century saw heavy Mexican immigration of mainly poor workers. The first Bracero programs—official, temporary importation of field hands—appeared. With increasing numbers, white-only signs, segregated housing and schools appeared, aimed now at Mexicans in addition to blacks. With increased risk of interaction and intermarriage, novels and newspaper writing reinforced the notion of these immigrants' baseness, simplicity, and inability to become assimilated.

The movies of this period depicted Latins as buffoons, sluts, or connivers; even some of the titles were disparaging: for example, *The Greaser's Gauntlet*. Films featured brown-skinned desperadoes stealing horses or gold, lusting after pure Anglo women, shooting noble Saxon heroes in the back, or acting the part of hapless buffoons. Animated cartoons and short subjects, still shown on television, featured tequila-drinking Mexicans, bullfighters, Speedy Gonzalez and Slowpoke Rodriguez, and clowns—as well as Castilian caballeras, light-skinned, upper class, and prone to wearing elaborate dresses and carrying castanets.

World War II brought the need for factory and agricultural workers and a new flood of immigrants. Images now softened to include "normal," or even noble, Mexicans, like the general played by Marlon Brando in *Viva Zapata*. Perhaps realizing it had overstepped, America diminished the virulence of its anti-Mexican imagery. Yet the Western genre, with Mexican villains and bandits, continues; and the immigrant speaking gibberish still makes an appearance. Even the most favorable novel and film of the post-war period, *The Milagro Beanfield War*, ends in stereotypes. A few writers found their own culture alienating or sick and sought relief in a more serene Southwest culture. As with the Harlem Renaissance, these creative artists tended to be more generous to Mexicans, but nevertheless retained the Anglo hero as the central figure or Samaritan who uplifts the Mexican from his or her traditional ignorance.

How Could They? Lessons from the History of Racial Depiction

The depiction of ethnic groups of color is littered with negative images, although the content of those images changes over time. In some periods, society needed to suppress a group, as with blacks during Reconstruction. Society then coined an image to suit that purpose—that of primitive, powerful, larger than life blacks, terrifying and barely under control. At other times, for example during slavery, society needed reassurance that blacks were docile, cheerful, and content with their lot. Images of sullen, rebellious blacks dissatisfied with their condition would have made white society uneasy. Accordingly, images of simple, happy blacks, content to do the master's work, were disseminated.[19]

The racism of other times and places does stand out, does strike us as glaringly and appallingly wrong. But this happens only decades or centuries later; we acquiesce in today's version with little realization that it is wrong, that a later generation will ask "How could they?" about *us*.

Racism forms part of the dominant narrative, the group of received understandings and basic principles that form the baseline from which we reason. How could these be in question? Recent scholarship shows that the dominant narrative changes very slowly and resists alteration. We interpret new stories in light of the old. Ones that deviate too markedly from our pre-existing stock are dismissed as extreme, coercive, political, and wrong. The only stories about race we are prepared to condemn, then, are the old ones giving voice to the racism of an earlier age, ones that society has already begun to reject.

Notes

1. We have identified the following: Alternative Museum, New York City, Prisoners of Image: Ethnic and Gender Stereotypes, curated by Robbin Henderson and Geno Rodriquez (1989); The Balch Institute for Ethnic Studies, Philadelphia, Ethnic Images in Advertising (1984), Ethnic Images in Comics (1986), Ethnic Images in World War I Posters (1988), Ethnic Images in Toys and Games (1990); Berkeley Art Center, Berkeley, Ethnic Notions: Black Images in the White Mind, The Janette Faulkner Collection of Stereotypes and Caricature of Afro-Americans (1982); Galeria de la Raza, San Francisco, Cactus Hearts/Barbed Wire Dreams: Media, Myths, and Mexicans, curated by Yolanda Lopez (1988) (telephone interviews with Phyllis Bischof, Librarian for African and African American Collections, U.C. at Berkeley; Jan Faulkner, Collector and Clinical Professor, Psychiatry, U.C.S.F.; Robbin Henderson, Director, Berkeley Art Center (Feb. 1992)). *See also* Jessie Smith, Images of Blacks in American Culture: Reference Guide to Information Sources 289 (1988) (listing collections of Black Americana).

2. Some of the works we found particularly helpful are the following: Arthur G. Pettit, Images of the Mexican American in Fiction and Film (1980); Catherine Silk & John Silk, Racism and Anti-Racism in American Popular Culture (1990); Raymond W. Stedman, Shadows of the Indian: Stereotypes in American Culture (1982); E. Wong, On Visual Media Racism: Asians in the American Motion Picture (1978); From Different Shores: Perspectives on Race and Ethnicity in America (Ronald Takaki ed., 1987); Split Image: African Americans in the Mass Media (Jannette L. Dates & William Barlow eds., 1990) [hereinafter Split Image]. For additional works, see bibliographies in Silk & Silk, *supra* (dealing with African-Americans). *See also* Edward W. Said, Orientalism (1985) (dealing with Asian-Americans).

3. The dandified image (the "Coon") showed the folly of the North's policy concerning freedom, while that of the happy Southern slave reassured whites that blacks were happiest in "their natural condition." *See* Split Image, *supra* at 7. The dandified urban "coon" image, played by white actors, reappeared in the 1920s and continued until the 1950s in the phenomenally popular radio serial "Amos 'n' Andy."

4. *See* The Classic Slave Narratives (H. Gates ed., 1987).

5. *See* Split Image, *supra* at 11, 39, 48–49. This obsession with matters sexual dates back to Puritan times in Massachusetts, and has surfaced in similar stereotyping of the four major racial groups in the United States. *See* Stedman, *supra* at 81; William L. Van Deburg, Slavery and Race in American Popular Culture 122–25 (1984) (on recurring image of the Negro as beast).

6. Silk & Silk, *supra* at 49.

7. Silk & Silk, *supra* at 121, 127, 135. Wilson's comment probably was intended as praise, for he added: "[O]ne of my regrets is that it is so horribly true."

8. 163 U.S. 537 (1896).

9. *See The Congo*, in The New Poetry 291 (H. Monroe ed., 1932).

10. Stedman, *supra* at 253 (noting descriptions that explorers Christopher Columbus and Amerigo Vespucci gave). For further writings on Columbus and his early impressions, see The Four Voyages of Columbus (J.M. Cohen trans. & ed., 1969).

11. Dee Brown, Bury My Heart at Wounded Knee 2–5 (1972); Fairfax Downey, Indian Wars of the U.S. Army (1776–1865) (1963); Robert A. Williams, The American Indian in Western Legal Thought (1990).

12. William Shakespeare, The Tempest (Stephen Orgel ed., Oxford University Press 1987) (1611).

13. James Fenimore Cooper, The Last of the Mohicans (William Chorvot ed., Houghton Mifflin 1958) (1826).

14. M. Rowlandson, The Sovereignty & Goodness of God, Together with the Faithfulness of His Promises Displayed: Being a Narrative of the Captivity and Restoration of Mrs. Mary Rowlandson (1682).

15. On Indians in films, see Jon Tuska, The Filming of the West (1976); John E. O'Connor, The Hollywood Indian: Stereotypes of Native Americans in Film (1980).

16. Stedman, *supra* at 108, 157. During this period, some of the titles, in themselves, tell the story. *E.g.,* On the Warpath (1909), The Flaming Arrows (1911), Poisoned Arrows (1911), Incendiary Indians (1911), The Indian Raiders (1910), The Cheyenne Raiders (1910), Attack by Arapahoes (1910), The Dumb Half-Breed's Defense (1910), Saved from the Redmen (1910), Love in a Tepee (1911), The Hair Restorer and the Indian (a "comedy" of 1911).

17. Stedman, *supra* at 58, 62–63, 183. See William Penn's Own Account of the Lenni Lenapi or Delaware Indians (A. Myers ed., 1970); Vine Deloria, Jr., *Identity and Culture,* in From Different Shores: Perspectives on Race and Ethnicity in America 94, 102 (Ronald Takaki ed., 1987).

18. *See* Richard Griffith & Arthur Mayer, The Movies 108 (1970); Joe Morella & Edward Epstein, The Films of World War II (1973); Lewis Jacobs, *World War II and the American Film,* 7 Cinema J. (1967–68). For two Supreme Court cases upholding curfews placed on Japanese-Americans, see Hirabayashi v. United States, 320 U.S. 81 (1943) and Korematsu v. United States, 323 U.S. 214 (1944). B. Hosokawa, Nisei: The Quiet Americans 292–301, 348 (1969); *see* Maisie Conrat & Richard Conrat, Executive Order 9066: The Internment of 110,000 Japanese Americans (1972) (internment a product of war hysteria and military alarmism).

19. Other ethnic groups, at various times and in response to different social needs, were depicted as: Charlie Chans; hapless, lazy Mexicans interested only in singing and dancing; conniving Indians or greasers; devious or superindustrious Asians willing to work inordinate hours; and so on, all depending on what society needed—immigration or the opposite, cheap or excess labor, suppression, indifference, guilt assuagement, and so on.

29

Back to the Future with *The Bell Curve:* Jim Crow, Slavery, and G

JACQUELINE JONES

According to Richard Herrnstein and Charles Murray, we live in an age and a country untainted by history, an age that springs full blown from *g*, or the "general intelligence" of the citizens who live here, now. In presenting their rigidly deterministic view that IQ is the major force shaping social structure in the United States today, the authors of *The Bell Curve* exude a smug complacency about late-twentieth-century American society: they argue that, judging from current housing and job patterns, people are pretty much where they should be—members of the so-called cognitive elite are ensconced in the wealthiest communities, while the poor (dubbed the "dull" or "very dull") languish, and deservedly so, in run-down, crime-ridden neighborhoods because they are unable to do any better for themselves. Yet even as the authors revel in the purity of a *g*-driven society, they hearken back to the supposedly glorious days of yesteryear, when poor people not only remained in their place, but also knew and understood that to be their place. As we read *The Bell Curve*, then, the past unfolds behind us, and beckons, full of promise for the future.

Among the more ludicrous claims of *The Bell Curve* is the authors' assertion that they are fearless scholars, venturing "into forbidden territory" (p. 10), into an intellectual no-man's land "between public discussion and private opinion" (p. 297). In fact, the book is simply the most recent in a long line of efforts to prove the congenital inferiority of poor people in general, and black people in particular. In the seventeenth century, settlers in the British colonies justified the enslavement of Africans because most blacks were non-Christian, non-English, and non-white. In the eighteenth century, white elites arranged that poor black people be permanently stigmatized, and forced to toil at the dirtiest jobs, so that white men could enjoy their republican liberties. In the late nineteenth century, southern politicians and landowners charged that the former slaves were lazy, immoral, and irresponsible; the federal government gave its blessing to efforts to keep black men and women disenfranchised, hard at work, and segregated from whites. In the early twentieth century, racists turned to scientific theories to bolster their contention that whites were superior to non-whites in culture and intelligence.

As a text revealing of our times, then, *The Bell Curve* pursues traditional ends via new means; it seeks to denigrate blacks and justify their exclusion from the best jobs. Well-paying, secure positions that include benefits like health care will remain the province of whites (and a few Asians), while the most menial jobs will remain reserved for blacks and the

"New Immigrants" from Latin American countries. According to *The Bell Curve*, persistent racial and class segregation of neighborhoods and workplaces will insure that the poor, with their bad morals and shiftless ways, will not contaminate the well-to-do. As a political program, these ideas have the added advantage of appealing to poor whites, who might otherwise have to compete with the darker-skinned "lower orders" for scarce resources.

Although the authors do not dwell explicitly on the alleged glories of days gone by, they do seem to envision a society that bears a striking resemblance to earlier periods in the nation's history, periods characterized by the legal and economic subordination of black people as a group. Indeed, the history-minded reader can discern that *The Bell Curve* begins by evoking the days of Jim Crow, and then moves back to the time of slavery, building toward a dramatic climax in the last chapter, when the authors wax eloquent about the virtues of the political ideology and social structure characteristic of the late eighteenth century.

As a blueprint for the good society, the period 1890 to 1915 has much to recommend it when viewed from the perspective of *The Bell Curve*. (Not coincidentally, it was during these years that intelligence testing came into vogue, no doubt in response to large-scale immigration from Eastern Europe; economic transformations often provoke new theories and systems of social control and racial inferiority.) During the late nineteenth and early twentieth centuries, the executive branch, Congress, and the Supreme Court sanctioned a system of racial segregation in public places and institutions. While the country was undergoing a process of urbanization and industrialization, the vast majority of black people were domestic servants and agricultural workers (that is, they worked at jobs befitting their low mental abilities, in the parlance of *The Bell Curve*). Judging from Herrnstein and Murray's overall conclusions, we can speculate that this must have been a Golden Age in American history, since even mentally deficient people found a productive place in a dynamic, growing society; "in a simpler America, being comparatively low in the qualities measured by IQ did not necessarily affect the ability to find a valued niche in society. Many such people worked on farms" (p. 536).

Though obviously ignorant of the far reaching value of IQ testing, the cognitive elite in the Jim Crow South recognized the folly of funding schools for black children; therefore, tax money for education was routinely diverted away from black schools and given to white ones. Around the turn of the century, the southern public-education system reflected a racial division of labor that limited African Americans to work in the fields. In 1900, fully 80 percent of Mississippi's black population were confined to agricultural labor, and another 15 percent to domestic service. In 1899, the state's governor, James K. Vardaman, observed, "people talk about elevating the race by education! It is not only folly, but it comes pretty nearly being [*sic*] criminal folly. . . . It is money thrown away." Foreshadowing *The Bell Curve*'s lament that too many black folks today are getting educational credentials they don't deserve, creating all sorts of unrealistic expectations, Vardaman was of the opinion that "literary education—the knowledge of books—does not seem to produce any substantial results with the negro, but serves rather to sharpen his cunning, breeds hopes that cannot be gratified, creates an inclination to avoid honest labor."

In the late nineteenth century, the rural South abided by a racial etiquette characterized by a superficial familiarity between members of the two races. And in order to do well— to buy land or obtain credit—individual blacks often had to look to a white patron, usually a man who could vouch for their honesty and testify to their hat-in-hand industry. Similarly, the authors of *The Bell Curve* suggest that a strict racial division of labor need not lead to hard feelings between individuals: "*We cannot think of a legitimate argument why any encounter between individual whites and blacks need be affected by the knowledge that an aggregate ethnic difference in measured intelligence is genetic instead of environmental"* (p. 313). In other words, there is no reason why a white lawyer need not engage in friendly banter with the custodian who cleans his office late at night; in the South, such easy familiarity was attributed to "good breeding" among whites.

The rural South, in a "simpler" America, was a time and place where "the community provided clear and understandable incentives for doing what needed to be done" (p. 537). Jim Crow courts often deferred to Judge Lynch in dealing with black men and women who resisted doing "what needed to be done." The authors in fact suggest explicitly that they yearn for "a society where the rules about crime are simple and the consequences are equally simple. Someone who commits a crime is probably caught—and almost certainly punished. The punishment almost certainly hurts. Punishment follows arrest quickly, within a matter of days or weeks" (p. 543). Those were the days, when lynch mobs stood ready to act as the efficient agents of the cognitive elite. Thus Jim Crow America meets *The Bell Curve*'s criteria for a place where "the stuff of community life had to be carried out by the neighborhood or it wouldn't get done" (p. 538). For all intents and purposes, federal authority did not exist; "local control" reigned supreme, and a small number of white men were in control of everything.

The days of Jim Crow were a bit more complicated than Herrnstein and Murray's simple-minded scenario would suggest. Stepping back from their historical idyll, we might note that the authors see the past, like the present, as static, as they blissfully ignore the complex interplay of political and economic factors that have always shaped social structure. In the postbellum South, and in the early twentieth-century North, white tradesmen and skilled workers gradually displaced the few black artisans who plied their trades. This process had nothing to do with intelligence and everything to do with the politics of discrimination; white trades unions served as gatekeepers to their crafts, and white craftsmen appealed to "race loyalty" in order to lure customers away from their black competitors. Employers had good reason to discriminate in hiring regardless of the qualifications of workers; black people were excluded from the position of department store clerk because store owners feared that white customers would not patronize their establishments.

In keeping with their wide-eyed, romantic view of the past, Herrnstein and Murray often get their facts wrong when they make tentative forays into the thicket of historical specificity. They refer to "the urbanizing process following slavery" (p. 328), ignoring the half century when the vast majority of former slaves and their children lived in the rural South, and toiled as sharecroppers, before the Great Migration beginning in 1916. The authors also assert that "the wealthy people have always been the most mobile" (p. 104), when in fact sharecroppers had extraordinarily high rates of residential mobility; every year or two, desperately poor families sought out a better deal, a better contract, down the road—or they were evicted by landlords who hoped to find more compliant tenants. The statement that "poverty among children has always been much higher in families headed by a single woman, whether she is divorced or never married" (p. 137) has little relevance to the history of sharecroppers; though they were among the poorest people in the nation, they by and large lived in two-parent households, and those rates of familial stability were the same for black as well as white families.

The Bell Curve proceeds, or rather, recedes, from Jim Crow back to the slave South. In order to refute the idea that a legacy of slavery has affected the IQ of African Americans in a negative way, the authors suggest that Africans as a group are "very dull"; they cite a researcher who reports "median black African IQ to be 75, approximately 1.7 standard deviations below the U.S. overall population average, about ten points lower than the current figure for American blacks" (p. 289). These data suggest to Herrnstein and Murray that "the special circumstances of American blacks" (p. 289) have not depressed the group's IQ scores at all. Indeed, we might assume that the authors mean to suggest just the opposite—that slavery was a school of sorts, an institution that helped mentally deficient Africans adapt to a superior way of living.

Many large slave-owning planters, as well as their early twentieth century scholarly apologists, would have agreed with this assessment. In 1856 the planter-politician William J. Garrison of South Carolina waxed poetic about the benefits of slavery as an educational institution, and about the pedagogical skills of slave owners: "Taught by the master's efforts, by his care / Fed, clothed, protected many a patient year, . . . / The Negroes schooled by slavery embrace / The highest portion of the Negro race." Samuel Cartwright, a New Orleans physician, agreed that the slave plantation was "gradually and silently converting the African barbarian into a moral, rational, and civilized being."

On the plantation, blacks and whites coexisted in a relatively peaceful way (though the peace was enforced with violence or the threat of it). Since black people often made bad parents—as *The Bell Curve* puts it—a planter no doubt felt justified in exercising paternalistic control over his workers, sending mothers and fathers to the field each day while an elderly slave woman minded their children; or perhaps he felt that it was in his best interest, and that of "society in general" if the children were separated from their parents and sold to another owner. Because the slave family had no legal standing, all slave children were illegitimate; hence their parents hardly deserved to have much control over them. Herrnstein and Murray argue that people with low IQs lack the personal qualities necessary for citizenship because they are not "civilized." They also suggest that dumb people commit more crimes than their smart counterparts; we might conclude, then, that the system of slavery was meant to control "uncivilized" people, since "civilized people do not need to be tightly constrained by laws or closely monitored by the organs of state" (p. 254). The slave plantation operated on the principle that all low-IQ persons (i.e., blacks) could work productively and should be taken care of accordingly—a virtue in any society (p. 547). If we extrapolate from Herrnstein and Murray's analysis—and understand the planter as a paternalistic smart white man overseeing lots of hardworking black males and fecund "wenches," and controlling the "Nats" predisposed to violent crime or rebellion—then the slave plantation takes on a more benevolent, or at least socially useful, cast.

Antebellum slavery rested on several ideological foundations—the notions that blacks were inherently inferior to whites, that some groups must do the dirty work while others govern, and that inequality of ability—and legal rights—was fundamental to an orderly, stable society. James Henry Hammond, a South Carolina slave owner, articulated the antebellum version of *The Bell Curve*. Hammond argued that all societies "have a natural variety of classes. The most marked of these must, in a country like ours, be the rich and the poor, the educated and the ignorant." Hammond, like Herrnstein and Murray, conflated poor people with those of limited intellectual abilities. And like his late-twentieth-century ideological successors, Hammond was convinced that the cognitive underclass had no part to play in government at any level; the beauty of slavery was that it rendered the issues of rights and representation among the poor and ignorant a moot question, since this benighted class was rightly "excluded from all participation in the management of public affairs."

Again, what is striking about *The Bell Curve* is the way it offers some very old ideas in the guise of fresh, statistics-based revelations. In their claims of scholarly disinterestedness the authors seem to have taken a page out of one of the weighty tomes written by Josiah Nott, a slavery apologist. In his book *Types of Mankind*, published in 1854, Nott argued that blacks were inherently inferior to whites and that statesmen, rather than wasting their time on issues related to "the perfectibility of races," might better "deal, in political argument, with the simple facts as they stand." Those "facts" included the idea that no "full-blooded Negro . . . has ever written a page worthy of being remembered."

Not content to tarry in antebellum Dixie, the authors of *The Bell Curve* continue their march back into time with a final chapter entitled "A Place for Everyone." Here the wisdom of the Founding Fathers is revealed; these slaveholding men inspire hope for the future not because they invented a rhetoric that has informed some of world's great struggles for human rights, but rather, for the opposite reason: because they "wrote frankly about the inequality of men" (p. 530). Jefferson, for example, according to the authors of *The Bell Curve*, "was thankful for a 'natural aristocracy' that could counterbalance the deficiencies of others, an 'aristocracy of virtue and talent, which Nature has wisely provided for the direction of the interests of society'" (p. 530). The new nation was founded by the cognitive elite, and it is to the social ideal that they represented that the nation must return; "in reminding you of these views of the men who founded America, we are not appealing to their historical eminence, but to their wisdom. We think they were right" (p. 532). The great lesson to be learned from the era of the Revolution was that "the ideology of equality has done some good. . . . But most of its effects are bad" (p. 533).

Herrnstein and Murray neglect to mention that Jefferson himself was one of the first white Americans to test the waters of scientific racism; in this respect his ideas served as a bridge between the seventeenth-century emphasis on blacks as dangerous people, to the antebellum view that blacks were dumb and immoral. During much of the colonial period, blacks were described as wily, cunning, thievish, and recalcitrant. They were described by privileged whites in the same terms used to describe a variety of other groups of subordinate workers, including Irish servants, imported English convicts, and Indian day workers. As a group, Africans and their descendants in this country were not so different from other groups of bound laborers; all of these groups resisted the demands imposed upon them by their masters, and all of them, either singly or collectively, posed threats to civil order. Thomas Jefferson, as one of the leading political theorists of his day, was able to mediate between old doctrines that justified the social control of potentially rowdy workers, and new theories of equality; he did this by arguing that black people were fundamentally different from white people.

Like Herrnstein and Murray, Jefferson was intrigued by "the real differences that nature has made" among different groups of people. Writing in *Notes on the State of Virginia*, first published in 1787, Jefferson suggested that blacks' "existence appears to participate more of sensation than reflection." Unlike those Southerners who, half a century later, would expand upon his views and offer a full-blown defense of slavery, Jefferson simply recorded his observations: "Comparing them by their faculties of memory, reason, and imagination, it appears to me, that in memory they are equal to the whites, in reason much inferior, as I think one could scarcely be found capable of tracking and comprehending the investigations of Euclid, and that in imagination they are dull, tasteless, and anomalous." Assuming that comprehension of "the investigations of Euclid" amounted to the eighteenth-century equivalent of an IQ test, it is clear that Jefferson shared with Herrnstein and Murray a contempt for the intellectual abilities of black people, and for their potential as members of the body politic. Jefferson's rhetoric about equality would later become appropriated by a number of different groups—by slaves and their abolitionist allies, and by women's rights advocates. Yet within the late-eighteenth-century social and political context, Jefferson was very much a man of his time, and his place, the slaveholding state of Virginia.

The Bell Curve calls for a devolution of America into a more simple time and place, one where the federal government has receded so that a *"wide range of social functions . . . [can] be restored to the neighborhood when possible and otherwise to the municipality"* (p. 540). The anti-Federalists would feel vindicated; but time was not on their side. Late-eighteenth-century Republicanism was predicated on a nation of sturdy, independent yeomen farmers, men deferential to their social betters. By the mid-nineteenth century the ideal of widespread landownership had already slipped out of the reach of many Americans; society was highly stratified, with large numbers of wage hands replacing small family farmers. Likewise, it is difficult to see how today's high-tech economy and global assembly line might be compressed to fit into the villages and plantations of late-eighteenth-century rural America.

Throughout the authors' stroll down the backroads and byways of America's past, women remain conspicuous for their absence, except as they make brief, unwanted appearances as the media of murder and mayhem—that is, as reproducers of the Cognitive Mudsill. Here Herrnstein and Murray boldly depart from the Founding Fathers' appreciation that slave women of child-bearing age were just as valuable as the strongest male field hands. Postindustrial America has no need for more dumb babies, and the authors make it clear that the federal government should stop subsidizing this kind of sociopathological activity. Gone are the days when a bumper tobacco or cotton crop could siphon off the potentially destructive energies of low-IQ people of all ages.

The Bell Curve furthers the currently fashionable agenda of demonizing poor women of both races. Indeed, the authors provide much fodder for the notion that unwed mothers are the root cause of everything that plagues this nation. These women, charge the authors, indulge themselves by living off the goodwill of long-suffering taxpayers. They produce low-birth-weight babies with low IQs, babies who will themselves grow up to become chronic welfare recipients and abusive parents—and if they are boys, violent criminals, and if they are girls, irresponsible citizens and the mothers of even more living social time bombs.

The Bell Curve focuses its ire on poor women; the authors suggest that "going on welfare really is a dumb idea, and that is why women who are low in cognitive ability end up there" (p. 201). Yet for all of their discussions of jobs and opportunity and civic responsibility, the authors shy away from confronting the political implications of the nation's largest group of dependent people—the middle-class wives and mothers who stay home full time with their children. Why are poor women who want to attend to their children a threat to the Republic, while middle-class women who do the same thing are heralded as guardians of the nation's "family values"? Why is it so important that welfare mothers betake themselves to the nearest employment office, while middle-class women who choose to work are decried as the embodiment of all neuroses? For all of their self-proclaimed intellectual derring-do, Herrnstein and Murray avoid these issues; instead, they favor glib generalizations that will no doubt prove fodder for any number of right-wing demagogues.

Herrnstein and Murray must deny history, and replace it with mythology, in order to justify a social structure that will keep black people disproportionately relegated to the jobs of nursing aides, orderlies and attendants, cleaners and servants, maids and horsemen. In *The Bell Curve* they suggest that the great threat to American society today is not radical socioeconomic inequality *per se,* but rather all of the loud and rude complaints that emanate from those who are resentful of this inequality. Though they coyly refrain from endorsing a "custodial state" ("we have in mind a high-tech and more lavish version of the Indian reservation for a substantial minority of the nation's population" [p. 526]), the authors put their implicit stamp of approval on policies that at least point in that direction. For example, they propose that the city of Washington, D.C., reject affirmative action and return "to a policy of hiring the best-qualified candidates" for its police department, a policy that will inevitably mean that "a smaller proportion of those new police would be black." Then, "the quality of the Washington police force is likely to improve, which will be of tangible benefit to the hundreds of thousands of blacks who live in that city" (p. 507). Here is the distilled essence of *The Bell Curve:* a call for a city composed largely of black workers to be controlled by white police officers. The notion that white cops will perform their jobs well by virtue of their relatively high IQs is absurd on the face of it; but more significantly, this vision of the well-ordered city exists outside the realm of history, and thus outside the realm of reason.

30

The Genetic Tie

DOROTHY E. ROBERTS

The Inheritability of Race

The genetic tie's prominence in defining personal identity arose in a racial caste system that preserved white supremacy through a rule of racial purity. In America, perhaps the most socially significant product of the genetic link between parents and children is still race. The inheritability of one's race—which determines one's social status—radically distorts the lens through which we view the biological relationship between generations. It is crucial to examine the historical interplay between concepts of race, social status, and genetic connection.

The Invention of Race

Scientific racism places great value on the genetic tie, as it understands racial variation as a biological distinction that determines superiority and inferiority.[1] Whites justified their enslavement of Africans by the idea of a hierarchical ordering of the races.[2] Only a theory rooted in nature could systematically explain the anomaly of slavery existing in a republic founded on a radical commitment to liberty, equality, and natural rights. In this view, the physical differences between Africans, Indians, and whites separated them into distinct "races" where whites were created superior to blacks and Indians.[3] For example, the racial myth asserted that nature had perfectly adapted Africans' bodies to the heavy agricultural labor needed in the South, and fitted their minds to bondage.

As late as the 1960s, judges and legislators subscribed to the notion of a natural separation between the races. For example, in a 1965 opinion, quoted by the Supreme Court in *Loving v. Virginia*, Circuit Court Judge Leon Bazile defended Virginia's antimiscegenation law as necessary to maintain racial purity:

> Almighty God created the races white, black, yellow, malay and red, and he placed them on separate continents. And but for the interference with his arrangement there would be no cause for such marriages. The fact that he separated the races shows that he did not intend for the races to mix.[4]

Scientific racism explained domination by one group over another as the natural order

62 U. Chi. L. Rev. 209 (1995). Originally published in the *University of Chicago Law Review*. Reprinted by permission.

of society. Blacks were biologically destined to be slaves, while whites were destined to be their masters. Whites invented the hereditary trait of race and endowed it with the concept of racial superiority and inferiority in order to resolve the contradiction between slavery and liberty.

The Genetic Tie and Social Status

The racial caste system required a clear racial demarcation between slaves and their masters. Whites maintained this line by enforcing a principle of racial purity and by making slave status inheritable from the mother.[5] The rule determining slave status departed from the traditional English view of the genetic tie in two ways. First, the inheritance of slave status violated the expectation that most English men and women were born free.[6] The English introduced into the American colonies various forms of white servitude for debtors, convicts, and poor people, and during most of the seventeenth century the legal status of Negro and white servants remained unsettled.[7] By the eighteenth century, however, whites had imposed a distinctive form of bondage on Africans. African chattel slavery, unlike white servitude, was a perpetual, lifelong condition passed on to the next generation. The law presumed that blacks were slaves and that whites were free. Under the American institution of slavery the genetic tie took on supreme importance. It determined the most critical feature of the human condition—whether a child would be deemed a free human being or chattel property.

Second, the principle of *partus sequitur ventrem*[8] violated the long-standing patriarchal tenet that the social status of the child followed the male line. If children took on the status of their fathers, the mulattoes produced by sexual liaisons between white men and their female slaves would have been born free. The slave system rejected this possibility. Under this system, black women bore children who were legally slaves and thus replenished the master's capital assets, while white women bore white children to continue the master's legacy. The racial purity of white women's children was guaranteed by a violently enforced taboo against sexual relations between white women and black men and by antimiscegenation laws that punished interracial marriages. Courts ignored the far more common sexual liaisons between white men and female slaves.

Race came to define an entire caste of second-class members of society: "While some blacks in the South ceased to be slaves, freedom only relieved them of the burdens of servitude; it could never lead to full equality."[9] Both Northern and Southern states denied free blacks many of the rights and privileges enjoyed by white citizens, such as voting, participation in certain professions, and liberty of movement. Such laws made every black person in America, free or slave, subordinate to every white person.

The Genetic Tie and Race

In eighteenth-century America, the genetic tie legally determined one's race, as well as one's status. Statutory definitions of race were based on ancestry, or genotype. A person's race depended on the proportion of white, black, and Indian blood he or she inherited. People with mixed black and white ancestry—mulattoes—were treated the same as Negroes and denied the rights and privileges of whites. As Winthrop Jordan observed, "the separation of slaves from free men depended on a clear demarcation of the races, and the presence of mulattoes blurred this essential distinction." Classifying mulattoes as black denied the fact of racial intermixture which—if acknowledged—would have undermined the logic of racial slavery.[10]

Courts and legislatures took pains to define the precise amount of black ancestry that barred inclusion in the white race. In 1705, for example, a Virginia statute that barred mulattoes, Negroes, Indians, and criminals from holding public office defined mulattoes as "the child of an Indian, or the child, grandchild, or great grandchild of a Negro."[11] Thus, a person with one-eighth Negro ancestry was legally mulatto and was excluded from white privileges. Even into the twentieth century, racial definitions ensured that "any trace of Negro blood would disqualify a person from being considered white under the law."

Legal racial classifications thus created and preserved racial *purity* and racial *domination*. They maintained the myth of a "pure white race," members of which alone were entitled to hold positions of power. The law paradoxically rendered the genetic tie at once supremely important and supremely insignificant. It determined one's most basic condition—free or slave—at birth and declared the black genetic tie, no matter how miniscule, both contaminating and subordinating. Despite the importance of biological descent in race-based slavery, people with predominantly white blood were held as slaves because they descended from a slave woman. The law made their white genetic tie invisible in the name of racial purity.

This racial hierarchy rested on the assumption that the genetic tie to a black parent automatically passed down a whole set of inferior traits. Racist ideology dictated that black bodies, intellect, character, and culture were all inherently vulgar.[12] The black genetic tie was not a valued promise for future generations, but an indelible mark that doomed a child to an inhumane future. Conversely, the white genetic tie was an extremely valuable attribute to be preserved and protected. The status of being white in America brings with it benefits and privileges that whites have come to expect. By ratifying these expectations, the law recognizes a property interest in whiteness.

The rigidly guarded racial line supported a view of whiteness as purity and blackness as pollution, taint, blemish, corruption, and contamination. For whites, racial intermingling "was stamped as irredeemably illicit; it was irretrievably associated with loss of control over the baser passions, with weakening of traditional family ties, and with breakdown of proper social ordering." White colonists described the sexual union of blacks and whites as the mixture of "bloods"—the intermingling of two radically and permanently distinct kinds of people.[13] They complained that interracial unions "polluted the blood of many amongst us," and "smutted our blood."[14] Thus, the meaning of the genetic tie in American law and culture was infused with the paramount objective of keeping the white bloodline free from black contamination.

Notes

1. *See* Nancy Stepan, The Idea of Race in Science: Great Britain, 1800–1960 (Archon, 1982). *See generally* Nancy Leys Stepan and Sandra L. Gilman, *Appropriating the Idioms of Science: The Rejection of Scientific Racism, in* Dominick LaCapra, ed., The Bounds of Race: Perspectives on Hegemony and Resistance 72 (Cornell, 1991); Stephen Jay Gould, The Mismeasure of Man (Norton, 1981). For a contemporary example of scientific racism, see J. Philippe Rushton, Race, Evolution, and Behavior: A Life History Perspective (Transaction, 1995).

2. *See generally* Winthrop D. Jordan, White Over Black: American Attitudes Toward the Negro, 1550–1812, 482–511 (North Carolina, 1969); Ronald T. Takaki, Iron Cages: Race and Culture in Nineteenth-Century America (Knopf, 1979).

3. *See* Takaki, Iron Cages at 47–48, 105. In recognition of the social invention of "races," some scholars surround the term with scare quotes. See, for example, K. Anthony Appiah, *Identity, Authenticity, Survival: Multicultural Societies and Social Reproduction, in* Amy Gutmann, ed., Multiculturalism: Examining the Politics of Recognition 149, 149 n.1 (Princeton, 1994).

4. Loving v. Virginia, 388 U.S. 1, 3 (1967). *See generally* Herbert Hovenkamp, *Social Science and Segregation Before* Brown, 1985 Duke L.J. 624.

5. American law enforced a rule of racial purity for nearly three centuries. A. Leon Higginbotham, Jr., and Barbara K. Kopytoff, *Racial Purity and Interracial Sex in the Law of Colonial and Antebellum Virginia,* 77 Georgetown L.J. 1967, 1967–68, 1971 (1989). The prohibition against interracial marriage in Virginia lasted from 1691 until the Supreme Court declared it unconstitutional in *Loving,* 388 U.S. 1.

6. Kenneth M. Stampp, The Peculiar Institution: Slavery in the Ante-Bellum South 193 (Knopf, 1956); A. Leon Higginbotham, In the Matter of Color: Race and the American Legal Process: The Colonial Period 42–45, 252 (Oxford, 1978).

7. Stampp, The Peculiar Institution at 15–16, 21–22.

8. The child inherits the condition of the mother. Stampp, The Peculiar Institution at 193.

9. Paul Finkelman, *The Centrality of the Peculiar Institution in American Legal Development,* 68 Chi.-Kent L. Rev. 1009, 1014 (1993).

10. Jordan, White Over Black, *supra* at 178.

11. *See* 3 Va. Stat. 4 Anne ch. IV (Hening 1823), quoted in Higginbotham and Kopytoff, 77 Georgetown L.J. at 1977.

12. Cornel West, Race Matters 85–86 (1993).

13. Jordan, White Over Black at 144.

14. *Id.* at 167, quoting James Fontaine, Memoirs of a Huguenot Family (G.P. Putnam & Sons, 1872) (Ann Aaury, trans).

Synopses of Other Important Works

Inventing Whiteness: Them and Us, Cowboys and Indians— Further Notes on the Role of Oppositionality

The Indian and Irish Analogy: Theodore Allen

In the introduction to his classic work *The Invention of the White Race*, Theodore Allen draws attention to the insights Irish history affords into American patterns of supremacy and racial oppression. The abuse and mean treatment afforded early Irish immigrants "present[ ] a case of racial oppression without reference to alleged skin color or . . . phenotype." It illustrates that racial oppression introduced a ruling-class policy even where it was not originally intended. The Irish case also shows how propertyless classes can be recruited first into an "intermediate stratum," and later into a system that embraces racial oppression and white supremacy. Allen also points out that a hallmark of racial oppression is the deliberate destruction of tribal affinities, customs, and bonds of the group in question; he shows how this happened not only with the Irish and African-Americans but with American Indians. Native American tribal relations and rights were assaulted and destroyed, their system of tribal ownership of land ignored. Like blacks, and to some extent the Irish, they were treated as an "undifferentiated mass," a race utterly unlike whites and ripe for exploitation.

The Black Shadow-Figure: George Fredrickson

In a series of books including *The Arrogance of Race: Historical Perspectives on Slavery, Racism, and Social Inequity* and *The Black Image in the White Mind*, Professor George M. Fredrickson of Stanford University describes the process by which white authors, songwriters, and other cultural purveyors coined stereotypes of blacks, both during and after slavery. Some of the stereotypes included docility—the "Sambo," for example, was happy and jovial, satisfied with his lot in life. At other times, society needed a different image—the Negro as brute or oversexed rapacious beast. The various media obligingly disseminated this second image to justify a different set of social needs—outright repression. Similar processes happened with Native Americans and with Mexicans. These images are functional, created by the dominant society to justify policies exploiting the subjugated group.

Whites as Enslaved? Leon Higginbotham

In his foundational work *In the Matter of Color: Race and the American Legal Process*, A. Leon Higginbotham, Jr., discusses the role of race in colonial times. In one section (p. 375 et seq.), Judge Higginbotham demonstrates that, although actual enslavement of whites was never legal in the colonies, Revolutionary leaders constantly described their plight at the hands of the British as being such. Quoting the diatribe of Governor Stephen Hopkins of Rhode Island against the Sugar Act of 1765, Higginbotham notes that the governor—without a trace of irony—asserted: "Liberty is the greatest blessing that men enjoy, and slavery the heaviest curse. . . ." John Adams of Massachusetts concurred: "[W]e are the most abject sort of slaves, to the worst sort of masters!" (p. 375). In a strange juxtaposition, the colonials saw themselves as defined, oppositionally, from their British overlords, to whom they were virtual slaves because of their economic dependence—and of course from African slaves, whose genuinely debased condition meant that the colonials were justified in revolting, lest they suffer something similar!

White Working-Class People and Immigrants: David Roediger

In his acclaimed book *Towards the Abolition of Whiteness*, Professor David R. Roediger of the University of Minnesota analyzes where white, working-class immigrants fit into the picture. Like that of the other authors summarized in this note, Roediger's thesis is subtle and not easily paraphrased. But it includes the idea that society (and the courts) constructed whiteness (and other races, as well) with an eye to class origins and also to what was deemed "common knowledge." In a treatment of "Not-Yet-White Ethnics" (p. 184 et seq.), Roediger amplifies the notion of in-betweenness that he treats elsewhere in this volume. He observes that "immigrants could be Irish, Italian, Hungarian and Jewish, for example, without being white. Many groups now commonly termed part of the 'white' or 'white ethnic' population were in fact historically regarded as nonwhite, or of debatable racial heritage, by the host American citizenry." Professor Roediger goes on to note that around 1850 "the racial status of Catholic Irish newcomers became the object of fierce, extended debate. The 'simian' and 'savage' Irish only gradually fought, worked and voted their ways into the white race. Well into the twentieth century, blacks were counted as 'smoked Irishmen' in racist and anti-Irish U.S. slang. Later, sometimes darker, migrants from Southern and Eastern Europe were similarly cast as nonwhite." The extent to which the experience of these other groups paralleled or did not parallel that of African-Americans, and the interplay between class (money) and race, are the topics of Roediger's book.

Real Whites; or, Cowboys and Other Heroes: Alexander Saxton

In a recent and much-cited book, *The Rise and Fall of the White Republic*, Alexander Saxton writes about class politics and mass culture in nineteenth-century America. Among other topics, Saxton addresses the construction of heroes (p. 321 et seq.), which he believes explains much about the ideological process in a racially and economically divided society. Saxton reviews images in popular culture of Revolutionary and Free Soil heroes, dime-novel stalwarts, Indian killers, and cowboys. This congeries of whites and super-whites, and the themes they are made to play out, tell us much about class consciousness and warfare, as well as about society's need to position whites vis-à-vis such villains as treacherous Mexicans or warlike Indians.

From the Editors: Issues and Comments

Do you agree with the authors in this part of the book that the white race did not exist until it was invented? Surely there were people who look like the Anglo-Americans of today, but were they conscious of themselves as a group or race? If so, who did the inventing, and why? What components went into the new invention? Is race—any race—an act of arrogance, or is it possible to be humble, quietly proud, neutral, or even negative about one's own race? Is it antidemocratic to identify oneself as a white, as Kathleen Cleaver insists—and, if so, is it not equally antidemocratic to call oneself black or Jewish?

Is it possible to identify oneself as a member of a certain race (white or anything else) without believing in physical (genetic) difference? And, if scientists conclusively showed that the genetic difference between your race and some other one were negligible, would you give up your identification as . . . white, black, or whatever you are?

Suppose that global environmental conditions change so that it is a major disadvantage to be white. Whites are now sickly, die earlier than other people, and contract certain dread diseases more frequently than members of other racial groups. Would everyone want to be nonwhite, and conceal their white genealogy?

Suggested Readings

Acuña, Rodolpho, OCCUPIED AMERICA: A HISTORY OF CHICANOS. 3d ed. (Harper & Row, 1988).

THE BIRTH OF WHITENESS: RACE AND THE EMERGENCE OF UNITED STATES CINEMA (Daniel Bernardi, ed., Rutgers University Press, 1996).

Dudziak, Mary, *Desegregation as a Cold War Imperative*, 41 STAN. L. REV. 61 (1988).

Fields, Barbara, *Slavery, Race, and Ideology in the United States of America*, 181 NEW LEFT REV. 95 (1990).

Gossett, Thomas, RACE: THE HISTORY OF AN IDEA IN NORTH AMERICA (1963).

Haney Lopez, Ian F., WHITE BY LAW (New York University Press, 1995).

THE INVENTION OF ETHNICITY (W. Sollers, ed., 1989).

"RACE," WRITING, AND DIFFERENCE (H. Gates, ed., 1985).

Roediger, David, TOWARDS THE ABOLITION OF WHITENESS: ESSAYS ON RACE, POLITICS AND WORKING CLASS HISTORY (Verso, 1994).

Williams, Robert A., Jr., THE AMERICAN INDIAN IN WESTERN LEGAL THOUGHT: THE DISCOURSES OF CONQUEST (Oxford, 1990).

Williams, Robert A., Jr., *Jefferson, the Norman Yoke, and American Indian Lands*, 29 ARIZ. L. REV. 165 (1987).

Young, Robert, WHITE MYTHOLOGIES: WRITING HISTORY AND THE WEST (1990).

Part IV

Whiteness: Law's Role

Everyone knows that the legal system has played a part in enforcing racial separation (e.g., in schooling) and also, from time to time, in requiring racial fairness. But the law played a role in something that is prior to that—namely, in constructing racial categories in the first place. Does law, as some writers believe, have the ability actually to change physical appearance and so reinforce the belief that races are biologically distinct? When the legal system sets out to redress racial discrimination does it just end up hardening lines and reinforcing the idea of racial Otherness? Does color blindness make matters worse?

Did law play a role in constructing the idea of the white race? In the idea of racial superiority and inferiority? In the naturalness of spatial separation, as in housing or public schools? Can it help us in moving toward a color-blind society, and would that be desirable?

31

White Law and Lawyers:
The Case of Surrogate Motherhood

PETER HALEWOOD

Much has been written on surrogate motherhood as an application of biotechnology which challenges conventional understandings of equality and the family. Surrogacy also challenges conventional notions of embodiment. Indeed, the law has responded to surrogacy by bracketing off the surrogate mother's embodiment—her factual experience of pregnancy—from the legal facts relevant to deciding disputes over custody arising from surrogacy arrangements. For example, even where the so-called surrogate is pregnant with her own fertilized ovum, she is defined not as the "biological" mother but as the "surrogate" mother, thus denying the biological and experiential fact that she is the mother.

Surrogacy raises issues of embodiment along multiple axes. For example, when the surrogate mother is a woman of color and the contracting parents are white, the intersectionality of race, class, and gender makes the equality analysis more complicated. Where, for example, the surrogate is African American but both egg and sperm are from a white couple, making her neither genetically nor even racially connected to the fetus she carries, novel and important moral, legal, and political issues arise. The basic point is that women of color are subjected to discrimination along intersecting trajectories of race and gender and that this intersection is not recognized by anti-discrimination law because of its conventional top-down perspective, which has produced an analysis based on *either* race or gender that does not recognize the dual identity of women of color. But the fact of this dual identity is a fact of embodiment: this duality is the lived concrete existence of women of color.

A liberal might argue that commercial surrogacy represents nothing more than a legitimate, marketable property interest in one's reproductive capacity. That is clearly a disembodied analysis, for it does not recognize that in surrogacy arrangements it will *always* be a female body and female reproductive capacity that are being purchased, often by the elevated earning power of a middle-class, white couple. Following this logic, many feminists have argued that surrogacy will always effect a degradation of women by commodifying their bodies and identities. For this reason, Margaret Radin has argued that reproductive capacity should be market-inalienable personal property—meaning that a woman's reproductive capacity is her property, but not property she is allowed to sell. Such regulation would protect the authenticity of female personhood.

From "White Men Can't Jump: Critical Epistemologies, Embodiment, and the Praxis of Legal Scholarship," 7 YALE J. L. AND FEMINISM 1 (1995). Originally published in the *Yale Journal of Law and Feminism*. Reprinted by permission.

In the famous Baby M case, Mary Beth Whitehead, a working-class white woman, contracted as a surrogate mother to bear a child conceived from her ovum fertilized by the
sperm of the husband in the middle-class contracting couple. After giving birth, Whitehead
decided to break the contract and keep the child. The New Jersey Superior Court held that
the contract was not illusory and that Whitehead was bound by its terms.[1]

The liberal analysis of this problem assumes the classic free-contract abstraction and agnosticism about the concrete details of the parties' experiences. The "father" was a consumer; Whitehead was a child "producer" in a mutually beneficial contract. The surrogate's
relation to her pregnancy was analyzed in market-oriented terms, denying the unique relationship of the surrogate to the fetus *inside her body*. If the analysis focuses on her embodied relationship with the fetus rather than on the cold, hard legal facts of contractual
transfer, the surrogate could be said to have a property interest in the experience of pregnancy greater than the rights assigned between the parties under contract. If one focuses
on embodiment as an index of legality here, the transfer of Whitehead's reproductive capacity is no longer neutral. It is deeply significant to an analysis of equality and exploitation that in surrogacy it is always a woman's body at stake—never a man's. This obvious
fact curiously disappears in a liberal, sex-neutral contract analysis. Here the normativity
of law does conceptual violence to Whitehead's narrative about what happened to her, removing her dignity and erasing her history. She did not rationally contract away a disembodied intellectual service—her case was simply an unfortunate attempt by a middle-class
couple to remove from her one of the most intimate forms of physical integrity and experience of embodiment.

Yet this is not the whole story of the commodification of women in surrogacy. Regina
Austin and Joan Williams have argued that commodification is not always a bad thing for
women or people of color. Indeed, Carol Rose has said that "women have not had enough
commodification."[2] Anti-commodification rhetoric in the family context has meant the allocation of money to men: fear of commodifying women has prevented courts from granting the wife a larger share of the husband's property following divorce. This is the result
of "anti-commodification anxiety": "anti-commodification rhetoric polices the borders of
traditional family allocation of resources."[3]

How could the commodification of women's bodies in commercial surrogacy be studied
and interpreted by a white male legal scholar in a manner which takes into account the
methodological cautions about epistemological standpoint? Do the feminist standpoint
epistemologies *preclude* me, a white man, from accurately analyzing and interpreting commodification of women's bodies, or do they merely indicate that I must approach the topic
with deference to women's experience? The task is to demonstrate how law erases the experience of subordinated groups, and to retrieve that experience and its relation to law in
our scholarship. How can a white male interpret gender commodification given the stated
problem of epistemological perspective, and how can one avoid appropriating or erasing the
voices of women in doing it?

Several points suggest themselves. First, the white male scholar must acknowledge that
surrogacy touches issues intimate to women's bodies, and respect his scholarly obligation
to treat with dignity those affected by his analysis—here, primarily women. Second, and
most importantly, I must openly acknowledge my own white male perspective as part of
the project (since being white and male often is intepreted as having no perspective), and
acknowledge that this is often the perspective of the powerful and privileged party in surrogacy commodification. It is important to acknowledge that as a white man, I am impli-

cated in this discussion (certainly in the pejorative sense indicated by Austin, Rose, and Williams' critique of the under-commodified family) and therefore should not pretend to a position of detachment and objectivity in my analysis. In this way, I remove myself from an attempt to explain or define, recognizing that I am not in the same epistemological plane as the subordinated group (women) which is the subject of scholarly inquiry. It is also important to point out the racial exploitation that some of the surrogacy cases evidence, that is, that some of the contracting parties have been white women contracting for the services of African-American women surrogates.

Third, I should not claim expertise, or claim to have intellectually mastered the theory of commodification or the analysis of surrogacy (though one must do one's best, of course, to be thoroughly familiar with both the issues and the legal literature on commodification). Rather, I should attempt to explore the insights of women scholars insofar as their embodied experience privileges their insight into the problems of surrogacy that are not evident to me (for example, the issue of exploitation of women in family law by under-commodification). I must become thoroughly familiar with the sociology and mechanics of surrogacy. Uninformed scholarship is potentially threatening to those women among the scholarly audience who may identify with the surrogate.

Most importantly, the scholar must first thoroughly learn about the commodification under examination. The white male scholar must acknowledge that he cannot intuit this perspective. However, perspectival epistemology does not mean that the subordinate perspective cannot be learned by a member of the dominant group, here the white male scholar himself, who may in turn incorporate it in his scholarship. One should try to build bridges from male experiences of commodification of the male body, for example, in the context of organ donation, or perhaps in fashion, exercise, and fitness, the fetishization of the slim, muscular male body. Though male and female experiences of commodification are dissimilar, male experiences of embodiment might nonetheless give men the basis of an understanding of commodification of their own bodies from which to extrapolate an empathetic scholarly interpretation of surrogacy and consequent problems of commodification of the female body by biotechnology and contract law.

Fourth, collaborative scholarship is especially appropriate to such forms of inquiry: surrendering one's leadership role to a female colleague who is more familiar with this complex set of practices, using women's concrete experiences as a test of one's scholarly propositions, and engaging in rigorous social contextualization of one's work. The Superior Court decision in the Baby M case illustrates the pitfalls of analyzing complex material without adequate context, and with insufficient humility. . . . A scholar could use the substance of the Baby M commercial surrogacy case to produce a critical understanding of the subtleties of gender inequality, gender commodification, and the situated epistemological perspectives which frame the legal inquiry. Why was this case framed and decided as one of *contract*- and not *sex*-based tortious harassment by the father? One might explore how such a decision might have been made. It might be the result of a pragmatic litigation strategy, given what is known about courts' sympathy for certain types of contract claims, and given the absence (then) of applicable statutes and regulations. Even if this is in fact pragmatic, is it a desirable way to approach such a case, given its misrepresentation of the surrogate's perception of her experience? How could such a process of misrepresentation have come about? One might suggest that, were Whitehead's lawyers (and the Superior Court judge) female, pregnancy would be a phenomenon more accessible to them than it would be to male attorneys and judges—it is at least potentially within all women's experience of embodiment. Men, by contrast, would have to work very hard to understand the significance of pregnancy and women's bodies in what, according to liberal jurisprudential analyses of surrogacy, is a simple contractual transfer of services.

But what of the *racial* aspects of surrogacy where the surrogate is African-American? Assume the plaintiff was represented by white, female, feminist attorneys—could they be expected to have better access to the "truth" of the sex discrimination suffered by an African-American woman than could male attorneys? Why? Or is there something about their experience as white women that might make them as blind as white men to racial discrimination? Might feminist attorneys downplay racial aspects of such a case in the interests of obtaining a broader precedent for all women? Do attorneys have a professional responsibility to present a case's intersectional aspect, even if this might mean the plaintiff would lose? How could such sensitivity to the plaintiff's experience be achieved?

Assume instead that such a plaintiff were represented by African-American male attorneys—would similar partial advantages of insight, problems, and responsibilities arise? Is it possible that a white male law firm, or a firm fully diverse along sex, ethnic, and other lines, could map an appropriate litigation strategy for such a plaintiff's case, one that would have given the plaintiff opportunity to fully articulate her experience and harm? Exploring these kinds of questions based on the case would make for a compelling inquiry into the bodily commodification involved in surrogacy. My purpose here is not to provide such an analysis of the issues surrounding surrogacy, but rather to suggest a situated reconstruction of the white male scholarly enterprise.

Notes

1. *In re* Baby "M," 217 N.J. Super. 313, 525 A.2d 1128 (1987), *aff'd in part* and *rev'd in part*, 109 N.J. 396, 537 A.2d 1227.

2. Regina Austin, Carol Rose, and Joan Williams, panel on commodification at the AALS Annual Meeting (January 5, 1995) (author's recollection; audio cassette on file with the AALS).

3. *Id.*

32

Social Science and Segregation before *Brown*

HERBERT HOVENKAMP

No historical legal policy can be evaluated without an understanding of the framework in which the policymakers viewed the world. If members of a society believe a particular scientific theory—for example, that interracial sex produces degenerate children—then they may be willing to sacrifice a great deal to avoid the consequences of interracial marriages. If they later discover that interracial marriages have no such consequences, then their views will probably change accordingly. In short, people's scientific view of the world determines in large part the social situation that they regard as optimal. The genetic determinism that dominated social science in the last part of the nineteenth century made strict racial segregation appear to be socially prudent. Later, when environmentalism gradually replaced genetic determinism as a theory of race, racial separation became less valuable to society as a whole. When that happened, certain competing values—such as Americans' more general concern with equality—began to weigh more heavily.

In discussing the history of the law of race relations, it is useful to distinguish two ways in which courts were influenced by scientific theories. Some scientific data were presented directly to the courts—as in Justice Brandeis's famous brief in *Muller v. Oregon*,[1] which used social science data to convince the Supreme Court that a state had the constitutional power to regulate the working hours of women even though it could not do so for men. A second influence was the "background" scientific information that formed part of a judge's perception of the world. A judge's views about the propriety of state-mandated segregation were necessarily a product of both sources of information. Each had an important yet distinctly different influence on the case law of race relations in the late nineteenth and early twentieth centuries.

In *Berea College v. Kentucky*,[2] decided only a few months after *Muller v. Oregon*,[3] the United States Supreme Court was for the first time directly confronted with social science data about race. Its decision in *Berea College* upheld as constitutional a Kentucky statute mandating statewide school segregation.

Berea College was a church school, a product of the evangelical antislavery movement of the 1830s. Its geographic setting, in one of the four slaveholding states that remained with the Union during the Civil War,[4] caused it to experience more difficulty than other small, struggling religious institutions. Berea College entered the post-Reconstruction period as an ideological rarity: a school committed to the integrated education of white and black students, but isolated in a southern, formerly slaveholding state.

1985 Duke L.J. 624. Originally published in the *Duke Law Journal*. Reprinted by permission.

The college managed to survive local opposition during and after Reconstruction—financial starvation, aggressive racial hostility, and occasional acts of violence against its faculty and students. It did not fare so well against the new science and politics of the Gilded Age. Before the turn of the century, a large number of scientific studies warned against the dangers of racial mixing. Both scientists and laypersons generally believed that Afro-Americans were inherently inferior, that they learned much more slowly than white persons, and that their close association with whites could contaminate and weaken the white race. After the Civil War, the possibility of substantial racial mixing became real; the prospect most feared was that of interracial marriage, or "miscegenation." Nearly everyone assumed that the way to prevent interracial sexual contact was to keep the races separated, particularly in institutions where young people's values were developed, such as the schools. In 1904 the Kentucky legislature passed a law prohibiting the operation of "any college, school or institution where persons of the white and negro race are both received as pupils for instruction."[5] The statute was aimed directly at Berea—Kentucky's only integrated college. Berea violated the new law, was fined $1000, and challenged the constitutionality of the statute.

The college advanced several constitutional arguments, some of which would later become law. Although the fourteenth amendment did not prohibit the state from using its police power to force segregation of public schools,[6] Berea was a private school. The college asserted that its students had the right to associate with whom they pleased as long as they did not interfere with the rights of outsiders. Furthermore, because integrated education was an important part of the Bereans' religious beliefs, Kentucky was interfering with the students' free exercise of that belief.

The Kentucky Court of Appeals held that the Constitution did not limit the police power of the state to pass segregation laws unless the laws were themselves unreasonable. In this case the Kentucky legislature had done no more than recognize an obvious scientific truth—that "[t]he separation of the human family into races . . . is as certain as anything in nature."[7] Integration of blacks and whites was "incompatible [with] the continued being of the races" and "repugnant to their instincts."[8] Furthermore, "[f]rom social amalgamation it is but a step to illicit intercourse, and but another to intermarriage."[9] The state clearly had a right to protect its citizens from the devastating effects of miscegenation. The court admitted that balancing the liberty promised to everyone against the need to preserve racial integrity "forms now one of the biggest questions being worked out by this great North American republic."[10] Here, however, the challenged regulation was minimal. No one was denying the freedman's basic right to an education. "[T]o assert separateness is not to declare inferiority in either. . . . It is simply to say that following the order of Divine Providence, human authority ought not to compel these widely separate races to intermix."[11]

Berea College also lost in the United States Supreme Court. Justice Brewer limited his analysis to the question of Kentucky's power to control its own private corporations, never addressing the question of individual rights under the fourteenth amendment. The most interesting aspect of *Berea*, however, is not to be found in the Supreme Court's opinion, but in the brief submitted by the Commonwealth of Kentucky in defense of the segregation statute. James Breathitt, Kentucky's Attorney General, prepared a "Brandeis Brief" somewhat like the one that Brandeis himself had used only three months earlier when he successfully defended the Oregon women's protective statute in *Muller v. Oregon*. Breathitt asked the Supreme Court to take notice of certain facts that were "so notorious and universally known as to form a part of the common information of mankind."[12] Then, just as Brandeis had done, the Kentucky Attorney General produced his "scientific" data. The data were not part of the "common information of mankind" at all; in fact, they were quite esoteric and controversial. Breathitt cited an important study by Dr. Sanford B. Hunt, a United States surgeon and pioneer in the field of anthropometrics—the study of the physical characteristics of the races of mankind. In the 1870s Hunt had discovered that the average Afro-American's brain weighed five ounces less than the average white person's brain. Hunt also found that the brain of the average mulatto was even smaller than that of the average black. Because it was assumed that brain weight was directly correlated with intelligence, Hunt concluded not only that blacks had far less mental capacity than whites, but that intermarriage of the races would produce offspring inferior even to the offspring of "pure-blooded" blacks; furthermore, these differences among racial types were either permanent or destined to evolve so slowly that it would take thousands of years for blacks to achieve intellectual equality with whites.

Sanford B. Hunt came from a line of American anthropometrists that began with Samuel George Morton, a Philadelphia physician who, in the 1820s, compared the cranial capacities of blacks and whites. Morton found differences in cranial capacity that approximated the differences in brain weights Hunt was to discover a half century later. Morton was also able to obtain the skulls of some 3000-year-old white Egyptians and their black slaves. He discovered approximately the same variations in cranial capacity. In three millennia blacks had come no closer to "catching up" with whites.[13]

Attorney General Breathitt argued that this evidence clearly showed that the state had an interest in maintaining racial separation. The anthropometric studies supported the long-held view that there was a substantial "mental gap" between African and Caucasian Americans. Breathitt also argued that the gap "is not the result of education, but is innate and God-given."[14] Science had shown that "education, culture, refinement and civilization [are] the result of the polishing of the inborn and God-given faculty. Training, culture and education never produce faculty. All these are but the growth, the enlargement and expansion of an inborn capacity."[15]

Attorney General Breathitt had entered an anthropological battle that had already been hot for a century. What was it that determined racial characteristics—heredity or environment? The theory of evolution by natural selection had greatly changed the nature of the battle when it began to influence anthropology in the 1870s. Far from solving the heredity/environment dispute, however, the theory of evolution made understanding racial characteristics a more difficult task than it had ever been before.

By the time Breathitt argued *Berea College* in 1908 there were three general positions on the nature of race. The traditional position had become the official view of many American churches, particularly after Charles Darwin published *On the Origin of Species* in 1859. This view was that racial characteristics were permanent—"innate and God-given," as Attorney General Breathitt argued. God created the species and races "after their kind," with the distinguishing features of each group part of its permanent nature. Heredity was the mechanism that ensured this permanence. The rule that "like begets like" was a part of natural law, and any tampering—such as the interbreeding of dissimilar organisms—could have ugly consequences. It is probably safe to say that in 1908 this was the view of racial characteristics adopted by most American non-scientists, and by a substantial minority of scientists as well. As the theory of natural selection became more popular, however, this group of scientists was gradually edged out of the mainstream of the scientific community.

A second group, which included the majority of scientists in 1908, were evolutionists, who placed a great emphasis on the role of genetics in determining racial features. For them, characteristics such as intelligence do in fact "evolve," so that perhaps someday the Afro-American would develop an intelligence equal to the Caucasian's. However, because the evolution of intelligence is a process that takes thousands of years, the intellectual differences between the races had to be regarded, for all intents and purposes, as permanent. Furthermore, most hereditary determinists argued, race mixing was bad for two reasons. First, it could slow the evolutionary progress of the more advanced race. Second, when organisms with dissimilar genes interbreed, this increases the possibility of producing bizarre, unhealthy offspring.

On two matters, these groups generally agreed. First, integrated education was bad because blacks learned much more slowly than whites. The presence of black children in a classroom would therefore retard the progress of the white children. Second, social integration of any kind was bad because race mixing would eventually lead to miscegenation. As the Kentucky Court of Appeals said, "[f]rom social amalgamation it is but a step to illicit intercourse, and but another to intermarriage."[16]

A third view of racial differences was held by a small number of scientists—the environmentalists—who were not to have a significant impact for almost a generation. Their views may have been altogether unknown to Attorney General Breathitt. These scientists agreed with the genetic determinists that some human physical characteristics were hereditary and would take a long time to change by evolution. The environmentalists, however, believed that other characteristics—such as behavior and intelligence—were determined largely by the outside influences that affect an individual during his developmental period. Thus the only true intellectual difference between blacks and whites was that blacks had not had the advantage of the white person's life situation, economic status, or education. More importantly, the genetic differences between the races were not nearly as great as the genetic determinists believed. If one plotted all the world's organisms on a chart, the different races of humanity would be genetically so close together that they would appear to be one. The environmentalists thus argued that, notwithstanding any negative social consequences, racial interbreeding would probably have no harmful biological consequences.

By 1908 the people in the first of these three groups—the religious anti-evolutionists—had produced an immense literature on the "mental gap" between blacks and whites and the dangers of racial mixing. Most of the assertions relied heavily on contemporary science. Frequently the scientific and religious arguments were so closely intertwined that it was hard to tell where one ended and the other began.

The hereditary determinists in the second group had also produced a large amount of literature, most of it fairly scientific. Attorney General Breathitt, however, was not a scientist; his perspective on the race problem came largely from popularizers, most of whom were quite religious and antagonistic toward the theory of evolution. Still, his view, and ones like it, carried the day. . . .

Social Science in a Racist Society

In the nineteenth century, it was customary to distinguish between political equality and social equality when discussing the rights of a black person. To have political equality was to have the same basic human rights against the state that the white person has—the right to own property, to vote, to plead in court, and to share equally in the costs and benefits of government. As a participating member of society, every person deserved these things, heredity and intelligence notwithstanding. Social equality, on the other hand, was measured not against the state, but against other individuals. The black person who wanted to vote was imposing on the state, but the black person who wanted to attend an integrated college was imposing his presence on the individuals who composed the majority, who did not want him there. The freedman could assert his social rights only at the obvious expense of the rights of someone else. "Every man has a natural and inherent right of selecting his own associates," Judge Dick wrote in 1875, "and this natural right cannot be properly regulated by legislative action, but must always be under the control of individual taste and inclination."[17] The fourteenth amendment imposed an obligation only on the states, not on private individuals. It had been designed to guarantee political equality, not to enforce social equality.

The fourteenth amendment concept of state action, which facilitated the Supreme Court's declaration that the 1875 Civil Rights Act was unconstitutional,[18] effectively determined the kind of race discrimination that was appropriate in the 1880s. White Americans could now deliver to the newly freed American black a measure of participation in the political process and a certain amount of access to the public facilities from which he traditionally had been excluded. On the other hand, the science of the day indicated that close racial mixing would impose social costs far greater than any benefits it might bring. Although that science had relatively little to say about political equality, it had a great deal to say about social equality.

A great deal of nineteenth-century science was implicit in Judge Dick's distinction between political and social equality. If politics had shown that the American state was flexible enough to accommodate a diverse citizenry, anthropology and sociology were beginning to show that human beings were extraordinarily inflexible in the matter of racial amalgamation. It was easy for the state to give the Afro-American the vote, but it was terribly difficult for the white person to share his seat with an African.

The Social Science of the Gilded Age

Anthropology became a science at a time when the sciences were obsessed with new developments in biology. To explain man's physical structure was to explain mankind. America's first great contributor to anthropology was Samuel George Morton, who developed a large following of scientists who believed that permanent differences separated racial types. Sanford Hunt, upon whom Kentucky's Attorney General Breathitt had relied in *Berea College*, was fascinated by Morton's findings. When Hunt was working for the United States Sanitary Commission during the Civil War he prepared a report on the physical, emotional, and mental characteristics of the black soldier. The first part of Hunt's report concluded that blacks were imitative, cheerful, rhythmical (they marched well at night), and not very intelligent. These characteristics made the Afro-American a good foot soldier but a bad officer.

The problem of black intelligence bothered Hunt. He wanted to be fair, yet he wanted his conclusions to be as universal as possible. Hunt concluded that artificial intelligence testing was unsatisfactory because the tests measured too many environmental influences. The typical black soldier was a former slave who had been forced into the kind of existence that would naturally tend to dull one's wits. Hunt decided that cranial capacity and brain weight would be much more accurate indicators of innate racial intelligence than any skills testing of living subjects. He studied the results of 405 autopsies of white and black soldiers and came to the conclusions that Attorney General Breathitt cited in his brief. Much of the physical anthropology of the second half of the century was derived from these data collected by Hunt and others during the Civil War.

The ease with which Hunt was able to separate genetic and environmental determinants of intelligence reveals a naïveté about human development that dominated social science until the twentieth century. By 1908, when Attorney General Breathitt used Hunt's anthropological data before the Supreme Court, the idea that one could measure intelligence simply by weighing brains was in disrepute. However, psychologists were only beginning to realize that the separation of genetic and environmental factors in race development could be an extremely complex task. Even if Breathitt had used the most up-to-date scientific data available he could still easily have concluded that blacks were inherently inferior to whites in intelligence, and that amalgamation of the two races could seriously threaten the integrity of the white race.

Most of the physical anthropologists of the Gilded Age were probably evolutionists. The immediate effect of Darwin's work was, however, to confirm and strengthen long-established ideas about black inferiority. The theory of evolution gave direction to the Jeffersonian notion that the African occupied a *fixed* position somewhere below the white man. For Gilded Age American anthropologist Lewis Henry Morgan, however, the black man was inferior to the white and was falling further behind every year. Morgan adapted Darwinian natural selection to a Spencerian notion of absolute cultural progress. He concluded that the different human races were in different stages of physical and cultural evolution. Morgan named the three general stages of human cultural achievement: savagery, barbarism, and civilization. In Morgan's view, "[t]he Aryan family represents the central stream of human progress, because it produced the highest type of mankind, and because it has proved its intrinsic superiority by gradually assuming the control of the earth."[19] The African race, on the other hand, was still in the middle stage of barbarism.

Like Darwin, Morgan believed that species or varieties of any organisms in close physical proximity compete with each other. Morgan applied this principle to cultural as well as to physical development. He believed that the human races differed from the lower animals in that they no longer relied on brute strength but on intelligence and inventiveness to survive. The more advanced the culture, the more mental powers had replaced physical strength as the basic survival weapon. In this respect the Afro-American was hopelessly outclassed, for when an inferior culture confronts a superior one the former must give way. Blacks sharing the same environment with whites were unable to compete.

The idea that the black race was so inferior that it would eventually become extinct was popular at the end of the nineteenth century. Anthropologist Frederick L. Hoffman believed that emancipation had been the worst thing that ever happened to the Afro-American. As freedmen, the Africans were not equipped to deal with the complexities of their new culture. Hoffman found evidence that after the Civil War the black mortality rate had increased, blacks had developed a much higher incidence of several diseases, and their general standard of living had declined. Turned loose in a civilized society, the African was doomed.

Many white Americans could have lived with that conclusion. To them, a nation without blacks was thinkable, if not appealing. But interracial marriage destroyed the simplicity of the evolutionary idea. Although social scientists generally agreed about the characteristics of the "pure" African, the hybrid was hotly debated in the late nineteenth century. Sanford Hunt believed that the mental capacity of the mulatto varied with the amount of white blood that flowed in his veins. Frederick Hoffman, however, thought all mulattoes were inferior to members of either race. Nathaniel Southgate Shaler, a prominent Harvard professor, believed that the mulatto was less healthy, shorter-lived, and less fertile than members of either the black or the white race. Shaler's research supported the popular idea that most mulattoes grow up with "disharmonic" features — large frames combined with small heart and kidneys, for example, or large teeth tightly crowded into an undersized mouth.

Worse yet were the mulatto's insoluble moral and psychological problems. "From the white he inherits a refinement unfitting him for all work which has not a certain delicacy about it," concluded Shaler; however, from his black parent the mulatto acquires "a laxity of morals which, whether it be the result of innate incapacity for certain forms of moral culture or the result of an utter want of training in this direction, is still unquestionably a negro characteristic."[20] In short, the mulatto was an outcast in both worlds—too civilized to be comfortable with the black, but too primitive to live with the white without giving offense.

Although many of the racists who opposed interracial sexual relations were evolutionists, they cast the problem in a scientific paradigm that was more Lamarckian than Darwinian. Jean-Baptiste Lamarck was a pre-Darwinian evolutionist who never hit upon the theory of natural selection. Rather, he explained evolutionary progress as the instinctive "unconscious striving" of each member of a species to better itself and its progeny. To this theory Lamarck coupled the notion of the inheritance of acquired physical characteristics.

During the late nineteenth century many biologists explained evolution in a modified Lamarckian paradigm. According to the neo-Lamarckian evolutionary theory, any organism's "unconscious striving" naturally attracts it to the most superior mate. Thus in many species the males fight among each other, and the winner gets first choice of the females. In this way the best characteristics of the best pair are united, and the species is improved.

Progressive Era racial theorists used the neo-Lamarckian theory to explain what to them seemed to be a universal phenomenon: the intense sexual attraction that blacks had for whites—particularly black males for white females. The whites, after all, were the superior strain. The black, on the other hand, occupied a lower rung on the evolutionary ladder. For the black, interracial mating meant evolutionary progress; for the white, it meant regression. To many racists this meant that the white race had a natural tendency to preserve its racial purity. The natural tendency of the black race, however, was to blend with the whites until the racial identity of the blacks entirely disappeared.

How to combat the black male's urge for the white female was a question of social control. Self-help, to be sure, was one method—and lynchings of black males accused of sexual misconduct were relatively common in the New South. In addition, statutory prohibitions of interracial marriage were universal in the South and relatively common in the North and the West. Statutory controls on interracial marriage and sexual relations were such an intrinsic part of the American value system during the Gilded Age that few people bothered to challenge their constitutionality. No miscegenation case reached the Supreme Court. However, in 1882 the Supreme Court dismissed a fourteenth amendment challenge to an Alabama law that made interracial adultery a much more serious offense than adultery of the ordinary variety.[21]

The social costs of racial mixing and miscegenation were perceived as so high that few seriously considered permitting the practices. In the scientific view of the day a racially mixed couple—no matter how happy they might be—were likely to produce inferior offspring that would be a lifetime burden on society and were guaranteed to weaken and contaminate both the white and the black races. In such a perspective, the costs of social integration far exceeded any benefits.

Social Planning: Responding to Social Science Data

In the first two decades of the twentieth century the popular horror of racial amalgamation reached its apogee. Progressive Era politicians supported a wider role for government in social planning than did their Gilded Age predecessors, and they looked for broader methods of social control than mere antimiscegenation statutes. The most obvious way to ensure separation was to force blacks and whites to live in different places. In 1910 Baltimore passed the ultimate antiamalgamation statute—an ordinance that zoned separate residential districts for blacks and whites. Within six years more than a dozen southern cities had followed suit.

The ordinance passed by the City of Louisville, Kentucky, was typical. It prevented any black person from moving into "any house upon any block upon which a greater number of houses are occupied . . . by white people than are occupied . . . by colored people."[22] The second section of the law likewise made it illegal for a white person to move onto a predominantly black block. With the statute in effect, Louisville would eventually have had no racially mixed residential blocks.

Shortly after Louisville enacted its ordinance, Robert Buchanan, a white man, contracted to sell his home to a black man named William Warley. At the time there were ten houses on Buchanan's block, eight of them occupied by whites. Under the new ordinance Warley could not occupy the house he had agreed to purchase. Warley refused to pay the price and Buchanan sued him. As a result the case came into the Kentucky court system in a peculiar posture. Warley, the black man, argued that the racial zoning statute was constitutional and that because of it he should be excused from performing his contract. Buchanan, the white man, on the other hand, argued that the statute was unconstitutional and could not provide Warley with a defense.

Judging from the speed with which the newly formed National Association for the Advancement of Colored People (NAACP) moved in and agreed to represent Anglo-Saxon Buchanan against African Warley, it is likely that the case had been "tailored" a bit in order to present it to the Supreme Court in the most attractive way: The case made it obvious that racially exclusive zoning could do as much damage to the property rights of white persons as to the rights of blacks.

Kentucky's highest court upheld the statute as a rational exercise of the state's police power, citing *Berea College*.[23] By the time the United States Supreme Court agreed to hear the case it had generated a great deal of publicity. Racial zoning ordinances were becoming very popular, and eventually most of the South and parts of the North would have passed them.

Moorfield Storey, a prominent Boston attorney and the national president of the NAACP, argued the plaintiff's case in April of 1916. Two attorneys working for the City of Louisville argued for the constitutionality of the statute. In his oral argument Storey insisted that racial mixing was essential to America's cultural vitality, and that *any* state policy of segregation was thus unreasonable. Consistent with this position, he was forced to acknowledge that he believed statutes forbidding interracial marriage and integrated schools were also unreasonable and unconstitutional uses of state police power.[24]

This argument for the wisdom of racial amalgamation intrigued the Court, and it held the case over for reargument. Stuart Chevalier and Pendleton Beckley, the attorneys representing the City of Louisville, told the Court in the April 1917 reargument that they had been astounded when Moorfield Storey tried to make the case turn on the reasonableness of racial amalgamation. To bolster his argument, Storey had "cited various scientific authorities" in support of racial mixing. The Louisville attorneys felt obliged to reply in kind.

Chevalier and Beckley modeled their reply brief after Brandeis's famous brief in *Muller v. Oregon*. The brief cited Brandeis for the proposition that certain commonly known facts could be brought to the Court's attention even though they had not been part of the fact findings at trial. Then the brief proceeded with one hundred pages of social science data, designed to prove that amalgamation of the races was clearly not in the best interests of either blacks or whites.

Many of the sources Chevalier and Beckley quoted were not social scientists at all. They included Henry W. Grady, editor of the *Atlanta Constitution*, Charles W. Eliot, former president of Harvard University, and Washington Gladden, a prominent liberal Protestant clergyman who was one of the leaders of the Social Gospel movement. These writers were quoted in the Louisville brief because they revealed that America's intellectual leaders and even one of its outstanding social liberals were opposed to the mixing of races. Without distinguishing among its authorities, the Louisville brief also quoted some of the South's most notorious bigots—such as John Vertrees, who believed that white solidarity could be maintained only if the white race retained a monopoly on political power.

The Louisville brief also cited many respectable scientific sources for the argument that the offspring of interracial marriages were inferior. Like Attorney General Breathitt in *Berea College*, Chevalier and Beckley relied heavily on William Benjamin Smith's *The Color Line*.[25] Smith in turn had drawn much of his evidence of mulatto degeneracy from Benjamin A. Gould, who had been hired by the United States Sanitary Commission to perform several anthropometric studies of the autopsy reports of black and white Civil War soldiers. He had discovered that the average lung capacity of a white soldier was 185 cubic inches, and of a black soldier 164 cubic inches. However, the average capacity of the lungs of the mulatto was only 159 cubic inches.[26] The result, according to Gould, was that mulattoes were chronically unhealthy and unfit for hard labor.

The Louisville brief also relied on the work of Scottish geologist and natural historian James Bryce, who had visited America in order to observe its race problem. Bryce concluded that when "similar" races, such as Caucasians and Chinese, intermarry the resulting stock can be quite healthy—as strong and intelligent as either parent. When "remote" races intermarry, however, they are so biologically different that genetic defects are sure to result.[27] Bryce viewed the American South as having the unusual problem that it was populated simultaneously by the highest and the lowest races of mankind. Any intermarriage between the two races could yield grossly inferior offspring.

The mere inferiority of the mulatto was not sufficient. Chevalier and Beckley also produced evidence that interracial marriage was on the rise. Alexander Harvey Shannon, chaplain of the Mississippi State Penitentiary and an ethnologist, had found that at the time of the Civil War mulattoes composed 13.2% of the black population. By 1890, however, 15.2% of the black population was mulatto, and indications were that their number was still growing. The figures seemed to confirm the theory that intelligence and fertility were inversely related. If encouraged by state toleration, the mulattoes would breed uncontrolled until they overran the country. In Shannon's view, mulattoes had lost their identity with any race; they had no culture and, as a result, no sense of social morality. Shannon concluded that "[t]hese figures are sufficient to warrant whatever discrimination may be found necessary in controlling the situation."[28]

In case the Supreme Court should think that this scientific justification of racism was a unique product of southern prejudice, Chevalier and Beckley also documented the existence of racial tension in the North. Racial prejudice, they found, had been growing in northern cities at an alarming rate since the Civil War. They relied on a remarkable study by Frank U. Quillin, a sociologist who in 1913 published a survey of racial prejudice in several Ohio cities. Quillin concluded that northern racial prejudice was much stronger in 1910 than it had been in 1865. Further, racial tensions seemed to grow as the proportion of blacks in an area increased. Quillin concluded that blacks in Ohio were economically worse off than blacks in the South; Ohio was much more heavily industrialized and unionized, but virtually every northern trade union excluded blacks from membership. In time northern racial attitudes would be no different from attitudes in the South, and then "the Negro problem" would take on national dimensions.[29]

The Supreme Court found the racial zoning statutes unconstitutional.[30] The Court based its decision on a rationale different from that which the social science data were intended to suggest. It expressly refused to hold that racial zoning was invalidated by any special protection that the fourteenth amendment gave to blacks. Rather, a unanimous Court held that the constitutionally protected right to own property "includes the right to acquire, use, and dispose of it."[31] This was a property case, not a race case, and Buchanan's right to sell his property to whomever he pleased had been unconstitutionally abridged: "The right which the ordinance annulled was the civil right of a white man to dispose of his property . . . to a person of color, and of a colored person to make such disposition to a white person."[32]

Notes

1. Brief for Defendant in Error, *Muller v. Oregon*, 208 U.S. 412 (1908), *reprinted in* 16 Land-mark Briefs and Arguments of the Supreme Court of the United States: Constitutional Law 63 (1975).

2. 211 U.S. 45 (1908).

3. 208 U.S. 412 (1908).

4. Kentucky, Maryland, Delaware, and Missouri.

5. Act of Mar. 22, 1904, ch. 85, 1904 Ky. Acts 181.

6. *See Plessy v. Ferguson*, 163 U.S. 537, 544 (1896).

7. *Berea College v. Commonwealth*, 123 Ky. 209, 221, 94 S.W. 623, 626 (1906), *aff'd*, 211 U.S. 45 (1908). Kentucky's stated public purpose in passing the statute, as well as other segregation laws, was to preserve race identity, to maintain the purity of blood, and to prevent amalgamation of races. *Berea College v. Kentucky*, 211 U.S. 45, 51 (1908).

8. *Berea College*, 123 Ky. at 221, 94 S.W. at 626.

9. *Id.* at 225–26, 94 S.W. at 628.

10. *Id.* at 222, 94 S.W. at 626.

11. *Id.* at 226, 94 S.W. at 628.

12. *See* Brief for Defendant in Error at 40, *Berea College v. Kentucky*, 211 U.S. 45 (1908).

13. Morton, *Observations on the Size of the Brain in Various Races and Families of Man*, 5 Proc. Acad. Nat. Sci. Philadelphia 1, 30–33 (1850); *see generally* S. Morton, Crania Aegyptica: Or, Observations on Egyptian Ethnography Derived from Anatomy, History and the Monuments (1854).

14. Brief for Defendant in Error at 40, *Berea College v. Kentucky*, 211 U.S. 45 (1908).

15. *Id.*

16. *Berea College v. Commonwealth*, 123 Ky. 209, 222, 94 S.W. 623, 626 (1906), *aff'd*, 211 U.S. 45 (1908).

17. Charge to Grand Jury — The Civil Rights Act, 30 F. Cas. 999, 1000 (C.C.W.D.N.C. 1875) (No. 18,258).

18. *The Civil Rights Cases*, 109 U.S. 3, 10–19 (1883).

19. L. Morgan, Ancient Society 553 (1877).

20. Shaler, *Our Negro Types*, 29 Current Lit. 47 (1900) (mulattoes are "general[ly] of feeble vitality, rarely surviving beyond middle age").

21. *Pace v. Alabama*, 106 U.S. 583, 585 (1882).

22. *Buchanan v. Warley*, 245 U.S. 60, 70–71 (1917).

23. *See Harris v. City of Louisville*, 165 Ky. 559, 571, 177 S.W. 472, 477 (1915) (citing Berea College v. Commonwealth, 123 Ky. 209 (1906), *aff'd*, 211 U.S. 45 (1908)).

24. *See* Supplemental and Reply Brief for Defendant in Error on Rehearing at 123, *Buchanan v. Warley*, 245 U.S. 60 (1917).

25. W. Smith, The Color Line: A Brief in Behalf of the Unborn 81 (1905).

26. *See* B. Gould, Investigations in the Military and Anthropological Statistics of American Soldiers 471 (1869).

27. Bryce, *Thoughts on the Negro Problem*, 153 N. Am. Rev. 641, 643–44, 647 (1891).

28. A. Shannon, Racial Integrity and Other Features of the Negro Problem 16–95 (1907).

29. *See* Supplemental and Reply Brief, *supra* at 182–98 (*quoting* F. Quillin, The Color Line in Ohio: A History of Race Prejudice in a Typical Northern State 1–11, 125–65 (1913)).

30. *Buchanan v. Warley*, 245 U.S. 60, 82 (1917).

31. *Id.* at 74.

32. *Id.* at 81. In 1926 the Supreme Court unanimously ruled that private restrictive covenants in deeds, by which persons agreed when they purchased property that they would not resell to blacks, raised no fourteenth amendment issues nor any other federal questions. For the following twenty years property developers and owners were therefore free to do by private agreement what states could not do by statute. *See Corrigan v. Buckley*, 271 U.S. 323, 330 (1926) (suit to enjoin conveyance of real estate dismissed for lack of jurisdiction), *distinguished in Shelley v. Kraemer*, 334 U.S. 1, 8–9, 13 (1948).

33

Mexican-Americans and Whiteness

GEORGE A. MARTINEZ

During slavery, the racial divide between black and white became a line of protection from the threat of commodification: whiteness protected one against being an object of property. Even after slavery ended, the status of being white continued to be a valuable asset, carrying with it a set of assumptions, privileges and benefits. Given this, it is hardly surprising that minorities have often sought to "pass" as white—i.e., present themselves as white persons. They did so because they thought that becoming white insured greater economic, political and social security. Becoming white, they thought, meant gaining access to a panoply of public and private privileges, while it insured that one would avoid being the object of others' domination.

In light of the privileged status of whiteness, it is instructive to examine how legal actors—courts and others—constructed the race of Mexican-Americans.[1] In *Inland Steel Co. v. Barcelona*,[2] an Indiana appellate court addressed the question of whether Mexicans were white. The court noted that the *Encyclopaedia Britannica* stated that approximately one-fifth of the inhabitants of Mexico are whites, approximately two-fifths Indians and the balance made up of mixed bloods, blacks, Japanese and Chinese. Given this, the court held that a "Mexican" should not necessarily be found to be a white person.[3]

The Texas courts also considered the same question. In *In re Rodriguez*,[4] a Texas federal court addressed whether Mexicans were white for purposes of immigration. At that time, the federal naturalization laws required that an alien be white in order to become a citizen of the United States. The court stated that Mexicans would probably be considered non-white from an anthropological perspective,[5] but went on to note that the United States had entered into certain treaties with Mexico. Those treaties expressly allowed Mexicans to become citizens of the United States. Thus, the court held that Congress must have intended that Mexicans were white within the meaning of the naturalization laws. *In re Rodriguez* reveals how racial categories can be constructed through the political process. Through the give and take of treaty making, Mexicans became "white."

Other cases show how politics operated to turn persons of mixed blood into whites or the opposite. In immigration cases, mixed race applicants often failed to establish their whiteness. For example, in *In re Camille*,[6] the court held that the son of a white Canadian father and an Indian mother was non-white, and therefore was denied the right of naturalization. Similarly, in *In re Young*,[7] the son of a German father and a Japanese mother was not a white person within the meaning of the immigration laws.[8] If these cases stand

for the proposition that mixed race persons were not white, Mexicans—a mixture of Spanish and Indian—should not have counted as white. The treaties nevertheless operated to
turn them into whites.

The issue of the race of Mexican-Americans also arose in connection with school segregation. In *Independent School District v. Salvatierra*,[9] plaintiffs sought to enjoin segregation of Mexican-Americans in the city of Del Rio, Texas. There, the court treated Mexican-Americans as white, holding that Mexican-Americans could not be segregated from
children of "other white races, merely or solely because they are Mexicans."[10] Significantly, the court did permit segregation of Mexican-Americans on the basis of linguistic
difficulties and migrant farming patterns.

Mexican-American jury participation and exclusion also show how the race of Mexican-
Americans is constructed. For example, in *Hernandez v. State*, a Mexican-American had
been convicted of murder. He sought to reverse his conviction on the ground that Mexican-Americans had been excluded from the grand jury and the petit jury. He relied on cases
holding that exclusion of blacks from jury service violated due process and equal protection. The court recognized only two classes as falling within the guarantee of the Fourteenth Amendment: the white race and the black race. It went on to hold that Mexican-
Americans are white for purposes of the Fourteenth Amendment. The court reasoned that
to say that the members of the various groups comprising the white race must be represented on grand and petit juries would destroy the jury system.[11] Since the juries that indicted and convicted the defendant were composed of members of his race—white persons—he had not been denied the equal protection of the laws.[12]

Federal agencies also constructed the race of Mexican-Americans. The federal govern-
ment has long compiled census data on persons of Mexican descent. In 1930, the Census
Bureau made the first effort to identify Mexican-Americans. The Bureau used the term
"Mexican" to classify Mexican-Americans, placing it under the rubric of "other races,"
which also included Indians, Blacks and Asians. According to this definition, Mexican-
Americans were not considered "whites." Interestingly, the Mexican government and the
United States Department of State both objected to the 1930 census definition of Mexican.
Thus, in the 1950 census Mexican-Americans were classified as "whites."[13] The Census
Bureau experience is significant in that it presents another example of how politics have
influenced the construction of a race. The Office of Management and Budget (OMB) has
set forth the current federal law of racial classification. In particular, Statistical Directive
No. 15, which governs the collection of federal statistics regarding the implementation of
a number of civil rights laws,[14] classifies Mexican-Americans as white.

White identity traditionally has served as a source of privilege and protection. Since
the law usually recognized Mexican-Americans as white, one might have expected that
social action would have reflected the Mexican-American's privileged legal status as
white. That, however, was not the case. Legal recognition of the Mexican-American as
white had only a slight impact on conduct. Far from having a privileged status, Mexican-
Americans faced discrimination very similar to that experienced by African-Americans.
Excluded from public facilities and neighborhoods and the targets of racial slurs, Mexican-
Americans typically lived in one section of town because they were not permitted to rent
or own property anywhere except in the "Mexican Colony."[15] Segregated in public schools,
Mexican-Americans also faced significant discrimination in employment. Mexican-
Americans were earmarked for exclusive employment in the lowest brackets of employ-
ment and paid less than Anglo-Americans for the same jobs.[16] Moreover, law enforce-

ment officials have committed widespread discrimination against Mexican-Americans, arresting them on pretexts and meting out harassment and penalties disproportionately severe compared to those imposed on Anglos for the same acts.[17] In all these respects actual social behavior failed to reflect the legal norms that defined Mexican-Americans as white. Although white as a matter of law, that law failed to provide Mexican-Americans with a privileged status.

The legal construction of Mexican-Americans as white thus stands as an irony—thoroughly at odds with the colonial discourses that developed in the American Southwest. As happened in other regions of the world the colonizers engaged in epistemic violence—i.e., produced modes of knowing that enabled and rationalized colonial domination from the standpoint of the West.[18]

In sharp contrast to their legal construction as white, writers and other Anglo opinion makers plainly construed Mexican-Americans as irreducibly Other. The historian David Weber writes:

> Anglo Americans found an additional element to despise in Mexicans: racial mixture. American visitors to the Mexican frontier were nearly unanimous in commenting on the dark skin of Mexican mestizos, who, it was generally agreed, had inherited the worst qualities of Spaniards and Indians to produce a 'race' still more despicable than that of either parent.[19]

Similarly, another commentator described how Anglo Americans drew a racial distinction between themselves and Mexican-Americans:

> Racial myths about Mexicans appeared as soon as Mexicans began to meet Anglo American settlers in the early nineteenth century. The differences in attitudes, temperament and behavior were supposed to be genetic. It is hard now to imagine the normal Mexican mixture of Spanish and Indian as constituting a distinct 'race,' but the Anglo Americans of the Southwest defined it as such.[20]

Likewise, the dean of Texas historians, Walter Prescott Webb, wrote:

> Without disparagement it may be said that there is a cruel streak in the Mexican nature, or so the history of Texas would lead one to believe. This cruelty may be a heritage from the Spanish of the Inquisition; it may and doubtless should be attributed partly to the Indian blood.[21]

Through this discourse on the Mexican-American, Anglo Americans also reformulated their white selves. Anglo judges, as we have seen, did the same, ruling that Mexicans were co-whites when this suited the dominant group—and non-white when necessary to protect Anglo privilege and supremacy.

Notes

1. Gary A. Greenfield & Don B. Kates, Jr., *Mexican-Americans, Racial Discrimination, and the Civil Rights Act of 1866*, 63 Cal. L. Rev. 662 (1975). Greenfield and Kates analyze the race of Mexican-Americans for purposes of the Civil Rights Act of 1866 and discuss some of the legal materials mentioned in this section. They, however, do not analyze the race of Mexican-Americans through the lens of social construction or critical theory—this essay seeks to do so.

2. 39 N.E.2d 800 (Ind. 1942).

3. *Id.* at 801.

4. 81 F. 337 (W.D. Tex. 1897).

5. *Id.* at 349.

6. 6 F. 256 (1880).

7. 198 F. 715 (1912).

8. *Id.* at 716–717. The court observed:

In the abstractions of higher mathematics, it may be plausibly said that the half of infinity is equal to the whole of infinity; but in the case of such a concrete thing as the person of a human being it cannot be said that one who is half white and half brown or yellow is a white person, as commonly understood.

198 at 717.

9. 33 S.W.2d 790 (Tex.Civ.App. 1930). *Salvatierra* was the first case to decide the issue of whether segregation of Mexican-Americans in public schools was permissible.

10. *Id.* at 795.

11. 251 S.W.2d 531, 532, 535 (Tex. 1952).

12. *Id.* at 536. In *Sanchez v. State*, 243 S.W.2d 700 (1951), a Mexican-American had been convicted of murder. He sought to challenge his conviction on the ground that his due process rights had been violated because the county had discriminated against Mexican-Americans in the selection of grand jurors. The Texas court held that Mexican-Americans are not a separate race, but are white people of Spanish descent. 243 S.W.2d at 701. Thus, the defendant's rights were not violated because whites were not excluded from the grand juries.

13. LEO GREBLER, JOAN W. MOORE & RALPH C. GUZMAN, THE MEXICAN-AMERICAN PEOPLE 601–02 (1970).

14. Directive No. 15, Race and Ethnic Standards for Federal Statistics and Administrative Reporting, 43 Fed. Reg. 19,260, 19,269 (Off. Mgmt. & Budget 1978).

15. P. KIBBE, LATIN AMERICANS IN TEXAS 123–24 (1946).

16. C. MCWILLIAMS, NORTH FROM MEXICO 167, 215–16 (1948); KIBBE, *supra* at 157.

17. U.S. COMM'N ON CIVIL RIGHTS, MEXICAN AMERICANS AND THE ADMINISTRATION OF JUSTICE IN THE SOUTHWEST (SUMMARY) 2 (1970).

18. RUTH FRANKENBERG, WHITE WOMEN, RACE MATTERS: THE SOCIAL CONSTRUCTION OF WHITENESS 16–17 (1993). See also ROBERT YOUNG, WHITE MYTHOLOGIES: WRITING HISTORY AND THE WEST 127, 158, 173 (1990); EDWARD W. SAID, ORIENTALISM 228 (1978).

19. FOREIGNERS IN THEIR NATIVE LAND: HISTORICAL ROOTS OF THE MEXICAN AMERICANS 59–60 (David J. Weber ed., 1973).

20. J. MOORE, MEXICAN AMERICANS 1 (1970). *See also* RODOLFO ACUÑA, OCCUPIED AMERICA: THE CHICANO'S STRUGGLE TOWARD LIBERATION (1972) at 7.

21. WALTER PRESCOTT WEBB, THE TEXAS RANGERS: A CENTURY OF FRONTIER DEFENSE xv (1965).

34

Race and the Core Curriculum in Legal Education

FRANCES LEE ANSLEY

[Professor Ansley taught the following material in a law school course. Ed.]

Race and the Constitution

It hardly needs saying that the Constitution represents contested and bloody ground. The celebration of the Constitution's bicentennial brought on a great debate about race and the Constitution. No doubt scholars of differing persuasions would have raised the race question during the bicentennial in any event, but a highly publicized speech by Justice Thurgood Marshall underscored the question in a dramatic fashion and provoked additional responses. Justice Marshall wrote:

> The focus of this celebration invites a complacent belief that the vision of those who debated and compromised in Philadelphia yielded the "more perfect Union" it is said we now enjoy.
>
> I cannot accept this invitation, for I do not believe that the meaning of the Constitution was forever "fixed" at the Philadelphia Convention. Nor do I find the wisdom, foresight, and sense of justice exhibited by the framers particularly profound. To the contrary, the government they devised was defective from the start, requiring several amendments, a civil war, and momentous social transformation to attain the system of constitutional government, and its respect for the individual freedoms and human rights, that we hold as fundamental today.[1]

Those in sympathy with Justice Marshall's sentiments rejoiced at his ringing words. Critics, on the other hand, accused Marshall of "blaming" the founders for "act[ing] immorally," of having made a "virulent" attack on the framers.[2] One author argued that Marshall had "bewilderingly given *Dred Scott* new life" by accepting the Court's representation of the framers' beliefs and instructed the justice to "give up the effort to revive this foul-smelling corpse."[3] The Washington Legal Foundation called for Marshall's resignation because his remarks displayed a "deepseated bitterness and dislike that impair his capacity."[4] William Bradford Reynolds, then Assistant Attorney General of the United States, stated that Marshall was "absolutely right to remind us" of "the most tragic aspects of the American experience" but expressed grave concern that the substance of Marshall's analysis was to consign the original unreconstructed Constitution "to the dustbin of history." In Reynolds' view such a move would itself be tragic because "[n]otwithstanding its very serious flaws, the Constitution in its original form constituted the greatest advance for human liberty in the entire history of mankind, then or since."[5]

After a brief sociolegal introduction to the institution of slavery, we began to explore the drafting of the Constitution with respect to slavery, what one author has called "the witch at the christening."[6] We looked first at the Declaration of Independence, a comfortably familiar document, but went on to read about a less well-known episode in the Declaration's history. When Thomas Jefferson first drafted the Declaration of Independence, he included a passage that was highly critical of George III for sanctioning the slave trade. However, the passage was eventually purged from the document.

The Constitution of 1787 is a monument to silence on the slavery question. Although the reality of eighteenth-century chattel slavery is built into the structure of the Constitution of 1787, the word "slavery" never appears in the document. It is quite possible for an uninformed twentieth-century reader to scan the entire 1787 Constitution with moderate care and never realize that slavery was an issue for the framers, let alone that the Constitution embodied a series of conscious and momentous decisions on the slavery question for the nascent republic.

In the three-fifths clause, "free Persons, including those bound to Service for a Term of Years, and excluding Indians not taxed" were counted for purposes of determining a state's representation in the House of Representatives (and for purposes of apportionment of direct taxes), while only three-fifths of "all other persons" were to be counted.[7] The "other persons" were slaves. This provision most often appears in contemporary popular rhetoric as proof that slaves were devalued by the Constitution of 1787 because each was counted as only three-fifths of a person—less than a full human being. Though the substance of the rhetorical point is well taken, nevertheless, the more each slave counted, the better for the perpetuation of slavery. Antislavery forces wanted slaves to count for nothing. Slaves, after all, would not vote or otherwise exercise political power. Therefore, each enslaved African-American who "counted" for anything simply helped to increase the representation of slaveholding states, in effect increasing the political clout of his or her master and tipping the balance of power in the Congress more toward the proslavery forces.

The slave trade clause forbade Congress to outlaw the slave trade until 1808.[8] Given the history of the issue, proponents of the trade had reason to fear federal action. Abolitionist forces had attacked the international slave trade early on as one of the most vulnerable components in the then-existing infrastructure of slavery, and this trade was subjected to restrictive regulation in various states, both North and South, from colonial times onward. Even some who supported slavery found it possible to condemn the international trade. The slave trade clause of the Constitution of 1787 ensured the trade continued until 1808, and article V put any shortening of that guaranteed time beyond all amendment.[9]

The fugitive slave clause required free states to recognize escaped slaves as the legal property of their owners and required them to return such fugitives into bondage.[10] It was this clause that eventually generated much of the abolitionist heat preceding the Civil War. Various other provisions of the 1787 Constitution related directly or indirectly to slavery, and constitutional scholars have proposed numerous ways to categorize and elucidate them. Other clauses frequently mentioned include those pertaining to the use of the militia to suppress insurrections, prohibition on export taxes, and the requirement that constitutional amendments could only be proposed by a two-thirds supermajority of Congress or of petitioning states. In class we looked at all these provisions. After listing and decoding them, however, we were faced with the more difficult task of evaluating and interpreting. What do these provisions mean? Why should anyone care about these arcane and coded messages now that the thirteenth amendment is the law of the land?

I introduced Thurgood Marshall's bicentennial speech, his act of interpretation. I also introduced the observations of Don Fehrenbacher, who views the Constitution of 1787 as a compromise that contained both proslavery and antislavery provisions but which at bottom "dealt only minimally and peripherally with slavery and was essentially open-ended on the subject."[11]

We began grappling with our varying and sometimes diametrically opposed reactions to the slavery compromise; students displayed a wide range of opinions. [The following statements are reactions by the students in Professor Ansley's class. Ed.]

> Of the readings that we have done, the ones that have surprised me the most are those that dealt with how the founding fathers dealt with the issue of slavery. I had never thought about how the framers had wrestled with this problem.

> I just wanted to say that I have never had a black professor in the seventeen years of my continuing education. It was not until this class that the Constitution and its Framers had ever been presented to me as anything but perfect, ingenious, and insightful. I am glad that I now know the Constitution has its flaws. . . . I'm shocked that this has never been pointed out to me before. Growing up within the inner circle, and being educated there—it's like a select existence which doesn't want to face the realities of those on the fringe. I feel lucky to be moving, although slowly, outward.

> I am a thirty-five year old, white, Anglo-Saxon Protestant. . . . I was born and raised . . . in the Northeast. I attended high school with a black population of some 80%. I was a minority. When racial violence struck Detroit, Newark, and many other cities in the 1960's, it struck my town as well. I have witnessed first-hand a black person get beaten up solely because he was black, and I have seen white persons get beaten simply because they were white. I know from experience that hatred exists in both white and black men. I have heard words spoken to the effect that the white man owes the black man something because of a thing called slavery. In response to those words I have always felt that the point was moot. I believed that what happened . . . should be forgotten, that it was a dead issue and not relevant in twentieth century America. I think I may have been mistaken.

> Unqualified praise of the Constitution's framers should cause uneasiness. That seems reasonable. Thurgood Marshall's apparent outrage (especially if it reflects shock on his part at the framers' duality of mindset and purpose) seems less so and is perhaps a bit disingenuous. The seeming (and at times, quite real) hypocrisy of politicians has long been recognized. . . .

> . . . The Constitution was an attempt to create a flexible framework for rational government in the context of a world filled with regimes exercising arbitrary power. . . . It indeed represented the naked self-interest of the white men who drafted and signed it. But it also represented an enlightened self-interest. It allowed for change at a later date and therein lies the "morality" of this or any such document.

> In all truthfulness, Marshall's speech angered me as I read it. However, I tried to put myself in "his shoes," but it is a viewpoint I have never had to experience. I never thought a July 4th celebration or a celebration for our Constitution would arouse such ill-feelings.

I know this probably sounds like "rose colored glasses" stuff, but I truly believe all persons are created equal. And even if the Framers of the Constitution were not sure who they meant when they used a similar phrase, I am.

Some students viewed the problem as one of inadequate information. Many thought that the framers simply had no way of knowing the evils that would result from slavery and had not been exposed to our now widely shared modern sensibilities on the subject of racial justice. Those who focused on economic realities drew radically different conclusions. Some expressed the view that the accommodation of slavery was "just economics," and therefore somehow had no real racial or moral dimension, while others thought that the economic motive made the moral dissonance all the more intense. Some perceived the basic question to be whether the framers, and the document they created, were "good" or "bad." Others were more willing to entertain the idea of an openly ambivalent response. Questions about the existence, meaning, and discoverability of original intent became unavoidable as we explored the motives and statements of various founders and studied their debates. The question of intent and its meaning led us to consider other possible values that might guide us in the process of constitutional interpretation.

We then turned to the heated debate that took place over a hundred years ago among abolitionists as to whether the 1787 Constitution was proslavery or antislavery. The Garrisonian wing of the abolitionist movement concluded that the Constitution was irretrievably proslavery and should be repudiated, by means of "disunion" if necessary. Another group preached that the Constitution permitted and even mandated immediate abolition of slavery. Others, including eventually Frederick Douglass, conceded that the Constitution did not mandate abolition but argued that there were antislavery features in the constitutional text itself that could provide a basis for antislavery politics and eventual victory within the union. Then as now, these disagreements about the framers generated much heat because they were seen as relevant to contemporaneous controversies that bitterly divided the public.

[The following are anonymous student comments on Professor Ansley's course. Ed.]

This has been one of the very few classes here that has stimulated independent thinking for me.

The class was simply a forum for blacks to vent their anger. White students' comments were passed over many times . . . or countered angrily or laughingly by black students. . . . [M]any whites felt they couldn't speak because the blacks would become so offended and angry. This class simply increased the racial tension between the students—instead of educating the students to differing viewpoints.

On the whole, this was an interesting course and I think the professor has a true commitment to anti-discrimination. It must be risky to stand in front of a class and hear people's opinions that are racist and not respond, or even harder, to respond. Several times I found it almost impossible not to jump up and leave because comments were made that were blatantly racist and should have been nixed!

White students who have had little opportunity to think and talk about these issues may be experiencing high levels of anxiety and conflict. One of my white students told me her perspective on this:

I have become more comfortable with the overall subject matter that is explored in this class. Getting off the slavery issue is in no small way responsible for this more comfortable feeling. I didn't have to examine myself very deeply to understand why this is true. I didn't have to consider if I am a "closet racist."

I feel that the reason for this is that we are now getting into issues about which I do not feel totally alienated. I have never been black, therefore, I couldn't possibly know the feelings of those who are and who feel that their color has played a major role in keeping them from doing whatever they chose to do. I seemed to experience the most problems when I did try to put myself in the shoes of others and sometimes felt that somewhere, somehow, I should have done something to try to make the situation better. Then the old guilt feelings took over and eventually I would become angry with myself and probably with the people for which I had been concerned, and I would think, I didn't do these things, then why should I feel like I owe anything to anybody. What emerged here was a vicious cycle of ill feelings, sometimes directed at others and sometimes directed at myself. I wanted to literally let out a giant WHEW when we moved on.

Similarly, members of racial minorities in a predominantly white group discussing matters of race often feel in a bind that few white people have imagined. One of my black students told me about his feelings:

In all candor I chose to take this course by default. . . . I had little desire to take a class about discrimination offered by a school where my race (African-American) comprised a numerical minority.

It has been my experience that most white people are really not very interested in hearing about the problems that black people face in this country because of their blackness. The scenario is an all too familiar one. First, the subject is opened. Next comes a rush of well-travelled clichés in an attempt either to prove the absence of bigotry in the speaker, or to demonstrate a deep understanding of the problem. Finally, conclusory and transitional statements ease the conversation into another more worthy direction. Attempts to re-open discussion and show that bigotry wears many faces, sometimes including the face that stares out of the mirror, are met with pained expressions and impatience. . . . These interfaces, though typically low-key, invariably result in ulcer-like abdominal pain for the African-American.

My experience has been that most white people aren't really very interested in hearing about the travails of the African in America. As an African-American, however, it's difficult for me not to speak about relevant facts in our history. . . .

Most black people know that most white people aren't particularly interested in hearing about their struggles. As a result, soon after they apprehend this, they simply don't initiate conversation on the subject. No one, black or white, enjoys having something which they hold in great esteem minimized.

Notes

1. The precise event was the Annual Seminar of the San Francisco Patent and Trademark Law Association in Maui, Hawaii, on May 6, 1987. See Thurgood Marshall, *Commentary: Reflections on the Bicentennial of the United States Constitution*, 101 HARV. L. REV. 1 (1987); Thurgood Marshall, *The Constitution: A Living Document*, 30 How. L.J. 915 (1987) (symposium issue celebrating bicentennial).

2. Don Fehrenbacher, author of the 1978 book *The Dred Scott Case: Its Significance in American Law and Politics*, chose thus to characterize Justice Marshall's thesis in a bicentennial speech at

the University of Tennessee. Address by Don Fehrenbacher, University of Tennessee (Sept. 19, 1988).

3. Erik M. Jensen, *Commentary: The Extraordinary Revival of Dred Scott*, 66 WASH. U. L.Q. 1, 2, 10 (1988).

4. Ted Gest, *Justice Marshall's Minority Report*, 102 U.S. NEWS & WORLD REP., May 18, 1987, at 12.

5. William Bradford Reynolds, *Another View: Our Magnificent Constitution*, 40 VAND. L. REV. 1343, 1345, 1346 (1987).

6. *See* William M. Wiecek, *The Witch at the Christening: Slavery and the Constitution's Origins*, in THE FRAMING AND RATIFICATION OF THE CONSTITUTION 167 (Leonard W. Levy & Dennis J. Mahoney eds., 1987).

7. U.S. CONST. art. I, § 2, cl. 3.

8. *Id.* § 9, cl. 1. The clause reads: "The Migration or Importation of Such Persons as any of the States now existing shall think proper to admit, shall not be prohibited by the Congress prior to the Year one thousand eight hundred and eight. . . . "

9. U.S. CONST. art. V ("[N]o Amendment which may be made prior to the Year One thousand eight hundred and eight shall in any Manner affect the first and fourth Clauses in the Ninth Section of the first Article. . . . ").

10. *Id.* art. IV, § 2, cl. 2. The clause reads:

A Person charged in any State with Treason, Felony, or other Crime, who shall flee from Justice, and be found in another State, shall on Demand of the executive Authority of the State from which he fled, be delivered up, to be removed to the State having Jurisdiction of the Crime.

11. Fehrenbacher identified the two major antislavery provisions as (1) the territory clause, which he believes gave Congress the power to exclude slavery from the territories, and (2) the commerce clause, under which he believes Congress could regulate or abolish the slave trade after the slave trade clause expired in 1807. *See* Don E. Fehrenbacher, *Slavery, the Framers, and the Living Constitution*, in SLAVERY AND ITS CONSEQUENCES 1, 13 (Robert A. Goldwin & Art Kaufman eds., 1988).

35

The Transparency Phenomenon, Race-Neutral Decisionmaking, and Discriminatory Intent

BARBARA J. FLAGG

In this society, the white person has an everyday option not to think of herself in racial terms at all. In fact, whites appear to pursue that option so habitually that it may be a defining characteristic of whiteness: to be white is not to think about it.[1] I label the tendency for whiteness to vanish from whites' self-perception the transparency phenomenon.[2] Because transparency is such a pervasive fact of whites' conceptualization of ourselves, we have reason to be skeptical of ostensibly race-neutral decisionmaking by white decisionmakers. I propose that white decisionmakers adopt that deliberate skepticism as well regarding their own criteria of decision.

The Transparency Phenomenon

On a recent trip to Washington, D.C., my life partner, who is white, was visiting a white friend and bringing her up to date on family events and activities. When she mentioned that I have been teaching a new course on Critical Race Theory, her friend appeared puzzled and surprised. "But," said the friend, "isn't she white?"[3]

White people externalize race. For most whites, most of the time, to think or speak about race is to think or speak about people of color, or perhaps, at times, to reflect on oneself (or other whites) in relation to people of color. But we tend not to think of ourselves or our racial group as racially distinctive. Whites' "consciousness" of whiteness is predominantly unconsciousness of whiteness. We perceive and interact with other whites as individuals who have no significant racial characteristics. In the same vein, the white person is unlikely to see or describe himself in racial terms, perhaps in part because his white peers do not regard him as racially distinctive. Whiteness is a transparent quality when whites interact with whites in the absence of people of color. Whiteness attains opacity, becomes apparent to the white mind, only in relation to, and contrast with, the "color" of nonwhites.[4]

I do not maintain that white people are oblivious to the race of other whites. As a powerful determinant of social status, race is always noticed, in a way that eye color, for example, is not. However, whites' social dominance allows us to relegate our own racial speci-

From "'Was Blind, but Now I See': White Race Consciousness and the Requirement of Discrimatory Intent," 91 Mich L. Rev. 953 (1993). Originally published in the *Michigan Law Review*. Reprinted by permission.

ficity to the realm of the subconscious. Whiteness is the racial norm. In this culture the black person, not the white, is the one who is different. Once an individual is identified as white, his distinctively racial characteristics need no longer be conceptualized in racial terms; he becomes effectively raceless in the eyes of other whites. Whiteness, once identified, fades almost instantaneously from white consciousness into transparency.

The best "evidence" for the pervasiveness of the transparency phenomenon will be the white reader's own experience: critically assessing our habitual ways of thinking about ourselves and about other white people should bring transparency into full view.[5] The questions that follow may provide some direction for the reader's reflections.

In what situations do you describe yourself as white? Would you be likely to include *white* on a list of three adjectives that describe you?[6] Do you think about your race as a factor in the way other whites treat you? For example, think about the last time some white clerk or salesperson treated you deferentially, or the last time the first taxi to come along stopped for you. Did you think, "That wouldn't have happened if I weren't white"? Are you conscious of yourself as white when you find yourself in a room occupied only by white people? What if there are people of color present? What if the room is mostly non-white?[7] Do you attribute your successes or failures in life to your whiteness? Do you reflect on the ways your educational and occupational opportunities have been enhanced by your whiteness? What about the life courses of others?

If your lover or spouse is white, how frequently do you reflect on that fact? Do you think of your white friends as your white friends, other than in contrast with your friends who are not white? Do you try to understand the ways your shared whiteness affects the interactions between yourself and your white partner, friends, and acquaintances? For example, perhaps you have become aware of the absence of people of color on some occasion. Did you move beyond that moment of recognition to consider how the group's uniform whiteness affected its interactions, agenda, process, or decisions? Do you inquire about the ways white persons you know have dealt with the fact, and privilege, of their whiteness?[8]

Imagine that I am describing to you a third individual who is not known to you. I say, for example, "She's good looking, but rather quiet," or "He's tall, dark, and handsome." If I do not specify the race of the person so described do you assume she or he is white?[9]

Race-Neutral Decisionmaking

Like most kids, I liked to color things with crayons. If you wanted to draw a person with Crayola crayons back then, you used the "Flesh" crayon, a pinkish color that is now labeled "Peach." You could also draw an Indian with one of the red colors, or use a shade of brown, but we knew those weren't really skin colors.[10]

Transparency casts doubt on the concept of race-neutral decisionmaking. Facially neutral criteria of decision formulated and applied by whites may be as vulnerable to the transparency phenomenon as is the race of white people itself. I suggest that whites should respond to the transparency phenomenon with a deliberate skepticism concerning race neutrality. At a minimum, transparency counsels that we not accept seemingly neutral criteria of decision at face value. Most whites live and work in settings that are wholly or predominantly white. Thus whites rely on primarily white referents in formulating the norms and expectations that become criteria of decision for white decisionmakers. Given whites' tendency not to be aware of whiteness, it's unlikely that white decisionmakers do not similarly misidentify as race-neutral personal characteristics, traits, and behaviors that are in fact closely associated with whiteness. The ways in which transparency might infect white decisionmaking are many and varied.

Three considerations, however, counsel against attempting to formulate a "rule" to distinguish transparent from authentically race-neutral criteria of decision. First, transparency is often difficult to recognize and analyze. Whites as a group lack the experiential foundation necessary even to begin to construct the analytic tools that would ground a comprehensive theory of transparency.

Second, transparency probably attaches more to word usages than to the words themselves. For example, *hostility* may not have a race-laden connotation in every instance in which a white decisionmaker employs it. The context of use—the combination of speaker, audience, decisionmaking process, and purpose—more likely supplies the racial content of the term *hostile* as applied. Thus, a general analysis of transparency might have to be, paradoxically, situation specific, with a concomitant exponential increase in the difficulty of the theoretical project.

Finally, the assumption that we can get better at identifying genuinely race-neutral decisionmaking presupposes that such a thing is possible. However, to repose any confidence in the concept of race neutrality is premature at best, because little supports it other than whites' subjective experience, itself subject to the transparency phenomenon. The available empirical evidence points in the opposite direction. Social scientists' work shows that race nearly always influences the outcomes of discretionary decisionmaking processes, including those in which the decisionmaker relies on criteria thought to be race-neutral. There is, of course, no conclusive evidence that no instances of genuine race neutrality exist, but neither is there conclusive evidence to the contrary. The pervasiveness of the transparency phenomenon militates against an unsupported faith by whites in the reality of race-neutral decisionmaking.

I recommend instead that whites adopt a deliberate and thoroughgoing skepticism regarding the race neutrality of facially neutral criteria of decision. This stance has the potential to improve the distribution across races of goods and power that whites currently control. In addition, skepticism may help to foster the development of an antiracist white racial identity that does not posit whites as superior to blacks.

Even when he looks for it, however, the white decisionmaker may not always be able to uncover the hidden racial content of the criteria he employs. In those instances, the skeptical stance may function to promote distributive justice in two different ways. First, the skeptical decisionmaker may opt to temper his judgment with a simultaneous acknowledgment of his uncertainty concerning nonobvious racial specificity. Second, white decisionmakers might choose to develop pluralistic criteria of decision as a guard against covert white specificity.

The skeptical stance may contribute to the development of a positive white racial identity by relativizing white norms. Even whites who do not harbor any conscious or unconscious belief in the superiority of white people participate in the maintenance of white supremacy whenever we impose white norms without acknowledging their whiteness. Any serious effort to dismantle white supremacy must include measures to dilute the effect of whites' dominant status, which carries with it the power to define as well as to decide. Because the skeptical stance prevents the unthinking imposition of white norms, it encourages white decisionmakers to consider adopting nonwhite ways of doing business, so that the formerly unquestioned white-specific criterion of decision becomes just one option among many. The skeptical stance thus can help develop a relativized white race consciousness, in which the white decisionmaker is conscious of the whiteness and contingency of white norms.

A Transparency-Conscious Look at the Discriminatory Intent Rule

In constitutional law, the threshold requirement in most of antidiscrimination law that the plaintiff prove discriminatory intent distinguishes between facially neutral but unconsciously race-specific white decisionmaking, on the one hand, and the deliberate use of race, whether overt or covert, on the other; only the latter is constitutionally impermissible. Relying on a distinction among discriminators' states of mind seems a curious strategy for implementing a colorblindness principle, because a racial criterion is equally present in either case. Indeed, the current rule appears more suited to drive the race specificity of white decisionmaking underground—out of whites' awareness—than to eradicate it altogether. However, the intent requirement might rest on either of two assumptions that, coupled with the perceived institutional costs of heightened scrutiny, provide ostensible justification for the decision to disapprove only the *purposeful* use of race in government decisionmaking. These foundational assumptions are, first, that unconsciously race-specific decisionmaking is relatively rare, or, second, that the conscious use of race as a factor in decisionmaking is more blameworthy than its unconscious use.

The transparency phenomenon counsels skepticism regarding the belief that truly race-neutral decisionmaking is the norm. In addition, the social science literature provides further evidence that unconscious race-specific decisionmaking is in fact relatively common, and the potential impact of transparency upon the research itself strengthens that conclusion.

The Court's decision [in *Washington v. Davis*, a major ruling that held that a plaintiff in a racial discrimination case must show that the defendant intended to discriminate against him or her on grounds of race. A mere showing that a defendant's *policy*—for example, insisting on a college diploma—has a disproportionate impact on minorities does not suffice. Ed.] to adopt a discriminatory intent rule that does not reach unconscious race-specific decisionmaking might rest on a belief that such discrimination does not commonly occur. Such a belief is, perhaps, the natural corollary of whites' widespread faith in the pervasiveness of race-neutrality. This faith views Klan and other overtly white supremacist attitudes as extreme, perhaps pathological, deviations from the norm of white racial thinking, as if those attitudes can be comprehended in complete isolation from the culture in which they are embedded. Similarly, whites tend to adopt the "things are getting better" story of race relations, which allows us to suppose that our unfortunate history of socially approved race discrimination is largely behind us. This white confidence in race neutrality might dictate that the law should treat the unconscious use of nonobviously race-specific criteria of decision as nothing more than the occasional deviation from the prevailing practice of race-neutral government decisionmaking. From this perspective, given that significant institutional costs are associated with judicial intervention, unconscious race specificity seems too rare to justify heightened review.

The transparency phenomenon provides two arguments against this view. At minimum, it counsels that we distrust any view that accepts race neutrality at face value, whether as a matter of fact or of frequency of occurrence. Second, transparency supports the stronger, affirmative argument that unconscious race-specific decisionmaking is so common that it is in fact the norm for white decisionmakers.

The belief that race-neutral decisionmaking is relatively common and unconsciously race-specific decisionmaking relatively uncommon stands analytically distinct from the belief that any particular instance of facially neutral decisionmaking is in fact what it seems. Even if the unconscious use of race were extremely rare, whites could still misperceive the true character of every one of the few instances in which race was a factor in the decision. Conversely, that whites frequently are unaware of the white-specific factors that may be used in white decisionmaking does not dictate one conclusion or another regarding the frequency with which such factors actually are employed. This analytic distinction notwithstanding, transparency counsels skepticism with respect to the frequency of race-neutral decisionmaking as well.

Because the transparency phenomenon creates a risk that whites will misapprehend the race-specific nature of apparently race-neutral decisionmaking, it simultaneously creates a risk that we will systematically underestimate the incidence of such decisionmaking. Each circumstance in which we fail to perceive accurately the racial content of our decisions contributes to the overall perception that race neutrality is the more common way of doing business. Thus, even though the conclusion that race specificity is the norm does not necessarily follow from transparency alone, we ought to adopt a healthy skepticism toward, rather than a blind faith in the pervasiveness of, race neutrality if we wish to be able more accurately to assess the role of race in white decisionmaking.[11]

Transparency also lends support to the stronger position that unconscious race-specific decisionmaking is so common that it is in fact the norm. This argument rests in part on an analysis of the outcomes of discretionary white decisionmaking. Numerous studies indicate that whites receive more favorable treatment than blacks in virtually every area of social interaction, including hiring and performance evaluations; mortgage lending, insurance redlining, and retail bargaining; psychiatric diagnoses; responses to patient violence in mental institutions; and virtually every stage in the criminal law process: arrest, the decision to charge, imprisonment, and capital sentencing.

Studies of the impact of race on white decisionmaking nearly always explain disparate race effects by focusing on negative assessments of, or undesirable outcomes for, nonwhites, rather than positive results for whites. That is, they adopt a conceptual framework in which unconscious race discrimination tends to be associated with bias or stereotyping rather than transparency. At the same time, each of the studies controls the data for race-neutral variables, so that the influence of race on the decisionmaking process can be assessed in isolation from other factors. The transparency phenomenon suggests that the selected independent variables may in fact be transparently white-specific. When they are, race effects, though different in kind from those conceptualized by the researchers, are present after all.

In sum, the social science literature indicates that race influences most white decisionmaking most of the time, and the researchers' own susceptibility to transparency suggests that unconscious discrimination may be even more prevalent than the studies acknowledge. It follows that faith in the commonality of race-neutral decisionmaking is a component of white race consciousness that lacks any solid empirical support.

Notes

1. *See* Robert W. Terry, *The Negative Impact on White Values*, in IMPACTS OF RACISM ON WHITE AMERICANS 119, 120 (Benjamin P. Bowser & Raymond G. Hunt eds., 1981) ("To be white in America is not to have to think about it.") (emphasis omitted); Judy H. Katz & Allen Ivey, *White Aware-*

ness: The Frontier of Racism Awareness Training, 55 PERSONNEL & GUIDANCE J. 485, 486 (1977) ("White people do not see themselves as white.") (emphasis omitted). Janet Helms concludes that "it appears that most Whites have no consistent conception of a positive White identity or consciousness. As a consequence, Whites may feel threatened by the actual or presupposed presence of racial consciousness in non-White racial groups." Janet E. Helms, *Toward a Model of White Racial Identity Development*, in BLACK AND WHITE RACIAL IDENTITY 50 (Janet E. Helms ed., 1990).

2. Any claim about whites as a group, like claims about nonwhite groups or about the category "women," raises potential concerns about essentialism. I suspect there is more homogeneity among whites' experience of transparency than there is among the experiences of whites or nonwhites regarding most other issues, but I do not ask the reader to accept this assertion on faith. Rather, I ask each white reader to verify in her own experience the claim that we tend to be unaware of whiteness.

3. This is a true story. For the reader who finds it distracting or irrelevant that I identify myself as lesbian in this story, I offer a brief explanation. In my view, though coming out as lesbian clearly plays a different role in the struggle against oppression than does the acquisition of self-consciousness of whiteness, each is crucial. Sexual orientation is no more irrelevant to personal identity than is race, or gender, or class.

4. *See* BELL HOOKS, YEARNING: RACE, GENDER, AND CULTURAL POLITICS 54 (1990).

5. Social scientists have studied what I call the transparency phenomenon, and some legal scholars have mentioned it as well. However, I do not rest my implicit claim that the transparency phenomenon is "real"—a better way of conceptualizing things—on the authority of social scientists or legal scholars, in part because they too must rely at bottom on the reported experience of white people. I believe we are more likely to take transparency seriously if we recognize it in our own lives than if our only acquaintance with it is third-hand "empirical" evidence.

6. Pat Cain reports that in her experience white women never include whiteness as one of the three adjectives. *See* Patricia A. Cain, *Feminist Jurisprudence: Grounding the Theories*, 4 BERKELEY WOMEN'S L.J. 191, 208 (1989–90).

7. Compare Justice Marshall's reflection: "[Y]ears ago, when I was a youngster, a Pullman porter told me that he had been in every city in this country . . . and he had never been in any city in the United States where he had to put his hand up in front of his face to find out he was Negro. I agree with him." Ruth Marcus, *Plain-Spoken Marshall Spars with Reporters*, WASH. POST, June 29, 1991, at A1, A10.

8. The transparency phenomenon appears across gender and class lines, though its manifestations may vary. Consider the last time a female sales clerk, secretary, or receptionist—someone you consider a functionary—behaved in a manner you found rude or discourteous. Did you attribute her behavior to race if she was black? If she was white?

9. I experienced an example of this phenomenon recently. My life partner and I purchased a house together, but I went alone to provide the necessary information and documents for the loan application; the loan officer was the one who actually filled out the application form. A space was provided at the bottom of the form for the applicants' race. Without asking any race-related questions about me or about my partner, whom he had never seen, the officer checked the designation "Caucasian" for each of us.

One social scientist was so confident of the presumption of whiteness that he incorporated it in his study design. White students were asked to compare a series of job candidates' résumés; researchers found it unnecessary to identify the race of the candidates described by these stimulus résumés. "Pilot testing had shown that white students in thesubject population assumed that résumés without pictures described white [candidates]." John B. McConahay, *Modern Racism and Modern Discrimination: The Effects of Race, Racial Attitudes, and Context on Simulated Hiring Decisions*, 9 PERSONALITY & SOC. PSYCHOL. BULL. 551, 553 (1983).

10. Crayola changed the "Flesh" label to "Peach" in 1962. Judith Newmark, *Solving Problem of Too Much Flesh*, ST. LOUIS POST-DISPATCH, Sept. 14, 1992, at D4. However, I don't mean by this

story to lend credence to the "things are getting better" conception of race relations. Even without the "Flesh" designation, I think most children, even if nonwhite, still would choose the same or a similar crayon if asked to pick out a skin color.

11. Accordingly, the Supreme Court ought not to rely on the perceived rarity of unconscious discrimination as a justification for the requirement of discriminatory intent. The transparency phenomenon suggests that if the Court desires to adopt the proposition that whites engage in race-neutral decisionmaking more often than not, it should do so only following a careful examination of the facts pertaining to the area of white decisionmaking under consideration. Because no such discussion appears in any Supreme Court disparate impact decision, to the extent the Court has employed this line of reasoning at all it seems to have done so on the basis of an unexamined faith in race neutrality, one that is unjustified from the perspective of transparency.

36

Toward a Black Legal Scholarship: Race and Original Understandings

JEROME McCRISTAL CULP, JR.

Initially, the law largely treated black slaves as non-beings.[1] Eventually, the law evolved into a paternalistic system that viewed blacks as lesser beings whom white masters and overseers needed to protect from their own ignorant, sloven, and evil nature. Finally, slave law provided for legal limitations on the activities of slaves and their masters; in other words, the state stepped between slaves and masters and imposed external rules.[2] Thus, slavery bequeathed three powerful constructions of law to legal interpretation—ignoring blacks altogether, treating blacks paternalistically, and creating limited legal rules to regulate white behavior toward blacks. The post-slavery period added a fourth powerful way of constructing race and law: The requirement that blacks, in participating in the legal environment, defer to the interests of the white majority. For this historical reason, American law continues to be unequal and separate with respect to the interests of blacks.

These four different ways of viewing black Americans are not simply an evolutionary progression: The law continues to embody all four elements in its interpretation of legal protections available to black Americans. In this sense, there is no past or future for the treatment of black citizens—instead there is only a mushy present that retains all of its past even as it alters the forms of black treatment.

In many ways, the legal process has come full circle. Black Americans, when they came to the United States, were ignored by the law. And judges, through the doctrine of color-blind neutrality, are again ignoring the concerns of blacks.

A recent example of this phenomenon is *Rankin v. McPherson*.[3] Ardith McPherson, a black woman, was working as a deputy constable. Ms. McPherson's position did not permit her to act as a licensed police officer. On the day that President Reagan was shot, she said to her boyfriend, who also was an employee of the constable's office, "[I]f they go for him [Reagan] again, I hope they get him." Ms. McPherson was fired from her job for making this statement and subsequently she sued to be reinstated.[4] The Supreme Court held that she was wrongfully fired because, given her job, the state's interest in dismissing an employee with such views did not outweigh the employee's first amendment interests. The most fascinating aspect of the case, however, is how the different justices dealt with Ms. McPherson's race.

Justice Marshall, who wrote the majority opinion, specifically mentioned that Ms. McPherson is black—a matter that neither Justice Powell nor Justice Scalia included in their opinions. Leaving race out of their opinions was not an accident. Both Justices Pow-

1991 Duke L.J. 39. Originally published in the *Duke Law Journal*. Reprinted by permission.

ell and Scalia believe that race is irrelevant—even when it is crucial to understanding the context that gives rise to a case. The law seems to take this color-blind approach most often when a color-conscious approach would lend perspective to the situation of a black participant in the legal process.

Why, then, does Justice Marshall mention that Ms. McPherson was black? The answer is clear from the perspective of the black experience. Much of the lives of black people are spent in anger over real and imagined slights by white landlords, supervisors, and bosses. In a country in which black perspectives are so out of line with those of the white majority,[5] our only power is to speak to ourselves. Justice Marshall often uses the dialect of black people—a voice that permits black people to criticize powerful people in a somewhat veiled fashion. Justice Marshall understood Ms. McPherson's comments in this light and he sought to infuse his opinion with a fact essential to the understanding of the context—Ms. McPherson's race.[6] Race matters to Justice Marshall just as it does not matter to his colleagues.

Judges do not always tell us when and for what purpose a fact is important, but the absence of race considerations in general is no accident; it reflects the judicial view that race is irrelevant to understanding the circumstances surrounding an incident, despite the fact that, in reality, race colors most situations in which whites and blacks interact. It is not simply that some white judges did not mention that Ms. McPherson was black. For those judges, that a party is black does not change the perspective from which any issue should be examined. However, because the world is implicitly examined from the perspective of the white majority, colorblindness actually discriminates. Justice Marshall understands that if the law is to be truly fair it must be in touch with the black experience.

Recent examples of the problem of white lack of awareness of racial involvement can be found in Justice Scalia's opinion in *Rankin*. Justice Scalia put the question in its clearest light at the very beginning of his dissenting opinion. He stated:

> I agree with the proposition, felicitously put by Constable Rankin's counsel, that no law enforcement agency is required by the First Amendment to permit one of its employees to "ride with the cops and cheer for the robbers. . . ." The issue in this case is whether Constable Rankin, a law enforcement official, is prohibited by the First Amendment from preventing his employees from saying of the attempted assassination of President Reagan—*on the job and within hearing of other employees*—"If they go for him again, I hope they get him."[7]

Why does Justice Scalia find it important that Ms. McPherson was on the job? Arguably, Ms. McPherson was not on the job but on her lunch break when she made the statement—and it was made in a way that makes it clear that Ms. McPherson did not intend for it to be "within the hearing of other employees." Why then does Justice Scalia reach out to find facts that are not there in order to make his case stronger?

A careful reading of Justice Scalia's dissenting opinion suggests that race is the determining factor in shaping how he perceives this case. The real reason he is concerned about the statement has nothing to do with the morale of the police force. Justice Scalia's real concern is that Ms. McPherson has overstepped the permissible bounds of her right to be black—by which I mean the right to take personally the political statements made by a white politician that seemed directed at black people.

It is important to realize that the vast majority of black Americans understand the statement of Ms. McPherson only as a part of the hyperbole to which black anger is limited in the United States. She did not mean for these statements, which were directed to her black fiancé, to be overheard by her white colleagues. It is also important to understand that black people speak more than one language, and the language at home is often angry and always different from the common language spoken in public.

Justice Marshall alone acknowledged this possibility in the majority opinion, yet he stopped short of an explicitly race-conscious perspective in *Rankin*. Instead, Marshall concluded:

> McPherson's employment-related interaction with the constable was apparently negligible. Her duties were clearly clerical and were limited solely to the civil process function of the Constable's office. There is no indication that she would ever be in a position to further—or indeed to have any involvement with—the minimal law enforcement activity engaged in by the Constable's office. Given the function of the agency, McPherson's position in the office, and the nature of her statement, we are not persuaded that Rankin's interest in discharging her outweighed her rights under the First Amendment.[8]

Justice Marshall's opinion focused on the nature of Ms. McPherson's job, concluding that her comment was so unimportant that the Court need not look at how much protection the first amendment provides for her statements. However, Marshall just as easily could have focused on the statements themselves, concluding that since they were insubstantial and not personal they were protected by the First Amendment, leaving for another day whether some statements made by some officers would amount to such a direct threat to the interests of an employer that those interests would have to be balanced against first amendment concerns. Justice Marshall's opinion urges judges to look at the status of employees in evaluating the protection given their speech. The Court's approach provided the most limited protection that could have been granted to black employees without permitting their discharge.

The Court implicitly, and Justice Scalia explicitly, asks black employees to subordinate their concerns to the conventional views of the white majority—if their employment status is sufficiently powerful to warrant such conformity. The concession only eliminates a small part of the possible discourse of black people—but the impact of that change is substantial for how black people react to employment. Black anger nonthreateningly addressed toward employers or other whites is now seen as a legitimate rationale for discipline and discharge. The growing number of cases that charge employers in racial discrimination cases with retaliation is stark evidence of this fact.

A similar issue of ignoring the concerns of blacks appears in the Supreme Court's most important recent examination of the death penalty and race. In *McCleskey v. Kemp*,[9] Justice Powell stated that the fact that blacks are executed more frequently than whites, and were executed at statistical rates several times greater when they kill whites than when they kill blacks or when whites kill other whites, does not call into question the basic fairness of the criminal justice system.

Race is viewed as irrelevant by the five-justice majority in *McCleskey*. They ignore black concerns—concerns that are considered irrelevant to the fairness of the death penalty. The Court argued that to accept any other approach would lead to a slippery slope from which the death penalty system would not be able to escape. The Supreme Court thus permitted the states to assume that black people do not have a right to be treated equally as long as the system seems fair to white victims. From the perspective of white victims, it is fair to hold black criminals to a higher and different standard. Being a black victim or a black perpetrator of crimes against black people does not count as heavily. Race plays a part in the sentencing of criminals everywhere in this country because race matters to the participants in the system, both black and white. The problem for black people is that white people use the imposition of the death penalty to keep black people in their place. This use is an improper one, and as Justice Brennan suggests, it is up to the state to provide a nonracist method of imposing the death penalty.

Notes

1. The Constitution referred to black slaves as "other persons." U.S. Const., art 1, § 2, cl. 3.

2. *See, e.g.*, Barbara Jeanne Fields, Slavery and Freedom on the Middle Ground 23–62 (1985).

3. 483 U.S. 378 (1987).

4. *Id.* at 380–82.

5. For example, in 1984, 63% of whites and only 11% of blacks voted for Ronald Reagan. *See* ABC News Exit Poll cited in Paul Light & Celinda Lake, *The Election: Candidates, Strategies, and Decisions*, in The Elections of 1984, at 106 (Michael Nelson ed., 1985).

6. *Rankin*, 483 U.S. at 382–86.

7. *Id.* at 394 (Scalia, J., dissenting).

8. *Id.* at 378, 392 (1986).

9. 481 U.S. 279 (1987).

37

Identity Notes, Part One:
Playing in the Light

ADRIENNE D. DAVIS

"What parts do the invention and development of whiteness play in the construction of what is loosely described as 'American'"?[1] And how does *binarism* affect law and legal study? ["Binarism" refers to the socially constructed, dualistic black/white paradigm of race, which is dominant in Western culture today. Ed.] The paradigm *appears* internally neutral, as though blacks and whites were equally situated within it. Yet the cases discussed below suggest that a primary motivation in the crafting of the American racial architecture may not have been a pure desire to have a taxonomy for classifying races, but to define and protect white identity.

This search for white identity has been documented by Nobel laureate Toni Morrison. She argues that whiteness as a discrete concept remains largely unexamined in American culture. Her readings of classic nineteenth-century literature indicate that whiteness became defined by its opposite: color, and more specifically, blackness.[2] In my seminars on race and law, I routinely ask the students to define "black culture." A variety of attributions pour out: emotion and soul, instinct and intuition, violence and passion, drive and pride, spirituality and strength. Yet when I ask for the attributes of "white culture" the students are stumped, sometimes disturbed. I have yet to have a student attach a meaning that does not refer to a more specific class-based or ethnic culture rather than a more broadranging racial culture of whiteness.

I emphasize the void around whiteness to illustrate the embeddedness of polarizing logic in the American racial paradigm. Other racial groups form their identity around shared cultural norms, common histories of immigration, mythologized homelands, or racial oppression. Non-Hispanic white American identity appears to be formed solely around the experience of being not black, Asian, or Latino/a. White Americans do not appear to have a sense of racial identity that is not linked to ethnicity or class, unless juxtaposing themselves against blacks, Asian Americans, or sometimes Latinos/as.[3] Hence, the social and legal construction of colored identities is critical to the maintenance of white identity. It is against this backdrop that I will examine two cases in which non-black groups of color negotiated the black/white paradigm in efforts to secure their own civil rights. The appearance of whiteness as an organizing legal principle becomes critical in understanding the maintenance of contradictory rules of law and race.

43 Am. U. L. Rev. 695 (1996). Originally published in the *American University Law Review*. Reprinted by permission.

Yearning to Be Free

One significant question in both cases is who will define and assign racial labels. This power of assigning race suggests a larger question about the role of white identity in these cases. In Virginia in 1806, two enslaved women, Hannah and her daughter, asserted their freedom against the man who claimed them as his slaves.[4] Prior to reaching the issue of their status, the court had to decide which party, the alleged slave or claiming master, bore the burden of proof. The political economy of slavery, including the requisite legal regime, sharply restricted the capacity of any black to participate in the production, use, and circulation of texts, especially any that would satisfy legal evidentiary standards. Hence, the designation of alleged slaves as the party with the burden of producing documents would deny to many of them a legal remedy of freedom for illegal enslavement.

In *Hudgins v. Wrights*, the Virginia Supreme Court considered the servitude status of Native Americans. Native Americans were held as slaves throughout the colonial era and early antebellum period. However, Virginia formally recognized by statute Native American enslavement only between the years 1679 and 1705. Because slavery descended matrilineally in the United States, an alleged slave would have to satisfy two prongs of a test in order to be entitled to freedom. First, the slave would have to demonstrate that he or she had a maternal ancestor who was Native American, opening the possibility that the ancestor legally was free. Second, the slave would have to demonstrate that the ancestor was not enslaved between 1679 to 1705, the period of legal Native American enslavement. Hannah and her daughter claimed their freedom through their mother/grandmother, Butterwood Nan. If Butterwood Nan had been held as a slave outside of the statutorily prescribed period in Virginia, the appellees would go free. The judges decided in *Hudgins v. Wrights* to allocate the burden of proof to the claiming master.[5] This meant that he had to prove either that Butterwood Nan was not Indian, but rather a member of a racial group that could be enslaved legally, or that she had been enslaved within the statutorily recognized period. He failed to do either, and Hannah and her child went free.

A close reading of this case reveals the extent to which the court's and parties' approach to the conflict was inextricably embedded within a political economy governed by the black/white paradigm. Although the court is attempting to locate three races within the racial map—Indian, negro, and white—its logic is solely binary in structure and subordinating in effect.

The court in *Hudgins* must have understood the potential impact of its procedural holding on the political economy of American chattel slavery. At issue was not just the economic ordering of society, but also the political and cultural negotiations of domination and subordination between masters and slaves. These engagements occurred largely beyond the regulation of the legal system, and it was in the interest of those who owned slaves to maintain this quasi-feudal authority over bondspeople by circumscribing access to the courts.

Two well-known Virginia jurists, Judges Tucker and Roane, each articulated rules to govern future cases in which a claim of mistaken racial identity might be made as a defense to being enslaved. These rules operated largely to protect Native Americans, and indirectly whites, but more permanently associated slavery with blackness and blackness with slavery. To reconcile this conflict, the judges employ two contradictory vectors of racial analysis. First, they establish a discretionary standard for allocating the burden of proof:

> In the case of a person visibly appearing to be a negro, the presumption is, in this country, that he is a slave, and it is incumbent on him to make out his right to freedom: but in the case of a person visibly appearing to be a white man, or an Indian, the presumption is that he is free, and it is necessary for his adversary to shew that he is a slave.[6]

Visible racial characteristics thus determine the preliminary procedural element of allocation of burden of proof.

I call this physical component scopic in that it relies on the scrutinizing gaze of a (white) individual to assign racial identity. "The distinguishing characteristics of the different species of the human race are so visibly marked, that those species may be readily discriminated from each other by mere inspection only."[7] Judges are appointed the proper practitioners of this new taxonomy; however, Judge Roane's opinion suggests that jurors (who were then only whites) also may be arbiters of racial designation in Virginia. Thus, in this era, only white men are endowed with this consummate power of racial assignation.[8]

This rule, and Judge Tucker's defense of it, removes any of the contingency that is present in any racial taxonomic practice. Instead, a white stance becomes the only subjective position possible for racial identification. Those excluded by law from juries and the judiciary are also excluded from this economy of racial surveillance, buttressed by the rule itself.

Both judges used the opportunity presented by the conflict to instill a phenotypic racial taxonomy with the force of the law:

> Nature has stampt upon the African and his descendants two characteristic marks, besides the difference of complexion, which often remain visible long after the characteristic distinction of color either disappears or becomes doubtful: a flat nose and woolly head of hair. The latter of these characteristics disappears the last of all: and so strong an ingredient in the African constitution is this latter character, that it predominates uniformly where the party is in equal degree descended from parents of different complexions, whether white or Indians; giving to the jet black lank hair of the Indian a degree of flexure, which never fails to betray that the party distinguished by it, cannot trace his lineage purely from the race of native Americans.[9]

Notice how the court gives legal substance to what was scientifically uncertain and socially contested. It establishes as an objective legal standard the individual judges' subjective perceptions of racial distinction.

The scopic/visual procedural rule stands in contrast to the more standard rule of determining race according to genealogy, or "blood." In fact, the formula of hypodescent stated that one's race would not be determined by appearance, but by ancestry.[10] [Hypodescent, the "one drop" rule, means that a person with any visible trace of black ancestry is deemed black for legal purposes. Ed.] However, the court employs this rule, too, in resolving Hannah's case. The court held that the appellees would go free if they could trace their lineage back to a Native American woman who transmitted free status to a child. Hence, ancestry, not appearance, governs.

The court adopts two conflicting modes of analysis in order to map race in early national Virginia. The rule of hypodescent runs along a formalist path of employing "objective" principles of genealogy and lineage. The other rule stems from subjective scopic determinations made by physical judicial inspection. These two rules appear irreconcilable on their face. However, the rules can be explained through attention to the subtext of the case: safeguarding various material interests of whites, especially the economic interests in slavery. Designating an individual as black subjected that person to a series of legal disabilities that made it more difficult to claim freedom.

But the conflict in *Hudgins* revealed a latent danger of slavery for whites: the loss of a liberty interest. The laws, designed to protect the economic and political interests of whites in their slaves, effectively prevented those claimed as slaves from contesting their status. As the quandary of the appellees in *Hudgins* suggested, however, whites also might find themselves on the accused end of being a slave. Judge Roane tellingly shares his concern: "In the present case it is not and cannot be denied that the appellees have entirely the appearance of white people: and how does the appellant attempt to deprive them of the blessing of liberty to which all such persons are entitled?"[11] Although on its face this case is about Native American enslavement, Judge Roane's main focus seems to be the safeguarding of whites from accidentally falling into the perils of slavery. This is done by coding legal rights to race and racializing the rhetoric of liberty interests.[12] Simultaneous protection of white economic and liberty interests is accomplished by differing modes of racial analysis and surveillance which, at their core, articulate white identity and code rights and liberty to it.

A second mechanism of the binary legal mode is an aspirational quality that masks a disciplining function. The following language from Judge Tucker isolates black Americans from both whites and Native Americans.

> Its operation is still more powerful where the mixture happens between persons descended equally from European and African parents. So pointed is this distinction between natives of Africa and the aborigines of America, that a man might as easily mistake the glossy, jetty cloathing [sic] of an American bear for the wool of a black sheep, as the hair of an American Indian for that of an African. Upon these distinctions as connected with our laws, the burthen of proof depends.[13]

Racial integrity of both whites and Native Americans is indicated by the power of black admixture to corrupt the purity of each of these "fragile" races and to thereby dilute the integrity of the color-based scopic/visual taxonomy.

More than rhetoric disciplined the Native American parties. Not only had blackness been coded to servitude, but whiteness had been coded to liberty rights. If considered white, the appellees could evade the burden of proof. This conundrum is reflected in the appellees' opening statement: "This is not a common case of mere *blacks* suing for their freedom; but of persons perfectly *white*."[14] The appellees, though claiming freedom substantively through Native American ancestry, employed the rhetoric of the scopic economy, hence invoking whites' fear of being accidentally enslaved.

In order to obtain freedom through laws structured to secure white economic and liberty interests, the appellees had to situate themselves as people who could be removed from chattel slavery without altering its fundamental order. The appellees' argument demonstrates that the creation of whiteness as something to be aspired to and blackness to be distanced from was already powerful in this early moment in national consciousness.

The appellant negotiated within the same binary logic, attempting then to distance the alleged slaves from the security of whiteness. The attorney insisted that the chancellor had been disabled by the appearance of appellees: "The circumstance of their being white operated on the mind of the chancellor."[15] He went on to warn the Supreme Court: "The circumstance of the appellees' being white, has been mentioned, more to excite the feelings of the court as men, than to address them as judges."[16] Thus each side inexorably negotiated within the confines of the black/white paradigm.

Ultimately, the binary logic of *Hudgins* reveals an implicit quality in the black/white paradigm that is often overlooked by legal racial theorists. The very label "black/white" suggests parity of the races within the paradigm. It evokes two equal poles on a line that together make up the category race. Hence race itself as a construct appears to be neutral; everyone has one, it is merely a matter of identification. The appearance of neutrality is critical in order to maintain the paradigm. But how neutral is it? *Hudgins* makes clear that the black/white paradigm arising from chattel slavery was not merely a neutral taxonomy, but a set of dynamic juxtapositions with their own internal hierarchy, elaborated through the assignment of rights.

The *Hudgins* opinion remains one of the most stark examples of the role of law in creating the national racial taxonomy. Its language illustrates how the national racial taxonomy took differences of phenotype and reified them into bases for legal and social discrimination. *Hudgins* employs the black/white paradigm to more firmly inscribe slave status onto blacks, ending any ambiguities of the racial coding of enslaved status that may have remained from colonial white servitude. In *Hudgins*, blackness is treated narrowly, limited in order to protect white liberty. Fifty years later, the same binary mode of reasoning led a court to define blackness far more expansively, and whiteness more narrowly. But the shift still secures white interests, albeit of a different sort. This shifting construction of both blackness and whiteness illuminates both the fluidity of racial classification and the inexorable nature of securing white rights.

In *Hudgins*, Native Americans argued their way out of chattel slavery by legally linking it to black Americans. Years later, in *People v. Hall*,[17] Chinese residents of California were situated within a completely different political economic structure. Yet, even across 3000 miles and half a century, a paradigm of binary racial reasoning functioned hegemonically to govern the judicial resolution of where to locate a third race. In *Hudgins*, Native Americans negotiated a shifting racial structure to secure freedom. Unlike *Hudgins*, in *Hall*, liberty interests were not at stake. Instead the conflict was over access to the courtroom. However, white interests still appeared paramount and were protected judicially along two axes.

At issue in *Hall* was a statute that coded rights to whites in an analogous fashion to *Hudgins v. Wrights*. The court had to racially locate Chinese within a prohibitory statute: "No black or mulatto person, or Indian, shall be permitted to give evidence in favor of, or against, a white person."[18] Hannah and her daughter aligned themselves with whiteness in order to gain freedom. For the Chinese in *Hall*, the taxonomic racial choices would be equally clear and stark. The state charged Hall, a white man, with the murder of Ling Sing, a Chinese man. Hall was convicted following a trial that included the testimony of three Chinese witnesses. The California Supreme Court reversed the conviction, because Chinese testimony had been improperly admitted under the statute. It held that the statute applied to all non-whites and that the Chinese were prohibited from testifying against whites.

The Chinese community was outraged. Implicated was not just the value of Chinese lives, but the access to the courtroom. The courts are where people go to assert their rights, from protection against violence to enforcement of contracts. The segregation of Chinese/white life also meant that Chinese might not have white witnesses to support legal claims they might make. When *Hall* was decided, Chinese residents of the United States were precluded from citizenship. In many areas of California they lived in segregated communities, Chinatowns. Thus courts provided one of the few public spaces in which Chinese could participate in mainstream American political life. They were able to exercise rights not only in an individual sense, but in the sense of a group asserting its collective right to be recognized as Americans. Chinese participation in rights discourse reminded Californians that the Chinese were more than mere temporary laborers whom they wished would leave during economic downturns. Many had come to stay.

Finally, for the Chinese, the act of speaking in the courtroom was itself significant. White Californians justified the exclusion of Chinese in part on language differences. Participation in legal discourse not only forced whites to encounter the Chinese voice as comprehensible, but injected Chinese interests and concerns into public life. Hence, the courtroom became a democratic space for white/Chinese engagement.

The challenge by Hall to his conviction dramatically contested Chinese participation. In interpreting the statute, the court said: "The evident intention of the Act was to throw around the [white] citizen a protection for life and property, which could only be secured by removing him above the corrupting influences of degraded castes."[19] Thus, in seeking their own justice (or defending themselves from others seeking it), whites were not to have to encounter noxious others. The case also demonstrates how white interests were again at the foreground of the *Hall* decision. In *Hudgins*, the main concern was to protect whites from chattel slavery. In *Hall* it was to safeguard the courtroom as a political space for the protection of white interests.

As mentioned earlier, the achievement of this space is done along two axes. Not only would whites be able to testify as a fundamental right of whiteness, but also they would be protected from having to engage with non-whites through the latter's testimony. Hence the statute grants to whites both the positive right to participate in a court of law and the negative right to be free, not just from challenges from people of color, but any racially integrated legal interaction. That testimony could not be offered in any civil case in which a white person was a party, or in any criminal case "in favor of, or against a white man," supports this conclusion.[20] The larger connotations of Chinese testimony for or against whites is suggested by the court: "The same rule which would admit them to testify, would admit them to all the equal rights of citizenship, and we might soon see them at the polls, in the jury box, upon the bench, and in our legislative halls."[21] Thus, what seems to be a moment of racial confusion, making the binary paradigm vulnerable to correction, again is resolved with primary attention to white interests.

As in *Hudgins*, American race is focused on white identity, the need to define it and protect it. Again this can only be done through classifying other groups. Although not directly implicated, blackness again becomes a pivotal concept in the racial designation of whiteness. The court begins by noting that the criminal and civil statutes employ different language: while the criminal code prohibits testimony against whites by "Black, or Mulatto person, or Indian," the civil code used the word "Negro" in place of "Black." The court concludes:

> The word "Black" may include all Negroes, but the term "Negro" does not include all Black persons.
>
> By the use of this term in this connection, we understand it to mean the opposite of "White," and that it should be taken as contradistinguished from all White persons.
>
> In using the words . . . the Legislature . . . adopted the most comprehensive terms to embrace every known class or shade of color, as the apparent design was to protect the White person from the influence of all testimony other than that of persons of the same caste. The use of these terms must, by every sound rule of construction, exclude every one who is not of white blood.[22]

Thus is blackness the residue left once whiteness has been defined and assigned.

Within this binary logic, there is no space for securing specifically Chinese rights. Not surprisingly, in the aftermath of the decision, the political arguments by the Chinese against their own subordination were influenced by the binary black/white paradigm. With whiteness coded to rights, they attempted to argue for their own cultural and legal distancing from the historically subjugated races targeted in the statute. Charles McClain reports that one "prominent San Francisco merchant" wrote in a letter to the governor expressing bitterness at their linkage to other non-whites:

> [O]f late days, your honorable people have established a new practice. They have come to the conclusion that we Chinese are the same as Indians and Negroes, and your courts will not allow us to bear witness. And yet these Indians know nothing about the relations of society; they know no mutual respect; they wear neither clothes nor shoes; they live in wild places and [in] caves.[23]

The law demanded that groups seeking rights reject and cast as inferior the non-white end of the pole. Sometimes they won rights, and sometimes they did not. Hannah and her daughter were able to win under a combination of a scopic and genealogical rule designed to protect white liberty and economic interests; the Chinese could not. The force of racial binarism links *Hudgins* and *Hall* across half a century. In each, the assertion of rights by the non-black colored plaintiff is governed by a paradigm of binary identity formation.

Notes

1. Toni Morrison, Playing in the Dark—Whiteness and the Literary Imagination 9 (1992).

2. Morrison, supra at 9, 31–59. Professor Ian Haney López makes an analogous point within law through close readings of late–nineteenth century cases. *See* Ian F. Haney López, White by Law, in Critical Race Theory—The Cutting Edge 542 (Richard Delgado ed., 1995); *see also* Stephanie M. Wildman, Privilege Revealed: How Invisible Preference Undermines America (1996) (with contributions by Margalynne Armstrong, Adrienne D. Davis & Trina Grillo).

3. For a discussion of white racial identity, *see generally* Andrew Hacker, Two Nations: Black and White, Separate, Hostile, Unequal (1992); David R. Roediger, Towards the Abolition of Whiteness: Essays on Race, Politics, and Working Class History (1994); David R. Roediger, Wages of Whiteness: Race and the Making of the American Working Class (1991).

4. *Hudgins v. Wrights*, 11 Va. (1 Hen. & M.) 134 (1806).

5. "All American Indians are prima facie free: and that where the fact of their nativity and descent, in a maternal line, is satisfactorily established, the burthen *[sic]* of proof thereafter lies upon the party claiming to hold them as slaves." *Hudgins*, at 139 (Tucker, J.).

6. *Hudgins*, at 141 (Roane, J.).

7. *Id.*

8. "Throughout much of the 19th century the position of women in our society was, . . . comparable to that of blacks under the pre–Civil War slave codes. Neither slaves nor women could hold office, serve on juries, or bring suit in their own names, ..." *Frontiero v. Richardson*, 411 U.S. 677, 685 (1973).

9. *Hudgins*, at 139 (Tucker, J.).

10. *See Neil Gotanda, A Critique of "Our Constitution Is Color Blind,"* 44 Stan. L. Rev. 1, 23–26 (1991)("Rule of descent: (a) Any person with a known trace of African ancestry is Black, notwithstanding that person's visual appearance.").

11. *Hudgins*, at 141.

12. Note that the court holds not only that whites and Indians do not have a burden of proof in such cases, but also dictates that those appearing negro shall remain in custody pending adjudication while those appearing otherwise will remain unfree. *Hudgins,* 11 Va. at 140.

13. *Hudgins,* at 139–40 (Tucker, J.).

14. *Id.* at 135 (italics in original).

15. *Id.* at 134.

16. *Id.* at 136.

17. 4 Cal. 399 (1854).

18. Act of Apr. 16, 1850, ch. 99, 14, 1850 Cal. Stat. 229, 230, amended by Act of Mar. 18, 1863, ch. 70, 1863 Cal. Stat. 69, repealed by omission from codification Cal. Penal Code 1321 (1872) (officially repealed, Act of Mar. 30, 1955, ch. 48, 1, 1955 Cal. Stat. 488, 489).

19. *Hall,* 4 Cal. at 403. "The European white man who comes here would not be shielded from the testimony of the degraded and demoralized caste, while the Negro, fresh from the coast of Africa, or the Indian of Patagonia, the Kanaka, South Sea Islander, or New Hollander, would be admitted upon their arrival, to testify against white citizens in our courts of law." *Id.* at 402.

20. *Hall,* 4 Cal. at 399.

21. *Id.* at 404.

22. *Id.* at 403.

23. *Charles J. McClain Jr., The Chinese Struggles for Civil Rights in Nineteenth Century America: The First Phase, 1850–1870,* 72 Cal. L. Rev. 529, 550 (1984) (footnotes omitted).

38

The Constitutional Ghetto

ROBERT L. HAYMAN, JR., AND NANCY LEVIT

Three themes characterize latter-day desegregation law.

First, *Plessy* originated, and recent decisions embrace, a concept of natural racism. This view holds that racism inheres in the human condition. Racism is innate and inevitable and, as a consequence, it must be tolerated—by the federal courts among others—as an unfortunate fact of human existence. The Constitution and the construing Court are powerless to alter the course of racial instincts; separation may not be equal, but it is entirely natural.

Second, recent decisions complete another cycle begun in *Plessy*: the discrediting of racism as a barrier to constitutional equality. In several ways, segregation itself becomes an ironic metaphor for this approach: the law of desegregation becomes an insular body of rules, separated from the remainder of equal protection doctrine; it regresses to treat segregation in education as a phenomenon unconnected to other social causes; and it creates a category of people isolated from the constitutional norm of equality.

Third, desegregation doctrine includes methodology of betrayal, of broken promises and of interpretive possibilities discarded. From its inception, desegregation law manifested a notable lack of candor. As the body of law developed, the test prescribed for determining liability immediately undercut the reach of the remedy. And now, Supreme Court jurisprudence attempts to convey that the promise of *Brown* has been met to the fullest possible extent; that those who placed their faith in *Brown* were doomed to disappointment by the unrealizable vision which inhered in *Brown*'s quixotic project; and that the shortcomings of desegregation are the failures not of the state, not of the courts, but of the American people themselves, who suffer only what they choose.

The Beginnings: Government-Sponsored Subordination

In *Plessy v. Ferguson*, the Supreme Court upheld a statute requiring racially segregated railway cars and ruled that these separate but equal accommodations did not offend the Constitution. Racial prejudice was viewed as a behavior unalterable by legislation; laws would be "powerless to eradicate . . . instincts."[1] The Court drew a sharp distinction between political and social equality, and relegated the success of social equality projects to "the result of natural affinities . . . and a voluntary consent of individuals."[2] Thus, the *Plessy* Court viewed racism as a "natural" state of affairs and commented that segregation reflected "established usages, customs and traditions of the people."[3] The

Court concluded that "[the Equal Protection Clause] could not have been intended to abolish distinctions based upon color."[4] For the *Plessy* majority, the differences between blacks and whites were inherent. And even if the "instincts" were not biological in origin, societal preferences embodied as majoritarian choices became the constitutional mandate.

The Promise of *Brown*

Brown v. Board of Education[5] was a marvelous statement of constitutional promise. *Brown* condemned segregation in education because it created a stigma of inferiority in black schoolchildren; a unanimous Court insisted that separation of the races "generates a feeling of inferiority as to [blacks'] status in the community that may affect their hearts and minds in a way unlikely ever to be undone."[6]

Brown was more than a command to dismantle segregated schools; it was a call to uproot deeply entrenched racism. On the doctrinal level, *Brown* represented a marked departure from prior patterns of assessing the equivalence of black and white institutions. *Brown* was also extraordinary in terms of its intended symbolic effect. *Brown's* overruling of *Plessy* articulated a reversal of the assumptions that supported *Plessy's* social inferiority thesis. *Brown* carried a message designed, at a minimum, to make the white majority less convinced of its own superiority.

Yet the *Brown* Court itself was troubled by the implications of its decision and waited for a consensus to develop. For one thing, the initial decision in *Brown* was delayed a year as the case was carried over from the 1953 Term to the 1954 Term. For another, the Court saved consideration of the relief issue for yet another year in *Brown II*.

If *Brown's* commitment was still to be taken seriously, the Court in *Brown II* certainly expressed discomfort with what it unleashed. Resistance was viewed as inevitable, recalcitrance almost invited. Lacking from *Brown II's* commands was a specific relief order; instead, the Court directed federal district courts to retain jurisdiction over the collected cases until each school district "achieve[d] a system of determining admission to the public schools on a nonracial basis."[7] The Court permitted consideration of local conditions and vested district courts with discretion to "take into account the public interest in the elimination of such obstacles in a systematic and effective manner."[8] Partly as a consequence, the oxymoronic "all deliberate speed" requirement did not turn into a mandate of "at once" or "now" until a decade later.

Narrowing of the Vision

In 1968, in *Green v. County School Board*,[9] the Court required a desegregation plan that "promises realistically to work now."[10] In *Green*, the Court disapproved of "freedom of choice" plans and held that school systems with de jure segregation [De jure segregation is segregation by law. De facto segregation arises through social conditions. Ed.] were "clearly charged with the affirmative duty to take whatever steps might be necessary to convert to a unitary system in which racial discrimination would be eliminated root and branch."[11]

Yet just as the Court demanded for the first time immediate response to its desegregation mandate, it both narrowed the scope and envisioned the end of that mandate. *Brown* could have been read either as a proscription of any segregation or only of segregation explicitly caused by purposeful government action. Decisions in the 1970s, beginning with

Green, and coincident with the actual enforcement of the *Brown* mandate, chose to read *Brown* as prohibiting only intentional segregation. *Green* also anticipated the end of court supervision. The Court provided components for district courts to examine in order to determine whether a school system remained dual or was unitary: student body, faculty, staff, transportation, extracurricular activities, and facilities.

These criteria exhibit a departure from both the promise of *Brown* and from its implicit contextualism. They focus narrowly on intraschool ingredients, rather than requiring consideration of such related elements as racially located government housing starts, provision of other government services in a race-conscious manner, employment statistics reflecting racial disparities, or patterns of race-based behavior in the community.

Although the 1970s cases contain glimmerings of a more contextual approach,[12] in the main they continued *Green*'s narrow focus on the discrete components of a dual school system, ignoring the effects of various social conditions, such as residential or housing patterns.[13] While the Court recognized that system-wide violations necessitated relief, it refused to require that schools reflect the racial balance of the population. The Court acknowledged the messages conveyed when local government units attempted to circumvent desegregation plans, yet urged district courts to exhibit "a sensitivity to local conditions."[14] While the Court made sweeping pronouncements that "[t]he measure of any desegregation plan is its effectiveness,"[15] the Court nevertheless permitted authorities to take into account "the practicalities of the situation."[16] In each case, aspiration was sharply undercut by the Court's acquiescence to current conditions.

By the time of *Swann v. Charlotte-Mecklenburg Board of Education,*[17] the tension between order and equality was patent. In *Swann,* the Court explicitly articulated the ambivalence of the prior cases, reflecting the Court's struggle with the obligation to do justice and the threat to racial order that fulfillment of that obligation clearly entailed. The *Swann* Court thus candidly acknowledges the interplay of educational and residential segregation, yet steers away from a more comprehensive resolution of racial segregation. *Swann* ultimately devolves to "a balancing of the individual and collective interests":[18] The approved measures include racial balancing ratios, minority-to-majority transfer policies, alteration of school attendance zones, and busing, but all are carefully qualified.

The hard-won unanimity of the Court in *Swann* lapsed the following term in *Wright v. Council of Emporia.*[19] Although the Court, by a 5–4 vote, prevented a city from seceding and constructing its own school district, which would have frustrated the county's desegregation order, a strong dissent revisited the theme that "the normal movement of populations could bring about . . . shifts [in the racial composition of schools] in a relatively short period of time."[20] Some racism was viewed as natural—implicit in the way people conducted their affairs and chose their residences—and thus untouchable by the Constitution.

The Formal Separation of State Responsibility

Keyes v. School District No. 1,[21] decided in 1973, presented a challenge to segregation in the Denver area schools. The district court found intentional segregative conduct, such as manipulation of attendance zones and racially premised teacher assignments, with respect to thirty-eight percent of the black student population. The Supreme Court approved system-wide relief on this showing of segregative actions in "a meaningful portion of the school system."[22]

Yet just as *Keyes* agreed that intentional actions in one part of a school district could be related to the existence of segregated schools in another part of it, it restricted relief in future cases by circumscribing what government conduct is reachable under the Equal Protection Clause. *Keyes* solidified the distinction between de jure and de facto segregation—between intentional actions of the government requiring desegregation and segregation arising from social conditions not directly tied to purposeful segregation by school authorities. The *Keyes* Court thus envisioned a binary universe, where conduct was either governmental in origin or not. The former was redressable under the Constitution; the latter—no matter the causative interplay of government and societal forces—was not.

Keyes and later cases expanded the effects of presumptions regarding intentional government conduct. These cases shifted attention toward the distinction between the intent of government action and the effects of that action, and away from broader focus on the systemic network of segregation's causal forces. Despite recognition that the harms of *de jure* and *de facto* segregation were indistinguishable,[23] and that official and social causes might not be readily separable,[24] the majority limited the corrective obligation of the government to racially motivated decision making by government officials.

While *Keyes* might have sent a mixed message, *Milliken v. Bradley*[25] signaled retrenchment from the promise of *Brown* and crippled the construction of viable desegregation remedies. In *Milliken,* the Detroit Board of Education had created racially drawn optional attendance zones, bused black students to predominantly black schools farther away from predominantly white schools which had available space, and engaged in racially segregative patterns of school construction. The district court determined that state government had engaged in racially disparate funding of public housing and that it would thus be impossible to desegregate the Detroit school system without including the suburbs.

The Supreme Court reversed, holding that, absent an interdistrict violation, "there is no constitutional wrong calling for an interdistrict remedy."[26] In response to the argument that the state had deliberately created an "inner core of Detroit [that] is now rather solidly black,"[27] the *Milliken* majority held that government responsibility ended at the school district boundary. Thus, without evidence that the state had discriminatorily drawn the district boundaries or created "a constitutional violation within one district that produces a significant segregative effect in another district,"[28] the Constitution pulls up short at the school district boundaries. The majority explained this reverence for district boundary lines: "No single tradition in public education is more deeply rooted than local control over the operation of schools; local autonomy has long been thought essential both to the maintenance of community concern and support for public schools and to quality of the educational process."[29]

The Rejuvenation of "Natural Racism"

Just a few short years after effective enforcement of *Brown, Pasadena City Board of Education v. Spangler*[30] heralded the end of the desegregation dream. In *Spangler,* the district court had required a school board under a desegregation order to conduct annual modification of attendance zones to adjust for resegregation due to changing patterns of residential demographics. The Supreme Court reversed and held that once the district court issued its racially-neutral plan, it could not order yearly readjustments to account for "[t]his quite normal pattern of human migration."[31]

Spangler did more than curtail the power of the federal judiciary to remedy race discrimination. In its ruling that federal courts are without power to reach private behavior, *Spangler* echoed the themes of *Swann* and *Milliken* that distinguished between private and governmental conduct. The Court reasserted that private and governmental conduct stand on different footings, and that, for constitutional purposes, the two spheres of conduct are isolated. More powerfully, and much more sadly, *Spangler* contains fatalistic conclusions about racism: It assumes that white flight from blacks is inevitable and unremediable; it assumes that changes in residential patterns are caused by factors outside government control; and it deems all this untouchable by the Constitution. Once integration has been achieved in certain, although not all, aspects of school administration, the obligation to desegregate has been satisfied.

The Color Line

Attempts to assess the desegregation effort—its successes and failures—are notably ahistorical, as if the story of "racism" began the day before *Brown*. Curiously absent from most such assessments is the story of the *segregation* effort, of the drawing of the color line. The suggestion apparently is that there is no story to tell: Nothing happened and no one did anything; the color line simply *was*.

Eluding the tale of the segregation effort affords a certain comfort. By ignoring its origins, the color line becomes an evolutionary truth, rooted in some undiscoverable primal moment. Forged this way by the mysterious forces of creation, the story of segregation becomes at once too profound and too elusive to tell. It also becomes irrelevant, and the sense of relief is compounded by the realization that the painful history of segregation is not one of "our" making: It just happened, it's nobody's fault, and it's nobody's responsibility.

But there is a story to tell, and the tale of the segregation effort contains some embarrassing truths both for those who have constructed it and for those who today deny its relevance. And if the story is painful, it is nonetheless empowering, for it suggests that the racism which pervades America's soul is no less an artifact than the laws that formalize it; that de facto segregation is as much a political construct as de jure segregation; and that the promises of *Brown*—challenged as they have been—remain today both viable and fully realizable. As Frederick Douglass said of slavery a century ago: "[W]hat man can make, man can unmake";[32] segregation, the history suggests, is for us now to unmake.

Consider, to begin with, the observation that color prejudice was not always a part of the encounters between Europeans and Africans. The ancient Egyptians, Greeks, Romans, and early Christians did not share the modern preoccupation with skin color. At least through the sixth century, the extensive contacts between black and white populations were largely unencumbered by philosophical, scientific, or religious notions of racial hierarchy. As late as the seventeenth century, European accounts of the African peoples acknowledged the curious difference in skin hues without attendant notions of relative superiority or inferiority. This essentially neutral disposition toward skin color appears also to describe the early American attitude toward race. Race was not, at the outset, a symbol of servitude: The modern equation of "black" and "slave" arose only as a practical exigency. Through the early part of the eighteenth century, colonial conceptions of involuntary servitude were, in terms of "race," all-embracing: They included Africans, Europeans, and Native Americans. For pragmatic reasons, the latter two groups proved poor choices as bondsmen; international events, meanwhile, radically altered the demographic composition of the servant class to increase the proportion of Africans. In short, Africans became the preferred bondsmen not through some perceived mandate—biological, philosophical, religious, or otherwise—but instead largely by default.

But if the empirical correlation of "black" and "bondsman" was largely accidental, the political correlation of "black" and "slave" certainly was not. The ambiguous nature of servile relationships through the seventeenth and early eighteenth centuries facilitated class alliances unencumbered by barriers of "race": The divisions between white indentured servant and black slave were far less clear than the divisions between master and bondsmen. The gradual change in demographics permitted a reversal of this emphasis; the master class, literally fearing for its survival, enacted statutory initiatives that formalized chattel slavery, compelled the social segregation of the races, and created a racial hierarchy of political and economic rights. The result, by the middle of the eighteenth century, was the isolation of the "black slave."

The modern picture was completed by the dominant culture's "natural" equation of "black" and "inferior." It was, perversely, the philosophical precepts of the movement for independence that ultimately demanded this subordination of African-Americans. The bourgeois ethic of the prerevolutionary era was not incompatible with slavery: Slavery required no justification because almost no one perceived it as wrong. But the dissonance between the liberal rhetoric that gave justification to the new republic and the realities of chattel slavery demanded formal reconciliation. Inevitably, this reconciliation had to be achieved through the construction of some "natural" hierarchy—a political philosophy that exalts "natural" liberty over political power could tolerate no less. And if the "natural" inequalities among men could serve to explain their relative positions in society, then surely the existence of master and slave could find its own "natural" explanation based with stunning elegance on the color of a man's skin.

A lie repeated with enough frequency and conviction can easily assume the guise of a truth. This was the case with the myths of racism. Generation after generation, the belief in natural race—in racial instincts, natural racial affinities, and racial supremacy and inferiority—pervaded the dominant culture. It tainted its science, its religion, its art, and its law, and left its malignant stain on the soul of Americans of all colors.

And of course, the myths infected the schools. Education had long been a privilege denied African-Americans; before the Civil War, every Southern state except Tennessee prohibited the instruction of slaves. There were glimmers of hope during Reconstruction in the extraordinary efforts of the freedmen to secure widespread access to education; in the work of the Reconstruction state legislatures to establish open educational systems; and in the national Republican party's attempt to guarantee by federal law the right to an integrated education. But on the whole, the promise far exceeded the reality, and soon even these modest gains were largely undone.

The Jim Crow system, which supplanted slavery—and which governed the lives of most black Americans through the first half of the twentieth century—filled the void left by the demise of the customs integral to the antebellum South. The rules changed, but the racial hierarchy remained the same. As before, the denial of equal opportunity was vital. The growth of the public schools necessitated acts to suppress black education: Some of these were legal, some extra-legal. As to the former, racial segregation—combined with grotesque disparities in the allocation of educational resources and radical differences in the focus and depth of the curricula—was pervasive. As to the latter, a scheme of orchestrated violence—directed principally at educated black Americans—achieved for white supremacy what laws alone could not. The message to black Americans was that education afforded no way out; the message for white Americans was that it was proper to hate. The myths, shielded by ignorance and brutality, were secure.

Maintaining the Color Line

The persistence of America's racism remains somewhat a mystery. If racism is neither innate nor inevitable, why—after Emancipation, Reconstruction, and a Second Reconstruction—does the color line persist? It does even though the color line which divides white and black America today is less distinct than the one which has historically prevailed. A recent survey of racial attitudes concludes that, at least in what they say, "white Americans are gradually becoming less prejudiced and more egalitarian."[33] Over the past four decades, negative stereotypes of black Americans have consistently faded, while pro-integration sentiments have consistently risen. By 1980, over ninety percent of white northerners and seventy-five percent of white southerners supported school integration; by 1982, the support for integration was at ninety percent for the entire national sample. An earlier survey, done in 1978, indicated that roughly three-quarters of the white population had no objection to their child being in a school where half the children were black; over forty percent had no objection if a majority of the children were black. And in a 1988 survey, more whites reported that they would prefer to live in a neighborhood racially mixed "half and half" than in a neighborhood with "mostly whites."

But there are reasons to be cautious. The surveys consistently reveal that a significant minority in the white population—roughly twenty percent—continues to demonstrate direct, traditional racial prejudice. Moreover, the surveys contain traces of ambivalence, indications that racial prejudice persists among white Americans, but in more subtle forms.

It is impossible to conclusively establish the relationship between these modern forms of racism and their more virulent historical counterparts. But the evidence strongly suggests that today's version represents just a stage in the evolutionary process: that modern racism is a direct descendant of the color line drawn nearly three centuries ago and is shaped and sustained by the same political forces. Modern racism,[34] like its predecessor, is not attributable to individual pathology. On the contrary, the cognitive processes that provide the foundation for individual racial prejudice—the ability to differentiate—is normal and quite benign. But while the individual may have an innate ability to differentiate based on "race," it is principally the work of sociocultural influences that makes "race" salient. Thus "race," itself largely a social construction, evokes the attitudes and attributes developed by social processes.[35]

Moreover, it is social norms that make specific differentiating behaviors either more or less acceptable. For example, research indicates that biased positive attitudes (e.g., by whites toward whites) are not invariably accompanied by equally biased negative attitudes (e.g., by whites toward blacks). Specific negative responses to differentiating characteristics seem to find expression where they enjoy social sanction. "Racism" is perpetuated, in this sense, by its own long-standing tradition.

We know that racism can be "unlearned" through the meaningful engagement of countervailing epistemological and moral truths. Epistemological premises for racist behavior can be refuted through interracial learning: When it is clear that the real meanings of "race" are social and not biological, the negative racial schema is substantially undone. However, such a result cannot be obtained merely through notions of "colorblindness." Rather, the contemporary insistence that "race" has no meaning resolves the dissonance between racial oppression and society's egalitarian ideals only through denial. Thus, one unfortunate consequence of race-neutral policies may actually be the entrenchment of racist beliefs.

The proclamation of competing moral truths *can* counter racist attitudes, but they must directly challenge the norms on which racism is constructed. Research suggests that appeals to the ethic of individualism do not meet the moral challenge; on the contrary, this ethic tends to increase negative racial attitudes, undermining interracial empathy and creating a tendency to discount the effects of racial discrimination. Thus, the reinforcement of the individualist ethos may actually exacerbate negative race-related tendencies.[36]

The set of norms that appears to provide an effective counter to racist tendencies is that which includes principles of fairness and equality. The race-neutral approach of modern racism, in fact, does not so much confront these norms as it does elude them. Since egalitarian norms are comparatively abstract, their effectiveness thus depends upon presentation in unambiguous terms; when the divorce between the norm and the racist behavior is made clear, the modern subject, who may not recognize the behavior as racist, can and does reject the behavior in favor of the egalitarian norm.

The norm must be unambiguous, however. The most significant feature of modern racism is its ability to assimilate an egalitarian framework while avoiding the practical implications of the normative mandate for equality. Thus, modern racism eludes the contradiction between racist behavior and egalitarian norms through such rationalizing devices as the diffusion of personal responsibility to realize equality and the attribution of racism to a larger social force. Of course, the subtle nature of modern racism does not make it any less debilitating for its victims. This suggests the need for a leadership that is insightful enough to recognize the subtle hand of racism, and dedicated enough to articulate the demands of equality in an unambiguous voice. In this recognition lies one of the truly heroic features of *Brown v. Board of Education*, and perhaps the legal system's most tragic failing.

Notes

1. *Plessy*, 163 U.S. at 551.

2. *Id.* The Court held that there is no constitutional relief "[i]f one race be inferior to the other socially." *Id.* at 551–52.

3. *Id.* at 550.

4. *Id.* at 544.

5. 347 U.S. 483 (1954).

6. *Id.* at 494.

7. *Brown II*, 349 U.S. 294, 300–01 (1955).

8. *Id.* "But it should go without saying," the Court continued, "that the vitality of these constitutional principles cannot be allowed to yield simply because of disagreement with them." *Id.*

9. 391 U.S. 430 (1968).

10. *Id.* at 439. *See also Griffin*, 377 U.S. at 234 ("The time for mere 'deliberate speed' has run out."); *Alexander v. Holmes County Bd. of Educ.*, 396 U.S. 19, 20 (1969) (stating that "the obligation of every school district is to terminate dual school systems at once").

11. *Green* at 437–38.

12. *Keyes v. School Dist. No. 1*, 413 U.S. 189, 196 (1973) (holding that in defining what constitutes a segregated school, courts must look at "the community . . . attitudes toward the school").

13. *Swann v. Charlotte-Mecklenburg Board of Education*, 402 U.S. 1, 22 (1971) ("We are concerned in these cases with the elimination of the discrimination inherent in the dual school systems, not with myriad factors of human existence which can cause discrimination in a multitude of ways on racial, religious or ethnic grounds.").

14. *Wright v. Council of Emporia*, 407 U.S. 451, 466 (1972).

15. *Davis v. Board of Sch. Comm'rs*, 402 U.S. 33, 37 (1971).

16. *Id.*

17. 402 U.S. 1 (1971).

18. *Id.* at 16.

19. 407 U.S. 451 (1972).

20. *Id.* at 474 (Burger, C.J., dissenting).

21. 413 U.S. 189 (1973).

22. *Id.* at 208.

23. *Keyes*, 413 U.S. at 230 n.14 (Powell, J., concurring in part, dissenting in part) ("If a Negro child perceives his separation as discriminatory and invidious, he is not, in a society a hundred years removed from slavery, going to make fine distinctions about the source of a particular separation.") (quoting ALEXANDER M. BICKEL, THE SUPREME COURT AND THE IDEA OF PROGRESS 119 (1970)).

24. *Id.* at 216 (Douglas, J., concurring) ("I think it is time to state that there is no constitutional difference between *de jure* and *de facto* segregation, for each is the product of state action or policies.").

25. 418 U.S. 717 (1974).

26. *Id.* at 745.

27. *Id.* at 759 (Douglas, J., dissenting).

28. *Id.* at 745.

29. *Id.* at 741–42.

30. 427 U.S. 424 (1976).

31. *Id.* at 436.

32. HOWARD ZINN, A PEOPLE'S HISTORY OF THE UNITED STATES 176 (1990).

33. John F. Dovidio & Samuel L. Gaertner, *Changes in the Expression and Assessment of Racial Prejudice*, in OPENING DOORS: PERSPECTIVES ON RACE RELATIONS IN CONTEMPORARY AMERICA 119 (Harry J. Knopke et al. eds., 1991). The authors reviewed surveys and nationwide polls spanning the period from 1942 to 1988 to complement the results of their own behavioral research.

34. "Modern racism" is used here to denote those attitudes and behaviors that correlate first, with a positive belief in racial inferiority or racial deviance and second, with a normative belief in "race-neutral" policies and practices that result in the perpetuation of racial hierarchy. It differs from "old-fashioned" race prejudice in that its prescriptions are not explicitly race based.

35. Significantly, it is not just white Americans who learn, through social interaction, that "race" matters: The experience of racism makes race more salient for African-Americans as well.

36. There exists a correlation between "political conservatism," marked principally by a commitment to individualistic ideologies, and conventionally racist attitudes, like, for example, the notion that African-Americans are more lazy and irresponsible than whites. *See* Paul M. Sniderman et al., *The New Racism*, 35 AM. J. POL. SCI. 423, 445 (1991). In addition, proponents of individualistic ideology are more likely than others to disavow institutional efforts to assist African-Americans. *Id.*

Synopses of Other Important Works

What Is Whiteness?

In *White by Law* (1995), Ian F. Haney López examines the legal and social origins of white racial identity in early Supreme Court cases having to do with naturalization. Decided at a time when whiteness was a condition of becoming a U.S. citizen, these cases show courts equivocating about what whiteness really is—whether it might stem from biology, common knowledge, or something else—and its relationship to cultural superiority. During later periods of relaxed restrictions on immigration, courts switched to a firm embrace of color blindness, in sharp contrast to their former intense preoccupation with skin tone and whiteness. Haney López shows how ordinary white citizens experience whiteness as transparent, and so remain blind to the racialized aspects of their identity; whiteness confers the privilege of not having to think about one's own race. Finding the concept of whiteness socially harmful and biologically false, Haney López urges white people to cast aside their claim to whiteness. He contends that doing so will benefit whites by enabling them to interact more naturally with other people and deal with them more fairly and equally.

From the Editors: Issues and Comments

Does law force people to identify themselves as white, black, or brown, etc.? Does it create those categories in the first place? And what of whiteness—did American courts invent the idea, as a number of our authors imply? Did it have a lot of help from its friends in the social sciences, as Professor Hovenkamp maintains? If someone invented a "Michael Jackson pill" and a prankster put one in a black person's drink, rendering her forever white when she was happy the way she was, would the once-black person be able to recover damages? For what? Are white women like blacks, either legally or socially? Are they both oppressed and thus kin? Or are white women more like white men?

Suggested Readings

Allen, Theodore, THE INVENTION OF THE WHITE RACE (Verso, 1994).

Delgado, Richard, *Rodrigo's Tenth Chronicle: Merit and Affirmative Action*, 83 Geo. L.J. 1711 (1995).

Finkelman, Paul, *The Color of Law*, 87 N.W. U. L. REV. 937 (1993).

Finkelman, Paul, *The Crime of Color*, 67 TUL. L. REV. 2063 (1993).

Gaden, Charles, *The Racial Barrier to American Citizenship*, 93 U. PA. L. REV. 237 (1945).

Gold, George, *The Racial Prerequisite in the Naturalization Law*, 15 B. U. L. REV. 462 (1935).

Horsman, Reginald, RACE AND MANIFEST DESTINY (Harvard University Press, 1981).

Massey, Douglas S., and Nancy A. Denton, AMERICAN APARTHEID (1993).

Roediger, David, TOWARDS THE ABOLITION OF WHITENESS: ESSAYS ON RACE, POLITICS AND WORKING CLASS HISTORY (Verso, 1994).

Part V

Whiteness: Culture's Role

Many authorities believe that one of the most pervasive ways in which racial ideas are conveyed and reinforced is through language—the narratives, tales, sayings, jokes, movie scripts, songs, children's stories, metaphors, and imagery we use in constructing our common culture. One living in our society finds it almost impossible to think of a Madonna or hero who is not white, or a villain who is not swarthy. Can you imagine a mass murderer or a general of the Huns' army, say, who looks like Robert Redford? Or the infant Jesus as a smiling black baby? The following selections deal with the role of culture and cultural artifacts, especially language, or "gaze," in creating stereotypes about race. One theme running through these materials is that once cultural ideas and expectations are internalized the individual begins to act, at a quite unconscious level, in accord with them. In selecting a residence, friend, movie, book, hero, or role model, one chooses in accord with one's sense of who (or what) is likely to turn out to be nice, valued, trustworthy, intelligent, and esteemed. If, as in our society, these traits are linked up with racial archetypes, it becomes almost impossible to act naturally in cross-race situations.

39

Do You Know This Man?

DANIEL ZALEWSKI

What did Jesus look like? Think for a second: Most likely, your mind will conjure up airbrushed golden locks, a silky beard, and baby blue eyes. Yet another reproduction of Warner Sallman's 1940 painting *Head of Christ* will have permeated your brain.

Sallman's portrait may be bad art (one critic has called it a "pretty picture of a woman with a curling beard"), but, for better or worse, the image has cornered our consciousness. How did Sallman's Savior become so popular? A new essay collection, *Icons of American Protestantism: The Art of Warner Sallman* (Yale), edited by Valparaiso art historian David Morgan, tries to answer that question. Rather than defend Sallman's work on aesthetic grounds, the essays trace the social history of one of American art's most beloved (and reviled) images.

Warner Sallman was a devout Christian and a commercial artist who designed everything from advertising flyers to magazine covers for religious publications. Though he attended the tony Art Institute of Chicago, Sallman was most comfortable with the language of advertising. (A shiny copyright symbol can be found emblazoned on the original canvas of *Head of Christ*.) In the Twenties, his commercial instincts found a welcome home in the evangelical movement—which understood that you had to sell the Savior to fill increasingly empty church pews.

Though Sallman's image might have been heavenly, his inspiration was terrestrial. The *Head* can be found in full-bodied form in French artist Leon Lhermitte's 1892 painting of Jesus, *The Friend of the Humble*. In the December 1922 issue of *Ladies' Home Journal*, Sallman saw a black-and-white print of the work and produced a colorized version before contacting the Golden Trumpet Company, a maker of Christian art objects that had been scouting around for a new trademark image. Over the years, Sallman and the Trumpeters produced an entire line of Jesus paintings with the same interchangeable head—often simply cutting the face from one picture and pasting it on the next.

Critics, particularly liberal Christian theologians, have long disparaged Sallman's Jesus as a cheap "matinee idol," and it's easy to see why. The Hollywood halo, the rigid studio pose, the honey-glazed lighting—the composition of *Head of Christ* comes straight from the devotional world of celebrity publicity stills. Sallman jettisoned all historical background and narrative detail from Lhermitte's painting, opting instead for a close-up of Christ, whose limpid eyes upturn with Garboesque glamour. Is it a coincidence, Morgan asks, that Sallman's *Head* was painted during the glory days of the movie-star pinup? In

Reprinted by permission from *Lingua Franca: The Review of Academic Life*, published in New York. E-mail: 76200.414 @ compuserve.com. Originally published in *Lingua Franca*, May/June 1996.

Morgan's view, the "photographic rhetoric" of Sallman's work largely accounts for its success: *Head of Christ* was frequently sold in wallet-size form (at 50 cents a dozen), to be tucked into one's billfold right next to family snapshots.

At its peak, Sallman's *Head of Christ* could be found stamped on bookmarks, calendars, and stickers—even night lights. And during World War II, the Salvation Army and the YMCA supplied millions of American servicemen with tiny reproductions of Sallman's painting, complete with a prayer on the back. While Sallman's detractors saw a feminized figure in *Head of Christ,* those who carried the image with them into foxholes and trenches perceived a manliness that contemporary eyes may find difficult to see. According to Utah religion professor Colleen McDannell, this strength-by-association allowed Sallman's depiction to break free from the limited women's market, becoming so successful that 14 million copies were sold by 1943. (By now, that number has passed one billion.)

To the liberal Christian clergy and seminary theologians, however, Sallman's success was a spiritual calamity. In 1956, the philosopher Paul Tillich fumed against what he called Sallman's "Sunday school art," declaring that "the religious art of capitalist society reduces the traditional religious symbols to the level of middle-class morality and robs them of their transcendence." Sally Promey documents the various ways in which liberal Christian leaders tried to ward off religious kitsch. The Methodist magazine *Motive,* for example, sponsored a sale of "Original Works of Art!" in 1958, in response to the "reprehensible custom of collecting art via the printing press." And Tillich, in conjunction with Yale theologian Theodore Green, organized an exhibition on "authentic religious art" at the Art Institute of Chicago.

Today's scholars find less to loathe in religious popular culture. As Morgan says, "We don't start with the assumption that liking Sallman's art makes you somehow a flawed Christian." In fact, Promey suggests that elitist concerns about the debasing effects of Sallman's art were ultimately unfounded: "Supporters of Sallman, in contrast to the liberals' focus on the *de*-humanizing potential of the images, reported highly individual and personalized responses to reproductions of Sallman's paintings."

The seminary set should be pleased to hear, however, that Sallman's popularity has finally started to fade. For example, McDannell reports that "Victorian angels and elaborate crosses" now outsell Sallman's wares at Christian bookstores. The reason has less to do with a new appreciation for "authentic art" than with demographics. In today's multicultural world, the lily-white Jesus depicted in *Head of Christ* doesn't look quite right. So who will be Sallman's successor? According to Morgan, "no image has really been able to fill this void, and it's hard to imagine one ever doing so again." Then again, he adds, maybe that's not *entirely* true: "Forty years ago, my young daughter probably would have had a Sallman on her bedroom wall. Instead, she's got Michael Jordan."

40

The Curse of Ham

D. MARVIN JONES

Society has created a connection between color and meaning. But what of black and white?

> Black is . . . the *total absence of color,* due to the absence or total *absorption* of light. . . . "White" is "fully luminous and devoid of any distinctive hues." That void is the point where white and black meet and reverse; for if white is an empty fullness (fully luminous but *void*), then black is a full emptiness (*total* absence).[1]

The fact that black and white represent a falling out of color represents the idea that ultimately black and white signify a falling out of meaning[2] and coherence.[3] Thus, as Anthony Appiah has stated, race has no real side referent.[4] Black and white may just be signifiers of each other before they are signifiers of any meaning. However paradoxical, Western culture has fixed blackness within the structure of language, firmly entrenching blackness as a symbol of negation. Frantz Fanon writes:

> In Europe . . . the Torturer is the black man, Satan is black, one talks of the shadow, when one is dirty one is black—whether one is thinking of physical dirtiness or moral dirtiness. . . . Blackness, darkness, shadow, shades, night, and the labyrinths of earth, abysmal depths, blacken someone's reputation; and on the other side, the bright look of innocence, the white dove of peace, magical, heavenly light.[5]

The root of this negative image of blackness in the English language is traceable to a religio-ethical tradition of associating whiteness with purity and blackness with sin. It is a tradition as old as Plato's narrative vision of the soul or Horace's association of blackness with a power of evil. Blackness has also been perceived as a mark of cursedness because "nearness" to the sun suggested a punishment of some kind.[6] Moreover, in the Christian tradition, white refers to innocence or wisdom (or both) and blackness is tied directly to sin:

> Many shall purify themselves, and make themselves white, and be refined; but the wicked shall do wickedly; and none of the wicked shall understand; but those who are wise shall understand.

> [L]earn to do good;
> seek justice, . . .
> plead for the widow. . . .
> [T]hough your sins are like scarlet,
> they shall be as white as snow. . . .[7]

From "DARKNESS MADE VISIBLE: LAW, METAPHOR, AND THE RACIAL SELF," 82 GEO. L.J. 437 (1993). Originally published in the *Georgetown Law Journal*. Reprinted by permission.

An English writer pondering the question of whether blacks were capable of salvation concluded that they were, but that in redemption they shed their color:

Quest.: Whether negroes shall rise on the last day?
Answer: The pinch of the Question only lies—Whether *White* or *Black* is the *better colour.* . . . [A]fter all . . . there is something natural in't. Black is the Colour of Night, Frightful, Dark, and Horrid; but White of the Day and Light, refreshing and lovely. Taking then this Blackness of the Negro to be an accidental imperfection . . . I conclude thence, that he shall not arise with that Complexion, but leave it behind him in the Darkness of the Grave, exchanging it for a brighter and a better, at his return again into the World.[8]

The imagery of blackness as sin continues today, in songs that are presently sung:

On the Cross at Cavalry,
Jesus died for you and me
There he shed His precious blood
That from sin we might be free
O cleansing stream does flow
And it washes *white* as snow.[9]

This symbolic framework drew together notions of spiritual equality and secular inferiority. This imagery was instrumental throughout the slave and colonial regimes in reconciling religious equalitarianism with institutions of colonial domination and slavery.[10] A variation on this theme of blackness as the absence of virtue is the idea that blackness represents the absence of intelligence. As a color, black does not reflect. As such it was an easy, if illogical, step to extend Gobineau's "Le noir ne reflechit pas" (the color of black does not reflect) to the notion that the black man does not "reflect" (i.e., think).[11] Color and mental qualities are thus conflated. Consequently, Hume could posit a fundamental identity between color, intellectual achievement, and intelligence. Hume wrote:

I am apt to suspect the negroes, and in general all the other species of men (for there are four or five different kinds) to be naturally inferior to the whites. There never was a civilized nation of any other complexion than white, nor even any individual eminent either in action or speculation. No ingenious manufactures amongst them, no arts, no sciences. . . . Such a uniform and constant difference could not happen, in so many countries and ages, if nature had not made an original distinction betwixt these breeds of men. Not to mention our colonies, there are NEGROE slaves dispersed all over EUROPE, of which none ever discovered any symptoms of ingenuity. . . . In JAMAICA indeed they talk of one negro as a man of parts and learning; but 'tis likely he is admired for very slender accomplishments, like a parrot, who speaks a few words plainly.[12]

Notes

1. CHRISTOPHER MILLER, BLANK DARKNESS 30–31 (1985).

2. Ralph Ellison, in his classic work, *Invisible Man,* presents a literary treatment of the consequences of race construction and humorously examines this point concerning the incoherence of color as a signifier. For example, he writes:

"Brothers and sisters, my text this morning is the 'Blackness of Blackness.'"
And a congregation of voices answered: "That blackness is most black, brother, most black . . ."
"In the beginning . . ."

"At the very start," they cried.
"... there was blackness ..."
"Preach it ..."
"... and the sun ..."
"The sun, Lawd ..."
"... was bloody red ..."
"Red ..."
"Now black is ..." the preacher shouted.
"Bloody ..."
"I said black is ..."
"Preach it, brother ..."
"... an' black ain't ..."
"Black will git you ..."
"Red, Lawd, red: He said it's red!"
"Amen, brother ..."
"Yes it will ..."
"... an, black won't ..."
"Black will make you ..."
"Black ..."
"... or black will un-make you."
"Ain't it the truth Lawd?"

RALPH ELLISON, INVISIBLE MAN 7–8 (1980) (1952).

   3. Christopher Miller explains:

Pure darkness is felt as a force so powerful that it must be repressed as a "criterion for evaluating men." The consequence of this, however, is that meaning itself will fall out of a secure grounding in symbolism and be forced always to point elsewhere. ...

   ... Black and white are to color what promiscuous concubinage, squeaking, and nakedness were to marriage, speech, and clothing: they negate the category they occupy.

MILLER, *supra* at 30–31.

   4. *See* Kwame Anthony Appiah, *The Conservation of Race*, in BLACK AMERICAN LITERARY FORUM 49–51 (Spring 1989).

   5. FRANTZ FANON, BLACK SKIN, WHITE MASKS 188–89 (Charles L. Markmann trans., 1967).

   6. WINTHROP JORDAN, WHITE OVER BLACK 13 (1968).

   7. Daniel 12:10; Isaiah 1: 17–18.

   8. JORDAN, *supra* at 258 (quoting THE ATHENIAN ORACLE, I, 435–36 (2d ed. 1704)); *see also* FRANK SNOWDEN, BLACKS IN ANTIQUITY 200 (1970) (stating that "Christ came into the world to make blacks radiantly white").

   9. *On the Cross of Calvary*, in SONG BOOK OF THE SALVATION ARMY 33 (1963) (emphasis added).

   10. *See, e.g.*, WILLIAM H. FOOTE, SKETCHES OF VIRGINIA 232–33 (2d ed. 1856) (recounting the preachings of Reverend Cary Allen).

   11. *See* MILLER, *supra* at 31.

   12. DAVID HUME, *Of National Characters*, in 1 THE PHILOSOPHICAL WORKS 252 n.1 (Thomas H. Green & Thomas H. Grose eds., 1964) (1874–75).

41

Los Olvidados: On the Making of Invisible People

JUAN F. PEREA

The Framers' Plan for a White America

According to its English conquerors, America was always meant to belong to white Englishmen. In 1788, John Jay, writing in the Federalist Number 2, declared: "Providence has been pleased to give this one connected country to one united people—a people descended from the same ancestors, speaking the same language, professing the same religion, attached to the same principles of government, very similar in their manners and customs. . . . "[1] Although Jay's statement was wrong—early American society was remarkably diverse—his wish that America be a homogeneous, white, English-speaking Anglo society was widely shared by the Framers of the Constitution and other prominent leaders.

Early on, Benjamin Franklin expressed his distaste for the Germans in Pennsylvania, who, by 1790, accounted for over one-third of the citizens of that state.[2] The presence of German colonists and their different language, in Franklin's eyes, threatened the English and their government. In his "Observations Concerning the Increase of Mankind," written in 1751, Franklin lamented the presence of Germans, other Europeans, and Africans, who would render impure or darken the "lovely White and Red" complexion of the English in America.[3] Regarding the Germans, Franklin wrote:

> [W]hy should the *Palatine Boors* be suffered to swarm into our Settlements and, by herding together, establish their Language and Manners, to the Exclusion of ours? Why should *Pennsylvania*, founded by the *English*, become a Colony of *Aliens*, who will shortly be so numerous as to Germanize us instead of our Anglifying them, and will never adopt our Language or Customs any more than they can acquire our Complexion?

Interestingly, Franklin thought that the Germans and other Europeans had a "swarthy complexion," different and inferior to the "lovely White and Red"[4] of the English. Franklin attributed racial differences in skin color to the Germans, differences that would probably not be perceptible today, because of his hostility toward their ethnic differences from the English. In this excerpt we can see one of the functions of racial difference: the assignment of an inferior position to a disliked other.

With respect to Africans, Franklin pronounced that "[a]ll *Africa* is black or tawny." He asked, rhetorically: "Why increase the Sons of *Africa*, by planting them in *America*, where

70 N.Y.U. L. Rev. 965, 972–78 (1995). Originally published in the *New York University Law Review*. Reprinted by permission.

we have so fair an Opportunity, by excluding all Blacks and Tawneys, of increasing the lovely White and Red?" Franklin's design for a white America called for excluding others of a different complexion, so that America might not darken its people.[5]

Like Franklin and Jay, Thomas Jefferson was also preoccupied with creating a homogeneous and white nation. In 1801, Jefferson wrote that

> it is impossible not to look forward to distant times, when our rapid multiplication will expand itself . . . & cover the whole northern, if not the southern continent, with a people speaking the same language, governed in similar forms, & by similar laws; *nor can we contemplate with satisfaction either blot or mixture on that surface.*[6]

The "blot or mixture" that concerned him was the presence of Africans in the United States. Jefferson worried that the black "blot" would lead to "mixture" and the "staining" of "the fine mixture of red and white."[7] Jefferson's solution was expulsion: the African was "to be removed beyond the reach of mixture," perhaps to Santo Domingo or perhaps back to Africa as a last resort.[8] For Jefferson, the lovely white, homogeneous republic must not allow its people to be stained and to become a nation of mulattoes.

Benjamin Rush, signer of the Declaration of Independence and leading educator and physician of his time, saw blackness as a disease, like leprosy, which was curable with proper treatment. Rush wanted to cure blacks of their blackness. While they recovered from their blackness, Rush proposed isolating and segregating blacks in internal domestic colonies, black farming communities, rather than expelling them from the country.[9]

Whites were no more willing to include Native Americans in their society than they were to include Africans. White hatred of the Indian was perhaps best personified by President Andrew Jackson, who viewed Indians as impulsive and lacking in discipline. He also feared Indian men as sexual threats to white women. Jackson described Indians as "savage bloodhounds" and "blood thirsty barbarians." He urged their extermination, encouraging his troops to commit acts of great cruelty and brutality against them. As President, Jackson was most responsible for the removal of Indians from their desirable lands in the eastern United States and their relocation west of the Mississippi.[10]

As different American leaders implemented their visions of a homogeneous white nation, peoples of color were inconvenient obstacles to be managed by any of several means: expulsion, isolation, removal, enslavement, even extermination. How, then, would the white nation deal with its Latinos—a hybrid people, a tiny portion part-Spanish, mostly Indian, many part-African, speaking Spanish, and embodying the very "blot and mixture" the Framers had thought so necessary to expel?[11]

The Early Conflict between White America and Latinos

As historian David Weber has written:

Despite the enduring myth that "Spaniards" settled the borderlands, it is quite clear that the majority of the pioneers were Mexicans of mixed blood. In New Spain, the three races of mankind, Caucasian, Mongol, and Negro, blended to form an infinite variety of blood strains, and this blending continued as Mexicans settled among aborigines [Indians] in the Southwest. Thus *mestizaje*, or racial mixture, was so common that today the vast majority of all Mexicans are of mixed blood.[12]

The imperative of establishing and preserving a pure white government still ran strong when Anglos first encountered Mexicans. Senator John Calhoun opposed United States annexation of Mexican lands on racial grounds:

> I know further, sir, that we have never dreamt of incorporating into our Union any but the Caucasian race—the free white race. To incorporate Mexico, would be the very first instance of the kind of incorporating an Indian race. . . . I protest against such a union as that! *Ours, sir, is the Government of a white race.*[13]

Both before and after the conquest of Mexico in 1846, the ideological stage had been set for the mutual dislike that Mexicans and white Americans had for each other. As David Weber has written: "American visitors to the Mexican frontier were nearly unanimous in commenting on the dark skin of Mexican mestizos who, it was generally agreed, had inherited the worst qualities of Spaniards and Indians to produce a 'race' still more despicable than that of either parent."[14] Rufus B. Sage, newspaperman and Rocky Mountain trapper, expressed the common view, describing residents of New Mexico in 1846:

> There are no people on the continent of America, whether civilized or uncivilized, with one or two exceptions, more miserable in condition or despicable in morals than the mongrel race inhabiting New Mexico. . . .
>
> . . . To manage them successfully, they must needs be held in continual restraint, and kept in their place by force, if necessary,—else they will become haughty and insolent.
>
> As servants, they are excellent, when properly trained, but are worse than useless if left to themselves.[15]

Lest one think this kind of thinking is a thing of the distant past, consider the views of historian Walter Prescott Webb, writing in 1935:

> The Mexican nation arises from the heterogeneous mixture of races that compose it. The Indian blood—but not Plains Indian blood—predominates, but in it is a mixture of European, largely Latin. The result is a conglomerate with all gradations from pure Spanish to pure Indian. There are corresponding social gradations with grandees at the top and peons at the bottom. The language is Spanish, or Mexican, the religion Catholic, the temperament volatile and mercurial.[16]

Both writers appear obsessed with the racial "blot and mixture" that so preoccupied white Americans, Framers, frontiersmen, and historians alike. Interestingly, in Webb's writing, the historian imposes racial hierarchy according to the relative amounts of "Spanish" (i.e., quasi-white) and Native American ancestry exhibited by Mexicans.

Today, an important part of the public image of the Latino is the Latino as alien: an immigrant, a recent arrival, a foreigner not really belonging to, or in, America. The irony and the proof of falsity in this public image are found in history. The Spanish language was introduced into Mexico in 1519 when explorers and conquerors claimed Mexico for the Spanish crown. The presence of the largest group of people we now call Latinos, Mexican Americans, has been continuous in the Southwest since the sixteenth century.

Of course, Mexicans formulated their own views of the Anglos that began entering their territories in Texas, New Mexico, and California. Jose Maria Sanchez, writing in 1828, described the living conditions of Anglos settled in Villa de Austin, on the Texas frontier:

> Its population is nearly two hundred persons, of which only ten are Mexicans, for the balance are all Americans from the North with an occasional European. Two wretched little stores supply the inhabitants of the colony: one sells only whiskey, rum, sugar, and coffee; the other, rice,

flour, lard, and cheap cloth. . . . The Americans from the North, at least the greater part of those I have seen, eat only salted meat, bread made by themselves out of corn meal, coffee, and home-made cheese. To these the greater part of those who live in the village add strong liquor, for they are in general, in my opinion, lazy people of vicious character. Some of them cultivate their small farms by planting corn; but this task they usually entrust to their negro slaves, whom they treat with considerable harshness.[17]

Juan Seguin, former mayor of San Antonio, was forced to flee Texas because of a huge influx of Anglo-Americans. In 1858, he described the painful irony of his new powerless-ness at the hands of the new Anglo rulers of San Antonio: "A victim to the wickedness of a few men, whose imposture was favored by their origin, and recent domination over the country; a foreigner in my native land; could I be expected stoically to endure their outrages and insults?"[18] Anglo-Americans thus turned Latinos into foreigners in their own lands.

White America and the English Language

The Framers' white America also had to be a predominantly English-speaking America in the words of John Jay and later echoed by Thomas Jefferson. Benjamin Franklin's dislike of the German language was palpable. I will use two examples to illus-trate the perceived need for a white and English-speaking America.

In 1807, Jefferson proposed the resettlement, at government expense, of thirty thousand presumably English-speaking Americans in Louisiana in order to "make the majority American, [and] make it an American instead of a French State."[19] The first governor of Louisiana, William Claiborne, unsuccessfully attempted to require that all the laws of Louisiana be published in English.

The saga of New Mexico's admission to statehood also illustrates the perceived need for a white and English-speaking America. Despite repeated attempts beginning in 1850, New Mexico did not became a state until 1912, when a majority of its population was English-speaking for the first time. Statehood was withheld from New Mexico for over sixty years because of Congress's unwillingness to grant statehood to a predominantly Spanish-speaking territory populated by Mexican people.

Notes

1. The Federalist No. 2, at 91 (John Jay) (Isaac Kramnick ed., 1988).

2. 2 Albert B. Faust, The German Element in the United States 14 (1909).

3. Benjamin Franklin, Observations Concerning the Increase of Mankind, Peopling of Countries, Etc. (1751), in 3 The Writings of Benjamin Franklin 63, 73 (Albert H. Smyth ed., 1905).

4. Id. at 72–73.

5. See id. at 72–73. These observations, including the comments on Germans, were deleted from all editions of Franklin's essay that appeared during his lifetime except the first edition. Id. at 63 n.1, 72 n.1.

6. Thomas Jefferson, Letter to James Monroe (Nov. 24, 1801), in Thomas Jefferson: Writings 1096, 1097 (Merrill D. Peterson ed., 1984) (emphasis added).

7. Thomas Jefferson, Notes on the State of Virginia, Query XIV (1844), reprinted in Thomas Jef-ferson: Writings, supra at 264–65.

8. Id. at 270; see also Ronald Takaki, Iron Cages: Race and Culture in Nineteenth-Century America 49–50 (1979) (describing Jefferson's thoughts about dealing with America's African population).

9. See Takaki, supra at 33–35.

10. Id. at 95–97.

11. It is understatement to note, as Judge Higginbotham wrote, that the English colonists had "difficulties in fostering a sense of community in a colony [Virginia] populated by Portuguese, Spanish, French, Turks, Dutch, blacks, and Indians." A. Leon Higginbotham, Jr., In the Matter of Color: Race and the Legal Process 29 (1978).

12. Foreigners in Their Native Land: Historical Roots of the Mexican Americans 33 (David J. Weber ed., 1973).

13. Cong. Globe, 30th Cong., 1st Sess., 98 (1848) (remarks of Sen. Calhoun), excerpted in Foreigners in Their Native Land, supra at 135 (emphasis added).

14. Foreigners in Their Native Land, supra at 59–60.

15. 2 Rufus B. Sage: His Letters and Papers, 1836–1847, at 82–87 (LeRoy R. Hafen & Ann W. Hafen eds., 1956), excerpted in Foreigners in Their Native Land, supra at 72, 74.

16. Walter P. Webb, The Texas Rangers: A Century of Frontier Defense 13–14 (2d ed. 1965), excerpted in Foreigners in Their Native Land, supra at 77.

17. Jose M. Sanchez, A Trip to Texas in 1828, 29 Sw. Hist. Q., Apr. 1926, at 270–71 (Carlos E. Castañeda trans.), excerpted in Foreigners in Their Native Land, supra at 81–82.

18. Juan N. Seguin, Personal Memoirs of John N. Seguin, From the Year 1834 to the Retreat of General Woll from the City of San Antonio, 1842, at iii–iv, 18–32 (1858), excerpted in Foreigners in Their Native Land, supra at 178.

19. Letter from Thomas Jefferson to John Dickinson (Jan. 13, 1807), in Thomas Jefferson: Writings, supra at 1169, 1169–70.

42

White Innocence, Black Abstraction

THOMAS ROSS

White Innocence

To understand the power of the theme of white innocence, one must begin with the cultural conception of innocence. To be innocent is important everywhere in our culture. The argument for the white person's innocence in matters of race connects with the cultural ideas of innocence and defilement. The very contrast between the colors, white and black, is often a symbol for the contrast between innocence and defilement. Thus, the theme of white innocence in the legal rhetoric of race draws its power from more than the obvious advantage of pushing away responsibility. It takes power from the cultural, religious, and sexual themes its terms suggest. [Professor Ross also discusses this idea in chapter 16. Ed.]

White and black often symbolize some form of good and bad. Black or darkness has served as the symbol of evil for many Western cultures. Darkness is a symbol of the anti-God, Satan by any name.[1] "Black magic" is often used to describe a perverse form of magic and worship. In Christian sects, darkened churches symbolize the days of Lent, whereas the glory of Easter is a time to throw open the windows and let in the light.

The sexual connotations of white innocence are many and complex. White often symbolizes innocence as chaste, whereas black symbolizes noninnocence, as in the defiled and the defiler. The white wedding dress is a double symbol of the connection between white and innocence and the significance of sexual innocence of women.

The black person is often depicted as the sexual defiler. Shakespeare's depiction of Othello, although an uncommonly rich portrait of a black person in literature, expressed the idea of the black as sexual defiler. [A more recent commentator has observed:]

> It is clear that among Englishman there was indeed a vague prejudice against blacks even before the first colonists set foot in North America. As a result of early contacts with Africa, Englishmen tended to associate blackness with savagery, heathenism, and general failure to conform to European standards of civilization and propriety. Contributing to this predisposition to look upon Negroes with disfavor were the conscious and unconscious connotations of the color black. The association of black with evil was of course deeply rooted in Western and Christian mythology; it was natural to think of Satan as the Prince of Darkness and of witchcraft as black magic. On the unconscious level, twentieth-century psychoanalysts have suggested, blackness can be associated with suppressed libidinous impulses. Carl Gustav Jung has even argued that the Negro became for European whites a symbol of the unconscious itself—of what he calls "the shadow"—the whole suppressed or rejected side of the human psyche.[2]

FROM "THE RHETORICAL TAPESTRY OF RACE: WHITE INNOCENCE AND BLACK ABSTRACTION," 32 WM. & MARY L. REV. 1 (1990). Originally published in the *William and Mary Law Review*. Reprinted by permission.

The contrast between black and white in its sexual aspect is most vividly captured in miscegenation statutes, always accompanied by images of the black man's defilement of the white woman. Commentators on southern culture have noted the recurring mythology of the black man as the oversexed, large, would-be defiler of the innocent white woman.[3] Griffith's epic motion picture *The Birth of a Nation* depicts the suicide of the innocent white woman seeking to avoid the touch of the black man, portrayed as a slobbering beast.

Our media's obsession with the violent sexual assault of a white woman by a group of blacks in the "Central Park jogger" case[4] suggests that the sexual connotation of white innocence persists. The notion of the black person as oversexed and dirty is part of our cultural stereotypes. The unconscious racism which our culture continues to teach expresses the terror of the black defiler of the innocent white. In 1967, *Loving v. Virginia*[5] finally declared unconstitutional our most vivid legal expression of this form of racism, the miscegenation statutes, although the Court's opinion lacked any real expression of outrage.

The rhetorical theme of white innocence thus connects with the cultural, religious, and sexual notions of innocence, sin, and defilement. The power of the rhetoric comes in part from its ability to conjure in us at some unconscious level the always implied contrast to white innocence—the black one who is both defiled and the potential defiler.

White innocence is thus a special rhetorical device. When nineteenth-century Supreme Court justices insisted on white innocence as part of the rhetorical veneer placed over the choices to subjugate the black in cases like *Dred Scott* and *Plessy*, they were inviting the reader to draw on the cultural themes of innocence. These cultural themes of innocence in the nineteenth-century texts invited images of the black as the sexual defiler, the very embodiment of sin or evil.

The irony is that the rhetoric of white innocence was arguably less powerful in its nineteenth-century version because these cultural connections and images were part of accepted public ideology and discourse. People spoke publicly of blacks as degenerate, dirty, and beast-like. The rhetoric of white innocence thus might have been merely an alternative way of expressing a widely accepted vision of blacks and whites—the vision of blunt and explicit racism.

On the other hand, the rhetoric of white innocence in its contemporary form may be rhetorically more powerful. Our public ideology and discourse are ones of nonracism. Judges cannot say out loud that blacks are inferior, nor can lawyers make arguments with the explicit premises of racism. When the contemporary rhetoric of white innocence invites the cultural connections and images, we may be tapping into a repressed vein of unconscious racism which cannot be expressed in any way but indirectly and metaphorically.

We ought to set aside the rhetoric of white innocence for several reasons. First, its family resemblance to the rhetoric of cases we now disavow makes it suspect. Second, when we consider the implicit premises of our claim to innocence, we see a much more complicated set of circumstances. Finally, when we consider the cultural connections that the rhetoric invites and the way those connections form part of the unconscious racism that persists in our culture, we have the most powerful reason of all to stop talking this way.

Black Abstraction

In various ways, legal rhetoric denied, or obscured, the full humanness of the black person. By doing so, we made legally coherent the nineteenth-century legal choices first to enslave and thereafter to segregate blacks. Slavery became legally coherent when the subject was not human. De jure segregation became legally coherent when whites supposed that blacks suffered no harm and experienced no stigma.

As in legal rhetoric, we also typically depicted blacks as something less than fully human in literature and art. With but several notable exceptions, American writers either ignored the black or depicted him as a simple, one-dimensional character. Until the public emergence of black writers in the twentieth century, American public literature was generally the product of white authors and generally depicted the black as either a saint, a suffering victim, or a wild beast. American art similarly depicted blacks as unidimensional figures. In most instances, black persons occupy the shadows, the periphery of paintings, or are depicted as one of several common stereotypes.

The denial of the full humanness of the black person has been a central and tragic part of our discourse. Black abstraction functioned as a lens through which we remade the setting in which our choices were played out. We abstracted away the pieces of reality that might have made those choices less comfortable.

Black abstraction also worked in another, equally tragic way. In law and elsewhere in our culture, black abstraction makes more difficult the empathic response of the white person to the suffering of the black. Empathy connotes the capacity to share, in some imperfect way, in the suffering of others. We easily can achieve some degree of empathy for the suffering of those whom we think of as familiar. Although the empathy may not move us to personal sacrifice or even to a lesser intervention in any particular case, we understand their suffering because we have an obvious and easily accessible analog, our own. We have a more difficult time achieving empathy for the suffering of people we think of as unfamiliar. We can separate ourselves more easily from their circumstances; we can simply not imagine that they suffer; we can suppose some sense of justice in whatever suffering we are forced to see.

When we see that white innocence and black abstraction fill our legal rhetoric of race, we have reason to doubt that our choices are any better than those that stain our legal history. We have reason to wonder whether our choices are made from any real sense of empathy with those who suffer. We have reason to doubt the justice of it all. White innocence and black abstraction comfort us in our choices. They provide a source of shelter that we should struggle to give up. We should try to see the problematic quality of white innocence and the "make believe" world depicted through black abstraction.

Changing the way we talk about race is not simply a matter of resolve. We cannot slough off the assumptions and attitudes that determine in part the language we use. White innocence and black abstraction never have been simply rhetorical structures that we made up by ourselves. They always have been a product of both the imagination of the rhetorician and the influences of history and culture. To change truly the way we talk about race requires a parallel change in attitudes and assumptions. Our language and our basic assumptions are inescapably intertwined. This close relation is what makes a change in language and rhetoric so powerful, and so difficult. It is thus a struggle. There are those who can help in this struggle. The storytellers are here. Justice Thurgood Marshall never ceased his insistence on narrative and his struggle against the abstract depiction of blacks. Hearing the stories will not provide any easy answers. It will, however, increase the chance that our choices on matters of race will not become a story of tragedy and a source of shame.

Notes

1. "Blackness and darkness are almost always associated with evil, in opposition to the association of whiteness and light with good." J. RUSSELL, THE DEVIL: PERCEPTIONS OF EVIL FROM ANTIQUITY TO PRIMITIVE CHRISTIANITY 64–65 (1977). "The Devil's blackness may derive from his association with darkness, which symbolizes death, annihilation, and the terrors of the night." J. RUSSELL, at 253. "Sometimes the devil wears green or grey, but mostly he is dressed in black. . . ." W. WOODS, A HISTORY OF THE DEVIL 185 (1973).

2. GEORGE FREDRICKSON, THE ARROGANCE OF RACE: HISTORICAL PERSPECTIVES ON SLAVERY, RACISM, AND SOCIAL INEQUALITY (1988), at 191.

3. "[T]he growing myth of the black man as a genetic sexual monster fanned the Negrophobia of the 1890s, a myth encouraged by novelists such as Thomas Nelson Page and later trumpeted by Thomas Dixon, Jr." J. KINNEY, AMALGAMATION! 153 (1985).

4. *See 3 Youths Guilty of Rape And Assault of Jogger,* N.Y. TIMES, Aug. 19, 1990, at 1, col. 1.

5. 388 U.S. 1 (1967).

43

Race and the Dominant Gaze: Narratives of Law and Inequality in Popular Film

MARGARET M. RUSSELL

In *The Birth of a Nation* (Epoch Pictures, 1915), frequently cited as a milestone in the history of American motion pictures, D. W. Griffith offered his vision of race relations in the United States. Originally entitled *The Clansman,* the film portrays a South ravaged by the Civil War, corrupted by Reconstruction, and eventually redeemed by the birth of the Ku Klux Klan. *The Birth of a Nation* conveys its blunt white supremacist message through a narrative chronicling the effect of the Civil War on the South Carolina plantation of the Cameron family. As the silent film begins, subtitles extol the virtues of the Camerons' tranquil way of life which "is to be no more." Benevolent masters are served by loyal slaves who contentedly pick cotton, perform domestic chores, and otherwise aim to please. By war's end, this felicitous social order has degenerated into lawlessness. The newly emancipated roam the streets and terrorize the white community; anarchic hordes take over the polls, disenfranchise white voters, and seize control of the Congress. Griffith's first black legislators are contemptible, priapean fools; swigging from whiskey bottles and gnawing on fried chicken legs, they conduct their first legislative session with shoes off and legs splayed carelessly across their desks. The film depicts emancipation as destructive of the private sphere as well; freedmen lust after Southern belles, and communities fall prey to "ruin, devastation, raping, and pillage." The saga climaxes with a dramatic, victorious ride to the rescue by the Klan, which defeats the black rebels and restores civilization.

The Birth of a Nation was advertised upon its release as a film that would "work audiences into a frenzy . . . it will make you hate."[1] The "you" to whom this exhortation was addressed, of course, was not a neutral or universal "you," but a specifically targeted one: the white viewer threatened by integration and fearful of black insurgency. Through a carefully constructed fusion of unprecedented technical wizardry and degrading racial stereotypes, Griffith sought to convince his audience that his was the "true" story of the old South and that white domination was necessary for their survival. To a great extent, he succeeded: The film's enormous popularity fueled the growing influence of the Klan, and *The Birth of a Nation* remains to this day one of the highest-grossing box office successes in Hollywood history. Thus, it continues to be important not only as an individual aesthetic statement or arcane historical artifact, but as a popular work which has profoundly affected both popular discourse and events concerning race relations in the United States.

15 LEGAL STUD. F. 243 (1991). Originally published in *Legal Studies Forum.* Reprinted by permission.

In this latter respect—as a text about race, dominance, and the American social/legal order—*The Birth of a Nation* exemplifies what I would call the "dominant gaze": the tendency of mainstream culture to replicate, through narrative and imagery, racial inequalities and biases which exist throughout society. I derive the term "dominant gaze" from Laura Mulvey's feminist critique of Hollywood movies, "Visual Pleasure and Narrative Cinema,"[2] in which she contends that popular film essentially serves the political function of subjugating female bodies and experiences to the interpretation and control of a heterosexual "male gaze." According to Mulvey, any observer's potential to experience visual and visceral pleasure from watching Hollywood movies is completely predicated upon acceptance of a patriarchal worldview in which men look and women are looked at, men act and women are acted upon. She further contends that this distinctly male-oriented perspective insidiously perpetuates sexual inequality by forcing the viewer (whether male or female) to identify with and adopt a perspective which objectifies and dehumanizes women. Finally, she asserts that only through concerted deconstruction and disruption of the male gaze can women achieve equality in societal relations and in the cultural representations which reinforce them.

Extending Mulvey's metaphor, I use the term "dominant gaze" to describe the tendency of American popular cinema to objectify and trivialize the racial identity and experiences of people of color, even when it purports to represent them. Like Mulvey's male gaze, the dominant gaze subtly invites the viewer to empathize and identify with its viewpoint as natural, universal, and beyond challenge; it marginalizes other perspectives to bolster its own legitimacy in defining narratives and images. As D. W. Griffith illustrated so effectively in *The Birth of a Nation*, the dominant gaze's power lies in projecting stereotypes and biases as essential "truths."

Intrigued by the relationship between law and popular culture in forging societal norms about race, I decided to explore the dominant gaze that pervades the representation of blacks in American cinema. Much as analyzing jurisprudential artifacts such as *Dred Scott v. Sandford* and *Plessy v. Ferguson* remains essential to a full understanding of the persistent effects of racism in our legal system, film classics such as *The Birth of a Nation* provide a useful starting point for analysis of the narratives and images that perpetuate legacies of bigotry in our popular culture and in our laws.

Doing the Hollywood Shuffle: Racial Stereotypes in American Popular Films

In 1941, in commenting on a demeaning and unintelligible line of dialogue written for her role as a mammy-ish maid in *Affectionately Yours*, black Hollywood actress Butterfly McQueen confessed: "I never thought I would have to say a line like that. I had imagined that since I was an intelligent woman, I could play any kind of role."[3] McQueen's dismay stemmed from the realization that Hollywood had no roles for an intelligent black woman—only ones for "toms, coons, mulattoes, mammies, and bucks."[4] Nearly fifty years later, black filmmaker Robert Townsend made a similar point in the 1987 comedy *Hollywood Shuffle*. Townsend lambastes the Hollywood film and television community as manipulative buffoons who use black actors only for roles as pimps, drug addicts, and prostitutes; accordingly, the film's black characters realize that their livelihood depends upon conforming to these debilitating images—that is, doing the "Hollywood Shuffle."

How has the dominant gaze operated to perpetuate the subordination of blacks in mainstream Hollywood films? Consider three distinct ways: (1) in the proliferation of degrading stereotypes which serve to dehumanize blacks' history, lives, and experiences; (2) in the marginalization or complete absence of indigenous perspectives on blacks' history, lives, and experiences; and (3) in the co-optation—or "Hollywood-ization"—of ostensibly "racial" themes to capitalize on the perceived trendiness or fashionableness of such perspectives. In marginalizing blacks and other minorities from popular discourse, the three trends frequently overlap in particular films. *The Birth of a Nation,* for example, both disseminates negative stereotypes and obscures indigenous perspectives; a more recent film such as *Driving Miss Daisy* might be seen as a benignly intended example of the second and third trends; and slick Eddie Murphy vehicles such as *Beverly Hills Cop* illustrate all three.

It is important to understand the history of exploitation of blacks in American films, for it is from this ideological cinema-scape that contemporary movies emerge. Over time, such distortion and erasure create damage both subtle and severe. The unchallenged transmission of racial stereotypes in films not only weakens resistance to their falsity, but also strengthens the legitimacy of their narrative source. With these concerns in mind, I must concede that I approach movies not only with an avid fan's enthusiasm and curiosity, but with a skeptic's critical eye as well. It was in this frame of mind that I first saw *Soul Man*—a fairytale romance of a white student who pretends to be black so that he can go to Harvard Law School.

Soul Man: Variations on the Gaze

"This is the Eighties! It's the Cosby decade—America LOVES black people!"

With these cheery words, the white protagonist of *Soul Man* attempts to reassure a doubting friend of the wisdom of his decision to "turn black" in order to win a minority scholarship to Harvard Law School. As the flippancy of this dialogue might suggest, *Soul Man* aims both stylistically and substantively to be very much in tune with the times. It sparkles with several (by now de rigueur) attributes bound to please the youthful, upwardly mobile movie-goer: a hip title; a musical soundtrack studded with soul, rock, and blues standards; and a plot featuring attractive, well-educated, and basically conventional young people. Its obvious theme of "twentysomething" self-interest is carefully tempered by the presence of a few prominent older stars to draw a wider audience. The slickly packaged story provides carefully measured doses of comedy, romance, sex, conflict, and moralizing before reaching a happy and uncomplicated denouement.

Not coincidentally, *Soul Man*'s narrative premise is also characteristic of its era; it is a post-*Bakke* fantasy about the dangerous possibilities of affirmative action, minority scholarships, and other race-conscious remedies. Mark Watson, an upper-middle-class, white male college graduate, fears that he will be prevented from attending the law school of his dreams. To obtain his "rightful" place at Harvard, he decides to fake being black so that he can win a minority scholarship. With the help of a friend, Mark obtains chemicals to darken his skin, interviews successfully for the scholarship, and—voilà!—embarks on his new life as a black man at Harvard.

Mark continues this ruse without hesitation until he falls in love with Sarah Walker, a brilliant and beautiful black law student, and learns that *she* would have received the scholarship if *he* had not happened along. Torn with guilt and driven by his desire to please the unknowing Sarah, Mark confesses his deception to a black law professor and submits to prosecution by the Harvard disciplinary council. After a climactic trial scene, he is exonerated and permitted to remain at Harvard Law School. As the film ends, a wiser and more sensitive Mark returns to his life as a white student, now accompanied by Sarah, who has forgiven his transgressions and realized her true, color-blind love for him.

As one might surmise from this synopsis, in many ways *Soul Man* is—beneath its hip, race-conscious veneer—simply another romantic comedy in the old-style Hollywood tradition: Boy Meets Girl, Boy Gets Girl, Boy Loses Girl, Boy Gets Girl Back. However, what renders this movie an especially revealing artifact of its era is its willingness (indeed eagerness) to use race explicitly as a gimmick to advance its old-fashioned story line. *Soul Man*'s comic effectiveness depends upon the viewer's willingness to accept racial stereotypes as comedy and racial identity as a gag. Significantly, the movie transmits its putative wisdom about black experience not through the eyes of its black characters but through the gaze of a white person aiming to carry out a self-serving schoolboy scheme. In using such a dominant gaze, the film undermines its own "enlightened" pretensions in commenting on law, race, and the reality of racial discrimination. To understand how this diminution is accomplished, it is helpful to clarify the perspective of race that permeates the film.

Watson's Plot: A View of the Bottom from the Top

Three early scenes in *Soul Man* set the stage for Mark's racial transformation. As the movie begins, the camera's eye introduces us to Mark Watson's world of collegiate ease and privilege: a student's messy bedroom, replete with carelessly strewn clothes, tennis balls, frisbees, and other sports paraphernalia. A radio blares blues music; a large kitschy figurine of a bikini-clad white woman decorates a corner. Mark has just awakened from the previous night's revelry to find a blonde woman asleep beside him. Suddenly, his roommate bursts loudly into the room, waving two letters from Harvard Law School! Before they can open the momentous letters, Mark offers his roommate, Gordon, a mock-solemn, man-to-man vow: "You're my best friend and I love you; but if you get into Harvard and I don't, I hope you rot in hell." They rip open the letters; both of them have been accepted! Joyous, fraternistic whooping follows. The "buddy" strand of the plot has been established.

The next scene brings us to Mark's parents' lavish Southern California home, where we are invited to share Mark's shock as his self-centered, nouveau–New Age father explains that he will not pay Mark's way through Harvard. Mark's subsequent conversation with friend Gordon invites us to commiserate with Mark; how will he ever obtain the $50,000 he needs to get through Harvard Law School? Thus, the moral urgency of Mark's dilemma has been established.

In the third major episode, Mark and Gordon desperately plow through the Harvard catalogue, trying to find scholarships that might solve Mark's problem. After dismissing several options, they find one that intrigues Mark—the Henry Bouchard Scholarship for the most qualified black student from the Los Angeles area. In a stroke of ingenuity, Mark makes himself "qualified" by making himself black. Gordon asks, Is Mark really ready to *be* a black person? Of course, Mark responds—"America loves black people!" Thus, the ethical rationale for Mark's behavior is established, and the viewer is invited to root for his "harmless" deception.

Once these introductory scenes have established the film's narrative framework, the rest of *Soul Man* focuses on Mark's blackface experience at Harvard Law. Notice that *Soul*

Man's central plot gimmick—a white protagonist in blackface—is hardly new; films such as *The Birth of a Nation* and *Uncle Tom's Cabin* featured white actors playing black roles, and vaudevillian blackface constituted a major entertainment form in the early part of the century. The effect of blackface in *Soul Man*—as in these earlier representations—is to create a disquieting narrative undercurrent, a disfunction between surface and substance. The viewer is expected not to question this dissonance, but to accept it as a gag for the purposes of being entertained.

In this respect, *Soul Man's* use of blackface more closely resembles these earlier regressive films than it does two more recent movies using blackface themes to advance serious points. *Watermelon Man* (1971) focuses on the tragicomic dilemma of a white character who wakes up one day and discovers that he has turned black overnight; however, a critical distinction between this film and *Soul Man* rests upon the viewer's knowledge that the white character is in fact played by a black actor, Godfrey Cambridge. *Black Like Me* (1965), based on the well-known book by John Howard Griffin, dramatizes the prejudice and hatred confronted by a white journalist who deliberately darkens his skin to learn first-hand the treatment of blacks in the South in the early 1960s. Unlike *Soul Man*, *Black Like Me* is a serious tale of degradation and cruelty; the protagonist cannot find lodging, work, transportation, or even a place to go to the bathroom. He suffers the indignities of racial slurs, ignorant comments, and outright threats of violence; his experience of life in the South is almost unremittingly somber and bleak.

Unlike *Watermelon Man* or *Black Like Me*, *Soul Man* uses blackface to portray the issue of crossing the color line as a farcical, frat-boy romp. Mark Watson's indignities seem to be limited to suffering the occasional bigoted apartment manager or tasteless racist joke from fellow students—hardly an inconvenience when compared to the "benefits" that he derives from being black. Moreover, *Soul Man* presents these incidents as comic fodder, intended to amuse rather than to provoke or disturb. As a result, the depiction of racist incidents in this film is stripped of affective power and validity and subsumed within Mark's dominant gaze.

In scene after scene, the plot trots out hoary old stereotypes and invites the viewer to find them amusing. In a pivotal scene, we watch Mark's tense visit to the home of a white Radcliffe student's wealthy and bigoted family, and are asked to observe the event through Mark's eyes. Through his gaze, we see racist stereotypes which Mark imagines are being projected upon him by the family: that he is a vicious drug addict and pimp who will abuse their pure daughter; or a lascivious island native who wants to seduce the mother; or a Prince-style, pelvis-thrusting rocker who will corrupt the young son. By filtering its parody of ignorance and bias through the eyes of Mark—hardly a true "victim" of prejudice—the scene lacks both the irony and the empathic power necessary to convey its ostensibly well-intended message. Instead, since Mark is clearly not black and not in a subordinate role to anyone, I was left with the sense that Mark's dilettantish exposure to racism in this scene was somehow equated with blacks' everyday experiences with racism, and that the hyperbolically bigoted whites were being equated with blacks' everyday experiences with racists. Such a message is not enlightened but distressingly discourages viewers from recognizing that often bigotry wears a mask not burlesque-style and latent, but subtle and insidious.

In defending his film *Do the Right Thing* (1989) against the criticism that it might make mainstream white audiences uncomfortable, Spike Lee asserted, "[T]hat's the way it is all the time for black people."[5] Lee's point was that the dominant gaze still prevails; "uncomfortable" perspectives are marginalized, criticized, or, worst of all, simply ignored. A film such as *Soul Man,* which capitalizes on an ostensibly alternative perspective to tell a tale about contemporary race relations, is ultimately fatally flawed by the dominance of its vision. By exploiting the effect of racial stereotypes without reminding the viewers of their continuing destructive force, *Soul Man* misses the opportunity to make—either seriously or comically—a truly instructive comment about the nature of racism in our society.

Notes

1. Donald Bogle, *Toms, Coons, Mulattoes, Mammies, and Bucks: An Interpretive History of Blacks in American Films* (New York: Viking Press, 1973), 11–12, 15.

2. Laura Mulvey, "Visual Pleasure and Narrative Cinema," *Screen* 16:3, August 1975, 6–18. See also Lorraine Gawnman and Margaret Marshman, eds., *The Female Gaze: Women as Viewers of Popular Culture* (Seattle: Real Comet Press, 1989).

3. Bogle, supra at 93.

4. Id. at 3–18.

5. bell hooks, *Yearning: Race, Gender, and Cultural Politics* (Boston: South End Press, 1990), 173.

44

Residential Segregation and
White Privilege

MARTHA R. MAHONEY

Residential segregation and white dominance are integrally related. White choices are not only the aggregation of individual preferences regarding proximity to blacks. Rather, governmental and private forces—in interaction with each other—in the past created a racialized process of urban/suburban development in which "good" neighborhoods were defined as white and whiteness was defined as good, stable, employed, and employable.

Racial segregation was systematically promoted during the 1930s, 1940s, and 1950s by federal programs like the Home Owners Loan Corporation (HOLC), which made loans to homeowners, and the Federal Housing Authority (FHA), which insured private-sector loans.[1] These programs refused to lend money to blacks. They also actively promoted systems of restrictive racial covenants. The greatest impact of these federal agencies in structuring the market, however, lay in the ranking system—the origins of redlining—that the government used to rank communities in their eligibility for federally financed or federally insured loans.

Using these guidelines, the HOLC and FHA actually refused to lend money or underwrite loans for whites if whites moved to areas where people of color lived. Private lenders adopted policies in line with federal guidelines. These programs reduced housing opportunities for blacks. But they also went considerably further in the process of socially constructing whiteness and blackness in urban areas. Redlining causes decline in majority-black areas, while at the same time preventing lending in majority-white areas where the presence of "inharmonious" racial groups causes lower rankings.

These federal policies, incorporated into private practices, enforced a system in which whiteness was both required and rewarded as a feature of development. Blacks had no choice to move to suburbia. Whites had no choice to move to integrated suburbia. Racism is so pervasive in America that the importance of the construction of whiteness is often overlooked in discussions of racial geography. Whites generally express preferences to live in neighborhoods shared with very low percentages of blacks. Blacks generally express preferences for living in neighborhoods that are more evenly mixed. If the preference for whiteness is addressed at all, it is raised in examining whether the use of racial steering or quotas to prevent white flight is permissible. The *construction* of this white preference for whiteness is not examined at all. Racism is treated as a natural and unexamined force.

Assume for a moment that whites generally tell the truth about their preference for liv-

From "SEGREGATION, WHITENESS, AND TRANSFORMATION," 143 U. PA. L. REV. 1659 (1995). Copyright © 1995 The University of Pennsylvania Law Review. Reprinted by permission.

ing in slightly desegregated communities. Lending policies of the HOLC, FHA, and private banks in the years of postwar suburban expansion actively discouraged such communities by forging a requirement that the neighborhood be uniformly white before investments would be made or insured. Any developer who had tried to accommodate a white taste for slight desegregation would have paid the heavy price of forfeiting access to the large number of buyers who required federal loans or insurance. Maintaining a development as all-white protected white buyers' ability to finance homes, and at the same time the developers' ability to sell them. It is difficult to overestimate the importance of this lesson—that whiteness equalled attractiveness, safeness, and financial security—in the postwar world. Suburban development came to mean white development, and whites came to see suburbs as naturally white. The enforcement of whiteness, therefore, prevented the sort of incremental desegregatory developments that might have changed the way suburbia itself was seen by whites.

The federal requirement of segregation in home financing placed a stamp of approval on private discrimination as well. Both real estate brokers and private lenders followed suit. Once racialized community development was institutionalized as federal policy, any private sector actor who went against the segregated norm would have compromised buyers and their neighbors. Both the ability of the current owners to sell to buyers with federally funded or insured mortgages on resale of the property, and the mortgage insurability of nearby properties, rested on maintaining whiteness in suburbia. Not only were white people socially reluctant to live near black people, but they were also economically rewarded for living near each other. Maintaining a white market paid. The incentives, enforcement mechanisms, and preferences for maintaining whiteness were systemic, not merely individual.

The Kerner Commission on Civil Disorders, inquiring into the causes of the racial riots of the late 1960s, did not find whites moving to the suburbs primarily to avoid blacks. The "more basic" reason for white migration to the suburbs was the "rising mobility and affluence of middle-class families."[2] The suburbs had better schools, living conditions, and affordable housing. But all those qualities of ease and comfort were associated with whiteness, and in turn these qualities increasingly defined whiteness. Jobs moved to the suburbs following the white work force and attracting more white workers.[3] Blacks incur higher time and money costs to commute; blacks possess less information about distant jobs; and suburban locations build employers' fear of white resentment if blacks arrive and remove pressures on employers to avoid discriminating.

Government-sponsored segregation helped inscribe in American culture the equation of "good neighborhoods" with white ones. In the process, of course, they made all ethnic groups that had access to these neighborhoods "white"—something that had at one historical moment or another been uncertain in terms of the social construction of some groups (such as Jews, Greeks, and Italians) that had been defined as "other." [See chapters 65 and 66. Ed.] The close correlation between employment opportunity and residential segregation meant that "black" was increasingly linked with "inner-city" and "unemployed or unemployable" in white consciousness; whiteness was identified with "employed or employable," stability and self-sufficiency. Residential segregation was both product and cause of racial constructions that tended to promote further preferences for whites and further exclusion for blacks. White neighborhoods increasingly seem to be suitable sites for investment, while black neighborhoods seem unsuitable.

I have heard many anecdotal reports indicating that, in applying for office jobs, well-qualified black applicants who put inner-city home addresses on applications or résumés had greater difficulty getting hired than the same individuals did if they used suburban home addresses. Recently, two sociologists were able to uncover employer attitudes by asking employers who would make good employees. The employers frankly revealed their biases,[4] listing race and inner-city residence as explicit parts of their consideration of applicants. Employers freely generalized about race and ethnicity, expressing negative opinions about people of color—especially African-Americans—and positive ideas about whites. For example, they believed that whites had a better work ethic than blacks. Employers' concepts of race and employability were nuanced by ideas about class—mostly signaled by the way employees dressed and spoke. Space was also important: "inner-city" was equated with "black, poor, uneducated, unskilled, lacking in values, crime, gangs, drugs, and unstable families." "Suburb" meant "white, middle-class, educated, skilled, and stable families." Public school attendance was less favorable than private school, and residence in public housing was also seen as a signal of status. Class and space distinguished among black applicants for employers, with inner-city blacks associated with lower classes and with undesirable characteristics as workers.[5] It makes sense, therefore, that blacks who live in white areas are to some extent identified by greater access to whiteness.[6] And indeed, a recent study showed that blacks in suburbs did better at finding jobs than blacks in inner cities.

The link between residential segregation and poverty therefore depends on the social construction of race. In particular, the social construction of whites as employed and employable will continue to attract employers and attract development, as well as discourage the employment of blacks. The problems that residential segregation brings—distance, inconvenience, lower tax base, more concentrated poverty—continue to be reproduced because of their role in reinforcing and reproducing the very idea of race.

[See Chapter 113 for Professor Mahoney's suggestions on how to attack race and housing segregation. Ed.]

Notes

1. For discussions of these federal programs, see CHARLES ABRAMS, FORBIDDEN NEIGHBORS: A STUDY OF PREJUDICE IN HOUSING 174–75 (1955) (arguing that the FHA and the Home Loan Bank System sanctioned and encouraged the refusal of New York City banks to provide loans to black neighborhoods); KENNETH T. JACKSON, CRABGRASS FRONTIER: THE SUBURBANIZATION OF THE UNITED STATES 190–218 (1985) (discussing the impact of various federal programs on housing patterns).

2. REPORT OF THE NATIONAL ADVISORY COMMISSION ON CIVIL DISORDERS 119 (1968).

3. On the suburbanization of jobs, see JOHN F. KAIN & JOHN M. QUIGLEY, HOUSING MARKETS AND RACIAL DISCRIMINATION: A MICROECONOMIC ANALYSIS 87–90 (1975) (detailing the interrelationships between the workplace and the residential choices of black workers); WILLIAM J. WILSON, THE TRULY DISADVANTAGED: THE INNER CITY, THE UNDERCLASS, AND PUBLIC POLICY 42, 100–01 (1987) (emphasizing structural problems creating inner-city joblessness).

4. See Joleen Kirschenman & Kathryn M. Neckerman, "We'd Love to Hire Them, But . . .": The Meaning of Race for Employers, in THE URBAN UNDERCLASS 203–04 (Christopher Jencks & Paul E. Peterson eds., 1991).

5. See Kirschenman & Neckerman, supra at 209–10, 213–17.

6. Note that in the family context whites lose their positions of privilege by marrying or living with blacks or by bearing or accompanying black children. White women with perceptibly black children are not as "white" as they were before they had black children. Interracial families are defined by the introduction of blackness rather than the other way around.

45

Mules, Madonnas, Babies, Bathwater: Racial Imagery and Stereotypes

LINDA L. AMMONS

Facts from a recent case help to illustrate how the conduct of a battered black woman is contrasted with the perception of how a battered white woman responds. A twenty-nine-year-old black woman, Pamela Hill, lived with her abusive boyfriend, Roy Chaney. At trial, the evidence revealed that police had been called to Hill's residence on five separate occasions to protect her. According to the police report, on the night in question, Chaney had been drinking and began slapping Hill. Hill got a knife and the two began struggling over it. Hill got control of the knife and suffered several cuts before fatally wounding Chaney. Hill told the police that she had been trying to kick Chaney out of her public housing apartment, "(b)ut she couldn't just throw him out into the cold." At trial, the prosecutor provided evidence that Hill had stabbed Chaney the year before, and therefore, in his opinion, the relationship was "mutually combative." In his closing argument, the prosecutor made this statement: "(A) lot of people would have you believe Pamela Hill is carrying the banner of Nicole Simpson."[1] The contrasts between the two cases could not be more stark.

The imagery and stereotypes that were raised by the prosecutor's comparison of Pamela Hill and Nicole Simpson cannot be missed. Nicole Simpson was white, beautiful, rich, portrayed as a good mother, and brutalized. Pamela Hill is black, poor, an unwed mother, and considered violent. Hill was convicted and received a sentence of five to twenty-five years. The prosecutor, in making the statement about Pamela Hill "carrying the banner of Nicole Simpson," wanted to make sure that the jurors had a picture in their minds of a real battered woman. However, without discounting the seriousness of the domestic violence conviction of O. J. Simpson, in comparing the situations of Nicole Brown Simpson and Pamela Hill, Hill's situation appears to be more desperate because of her lack of resources and options. Why, then, was she treated so harshly?

The subtlest and most pervasive of all influences are those which create and maintain the repertory of stereotypes. We are told about the world before we see it. We imagine most things before we experience them. And those preconceptions, unless education has made us acutely aware, govern deeply the whole process of perception.[2]

> Next comes a warmer race, from sable sprung,
> To love each thought, to lust each nerve is strung;
> The Samboe dark, and Mulatto brown,

1995 Wis. L. Rev. 1003. Copyright © 1995, by the Board of Regents of the University of Wisconsin System. Reprinted by permission of *Wisconsin Law Review*.

The Mestize fair, the well-limb'd Quaderoon,
And jetty Afric, from no spurious sire,
Warm as her soil, and as her sun—on fire.
These sooty dames, well vers'd in Venus' school,
Make love an art, and boast they kiss by rule.[3]

White girls are pretty funny,
sometimes they drive me mad,
black girls just want to get fucked all night
I just don't have that much jam.[4]

A stereotype is a fixed impression that "conforms very little to the facts . . . and results from our defining first and observing second,"[5] "an exaggerated belief associated with a category. Its function is to justify (rationalize) our conduct in relation to that category."[6] Stereotypes are "the language of prejudice";[7] as such, they are a part of the social heritage of a society. They appear in a range of materials from academic sources to rock-and-roll lyrics. For example, although the above quotation cited by historian Winthrop Jordan and the lyrics by The Rolling Stones were written more than 200 years apart, the statements promote the same stereotype about black women: they are sexually available.

By the time a child is four or five, he or she has learned the significance of skin color and racial membership. Writer Audre Lorde recalls how one day, while wheeling her two-year-old daughter around in the shopping cart, she passed a white woman and her little girl in the aisle. The little white girl "called out excitedly, 'Oh, look Mommy, a baby maid.'"[8] Whites have been taught either expressly or implicitly that they are better than blacks. Kimberlè Crenshaw has provided the following chart to illustrate how the negative image of blacks corresponds with the image of whites:

White Images	Black Images
Industrious	Lazy
Intelligent	Unintelligent
Moral	Immoral
Knowledgeable	Ignorant
Enabling Culture	Disabling Culture
Law-Abiding	Criminal
Responsible	Shiftless
Virtuous/Pious	Lascivious[9]

Even when adults conform their public behavior to what is socially acceptable, because of the changing laws and/or mores the indoctrination of childhood can create psychological conflicts.[10] Psychologist Thomas Pettigrew provides an example: "(m)any Southerners have confessed to me, for instance, that even though in their minds they no longer feel prejudice against blacks, they still feel squeamish when they shake hands with [one]."[11]

Scientists exploring stereotypes about African-Americans repeatedly find that blacks consistently receive the most unfavorable attributions. Among those that were created to keep black women marginalized were Mammy, the asexual nursemaid of white children; Aunt Jemima, the mammy-cook with a name; and Jezebel, the black seductive temptress. Modern caricatures include Sapphire, an emasculating, hateful, stubborn woman; the matriarch, the strong, single mother with no needs; and the welfare queen, the overbreeding, lazy, cheating, single black mother. These representations are so powerful that the sight of a woman of African descent can trigger responses of violence, disdain, fear, or invisibility. Black women know that public humiliation can strike at any moment just because of who they are. For example, the sociologist Joe Feagin interviewed two black women. The first said:

> (I have faced) harassment in stores, being followed around, being questioned about what are you going to purchase here. . . . There are a few of those white people that won't put change in your hand, touch your skin—that doesn't need to go on.

A second reported:

> Because I'm a large black woman and I don't wear whatever class status I have, or whatever professional status (I have) in my appearance when I'm in the grocery store, I'm part of the mass of large black women shopping. . . . That means that they are free to treat me the way they treat most poor black people because they can't tell by looking at me that I differ from that.[12]

Black women are trapped between sub- and super-human imagery and expectations. Even attributes such as strength, that should be considered positive when applied to black women, can be detrimental. For example, African-American women who are strong and independent may be blamed for the breakup of their families—or for the failure of their men. If these stereotypes can affect public policy, routine transactions, and normal discourse, to what extent is the African-American female defendant at a disadvantage when she is brought to trial for a violent crime—even if she claims that she acted in self-defense because she was being battered? Recall what happened to Pamela Hill.

When African-Americans are brought to trial, the question of how extra-legal factors alter their ability to get a fair trial lingers on, raising the possibility that different standards of justice exist for people who are of European descent and those who are not. Racial bias in the courtroom is *de jure* illegal, but malevolent *de facto* bias is not dead.

Notes

1. *See* James Ewinger, Women Gets Prison in Boyfriend's Killing. Cleveland Plain Dealer, Sept. 20, 1994, at 3B.

2. Walter Lippmann, Public Opinion 59 (1922).

3. Jamaica, a Poem in Three Parts, quoted in Winthrop D. Jordan, White Over Black: American Attitudes Toward the Negro 150 (1968).

4. The Rolling Stones, Some Girls, on Some Girls (WarnerCommunications 1978).

5. John C. Brigham, Ethnic Stereotypes, 76 Psychol. Bull. 15, 17 (1971).

6. Gordon Allport, The Nature of Prejudice 191 (1979). bell hooks defines a stereotype as "a fantasy, a projection onto the Other that makes them less threatening." bell hooks, Representations of Whiteness in the Black Imagination, in Black Looks, Race And Representation 165, 170 (1992).

7. Howard J. Ehrlich, The Social Psychology of Prejudice 21 (1973).

8. Audre Lorde, Sister Outsider 126 (1984). *See also* Marc Elrich, The Stereotype Within: Why Students Don't Buy Black History Month, Wash. Post, Feb. 13, 1994, at C1. Elrich, a sixth grade teacher, gave a contemporary example of how young black students have internalized racism. A black student told Elrich, "Everybody knows that black people are bad. That's the way we are." Id.

9. Kimberlè Crenshaw, *Race, Reform and Retrenchment: Transformation and Legitimation in Antidiscrimination Law,* 101 Harv. L. Rev. 1331, 1373 (1988). Crenshaw also explains how racism and oppression work. "Racism serves to single out Blacks as one of these groups 'worthy' of suppression. . . . The most significant aspect of Black oppression seems to be what is believed about Black Americans, not what Black Americans believe." Id. at 1358.

10. Sometimes the unconscious may take control when public demeanor would dictate otherwise.

For example, while on the 1980 presidential campain trail, Nancy Reagan telephoned her husband, after attending a Chicago fundraiser, and said to him that "she wished he could be there to see all these beautiful white people." See On Reagan Campaign: "There Goes Connecticut," Wash. Post, Feb. 18, 1980, at A2. Upon realizing that she had been overheard, the soon-to-be First Lady amended her comment to "beautiful black and white people." Id. Later she told a reporter that she was sorry and did not mean the comment. Id.

11. Daniel Coleman, *Useful Modes of Thought Contribute to the Power of Prejudice*, N.Y. Times, May 12, 1987, at C-1 (quoting Pettigrew).

12. Joe R. Feagin, *The Continuing Significance of Race: Antiblack Discrimination in Public Places*, 56 Am. Soc. Rev. 101, 107 (1991).

46

The Other Pleasures:
The Narrative Function of Race
in the Cinema

ANNA EVERETT

Even with the phenomenal influence of cultural studies and of cognitive and feminist theories, there remains a conspicuous absence of theorizing about the narrative function of race *qua* race in contemporary films. I contend that *Scenes from the Class Struggle in Beverly Hills* (1988), *The Player* (1992), *Cool Runnings* (1993), *Blue Chips* (1994), *The Nightmare before Christmas* (1993), and *The Perfect Woman* (1993) all, in varying degrees, devise narrative situations that rely on race to authorize their speaking the unspeakable, performing the prohibited, defiling the sacred, and generally transgressing most sanctioned codes of social conduct. These films deploy racialized archetypal characters to underwrite audiences' suspended disbelief and thereby ensure what Peter Brooks has termed film's "textual erotics."

Because race functions in these films to reify established hierarchies, its influence often proceeds undetected or, at the least, unchallenged. By covertly voicing the ideology of race in popular entertainment vehicles, filmmakers assure perpetuation of racist attitudes throughout our society. And because of counter movements such as multiculturalism and pluralism, which resist the ideology of racial supremacy, narrating race in this way becomes the means of choice for recruiting and sustaining adherents. This is especially true for young children. Consider, for instance, the treatment of race in *The Nightmare before Christmas*. This animated film, significant for its dual address to both adults and children, features an embedded "nightmare," or what Roland Barthes would term a nested narrative, implicitly named as blackness. The villain, who imperils the film's protagonist, Jack, and who functions as narrative disruption, is codified in terms of racial otherness.

Far from being a mere descriptor of physiognomy, race must be acknowledged for its structural as well as thematic centrality to the narrative situations of popular films today. Consider, for example, the narrative structures of *The Player, Scenes from the Class Struggle in Beverly Hills, The Perfect Woman, The Nightmare before Christmas, Cool Runnings*, and *Blue Chips*. In studying these particular filmic texts, I have found three types of racial inscription in narratives that organize spectatorial pleasure around notions of racial blackness and whiteness. I call these *segregated, partially integrated*, and *fully integrated*

20 FILM CRITICISM, no. 1–2 (1995–96), p. 26. Originally published in *Film Criticism*. Reprinted by permission. Excerpted from THE OTHER PLEASURES: THE NARRATIVE FUNCTION OF RACE IN THE CINEMA. Copyright © 1994 by Anna Everett.

narrative structures, based on the racial identities of the film's significant characters and their interrelationships. I have found that each of these structural modalities imposes narrative conditions on the fulfillment of pleasure for its privileged or ideal spectators. Further, the racialized inscriptions in these films suggest that it is still the white, bourgeois male to whom these narratives are addressed. However, I hasten to add that these films do cast a wide enough narrative net so as to snare the not-privileged spectators as well. These spectator positions are dependent on the hegemonizing nature of racialized cinematic narratives wherein spectatorial identification is achieved via the lure of highly desirable racialized characters as ego-ideals. Protagonists and antagonists in these six films are little more than stock racial stereotypes updated so as to avoid character anachronisms. These narratives construct a preferred reading of the narrative events which, accordingly, require the construction of a preferred spectator to interpret the given work.

What does it mean, for example, when a film widely publicized and received as being conceived outside the political maelstrom of Hollywood finds it necessary and indeed desirable to devise a racially constructed arch-villain as well as a racially spatialized underground never-never land as plot points *par excellence*, wherein race, specifically blackness, functions as the perfect narrative interruptus? I am referring here to Tim Burton's *The Nightmare before Christmas*. In having his arch-villain speak in a constructed black dialect, Burton is little concerned with representing the polyphony of voices that are the American vernacular. Rather, it is clear that this particularized instance of "blackspeak" has the narrative intent of invoking existing notions of black male criminality. Moreover, when contrasted to all other speech representations that signify normative "whitespeak" in this film, this insidious use of cinematic blackspeak renders untenable the recourse to pleas of misconstrued irony on behalf of the filmmaker and his target audiences (interestingly, irony and satire are favored terms for rationalizing or excusing white racist utterances, but few would argue that Leonard Jeffries or Louis Farrakhan is simply being ironic). Solidifying the racial theme in *The Nightmare before Christmas* is a jazz-like music that heightens the racial impact of this otherwise charming film. This issue is crucial because it uncovers the veiled function of race in this film's narrative structure. The subterfuge is that the blackened arch-villain is not drawn with what could be thought of as black features or even coloration, but his speech, his environment, and his function as narrative obstacle clearly deploy social constructions of racial blackness and thus racial undesirability: threatening racialized speech, "jungle music" signifying a debased culture's jazziness, and the villain's underground cave is the virtual heart of darkness for this script.

Those films constituting our first narrative modality, the segregated film texts, at first glance seem the most transparent, thereby lacking in any depth that might suggest the need for further explication beyond surface appearances—evoking a "what you see is what you get" literal interpretative strategy. When audiences opt for an interpretation of films in this transparency mode in spite of textual evidence to the contrary, their disengagement with encoded motifs of racial difference implicates them in these films' ability to smuggle racist values into the narrative transaction without censure. Consider *The Nightmare before Christmas* and *The Perfect Woman*, for example. On the surface, the segregated mode seems to bare its narrative intent when its significant characters are racially homogeneous. Thus a visible absence of black characters in other than supernumerary roles, as in the above two films, might suggest an absence of thematic or structural blackness in narrative terms. A transparent reading of *The Nightmare before Christmas* and *The Perfect Woman* might hold this as indeed the case. However, this structured absence of blackness is predicated paradoxically on the very presence of a covert blackness conjurable at the perfect moment of narrative exigency. Therefore when the "perfect woman," in direct address to the camera, remarks satirically that she is thrilled that her implied spectator-lover could "go on so long" in spite of being "a white man," she turns to the audience with a knowing wink of racial difference. In doing so, her speech act participates in a socially destructive link of race-signifying chains, and its humor as textual erotica is purchased at the price of encouraging racist complicity in the implied spectator. Moreover, such a racialized statement stands out even more prominently when the entire female cast and the upscale setting are held as representing normative whiteness, albeit humorously. The fact is that in both *The Nightmare before Christmas* and *The Perfect Woman* we are confronted with films that advance their racialized narrative emplotments through the disarming genre of comedy, which makes their racialized discourse appear less objectionable, pointed, or pedantic, and therein lies their efficacy. The implied spectator is expected to comprehend—and is rewarded with textual pleasure for comprehending—the narration of race, thereby lessening the disparities of textual knowledge between implied author and implied reader.

The second approach is the partially integrated text. *The Player* and *Scenes from the Class Struggle in Beverly Hills* are typical. These two films display multiracial casts as main characters, engaging race by marrying it to class. Conjoined in this way, race and class work to maintain black characters fictionally in class positions that simultaneously reflect and reaffirm their subordinate socio-economic status in the real world. Most significant for us is that *The Player* and *Scenes* both depend on today's racial discourse to construct their narrative emplotments.

From the outset, race is foregrounded in *The Player*. Right from the start, the camera promises ocular plenitude to its actual spectator/voyeur. Since the camera is not moored to any of the characters' points-of-view, its peering through a shrub-obstructed window to procure a glimpse of our hero, Griffin, at work positions the actual spectator as the character who can eavesdrop on this all-important "pitch" meeting. The dialogue proceeds thus:

> Woman Writer: "Goldie goes to Africa . . . is found by this tribe of small people . . . and they worship her . . ."
> Griffin: "I see. It's kind of like a *Gods Must Be Crazy*, except the coke bottle is a television actress."
> Woman Writer: "Exactly; it's *Out of Africa* meets *Pretty Woman*. And she has to decide whether to stay with the TV show or save this entire African tribe.

Immediately, we are put on notice that racial blackness will be an important issue in this film. Effecting the film's second plot point, or narrative reversal, is Whoopi Goldberg's detective character. Detective Avery is the agglomeration of many pernicious stereotypes of African American womanhood in the American imaginary. As in our society's discourse agreement on black sexuality, *The Player* constructs Whoopi's black female detective as the most radical alterity to her other, the essentialized Anglo-American woman as femininity incarnate. In contrast to her white female subordinate, we must recognize the nation's discourse agreement about black female promiscuity which informs Whoopi's character pronouncement to her male and female colleagues that the "slender-regular" tampons belonging to her white co-worker are inadequate because she requires the jumbo size. This scene works for privileged spectators because it conflates the real existence of "slender-regular" tampons with the non-existent "jumbo" size in a narratological sleight of hand that reifies the myth of black female hypersexuality. Here is another case of textual erotics hot-wired to race.

Finally, in Griffin's meeting with the white writer who will ultimately bring his own narrative of otherness and alterity into this fictive Hollywood world, racial blackness once again provides narrative synergy. It is the white male writer, himself marked as other, as "Eurotrash," who gets to enounce the tropes of reverse discrimination at the heart of this idea for a perfect film story. Describing a lone black woman protestor, this white writer continues: her "face is illuminated like a spirit." The fictional black character he describes is demonstrating to save her son from the death sentence. "Black, 19, and definitely guilty," the writer adds, "we're in the greatest democracy in the world, 36% of the defendants on death row are black, poor, disadvantaged, black. This D.A. believes in the death penalty. He swears the next person he sees executed will be smart, rich, and white—you, me, the whole world. . . . Cut from D.A. to upscale white neighborhood." With that, the white writer concludes his pitch by revealing that there will be a white woman victim on death row, erroneously convicted of her husband's death: "She's innocent, she dies—'cause that's the reality, the innocent die . . . this is a tough story, an innocent dies, because that is the reality" *(The Player)*. Functionally, this scene has narrative centrality to this film. For it is this racialized story pitch that becomes the big idea for the film within the film. Recall "Goldie Goes to Africa"? Well, that early narrative setup has returned according to form as narrative event payoff, except that Goldie is now Julia Roberts, and Africa is now the predominantly black penitentiary.

Scenes from the Class Struggle in Beverly Hills, the other partially integrated film text in our narrative schematic, uses race as the motive force behind most of its plot reversals, as exemplified by the film's treatment of a dysfunctional interracial marriage. Tobel, the African American wife character, is yet another cinematic construction of the oversexed, unprincipled black "ho," who, in addition to having symbolic sex with a dog named Bojangles, must conceal her appearance in a pornographic film from her white husband and his wealthy family. She is aided in her deception by her white adolescent nephew-in-law, Willie, whom she sexually rewards later. Tobel's discursive space functions as one of this film's main sites for articulating the profane and vulgar. Tobel responds to her husband: "yesterday, I fucked the houseboy, in complete daylight." Her husband, Peter, responds: "you cheap, black whore, [white] Claire here is a real woman, she likes to wash everywhere, with soap!" Tobel: "it was so degrading, I felt like some fabulous farm animal." Willie: "my aunt [Tobel] told me that compared to my daddy, I was hung like a rhino" *(Scenes)*. Of the many dangerous liaisons constructed in this narrative, none is more striking for its rearticulation of the American miscegenation taboo. Furthermore, the disparity of knowledge between author and reader/spectator is relatively high because the implied spectator is never really apprised of why and how a leading character in the film, Juan, gets mixed up with the black and Asian loan sharks who attempt to kill him. Due to its participation in the national discourse agreement on minority criminality, and since Juan is a Mexican character, perhaps this narrative absence is an actual presence of the unspoken American assumption that "minority" criminality needs no explication, it just is.

Our last type is the fully integrated film narrative, wherein the racial breakdown of the cast tends to achieve some degree of parity between white characters and others. *Blue Chips* and *Cool Runnings* are examples. In this mode, spectatorial pleasure is inscribed to the extent that socially accepted racial categories are not upset or challenged sufficiently. This results in black and white characters never achieving qualitative parity in the narrative. In effect, these narratives hinge on the racial discourse of black-brute-force meets with white-rational-intellect. From the very beginning, these narratives are preconditioned on a racial-ized character hierarchy wherein the infantilization of blacks is naturalized vis-à-vis their character positions as athletes, just as white paternalism is reified vis-à-vis the privileged-character status of coaches. Even though these films feature fully integrated casts in sig-nificant character roles, it is important to note the narrative convolutions that these film texts devise to separate their characters in terms of racialized spheres of character influence within the world.

Blue Chips is instructive for its fictional engagement with real life sports intrigue. Also tak-ing its cue from actual news events (which is true of *Cool Runnings* as well), this film cen-ters on corruption in college athletics and the controversial debates about affirmative action, black and working-class athletes, and universities' responsibilities to them beyond their play-ing years. In a tone that recalls *The Player*'s discursive strategy on race, crime, and punish-ment, this film similarly posits the victim as white. *Blue Chips*' established narrative equi-librium is disrupted when Nick Nolte's coach character is wrongly accused of a major NCAA infraction actually committed by the coach's favorite black athlete–son, Tony. When Nolte's character is in the process of discovering his betrayal (propelling a narrative reversal), he is surrounded by his black assistant coaches, who, not surprisingly, try to cover up Tony's role in this gambling debacle, which is the narrative's *raison d'être*. When confronted, Tony's ig-norance of and indifference to the severe consequences his actions bring upon his coach-fa-ther (who functions as a father-figure when Tony's black girlfriend gets pregnant) is ascribed naturally to his greed, his naïveté, his inability to separate right from wrong, and ultimately his narratological blackness. Tony's decision to make a few extra bucks has jeopardized the coach's entire career at the same time that it has created narrative displeasure for the implied racialized spectator. Should one wonder why this fiction displaces the reality of the institu-tional corruption in college sports onto the single black athlete, I contend that such enter-tainment narratives at once reflect and influence public attitudes on these important social is-sues, their "entertainment value" obfuscating the real facts and lessening the cognitive dissonance of such reality/fiction clashes. Patricia Williams sums up this situation best when she argues, in *The Alchemy of Race and Rights,* that "statistically, and corporeally, blacks as a group are poor, powerless, and a minority. It is in the minds of whites that blacks become large, threatening, powerful, uncontrollable, ubiquitous, and supernatural."

Consider also the function of whiteness in *Blue Chips*. Harkening back to the anti–affirmative action discourse in *The Player*, the white basketball recruit in *Blue Chips* is able to say to the white coach, who functions in this cinematic relationship only as a coach and not as a father-figure (for in this white sphere of influence the biological father is present), "as a white player, I expect. . ." and he goes on to list financial kickbacks he expects to re-ceive for his father and himself. Clearly, the nation's anti–affirmative action and reverse-discrimination tropes legitimate this narrative utterance with its implied white spectators, who are expected to "get it."

The films under discussion, although targeted at the white spectator (these are main-stream Hollywood films, after all), have also taken advantage of their racially integrated casts to appeal to black spectators. Following the lead of advertisers (Nike, Reebok, Wheaties, etc.) who understand the profit to be made in consuming the other, filmmakers understand the narratological function of race even if we consumers do not. And at the very moment when black media images are being most defiled, criminalized, bestialized, and in-fantilized, these films must be discussed honestly because of how they participate in the selling of otherness.

Synopses of Other Important Works

Culture and Mass Culture: How We Create and Maintain Racial Lines

Many other commentors have written incisively on the role of culture in creating color categories and relations of class supremacy. Here is a sampling of opinion.

The Black Disease

Ronald Takaki, in *Iron Cages* (Knopf, 1979), describes how early opinion makers like Benjamin Rush, a signer of the Declaration of Independence, went about teaching that African-Americans were afflicted by a kind of disease of the body that accounted for their color (p. 30 et seq.) and by bad habits of mind as a result of slavery. Rush, a physician, warmly sympathized with Negro causes and favored emancipation. Nevertheless, he considered negritude an unfortunate affliction related to leprosy and warned that whites who were too close to Negroes could become infected.

The White Lie

James Baldwin is most famous for his novels, such as *Another Country*, and for his essays, such as those collected in *The Price of the Ticket*. In a short piece written toward the end of his life, "On Being 'White' . . . and Other Lies" (*Essence*, April 1984), he advances this thesis: "No one was white before he/she came to America. It took generations, and a vast amount of coercion, before this became a white country." Immigrant groups like Irish, Germans, Jews, and Italians paid a terrible price for becoming white—even if some of them paid it willingly. Each group bought into a lie—a genocidal practice that ruthlessly subordinated blacks, poisoned the wells of Native Americans, and raped the women of both races. According to Baldwin,

> This moral erosion has made it quite impossible for those who think of themselves as white in this country to have any moral authority at all—privately or publicly. The multitudinous bulk of them sit, stunned, before their TV sets, swallowing garbage that they know to be garbage, and . . . pay a vast amount of attention to athletics. . . . They are either relieved or embittered by the presence of the Black boy on the team. I do not know if they remember how long and hard they fought to keep him off it. I know that they do not dare have any notion of the price Black people . . . paid and pay. They do not want to know the meaning, or face the shame. . . .

Baldwin considers that failure to face America's genocidal history—its "lie"—amounts to cowardice and that it "has placed everyone now living into the hands of the most ignorant and powerful people the world has ever seen. And how did they get that way? . . . By deciding that they were white. By opting for safety instead of life. By persuading themselves that a black child's life meant nothing compared with a white child's life."

Hegemony

Kimberlè Crenshaw, professor of law and cofounder of the school of thought known as critical race theory, in a famous article ("Race, Reform, and Retrenchment," 101 *Harvard Law Review* 1331 [1988]), argues that liberal strategies of race reform (litigation, sit-ins, etc.) have both advanced and impeded the cause of black justice. For Crenshaw, white people's race consciousness

> is central not only to the domination of blacks, but also to whites' acceptance of the legitimacy of hierarchy and to their identity with elite interest. Exposing the centrality of race consciousness is crucial to identifying and delegitimating beliefs that present hierarchy as inevitable and fair.

She therefore calls for a "realignment of the Critical project [civil rights. Ed.] to incorporate race consciousness [and] beliefs about blacks in American society." This new focus will show "how these beliefs legitimize racial coercion"; at the same time, it will liberate whites from false identification with their own class oppressors.

Snow-White

In his essay "Language and Prejudice Toward Negroes"—reprinted in the anthology *White Racism,* edited by Barry Schwartz and Robert Disch (Dell, 1970; pp. 385–91)—Simon Podair offers several rich accounts of how language embraces and maintains color lines and imagery. Why is a wild, outcast member of a family a "black sheep"? Why is a competitor with little chance of winning a "dark horse"?

The author invites his readers to consider phrases and words such as (p. 388):

> blackball—to exclude from membership
> black book —containing names that are out of favor or in disgrace
> blacken—to defame or sully
> blackguard—one who uses scurrilous language or treats others with foul abuse
> black-letter—unlucky, inauspicious
> blacklist—regarded as suspect
> blackmail—extortion by intimidation
> blackly—gloomily, threateningly, atrociously

Other terms examined are black looks, black mark, black market, and black lie.

> Language is the mirror of society, reflecting its attitudes and thinking. As a society changes its concepts through political action and education, its language patterns may be modified. Thus, in years to come, the symbols "black" and "white" may no longer take on divergent meanings. . . . In [their] place, there may be substituted a more honest appraisal of color, with a resultant favorable effect upon race relations. (p. 391)

[These lines were written almost thirty years ago. Has the hoped-for improvement occurred? Has the political-correctness movement gone too far in the other direction? Ed.]

Mau-Mau Movies

Richard Dyer, writing in *Screen* magazine ("White," vol. 29, no. 4, p. 44 et seq.), discusses the representation of whiteness as an ethnic category in motion pictures. Films depict whiteness as "the norm" and as embodying such favorable attributes as power and safety. This is seen most easily by examining Mau-Mau, Jezebel, and horror movies that feature nonwhite characters playing a significant role. In *Simba, Jezebel,* and *Night of the Living Dead,* Dyer shows how cinematic conventions (even gory ones) depict and reflect basic cultural values about who is esteemed and in control and who is not.

Dr. Doolittle, and Others

The reader wishing to explore the contribution of children's stories to race consciousness, the imagery of skin color, and notions of inferiority and superiority will find a copious literature. Two excellent pieces are Harold R. Isaacs's classic "Blackness and Whiteness" (*Encounter,* August 1963, p. 12 et seq.) and David Milner, *Children and Race: Ten Years On* (Ward Lock Educational Press, 1983). Isaacs shows how the terms and names for Africans in the United States changed with the times and with the changing status of the Negro vis-à-vis whites (who began to be constructed in terms opposite of those reserved for blacks). According to one author quoted,

> The Anglo-Saxon civilisation is the highest and best yet evolved in the history of the human race. . . . The word "Negro" originally referred to a native African black, who was a barbarian and a savage. . . . "Negro" calls up a black, kinky-haired and heavy-featured being. . . . [It] suggests physical and spiritual kinship to the ape. (p. 12)

Isaacs also goes over how races are depicted in the Bible, in children's tales like Dr. Doolittle and the "Sleepy-Time Stories," and in *Othello* and other Shakespearean plays.

David Milner reviews racism in children's literature (p. 76 et seq.) and how it devalues "dark" people and celebrates light ones, relegating heroes and villains to the predictable categories. In his view:

> It would be easy indeed to emerge from a childhood spent with some of these books believing that Africans seldom come out of the jungle, Chinese men wear pigtails, and French men (who affect droopy moustaches and dress only in striped jerseys and black berets) dine exclusively on frogs and snails.

One heroine of a fairy tale was "a beauty . . . Marusia the Fair they called her. Her skin was as white as milk. . . . And what's more, Marusia was kind and good natured as she was pretty." Another volume is a moral tale of Ellie, "a clean, white, good little darling" of a wealthy family. When Tom, a young chimney sweep, enters her room by mistake, he finds that

> [t]he room was all dressed in white; white window-curtains, white bed-curtains, white furniture and white walls, with just a few lines of pink here and there. . . . Under the snow-white coverlet, upon the snow-white pillow lay the most beautiful little girl that Tom had ever seen. Her cheeks were almost as white as the pillow and her hair was like threads of gold. . . . [Tom] stood staring at her as if she had been an angel out of heaven. (p. 80)

Milner goes on to say of his findings: "The issue is whether *colour* values in any way determine racial values. The experiments described show that the two sets of values are congruent; they point in the same direction. . . . People who [come to] rate the colour black negatively also rate the concepts 'black person' and 'Negro' negatively . . ." (p. 100).

From the Editors: Issues and Comments

Is it possible to imagine Eve, Jesus, the Virgin Mary, or Joan of Arc as black? If you could buy a bar of black soap or white soap (otherwise identical), would you buy the black soap? If it were cheaper? Five percent more effective at cleaning and killing germs? In our society, do films, stories, and songs always take the white point of view? Even if the performer or director is nonwhite? Can a white person write a story or novel about a black, and vice versa, so convincingly or well that you, the reader, would not know it? Suppose a friend of yours said, "I met someone the other day who. . . ." Do you assume, in the absence of other information, that the person is white? Why or why not? Suppose the other person is described as a professor, a senator, or a concert violinist? Do you do a double take when you pass an interracial couple on the sidewalk? When you see a black or brown doll?

Suggested Readings

Allen, Theodore, THE INVENTION OF THE WHITE RACE (Verso, 1994).

Delgado, Richard, and Jean Stefancic, *Scorn*, 35 WM. & MARY L. REV. 1061 (1994).

Goldberg, Theo, *The Semantics of Race*, 15 ETHNIC & RACIAL STUD. 543 (1992).

Haney López, Ian F., *Community Ties, Race, and Faculty Hiring: The Case for Professors Who Don't Think White*, 1 RECONSTRUCTION no. 3, 1991, at 46.

ICONS OF AMERICAN PROTESTANTISM: THE ART OF WARNER SALLMAN (D. Morgan, ed., Yale University Press, 1996).

Ikemoto, Lisa, *Traces of the Master Narrative in the Story of African American/Korean American Conflict: How We Constructed "Los Angeles,"* 66 S. CAL. L. REV. 581 (1993).

Omi, Michael, and Howard Winant, RACIAL FORMATION IN THE UNITED STATES (1986).

Perea, Juan F., *Demography and Distrust: An Essay on American Language, Cultural Pluralism, and Official English*, 77 MINN. L. REV. 269 (1992).

Riggs, Marlon, COLOR ADJUSTMENT (1991, documentary).

Riggs, Marlon, ETHNIC NATIONS (1987, documentary).

Saxton, Alexander, THE RISE AND FALL OF THE WHITE REPUBLIC (Verso, 1990).

Part VI

White Privilege

Does being white bring prerogatives—or detriments and liabilities? Black entertainers and athletes get all the attention, and affirmative action certainly benefits persons of minority race (and women) and not white men, at least in individual cases. But few passersby on a dark sidewalk would cross the street to avoid coming face to face with an average-looking, presentably dressed white. Whites are hassled by the police less than blacks, given the benefit of the doubt in commercial transactions, and favored in many other ways as well. The readings in this part explore whether there is such a thing as white privilege and what its content might be. Is it hard to see, and if so why? Do minority communities themselves dispense a privilege based on color, preferring members of their own groups who are light skinned? How much of a boost, an advantage, an entré is it to be white?

47

White Privilege and Male Privilege: A Personal Account of Coming to See Correspondences through Work in Women's Studies

PEGGY McINTOSH

Through work to bring materials and perspectives from Women's Studies into the rest of the curriculum, I have often noticed men's unwillingness to grant that they are over-privileged in the curriculum, even though they may grant that women are disadvantaged. Denials which amount to taboos surround the subject of advantages which men gain from women's disadvantages. These denials protect male privilege from being fully recognized, acknowledged, lessened, or ended.

Thinking through unacknowledged male privilege as a phenomenon with a life of its own, I realized that since hierarchies in our society are interlocking, there was most likely a phenomenon of white privilege which was similarly denied and protected, but alive and real in its effects. As a white person, I realized I had been taught about racism as something which puts others at a disadvantage, but had been taught not to see one of its corollary aspects, white privilege, which puts me at an advantage.

I think whites are carefully taught not to recognize white privilege, as males are taught not to recognize male privilege. So I have begun in an untutored way to ask what it is like to have white privilege. This paper is a partial record of my personal observations, and not a scholarly analysis. It is based on my daily experiences within my particular circumstances.

I have come to see white privilege as an invisible package of unearned assets which I can count on cashing in each day, but about which I was "meant" to remain oblivious. White privilege is like an invisible weightless knapsack of special provisions, assurances, tools, maps, guides, codebooks, passports, visas, clothes, compass, emergency gear, and blank checks.

Since I have had trouble facing white privilege, and describing its results in my life, I saw parallels here with men's reluctance to acknowledge male privilege. Only rarely will a man go beyond acknowledging that women are disadvantaged to acknowledging that men have an unearned advantage, or that unearned privilege has not been good for men's development as human beings, or for society's development, or that privilege systems might ever be challenged and *changed*.

I will review here several types or layers of denial which I see at work protecting, and preventing awareness about, entrenched male privilege. Then I will draw parallels, from my own experience, with the denials which veil the facts of white privilege. Finally, I will list 46 ordinary and daily ways in which I experience having white privilege, within my life situation and its particular social and political frameworks.

Writing this paper has been difficult, despite warm receptions for the talks on which it is based.[1] For describing white privilege makes one newly accountable. As we in Women's Studies work reveal male privilege and ask men to give up some of their power, so one who writes about having white privilege must ask, "Having described it, what will I do to lessen or end it?"

The denial of men's overprivileged state takes many forms in discussions of curriculum change work. Some claim that men must be central in the curriculum because they have done most of what is important or distinctive in life or in civilization. Some recognize sexism in the curriculum but deny that it makes male students seem unduly important in life. Others agree that certain *individual* thinkers are blindly male-oriented but deny that there is any systemic tendency in disciplinary frameworks or epistemology to over-empower men as a group. Those men who do grant that male privilege takes institutionalized and embedded forms are still likely to deny that male hegemony has opened doors for them personally. Virtually all men deny that male overreward alone can explain men's centrality in all the inner sanctums of our most powerful institutions. Moreover, those few who will acknowledge that male privilege systems have over-empowered them usually end up doubting that we could dismantle these privilege systems. They may say they will work to improve women's status, in the society or in the university, but they can't or won't support the idea of lessening men's. In curricular terms, this is the point at which they say that they regret they cannot use any of the interesting new scholarship on women because the syllabus is full. When the talk turns to giving men less cultural room, even the most thoughtful and fair-minded of the men I know well tend to reflect, or fall back on, conservative assumptions about the inevitability of present gender relations and distributions of power, calling on precedent or sociobiology and psychobiology to demonstrate that male domination is natural and follows inevitably from evolutionary pressures. Others resort to arguments from "experience" or religion or social responsibility or wishing and dreaming.

After I realized, through faculty development work in Women's Studies, the extent to which men work from a base of unacknowledged privilege, I understood that much of their oppressiveness was unconscious. Then I remembered the frequent charges from women of color that white women whom they encounter are oppressive. I began to understand why we are justly seen as oppressive, even when we don't see ourselves that way. At the very least, obliviousness of one's privileged state can make a person or group irritating to be with. I began to count the ways in which I enjoy unearned skin privilege and have been conditioned into oblivion about its existence, unable to see that it put me "ahead" in any way, or put my people ahead, overrewarding us and yet also paradoxically damaging us, or that it could or should be changed.

My schooling gave me no training in seeing myself as an oppressor, as an unfairly advantaged person, or as a participant in a damaged culture. I was taught to see myself as an individual whose moral state depended on her individual moral will. At school, we were not taught about slavery in any depth; we were not taught to see slaveholders as damaged people. Slaves were seen as the only group at risk of being dehumanized. My schooling followed the pattern which Elizabeth Minnich has pointed out: whites are taught to think of their lives as morally neutral, normative, and average, and also ideal, so that when we work to benefit others, this is seen as work which will allow "them" to be more like "us." I think many of us know how obnoxious this attitude can be in men.

After frustration with men who would not recognize male privilege, I decided to try to work on myself at least by identifying some of the daily effects of white privilege in my life. It is crude work, at this stage, but I will give here a list of special circumstances and conditions I experience which I did not earn but which I have been made to feel are mine by birth, by citizenship, and by virtue of being a conscientious law-abiding "normal" person of good will. I have chosen those conditions which I think in my case *attach somewhat more to skin-color privilege* than to class, religion, ethnic status, or geographical location, though of course all these other factors are intricately intertwined. As far as I can see, my Afro-American co-workers, friends, and acquaintances with whom I come into daily or frequent contact in this particular time, place, and line of work cannot count on most of these conditions.

1. I can if I wish arrange to be in the company of people of my race most of the time.
2. I can avoid spending time with people whom I was trained to mistrust and who have learned to mistrust my kind or me.
3. If I should need to move, I can be pretty sure of renting or purchasing housing in an area which I can afford and in which I would want to live.
4. I can be pretty sure that my neighbors in such a location will be neutral or pleasant to me.
5. I can go shopping alone most of the time, pretty well assured that I will not be followed or harassed.
6. I can turn on the television or open to the front page of the paper and see people of my race widely represented.
7. When I am told about our national heritage or about "civilization," I am shown that people of my color made it what it is.
8. I can be sure that my children will be given curricular materials that testify to the existence of their race.
9. If I want to, I can be pretty sure of finding a publisher for this piece on white privilege.
10. I can be pretty sure of having my voice heard in a group in which I am the only member of my race.
11. I can be casual about whether or not to listen to another woman's voice in a group in which she is the only member of her race.
12. I can go into a music shop and count on finding the music of my race represented, into a supermarket and find the staple foods which fit with my cultural traditions, into a hairdresser's shop and find someone who can cut my hair.
13. Whether I use checks, credit cards, or cash, I can count on my skin color not to work against the appearance of financial reliability.
14. I can arrange to protect my children most of the time from people who might not like them.
15. I do not have to educate my children to be aware of systemic racism for their own daily physical protection.
16. I can be pretty sure that my children's teachers and employers will tolerate them if they fit school and workplace norms; my chief worries about them do not concern others' attitudes toward their race.
17. I can talk with my mouth full and not have people put this down to my color.
18. I can swear, or dress in second hand clothes, or not answer letters, without having people attribute these choices to the bad morals, the poverty, or the illiteracy of my race.
19. I can speak in public to a powerful male group without putting my race on trial.
20. I can do well in a challenging situation without being called a credit to my race.
21. I am never asked to speak for all the people of my racial group.

22. I can remain oblivious of the language and customs of persons of color who constitute the world's majority without feeling in my culture any penalty for such oblivion.

23. I can criticize our government and talk about how much I fear its policies and behavior without being seen as a cultural outsider.

24. I can be pretty sure that if I ask to talk to "the person in charge," I will be facing a person of my race.

25. If a traffic cop pulls me over or if the IRS audits my tax return, I can be sure I haven't been singled out because of my race.

26. I can easily buy posters, post-cards, picture books, greeting cards, dolls, toys, and children's magazines featuring people of my race.

27. I can go home from most meetings of organizations I belong to feeling somewhat tied in, rather than isolated, out-of-place, outnumbered, unheard, held at a distance, or feared.

28. I can be pretty sure that an argument with a colleague of another race is more likely to jeopardize her chances for advancement than to jeopardize mine.

29. I can be pretty sure that if I argue for the promotion of a person of another race, or a program centering on race, this is not likely to cost me heavily within my present setting, even if my colleagues disagree with me.

30. If I declare there is a racial issue at hand, or there isn't a racial issue at hand, my race will lend me more credibility for either position than a person of color will have.

31. I can choose to ignore developments in minority writing and minority activist programs, or disparage them, or learn from them, but in any case, I can find ways to be more or less protected from negative consequences of any of these choices.

32. My culture gives me little fear about ignoring the perspectives and powers of people of other races.

33. I am not made acutely aware that my shape, bearing, or body odor will be taken as a reflection on my race.

34. I can worry about racism without being seen as self-interested or self-seeking.

35. I can take a job with an affirmative action employer without having my co-workers on the job suspect that I got it because of my race.

36. If my day, week, or year is going badly, I need not ask of each negative episode or situation whether it has racial overtones.

37. I can be pretty sure of finding people who would be willing to talk with me and advise me about my next steps, professionally.

38. I can think over many options, social, political, imaginative, or professional, without asking whether a person of my race would be accepted or allowed to do what I want to do.

39. I can be late to a meeting without having the lateness reflect on my race.

40. I can choose public accommodation without fearing that people of my race cannot get in or will be mistreated in the places I have chosen.

41. I can be sure that if I need legal or medical help, my race will not work against me.

42. I can arrange my activities so that I will never have to experience feelings of rejection owing to my race.

43. If I have low credibility as a leader, I can be sure that my race is not the problem.

44. I can easily find academic courses and institutions which give attention only to people of my race.

45. I can expect figurative language and imagery in all of the arts to testify to experiences of my race.

46. I can choose blemish cover or bandages in "flesh" color and have them more or less match my skin.

I repeatedly forgot each of the realizations on this list until I wrote it down. For me, white privilege has turned out to be an elusive and fugitive subject. The pressure to avoid it is great, for in facing it I must give up the myth of meritocracy. If these things are true, this is not such a free country; one's life is not what one makes it; many doors open for certain people through no virtues of their own. These perceptions mean also that my moral condition is not what I had been led to believe. The appearance of being a good citizen rather than a troublemaker comes in large part from having all sorts of doors open automatically because of my color.

A further paralysis of nerve comes from literary silence protecting privilege. My clearest memories of finding such analysis are in Lillian Smith's unparalleled *Killers of the Dream* and Margaret Andersen's review of Karen and Mamie Fields' *Lemon Swamp*. Smith, for example, wrote about walking toward black children on the street and knowing they would step into the gutter; Andersen contrasted the pleasure which she, as a white child, took on summer driving trips to the South with Karen Fields' memories of driving in a closed car stocked with all necessities lest, in stopping, her black family should suffer "insult, or worse." Adrienne Rich also recognizes and writes about daily experiences of privilege, but in my observation, white women's writing in this area is far more often on systemic racism than on our daily lives as light-skinned women.[2]

In unpacking this invisible knapsack of white privilege, I have listed conditions of daily experience which I once took for granted, as neutral, normal, and universally available to everybody, just as I once thought of a male-focused curriculum as the neutral or accurate account which can speak for all. Nor did I think of any of these perquisites as bad for the holder. I now think that we need a more finely differentiated taxonomy of privilege, for some of these varieties are only what one would want for everyone in a just society, and others give license to be ignorant, oblivious, arrogant, and destructive. Before proposing some more finely-tuned categorization, I will make some observations about the general effects of these conditions on my life and expectations.

In this potpourri of examples, some privileges make me feel at home in the world. Others allow me to escape penalties or dangers which others suffer. Through some, I escape fear, anxiety, or a sense of not being welcome or not being real. Some keep me from having to hide, to be in disguise, to feel sick or crazy, to negotiate each transaction from the position of being an outsider or, within my group, a person who is suspected of having too close links with a dominant culture. Most keep me from having to be angry.

I see a pattern running through the matrix of white privilege, a pattern of assumptions which were passed on to me as a white person. There was one main piece of cultural turf; it was my own turf, and I was among those who could control the turf. I could measure up to the cultural standards and take advantage of the many options I saw around me to make what the culture would call a success of my life. *My skin color was an asset for any move I was educated to want to make.* I could think of myself as "belonging" in major ways, and of making social systems work for me. I could freely disparage, fear, neglect, or be oblivious to anything outside of the dominant cultural forms. Being of the main culture, I could also criticize it fairly freely. My life was reflected back to me frequently enough so that I felt, with regard to my race, if not to my sex, like one of the real people.

Whether through the curriculum or in the newspaper, the television, the economic system, or the general look of people in the streets, we received daily signals and indications that my people counted, and that others *either didn't exist or must be trying, not very successfully, to be like people of my race.* We were given cultural permission not to hear voices of people of other races, or a tepid cultural tolerance for hearing or acting on such voices. I was also raised not to suffer seriously from anything which darker-skinned people might say about my group, "protected," though perhaps I should more accurately say *prohibited,* through the habits of my economic class and social group, from living in racially mixed groups or being reflective about interactions between people of differing races. In proportion as my racial group was being made confident, comfortable, and oblivious, other groups were likely being made unconfident, uncomfortable, and alienated. Whiteness protected me from many kinds of hostility, distress, and violence which I was being subtly trained to visit in turn upon people of color.

For this reason, the word "privilege" now seems to me misleading. Its connotations are too positive to fit the conditions and behaviors which "privilege systems" produce. We usually think of privilege as being a favored state, whether earned, or conferred by birth or luck. School graduates are reminded they are privileged and urged to use their (enviable) assets well. The word "privilege" carries the connotation of being something everyone must want. Yet some of the conditions I have described here work to systematically overempower certain groups. Such privilege simply *confers dominance,* gives permission to control, because of one's race or sex. The kind of privilege which gives license to some people to be, at best, thoughtless and, at worst, murderous should not continue to be referred to as a desirable attribute. Such "privilege" may be widely desired without being in any way beneficial to the whole society.

Moreover, though "privilege" may confer power, it does not confer moral strength. Those who do not depend on conferred dominance have traits and qualities which may never develop in those who do. Just as Women's Studies courses indicate that women survive their political circumstances to lead lives which hold the human race together, so "underprivileged" people of color who are the world's majority have survived their oppression and lived survivors' lives from which the white global minority can and must learn. In some groups, those dominated have actually become strong through *not* having all of these unearned advantages, and this gives them a great deal to teach the others. Members of so-called privileged groups can seem foolish, ridiculous, infantile or dangerous by contrast.

I want, then, to distinguish between earned strength and unearned power conferred systematically. Power from unearned privilege can look like strength when it is in fact permission to escape or to dominate. But not all of the privileges on my list are inevitably damaging. Some, like the expectation that neighbors will be decent to you, or that your race will not count against you in court, should be the norm in a just society and should be considered as the entitlement of everyone. Others, like the privilege not to listen to less powerful people, distort the humanity of the holders as well as the ignored groups. Still others, like finding one's staple foods everywhere, may be a function of being a member of a numerical majority in the population. Others have to do with not having to labor under pervasive negative stereotyping and mythology.

We might at least start by distinguishing between positive advantages which we can work to spread, to the point where they are not advantages at all but simply part of the normal civic and social fabric, and negative types of advantage which unless rejected will always reinforce our present hierarchies. For example, the positive "privilege" of belonging, the feeling that one belongs within the human circle, as Native Americans say, fosters development and should not be seen as privilege for a few. It is, let us say, an entitlement which none of us should have to earn; ideally it is an *unearned entitlement.* At present, since only a few have it, it is an *unearned advantage* for them. The negative "privilege" which gave me cultural permission not to take darker-skinned Others seriously can be seen as arbitrarily conferred dominance and should not be desirable for anyone. This paper results from a process of coming to see that some of the power which I originally saw as attendant on being a human being in the U.S. consisted in *unearned advantage* and *conferred dominance,* as well as other kinds of special circumstance not universally taken for granted.

In writing this paper I have also realized that white identity and status (as well as class identity and status) give me considerable power to choose whether to broach this subject and its trouble. I can pretty well decide whether to disappear and avoid and not listen and escape the dislike I may engender in other people through this essay, or interrupt, take over, dominate, preach, direct, criticize, or control to some extent what goes on in reaction to it. Being white, I am given considerable power to escape many kinds of danger or penalty as well as to choose which risks I want to take.

There is an analogy here, once again, with Women's Studies. Our male colleagues do not have a great deal to lose in supporting Women's Studies, but they do not have a great deal to lose if they oppose it either. They simply have the power to decide whether to commit themselves to more equitable distributions of power. They will probably feel few penalties whatever choice they make; they do not seem, in any obvious short-term sense, the ones at risk, though they and we are all at risk because of the behaviors which have been rewarded in them.

Through Women's Studies work I have met very few men who are truly distressed about systemic, unearned male advantage and conferred dominance. And so one question for me and others like me is whether we will be like them, or whether we will get truly distressed, even outraged, about unearned race advantage and conferred dominance and if so, what we will do to lessen them. In any case, we need to do more work in identifying how they actually affect our daily lives. We need more down-to-earth writing by people about these taboo subjects. We need more understanding of the ways in which white "privilege" damages white people, for these are not the same ways in which it damages the victimized. Skewed white psyches are an inseparable part of the picture, though I do not want to confuse the kinds of damage done to the holders of special assets and to those who suffer the deficits. Many, perhaps most, of our white students in the U.S. think that racism doesn't affect them because they are not people of color; they do not see "whiteness" as a racial identity. Many men likewise think that Women's Studies does not bear on their own existences because they are not female; they do not see themselves as having gendered identities. Insisting on the universal *effects* of "privilege" systems, then, becomes one of our chief tasks, and being more explicit about the *particular* effects in particular contexts is another. Men need to join us in this work.

In addition, since race and sex are not the only advantaging systems at work, we need to similarly examine the daily experience of having age advantage, or ethnic advantage, or physical ability, or advantage related to nationality, religion, or sexual orientation. Prof. Marnie Evans suggested to me that in many ways the list I made also applies directly to heterosexual privilege. This is a still more taboo subject than race privilege: the daily ways in which heterosexual privilege makes married persons comfortable or powerful, providing supports, assets, approvals, and rewards to those who live or expect to live in heterosexual pairs. Unpacking that content is still more difficult, owing to the deeper imbeddedness of heterosexual advantage and dominance, and stricter taboos surrounding these.

But to start such an analysis I would put this observation from my own experience: The fact that I live under the same roof with a man triggers all kinds of societal assumptions about my worth, politics, life, and values, and triggers a host of unearned advantages and powers. After recasting many elements from the original list I would add further observations like these:

1. My children do not have to answer questions about why I live with my partner (my husband).
2. I have no difficulty finding neighborhoods where people approve of our household.
3. My children are given texts and classes which implicitly support our kind of family unit, and do not turn them against my choice of domestic partnership.
4. I can travel alone or with my husband without expecting embarrassment or hostility in those who deal with us.
5. Most people I meet will see my marital arrangements as an asset to my life or as a favorable comment on my likability, my competence, or my mental health.
6. I can talk about the social events of a weekend without fearing most listeners' reactions.
7. I will feel welcomed and "normal" in the usual walks of public life, institutional and social.
8. In many contexts, I am seen as "all right" in daily work on women because I do not live chiefly with women.

Difficulties and dangers surrounding the task of finding parallels are many. Since racism, sexism, and heterosexism are not the same, the advantaging associated with them should not be seen as the same. In addition, it is hard to disentangle aspects of unearned advantage which rest more on social class, economic class, race, religion, sex, and ethnic identity than on other factors. Still, all of the oppressions are interlocking, as the Combahee River Collective statement of 1977 continues to remind us eloquently.[3]

One factor seems clear about all of the interlocking oppressions. They take both active forms which we can see and embedded forms which as a member of the dominant group one is taught not to see. In my class and place, I did not see myself as racist because I was taught to recognize racism only in individual acts of meanness by members of my group, never in invisible systems conferring unsought racial dominance on my group from birth. Likewise, we are taught to think that sexism or heterosexism is carried on only through individual acts of discrimination, meanness, or cruelty toward women, gays, and lesbians, rather than in invisible systems conferring unsought dominance on certain groups. Disapproving of the systems won't be enough to change them. I was taught to think that racism could end if white individuals changed their attitudes; many men think sexism can be ended by individual changes in daily behavior toward women. But a man's sex provides advantage for him whether or not he approves of the way in which dominance has been conferred on his group. A "white" skin in the United States opens many doors for whites whether or not we approve of the way dominance has been conferred on us. Individual acts can palliate, but cannot end, these problems. To redesign social systems we need first to acknowledge their colossal unseen dimensions. The silences and denials surrounding privilege are the key political tool here. They keep the thinking about equality or equity incomplete, protecting unearned advantage and conferred dominance by making these taboo subjects. Most talk by whites about equal opportunity seems to me now to be about equal opportunity to try to get into a position of dominance while denying that *systems* of dominance exist.

It seems to me that obliviousness about white advantage, like obliviousness about male advantage, is kept strongly inculturated in the United States so as to maintain the myth of meritocracy, the myth that democratic choice is equally available to all. Keeping most people unaware that freedom of confident action is there for just a small number of people props up those in power, and serves to keep power in the hands of the same groups that have most of it already. Though systemic change takes many decades, there are pressing questions for me and I imagine for some others like me if we raise our daily consciousness on the perquisites of being light-skinned. What will we do with such knowledge? As we know from watching men, it is an open question whether we will choose to use unearned advantage to weaken hidden systems of advantage, and whether we will use any of our arbitrarily-awarded power to try to reconstruct power systems on a broader base.

Notes

1. This paper was presented at the Virginia Women's Studies Association conference in Richmond in April 1986 and the American Educational Research Association conference in Boston in October 1986 and discussed with two groups of participants in the Dodge Seminars for Secondary School Teachers in New York and Boston in the spring of 1987.

2. Andersen, Margaret, "Race and the Social Science Curriculum: A Teaching and Learning Discussion." RADICAL TEACHER, November 1984, pp. 17–20. Smith, Lillian, KILLERS OF THE DREAM, New York, 1949.

3. "A Black Feminist Statement," The Combahee River Collective, pp. 13–22 in Hull, Scott, Smith, eds., ALL THE WOMEN ARE WHITE, ALL THE BLACKS ARE MEN, BUT SOME OF US ARE BRAVE: BLACK WOMEN'S STUDIES. The Feminist Press, 1982.

48

From Practice to Theory, or What Is a White Woman Anyway?

CATHARINE A. MacKINNON

And ain't I a woman?
Sojourner Truth[1]

Black feminists speak as women because we are women . . .
Audre Lorde[2]

In recent critiques of feminist work for failing to take account of race or class, race and class are regarded as unproblematically real and not in need of justification or theoretical construction.[3] Only gender is not real and needs to be justified.[4] Although many women have demanded that discussions of race or class take gender into account, typically these demands do not take the form that, outside explicit recognition of gender, race or class do not exist. That there is a diversity to the experience of men and women of color, and of working-class women and men regardless of race, is not said to mean that race or class are not meaningful concepts. I have heard no one say that there can be no meaningful discussion of "people of color" without gender specificity. Thus the phrase "people of color and white women" has come to replace the previous "women and minorities," which women of color rightly perceived as not including them twice, and embodying a white standard for sex and a male standard for race. But I hear no talk of "all women and men of color," for instance. It is worth thinking about that when women of color refer to "people who look like me," it is understood that they mean people of color, not women, in spite of the fact that both race and sex are visual assignments, both possess clarity as well as ambiguity, and both are marks of oppression, hence community.

In this connection, it has recently come to my attention that the white woman is the issue here, so I decided I better find out what one is. This creature is not poor, not battered, not raped (not really), not molested as a child, not pregnant as a teenager, not prostituted, not coerced into pornography, not a welfare mother, and not economically exploited. She doesn't work. She is either the white man's image of her—effete, pampered, privileged, protected, flighty, and self-indulgent—or the black man's image of her—all that, plus the "pretty white girl" (meaning ugly as sin but regarded as the ultimate in beauty because she is white). She is Miss Anne of the kitchen, she puts Frederick Douglass to the lash, she cries rape when Emmett Till looks at her sideways, she manipulates white men's very real power with the lift-

This is an excerpt from a speech on theory and practice that appeared in 4 YALE J. L. AND FEMINISM 13 (1991). Originally published in the *Yale Journal of Law and Feminism.* Copyright © 1991 by Catharine A. MacKinnon. Reprinted by permission.

ing of her very well-manicured little finger. She makes an appearance in Baraka's "rape the white girl,"[5] as Cleaver's real thing after target practice on black women,[6] as Helmut Newton's glossy upscale hard-edged, distanced vamp,[7] and as the Central Park Jogger, the classy white madonna who got herself raped and beaten nearly to death. She flings her hair, feels beautiful all the time, complains about the colored help, tips badly, can't do anything, doesn't do anything, doesn't know anything, and alternates fantasizing about fucking black men with accusing them of raping her. As Ntozake Shange points out, all Western civilization depends on her.[8] On top of all of this, out of impudence, imitativeness, pique, and a simple lack of anything meaningful to do, she thinks she needs to be liberated. Her feminist incarnation is all of the above, and guilty about every single bit of it, having by dint of repetition refined saying "I'm sorry" to a high form of art. She can't even make up her own songs.

There is, of course, much to much of this, this "woman, modified," this woman discounted by white, meaning she would be oppressed but for her privilege. But this image seldom comes face to face with the rest of her reality: the fact that the majority of the poor are white women and their children (at least half of whom are female); that white women are systematically battered in their homes, murdered by intimates and serial killers alike, molested as children, actually raped (mostly by white men), and that even black men, on average, make more than they do.[9] If one did not know this, one could be taken in by white men's image of white women: that the pedestal is real, rather than a cage in which to confine and trivialize them and segregate them from the rest of life, a vehicle for sexualized infantilization, a virginal set-up for rape by men who enjoy violating the pure, and a myth with which to try to control black women. (See, if you would lie down and be quiet and not move, we would revere you, too.) One would think that the white men's myth that they protect white women was real, rather than a racist cover to guarantee their exclusive and unimpeded sexual access—meaning they can rape her at will, and do, a posture made good in the marital rape exclusion and the largely useless rape law generally. One would think that the only white women in brothels in the South during the Civil War were in *Gone with the Wind*.[10] This is not to say there is no such thing as skin privilege, but rather that it has never insulated white women from the brutality and misogyny of men, mostly but not exclusively white men, or from its effective legalization. In other words, the "white girls" of this theory miss quite a lot of the reality of white women in the practice of male supremacy.

Beneath the trivialization of the white woman's subordination implicit in the dismissive sneer "straight white economically privileged women" (a phrase which has become one word, the accuracy of some of its terms being rarely documented even in law journals) lies the notion that there is no such thing as the oppression of women as such. If white women's oppression is an illusion of privilege and a rip-off and reduction of the civil rights movement, we are being told that there is no such thing as a woman, that our practice produces no theory, and that there is no such thing as discrimination on the basis of sex. What I am saying is, to argue that oppression "as a woman" negates rather than encompasses recognition of the oppression of women on other bases, is to say that there is no such thing as the practice of sex inequality.

Let's take this the other way around. As I mentioned, both Mechelle Vinson and Lillian Garland are African-American women. [Vinson and Garland were plaintiffs in landmark sex-discrimination cases. Ed.] Wasn't Mechelle Vinson sexually harassed as a woman? Wasn't Lillian Garland pregnant as a woman? They thought so. The whole point of their cases was to get their injuries understood as "based on sex," that is, because they are women. The perpetrators, and the policies under which they were disadvantaged, saw them as women. What is being a woman if it does not include being oppressed as one? When the Reconstruction Amendments "gave blacks the vote," and black women still could not vote, weren't they kept from voting "as women"? When African-American women are raped two times as often as white women, aren't they raped as women? That does not mean their race is irrelevant and it does not mean that their injuries can be understood outside a racial context. Rather, it means that "sex" is *made up of* the reality of the experiences of all women, including theirs. It is a composite unit rather than a divided unitary whole, such that each woman, in her way, is all women. So, when white women are sexually harassed or lose their jobs because they are pregnant, aren't they women too?

The treatment of women in pornography shows this approach in graphic relief. One way or another, all women are in pornography. African-American women are featured in bondage, struggling, in cages, as animals, insatiable. As Andrea Dworkin has shown, the sexualized hostility directed against them makes their skin into a sex organ, focusing the aggression and contempt directed principally at other women's genitals.[11] Asian women are passive, inert, as if dead, tortured unspeakably. Latinas are hot mommas. Fill in the rest from every demeaning and hostile racial stereotype you know; it is sex here. This is not done to men, not in heterosexual pornography. What is done to white women is a kind of floor; it is the best anyone is treated and it runs from *Playboy* through sadomasochism to snuff. What is done to white women can be done to any woman, and then some. This does not make white women the essence of womanhood. It is a reality to observe that this is what can be done and *is* done to the most privileged of women. This is what privilege as a woman gets you: most valued as dead meat.

I am saying, each woman is in pornography as the embodiment of her particularities. This is not in tension with being there "as a woman," *it is what being there as a woman means*. Her specificity makes up what gender *is*. White, for instance, is not a residual category. It is not a standard against which the rest are "different." There is no generic "woman" in pornography. White is not unmarked; it is a specific sexual taste. Being defined and used in this way defines what being a woman means in practice. Robin Morgan once said, "pornography is the theory, rape is the practice."[12] This is true, but Andrea Dworkin's revision is more true: "Pornography is the theory, pornography is the practice."[13] This approach to "what is a woman" is reminiscent of Sartre's answer to the question "what is a Jew?" Start with the anti-Semite.[14]

In my view, the subtext to the critique of oppression "as a woman," the critique that holds that there is no such thing, is dis-identification with women. One of its consequences is the destruction of the basis for a jurisprudence of sex equality. An argument advanced in many critiques by women of color has been that theories of women must include all women, and when they do, theory will change. On one level, this is necessarily true. On another, it ignores the formative contributions of women of color to feminist theory since its inception. I also sense, though, that many women, not only women of color and not only academics, do not want to be "just women," not only because something important is left out, but also because that means being in a category with "her," the useless white woman whose first reaction when the going gets rough is to cry. I sense here that people feel more dignity in being part of any group that includes men than in being part of a group that includes that ultimate reduction of the notion of oppression, that instigator of lynch mobs, that ludicrous whiner, that equality coat-tails rider, the white woman. It seems that if your oppression is also done to a man, you are more likely to be recognized as oppressed, as opposed to inferior. Once a group is seen as putatively human, a process helped by including men in it, an oppressed man in that group falls from a human standard.[15] A woman is just a woman—the ontological victim—so not victimized at all.

Unlike other women, the white woman who is not poor or working class or lesbian or Jewish or disabled or old or young *does not share her oppression with any man*. That does not make her condition any more definitive of the meaning of "women" than the condition of any other woman is. But trivializing her oppression, because it is not even potentially racist or class-based or heterosexist or anti-Semitic, does define the meaning of being "anti-woman" with a special clarity. How the white woman is imagined and constructed and treated becomes a particularly sensitive indicator of the degree to which women, as such, are despised.

If we build a theory out of women's practice, comprised of the diversity of all women's experiences, we do not have the problem that some feminist theory has been rightly criticized for. When we have it is when we make theory out of abstractions and accept the images forced on us by male dominance. I said all that so I could say this: the assumption that all women are the same is part of the bedrock of sexism that the women's movement is predicated on challenging. That some academics find it difficult to theorize without reproducing it simply means that they continue to do to women what theory, predicated on the practice of male dominance, has always done to women. It is their notion of what theory is, and its relation to its world, that needs to change.

If our theory of what is "based on sex" makes gender out of actual social practices distinctively directed against women as women identify them, the problem that the critique of so-called "essentialism" exists to rectify ceases to exist. And this bridge, the one from practice to theory, is not built on anyone's back.

Notes

1. BLACK WOMEN IN NINETEENTH-CENTURY AMERICAN LIFE: THEIR WORDS, THEIR THOUGHTS, THEIR FEELINGS 235 (Bert J. Loewenberg & Ruth Bogin eds., 1976).

2. AUDRE LORDE, SISTER OUTSIDER 60 (1984). The whole quotation is "Black feminists speak as women because we are women and do not need others to speak for us."

3. I am thinking in particular of ELIZABETH SPELMAN, INESSENTIAL WOMAN (1988), and Marlee Kline, *Race, Racism and Feminist Legal Theory*, 12 HARV. WOMEN'S L.J. 115 (1989), although this analysis also applies to others who have made the same argument. Among its other problems, much of this work tends to make invisible the women of color who were and are instrumental in defining and creating feminism as a movement of women in the world, as well as a movement of mind.

4. This is by contrast with the massive feminist literature on the problem of class, which I discuss and summarize as a foundational problem for feminist theory in TOWARD A FEMINIST THEORY OF THE STATE (1989).

5. LEROI JONES, *Black Dada Nihilismus*, in THE DEAD LECTURER 61, 63 (1964).

6. "I became a rapist. To refine my technique and *modus operandi*, I started out by practicing on black girls in the ghetto . . . and when I considered myself smooth enough, I crossed the tracks and sought out white prey." ELDRIDGE CLEAVER, SOUL ON ICE 14 (1968). "[R]aping the white girl" as an activity for black men is described as one of "the funky facts of life," in a racist context in which the white girl's white-girlness is sexualized—that is, made a site of lust, hatred and hostility—for the black man through the history of lynching. *Id.* at 14–15.

7. HELMUT NEWTON, WHITE WOMEN (1976).

8. NTOZAKE SHANGE, THREE PIECES 48 (1981).

9. In 1989, the median income of white women was approximately one-fourth less than that of

black men; in 1990 it was one-fifth less. U.S. Bureau of the Census, Current Population Rep., Ser. P-60, No. 174, Money Income of Households, Families, and Persons in the United States: 1990, at 104–05 (tbl. 24) (1991).

10. This is an insight of Dorothy Teer.

11. Andrea Dworkin, Pornography: Men Possessing Women 215–16 (1981).

12. Robin Morgan, Going Too Far 169 (1978).

13. Personal communication with Andrea Dworkin. *See also* Andrea Dworkin, Mercy 232, 304–07 (1991).

14. "Thus, to know what the contemporary Jew is, we must ask the Christian conscience. And we must ask, not 'What is a Jew?' but *'What have you made of the Jews?'*"

15. "The Jew is one whom other men consider a Jew: that is the simple truth from which we must start. In this sense . . . it is the anti-Semite who makes the Jew." Jean Paul Sartre, Anti-Semite and Jew 69 (George J. Becker trans., 1948).

15. I sense a similar dynamic at work in the attraction among some lesbians of identification with "gay rights" rather than "women's rights," with the result of obscuring the roots in male dominance of the oppression of both lesbians and gay men.

49

Racial Construction and Women as Differentiated Actors

MARTHA R. MAHONEY

What is race? A social construct, a concept having no natural truth, no truth separate from historical development, and possibly no truth comprehensible apart from domination. The term has meant different things in this country over time; and its social and cultural meanings continue to change within our own time. In law as well as elsewhere in society the term "race" has been used to stand for several different concepts. Even the Supreme Court, when faced with the question, had to recognize that "race" was a contingent category that shifted over time.[1]

Race is a social construct. However, that does not mean race is not real or that we can "just stop doing it." Even if race is a set of beliefs and cultural meanings subject to change, it is not "just" an idea. The question is, What does it mean for race to be socially constructed? Race is not only skin color. Social and legal rules have determined racial identification as black when people are phenotypically white,[2] and some dark-skinned groups are not consistently socially defined as black in this country. The existence of the concept of "passing for white"—the word "passing"—is itself evidence that color is not race.

"Race" is partly about culture: some European cultures have experienced something like racism from people with different cultures but similar skin color. Race is partly about skin color: in the United States "race" has been anchored to an obsession with skin color and phenotype. And it is insistently about domination: the dominant culture uses its power to attempt to define and subjugate the "other." Perhaps dominance is actually the key here. The official rules that define "race" in America have been the white rules, even though the meaning of race has been contested in many ways, and even though African-American culture has had a great, though generally unacknowledged, impact on white culture and perhaps on concepts of race as well.

If dominance/subordination is what turns "culture" into "race," does this then define the oppressed person or group as the mere object of the process of social construction? White use of the term "race" is based on definitions of the "other" which imply a normal, neutral, objective, culture-less stance toward whiteness. This does not mean that white culture actually fully succeeds in defining the "other." African-American self-assertions in black culture have a long history in the United States; white appropriation, commercialization, and transformation of parts of that culture have a complex history as well. Nor does it mean only that whites concoct the dominant definition of "other," imposing on society

From "Whiteness and Women, in Practice and Theory," 5 Yale J. L. and Feminism 217 (1993). Originally published in the *Yale Journal of Law and Feminism.* Reprinted by permission.

our vision of people of color. Whites also define whiteness, albeit in ways that we cannot fully see, and then impose that vision on the world as much as we can. If this process does not entirely persuade the rest of the world that our vision is "truth," it surely protects our own perceptions.

In a much cited working paper, Peggy McIntosh conceptualizes her white privilege as an invisible, weightless "knapsack" of special provisions, assurances, and blank checks.[3] Her knapsack includes both unearned assets (things that should be entitlements of humanity and that everyone should have in a just society, but which in fact are awarded to the dominant race) and unearned power that is systematically conferred (those things that are damaging in human terms even as they bring advantage and are associated only with dominance, such as the freedom not to be concerned about the needs, culture, or reality of others). [See chapter 47. Ed.]. American cities have developed around invisible conveniences that are a social, physical analogue to this invisible knapsack—location of transit and other municipal services, and even the plotting of streets, have often been planned to serve white neighborhoods and preserve their whiteness.

Part of white privilege, therefore, is not seeing all we have and all we do, and not seeing how what we do appears to those defined as "other." Whites cannot just opt out of the process of formation of this racial consciousness that takes the form of unconsciousness. This can be painful. For example, note the feeling of exclusion that arises when white college students notice that black students all sit together—but don't also notice that the white students all sit together. And whiteness can re-create itself without the conscious will to exclude, as when people interview and hire through friends and acquaintances and find desirable candidates to be similar to themselves.

This country is both highly segregated and based on a concept of whiteness as "normal." It is therefore hard for white folks to see whiteness both when we interact with people who are not socially defined as white and when we interact with other white people, when race doesn't seem to be involved. White women see ourselves as acting as individuals rather than as members of a culture in part because we do not see much of the dominant culture at all. Our own lives are therefore part of a racialized world in ways we do not see. This happens when we interact with people of color thinking we are acting as individuals but are in fact acting as part of a white pattern. It also happens when we interact with other white people in ways that seem attached to individuality, humanity, or personhood, but that are not consistently accorded to people who are not white. These interactions with other whites are a circumstance that arises with some frequency because of urban, occupational, and social segregation.

This is where the difficulty of seeing whiteness intersects the definitions of gender that focus on what is taken from women. Both contribute to perpetuating the invisibility to ourselves of our particular experience of privilege as white women. Seeing only harm hampers our vision of women as actors. Further, seeing women's work in social reproduction (cleaning, cooking, caring, and more) as inherently inauthentic contributes to denying dignity in this work.[4] Treating social reproduction as unimportant hides the ways in which this labor has been racially structured as a result of the efforts of white women to minimize its oppressiveness to ourselves.

To better understand women as actors differentiated by race, I want to look at areas in which women have historically been oppressed and have tried to solve the problems posed by that oppression: housework, and access to money and credit. Housework is a human need—one that is oppressively assigned to women. Domestic services are often brutally enforced within marriages and in social expectation. To cope with the oppressive assignment of household work to women, some women employ other women to do significant amounts of household work. Some white women have employed women of color for this purpose. Historically, the domestic employment of women of color by white women has been culturally important to many women of color, and women of color have fought hard to keep their daughters from going into household employment. This racial employment relationship was important in the experience of women of color in ways that were not comparable for all white women. First, the world of relatively economically privileged white women who employ women of color to do housework will be generally invisible to the many white women who never employ household help. Second, white women who did employ household help could generally maintain the almost magical invisibility of dominance to itself—household workers, not their white employers, were the issue for these white women.

Privileged identity requires reinforcement and maintenance, but not seeing the mechanisms that reinforce and maintain privilege is an important component of this identity. Cathy Powell recounted the experience of her grandmother, a black woman who had little contact with white women while growing up in a family that survived on subsistence farming, "until she later moved to New York where she worked as a domestic for a wealthy white family. She has told me how degrading this experience was in both gender and racial terms."[5] Although employment of people of color to perform domestic service has been important to white dominance, it seems unlikely that women from the wealthy white family would tell their grandchildren about the employment of the black domestic worker as an important part of their experience of their race and gender. These different learned cultural truths have made it possible for white women not to see the ways in which women of color have experienced employment interactions with white women.

In an essay in Alice Childress's book *Like One of the Family*, a domestic worker describes a white woman who fiercely clutches her purse whenever the black housekeeper is anywhere on the premises.[6] This white woman's behavior is so patently ugly that it is almost too easy an example of racism. It shows her hostility, her fear, and her privilege to act on them offensively. It is consistent with a stereotype of black people as dishonest and dangerous.

But the white woman could conceivably have seen herself as motivated not by race at all. She could think, maybe without self-delusion, that she would also grab her purse when a white household worker came in—and not think about whether she would learn to hide her purse to avoid embarrassing that white woman. She could think these things and not see where she fit in a world of white people who treat black people as dishonest and dangerous. She could protect her purse without seeing where she fit in a world of white power which creates different job paths for black women and white women, so that black women were for many years forced into domestic work by exclusion from many other forms of employment. Especially important, she could act without seeing where she fit among the several simultaneous white employers of that particular black woman.

Those attributes of whiteness were invisible to that white woman. She could possibly think to herself, "I never let anyone else (strangers, delivery people, maybe even neighbors) stay in the room with my purse." But she also never let anyone else have the mobility in her home without trust that many domestic workers have.

Each white woman may see herself acting as an individual in response to a dangerous other, but these examples have collective aspects. In each case, there is an aspect of what we usually call racism: the white woman is acting on her sense of black people and react-ing to black people. However, privilege also often exists for the white woman as an indi-vidual (for example, being waited on promptly in stores, or not being assumed to be a rep-resentative of her race) when she need not see the event as a matter of "race" at all.

One of the most important characteristics of whiteness in modern society is the way in which white people can have little contact with people of color. We live in a society that is profoundly geographically segregated. Many white people live predominantly white lives without being more than intermittently conscious of "choosing" whiteness—or may live this way without ever consciously choosing whiteness if instead the person is choosing a "good neighborhood." The cultural values surrounding this segregation—the set of values in which white neighborhoods and "good" neighborhoods come together—are part of the oppression of people of color and part of the construction of race itself.[7]

Therefore, part of the experience of white women is that we may live where we have minimal interactions with people of color. Then the issue is one of the *social* construction of race: how living this way shapes white women and shapes a cultural phenomenon of whiteness. This can be particularly important because of our feeling of vulnerability as women, which leads to a quest for safety that we cannot really achieve and tends to rein-force emphasis on "good neighborhoods." In seeking to avoid men and the dangers they pose, we may accept social markers that treat "safety" as equivalent with whiteness, thereby reinforcing racism.

Women have historically lacked access to money and property, so much so that equal access to credit was a prime component of the modern women's movement. Once money, checking accounts, or credit cards have been secured, however, their usefulness and the experience of using them differentiates by race. Imagine a line of women with check-books in hand at a cash register. The white woman writes a check or pulls out her credit card and charges a purchase. Black women often encounter much more difficulty in or-dinary commercial transactions, and the black woman who comes to the cash register next has her identity and her credit card questioned. In the first transaction, the woman cashing the check is actually experiencing life as a white woman—but from her vantage point, all she did was cash a check, not conduct a racial transaction. In the second trans-action, the black woman who has trouble cashing the check is more likely to know it as a racial transaction, or constantly be forced to suspect it or to ignore the issue of why this happened this time—and all these levels of consciousness are part of that experience of a black woman cashing a check.[8] Part of the first transaction was the white woman's whiteness—and that is the invisible part of privilege. Both of these transactions are part of the construction of race, but white people have difficulty seeing exchanges with other white people as race-charged.

As a white single mother, my parenting was often socially suspect. Compared with black single mothers I knew, however, my suspect competence seemed less policed. Both my white experience and my black friends' experiences were particular to the social construc-tion of our identities. But mere recognition of diversity of experience does not fill in the picture: I did not see myself as a "white single mother," and I believe the privilege of not noticing one's race as a single mother is absent for black women. My status had no com-mon race-specific phrase. Although my whiteness was invisible, many events and interac-tions showed me that I faced stigma and struggle as a woman. Most important, nothing would have told me that I was experiencing "privilege," and nothing would have shown me that whiteness was part of the picture, had I not been simultaneously hearing the experience of women of color. Like the white woman cashing a check, I would know only whatever it took for me to get there, and I would take the money and go.

Notes

1. St. Francis College v. Al-Khazraji, 481 U.S. 604, 606–13 (1987); Shaare Tefila Congregation v. Cobb, 481 U.S. 615, 617–18 (1987) (discussing whether Arabs and Jews were "distinct races" and thus "within the protection of" civil rights statutes). Confronted by the indeterminacy of the concept of "race," the Court decided that the important question today is what legislators thought race was when the statutes were enacted. *St. Francis* and *Shaare Tefila* therefore stand for the proposition that the relevant social construction for civil rights law today is the archaic one.

2. Race is built around skin color, yet skin color is not really determinative of race. Not all dark-skinned people are "black" and not all light-skinned people are "white."

3. Peggy McIntosh, White Privilege and Male Privilege: A Personal Account of Coming to See Correspondences Through Work in Women's Studies (Wellesley College Center for Research on Women. Working Paper No. 189, 1988), at 2. [Reprinted as Chapter 47 of this book. Ed.]

4. bell hooks, *Re-thinking the Nature of Work, in* Feminist Theory from Margin to Center, 95, 102–05 (1984).

5. Letter from Cathy Powell, *Open Letters to Catharine MacKinnon*, 4 Yale J. L. & Feminism 189 (1991).

6. Alice Childress, *The Pocketbook Game, in* Like One of the Family: Conversations from a Domestic's Life 26 (1956).

7. The concept of "white" as employed, employable, and competent is in part a product of the access to employment in white neighborhoods; the concept of black as unemployed/unemployable follows patterns of urban development that segregated urban areas by race, deprived black neighborhoods of jobs, and then defined these neighborhoods as filled with unemployables known by their blackness. *See generally* William Julius Wilson, The Truly Disadvantaged (1987); Martha Mahoney, Note, *Law and Racial Geography: Public Housing and the Economy in New Orleans*, 42 Stan. L. Rev. 1251 (1990).

8. Consider situations in which white women walking down the street clutch their purses when a black man approaches. Many white women tell me in conversation that they clutch their purses when any man who is not perceptibly elderly approaches. Even if these women accurately perceive their own patterns of behavior (and do not underestimate the times they fail to notice white men on the street, for example), their actions have social meanings created by the actions of others and of society. To white men walking down the street, these actions are usually not part of a pattern of fearful-acting white women nor a pattern of social treatment of these men as dishonest, dangerous, criminal. To black men walking down the street, the women's actions are part of those patterns *and* part of a social script about the dangers of black men to white women.

50

The GI Bill: Whites Only Need Apply

KAREN BRODKIN SACKS

The GI Bill of Rights, as the 1944 Serviceman's Readjustment Act was known, was arguably the most massive affirmative action program in U.S. history. It was created to develop needed labor-force skills, and to provide those who had them with a life-style that reflected their value to the economy. The GI benefits ultimately extended to sixteen million GIs (veterans of the Korean War as well) included priority in jobs— that is, preferential hiring, but no one objected to it then—financial support during the job search; small loans for starting up businesses; and, most important, low-interest home loans and educational benefits, which included tuition and living expenses. This legislation was rightly regarded as one of the most revolutionary postwar programs. I call it affirmative action because it was aimed at and disproportionately helped male, Euro-origin GIs.

GI benefits, like the New Deal affirmative action programs before them and the 1960s affirmative action programs after them, were responses to protest. Business executives and the general public believed that the war economy had only temporarily halted the Great Depression. Many feared its return and a return to the labor strife and radicalism of the 1930s. "[M]emories of the Depression remained vivid and many people suffered from what Davis Ross has aptly called 'depression psychosis'—the fear that the war would inevitably be followed by layoffs and mass unemployment."[1]

It was a reasonable fear. The eleven million military personnel who were demobilized in the 1940s represented a quarter of the U.S. labor force. In addition, ending war production brought a huge number of layoffs, growing unemployment, and a high rate of inflation. To recoup wartime losses in real wages caused by inflation as well as by the unions' no-strike pledge in support of the war effort, workers staged a massive wave of strikes in 1946. More workers went out on strike that year than ever before, targeting all the heavy industries: railroads, coal mining, auto, steel, and electrical. For a brief moment, it looked like class struggle all over again. But government and business leaders had learned from the experience of bitter labor struggles after World War I just how important it was to assist demobilized soldiers. The GI Bill resulted from their determination to avoid those mistakes this time. The biggest benefits of this legislation were for college and technical school education, and for very cheap home mortgages.

It is important to remember that prior to the war a college degree was still very much a "mark of the upper class."[2] Colleges were largely finishing schools for Protestant elites. Before the postwar boom, schools could not begin to accommodate the American masses.

Even in New York City before the 1930s, neither the public schools nor City College had room for more than a tiny fraction of potential immigrant students.

Not so after the war. The almost eight million GIs who took advantage of their educational benefits under the GI bill caused "the greatest wave of college building in American history."[3] White male GIs were able to take advantage of their educational benefits for college and technical training, so they were particularly well positioned to seize the opportunities provided by the new demands for professional, managerial, and technical labor. "It has been well documented that the GI educational benefits transformed American higher education and raised the educational level of that generation and generations to come. With many provisions for assistance in upgrading their educational attainments veterans pulled ahead of nonveterans in earning capacity. In the long run it was the nonveterans who had fewer opportunities."[4]

Just how valuable a college education was for white men's occupational mobility can be seen in John Keller's study of who benefited from the metamorphosis of California's Santa Clara Valley into Silicon Valley. Formerly an agricultural region, in the 1950s the area became the scene of explosive growth in the semiconductor electronics industry. This industry epitomized the postwar economy and occupational structure. It owed its existence directly to the military and to the National Aeronautics and Space Administration (NASA), who were its major funders and its major markets. It had an increasingly white-collar work force. White men, who were the initial production workers in the 1950s, quickly transformed themselves into a technical and professional work force thanks largely to GI benefits and the new junior college training programs designed to meet the industry's growing work-force needs. Keller notes that "62 percent of enrollees at San Jose Junior College (later renamed San Jose City College) came from blue-collar families, and 55 percent of all job placements were as electronics technicians in the industrial and service sectors of the county economy."[5] As white men left assembly work and the industry expanded between 1950 and 1960, they were replaced initially by Latinas and African-American women, who were joined after 1970 by new immigrant women. Immigrating men tended to work in the better-paid unionized industries that grew up in the area.

Postwar expansion made college accessible to the mass of Euromales in general and to Jews in particular. My generation's "Think what you could have been!" answer to our parents became our reality as quotas and old occupational barriers fell and new fields opened up to Jews. The most striking result was a sharp decline in Jewish small businesses and a skyrocketing of Jewish professionals. For example, as quotas in medical schools fell the numbers of Jewish doctors mushroomed. If Boston is an indication, just over 1 percent of all Jewish men before the war were doctors, compared to 16 percent of the postwar generation. A similar Jewish mass movement took place into college and university faculties, especially in "new and expanding fields in the social and natural sciences."[6] Although these Jewish college professors tended to be sons of businesspersons and professionals, the postwar boom saw the first large-scale class mobility among Jewish men. Sons of working-class Jews now went to college and became professionals themselves, according to the Boston survey, almost two-thirds of them. This compared favorably with three-quarters of the sons of professional fathers.

Even more significantly, the postwar boom transformed the U.S. class structure—or at least its status structure—so that the middle class expanded to encompass most of the population. Before the war, most Jews, like most other Americans, were working class. Already upwardly mobile before the war relative to other immigrants, Jews floated high on this rising economic tide, and most of them entered the middle class. Still, even the high tide missed some Jews. As late as 1973, some 15 percent of New York's Jews were poor or near-poor, and in the 1960s, almost 25 percent of employed Jewish men remained manual workers.

Educational and occupational GI benefits really constituted affirmative action programs for white males because they were decidedly not extended to African Americans or to women of any race. White male privilege was shaped against the backdrop of wartime racism and post-war sexism. During and after the war, white racist violence broke out against black servicemen in public schools, and in the KKK, which spread to California and New York. The number of lynchings rose during the war, and in 1943 antiblack race riots flared in several large northern cities. Although there was a wartime labor shortage, black people were discriminated against in access to well-paid defense industry jobs and in housing. In 1946 white riots against African Americans spread across the South, and broke out in Chicago and Philadelphia as well. Gains made as a result of the wartime Civil Rights movement, especially employment in defense-related industries, were lost with peacetime conversion as black workers were the first fired, often in violation of seniority. White women also suffered lay-offs, ostensibly to make jobs for demobilized servicemen, losing most of the gains they had made in wartime. We now know that women did not leave the labor force in any significant numbers but instead were forced to find inferior jobs, largely nonunion, part-time, and clerical.

Although the program was theoretically available to all veterans, in practice women and black veterans did not get anywhere near their share of GI benefits. Because women's units were not treated as part of the military, women in them were not considered veterans and were ineligible for Veterans' Administration (VA) benefits. The barriers that almost completely shut African-American GIs out of their benefits were more complex. Black GIs anticipated starting new lives, just like their white counterparts. Over 43 percent hoped to return to school and most expected to relocate, to find better jobs in new lines of work. The exodus from the South toward the North and far West was particularly large. So it wasn't a question of any lack of ambition on the part of African-American GIs.

Rather, the military, the Veterans' Administration, the U.S. Employment Service, and the Federal Housing Administration (FHA) effectively denied African-American GIs access to their benefits and to the new educational, occupational, and residential opportunities. Black GIs who served in the thoroughly segregated armed forces during World War II served under white officers, usually southerners. African-American soldiers were disproportionately given dishonorable discharges, which denied them veterans' rights under the GI Bill. Thus between August and November 1946, 21 percent of white soldiers and 39 percent of black soldiers were dishonorably discharged. Those who did get an honorable discharge then faced the Veterans' Administration and the U.S. Employment Service. The latter, which was responsible for job placements, employed very few African Americans, especially in the South. This meant that black veterans did not receive much employment information, and that the offers they did receive were for low-paid and menial jobs. "In one survey of 50 cities, the movement of blacks into peacetime employment was found to be lagging far behind that of white veterans: in Arkansas 95 percent of the placements made by the USES for Afro-Americans were in service or unskilled jobs." African Americans were also less likely than whites, regardless of GI status, to gain new jobs commensurate with their wartime jobs, and they suffered more heavily. For example, in San Francisco by 1948, black Americans "had dropped back halfway to their pre-war employment status."[7]

Black GIs faced discrimination in the educational system as well. Despite the end of restrictions on Jews and other Euroethnics, African Americans were not welcome in white colleges. Black colleges were overcrowded, and the combination of segregation and prejudice made for few alternatives. About twenty thousand black veterans attended college by 1947, most in black colleges, but almost as many, fifteen thousand, could not gain entry. Predictably, the disproportionately few African Americans who did manage to use educational benefits were able, like their white counterparts, to become doctors and engineers, and to enter the black middle class.

Notes

1. Neil A. Wynn, *The Afro-American and the Second World War*, Elek, London, 1976, p. 15.

2. June A. Willenz, *Women Veterans: America's Forgotten Heroines*, Continuum, New York, 1983, p. 165.

3. Gary B. Nash et al., *The American People: Creating a Nation and a Society*, Harper and Row, New York, 1986, p. 885.

4. Willenz, *Women Veterans*, p. 165.

5. John F. Keller, "The Division of Labor in Electronics," in J. Nash and M. P. Fernandez-Kelly, eds., *Men, Women, and the International Division of Labor*, SUNY Press, Albany, 1983, p. 363.

6. Stephen Steinberg, *The Ethnic Myth: Race, Ethnicity, and Class in America*, 2nd ed., Beacon, Boston, 1989, p. 137.

7. Wynn, *The Afro-American and the Second World War*, pp. 114, 116.

51

Making Systems of Privilege Visible

STEPHANIE M. WILDMAN WITH

ADRIENNE D. DAVIS

How Language Veils the Existence of Systems of Privilege

Race and gender are, after all, just words. Yet when we learn that someone has had a child, our first question is usually "Is it a girl or a boy?" Why do we ask that, instead of something like "Are the mother and child healthy?" We ask, "Is it a girl or a boy?" according to philosopher Marilyn Frye, because we do not know how to relate to this new being without knowing its gender.[1] Imagine how long you could have a discussion with or about someone without knowing her or his gender. We place people into these categories because our world is gendered.

Similarly, our world is also raced, and it is hard for us to avoid taking mental notes as to race. We use our language to categorize by race, particularly, if we are white, when that race is other than white. Marge Shultz has written of calling on a Latino student in her class.[2] She called him Mr. Martinez, but his name was Rodriguez. The class tensed up at her error; earlier that same day another professor had called him Mr. Hernandez, the name of the defendant in the criminal law case under discussion. Professor Shultz talked later with her class about her error and how our thought processes lead us to categorize in order to think. She acknowledged how this process leads to stereotyping that causes pain to individuals. We all live in this raced and gendered world, inside these powerful categories, that make it hard to see each other as whole people.

But the problem does not stop with the general terms "race" and "gender." Each of these categories contains the images, like an entrance to a tunnel with many passages and arrows pointing down each possible path, of subcategories. Race is often defined as black and white; sometimes it is defined as white and "of color." There are other races, and sometimes the categories are each listed—for example, as African American, Hispanic American, Asian American, Native American, and White American, if whiteness is mentioned at all. All these words, describing racial subcategories, seem neutral on their face, like equivalent titles. But however the subcategories are listed, however neutrally the words are expressed, these words mask a system of power, and that system privileges whiteness.

Other words we use to describe subordination also mask the operation of privilege. Increasingly, people use terms like "racism" and "sexism" to describe disparate treatment and the perpetuation of power. Yet this vocabulary of "isms" as a descriptive shorthand for undesirable, disadvantaging treatment creates several serious problems.

First, calling someone a racist individualizes the behavior and veils the fact that racism can occur only where it is culturally, socially, and legally supported. It lays the blame on the individual rather than the systemic forces that have shaped that individual and his or her society. Whites know they do not want to be labeled racist; they become concerned with how to avoid that label, rather than worrying about systemic racism and how to change it.

Second, the isms language focuses on the larger category, such as race, gender, sexual preference. Isms language suggests that within these larger categories two seemingly neutral halves exist, equal parts in a mirror. Thus black and white, male and female, heterosexual and gay/lesbian appear, through the linguistic juxtaposition, as equivalent subparts. In fact, although the category does not take note of it, blacks and whites, men and women, heterosexuals and gays/lesbians are not equivalently situated in society. Thus the way we think and talk about the categories and subcategories that underlie the isms allows us to consider them parallel parts, and obscures the pattern of domination and subordination within each classification.

Similarly, the phrase "isms" itself gives the illusion that all patterns of domination and subordination are the same and interchangeable. The language suggests that someone subordinated under one form of oppression would be similarly situated to another person subordinated under another form. Thus, a person subordinated under one form may feel no need to view himself or herself as a possible oppressor, or beneficiary of oppression, within a different form. For example, white women, having an ism that defines their condition—sexism—may not look at the way they are privileged by racism. They have defined themselves as one of the oppressed.

Finally, the focus on individual behavior, the seemingly neutral subparts of categories, and the apparent interchangeability underlying the vocabulary of isms all obscure the existence of systems of privilege and power. It is difficult to see and talk about how oppression operates when the vocabulary itself makes these systems of privilege invisible. "White supremacy" is associated with a lunatic fringe, not with the everyday life of well-meaning white citizens. "Racism" is defined by whites in terms of specific, discriminatory actions by others. The vocabulary allows us to talk about discrimination and oppression, but it hides the mechanism that makes that oppression possible and efficient. It also hides the existence of specific, identifiable beneficiaries of oppression, who are not always the actual perpetrators of discrimination. The use of isms language, or any focus on discrimination, masks the privileging that is created by these systems of power.

Thus the very vocabulary we use to talk about discrimination hides these power systems and the privilege that is their natural companion. To remedy discrimination effectively we must make the power systems and the privileges they create visible and part of the discourse. To move toward a unified theory of the dynamics of subordination, we have to find a way to talk about privilege. When we discuss race, it needs to be described as a power system that creates privileges in some people as well as disadvantages in others. Most of the literature has focused on disadvantage or discrimination, ignoring the element of privilege. To really talk about these issues, privilege must be made visible.

What Is Privilege?

When we try to look at privilege we see several elements. First, the characteristics of the privileged group define the societal norm. Second, privileged group members can rely on their privilege and avoid objecting to oppression. For both reasons, privilege is rarely seen by the holder of the privilege.

The characteristics and attributes of those who are privileged group members are described as societal norms—as the way things are and as what is normal in society. This normalization of privilege means that members of society are judged, and succeed or fail, measured against the characteristics that are held by those privileged. The privileged characteristic is the norm; those who stand outside are the aberrant or "alternative."

Members of the privileged group gain greatly by their affiliation with the dominant side of the power system. This affiliation with power is not identified as such; often it may be transformed into and presented as individual merit. Legacy admissions at elite colleges and professional schools are perceived to be merit-based, when this process of identification with power and transmutation into qualifications occurs. [Legacy admissions give preference to sons and daughters of wealthy alumni or donors. Ed.] Achievements by members of the privileged group are viewed as the result of individual effort, rather than privilege.

Members of privileged groups can opt out of struggles against oppression if they choose. Often this privilege may be exercised by silence. Recently, I was called to jury service. During *voir dire* [preliminary hearings by the court and attorneys to determine prospective jurors' qualifications. Ed.], each prospective juror was asked to introduce herself or himself. The plaintiff's and defendant's attorneys then asked additional questions. I watched the defense attorney ask each Asian-looking male prospective juror if he spoke English. No one else was asked. The judge did nothing. The Asian American man sitting next to me smiled and flinched as he was asked the question. I wondered how many times in his life he had been made to answer it. I considered beginning my own questioning by saying, "I'm Stephanie Wildman, I'm a professor of law, and yes, I speak English." I wanted to focus attention on the subordinating conduct of the attorney, but I did not. I exercised my white privilege by my silence. I exercised my privilege to opt out of engagement, even though this choice may not always be consciously made by someone with privilege.

Depending on the number of privileges someone has, she or he may experience the power of choosing the types of struggles in which to engage. Even this choice may be masked as an identification with oppression, thereby making the privilege that enables the choice invisible. The holder of privilege may enjoy deference, special knowledge, or a higher comfort level to guide societal interaction. Privilege is not visible to its holder; it is merely there, a part of the world, a way of life, simply the way things are.

Although different privileges bestow certain common characteristics (membership in the norm, the ability to choose whether to object to the power system, and the invisibility of its benefit), the form of a privilege may vary. White privilege derives from the race power system of white supremacy. Male privilege and heterosexual privilege result from the gender hierarchy. Class privilege derives from an economic, wealth-based hierarchy. Examining white privilege from the perspective of one who benefits from it, Peggy McIntosh has found it "an elusive and fugitive subject. The pressure to avoid it is great." She defines white privilege as

> an invisible package of unearned assets which [she] can count on cashing in each day, but about which [she] was "meant" to remain oblivious. White privilege is like an invisible weightless knapsack of special provisions, assurances, tools, maps, guides, codebooks, passports, visas, clothes, compass, emergency gear, and blank checks.[3]

McIntosh identified forty-six advantages available to her as a white person that her African

American coworkers, friends, and acquaintances could not count on. Some of these include being told that people of her color made American heritage or civilization what it is; not needing to educate her children to be aware of systemic racism for their own daily protection; and never being asked to speak for all people of her racial group.[4] [Peggy McIntosh's essay is reprinted as Chapter 47 of this book. Ed.]

The identification of class structures and class privilege is rendered difficult in modern American society because of the myth that the United States is a classless society. Discrimination based on race, sex, and other power systems is considered illegal, but discrimination based on wealth has been interpreted as permissible by the Constitution. In a society where basic human needs, such as food, clothing, and shelter, can be met only with money, the privilege of class and wealth seems clear.

In spite of the pervasiveness of privilege, antidiscrimination practice and theory have generally not examined it and its role in perpetuating discrimination. One notable exception is Kimberlè Crenshaw, who has explained, using the examples of race and sex, that

> Race and sex . . . become significant only when they operate to explicitly *disadvantage* the victims; because the *privileging* of whiteness or maleness is implicit, it is generally not perceived at all.[5]

Antidiscrimination advocates focus only on one portion of the power system, the subordinated characteristic, rather than seeing the essential links between domination, subordination, and the resulting privilege.

Adrienne Davis writes:

> Domination, subordination, and privilege are like three heads of a hydra. Attacking the most visible heads, domination and subordination, trying bravely to chop them up into little pieces, will not kill the third head, privilege. Like a mythic multi-headed hydra, which will inevitably grow another head if all heads are not slain, discrimination cannot be ended by focusing only on subordination and domination.[6]

Subordination will grow back from the ignored head of privilege, yet the descriptive vocabulary and conceptualization of discrimination hinder our ability to see the hydra head of privilege. What is not seen cannot be discussed or changed. Thus to end subordination, one must first recognize privilege. Seeing privilege means articulating a new vocabulary and structure for antisubordination theory. Only by visualizing this privilege and incorporating it into discourse can people of good faith combat discrimination.

Visualizing Privilege

For me the struggle to visualize privilege has most often taken the form of the struggle to see my white privilege. Even as I write about this struggle, I fear that my own racism will make things worse, causing me to do more harm than good. Some readers may be shocked to see a white person contritely acknowledge that she is racist. I do not say this with pride. I simply believe that no matter how hard I work at not being racist, I still am. Because part of racism is systemic, I benefit from the privilege that I am struggling to see.

Whites do not look at the world through a filter of racial awareness, even though whites are, of course, members of a race. The power to ignore race, when white is the race, is a privilege, a societal advantage. The term "racism/white supremacy" emphasizes the link between discriminatory racism and the privilege held by whites to ignore their own race. As bell hooks explains, liberal whites do not see themselves as prejudiced or interested in domination through coercion, yet "they cannot recognize the ways their actions support and affirm the very structure of racist domination and oppression that they profess to wish to see eradicated."[7] All whites are racist in this use of the term, because we benefit from systemic white privilege. Generally whites think of racism as voluntary, intentional conduct, done by horrible others. Whites spend a lot of time trying to convince ourselves and each other that we are not racist. A big step would be for whites to admit that we are racist and then to consider what to do about it.

Privilege can intersect with subordination or other systems of privilege. Seeing privilege in this way is complicated by the fact that there is no purely privileged or unprivileged person. Most of us are privileged in some ways and not in others. A very poor person might have been the oldest child in the family and exercised power over his siblings. The wealthiest African American woman, who could be a federal judge, might still have racial, sexist epithets hurled at her as she walks down the street. The experience of both privilege and subordination in different aspects of our lives causes the experiences to be blurred, and the presence of privilege is further hidden from our vocabulary and consciousness. An African American woman professor may act from the privilege of power as a professor to overcome the subordination her white male students would otherwise seek to impose on her. Or a white female professor may use the privilege of whiteness to define the community of her classroom, acting from the power of that privilege to minimize any gender disadvantage that her students would use to undermine her classroom control. Because the choice to act from privilege may be unconscious, the individual, for example, the white female professor, may see herself as a victim of gender discrimination, which she may in fact be. But she is unlikely to see herself as a participant in discrimination for exploiting her white privilege to create the classroom environment.

Imagine intersections in three dimensions, where multiple lines intersect. From the center one can see in many different directions. Every individual exists at the center of these multiple intersections, where many strands meet. No individual really fits into any one category; rather, everyone resides at the intersection of many categories. Categorical thinking makes it hard or impossible to conceptualize the complexity of an individual. The cultural push has long been to choose a category. Yet forcing a choice results in a hollow vision that cannot do justice.

Justice requires that we see the whole person in her or his social context, but the social contexts are complicated. Subordination cannot be adequately described with ordinary language, because that language masks privilege and makes the bases of subordination themselves appear linguistically neutral. As a result the hierarchy of power implicit in words such as "race," "gender," and "sexual orientation" is banished from the language. Once the hierarchy is made visible, the problems remain no less complex, but it becomes possible to discuss them in a more revealing and useful fashion.

Notes

1. See Marilyn Frye, The Politics of Reality: Essays in Feminist Theory 19–34 (1983) (discussing sex marking, sex announcing, and the necessity to determine gender).

2. Angela Harris and Marge Shultz, *"A(nother) Critique of Pure Reason": Toward Civic Virtue in Legal Education*, 45 STAN. L. REV. 1773, 1796 (1993).

3. Peggy McIntosh, *Unpacking the Invisible Knapsack: White Privilege*, CREATION SPIRITUALITY, Jan./Feb. 1992, at 33. Martha Mahoney has also described aspects of white privilege. Martha Mahoney, *Whiteness and Women, in Practice and Theory: A Reply to Catharine MacKinnon*, 5 YALE J. L. & FEMINISM 217 (1993).

4. McIntosh, *Unpacking the Invisible Knapsack*, at 34.

5. Kimberlè Crenshaw, *Demarginalizing the Intersection of Race and Sex: A Black Feminist Critique of Antidiscrimination Doctrine, Feminist Theory and Antiracist Politics*, 1989 U. CHI. LEGAL F. 139, 151. Another important exception, Mari Matsuda, urges those who would fight subordination to "ask the other question," showing the interconnection of all forms of subordination:

> The way I try to understand the interconnection of all forms of subordination is through a method I call "ask the other question." When I see something that looks racist, I ask, "Where is the patriarchy in this?" When I see something that looks sexist, I ask, "Where is the heterosexism in this?"

Mari Matsuda, *Beside My Sister, Facing the Enemy: Legal Theory Out of Coalition*, 43 STAN. L. REV. 1183, 1189 (1991).

6. Adrienne D. Davis, *Identity Notes Part One: Playing in the Light*, 45 AM. U. L. REV. 695 n. 51(1996).

7. bell hooks, *overcoming white supremacy: a comment*, in TALKING BACK: THINKING FEMINIST, THINKING BLACK 113 (1989).

52

Race and Racial Classifications

LUTHER WRIGHT, JR.

In 1983, Susie Phipps' five-year, $49,000 legal battle to have her birth certificate's "erroneous" racial classification changed ended with the court denying her petition.[1] Six years later, Mary Walker's fight to have her racial classification changed on her birth certificate ended with the court granting the change she sought.[2] Why did these two cases, seemingly very similar, have totally opposite outcomes? First, Susie Phipps sought to have her racial classification changed from "black" to "white," while Mary Walker sought a change from "white" to "black."[3] Second, Susie Phipps' home state, Louisiana, was the only one with a statute legally defining the "black" racial classification. Mary Walker's claim, brought in Colorado, was not subject to any statutory definition. Neither woman challenged the "erroneous" classifications on their birth certificates until both faced some tangible loss because of their racial classifications: jobs and social status.[4]

Even though the Louisiana statute was highly biased toward white purity, it was the last rule in the modern era with some notion of a bright-line definition. However, all states still require racial data at birth for statistical purposes such as monitoring population migration, disease, and fertility among racial groups. These statutory requirements mandate that a racial classification be selected at the time of birth. No standards oversee this classification procedure. Instead, parents choose the race of their children based on how they classify themselves. Since birth certificates and other state documents are often used as proof of race, the current standard for racial classification seems to be self-definition.

The Modern Era

While American society may like to believe that limitations and disabilities based on race no longer exist, the reality is otherwise. Studies reveal that criminals who perpetrate crimes against white victims are frequently punished more severely than those who victimize blacks, suggesting that the lives and rights of white victims are valued more highly than the lives of victims of other races.[5] Black orphans are far less likely to be adopted than whites. Minorities are discriminated against in jury selection, often depriving minority group members of one of their most significant constitutional rights. Blacks are still routinely discriminated against in obtaining mortgage loans, and in other significant economic situations such as the purchase of an automobile.[6] In Florida, a white woman was awarded

From "Who's Black, Who's White, and Who Cares: Reconceptualizing the United States's Definition of Race and Racial Classifications," 48 Vand L. Rev. 513 (1995). Originally published in the *Vanderbilt Law Review*. Reprinted by permission.

full worker's compensation disability for her phobia of black men after she was attacked by someone she believed to be black.[7] This century's efforts to achieve voting rights and school desegregation illustrate the continued presence of racial limitations in modern society.

Ian Haney López asserts that race dominates our personal lives because it manifests itself in our speech, dance, neighbors, and friends, and in our ways of talking, walking, eating, and dreaming. He writes that race determines our economic prospects, screening and selecting us for manual jobs and professional careers, red-lining financing for real estate, and green-lining access to insurance. Race permeates politics by altering electoral boundaries, shaping the disbursement of local, state, and federal funds, fueling the creation and collapse of political alliances, and affecting efforts of law enforcement. In short, race permeates every aspect of our lives.[8]

At the federal, state, and local levels, both intentional and benign measures have made race legally significant in the routine activities of everyday life. Minority communities, many established due to discrimination, are often deprived of the basic protections of zoning ordinances. Residents so deprived fear for the safety, quality, and integrity of their communities due to toxic hazards, vile odors, traffic congestion, and blighting appearance. Communities that are nearly one hundred percent black are often deprived of adequate street paving, sanitary sewers, surface water drainage, street lighting, water mains, and fire hydrants. These examples of race-conscious zoning and residential services demonstrate how racial classifications can plague entire urban areas and seriously impair the quality of life in minority areas.

Unfortunately, sometimes even benevolent programs designed to help improve the blighted communities only exacerbate race-conscious deprivation. A fourteen-month investigation during the mid-1980s found that in non-integrated federal rent-subsidy housing, the residential services and privileges were far better than those in the minority areas. Similarly, the Federal Slum Clearance and Urban Renewal Program uprooted thousands of black families, most often relocating them in deprived areas.

The Modern Court's Approach to Race

Neil Gotanda offers four types of racial doctrines that track how society and the courts have viewed race: (1) status-race; (2) formal-race; (3) historical-race; and (4) cultural-race. Under the status-race doctrine, the notion that the black race is inferior allows private individuals to discriminate on the basis of this belief. The formal-race doctrine employs a definition of race that removes all social and historical experiences and views race in isolation, as merely a difference in appearance. The historical-race doctrine defines race in terms of its relationship to oppression and unequal power. Finally, the cultural-race doctrine incorporates all aspects of culture, community, and consciousness.[9]

The significance of these four doctrinal orientations cannot be overemphasized. The Court routinely uses all of these doctrines at its convenience. In the private sector, the Court allows a status-race definition to control. Private individuals are welcome to use an inferiority-based definition of race. In remedial cases, the Court uses the formal-race definition, requiring particularized proof of intentional discrimination on the basis of differences in appearance.[10] The historical approach has been referred to in jury selection, but only after a clear showing of bias, converting the historical approach into a formal-race case. Lastly, the cultural situation seems to apply in diversity cases only, usually not the kind of cases that will affect the rights of the masses. These approaches are problematic because viewing race outside of its historical and cultural context will almost always lead to negative results. As a policy matter, lower courts have seemingly decided that definitions of race must depend on the context in which they are used. The Supreme Court, however, determines what the setting is and, therefore, determines the outcome based on how it frames issues. This lack of consistency simply adds to the confusion in the struggle to define race.

Notes

1. Art Harris, *Louisiana Court Sees No Shades of Gray in Woman's Request*, Wash. Post A3 (May 21, 1983) (recounting how a woman whose birth record declared her to be "black" was classified as such under Louisiana law, even though only her great-great-great-great-grandmother was black).

2. See *Rewriting Her Story*, Nat'l L. J. 51 (Sept. 18, 1989). Mary Christine Walker's birth certificate was issued in the state of Kansas. Years after her birth, the state began issuing birth certificates that did not indicate race. In the end, Walker was allowed to have a new birth certificate issued that did not designate her race.

3. All of the racial statutes favored the notion of white racial purity. Consequently, a person's admission of black ancestry would probably be enough to have that person declared black. Conversely, the notion of white racial purity would make it much harder to prove that a person was white instead of black.

4. See *Rewriting Her Story*, Nat'l L. J. at 51. In the Louisiana case, Susie Phipps did not question the classification on her birth certificate until she needed a copy to receive her passport. Apparently fearful of her wealthy husband's reaction to her racial classification (black), she skipped the trip and spent $20,000 of her "allowance" to have her birth certificate changed. She paid her lawyer with cashier's checks so that her husband would not find out about her birth certificate. See Harris, Wash. Post at A3.

Mary Walker did not challenge her racial classification until her prospective employer accused her of falsely listing her race as black to take advantage of minority hiring policies. Ms. Walker apparently knew that her parents (one black, one mixed heritage) had listed her race as white on her birth certificate so that she could "make it." See *Rewriting Her Story*, Nat'l L. J. at 51.

5. See *McCleskey v. Zant*, 499 U.S. 467, 503–06 (1991) (alleging race discrimination in death penalty sentencing); *Wisconsin v. Mitchell*, 113 S. Ct. 2194 (1993) (upholding sentence of black defendant punished more severely for attacking a white victim pursuant to a state statute stiffening penalties for racially motivated crimes).

6. See generally Ian Ayres, *Fair Driving: Gender and Race Discrimination in Retail Car Negotiations*, 104 Harv. L. Rev. 817 (1991).

7. William Booth, *Phobia About Blacks Brings Workers' Compensation Award*, Wash. Post A3 (Aug. 13, 1992).

8. Ian Haney López, *The Social Construction of Race*, 29 Harv. C.R.–C.L. L. Rev. 1, 3 (1994).

9. Neil Gotanda, *A Critique of "Our Constitution Is Color-Blind,"* 44 Stan. L. Rev. 1 (1991).

10. In his dissent in *Bakke*, Justice Thurgood Marshall wrote:

It is unnecessary in 20th-century America to have individual Negroes demonstrate that they have been victims of racial discrimination; the racism of our society has been so pervasive that none, regardless of wealth or position, has managed to escape its impact. The experience of Negroes in America has been different in kind, not just in degree, from that of other ethnic groups. It is not merely the history of slavery alone but also that a whole people were marked as inferior by the law. And that mark has endured.

Bakke, 438 U.S. at 400 (Marshall, J., dissenting). Viewing race from this historical perspective would most likely change the outcome in the remedial cases.

53

Reflections on Whiteness:
The Case of Latinos(as)

STEPHANIE M. WILDMAN

Imagine that a plane crashes, and in the wreckage we discover a book. Nothing on its cover gives any indication of its contents. But when we open it up, it reveals all the secrets of how to behave as if you rule the world. Suddenly we have an explanation for why so many of them *seem to behave the same way and also why they just don't get it: This handbook teaches them all how to be who they are and makes them so they can't hear us or see us, so much of the time. These are the rules we always feel so outside of and don't understand until we trip over them. These are the rules we didn't make.*

We discover chapters on how to saunter into a room and sit in your chair taking up as much space as possible, and information on how to act like no one says anything of any importance until you rise to speak. We find lessons on how not to see or hear any women or any men of color or any issues that might concern them, but to say exactly what they said (if it was a good idea) without giving them credit or acting as if they had just said precisely the same thing.

A special chapter on white boys in the legal academy explains how to decide what books and articles to recommend to students to read, how to be exclusive about who to cite, and how to discern what is good scholarship and what is drivel, justifying the likeness of good to everything like yourself. The book also contains, of course, chapters on white women as white boys, and men of color as white boys, but you get the idea. (Two friends, Trina Grillo and Adrienne Davis, and I discussed writing such a book.)

Not long ago, I was invited to speak at the University of Texas. The university has a reimbursement request form, which the law journal had filled out, so that they could be reimbursed for sending me an airplane ticket. A state school, Texas devoted a portion of the form to questions about race and ethnicity. In an effort to be helpful, the student filling out my form had entered my race for me. She had checked black. Now here was a lose-lose situation if ever there was one. I don't feel antipathy at being regarded as black, but the fact is I'm not. So next to the box I wrote, "Sadly, not." But I thought it was interesting that people would think I couldn't be white, perhaps because of the things I say and write.

Looking at me you would imagine that most of my life people have assumed that I *am* white, unless I am in a setting where they are inquiring if I am Jewish, which I also am.

Then I am still white, but it's white and. . . . Whiteness, unmodified, remains the dominant cultural norm. Professor Rene Nunez described the history of Anglo-Saxonization that was accompanied by Christianity as part of the formation of this dominant culture. In this vision I am white as long as I "pass" as a real white. And I do get many unsought privileges for that whiteness. I won't be followed around when I enter a store or a bank, the emergency room in the hospital will pay attention when my child is brought in with a broken wrist and won't ask her if she has been abused. I receive these privileges because appearance places me within the dominant fold.

Studying whiteness from a critical perspective reveals a lot about the construction of hierarchy and power, insiders and outsiders. Because whiteness is considered the norm of the dominant culture, it remains mostly invisible, taken as a given. Whiteness is rarely named in conversations about race, except when it is discussed as the opposite of black. Discussions about race are usually constructed along this bipolar axis, making many of the dynamics of the social construction of race invisible and thereby perpetuating white privilege.

This invisibility works in curious ways when Latinas/os are added to the discussion. The bipolar construction of race—blacks versus whites—eliminates them from conversations about race. As a group, Latinas/os span many racial sets of different colors, including white; yet they are not positioned with whites in the bipolar conversation. Latinas/os are defined as nonwhite or other by the dominant culture. Even the history of how to name the group shows that they are not the powerful. The fight for some kind of recognition in the census, to make adequate funding requests for education and other programs possible, led to the use of the category "Hispanic."[1] Recognition in the census was a form of political victory, but the power to self-name remained elusive.

There is a downside to naming Latinas/os as a group, because this act of naming essentializes a highly diverse population, making it appear as a homogeneous whole. The term essentializes many different communities—the Cubanos, Puerto Ricanos, Chicanos—all into one lump. To talk about Latinas/os means ignoring the diverse and many-faceted groups encompassed in the term. The error of this homogenization is perhaps best illustrated by Berta Hernández's story about trying to order a tortilla in New Mexico, thinking she would get an omelette and receiving instead a white pancake-like bread. As she explained, "Same word, same language, different meaning." [2]

Naming Latinas/os, being strategically essentialist, instead of relying on the umbrella category "race" or "people of color" can help us to reveal the hierarchies that exist within the category called race. My friend Julianna Alvarez, who was born in Nicaragua, tells a story of working for a white woman from South Africa. This woman began an argument in which she was particularly abusive to Julianna, who responded, "My skin may be dark, but I'm not black. You can't treat me like that." After her anger had subsided, my friend realized she should have said, "You can't treat me like that just because I'm Latina and a person of color." Although she would not use these words to describe what she had done, she had incorporated the bipolar, dominant discourse into her gut reaction. Such a reaction reinforced the privileging of whiteness. But she realized that she did not want to benefit from using a racial hierarchy, from positioning herself above other people of color.

Being strategically essentialist in this way, naming Latinas/os as a particular community to be examined, ironically creates a less essentialist conversation within race theory in two significant ways: It illuminates that there are different issues for different people of color, and it reminds us that gender matters and is linked to the racial discourse. Of course critical race theorists never claimed all races were alike or that gender didn't matter. But the problems of our language, the very word "race," encourage us to forget the complexity that must be part of the conversation.[3]

Peggy McIntosh pinpointed white privilege when she listed conditions she could count on that her African American co-workers, friends, and acquaintances could not count on most of the time.[4] Many of these conditions on her list of 46 apply to Latinas/os as well, such as:

- I can if I wish arrange to be in the company of people of my race most of the time.
- When I am told about our national heritage or about "civilization," I am shown that people of my color made it what it is.
- I can be sure that my children will be given curricular materials that testify to the existence of their race.

And so I have been thinking about what conditions I can count on that are specific to dominant cultural white privilege, with respect to my Latina/o friends, acquaintances, and colleagues. And I am beginning such a list:

- People seeing me and hearing my name will assume that I, and my children, speak fluent English. People will not be surprised if I speak English well.
- People seeing me, in this country, will assume that I am white (the University of Texas notwithstanding).
- People seeing me will assume I am a citizen of the United States. They will probably voice this by assuming I am an American, an assumption they ironically will not make for people from Central and South America, who of course are equally entitled to claim that word. People will never assume that I or my children are illegal immigrants.
- People will assume that I was born in this country, and will be surprised to learn that my mother was not.
- Stereotyped assumptions will not be made about my class and educational background (or my likely form of employment, if I were a man).
- People will not comment about my sense of time, if I am prompt or late, unless I am unusually late. Then people will assume that I have an individual, personal reason for being late. My lateness will not be dismissed as a joke about white time.
- People will not assume that I have a low IQ.
- People will pronounce my name correctly or politely ask about the correct pronunciation. They will not behave as if it is an enormous imposition to get my name right.[5]
- People will not question my objectivity concerning questions of race.[6]

All of these conditions are related to the assumption that I belong and will fit into the social norm. Since so many Latinas/os are also white, considering these conditions reveals the construction of race as not about race at all, but about power. These assumptions about me, made in my list of conditions—that I belong—show the power of the dominant culture's value in assimilation; belonging is everything, belonging is defined as sameness and in not being the other. This empty value in assimilation reveals why a multicultural perspective, one that honors difference and does not require assimilation, is so important. It is an incredible strength to be bi- or tri-lingual, to understand more cultures than just the dominant one. These real advantages possessed by Latinas/os are used by the dominant culture as disadvantages. This is a crime.

Consider the notion of so-called merit. What if we defined as an aspect of merit for law school admissions the ability to speak more than one language—the ability to be bi- or tri-lingual? What if we required knowledge of a language other than English as part of graduation requirements, so students could serve a wider client base? Who would be the experts sought after in study groups then? The operation of white privilege makes such a scenario unlikely, but would not promoting such requirements make sense?

Recently, at a conference about including these issues within our classrooms (where the audience was a group especially receptive to these concerns rather than the usual audience of law professors), Professor Margaret Montoya rose and spoke in Spanish and English. She described the difficulty of finding her voice at this conference of supposed compañeros which was so alienating to her. She talked about the speech patterns that favor those who are pushy and jump in front of others, of the lack of time to be thoughtful, to process and really hear what people were saying. She said that these patterns excluded voices like her own—Latina voices.

As I listened, tears streamed down my face, because I too have a history of trouble in making my voice heard, in classrooms as a student and teacher, at conferences, and at meetings. We all need to fight against the internalized manual inside our heads defining insiders and outsiders.

Notes

1. Michael Omi & Howard Winant, Racial Formation in the United States: From the 1960s to the 1980s 76 (1986).

2. *See* Berta Esperanza Hernández Truyol, *Building Bridges—Latinas and Latinos at the Crossroads: Realities, Rhetoric and Replacement*, 25 Colum. Hum. Rts. L. Rev. 369, 381, 406–07 (1994).

3. *See Making Systems of Privilege Visible, in* Stephanie M. Wildman (with contributions by Margalynne Armstrong, Adrienne D. Davis, and Trina Grillo), Privilege Revealed (1996).

4. Peggy McIntosh, *White Privilege and Male Privilege: A Personal Account of Coming to See Correspondences through Work in Women's Studies, in* Power, Privilege, and the Law: A Civil Rights Reader (Leslie Bender & Dan Braveman eds., 1995). [Reprinted as Chapter 47 in this book. Ed.]

5. Thanks to Catharine Wells for this idea.

6. Thanks to Margalynne Armstrong for this idea.

54

Stirring the Ashes: Race, Class, and the Future of Civil Rights Scholarship

FRANCES LEE ANSLEY

The "class model" of white supremacy portrays it as a means to justify and enhance class dominance and thus to strengthen existing relations of economic power. This function gives racism its central status in American political life and assures its survival. This is the source of racism's strength and resilience. The class model addresses how, in a white supremacist system, the poor people of all races come out on the short end while the people of the dominant classes appear to extract extraordinary benefits.

The "class domination model" sees racism as an economic tool of the dominant classes, assuring the existence of a reserve army of labor. Minorities are forced into a marginal underclass, cutting them off from their natural class allies and making them vulnerable to abuses and economic manipulation. This system of super-exploitation sanctions extra profit and creates an underclass that can be summoned, moved, or rebuffed almost at will, thereby facilitating the mobility of capital and improving the system's ability to control and channel investment. Economic realities such as the great migrations of black labor earlier in this century, the marginal character of many black jobs, the high unemployment among minorities, and the low wages of many people of color support this picture of white supremacy.

The class domination model also has a "political face," which posits that white supremacy not only allows super-exploitation of blacks, but also blocks potential class-based action by splitting the working class. Exploited classes divided against each other have less power compared to the relatively united exploiting classes. The constant reminder to whites that others are willing to work for less makes minority workers a helpful instrument of discipline to be used against their relatively privileged white counterparts. Concrete historical examples confirm this divide-and-conquer pattern. The frequent use of blacks as strike-breakers during Jim Crow days and the well-known contributions of racism to breaking unions in the South and elsewhere are two instances where this dynamic operates.

As changes have occurred in our economy and in public opinion, civil rights scholars have found cause for both hope and fear. A deep shift away from industrial production, increasing automation, and a decrease in the domestic demand for unskilled labor are making the old economic uses of racial oppression look less and less functional. The effectiveness of race as a dividing wedge has not disappeared, but changed. For example, overt bigotry, despite its resilience and undeniable presence, has suffered significant blows in popular consciousness as a result of the civil rights struggle.

Meanwhile, the *costs* of racism to our system have dramatically increased since the close of World War II. These costs include domestic unrest and damage to our national prestige in a post-Nazi, Cold War, and decolonizing world. The fate of blacks in this country has been an international question since the American slave trade began, but we have often lost sight of that dimension.

Civil rights scholars have noted these changes and have drawn different conclusions about them. Adolph Reed recognizes the altering landscape but still pictures economic realities as the driving force behind race policy. Sidney Willhelm sees the change in economic conditions as evidence of a worse fate for blacks who, rather than being liberated, are now expendable: "[B]lack labor is no longer necessary to economic needs of capitalism or for the state economy; black people are increasingly becoming superfluous. . . . [T]here is no white need for blacks. . . . [We are now confronted with] an economy of uselessness."[1]

On the other hand, some civil rights scholars have found hope in the changing geopolitical pressures and in the rising costs of white supremacy to those in power. For example, the NAACP argued to the Supreme Court in *Brown v. Board of Education*[2] that visible race remediation would help the United States defeat Communism in the war "for the hearts and minds of Third World people. . . ."[3] Their arguments clearly expressed the hope that racism and our economic system could be uncoupled, and that such an uncoupling would serve the long-term interests of the existing order.

At any rate, a number of developments challenge the class domination model. Traditional benefits of white supremacy appear to be waning while costs increase. Meanwhile, during recent decades of civil rights struggle, many members of dominant elites have aligned themselves with the opponents of old-style racism. How then does one explain the continued force of racial division?

The class domination model's answer questions the "obsolescence" notion itself. In its view, the economic system still needs, and will continue to defend, white supremacy, particularly when the global economy is taken into account. Regardless of whether class and race could ever be disconnected, they show no signs of being so to date. The role of color in producing and assuring sizeable stable profits for those in a position to enjoy capturing them is hardly over. We may have witnessed a *change* in white supremacy, but not its withering away, and certainly not the end of its economic usefulness.

[This passage is excerpted from an article in which Professor Ansley sets out "two polar theories that offer opposing explanations" of the staying power of white supremacy. She concedes that they are oversimplified and schematic fictions, but voices the hope that they will advance discussion and analysis. The two polar theories are: the "class model" (itself further divided into "class domination" and "class legitimation" variants), and the "race model." The first model Ansley dubs White Supremacy as a Feature of Class Domination, and the second, White Supremacy for Its Own Sake. She ultimately concludes that neither model is satisfactory. "Rather, the inadequacies of each demonstrate the importance of race *and* class to a full understanding of white supremacy and to a viable plan for overcoming it." Ed.]

Notes

1. Derrick Bell, *A Hurdle Too High: Class-Based Roadblocks to Racial Remediation*, 33 Buffalo L. Rev. 1 at 25, 26 (Sidney Willhelm speaking).

2. 349 U.S. 294 (1955).

3. Derrick Bell, And We Are Not Saved: The Elusive Quest for Racial Justice 62 (1987).

One episode of the television documentary *Eyes on the Prize* (six-part documentary, produced by Blackside, Inc., first aired on Public Broadcasting Service, 1987) makes this point graphically. The narrator recounts the history of the desegregation campaign in Birmingham, which culminated in mass demonstrations. The camera moves from footage of the demonstrations to a sequence of photographs and articles published at that time in the international press featuring children being attacked with dogs and fire hoses under the direction of then police chief Bull Connor. Following this montage, the viewer watches Alabama Governor George Wallace's reaction to the international coverage. While the governor vociferously maintains supreme unconcern about world opinion, we are led to the firm conclusion that worry about the "outside world" provided protest leaders with important leverage for change.

55

The Social Construction of Whiteness

MARTHA R. MAHONEY

Race is a phenomenon always in formation. Therefore whiteness, like other racial constructions, is subject to contest and change. Whiteness is historically located, malleable, and contingent. Arguments about the contingency of white privilege, and its dysfunctionality for white working people, may seem counterintuitive. Most writers emphasize what whites gain—the existence and benefits of privilege—or what whites lose—the costs of change for whites—rather than looking at transformative interests for whites. Yet some struggles that brought antiracist consciousness to the defense of shared class interest succeeded, historically, even under the formidable difficulties of formal segregation, and fomentation of race hatred.[1] My goal is to identify those points about whiteness that are most susceptible to change—especially those points that reveal potential for undermining the construction of privilege and subordination and for uniting whites, along with people of color, in opposition to privilege.

Although race is not "a natural division of human-kind,"[2] race derives much of its power from seeming to be a natural or biological phenomenon or, at the very least, a coherent social category. For whites, residential segregation is one of the forces giving race a "natural" appearance: "good" neighborhoods are equated with whiteness, and "black" neighborhoods are equated with joblessness. This equation allows whiteness to remain a dominant background norm, associated with positive qualities for white people, at the same time that it allows unemployment and underemployment to seem like natural features of black communities.

Race is also a relational concept. It describes social and cultural groups in relation to each other.[3] The concept of race acquires meaning only in the context of historical development and existing race relations. Therefore, the construction of whiteness as "naturally" employed and employable, and blackness as "naturally" unemployed and unemployable, are both examples of the way in which concepts of whiteness and blackness imply whiteness as dominant and blackness as "Other." Both become part of the way of thinking about race in America.

Recently, social and legal theorists have begun to "interrogate whiteness,"[4] a project made difficult in part because explicit discussion of whiteness is usually associated only with white supremacists. We especially need to identify those moments in time and points in social understanding at which shared social interests exist, rather than treat white privilege as a fixed and frozen artifact. Ruth Frankenberg divides whiteness into a set of "linked dimensions": a location of structural advantage and race privilege; a "standpoint" from which white people look at themselves, at others, and at society; and a set of cultural practices that are usually unmarked and unnamed. She explores the ways in which material existence and the way we understand and describe it are interconnected in the construction of whiteness. The interaction of the material world and the ways we explain and understand it "generates experience" and, therefore, the "experience" of lived whiteness is something continually constructed, reconstructed, and transformed for white people.

Whites have difficulty perceiving whiteness, both because of its cultural prevalence and because of its cultural dominance. Anthropologist Renato Rosaldo describes "culture" as something perceived in someone else, something one does not perceive oneself as having.[5] What we ourselves do and think does not appear to us to be "culture," but rather appears to be the definition of what is normal and neutral, like the air we breathe, transparent from our perspective. Like culture, race is something whites notice in themselves only in relation to others.[6] Privileged identity requires reinforcement and maintenance, but protection against seeing the mechanisms that socially reproduce and maintain privilege is an important component of the privilege itself. Peggy McIntosh conceptualizes white privilege as "an invisible weightless knapsack" of provisions, maps, guides, codebooks, passports, visas, compasses, and blank checks.[7] [See Chapter 47. Ed.] The privilege that facilitates mobility and comfort in ordinary life is particularly difficult for whites to see. From the position of people of color, white privilege is neither transparent nor invisible, its reproduction through many conscious and unconscious acts not at all mysterious. Opening a bank account appears routine, as does air travel without police stops, or shopping without facing questions about one's identification—unless the absence of suspicion is a privilege of whiteness.

White privilege therefore includes the ability to not-see whiteness and its privileges. Whites not only fail to see themselves clearly, they also fail to see the way white privilege appears to those defined into the category of "Other." Among other whites, white people generally perceive that no race at all is present. "Race" itself comes to mean "Other" or "Black." In the context of housing and urban development, terms like "racially identifiable" generally refer to locations that are racially identifiably black. Dominant culture remains transparent to those inside it.

Because the dominant norms of whiteness are not visible to them, whites are free to see themselves as "individuals," rather than as members of a culture. Individualism in turn becomes part of white resistance to perceiving whiteness and indeed to being placed in the category "white" at all. The shift in vision that makes whiteness perceptible is thus doubly threatening for whites: It places whites in a category that their whiteness itself requires them to be able to ignore, at the same time that it asks them to admit the perceptions of those defined outside the circle of whiteness.

Whiteness is visible to whites, however, when it appears to be the basis on which well-being is threatened. Whites perceive racism against themselves when, through interventions in the norm of transparency, whites are forced to experience the consciousness of whiteness. In the logic of white privilege, making whites feel white equals racism. A recent poll of young people between the ages of fifteen and twenty-four showed that 68% of blacks felt that blacks were discriminated against on the basis of race, 52% of Hispanics felt Hispanics were discriminated against on the basis of race, and 49% of white people felt that whites were being discriminated against on the basis of race.[8] Many whites explain the gap between black and white earnings not by invoking inequality and prejudice, but by relying on "individualistic" explanations about thrift, hard work, and other factors—all of which tend to explain white success through white merit and equate whiteness with stability and employability.

In work on desegregation and urban development, the routine acceptance of whiteness as a dominant background norm is apparent in attitude surveys that inquire about the percentage of blacks whom whites would be willing to tolerate as neighbors. Whites are seldom asked how many whites they require as neighbors in order to feel comfortable. The accepted concept of "neighbors" or "area residents" is one that is white. On the other hand, defensive white self-awareness manifests itself quickly during times of racial transition in an area, or in relation to nearby groups in "other" neighborhoods.

Notes

1. For example, even in bastions of racism at times of great white resistance to civil rights for African-Americans, white working-class southerners sometimes proved capable of working for change in the areas of race and class. *See generally* JASON BERRY, AMAZING GRACE (1973); MICHAEL HONEY, SOUTHERN LABOR AND BLACK CIVIL RIGHTS (1993); Martha R. Mahoney, White Working Men, Law, and Politics: Transformation and the Social Construction of Race (March 10, 1995) (unpublished manuscript, on file with author).

2. Peter Jackson, *The Idea of "Race" and the Geography of Racism, in* RACE AND RACISM: ESSAYS IN SOCIAL GEOGRAPHY 3, 6 (Peter Jackson ed., 1987).

3. The concepts of "white" and "black" races (and, indeed, "brown," "yellow," or "red" races) could not exist without each other. Otherwise, we would experience the many diverse people, cultures, skin tones, and languages that comprise each "race" without using the concept of race to group them together.

4. *See, e.g.,* BELL HOOKS, YEARNING: RACE, GENDER, AND CULTURAL POLITICS 54 (1990) (discussing the need to "interrogate[ ] whiteness"). Ruth Frankenberg defines "whiteness" as the cumulative way that race shapes the lives of white people. *See* RUTH FRANKENBERG, WHITE WOMEN, RACE MATTERS: THE SOCIAL CONSTRUCTION OF WHITENESS 1 (1993).

5. *See* RENATO ROSALDO, CULTURE AND TRUTH: THE REMAKING OF SOCIAL ANALYSIS 198 (1989) ("In 'our' own eyes, 'we' appear to be 'people without culture.' By courtesy, 'we' extend this noncultural status to people who ('we' think) resemble 'us.'"). *Cf.* Mari J. Matsuda, *Voices of America: Accent, Antidiscrimination Law, and a Jurisprudence for the Last Reconstruction,* 100 YALE L.J. 1329, 1360–67 (1991) (indicating that we hear accent in others but not in ourselves).

6. Often, we evaluate our own whiteness obliquely, without mentioning it. For example, when whites express beliefs that blacks are less moral or take poor care of their homes, this is an indirect statement that whites are moral and whites do take care of their homes. *Cf.* DOUGLAS S. MASSEY & NANCY A. DENTON, AMERICAN APARTHEID: SEGREGATION AND THE MAKING OF THE UNDERCLASS 94–95 (1993) (citing several studies showing that significant percentages of whites believe that blacks are more likely than whites to fail to care for their homes properly and more likely to lie, cheat, steal, and commit sex crimes); Joleen Kirschenman & Kathryn M. Neckerman, *"We'd Love to Hire Them, But . . .": The Meaning of Race for Employers, in* THE URBAN UNDERCLASS 203, 203–04 (Christopher Jencks & Paul E. Peterson eds., 1991) (observing that black race and ethnicity reinforces various other characteristics, such as instability, uncooperativeness, and dishonesty, in employers' eyes).

7. *See* Peggy McIntosh, *White Privilege and Male Privilege: A Personal Account of Coming to See Correspondences through Work in Women's Studies* 2 (Wellesley College Center for Research on Women, Working Paper No. 189, 1988). For a related discussion of "shopping stories" about and for blacks, see generally Regina Austin, *"A Nation of Thieves": Securing Black People's Right to Shop and to Sell in White America,* 1994 UTAH L. REV. 147.

8. *See* George E. Curry, *Young Find Race Relations Troubling,* CHI. TRIB., Mar. 17, 1992, at 3C

(describing a poll conducted by People for the American Way in which half of the 1,170 white, black, and Hispanic youths polled describe race relations in the United States as "generally bad"). In this framework, individual white success becomes defined as triumph over racial adversity. Most people polled expressed opposition to racial separation, but their opposition may be inflected by their fear of discrimination against whites. *See id.* (noting that a majority of all youths surveyed disagreed with the statement "It's okay to have a country where the races are basically separate from one another, as long as they all have opportunities," but that 49% of the white youths questioned believe that whites are "denied opportunity"). A smaller percentage (18%) of whites said they had themselves been the victim of discrimination. *See Racial Stereotypes Keep Strong Grip on Young America,* SAN DIEGO UNION-TRIB., Mar. 17, 1992, at A4 (presenting figures from the same People for the American Way poll).

Synopses of Other Important Works

Contesting Privilege: David Roediger

In *The Wages of Whiteness* (Verso, 1991), the University of Minnesota historian David Roediger amplifies the interaction of race, social construction, and class explored elsewhere in this volume. In the fifth chapter of his book ("Class, Coons, and Crowds in Antebellum America"), Roediger shows how the emerging morality of capitalism—including punctuality, abstention from alcohol except on weekends, and separation of work from pleasure and the rest of life—created guilt, anxiety, and a degree of longing on the part of an American working class called upon to give up its former ways. These repressed longings found ready outlet in minstrel shows and other cultural images depicting—directly through various aesthetic genres and physical stereotypes and indirectly through the psychological mechanism of projection—blacks as possessing all the qualities (leisure, music, sexuality, etc.) that white blue-collar workers were forced to give up.

From the Editors: Issues and Comments

Are white people privileged? Un-privileged? Privileged in some respects and not in others? Is it an aspect of white privilege not to have to think about one's privilege, or to be able blandly to deny it? Do clerks follow you around when you go in a store? Do police officers hassle you? When you take a car trip through certain parts of the country, do you take extraordinary precautions so that your car does not break down or you are stranded? Do you carefully make telephone reservations in advance for every place you plan to spend the night? Would you feel comfortable living in a middle-class neighborhood where ten percent of your neighbors were black if you are white, and vice versa? Fifty percent? Ninety percent? If blacks or Chicanos prefer to date light-skinned members of their own groups, are they racist? The United States Census currently has no category for biracial people—sons or daughters of, for example, a black mother and a white father. If such a person checks a box (say, white), does that mean he or she is rejecting the heritage of the other parent? Is the U.S. Census, then, racist?

Suggested Readings

Bowser, Benjamin B., and Raymond G. Hunt, IMPACTS OF RACISM ON WHITE AMERICANS (Sage, 2d ed., 1996).

Cose, Ellis, THE RAGE OF A PRIVILEGED CLASS (1993).

Culp, Jerome M., *Posner and Duncan Kennedy and Racial Differences*, 1991 DUKE L.J. 1095.

Flagg, Barbara, BROKEN PROMISES AND (NOT SO) LITTLE WHITE LIES: WHITE RACE CONSCIOUSNESS AND LAW (New York University Press, 1997).

Frankenburg, Ruth, *Growing Up White*, 45 FEMINIST STUDIES 51 (1993).

Harris, Angela, *Race and Essentialism in Feminist Legal Theory*, 42 STAN. L. REV. 582 (1990).

Kline, Marlee, *Race, Racism, and Feminist Theory*, 12 HARV. WOMEN'S L.J. 115 (1989).

Levine, J., *The Heart of Whiteness: Dismantling the Master's House*, 128 VOICE LITERARY SUPPLEMENT 11 (1994).

Ware, Vron, BEYOND THE PALE: WHITE WOMEN, RACISM, AND HISTORY (Verso, 1991).

Wildman, Stephanie, WHITE PRIVILEGE (New York University Press, 1996).

Part VII

The Ladder of Whiteness

Our society prides itself on the way it holds out the promise of upward mobility to all groups, including immigrants. The lines etched on the base of the Statue of Liberty ("Give me your tired, your poor, / Your huddled masses, yearning to breathe free") imply that all are welcome and that anyone who works hard can enter the mainstream of society and achieve the American dream. Yet many immigrant groups have found the going tough. Some, such as the Irish, were surprised to find that they were considered nonwhite; others were puzzled that working hard and attaining high occupational prestige did not enable them to cast off working-class origins and worries after all. And what of merit? Can a white with extremely high test scores, for example, make his or her way in the world if he or she lacks a mentor and is excluded, by reason of lower-class origins, from networks of influence and information? Can he or she cast off blue-collar or "ethnic" origins and fit easily into upper-class society? What of those bastions of white privilege and Anglo-Saxon supremacy, Ivy League schools? Can one get as good an education at a state university, and rise as far in the world?

56

The Mind of the South

W. J. CASH

There remain the people who, under the classical interpretation, were lumped together as poor whites—the non-slaveholding masses of the South. Who were they? Obviously and simply, in the large and outside the oldest regions, the residue of the generally homogeneous population of the old backwoods of the eighteenth century, from which the main body of the ruling class had been selected out. The relatively and absolutely unsuccessful, the less industrious and thrifty, the less ambitious and pushing, the less cunning and lucky—the majority here as everywhere. The weaker elements which, having failed in the competition of the cotton frontier, or having perhaps never entered it, were driven back inexorably by the plantation's tendency to hog the good cotton lands into a limited number of large units, to the lands that had been adjudged as of little or no value for the growing of the staple.

But driven back in degree, of course. Thousands and ten thousands—possibly the majority of non-slaveholders were really yeoman farmers. Some of these occupied the poorer cotton lands; but by far the greater number of them were planted on lands which, while they were reckoned as of no account for cotton, were fertile enough for other purposes. Nearly all of them enjoyed some measure of a kind of curious half-thrifty, half-shiftless prosperity—a thing of sagging rail fences, unpainted houses, and crazy barns which yet bulged with corn. And if they are to be called poor whites, then it is not at all in the ordinary connotation of the term, but only in a relative and broad sense—only as their estate is compared with that of the larger planters, and, what is more important, only as they may be thought of as being exploited, in an indirect and limited fashion, by the plantation system.

But I must pause to explain more fully what I mean by this exploitation. It involved the fact, not only that the plantation system had driven these people back to the less desirable lands, but also that it had, to a very great extent, walled them up and locked them in there—had blocked them off from escape or any considerable economic and social advance as a body. (No, not even by flight beyond the Mississippi since the cotton planters, with their appetite for gain merely whetted by what they had already won, were presently seizing the best lands there, too—were moving out upon Arkansas and Texas armed with plentiful capital and solid battalions of slaves.) For this system, once on its feet, was a static one, the tendency of which was to hold each group rigidly in the established equilibrium.

Moreover, having driven these people back, it thereafter left them virtually out of account. Wholly dominant, possessing, for practical purposes, absolute control of government and every societal engine, it took its measures solely with an eye to its own inter-ests—which were not the interests, clearly, of most of the non-slaveholders. Worse yet, it concerned itself but little if at all about making use of them as economic auxiliaries—as feeders of those things which the plantation had need of but did not produce in sufficient quantities. It would be nonsense, certainly, to suggest that it had no traffic with them, or that it did not, in fact, furnish them a considerable market. Nevertheless, it is true that, in following its own interests alone, it always preferred to buy a great part of its hay and corn and beef and wool from the North or the Middle West rather than go to the trouble and expense of opening up the backcountry adequately. Roads, railroads, transportation facili-ties generally, were provided mainly with regard to the movement of cotton. And so, though the slaveless yeomen might wax fat in the sort of primitive prosperity which con-sisted in having an abundance of what they themselves could produce, they could not go much further than that—were left more or less to stagnate at a level but a step or two above the pioneers.

The poor whites in the strict sense were merely the weakest elements of the old back-country population, in whom these effects of the plantation had worked themselves out to the ultimate term; those who had been driven back farthest—back to the red hills and the sandlands and the pine barrens and the swamps—to all the marginal lands of the South; those who, because of the poorness of the soil on which they dwelt or the great inaccessi-bility of markets, were, as a group, most completely barred off from escape or economic and social advance. They were the people to whom the term "cracker" properly applied—the "whitetrash" and "po' buckra" of the house-niggers, within the narrowest meaning of those epithets, which, however, were very far from being always used with nice discrimi-nation.

They exhibited some diversity of condition, beginning at the bottom with a handful of Jukes and Kallikaks with all the classical stigmata of true degeneracy, and scaling up to, and merging at the top with, the lower type of yeoman farmer. Not a few of the more abject among them were addicted to "dirt-eating," but the habit was by no means so universal as has sometimes been claimed. [Poor Southerners, especially pregnant ones, formerly sup-plemented their iron-deficient diets by eating red clay. Ed.] Some of them were masters of hundreds of acres of a kind. Others had no claim to their spot of earth save that of the squat-ter. The houses of the better sort were crude shells of frame or logs, with as many as seven or eight rooms at times. Those of the run were mere cabins or hovels, with shutters for windows, with perhaps no other door than a sack, and with chinks wide open to the wind and the rain. Very often an entire family of a dozen, male and female, adult and child, slept, cooked, ate, lived, loved, and died—had its whole indoor being—in a single room.

But whatever their diversity, their practice of agriculture was generally confined to a lit-tle lackadaisical digging—largely by the women and children—in forlorn corn-patches. The men might plow a little, hunt a little, fish a little, but mainly passed their time on their backsides in the shade of a tree, communing with their hounds and a jug of what, with a fine feeling for words, had been named "bust-head." And finally, as the very hallmark of the type, the whole pack of them exhibited, in varying measure, a distinctive physical char-acter—a striking lankness of frame and slackness of muscle in association with a shambling gait, a boniness and misshapeliness of head and feature, a peculiar sallow swartness, or al-ternatively a not less peculiar and a not less sallow faded-out colorlessness of skin and hair.

This is the picture—often drawn more or less as I have drawn it here—which no doubt has given rise to the whole classical notion of the poor white as belonging to a totally different stock from the run of Southerners and particularly from the ruling class, and which has persuaded so many eminent historians that he must be explained by the convict servants and redemptioners of old Virginia. But, quite apart from the considerations I have already urged against it, that theory can be fully disposed of by a moment's reflection on what it is one is asked to believe in order to swallow it; to wit: that some fifty thousand indentured servants set down in tidewater Virginia in the seventeenth century account in the nineteenth for at least two million crackers, scattered all the way from the Great Dismal Swamp to the Everglades and from the Atlantic to the Mississippi and beyond—that these servants and their progeny were so astoundingly inferior that through two centuries they spread over the land, past a dozen frontiers and through vast upheavals, without ever in the slightest losing their identity, without ever marrying and intermingling with the generality, and breeding steadily only with their own.

Actually, there is nothing in the description of the cracker to give us pause—nothing which need raise any doubt that he derived from like sources with the mass of Southerners of whatever degree—nothing that is not readily to be explained by the life to which the plantation had driven him back and blocked him in. For this life, in its essence, was simply a progressively impoverished version of the life of old backwoods. The forest, which had been the rock upon which that life had been built, was presently in large part destroyed by the plantation and the prevailing wastefulness. Hence the hunter who had formerly foraged for larder while his women hoed the corn found himself with less and less to do. Lacking lands and markets which would repay any extensive effort as a farmer, lacking any incentive which would even serve to make him aid the women at tasks which habit had fixed as effeminate, it was the most natural thing in the world for him to sink deeper and deeper into idleness and shiftlessness. More, the passing of the forest increasingly deprived his table of the old abundant variety which the teeming wild life had afforded. Increasingly his diet became a monotonous and revolting affair of cornpone and the flesh of razorback hogs. And so, increasingly, he was left open to the ravages of nutritional disease (long since proved to be the cause of "dirt-eating") and of hookworm and malaria.

Take these things, add the poorness of the houses to which his world condemned him, his ignorance of the simplest rules of sanitation, the blistering sun of the country, and apply them to the familiar physical character of that Gaelic (maybe a little Iberian) strain which dominated in so large a part of the original Southern stocks—to this physical character as it had already been modified by the backwoods into the common Southern type— and there is no more mystery about even the peculiar appearance of the cracker. A little exaggerating here, a little blurring there, a little sagging in one place and a little upthrusting in another—and *voilà!* . . . Catch Calhoun or Jeff Davis or Abe Lincoln (whose blood stemmed from the Carolina foothill country, remember) young enough, nurse him on "bust-head," feed him hog and pone, give him twenty years of lolling—expose him to all the conditions to which the cracker was exposed—and you have it exactly.

The matter of the derivation of the poor white, indeed, goes further than I have yet said. Not only is it true that he sprang from the same general sources as the majority of the planters, but even that, in many cases, he sprang from identical sources—that he was related to them by the ties of family. In any given region the great planter who lived on the fertile lands along the river, the farmer on the rolling lands behind him, and the cracker on the barrens back of both were as often as not kindred. And in sections half a thousand miles apart the same connection could be traced between people of the most diverse condition.

The degree of consanguinity among the population of the old Southern backcountry was very great. As I have suggested, economic and (for all the considerable variation in original background) social distinctions hardly existed prior to the invention of the cotton gin; certainly few existed to the point of operating as an effective barrier to intermarriage. And the thin distribution of the people often made it necessary for the youth, come of marrying age, to ride abroad a considerable way for a wife. Hence by 1800 any given individual was likely to be cousin, in one degree or another, to practically everybody within a radius of thirty miles about him. And his circle of kin, of course, overlapped more or less with the next, and that in turn with the next beyond, and so on in an endless web, through the whole South.

What happened when the cotton gin tossed the plantation ferment into this situation is obvious. Given a dozen cousins—brothers, if you wish—one or two would carve out plantations at home (in the Carolinas or Georgia, say); another or two, migrating westward, might be lucky enough to do the same thing there; four or five, perhaps attempting the same goal, would make just enough headway to succeed as yeoman farmers; and the rest would either fail in the competition, or, being timid and unambitious, would try the impossible feat of standing still in this world of pushing men—with the result that, by processes I need not describe, they would gradually be edged back to poorer and poorer lands. In the end, they—or the weakest and least competent of their sons—would have drifted back the whole way: would definitely have joined the ranks of the crackers. And once there, they would be more or less promptly and more or less fully forgotten by their more prosperous kinsmen.

That this is really what took place is a proposition which does not depend on mere supposition or dogmatic statement. Whoever will take the trouble to investigate a little in any county in the South—outside the areas occupied by the colonial aristocracies, at any rate—will be immediately struck by the fact that the names of people long prominent locally, people emphatically reckoned as constituting the aristocracy, are shared by all sorts and conditions of men. Stay awhile in any town of the land, and presently some gentleman native to the place will point you out a shuffling, twisted specimen, all compact of tangled hair, warts, tobacco stains, and the odor of the dung-heap, and with a grandiloquent wave of the hand and a mocking voice announce: "My cousin, Wash Venable!" What he means, of course, is what he means when he uses the same gesture and the same tone in telling you that the colored brother who attends to his spittoons is also his cousin—that you will take him seriously at your peril. What he means is that the coincidence of names is merely a little irony of God, and that the thing he says is clearly not so.

But, though he may know it only vaguely if at all, it more often than not is so just the same. It is not necessary to rest on the reflection that, while it is plausible enough that some such coincidences should arise from mere chance, it seems somehow improbable that a hundred such coincidences in the same county, ten thousand such coincidences in the South generally, can be so explained. If one gets out into the countryside where the "cousin" lives, one is pretty sure to come upon definite and concrete evidence. Maybe there will be an old woman—there nearly always is an old woman—with a memory like a Homeric bard's, capable of moving easily through a mass of names and relationships so intricate that the quantum theory is mere child's play in comparison. And scattered here and there all about the South are one-gallus genealogists, somewhat smelly old fellows with baggy pants and a capacity for butchering the king's English, but shrewd withal and, like the old woman, capable of remarkable feats of memory. From such sources one may hear the whole history of the Venables, beginning with Big John, who used to catch squirrels with his hands and whoop with laughter when they bit him, down to seventh cousin Henry's third wife and the names that had been selected for the babies that were born dead. One may discover, indeed, that the actual relationship between the mocking gentleman in the town and "Cousin Wash" is somewhat remote. But—it was not so remote in the Old South.

Perhaps there are limits beyond which this should not be pushed, but they are not narrow. I am advised by those who know Virginia better than I do that even there, if only one goes back far enough, it is often quite possible to establish such connections. And I have myself traced the origin of many of the names ensconced in the beautiful old red brick houses which dot the lovely landscape of bluegrass Kentucky to a group of families in the piedmont country of North Carolina—families which, to my personal knowledge, perfectly illustrate, in their native habitat, the account I have set down here. . . .

If the yoke of law and government weighed but lightly, so also did that of class. Prior to the last ten or fifteen years before Secession, the Old South may be said, in truth, to have been nearly innocent of the notion of class in any rigid and complete sense. And even when the notion did come into use, it was always something for philosophers bent on rationalizing an economic system to bandy about rather than something which was really an integral part of Southern thinking in general.

Here, manifestly, I do not infer that the Old South was ever egalitarian, as, say, the U.S.S.R. is egalitarian, or that the backcountry's lack of distinctions was brought over into the plantation order without modification. From what I have already recorded, from the reports of every contemporary observer, it is clear that, from an early time, there was a great deal of snobbish feeling; that an overweening pride in the possession of rich lands and slaves, and contempt for those who lacked them, quickly got to be commonplaces; and that the *nouveaux*, fired by the example of the Virginians and their high pride of birth and breeding, were eagerly engaged in heaping distinction upon distinction and establishing themselves in the role of proper gentlemen. Nowhere else in America, indeed, not forgetting even Boston, would class awareness in a certain very narrow sense figure so largely in the private thinking of the master group. And not only in the private thinking of the master group, for that matter. Everybody in the South was aware of, and habitually thought and spoke in terms of, a division of society into Big Men and Little Men, with strict reference to property, power, and the claim to gentility.

Nevertheless, the Southerner's primary approach to his world was not through the idea of class. He never really got around in his subconsciousness to thinking of himself as being, before all else, a member of a caste, with interests and purposes in conflict with the interests and purposes of other castes. And certainly he never felt even the premonitory twinges of class awareness in the full sense—of that state in which the concept of society as divided into rigid layers and orders burrows into the very tissues of the brain and becomes the irresistible magnetic pole for one's deepest loyalties and hates, the all-potent determiner of one's whole ideological and emotional pattern. Rather, he saw with essentially naïve, direct, and personal eyes. Rather, his world, as he beheld it, remained always, in its basic aspect, a single aggregation of human units, of self-contained and self-sufficient entities, whose grouping along class lines, though it might and would count tremendously in many ways, was yet not a first thing.

Perhaps this will seem amazing in view of what I have already said about the effect of the plantation system in driving back and blocking up poor white and farmer. That might have been expected to generate resentment and even hate—to set off class conflict and make class feeling a prevailing emotion. Yet when one carefully examines the whole of the curious situation which existed in the plantation world, there is nothing amazing here.

The groundwork in this case as elsewhere, it must be borne firmly in mind, was the tradition of the backcountry and the more or less fresh—the never entirely obliterated—remembrance of the community of origins: factors operating, of course, for the preservation of the old basic democratic feeling. It is perfectly plain, indeed, that if, being a poor white or a farmer, you knew that your planter neighbor was a kinsman, you were normally going to find it as difficult to hate him as to think of him as being made of fundamentally different stuff from yourself—a "shining one" begotten by God for the express purpose of ruling you. You might defer to him as a rich man, and you might often feel spite and envy; but to get on to genuine class feeling toward him you would have to have an extraordinarily vivid sense of brutal and intolerable wrong, or something equally compulsive.

Similarly, if you were a planter, and recalled that you had played about a cabin as a boy, that as a youth you had hunted the possum with that slouching fellow passing there, or danced the reel with the girl who had grown up unbelievably into the poke-bonneted, sun-faded woman yonder (had maybe kissed her on that moon-burning, unutterable, lost night when you rode away to New Orleans with Andy Jackson), why, the chances were that, for all your forgetfulness when your ambition was involved, for all your pride in your Negroes, and your doctrinaire contempt for incompetence, there was still at the bottom of you a considerable community of feeling with these people—that, in truth, it would unconsciously dominate you and keep class awareness from penetrating below your surface and into the marrow of your bones, so long as those below did not rouse to a sense of wrong and begin to strike back.

But now behold with what precision the plantation conspired—and quite without the intervention of feeble human wit—to see that this sense of wrong did not develop.

In the first place, if the plantation system had robbed the common Southern white of much, it had not, you will observe, robbed him completely. Since it was based on Negro slavery, and since Negro slavery was a vastly wasteful system and could be made to pay only on rich soils, it had practically everywhere, as I have implied, left him some sort of land and hence some sort of subsistence. And in doing that, it had exempted him from all direct exploitation, specifically waived all claim to his labor (for the excellent reason, of course, that it had no use for it), and left his independence totally unimpaired. So long, indeed, as the "peculiar institution" prevailed, he might rest here forever, secure in the knowledge that his estate in this respect would never grow worse—after his fashion, as completely a free agent as the greatest planter of the country.

In this regard, it seems to me, the Old South was one of the most remarkable societies which ever existed in the world. Was there ever another instance of a country in which the relation of master and man arose, negligible exceptions aside, only with reference to a special alien group—in which virtually the whole body of the natives who had failed economically got off fully from the servitude that, in one form or another, has almost universally been the penalty of such failure—in which they were *parked*, as it were, and left to go to the devil in the absolute enjoyment of their liberty?

Again, if the Southern social order had blocked in the common Southerner, it had yet not sealed up the exit entirely. If he could not escape *en masse*, he could nevertheless escape as an individual. Always it was possible for the strong, craving lads who still thrust up from the old sturdy root-stock to make their way out and on: to compete with the established planters for the lands of the Southwest, or even—so close to the frontier stage did the whole country remain, so little was the static tendency realized, so numerous were the bankruptcies, with such relative frequency did many estates go on changing hands, and above all, perhaps, so open an opportunity did the profession of law afford—to carve out wealth and honor in the very oldest regions. Thus, of the eight governors of Virginia from 1841 to 1861, only one was born a gentleman, two began their careers by hiring out as plow-hands, and another (the son of a village butcher) as a tailor.

But in their going these emergent ones naturally carried away with them practically the whole effective stock of those qualities which might have generated resentment and rebellion. Those who were left behind were the simplest of the simple men of this country—those who were inclined to accept whatever the day brought forth as in the nature of things—those whose vague ambition, though it might surge up in dreams now and then, was too weak ever to rise to a consistent lust for plantations and slaves, or anything else requiring an extended exercise of will—those who, sensing their own inadequacy, expected and were content with little.

Moreover, they were in general those in whom the frontier tradition was likely to run strongest; which is to say that they were often almost indifferent, even in their dreams, to the possession of plantations and slaves and to the distinctions which such possessions set up. For it is characteristic of the frontier tradition everywhere that it places no such value on wealth and rank as they command in an old and stable society. Great personal courage, unusual physical powers, the ability to drink a quart of whisky or to lose the whole of one's capital on the turn of a card without the quiver of a muscle—these are at least as important as possessions, and infinitely more important than heraldic crests. In the South, if your neighbor overshadowed you in the number of his slaves, you could outshoot him or outfiddle him, and in your own eyes, and in those of many of your fellows, remain essentially as good a man as he.

Once more, the escape of the strong served potently to perpetuate in the weak the belief that opportunity was still wholly free and unlimited. Seeing the success of these, and recalling obscurely that somewhere out there beyond the horizon were fertile lands to be had for the taking, it was the easiest thing for men steeped in the tradition of the frontier to harbor the comfortable, the immensely soothing, faith that if only they chose . . . that if only they chose . . .

But all these considerations are in some sense only negative. And there was in fact a very positive factor at work in the situation. If the plantation had introduced distinctions of wealth and rank among the men of the old backcountry, and, in doing so, had perhaps offended against the ego of the common white, it had also, you will remember, introduced that other vastly ego-warming and ego-expanding distinction between the white man and the black. Robbing him and degrading him in so many ways, it yet, by singular irony, had simultaneously elevated this common white to a position comparable to that of, say, the Doric knight of ancient Sparta. Not only was he not exploited directly, he was himself made by extension a member of the dominant class—was lodged solidly on a tremendous superiority, which, however much the blacks in the "big house" might sneer at him, and however much their masters might privately agree with them, he could never publicly lose. Come what might, he would always be a white man. And before that vast and capacious distinction, all others were foreshortened, dwarfed, and all but obliterated. . . .

If the common white was scorned, yet that scorn was so attenuated and softened in its passage down through the universal medium of this manner, struck at last so obliquely upon his ego, that it glanced off harmless. When he frequented public gatherings, what he encountered would seldom be naked hauteur. Rather, there would nearly always be a fine gentleman to lay a familiar hand on his shoulder, to inquire by name after the members of his family, maybe to buy him a drink, certainly to rally him on some boasted weakness or treasured misadventure, and to come around eventually to confiding in a hushed voice that that damned nigger-loving scoundrel Garrison, in Boston—in short, to patronize him in such fashion that to his simple eyes he seemed not to be patronized at all but actually deferred to, to send him home, not sullen and vindictive, but glowing with the sense of participation in the common brotherhood of white men. . . .

Another obscuring factor we must note is that if the common whites were being deprived of their former liberty and, in large numbers, brought within the scope of direct exploitation, it was rather through the impersonal working out of social and economic forces than through any will or purpose to that end on the part of anybody. So far as the planters were concerned, in truth, they had almost as little actual need for the labor of the common whites now [after the Civil War. Ed.] as in the Old South. If there were not Negroes enough in the land—and Negroes easily made available—to furnish the entire required quota of tenants and croppers, then there were nearly enough. As witness the fact that from the time of the appearance of the white tenant and cropper, we find growing up in the South a body of Negroes at loose ends, without any definite place in the economic order or any settled means of support. Moreover, many of the landlords undoubtedly preferred black labor, as being more docile.

Some there were, to be sure, who felt the other way about it. There were local shortages of blacks, too. And like employers everywhere, practically the whole lot of the landowners looked on the creation of a reasonable surplus of labor as a very fine thing in itself. But this wholesale falling down of the masses into availability—this was anything on earth but their desire.

In large measure, and in literal fact, they came to the use of white tenants only through the operation of race loyalty and the old paternalism. They felt, mind you, not the slightest responsibility for what had happened to the dispossessed. They despised them now, as a rule, with an even greater doctrinal contempt than they had felt for them in the old days when they could not achieve rich lands and Negroes. Yet . . . here they were, willy-nilly. Under our planter eyes. Men we have known all our days, laughed with, hunted with, and, in many a case, fought side by side with. Human. White. With white women and white children. And having to find employment—or starve.

And if we feel no responsibility for their having landed in this condition, yet it is the law of our personally humane tradition, you will recall, that none must be allowed to starve—certainly not under our eyes—certainly no white man; an essential part of our high profession, of the profoundest conviction in many of us, that it is our duty to look after these weaker brethren, to the extent at least of seeing that they have some such living as they have been accustomed to.

Give them special advantages? We shall do nothing of the kind. We shall give them the same terms we give the Negro. We shall carry over into our dealing with them very much of the attitude toward labor fixed by slavery. We shall curse them roundly for no-'count, trifling incompetents who richly deserve to starve—always in our peculiar manner, which draws the sting of what we say. But look after them we must and will.

More—the finest and best among us, while holding fast to those same legal terms originally set for the black man, not only will discharge those terms to the letter, but will soften the bargain by spontaneous gifts from our own larders: by the perpetuation and even the extension of that personal care and interest we exhibited toward our poorer neighbor in the Old South. And of course many of us will make precious little profit out of these whites, as out of the blacks. They are going to live hard, but so in this lean world and these lean times are we.

The issue of this is manifest, I take it. Coming to the use of these whites as men conferring a favor, the landlords of the South naturally did not see themselves as any wicked oppressors out of a Marxist legend but as public benefactors; they swelled with pride in it, had their ancient complacency and self-approval increased, their confidence in their paternalistic prerogative as necessary to the happiness of everybody concerned bolstered. And the common whites saw it and responded to it in cognate fashion. Instead of anger and resentment, the dominant emotion of the white cropper or tenant toward the more fortunate neighbor on whose land he found himself planted, under whose mastery he found himself lodged, was likely to be gratefulness.

Even the case of the supply merchant was obscure. For one thing, few of his customers had any notion of what charges they were being subjected to. For another, he himself was likely to approach his calling from within the universal Southern habit of high profession; however cynical his deeds may seem, he almost invariably thought of himself as a great public patron and came to his clients with the manner and the conviction of conferring inestimable benefits. And, in fact, hadn't he made it possible for you to grow cotton? Didn't he enable you to keep on in that pursuit year after year? And if in the end he sold you out, would you, stout individualist, have done otherwise in his place? Wasn't he kind about it? Didn't he often see to it that you got a good place as tenant, either on his own expanding acres or elsewhere? Grumble at him, hate him spasmodically—you would, of course. But you would never get up tenacious resentment enough even to keep alive the co-operative stores the Alliance was setting up against him. [Locally based Farmers' Alliances were the forerunners of the national Populist Party of the 1890s. Ed.]

But there was in operation here something more potent than any of this. We have to observe explicitly that the loss of economic independence, the passing of that old freedom from exploitation which had been so primary for the Southern pattern, took place at a time when the longwaging battle of Reconstruction had already done its work—when patriotism to the South had been raised to the ultimate pitch, when the determination to maintain this South in its essential integrity burned at white heat in every proper Southern breast, and when, as the heart of it all, the ancient fixation on [the] Negro, always perhaps the single most primary thing, had been drawn to consuming monomania: when the white man's pride and will, and particularly the common white man's, had concentrated on the maintenance of superiority to that black man as the paramount thing in life.

For, coming to the matter from this position, the common white inevitably had his attention taken, not so much by the fact that he had now to submit himself to the will of another, to take orders from a boss, to work when he would not himself have chosen to work—bitter though this might be. What fixed his gaze to the eclipse of everything else was the spectacle of himself being reduced to working side by side, and on the same place, with the black man; his Proto-Dorian rank, his one incontestable superiority, threatening to plunge finally and irretrievably down to extinction. What every white tenant and cropper, every white man in peril of becoming such, was crying out for first of all in these years was to have this threat somehow stayed.

57

Old Poison in New Bottles:
The Deep Roots of Modern Nativism

JOE R. FEAGIN

Dating back at least two centuries, anti-immigrant nativism has profoundly shaped the history and present demography of this nation. For instance, the 1990 census revealed that *only twelve* of the world's nearly two hundred countries were checked off by as much as one percent of Americans as countries of national origin: Britain, Ireland, Canada, Italy, Russia, Poland, France, Netherlands, Sweden, Germany, Norway, and Mexico. From 1607 to 1990 the major waves of immigrants to this country came from Great Britain and certain other European countries (all but one in northern Europe), and from Africa and Mexico. Conspicuously absent from the list are *any* countries in the Middle East, Asia, South America, or post-colonial Africa.

For the most part, both immigration and the shape of the U.S. population reflect the desires, interests, and purposes of Americans of European descent. Indeed, if the United States had not had a Euro-American nativist movement from the 1880s to 1920s, there would not have been a Chinese Exclusion Act (1882), an anti-Japanese "Gentleman's Agreement" (1907–1908), or a series of immigration acts from 1917 to 1924 designed to keep out southern and eastern Europeans. In addition, there would not have been a 1924 Immigration Act sharply reducing the number of Catholic immigrants from countries like Italy and Poland and the number of Jewish immigrants from eastern Europe—and excluding Asian immigrants. If these regulations and laws had not been in effect, the current U.S. population would likely include far more Asian Americans and have a majority composed of Catholic and Jewish Americans.

Battles over immigration, then, are struggles over the composition and character of the nation. The same is true today, as many native-born Americans are rising to assert their desire to shape the U.S. population, once again in narrow cultural or racial terms. As in the past, most of the new American nativists wish to keep the nation predominantly white and European.

The foundation for aggressive nativism in North America begins in the expansion of European capitalism. By the sixteenth and seventeenth centuries several European nations, especially the Netherlands, France, and England, had spurred the globalization of capitalism. In the process they created a type of colonialism with fundamental inequalities between colonizers and the newly colonized. Beginning in the 1600s, English immigrants began a major colonization of North America, taking over Native American lands in four distinctive waves. The first to come were English Puritans, who settled in New England and brought dissenting Protestant churches. A second wave, consisting of a few Royalists and many indentured servants, came to Virginia in the mid-17th century and established a hierarchical colony with Anglican churches. A third wave of English Quakers came to the Delaware Valley between 1675 and 1725 and established a pluralistic system based on spiritual and social equality and an intense work ethic. The fourth wave came to the Appalachian backcountry from the borderlands of Britain between 1718 and 1775; this group represented English, Scotch, and Scotch-Irish ancestries and was mostly Protestant. While each group had a distinctive type of English or Scottish culture, for the most part they shared a commitment to an Anglo-Protestant culture, central to which were variants of the English language.[1]

This fierce commitment to English norms, values, and ways of operating begins the trail to modern nativism. In particular, the famous Puritans built a base for the ethnocentrism and parochialism of the newly emerging U.S. republic. They developed, as Joel Kovel has noted, "a powerful tradition of hating strangers, foreigners, and subversives."[2] This tradition was honed in the bloody attacks by Puritans on the native population. The Puritan immigrants created the first colonial settler-society, one animated by the arrogant notion that these English settlers would make better use of what they saw as undeveloped "wilderness" than "wild savages" who were the present occupants. Commenting on this English settler perspective, Kovel has noted that "The land wasn't densely settled, but it was settled everywhere, and everywhere the whites went they had to get rid of highly developed and very profoundly interesting cultures that had achieved a kind of equilibrium with the land over millennia."[3] English immigrants' destruction or oppression of highly civilized Native American communities was soon coupled with the importation and oppression of Africans brought to the new immigrant colonies in the slave trade.

Early European interpretations of the colonial enterprise could be found both in popular sentiment and in the systematic perspectives developed by intellectuals and political leaders. From the fifteenth century onward European and Euro-American intellectual and political elites defended the racism and exploitation of the imperialist enterprises. Scholars, theologians, and politicians in Europe and the new American colonies developed theories of the superiority of white Europeans and of the animal-like inferiority of native peoples. These views buttressed popular feelings about certain outgroups. Common to most societies is ethnocentrism—the perspective that sees one's own group as the center and evaluates outgroups with reference to that center. However, a distinctively negative ethnocentrism in regard to outsiders developed in the American colonies and, later, the United States. Europeans distinguished themselves from the "savages," and colonized peoples were demonized as replete with vices Europeans feared in themselves: wildness, brutishness, cruelty, laziness, and heathenism. "Far from English civilization, [the Europeans] had to remind themselves constantly what it meant to be civilized—Christian, rational, sexually controlled, and white. And they tried to impute to peoples they called 'savages' the instinctual forces they had within themselves."[4] By the 1700s and 1800s well-developed theories of the cultural and racial inferiority of the "uncivilized savages" were common in both England and the new United States.

From the 1700s onward Euro-American views of savage outsiders were directed not only at Americans of color but also at certain new immigrants of European origin. The new immigrants were often needed to meet the labor needs of U.S. employers, and many native-born Americans profited from the economic impact of immigration. At the same time, many Americans viewed the new immigrants as a major threat to the nation's Anglo culture and institutions.

If immigrants could not be excluded, restricted, or discouraged, the next best thing was to assimilate them, in a one-way adaptation pattern, to the dominant Anglo-Protestant culture. As one writer put it: "If there is anything in American life which can be described as an overall American culture which serves as a reference point for immigrants and their children, it can best be described, it seems to us, as the middle-class, cultural patterns of, largely, white Protestant, Anglo-Saxon origins."[5]

In the first decades of the 19th century nativists honed their anti-foreign perspective further, with increasing emphasis on anti-Catholicism and white supremacy. Many nativists targeted Irish Catholic immigrants and their children. In the early 19th century industrial capitalists faced a shortage of labor. Native-born workers resisted the oppressive conditions of the new industrial enterprises, and capitalists increasingly recruited workers for building transportation projects and manufacturing mills from overseas. By the mid-nineteenth century Irish and German immigrants were critical to many new industrial enterprises, including textile mills, railroad lines and shops, and foundries. Major capitalists aggressively sought the new immigrant workers, while other Americans wished to see this immigration reduced if not curtailed. Over the course of U.S. history capitalists and exclusionary nativists have periodically found themselves at odds on the matter of immigration. Indeed, every time that nativists have succeeded in getting restrictive legislation, business interests needing cheap labor have found ways around the laws. Laws have never stopped immigration when powerful interests desire it, especially in times of labor shortage.[6]

English American resistance to Irish immigrants dates from the seventeenth century, but it was the nineteenth-century Catholic immigrants from famine-ridden Ireland who were attacked viciously under the new banners of nativism. Anglo-Protestant nativist organizations played a major role. Catholics were hated not only because they were "foreign" immigrants but because of Protestant stereotypes of Catholic "popery." The large number of Catholic immigrants from Ireland (and to a lesser extent Germany) in the mid-19th century brought new targets for the anti-immigrant nativists among Anglo-Protestant Americans.

By the mid-19th century a racist perspective joined anti-Catholicism. Initially, the racial supremacy perspective took the form of accenting the superiority of those Americans whose ancestors came from the dominant "race" of northern Europe. Other north European Protestants often joined together with British Americans to celebrate a "superior Anglo-Saxon race." By the 1840s and 1850s Anglo-Saxonism was forcefully targeting not only white immigrants, but people of color, whose lands were still coveted by white colonizers.

In the eighteenth and nineteenth centuries the "white race" emerged as a constructed social group for the first time in history. In this period the Anglo-Protestant ruling elite developed the ideology of a superior "white race" as one way of providing racial privileges for poorer European Americans and keeping the latter from joining with black Americans in worker organizations. White nationalism grew dramatically. By the mid-19th century not only later English immigrants but also immigrants from Scotland and Scandinavia, Ireland, and Germany had come to accept a place in this socially constructed "white race," whose special racial privileges included the rights of personal liberty, travel, and voting.[7]

After the U.S. Civil War the federal government generally encouraged immigration, particularly from Europe. Following its lead, industrial employers and land companies sent agents to Europe and Asia to recruit labor. As of 1900, the major source of new labor for expanding industries was southern and eastern European immigrants. Indeed, between

1881 and 1920 the majority of the 21 million immigrants emigrated from southern and eastern Europe.[8]

In spite of the crucial role U.S. business played in generating much of this migration, many Americans at all class levels were becoming opposed to these new immigrants, an opposition that intensified during and after World War I. The renewed nativism of the late 1910s and 1920s made use of the sciences of biology, anthropology, and psychology. Racial eugenics thinking spread from European intellectuals to U.S. leaders. Promulgated in many articles in the media, this perspective accented the importance of breeding the right racial groups. For most U.S. nativists, immigrants from southern and eastern Europe did not represent the "superior races."

Among the favorite targets of these nativists were Italian Catholic immigrants, a "racial stock" that nativists saw as "inferior and degraded." They also echoed an old nativist theme, that the new stock will "not assimilate naturally or readily with the prevailing 'Anglo-Saxon' race stock of this country; that intermixture, if practicable, will be detrimental; that servility, filthy habits of life, and a hopelessly degraded standard of needs and ambitions have been ingrained in Italians by centuries of oppression and abject poverty."[9] Racial indictments of Italian Americans appeared in national magazines. In the 1888 *North American Review* labor activist T. V. Powderly alleged that southern Europeans lived immoral lives centered in liquor.[10] Like poor immigrants before and after them, the Italians were blamed for destroying the moral fabric of the nation and for increasing the costs of government, particularly in relation to crime and poverty.

For many of the same reasons, Jewish immigrants from eastern Europe were also major targets by the early 1890s. Widely accepted racial stereotypes caricatured Jewish immigrants in the national and local media. Jews were seen as immoral and as unscrupulous business competitors. They were accused of taking the jobs of "Americans." By the early 1900s riots erupted among Gentile workers against Jewish American workers brought into factories. In Georgia, the Jewish part-owner of a pencil factory was convicted of killing a girl employee, though evidence pointed elsewhere. After being beaten up in prison, he was lynched by a white Gentile mob. Moreover, by the 1920s a revived Ku Klux Klan waged violence against both Jewish and Catholic immigrants and their children. Crosses were burned on Jewish property, and synagogues were desecrated and vandalized.[11]

British Americans in Boston formed the Immigration Restriction League to try to curtail immigration. Working in several different arenas, the League pressed the U.S. Congress to pass literacy restrictions on immigrants. Southern and eastern Europeans faced other anti-immigrant organizations as well. Oddly enough, these organizations were made up of the descendants of earlier immigrants. In the late 19th century the American Protective Association (APA) and a revived Ku Klux Klan were working aggressively against immigration of southern and eastern European and Asian workers. The membership of these groups included many business people, white-collar workers, and fundamentalist Protestants. The often racist anti-immigrant agitation led to restrictive laws; between 1875 and 1917 the U.S. Congress passed laws excluding "immoral" aliens, those with diseases, political radicals, and the illiterate. Congress overrode a presidential veto to enact a law excluding persons of "psychopathic inferiority," vagrants, and illiterate adults.[12]

By the 1920s the anti-immigrant hysteria had taken on major proportions, and in many areas aliens were prohibited from practicing certain jobs or professions, including medicine, engineering, and law. In the heat of postwar fears of "foreigners" taking jobs from demobilized soldiers, and of the U.S. being inundated by inferior races, the first major law restricting immigration across the board was passed. While temporary, it was the first to impose numerical limits on immigrants by means of a nationality quota system. It limited European immigrants to about 3 percent of the number of foreign-born from each country present in the United States in 1910. The total limit was about 350,000, with most slots reserved for northern Europeans. This law remained in effect until the even more restrictive 1924 law was enacted.[13]

This overtly racist law established small quotas for southern and eastern Europeans. For example, the annual quota for Italian immigrants was about 5,800, compared with nearly 66,000 for Great Britain and nearly 26,000 for Germany. The British, Germans, Irish, and Scandinavians got most of the total allowance. As a result of these skewed quotas, Allan Chase estimates, about six million people from southern and eastern Europe, including many who would die in Adolf Hitler's concentration camps, were excluded. The nativists' greatest victory, a racist immigration law, would stay in effect until the mid-1960s.

While some nativists wished to exclude all or most immigrants who were not English, other influential Americans wanted the immigrants to be allowed in, but only on anglocentric terms. Indeed, the view that immigrants must quickly "Americanize" was widely shared by powerful U.S. capitalists. The nation's most famous capitalist, Henry Ford, pressed strongly for immigrant Americanization. Working with his firm's executives, Henry Ford recruited southern and eastern European immigrants for his auto plants. The company then set up a "Sociological Department" with investigators who visited workers' homes, providing advice on family matters and personal morality. In addition, the immigrant workers had to attend a "melting pot school," where they learned English and certain Anglo-Protestant values of great concern to men like Ford. Remarkably, during graduation ceremonies Ford's employees, at first dressed as in their home countries, walked through a big pot labeled "melting pot" and emerged in business suits holding American flags.[14] Although this process was labeled "melting pot" assimilation, the actual model is one-way assimilation to the dominant culture.

Over the entire course of U.S. history we can see that one-way assimilation to an Anglo-Protestant core culture—consisting of an Anglo-British legal system, Anglo-Protestant religious values, an English language, and an Anglo-capitalist economic system—has been both the norm and the reality for new immigrants. Immigrants have been cajoled or forced into modelling themselves and their children on the norms of this core culture, which modelling has included accepting the "places"reserved for those defined as "whites" (a favored place) and for those defined as "not-whites" (a subordinated place). Increasingly, as we move into the 21st century this Procrustean bed of assimilation will be challenged, as the demographic composition of this nation changes dramatically and those in subordinated places, people of color, become the majority group.

Notes

1. David Hackett Fischer, *Albion's Seed: Four British Folkways in America* (New York: Oxford University Press, 1989), pp. 6, 13–205, 785–786, and passim.

2. Quoted in Gerry O'Sullivan, "Mythmaking in the Promised Land; An Interview with Joel Kovel," *Humanist*, September, 1994, p. 18.

3. Ibid.

4. Ronald Takaki, *Iron Cages* (New York: Oxford University Press, 1990), p. 12.

5. Milton M. Gordon, *Assimilation in American Life* (New York: Oxford University Press, 1964), pp. 72–73.

6. See Aristide R. Zolberg, "Reforming the Back Door: The Immigration Reform and Control Act of 1986 in Historical Perspective," in *Immigration Reconsidered*, ed. by Virginia Yans-McLaughlin (New York: Oxford University Press, 1990), pp. 315–335.

7. Theodore W. Allen, *The Invention of the White Race* (New York: Verso, 1994), pp. 21, 184.

8. Douglas F. Dowd, *The Twisted Dream* (Cambridge, Mass.: Winthrop, 1977), pp. 146–147.

9. Eliot Lord, John J. D. Trenor, and Samuel J. Barrows, *The Italian in America*, reprint ed. (San Francisco: R & E Associates, 1970), pp. 17–18.

10. Quoted in Luciano J. Iorizzo and Salvatore Mondello, *The Italian-Americans* (New York: Twayne, 1971), p. 64

11. See Henry L. Feingold, *Zion in America* (New York: Twayne, 1974), pp. 143–144; C. Vann Woodward, *Tom Watson* (New York: Oxford University Press, 1963), pp. 435–445.

12. See Rufus Learski, *The Jews in America* (New York: KTAV Publishing House, 1972), pp. 290–293.

13. John Higham, *Strangers in the Land* (New York: Atheneum, 1963), pp. 301–313.

14. James J. Fink, *The Car Culture* (Cambridge, Mass.: MIT Press, 1975), pp. 88–90.

58

The First Word in Whiteness:
Early Twentieth-Century
European Experiences

DAVID ROEDIGER

A character in Chester Himes' 1945 novel, *If He Hollers Let Him Go,* has a "funny thought." He begins to "wonder when white people started to get white—or rather, when they started losing it." The narrower question of when new immigrants "started to get white" and of what they lost in doing it has received passionate and varied treatment within African-American thought. That treatment provides the best points of entry to the question of white identity among new immigrants to date.

The simplest and perhaps most celebrated answer to how the whiteness of new European immigrants came about appears in the epilogue to Malcolm X's *Autobiography.* His collaborator, Alex Haley, describes being in a U.S. airport with Malcolm and admiring an arriving family of European immigrants. They are, Malcolm predicts, about to learn their first word of English: *nigger.* Malcolm's one-liner, which recalls images of the Gads Hill minstrel show, is so precisely repeated (without credit) in the works of black artists from John Oliver Killens to Richard Pryor—and Toni Morrison counts *nigger* as the second word in the immigrant's English vocabulary, with only *okay* coming before—as to raise the possibility that each teller of the joke drew it from black folk humor. Like the most enduring folklore, it distills a sharp point and operates on a variety of levels. Pessimistic to the point of rancor, the joke's logic resembles that of African-American usages of *hunky* and *honky,* the mixing up and evolution of which imply that the new eastern European immigrants slurred by the former term could come to exemplify the white oppressors identified by the latter in a remarkably short time. But however bitter, the joke does not make immigrant racism a product of the essential "white" characteristics of the newcomers. The weight of U.S. racial division must be learned—and the immigrants' beauty, or as Baldwin has it "soul," lost—on this view. The tragedy arises from the knowledge that American realities were such brutal and effective teachers of that division and that immigrants were such apt and ready learners of it.

Coexisting with the bitterness of Malcolm's joke is a much more lyrical tradition of black commentary on new immigrant whiteness—a tradition which is, however, equally premised on a deep sense of tragedy. In William Attaway's soon-to-be canonical 1941 proletarian novel, *Blood on the Forge,* Melody and his half-brother, Chinatown, disagreed on the merits of the music made by Slavic immigrants with whom they worked in Pittsburgh's steel mills. Chinatown heard nothing in it but a "yowl," adding that "a man can't understand one word they yowlin'." But Melody, who lived to play the blues and who could "hear music in a snore," knew better. He had heard some of these people from the Ukraine singing. He hadn't understood one word. Yet he didn't have to know the words to understand what they were wailing about. Words didn't count when the music had a tongue. The field hands of the sloping red-hill country in Kentucky sang that same tongue. Hearing the wails of his (and Chinatown's) old Kentucky home in Ukrainian music, Melody echoed Frederick Douglass' observations of almost a century earlier. During his 1845–46 tour of Ireland, Douglass heard the "wailing notes" of the music of the oppressed and famished Irish people as close kin of the "wild notes" of the slaves' sorrow songs.

For the jazz musician Mezz Mezzrow, it was weeping and wailing that united black and new immigrant musics. In a remarkable section of his autobiographical *Really the Blues*, Mezzrow recalled a prison term he served for selling drugs. Having convinced himself that, despite Jewish-American origins, he was in fact black, Mezzrow likewise convinced prison officials, who allowed him to be confined in the segregated African-American section of the prison. Nonetheless, when white Catholic prisoners organized Christmas caroling, the response of Jewish inmates was to ask Mezzrow to lead them in song. Professing surprise that he, "a colored guy," would be chosen to direct a Jewish chorus, Mezzrow learned "once more how music of different oppressed peoples blends together." He did not "know the Hebrew chants," but a "weepy blues inflection" made his interpretation of their "wailing and lament" a huge success.

On one level, these African-American commentaries on the soul of the music of oppressed Europeans underline the affinities of blacks and "inbetween" immigrants suggested by Jane Addams' look at Hull House residents looking at Dr. Du Bois. Indeed, Mezzrow's comments could tempt us to imagine Jewish jazz great Benny Goodman, who learned to play at Hull House, providing the background music as Du Bois lectured on African-American spirituals. But Mezzrow, Douglass, and Attaway all were as intent to invoke tragedy as possibility in discussing new immigrant relations with nonwhite Americans. Mezzrow disdained appeals to Jewish "racial" solidarity in the entertainment world, seeing such "jive" as a betrayal of "colored musicians" who were his "real brothers." Douglass lingered over the wails of the Irish to emphasize the tragedy of Irish-American racism, seconding Irish nationalist leader Daniel O'Connell's longstanding point that this was "cruelty" not learned in Ireland and was utterly inappropriate to the Irish experience. Morrison makes much the same point in telling of her own brief, innocent, and tragic relationship with a schoolmate in her Pennsylvania home town. The immigrant child learned to speak and read English in large part from Morrison, who was his best friend until he also learned the word *nigger* and his country's racial ground rules. His American education taught him not to learn about language from Toni Morrison.

Attaway portrayed common oppression at every turn. Blacks and Bohunks shared a wrenching from the land, lived in comparable squalor, and died in the same industrial accidents. The same profit motive and the same Irish-American petty bosses pitted African Americans against hunkies. Even the breaching of racial categories took tragic form. When Big Mat, Melody's half-brother, saved an Irish-American foreman's life by "laying out" a young "hayseed," the Irish bosses and hearth workers rechristened him as "black Irish," adding that "lots of black fellas have Irish guts." Mat makes "a whole lot better Irisher than a hunky or a ginny," at whose expense the juggling of racial hierarchies occur. Nor does

Big Mat actually profit from his recategorization. He cannot bear to come near those praising him. "Full of savage pressure," he escapes to the "pleasant" thought of "dogs tearing
at each other" and adjourns to the dog fights. Big capital and petty bosses constantly structured working class life as a dogfight in *Blood on the Forge*, often by taking advantage of
immigrant hatred of black workers. The solidarities Melody heard in music remain largely
and sadly absent from labor mobilizations and from everyday life.

James Baldwin's indispensable essays on the whitening of new immigrants bring together
the acerbity of Malcolm's joke and the attuned-to-tragedy humanism of Attaway and Douglass.
Especially in " 'On Being White' and Other Lies" and in "White Man's Guilt," Baldwin pairs
the embrace of whiteness with the immigrants' losses of contact with land and with community. Reminding readers that folks in Norway did not preen themselves on how white
they were, Baldwin makes the taking up of whiteness a product and cause of the new immigrants' "losing it" in terms of humanity. As insistently (and far less wrongheadedly) as
Stanley Elkins wrote of the slave trade's devastation of the African's personality, Baldwin
saw a loss of humanity among those wrenched from European villages and then whitened.
Regimented by necessity into industrial work, these new immigrants also chose to enter the
imprisoning confines of whiteness, which Baldwin suggestively terms a "factory." At times
Baldwin posits an almost immediate sea change to a white identity. Elsewhere he describes
a process which "took generations and a vast amount of coercion." In that process he emphasizes that the joining in racial victimization and the committing of atrocities against nonwhites affirmed the immigrants' whiteness over time. Deep empathy and disquiet run
through every line of Baldwin's writings as he shouts out to those in the factory: "So long
as you think you are white, there's no hope for you."

Attaway, Killens, Pryor, Malcolm X, and Douglass were not commenting principally on
the European immigrant experience, and when Baldwin did so he did not write more than a
few thousand words. Even so, their work poses the drama and importance of race within the
new immigrant experience in ways in which even the best of immigration history has only
begun to approach. For that reason, the best reaction to their insights is not to quibble about
what is mistaken or omitted in the ground they cover. Rather, it is to address urgently the
issues that are raised but not settled in their remarks. These include the question of when
and how whiteness was learned, of who taught it, of whether learning to call others *nigger*
meant being ready or able to call oneself white, of why those whose musical wails were close
cousins of African-American sorrow songs came to march to the tune of whiteness.

59

Life on the Color Line

GREGORY WILLIAMS

"Billy!" Dad said sharply as he leaned across the aisle. I looked into his face. The Greyhound's air brakes hissed as it slowed for the junction with State Highway 201. In a somber voice he continued. "Boys, I've got some bad news for you." He paused. We leaned forward, anxiously. The wool of the seat made me itch. "We're not going to stay with Grandpa and Grandma Cook when we get to Muncie."

The gears clunked and the bus shuddered to a stop at an intersection.

"Why not?" I demanded.

"Your mother and I are getting a divorce. We can't stay with them."

Straightening my back, I turned toward him. He tightened his lips. My stomach rumbled with anger. I refused to believe we could not live with Grandpa and Grandma! They would end all the worries about food, clothes, and lunch money. If Dad thought Grandpa and Grandma didn't want us, he was wrong! Reassured, I leaned against the seat. As the bus bumped into gear, I felt a tinge of doubt. He leaned closer and spoke very softly. "There's something else I want to tell you."

"What?" I groaned.

"Remember Miss Sallie who used to work for us in the tavern?"

Dad's lower lip quivered. He looked ill. Had he always looked this unhealthy, I wondered, or was it something that happened on the trip? I felt my face—skin like putty, lips chapped and cracked. Had I changed, too?

"It's hard to tell you boys this." He paused, then slowly added, "But she's really my momma. That means she's your grandmother."

"But that can't be, Dad! She's colored!" I whispered, lest I be overheard by the other white passengers on the bus.

"That's right, Billy," he continued. "She's colored. That makes you part colored, too, and in Muncie you're gonna live with my Aunt Bess. . . . "

I didn't understand Dad. I knew I wasn't colored, and neither was he. My skin was white. All of us are white, I said to myself. But for the first time, I had to admit Dad didn't exactly look white. His deeply tanned skin puzzled me as I sat there trying to classify my own father. Goose bumps covered my arms as I realized that whatever he was, I was. I took a deep breath. I couldn't make any mistakes. I looked closer. His heavy lips and dark brown eyes didn't make him colored, I concluded. His black, wavy hair was different from Negroes' hair, but it was different from most white folks' hair, too. He was darker than most whites, but Mom said he was Italian. That was why my baby brother had such dark skin and curly hair. Mom told us to be proud of our Italian heritage! That's it, I decided. He was Italian. I leaned back against the seat, satisfied. Yet the unsettling image of Miss Sallie flashed before me like a neon sign.

Colored! Colored! Colored!

He continued. "Life is going to be different from now on. In Virginia you were white boys. In Indiana you're going to be colored boys. I want you to remember that you're the same today that you were yesterday. But people in Indiana will treat you differently."

I refused to believe Dad. I looked at Mike. His skin, like mine, was a light, almost pallid, white. He had Dad's deep brown eyes, too, but our hair was straight. Leaning toward Dad, I examined his hands for a sign, a black mark. There was nothing. I knew I was right, but I sensed something was wrong. Fear overcame me as I faced the Ohio countryside and pondered the discovery of my life.

"I don't wanta be colored," Mike whined. "I don't wanta be colored. We can't go swimmin' or skatin'," he said louder. Nearby passengers turned toward us.

"Shut up, Mike." I punched him in the chest. He hit me in the nose. I lunged for him. We tumbled into the aisle. My knee banged against a sharp aluminum edge. The fatigues ripped. I squeezed his neck. His eyes bulged. I squeezed harder. *Whap!* Pain surged from the back of my head. Dad grabbed my shirt collar and shoved me roughly into the seat. Mike clambered in beside me, still sniffling.

"Daddy, we ain't really colored, are we?" he asked quietly.

No! I answered, still refusing to believe. I'm not colored, I'm white! I look white! I've always been white! I go to "whites only" schools, "whites only" movie theaters, and "whites only" swimming pools! I never had heard anything crazier in my life! How could Dad tell us such a mean lie? I glanced across the aisle to where he sat grim-faced and erect, staring straight ahead. I saw my father as I never had seen him before. The veil dropped from his face and features. Before my eyes he was transformed from a swarthy Italian to his true self—a high-yellow mulatto. My father was a Negro! We were colored! After ten years in Virginia on the white side of the color line, I knew what that meant.

Again Dad spoke in a whisper. "You boys are going to have to learn to live with it, and living with it in Muncie won't be easy. But Indiana is only temporary. Once I settle up the business, we'll head to California and start over. We can still be white, but not in Muncie. The town is full of the Ku Klux Klan. Once they know who you are and what you are, they'll do everything humanly possible to keep you 'in your place.'"

The mention of the Klan stirred up frightful memories. At the tavern I heard many stories about beatings, shootings, and murders of blacks, Catholics, and Jews by the Klan. In Virginia Dad was known as a protector of the Gypsies who plied their craft as painters, roofers, and septic tank men up and down U.S. 1. Much to the consternation of the local police and our white neighbors, the Gypsies often camped in our one-acre parking lot while working in the area. One summer we discovered the Klan was angry at us for shielding the Gypsies, but Dad paid little attention until he noticed a group of white men parked across the highway from us several evenings in a row. Late one night, just before closing, a gunshot shattered our front plate glass window. Dad sat up the rest of the night clutching his German Luger pistol. Raymond borrowed a shotgun from a friend in Gum Springs, and Harvey joined the vigil with his trusty baseball bat. I stayed with them until I couldn't hold my eyes open any longer.

Dad said he planned to return to Virginia to tie up loose ends. Soon, we'd all be together. He called us the "Three Musketeers." In the meantime, we'd live with Aunt Bess.

Questions whirled through my mind, but I did not dare to ask them. I feared the answers. Who was Aunt Bess? Was she colored? Would Grandma and Grandpa Cook take us? Were they prejudiced? Suddenly, I recalled Grandma's quip about the "little niggers" on East Jackson Street one afternoon the past summer as she drove Grandpa to work. But we were different from those kids playing on the street corner. We were her own flesh and blood!

"Dad," I haltingly asked, "if you and Mom get a divorce, will we still be related to Grandpa and Grandma Cook?"

"Sure, Billy, they're your grandparents. They love you too much to forget about you."

The bus pulled into the Dayton terminal. We moved sluggishly to the front. There was a two-hour wait for the ABC Coach Line connection to Muncie. Dad, a step ahead of us, passed through double doors into the cavernous hall. A crackling loudspeaker filled the air. "Hamilton and Cincinnati now boarding at . . ." A crowd converged. A soldier lingered near the doors, kissing his girlfriend good-bye. Earlier, Mike and I would have gaped at them, but now we had too much to ponder. We passed the familiar green Traveler's Aid cubicle. At the lunch counter at the far end of the building we stood quietly while the waitress reached into a glass case for a cold roast beef sandwich. She punched the register keys while Dad split the sandwich in two. It was our first food since Harvey bought us a candy bar at the bus station in Washington the day before. Dad led us to an isolated wooden bench and dropped the small, tattered canvas bag holding all our belongings. "Wait here," he ordered. "I'll be right back."

He strolled across the room as I hungrily ripped a bite from the sandwich. When Dad disappeared through the terminal doors, I panicked. I felt like I was standing alone at the center of the universe. With the bag in one hand and the sandwich in the other, I shouted for Mike. We raced across the concourse, pushing our way past soldiers and sailors. On the sidewalk I looked north, then south—Dad had vanished. I had no idea what to do. Finally, I saw his tall lanky figure enter a tavern a block away. Half dragging and half carrying our bag, I led Mike down the street. Comforted by the knowledge that Dad was inside, we huddled in the tavern doorway.

After devouring the sandwich, Mike and I began our vigil. Every few minutes I peered into the tavern window to check the time on the Schlitz Beer clock. An hour and a half dragged by. We grew cold and restless. Mike kicked beer bottle caps along the sidewalk. Empty bottles lined the bar in front of Dad. I recognized his familiar gestures punctuating a pronouncement on some public event. Drunk! Five minutes passed, then ten. I pressed my face to the cold plate glass window, hoping he would walk outside to scold me. Just when I was certain we would miss our bus, a heavyset man in a denim jacket approached the doorway. Summoning all my courage, I begged, "Mister, will you tell the man in the brown derby we gotta catch the bus?"

Just five minutes before departure, Dad strode from the tavern and grabbed the bag.

"Come on boys, let's double-time it!"

Mike and I raced behind him, struggling to keep up with his long legs. Though I feared what lay ahead of us, I knew it couldn't be any worse than what we had left behind in Virginia.

60

Others, and the WASP World They Aspired To

RICHARD BROOKHISER

In its brief history, America has experienced the greatest population transfer the Western world has known since the fall of Rome, with happier results.

This human tsunami has been seen as a simple transfer, not an amalgamation: a shift of bodies, not souls. Michael Novak called ethnics unmeltable. Father Andrew Greeley, the novelist and pollster, pops up every few years with a study showing how different Catholic and Protestant Americans continue to be (and justifying, incidentally, the existence of priestly pollsters).

Many WASPs have made similar assumptions about the tenacity of immigrant behavior and have brooded about the effects it would have on their way. "It is an axiom," Captain John B. Trevor, a lobbyist for restricted immigration, warned Congress in 1924, "that government not imposed by external force is the visible expression of the ideals, standards, and social viewpoint of the people over which it rules." Trevor got his rank in military intelligence, for which he had monitored the activities of radical groups in New York after World War I, an experience that made him suspicious of the people America had recently been getting. "The races [*sic*] from southern and eastern Europe . . . cannot point during a period of seven centuries since Magna Charta to any conception of successful government other than a paternal autocracy." Trevor's first sentence was no fallacy, it was pure Tocqueville; and though one could quarrel with "paternal autocracy" in the second, one could not challenge the larger point: that, whatever form government took in the old countries of Southern and Eastern Europe, from city state to *shtetl*, it did not have a lot to do with the Magna Carta. "If, therefore," Trevor concluded, "the principle of individual liberty guarded by constitutional government"—the way of the WASP—"is to endure, the basic strain of our population must be maintained."[1] So sell the Statue of Liberty for scrap.

But Trevor's conclusion does not necessarily follow from his premises. The trouble with his fears, and with ethnic pride, is that they both underestimate the psychological rupture of immigration. The leap from an old country that any immigrant makes is sundering. The new country confronts him with new ideals, standards, and social viewpoints. Under any circumstances, the pressure of the new ideals and standards will be compelling. If they happen to be, in crucial respects, superior to the immigrants' old ones, the attraction will be doubly powerful.

Immigrants have brought thousands of things here, in their baggage or in their minds, from snacks to religions. What none of them has successfully established is a rival way of life. For most of the history of American immigration, the dock or the tarmac was the first step in becoming WASPs.

The others—who are by now the vast majority of Americans—came in four great swells, each composed of smaller distinct currents.

Germans and Irish—Irish-Irish, in addition to Scotch-Irish—began arriving in colonial times, hit a peak with the famines and revolutions of the 1840s, and continued at that level for some decades. In the last third of the century they were joined, then surpassed, by people from every other country of Europe, from Portugal to Finland. This wave, interrupted by World War I, was virtually halted by the immigration laws of the 1920s that Captain Trevor was so keen to pass. The West Coast experienced its own influx of Chinese and Japanese earlier, beginning with the Gold Rush and ending with earlier restrictive acts. In 1965, after a forty-year lull, the gates opened again. Attorney General Robert Kennedy, testifying before Congress in 1964, expected five thousand immigrants from the "Asia-Pacific triangle" in the first year of the proposed law, "after which immigration from that source would virtually disappear."[2] The attorney general was mistaken. The last twenty-five years have seen a rush of newcomers, legal and illegal, from the triangle, as well as from Latin America and the Caribbean, from West Africa, and from some oldtime spots of Europe—Ireland, Russia—that were getting a second wind. A New Yorker buys his fruit from Koreans, his newspapers from Indians, and his umbrellas, when he is caught on Fifth Avenue without one, from Senegalese peddlers. Knowing that Senegal was a former French colony, the police in the early eighties assigned a francophone cop to deal with the peddlers, only to discover that the only language they spoke was the African tongue Wolof. The social service ads in the subways, more savvily, assure Haitians *nou pale kreyol*. When Washingtonians tire of Vietnamese restaurants, they go to Afghan ones. (Lose a country, gain a cuisine.) Cinco de Mayo is a holiday in South Texas, the Bay of Pigs is a day of infamy in Miami. One of the last places on earth where Aramaic, the language of Jesus, is used is Hackensack, New Jersey. The experiences of at least the European immigrants of the first two waves have been thoroughly, in some cases obsessively, recorded. The third wave is sure to get similar treatment. To these must be added the journeying of American blacks, in two stages, one compulsory, one internal: the slave trade, which lasted from the early seventeenth century to 1808; then, beginning in the 1920s, the migration of blacks from south to north, sucked like leaves by the furnace of industry.

Some of these groups of others slid into WASPhood with remarkably little trouble. The first and largest European immigrant group, the Germans, showed an extreme of docility. Though they did not speak the language, and though they had certain unWASPy habits—they drank regularly and to moderation, and they knew something about music—they fitted in without much ado. It has been suggested that this happened because they were such a heterogeneous lot to begin with—farmers and city folk, laborers and intelligentsia, Protestants, Catholics, and Jews. "They reflected," Nathan Glazer and Daniel Moynihan wrote, "an entire modern society, not simply an element of one."[3] They maintained numerous parallel institutions—churches, schools, newspapers (twenty-seven German-language dailies by 1860). But when in this century America twice fought Germany, the Germans simply closed the parallel institutions down. Many anglicized their names. Many had already done so—Dink Stover's parents or grandparents had probably spelled it Stouffer.

Other groups had serious problems of adjustment, though they managed to keep them to themselves. The Sicilians in America, wrote Luigi Barzini, the Milanese journalist who lived here for five years in the twenties, "as they had done since the days of Homer, neatly divided human beings into friends, enemies, and neutrals. Their rule (which is also a Spanish proverb) was 'To friends, everything; to enemies, the law.' . . . The family and its allies then became a Macedonian phalanx going through American society as if through butter."[4] In the service of their families, Italians reimmigrated in larger numbers than any other group. Though more than 2 million Italians arrived here in the first decade of the twentieth century, the 1910 census counted scarcely more than a million in the country. The reason was that as soon as they had made some money, most of the new arrivals promptly sent it, and themselves, back to the home folks. Yet this intense—and, in the WASP world, inordinate—family loyalty, except when it was turned to crime, had no negative social effects (except, it may be, on Italians themselves). The Italians who settled down here lived peaceably with non-Italian neighbors: Jews and Chinese in New York, blacks in Louisiana. Howard Beach and Bensonhurst were headlines in the eighties, but they are historical anomalies. Italians have shown only moderate skill in running ethnic political machines, and scant interest in home country politics. The Italians' intense involvement in their families violated the imperative of civic-mindedness, but it permitted a passive conformity with other WASP ways.

But for some groups of others, fitting into the WASP world was a process fraught with turmoil. The experience of the Irish—not the dour Orange garrison of Ulster, but the Irish the word usually conjures up—offers an extreme case of the difficulties of blending in, and of success even in spite of difficulties.

To other newcomers, the Irish seem at a distance to be WASPs. Novak excluded them from his book on the grounds that they were not ethnic enough. To American Catholics from Eastern Europe, he noted, any parish without a national prefix—Polish, Slovak, whatever—was assumed to be Irish. The Irish, in other words, needed no arrivals' identifier; they were established. "The nuances of the regional Irish-Yankee feud [in Boston] escaped Brad" Schaeffer, a character in an Updike story, "since to his Midwestern eyes the two inimical camps were very similar—thin-skinned, clubby men from damp green islands, fond of a nip and long malicious stories."[5]

The perception of congruence was based on powerful WASP-Irish similarities. The Irish knew the language. They were familiar with the English half of Anglo-American liberties, even if only by being deprived of them. Temperamentally, they made an excellent fit with certain aspects of the way of the WASP. The Irish are even more puritanical than the Puritans. "I inclined his young mind," a character in *Molloy* says of his son, "towards that most fruitful of dispositions, horror of the body and its functions."[6] The Irish handle drink in the same way as WASPs: alcoholism or teetotaling.

Yet the Irish record in America is filled with problems. In terms of average income, the Irish advanced slowly relative to later immigrant groups. The Irish ran urban and statewide political machines, a sign of power but also of parochialism and segregation. Many of the pathologies associated with the crackheads and AFDC families of today were rife in the Irish slums of the early nineteenth century; the worst riot in American history, the New York City draft riot of 1863, which left nearly a thousand people dead, was an Irish outbreak against a system of conscription that oppressed them.

These are statistics and headlines; symptoms, not causes. The source of Irish difficulties—difficulties experienced, to some degree, by many newcoming others—was a fundamental problem they had with the way of the WASP.

For years the Irish maintained a dual political loyalty, a consuming interest in the affairs of another country. In 1870 a private army of Irishmen attacked Canada from Vermont.

Twelve decades later, aged bomb-throwers still march in St. Patrick's Day parades. The meddling in Irish and British politics is now mostly ritual, but sentiments of grievance against the former oppressor, difficult for a WASP to credit, remain. "The Irish," as John Roche puts it, "wear bandages to remind themselves where their wounds were."[7]

They also indulged in intergroup vendettas here. Their partners in uproar until they disappeared as an identifiable ethnic group were the Scotch-Irish. Green-Orange riots and brawls regularly accompanied celebrations of St. Patrick's Day and the Battle of Boyne in the nineteenth century. The Irish also picked fights with non-Irish immigrant groups among whom they lived—Jews, blacks, Germans, Chinese, Italians. . . .

All this indicates a deficiency in the cardinal WASP public virtue, civic mindedness. In its place the Irish showed clan-mindedness. It was based, in part, on a plausible suspicion of the justice of any social system, fostered by their experience in Ireland. But it persisted long after they had left Ireland behind. The Irish wished to, and did, escape in the flesh. The escape of the mind was more difficult.

What about the keystone of the WASP's private life—conscience? The keeper of Irish conscience was, until quite recently, the Roman Catholic Church. For a century the Irish ruled it, and it ruled them. One of the French clerics who still ran the American church at the end of the eighteenth century referred to the Irish members of his flock as *canaille*. By the end of the nineteenth century, their grip on its institutions and hierarchy was so strong that non-Irish American Catholics complained all the way to Rome.

Many WASPs doubted, and some loudly denied, that large numbers of newcomers, obedient to an institution that was so much older than the United States, and so inimical, as it seemed, to republican government, could live in peace here. It is one of the pleasant surprises of the Irish experience that Catholicism adapted so well. The reason is plain. The Catholic Church in America became Americanized—that is, WASPized. The Catholic Church arrived as the one true faith, outside which there was no salvation, and it became a denomination. It was still the one true faith, of course, but then so were all the others. It never pushed its claims politically, and it learned to be polite about pushing its claims polemically. When a WASP controversialist challenged Al Smith, on the eve of the 1928 election, to affirm or reject the triumphalist implications of certain papal encyclicals, Smith is said to have asked his advisers, "Will someone tell me what the hell a papal encyclical is?"[8] Quoted out of context, it reads like a joke on Smith's ignorance of theology. Properly understood, it is a sad, almost tragic joke on the completeness of Irish Catholicism's assimilation. Will someone tell me, Smith was asking, what the hell a papal encyclical that is contrary to the spirit of American politics *could be*? Such a thing, he assumed in the strength of his faith—his double faith: in his church, and in the ways of his country—could not exist. The church of the Irish quickly acquired an attitude toward public expressions of conscience indistinguishable from that of its suspicious neighbors.

The domestication of the Irish Catholic Church is important, because it shows how assimilation works. Others do not assimilate to the way of the WASP by learning the language or getting a job, though these are important. The process is more than a matter of recognizing that life here is better than it was at home. The immigrant knew that when he arrived, sometimes before he arrived. Assimilation occurs when the outsider intuits the character traits that *make* life here better for him. "One man prefers the Republic," Mencken remarked, "because it pays better wages than Bulgaria. . . . Another because there is a warrant out for him somewhere else."[9] As usual, Mencken is jeering. But drain away the spleen, and it turns out that he is talking about economic opportunity and political freedom. Internal assimilation—the only important kind—occurs when the job seeker and the refugee understand, intellectually or unconsciously, why the way of the WASP leads to higher wages and fewer warrants. For Irish and other Catholics, America offered something almost unknown in the post-Reformation history of their church: a country, filled with non-Catholics, which placed no penalties on the faithful. They immediately saw that this was better than being persecuted; they came to see, based on the enormous strides their church made—by 1850, it was the largest in America, a position it has held to this day—that WASP ideals of conscience and civic-mindedness were even preferable to those of societies in which Catholics themselves ruled and persecuted. Once they saw that, they were well on the way to becoming the only kind of WASP that counts: WASPs by conviction.

The Roman Catholic Church was the one immigrant institution which had the numbers, the force of tradition, and the intellectual weight to have deflected the American character, or at least split it. The fact that it did not, and that good Catholics became good Americans, which is to say, good WASPs, is the most dramatic proof of the gravitational power of the WASP world.

Literal WASPs were not passive spectators of these assorted perplexities and achievements. They involved themselves directly in their neighbors' affairs and experienced strong reactions to their presence. The involvement and the reactions fell, unsurprisingly, into two broad categories: hostile and welcoming. For half a century the hostility became so rancorous that many WASPs slid into clan-mindedness, behaving like any other imperfectly adjusted ethnic group.

Hostility was as old as immigration. The second American third party, after the Anti-Masons, was the Know-Nothings, or the American party. Its enemies were the Irish, and it distrusted them because of their combination of Catholicism and political skill. The Know-Nothings swelled and burst in a matter of years; their one presidential candidate, the hapless Millard Fillmore, who rejected their program, carried only one state in 1856. But anti-Catholicism lingered on—lingers today. Jimmy Swaggart assured his viewers in the 1980s that all Mother Teresa's care for beggars wouldn't keep her out of Hell.

The long and various second wave (which coincided with the Irish assumptions of control over the big-city machines they had formerly supported) became the occasion for more complicated hostilities. Anti-Semitism appeared in American life in the 1870s. The phenomenon was sudden, unprecedented, and sometimes ironic in its workings. Digby Baltzell tells the story of Jesse Seligman, a founder of the Union League Club, one of the stuffiest upper-crust preserves in New York, who resigned his membership in 1893 when his own son was blackballed.[10] The South, which had enjoyed a false dawn of legal racial equality under Reconstruction and under the Democratic grandees who took over when the Federal troops left, began imposing Jim Crow in the 1880s and 1890s. All these strains—anti-Catholic, anti-Jewish, antiblack—were brought together in the second Ku Klux Klan of the 1920s, which, unlike its predecessor and its successors, was neither an all-Southern group nor a fringe of lowlifes and skinheads, but a national organization with strength in the North and the Midwest. At the Democratic convention of 1924, a pro-Klan candidate hung in the race through one hundred ballots.

Feelings of WASP dislike and dismay were not confined to troglodytes. Jokes about Irishmen and their boggy feet disfigure *Walden*. Genteel urban reformers were as alarmed as the Invisible Empire by the foreignness of their opponents. One of Margaret Sanger's motives in campaigning for birth control was to limit the breeding of lesser breeds. Madison Grant, a founder of the New York Zoological Society and the Save the Redwoods League, was author of *The Passing of the Great Race in America,* an anti-immigration scare book which Jay Gatsby's Long Island neighbor, Tom Buchanan, seems to have read.

More than motiveless malignity lay behind these reactions. We have already examined the political argument against taking in large numbers of others—John Trevor's. WASPs also feared economic competition from transplanted businessmen at the top and from toiling masses below. Immigrants, as the Imperial Wizard of the twenties' Klan put it, "fill the lower rungs of the ladder of success." This is, in the aggregate, a fallacy—new labor floats an economy, it does not sink it—though there will always be individuals displaced by those who work harder and better or who hold lower expectations. WASPs were not the only ones who feared displacement. At the height of the second wave, the United Garment Workers of America, no WASP coterie, deplored "the overstocking of the labour market" with those "unfitted to battle intelligently for their rights." Last one in raise the drawbridge.[11]

There was, finally, a sense among WASPs that the psychological burden of assimilation did not lie only on the assimilating. The melters had difficulties of which the melted were unaware. Tolerance, a writer in the *Christian Century* pointed out in 1945, twenty years after the second wave had been halted, "is chiefly Protestant tolerance. Whatever degree of tolerance (if any) [that] is produced in the other groups is hardly more than academic and sentimental, because, being a minority, they have no concrete occasion to exercise it."[12] One can almost see the wan smile of the host who was happy, at eight o'clock, to throw a party, but who, at two in the morning, with the guests still filling his sofa and the ring marks multiplying on his tables, is less happy.

One effect of these hostilities, and the lack of confidence they betoken, was to create in many WASPs, from the 1880s to the 1920s, an ethnic consciousness, with all its attendant problems. Clubs, schools, and political movements became preoccupied with "stock," as if they were dealing with horses rather than humans. There even developed a dual loyalty among many WASPs to England: the Anglo-Saxon fad. George Apley wrote during World War I of "our former Mother Country . . . saving civilization for posterity," [13] and let his daughter be wooed by a con man posing as an English officer.

Hostility continually recurs, and is therefore important. Equally important is its recurring shallowness. WASP ethnicity was an episode. So were other manifestations of clannishness. We have already noted the brief and inglorious history of the Know-Nothings. The Democratic party the Klan fought to control seventy years later was a minority party, and the Klan lost the fight. Immigration from Southern and Eastern Europe was restricted for only forty-one years; Japanese and Chinese immigrants were blocked for only decades more. Every acrid reference in WASP letters or diaries to "alien vermin" swarming out of "steerage" can be matched by a paean: "the inner light of Pilgrim and Quaker colonists . . . gleams no less in the faces of the children of Russian Jew immigrants today."[14]

The large fact, larger than exclusion, is that non-WASPs were welcome—welcome enough, anyway, that most of them stayed, and more kept coming. The practical motives for WASP hospitality were supplied by industry and use. A country so big and booming needed people. The magnates who, as clubmen, blackballed the Seligmans of the world profited, as businessmen, from the immigration of their cousins. The treatment accorded newcomers once they arrived was dictated, for the most part, by civic-mindedness. The liberties WASPs had devised for themselves applied to everyone. By itself, Bartholdi's statue, "Liberty Enlightening the World," is Gallic and abstract. In New York Harbor, a stone's throw from Ellis Island, where the world flowed in beneath it, it expressed an American reality.

The exception, the special case, as always, is blacks, slaves for two centuries, second-class citizens for a century more. To which one can only say that the war which emancipated them was not nothing; neither is the money that has been spent on the black poor in the last twenty-five years. Whether it has been spent to anyone's benefit is another matter.

The only price even the most inclusive WASPs exacted was that newly arrived others should become exactly like themselves. Theodore Roosevelt, in the thick of the immigration debates sparked by the second wave, put it most simply. Roosevelt accepted the economic argument against unrestricted inflow, and he also believed there was such a thing as "races [*sic* again] which do not readily assimilate with our own." Against the sweep of his premises, these reservations shrink to cavils. "Where immigrants, or the sons of immigrants, do not heartily and in good faith throw in their lot with us, but cling to the speech, the customs, the ways of life, and the habits of thought of the Old World which they have left, they thereby do harm both to themselves and us." But those who "become completely Americanized . . . stand on exactly the same plane as descendants of any Puritan, Cavalier, or Knickerbocker among us, and do their full and honorable share of the nation's work."[15] They stand, Roosevelt (descendant of a Knickerbocker) was saying, on exactly the same plane as himself.

One reason for WASP complacency is surely that none of the non-WASP others separately, nor all of them together, offered any coherent or attractive alternative way of life. Where there is no threat, there should be no anxiety. Foreign things—bagels, banjos, burritos, beer steins—posed no threat at all. You can change a menu without changing your taste, and for most of American history that is what WASPs did, with strange words, skills, objects, edibles. New things, after all, might be useful, in which case it would be wrong not to use them. Many new things burrowed into American life so securely that they were absorbed and reexported, with the label "MADE IN THE USA." Thus, on the outskirts of Panama City one finds a Taco Bell.

Cultural contributions that were more than random items were more problematic. An activity or a belief that implies or proclaims a different view of the world is less easy to make use of than pizza or Santa Claus. Yet even here WASPs exercised considerable adaptive powers. If a potentially alien force could be seen as unserious, and therefore beneath notice, it could be allowed to fill a gap in the national pattern without disturbing the pattern. It ran free in WASP backyards as fun (the fate of jazz). Counter-philosophies that were unmistakably earnest were made to conform in their externals. Their domestic affairs, so to speak, may have remained unchanged, but their foreign policy was transformed (the fate of the Catholic Church). Ideas that did not slip into the mainstream bobbed in it, insoluble and unabsorbed. Socialism offers a case in point. There is an indigenous WASP radicalism, of the Populists and *Looking Backward;* a little earlier, of abolition and women's suffrage. European socialism, as practiced by Jews in New York and Germans in Milwaukee, was a political curiosity, less significant than Prohibition. The modern Socialist party used as its front man Norman Thomas, a former Presbyterian minister.

The fact is, there was no challenge that non-WASPs were capable of mounting that could have undermined the cultural hegemony of a group as large, as central, and as entrenched as the WASPs in America. The great majority of others, preoccupied with becoming a part of the WASP world themselves, offered no such challenge.

But, of course, challenges do not come only from outside.

Notes

1. Quoted in Margo J. Anderson, *The American Census* (New Haven: Yale University Press, 1988), p. 146.

2. Nathan Glazer and Daniel P. Moynihan, *Beyond the Melting Pot* (Cambridge, Mass.: MIT Press, 1970), p. 56.

3. *Ibid.*, p. 312.

4. Luigi Barzini, *O America* (New York: Penguin, 1977), pp. 174–75.

5. John Updike, *Trust Me* (New York: Knopf, 1987), p. 198.

6. Samuel Beckett, *Molloy* (New York: Grove Press, 1955), p. 161.

7. Interview with John Roche.

8. Glazer and Moynihan, p. 275.

9. H. L. Mencken, *Prejudices: A Selection* (New York: Vintage Books, 1958), pp. 124–25.

10. E. Digby Baltzell, *The Protestant Establishment* (New Haven: Yale University Press, 1987), p. 138.

11. Sydney E. Ahlstrom, *A Religious History of the American People* (New Haven: Yale University Press, 1972), p. 917, and John Lukacs, *Outgrowing Democracy* (Garden City, N.Y.: Doubleday, 1984), p. 252.

12. Will Herberg, *Protestant-Catholic-Jew* (Garden City, N.Y.: Doubleday, 1960), p. 252.

13. John P. Marquand, *The Late George Apley* (New York: Washington Square Press, 1963), p. 235.

14. Lukacs, pp. 134, 150. The vermin line is Owen Wister's; the inner light, Bliss Perry's.

15. Peter Schrag, *The Decline of the WASP* (New York: Simon & Schuster 1970), p. 188.

61

Beyond the Melting Pot

NATHAN GLAZER AND
DANIEL PATRICK MOYNIHAN

It was reasonable to believe that a new American type would emerge, a new nationality in which it would be a matter of indifference whether a man was of Anglo-Saxon or German or Italian or Jewish origin, and in which indeed, because of the diffusion of populations through all parts of the country and all levels of the social order, and because of the consequent close contact and intermarriage, it would be impossible to make such distinctions. After all, in 1960 almost half of New York City's population was still foreign-born or the children of foreign-born. Yet it is also true that it is forty years since the end of mass immigration, and new processes, scarcely visible when our chief concern was with the great masses of immigrants and the problems of their "Americanization," now emerge to surprise us. The initial notion of an American melting pot did not, it seems, quite grasp what would happen in America. At least it did not grasp what would happen in the short run, and since this short run encompasses at least the length of a normal lifetime, it is not something we can ignore.

It is true that language and culture are very largely lost in the first and second generations, and this makes the dream of "cultural pluralism"—of a new Italy or Germany or Ireland in America, a League of Nations established in the New World—as unlikely as the hope of a "melting pot." But as the groups were transformed by influences in American society, stripped of their original attributes, they were re-created as something new, but still as identifiable groups. Concretely, persons think of themselves as members of that group, with that name; they are thought of by others as members of that group, with that name; and most significantly, they are linked to other members of the group by new attributes that the original immigrants would never have recognized as identifying their group, but which nevertheless serve to mark them off, by more than simply name and association, in the third generation and even beyond.

The assimilating power of American society and culture operated on immigrant groups in different ways, to make them, it is true, something they had not been, but still something distinct and identifiable. The impact of assimilating trends on the groups is different in part because the groups are different—Catholic peasants from Southern Italy were affected differently, in the same city and the same time, from urbanized Jewish workers and merchants from Eastern Europe. We cannot even begin to indicate how various were the characteristics of family structure, religion, economic experience and attitudes, educational experience and attitudes, political outlook that differentiated groups from such different backgrounds. Obviously, some American influences worked on them in common and with the same effects. But their differences meant they were open to different parts of American experience, interpreted it in different ways, used it for different ends. In the third generation, the descendants of the immigrants confronted each other, and knew they were both Americans, in the same dress, with the same language, using the same artifacts, troubled by the same things, but they voted differently, had different ideas about education and sex, and were still, in many essential ways, as different from one another as their grandfathers had been.

The initial attributes of the groups provided only one reason why their transformations did not make them all into the same thing. There was another reason—and that was the nature of American society itself, which could not, or did not, assimilate the immigrant groups fully or in equal degree. Or perhaps the nature of human society in general. It is only the experience of the strange and foreign that teaches us how provincial we are. A hundred thousand Negroes have been enough to change the traditional British policy of free immigration from the colonies and dominions. Japan finds it impossible to incorporate into the body of its society anyone who does not look Japanese, or even the Koreans, indistinguishable very often in appearance and language from Japanese. And we shall test the racial attitudes of the Russians only when there are more than a few Negroes passing through as curiosities; certainly the inability of Russians to get over anti-Semitism does not suggest they are any different from the rest of mankind. In any case, the word "American" was an unambiguous reference to nationality only when it was applied to a relatively homogeneous social body consisting of immigrants from the British Isles, with relatively small numbers from nearby European countries. When the numbers of those not of British origin began to rise, the word "American" became a far more complicated thing. Legally, it meant a citizen. Socially, it lost its identifying power, and when you asked a man what he was (in the United States), "American" was not the answer you were looking for. In the United States it became a slogan, a political gesture, sometimes an evasion, but not a matter-of-course, concrete social description of a person. Just as in certain languages a word cannot stand alone but needs some particle to indicate its function, so in the United States the word "American" does not stand by itself. If it does, it bears the additional meaning of patriot, "authentic" American, critic and opponent of "foreign" ideologies.

The original Americans became "old" Americans, or "old stock," or "white Anglo-Saxon Protestants," or some other identification which indicated they were not immigrants or descendants of recent immigrants. These original Americans already had a frame in their minds, which became a frame in reality, that placed and ordered those who came after them. Those who were like them could easily join them. It was important to be white, of British origin, and Protestant. If one was all three, then even if one was an immigrant, one was really not an immigrant, or not for long.

Thus, even before it knew what an Italian or Jew or an Irishman was like, the American mind had a place for the category, high or low, depending on color, on religion, on how close the group was felt to be to the Anglo-Saxon center. There were peculiarities in this placing. Why, for example, were the Germans placed higher than the Irish? There was of course an interplay to some extent between what the group actually was and where it was placed, and, since the German immigrants were less impoverished than the Irish and somewhat more competent craftsmen and farmers, this undoubtedly affected the old American's image of them. Then ideology came in to emphasize the common links between Englishmen and Germans, who, even though they spoke different languages, were said to be really closer to each other than the old Americans were to the English-speaking, but Catholic and Celtic, Irish. If a group's first representatives were cultured and educated, those who came after might benefit, unless they were so numerous as to destroy the first image. Thus, German Jews who arrived in the 1840's and 1850's benefited from their own characteristics and their link with Germans, until they were overwhelmed by the large number of East European Jewish immigrants after 1880. A new wave of German Jewish immigrants, in the 1930's, could not, regardless of culture and education, escape the low position of being "Jewish."

The ethnic group in American society became not a survival from the age of mass immigration but a new social form. One could not predict from its first arrival what it might become or, indeed, whom it might contain. The group is not a purely biological phenomenon. The Irish of today do not consist of those who are descended from Irish immigrants. Were we to follow the history of the germ plasm alone—if we could—we should find that many in the group really came from other groups, and that many who should be in the group are in other groups. The Protestants among them, and those who do not bear distinctively Irish names, may now consider themselves, and be generally considered, as much "old American" as anyone else. The Irish-named offspring of German or Jewish or Italian mothers often find that willy-nilly they have become Irish. It is even harder for the Jewish-named offspring of mixed marriages to escape from the Jewish group; neither Jews nor non-Jews will let them rest in ambiguity.

Parts of the group are cut off, other elements join as allies. Under certain circumstances, strange as it may appear, it is an advantage to be able to take on a group name, even of a low order, if it can be made to fit. It is better in Oakland, California, to be a Mexican than an Indian, and so some of the few Indians call themselves, at certain times, for certain occasions, "Mexicans." In the forming of ethnic groups subtle distinctions are overridden; belonging to a big group confers advantages, even if it is looked down upon. West Indian Negroes achieve important political positions, as representatives of Negroes; Spaniards and Latin Americans become the representatives of Puerto Ricans; German Jews rose to Congress from districts dominated by East European Jews.

Ethnic groups then, even after distinctive language, customs, and culture are lost, as they largely were in the second generation, and even more fully in the third generation, are continually re-created by new experiences in America. The mere existence of a name itself is perhaps sufficient to form group character in new situations, for the name associates an individual, who actually can be anything, with a certain past, country, race. But as a matter of fact, someone who is Irish or Jewish or Italian generally has other traits than the mere existence of the name that associates him with other people attached to the group. A man is connected to his group by ties of family and friendship. But he is also connected by ties of *interest.* The ethnic groups in New York are also *interest groups.*

This is perhaps the single most important fact about ethnic groups in New York City. When one speaks of the Negroes and Puerto Ricans, one also means unorganized and unskilled workers, who hold poorly paying jobs in the laundries, hotels, restaurants, small factories or who are on relief. When one says Jews, one also means small shopkeepers, professionals, better-paid skilled workers in the garment industries. When one says Italians, one also means homeowners in Staten Island, the North Bronx, Brooklyn, and Queens.

If state legislation threatens to make it more difficult to get relief, this is headline news in the Puerto Rican press—for the group is affected—and news of much less importance to the rest of the press. The interplay between rational economic interests and the other interests or attitudes that stem out of group history makes for an incredibly complex political and social situation. Consider the local laws against discrimination in housing. Certain groups that face discrimination want such laws—Negroes, Puerto Ricans, and Jews. Jews meet little discrimination in housing in New York but have an established ideological commitment to all antidiscrimination laws. Apartment-house owners are against any restriction of their freedom or anything that might affect their profits. In New York, this group is also largely Jewish, but it is inhibited in pushing strongly against such laws by its connections with the Jewish community. Private homeowners see fair-housing laws as a threat to their homogenous neighborhoods. This is particularly so for the German, Irish, and Italian, whose ethnic background as homeowners links them to communities with a history of anti-Negro feelings. The Irish and Italian immigrants have both at different times competed directly with Negro labor.

In the analysis then of the conflict over antidiscrimination laws, "rational" economic interests and the "irrational" or at any rate noneconomic interests and attitudes tied up with one's own group are inextricably mixed together. If the rational interests did not operate, some of the older groups would by now be much weaker than they are. The informal and formal social groupings that make up these communities are strengthened by the ability of Jews to talk about the garment business, Irish about politics and the civil service, Italians about the state of the trucking or contracting or vegetable business.

In addition to the links of interest, family and fellowfeeling bind the ethnic group. There is satisfaction in being with those who are like oneself. The ethnic group is something of an extended family or tribe. And aside from ties of feeling and interest, there are concrete ties of organization. Certain types of immigrant social organization have declined, but others have proven as ingenious in remolding and re-creating themselves as the group itself. The city is often spoken of as the place of anonymity, of the breakdown of some kind of preexisting social order. The ethnic group, as Oscar Handlin has pointed out, served to create a new form of order. Those who came in with some kind of disadvantage, created by a different language, a different religion, a different race, found both comfort and material support in creating various kinds of organizations. American social services grew up in large part to aid incoming immigrant groups. Many of these were limited to a single religious or ethnic group. Ethnic groups set up hospitals, old people's homes, loan funds, charitable organizations, as well as churches and cultural organizations. The initial need for a separate set of welfare and health institutions became weaker as the group became more prosperous and as the government took over these functions, but the organizations nevertheless continued. New York organizational life today is in large measure lived within ethnic bounds. These organizations generally have religious names, for it is more acceptable that welfare and health institutions should cater to religious than to ethnic communities. But of course religious institutions are generally closely linked to a distinct ethnic group. The Jewish (religious) organizations are Jewish (ethnic), Catholic are generally Irish or Italian, now with the Puerto Ricans as important clients; the Protestant organizations are white Protestant—which means generally old American, with a smaller German wing—in leadership, with Negroes as their chief clients.

Thus many elements—history, family and feeling, interest, formal organizational life—operate to keep much of New York life channeled within the bounds of the ethnic group. Obviously, the rigidity of this channeling of social life varies from group to group. For the Puerto Ricans, a recent immigrant group with a small middle class and speaking a foreign language, the ethnic group serves as the setting for almost all social life. For Negroes too, because of discrimination and poverty, most social life is limited to the group itself. Jews and Italians are still to some extent recent immigrants, and despite the growing middle-class character of the Jewish group, social life for both is generally limited to other members of the group. But what about the Irish . . . ?

The Irish

New York used to be an Irish city. Or so it seemed. There were sixty or seventy years when the Irish were everywhere. *They* felt it was their town. It is no longer, and they know it. That is one of the things bothering them.

The Irish era began in the early 1870's, about the time Charles O'Conor, a New York lawyer, began the prosecution of Honorable William March Tweed. It ended in the 1930's. A symbolic point might be the day ex-Mayor James J. Walker sailed for Europe and exile with his beloved, but unwed, Betty.

Boss Tweed was the last vulgar white Protestant to win a prominent place in the city's life. The Protestants who have since entered public life have represented the "better element." Tweed was a roughneck, a ward heeler, a man of the people at a time when the people still contained a large body of native-born Protestant workers of Scotch and English antecedents. By the time of his death in the Ludlow Street jail this had all but completely changed. The New York working class had become predominantly Catholic, as it has since remained. The Irish promptly assumed the leadership of this working class. "Honest John" Kelly succeeded Tweed as leader of Tammany Hall, formalizing a process that had been steadily advancing.

In 1880 Tammany Hall elected the city's first Irish Catholic mayor, William R. Grace of the shipping line. This ascendancy persisted for another half century, reaching an apogee toward the end of the twenties when Al Smith ran for President and Jimmy Walker "wore New York in his buttonhole." The crash came suddenly. In June 1932 Smith was denied the Democratic renomination. The Tammany delegates left Chicago bitter and unreconciled. Two months later Mayor Walker resigned in the face of mounting scandal, and decided to leave the country with his English mistress. A few days before his departure, Franklin Roosevelt had been elected President. The next man to be elected Mayor of New York City would be Fiorello H. La Guardia. Next, a Jewish world heavyweight champion. DiMaggio became the new name in baseball; Sinatra the new crooner. So it went. The almost formal end came within a decade. In 1943 Tammany Hall itself, built while Walker was Mayor at the cost of just under one million dollars, was sold to Local 91 of the International Ladies' Garment Workers' Union. Tammany and the New York County Democratic Committee went their separate ways. The oldest political organization on earth was finished. So was the Irish era.

This is not to say the Irish have disappeared. They are still a powerful group. St. Patrick's Day is still the largest public observance of the city's year. On March 17 a green line is painted up Fifth Avenue and a half-million people turn out to watch the parade. (In Albany the Legislative Calendar is printed in green ink.) The Irish have a position in the city now as they had before the 1870's, but now, as then, it is a lopsided position. "Slippery Dick" Connoly and "Brains" Sweeney shared power and office with Tweed, as did any number of their followers. But, with few exceptions, they represented the *canaille*. With the coming of the Gilded Age, middle-class and even upper-class Irish appeared. For a period they ranged across the social spectrum, and in this way seemed to dominate much of the city's life. The Tweed ring was heavily Irish, but so was the group that brought on its downfall. This pattern persisted. The Irish came to run the police force *and* the underworld; they were the reformers and the hoodlums; employers and employed. The city entered the era of Boss Croker of Tammany Hall and Judge Goff of the Lexow Committee which investigated him; of business leader Thomas Fortune Ryan and labor leader Peter J. McGuire; of Reform Mayor John Purroy Mitchel and Tammany Mayor John F. "Red Mike" Hylan. It was a stimulating miscellany.

All this is past. The mass of the Irish have left the working class, and in considerable measure the Democratic party as well. But the pattern of egalitarian politics they established on the whole persists, so that increasingly the Irish are left out. Their reaction to this is one of the principal elements of the Irish impact on the city today.

The basis of Irish hegemony in the city was established by the famine emigration of 1846–1850. By mid-century there were 133,730 Irish-born inhabitants of the city, 26 per cent of the total population. By 1855, 34 per cent of the city voters were Irish. By 1890, when 80 per cent of the population of New York City was of foreign parentage, a third of these (409,924 persons of 1,215,463) were Irish, making more than a quarter of the total population.[1] With older stock included, over one-third of the population of New York and Brooklyn at the outset of the Gay Nineties was Irish-American.

The older stock went far back in the city's history. Ireland provided a continuing portion of the emigration to North America during the seventeenth and eighteenth centuries. Much of it was made up of Protestants with English or Scottish antecedents, but there were always some Celtic Irish of Protestant or Catholic persuasion. The Catholic Irish were kept out of the political life of the city for almost a century. It began a long tradition of denying rights to Irish Catholics on grounds that they wished to do the same to English Protestants. To this day the most fair-minded New York Protestants will caution that Irish Catholics have never experienced the great Anglo-Saxon tradition of the separation of church and state, although indeed they have known nothing but.

At the first New York Constitutional Convention in 1777, John Jay even proposed that Roman Catholics be deprived of their civil rights and the right to hold land until taking an oath that no Pope or priest could absolve them from sin or from allegiance to the state. This proposal was rejected, but Jay did succeed in including a religious test for naturalization in the Constitution which remained in force until superseded by a federal naturalization statute in 1790. It was not until 1806 that a similar oath required for officeholders was repealed, permitting the first Irish Catholic to take his seat in the Assembly. In 1798 another of the native Irish revolts took place, and failed. In its aftermath came the first of a long trail of Irish revolutionaries, Catholic and Protestant, who disturbed the peace of the city for a century and a quarter. These were educated professional men who had risked their lives for much the same cause that had inspired the Sons of Liberty in New York a generation earlier. In general they were received as such.

In the early nineteenth century a sizable Irish-Catholic community gathered in New York. By the time of the great migration it was well enough established. For some time prior to the potato famine the basic patterns of Irish life in New York had been set. The hordes that arrived at mid-century strengthened some of these patterns more than others, but they did not change them nearly so much as they were changed by them. They got off the boat to find their identity waiting for them: they were to be Irish-Catholic Democrats.

Tammany was organized in New York a few weeks after Washington was inaugurated at Federal Hall on April 30, 1789. The principal founder was one William Mooney, an upholsterer and apparently by birth an Irish Catholic. Originally a national organization, from the first its *motif* was egalitarian and nationalist: the Sons of St. Tammany, the American Indian chief, as against the foreign ties of the societies of St. George and St. David (as well, apparently, of the Sons of St. Patrick), or the aristocratic airs of the Sons of the Cincinnati. Its members promptly engrossed themselves in politics, establishing the New York Democratic party.

The original issues on which the New York political parties organized concerned the events of the French Revolution. Jefferson and his Democratic followers were instinctively sympathetic to France. Hamilton, Jay, and the Federalists looked just as fervently to England. This automatically aligned the Irish with the Democrats: the French Revolution had inspired the Irish revolt of 1798, and the French had sent three expeditions to aid it. The Federalists reacted with the Alien and Sedition Acts of 1798, designed in part to prevent the absorption of immigrants into the Jeffersonian party, but which only strengthened their attachment to it. In 1812 the Federalists bitterly, but unsuccessfully, opposed the establishment of more-or-less universal white suffrage, certain it would swell the immigrant Irish vote of New York City.

So it did, and in no time the Irish developed a powerful voting bloc. In the 1827 city elections, a prelude to the contest between John Quincy Adams and Andrew Jackson, the Irish sided mightily with Jackson, himself the son of poor Irish immigrants, and thereupon entered wholeheartedly into the politics of the Jacksonian era. The contest for the "Irish vote" became an aspect of almost every New York election that followed. In 1884 Republican candidate James G. Blaine, who had been making headway with the Irish, lost New York by 1,077 votes, and thereby the election, which ended the Republican rule of post–Civil War America. By this time the New York City Irish were not only voting for the Democratic party but thoroughly controlled its organization. Apart from building their church, this was the one singular achievement of the nineteenth-century Irish.

New York became the first great city in history to be ruled by men of the people, not as an isolated phenomenon of the Gracchi or the Commune, but as a persisting, established pattern. Almost to this day the men who have run New York City have talked out of the side of their mouths. The intermittent discovery that New York did have representative government led to periodic reform movements. But the reformers came and went; the party remained. The secret lay in the structure of the party bureaucracy, which ever replenished and perpetuated itself.

In politics, as in religion, the Irish brought many traits from the Old Country. The machine governments that they established in New York (as in many Northern cities) show a number of features characteristic of nineteenth-century Ireland. The exact nature of the relationship is not clear. But the coincidence is clear enough to warrant the proposition that the machine governments resulted from a merger of rural Irish custom with urban American politics. But in nineteenth-century New York events did not permit one system gradually to recede as the other slowly emerged. The ancient world of folkways and the modern world of contracts came suddenly together. The collision is nicely evoked by the story of Congressman Timothy J. Campbell of New York, a native of Cavan, calling on President Grover Cleveland with a request the President refused on the ground that it was unconstitutional. "Ah, Mr. President," replied Tim, "what is the Constitution between friends?"[2]

Four features of the machine government are particularly noticeable in this respect:

First, there was an indifference to Yankee proprieties. To the Irish, stealing an election was rascally, not to be approved, but neither quite to be abhorred. It may be they picked up some of this from the English. Eighteenth-century politics in Ireland were—in Yankee terms—thoroughly corrupt.

But the Irish added to the practice, from their own social structure, a personal concept of government action. Describing the early period of Irish self-government, Conrad M. Arensberg relates that

> . . . At first, geese and country produce besieged the new officers and magistrates; a favourable decision or a necessary public work performed was interpreted as a favour given. It demanded a direct and personal return. "Influence" to the countryman was and is a direct personal relationship, like the friendship of the countryside along which his own life moves.[3]

Second, the Irish brought to America a settled tradition of regarding the formal government as illegitimate, and the informal one as bearing the true impress of popular sovereignty. The Penal Laws of eighteenth-century Ireland totally proscribed the Catholic religion and reduced the Catholic Irish to a condition of *de facto* slavery. Cecil Woodham-Smith holds with Burke that the lawlessness, dissimulation, and revenge which followed left the Irish character, above all the character of the peasantry, "degraded and debased."

> His religion made him an outlaw; in the Irish House of Commons he was described as "the common enemy," and whatever was inflicted on him he must bear, for where could he look for redress? To his landlord? Almost invariably an alien conqueror. To the law? Not when every person connected with the law, from the jailer to the judge, was a Protestant. . . .
>
> In these conditions suspicion of the law, of the ministers of the law and of all established authority "worked into the very nerves and blood of the Irish peasant," and since the law did not give him justice he set up his own law. The secret societies which have been the curse of Ireland became widespread during the Penal period . . . dissimulation became a moral necessity and evasion of the law the duty of every God-fearing Catholic.[4]

This habit of mind pervaded Tammany at its height. City Hall as such was no more to be trusted than Dublin Castle. Alone one could fight neither. If in trouble it was best to see The McManus. If the McMani were in power in City Hall as well as in the Tuscarora Regular Democratic Organization of the Second Assembly District Middle—so much the better.

Third, most of the Irish arrived in America fresh from the momentous experience of the Catholic Emancipation movement. The Irish peasants, who had taken little part in Gaelic Ireland's resistance to the English (that had been a matter for the warrior class of an aristocratic society) arrived in America with some feeling at least for the possibilities of politics, bringing with them, as a fourth quality, a phenomenally effective capacity for political bureaucracy.

Politics is a risky business. Hence it has ever been the affair of speculators with the nerve to gamble and an impulse to boldness. These are anything but peasant qualities. Certainly they are not qualities of Irish peasants who, collectively, yielded to none in the rigidity of their social structure and their disinclination to adventure. Instead of letting politics transform them, the Irish transformed politics, establishing a political system in New York City that, from a distance, seems like the social system of an Irish village writ large.

The Irish village was a place of stable, predictable social relations in which almost everyone had a role to play, under the surveillance of a stern oligarchy of elders, and in which, on the whole, a person's position was likely to improve with time. Transferred to Manhattan, these were the essentials of Tammany Hall. By 1817 the Irish were playing a significant role in Tammany. Working from the original ward committees, they slowly established a vast hierarchy of party positions descending from the county leader at the top down to the block captain and beyond, even to building captains. Each position had rights and responsibilities that had to be observed. The result was a massive party bureaucracy. The county committees of the five boroughs came to number more than 32,000 persons. It became necessary to hire Madison Square Garden for their meetings, and to hope that not more than half would come. The system in its prime was remarkably stable. Kelly, Richard Croker, and Frank Murphy in succession ran Tammany for half a century. Across the river Hugh McLaughlin ran the Brooklyn Democratic party and fought off Tammany for better than forty years, from 1862 to 1903. He was followed shortly by John H. McCooey, who ruled from 1909 until his death a quarter century later in 1934. Ed Flynn ran the Bronx from 1922 until his death in 1953.

The stereotype of the Irish politician as a beer-guzzling back-slapper is nonsense. Croker, McLaughlin, and *Mister* Murphy were the least affable of men. Their task was not to charm but to administer with firmness and predictability a political bureaucracy in which the prerogatives of rank were carefully observed. The hierarchy had to be maintained. For the group as a whole this served to take the risks out of politics. Each would get his deserts—in time.

It would also seem that the term "Boss" and the persistent attacks on "Boss rule" have misrepresented the nature of power in the old machine system. Power was hierarchical in the party, diffused in the way it is in an army. Because the commanding general was powerful, it did not follow that the division generals were powerless. Tammany district leaders were important men, and, right down to the block captain, all had rights.

The principle of Boss rule was not tyranny, but order. When Lincoln Steffens asked Croker, "Why must there be a boss, when we've got a mayor and—a council and—" "That's why," Croker broke in. "It's because there's a mayor *and* a council *and* judges—*and* a hundred other men to deal with."[5]

At the risk of exaggerating, it is possible to point to any number of further parallels between the political machine and rural Irish society. The incredible capacity of the rural Irish to remain celibate, awaiting their turn to inherit the farm, was matched by generations of assistant corporation counsels awaiting that opening on the City Court bench. Arensberg has described the great respect for rank in the Irish peasantry. Even after an Irish son had taken over direction of the farm, he would go each morning to his father to ask what to do that day. So was respect shown to the "Boss," whose essential demand often seemed only that he be consulted.

The narrow boundaries of the peasant world were ideally adaptable to precinct politics. "Irish familism is of the soil," wrote Arensberg. "It operates most strongly within allegiances to a definite small area."[6] Only men from such a background could make an Assembly district their life's work.

The parallel role of the saloonkeeper is striking. Arensberg writes of the saloonkeeper in Ireland:

> . . . the shopkeeper-publican-politician was a very effective instrument, both for the countryside which used him and for himself. He might perhaps exact buying at his shop in return for the performance of his elective duties, as his enemies charge: but he also saw to it that those duties were performed for the very people who wished to see them done. Through him, as through no other possible channel, Ireland reached political maturity and effective national strength.[7]

It used to be said the only way to break up a meeting of the Tammany Executive Committee was to open the door and yell "Your saloon's on fire!" At the same time a mark of the successful leaders was sobriety. George Washington Plunkitt, a Tammany district leader, related with glee the events of election night 1897 when Tammany had just elected—against considerable odds—the first mayor of the consolidated City of New York:

> Up to 10 P.M. Croker, John F. Carroll, Tim Sullivan, Charlie Murphy, and myself sat in the committee-room receivin' returns. When nearly all the city was heard from and we saw that Van Wyck was elected by a big majority, I invited the crowd to go across the street for a little celebration. A lot of small politicians followed us, expectin' to see magnums of champagne opened. The waiters in the restaurant expected it, too, and you never saw a more disgusted lot of waiters when they got our orders. Here's the orders: Croker, vichy and bicarbonate of soda; Carroll, seltzer lemonade; Sullivan, apollinaris; Murphy, vichy; Plunkitt, ditto. Before midnight we were all in bed, and next mornin' we were up bright and early attendin' to business while other men were nursin' swelled heads. Is there anything the matter with temperance as a pure business proposition?[8]

As a business proposition it all worked very well. But that is about as far as it went. The Irish were immensely successful in politics. They ran the city. But the very parochialism and bureaucracy that enabled them to succeed in politics prevented them from doing much with government. In all those sixty or seventy years in which they could have done almost anything they wanted in politics, they did very little. Of all those candidates and all those campaigns, what remains? The names of two or three men: Al Smith principally (who was a quarter English, apparently a quarter German, and possibly a quarter Italian), and his career went sour before it ever quite came to glory.

In a sense, the Irish did not know what to do with power once they got it. Steffens was surely exaggerating when he suggested the political bosses kept power only on the sufferance of the business community. The two groups worked in harmony, but it was a symbiotic, not an agency relationship. The Irish leaders did for the Protestant establishment what it could not do for itself, and could not do without. But the Irish just didn't know what to do with their opportunity. They never thought of politics as an instrument of social change—their kind of politics involved the processes of a society that was not changing. Croker alone solved the problem. Having become rich he did the thing rich people in Ireland did: he bought himself a manor house in England, bred horses, and won the Derby. The King did not ask him to the Derby Day dinner.

Notes

1. Eleventh Census 1890, Part 1, pp. cixii, cixix. New York City did not then include Kings, Queens, or Richmond Counties. However, the proportion generally carried over. In 1890 three quarters of the Brooklyn Assemblymen were Irish, as against slightly less than half those from Manhattan.

2. In his autobiography, George B. McClellan, Jr., states that Cleveland told him the story was apocryphal. George B. McClellan, Jr., *The Gentleman and the Tiger*, Harold C. Syrett, Ed., Philadelphia: J. B. Lippincott Co., 1956, p. 311.

3. Conrad M. Arensberg, *The Irish Countryman*, London: The Macmillan Company, 1937, p. 178.

4. Cecil Woodham-Smith, *The Great Hunger*, New York: Harper & Row, 1962, pp. 27 ff.

5. Lincoln Steffens, *Autobiography*, New York: Harcourt, Brace and Co., 1931, p. 236.

6. Arensberg, *op. cit.*, p. 107.

7. *Ibid.*, p. 179.

8. William L. Riordon, *Plunkitt of Tammany Hall*, New York: Knopf, 1948, pp. 107–108.

62

The Economic Payoff of Attending an Ivy-League Institution

PHILIP J. COOK AND ROBERT H. FRANK

Many of our best and brightest high-school seniors know what most of our higher-education leaders have been reluctant to admit: An increasingly small number of colleges and universities have become the gatekeepers for society's top-paying jobs.

Look at the legal profession. Lawyers who deal with mergers and business acquisitions, for example, receive just a small percentage of the money that changes hands in the transactions that they negotiate, but their fees can amount to millions of dollars in multibillion-dollar deals. Not surprisingly many bright and ambitious young people ask themselves, "How can I get a job as a Wall Street lawyer?"

Wall Street law firms typically are inundated with applications for each entry-level position and will not grant interviews to graduates of any but the top law schools. And how does one gain admission to such a school? The surest route is to have been an outstanding student at one of a handful of prestigious colleges and universities.

In past decades, many of our best students attended state universities close to home, where they often received an excellent education at reasonable cost. Today, such students are likely to be vying for admission to the nation's most elite colleges and universities. Does this widening of the "prestige gap" between elite and lower-tier institutions, this "tracking" of students into educational institutions by their ability, raise matters of public concern? Or are these shifts simply of interest to institutions at or near the top? We think they raise issues of general social importance.

The increased interest of top students in attending the most prestigious institutions is easily documented. During the 1980s for example 59 per cent of the finalists in the Westinghouse Science Talent Search (one of the nation's premier academic contests for high-school students) chose to enroll at one of just seven institutions—Cornell, Harvard, Princeton, Stanford, and Yale universities, the California Institute of Technology, and the Massachusetts Institute of Technology. The same seven institutions led the list in the 1970s, but enrolled only 48 per cent of the Westinghouse finalists.

Further, by 1990, about 43 per cent of students scoring above 700 on the verbal section of the Scholastic Assessment Test chose one of the 30 "most competitive" colleges listed in *Peterson's Guide to Four Year Colleges*, up from 32 per cent in 1979. And Richard Spies, vice-president for finance at Princeton, has estimated that from 1976 to 1987, the probability increased by about half that a student with a combined S.A.T. score above 1,200

CHRON. HIGHER ED., January 5, 1996, at B3. Originally published in the *Chronicle of Higher Education*. Reprinted by permission of the authors.

would apply to one of the 33 elite private institutions belonging to the Consortium on Financing Higher Education. This trend in applications has continued into the 1990s.

The quest for a high-paying job is clearly not the only cause of the increased concentration of top students at prestigious colleges and universities. Travel costs are lower now, and elite institutions have increased their efforts to attract talented students from outside their traditional applicant pools. Even more important, demographic and economic trends have made elite institutions increasingly affordable and therefore attractive to more families.

Households headed by well-educated older workers—which provide a disproportionate share of the top students—have enjoyed substantial growth in income since the early 1970s. This period also has witnessed a steep decline in the average number of children in the families of college-age youths. Thus despite a doubling of tuition (in constant dollars) since 1979 in the Ivy League, for example, an elite private education has actually become more affordable for a substantial share of the relevant market. But we cannot escape the conclusion that the growing economic payoff of obtaining a degree from an elite college is driving the concentration of top students at such institutions.

In our recent book, *The Winner-Take-All Society* (The Free Press, 1995), we document a large increase in inequality of earnings *within* every white-collar profession. The number of Americans earning more than $120,000 a year (in 1989 dollars) doubled during the 1980s. While median earnings were stagnant in most of the white-collar professions during that time, more than 60 per cent of the increased number of Americans earning more than $120,000 a year had incomes at the top end of the salary scales for executives, physicians, lawyers, sales representatives, and other professionals. Thus, people in those occupations had a greater chance of earning a six-figure income not because of general growth in earnings in their profession, but because of increased compensation for those at the top. A degree from an elite college long has helped graduates gain high-status jobs—and the payoff of those jobs has grown sharply.

A self-reinforcing process of the "rich get richer" sort also underlies the concentration of top students at a few institutions. Athletics directors understand this process well, knowing that a successful football season one year will make it easier to recruit top players the next. On the academic side, as more and more top students have chosen elite institutions the gap in academic prestige between Ivy U. and State U. has widened. This, in turn, has provided an even more compelling reason for students to choose an elite college.

As Thomas Ehrlich, provost of the University of Pennsylvania during the mid-1980s, has put it: "The wonderful thing is that the more successful you are, the more successful you are. The more you hear Penn is the institution of choice the more you want to come." This process is strengthened by the now-ubiquitous rankings of undergraduate colleges, and by the way the quality of an institution's students affects its ability to recruit the best faculty members. Further, the amount of income earned by alumni affects the amount of alumni giving, reinforcing an institution's desire to attract students likely to earn high incomes.

But we should recognize that the increased concentration of top students at elite institutions entails both benefits and costs. Perhaps the most important benefit is that gifted students have access not only to the best faculty members, but also to one another. To the extent that society's top jobs always have been filled through networks of contacts that originate in elite universities, such jobs now are more likely to be filled by our most able students. If so, America's standing in the global economy will benefit.

But obvious concerns about equity remain. If America aspires to be the land of the second chance, we lose something important when so many top jobs are closed to students unable to attend a prestigious institution. Able youths who do not grow up in an environment conducive to academic excellence or who bloom intellectually after high school are at a greater disadvantage now, when a degree from the local state university leaves them economically further behind Ivy League graduates than would have been the case a generation ago. We are troubled by the image of an "overclass" of high achievers propelled by their elite credentials while graduates from other colleges find it increasingly difficult to compete.

Concerns about equity will be mitigated as long as many elite institutions retain their commitment to "need-blind" admissions, offering financial aid that meets the needs of all admitted students, while generally avoiding merit-based scholarships. If a college admits students without regard to their financial standing and provides them with whatever aid they need, no top student will be prevented from attending an elite institution because of financial concerns. On the other hand, if such institutions use financial aid to compete with one another for the very best students—regardless of family income—little money may be left for the poor or middle-class students of slightly less academic merit who nonetheless qualify for admission.

Will elite institutions continue to follow need-blind policies and to shun merit-based awards? To attract better students a number of public and private second-tier institutions already have modified their approach to financial assistance, increasingly awarding aid based on academic merit rather than financial need. We doubt that the top-tier institutions will stick to their democratic commitment in the face of this competition. We may see some of them reduce financial aid to needy students who are not of star quality, in order to put more money into merit scholarships.

Just as a college or university can improve its standing by bidding for star faculty members, so can it improve by bidding for top students. Indeed, sought-after students already have begun to negotiate with competing institutions over the terms of their financial-aid packages. At the nation's leading business schools, for example, financial aid for non-minority students already is based almost totally on merit.

It is highly likely that the increased concentration of the most-talented students at prestigious institutions will continue. Look at the case of Jim Besaw. In the spring of 1994, as a top senior at a Minnesota public high school, he turned down a full scholarship to Carleton College, a small, highly selective liberal-arts college in his native state. Although his father was retired and his mother earned only $8,000 a year, he enrolled at Yale.

"I'm willing to lose some money now and take out a loan," he explained, "because I feel I might get a better job if I go to one of the more prestigious schools." Many other students apparently agree; Yale's applications rose 21 per cent that year and continued at the same level in 1995.

What can we do about this situation? No easy solutions suggest themselves, because what we're experiencing grows out of a complex mix of economic, demographic, and social factors. But we at least need to begin talking openly about the fact that it is occurring—and about its social costs.

63

Useful Knowledge

MARY CAPPELLO

To Whom It May Concern: I am not what I have tried to be! Will I ever be able to write a few words correctly? Will I ever learn not to misspell words? No. Never. I am a cobbler.
    From the journal of my grandfather, John Petracca

In the process of becoming official, of gaining the authority to reproduce knowledges about the history of private and public utterances in the United States, in entering the academy as an assistant professor of English, I have experienced in many ways the not-so-subtle necessity of having to move as far away as possible from who I am. When I think "working class," pictures come to me more readily than words, thus signaling this aspect as perhaps the most unspeakable feature of my identity in academe. I am, after all, much more aware of how even my lesbianism, an obvious site of censorship, shapes my interpretations of literature in and out of the classroom than I am of how my working-class upbringing does. My working-class background may be my best kept secret.

Woman/lesbian/feminist/Italian American no doubt intersect *working class*, and yet I only narrate myself as working class through the figure of once-within-a-place. Insofar as I have learned to affiliate my class position (in contradistinction to other subject positions) with its material evidence, its signs, it makes sense that *working class* in my story conjures architectures: row home; playgrounds like minefields of unsuspected debris, rusted shopping carts that scarred faces and legs; resounding edifice of Catholic church and Catholic school, hallowed heights and peculiar smells of incense or the sawdust meant to quell the tang of vomit. Yet I also suspect that my affiliation of class with the somewhere that I left when I entered this profession is the fresh retelling of its sequestering by the middle-class authority of the academy.

Why have I not, after five years in graduate school and four years as an assistant professor at both a prestigious private and a sprawling state university, been able or compelled to position myself as from the working class? Are there ways of imagining working-class experience vis-à-vis higher education that wouldn't presuppose a movement up? (Up and away?) What's at stake in the refusal to implicate one's working-class markings in the work of teaching people how to reinterpret the representations that shape their real lives? What happened in the university—undergraduate studies at Dickinson College, graduate work at SUNY-Buffalo, tenure-track positions at the University of Rochester and the University of Rhode Island—must not be imagined as antithetical to what happened in Darby, Pennsylvania, where I grew up. Even though each locale played its part in negating the other, each was and is always complicit with the other. Each was and is equally threatening to the other though not equally damaging or devastating, for the violence with which academe keeps working-class people from entering its domain is not exactly equivalent to the resistance that working-class people might have to that space.

My father, a sheet-metal worker at the Philadelphia Naval Shipyard for forty years, suffers from asbestosis as a result of one of his jobs. My mother was a housewife/poet and closet political activist who suffered from agoraphobia for many years. Credentials aside, what I remember and affiliate my working-class identity with are (too thin) walls and broken, split-open bodies accompanied by the eventual dawning of the illusion of upward mobility. To be working class was always to be in a simultaneous state of surround and transparency. Surround: my neighborhood was cacophonous with the noise of work and rage. Someone inevitably had his visor lowered to extra welding in his garage on the weekends; or a hammering job that threatened to split the fragile foundations of the neighborhood would pound out from the small fenced-in patch that was an amateur boxer's backyard. Houses did not communicate with one another so much as they interfered in their married proximity with one another. No community to speak of, except at church, where contributions were the key to success no one could purchase. Transparency: being astonished and embarrassed to discover that I could see my family's unselfconscious movements from the window of my friend's house across the street.

But the violence of seeing and being seen and of being forced to listen and being wholly heard was outdone by the violence of body opening body, of male against male or male against female. He spun him round and threw him onto the cement; he grabbed him by the shirt collar and threatened to choke him; the father beat the small boy/as the boy grew older, he ordered the father to beat him; the boxer smashed the face of a gang member in a public place/the victim's buddies sought revenge and "accidentally" shot the boxer's little girl (age eight) through the back of her head. Such violence was not, as is stereotypically assumed in the United States, a way of life for Italian Americans per se. The neighborhood was mostly populated by Anglo, Irish, and African Americans who shared, though never exactly or equivalently, a rage-inducing class status. On Concord Road, my family were the minority "wops" among wasps. Take, for example, an incident I recall from elementary-school English class. We were learning about characterization in literature, and the teacher, Miss DiBonaventura, asked David Lemon to characterize me: "She has little feet, curly hair, and she's a wop," he said. Obviously, he had never considered that our teacher's mellifluous name might have a Mediterranean origin, and so he was forced to apologize to her and to me.

This is the narrative that brought me to school: escape, study, read, apply, and the world of the Ivy League will open up to you its contemplative flower and the noise will subside. Following a dominant mythology that persists in our national consciousness today, I had equated higher education with the Ivy League, picturing the Ivy League as a world of richer textures and finer sounds than those I knew. It was a fantasy reserved for a select number of us in high school. One inspiring English teacher who was deeply connected to certain of nearby Philadelphia's pulses, film and theater in particular, occasionally chose a few of us for the golden opportunity to join her on excursions to such events. *The* university from our parochial point of view was Penn; Princeton, though, was not far off. Its flower, I thought, would open up to me. I was sensitive and it deserved to be mine.

The flower crumpled in one short interview and one clipped rejection—two out of three of my postsecondary-school options, for my family could only afford for me to apply to three schools. Nearby Swarthmore College had sent a representative to our high school (Darby-Colwyn) to interview those of us at the top of the class. We were told they had a full four-year scholarship that might be offered to one of us. At my interview's end, my interlocutor jokingly asked, "Do you play football?" then went on to offer his evaluation of me to our guidance counselor: "She's short but perky," he said. There must have been something wrong: I'd worked hard, I was the class valedictorian and a class leader. Soon after this disappointment, I received a rejection from Princeton University, only to learn that a less scholastically able football player at my high school was accepted there. The repetition made the message clear. Not only was passage to higher education going to be rare, but the only ticket in might be the body, and at that, only a particular version of the body: the brawniest child of labor, the buxom male body burst from the working-class frame was recruited to carry the transcendent-of-class Latinate insignia.

Ever after this and in spite of the richly creative years I have known in higher education, there always has lurked a feeling of lack of fit between the contours of my knowledge and the academician's garb. I falter in announcing it, however, for a subordinate class position is already over-accompanied by that most impoverished of emotions, pity. Sympathy, understanding, will not do. The borderline state, the sense of being neither here nor there persists: the working-class academic can never fully "move in." The people from your former life refuse to understand what you do; in your new one, what happens at the dinner table will always give you away: arranging silverware was not part of your training. You know and you don't know, and what you don't know is worth more to your professional position. You know how to play Italian folksongs on the mandolin; you know how to play beeries and basketball; you know how to plant an unpatterned garden (weeds can be beneficial too); you know what a gunshot sounds like; you know the fear of impending violence, the padding of feet down a corridor of no return; you know to expect the spillage of somebody's pain into the festivities. You don't know how to color-coordinate your wardrobe; you've never found glasses to fit your face; you don't know how to play tennis. You know how to shut out external noise, yet you don't know how to shut out demands that will exploit you as a junior woman faculty member at any university. You feel you have missed something. All the awards and honors cannot convince you "you're in." You still think analogically in a profession that welcomed you into its precincts for your clarity and logic.

This is where some new vantage is required, where the fissures created by the narrative of was and is need to be puzzled out without being figured into a middle-class penchant for neatness. The most obvious observation I can make about the preceding diagnostic profile is its emphasis on lack. Feminist writers especially have exposed the myth of lack as it has been applied for centuries to the marginalized—women, African Americans, and the working class, among other subalterns. We're told women lack aptitude for the public sphere; blacks lack the ambition to better their position; working-class people lack consciousness of their condition. These are some of the readiest instances of dominant displacement, and while they are easily enough exposed for their invalidity, easily enough indicative of the fragility of the center that insists upon them, they have wreaked havoc in people's psychological dispositions that are none too easily repaired or are all too easily given over to the "cures" of the systems that oppress. Higher education in the United States has done much to reinforce lack across the bodies and minds of women, working-class people, and people of color, in part by insisting that they sever themselves from an identity designated as "prior" to their entry into academe, as though it were as simple as leaving one's baggage at the door.

But what had been deemed lack is now better understood as delegitimized knowledge, knowledge that needs to be acknowledged—a task that is difficult for student and teacher alike. As a working-class student, I should have been encouraged to interrogate aloud the homogeneous student body that I was ever aware of—redundantly thin and appallingly white. Rather than quiet the noise of the working-class neighborhood now internalized along with other cultural voices, rather than transmute the distracting din into a convincingly serene Muzak, we might learn to mine such sounds for their worth, their instructive tension. I am reminded of Henry James's governess in *The Turn of the Screw*, whose escape from lower to upper class provokes hallucinations. Shocked by the repressions exacted by her new world and by the disillusion of the so-called real world she's entered, she starts to "see things." I want to suggest that we can't afford to get sick like the governess on realizing how the middle class uses the working class as a screen for what's most aberrant about itself; we can't afford to work our psyches into a permanent grimace because of the lack of fit of working-class face to middle-class mask. Instead, we need to tell the things we see as what we know: a knowledge that is just as valid as any and possibly more instructive than most. But this would require from the outset that students be encouraged NOT to assume they already know everything about themselves, the student sitting next to them, their teacher, and the texts we put in front of them. Students become disappointed and confused to learn that their teachers—people whom they've come to enjoy and respect and who may even have changed their lives—might not share their upper-crust background or their heterosexual disposition.

A year or so ago I was asked to serve on a board at the University of Rochester consisting of faculty and administrators who were to evaluate a questionnaire meant to measure the university's strengths and weaknesses in the eyes of seniors exiting the university. I took issue at the contradistinction embedded in these two questions: "To what extent have you learned to appreciate literature, music and art?" and "To what extent have you learned to understand the role of science in society?" Since I had been teaching my students to deconstruct binaries like "appreciate and understand," "art and science," and especially to analyze literature in terms of its material circumstance and ideological implications, I felt that the questionnaire would misrepresent what I do. I also hoped that any student who had studied with me would not have known how to answer the questions. When I announced my position to the group, they looked confused and aghast. I tried putting it another way: "I don't teach literature so that my students will know what play to go to in their leisure time after a hard day in the lab." Rather than persuading my audience with clarity, I provoked further disdain as another faculty member retorted that surely I must know that we have an obligation to help our students to "become bourgeois." (He wasn't kidding.) Another responded that it would be a crime if we didn't help our students to "enjoy fine music." Now I would never deny that as an educator I am complicit with the middle-class establishment. Education is pretty high on Althusser's list of "ideological state apparatuses," and I do enjoy the privileges of the middle class: a space that shelters me from pain and enables me to escape oppressive forms of labor, a space for making my version of class intelligible and valid, enough room to make choices in, material comfort, and mobility. But I also still have hope that the university can be an agent for social change even if my working-class students (though it's hard to know who they are) may want this kind of knowledge least, and I feel most disabled when it comes to finding ways to use precisely the space of this privilege to meet my working-class kin where they live. . . .

My family is dark complexioned and curly-haired, except for my grandmother, who always expressed a feeling of good fortune at having fair skin and blue eyes. "Most people" she would proudly announce, "think that I'm Irish." Even if the formation of Italian American immigrant identities can in no way be compared with the history of the African or Chicano in the United States, shared class affiliation and broadly conceived ethnic features within white hegemony render us familiar. It may be that in the United States we *really* and not just imaginatively have lives in common. Nevertheless, I am not aware of any work in cultural studies on the real and fantasized identifications forged between people of color and Italian Americans in the United States, and film director Spike Lee's attempts to represent serious neighborhood rivalries in New York City between blacks and Italians unfortunately depend upon brutish fabulations of Italian-American sensibility, now reduced to a rude or beautiful face.

In popular cultural representations of the Italian American, words fail her or make him out to be dumbly poetic. Indeed, the ideological linkage of my particular ethnic identity with my class made me a highly unlikely candidate for higher education, even if my own experience of being Italian in America was daily marked by my family's unfailing attention to the nuance, power, and range of voice, an unacknowledged literacy.

To return to the epigraph from my grandfather John Petracca's (1900–1972) journal, a kind of letter to the world: "To Whom It May Concern: I am not what I have tried to be! Will I ever be able to write a few words correctly? Will I ever learn not to misspell words? No. Never. I am a cobbler." The "No. Never" in this passage haunts me. It's a dead weight that contradicts my grandfather's life's work—the mountains of lore, short stories, letters, aphorisms that he composed in his shoe repair shop and jotted onto the material of his trade, whole treatises squeezed onto the backs of the tabs used to mark down what part of the shoe needed fixing, with a word inevitably broken by the hole-punched O at the top or bottom of the tab. My grandfather hoped to be a writer, and he was. My grandfather hoped to express his thoughts and feelings in the language of the new culture he had entered, but this presented a variety of problems. To be a laborer and a writer in this culture was not allowed; there were no means by which his writing could become public. He wore the mantle of English uncomfortably; sometimes English simply was not adequate to his task. Two generations later, I am unable to read the passages he produced in Italian: the language, and with it, the ineffable and therefore perhaps most pressing aspects of my familial and class identity have been erased from the realm of useful knowledge.

In spite of what I have yet to know, I remain sure that speech, song, and the written word were survival tactics for my family. In the Depression years, my grandfather seems to have used irony in his journal as a strategy for getting by and as a tool for restaking his dislodged self:

> It is cloudy and warm. The water company served notice threatening to close my supply of water if I don't pay my bill! Is it not grand? And to think that here we have no public water places where I could fetch it home! 1 PM—The Gas and Electric Company has sent its two cents in. I must be a prominent person, for everyone points his finger at me!

While my grandmother suffered through multiple pregnancies, my great-grandmother told her comic tales from her peasant town to make her laugh and danced for her to ease the pain. My mother gave to my father some of the most impassioned and persuasive speeches on civil rights that I have ever heard. In the early seventies, she wrote feminist sermons for a progressive parish priest; she used her poetry to leave the church and the bad marriage to which it yoked her and to enter a new, more various, city-bound community as a small-press editor and an organizer of readings and forums. But, powerful as writing, music, or the spoken word might be, none of these media could ever really materialize as divining rod. If the water company turns the water off, so shall it be. Poetry readings won't bring the bacon home, so my mother struggles daily as a legal secretary against the delegitimizing of her experience and knowledge, her identity. A working-class person's daily thoughts, a shoemaker's poetry, may be just the resources higher education needs to divine itself, to plumb the depths of its mechanisms of exclusion, its refusals to know or to find marginal knowledge(s), in the best sense of the word, useful.

64

Stupid Rich Bastards

LAUREL JOHNSON BLACK

Sunday morning, six o'clock. Dad knocks on my door and in a stage whisper tells me to get up and get going. Trying not to wake up my sister, I crawl out of bed into the chilly Massachusetts air and pull on jeans, a T-shirt, a sweatshirt, and sneakers. Nothing that can't get dirty. This isn't church, but it might as well be, an education full of rituals, its own language, its mystery and rewards, its punishments for falling away.

Every Sunday, each child in turn went with Dad to the flea markets, the yard sales, the junk yards, the little stores with names like "Bob's Salvage," "Junk n Stuff," or "The Treasure House." Even in winter, when the outdoor flea markets closed down and leaves spun with litter in circles in the yards, the salvage stores stood waiting for us, bleak and weathered, paint hanging in little flaps from the concrete-block walls, and our breath hanging in the still, frigid air surrounding the old desks and radio tubes, the file cabinets and chandeliers. In each place the man behind the counter would grab the lapels of his old wool coat and pull them tighter around him, saying how one day he'd like to heat the joint. Dad would tell him about the great buy we just saw at the last place but had to pass up this time and then ask him what was new. And each time the answer was, "In heayah? Nothin's evah new! But I got some stuff I didn't have befoah!" They'd laugh with one another, and I would trace my initials next to someone else's in the dust on the display cabinet.

In summer, we passed by the vendors who hawked T-shirts, socks, perfume, or cheap jewelry and walked to the tables covered with stuff from home, tables full of things that someone had wanted and needed for a long time until they needed money more, to pay their rent, fix their car, or feed the next child. Wall hangings, little plaques, beverage glasses with superheroes on them, ashtrays, bedspreads, tricycles, lawn mowers, table lamps, kitchen pots and pans, picture frames, shoes, a spice rack. Always behind one of these tables stood an older man, deeply tanned and showing muscles from long years of hard work, gray-haired and with a cigarette and a hopeful smile, always willing to come down a little on an item, even though it meant a lot to him. Sometimes his wife would also be there, heavy, quiet, holding a styrofoam cup of coffee, sitting in a webbed lawn chair set back a little from the table, judging those who would judge the things she had loved and used for so long.

We touched these items carefully, with respect, because we were that child who needed to be fed, because we knew what it felt like to have your things laid on such a table, touched by many hands and turned over and over while the dew burned off and the pavement heated up and people began to move as though through water, their legs lost in the shimmering heat that slipped sticky arms around buyers, sellers, lookers, and dreamers. And the *language* of these people behind the tables, and those who respected them and understood why they were there, filled the air like the smell of French fries from the dirty little restaurant next door and hung in my mind and sifted down into my heart. . . .

Language for me has always been inseparable from what I am, from what and who people are. My house was filled with the language I associate with the working class and the poor, people who haven't the means to keep all the "dirty" parts of life at bay and who see no reason to do so with words. Shouting to each other across the yards in the old mill town where I grew up, my mother and her friends Pat and Barbara kept up their friendship and shared gossip and complaints about their lives. They wove their voices into the fabric of words and life I knew. As we played after school in the stand of woods along the river down behind the factory, we heard our names called for supper. The more time we took to get home to the table, the sharper the tone became and the longer the wonderful string of curses stretched out, echoing off the brick walls.

We talked about whatever had touched us as we sat down to eat—who had stopped up the upstairs toilet, who had fought in the hallway at school, the girl who was stabbed in the head with a fork in the lunchroom, name calling on the bus, whether the home economics teacher was having an affair with the phys. ed. teacher, what my father saw in the house he'd just put a tub in, who we knew who'd been arrested. Bodily functions, secretions, garbage, crimes and delinquency, who got away with what were as much a part of our language as they were of our lives. They were part of the humor that filled my home. My father rising up from his chair to fart, shouting out in mock seriousness, " 'Repoaht from the reah!' the sahgent replied," set us off in hysterics, imitations, and stories of passed gas and the contexts that made them so funny. Swearing was also a part of our lives—among adults, among kids away from their parents, and in the bad kids' homes, everyone swore fluently before they were eighteen or out of school. "Damn" and "shit" were every other word and so became like "and" and "well" to us as we talked with each other.

I lived in a web of narrative, something I've missed in graduate school. My father was a storyteller and a traveler, would go away for a week or two at a time on "business" of an undetermined nature. When he came back, he didn't bring presents but stories. Only a few years ago did I realize why the tale of Odysseus had seemed so familiar to me in the eighth grade and again as an undergraduate. In the tales told by my father and the men he bartered with, the "stupid rich bastards" almost always "got it" in the end, outwitted by the poor little guy. I learned that the stupid rich bastards always underestimated us, always thought we were as dumb as we were poor, always mistook our silence for ignorance, our shabby clothes and rusted cars for lack of ambition or enterprise. And so they got taken, and sharing stories about winning these small battles made us feel better about losing the war.

My father knew all the regular merchants at the flea markets. As we wandered along the aisles he'd yell over to Tony, a heavy man with thinning black hair patted into an ugly, oily arc across his head, "Hey! Ya fat Guinea! Ya still sellin' the same old junk? Huh? I've seen stuff move fasta in the toilets I unplug!" Tony would wave him off, turning a little away from him and throwing back over his shoulder, "What would you know about merchandise, ya stupid Swede? Huh? Shit for brains!" He'd touch his forehead with his middle finger, grin maliciously, and so would my father. As we worked our way closer to Tony, past the booth with old tools, past the book booth, Dad would ask, "So why haven't the cops bustid ya yet for alla this, Tony? What, you got a captain on ya payroll? This stuff is hot enough to burn ya hands off!" He'd blow on his fingers and wave them in the air, grinning. Tony grinned back at the compliment. "Naah, I buy this legit." He'd widen his eyes and look cherubic. "Really." They'd both laugh.

During the week, my father was a sometimes plumber, sometimes car salesman, sometimes junkman. My mother worked as a cook, a school crossing guard, a McDonald's clerk. It was never enough. I remember one Saturday afternoon in August, my father was melting down old lead pipes. All afternoon he cut the soft pipes into small pieces and fed them into the heat of the kettle, then poured the liquid metal out into the little cupcake-shaped molds he'd set in the dirt of the driveway. Late in the afternoon, the heavy clouds broke and rain began spattering down on his back and shoulders. While I watched from the kitchen he kept working, the rain hissing and turning into steam as it struck the melting lead. Over and over, he reached forward to drop chunks of pipe in to melt, and his arms, then shoulders, then head disappeared in the fog of metal and mist. He became that man to me, the half-man in steam. He was the back I saw sometimes wearily climbing the stairs to sleep for a few hours. He was the chains rattling in the truck as it bounced down the pitted driveway and whined back up late at night as he came home. It wasn't enough. A stack of dunnings and notices littered the end of the old stereo.

I remember when the man from the bank came to repossess our car. I had just broken my foot, and I hung onto the car door handle while my mother stood next to me talking to the man who wanted to take the car. Her voice was high, and with one hand she opened and closed the metal clasp on her purse. Finally she opened the car door, pushing me in and sliding in next to me. The man from the bank stepped back as she started the engine, and she rolled up the window as he leaned over to say something to us. She gunned it, careening wildly backward across the yard out into the street, crying. "So this is what we've got," she said. "This is it."

Working poor, we were alternately afraid and ashamed and bold and angry. We prayed to nothing in particular that no one would notice our clothes or that the police wouldn't notice the car didn't have a valid inspection sticker. My mother had to decide between a tank of gas and an insurance payment. She had to decide whether or not we really needed a doctor. We shopped as a group so that if my new dress for the year cost two dollars less than we had thought it would, my sister could get one that cost two dollars more. We didn't say such things out loud, though we thought them all the time. If I ate seconds, maybe I was eating my sister's dress. If Susan was really sick, then maybe I couldn't get new shoes. But if anyone ever said those things, it would all come crashing in. All of it—the idea that working hard would get you some place better, that we were just as good as anyone else— would crash to the floor like some heirloom dish that would never be the same again, even if we could find all the shards.

At some point in my life, when I was very young, it had been decided that I would be the one who went on to college, who earned a lot of money, who pulled my family away from the edge of the pit, and who gave the stupid rich bastards what they had coming to them. I would speak like them but wouldn't be one of them. I would move among them, would spy on them, learn their ways, and explain them to my own people—a guerrilla fighter for the poor. My father had visions of litigation dancing in his head, his daughter in a suit, verbally slapping the hell out of some rich asshole in a courtroom.

As I was growing up, the most important people I knew, the ones I most respected, were my teachers. I wanted to be like them. They had made the supreme sacrifice, had gone away and succeeded, but had chosen to come back to help us. They drove cars I could imagine appearing occasionally in my father's lot. They wore scuffed shoes and shopped at K-Mart.

They didn't belong to a country club, didn't refuse to teach us because we were poor, didn't treat us with pity or condescension. They often worked year round, teaching summer school or even, as with my history teacher, driving a beer truck from June through August.

They were the only people I knew and trusted who might be able to teach me to speak like and understand the stupid rich bastards who held our lives in their hands and squeezed us until we couldn't breathe: doctors who refused to treat us without money up front; lawyers who wrote short, thick, nasty letters for credit companies; insurance agents who talked in circles and held up payment; loan officers who disappeared into the backs of banks and didn't look at us when they told us we were too much of a risk; police and town selectmen who told us to get rid of our cars and clean up our disgraceful yards and lives—all the people who seemed always to be angry that they had to deal with us in any way. My teachers moved, I thought, with ease between my world and this other world. I hoped they would help me do the same.

My teachers tried to bridge the gap with speech. "In other words," they said, looking from the text to us, "what they're saying is . . ." They tried to bridge the gap with their bodies, one hand pointing to the board, the other hand stretched out palm up, fingers trying to tug words from mouths contorted with the effort to find the right speech. We were their college-bound students, the ones who might leave, might be them again, might even do better. They were like our parents in their desire to have us succeed, but they had skills and knowledge that counted to the white-shirted men who sat behind the glass windows at the savings and loan, to the woman who handled forms for free butter, cheese, and rice.

I wanted to be like my teachers, but I was afraid of standing up before a classroom filled with students like the ones who laughed in the back of the classroom. The only writing these students did was carving names and sexual slurs or boasts on their desks, and their dreams, I imagined, were of lives like they already knew. I was afraid, too, that when I had become like these teachers I admired so much, I would still drive down the main street of a rotting industrial town and go into the 7-Eleven and somehow I would be no different than I was now. The very ones I admired most I also most suspected: if my teachers were such successes, why were they back here? Why did they make so little money? Drive those cars? I was afraid I would have nothing to say or show to the students who sat in the back, afraid that if they actually asked what I only thought—"So what?"—I would have no answer. . . .

I decided on three colleges, all small, private ones because I was afraid of the throngs of students in the brochures for the state schools. Some of the schools had said they were "teaching institutions"; I avoided those too, believing that I would have to become a teacher if I went there. I was going to be a lawyer, was going to fulfill my father's vision. I was going to go where the kids of lawyers went. I filled out forms largely on my own, knowing that my parents didn't understand the questions and would be embarrassed at not being able to help. I took all the standardized tests and did only okay, confused by analogies of bulls and bears (I thought they referred to constellations, not the stock market) and questions about kinds of sailing boats.

When my first-choice college sent me a letter telling me I was on their waiting list, my mother hugged me and told me how proud she was. My father asked me how long I'd have to wait and if I'd work in the meantime. My mother thought that merely making the waiting list was an achievement, something she could brag about to Pat and Barbara and the mailman, while my father thought that there was only a limited number of spaces in colleges all over the country and each student waited in turn to get in. I went upstairs and cried for hours. When I came back down for supper, my mother had fixed a cake in celebration.

I was in my first English class at my second-choice school, never having made it off the waiting list at the first one. I'd never visited this college and knew little about it. I hadn't gone to orientation, begging off because of work. Actually, I had begun to look at those smiling catalogue faces and bodies and then to look at myself. I had crooked teeth. I wore makeup. I wasn't tanned and lithe from summers of tennis and sailing. I wore old jeans patched at the thighs and ragged around the cuffs. I wore T-shirts and work boots, not clothing from L. L. Bean's. I read statements from the happy students, moving my lips and trying to make the words sound like they could be mine, but I realized that it was wrong, that I was wrong. What could I say to all these people? What could they say to me? And what people did I belong to? . . .

Now I was here, dropped off by my sister and brother, who had turned the car around and headed for home after dumping off my box and bag. My roommate was crying because she couldn't fit all her Pendleton wools in her closet and drawers and had taken over some of mine. Her father, a successful lawyer, sized up the situation, watching me sit in silence in my flannel shirt and unfashionable jeans. "What should we call you?" he asked politely. I thought for a moment. "Johnson." He laughed delightedly. "Johnson? That's great! Sue, this'll be good for you," he chortled as he led his sniffling daughter and perfectly coiffed wife out to get lunch.

Now I was being asked to write editorials, but I didn't know what one was. My family had always bought the newspaper with the big photos in it, and the little local weekly had columns about who'd been arrested and what stores had gone out of business. I didn't understand the articles I had to read in order to write my editorials. I summarized what I'd read in two major paragraphs and turned it in, over and over, week after week. I got a B each time, no comments.

In French government class, students talked excitedly about their travels abroad. I felt the chip on my shoulder getting heavier and heavier. I'd been through all of New England; they'd been to France. Big fucking deal. Lions, Lee-ons, Lyons, it's all the same. Unless someone laughs at you for not knowing how to say what everyone else can not only say but describe from personal experience. Poetry class. I describe in a long narrative poem what things I see around my neighborhood. The teacher gushes over it. It reminds him of T. S. Eliot, he says, and when I say, "Who's that?" he is astounded. He decides he has a diamond in the rough; he calls me a lump of coal with lots of potential. (Later, he asks me if I want to sleep with him.)

I understand my students where I now teach. I understand their fear of poverty, of sliding backwards, of not being as successful as their very successful parents. They recoil in disgust and loathing from the poor, from the working class, and that, too, is familiar to me. They insist that if we all just try hard enough, everyone can succeed. But until then, they don't want to live with those who haven't really made it, who haven't tried. I understand how deep and visceral that fear of failure is. It keeps them in college. . . .

In the dormitories at night the girls gathered into groups in the lounges or on the hallway floors and told stories about their lives. I was silent, stricken dumb with fear. What would I tell them when my turn came? The truth? A lie? But I needn't have worried. My turn never came. I don't know whether it was out of compassion or snobbishness, but no one ever asked me about my family, my home, my friends, even my major or my hoped-for career. And as much as I hated myself for being ashamed of my life, I hated the girls more for knowing it. In my conferences with teachers I sat mute, nodding weakly when it seemed called for, when their voices rose as if in a question. Whatever they suggested was right. In lectures, I took notes furiously, narrative notes, full sentences, trying to get the exact words spoken by the teacher. I knew if I took down just a word here and there I would have to fill in the gaps with my own words, and those words were horribly wrong. I was horribly wrong.

Maybe my mother knew. She's dead now and I never asked her. But she wrote me letters every now and then, and not once did she say she'd like me back. Not once did she explicitly give me the option of returning. After one letter in which I came close to admitting my despair, she wrote back, "We love you and we're proud of you. Don't show your face in the door until you're supposed to."

I had gotten an F+ on an English paper. On the bottom of the last page, Dr. B. had written, "Come and see me about this." I was now a second-semester sophomore and still had not gotten an A in my major, English; in fact, I had barely survived the drinking and class cutting of my first year. My parents had never seen my grade report, only knew that I was allowed to come back a second year, more reason for pride. I had learned to buy my classmates' thrown-away clothes at the local thrift store, and if I kept my mouth shut I could pass as one of them in most of my classes. I stopped wearing makeup, even stopped sitting in the groups in the dorms. Instead, I worked in the library on Friday nights and Saturday mornings, which gave me an excuse (I imagined one day I would need one) for never going out and spending money with anyone on weekends. Now, though, I had to hide from teachers, the people I had once wanted so much to be like.

I went to Dr. B.'s office about one minute before his office hours were over. I made sure the secretary saw me and that I had a piece of paper to write a note like: "Stopped by to talk about my paper. I'll catch you some other time." I inched my way down the hall toward his door, reading the numbers so I could pretend I had missed him because I had gotten lost.

Dr. B. was still in his office. He welcomed me in, appearing surprised. He pulled his chair over next to mine, took my paper, and began to go over it, line by line, word by word. He peered over his little glasses, sometimes giving his head a violent nod so they would drop down on his chest and he could sit back and watch my reactions to his statements. I couldn't breathe. My chest felt like it was full, but I had no air. I didn't dare blink because my eyes were full of tears. I kept my head bent, my chin in my hand, and stared at my paper.

He sighed. Finally, he said something like, "Look. See this paragraph? This is a good one. There's a good idea in here. That's your idea. But it's not phrased well. Listen to it phrased this way." And he reread my idea in words that sounded like all my professors. Words that could have kept a stupid rich bastard listening. My idea. His words. But they were connected then. For the first time, I felt like I might make it through. I choked out a thank you, and he looked up, surprised. The conference wasn't over, but I was standing up. I thanked him again, stuffing the paper into my bookbag, and left before the tears came pouring down my face. I didn't know why I was crying, whether it was because I was so stupid that I got an F+ and had to sit there and make a nice man frustrated or because I felt that I could take that one paragraph and begin again, begin learning how to speak about what I thought and felt to people who weren't like me. Stupidity and relief. They've dogged me ever since. . . .

The phone rang at two in the morning. It was my little sister, sobbing and nearly hysterical. Her boyfriend, drunk or high on something, had leaped from a closet and attacked her. She had beaten him off, clubbing him with a brass statue that my mother had given her. Now, while two friends tried to stop her bleeding—she had a broken nose, broken ribs, a broken foot—she choked out why she had called.

"He said the apahtment was in his name an' I gotta be outta heyah tomorrow mohnin' or he's takin' all the stuff heyah an' sellin' it an' he'll keep the dog too! An' I OWN this stuff, I paid fuh it an' I pay the rent but I don't got anywayah to go. You know legal stuff, right? Laurel, ya gotta help me!" I searched my brain for what little I remembered from my pre-law days at college, a decade earlier. Now in a Ph.D. program in composition and rhetoric, far away from the gritty New England town where my sister lived and near which we grew up, I felt useless. Again. I began to ask her about her lease, to tell her about the Legal Aid Society; I even began to think out loud through cases from a textbook I remembered. Suddenly she interrupted me, screaming over the line, "Fuck you! Fuck you! Don't talk to me like college, talk to me like a sista!"

I remember the first time I chose to say to a professor, "Really!" instead of the more natural (to me), and what others might think of as more colorful, "Get outta heyah!" I remember when I began to believe that I might go into English and not law. It was a course on realism and naturalism. I began to tremble when I read *McTeague* [an 1899 novel by Frank Norris. Ed.]. Here were people I recognized! Here were characters who spoke like I did, who swore and hoped and dreamed for so damn little, for a place to stay that was clean, for respect, for something of their own that would last. Here were novels that showed that the poor weren't poor because they wanted to be, because they were lazy, but because of economic forces that smashed them down and kept them down, and here were stupid rich bastards shown as they were in my own life. Here were writers who had words that spoke to me, that invited me not to join in some fantasy world but to confront and describe my own *real* world.

My parents (and in some ways, my whole family) never got over my defection from law. I tried to soften the blow by going into archeology; while it paid little, it was at least exotic and held out the hope of discovering some kind of lost treasure—imagine, money without working! But it was reconstructing lives and words, not ancient cultures but my own culture, that I kept being drawn to. I have come through poetry, sales, admissions, and finally composition, where first-year students begin to learn how their words hurt and heal, probe and hide, reshape, connect, embrace, and gag. It is a field that feels like work, where the texts are of a home and life so close to the world that the arguments mean something. They are like "sista," not "college."

No one in my family has ever read what I write. No one has visited my office or my classroom. I tell my students about my family, though; I talk to them in my language to show them there are many ways to say things. When we share our writing, I share a letter to home, full of swear words, little jokes, scatological humor, assertions that will be accepted without evidence solely because my sister and I "know" what stupid rich bastards are like and what they will say and do. And then we look at an essay I've written and then a poem, all dealing with my life, with words. They begin to feel their own words working in different ways, different contexts, begin to value the phrases and words that make them one thing and understand that these same words make it hard to be another thing. For most of my students, these exercises are often just an interesting diversion from reading literature. Some of them write in their journals of their relief. They, too, are first-generation college students, working class, afraid and silent. They appear at my door, ready to talk, knowing that I have been there and do not entirely want to leave.

When I work with my colleagues, with "real" faculty, I say little. I rehearse what I will say if I can predict the course of a meeting, and I miss some of what is going on while I hold my speech in my head, waiting for the opening in which I will speak like them long enough to fool them into thinking I *am* one of them. I am and I am not. My father's dream of how I would live and move between two worlds, two ways of speaking and knowing, haunts me. I used to sit on the school bus on the way home from high school and look around at my classmates and wonder who would still be in my town in twenty years, who would go on, get out, succeed in ways that no one dreamed of. I used to think I would be one of those. Now I sometimes sit in meetings and classrooms and wonder who else would like to cut the shit and say what they feel. I feel suspended, dangling. If I put my toe down at any point, I might root there. I cannot move among the rich, the condescending, the ones who can turn me into an object of study with a glance or word, cannot speak like them, live in a house like them, learn their ways, and share them with my family without being disloyal to someone. I thought learning would make it easier for me to protect and defend my family, myself, but the more I learn the harder it is to passionately defend anything.

I am seeking a way to keep the language of the working class in academia, not just in my office with my working-class office mate, to nurture its own kind of vitality and rawness and directness, its tendency to ask "Why?" even as it says "Ah, what the fuck." I would like my colleagues to listen for the narratives embedded in their own writing, to feel the power of that movement forward just as they feel the power of the turning concept, the academic idea. And I would like my colleagues to turn my language over in their mouths with the same respect that my father and I turned over the items on those flea market tables.

65

How Did Jews Become White Folks?

KAREN BRODKIN SACKS

The late nineteenth and early decades of the twentieth centuries saw a steady stream of warnings by scientists, policymakers, and the popular press that "mongrelization" of the Nordic, or Anglo-Saxon, race—the real Americans—by inferior European races (as well as inferior non-European ones) was destroying the fabric of the nation. I continue to be surprised to read that America did not always regard its immigrant European workers as white, that it thought people from different nations were biologically different. My parents, first-generation U.S.-born eastern European Jews, are not surprised. They expect anti-Semitism to be part of the fabric of daily life, much as I expect racism to be part of it. They came of age in the 1920s and 1930s at the peak of anti-Semitism in the United States. Proud of their upward mobility, they think of themselves as pulling themselves up by their own bootstraps. I grew up during the 1950s in the Euro-ethnic New York suburb of Valley Stream, where Jews were simply one kind of white folks and where ethnicity meant little more to my generation than food and family heritage. Part of my familized ethnic heritage was the belief that Jews were smart and that our success was the result of our own efforts and abilities, reinforced by a culture that valued sticking together, hard work, education, and deferred gratification. Today, this belief in a Jewish version of Horatio Alger has become an entry point for racism by some mainstream Jewish organizations against African Americans and for opposition to affirmative action for people of color.

The United States has a long history of anti-Semitism and of beliefs that Jews were members of an inferior race. But American anti-Semitism was part of a broader pattern of late-nineteenth-century racism against all southern and eastern European immigrants, as well as against Asian immigrants. These views justified all sorts of discriminatory treatment, including closing the doors to immigration from Europe and Asia in the 1920s. This picture changed radically after World War II. Suddenly the same folks who promoted nativism and xenophobia were eager to believe that the Euro-origin people whom they had deported, reviled as members of inferior races, and prevented from immigrating only a few years earlier were now model middle-class white suburban citizens.

It was no epiphany that made those in power change their hearts, their minds, and our race. Instead, it was the biggest and best affirmative action program in the history of our nation, and it was for Euro-males. There are similarities and differences in the ways each of the European immigrant groups became "whitened." I want to tell the story in a way that links anti-Semitism to other varieties of anti-European racism, because this foregrounds what Jews shared with other Euro-immigrants and shows changing notions of whiteness to be part of America's larger system of institutional racism.

The U.S. "discovery" that Europe had inferior and superior races came in response to the great waves of immigration from southern and eastern Europe in the late nineteenth century. Before that time, European immigrants—including Jews—had been largely assimilated into the white population. The twenty-three million European immigrants who came to work in U.S. cities after 1880 were too many and too concentrated to disperse and blend. Instead, they piled up in the country's most dilapidated urban areas, where they built new kinds of working-class ethnic communities. Since immigrants and their children made up more than 70 percent of the population of most of the country's largest cities, urban America came to take on a distinctly immigrant flavor. The golden age of industrialization in the United States was also the golden age of class struggle between the captains of the new industrial empires and the masses of manual workers whose labor made them rich. As the majority of mining and manufacturing workers, immigrants were visibly major players in these struggles.

The Red Scare of 1919 clearly linked anti-immigrant to anti-working-class sentiment—to the extent that the Seattle general strike of native-born workers was blamed on foreign agitators. The Red Scare was fueled by economic depression, a massive postwar strike wave, the Russian revolution, and a new wave of postwar immigration. Strikers in steel, and the garment and textile workers in New York and New England, were mainly new immigrants. "As part of a fierce counteroffensive, employers inflamed the historic identification of class conflict with immigrant radicalism." Anti-Communism and anti-immigrant sentiment came together in the Palmer raids and deportation of immigrant working-class activists. There was real fear of revolution. One of President Wilson's aides feared it was "the first appearance of the soviet in this country."[1]

Not surprisingly, the belief in European races took root most deeply among the wealthy U.S.-born Protestant elite, who feared a hostile and seemingly unassimilable working class. By the end of the nineteenth century, Senator Henry Cabot Lodge pressed Congress to cut off immigration to the United States; Teddy Roosevelt raised the alarm of "race suicide" and took Anglo-Saxon women to task for allowing "native" stock to be outbred by inferior immigrants. In the twentieth century, these fears gained legitimacy thanks to the efforts of an influential network of aristocrats and scientists who developed theories of eugenics—breeding for a "better" humanity—and scientific racism. Key to these efforts was Madison Grant's influential *Passing of the Great Race*, in which he shared his discovery that there were three or four major European races, ranging from the superior Nordics of northwestern Europe to the inferior southern and eastern races of Alpines, Mediterraneans, and, worst of all, Jews, who seemed to be everywhere in his native New York City. Grant's nightmare was race mixing among Europeans. For him, "the cross between any of the three European races and a Jew is a Jew."[2] For Grant, race and class were interwoven: the upper class was racially pure Nordic, and the lower classes came from the lower races.

Far from being on the fringe, Grant's views resonated with those of the nonimmigrant middle class. A *New York Times* reporter wrote of his visit to the Lower East Side:

> This neighborhood, peopled almost entirely by the people who claim to have been driven from Poland and Russia, is the eyesore of New York and perhaps the filthiest place on the western continent. It is impossible for a Christian to live there because he will be driven out, either by blows or the dirt and stench. Cleanliness is an unknown quantity to these people. They cannot

be lifted up to a higher plane because they do not want to be. If the cholera should ever get among these people, they would scatter its germs as a sower does grain.[3]

Such views fell well within the mainstream of the early-twentieth-century scientific community. Grant and eugenicist Charles B. Davenport organized the Galton Society in 1918 to foster research and to otherwise promote eugenics and immigration restriction. Lewis Terman, Henry Goddard, and Robert Yerkes, developers of the so-called intelligence test, believed firmly that southeastern European immigrants, African Americans, American Indians, and Mexicans were "feebleminded." And indeed, more than 80 percent of the immigrants whom Goddard tested at Ellis Island in 1912 turned out to be just that. Racism fused with eugenics, the latter overlapping with the nativism of WASP aristocrats. During World War I, racism shaped the army's development of a mass intelligence test. Psychologist Robert Yerkes, who developed the test, became an even stronger advocate of eugenics after the war. Writing in the *Atlantic Monthly* in 1923, he noted:

> If we may safely judge by the army measurements of intelligence, races are quite as significantly different as individuals . . . [and] almost as great as the intellectual difference between negro and white in the army are the differences between white racial groups. . . .
>
> For the past ten years or so the intellectual status of immigrants has been disquietingly low. Perhaps this is because of the dominance of the Mediterranean races, as contrasted with the Nordic and Alpine.[4]

By the 1920s, scientific racism sanctified the notion that real Americans were white and came from northwest Europe. Racism animated laws excluding and expelling Chinese in 1882, and then closing the door to immigration by virtually all Asians and most Europeans in 1924. Northwestern European ancestry as a requisite for whiteness was set in legal concrete when the Supreme Court denied Bhagat Singh Thind the right to become a naturalized citizen under a 1790 federal law that allowed whites the right to become naturalized citizens. Thind argued that Asian Indians were the real Aryans and Caucasians, and therefore white. The Court countered that the United States only wanted blond Aryans and Caucasians, "that the blond Scandinavian and the brown Hindu have a common ancestor in the dim reaches of antiquity, but the average man knows perfectly well that there are unmistakable and profound differences between them today."[5] The 1930 census added its voice, distinguishing not only immigrant from "native" whites but also native whites of native white parentage, and native whites of immigrant (or mixed) parentage. In distinguishing immigrant (southern and eastern Europeans) from "native" (northwestern Europeans), the census reflected the racial distinctions of the eugenicist-inspired intelligence tests.

As the first of the Euro-immigrant groups to enter colleges in significant numbers, it wasn't surprising that Jews faced the brunt of discrimination there. The Protestant elite complained that Jews were unwashed, uncouth, unrefined, loud, and pushy. Harvard University President A. Lawrence Lowell, also a vice president of the Immigration Restriction League, was openly opposed to Jews at Harvard. The Seven Sisters schools had a reputation for "flagrant discrimination." M. Carey Thomas, Bryn Mawr president, may have been a feminist of a kind, but she also was an admirer of scientific racism and an advocate of immigration restriction. She "blocked both the admission of black students and the promotion of Jewish instructors."[6]

Anti-Semitic patterns set by these elite schools influenced standards of other schools, made anti-Semitism acceptable, and "made the aura of exclusivity a desirable commodity for the college-seeking clientele."[7] Fear that colleges "might soon be overrun by Jews" were publicly expressed at a 1918 meeting of the Association of New England Deans. In 1919 Columbia University took steps to decrease the number of entering Jews by a set of practices that soon came to be widely adopted. The school developed a psychological test based on the World War I army intelligence tests to measure "innate ability—and middle-class home environment" and redesigned the admission application to ask for religion, father's name and birthplace, a photo, and a personal interview.[8] Other techniques for excluding Jews, like a fixed class size, a chapel requirement, and preference for children of alumni, were less obvious. Sociologist Jerome Karabel has argued that these exclusionary efforts provided the basis for contemporary criteria for college admission that mix grades and test scores with criteria for well-roundedness and character, as well as affirmative action for athletes and children of alumni, which allowed schools to select more affluent Protestants. Their proliferation in the 1920s caused the intended drop in the number of Jewish students in law, dental, and medical schools; the period also saw the imposition of quotas in engineering, pharmacy, and veterinary schools.

Columbia's quota against Jews was well known in my parents' community. My father is very proud of having beaten it and of being admitted to Columbia Dental School on the basis of his sculpting skill. In addition to demonstrating academic qualifications, he was asked to carve a soap ball, which he did so well and fast that his Protestant interviewer was willing to accept him. Although the high cost of dental school tuition drove him to become a teacher instead, he took me to the dentist every week of my childhood, prolonging the agony by discussing the finer points of tooth filling and dental care. My father also almost failed the speech test required for his teaching license because he didn't speak "standard"— that is, nonimmigrant, nonaccented—English. For my parents and most of their friends, English was a second language learned when they went to school, since their home language was Yiddish. They saw the speech test as designed to keep all ethnics, not just Jews, out of teaching. In an ironic twist, my mother was always urging me to speak well and correctly, like her friend Ruth Saronson, a speech teacher. Ruth remained my model for perfect diction until I went away to college. When I talked to her on one of my visits home, I heard just how New York–accented my version of "standard" English was now that I had met the Boston academic version.

My parents' conclusion is that Jewish success, like their own, was the result of hard work and of placing a high value on education. They went to Brooklyn College during the Depression. My mother worked days and started school at night, and my father went during the day. Both their families encouraged them. More accurately, their families expected this effort from them. Everyone they knew was in the same boat—Jews who advanced as they did. In 1920, Jews made up 80 percent of the students at New York's City College, 90 percent of Hunter College, and before World War I, 40 percent of private Columbia University. By 1934, Jews made up almost 24 percent of all law students nationally, and 56 percent of those in New York City. Still, more Jews became public school teachers, like my parents and their friends, than doctors or lawyers. Stephen Steinberg has debunked the myth that Jews advanced because of the cultural value placed on education. This is not to say that Jews did not advance. They did. "Jewish success in America was a matter of historical timing. . . . [T]here was a fortuitous match between the experience and skills of Jewish immigrants, on the one hand, and the manpower needs and opportunity structures, on the other."[9] Jews were the only ones among the southern and eastern European immigrants who came from urban, commercial, craft, and manufacturing backgrounds, not least of which was garment manufacturing. They entered the United States in New York, center of the nation's booming garment industry, soon came to dominate its skilled (male) and "unskilled" (female) jobs, and found it an industry amenable to low-capital entrepreneurship. As a result, Jews were the first of the new European immigrants to create a middle class of small businesspersons early in the twentieth century. Jewish educational advances followed this business success, depending on, not creating, it.

In the early twentieth century, Jewish college students entered an arena in which the elite social mission was under challenge by a newer professional training mission. Pressure for change had begun to transform the curriculum and reorient college from a gentleman's bastion to a training ground for the middle-class professionals needed by an industrial economy. "The curriculum was overhauled to prepare students for careers in business, engineering, scientific farming, and the arts, and a variety of new professions such as accounting and pharmacy that were making their appearance in American colleges for the first time."[10] Occupational training was precisely what drew Jews to college. In a setting where disparagement of intellectual pursuits and the gentleman's C were badges of distinction, it was not hard for Jews to excel.

How we interpret Jewish social mobility in this milieu depends on whom we compare Jews to. Compared with other immigrants, Jews were upwardly mobile. But compared with that of nonimmigrant whites, their mobility was very limited and circumscribed. Anti-immigrant racist and anti-Semitic barriers kept the Jewish middle class confined to a small number of occupations. Excluded from mainstream corporate management and corporately employed professions, except in the garment and movie industries, which they built, Jews found themselves almost totally excluded from university faculties (and the few that made it had powerful patrons). Jews were concentrated in small businesses, and in professions where they served a largely Jewish clientele.

We shouldn't forget Jews' success in organized crime in the 1920s and 1930s as an aspect of upward mobility. Arnold Rothstein "transformed crime from a haphazard, small-scale activity into a well-organized and well-financed business operation." Consider also Detroit's Purple Gang, Murder Incorporated in New York, and a host of other big-city Jewish gangs in organized crime—and, of course, Meyer Lansky.[11]

Although Jews were the Euro-ethnic vanguard in college and became well established in public school teaching, as well as being visible in law, medicine, pharmacy, and librarianship before the postwar boom, these professions should be understood in the context of their times. In the 1930s they lacked the corporate framework they have today, and Jews in these professions were certainly not corporation based. Most lawyers, doctors, dentists, and pharmacists were solo practitioners and were considerably less affluent than their postwar counterparts.

Compared to Jewish progress after the war, Jews' prewar mobility was also highly limited. It was the children of Jewish businessmen, not those of Jewish workers, who flocked to college. Indeed, in 1905 New York, the children of Jewish workers had as little schooling as children of other immigrant workers. My family was quite modal in this respect. My grandparents did not go to college, but they did have a modicum of small-business success. My father's family owned a pharmacy. Although my mother's father was a skilled garment worker, her mother's family was large and always had one or another grocery or deli in which my grandmother participated. It was the relatively privileged children of upwardly mobile Jewish immigrants like my grandparents who began to push on the doors to higher education even before my parents were born. Especially in New York City—which had almost 1.25 million Jews by 1910 and remained the site of the biggest concentration of the nation's 4 million Jews in 1924—Jews built a small-business-based middle class and began to develop a second-generation professional class in the interwar years. Still, despite the high percentages of Jews in Eastern colleges, most Jews were not middle class, and fewer than 3 percent were professionals, compared to somewhere between 20 and 32 percent in the 1960s.

My parents' generation believed that Jews overcame anti-Semitic barriers because Jews are special. My belief is that the Jews who were upwardly mobile were special among Jews (and were also well placed to write the story). My generation might well counter our parents' story of pulling themselves up by their own bootstraps with, "But think what you might have been without the racism and with some affirmative action!" And that is precisely what the postwar boom, the decline of systematic, public anti-immigrant racism and anti-Semitism, and governmental affirmative action extended to white males.

By the time I was an adolescent, Jews were just as white as the next white person. Until I was eight, I was a Jew in a world of Jews. Everyone on Avenue Z in Sheepshead Bay was Jewish. I spent my days playing and going to school on three blocks of Avenue Z, and visiting my grandparents in the nearby Jewish neighborhoods of Brighton Beach and Coney Island. There were plenty of Italians in my neighborhood, but they lived around the corner. They were a kind of Jew, but on the margins of my social horizons. Portuguese were even more distant, at the end of the bus ride, at Sheepshead Bay. The *schul*, or temple, was on Avenue Z, and I begged my father to take me like all the other fathers took their kids, but religion wasn't part of my family's Judaism. Just how Jewish my neighborhood was hit me in first grade, when I was one of two kids in my class to go to school on Rosh Hashanah. My teacher was shocked—she was Jewish too—and I was embarrassed to tears when she sent me home. I was never again sent to school on Jewish holidays. We left that world in 1949 when we moved to Valley Stream, Long Island, which was Protestant, Republican, and even had farms until Irish, Italian, and Jewish exurbanites like us gave it a more suburban and Democratic flavor. Neither religion nor ethnicity separated us at school or in the neighborhood. Except temporarily. In elementary school years, I remember a fair number of dirt-bomb (a good suburban weapon) wars on the block. Periodically one of the Catholic boys would accuse me or my brother of killing his God, to which we would reply, "Did not" and start lobbing dirt-bombs. Sometimes he would get his friends from Catholic school, and I would get mine from public school kids on the block, some of whom were Catholic. Hostilities lasted no more than a couple of hours and merely punctuated an otherwise friendly relationship. They ended by junior high years, when other things became more important. Jews, Catholics, and Protestants; Italians, Irish, Poles, and "English" (I don't remember hearing WASP as a kid) were mixed up on the block and in school. We thought of ourselves as middle class and supremely enlightened because our ethnic backgrounds seemed so irrelevant to high school culture. We didn't see race (we thought), and racism was not part of our peer consciousness, nor were the immigrant or working-class histories of our families.

Like all chicken and egg problems, it's hard to know which came first. Did Jews and other Euro-ethnics become white because they became middle class? That is, did money whiten? Or did being incorporated in an expanded version of whiteness open up the economic doors to middle-class status? Clearly, both forces were at work. Some of the changes set in motion during the war against fascism led to a more inclusive version of whiteness. Anti-Semitism and anti-European racism lost respectability. The 1940 census no longer distinguished native whites of native parentage from those, like my parents, of immigrant parentage, so that Euro-immigrants and their children were more securely white by submersion in an expanded notion of whiteness. (This census also changed the race of Mexicans to white.) Theories of nurture and culture replaced theories of nature and biology. Instead of dirty and dangerous races who would destroy U.S. democracy, immigrants became ethnic groups whose children had successfully assimilated into the mainstream and risen to the middle class. In this new myth, Euro-ethnic suburbs like mine became the measure of U.S. democracy's victory over racism. Jewish mobility became a new Horatio Alger story. In time and with hard work, every ethnic group would get a piece of the pie, and the United States would be a nation with equal opportunity for all its people to become part of a prosperous middle-class majority. And it seemed that Euro-ethnic immigrants and their children were delighted to join middle America.

Notes

1. John Higham, *Strangers in the Land*, Rutgers University Press, New Brunswick, 1955, p. 226.

2. Id. at 156.

3. Allon Schoener, *Portal to America: The Lower East Side, 1870–1925*, Verso, London, 1967, p. 58.

4. Lewis H. Carlson and George A. Colburn, *In Their Place: White America Defines Her Minorities, 1850–1950*, Wiley, New York, 1972, pp. 333–34.

5. Ronald Takaki, *Strangers from a Different Shore*, Little, Brown, Boston, 1989, pp. 298–299.

6. Marcia Graham Synott, "Anti-Semitism and American Universities: Did Quotas Follow the Jews?" in *Anti-Semitism in American History*, ed. David A. Gerber, University of Illinois Press, Urbana, 1986, pp. 233, 238, 239, 249–50.

7. Id. at 250.

8. Id. at 239–40.

9. Stephen Steinberg, *The Ethnic Myth: Race, Ethnicity, and Class in America*, 2d ed., Beacon, Boston, 1989, p. 103.

10. Id. at 229.

11. Charles Silberman, *A Certain People: American Jews and Their Lives Today*, Summit, New York, 1985, pp. 127–30.

66

How White People Became White

JAMES R. BARRETT AND DAVID ROEDIGER

> By the eastern European immigration the labor force has been cleft
> horizontally into two great divisions. The upper stratum includes what is
> known in mill parlance as the English-speaking men; the lower contains the
> "Hunkies" or "Ginnies." Or, if you prefer, the former are the "white men," the
> latter the "foreigners."
>
> John Fitch, *The Steel Workers*

In 1980, Joseph Loguidice, an elderly Italian-American from Chicago, sat
down to give his life story to an interviewer. His first and most vivid childhood recollection was of a race riot that had occurred on the city's near north side. Wagons full of policemen with "peculiar hats" streamed into his neighborhood. But the "one thing that
stood out in my mind," Loguidice remembered after six decades, was "a man running down
the middle of the street hollering . . . 'I'm White, I'm White!'" After first taking him for
an African-American, Loguidice soon realized that the man was a white coal handler covered in dust. He was screaming for his life, fearing that "people would shoot him down."
He had, Loguidice concluded, "got caught up in . . . this racial thing."[1]

Joseph Loguidice's tale might be taken as a metaphor for the situation of millions of "new
immigrants" from Eastern and Southern Europe who arrived in the United States between
the end of the nineteenth century and the early 1920s. That this episode made such a profound impression is in itself significant, suggesting both that this was a strange, new situation and that thinking about race became an important part of the consciousness of immigrants like Loguidice. How did this racial awareness and increasingly racialized
worldview develop among new immigrant workers? Most did not arrive with conventional
U.S. attitudes regarding "racial" difference, let alone its significance and implications in industrial America. Yet most, it seems, "got caught up in . . . this racial thing." How did this
happen? If race was indeed socially constructed, then what was the raw material that went
into the process?

How did these immigrant workers come to be viewed in racial terms by others—employers, the state, reformers, and other workers? Like the coal handler in Loguidice's story,
their own ascribed racial identity was not always clear. A whole range of evidence—laws,
court cases, formal racial ideology, social conventions, and popular culture in the form of
slang, songs, films, cartoons, ethnic jokes, and popular theatre—suggests that the native
born and older immigrants often placed the new immigrants not only *above* African- and

Asian-Americans, for example, but also *below* "white" people. Indeed, many of the older immigrants, and particularly the Irish, had themselves been perceived as "nonwhite" just a generation earlier. As labor historians, we are interested in the ways in which Polish, Italian, and other European artisans and peasants became American workers, but we are equally concerned with the process by which they became "white." Indeed, in the U.S. the two identities merged, and this explains a great deal of the persistent divisions within the working-class population. How did immigrant workers wind up "inbetween"? . . .

We make no brief for the consistency with which "race" was used, by experts or popularly, to describe the "new immigrant" Southern and East Europeans who dominated the ranks of those coming to the U.S. between 1895 and 1924 and who "remade" the American working class in that period. We regard such inconsistency as important evidence of the "inbetween"[2] racial status of such immigrants. The story of Americanization is vital and compelling, but it took place in a nation also obsessed by race. For new immigrant workers the processes of "becoming white" and "becoming American" were connected at every turn. The "American standard of living," which labor organizers alternately and simultaneously accused new immigrants of undermining and encouraged them to defend via class organization, rested on "white men's wages." Political debate turned on whether new immigrants were fit to join the American nation and "American race." Nor do we argue that new immigrants from Eastern and Southern Europe were in the same situation as non-whites. Stark differences between the racialized status of African-Americans and the racial inbetween-ness of new immigrants meant that the latter *eventually* "became ethnic" and that their trajectory was predictable. But their history was sloppier than their trajectory. From day to day they were, to borrow from E. P. Thompson, "proto-nothing," reacting and acting in a highly racialized nation.[3]

Inbetween in the Popular Mind

America's racial vocabulary had no agency of its own, but rather reflected material conditions and power relations—the situations that workers faced on a daily basis in their workplaces and communities. Yet the words themselves were important. They were not only the means by which native born and elite people marked new immigrants as inferiors, but also those by which immigrant workers came to locate themselves and those about them in the nation's racial hierarchy. In beginning to analyze the vocabulary of race, it makes little sense for historians to invest the words themselves with an agency that could be exercised only by real historical actors, or meanings that derived only from the particular historical contexts in which the language was developed and employed.

The word *guinea,* for example, had long referred to African slaves, particularly those from the continent's northwest coast, and to their descendants. But from the late 1890s, the term was increasingly applied to southern European migrants, first and especially to Sicilians and southern Italians, who often came as contract laborers. At various times and places in the United States, *guinea* has been applied to mark Greeks, Jews, Portuguese, Puerto Ricans, and perhaps any new immigrant.[4]

Likewise, *hunky,* which began life, probably in the early twentieth century, as a corruption of "Hungarian," eventually became a pan-Slavic slur connected with perceived immigrant racial characteristics. By World War I the term was frequently used to describe any immigrant steelworker, as in *mill hunky.* Opponents of the Great 1919 Steel Strike, including some native born skilled workers, derided the struggle as a "hunky strike." Yet Josef Barton's work suggests that for Poles, Croats, Slovenians, and other immigrants who often worked together in difficult, dangerous situations, the term embraced a remarkable, if fragile, sense of prideful identity across ethnic lines. In *Out of This Furnace,* his epic novel of 1941 based on the lives of Slavic steelworkers, Thomas Bell observed that the word *hunky* bespoke "unconcealed racial prejudice" and a "denial of social and racial equality." Yet as these workers built the industrial unions of the late 1930s and took greater control over their own lives, the meaning of the term began to change. The pride with which second- and third-generation Slavic-American steelworkers, women as well as men, wore the label in the early 1970s seemed to have far more to do with class than with ethnic identity. At about the same time, the word *honky,* possibly a corruption of *hunky,* came into common use as black nationalism reemerged as a major ideological force in the African-American community.[5]

Words and phrases employed by social scientists to capture the inbetween identity of the new immigrants are a bit more descriptive, if more cumbersome. As late as 1937, John Dollard wrote repeatedly of the immigrant working class as "our temporary Negroes." More precise, if less dramatic, is the designation "not-yet-white ethnics" offered by immigration historian John Bukowczyk. The term not only reflects the popular perceptions and everyday experiences of such workers, but also conveys the dynamic quality of racial formation.[6]

The examples of Greeks and Italians particularly underscore the new immigrants' ambiguous positions with regard to popular perceptions of race. When Greeks suffered as victims of an Omaha race riot in 1909 and when eleven Italians died at the hands of lynchers in Louisiana in 1891, their less-than-white racial status mattered alongside their nationalities. Indeed, as Loguidice's coal handler shows, their ambivalent racial status put their lives in jeopardy. According to Gunther Peck's fine study of copper miners in Bingham, Utah, the Greek and Italian immigrants were "nonwhite" before their tension-fraught cooperation with the Western Federation of Miners during a 1912 strike ensured that "the category of Caucasian worker changed and expanded." Indeed, the work of Dan Georgakas and Yvette Huginnie shows that Greeks and other Southern Europeans often "bivouacked" with other "nonwhite" workers in Western mining towns. Pocatello, Idaho, Jim-Crowed Greeks in the early twentieth century and in Arizona they were not welcomed by white workers in "white men's towns" or "white men's jobs." In Chicago during the Great Depression, a German-American wife expressed regret over marrying her "half-nigger," Greek-American husband. African-American slang in the 1920s in South Carolina counted those of mixed American Indian, African-American, and white heritage as *Greeks.* Greek-Americans in the Midwest showed great anxieties about race, and were perceived not only as Puerto Rican, mulatto, Mexican, or Arab, but also as non-white *because of* being Greek.[7]

Italians, involved in a spectacular international diaspora in the early twentieth century, were racialized as the "Chinese of Europe" in many lands.[8] But in the U.S. their racialization was pronounced and, as *guinea*'s evolution suggests, more likely to connect Italians with Africans. During the debate at the Louisiana state constitutional convention of 1898 over how to disfranchise blacks, and over which whites might lose the vote, some acknowledged that the Italian's skin "happens to be white" even as they argued for his disfranchisement. But others held that "according to the spirit of our meaning when we speak of 'white man's government,' [the Italians] are as black as the blackest negro in existence."[9] More than metaphor intruded on this judgment. At the turn of the century, a West Coast construction boss was asked, "You don't call the Italian a white man?" The negative reply assured the questioner that the Italian was "a dago." Recent studies of Italian- and Greek-Americans make a strong case that racial, not just ethnic, oppression long plagued "non-white" immigrants from Southern Europe.[10]

The racialization of East Europeans was likewise striking. While racist jokes mocked the black servant who thought her child, fathered by a Chinese man, would be a Jew, racist folklore held that Jews, inside-out, were "niggers." In 1926 Serbo-Croatians ranked near the bottom of a list of forty "ethnic" groups whom "white American" respondents were asked to order according to the respondents' willingness to associate with members of each group. They placed just above Negroes, Filipinos, and Japanese. Just above them were Poles, who were near the middle of the list. One sociologist has recently written that "a good many groups on this color continuum [were] not considered white by a large number of Americans."[11] The literal inbetween-ness of new immigrants on such a list suggests what popular speech affirms: The state of whiteness was approached gradually and controversially. The authority of the state itself both smoothed and complicated that approach.

Notes

1. The epigraph is from John A. Fitch, THE STEEL WORKERS (New York, 1910), 147. Joe Sauris, Interview with Joseph Loguidice, July 25, 1980, Italians in Chicago Project, copy of transcript, Box 6, Immigration History Research Center, University of Minnesota, St. Paul, Minn.

2. We borrow "inbetween" from Robert Orsi, "The Religious Boundaries of an Inbetween People: Street Feste and the Problem of the Dark-Skinned 'Other' in Italian Harlem, 1920–1990," AMERICAN QUARTERLY, 44 (September 1992): passim, and also from John Higham, STRANGERS IN THE LAND: PATTERNS OF AMERICAN NATIVISM, 1860–1925 (New York, 1974), 169.

3. Lawrence Glickman, "Inventing the 'American Standard of Living': Gender, Race and Working-Class Identity, 1880–1925," LABOR HISTORY, 34 (Spring–Summer, 1993): 221–35; David Montgomery, BEYOND EQUALITY: LABOR AND THE RADICAL REPUBLICANS, 1862–1872 (Urbana, Ill., 1981), 254.

4. On guinea's history, see David Roediger, "Guineas, Wiggers and the Dramas of Racialized Culture," AMERICAN LITERARY HISTORY, 7 (1995): 654. On post-1890 usages, see William Harlen Gilbert, Jr., "Memorandum Concerning the Characteristics of the Larger Mixed-Blood Islands of the United States," SOCIAL FORCES, 24 (March 1946): 442; OXFORD ENGLISH DICTIONARY, 2d ed. (Oxford, 1989), 6:937–38; Frederic G. Cassidy and Joan Houston Hall, eds., DICTIONARY OF AMERICAN REGIONAL ENGLISH (Cambridge and London, 1991), 2: 838.

5. Tamony's notes on hunky (or hunkie) speculate on links to honky (or honkie) and refer to the former as an "old labour term." By no means did Hun refer unambiguously to Germans before World War I. See, e.g., Henry White, "Immigration Restriction as a Necessity," AMERICAN FEDERATIONIST, 4 (June 1897): 67; Paul Krause, THE BATTLE FOR HOMESTEAD, 1880–1892: POLITICS, CULTURE AND STEEL (Pittsburgh, 1992), 216–17; David Brody, STEELWORKERS IN AMERICA (New York, 1969), 120–21. See also the MILL HUNKY HERALD, published in Pittsburgh throughout the late 1970s.

6. Dollard, CASTE AND CLASS IN A SOUTHERN TOWN, 2d ed. (Garden City, N.Y., 1949), 93; Barry Goldberg, "Historical Reflections on Transnationalism, Race, and the American Immigrant Saga" (unpublished paper delivered at the Rethinking Migration, Race, Ethnicity, and Nationalism in Historical Perspective Conferences, New York Academy of the Sciences, May, 1990).

7. Albert S. Broussard, "George Albert Flippin and Race Relations in a Western Rural Community," THE MIDWEST REVIEW, 12 (1990): 15, n. 42; J. Alexander Karlin, "The Italo-American Incident of 1891 and the Road to Reunion," JOURNAL OF SOUTHERN HISTORY, 8 (1942); Gunther Peck, "Padrones and Protest: 'Old' Radicals and 'New' Immigrants in Bingham, Utah, 1905–1912," WEST-

ᴇʀɴ Hɪsᴛᴏʀɪᴄᴀʟ Qᴜᴀʀᴛᴇʀʟʏ, (May 1993): 177; Dan Georgakas, Gʀᴇᴇᴋ Aᴍᴇʀɪᴄᴀ ᴀᴛ Wᴏʀᴋ (New York, 1992), 12 and 16–17; Yvette Huginnie, Sᴛʀɪᴋɪᴛᴏs: Rᴀᴄᴇ, Cʟᴀss, ᴀɴᴅ Wᴏʀᴋ ɪɴ ᴛʜᴇ Aʀɪᴢᴏɴᴀ Cᴏᴘᴘᴇʀ Iɴᴅᴜsᴛʀʏ, 1870–1920, Thesis (Ph.D.) Yale University, 1991.

8. Donna Gabaccia, "The 'Yellow Peril' and the 'Chinese of Europe': Italian and Chinese Labourers in an International Labour Market" (unpublished paper, University of North Carolina at Charlotte, c. 1993).

9. George E. Cunningham, "The Italian: A Hindrance to White Solidarity in Louisiana, 1890–1898," Jᴏᴜʀɴᴀʟ ᴏғ Nᴇɢʀᴏ Hɪsᴛᴏʀʏ, 50 (January 1965): 34, includes the quotes.

10. Higham, Sᴛʀᴀɴɢᴇʀs ɪɴ ᴛʜᴇ Lᴀɴᴅ, 66; Gary R. Mormino and George E. Pozzetta, Tʜᴇ Iᴍᴍɪ-ɢʀᴀɴᴛ Wᴏʀʟᴅ ᴏғ Yʙᴏʀ Cɪᴛʏ: Iᴛᴀʟɪᴀɴs ᴀɴᴅ Tʜᴇɪʀ Lᴀᴛɪɴ Nᴇɪɢʜʙᴏʀs ɪɴ Tᴀᴍᴘᴀ, 1885–1985 (Urbana, Ill., 1987), 241; Micaela DiLeonardo, Tʜᴇ Vᴀʀɪᴇᴛɪᴇs ᴏғ Eᴛʜɴɪᴄ Exᴘᴇʀɪᴇɴᴄᴇ (Ithaca, N.Y., 1984), 24, n. 16; Georgakas, Gʀᴇᴇᴋ Aᴍᴇʀɪᴄᴀ ᴀᴛ Wᴏʀᴋ, 16. See also Karen Brodkin Sacks' superb "How Did Jews Become White Folks?" in Steven Gregory and Roger Sanjek, eds., Rᴀᴄᴇ (New Brunswick, N.J., 1994). [Reprinted as Chapters 50 and 65 of this book. Ed.]

11. Quoted in Brody, Sᴛᴇᴇʟᴡᴏʀᴋᴇʀs, 120; W. Lloyd Warner and J. O. Low, Tʜᴇ Sᴏᴄɪᴀʟ Sʏsᴛᴇᴍ ᴏғ ᴛʜᴇ Mᴏᴅᴇʀɴ Fᴀᴄᴛᴏʀʏ. Tʜᴇ Sᴛʀɪᴋᴇ: A Sᴏᴄɪᴀʟ Aɴᴀʟʏsɪs (New Haven, 1947), 140; Gershon Legman, Tʜᴇ Hᴏʀɴ Bᴏᴏᴋ (New York, 1964), 486–87; Aɴᴇᴄᴅᴏᴛᴀʟ Aᴍᴇʀɪᴄᴀɴᴀ: Fɪᴠᴇ Hᴜɴᴅʀᴇᴅ Sᴛᴏʀɪᴇs ғᴏʀ ᴛʜᴇ Aᴍᴜsᴇᴍᴇɴᴛ ᴏғ Fɪᴠᴇ Hᴜɴᴅʀᴇᴅ Nᴀᴛɪᴏɴs ᴛʜᴀᴛ Cᴏᴍᴘʀɪsᴇ Aᴍᴇʀɪᴄᴀ (Nᴇᴡ Yᴏʀᴋ, 1933), 98.

67

Paths to Belonging:
The Constitution and Cultural Identity

KENNETH L. KARST

Virtually every cultural minority in America has had to face exclusion, forced conformity, and subordination. All these patterns are variations on the same theme: those who are different cannot belong as full members of the community. The victims of cultural domination, therefore, face a serious problem: they must necessarily live their lives within the larger society, and in order to define themselves they must satisfy their basic needs for connection. They may choose to turn inward to the solidarity of the excluded group, banding together to confront the larger society. Alternatively, individual members of the cultural minority may, as to some aspects of their lives and in varying degrees, be assimilated into the culture of the larger society.

Cultural Politics: From Solidarity to Integration

Although most people have their cultural identities ascribed to them at birth, a great many people find their cultural identities thrust upon them. One principal source of cultural identity in America has always been the perceived need to band together in defense against domination or hostility. Indeed, the outside world plays an important part in the very definition of a group's cultural identity. The immigrants from a single European country typically came from different regions with marked cultural distinctions, but in America the people from a given village or region generally were few in number; naturally, they sought association with others of the same religion or from the same country. Natural affinities, of course, did exist: a common language, or a common religion, or both. However, much of the sense of community felt by the members of an American ethnic group today originated in the ways in which the members' ancestors were labeled—for example, as "Italians" or as "Jews"—and, by those labels, set apart as outsiders.[1]

"Defensive" identification with an ethnic or religious group has always been a major source of cultural pluralism in America; the victims of domination become bound together in a community, a "fraternity of battle."[2] Yet when the members of cultural minorities have intensified their group attachments by living in ethnic neighborhoods, or focusing their economic dealings within the ethnic communities,[3] or founding ethnic social or political organizations,[4] the outside world has been ready to call them "clannish" and unas-

64 N.C. L. Rev. 303 (1986). Originally published in the *North Carolina Law Review*. Reprinted by permission.

similable. Like many another process of social subordination, this one is circular. The exclusion of members of a cultural minority from full participation in the larger society causes them to focus their need to belong on the cultural group itself; and this very solidarity stimulates further outside suspicion and hostility.

Racial and ethnic domination has often led to defensive separatism. Black separatist movements, from the explicit black nationalism of Marcus Garvey[5] to the more ambiguous "Black Power" and "community control" movements of recent years, have origins that seek to replace the skepticism, frustration, and resentment produced by domination with a revitalized sense of pride.[6]

The hostility of the outside world is by no means the only source of ethnic solidarity in America. The very openness of American society, for all its assimilative power, also can impel some people to seek the solidarity of a cultural group. An ethnic group can offer shelter from the insecurity that stems from a sense of isolation in a crowd of strangers, even when the strangers are not hostile but indifferent. Yet, when an individual feels fenced out of the larger society or mistreated by it, the ethnic community may serve "as a solace for exclusion, a retreat from slights and prejudice."[7] The cultural group serves as a defense against a world that "measure[s] acceptability by appearances—skin color, dress, deportment—and by customs—language, family governance, religious ritual—according to broad racial and nationality stereotypes."[8] Facing either hostility or indifference, the members of a cultural minority may conclude that they will fare better if they act as a group, particularly when their aims can be satisfied only by participation in the larger community.

A quarter-century ago, in a study of black leaders in Chicago, James Q. Wilson distinguished between status goals and welfare goals.[9] By welfare goals Wilson meant tangible improvements such as better schools, new public housing, and better access to health services. Status goals focused on the principle of equality and on the integration of blacks into the general community: school integration, open occupancy in housing, and equal treatment of blacks in the allocation of public offices and honors. With respect to many immediate welfare goals, little distinguishes a cultural group from any other interest group. An ethnic neighborhood has the same interest in getting the city to repair street lights as any other neighborhood would have. A cultural group's status goals, however, differ from those of many other interest groups. The cultural minority seeks to replace discrimination and domination with acceptance, recognition, and equal citizenship. The concern for status arises out of a basic psychological need not only to belong, but to be respected for one's self. The cultural outsider wants the freedom to be allowed to keep a "primordial" identity and also to be accepted as one who belongs to the larger society.

Correspondingly, members of the dominant cultural group may see themselves as having an interest in maintaining existing "pecking orders" associated with race, ethnicity, and religion. In other words, dominance itself—preventing cultural outsiders from belonging—may be someone else's status goal.

In the short term, the distinction between welfare and status goals can be blurred. Poverty that is degrading, for example, may deprive its victims of effective participation as equal members of society.[10] To be unemployed is to be deprived of more than wages.[11] Thus, a series of antidiscrimination measures focused on welfare goals may, in the aggregate, work important changes in the status of a previously dominated group. However, the distinction between status and welfare goals retains utility, at least in the short run. Some

immediate issues are centered on material well-being, while others are centered on the
need for belonging and the dignity of equal citizenship.

The "emotionally charged" quality of American cultural politics arises out of conflicts
over status, with one group's anger matched against another group's fear. The cultural issues that recently have aroused the most fervor—abortion, immigration, religion in the
schools, affirmative action, and bilingualism—are all status issues, touching the heart because they touch the sense of self. When members of a cultural group join in taking a stand
on an issue, one of their main concerns is the recognition of their own cultural identity and
even of their status as citizens, whose voices count for something. Ethnic politics is a historically validated avenue to recognition and acceptance for members of minority cultures
and especially for their leaders.

A constant concern of ethnic leadership is group solidarity. Ethnic groups are, in some
sense, "the creation of their leaders";[12] no clear boundaries define the groups, and the openness of American society is a continuing invitation for marginal members to define themselves outside the group. The leaders themselves are apt to be people whose successes in
the larger society make them acceptable in that society, and, in the same degree, marginal
to the group. Each success for the group in the politics of the wider community, each material advance, integrates more and more members of the group into the institutions and
processes of the dominant culture.[13]

If the story of ethnic leadership in modern America is one of "a certain decline,"[14] the
main reason is that cultural assimilation follows modernization and advances in a market
economy. Solidarity politics, "organizing around in-group concerns and encouraging a bloc
vote," is likely to be seen as a practical necessity for a group that is just emerging from severe conditions of domination.[15] This quest for internal cohesion, however, will limit the
group to local successes. To carry its influence outside ethnic enclaves—a step necessary to
achieve both status goals and welfare goals—the group must form coalitions with other interests. Irony attends this "broker politics."[16] The ethnic leaders become integrated into
larger organizations and thus are drawn even further toward the margins of the group. The
achievement of the group's goals opens progressively more opportunities for members of
the group in the larger society, with the inevitable result that the group declines as a separate political force. Observers of ethnic politics have noticed that as ethnic bloc voting increases, ethnic identification decreases. In the nineteenth century, Edward Beecher spoke
about the antagonism between Catholicism and American democracy: "The systems are
diametrically opposed: one must and will exterminate the other."[17] In 1960 American voters, sensing that the Catholics' assimilation into American life was an accomplished fact,
elected John F. Kennedy as the Nation's first Catholic President. In the century that had
intervened between those two events, the Irish had been the Nation's foremost practitioners of cultural politics.

A cultural group's active participation in politics is a step along the path to assimilation.
The personalism, even nepotism, that has characterized politics among immigrant groups
throughout the Nation's history may look like no more than a reinforcement of intragroup
solidarity, but it also constitutes a first step in the process leading to a sense of belonging
to the Nation. Political party activity makes people feel like insiders. The parties themselves
both connect different groups and serve as "carriers of certain basic values that large numbers of citizens [can] accept as common American beliefs."[18] Local ethnic power produces
the belief that "the system works for us," further strengthening national allegiance.[19] Cul-

tural politics thus begins in the defensive solidarity of the cultural group, but ends in integration.

Participation and Assimilation

The assimilation of white immigrants' descendants into the cultural mainstream is undeniable. Assimilation means change—specifically, a change in cultural norms. These changes are most visible in behaviors such as the adoption of a language or a style of dress. Assimilation also implies change in self-identification, not so much a behavior pattern as a state of mind. Some such changes can be seen in first-generation Americans, but the typical immigrant is not inclined to undertake the wrenching transformation involved in adopting the ways of a new culture. Assimilation does not take place primarily within any individual. Mostly, it is visible as a group phenomenon, a change from one generation to another.

Like ethnicity itself, the process of assimilation is both subtle and complex. Even from generation to generation the movement from "community" to "society," from "primordial" association to contractual association, from ethnic identity to occupational identity is not a straight line. Rather, these types of association and identity exist side by side in the same individual; there is an "interaction . . . of communal and noncommunal ways in the lives of us all."[20] It would seem odd, for example, to say that fourth-generation Americans are assimilated. Rather, they are what they are; because they have grown up under certain circumstances, they lack the characteristics that once set their immigrant great-grandparents apart from the American cultural mainstream. For the individual, "assimilation," or its absence, is just a label that we attach to the product of myriad decisions made by that individual and by others, including ancestors and acquaintances and government officials.

Although an exact definition of assimilation appears to be impossible, observers can agree on certain measures of assimilation: language usage, educational integration, occupational dispersal, residential dispersal, and intercultural marriage. To an immigrant, some degree of assimilation might be indicated by activities that others would see differently:

> The peasant who had become a Polish Falcon or a Son of Italy, in his own view, was acting as an American; this was not a step he could have taken at home. To subscribe to a newspaper was the act of a citizen of the New World, not of the Old, even if the journal was [written in his native language].[21]

By these tests, it is plain that a common pattern prevails for nearly all the ethnic groups in American history: eventually they become largely integrated into the American cultural mainstream.[22]

What causes assimilation to take place? First, the commonly assumed assimilating effects of occupational mobility in an open society illustrate a larger truth: assimilation is advanced when the members of a cultural minority take part in the institutions and activities of the larger society. It is often said that assimilation is promoted by such behavior as speaking English, attending the public schools, listening to the national broadcast media, entering the job market, joining a union, moving away from the ethnic neighborhood, and voting in public elections. But a person who engages in a significant number of these kinds of behavior *is* assimilated. The various forms of behavior that indicate assimilation tend to reinforce each other, accelerating assimilation. The reinforcement takes place in people's minds. The more a person engages in "mainstream" behavior, the more that person is apt to perceive himself or herself as part of the wider American culture and to be disposed to participate in it still further.

Because participation and mobility are important to the process of assimilation, the ability to make choices about ethnic identification is, to a marked degree, dependent on the material resources available to an individual or to a family. In a market, resources mean opportunities, including opportunities to interact with widening circles of people in a variety of ways, provided, for example, by neighborhoods, schools, and social activities. The point has validity for cultural groups defined by race. No one chooses to be black, or Asian, or American Indian; yet, for people in all these groups, middle-class status permits a great many choices about participation in the wider society, choices that are unavailable to poor people.

Thus, the second generalization about assimilation is that it is closely associated with economic class. Most immigrants, whatever their class, remain largely unassimilated. In succeeding generations, however, middle-class families tend to live in the suburbs and to send their children to college. Higher education not only provides access to elite occupations, but also erodes social barriers to the point that ethnic intermarriage is now common among young people of the middle class.[23] Furthermore, the openness of American society tends to distribute the members of a cultural group over a range of levels of income and status, with the inevitable effect of weakening that group's internal cohesion.

The third engine driving assimilation is the complexity of our modern society, which presses nearly everyone into a fragmentation of roles and thus of norms. This fragmentation makes it virtually impossible for an individual to focus either loyalties or identity single-mindedly on an ethnic group. Our "primordial affinities," after all, are not our only attachments to groups. We also identify with those who share our occupations, our economic classes, the causes or institutions we support, the places where we live, and even our leisure activities. Each of us interacts with others in relation to different sets of expectations, one to govern each sub-part of society in which we see ourselves as members. Because individuals find different sets of "allies" for different types of conflict, society avoids the breakdown that would be threatened if its members saw themselves as divided into only two groups. One of the most pernicious features of the system of Jim Crow was that it fed on itself, polarizing Southern society and inhibiting the diversification of identities and attachments. To foster that diversified sharing and those multiple loyalties is to nourish the growth of tolerance.

Notes

1. The case of the Indian nations is different, and it is tragic. Hundreds of native cultures were present when the first European settlers arrived in America. Except for an early period of uneasy dealings on a basis of equality, the history of white-Indian relations in this country is a story of virtually unrelieved dispossession and even extermination of the Indian peoples justified by racist assumptions. *See generally* W. HAGAN, AMERICAN INDIANS (rev. ed. 1979).

2. W. McWILLIAMS, THE IDEA OF FRATERNITY IN AMERICA 542 (1974). Correspondingly, as the need for defense declines, group attachment weakens. Church attendance among Catholics has declined 23% since 1958. HARPER'S MAG., Mar. 1985, at 19. Enrollment in Catholic parochial schools has declined from about 5.6 million students in 1965 to about 2.9 million in 1985. Chandler, *Parochial School Enrollment Dwindling*, L.A. TIMES, May 20, 1985, § I, at 19, col. 1.

3. Personalism and nepotism have been seen as ways of surviving in a hostile environment. Some

forms of economic activity are suited for this kind of defensive response to adversity, for they are "located within a particular kind of social network: close quarters, daily routines, local connections, personal service, familial cooperation." M. WALZER, SPHERES OF JUSTICE 161 (1983); *see also* I. LIGHT, ETHNIC ENTERPRISE IN AMERICA 7–10 (1972).

4. On ethnic militia units, see M. JONES, AMERICAN IMMIGRATION 155–56, 158–59 (1960). On ethnic politics, see ETHNIC LEADERSHIP IN AMERICA (J. Higham ed. 1979); N. GLAZER & D. MOYNIHAN, BEYOND THE MELTING POT 134 (2d ed. 1970).

5. Garvey started the Universal Negro Improvement Association, a movement founded on the need to instill black pride and dignity. Garvey denounced assimilation and urged blacks to "return" to Africa. He scorned the existing black leadership and found his main support among the blacks who were the poorest of all. After impressive early successes, the movement collapsed in the 1920s.

6. Elijah Muhammad, one of Garvey's workers in Detroit, later founded the Nation of Islam. On this more recent black separatist movement, see J. BALDWIN, THE FIRE NEXT TIME 67–113 (1963); K. CLARK, KING, MALCOLM, BALDWIN: THREE INTERVIEWS 34, 45 (rev. ed. 1985) (quoting Malcolm X in 1963 as favoring "complete separation" and as saying, "My father was a Garveyite"). Malcolm X saw integration as a hoax, a sophisticated form of domination. MALCOLM X, THE AUTOBIOGRAPHY OF MALCOLM X 275–81 (1966).

Some blacks who do not opt for separatism have expressed skepticism about integration. James Baldwin asked, "Do I really want to be integrated into a burning house?" and remarked, "Why—especially knowing the family as I do—I should *want* to marry your sister is a great mystery to me." J. BALDWIN, *supra,* at 108, 111 (1963). Yet in the same breath Baldwin added, "[W]e, the black and the white, deeply need each other here if we are really to become a nation—if we are really, that is, to achieve our identity, our maturity, as men and women." *Id.* at 111. Other blacks have registered skepticism about the willingness of whites to carry out the process of integration unless they are made to see integration as advantageous to themselves. *See, e.g.,* Bell, *A Hurdle Too High: Class-based Roadblocks to Racial Remediation,* 33 BUFFALO L. REV. 1 (1984); Bell, *Brown v. Board to Education and the Interest-Convergence Dilemma,* 93 HARV. L. REV. 518 (1980).

7. W. MCWILLIAMS, *supra* at 102.

8. R. WIEBE, THE SEGMENTED SOCIETY: AN INTRODUCTION TO THE MEANING OF AMERICA 32 (1975).

9. J. WILSON, NEGRO POLITICS: THE SEARCH FOR LEADERSHIP 185–213 (1960).

10. *See* Matza, *The Disreputable Poor,* in SOCIAL STRUCTURE AND MOBILITY IN ECONOMIC DEVELOPMENT 310–19 (N. Smelser & S. Lipset eds. 1966); Michelman, *In Pursuit of Constitutional Welfare Rights: One View of Rawls' Theory of Justice,* 121 U. PA. L. REV. 962, 983–91 (1973); Plamenatz, *Diversity of Rights and Kinds of Equality,* in NOMOS IX: EQUALITY 79, 91–92 (J. Pennock & J. Champman eds. 1967).

11. On the destructive quality of unemployment and marginal employment, see E. LIEBOW, TALLY'S CORNER 29–71 (1967).

12. Higham, Preface to ETHNIC LEADERSHIP IN AMERICA, *supra* at ix. Indeed, political leaders may even play a distinctive role in the construction of ethnicity itself.

13. Consciousness of ethnicity, which is shared widely at all socio-economic levels, decreases as a factor influencing behavior for people in the middle class. D. SCHNEIDER & R. SMITH, CLASS DIFFERENCES AND SEX ROLES IN AMERICAN KINSHIP AND FAMILY STRUCTURES 35–36 (1973).

14. Higham, *Introduction: The Forms of Ethnic Leadership,* in ETHNIC LEADERSHIP IN AMERICA, *supra* at 1, 11.

15. A cultural group's very insularity may, in fact, enable it to act as a cohesive body and thus to carry more weight in the political process than would an equally large group that is dispersed and largely invisible. For discussion of this point, see Ackerman, *Beyond* Carolene Products, 98 HARV. L. REV. 713, 722–28 (1985).

16. The notion of cultural "broker politics" is an old one in this country. On the nineteenth-century version of ethnic politics, see R. WIEBE, *supra* at 139–40.

17. *Quoted* in R. WIEBE, *supra* at 68.

18. R. Wiebe, *supra* at 140. On local politics in the early twentieth century as a "substitute for community," see *id.* at 69.

19. J. Higham, *supra* at 185. Correspondingly, when members of a cultural minority see little benefit from political participation, they are not apt to participate, even by voting.

20. T. Bender, Community and Social Change in America 43 (1978).

21. O. Handlin, The Uprooted 250–51 (2d ed. 1973).

22. Until recently, the one obvious exception to this general trend has been found among black people. The overwhelming majority of black Americans still live in separate communities and send their children to predominantly black schools, a situation that is euphemistically called "racial isolation." *See, e.g.*, 1 U.S. Civil Rights Comm'n, Racial Isolation in the Public Schools 109–14 (1967). The intermarriage of blacks and whites is still uncommon. Because the black community suffers today from disastrously high rates of unemployment, most blacks have little hope for moving out of the ghetto. In short, race has long been a great divide in American society, and there is no reason to assume that it will lose its significance in the near future.

23. According to the 1980 census, 8% of persons of Italian descent born before 1920 were of mixed ancestry; 70% of those born after 1920 were of ethnically mixed parentage. Some 72% of all married persons of Asian ancestry were married to other Asians—which means that about 28% are married to non-Asians. Herbert J. Gans, a sociologist, has commented that these and other census data illustrate that "among economically secure middle-class whites, ethnic background is no longer the source of conflict that it once was." *Quoted in* Collins, *A New Look at Intermarriage in the U.S.*, N.Y. Times, Feb. 11, 1985, at C13, col. 2.

Black-white marriages are not common. The 1980 census showed that only 1.3% of married couples in the United States were interracial couples. Here, however, as with other ethnic groups, there has been a significant generational shift. Of black married men born before 1920, 0.8% were in interracial marriages, mostly to whites; for black married men born after 1950, 6% were interracially married—almost an eightfold increase. There are, however, many children of racially mixed parentage whose parents were not married.

68

Is the Radical Critique of Merit Anti-Semitic?

DANIEL A. FARBER AND SUZANNA SHERRY

[According to critical race theory,] a group's success cannot be justified on the basis of any presumed excellence in the performance of its members. [Critical race theory holds that notions of merit are manipulable and based on culture. Ed.] As applied to so-called "model minorities" like Jews or some groups of Asian Americans, however, this creates a paradox, for these groups seem to have succeeded in important social arenas beyond the average achievements of the dominant majority of white Gentiles. In 1970, Jewish family income was 172% of the average American income, Japanese-American family income was 132% of the average, and Chinese-American family income was 112% of the average. By 1980, native-born Chinese Americans were earning 150% of the non-Hispanic white average, with Japanese- and Korean-American families not far behind the Chinese Americans. As of that year, unemployment rates for Chinese, Japanese, and Korean Americans were approximately half that of the general population. Poverty rates are also significantly lower for some Asian-American groups.[1] More recent data similarly reveal that Jewish family income remains well above the average income for Gentile families.

Educational attainment accompanies this economic success. Jews and Asian Americans are disproportionately represented in higher education: In 1982, Jews obtained undergraduate degrees at nearly twice the rate of the general American population; in 1990, the percentage of Jews with some college education was almost twice that of the general population.[2] Asian Americans also completed college at twice the rate of the general population. Americans of Japanese, Chinese, and Korean ancestry comprise approximately one-fifth of the student body at some prestigious universities, even though they are less than two percent of the national population.[3] Although many universities implemented quotas to limit Jewish students and faculty from the early 1920s through at least the early 1960s,[4] by 1975 Jews "constituted 10 percent of all faculty members but 20 percent of those teaching at elite universities."[5] If there is no such thing as merit, what explains the success of these two groups, both of whom, like blacks, have been victims of discrimination by white Gentile America?[6]

Focusing on Jews, we can identify only a few conceivable explanations unconnected with merit. If merit is wholly irrelevant, the four possible explanations for Jewish success are: (1) that a Jewish conspiracy exists; (2) that Jews are parasitic on American culture; (3) that American culture is essentially Jewish; or (4) that there is no such thing as a distinct Jewish culture or identity. Without evaluating any of the explanations, we will note their anti-

Semitic overtones. Unless there is yet another explanation besides merit for Jewish success in a Gentile world, denying the role of merit has clear anti-Semitic implications.

The first theory is that Jews succeed as a consequence of a powerful and pervasive Jewish conspiracy. Some Americans believe that there is a Jewish or Zionist conspiracy, which has been posited as an explanation for everything from violence on television to the spread of AIDS. The existence of a powerful Jewish conspiracy would certainly explain why Jews as a group are successful even if success has nothing to do with merit. It is also one of the most ancient anti-Semitic myths. With roots dating back at least to medieval Christianity, the Jewish conspiracy theory persisted through the Reformation and into modernity.[7] Martin Luther, for example, viewed Jews as a menace to Christianity and as the "storm troops of the devil's forces."[8]

The Jewish conspiracy theory both feeds on and fosters anti-Semitism, portraying Jews as using devious or evil means to gain power over innocent non-Jews. It has spawned various myths, including the belief that Jews used the blood of Christian babies in the Passover seder and that Jews caused the Black Death by poisoning wells.[9] It takes its most powerful modern form in the fraudulent *Protocols of the Elders of Zion*, which purports to document a Jewish conspiracy to destroy the Christian world.[10] Although the *Protocols* have been thoroughly discredited, and were admitted to be a forgery by their publisher, some still believe in them.

Similar myths of an Asian conspiracy also abound. Fears of a "yellow peril," an Asian conspiracy to obliterate white civilization, were rampant in the first decades of this century. During World War II, Japanese were depicted as single-mindedly conspiring toward world conquest. Even today, Japan's economic success is sometimes attributed to deviousness or a desire to dominate the world.[11] The *Protocols of the Elders of Zion* finds its anti-Asian counterpart in the *Tanaka Memorial*, a document purportedly presented by Prime Minister Tanaka to Emperor Hirohito in 1927, outlining Japanese plans for world domination. Like the *Protocols*, it was widely accepted as genuine, although it was almost certainly fraudulent.[12]

Conspiracy theories are a powerful tool for those who wish to portray themselves as innocent victims of the successful or feared Other. Such theories have been used to justify everything from university quotas on both Jews and Asian Americans to the Holocaust[13] and the forced relocation and internment of Japanese Americans during World War II.[14] Conspiracy theories were also used, with tragic success, to justify increasingly harsh treatment of black slaves in order to prevent slave revolts.[15]

A second conceivable explanation for disproportionately high rates of success among Jews is that they are chameleons who, with no culture of their own, take on the cultural coloration of the society around them. They are so successful at imitating cultural norms that they outperform "authentic" members of the society. The negative aspect of this stereotype is not the purported adaptability, which could be considered a positive trait. Rather, it is the specific form of that adaptation, which is described as purely imitative with no creative component.

This negative portrayal of Jews as parasitic, unimaginative imitators who succeed on the backs of the truly deserving is typical of anti-Semitism. Historically, Jews have been portrayed as soulless parasites on the surrounding culture. In the mid–nineteenth century, French scholar Ernest Renan wrote that Jews had "no mythology, no epic, no science, no philosophy, no fiction, no plastic arts, no civic life; there is no complexity, nor nuance; an exclusive sense of uniformity."[16] Pierre-Joseph Proudhon, an early French socialist, characterized "the Jew" as "unproductive," and "an intermediary, always fraudulent and parasitical, who operates in business as in philosophy, by forging, counterfeiting, sharp practices."[17] The composer Richard Wagner similarly portrayed Jews—especially assimilated Jews—as "the most heartless of all human beings," lacking passion, soul, music, or poetry.[18] In the early twentieth century, an American anti-Semite belittled Jewish academic success as "simply another manifestation of the acquisitiveness of the race," describing Jews as "clever, acute, and industrious rather than able in the highest sense."[19] In publications that have now become notorious, the deconstructionist Paul de Man took a similar position during World War II about the contribution of Jews to Western literature.[20]

Asians, especially the Japanese, have similarly been described as imitative and without a culture of their own. In 1944, an American missionary in Japan wrote: "The Japanese have lost much irreparably by not having a great art, a great poetry, a great drama, to introduce to the Western world."[21] A U.S. Navy publication of the same era described even premodern Japan as a "third-hand culture . . . borrowing this and copying that, never inventing, but always adapting western machines, western arms, and western techniques to their own uses."[22] Portrayals of the Japanese as primarily good mimics continued after World War II, and are still found today. The prevalent modern American stereotype of Asian Americans as technically skilled but without leadership abilities might be at least partly derived from the longstanding belief that many Asians lack cultural or creative abilities. This supposed deficiency explains the ability of both Jews and Asian Americans to abandon any independent cultural identity and assume the character of the dominant culture.[23]

A third possible explanation for Jewish success, and the converse of the parasitic explanation, is that mainstream American culture and standards are in their essence not white but Jewish. Jews succeed because American culture has taken on Jewish characteristics.

The strong version of this theory is that Jews have somehow infiltrated American culture. Blaming Jews for the evils of mainstream culture has a long historical pedigree. The rise of both capitalism and communism have been blamed on Jews. Marx portrayed capitalism as essentially Jewish and predicted that Jews would disappear under socialism, which would "abolish the preconditions and thus the very possibility of huckstering" and thereby "make the Jew impossible."[24] In the early twentieth century, Germans and Austrians—in countries where anti-Semitism had always flourished and would soon explode—lamented the "Judaisation" of German and Austrian culture. Not surprisingly, given the role of Jews in important cultural institutions such as the academy and the movie industry, the same charges have been made about American culture.

Attributing societal problems to despised minorities is common. In the nineteenth century, Chinese immigrants were sometimes accused of threatening to destroy the American working class and its culture. Blacks have been blamed for causing cultural decay by introducing Americans to everything from crime and drugs to family breakdown. Like the first two explanations of Jewish success, then, this theory portrays Jews negatively and rests on an analysis common to racist arguments used against other minorities.

Suggesting that the fundamental "Jewishness" of American culture explains Jewish success also creates more questions than it answers. Considering that Jews are less than three percent of the population, how did Jewish culture become so dominant? Either Jewish culture happened to have features that were more meritorious than the majority culture or Jews insidiously remade that culture in their own image.

A milder version of the "Judaisation" argument is that Jewish (and Asian) culture happens to emphasize many of the values that are needed in modern society, such as education, initiative, and enterprise. These groups are thus more likely than some other minorities to play the game successfully by the white rules, and are more comfortable doing so. Such a proposition does not appear to be necessarily anti-Semitic, and could conceivably explain the relative success of Jews and Asian Americans (who presumably also share the same "white" values) as compared to African Americans, whose cultural values might be more distinctive. This benign explanation suggests that standards and values are developed by cultures for a variety of reasons, not the least of which is that they appear to be adaptive to the culture's environment. Stripped of its benign interpretation, the Judaisation argument retains only anti-Semitic components: to the extent that Jews share the (oppressive and racist) values of powerful white Gentiles, their "hyper-acceptance" of these values only makes them even "worse" than other whites.

The final conceivable explanation for Jewish success—that such success is nothing more than a statistical anomaly—is in many ways the most damaging, because it amounts to a denial that Jews exist as a distinct or identifiable group. Under this theory, it is no more than random chance that *any* three percent of the white American population will disproportionately exhibit any particular characteristics, from financial success to alcoholism. If being Jewish is an essentially insignificant trait, then any characteristics Jews exhibit are the result of random differences among the white population. It is thus misleading to point to "Jewish" success as a phenomenon in need of explanation.

Like the other theories, this purported explanation is analogous to historical forms of anti-Semitism. As early as the French Revolution, anti-Semitic Enlightenment thinkers had urged the removal of the pervasive restrictions on Jews with the hope that Judaism would be eliminated, because Jews' only common identity derived from their oppressed status: "The Jews were not to be emancipated as a community but as *individual* human beings, the assumption being that, once oppression was removed, their distinctive group identity would disappear."[25] To deny that Jews are a culturally distinct group is to ignore over 5,000 years of history, during which Jews kept their identity alive in the face of persecution, dispersal, and genocide.

It is troubling, but not unprecedented, that one of the pivotal propositions of this branch of critical theory—that merit is constructed to serve the powerful—has anti-Semitic implications. Critics of the existing order have often ended up targeting Jews, whether intentionally or not.[26] Anti-Semitism has served as "a convenient way of attacking the existing order without demanding its total overthrow and without having to offer a comprehensive alternative."[27] Sadly, like some of its radical predecessors through the ages,[28] radical constructivism is not altogether lacking in the potential to fall into the grips of this, "the longest hatred."[29]

Notes

1. THOMAS SOWELL, ETHNIC AMERICA: A HISTORY 5 (1981); U.S. COMMISSION ON CIVIL RIGHTS, THE ECONOMIC STATUS OF AMERICANS OF ASIAN DESCENT: AN EXPLORATORY INVESTIGATION 29, 61–62 (1988) [hereinafter Economic Status]; *see also* STANLEY LIEBERSON & MARY C. WATERS, FROM MANY STRANDS: ETHNIC AND RACIAL GROUPS IN CONTEMPORARY AMERICA 138–39 (1988); U.S. GENERAL ACCOUNTING OFFICE, ASIAN AMERICANS: A STATUS REPORT 23 (1990).

2. Sidney Goldstein, *Profile of American Jewry: Insights from the 1990 Jewish Population Survey, in* AMERICAN JEWISH YEARBOOK 1992, at 77, 110–11 (David Singer & Ruth R. Seldin eds., 1992).

3. HENRY ROSOVSKY, THE UNIVERSITY: AN OWNER'S MANUAL 67 n.12 (1990). *See also* ECONOMIC STATUS, *supra* at 26, 55.

4. NATHAN C. BELTH, A PROMISE TO KEEP: A NARRATIVE OF THE AMERICAN ENCOUNTER WITH ANTI-SEMITISM 96–110, 185–97 (1979); LEONARD DINNERSTEIN, ANTISEMITISM IN AMERICA 84–87 (1994); ALAN M. DERSHOWITZ, CHUTZPAH 66–71 (1991) (discussing Harvard's efforts at reducing Jewish matriculation in the 1920s).

5. CHARLES E. SILBERMAN, A CERTAIN PEOPLE: AMERICAN JEWS AND THEIR LIVES TODAY 144 (1985). Moreover, Jews tend to publish at higher rates than their colleagues: In 1975, 24% of those academics who had published twenty or more articles were Jewish. *Id.*

6. For accounts of past and present discrimination against Asian Americans, see, e.g., RONALD TAKAKI, STRANGERS FROM A DIFFERENT SHORE: A HISTORY OF ASIAN AMERICANS 101–03, 479–84 (1989); Pat K. Chew, *Asian Americans: The "Reticent" Minority and Their Paradoxes*, 36 WM. & MARY L. REV. 1, 9–24, 54 (1994). For accounts of discrimination against Jews, see, e.g., DINNERSTEIN, *supra*; ROBERT S. WISTRICH, ANTISEMITISM: THE LONGEST HATRED 114–25 (1991). Indeed, American prejudices against African Americans on the one hand and Asian Americans and Jews on the other have much in common. Asian Americans have often been included with African Americans as the subject of particular discriminatory laws and stereotypes. *See, e.g.,* JOHN W. DOWER, WAR WITHOUT MERCY: RACE AND POWER IN THE PACIFIC WAR 147–80 (1986).

7. WISTRICH, *supra* at 29–32 (describing medieval anti-Semitic myths); JOEL CARMICHAEL, THE SA-TANIZING OF THE JEWS: ORIGIN AND DEVELOPMENT OF MYSTICAL ANTI-SEMITISM 44–93 (1992).

8. HEIKO A. OBERMAN, THE ROOTS OF ANTISEMITISM IN THE AGE OF RENAISSANCE AND REFORMA-TION 117 (James I. Porter trans., 1984).

9. *See, e.g.,* CARMICHAEL, *supra* at 74; DINNERSTEIN, *supra* at xxii–xxv; WISTRICH, *supra* at 29, 32–33; *see also* David Berger, *Anti-Semitism: An Overview, in* HISTORY AND HATE: THE DIMENSIONS OF ANTI-SEMITISM 3, 7 (David Berger ed., 1986) (noting belief that Jewish doctors poisoned their patients).

10. *See, e.g.,* NORMAN COHN, WARRANT FOR GENOCIDE: THE MYTH OF THE JEWISH WORLD-CON-SPIRACY AND THE PROTOCOLS OF THE ELDERS OF ZION (1966); CARMICHAEL, *supra* at 138–40; DINNER-STEIN, *supra* at 80–83 (providing the history of the publication and circulation of the *Protocols*); WISTRICH, *supra* at 253–54 (discussing the adoption of the *Protocols* into current Arab thought).

11. *See* DOWER, *supra* at 20–21, 83–84, 156–64, 172–73, 313–14.

12. John J. Stephan, *The Tanaka Memorial (1927): Authentic or Spurious?,* 7 MOD. ASIAN STUD. 733, 733, 739–43 (1973).

13. *See, e.g.,* CARMICHAEL, *supra* at 152–80; COHN, *supra* at 194–215.

14. *See, e.g.,* DOWER, *supra* at 79–81; TAKAKI, *supra* at 388–405.

15. *See* JOHN LOFTON, INSURRECTION IN SOUTH CAROLINA: THE TURBULENT WORLD OF DENMARK VESEY 138, 196–97 (1964).

16. WISTRICH, *supra* at 47. Renan also claimed that Jews lacked creativity. *Id.*

17. CARMICHAEL, *supra* at 117.

18. WISTRICH, *supra* at 56.

19. DINNERSTEIN, *supra* at 64.

20. Paul de Man, *The Jews in Contemporary Literature,* LE SOIR, Mar. 4, 1941, reprinted in DAVID LEHMAN, SIGNS OF THE TIMES: DECONSTRUCTION AND THE FALL OF PAUL DE MAN 269–71 app. (1991).

21. DOWER, *supra* at 97.

22. *Id.* at 98.

23. A similar charge has also been made against whites: "Euro-Americans steal and co-opt vast portions of African-American culture, usually without attribution." John E. Morrison, *Colorblind-ness, Individuality, and Merit: An Analysis of the Rhetoric Against Affirmative Action,* 79 IOWA L. REV. 313, 359 (1994).

24. KARL MARX, *On the Jewish Question, in* EARLY WRITINGS 1, 34, 35–39 (T.B. Bottomore ed. & trans., 1963).

25. Wistrich, *supra* at xxi; *see also id.* at 44–45 (noting that Enlightenment thinkers were anti-Semitic).

26. In particular, African Americans, who have the greatest reason to be dissatisfied with the status quo, have often lashed out at Jews. Various studies have found blacks to be more anti-Semitic than whites. *See, e.g.,* Dinnerstein, *supra* at 209–10; Jonathan Kaufman, Broken Alliance: The Turbulent Times Between Blacks and Jews in America 273–74 (1988). Current tensions between African Americans and Jews, two groups that were historically allies, are disheartening.

27. Shulamit Volkov, The Rise of Popular Antimodernism in Germany: The Urban Master Artisans, 1873–1896, at 317 (1978).

28. *See, e.g.,* Marx, *supra* at 3–40; de Man, *supra* at 269–71.

29. The quotation is taken from the subtitle of Wistrich, *supra*.

Synopses of Other Important Works

How the Irish Became White: Noel Ignatiev

In this landmark book, the writer (and editor of *Race Traitor* magazine) Noel Ignatiev expounds on a central theme in his work. Race is constructed, white-looking people regard whiteness as a good, and they struggle to get themselves defined that way. For the members of one ethnic group, however, the achievement of whiteness only "meant at first that they could sell themselves piecemeal instead of being sold for life, and later that they could compete for jobs in all spheres. . . . In becoming white the Irish ceased to be Green" (pp. 2–3). Readers interested in labor history and the personal, political consequences of assuming—or shrugging off—a white identity will find *How the Irish Became White* sobering reading. (Please see Chapter 100 for an interview with Mr. Ignatiev.)

Human Belief and "Race": Ian F. Haney López

In "The Social Construction of Race," 29 *Harv. C.R.–C.L. L. Rev.* 1 (1994), Ian F. Haney López takes issue with "ethnicity theorists," who hold that blacks and other minorities of color are just like Italians and Irish and should be able to rise by hard work and diligent assimilation of American values. Constructed and treated radically differently, African-Americans and "white ethnics" have greatly different life chances, possibilities of intermarriage, and opportunities for assimilation. None of this difference is biologically based, however. Haney López points out that no genetic characteristic is possessed by every black but not by nonblacks. By the same token, no set of genes uniquely characterizes whites but not nonwhites: The lighest black is lighter than the darkest white, and vice versa. Small population groups, such as the Xhosa or the Basques, share certain physical traits among themselves, but these are not unique to them. The belief that humanity can be divided into five (or some other number of) great races reveals more about human belief than it does about race. In showing how law has been used to reinforce racial subordination, Haney López reveals how racial divisions are relatively new constructions, subject to constant change.

From the Editors: Issues and Comments

Can anyone get ahead in our society if he or she is willing to work hard? Is the price of doing so assimilation—giving up one's distinctive Irishness, Mexicanness, blackness, and so on? If you suddenly developed an allergy to some substance found only in the United States, and so you had to emigrate to another country, which one would you choose? How would you expect to be treated? Suppose you were frowned at for identifying with your Americanness? Are working-class whites who get scholarships, go to Ivy League schools, and become professors ever completely accepted? Are they always destined to be sub-whites? Are Jews white if they look white? For selections dealing with "passing for white" and describing the experiences of darker skinned people who look white (or vice versa), see Part VIII.

Suggested Readings

Delgado, Richard, *Rodrigo's Tenth Chronicle: Merit and Affirmative Action*, 83 Geo L.J. 1711 (1995).

Freeman, Alan, *Race and Class: The Dilemma of Liberal Reform*, 90 Yale L.J. 1880 (1981).

From Different Shores: Perspectives on Race and Ethnicity in America (Ronald Takaki, ed., 1987)

Higham, John, Strangers in the Land (1966).

The Invention of Ethnicity (W. Sollors, ed., 1989).

Karst, Kenneth, Belonging to America: Equal Citizenship and the Constitution (1989).

Lieberson, Stanley, A Piece of the Pie? Black and White Immigrants Since 1880 (1980).

Morgan, Edmund S., American Slavery, American Freedom: The Ordeal of Colonial Virginia (1975).

Waters, Mary, Ethnic Options: Choosing Identities in America (1990).

White Ethnics: Their Life in Working Class America (J. Ryan, ed., 1975).

Wilentz, Sean, Chants Democratic: New York City and The Rise of the American Working Class, 1788–1850 (1984).

Part VIII

The Color Line: Multiracial People and "Passing for White"

If you were black and could become white by taking a magic pill, would you do so? If you were of mixed race, your skin a medium color of brown so that you could identify either as white or as a person of color, which would you do? Who gives you the choice? Is it a liberatory act of defiance to chart one's own course, or is it a sign of deep role confusion? What should we make of minority communities who favor light-skinned members—or who display enmity and distrust toward other groups of color? In this part, you will read about all these scenarios, and about the life experience of white blacks, black whites, and light-skinned Latinas who lived to tell the tale.

69

Passing for White, Passing for Black

ADRIAN PIPER

[T]racing the history of my family is detective work as well as historical research. To date, what I *think* I know is that our first European-American ancestor landed in Ipswich, Massachusetts, in 1620 from Sussex; another in Jamestown, Virginia, in 1675 from London; and another in Philadelphia, Pennsylvania, in 1751 from Hamburg. Yet another was the first in our family to graduate from my own graduate institution in 1778. My great-great-grandmother from Madagascar, by way of Louisiana, is the known African ancestor on my father's side, as my great-great-grandfather from the Ibo of Nigeria is the known African ancestor on my mother's whose family has resided in Jamaica for three centuries.

I relate these facts and it doesn't seem to bother my newly discovered relatives. At first I had to wonder whether this ease of acceptance was not predicated on their mentally bracketing the implications of these facts and restricting their own immediate family ancestry to the European side. But when they remarked unselfconsciously on the family resemblances between us, I had to abandon that supposition. I still marvel at their enlightened and uncomplicated friendliness, and there is a part of me that still can't trust their acceptance of me. But that is a part of me I want neither to trust nor to accept in this context. I want to reserve my vigilance for its context of origin: The other white Americans I have encountered—even the bravest and most conscientious white scholars—for whom the suggestion that they might have significant African ancestry as the result of this country's long history of miscegenation is almost impossible to consider seriously.

She's heard the arguments, most astonishingly that, statistically, . . . the average white American is 6 percent black. Or, put another way, 95 percent of white Americans are 5 to 80 percent black. Her Aunt Tyler has told her stories about these whites researching their roots in the National Archives and finding they've got an African-American or two in the family, some becoming so hysterical they have to be carried out by paramedics.

Perry, *Another Present Era*

Estimates ranging up to 5 percent, and suggestions that up to one-fifth of the white population have some genes from black ancestors, are probably far too high. If these last figures were correct, the majority of Americans with some black ancestry would be known and counted as whites!

Davis, *Who Is Black?*

The detailed biological and genetic data can be gleaned from a careful review of *Genetic Abstracts* from about 1950 on. In response to my request for information about this, a white biological anthropologist once performed detailed calculations on the African admixture of five different genes, comparing British whites, American whites, and American blacks. The results ranged from 2 percent in one gene to 81.6 percent in another. About these results he commented, "I continue to believe five percent to be a reasonable estimate, but the matter is obviously complex. As you can see, it depends entirely on which genes you decide to use as racial 'markers' that are supposedly subject to little or no relevant selective pressure." Clearly, white resistance to the idea that most American whites have a significant percentage of African ancestry increases with the percentage suggested.

> *"Why, Doctor," said Dr. Latimer, "you Southerners began this absorption before the war. I understand that in one decade the mixed bloods rose from one-ninth to one-eighth of the population, and that as early as 1663 a law was passed in Maryland to prevent English women from intermarrying with slaves; and, even now, your laws against miscegenation presuppose that you apprehend danger from that source."*
>
> Harper, *Iola Leroy*

> *(That legislators and judges paid increasing attention to the regulation and punishment of miscegenation at this time does not mean that interracial sex and marriage as social practices actually increased in frequency; the centrality of these practices to legal discourse was instead a sign that their relation to power was changing. The extent of uncoerced miscegenation before this period is a debated issue.)*
>
> Eva Saks, "Representing Miscegenation Law," *Raritan*

The fact is, however, that the longer a person's family has lived in this country, the higher the probable percentage of African ancestry that person's family is likely to have—bad news for the DAR, I'm afraid. And the proximity to the continent of Africa of the country of origin from which one's forebears emigrated, as well as the colonization of a part of Africa by that country, are two further variables that increase the probability of African ancestry within that family. It would appear that only the Lapps of Norway are safe.

In Jamaica, my mother tells me, that everyone is of mixed ancestry is taken for granted. There are a few who vociferously proclaim themselves to be "Jamaican whites" having no African ancestry at all, but no one among the old and respected families takes them seriously. Indeed, they are assumed to be a bit unbalanced, and are regarded with amusement. In this country, by contrast, the fact of African ancestry among whites ranks up there with family incest, murder, and suicide as one of the bitterest and most difficult pills for white Americans to swallow.

> *"I had a friend who had two beautiful daughters whom he had educated in the North. They were cultured, and really belles in society. They were entirely ignorant of their lineage, but when their father died it was discovered that their mother had been a slave. It was a fearful blow. They would have faced poverty, but the knowledge of their tainted blood was more than they could bear."*
>
> Harper, *Iola Leroy*

> *There was much apprehension about the unknown amount of black ancestry in the white population of the South, and this was fanned into an unreasoning fear of invisible blackness. For instance, white laundries and cleaners would not accommodate blacks because whites were afraid they would be "contaminated" by the clothing of invisible blacks.*
>
> Davis, *Who Is Black?*

> *Suspicion is part of everyday life in Louisiana. Whites often grow up afraid to know their own genealogies. Many admit that as children they often stared at the skin below their fingernails*

and through a mirror at the white of their eyes to see if there was any "touch of the tarbrush."
Not finding written records of birth, baptism, marriage, or death for any one ancestor exacer-
bates suspicions of foul play. Such a discovery brings glee to a political enemy or economic ri-
val and may traumatize the individual concerned.

Domínguez, *White by Definition*

A number of years ago I was doing research on a video installation on the subject of racial identity and miscegenation, and came across the Phipps case of Louisiana in the early 1980s. Susie Guillory Phipps had identified herself as white and, according to her own testimony (but not that of some of her black relatives), had believed that she was white, until she applied for a passport, when she discovered that she was identified on her birth records as black by virtue of having one thirty-second African ancestry. She brought suit against the state of Louisiana to have her racial classification changed. She lost the suit but effected the overthrow of the law identifying individuals as black if they had one thirty-second African ancestry, leaving on the books a prior law identifying an individual as black who had any African ancestry—the "one-drop" rule that uniquely characterizes the classification of blacks in the United States in fact even where no longer in law. So according to this longstanding convention of racial classification, a white who acknowledges any African ancestry implicitly acknowledges being black—a social condition, more than an identity, that no white person would voluntarily assume, even in imagination. This is one reason that whites, educated and uneducated alike, are so resistant to considering the probable extent of racial miscegenation.

This "one-drop" convention of classification of blacks is unique not only relative to the treatment of blacks in other countries but also unique relative to the treatment of other ethnic groups in this country. It goes without saying that no one, either white or black, is identified as, for example, English by virtue of having some small fraction of English ancestry. Nor is anyone free, as a matter of social convention, to do so by virtue of that fraction, although many whites do. But even in the case of other disadvantaged groups in this country, the convention is different. Whereas any proportion of African ancestry is sufficient to identify a person as black, an individual must have *at least* one-eighth Native American ancestry in order to identify legally as Native American.

Why the asymmetry of treatment? Clearly, the reason is economic. A legally certifiable Native American is entitled to financial benefits from the government, so obtaining this certification is difficult. A legally certifiable black person is *disentitled* to financial, social, and inheritance benefits from his white family of origin, so obtaining this certification is not just easy but automatic. Racial classification in this country functions to restrict the distribution of goods, entitlements, and status as narrowly as possible to those whose power is already entrenched. Of course this institutionalized disentitlement presupposes that two persons of different racial classifications cannot be biologically related, which is absurd.

This [one-drop] definition of who is black was crucial to maintaining the social system of
white domination in which widespread miscegenation, not racial purity, prevailed. White
womanhood was the highly charged emotional symbol, but the system protected white eco-
nomic, political, legal, education and other institutional advantages for whites. . . . American
slave owners wanted to keep all racially mixed children born to slave women under their con-
trol, for economic and sexual gains. . . . It was intolerable for white women to have mixed chil-
dren, so the one-drop rule favored the sexual freedom of white males, protecting the double
standard of sexual morality as well as slavery. . . . By defining all mixed children as black and
compelling them to live in the black community, the rule made possible the incredible myth

among whites that miscegenation had not occurred, that the races had been kept pure in the
South.

Davis, *Who Is Black?*

But the issues of family entitlements and inheritance rights are not uppermost in the minds of most white Americans, who wince at the mere suggestion that they might have some fraction of African ancestry and therefore be, according to this country's entrenched convention of racial classification, black. The primary issue for them is not what they might have to give away by admitting that they are in fact black, but rather what they have to lose. What they have to lose, of course, is social status—and, insofar as their self-esteem is based on their social status as whites, self-esteem as well.

"I think," said Dr. Latrobe, proudly, "that we belong to the highest race on earth and the ne-
gro to the lowest."
*   "And yet," said Dr. Latimer, "you have consorted with them till you have bleached their*
faces to the whiteness of your own. Your children nestle in their bosoms; they are around you
as body servants, and yet if one of them should attempt to associate with you your bitterest
scorn and indignation would be visited upon them."

Harper, *Iola Leroy*

No reflective and well-intentioned white person who is consciously concerned to end racism wants to admit to instinctively recoiling at the thought of being identified as black herself. But if you want to see such a white person do this, just peer at the person's facial features and tell her, in a complimentary tone of voice, that she looks as though she might have some black ancestry, and watch her reaction. It's not a test I or any black person finds particularly pleasant to apply (that is, unless one dislikes the person and wants to inflict pain deliberately), and having once done so inadvertently, I will never do it again. The ultimate test of a person's repudiation of racism is not what she can contemplate *doing* for or on behalf of black people, but whether she herself can contemplate calmly the likelihood of *being* black. If racial hatred has not manifested itself in any other context, it will do so here if it exists, in hatred of the self as identified with the other—that is, as self-hatred projected onto the other.

Since Harry had come North he had learned to feel profound pity for the slave. But there is
difference between looking on a man as an object of pity and protecting him as such, and be-
ing identified with him and forced to share his lot.

Harper, *Iola Leroy*

Let me tell you how I'd get those white devil convicts and the guards, too, to do anything I
wanted. I'd whisper to them, "If you don't, I'll start a rumor that you're really a light Negro
just passing as white." That shows you what the white devil thinks about the black man. He'd
rather die than be thought a Negro!

The Autobiography of Malcolm X

When I was an undergraduate minoring in medieval and Renaissance musicology, I worked with a fellow music student—white—in the music library. I remember his reaction when I relayed to him an article I'd recently read arguing that Beethoven had African ancestry. Beethoven was one of his heroes, and his vehement derision was completely out of proportion to the scholarly worth of the hypothesis. But when I suggested that he wouldn't be so skeptical if the claim were that Beethoven had some Danish ancestry, he fell silent. In those days we were very conscious of covert racism, as our campus was exploding all around us because of it. More recently I premiered at a gallery a video installation exploring the issue of African ancestry among white Americans. A white male viewer commenced to kick the furniture, mutter audibly that he was white and was going to stay that way, and start a fistfight with my dealer. Either we are less conscious of covert racism twenty years later, or we care less to contain it.

Among politically committed and enlightened whites, the inability to acknowledge their probable African ancestry is the last outpost of racism. It is the litmus test that separates those who have the courage of their convictions from those who merely subscribe to them and that measures the depth of our dependence on a presumed superiority (of any kind, anything will do) to other human beings—anyone, anywhere—to bolster our fragile self-worth. Many blacks are equally unwilling to explore their white ancestry—approximately 25 percent on average for the majority of blacks—for this reason. For some, of course, acknowledgment of this fact evokes only bitter reminders of rape, disinheritance, enslavement, and exploitation, and their distaste is justifiable. But for others, it is the mere idea of blackness as an essentialized source of self-worth and self-affirmation that forecloses the acknowledgment of mixed ancestry. This, too, is understandable: Having struggled so long and hard to carve a sense of wholeness and value for ourselves out of our ancient connection with Africa after having been actively denied any in America, many of us are extremely resistant to once again casting ourselves into the same chaos of ethnic and psychological ambiguity that our diaspora to this country originally inflicted on us.

Thus blacks and whites alike seem to be unable to accord worth to others outside their in-group affiliations without feeling that they are taking it away from themselves. We may have the concept of intrinsic self-worth, but by and large we do not understand what it means. We need someone else whom we can regard as inferior, to whom we can compare ourselves favorably, and if no such individual or group exists, we invent one. For without this, we seem to have no basis, no standard of comparison, for conceiving of ourselves favorably at all. We seem, for example, truly unable to grasp or take seriously the alternative possibility of measuring ourselves or our performances against our own past novicehood at one end and our own future potential at the other. I think this is in part the result of our collective fear of memory as a nation, our profound unwillingness to confront the painful truths about our history and our origins, and in part the result of our individual fear of the memory of our own pasts—not only of our individual origins and the traumas of socialization we each suffered before we could control what was done to us, but the pasts of our own adult behavior—the painful truths of our own derelictions, betrayals, and failures to respect our individual ideals and convictions.

When I turned forty a few years ago, I gave myself the present of rereading the personal journals I have been keeping since age eleven. I was astounded at the chasm between my present conception of my own past, which is being continually revised and updated to suit present circumstances, and the actual past events, behavior, and emotions I recorded as faithfully as I could as they happened. My derelictions, mistakes, and failures of responsibility are much more evident in these journals than they are in my present, sanitized, and virtually blameless image of my past behavior. It was quite a shock to encounter in those pages the person I actually have been rather than the person I now conceive myself to have been. My memory is always under the control of the person I now want and strive to be, and so rarely under the control of the facts. If the personal facts of one's past are this difficult for other people to face too, then perhaps it is no wonder that we must cast about outside ourselves for someone to feel superior to, even though there are so many blunders and misdeeds in our own personal histories that might serve that function.

For whites to acknowledge their blackness is, then, much the same as for men to acknowledge their femininity and for Christians to acknowledge their Judaic heritage. It is to reinternalize the external scapegoat through attention to which they have sought to escape their own sense of inferiority.

Now the white man leaned in the window, looking at the impenetrable face with its definite strain of white blood, the same blood which ran in his own veins, which had not only come to the negro through male descent while it had come to him from a woman, but had reached the negro a generation sooner—a face composed, inscrutable, even a little haughty, shaped even in expression in the pattern of his great-grandfather McCaslin's face. . . . He thought, and not for the first time: I am not only looking at a face older than mine and which has seen and winnowed more, but at a man most of whose blood was pure ten thousand years when my own anonymous beginnings became mixed enough to produce me.

Faulkner, *Go Down, Moses*

I said . . . that the guilt of American whites included their knowledge that in hating Negroes, they were hating, they were rejecting, they were denying, their own blood.

The Autobiography of Malcolm X

It is to bring ourselves face to face with our obliterated collective past, and to confront the continuities of responsibility that link the criminal acts of extermination and enslavement committed by our forefathers with our own personal crimes of avoidance, neglect, disengagement, passive complicity, and active exploitation of the inherited injustices from which we have profited. Uppermost among these is that covert sense of superiority a white person feels over a black person which buttresses his enjoyment of those unjust benefits as being no more or less than he deserves. To be deprived of that sense of superiority to the extent that acknowledgment of common ancestry would effect is clearly difficult for most white people. But to lose the social regard and respect that accompanies it is practically unbearable. I know—not only because of what I have read and observed of the pathology of racism in white people, but because I have often experienced the withdrawal of that social regard firsthand.

For most of my life I did not understand that I needed to identify my racial identity publicly and that if I did not I would be inevitably mistaken for white. I simply didn't think about it. But since I also made no special effort to hide my racial identity, I often experienced the shocked and/or hostile reactions of whites who discovered it after the fact. I always knew when it had happened, even when the person declined to confront me directly: the startled look, the searching stare that would fix itself on my facial features, one by one, looking for the telltale "negroid" feature, the sudden, sometimes permanent withdrawal of good feeling or regular contact—all alerted me to what had transpired. Uh-oh, I would think to myself helplessly, and watch another blossoming friendship wilt.

In thus travelling about through the country I was sometimes amused on arriving at some little railroad-station town to be taken for and treated as a white man, and six hours later, when it was learned that I was stopping at the house of the coloured preacher or schoolteacher, to note the attitude of the whole town change.

Johnson, *The Autobiography of an Ex-Coloured Man*

Sometimes this revelation would elicit a response of the most twisted and punitive sort: for example, from the colleague who glared at me and hissed, "Oh, so you want to be black, do you? Good! Then we'll treat you like one!" The ensuing harassment had a furious, retaliatory quality that I find difficult to understand even now: as though I'd delivered a deliberate and crushing insult . . .

70

Black Like Me

JOHN HOWARD GRIFFIN

[In 1959 award-winning journalist John Howard Griffin decided to investigate race relations in the South. Taking medications to darken his skin, he assumed a black physical identity and recorded his experiences traveling in that region. Ed.]

November 6

For the past four days, I had spent my time at the doctor's or closed up in my room with cotton pads over my eyes and the sun lamp turned on me. They had made blood tests twice and found no indication of damage to the liver. But the medication produced lassitude and I felt constantly on the verge of nausea.

The doctor, well-disposed, gave me many warnings about the dangers of this project in so far as my contact with Negroes was concerned. Now that he had had time to think, he was beginning to doubt the wisdom of this course, or perhaps he felt strongly his responsibility. In any event, he warned me that I must have some contact in each major city so my family could check on my safety from time to time.

"I believe in the brotherhood of man," he said. "I respect the race. But I can never forget when I was an intern and had to go down on South Rampart Street to patch them up. Three or four would be sitting in a bar or at a friend's house. They were apparently friends one minute and then something would come up and one would get slashed up with a knife. We're willing enough to go all the way for them, but we've got this problem—how can you render the duties of justice to men when you're afraid they'd be so unaware of justice they may destroy you?—especially since their attitude toward their own race is a destructive one." He said this with real sadness. I told him my contacts indicated that Negroes themselves were aware of this dilemma and they were making strong efforts to unify the race, to condemn among themselves any tactic or any violence or injustice that would reflect against the race as a whole.

"I'm glad to hear that," he said, obviously unconvinced.

He also told me things that Negroes had told him—that the lighter the skin the more trustworthy the Negro. I was astonished to see an intelligent man fall for this cliché, and equally astonished that Negroes would advance it, for in effect it placed the dark Negro in an inferior position and fed the racist idea of judging a man by his color.

When not lying under the lamp, I walked the streets of New Orleans to orient myself.

Each day I stopped at a sidewalk shoeshine stand near the French Market. The shine boy was an elderly man, large, keenly intelligent and a good talker. He had lost a leg during World War I. He showed none of the obsequiousness of the Southern Negro, but was polite and easy to know. (Not that I had any illusions that I knew him, for he was too astute to allow any white man that privilege.) I told him I was a writer, touring the Deep South to study living conditions, civil rights, etc., but I did not tell him I would do this as a Negro. Finally, we exchanged names. He was called Sterling Williams. I decided he might be the contact for my entry into the Negro community.

November 10–12

On Chartres Street in the French Quarter I walked toward Brennan's, one of New Orleans' famed restaurants. Forgetting myself for a moment, I stopped to study the menu that was elegantly exposed in a show window. I read, realizing that a few days earlier I could have gone in and ordered anything on the menu. But now, though I was the same person with the same appetite, the same appreciation and even the same wallet, no power on earth could get me inside this place for a meal. I recalled hearing some Negro say, "You can live here all your life, but you'll never get inside one of the great restaurants except as kitchen boy." The Negro often dreams of things separated from him only by a door, knowing that he is forever cut off from experiencing them.

I read the menu carefully, forgetting that Negroes do not do such things. It is too poignant, like the little boy peering in the candy store window. It might affect the tourist. I looked up to see the frowns of disapproval that can speak so plainly and so loudly without words. The Negro learns this silent language fluently. He knows by the white man's look of disapproval and petulance that he is being told to get on his way, that he is "stepping out of line."

It was a day of giving the gracious smile and receiving the gracious rebuff as I asked again and again about jobs. Finally, I gave up and went to the shine stand. From there I set out to return at dusk to Dryades. But I had walked too far. My legs gave out. At Jackson Square, a public park, I found a long, curving bench and sat down to rest for a moment. The park appeared deserted. A movement through the bushes attracted my attention. I looked to see a middle-aged white man across the park slowly fold the newspaper he was reading, get to his feet and amble toward me. The fragrance of his pipe tobacco preceded him, reassuring me. Racists are not the pipe-smoking type, I thought to myself.

With perfect courtesy he said, "You'd better find yourself someplace else to rest."

I took it as a favor. He was warning me I could get out before someone insulted me. "Thank you," I said. "I didn't know we weren't allowed in here."

Later, I told the story at the Y, and discovered that Negroes have the right to sit in Jackson Square. This individual simply did not want me there.

But at the time I did not know it. I left, sick with exhaustion, wondering where a Negro could sit to rest. It was walk constantly until you could catch a bus, but keep on the move unless you have business somewhere. If you stop to sit on the curb, a police car will pass and probably ask you what you're doing. I have heard none of the Negroes speak of police harassment, but they have warned me that any time the police see a Negro idling, especially one they do not recognize, they will surely question him. This is worrisome, certainly an experience any Negro wants to avoid.

I walked over to Claiborne and caught the first bus that passed. It took me out to Dillard University, a beautiful campus. I was too tired to explore it, however, and sat on the bench waiting to catch another bus into town. Buses were inexpensive to ride and it was a good way to rest.

Night was near when I finally caught the bus going toward town. Two blocks before Canal, the bus makes a left turn off Claiborne. I rang the bell to get off at this stop. The driver pulled to a halt and opened the door. He left it open until I reached it. I was ready to step off when the door banged shut in my face. Since he had to remain there waiting for a clear passage through traffic, I asked him to let me off.

"I can't leave the door open all night," he said impatiently.

He waited another full minute, but refused to open the door.

"Will you please let me off at the next corner, then?" I asked, controlling my temper, careful not to do or say anything that would jeopardize the Negroes' position in the area.

He did not answer. I returned to my seat. A woman watched me with sympathetic anger, as though she in no way approved of this kind of treatment. However, she did not speak.

At each stop, I sounded the buzzer, but the driver continued through the next two stops. He drove me eight full blocks past my original stop and pulled up then only because some white passengers wanted to get off. I followed them to the front. He watched me, his hand on the lever that would spring the doors shut.

"May I get off now?" I asked quietly when the others had stepped down.

"Yeah, go ahead," he said finally, as though he had tired of the cat-and-mouse game. I got off, sick, wondering how I could ever walk those eight blocks back to my original stop.

In all fairness, I must add that this is the only example of deliberate cruelty I encountered on any of the city buses of New Orleans. Even though I was outraged, I knew he did not commit this indignity against me, but against my black flesh, my color. This was an individual act by an individual, and certainly not typical.

November 19

I arrived by bus in Biloxi too late to find any Negroes about, so I walked inland and slept, half-freezing, in a tin-roofed shed with an open south front. In the morning I found breakfast in a little Negro café—coffee and toast—and then walked down to the highway to begin hitching. The highway ran for miles along some of the most magnificent beaches I have ever seen—white sands, a beautiful ocean; and opposite the beach, splendid homes. The sun warmed me through, and I took my time, stopping to study the historic markers placed along the route.

For lunch, I bought a pint of milk and a ready-wrapped bologna sandwich in a roadside store. I carried them to the walk that runs along the shallow sea wall and ate. A local Negro stopped to talk. I asked him if the swimming were good there, since the beaches were so splendid. He told me the beaches were "man-made," the sand dredged in; but that unless a Negro sneaked off to some isolated spot, he'd never know how the water was, since Negroes weren't permitted to enjoy the beaches. He pointed out the injustice of this policy, since the upkeep of the beaches comes from a gasoline tax. "In other words, every time we buy a gallon of gas, we pay a penny to keep the beach up so the whites can use it," he said. He added that some of the local Negro citizens were considering a project to keep an account of the gasoline they purchased throughout the year and at the end of that time demand from the town fathers either a refund on their gasoline tax or the privilege of using the beaches for which they had paid their fair part.

After a time I walked again on legs that grew weak with weariness. A car pulled up beside me and a young, redheaded white man told me to "hop in." His glance was friendly, courteous, and he spoke with no condescension. I began to hope that I had underestimated the people of Mississippi. With what eagerness I grasped at every straw of kindness, wanting to give a good report.

"Beautiful country, isn't it?" he said.

"Marvelous."

"You just passing through?"

"Yes sir . . . I'm on my way to Mobile."

"Where you from?"

"Texas."

"I'm from Massachusetts," he said, as though he were eager for me to know he was not a Mississippian. I felt the keenest disappointment, and mentally erased the passages I had mentally composed about the kindness of the Mississippian who gave the Negro a ride. He told me he had no sympathy for the "Southern attitude."

"That shows," I said.

"But you know," he added, "these are some of the finest people in the world about everything else."

"I'm sure they are."

"I know you won't believe it—but it's really the truth. I just don't ever talk to them about the race question."

"With your attitude, I can understand that," I laughed.

"They can't discuss it," he said. "It's a shame but all they do is get mad whenever you bring it up. I'll never understand it. They're blocked on that one subject. I've lived here over five years now—and they're good neighbors; but if I mention race with any sympathy for the Negro, they just tell me I'm an 'outsider' and don't understand about Negroes. What's there to understand?"

I walked what—ten, fifteen miles? I walked because one does not just simply sit down in the middle of a highway, because there was nothing to do but walk.

Late in the afternoon, my mind hazed with fatigue. I concentrated all my energy in putting one foot in front of the other. Sweat poured down into my eyes and soaked my clothes and the heat of the pavement came through my shoes. I remember I stopped at a little custard stand and bought a dish of ice cream merely to have the excuse to sit at one of the tables under the trees—none of which were occupied. But before I could take my ice cream and walk to one of them some white teen-agers appeared and took seats. I dared not sit down even at a distant table. Wretched with disappointment I leaned against a tree and ate the ice cream.

Behind the custard stand stood an old unpainted privy leaning badly to one side. I returned to the dispensing window of the stand.

"Yes sir," the white man said congenially. "You want something else?"

"Where's the nearest rest room I could use?" I asked.

He brushed his white, brimless cook's cap back and rubbed his forefinger against his sweaty forehead. "Let's see. You can go on up there to the bridge and then cut down the road to the left . . . and just follow that road. You'll come to a little settlement—there's some stores and gas stations there."

"How far is it?" I asked, pretending to be in greater discomfort than I actually was. "Not far—thirteen, maybe fourteen blocks."

A locust's lazy rasping sawed the air from the nearby oak trees.

"Isn't there anyplace closer?" I said, determined to see if he would not offer me the use of the dilapidated outhouse, which certainly no human could degrade any more than time and the elements had.

His seamed face showed the concern and sympathy of one human for another in a predicament every man understands. "I can't think of any . . ." he said slowly.

I glanced around the side toward the outhouse. "Any chance of me running in there for a minute?"

"Nope," he said—clipped, final, soft, as though he regretted it but could never permit such a thing. "I'm sorry." He turned away.

"Thank you just the same," I said.

By dark I was away from the beach area and out in the country. Strangely, I began getting rides. Men would pass you in daylight but pick you up after dark.

I must have had a dozen rides that evening. They blear into a nightmare, the one scarcely distinguishable from the other.

It quickly became obvious why they picked me up. All but two picked me up the way they would pick up a pornographic photograph or book—except that this was verbal pornography. With a Negro, they assumed they need give no semblance of self-respect or respectability. The visual element entered into it. In a car at night visibility is reduced. A man will reveal himself in the dark, which gives an illusion of anonymity, more than he will in the bright light. Some were shamelessly open, some shamelessly subtle. All showed morbid curiosity about the sexual life of the Negro, and all had, at base, the same stereotyped image of the Negro as an inexhaustible sex-machine with oversized genitals and a vast store of experiences, immensely varied. They appeared to think that the Negro has done all of those "special" things they themselves have never dared to do. They carried the conversation into the depths of depravity. I note these things because it is harrowing to see decent-looking men and boys assume that because a man is black they need show him none of the reticences they would, out of respect, show the most derelict white man. I note them, too, because they differed completely from the "bull sessions" men customarily have among themselves. These latter, no matter how frank, have generally a robust tone that says: "We are men, this is an enjoyable thing to do and to discuss, but it will never impugn the basic respect we give one another; it will never distort our humanity." In this, the atmosphere, no matter how coarse, has a verve and an essential joviality that casts out morbidity. It implies respect for the persons involved. But all that I could see here were men shorn of respect either for themselves or their companion.

In my grogginess and exhaustion, these conversations became ghoulish. Each time one of them let me out of his car, I hoped the next would spare me his pantings. I remained mute and pleaded my exhaustion and lack of sleep.

"I'm so tired, I just can't think," I would say.

Like men who had promised themselves pleasure, they would not be denied. It became a strange sort of hounding as they nudged my skull for my sexual reminiscences.

"Well did you ever do such-and-such?"

"I don't know . . ." I moaned.

"What's the matter—haven't you got any manhood? My old man told me you wasn't really a man till you'd done such-and-such."

Or the older ones, hardened, cynical in their lechery. "Now, don't try to kid me. I wasn't born yesterday. You know you've done such-and-such, just like I have. Hell, it's good that way. Tell me, did you ever get a white woman?"

"Do you think I'm crazy?" I tacitly denied the racist's contention, for he would not hesitate to use it against the Negroes in his conversations around town: "Why, I had one of them admit to me just last night that he craves white women."

"I didn't ask if you was crazy," he said. "I asked if you ever had one—or ever really wanted one." Then, conniving, sweet-toned, "There's plenty white women would like to have a good buck Negro."

"A Negro'd be asking for the rope to get himself mixed up with white women."

"You're just telling me that, but I'll bet inside you think differently . . ."

"This is sure beautiful country through here. What's the main crop?"

"*Don't you?* You can tell me. Hell, I don't care."

"No sir," I sighed.

"You're lying in your teeth and you know it."

Silence. Soon after, almost abruptly he halted the car and said, "Okay, this is as far as I go." He spoke as though he resented my uncooperative attitude, my refusal to give him this strange verbal sexual pleasure.

I thanked him for the ride and stepped down onto the highway. He drove on in the same direction.

71

The Michael Jackson Pill: Equality, Race, and Culture

JEROME MCCRISTAL CULP, JR.

The Chronicle of the Michael Jackson Pill

I was leaving Langdell Hall, after having feasted too fervently at my fifteenth law school reunion, when I noticed what looked like a very ancient document pushed down in the trash can. The ancient scroll seemed out of place so carelessly thrown away outside the world's largest law school library. I picked it up and was surprised to discover that there, very near Derrick Bell's former office, I had found another of the scrolls that Professor Bell's friend Geneva had revealed to him before she joined the celestial curia. What was this wondrous document doing in Langdell Hall? Maybe it was some further message from Geneva Crenshaw that had been dropped there for me to discover. I rushed to find Professor Bell to tell him of my good luck.

As I approached the office that had once belonged to Professor Bell, I noticed a group of six black men standing together in the hallway. Much to my surprise and delight, I recognized among them the five faculty members at Harvard Law School who are both black and male. The sixth man was not Professor Bell, nor did I know him from Harvard, but he looked familiar and unmistakably professorial. Seeing this group gathered there confirmed the only possible interpretation of my discovery—I had been given the opportunity to share it with those at Harvard who would most appreciate its significance and, perhaps, explain it to me.

"Hey guys! What are you doing here?" I asked, chuckling secretly to myself about my discovery. However—as I was about to say some new version of "Guess what I found?"—I noticed that they all held scrolls that looked markedly like mine. Without an additional word we all opened our scrolls to find identical statements:

Dr. Michael Jackson, a doctor educated at Motown University and now a professor of medical appearance at Hollywood University, has invented a pill that if taken by black people will remove all vestiges of being black. Black features will disappear from black people who take the pill, and they will be given a random selection of names that white people in America have. Black speech patterns and ways of organizing expression will go away. To every outside appearance, all black people who take the pill will become white.

The legislature of the Commonwealth of Massachusetts has passed Massachusetts General

92 Mich. L. Rev. 2613 (1994). Originally published in the *Michigan Law Review*. Reprinted by permission.

Law 1619.28, requiring all black residents of the state to take the Michael Jackson Pill. Black residents who do not take the pill are subject to fines of up to $ 2,000. Sonny Flynn, speaker of the Massachusetts Assembly, said, "This bill will for all time remove the vestiges of slavery that have plagued this great commonwealth." The NAACP objects to the application of this statute to black residents of Massachusetts and asks the five black Harvard faculty members and Professor Derrick Bell to write a brief and argue the case. Representative King, one of three African Americans in the Massachusetts House of Representatives, has pointed out that evidence suggests that white people who take the pill will become black. He argues that black is beautiful and that we ought to make all white people take the pill. Marjorie Jones, a white professor of political economy at the Kennedy School, has noted that it is cheaper to have black people take the pill and that the problems with race are basically confined to the unfortunate segment that is black. "We, the white citizens of Massachusetts, are willing to welcome black people to that great white melting pot," she adds.

We were all instantly removed to a conference room nearby, with Derrick Bell at one end of the table and at the other an empty chair. Several of the faculty began to talk simultaneously when a deep but very feminine voice, belonging unmistakably to Geneva Crenshaw, interrupted . . .

Geneva Crenshaw: Excuse me—Excuse me. I see that you are all here. I have called all of you here today to discuss whether black people should take this pill. Can we be saved by a pill that transforms all black people into white people? Derrick has been making trouble by questioning whether some of you even want to be white, but Dr. Jackson has given all black people that opportunity.

Professor Bell: Gee—I think I need to know a little bit more about this pill.

Geneva Crenshaw: You mean you want to know whether you still will have rhythm after you take the pill.

Professor Culp: We all know your penchant for hyperbole, Ms. Crenshaw, but hasn't this description of the pill been simplistic? Eliminating blackness may exact a heavy price, and personally, I like being black.

Geneva Crenshaw: I don't know who you are—though there must be a reason for you to be here—but the point is this: You take the pill and you aren't black anymore—though some of you may have to take it twice. The pill doesn't eliminate class or other characteristics.

Professor Bell: I think we ought to start with a vote to see how many people think that all black people ought to be required to take this pill.

[The black male faculty look around at each other. Some raise their hands—most of them slowly. Others look disturbed but do not raise their hands.

Professor Culp keeps raising and lowering his hand.

One by one they each start to speak, asking questions of Geneva Crenshaw and of one another and beginning a debate that continues for some time. After listening to his compatriots carry on for a while, the strange-yet-familiar professor joins the conversation . . .]

Professor Not-Professor-Bell: I don't understand your ambivalence, Professor Culp. This pill washes away all the manifestations of racial difference. You have pointed out in your writing the importance of race as a cause of our nation's problems. Race will be no more, and therefore racial problems will be no more.

Professor Culp: I'm sorry, but the issue is still not clear to me. I gain from being black. My parents have strength of character that aids me in my work. The history of my family has an importance that would be erased if there were no culture or language or notion of place that was connected with being black.

Professor Not-Professor-Bell: Race is simply a cultural creation. As Professor Kendall Thomas of Columbia Law School is fond of saying, black people are raced. The pill removes the power of white people to race us.

Professor Culp: I understand that we are raced by society, but culture means something positive to me. People are raced, but people are also cultured and the two are interdependent. Black people invent themselves as black people through culture and history. Race, in other words, has a positive side.

Professor Not-Professor-Bell: We're all lawyers here, not cultural critics. Race will not matter in the job market when black people have taken the pill and become white. Being black doesn't make one a better janitor or law professor. Culture is a social creation: with this pill, those of us who want to love jazz or basketball or Toni Morrison or Gwendolyn Brooks can do so without the handicap of difference. Race doesn't matter, so taking it away shouldn't matter either. Indeed—what we want to eliminate are the transient and unimportant things that get in the way of equality.

Professor Culp: I'm not sure race is so easily disconnected from our notion of what a law professor is. I was pushing a garbage cart toward my office one evening when the child of two of my black colleagues asked me whether I had to hold a second job. My colleagues' child understood that what you do is closely connected with your race. Black people clean and wash toilets, and if they are special, like her parents, they may get to teach at a law school. Her fear—consistent with her experience—was that all black people secretly had to be cleaning people.

Geneva Crenshaw: You may be right, Professor Culp, but not completely. You see race from a patriarchal perspective. This very male room may be willing to take the pill without understanding the implications of culture. However, gender and other notions of identity cannot be separated from race, and culture holds gender and race together. Black men always think that if their apparent problem were solved—if only they weren't black—then the problems of black people would go away. The point is that black problems are more than simply race as defined by what black men are concerned about.

Professor Culp: But Geneva, black men are oppressed. They are jailed and die at an alarming rate.

Geneva Crenshaw: You don't have to tell black women about black men. The problem is that black men want to define the problem of black people only from their own perspective. Black women are oppressed by both race and gender, and this pill does nothing about this multiple oppression.

Professor Not-Professor-Bell: Isn't that the point, Ms. Crenshaw? This pill will eliminate any intersection between race and gender.

Professor Culp: The intersection will only be eliminated if we also remove the economic and other concerns produced by the interaction of race and gender.

Geneva Crenshaw: Close, but only a B- for theoretical rigor. The intersection of race and gender or of race, class, and gender cannot be reduced either to separate concerns or to a combination of concerns that are measured in economic values. Black women will always be women with the additional oppression of blackness. This oppression, however, is not simply added on. Oppressions, like rabbits, multiply exponentially when they are combined.

Professor Not-Professor-Bell: But taking the race pill will eliminate that multiplication by eliminating race, Geneva.

Professor Culp: That will be true only if we know what race is and what happens when we eliminate that social construction. It may take a race-gender pill to eliminate the intersections if race and gender add together to form something more powerful . . .

Geneva Crenshaw: Before you get to a race, gender, class, or sexual orientation oppression pill, deal with the problem we have before us. You have not answered the question of whether you think the law ought to require black people to take the Michael Jackson Pill. It might be true that we should not desire that black people give up jazz and storytelling, but there are white people who play jazz and who tell stories. Haven't you, Professor Culp, fallen into the trap of essentialism? You assume that race exists when it is in fact a political illusion.

Professor Culp: I am not naïve. I read the biological and historical literature. I know that people have argued that there is no meaningful biological basis for race, but that does not mean that we cannot worry about its social consequences.

Professor Bell: I argued in a recent book that racism is a permanent phenomenon.[1] The problem I see is that this pill cures race but not racism.

Professor Not-Professor-Bell: Notice that the elimination of race also eliminates white communities opposed to change. After all, the Ku Klux Klan is a racially created community for keeping the racial status quo.

Professor Culp: Indeed, the Democratic party was at times a racially created community to prevent change in the black community, particularly in the South. However, this pill doesn't eliminate the white community; it simply permits those who take the Michael Jackson Pill to enter it. If the white community contains elements of oppression, it may reinvent other subcommunities of people to oppress—people who tan too well or who have other characteristics. And for those black people who choose to stay black, race will still exist, as will racism.

Professor Not-Professor-Bell: The courts limit the notions of equality that the legislature or Congress can use, but they do not eliminate the ability of those institutions to make changes. What this pill does is provide choice to black people in the same way that *Roe v. Wade*[2] provides choice to women about pregnancy.

Professor Culp: One of my white male students wondered whether he could challenge a minority clerkship that was created for black first-year law students in a large southern law firm without many black associates and partners. He questioned whether such a program was fair or legal. My answer was that the program is probably legal, but as the market becomes tighter, it is going to be more difficult to prevent courts from overturning any victory accomplished in Congress or state legislatures or local governments or by community groups. The Court's jurisprudence in *Croson,*[3] *Hicks,*[4] and *Shaw v. Reno*[5] bears me out. When black people engage fairly in the governing process, their views are found to be inappropriate if they alter the racial status quo. Such alteration threatens white supremacy, which the Supreme Court is not willing to eradicate.

Professor Not-Professor-Bell: Aren't you making this student out to be a villain when he is simply trying for fairness? Why should the son of a black doctor get a job instead of the son or daughter of a white mechanic?

Professor Culp: You miss the point, just as that student and, too often, the Court do. Racial communities have played the same role regarding problems of class that the gay community has in the AIDS health crisis. We know that a class and poverty problem exists in this country primarily because we see evidence of it in the black community. The gay community's involvement with AIDS allowed us to understand the existence of the AIDS health crisis much earlier than we would have otherwise. Communities and the differences those communities produce have importance and power that individuals do not—for good as well as evil. A large part of the power behind change for the poor comes, not from the larger white poor community, but from the black poor, who are fairly egalitarian about the change they support.

Geneva Crenshaw: This sounds like the argument often heard in black literary and political circles—that blacks have some mythic ability to suffer and to redeem white America.[6]

Professor Culp: No, I don't believe pain is good for the soul or necessarily leads to redemption. I see too much pain in our poor communities of color and too little redemption there. The redemption thesis assumes that we can only see the world through the lenses of the majority. I would like to see it through the lenses of the black minority and the other communities of color. In those communities we can form action, not as an example of pain or as victims of oppression, but as positive forces for change.

Geneva Crenshaw: Does this mean that you think that the black community alone will solve the problems of poverty and race?

Professor Culp: My point is that one of the few forces for change in our society comes from the politics surrounding race. If we eliminate that positive force it will be even more difficult to accomplish change in the world.

Professor Not-Professor-Bell: I agree with you that community is important, but why does it have to be *black* community? Isn't it possible that the reason other communities are not forces for change is that race gets in the way? If that's true, removing the notion of race not only will eliminate that impediment but also may allow new, more effective, nonracial communities to come into existence.

Professor Culp: What you say is theoretically possible, but the truth is that the most effective communities have been those that have some notion of identity that empowers change. This has been true for ethnic groups—Jews and Italians, for example—as well as for some Asian groups and some religious groups—including Mormons and Catholics. All these groups have used a sense of community to accomplish social and economic progress.

Professor Bell: You're saying that the very idea behind the pill runs counter to the forces that have produced change in America and that we will not be able to accomplish change without some notion of community.

Professor Culp: People are not identity-less automatons. If we eliminate people's race and the communities in which they exist, can they be whole?

Geneva Crenshaw: As I understand it, the Michael Jackson Pill creates a person who is not raceless but white. Aren't you simply doing what you criticize in others, Professor Culp, by assuming that white people don't have a race?

Professor Culp: You may be right. What I meant to say is that we cannot make black people into white people without losing something important.

Professor Not-Professor-Bell: How can that be? Race has no meaning. Professor Culp, you're looking for a form of essentialism that replaces race with culture. More importantly, aren't you falling into the trap set by the Afrocentric essentialists, who argue for a superior black culture? They would replace white supremacy with black supremacy. Aren't you arguing for a milder version of that pill? If race doesn't matter, then the community we replace the black community with will be better than the one that exists.

Professor Culp: Isn't that just assuming that race doesn't matter or that white is superior to black? Why not require white people to take a pill to change their race? After all, most of the world is made up of people of color.

Professor Not-Professor-Bell: If race doesn't matter, then whether we have black people take the Michael Jackson Pill—the cheaper solution—or whether white people take the Michael Jackson Pill, the results will be the same. Would you make the same argument if we were talking about a pill to make people thin? The First Circuit has, correctly, found obesity to be a disability under the Americans With Disabilities Act. Are we going to have communities of the disabled blocking us from giving fat people pills to eliminate obesity because some people think there is a fat community or a community of disabled people? It seems to me that we have to be able to allow law to make people normal. Law reflects norms and the status quo. We cannot escape these norms, and it is fruitless to try. The fat have no more right to be fat than those who won't work have to get paid.

Professor Culp: I take it your point is that race and fatness can be defined by society as bad and that we should accept those community-imposed norms.

Professor Not-Professor-Bell: Yes, law has to reflect the decisions of society. Those decisions may change over time as society changes, but no society can exist that cannot impose its own norms on those it identifies as "deviants."

Professor Culp: The problem is that you are defining race as deviance and the black community as wrong. We all suffer when we allow law to be just an enforcement of community norms. Law also has to be able to live with difference.

Geneva Crenshaw: Professor Culp, you've criticized the solutions others have suggested for reaching racial equality. The color-blindness pill won't work, you say, because we can peek at color. The assimilation pill won't work because it is too damaging to the black psyche and because white society really is not able fully to assimilate black people. And the antidiscrimination pill won't work because the enforcers of the process are also racist. What pill would you suggest? It's easy to criticize but harder to help us construct a better future.

Professor Culp: I think the ultimate problem is to think that this kind of micropill will ever work to attack race or racism. Indeed, the problem I see at the heart of our legal system is a reliance on microchoices that leave unresolved macroproblems. I think we've described the problem in the wrong way. The real problem with these pills as a solution is not what is changed but what isn't. Black employees are given the choice to change their hair, their mannerisms, and their neighborhoods in order to fit in, but even those choices are not likely to be enough to ensure a change in the status quo. As long as race is connected to crime, poverty, and unemployment, no black person can escape the impact of racism no matter what microchoices she makes, including in the job market.

Notes

1. *See* DERRICK BELL, FACES AT THE BOTTOM OF THE WELL: THE PERMANENCE OF RACISM 13 (1992).

2. 410 U.S. 113 (1973).

3. *City of Richmond v. J.A. Croson Co.,* 488 U.S. 469 (1989) (striking down a Richmond set-aside program for minorities).

4. *St. Mary's Honor Ctr. v. Hicks,* 113 S. Ct. 2742 (1993) (making disparate treatment discrimination under Title VII harder to prove).

5. 113 S. Ct. 2816 (1993) (holding that a race-conscious redistricting plan that is so irregular on its face that it can only be explained as an effort to separate voters into different districts on the basis of race may violate the Fourteenth Amendment).

6. *See* WILSON J. MOSES, BLACK MESSIAHS AND UNCLE TOMS: SOCIAL AND LITERARY MANIPULATIONS OF A RELIGIOUS MYTH 1–48 (rev. ed. 1993).

72

Did the First Justice Harlan Have a Black Brother?

JAMES W. GORDON

On September 18, 1848, James Harlan, father of future Supreme Court Justice John Marshall Harlan, appeared in the Franklin County Court for the purpose of freeing his mulatto slave, Robert Harlan. This appearance formalized Robert's free status and exposed a remarkable link between this talented mulatto and his prominent lawyer-politician sponsor.

This event would have little historical significance but for Robert Harlan's being no ordinary slave. Born in 1816, and raised in James Harlan's household, blue-eyed, light-skinned Robert Harlan had been treated by James Harlan more like a member of the family than like a slave. Robert was given an informal education and unusual opportunities to make money and to travel. While still a slave in the 1840s, he was permitted sufficient freedom to have his own businesses, first in Harrodsburg, Kentucky, and then later in Lexington, Kentucky. More remarkably still, he was permitted to hold himself out to the community as a free man of color at least as early as 1840, not only with James Harlan's knowledge, but apparently with his consent. After making a fortune in California during the Gold Rush, Robert moved to Cincinnati in 1850, where he invested his money in real estate and a photography business. In the years that followed, he became a member of the Northern black elite, and, in the period after 1870, established himself as one of the most important black Republican leaders in Ohio.

Although a humane master, James Harlan's treatment of Robert was paradoxical. James' tax records show that he bought and sold slaves throughout his life. The slave census of 1850 lists fourteen slaves in James Harlan's household, ranging in age from three months to seventy years. The census for 1860 lists twelve slaves ranging in age from one to fifty-three years. James neither routinely educated nor often emancipated his slaves, although his ambivalence about the "peculiar institution" was well enough known to become a political liability in Kentucky, a state which was firmly committed to the preservation of slavery.

What about Robert Harlan was so special as to lead to such exceptional treatment by James? In the view of two scholars, the peculiarity of James Harlan's relationship with Robert Harlan is easily explained. Robert Harlan, they assert, was James Harlan's son. If true, this means that another of James' sons, the first Justice John Marshall Harlan, had a black half-brother.

When James emancipated Robert, John Harlan was fifteen years old. Thereafter, James and Robert continued to have contacts. After James' death in 1863, John and Robert re-

15 W. New Eng. L. Rev. 159 (1993). Originally published in the *Western New England Law Review*. Reprinted by permission.

mained in touch. Robert was an anomalous feature of John's childhood in slaveholding Kentucky and remained a part of his perception of blacks as an adult.

John deeply loved and respected his father, James. He lived in his father's house until after his own marriage. James taught John law and politics. In both arenas, father and son were partners and seem to have confided freely in one another. James remained the most important influence in John's life until the older man died in 1863, when John was thirty years old.

James Harlan's ambivalent, but generally negative, feelings about slavery surely influenced John's views on the subject. But even more importantly, James' peculiar relationship with Robert during John's youth, and the ongoing contacts between James, John, and Robert after Robert's emancipation, must have affected John's attitudes toward blacks. Robert was smart and ambitious, but lived his life in the twilight between two worlds, one black, the other white. Never completely at home in either, Robert's lifelong experience of the significance of the color line became, vicariously, a part of John's. Robert was also a continuing example of something John Harlan could not later, as a Supreme Court Justice, bring himself to deny—the humanity of blacks, and the profound unfairness of their treatment by a racist America.

Given his connection to Robert, Justice John Harlan's progressive views on race, views which he repeatedly articulated in his famous dissents as an Associate Justice of the United States Supreme Court, become more comprehensible. Indeed, it is reasonable to assume that we will never understand fully the sources of Justice Harlan's advanced views on race until we better understand his relationship with the black man who might have been his half-brother. Justice Harlan argued repeatedly that the Civil War Amendments had given black Americans the same civil rights as whites:

> [T]here cannot be, in this republic, any class of human beings in practical subjection to another class, with power in the latter to dole out to the former just such privileges as they may choose to grant. The supreme law of the land has decreed that no authority shall be exercised in this country upon the basis of discrimination, in respect of civil rights, against [free men] and citizens because of their race, color, or previous condition of servitude.[1]

Harlan further denied that blacks constituted

> a class which may still be discriminated against, even in respect of rights of a character so necessary and supreme, that, deprived of their enjoyment in common with others, a [free man] is not only branded as one inferior and infected, but, in the competitions of life, is robbed of some of the most essential means of existence.[2]

In *Plessy v. Ferguson*, Harlan, standing alone against the rest of the Court, again dissented:

> In respect of civil rights, common to all citizens, the Constitution of the United States does not . . . permit any public authority to know the race of those entitled to be protected in the enjoyment of such rights. . . . I deny that any legislative body or judicial tribunal may have regard to the race of citizens when the civil rights of those citizens are involved.[3]

Elsewhere in the same opinion, in words that have since become famous, Harlan wrote,

> in view of the Constitution, in the eye of the law, there is in this country no superior, dominant, ruling class of citizens. There is no caste here. Our Constitution is color-blind, and neither knows nor tolerates classes among citizens. In respect of civil rights, all citizens are equal before the law.[4]

If Robert and John were brothers, a provocative dimension for contemplation is opened.

The careers of these two talented, ambitious men offer us parallel examples of life on different sides of the color line in nineteenth-century America. They grew up in the same household, and, if brothers, carried many of the same genes. Each was given every opportunity that his status and skin color permitted. Each succeeded to a remarkable extent, again, within the limits imposed upon him by the society in which they both lived. Each man was shaped by his own perceptions of these limits and by their reality. In the end, John Harlan climbed as high as his society permitted *any man*. Robert Harlan climbed as high as his society permitted *any black man*. Although in the end Robert did not rise as high as did John, his achievements were, upon reflection, equally impressive.

John Marshall Harlan (1833–1911)

John Harlan was born on June 1, 1833, near Danville on the family farm, Harlan Station. His father, James, was by then an established lawyer and a rising politician, having already served as Commonwealth's Attorney in the circuit court. John received local primary schooling and then attended Presbyterian Centre College. After he graduated from Centre in 1850, he attended Transylvania Law School, in Lexington, and then completed his legal training in his father's law office in Frankfort. John practiced with his father until 1860, when he moved to Louisville to expand his professional opportunities. John received his political baptism in the mid-1850s as a successful stump speaker, and quickly became a rising political star. Following the Civil War, he reluctantly joined the Republican Party, and, in partnership with men like his law partner Benjamin Bristow, became one of the "Great Men" of the party in Kentucky.

By switching the Kentucky delegation from Bristow to Rutherford B. Hayes in the 1876 Republican National Convention after it became clear that Bristow could not be nominated, Harlan earned Hayes' gratitude. This gratitude eventually led Hayes to nominate John Harlan to be an Associate Justice of the United States Supreme Court in 1877, and to give Harlan the platform from which to proclaim that blacks deserved the full rights of American citizens under our "color-blind" Constitution.

Robert Harlan (1816–1897)

Much less is known for certain about Robert Harlan than about John. Black men and women, as individuals, were nearly invisible in Kentucky during the slavery period. Surviving accounts almost invariably treat blacks in the aggregate, noting few personal characteristics. Individual slaves had less personal history than fast horses or pedigreed dogs. Writers took little notice of them as individuals, and they rarely appeared in public records other than the minute books of the county courts, where individuals occasionally brushed against local authorities. Robert Harlan lived the first thirty-four years of his life as a member of this faceless human scenery. For this reason, his years in Kentucky are obscure. Most of the reliable information about him comes from his years in Cincinnati—after he acquired wealth and became active in Republican politics.

The most important narrative source of information about Robert Harlan's life is a brief sketch written by William J. Simmons, a black educator, and published in 1887 in Simmons' collection of biographies of notable black Americans, *Men of Mark: Eminent, Pro-*

gressive and Rising.[5] At the time, Robert Harlan was in the Ohio legislature serving as one of the first elected black members of the state House of Representatives. Simmons reports that Robert Harlan was born in Mecklenburg County, Virginia, December 12, 1816, the son of a white father and a slave mother who was "three-parts" white. Simmons further states that Robert was brought to Kentucky at the age of eight and raised by James Harlan, the "father of the Hon. John M. Harlan, . . . associate justice of the Supreme Court of the United States."

Whatever may be the truth about the place of his birth, there is no doubt about his exceptional treatment at the hands of James Harlan. Intelligent and ambitious, Robert was given some education in the Harlan household. Although Kentucky, unlike her sister states further South, never made it a crime to teach slaves to read and write, such behavior was not encouraged. Most slaveholders believed that a slave who could read would prove less manageable than one who could not. Slaves who could write were a direct threat to the slave system because that system relied upon written passes to restrict a slave's mobility. A slave who could write could forge passes facilitating his own flight to freedom or assisting others in theirs.

Simmons wrote that James Harlan attempted to send Robert to school with James' own sons, but that Robert was "discovered" to be black and sent home, where he was thereafter educated by James' older sons. Surviving examples of Robert's speeches and letters show that he learned a great deal from these informal educational opportunities, although his polished work displays much more refinement than do his private letters. Because of his light skin and his education, Robert was almost certainly a house slave who spent much time with the Harlan family. Simmons wrote that Robert was trained as a barber, subsequently opened a barber shop in Harrodsburg, and later a grocery in Lexington.

Robert also seems to have been permitted to travel while still formally a slave. Simmons asserted that Robert had visited "almost every state in the Union [and Canada]," "with the consent of his owner" and "without restriction." This would represent remarkable freedom of movement for a man who was still nominally a slave. It is certain that he traveled widely after formal emancipation, and the restlessness he displayed later—visiting California in 1849 and later Europe—coupled with his early interest in horse racing, offer some support for Simmons' report. Permitting such travel would have been consistent with James' other extraordinary treatment of Robert, although it entailed some risk of Robert being swept up by white patrollers.

In 1848, James formally emancipated Robert. John was fifteen at the time. Frankfort was a small community in 1848. It seems likely that John knew what his father intended to, and did, do that September morning before the county court. County records show that emancipations were unusual events, and it is likely that this one, especially since it concerned a slave who was already believed to be a free man, elicited comment from James' neighbors. Surely John would have discussed Robert's unique status with his father at this time.

In late 1848, or early 1849, after reconnecting publicly with James Harlan long enough to be formally emancipated, Robert left his family and went to California in search of wealth.[6]

Robert went no farther than San Francisco, where he amassed a fortune of $45,000 in less than two years. Simmons does not state how Harlan made his money in California. One account says he opened a store in San Francisco and made his fortune through trade. If this were true, Simmons would probably have reported it. It also seems unlikely that Harlan could have accumulated so much money so quickly in this fashion. He may have obtained this money by gambling, by running either a faro or monte table in a San Francisco saloon. This seems confirmed by an admission later elicited from Robert by one of his political enemies, that gambling was the foundation of his wealth.[7]

When Harlan returned East in 1850, to settle in Cincinnati, Ohio, he was a very rich man. Robert's Kentucky wife had died during his absence, but as soon as he was established in Cincinnati he sent for his three surviving daughters and their grandmother. Legally free and with money to invest, he bought real estate and a photography business. As a man of leisure, he began to concentrate on what was apparently the first love of his life, horse racing. It stretches belief to imagine that Robert could have restrained himself from communicating his financial good fortune to his former master. If Robert informed James Harlan of his dramatic change of circumstances, such startling news would have been made known to John as well. John was living in his father's house during many of these years (he did not marry Malvina French Shanklin until 1856) and practicing law and politics at his father's side.

By 1852, Robert had remarried. Robert's first son was born in 1853 and was named Robert James Harlan.[8] That his son should be named after both Robert and Robert's benefactor is not surprising. It suggests that Robert felt good will toward James. It may also hint that Robert privately made a claim to a closer relationship to James than any he put forward in public. It would be remarkable if Robert had not announced to James Harlan the birth of a child named for him. This also suggests that contact between the Frankfort Harlans and the Cincinnati Harlans was maintained. Within a few months of the birth of his son, Robert Jr., Robert's second wife, Josephine M. Harlan, died. . . .

Perhaps it was the emotional impact of the United States Supreme Court's infamous *Dred Scott* decision, issued in 1857, that prompted Harlan to give up on the United States. This decision validated federal protection for the South's "peculiar institution" and sketched, in unmistakably bleak terms, the withered prospects for American blacks, North or South, slave or free. It might have been, instead, the raising and then dashing of hope nearer home which finally convinced Robert Harlan that he had no future in his own country. In 1857, in apparent reaction to the *Dred Scott* decision, the Ohio legislature—under Republican leadership—enacted three new statutes granting blacks important rights. This must have taken some of the sting out of the Supreme Court opinion and the federal commitment to the apprehension of fugitive slaves. However, the next year, the Republican Party lost control of both houses of the Ohio legislature. The new Democratic majority quickly repealed all three of the 1857 acts, and passed a "visible admixture" law which made it a criminal offense for election officials to allow people with a "visible admixture of Negro blood" to vote. For Harlan, who was seven-eighths white, this must have seemed a burning, personal affront, since it disenfranchised him.

Robert Harlan lived abroad for ten years, from late 1858 or early 1859, until 1869. He missed most of the turbulent decade of the 1860s, returning to Cincinnati in 1869, having lost most of his financial resources due to the dislocation of his investments during the Civil War. His financial decline was almost certainly exacerbated by gambling losses and the failure of his horse-racing ventures in Great Britain. It is possible that the passage of a bill granting suffrage to Ohio blacks in 1869 played a part in inducing Robert to return to Cincinnati.[9]

Whatever prompted his return, Cincinnati at that time offered to talented, ambitious black men opportunities that had never before been available. The triumph of the North in the Civil War, the ratification of the Fifteenth Amendment guaranteeing northern blacks the vote, and the partisan interests of the Republican Party combined to open apparently breath-taking opportunities for prominent blacks. All they need do was to attach the new black voters to the Republican electoral machine—*attach* them to the party, not *integrate* them into it. Robert Harlan recognized these possibilities and, in early 1870, threw himself into politics as a vocation. He set about making himself useful to the white Republican leadership of the city and the state, and quickly became a thoroughgoing party man.

By 1871, Robert was deeply enmeshed in Republican politics in Ohio. He was given serious consideration as a candidate for the state legislature from Cincinnati in 1871, and acquired substantial support before being defeated in the county convention. He met President Grant in the summer of 1871, and became one of Grant's most important adherents in the Ohio black community. In 1872, Harlan was one of two representatives from Cincinnati elected to the Republican State Central Committee, becoming the second black man ever to serve in this capacity. Also in 1872, he attended the national Republican convention, held in Philadelphia, as one of six Ohio alternates at-large. In this delegation, as a delegate at-large, was future President Rutherford B. Hayes. In the presidential election of that year, Robert worked hard for Grant's re-election.

For his efforts on behalf of the party, Harlan received the first significant federal patronage position given to an Ohio black man: appointment in 1873 as Special Inspector of the United States Post Office at Cincinnati. The 1873 register of federal employees lists Harlan as a Special Agent for "mail depredations."[10] The postal laws and regulations that were in effect in 1873 fixed a special agent's salary at $1600 per year, and a Post Office *Register* entry for 1873 lists Harlan's compensation in this amount. The regulations also provided for the payment of five dollars per day "for traveling and incidental expenses, while actually employed in the service." Robert had found in politics the additional income he needed to again enjoy "the good life." But, his good fortune was short-lived. It appears that he was removed from office in January or February 1875.

In these years Robert also saw to the education and support of his son, Robert Jr. He sent him to Woodward High School—a white school—where William Howard Taft was a classmate. Robert Jr. attended the Cincinnati Law College, and worked as a clerk from 1872 until 1878, when the younger man was appointed a deputy United States internal revenue collector. In 1887, Robert Jr.'s occupation was listed for the first time as "attorney" in the Cincinnati directory, and he was listed in the same way in the directories for 1890 and 1891.

Meanwhile, Robert attended Ohio state Republican conventions throughout the 1870s and 1880s. He also attended the national Republican conventions held in 1884 and 1888 in Chicago, serving in the Ohio delegations with future President William McKinley, Jr., in 1884, and with Governor, later United States Senator, Joseph B. Foraker in 1888. In the late 1870s, Robert Harlan aligned himself with the Garfield forces in Ohio and nationally. In the 1880s, after President Garfield's assassination, he supported Joseph Foraker, defending him against charges that Foraker was cool in his support of black rights.

After nearly winning a seat in the state legislature from Cincinnati in 1880, Robert succeeded in obtaining a second federal patronage job in 1882, when he was appointed Special United States Customs Inspector at Cincinnati by President Chester A. Arthur. Harlan's application and recommendation file[11] has survived and opens a small window into his political life. Applying originally for reappointment to the position as special postal agent that he had held under Grant, Harlan solicited and received letters of support from many important Republican politicians.

Robert was able to obtain letters of recommendation from former President Grant, as well as from prominent local and state Ohio Republicans. Grant's letter, dated December

6, 1881, states, "I know the Colonel very well. . . . I think him in every way well qualified for the place."[12] In addition to the recommendation from Grant, Harlan's application file contains letters from William Lawrence, who calls Harlan "my friend" and writes,

> [h]is long service as a Republican, his capacity for usefulness and the fact that he is a representative man of his race give him strong claims which I hope you can find it practical to recognize—His many friends, of whom I am one, would be gratified if this can be done.[13]

Both Cincinnati Republican Congressmen, Thomas L. Young and Benjamin Butterworth, supported Harlan's appointment, as did Ohio United States Senator George H. Pendleton of Cincinnati, and eleven other Ohio congressmen. Butterworth pressed repeatedly and hard for Harlan's appointment. All of these men commented upon Harlan's service and usefulness to the Republican party. A number noted the importance of appointing a black man to office. Halstead, the long-time editor and publisher of the *Cincinnati Commercial*, the leading Republican newspaper in southern Ohio, wrote in support of Harlan's appointment, as did Alphonso Taft, the father of future President and Chief Justice William Howard Taft.

The list of references is remarkable, demonstrating both Harlan's sophistication about who controlled federal patronage in Ohio and his ability to obtain support from southern Ohio's most important Republican officials. There is no reference from John Marshall Harlan in the file, but given Robert's clout in Ohio Republican circles this fact is less surprising than it would have been in 1873. By now, Robert Harlan had a long political reach of his own. In 1877, when John Harlan's name was being suggested for appointment to the Supreme Court, John apparently asked Robert to support his nomination among Robert's Ohio contacts. Robert made overtures to his friends (who were friends of President Hayes) and wrote to John to reassure him that his name would be submitted.[14] Robert had less reason to appeal to John for help now than he had in 1873, and John may well have been less well-placed to provide written assistance of this kind once he took his place on the United States Supreme Court in 1877. Certainly, he did not have the same private connection to the Arthur administration that Bristow at first had provided him to Grant.

In 1886, after fifteen years of effort, Robert Harlan won a seat in the Ohio legislature, the second black man so elected—the first being attorney George Washington Williams in 1880—and the fourth ever elected to the state House of Representatives. Harlan listed his occupation as "Horseman."[15]

Robert Harlan had struggled his entire life to obtain a shadow of the opportunities presented to John Harlan at birth. Robert had been forced to swim against the current of racism in both Kentucky and Cincinnati. He learned what was necessary in order to maximize the limited autonomy Kentucky society permitted blacks, and he succeeded in finding a niche in the power structure of Cincinnati. He seized opportunities whenever they presented themselves, both for himself and for his son, Robert Jr. Robert was strong enough to make a reasonably good life for himself and his family, but he also suffered from the personal flaws that were produced in him by lifelong oppression. As an illegitimate son, he craved recognition, and sought the respect of people who would never give it to a black man. He suffered racist abuse even from his Republican allies in Cincinnati, receiving the message over and over again that he was important not as an individual but as an instrument. Even in post-war Ohio, he was not a person but a thing.

He lived by his wits, and when necessary did so at the expense of others. His success was a reflection of his intelligence and his willingness to seize the main chance. His restlessness is apparent from the range of his wanderings. He seems to have been a man who never quite got what he wanted, though he often came close. His influence depended on his ability to be useful. He surely must have experienced the insecurity that awareness of this would bring.

He was as courageous, in his own way, as James or John Harlan. Despite being white enough to "pass," he seems never to have made the attempt. His position throughout his life enabled him to see far across the color line. He knew the possibilities of life on the white side of that line and yet chose to remain "black" and struggle against the prejudices and handicaps he could have left behind. In all of his contacts with white politicians, he seems to have emphasized his black status, and to have appealed to them as a representative of the black community. For a relatively brief period, in the 1870s, his skin color became an asset instead of an unmitigated liability. Thereafter, he was trapped in the role when the circumstances of the country changed in the last two decades of the nineteenth century. The national Republican Party shifted its focus from race to economics, and the country reverted to its ante-bellum racist consensus. As a result, Robert's influence waned. He was unable to transfer that influence intact to his son, who found that the strategies that had worked for his father in the 1870s worked no longer.

Who Was Robert Harlan's Father?

Robert Harlan was born into a biracial Southern world in which whites owned human beings and blacks were forced to submit to nearly absolute white authority or die. It was a society in which the races were separated by a strict caste line that was supported by profound social, economic, and ideological differences between the races. But it was also a society in which blacks and whites were constantly brought into intimate contact with each other by the slave system.

The racial intimacy required by the slave system and the profound vulnerability of blacks when presented with demands from white masters and satellite whites produced common, if disapproved, interracial sexual encounters. These encounters in turn produced large numbers of mulatto offspring. Robert Harlan was one of these children. If Robert Harlan's mother was one-quarter black, a "quadroon," and his father was a white man, Robert was one-eighth black, an "octoroon"—he had one black great-grandparent—like Plessy in the famous "separate but equal" case, *Plessy v. Ferguson*. Perhaps it was more than coincidence that led John Marshall Harlan to write one of his most famous and impassioned dissents in defense of the civil rights of black Americans on Plessy's behalf. Because of the character of Robert's birth and the scarcity of historical records on slave births, we will never know the names of his parents with certainty.[16]

Is it possible that Robert knew or suspected that he had a Harlan father and chose to conceal this fact from the public during his lifetime? If he had claimed his patrimony publicly, at any time, the claim would have been doubted in the absence of acknowledgment by James or some other member of the white Harlan family. It seems likely that Robert was genuinely grateful to James for his humane treatment, and that there were bonds of affection between these men that prevented the younger man from publicly proclaiming their blood tie. Affection and gratitude for James is suggested by Robert's naming his only son after his former master. Affection also comes through occasionally in Robert's letters to John. When John agreed to serve on the Louisiana election commission in April 1877, Robert wrote him:

I beg to repeat to you the words of an old colored man that formerly belong [*sic*] to your father—they were do-do-take care.

I do not care which way you may decide the Louisiana question your [*sic*] bound to make enemies especially if you take a leading part in the matter.[17]

Disclosure would certainly have embarrassed James and John, and deeply hurt their family. It also would have damaged James' own political prospects and those of his legitimate
son, John. It is possible that there were conditions attached to James' generosity toward, and
sponsorship of, Robert—one condition being that Robert never publicly claim the blood relationship. It is possible that any secret assistance Robert may have received from John Harlan later was given upon the same terms. All of these possibilities rest on speculation, but
the point is that there may have been reasons for Robert to consistently maintain a lie about
the circumstances of his birth. There is a reference in one of Robert's letters to John that
suggests that some of Robert's political associates in Cincinnati were aware of some connection between Robert and John. In a letter dated October 4, 1873, Robert invited John to
make a campaign speech in Cincinnati in support of Republican candidates. In the letter
Robert explained, "The campaign committee requested me to write you thinking I might
have more influence with you than they had."[18] This reference does not necessarily relate
to a claim of blood ties, but it does suggest that there was an awareness, at least in some Republican circles in Cincinnati, that Robert had a special relationship with John.

Was James Harlan Robert Harlan's Father? Physical Characteristics

Although by no means conclusive, Robert's size and physical resemblance to the "Big Red" branch of the Harlan family argue strongly against the paternity
of a stranger to that clan. Robert Harlan was a big man. He stood over six feet tall and
weighed more than 200 pounds. With blue-grey eyes, light skin, and black, straight hair,
he was physically vigorous and healthy his whole life and traveled extensively. When
Robert died in 1897, at age eighty, the average life expectancy for a black man was thirty-
two years. That of white males was only forty-eight. Robert Harlan's son, Robert Jr., also
lived at least into his late seventies. Both men were long-lived, and modern mortality studies indicate that heredity is an important factor in family longevity.

A number of portraits of Robert Harlan were published during his lifetime. The best of
these appeared in 1886 in an Ohio newspaper.[19] In this detailed etching, which is captioned
"Col. Robert Harlan, Member of the Ohio Legislature," Harlan's fine features stare out in
a right full-face profile. His most prominent features are a rounded pate with a high, full
forehead crowned by a receding hairline of short, straight hair which has reached the peak
of his head. He has large ears with full earlobes and a firm, well-defined jawline. A large, full
mustache sitting below a straight, slightly bulbous nose dominates the face and covers the
mouth, preventing any view of the lips. The smooth skin of the face—remarkably wrinkle-
free given his age—ends in a pointed chin. Heavy brows cover narrow eyes which turn
down at the outside, imparting almost a squinting expression. The entire face is lean and
shows strength.

When I first saw this picture, I was struck by the similarity it bore to a famous picture
of Justice John Marshall Harlan taken while he was a member of the Supreme Court. In
that picture, John Harlan's rounded dome of a head, with its crowning fringe of hair, displays, it seems to me, a number of the same features. The shape of the head is similar. The

large forehead is similar. The receding hairline, the short, straight hair (which had been red in his youth), and the large ears are there, as is the large earlobe and the strong jaw. The nose is the same, though fuller and more bulbous. The smooth skin, the heavy brows, the squinting eyes—also blue—and the pointed chin, are all there. The wide mouth, with its narrow lips and distinctive scowl, made me long for the look behind Robert Harlan's mustache that I will never have. Although John Harlan's face is fuller—John was overweight in his later years—I thought, they could be brothers. Of course, my "perception" may have been affected by my knowledge that Robert had grown up in James Harlan's household.

The only portrait of James Harlan, John's father, with which I am familiar is an oil painting by an unknown artist, in the collection of the Kentucky State Historical Society's museum at the Old Statehouse in Frankfort, Kentucky. That portrait shows a middle-aged man with a high forehead and thinning straight red hair, with the familiar Harlan nose and strong jawline. His eyes appear to be grey or hazel, although it is difficult to tell what color the artist intended. They look out from behind wire-rimmed antique glasses and heavy brows. The lobe of the left ear, just visible below the long hair on the side of James' head, is large. The mouth is firmly set and surrounded by thin lips; the face ruddy and thinner than John Harlan's—in this respect more resembling Robert's than John's—but the resemblance between father and son, between James and John, is pronounced.

Both James Harlan and John Marshall Harlan, like Robert Harlan, were big men. James was over six feet tall. John was six feet two. James probably had grey or hazel eyes. John's eyes were blue. Both men had ruddy complexions and sandy red hair.

The factors discussed here do not prove a blood relationship between James Harlan and Robert Harlan. Physical resemblance is a matter of opinion, and the presence of blue eyes, straight hair, and large size do not establish blood relationship. Their cumulative effect, as with so much else about this tale, is suggestive. When considered along with other factors, they become more so.

James Harlan's Treatment of Robert Harlan

In his powerful treatment of slavery, *Roll, Jordan, Roll*, Eugene Genovese concluded that "[t]hose mulattoes who received special treatment usually were kin to their white folks."[20] While by no means conclusive, evidence of Robert's special treatment by James is important to any consideration of the relationship between these two men.

Sometimes little things escape notice. Robert Harlan lived under that name throughout his life (as far as public records can establish this fact), and as Paul McStallworth[21] indicated, it was no small thing for Robert to have been permitted to take the Harlan family name and use it while still a slave.

Although it was common for freed slaves to take the family name of their former masters after the Civil War, this practice was rarer in the ante-bellum South. Perhaps this was simply because the planter families frowned upon it. Perhaps they did so for no more obscure reason than that use of the family name bestowed more humanity upon slaves than most owners found comfortable. One could call many other chattels by name, a horse or a dog, for example, but few of these "things" had two names, one of which associated it directly with the master's family. Perhaps it was this public association that was unacceptable, because it invited speculation and rumors that a family with self-respect and social position preferred to prevent. It was a rare thing indeed for a slave to be permitted to use the family name while still in bondage. Such permission came very close to an informal acknowledgment of familial connection. But allowing Robert Harlan to use the Harlan family name was not the only unusual privilege which James Harlan extended to his slave, Robert.

At least as early as 1840—eight years before his formal emancipation—Robert Harlan appears in the public records of Lexington, Kentucky, with the designation "free man of color" next to his name.[22] Accounts of Robert's life state that James Harlan permitted Robert to set up in Harrodsburg as a barber in the 1830s and as a grocer in Lexington in the 1840s. While in Harrodsburg, Robert might still have been living in James' household. However, James moved to Frankfort in 1840 to become Secretary of State, and Robert established himself in Lexington that same year. Robert must have been living on his own in Lexington. The city tax records for Lexington support this hypothesis. The records listed heads of household and independent individuals only. Robert's "household" appears in the records in the years 1841–1848. Robert lived with a free woman "of color" throughout the 1840s, and she bore him five daughters between 1842 and 1848, when Robert disappeared from the Lexington records.

Robert's status as a "non-slave" is especially surprising since it was illegal under the laws of Kentucky for Robert to live as a free man, working for his own account in Harrodsburg and Lexington. It was a criminal offense for James Harlan to permit him to do so and James could not have been ignorant of this fact.

The risks for James grew more immediate in 1847. Robert was living in Lexington and James in Frankfort, twenty miles away. James could no longer provide Robert with the informal protection possible when they both lived in Harrodsburg in the 1830s. Now, too, James' visibility as a Whig leader in the state made both men more vulnerable to James' political enemies. This point must have been driven home to James when the court of appeals handed down its decision in *Parker v. Commonwealth*,[23] in December 1847.

In *Parker*, the court sustained a verdict against a slaveholder under an indictment that was challenged as insufficient. The slaveholder was indicted for permitting her slave, Clarissa, "to go at large and hire herself by permission of the plaintiff in error, who was her owner."[24] It is possible that the Parker decision influenced James to convert Robert's de facto emancipation into formal, de jure manumission in September 1848. However, it must have been Robert's decision to leave the state—and James' protection—for the California gold fields which made legal emancipation absolutely necessary.

Robert remained in contact with John's brother James. James had practiced law with John in Louisville in the 1870s and served later as a judge in Louisville. However, James appears to have been an alcoholic and to have suffered a tragic decline. His correspondence with John about his circumstances and his need for money is agitated and moving. John apparently tried to assist James in ways which would not result in supplying his brother with liquor. In July of 1888 James' fortunes took a turn for the better, and he wrote John a newsy letter from James' new home in the Indian (soon to be Oklahoma) Territory. In it he told John that "Bob Harlan has for two years been unusually kind to me, not however putting me under obligation."[25]

Surely James would not have turned to Robert for money unless he believed the older man had financial means. It is possible, of course, that James turned to Robert not as a family member, but as a former family slave who owed the Harlan family a great debt of gratitude. However, from the content of James' surviving letters to John it appears that his appeals for financial help were directed primarily at family or very close friends of the family, like John's former law partner, Augustus Willson. That James maintained contact with Robert and looked to him for financial assistance is suggestive. The anguish James felt when driven to ask for Robert's assistance, and his assumption that such an appeal would discomfit John enough to wring money from the Justice, offers support for the family connection hypothesis when added to the rest of the evidence.

Did Robert Harlan Help to Shape John Marshall Harlan's Views on Race?

Most of the scholarly writings about the first Justice Harlan offer, at best, tentative explanations for his behavior. We need more studies of the details of his life and personal relationships if we are to understand better this complex and important Justice. One of the most important enigmas about John Harlan is the source of his progressive attitude concerning the legal rights of America's black citizens.

My own research has convinced me that one of the keys to understanding the sources of John Harlan's personal and judicial values is his relationship with his father, James. John Harlan loved and respected his father. Through James' relationship with Robert Harlan, and through John's own contacts with Robert, Robert was well situated to influence John's understanding of race. John's own contacts with Robert began in childhood and continued at least until the time of John's appointment to the Supreme Court. John's experiences with Robert were different in quality from those he had with other blacks because of Robert's special relationship with James Harlan. If the blood tie I have suggested existed, and if John knew it, then Robert's effect on John would have been profound. Even if my hypothesis of a blood relationship is rejected, the duration and intensity of contacts between John, James, and Robert is certain to have had some impact on the future Justice and should be explored as fully as the surviving sources permit.

At the very least, John's connection to Robert would have made empty abstractions about race impossible for John. Robert humanized, for John, all cases having to do with the rights of black Americans. John knew through personal experience what the legal disabilities imposed upon blacks—the disabilities against which John Harlan raged in his Supreme Court opinions—meant in people's lives. At the very least, Robert put a face on the millions of human beings forced to live their lives in the shadow of the Supreme Court's racist opinions. Robert made John see the human beings behind the briefs. This must certainly have been true in a case like *Plessy v. Ferguson,* where the plaintiff was seven-eighths white—like Robert. Once John Harlan could see blacks as individual persons, his religious convictions compelled him to extend to them the rights all human beings deserved. This alone might have set John Harlan apart from his fellow Justices, for whom race was largely an abstract matter.

Through Robert, John would also have experienced, vicariously, the consequences of the color line. Robert was raised in the household of a humane slaveholder. He had money and great opportunity for a man of color in his time. Despite these "advantages," Robert was denied all of the opportunities that were John's from birth. Through Robert, John could experience the frustration of butting doors which would never open no matter how meritorious he might be as an individual. In reviewing the story of Robert's life, John must have been acutely aware of the significance of the color line. Robert's slightly brown skin had rendered his considerable talents largely irrelevant to a color-conscious society. Indeed, this circumstance alone had robbed Robert of the Harlan birthright which helped John to prosper throughout his life.

If Robert Harlan helped to shape John Harlan's views about race in any of these ways, he made a lasting contribution to John's fame. Through John's words, Robert also left a mark on his country. He helped to start America's eventual, painful re-examination of the assumptions underlying its racist consensus. In this way, Robert left his descendants and his country a wonderful legacy.

Notes

1. *Civil Rights Cases*, 109 U.S. at 62 (Harlan, J., dissenting).
2. *Id.* at 39–40.
3. *Plessy*, 163 U.S. at 554–55 (Harlan, J., dissenting).
4. *Id.* at 559.
5. WILLIAM J. SIMMONS, MEN OF MARK: EMINENT, PROGRESSIVE AND RISING (Ebony Classics 1970) (1887).
6. *Id.* at 421.
7. *Colonel Harlan Visits the West End and Attends a Meeting—A Bit of His Political History By One Who Knows and Other Matters of Interest*, CINCINNATI COMMERCIAL, Sept. 4, 1871, at 8.
8. DICTIONARY OF AMERICAN NEGRO BIOGRAPHY 288 (Rayford W. Logan and Michael R. Winston eds. 1983).
9. BLACKS IN OHIO HISTORY: A CONFERENCE TO COMMEMORATE THE BICENTENNIAL OF THE AMERICAN REVOLUTION 18 (Ruben F. Weston ed., n.d.) (In the collection of the National Afro-American Museum and Cultural Center of Wilberforce, Ohio).
10. REGISTER OF THE OFFICERS AND AGENTS, CIVIL, MILITARY, AND NAVAL, IN THE SERVICE OF THE UNITED STATES, ON THE THIRTIETH OF SEPTEMBER, 1873, at 438.
11. Record Group 56, Special Agents Applications and Recommendations File for Robert J. Harlan (available in General Records of the Treasury Department, National Archives).
12. Letter from Ulysses S. Grant to Charles J. Folger, Secretary of the Treasury (Dec. 6, 1881) (in Record Group 56, Special Agents Applications and Recommendations File for Robert J. Harlan (available in General Records of the Treasury Department, National Archives)).
13. Letter from William Lawrence to Chester A. Arthur (Dec. 3, 1881) (in Record Group 56, Special Agents Applications and Recommendations File for Robert J. Harlan (available in General Records of the Treasury Department, National Archives)).
14. "[A]s regards your matter I spoke to John W. Heron about it. He informed me that he and others had spoke [*sic*] to the President while here in your favor, and that he had no doubt that you would be appointed." Letter from Robert Harlan to John Marshall Harlan (Oct. 10, 1877) (available in John Marshall Harlan Papers, Library of Congress). Robert may have been one of the first people to write to John about the younger man's appointment to the high court. In a letter written in early March 1877, Robert reported,

> Mr. Halstead [the editor/publisher of the Republican *Cincinnati Commercial*] said to me this afternoon that Hayes told him that you were on his Slate for anything you wanted—he further said that he could not understand it in way [*sic*] others worry that Hayes intended to offer you Judge Davis's place on the bench.

Letter from Robert Harlan to John Marshall Harlan (Mar. 7, 1877) (available in John Marshall Harlan Papers, Library of Congress).
15. BLACKS IN OHIO HISTORY, *supra* at 19.
16. The breadth of this problem is well illustrated by the examples of the two most prominent mulattoes in nineteenth-century America. Neither Frederick Douglass, the great black abolitionist orator, nor Booker T. Washington, the founder of Tuskegee Institute and Douglass' successor as spokesman for black America, ever identified their white fathers. In both of these cases, neither man seems to have known who his father was, and there is no existing evidence which would permit bi-

ographers to fill in this important blank. The problem becomes obviously even more pronounced when one seeks information about less prominent mulattoes.

17. Letter from Robert Harlan to John Marshall Harlan (Apr. 14, 1877) (available in John Marshall Harlan Papers, Library of Congress).

18. Letter from Robert Harlan to John Marshall Harlan (Oct. 4, 1873) (available in John Marshall Harlan Papers, Library of Congress).

19. *Honorable Robert Harlan*, CINCINNATI GAZETTE, May 1, 1886.

20. EUGENE D. GENOVESE, ROLL, JORDON, ROLL 429 (1972).

21. DICTIONARY OF AMERICAN NEGRO BIOGRAPHY, *supra* at 287.

22. *See* FAYETTE COUNTY [KENTUCKY] MARRIAGE BONDS "COLORED," 1823–1874 (Nov. 19, 1840); LEXINGTON, KENTUCKY, CITY TAX RECORDS, 1841–1848 (1840).

23. 47 Ky. (8 B. Mon.) 30 (1847).

24. *Id.* at 30.

25. Letter from James Harlan to John Marshall Harlan (July 27, 1888) (available in John Marshall Harlan Papers, University of Louisville Law School).

73

Learning How to Be Niggers

GREGORY WILLIAMS

"Come on boys. Let's go to Aunt Bess's."

We followed the alley to Monroe Street. As we trudged south, I realized I'd never seen so many black people in Muncie before. What bothered me most, however, was the tattered, down-at-the-heels feel of the neighborhood. The contrast with Grandpa and Grandma Cook's sparkling white two-story home in the new Mayfield Addition was striking. Here, gloomy weather-beaten houses tottered on crumbling foundations. Exposed two-by-fours propped sagging porches. Jagged glass shards were all that remained in many windows. Graffiti-covered plywood sheets partially covered doorways. The yards were small, littered, and unkempt. Across First Street the run-down houses were replaced by a series of flat-roofed two-story concrete block buildings, all a sickly mustard color. There wasn't a blade of grass in sight, just concrete, mud, and gravel.

"This is the Projects, boys," Dad explained. "Colored families live on this side of Madison, and crackers on the other. Stay outta there. If the crackers learn you're colored, they'll beat the hell out of you. You gotta be careful here, too. Coloreds don't like half-breeds either."

An electrical charge surged through my body. Never before had I thought of myself as a "half-breed." TV westerns taught me half-breeds were the meanest people alive. They led wild bands of Indians on rampages, killed defenseless settlers, and slaughtered innocent women and children. Nobody liked the half-breeds—not the whites, not the Indians. A half-breed! Turning it over and over in my mind, I forced my feet to follow Dad up a long hill, barely noticing a sand-and-gravel playground at the edge of the Projects. We skirted it quickly, and Dad opened the gate of a sooty one-story clapboard house. The ancient wooden porch swayed under our weight as the three of us stood expectantly at the door.

A heavy, big-boned woman, almost six feet tall, with light coffee-colored skin, angular features, and long black braids came to the door. She looked more like an Indian than a colored lady. A calf-length dress hung loosely over her thick body and sagging breasts.

The aroma of cooking grease wafted from the house. Peeking from behind her was a thin, dark-brown-skinned girl about my age.

"Boys, this is Aunt Bess," said Dad.

"How you boys doin'?" she said in a slow drawl. Both Mike and I uttered a weak "Fine."

"This is Mary Lou," she said, pulling the girl to her side. She popped quickly back behind her. "Say hi to your cousins, Mary Lou."

Cousins! I winced as a muffled "Hi" floated from behind the large flowered dress.

"Ain't no need to be standin' in the cold. Come on inside and rest your bones," she said, throwing open the door.

Raising my eyes, I stole another glance at Aunt Bess and Mary Lou. Colored! But that didn't make *me* colored, I decided. I didn't look anything like them. I didn't know them, and didn't want to know them.

Secretly, I examined the shabby room. A tattered couch nudged against a wall. Cotton stuffing spilled from the armrest of a faded green brocade chair. There was no television, just an old-fashioned Philco radio almost four feet tall. I turned to the window looking for an escape. Next to it hung a large collage of snapshots almost two feet square. My eyes scanned the dark faces, recognizing no one. Suddenly a photo leaped at me from the corner. White faces. I wondered why they were there. My mouth dropped open as my eyes fastened onto images resembling Mom and Dad. Certain my mind was playing tricks on me, I leaned forward. It *was* Mom and Dad! And Mike and I were right between them! Stepping closer, I recognized the concrete bench in front of the Open Air Theatre. Then I remembered when the picture was taken. Dad made me and Mike walk across U.S. Route 1 barefoot and in our underwear because he was in such a hurry to take that picture. I sank into the faded green chair. Was I really colored?

Aunt Bess's booming voice interrupted my lament. "You boys hungry?" Looking into her brown jowly face, I realized hours had passed since Mike and I shared the roast beef sandwich in Dayton. We nodded eagerly.

"Come on, then," she said. We followed her through a sitting room and into the kitchen. The crisp smell of burning wood filled the air. In front of an old soot-stained stove, she picked up tongs, inserted them into a large circular piece of iron, and expertly slid it across the stove. Flames leaped from the gaping hole. She dropped wood inside, and then with a clank shoved the covering back into place. She motioned us to a window while she sliced corn bread at the kitchen sink.

I stared at the playground we had passed. It was a full block square, mostly taken up by a gritty sand-and-gravel baseball diamond. A ten-foot wire baseball backstop stood in the corner nearest the house. Wire drooped from its top support, leaving a big gaping hole. An empty swimming pool with cracked walls and peeling paint sat in the far corner of the block. Brown weeds sprouted in its crevices.

Aunt Bess placed steaming bowls of navy beans in front of us. When Mom cooked beans I refused to eat them, but in the last six months I had learned to eat anything that was offered. The beans disappeared in minutes. For dessert we devoured strawberry Jell-O mixed with bananas.

When finished, I timidly asked to use the bathroom. "The slop jar's on the back porch, and the toilet's outside. Take the broom, if you go out."

Puzzled, I stared at the corner sink in the dimly lit kitchen. I noticed black holes in the white porcelain where faucets should have been. Some of the houses in Gum Springs didn't have indoor plumbing, but that was different. This was Indiana. Muncie was a big city. It was 1954. I stared again. Paper bags were stacked in the double sinks. I had not misunderstood. She was talking about an outhouse. Heading for the back room, I pondered, "Slop jar?" As I stepped into a cold, enclosed porch I was engulfed by the pungent odor of stale urine. I snatched the broom and stumbled out the back door, transported instantaneously to an urban barnyard. A six-foot mesh fence surrounded the entire area.

Chickens ran in and out of a henhouse. Rabbits scampered behind the wire screen of a hutch. Hay, grain, and farm tools were visible inside a shed. An early morning drizzle had turned the bare earth into a giant mud puddle. Wood plank walkways slick with water, mud, and chicken droppings snaked through the yard. My eyes searched for the toilet, but I couldn't find it. All the buildings blended into a gloomy barnyard gray. Again I wondered: Why the broom?

"Cock-a-doodle-doo!" pierced the air. I whirled to my left. A rooster stood directly between me and what I now recognized as the outhouse. Turning to retreat to the slop jar, I hesitated as I recalled the stench of urine. The rooster scurried toward me, his neck feathers bristled. I tried to wave him off. He came faster, his yellow talons almost a blur. Now only five feet away, I shook the broom at him, but he didn't stop. I poked again. He screeched, beak open, feathers on end. Now he was within striking distance. Dad said we had to fight the whites and the coloreds. He didn't say anything about roosters. I jabbed.

He fell on his side. His fluttering wings showered me with mud and water. I relaxed and whisked him into the mud once more. He screeched, "Nawk! Nawk!" I waved him off, but he kept after me. I grabbed the broom with both hands and waited. When he was three feet away, I swung it like a baseball bat and sent him flying sideways. He began another charge. I turned the hard wood handle toward him. I swung and missed his head, but grazed a yellow talon, spinning him head over heels into the mud once more. I stepped off the wooden walk, sinking into the muck. He frantically sought a grip in the dark water of the yard, trying to flee. I gritted my teeth and raised the broom handle over my head, watching him draw his last breath.

The back door swung open.

"Whoa, boy! Don't ya be killin' my chickens! I'm the only one 'round here that does that!" Shamefully, I looked at Aunt Bess and lowered the broom to my side.

"Just a little tap gets 'em out of the way." She paused. "Look at you. Don't be tracking mud back into the house either. Leave them shoes on the porch. Now go an' do your business."

The rooster and I hobbled away from one another.

An elderly black man sat at the head of the table when I returned to the kitchen. Dad introduced Uncle Osco Pharris. Osco's face beamed as Dad recounted how he had been one of the strongest hands at Broderick's Foundry for thirty years. Dad bragged about him, now pushing sixty, still peerless among the younger men before the flaming open-hearth furnace. Dad raved about Osco's physical prowess for almost half an hour, then asked for a beer.

"Buster, I don't drink no more."

"Don't drink no more?" Dad challenged. "I remember when you used to put away Speck Johnson's corn likker like it was goin' out of style. Hell, you got so drunk I saw you staggering up Monroe Street with a smile on your face and your dick stickin' straight outta your pants."

"Whoa, Buster. Hold up. Don't you be talking like that in my house."

"Sorry, Osco," said Dad soothingly, "I guess I'm just feeling the need for a little dram myself. Don't suppose you got any in the house for colds, do you?"

Osco shook his head.

"Anyway," Dad continued, unable to conceal his disappointment, "tell me how Wayne and Louise are doing in Cincinnati."

Soon I tired of the stories, walked into the sitting room, and dragged an old rocking chair across the sagging linoleum floor to the warmth of the coal stove.

That night, Mike and I crowded together on the sitting room bed while Dad slept on the living room couch. Mike kicked and squirmed, and I was unable to sleep. As I pushed his leg off me, I realized that we had shared a bed only once, on a vacation to Atlantic City when the hotel had only one room with two double beds.

Lying there in the darkness of the night, I remembered Harvey and Raymond standing behind the Greyhound bus as we waved good-bye. I was almost certain Harvey cried. Maybe it was my own tears. Harvey was too big to cry. As I lay in the strange bed in a strange house, trying to adjust to all the different sounds and smells, I wondered if I would ever see them again. Our lives were changing already. Here in Muncie, Aunt Bess and Uncle Osco called Dad "Buster." In Virginia he had been Tony. I wondered if Mike and I would have different names, too. Would I be Billy, Greg, or "Rooster"?

As I lay there, I was startled by the shuffle of slippers across the creaky linoleum. Rising up on my elbows, I saw Uncle Osco heading toward the back porch. Soon the buzz of urine rang out against the side of the steel slop jar. A minute later I heard a plop. Within seconds the nauseating odor swept over me. I prayed Grandma and Grandpa Cook would come for us as I pulled the covers over my head and tried to will myself to sleep. When it finally came, I was plagued by nightmares. Roosters attacked from all sides and I had no broom. . . .

January 26, 1954, Dad roused us for our first trip to Garfield Elementary School. My biggest worry was that it would be a "colored" school. I did not fear being in classes with black children, but I couldn't shake the memories of the ramshackle school buildings and ancient playground equipment I had seen when accompanying Raymond to collect his nieces and nephews from the all-black Fairfax County schools. It was a great relief to see a new bright-red brick building, and both white and black children milling about the schoolyard.

In the office I peered over Dad's shoulder while he laboriously printed "J. Anthony Williams" in the enrollment form box for "Father." In the blank for occupation he listed "U.S. Army." When he scrawled a "W" in the space for race, I nudged him. He frowned sharply. Rebuked, I joined Mike, who slouched at the door.

The secretary ushered us into the principal's office. A slightly balding man rose from behind a desk stacked high with folders. With little more than a curt "Good morning," he led us from the office. Just down the hall we stopped at Mike's new room. "Lehman," the principal said sternly, "come along." Mike hesitated, hiding behind Dad, his wide brown eyes on the verge of tears. "Go ahead, Mike," Dad said gently, and nudged him forward. As the principal guided Mike through the door, Dad whispered, "Good luck, son. Billy will be waiting on you after school." Mike returned a forlorn nod.

School had been difficult for Mike. He failed the first grade in Virginia, and he was struggling in the second. I knew he wasn't dumb, but I didn't know what was wrong. None of us did. As we stood in the hallway that morning, I hoped Indiana would be better for him. But I worried as he followed the principal to the front of the room, and giggles filtered out to the hallway when his classmates saw the small holes in the seat of his threadbare trousers.

Dad and I were hustled down green concrete steps to the basement. A tall, overweight man with horn-rimmed glasses huffed as he climbed the stairway toward us. His suit nearly burst at the seams. Mr. Hunt, my new fourth grade teacher, perhaps noticing I was tall for my age, asked eagerly, "Do you like basketball?" I searched my mind for something called basketball. In Virginia I played baseball, football, and even volleyball. Suddenly, I remembered a game called "medicine ball." Maybe that was it. The heavy ball was impossible to lift. No one in my gym class enjoyed it. You couldn't throw it, kick it, or run with it. No, I don't like it, I thought. Yet three adults stared intently waiting for an answer. I gulped and muttered, "Yes."

We entered a basement classroom reminiscent of a World War II bunker. Everything was solid concrete except for two small rectangular windows at the very top of the outside wall. From my assigned seat near the back I surveyed my new classmates. A fat boy spilled over the seat in front of me. Two rows over, a girl with horn-rimmed glasses was perfecting the studious look of one in pursuit of the "teacher's pet" prize. I counted five black children around the classroom. Though I had many black playmates in Gum Springs, we never attended school together. I wondered what it would be like. Then I remembered Dad on the bus: "Billy, you're part colored." I wondered if I looked any different. I wondered if anyone else could tell. I wondered if I would have any friends . . . black or white.

Two aisles away near the wall I spied bouncing blond curls and the twinkle of blue eyes gazing at me.

"Get to work!" the teacher shouted from the front of the room. I lowered my head, desperate to appear busy even though I had no assignment. He lumbered down the aisle toward me. I cringed. Mr. Hunt paused three seats in front of me, beside a brown-haired boy with thick glasses.

"Are you going to take all day, Donald?" He glared.

Silence.

"You've got the right name, Donald, because Donald Dolittle does little." He smiled, congratulating himself on his wit, reached across two students, and thrust a mimeographed math assignment toward me. His sharp tongue made me glad I lied about basketball. Though I solved the long division problems in less than two minutes, I continued to hover over my paper to avoid calling attention to myself. At recess we filed out the rear of the building onto a large shiny blacktop play area complete with swing sets, a jungle gym, monkey bars, and even a sandbox. Students from other classes filled the playground, and I searched for Mike among them. Unable to find him, I drifted toward my new classmates.

"Where you from?" asked Dolittle as we stood in line for a swing. Classmates gathered around as I talked about Virginia and seeing President Eisenhower once when Dad drove us by the White House. Dolittle's eyes glazed as I rambled on about Mount Vernon, but the girl with the blond curls edged closer. Her name was Molly. A head shorter than I, she had the rosiest cheeks I had ever seen. I could hardly take my eyes off her as she introduced her friend, Sally. Tall for a girl, Sally looked me straight in the eye. Her bobbed brown hair swished back and forth as her eyes flitted between Molly and me. For the first time since we stepped off the bus on South Walnut Street twenty-four hours earlier, I dared to smile.

Schoolwork was much easier than it had been in Virginia. That first week I received the teacher's praise several times. What I valued more was the friendship of Molly and Sally. The three of us soon became inseparable. They quizzed me endlessly about Washington. I described the Cherry Blossom Festival and the Lincoln and Jefferson memorials in elaborate detail. They only appeared to lose interest when I babbled at length about seeing the wreckage of the first airplane collision over National Airport.

One afternoon during our second week in Muncie my cousin Mary Lou ran to catch up with Mike and me as we walked to Aunt Bess's. That day was the first time I had seen her on the playground. She skipped back and forth in front of me as we made our way down Monroe Street, her toothy smile inches from my face, chanting, "Billy likes a white peck! Billy likes a white peck!"

"No, I don't." I spat. "She's just in my class. I can talk to white kids."

She put her hands on her hips and blocked my way.

"I bet she wouldn't talk to you if she knew you was colored."

"Yes she would. Color don't have nothing to do with it!" I protested.

"That's what you think, Mr. Bigshot!"

Ever since we arrived at Garfield, Mary Lou had told anyone who would listen that we were her cousins. I really didn't like it, but when black children asked, "Are you related to Mary Lou?" I didn't deny it. It was only when I saw the revulsion it produced in white kids that I became very nervous.

The next day after lunch at Aunt Bess's, I pulled on my tattered fatigue jacket and headed to school. Opening the gate, I glanced down the hill toward the busy Monroe and Willard Street intersection. No white families lived north of Willard, so normally only various shades of black and brown faces were on the corner. That day was different. Two white faces stood out from the crowd—Molly and Sally. Even from a distance I saw shock register on their faces. They turned toward each other. Molly stared up the hill once more. A final glance, then she darted from the intersection, her blond curls disappearing behind the corner grocery store.

That afternoon Molly and Sally sat in their seats on the far side of the room. As I walked through the door, their heads snapped toward the small window. I slumped at my desk for an endless hour of math problems. When it was time for recess I kept my head down. Mr. Hunt had to order me outside.

On the playground I took a deep breath and moved haltingly toward Molly and Sally, desperately concocting a story about being at Aunt Bess's. I decided to say she was our maid and that Mike and I just ate lunch there. I never had a chance to lie. When the girls saw me approach, they turned their backs to me. I retreated to the safety of the fire escape, feigning indifference. Heads bobbed up and down as they chattered animatedly with other white girls. Some of them stole glances in my direction. I hunched over and hid my face.

After school that afternoon I caught their burning stares once more as I stood alone outside the school door waiting for Mike. The disgust on their faces made me feel like I had committed some grievous wrong. Mike never came out of the building, and I trudged home forlorn, feeling the weight of the world on my shoulders. Mike lay on Aunt Bess's couch with a large white cotton bandage taped to his forehead. He raised himself up on his elbows and thrust his oily face toward me.

"I fell off the fire escape during the fire drill. The principal took me to get stitches. Then he drove me home. He didn't believe we lived here. He was gonna drive off till Aunt Bess waved him down and told him we was colored boys."

A month dragged by and Dad did not return from Virginia. I was furious with him and felt abandoned, and I wasn't alone in my anger. The mere mention of his name caused Uncle Osco to snarl, and his bad humor spilled over into the household. When Mike tracked mud in from the backyard, Aunt Bess gave him a switching. When I sloshed water while carrying it from the outdoor faucet, she swatted me with the "rooster" broom. Every day after school I withdrew into my private corner of the sitting room and played with a small bag of clay. Hours passed while I molded imaginary soldiers who killed, maimed, bombed, and demolished everything in their path. Men, women, and children all died; ships sank; towns were leveled—everything was destroyed.

One afternoon Aunt Bess tired of me being underfoot and ordered me outside. I sat at the edge of the playground. Mike was playing football with boys from the Projects. I smiled as he streaked across the gravel field with the ball tucked under his arm. A chocolate-skinned boy in a blue cotton cowboy suit complete with fringed pant legs gave chase. He grabbed Mike's arm and jerked him to the ground. Mike slid across the gravel as the ball bounced crazily into the street. I leaped to my feet. Mike lay motionless for several seconds, then finally pushed himself up from the hard ground.

"What'd you knock me down for?" he demanded.

"This is tackle. We get you down any way we can," the boy growled in response. "It ain't two-handed touch like you crackers play."

"Tell him, Reggie," crowed a boy I recognized from Garfield School.

Mike brushed the gravel from his clothes and nodded. From then on, every time Reggie's team ran in Mike's direction, he fiercely blocked Mike. Even when runners headed in the opposite direction, Reggie swung at Mike. Finally, red-faced and exasperated, Mike lunged at his attacker. Reggie punched him in the face. Mike fell backward. The other boys surrounded them, shouting, "Whip him! Kick his butt, Reggie! Kill that cracker!" I raced to Aunt Bess's for help.

"Aunt Bess, Aunt Bess, some colored boys is beatin' up Mike!" She sauntered to the window overlooking the playground. "Come on! Come on! Mike needs help!" I shouted, tugging at her apron.

"Let go, boy." She pushed me away. "You better get on over there and help him. He's your brother. You the one gotta take care of him."

I hesitated.

"Whatcha waitin' for, boy? Do you wanna fight me or them? Git!" she shouted one final time, and reached for the buggy whip in the corner near the stove.

Tears filled my eyes as I realized no one was going to help Mike. Not Mom, not Dad, not Aunt Bess. We were on our own. I ran through the house and leaped off the porch. As I reached the crowd, Mike lay on the ground shielding his face. Blood seeped between his fingers as he twisted and turned, trying to dodge the hail of fists. Reggie grinned at the laughing crowd. "Guess I showed that cracker. . . . " I pushed through the boys and grabbed him by the neck, pulling him off Mike. He tumbled backward on the gravel. I kneed him in the stomach. A fist to the mouth. Then all over his head, the same way he hit Mike. Soon his nose bled. The crowd fell silent. "That white mothafucka's kicking Reggie's ass," I heard. "Let's get him."

The sound of shoes shuffling across the gravel distracted me. Then a crack filled the air. With my hands gripped around Reggie's neck, I looked over my shoulder. Aunt Bess was lashing her buggy whip.

"Don't you all bother him!" she shouted. "If you do, I'm gonna put this here whip across your little black butts!"

"Miss Bessie, that white boy's gonna kill Reggie!" protested one boy.

"They ain't no white boys," responded Aunt Bess. "They niggers just like you. They got the same right to be here! Come on, Billy, git Mike and let's go on back to the house."

I left Reggie holding his nose and pulled Mike to his feet. There was yet another long rip in the sleeve of his army fire sale jacket. We followed Aunt Bess across the gravel playground. Maybe, I thought, there is somebody in the world who cares about us.

The next Saturday morning a tall, golden-skinned boy of sixteen arrived at the house. Aunt Bess called Mike and me into the living room and said, "Boys, this is your brother Jimmy."

As I surveyed the young stranger, I tried to absorb Aunt Bess's startling pronouncement. Neither Mom nor Dad had ever mentioned him. Yet his prominent nose and dark brown eyes bore a remarkable resemblance to Dad. He also had Dad's lanky build. In fact, he looked more like our father than either Mike or I. I wondered why we had never heard of him before. But if Jimmy had been forgotten he was not unfriendly.

"Glad to meet you, brother Billy," Jimmy said, cheerfully extending his hand.

Jimmy, a drummer for the Muncie Central High School Bearcats band, wore black pants, a long wool coat with brass buttons, and a purple-and-white cape. He was on the way to a high school pep rally and invited us along. As a result of my teacher's obsession with basketball, I learned a lot about it. In fact, our class spent more time discussing Muncie basketball teams than any other subject. Although there were two high schools in Muncie, only Central counted when it came to basketball. Central had won four state championships and was the odds-on favorite to capture a fifth in March 1954. The Muncie Fieldhouse, where the Bearcats played, seated over seven thousand people and was packed for every game. Folks waited years to buy season tickets. The Bearcats were ultimately derailed that year by a team from a tiny Indiana town called Milan. Later, the saga of Milan's march to the state championship and final victory over Muncie Central was the basis for the popular movie *Hoosiers*.

That morning Jimmy urged us to go to the rally and then "to Whitely and see Uncle Sam and Aunt Ceola."

The new names and places were strange and unfamiliar, but Mike and I eagerly followed Jimmy downtown. Purple-and-white team posters were prominently displayed in every window, and purple-and-white banners stretched high across South Walnut Street. Names of Bearcat team members like Jimmy Barnes, "Big John" Casterlow, and George Burks were whispered as if they were gods. In spite of the huge crowd gathered at the fieldhouse, and a boisterous pep rally, basketball still held little interest for me, and I was glad when we left the gathering.

Broadway curved northeast away from downtown Muncie to McCulloch Park. Directly east of the park was Whitely, the home of Muncie's second-largest concentration of blacks. Bounded on the north by Centennial Road, on the south by the White River, and on the east by the Nickel Plate Railroad tracks, it was isolated from the rest of Muncie. The tracks edged along the eastern border of Whitely for almost twenty blocks without one street connecting it with the adjacent white areas.

Jimmy led us to a small grocery store at the corner of Lowell and Penn. The sign over the door said SAM WHEELER'S GROCERIES, THE COUNTRY STORE THAT'S GOING TO TOWN. The store shelves were crammed with canned goods, breads, cookies, and potato chips. A near empty glass meat case stretched across the rear of the wooden-floored room. Behind it stood two large glass-doored freezers. A light golden-skinned woman in her mid-forties stood at the checkout counter. Jimmy introduced her as Aunt Ceola.

"Hi, boys," she said in a cheerful voice. "I'm so glad to see you. Jimmy's been talking about you all week." She reached under the counter and handed Mike and me each a candy bar.

We gushed thanks and ripped off the wrappers. She turned behind the counter and drew back a cloth curtain that opened onto a small living area. I heard a television from within.

"Boys, you all come on out here. I got somebody I want you to meet."

Two dark-brown-skinned boys our age walked from the room. Though the older boy and I were the same height, he outweighed me by at least thirty pounds. His thick shoulders and full, square face resembled those of a boxer. The younger boy was about the same size and weight as Mike.

Aunt Ceola explained that the boys were related to her and to Jimmy and, therefore, probably to us. It all sounded so complicated, but the boys seemed to accept our relationship without question.

"Why don't you run up to Longfellow and play some ball?" said Aunt Ceola. "Boys, show Mike and Billy the playground."

Recalling my last playground fight, I mumbled softly, "I don't wanna go."

Jimmy, no doubt sensing my fear, accompanied us.

Longfellow School playground was almost a mirror image of Madison Street—mostly sand and gravel. All of the children were black. That is, none of them were white. There was every imaginable hue of brown, ranging from deep chocolate to the color of the speckled light brown eggs we found in Aunt Bess's henhouse. And now two palefaces—Mike and me.

As we stood at the edge of the basketball court, an unusually short light-brown-skinned boy approached us. Though his skin color fit in with the rest of the boys, he seemed a bit out of place. All at once I realized that his hair was different. It was the same as Mike's and mine—long, dark, and straight. I towered over him by at least six inches, but he stood squarely in front of me and demanded, "What you white boys doing here?"

I was ready to quip, "None of your business, Shorty," when Jimmy interjected.

"They're my brothers, Pancho! Don't mess with them or I'll kick your little Mexican butt back across the street. Anyway, what you bothering them for? They're your cousins, too."

I tried to conceal my amazement, wondering how many more surprises the day would hold.

"No way," protested Pancho. "I'm Mexican John Vargas's boy. We don't have no crackers."

"Yeah, but Ruth Vargas used to be a Williams, which makes us cousins with all the Vargases."

Pancho shrugged his shoulders, tapped the basketball, and said, "Let's play ball!"

With the growing list of honey, brown, and chocolate relatives, it was becoming harder and harder to perceive myself as white. Yet I knew I also had two white grandparents, three white uncles, two white aunts, and a houseful of white cousins. They were less than one mile away, just across the Nickel Plate Railroad steel barrier that separated Whitely from white Muncie. Not one of them had come for us.

74

What Does a White Woman Look Like?
Racing and Erasing in Law

KATHERINE M. FRANKE

[This essay appeared as part of a collection of short articles discussing favorite Supreme Court opinions. Ed.]

In significant ways, legal texts produce a narrative of national identity. They weave stories about who we are, what we are committed to, and what we expect of one another, individually and collectively. Certain foundational fictions, like "We the People," provide the glue that over time binds a people to its past and to one another as a nation. But should law play the same role with respect to other aspects of human identity? I think not. Current debates surrounding affirmative action, congressional redistricting, the Million Man March, and the appointment of Clarence Thomas to the Supreme Court all represent cultural flashpoints in an ongoing national discussion about two fundamental questions: what does it mean to have a race or be a member of a particular race, and who has the authority to decide?

In the service of enslaving, segregating, and subordinating African Americans, law has claimed for itself the authoritative license to tell the story of racial meaning in this country—whether by declaring a certain race of people the status of property, by defining as negro any person who has one drop of negro blood, or by determining that race is a factor that may not be taken into account in the distribution of social goods or political rights because our Constitution is color-blind.

Sunseri v. Cassagne[1] represents an absolutely fascinating judicial confrontation with the problems of proof that arise when racial identity is litigated in a manner similar to that of, say, property rights. In *Sunseri* the Louisiana Supreme Court considered an appeal from a trial court order granting the request of Cyril Sunseri, a white man, that his marriage be annulled because, he maintained, his wife was legally negro. Verna Cassagne, the woman Sunseri married and who all agreed was phenotypically white, sought a divorce and alimony because, she insisted, she was white. In 1935, when the couple was married, the state of Louisiana prohibited and rendered void the marriage of any white person to any person having a trace of negro blood.

The court was thus faced with adjudicating Verna Cassagne's racial identity. It was presented with this problem only because it took it as given that *looking like* and *identifying* as a white person did not mean that one was a white person. Several interesting conse-

74 TEXAS L. REV. 1231 (1996). Originally published in the *Texas Law Review*. Copyright © 1996 by the Texas Law Review Association. Reprinted by permission.

quences flow from this conception of racial identity: If a person could look white, but not be white, then what does it mean to be white? Could one be white but not look white? Perhaps looking white is a necessary yet not sufficient condition of being white. What does a white woman look like anyway? If phenotype is not what racial identity means, then is how you look a *representation* of racial identity? If so, a representation of what? Finally, who should decide the answers to any of these questions?

In determining whether Cassagne possessed a trace of negro blood, the court rejected the reliability of Cassagne's white looks and denied her the authority to declare her own race. Thus, the court had to look to other evidence to prove her "true race"—statutorily defined in sanguinary terms. Because there is no scientific test to determine either the racial makeup of particular blood samples or the percentage of a particular kind of racialized blood that a person has in her veins, racial identity quickly reveals itself to be a metaphor, essentialized through the sign of blood. But how does one go about proving a metaphor? By resorting to anecdote masquerading as objective fact. Given the statute at issue, Cassagne's racial identity was to be resolved atavistically, that is, by focusing upon the racial identity of Verna Cassagne's relatives, particularly her great-great-grandmother Fanny Ducre, a slave. Sunseri maintained she was "a full-blooded negress," while Cassagne swore she was an Indian.[2]

Both parties relied heavily on anecdotal testimony to show the race of Cassagne's relatives. Cassagne showed that her mother was christened and confirmed as a white person in a white church, educated as a white girl in a white school, registered as a white Democratic voter, patronized hotels as a white woman, and traveled as a white person in buses, railroad cars, and streetcars. When Verna was born, her mother was assigned to the white maternity ward.[3] And, if that weren't enough, the court noted that all of Verna's parents' friends and associates were white. The court thus observed that "the overwhelming testimony [is] that [Verna] and her immediate associates have always been regarded as members of the white race and have associated with persons of that race."[4]

Yet, proof of this nature demonstrates the social, not legal, race of Cassagne and her relatives. Given the impossibility of proving legal race according to the statute's sanguinary formula, what else could she look to? While the court did not address the issue, proof of social race was relevant to a determination of legal race on two primary grounds: First, one might believe that social race bears a "stands for" relationship to legal or true race. In this sense, social race was indirect proof of the thing itself. Second, one might argue that notwithstanding her actual sanguinary pedigree or lack thereof, the community or an intimate associate such as a husband, or both, were prevented from denying Cassagne's whiteness where she and her relatives had relied, over generations, on the community's and her husband's acquiescence in and acceptance of her identity as white. Given the great social significance of and investment in rigid racial boundaries, the court was not prepared to allow the conduct of some members of the community to bind the larger culture by permitting a kind of racial amnesty for people like Cassagne who could pass. Passing was not and could not be the same thing as being white.

Ultimately, the court determined that the question of Cassagne's true race turned on the contents of three legal documents: Cassagne's birth certificate, which registered her as colored, and the marriage license applications of her mother's sisters, which had been stamped "colored." The court then proceeded to cite approvingly the testimony of two white men who testified that they "knew" that many of Cassagne's relatives were negro and that they had always been so regarded in the community. Based upon this, the court concluded that it had no alternative but to affirm the annulment of the marriage of Sunseri and Cassagne because there was "no room for doubt" that Cassagne was legally negro.[5]

This case shows the authority of law to race bodies through what Eva Saks calls an autonomous miscegenous discourse[6]—autonomous in the sense that the legal meaning of race stands independent of and often in opposition to the social meaning of race. As such, in cases like *Sunseri* a person who is socially white can be declared legally black. Verna Cassagne told a story about her racial identity that was authentic—for her. The court and Cyril Sunseri, however, had another story of what it meant to be a white woman in Louisiana in 1940. Many may agree that racial identity is not something that we can take literally at face value, but rather is something that needs interpretation. What then emerges is a struggle over whose interpretation counts—law's "official" story or that of the party to be raced?

At stake in the current debates about affirmative action, racial redistricting, Justice Thomas's ascension to the Supreme Court, and the Million Man March are fundamental questions about what it means to be African American and who gets to decide. There are many who insist that Justice Thomas is not really black, or that he has betrayed his black identity. Many have criticized the vision of African-American masculinity that was promoted by the leaders of the Million Man March in Washington last year. What was powerful about the event, however, was the wresting of control of the instruments of identity away from government and the assertion of a degree of agency by some African Americans with respect to what it means to be an African-American man, at this time, in this culture.

The power to name oneself is fundamentally critical to any individual and to any civil rights movement. One of the negative consequences of affirmative action has been the degree to which control over the meaning of racial difference and identity has been ceded to government for the purpose of achieving remedial redistribution of resources. The government now has interpreted the goal of our constitutional and statutory equality principles to be the creation of a color-blind society. The call for children to be judged by the content of their characters and not by the color of their skin has been taken to mean that we should aspire to a world in which racial differences are understood as equivalent to differences in hair color—that is, meaningless. The radical individualism of this normative vision of the Fourteenth Amendment has frustrated the empowerment of peoples of color in this country. A politics of empowerment, as contrasted with an ethic of formal equality, requires a thick conception of racial identity produced through a fluid cultural, nonlegal process of self-definition engaged in by the communities to be empowered. Law is ill-suited to this task because racial meanings are always local and partial.

Whether the state invokes its power to reinforce the salience of race, as it did in *Sunseri*, or to erase the salience of race, as it has with contemporary equality jurisprudence, the state renders legally static that which must remain contested and fluid. The cultural contestation of racial meaning and identity must be reclaimed from government as a significant foundation of our struggles for racial empowerment. Empowerment requires not only that we demand what we want, but also that we define who "we" are.

Notes

1. 196 So. 7 (La. 1940).
2. *Sunseri v. Cassagne,* 185 So. 1, 2 (La. 1938).
3. *Id.* at 4–5.

4. *Sunseri II,* 196 So. 7, 9 (La. 1940).

5. *Id.* at 7–9.

6. *See* Eva Saks, *Representing Miscegenation Law,* RARITAN, Fall 1988, at 39, 40 ("[M]iscegenation cases have a relative autonomy from other social definitions of miscegenation. This autonomy, along with their internal cohesiveness and cross-references, allow them to be analyzed as a genre: miscegenation discourse.").

75

La Güera

CHERRÍE MORAGA

It requires something more than personal experience to gain a philosophy or point of view from any specific event. It is the quality of our response to the event and our capacity to enter into the lives of others that help us to make their lives and experiences our own.

Emma Goldman[1]

I am the very well-educated daughter of a woman who, by the standards in this country, would be considered largely illiterate. My mother was born in Santa Paula, Southern California, at a time when much of the central valley there was still farm land. Nearly thirty-five years later, in 1948, she was the only daughter of six to marry an anglo, my father.

My mother is a fine story-teller, recalling every event of her life with the vividness of the present, noting each detail right down to the cut and color of her dress. I remember stories of her being pulled out of school at the ages of five, seven, nine, and eleven to work in the fields, along with her brothers and sisters; stories of her father drinking away whatever small profit she was able to make for the family; of her going the long way home to avoid meeting him on the street, staggering toward the same destination. I remember stories of my mother lying about her age in order to get a job as a hat-check girl at Agua Caliente Racetrack in Tijuana. At fourteen, she was the main support of the family. I can still see her walking home alone at 3 A.M., only to turn all of her salary and tips over to her mother, who was pregnant again.

The stories continue through the war years and on: walnut-cracking factories, the Voit Rubber factory, and then the computer boom. I remember my mother doing piecework for the electronics plant in our neighborhood. In the late evening, she would sit in front of the T.V. set, wrapping copper wires into the backs of circuit boards, talking about "keeping up with the younger girls." By that time, she was already in her mid-fifties.

Meanwhile, I was college-prep in school. After classes, I would go with my mother to fill out job applications for her, or write checks for her at the supermarket. We would have the scenario all worked out ahead of time. My mother would sign the check before we'd get to the store. Then, as we'd approach the checkstand, she would say—within earshot of the cashier—"oh honey, you go 'head and make out the check," as if she couldn't be bothered with such an insignificant detail. No one asked any questions.

I was educated, and wore it with a keen sense of pride and satisfaction, my head propped up with the knowledge, from my mother, that my life would be easier than hers. I was educated; but more than this, I was "la güera": fair-skinned. Born with the features of my Chicana mother, but the skin of my Anglo father, I had it made.

No one ever quite told me that light was right but I knew that being light was something valued in my family (who were all Chicano, with the exception of my father). In fact, everything about my upbringing attempted to bleach me of what color I did have. Although my mother was fluent in it, I was never taught much Spanish at home. I picked up what I did from school and from overheard snatches of conversation among my relatives and mother. She often called other lower-income Mexicans "braceros," or "wet-backs," referring to herself and her family as "a different class of people." And yet, the real story was that my family, too, had been poor (some still are) and farmworkers. My mother can remember this in her blood as if it were yesterday. But this is something she would like to forget (and rightfully), for to her, on a basic economic level, being Chicana meant being "less." It was through my mother's desire to protect her children from poverty and illiteracy that we became "anglocized"; the more effectively we could pass in the white world, the better guaranteed our future.

From all of this, I experience, daily, a huge disparity between what I was born into and what I was to grow up to become. Because these stories my mother told me crept under my "güera" skin. I had no choice but to enter into the life of my mother. *I had no choice*. I took her life into my heart, but managed to keep a lid on it as long as I feigned being the happy, upwardly mobile heterosexual.

When I finally lifted the lid to my lesbianism, a profound connection with my mother reawakened in me. It wasn't until I acknowledged and confronted my own lesbianism in the flesh, that my heartfelt identification with and empathy for my mother's oppression—due to being poor, uneducated, and Chicana—was realized. My lesbianism is the avenue through which I have learned the most about silence and oppression, and it continues to be the most tactile reminder to me that we are not free human beings.

You see, one follows the other. I had known for years that I was a lesbian, had felt it in my bones, had ached with the knowledge, gone crazed with the knowledge, wallowed in the silence of it. Silence *is* like starvation. Don't be fooled. It's nothing short of that, and felt most sharply when one has had a full belly most of her life. When we are not physically starving, we have the luxury to realize psychic and emotional starvation. It is from this starvation that other starvations can be recognized—if one is willing to take the risk of making the connection—if one is willing to be responsible to the result of the connection. For me, the connection is an inevitable one.

What I am saying is that the joys of looking like a white girl ain't so great since I realized I could be beaten on the street for being a dyke. If my sister's being beaten because she's black, it's pretty much the same principle. We're both getting beaten any way you look at it. The connection is blatant; and in the case of my own family, the difference in the privileges attached to looking white instead of brown are merely a generation apart.

In this country, lesbianism is a poverty—as is being brown, as is being a woman, as is being just plain poor. The danger lies in ranking the oppressions. *The danger lies in failing to acknowledge the specificity of the oppression.* The danger lies in attempting to deal with oppression purely from a theoretical base. Without an emotional, heartfelt grappling with the source of our own oppression, without naming the enemy within ourselves and outside of us, no authentic, non-hierarchical connection among oppressed groups can take place.

When the going gets rough, will we abandon our so-called comrades in a flurry of racist/heterosexist/what-have-you panic? To whose camp, then, should the lesbian of color retreat? Her very presence violates the ranking and abstraction of oppression. Do we merely live hand to mouth? Do we merely struggle with the "ism" that's sitting on top of our own heads?

The answer is: yes, I think first we do; and we must do so thoroughly and deeply. But to fail to move out from there will only isolate us in our own oppression—will only insulate, rather than radicalize us.

To illustrate: a gay male friend of mine once confided to me that he continued to feel that, on some level, I didn't trust him because he was male; that he felt, really, if it ever came down to a "battle of the sexes," I might kill him. I admitted that I might very well. He wanted to understand the source of my distrust. I responded, "You're not a woman. Be a woman for a day. Imagine being a woman." He confessed that the thought terrified him because, to him, being a woman meant being raped by men. He *had* felt raped by men; he wanted to forget what that meant. What grew from that discussion was the realization that in order for him to create an authentic alliance with me, he must deal with the primary source of his own sense of oppression. He must, first, emotionally come to terms with what it feels like to be a victim. If he—or anyone—were to truly do this, it would be impossible to discount the oppression of others, except by again forgetting how we have been hurt.

And yet, oppressed groups are forgetting all the time. There are instances of this in the rising black middle class, and certainly an obvious trend of such "unconsciousness" among white gay men. Because to remember may mean giving up whatever privileges we have managed to squeeze out of this society by virtue of our gender, race, class, or sexuality.

Within the women's movement, the connections among women of different backgrounds and sexual orientations have been fragile, at best. I think this phenomenon is indicative of our failure to seriously address ourselves to some very frightening questions: How have I internalized my own oppression? How have I oppressed? Instead, we have let rhetoric do the job of poetry. Even the word "oppression" has lost its power. We need a new language, better words that can more closely describe women's fear of and resistance to one another; words that will not always come out sounding like dogma.

What prompted me in the first place to work on an anthology by radical women of color was a deep sense that I had a valuable insight to contribute, by virtue of my birthright and background. And yet, I don't really understand first-hand what it feels like being shitted on for being brown. I understand much more about the joys of it—being Chicana and having family are synonymous for me. What I know about loving, singing, crying, telling stories, speaking with my heart and hands, even having a sense of my own soul comes from the love of my mother, aunts, cousins . . .

But at the age of twenty-seven, it is frightening to acknowledge that I have internalized a racism and classism, where the object of oppression is not only someone outside of my skin, but the someone inside my skin. In fact, to a large degree, the real battle with such oppression, for all of us, begins under the skin. I have had to confront that much of what I value about being Chicana, about my family, has been subverted by anglo culture and my own cooperation with it. This realization did not occur to me overnight. For example, it wasn't until long after my graduation from the private college I'd attended in Los Angeles, that I realized the major reason for my total alienation from and fear of my classmates was rooted in class and culture. CLICK.

Three years after graduation, in an apple-orchard in Sonoma, a friend of mine (who comes from an Italian Irish working-class family) says to me, "Cherríe, no wonder you felt like such a nut in school. Most of the people there were white and rich." It was true. All along I had felt the difference, but not until I had put the words "class" and "color" to the experience did my feelings make any sense. For years, I had berated myself for not being as "free" as my classmates. I completely bought that they simply had more guts than I did—to rebel against their parents and run around the country hitch-hiking, reading books and studying "art." They had enough privilege to be atheists, for chrissake. There was no one around filling in the disparity for me between their parents, who were Hollywood film-makers, and my parents, who wouldn't know the name of a filmmaker if their lives depended on it (and precisely because their lives didn't depend on it, they couldn't be bothered). But I knew nothing about "privilege" then. White was right. Period. I could pass. If I got educated enough, there would never be any telling.

Notes

1. Alix Kates Shulman, "Was My Life Worth Living?" *Red Emma Speaks* (New York: Random House, 1972), p. 388.

76

Notes of a White Black Woman

JUDY SCALES-TRENT

[What follows is an introduction to a longer work. Ed.]

We Americans have been talking about race for a long time. It is a constant theme in our lives and in our common language. Although the specific topic changes over the years—varying all the way from fugitive slave laws to affirmative action—the theme remains. Ideas about race lie at the core of the American character and the American dream.

In general, discussions about race center on the state of relations between black Americans and white Americans. They focus on who will control the resources: freedom, jobs, schools, housing, medical care. In some of this debate, black people call white people mean and ignorant and hateful, and white people call black people the same. At other times, we wonder whether there will ever be harmony between the races, and whether there is anything we can do to hasten the arrival of that day. Groups that might appear to be outside this debate are nonetheless connected to it. For example, people ask how Jews situate themselves with respect to the black-white drama: Which side are they on? How about Native peoples? And what does it mean that there will be more Mexican Americans than African Americans by the year 2010? How will that affect the great black/white racial divide so familiar to us all? Among the millions of Americans who participate in this discussion, points of view differ drastically. There seems to be profound agreement, however, with the notion that race is a serious matter in America, and always has been.

The most important premise of these discussions is the existence of "race" itself. We all simply know that "race" exists. It is obvious, it is real, it has its own independent presence. You can just look around and see how the world is split up—black people sitting over there at that table, white people walking together down that hall, maybe a table with black people and white people sitting together. Our eyes tell us this truth. Thus, racial identity is simply assumed. It is not questioned. It is not noticed or seen or discussed. It just is.

In these essays, I take my place in the debate on racial matters in America by moving the discussion back a step, to talk about the creation of "race" itself. What do we mean by "race" in this country? How is "race" created? Who creates it? How is racial identity maintained? What is the law of racial purity that America uses to create and maintain racial identity? And how does it work? I address these questions by showing the operation of America's racial purity law on my life—that is, on the life of one American.

Because I am a black American who is often mistaken for white, my very existence demonstrates that there is slippage between the seemingly discrete categories "black" and "white." This slippage is important and can be helpful to us, for it makes the enterprise of categorizing by race a more visible—hence, a more conscious—task. It is at this point, then, that we can pause and look carefully at what we are doing. It is at this point of slippage that we can clearly see that "race" is not a biological fact but a social construct—and a clumsy one, at that. Stories about my life as a white black American also show that creating and maintaining a racial identity takes a lot of effort on my part, and on the part of other Americans. "Race" is not something that just exists. It is a continuing act of imagination. It is a very demanding verb.

Many are surprised to discover that America has racial purity laws. We know that Nazi Germany and South Africa once did. Some even know that such formal, written laws existed in America from the earliest days of the colonies through at least the 1980s. One example is Virginia's 1924 law, which says:

> The term "white person" shall apply only to the person who has no trace whatsoever of any blood other than Caucasian, but persons who have one-sixteenth or less of the blood of the American Indian, and no other non-Caucasic blood shall be deemed white persons.

But racial purity laws would have to exist in this country, as they do in every culture that uses racial definitions: where race is important, there must be a way to sort by race. Thus, to the extent that we talk about race in America, we are basing our talk on notions of racial purity. The concept of race cannot exist without the concept of racial purity.

The need for racial purity laws arose in America as soon as an African and a European had sexual relations here and produced a child. Was the child African? European? Something else? It is not surprising, then, that the question was raised early. At the beginning of the seventeenth century, when sexual contact between these two groups took place, it was generally between enslaved and free blacks, and white indentured servants, in the colonies of Maryland and Virginia. Initially, the status of these relationships—and of the children born of these relationships—was uncertain. But by 1662 the state of Virginia, troubled by these relationships, passed its first law banning miscegenation.

By the early 1700s, the upper South had begun to formulate the social rule that held that all children with African ancestry would be considered "black." In making this decision, white Southerners rejected several other possibilities. For example, they could have considered these children "white"; they could have created a third racial category; and indeed, they could have eliminated the concept of race altogether. Instead, the upper South decided that the taint of Africa was so strong that one ancestor from Africa ("one drop of black 'blood'") would mark a child "black." (This rule is popularly called "the one black ancestor rule" or "the 'one-drop' rule"; anthropologists call it "hypodescent," which means that racially mixed people are assigned the status of the subordinate group. This rule applies only to African Americans in the United States and apparently also exists only in this country.) Early on support for this rule spread throughout the South. Eventually this social norm was codified into law.

The laws, however, were not uniform. They varied from state to state; they often varied, as well, within a given state over time. Hence, a person might be white in one state and black in another. Or a person might be black under state law one day, and the next day white—or vice versa. Nonetheless, well before the Civil War the "one-drop rule" was widespread in the North and in most of the South. Today, although as a general rule racial purity laws are no longer codified in formal laws, they have not disappeared. They remain in effect as very strong social norms in the United States. And the "one-drop rule" of racial purity is generally accepted by both black and white communities in America.

That is a brief history of the development and spread of the rule of hypodescent, which controls racial identity in America today. It is important to realize, however, that the creation and enforcement of this rule has had a powerful effect not only *on* the African American community but also *within* the African American community. In order to understand the impact of this rule within the African American community, we must return to the plantations.

As slavery developed in the black-belt plantations, ownership of African women soon included owning their sex life also. Thus, it was common for African women who were enslaved to be sexually assaulted, raped, made concubines. It was also common for the master (or other males in the master's family) to bring a particular slave woman to live and work in his home, in order to facilitate his sexual attacks. One result of this move to the master's house was that these enslaved women—and the children they had with the slave owners—were in close enough contact with European Americans to learn their language, habits, and beliefs. Some of the children were able to gain an education; the boys were often apprenticed to artisans, from whom they learned skilled trades. This did not mean that these women and children were not still slaves and still treated cruelly, but it did mean that members of the slave master's black family were often able to acquire certain skills because they lived in close proximity to the slave master's white family. Indeed, some slave owners freed the children they had with slave women.

These skills became an important way for slaves to find extra work, and thus earn enough money to buy their freedom and that of their loved ones. The skills were also important when the slaves were manumitted, or when they escaped, or after the Civil War. And then, because we are talking about the children of African and European parents, all this—the skills in a craft and in European ways, the chance to get free, freedom itself—all this was conflated with light skin. And because over the generations, as the men in the slave master's family had sex with the slaves with dark skin, and then with slaves with lighter skin, the offspring of these unions became even lighter. So it was not very long before widespread sexual contact between Africans and Europeans, and the rule of hypodescent, combined to create a group of free blacks and slaves and former slaves with very light skin— black people with green eyes and red hair, or blue eyes and light brown skin, or brown eyes and straight hair.

Some of this group, when freed, moved to cities, where their light skin and cultural attributes—language, education, skills—made possible the creation of a light-skinned black elite. And because light skin then, as now, was the most important marker of status in this country, many of this group came to use light skin as an independent mark of status. Historians also tell us that dark-skinned blacks who had other attributes of high status—a skill, a formal education, wealth—were often excluded from the social life of these elite communities because of their dark skin.

In the early years of slavery, there was some tendency for white Americans to see light-skinned African Americans—whether slave or free—as a separate group with a distinct political and social status that lay somewhere between the status afforded the black and white groups. This was especially true in South Carolina and Louisiana, where the legal system formalized this tripartite scheme of racial classification. This tendency ended, however, by the middle of the nineteenth century, as pressure on the South with respect to slavery caused it to intensify its control over the entire slave community. During this period, then, there was less tolerance of manumission, and less tolerance of any other special treatment for slaves with light skin. At the same time, the "one-drop rule" gained even more support nationwide as it helped defend the notion that Africans were "natural slaves." Thus, as the white community began to withdraw privileges from the light-skinned black community in the mid–nineteenth century, the light-skinned group started to seek out alliances with darker blacks. This new sense of unity accelerated during the Civil War and Reconstruction and was solidified during the Jim Crow era and the Black Pride movement of the 1960s.

The history that surrounds issues of race and color is, of course, much more complicated and interesting than is suggested in this brief introduction, which is almost misleading in its brevity. But there is a sense in which, even if this brief historical sketch shades into stereotype, it is the story that most black Americans know about race and color. And it is a history that scars us all. Just as the forced migration of millions of Yoruba and Ibo wrought destruction on those cultures in Africa as well as in America, so has this newly created African American community been devastated by a vision of the world in which light skin and dark skin are seen as mediations on good and evil, civilization and savagery, intelligence and ignorance. This cruel lesson has not only affected how we see ourselves in comparison with white Americans; it has also informed how we look at each other within our own community.

Because black and white Americans talk and write about race so much, I can say, with some assurance, that at any given time many blacks hate, fear, and despise white Americans, and that many whites hate, fear, and despise black Americans. And even though black Americans rarely talk or write about the color distinctions we make within our own community, I also think it safe to say that, at any given time, many light-skinned black Americans and dark-skinned black Americans despise, are attracted to, fear, reject, and are rejected by each other simply because of the color of their skin.

And it was into this America that I was born, in the fall of 1940.

Like my parents, I am a black American with white skin, an African American with both African and European ancestors. Thus, I live a life that is often disjointed, troubling. I also see the world in a different way. There is something about living on the margins of race that gives me a unique view of the categories "black" and "white," that presents a different picture of white Americans and black Americans, of America itself. For my position does not allow me the luxury of thinking that the notion of race makes any sense. If you are black and white at the same time, once you finally realize that it is not *you* that is strange, you realize that something very strange is going on in this society. Perhaps more directly and more starkly than other Americans, I understand "race" as a socially created metaphor, for my very existence unsettles expectations of "race." It is no longer a tangible reality as reflected through color. Indeed, my existence raises troubling questions. Suppose race really *does* have nothing to do with color? What, then, is it all about?

Skinwalkers, Race, and Geography

In Navajo cosmology there exist certain powerful creatures who, although they appear to be mere humans, can change shape whenever they wish by taking on animal form. These are supernatural beings, not like you and me. They are called "skinwalkers."

And I think about them, and this name, when I think about how we all "skinwalk"— change shapes, identities, from time to time, during the course of a day, during the course of our lives. I think about how we create these identities, how they are created for us, how they change, and how we reconcile these changes as we go along.

A young woman leaves her family on the farm and goes to medical school, where she learns a new language, a new culture. She tells me that she feels like an immigrant in a new land. She feels as if she is changing skin, shifting shape, and will be forever shifting as she travels back and forth between these two worlds. A young man goes to visit his parents with a wife and new child. He visits, however, in a complicated way, as he is now not only a son but also a husband and a father. And he shifts identities during the visit, mediating between these different roles within his newly structured family. A child whose parents have different religious beliefs—the father Methodist, the mother Episcopalian; the mother Roman Catholic, the father Greek Orthodox; the father Reform Jew, the mother Buddhist—this child learns to change shape as she communicates in two languages with her parents, as she visits with different sets of grandparents, aunts and uncles, cousins, during the holidays. And I, when I moved from a predominantly black civil rights community in Washington, D.C., to a predominantly white university in Buffalo, I too was a "skin-walker." In Washington, in the black community within a black city, I was a woman who just happened to be black. But in the Buffalo academic world, in this white community within a white city, I became a black person who just happened to be a woman.

All of these examples involve moving from one place to another, from one life to another, from one culture, one role, to another. But sometimes you can change identities while you are doing absolutely nothing at all. Things change around us. Society changes its rules and its boundaries, and suddenly you take on a different form: you become a heron, or forsythia, or your ancestor.

I have been thinking for a long time about two young girls, girls who were skinwalkers, sisters who never met.

The first, Marie, lived in Thionville, a small village in eastern France, in 1871. Like all good French girls, she went to Mass with her family, went to confession, and wore a beautiful white dress to her first Communion. Because her family had a prosperous farm, she also went to a small school, where she studied the French kings and queens, read the plays of Corneille and Racine, and learned the old songs of the region. Then one bright fall day, one day while she was in the kitchen with her mother putting bread on the table for the midday meal, somewhere far away, in some office or lawmaking place, one of the people who get to draw the lines wrote something down on a piece of paper—and suddenly Marie had a different identity. She was no longer French. She was German.

How could she comprehend this? Was she really supposed to unlearn everything she had ever learned about who she was? About who her people were? That must be so, because Germany immediately installed German schools in its new territory, the former French province of Lorraine. And suddenly Marie, now German, was required to speak only German and study the glory of German history.

The second young girl, Hannah, lived on her family farm in the Tidewater area of Virginia in 1785. Both her parents were free Negroes. Her father worked as a carpenter, and the whole family worked their small farm, a farm that provided a good life for Hannah and her two sisters. With the other black children in the community, the girls learned reading and writing and Bible verses in classes held in the nearby black church—the center of religion, culture, and community for all Negroes, free and enslaved, who lived in the Tidewater area in those days. And after classes, the children played circle games together, and they sang the old work songs and spirituals their grandparents had taught them. Then one day, one muggy summer's day while Hannah was sitting at the kitchen table with her mother stringing beans for dinner, something happened miles away, something that would change her life forever. The Virginia legislature changed the line between black and white. Now before this time, Hannah and her sisters were black, because one of their great-grandparents was black. They thus met the statutory definition of "Negro" in 1784. But in 1785 the legislators redefined "Negro" to mean anyone who had one black grandparent. And this, Hannah didn't have. All her grandparents were white. So on that simple summer's day, while she was at her home on the farm, someone somewhere wrote three sentences on a piece of paper and, magically, supernaturally, Hannah, a "skinwalker," became "white."

Thinking about the lives of these two young girls—one whose life was thrown into disarray by lines drawn on a map; the other, who was turned inside out by lines marked down in a book of rules—thinking about these two girls makes me think about the relationship between race and geography.

In both instances, we are talking about an exercise in drawing lines, lines to separate Here from There. The line-makers are marking boundaries, borders, creating Insiders and Outsiders. They are creating an "us" and a "them." They are creating the Other. Also, in both instances, those who draw these lines are drawing pictures of the world. They are showing what the world looks like, how the world *should* look, what looks right to them. So if you study their picture, you will know who you are—black or white, French or German, "us" or "them."

All this means, of course, that the line-drawers have the authority to describe the world for everyone in it. They are exercising enormous power, power they have grabbed or earned or received or simply found. But they have it, this power to locate the line, to decide who stands where in relationship to the line, and to divide community resources based on that decision.

Thus, whether we are talking about race or geography, marking boundaries creates property rights, for it is the boundaries that define who gets what—who gets the most, who gets less, who gets nothing—who takes, and who gets taken. And whether we are talking about race or geography, both imply war, as property rights always do. For those who somehow have the power to draw these lines, the power to say that they will get the most, will then have to, in fact *must*, fight to maintain those lines. And that means war.

Race and geography have one more important trait in common. They are both equally arbitrary systems of (dis)organization. Whether a person is sitting at a desk drawing lines on a piece of paper that represents the surface of this planet, or putting marks on a piece of paper that form words telling how to separate humans one from the other—no matter which task one is engaged in, it is simply and only a task. It is not a given, not a fact, not an eternal truth. Also, it is a task that leads to other tasks. For after creating this idea and drawing this line, the line-drawers must then convince a lot of people that this is the right line to draw and an important line to draw. And then they must develop a system to maintain these lines.

This is a lot of work.

Just think of the time, energy, and resources that a country uses to create and maintain the lines between its tribe and the tribe on the other side of the line. First, there are probably wars to establish the lines. Then you have to have guards on patrol at all times to make sure that only certain people cross the line. And there are immigration rules and lawyers and border patrols and enforcement agencies and soldiers and sailors and pilots and planes and bombs. The country also spends enormous sums of money teaching its youth about the importance, the "rightness" of the tribal line, so they will be eager to guard the line when it is their turn to patrol.

Then realize that this is the same amount of time and energy we expend to maintain the lines of racial purity in this country. And it is done the same way. There have been fights on the battlefield. And there are still fights—in the courts, in legislatures, on the streets of

America—a continuing struggle to maintain the line between black and white, to reinforce its validity and power. The country has published rules, drafted forms, hired census-takers, created grandfather clauses and gerrymandering and segregated water fountains and back-of-the-bus and "cordons sanitaires." It has deputized all Americans who are not black to engage in this battle as soon as the boat brings them here from Peru, from Ireland, from Japan. Similarly, white America expends enormous resources in school and in the media to teach its youth about the intrinsic rightness of this line, so that they will not question its value when they reach the age to stand guard.

One task is overt; the other, covert. But line-drawing is line-drawing. It is the same task.

So the next time you say "black" or "white," the next time you hear someone use a racial designation, think about geography. And when you think about geography, see this picture:

There is a small group of men in a tent, and it is night. These men, lieutenants and cartographers, are sitting, standing around a small table, trying to calculate where to put the line. An oil lamp on the table reflects its yellowish light on their tired faces, on papers strewn about. The men are concentrating on one of these papers—a heavy parchment scroll, its red wax seal broken. The scroll is from the generals at the front, claiming victory, and it tells the mapmakers what to do. The scroll says this:

> Draw the line here.
> We have taken more land.
> This much is ours.

77

Our Next Race Question: The Uneasiness between Blacks and Latinos

JORGE KLOR DE ALVA, EARL SHORRIS, AND CORNEL WEST

The angry and confused discourse about American race relations that followed the O. J. Simpson trial may have been passionate, but it blindly assumed (as if the year were 1963 or 1861) that the only major axis of racial division in America was black-white. Strangely ignored in the media backwash was the incipient tension between the country's largest historical minority, blacks, and its largest future one, Latinos.

In fifteen years, Latinos (known to the U.S. Census as Hispanics) will outnumber blacks, as they already do in twenty-one states. Each group constitutes an ever greater percentage of the total population; each is large enough to swing a presidential election. But do they vote with or against each other, and do they hold the same views of a white America that they have different reasons to distrust?

Knowing that questions of power and ethnicity are no longer black-and-white, *Harper's Magazine* invited three observers—a black, a Latino, and a white moderator—to open the debate.

EARL SHORRIS: To begin, would you both answer one question with a yes or no, no more than that? Cornel, are you a black man?

CORNEL WEST: Yes.

SHORRIS: Jorge, do you think Cornel is a black man?

JORGE KLOR DE ALVA: No, for now.

SHORRIS: Apparently we have something to talk about. Jorge, can you tell me why you say, "No, for now?"

KLOR DE ALVA: To identify someone as black, Latino, or anything else, one has to appeal to a tradition of naming and categorizing in which a question like that can make sense— and be answered with a yes or a no. In the United States, where unambiguous, color-coded identities are the rule, Cornel is clearly a black man. Traveling someplace else, perhaps in Africa, Cornel would not necessarily be identified as black. He might be seen as someone of mixed African descent, but that's different from being identified as black.

Cornel is only black within a certain reductionist context. And that context, where color is made to represent not so much the hue of one's skin as a set of denigrated experiences—and where these experiences are applied to everyone who ever had an African ancestor—is one I consider to be extremely negative.

WEST: I think when I say I am a black man, I'm saying first that I am a modern person, because black itself is a modern construct, a construct put forward during a particular moment in time to fit a specific set of circumstances. Implicit in that category of "black man" is American white supremacy, African slavery, and then a very rich culture that responds to these conditions at the level of style, mannerism, orientation, experimentation, improvisation, syncopation—all of those elements that have gone into making a new people, namely black people.

A hundred years ago I would have said that I was a "colored man." But I would still have been modern, I'd still have been New World African, I'd still have been dealing with white supremacy, and I would still have been falling back on a very rich culture of resistance, a culture that tried to preserve black sanity and spiritual health in the face of white hatred and job ceilings. I think Jorge and I agree that we're dealing with constructs. And I think we agree in our objections to essentialist conceptions of race, to the idea that differences are innate and outside of history.

KLOR DE ALVA: What advantage has it been, Cornel, for blacks to identify themselves as blacks?

WEST: For one, that identification was imposed. We were perceived as a separate people—enslaved, Jim Crowed, and segregated. To be viewed as a separate people requires coming to terms with that separateness. This category "black" was simply a response to that imposition of being a separate people, and also a building on one's own history, going back to Africa, yes, but especially here in the United States. So when I say, for example, that jazz is a creation of black people, I'm saying that it's a creation of modern people, New World African people. And we've come up with various categories, including black, as a way of affirming ourselves as agents, as subjects in history who create, initiate, and so forth. So in that sense there have actually been some real benefits.

KLOR DE ALVA: When the Europeans arrived in Mexico, they confronted people whose level of social organization was not unlike that of the Romans. Before millions died from newly introduced diseases, the Europeans called them *naturales*, or "natural people." Afterwards the survivors came to be called "Indians," a term the natives did not use until the nineteenth century, preferring to identify themselves by their tribal group. And to the extent that they were able to do that, they managed to maintain a degree of cultural integrity as separate groups. When that ended, they were all seen as despised Indians.

The general label only helped to promote their denigration. Now, I agree that group designations help build a sense of community, but as free and enslaved Africans took on the general labels that oppressed them, they also helped to legitimize their being identified as one irredeemable people. In the United States this unwillingness to challenge what has come to be known as the one-drop rule—wherein anyone who ever had an African ancestor, however remote, is identifiable only as black—has strengthened the hand of those who seek to trap them, and other so-called people of color, in a social basement with no exit ladder.

WEST: When we talk about identity, it's really important to define it. Identity has to do with protection, association, and recognition. People identify themselves in certain ways in order to protect their bodies, their labor, their communities, their way of life; in order to be associated with people who ascribe value to them, who take them seriously, who respect them; and for purposes of recognition, to be acknowledged, to feel as if one actually belongs to a group, a clan, a tribe, a community. So that any time we talk about the identity of a particular group over time and space, we have to be very specific about what the credible options are for them at any given moment.

There have been some black people in America who fundamentally believed that they were wholehearted, full-fledged Americans. They have been mistaken. They tried to pursue that option—Boom! Jim Crow hit them. They tried to press that option—Boom! Vanilla suburbs didn't allow them in. So they had to then revise and recast their conception of themselves in terms of protection, association, and recognition. Because they weren't being protected by the police and the courts. They weren't welcome in association. Oftentimes they were not welcome in white suburbs. And they weren't being recognized. Their talents and capacities were debased, devalued, and degraded. "Black" was the term many chose. Okay, that's fine, we can argue about that. But what are the other options? "Human being?" Yes, we ought to be human beings, but we know that's too abstract and too vague. We need human communities on the ground, not simply at the level of the ideal.

Constructing Humans

KLOR DE ALVA: Nobody is born black. People are born with different pigmentation, people are born with different physical characteristics, no question about that. But you have to learn to be black. That's what I mean by constructedness.

WEST: But are people born human? Is "human" itself constructed, as a category?

KLOR DE ALVA: Certainly as a category, as a social, as a scientific category, of course it's a construct. The species could have been identified in some other fashion. Since Columbus's landfall you had very extensive debates as to whether indigenous peoples in the Americas were human, like Europeans, or not. The priest Montesinos posed that question to the Spanish colonists in 1511, and Las Casas, a fellow priest, and the theologian Sepúlveda debated the issue at mid-century before Emperor Charles V.

WEST: You see, this historical process of naming is part of the legacy not just of white but of class supremacy. Tolstoy didn't believe his peasants were actually human until after he underwent conversion. And he realized, "My God, I used to think they were animals, now they're human beings, I have a different life and a new set of lenses with which to view it." So it is with any talk about blackness. It's associated with subhumanness, and therefore when we talk about constructed terms like "black" or "peasant" or "human," it means that the whole thing's up for grabs in terms of constructedness. And if that's so, then all we have left is history.

KLOR DE ALVA: All identities are up for grabs. But black intellectuals in the United States, unlike Latino intellectuals here, have an enormous media space within which to shape the politics of naming and to affect the symbols and meanings associated with certain terms. Thus, practically overnight, they convinced the media that they were an ethnic group and shifted over to the model of African-American, hyphenated American, as opposed to being named by color. Knowing what we know about the negative aspects of naming, it would be better for all of us, regardless of color, if those who consider themselves, and are seen as black intellectuals, were to stop participating in the insidious one-drop-rule game of identifying themselves as black.

WEST: If you're saying that we are, for the most part, biological and cultural hybrids, I think you're certainly right. But at the same time there's a danger in calling for an end to a certain history if we're unable to provide other options. Now, because I speak first and foremost as a human being, a radical Democrat, and a Christian, I would be willing to use damn near any term if it helped to eliminate poverty and provide adequate health care and child care and a job with a living wage, some control at the workplace, and some redistribution of wealth downward. At that point, you can call all black people colored. That's fine with me.

SHORRIS: Are you saying that you're willing to disappear?

WEST: Well, I would never disappear, because whatever name we would come up with, we're still going to have the blues and John Coltrane and Sarah Vaughan and all those who come out of this particular history. And simply because we change the name wouldn't mean that we would disappear.

KLOR DE ALVA: I think that's the wrong emphasis. I think what has happened is that much of the cultural diversity that Cornel mentions has, in fact, disappeared behind this veil that has transformed everybody with one drop of African blood into black. That reductionism has been a much more powerful mechanism for causing diversity to disappear.

WEST: Well, what do you mean by disappearance at this point?

KLOR DE ALVA: Let me answer your question from a slightly different perspective. We have, in the United States, two mechanisms at play in the construction of collective identities. One is to identify folks from a cultural perspective. The other is to identify them from a racial perspective. Now, with the exception of black-white relations, the racial perspective is not the critical one for most folks. The cultural perspective was, at one time, very sharply drawn, including the religious line between Catholics and Protestants, Jews and Protestants, Jews and Catholics, Jews and Christians. But in the course of the twentieth century, we have seen in the United States a phenomenon that we do not see anyplace else in the world—the capacity to blur the differences between these cultural groups, to construct them in such a way that they became insignificant and to fuse them into a new group called whites, which didn't exist before.

WEST: Yes, but whiteness was already in place. I mean, part of the tragedy of American civilization is precisely the degree to which the stability and continuity of American democracy has been predicated on a construct of whiteness that includes the subordination of black people, so that European cultural diversity could disappear into American whiteness while black folk remain subordinated.

KLOR DE ALVA: But everything, even whiteness, must be constructed and is therefore subject to change.

WEST: Categories are constructed. Scars and bruises are felt with human bodies, some of which end up in coffins. Death is not a construct. And so, when we're talking about constructs having concrete consequences that produce scars and bruises, these consequences are not constructed, they're felt. They're very real. Now, in light of that, I would want to accent the strengths of the history of black resistance. One of the reasons why black people are so integral a part of American civilization is because black people have raised a lot of hell. That's very important, especially in a society in which power and pressure decide who receives visibility. By raising hell I mean organization, mobilization, chaos-producing capacity, as in rebellion. That's a very important point. Why is it important? It's important for me because what's at stake is the quality of American civilization, whether it actually survives as a plausible idea.

That's why a discourse on race is never just that. Richard Wright used to say that the Negro is America's metaphor. It means you can't talk about one without talking about the nature of the other. And one of the reasons we don't like to talk about race, especially as it relates to black folk, is because we're forced to raise all the fundamental questions about what it means to be an American, what it means to be a part of American democracy. Those are exhausting and challenging questions.

The best of the black intellectual and political tradition has always raised the problem of evil in its concrete forms in America. People like Frederick Douglass, Martin Luther King, and Ella Baker never focused solely on black suffering. They used black suffering as a springboard to raise issues of various other forms of injustice, suffering, and so forth, that relate to other groups—black, brown, white workers, right across the board, you see. During the Eighties, the major opposition to right-wing Reaganism was what? Jesse Jackson's campaigns. Opening up to workers, gay brothers, lesbian sisters, right across the board. Black suffering was a springboard. Why? Because a question of evil sits at the heart of the American moral dilemma. With the stark exception of its great artists—Melville, Faulkner, Elizabeth Bishop, Coltrane, Toni Morrison—American society prefers to deny the existence of its own evil. Black folk historically have reminded people of the prevailing state of denial.

Anglos May Be of Any Race

SHORRIS: We've just demonstrated one of the tenets of this conversation. That is, we have discussed almost exclusively the question of blacks in this society. But we started out saying we would have a black-brown dialogue. Why does that happen? And not only in the media. Why did it happen here, among us?

KLOR DE ALVA: Part of the answer, as Cornel was pointing out, is that blacks are the central metaphor for otherness and oppression in the United States. Secondly, in part I take your question, when focused on Latinos, to mean, Don't Latinos have their own situation that also needs to be described if not in the same terms, then at least in terms that are supplementary?

I'm not sure. The answer goes to the very core of the difference between Latinos and blacks and between Cornel and myself: I am trying to argue against the utility of the concept of race. Why? Because I don't think that's the dominant construct we need to address in order to resolve the many problems at hand. Cornel wants to construct it in the language of the United States, and I say we need a different kind of language. Do you know why, Earl? Because we're in the United States and blacks are Americans. They're Anglos.

WEST: Excuse me?

KLOR DE ALVA: They're Anglos of a different color, but they're Anglos. Why? Because the critical distinction here for Latinos is not race, it's culture.

WEST: Speaking English and being part of American culture?

KLOR DE ALVA: Blacks are more Anglo than most Anglos because, unlike most Anglos, they can't directly identify themselves with a nation-state outside of the United States. They are trapped in America. However unjust and painful, their experiences are wholly made in America.

WEST: But that doesn't make me an Anglo. If I'm trapped on the underside of America, that doesn't mean that somehow I'm an Anglo.

KLOR DE ALVA: Poor whites similarly trapped on the underside of America are also Anglos. Latinos are in a totally different situation, unable to be captured by the government in the "five food groups" of racial classification of Americans. The Commerce Department didn't know what to do with Latinos; the census takers didn't know what to do with Latinos; the government didn't know what to do with Latinos, and so they said, "Latinos can be of any race." That puts Latinos in a totally different situation. They are, in fact, homologous with the totality of the United States. That is, like Americans, Latinos can be of any race. What distinguishes them from all other Americans is culture, not race. That's where I'm going when I say that Cornel is an Anglo. You can be a Latino and look like Cornel. You can be a Latino and look like you, Earl, or like me. And so, among Latinos, there's no surprise in my saying that Cornel is an Anglo.

WEST: But it seems to me that "Anglo" is the wrong word.

KLOR DE ALVA: Hey, I didn't make it up, Cornel.

WEST: "Anglo" implies a set of privileges. It implies a certain cultural formation.

KLOR DE ALVA: I'm trying to identify here how Chicanos see "Anglos."

WEST: But I want to try and convince those Latino brothers and sisters not to think of black folk as Anglos. That's just wrong. Now, they can say that we're English-speaking moderns in the United States who have yet to be fully treated as Americans. That's fine.

KLOR DE ALVA: My friend, Cornel, I was speaking of one of the more benign Latino names for blacks.

WEST: Let's hear some of the less benign then, brother.

What Color Is Brown?

KLOR DE ALVA: Do you think of Latinos as white?

WEST: I think of them as brothers and sisters, as human beings, but in terms of culture, I think of them as a particular group of voluntary immigrants who entered America and had to encounter this thoroughly absurd system of classification of positively charged whiteness, negatively charged blackness. And they don't fit either one: they're not white, they're not black.

SHORRIS: What are they?

WEST: I see them primarily as people of color, as brown people who have to deal with their blackness-whiteness.

SHORRIS: So you see them in racial terms.

WEST: Well, no, it's more cultural.

SHORRIS: But you said "brown."

WEST: No, it's more cultural. Brown, for me, is more associated with culture than race.

SHORRIS: But you choose a word that describes color.

WEST: Right. To say "Spanish-speaking" would be a bit too vague, because you've got a lot of brothers and sisters from Guatemala who don't speak Spanish. They speak an indigenous language.

KLOR DE ALVA: You have a lot of Latinos who aren't brown.

WEST: But they're not treated as whites, and "brown" is simply a signifier of that differential treatment. Even if a Latino brother or sister has supposedly white skin, he or she is still Latino in the eyes of the white privileged, you see. But they're not treated as black.

They're not niggers. They're not the bottom of the heap, you see. So they're not niggers, they're not white, what are they? I say brown, but signifying culture more than color. Mexicans, Cubans, Puerto Ricans, Dominicans, El Salvadorans all have very, very distinctive histories. When you talk about black, that becomes a kind of benchmark, because you've got these continuous generations, and you've got very common experiences.

Now, of course, blackness comprises a concealed heterogeneity. You've got West Indians, you've got Ethiopians. My wife is Ethiopian. Her experience is closer to browns'. She came here because she wanted to. She was trying to get out from under a tyrannical, Communist regime in Ethiopia. She's glad to be in a place where she can breathe freely, not have to hide. I say, "I'm glad you're here, but don't allow that one side of America to blind you to my side."

So I've got to take her, you know, almost like Virgil in Dante's *Divine Comedy*, through all of this other side of America so that she can see the nightmare as well as the dream. But as an Ethiopian, she came for the dream and did a good job of achieving it.

KLOR DE ALVA: So you are participating in the same process as the other Americans, other Anglos—to use that complicated term—that same song and dance of transforming her into a highly racialized American black.

WEST: It wasn't me. It was the first American who called her "nigger." That's when she started the process of Americanization and racialization. She turned around and said, "What is a nigger?"

KLOR DE ALVA: And you're the one who explained it.

LBJ's Other Dilemma

SHORRIS: How do you see yourself, Jorge?

KLOR DE ALVA: I'm an American citizen. What are you, Cornel?

WEST: I am a black man trying to be an American citizen.

KLOR DE ALVA: I'm an American citizen trying to get rid of as many categories as possible that classify people in ways that make it easy for them to be oppressed, isolated, marginalized. Of course, I'm a Chicano, I'm a Mexican-American. But for me to identify myself that way is not much help. More helpful is my actually working to resolve the problems of poor folks in the United States.

If I were black, I would heighten the importance of citizenship. Why? Because every time we've seen huge numbers of immigrants enter the United States, the people most devastated by their arrival, in terms of being relegated to an even lower rung on the employment ladder, have been blacks.

SHORRIS: Are you defining "black" and "Latino" as "poor"?

KLOR DE ALVA: No, no. I'm not defining them that way at all.

WEST: What's fascinating about this issue of race is the degree to which, in the American mind, black people are associated with instability, chaos, disorder—the very things that America always runs from. In addition, we are associated with hypersexuality, transgressive criminal activity—all of the various stereotypes and images.

SHORRIS: We all know LBJ's comment about affirmative action. He said that it's the right thing to do but that it will destroy the Democratic Party. There certainly is every likelihood that it has destroyed the Democratic Party as it's traditionally been understood, that the Democratic Party's base in the South has disappeared, that the white South now votes Republican and many blacks don't vote at all. What does this mean about America and the likelihood of any kind of affirmative action, or any program for social justice, succeeding, either for blacks or for Latinos?

KLOR DE ALVA: No matter what kind of policy you set in place, there has to be something in it for everybody or the policy is not going to last very long. And I'm not even going to get into the issue that affirmative action has been essentially an African-American thing, not a Latino thing.

WEST: But who have the major beneficiaries been? White women. And rightly so. More of them have been up against the patriarchy than black and brown people have been up against racism.

KLOR DE ALVA: If you're right that white women are the main beneficiaries, and if I'm right that African-Americans were meant to be the primary beneficiaries, then we have to ask if affirmative action is an effective strategy for the resolution of the Latinos' problems. And has the failure of class organization been due primarily to the racial divisions in the society? If so, then race is a lamentable category for any kind of progressive organization, and we need an alternative to affirmative action. I would remove the government from participation in the naming game and its divisive racializing of identities.

WEST: To the degree to which the Democratic Party cuts against a strong white supremacist grain in America and identifies with black people unequivocally, it will be destroyed. That's essentially what the Republican strategy has been since 1968. The question then becomes, How do we talk about these issues of class while also recognizing that any silence with respect to the de facto white supremacy results in institutions that ought to be changed because they have little moral content to them? If you're going to have a spineless, milquetoast Democratic Party that can't say a word against racism, it doesn't deserve to exist anyway.

KLOR DE ALVA: Affirmative action has had the capacity to create a black middle class. Many of these folks also have been the dominant group in the civil rights arena and in other human rights areas. The net effect has been to create a layer, essentially of African-Americans, within the public sphere that has been very difficult for Latinos to penetrate and make their complaints known.

WEST: That's true, and I think it's wrong. But at the same time, blacks are more likely to register protests than Latinos are. That's what I mean by raising hell, you see. Black people are more likely to raise hell than brown people.

KLOR DE ALVA: But having been blocked from the public sector, I am concerned that Latinos turning to the private one will buy deeply into U.S. concepts of race and will be even less willing than Anglos to employ blacks. So for me, any new social or public policy must begin with dismantling the language of race.

WEST: It's important not to conflate overcoming racial barriers with dismantling racial language. I'm all for the former; I'm not so sure about the latter, because it ignores or minimizes the history of racism. Most of human history is a history of oligarchs, unaccountable elites, manipulating anger, rage, setting working people against one another to enable those elites to maintain their position. That's why democracies are so rare in human history.

SHORRIS: Let me ask you a question about oligarchies. There are wealthy blacks, middle-class blacks, and many poor blacks. There are wealthy browns, middle-class browns, many poor browns. Are we talking about two groups or six? Are we talking about economic self-interest being greater than any kind of cultural or racial self-interest?

WEST: There is always going to be self-interest operating. The question is, How does it relate to the common good and contribute to the production, distribution, and consumption of goods and services so that there's some relative equality? Now, the six groups that you're talking about have to do with class divisions within brown and black America. The class divisions are there. And they're going to increase, there's no doubt about that. We're going to see more conservatives in black America, more conservatives in brown America, because the country in general is tilting in that direction and it's nice to be on the bandwagon. Even though we claim to be with the underdog, it's very American to want to be with the winners. So as those class divisions escalate, you're going to get class envy and class hatred within brown America as well as within black America. One of the purposes of a black-brown dialogue is to head off precisely these kinds of hatreds and various forms of bigotry.

KLOR DE ALVA: At the level of the working class, we're seeing a great deal of cooperation, but as you move up the economic scale you have progressively more turf wars—how many slots blacks get for this, how many slots Latinos get for that. Once you get to mayors of towns or cities, you have Latinos who aren't going to do terribly much for the black community or, if they're black, not very much for the Latino community. Hence my emphasis on a solution that addresses economics rather than race.

WEST: We do have some data in terms of voting behavior when it comes to brown-black contrast. Ninety percent of whoever votes in the black community still votes Democratic, right? Cubans, a million Cubans in America, vote for Republicans. We have 2.8 million Puerto Ricans. They vote Democratic roughly 60–40. We have 17.1 million Mexicans. They vote, the majority, for the Democratic Party. Black Americans tilt much more toward the Democratic Party than any other group, à la LBJ's idea: It's going to destroy this party, all these black folk over here. You see, once you get that racial divide, you can promote white anxieties and white fears, and you can use that for all it's worth. And the Republicans are going to use that into the twenty-first century. There's no doubt about it.

KLOR DE ALVA: Cornel, you're going back to the question of this evil empire.

WEST: No, it's not evil. It's a civilization in which there is a problem of evil.

KLOR DE ALVA: All civilizations have a problem with evil.

WEST: But some—like the United States—are in sustained denial even as they view themselves as the embodiment of good.

KLOR DE ALVA: I don't agree with that. I would say that one of the significant ideological possibilities, a door that's always open in the United States—and it goes back to that old contrast between Mexico and the United States—is that the United States has an epic vision, a vision of good against evil. Latinos supposedly have a tragic vision—a conflict between two goods. But in the United States, evil is always right there, and its defeat, like its creation, can therefore be imagined. Cornel, you represent evil if you take off your three-piece suit and walk out into the street at three o'clock in the morning.

WEST: Brother, I represent evil now, as a savage in a suit. Because this is black skin, what we started with. So I don't need to take off my suit. But the difference is this: The tragic view—of Unamuno or Melville or Faulkner or Morrison or Coltrane—is a much more morally mature view of what it is to be human. The triumphant view of good over evil, which is Manichaean, is sophomoric, childish. It has been dominant in America because our civilization is so spoiled.

KLOR DE ALVA: I would like to agree with you were it not for the fact that that tragic vision is also a kind of Hamlet vision. It makes it very difficult to move, to overcome evil.

WEST: But better Hamlet than Captain Ahab in *Moby-Dick*. And that's precisely what Melville was getting at—this tremendous voluntaristic view of the world in which a will to power, based on an absolute conception of good over evil, allows one to lead toward what? Nihilism, self-destruction. I'd go with Hamlet any day.

KLOR DE ALVA: Not me, not at the price of indecision and paralysis.

WEST: Now, Martin Luther King was neither Hamlet nor Captain Ahab, you see. King was something else. King actually comes out of a black tradition with a profound sense of the tragic. When he has Mahalia Jackson sing "Precious Lord," that's not triumphalism. That is the deepest sense of the tragic nature of this civilization, the same tragic sense at work in the spirituals and the blues and jazz. King was not in any way a triumphalist. The great King insight is that because he rejects triumphalism he knows that the evil is not simply external, that it's in him. He knew that there was white supremacy in him. That's what allowed him to love Bull Connor even as he opposed Connor's white supremacy. That's the great Christian insight.

KLOR DE ALVA: I agree with you. The evil is here in the United States, but it can be challenged.

One Night of Love

SHORRIS: Cornel, what do you most worry about in the future?

WEST: I think my fundamental concern is the disintegration of American civilization as black people become more and more insulated, isolated, targeted, and hence subjected to the most brutal authoritarian rule in the name of democracy. And that's exactly where we're headed, so it's not just a fear.

KLOR DE ALVA: I would say that what you've described for America would be true of just about any nation I know, particularly any multicultural nation. It's not something that's unique to the United States. My biggest fear, as this nation moves into an inevitable browning, or hybridization, is that there will be a very powerful minority, overwhelmingly composed of Euro-Americans, who will see themselves in significant danger as a consequence of the way democracy works: winner-take-all. And they will begin to renege on some of the basic principles that created the United States and made it what it is.

SHORRIS: We've been talking about conflicts. Let's stipulate, unless you disagree, that the advantage to the people in power of keeping those at the bottom at each other's throats is enormous. That's the case in all societies. So we have blacks and browns, for the most part, at the bottom. And they are frequently at each other's throats. They're fighting over immigration, fighting over jobs, and so on. A group of young people comes to you and says, "Tell us how to make alliances, give us a set of rules for creating alliances between blacks and browns." What would you answer?

WEST: I'd appeal to various examples. Look at Ernesto Cortés and the Industrial Areas Foundation in Texas or the Harlem Initiatives Together in New York City, which have been able to pull off black-brown alliances of great strength, the "breaking bread" events of the Democratic Socialists of America. Or I'd talk about Mark Ridley-Thomas in South-Central Los Angeles and the ways in which he speaks with power about brown suffering as a black city councilman, the way in which he's able to build within his own organization a kind of black-brown dialogue. Because what you really see then is not just a set of principles or rules but some momentum at work.

SHORRIS: But how do you do that? What's the first step?

WEST: Well, it depends on what particular action you want to highlight. You could, say, look at the movement around environmental racism, where you have a whole host of black-brown alliances. With Proposition 187 you had a black-brown alliance among progressives fighting against the conservatives who happened to be white, black, and brown. In the trade-union movement, look at 1199, the health-care workers union, here in New York City. You've got brown Dennis Rivera at the top, you've got black Gerry Hudson third in charge, running things. That's a very significant coordinated leadership of probably the most important trade union in the largest city in the nation. So it depends on the particular issue. I think it's issue by issue in light of a broad vision.

SHORRIS: What is the broad vision?

WEST: Democracy, substantive radical democracy in which you actually are highlighting the empowering of everyday people in the workplace and the voting booth so that they can live lives of decency and dignity. That's a deeply democratic sensibility. And I think that sensibility can be found in both the black and brown communities.

KLOR DE ALVA: Unless there's a dramatic shift in ideology, linkages between people who are identified as belonging to opposing camps will last only for the moment, like the graffiti I saw during the L.A. riots: "Crips. Bloods. Mexicans. Together. Forever. Tonite [*sic*]," and then next to that, "LAPD" crossed out and "187" underneath. That is, the alliances will work only as long as there's a common enemy, in this case the L.A.P.D., whose death the graffiti advocated by the term "187," which refers here to the California Criminal Code for homicide.

As long as we don't have a fundamental transformation in ideology, those are the kinds of alliances we will have, and they will be short-lived and not lead, ultimately, to terribly much. Clearly, the progressive forces within the United States must be able to forge ideological changes that would permit lasting linkages. At the core of that effort lies the capacity to address common suffering, regardless of color or culture. And that cannot be done unless common suffering, as the reason for linkages across all lines, is highlighted in place of the very tenuous alliances between groups that identify themselves by race or culture.

SHORRIS: Let's see if anything happened in this conversation. Cornel, are you a black man?

WEST: Hell yes.

SHORRIS: Jorge, is he a black man?

KLOR DE ALVA: Of course not.

78

A Review of *Life on the Color Line*

MARTHA CHAMALLAS AND PETER M. SHANE

In 1954, at the age of ten, Greg Williams took an unforgettable journey to Muncie, Indiana. Until that time, Greg and his younger brother Mike had lived in Virginia as white children. Their mother was white, and their father (then called Tony, later Buster) told everyone that he was Italian. But when the marriage broke up and Tony's financial ventures failed, he pushed Greg's life over the color line. He moved the boys to the black section of Muncie, where he had been raised. "In Virginia you were white boys," he told Greg and Mike. "In Indiana you're going to be colored boys" (page 33).

Life on the Color Line is Greg Williams's compelling memoir of his childhood and adolescence. On one level an intensely personal account of a young boy's discovery of himself and of a son's coming to terms with his father, at another it is a slice of American social history during the '50s and '60s, a documentary of the cruelties inflicted by racial hierarchy. Most profoundly, the memoir is a meditation on the social construction of identity, exploring the complexity of the meaning of race and racial identity.

Gregory Howard Williams, now the dean of the Ohio State University College of Law, was our colleague on the University of Iowa law faculty for twelve years. One of the first observations white people often make about Greg is that although he looks white, he is "really" black. It now seems startling to us that, over the years, we never understood how revealing that description was of Greg's identity. At Iowa, Greg's blackness was shown by his actions, interests, and affiliations. When he was director of admissions, he recruited record numbers of African-American students to law school and worked hard to find financial support for them; as an associate vice president, he exerted behind-the-scenes pressure to encourage departments to diversify their faculties; and as a classroom teacher, he taught about race and the criminal justice system. But occasionally someone who did not know Greg or who was unaware of his work would be astonished to learn that he was black and would question what it meant to "be" black and yet look like Greg Williams. *Life on the Color Line* responds to that central question of identity.

For the first ten years of his life, Greg (who was then called Billy) lived in Virginia with his parents, his brother Mike, and a younger brother and sister. Neither parent ever told the children about their background. Life was not easy for Greg: his father drank heavily and brutalized his mother. Tony's financial fortunes rose and fell as quickly as his moods. One year he made over $50,000, had an exclusive townhouse in Alexandria, and drove a Cadillac; the next year he was penniless and totally incapable of providing for his children.

The major trauma of Greg's childhood occurred when his mother abandoned him and Mike, taking the younger children with her as she fled from Tony. Greg and Mike were vir-

46 J. OF LEGAL ED. 1 (1996). Originally published in the *Journal of Legal Education*. Reprinted by permission.

tually left to fend for themselves. Shortly before they left for Muncie, their situation was desperate: their clothes were tattered and dirty, they were hungry all the time, and they were devastated by their inability to understand why such terrible things were happening to them. Greg recounts how the brothers coped with their fear and emotional deprivation:

> When school started in September, my hand shook with doubt as I penciled her name over "Mother" on my enrollment form. Reaching into my book bag, I grabbed an ink pen, and I traced over "Mary Williams" so she couldn't sneak into the school at night and erase her name. Homework kept me occupied, but Mike lost interest in school. Every evening he sat perched on the tavern steps like a motherless bird, eyes darting up and down Route 1, hoping Mom would arrive in the next car drifting into our parking lot (25).

Even before Greg crossed the color line, the pain of rejection was a central force in his life.

Greg began his life as a black boy when Tony decided to leave the boys with his mother in Muncie. [See Chapter 59. Ed.] Perhaps the most dramatic part of the book is Greg's description of his transition to Muncie, a violent one in which he and Mike were forced to cope with intense poverty, neglect, and bewilderment over their place in the world. Everything was different: Tony was now called Buster, and the tall, thin, brown-skinned woman whom Greg had known in Virginia as simply one of the hired help was revealed to be his grandmother, Sallie. The squalor surrounding the lives of Greg's relatives was shocking to the young boy. At first Greg thought Sallie's house was a tool shed. He was revolted by the smell of the outhouse, scared by the nasty rooster patrolling the yard, and even more afraid of the drunk and boisterous folks that hung out every night at Sallie's house.

Muncie reinforced the pain of rejection in the boys' lives. Their white relatives in town refused to acknowledge them. Even though it was obvious that Sallie's house was unsafe for the boys, none of Greg's relatives from his mother's side offered any help. Instead, the boys' lives were literally saved by a stranger—Miss Dora—a neighbor who took the boys into her home and paid for everything out of the $25 she earned weekly as a maid. The love and gratitude Greg felt for Miss Dora is evident throughout the book. He touchingly refers to her as his "truly mother" and is enraged because white people cannot seem to comprehend why a woman who was not a blood relation would ever choose to care for needy children.

Unlike much else in Muncie at the time, the public schools were racially integrated; race-based rejection was not written into Indiana education law as blatantly as in the Southern states. But race discrimination was efficiently managed by powerful informal mechanisms. For example, there was an unwritten rule at Greg's school that the sixth-grade academic achievement award was reserved for white children. In an especially painful passage, Greg recounts the assembly in which he learned that he had been robbed of the honor he had earned as the top student in the class (125–26).

The sting of being passed over unfairly is what many people probably identify as the crux of invidious discrimination. But much of the power of this memoir lies in the different message Greg Williams conveys about the experience of discrimination. Though the line is a fine one to draw, the anger and shame that discrimination engenders, in Greg's experience, seem not to stem principally from an internalized sense of frustration or blatant unfairness. It is the experience of discrimination as *rejection*, a motif in Greg's life from the moment his mother abandoned him, that is its hallmark.

Some of the rejection Greg endured followed the familiar script of white supremacy before the civil rights movement. [See Chapter 73. Ed.] Greg recounts how two little white girls who had initially befriended him in school turned away in disgust when they discovered he was black. His white appearance was often more problematic than liberating. Greg soon learned that his "very existence made people uncomfortable and shattered too many racial taboos" (166). He recalls watching a Ku Klux Klan leader on TV shortly after *Brown v. Board of Education* was decided:

> [H]is nasal repetition of "mongrel mulatto" finally hit me like a thunder-bolt. He was talking about me. I was the Klan's worst nightmare. I was what the violence directed against integration was all about. I was what they hated and wanted to destroy. And that was the biggest puzzle in the world to me because I had absolutely nothing (91).

Some of the rejection Greg endured was of a sort not well documented in the familiar cultural scripts, perhaps because it came from black children. The playgrounds in Muncie were racially segregated but, even so, there was no peace for Greg and his brother. Some of the black kids would taunt them because they looked white, and Greg often found himself getting into fights and screaming, "I ain't white" (119).

Buster had warned Greg that his relations with other black people would be difficult. On their trip to Muncie, Buster told his son that Greg would have to be very careful in his new life because neither whites nor blacks liked "half-breeds" (38). That proved to be not quite true. Although many blacks were willing to accept Greg only gradually, and only after he proved his allegiance to the black community, whites were far more threatened by Greg and his "deceptive" appearance. Indeed, the harassment he experienced from some blacks was different from the hostility of white teachers and classmates and had a different origin. As Greg describes it, the anger blacks felt toward whites was a response to hurt:

> Though I continued to endure barbed teasing about my white relatives, I began to take some solace in the belief that there were many more members of the black community who wanted to ignore white relatives than one might imagine. Denial of their full heritage was due less to anger and prejudice toward their white families than the total and absolute rejection of their existence by them (123).

In junior high, the color line intensified as teachers and administrators tried to prevent black boys from dating white girls. The only "guidance" Greg ever received from his school counselor was to stay away from a white girl who had been pursuing him. The cruel irony was that when Greg chose to date a dark-skinned girl, they both were met with jeers of "nigger lover." The combination of racial and sexual taboos in Muncie made dating for Greg "like swimming in shark-infested waters" (166). His brother Mike, however, followed their father's example and recklessly pursued both black and white girls, undeterred by the many stories he and Greg heard about false claims of interracial rape. In contrast, Greg became cautious about girls, repeatedly vowing to devote all his energy to school and athletics.

The racial battlegrounds at school and on the playground did not pose the biggest problem for Greg. That was how to handle his father, whose drinking and abuse had by this time gotten totally out of control. Greg's portrayal of his father makes clear that he sees the source of his father's cruelty in the rejection and pain that Buster also suffered. Buster's own father, a wealthy white man, never had anything to do with him. Buster's mother had worked for his father as a maid; he fired her when she became pregnant. Both blacks and whites taunted her "white nigger" baby and demanded she leave town. When Buster was an adult, he went in search of his father and tried to confront him. He found he could not even bring himself to face his father and say, "I am your son."

What is most compelling about Greg's portrayal of his father is the way he traces the impact of racial oppression on the development of his father's character. Buster Williams was highly intelligent, one of Muncie's first blacks to go to Howard University. A talented writer whose skills were used by the local white politicians to draft campaign leaflets and speeches, his only reward from City Hall was a janitor's job. Buster finally left Muncie when he was roughed up by police, arrested on suspicion of burglary, and jailed for seven days. Buster's political connections counted for nothing; as a black man, he could always be put in his place. Even for a dreamer and hopeless optimist, it was hard not to give in and give up.

The pain in Buster's life made itself manifest in many ways in the lives of his sons. Perhaps most cruelly, he could not bring himself to offer any hope or encouragement to Mike. In a wrenching episode, Buster makes his sons fight for bets in a ribs joint: "Boys, now square off! We're gonna see who is the best man. The nigger or the white boy" (154). His description of his sons was telling; he basically wrote off his academically less talented son as doomed to a life of hustling. He told Greg that Mike's "gonna be a no-'count black bastard just like me" (156).

The sting of rejection does not disappear over time. Greg Williams describes how it is possible to detest the white part of your heritage because it represents rejection and dispossession, and yet continue to hunger for recognition from all your blood relatives. Greg's decision to live his life as a black man never erased the longing for his mother or his desire to have her realize the enormity of what he had to live through. His memoir documents, in excruciating clarity, the cruelty of racism and its cost to the human spirit.

The complexities of race also form the primary backdrop for Greg Williams's search for identity. Lately biracialism and the meaning of race itself have been in the forefront of public discourse, from the debate about the categories used in the U.S. census to the controversies over affirmative action and mixed-race adoptions. The memoir has much to say about these issues, because it represents a life work as well as an extraordinary life. We began to appreciate the subtleties of Greg Williams's account of racial identity when we considered the puzzle posed by his subtitle: *The True Story of a White Boy Who Discovered He Was Black.* How could Greg have been a "white boy" and then, later, a "black boy"? Was he both "white" and "black" all along? The move to Muncie changed nothing about either Greg's genes or his genealogy. Could Greg have discovered he was a "black boy" without moving to Muncie? These dilemmas are most puzzling if we insist on thinking of race and racial identity as immutable characteristics. Of course, Greg's story is unusual because few people change their understanding of their own and their families' identity as radically and as rapidly as Greg did on that fateful trip to Muncie. But *Life on the Color Line* does reveal a more universal insight: namely, that it is a constellation of circumstances, of which skin tone is but one, that creates the potential for racial identity. Within the potential range of identities, a single person can experience racial identity in plural form; in some forms, racial identity is something people choose—and choose deliberately—at a number of points in their lives.

Greg initially acquired the potential for a new racial identity through his father's disclosure of the truth about himself. Greg's new knowledge allowed him to see his father in a different light and to reposition himself in a changed world. His reaction demonstrates dramatically that race is not a fixed trait apart from people's perceptions:

> I saw my father as I never had seen him before. The veil dropped from his face and features. Before my eyes he was transformed from a swarthy Italian to his true self—a high-yellow mu-

latto. My father was a Negro! We were colored! After ten years in Virginia on the white side of the color line, I knew what that meant (34).

But Greg's potential for a black identity also depended on his experience with black people and on his pursuit of this new knowledge. His father's disclosures inspired Greg to look more closely at black children and develop a more complex understanding of color, to break down the dichotomous view of black and white into a spectrum or continuum of difference. On the playground of "black" children there was suddenly "every imaginable hue of brown, ranging from deep chocolate to the color of the speckled light brown eggs we found in Aunt Bess's henhouse. And now two palefaces—Mike and me" (51).

Greg Williams clearly came to identify himself as a black man, rather than as a white man or biracial man. But Greg's "discovery" that he was black did not occur in the single moment he learned of his father's biracial background. He repositioned himself as a black person only gradually, influenced by forces far deeper than the recognition that he had many "honey, brown, and chocolate" relatives. *Life on the Color Line* teaches that, as experienced by the individual, racial identity is relational and emotional, dependent on personal experience and practical human need. Greg "became" black because of two important factors. First, at key points in his life crucial black people embraced him and gave him a sense of belonging while, for the most part, white people rejected him. Buster, for all his shortcomings, was probably the most important strength in Greg's early life. Emotionally, Miss Dora, not Mary Williams, was Greg's mother. The rejection by his mother and her relatives not only produced anger and pain; it altered Greg's sense of himself. Even for a ten-year-old child, the sense of self was dependent on reinforcement from his family and from those who loved him.

Second, the more Greg came to understand the situation of American blacks, the more their history of rejection, perseverance, and achievement came to provide a narrative within which he could make sense of his life. Among the most revealing passages in the book is Greg's response to his father after Buster suggests that when Greg leaves Muncie, he too can pass for white:

> I hadn't wanted to be colored, but too much had happened to me in Muncie to be a part of the white world that had rejected me so completely. I believed that most of Dad's problems stemmed from his attempt to "pass for white" in Virginia. . . . If Walter White could choose to remain in the black community and make a difference, so could I. . . . I knew who I was and what I wanted to be (157). [A blue-eyed, blond African-American, White headed the NAACP for more than two decades. Ed.]

This is not to suggest that, in all aspects, the acquisition of racial identity is a matter of choice. An obvious question is why Greg had to be rigidly classified by so many people as either white or black, given that he had one white and one biracial parent. The answer is plain: there was little space for biracialism in segregated Muncie in the 1950s and early 1960s. In the public realm, personal choice about racial identity had little room to operate. As a youngster, Greg was offered choices so constrained as not to be meaningful.

Although Greg's pale skin made it possible for others sometimes to think of him as white, the ideology of white supremacy in Muncie made it practically impossible for him to "be" white and survive. Whites would not tolerate anyone known to have black relatives, as Greg painfully discovered when his two white friends in elementary school abandoned him. Moreover, the policing of the color line made it inevitable that people would find out about him. The teachers from the elementary school made sure that the staff at the junior high school were not fooled by Greg's appearance. On Greg's confidential high school record appeared a notation that his father was "colored," even though "from outward appearance" Greg looked white (257).

By the time Greg was in high school, he had already had considerable experience negotiating the dilemma of looking white and being black. When he had to select where to sit in the auditorium, with whites on one side and blacks on the other, he joined the black students, realizing that he "had no real decision to make" (191). One of his black classmates astutely analyzed Greg's decision to sit with the black students as making his life "less complicated" because, sooner or later, the white students would find out about and reject him. Choosing to sit with the black students assured that Greg would not find himself an outcast.

Greg Williams does not stake the case for the authenticity of his blackness on exclusion of whites from his life. The emphasis here is on active lived-out relationships, and displays of love and a sense of belonging, rather than biology or genetics. We learn in the memoir that Sara, his true love in high school and now his wife, is white. And now that their two biological children are grown, Greg and Sara have adopted two boys from Honduras. What Greg's life seems to say, as eloquently as it can be said, is that identity depends on those who accept and love you and provide you with the strongest sense of yourself.

79

What Is Race, Anyway?

TOD OLSON

In the winter of 1993, the small town of Wedowee, Alabama, became a flashpoint of racial tension. The white principal of Randolph County High School had gathered the student body together to find out how many students planned to attend the prom with dates "outside their race." When several students raised their hands, he canceled the event. "How would that look at a prom, a bunch of mixed couples?" he scolded. From the stunned audience, a single voice responded. Junior-class president Revonda Bowen, daughter of a white father and an African-American mother, asked, "Who am I supposed to take to the prom?"

Revonda Bowen's question served notice in a divided town that the issue of race is not just black and white. Although we like to place ourselves neatly in boxes—black, white, Asian-American, etc.—the fact is that not everyone fits. Interracial marriages have quadrupled in the last 20 years, producing nearly 1.5 million kids of mixed race. A new wave of immigrants from Latin America and Asia has added more complexity to the mix. More Americans are foreign born than ever before, and their kids often marry outside their nationality.

Even as intermarriage blurs the lines between races, we seem to grow more obsessed with our ethnic and racial categories. The national census places every American into one of four basic groups: white, black, Asian or Pacific Islander, and American Indian or Alaskan Native. Last year, at Congressional hearings on proposed changes to the census, various ethnic groups sought to add more categories to the census form. Arab-Americans wanted a new listing for Middle Easterners; Hispanics wanted at least six subgroups to reflect their diversity; and multiracial people wanted a category besides "other" for themselves.

In the midst of all this race consciousness, scientists are suggesting that race may have no scientific basis at all. The races, they say, are just arbitrary groupings of people who happen to look similar and have ancestors who come from the same geographic area. While ethnic groups clamor for recognition, experts are wondering whether racial distinctions make sense at all. Current census categories are based on an old theory that has not changed much since 1758. That was the year when Swedish botanist Carolus Linnaeus divided the species Homo sapiens (human beings) into four basic varieties: Americanus, Europaeus, Asiaticus, and Afer. Linnaeus's idea was that people in various regions—America, Europe, Asia, and Africa—tended to have children only with each other. Their genes passed on characteristics we associate with race, such as skin color, facial features, and hair texture. Each region acted as a kind of bushel basket containing the genetic material of each race.

Africa's basket contained genes for tightly curled black hair and dark skin, Europe's had genes for straight hair and lighter skin, and so on.

In the past few decades, however, this scheme has begun to fall apart. The problem is that appearance is only one of thousands of genetically determined characteristics we could use to divide up the human race. The vast majority of genes don't fall neatly into one regional basket or another. Suppose, for instance, we divided people up according to whether or not they have a gene that protects against the disease malaria. Nearly all Africans have curly hair and dark skin, but only some of them have the antimalarial gene. In southern Africa, where the disease is not common, the Xhosa people don't have the gene. Neither do most northern Europeans. So the dark-skinned Xhosas would end up in the same race as lightskinned Swedes and Norwegians. The same kind of problems arise when you consider fingerprints, height, and a host of other traits. According to recent studies, only a small percentage of the differences between human beings are accounted for by genes we now associate with race.

So, if racial categories have such a shaky scientific basis, then why do we measure them at all? Ironically, racial classification is now used to protect the same groups it has harmed in the past. The government relies heavily on racial data to enforce antidiscrimination measures like the Voting Rights Act and Equal Employment Opportunity regulations. In 1992, for instance, federal officials used racial data to determine that blacks and Hispanics were denied housing loans at twice the rate of whites. In other cases, the government sets aside funds for businesses owned by minorities. The hope is that by helping these groups achieve economic equality, the nation can eventually make racial distinctions less important. Says Robert A. Hahn, a medical researcher who studies race and health care: "We need these categories essentially to get rid of them."

Still, some experts argue that we shouldn't use racial categories at all. Yehudi Webster, a sociologist, thinks our obsession with measuring race merely deepens racial divisions. "It is not race but a practice of racial classification that bedevils the society," he says. Many advocates for specific racial and ethnic groups disagree. "You can't erase differences between people by ignoring them," says Carlos Fernandez, president of the Association of Multi-Ethnic Americans. The categories will become irrelevant, he claims, only when interracial marriages are as common as same-race unions. "Eventually," he adds, "it will happen."

In the meantime, forms will continue to ask your race. Places like Wedowee, Alabama, will continue to split into hostile camps. And for people like the principal of Randolph High, the question of who people like Revonda Bowen take to the prom will continue to present problems.

Synopses of Other Important Works

Race Traveling

"A Constant and Intense Debate": Michael Omi and Howard Winant

In a modern classic, *Racial Formation in the United States: From the 1960s to the 1980s*, Michael Omi and Howard Winant theorize about how and why American society draws racial categories. In their fourth chapter ("Racial Formation"), they recount the case of Susie Guillory Phipps, who unsuccessfully sued the Louisiana Vital Records Bureau in 1982 to have her racial classification changed from black to white. A descendant of an eighteenth-century planter and his slave, Phipps had been listed as black on her birth certificate under a 1970 law specifying that anyone with at least one thirty-second Negro blood is legally black. Assistant Attorney General Ron Davis of Louisiana defended the law as necessary to comply with federal record-keeping requirements and to enable the state to track people at risk for genetic diseases. Phipps argued that assigning racial categories on birth certificates is unconstitutional and that the one thirty-second rule was inaccurate. The trial featured expert testimony that most whites have one-twentieth or more Negro ancestry. Nevertheless, Phipps lost. The court found nothing wrong with assigning individuals to specific racial groupings on the basis of ancestry.

As social constructionists, Omi and Winant find the case instructive:

> [It] illustrates the continuing dilemma of defining race and establishing its meaning in institutional life. Today, to assert that variations in human physiognomy are racially based is to enter a constant and intense debate. Scientific interpretations of race have not been alone in sparking heated controversy; religious perspectives have done so as well. Most centrally, of course, race has been a matter of political contention. This has been particularly true in the United States, where the concept of race has varied enormously over time without ever leaving the center stage of U.S. history (p. 59).

The authors go on to explain that race is a "pre-eminently sociohistorical concept" whose meaning is given concrete expression by specific social relations. In the United States, any degree of intermixture essentially renders one nonwhite, as Phipps learned when she sued in Louisiana. Omi and Winant contrast the U.S. situation with that in various areas of Latin America, where, since the abolition of slavery, sharply defined racial groups do not exist. Brazil, for example, subscribes informally to a variety of "intermediate" racial categories (p. 60). The same family may easily contain close members who are seen as representatives of opposite racial types.

Passing for White, Passing for Black: Adrian Piper

In a long, finely written article in *Transition* (vol. 58, no. 4 [1992]), the philosophy professor Adrian Piper recounts some of her experiences as a very light-skinned black. Her article, a portion of which appears as Chapter 69 of this book, well rewards reading in its entirety for its inventory of such events as:

- A graduate student reception in which an eminent professor confronted her, a newly minted member of her class, and demanded to know why she considered herself black (p. 58);
- Childhood encounters with dark-skinned black teenagers and classmates who accuse her of acting white (p. 6) or of not having suffered enough (p. 7);
- The awkwardness and outrage of some whites, including friends and colleagues, on learning for the first time that she considers herself black (pp. 9–11, 19, 22–23);
- Whites who spoke disparagingly of blacks in her presence, unaware of her racial identification (pp. 26–28).

Piper writes of her experiences:

I've learned that there is no "right" way of managing the issue of my racial identity, no way that will not offend or alienate someone, because my designated racial identity itself exposes the very concept of racial classification as the offensive and irrational instrument . . . it is. We see this in the history of the classifying terms . . . : first "blacks," then "darkies," then "Negroes," then "colored people," then "blacks" again, now "Afro-Americans." Why is it that we can't seem to get it right, once and for all? The reason . . . is that it doesn't really matter what term we use . . . , because whatever term is used will eventually turn into a term of derision and disparagement by virtue of its reference to those who are derided and disparaged (p. 30).

Even when they are used without racial animus, "[t]he fact is that the racial categories that purport to designate any of us are too rigid and oversimplified to fit anyone accurately" (p. 31).

From the Editors: Issues and Comments

Can a person fully "pass for white"? Can he or she fool everyone? Including himself or herself? Can a person have variable race—that is, live as a black for the first half of his or her life, and then as a white the rest? A number of our writers describe themselves as white blacks, so light-skinned that everyone on meeting them assumes they are white. But if everyone treats them as white, are they not then white? That is, if race is a social construct, and if everyone in society decides one is white, does it not follow that one is simply mistaken about one's own identity? If you were head of a black advocacy group, would you hail or deplore the proposed multiracial census category? Suppose you are a peace-loving, tolerant white? Suppose you were, in fact, multiracial—where would you stand? Would you want the government to offer such a category, and would you choose it for yourself?

Suggested Readings

Alba, Richard, ETHNIC IDENTITY: THE TRANSFORMATION OF WHITE AMERICA (1990).

Appiah, Anthony, *Are We Ethnic?* 20 BLACK AM. LIT. F. 209 (1986).

Davis, F. James, WHO IS BLACK? ONE NATION'S DEFINITION (1991).

Dominguez, Virginia, WHITE BY DEFINITION: SOCIAL CLASSIFICATION IN CREOLE LOUISIANA (1986).

Forbes, Jack D., *The Manipulation of Race, Caste, and Identity: Classifying AfroAmerican, Native American, and Red-Black People,* 17 J. ETHNIC STUD. 1 (1990).

Halsell, Grace, IN THEIR SHOES (1996).

Haney López, Ian F., WHITE BY LAW (New York University Press 1995).

Lee, Sharon M., *Racial Classifications in the U. S. Census: 1890–1990,* 16 ETHNIC & RACIAL STUD. 75 (1993).

LURE AND LOATHING: ESSAYS ON RACE, IDENTITY, AND THE AMBIVALENCES OF ASSIMILATION (G. Early, ed., 1993).

Matsuda, Mari, *Voices of America,* 100 YALE L.J. 1329 (1991).

Michaels, Walter Benn, *Race into Culture: A Critical Genealogy of Cultural Identity,* 18 CRIT. INQ. 655 (1992).

Morgenthau, Tom, *What Color Is Black?* NEWSWEEK, February 13, 1995, at 63.

Norment, Lynn, *Who's Black and Who's Not?* EBONY, March 1990, at 134.

Robinson, Amy, *It Takes One to Know One: Passing and Communities of Common Interest,* 20 CRIT. INQ. 715 (1994).

Russell, Kathy, Midge Wilson, and Ronald Hall, THE COLOR COMPLEX: THE POLITICS OF SKIN COLOR AMONG AFRICAN AMERICANS (1992).

Wright, Lawrence, *One Drop of Blood,* NEW YORKER, July 25, 1994, at 46.

Part IX

Biology and Pseudoscience

Are races real, innate, the product of physical and genetic differences? Are they arrayed in a hierarchy of intelligence and ability by race—with one's own race, presumably, at the top? Is complex behavior, such as criminality, genetically determined? Most scientists say emphatically no to these questions. Yet one of the most persistent strains of thought holds that races are distinct, with whites at the top in intelligence, morals, and other desirable attributes. The recent publication of *The Bell Curve*, by Richard Herrnstein and Charles Murray, has focused attention on all these issues. And what of the question of selective breeding? Minority families often have several children, elite whites only one or two. Does that mean that a precious gene pool will inevitably decline?

80

The Misleading Abstractions of Social Scientists

JEROME KAGAN

Five-month-old infants who stare at surprising events for a long time, 5-year-old children with large vocabularies, and 50-year-old adults who invent new computer programs are all described as intelligent. The use of the same adjective implies that the same process is operating in all three situations. But we have no good evidence to support the idea that the psychological processes that produce an attentive infant are the same as those that produce a creative computer programmer. Moreover, a small number of psychologists—including J. P. Guilford, Howard Gardner, and Robert Sternberg—have argued persuasively against the usefulness of the notion of a single, general cognitive ability.

The difficulty in defining intelligence illustrates a broad and serious problem with the kinds of words that social scientists use to describe their work. In psychology, sociology, anthropology, and economics, too many abstract concepts that describe social, emotional, and intellectual phenomena assume that the process operates the same way in all people. Thus, psychologists classify a person's decisions and actions as intelligent or not, without ever specifying the age or cultural background of the person, the type of mental activity involved, or the context in which it occurs. The rancor produced by *The Bell Curve* illustrates the mischievous consequences for public policy when social scientists assume the validity of an abstract notion of "general intelligence."

The book stirred controversy because of its argument that black children score lower on intelligence tests than children of other ethnic groups do, and, therefore, that programs such as Head Start cannot permanently raise their intelligence. However, if intelligence is not a clear-cut characteristic in the same way that height and weight are, all conclusions about intelligence must be treated skeptically.

The results of government programs such as Head Start and free meals for children typically are evaluated by research teams that base their conclusions on how the children score on standardized intelligence tests. These tests assume the validity of a characteristic called "intelligence." The investigators do not set out to assess a set of different skills—for example, the ability to convey one's thoughts, to invent a story, or to remember accurately events from the recent past. Because the evaluations of Head Start found that it made no permanent change in the I.Q. scores of children in the program, some of the early enthusiasm for the program waned. However, if Congress had asked for evaluations that assessed

CHRON. HIGHER ED., January 12, 1996, at A52. Originally published in the *Chronicle of Higher Education*. Reprinted by permission of the author.

a half-dozen or more particular talents, I believe lawmakers would have seen some stable, permanent gains in children who participated in Head Start.

The word "compete" provides a second example of a concept that social scientists too often use abstractly. They apply it to the actions of adolescent gangs, multinational companies, universities, and athletic teams, even though the motives, emotions, and strategies of each group are vastly different. Sociologists make the same error when they assume that being poor has similar consequences, regardless of a person's ethnicity, family history, or the region of the country in which he or she lives. For example, many poor whites living on welfare in the isolated hollows of eastern Kentucky may have a more coherent family and community structure than many poor African Americans living in large, urban ghettos.

Natural scientists use terms that imply a specific object and a context when they describe their work. When biologists use the word "bleach," for example, their colleagues understand that it refers to pigment changes in sensory cells of the retina under the stimulus of light. No biologist would use "bleach" to describe the lightening of a salamander's skin under threat or the facial pallor of a tubercular patient.

Everyday conversation often includes similar distinctions, especially when what is being described has strong emotional implications. For example, most speakers convey important information on the context, age, and intention of the people concerned when they select among the words "love," "seduce," "rape," or "abuse" to describe a sexual act.

The habit of assuming that a particular process is the same in very different individuals and situations is holding up progress in many fields. Many scholars working on personality assume that the individual qualities called extroversion, agreeableness, conscientiousness, emotional stability, and curiosity are unities that are consistent, regardless of time and location. These scholars incorrectly assume that a person who is agreeable at work with a superior is also agreeable at home with a spouse, and that the tendency to be agreeable will be as salient a trait in individuals living in a poor urban neighborhood as in those living in rural areas. But a personality trait, by definition, refers to a style of behavior or mood that distinguishes one person from another. Because contemporary theorists of personality are insufficiently sensitive to cultural variation in behavior, their writings have tempted younger scholars to assume that one set of traits fits all.

To give another example, some educational researchers have become enthusiastic about the concept of "self-esteem." It is true that all older children and adults engage in conscious evaluations of their personal qualities relative to other people in their communities. However, each person makes separate judgments for each of a variety of qualities, including academic skills, memory, courage, physical attractiveness, popularity, athletic talent, morality, wealth, and social status. No one computes an average of the many different characteristics to arrive at a general self-concept. Thus, it is an error for educators to argue that they can raise children's self-esteem merely by praising them. If a 6-year-old child who is poorly prepared to learn to read feels ashamed because he or she is lagging behind other children, it is unlikely that a teacher's praise alone, without tutoring in reading, will enhance the child's self-esteem.

Scholars' reluctance to take account of the type of agent or the nature of a situation stems, in part, from a praiseworthy, egalitarian motive—the desire to regard all humans as fundamentally similar. Because of the strong individualistic streak in Western thought, many Western scholars, in particular, want to locate the primary origin of actions and desires within the individual, rather than between the person and his or her environment.

European and American psychologists use the word "dependent" to describe someone who seeks psychological support from someone else. The Japanese use the term *amae* to refer to a mutual relationship between someone who seeks support and someone who provides it. *Amae* implies that the former knows he can trust the latter, and that the latter accepts responsibility for the psychological state of the former and feels obligated to respond in a helpful manner. English has no word for this idea, because *amae* denotes relations between two individuals, not a motive within one person.

Recent advances in genetics and neurobiology have tempted many scholars, as well as non-academics, to award each person an inherent set of abilities, emotions, and symptoms. We forget that the actual development and expression of those characteristics require a cooperative environment; if the environment is altered, the person's development will proceed in a different direction. It is time for social scientists to invent concepts acknowledging that every description of a human quality must specify the type of person being studied and the setting in which that person behaves. For example, four-month-old infants who reacted to new sights, sounds, and smells with very little motor activity and no crying were, later, during their preschool years, more likely than most other children to be sociable and outgoing with strangers. But the sex of the child, and the types of strangers encountered, make a difference. Infant boys who did not cry and exhibited low motor activity are more likely at age four to be very sociable with unfamiliar boys but less so with an unfamiliar adult. Infant girls who were low in arousal are more likely at age four to be very sociable with unfamiliar adults, but less so with unfamiliar girls. Thus, we describe the child's personality more accurately when we specify its sex and exact social situation than when we simply say some children are sociable.

If nature pays such careful attention to the details, it behooves scholars to do the same.

81

Caste, Crime, and Precocity

ANDREW HACKER

I have no problem accepting *The Bell Curve*'s finding that Americans with European forebearers average better on IQ tests than citizens with African ancestries. And for present purposes, I will concede the authors' claim that the capacity for scoring well via the multiple-choice method is "substantially heritable."

Yet Herrnstein and Murray also warn that while individuals get their genes through their parents, this inheritance does not entitle us to make race-based generalizations. "That a trait is genetically transmitted in individuals," they write, "does not mean that group differences in that trait are also genetic in origin."

Really? Surely what we know about gene pools suggests that when identifiable groups of human beings live and procreate with one another for considerable periods, certain traits will come to predominate and be reproduced. For a long time, and even now, people we call Koreans have been more likely than not to mate with one another. If this process passes on pigmentation and physical features, why not also the quality and contours of their cognitive capacities?

My aim here will be quite modest. It is to carry Herrnstein and Murray's premise a step further, by applying it to the persons who make up the race they call "white." What I found curious about their analysis is that they treat this extremely large catchment—more than 200 million people according to the last Census—as a singular genetic group. Yet it would seem self-evident that so capacious a conglomerate will contain vital variations. Much more might have been learned had they divided the white population into several sub-races—perhaps by pigmentation or physiognomy—then surveyed the average intelligence of these cohorts.

Of course, the authors might reply that such information is not available. Nor is this surprising. For the last half-century, this country has had an unstated understanding that it not draw genetic distinctions among Americans who have been allowed to identify themselves as white. Religious differences are obviously acknowledged, as are those of national origin. Even so, regardless of whether their forebears came from Stockholm or Sofia or Salerno, all whites are presumed to belong to a single gene pool and thus have equal status in the Caucasian category. And while we also take note of social disparities, even the lowest classes of whites are not given a diminished designation. (Epithets like "redneck" and "white trash," once commonly heard, have all but disappeared.) In a similar vein, Hugh Pearson has wondered why no attempt was made to discover whether lighter blacks register higher IQs. Such a study would not be difficult. One could compare the scores of a pool of people resembling Harry Belafonte and Colin Powell with a group more similar to Sidney Poitier and Clarence Thomas. This decision of whites to stand together colors the race-based analysis in *The Bell Curve*.

This was not always the case. Earlier in the century, such social scientists as Henry Goddard and Carl Brigham saw nothing untoward in identifying regional races within Europe which had varying mental capacities. Thus they felt free to pronounce the intellectual primacy of persons of "Nordic" stock, while citing the stunted facilities of swarthier "Mediterranean" and "Alpine" strains. And to sequester the best, they opposed intermarriage. That they rated African Americans even lower goes without saying, as does the happenstance that both of these scholars fell into the Nordic category Addressing a related concern, they pointed to white families like the "Jukes" and "Kallikaks" as a warning that inbreeding could ravage even Caucasians.

Due to lack of studies based on smaller gene pools, I have had to avail myself of an alternative measure. The Census provides quite reliable information on the number of persons who have entered and completed college. The following figures refer to the proportion of Americans of various European ancestries who have received bachelor's degrees.

Nature or Culture?
Proportions of Americans Who Have Completed College by Self-Identified Ancestries

French-Canadian	16.7%	Danish	27.4%
Dutch	18.5%	Swedish	27.4%
Italian	21.0%	Scotch-Irish	28.2%
Irish	21.2%	English	28.4%
German	22.0%	Welsh	31.8%
Finnish	24.2%	Scottish	33.6%
Norwegian	26.0%	Russian	49.0%

Even granting that some groups arrived here earlier, all of those on the list are at least third-generation, which should be sufficient time for their members to enter the college cohort. We can also agree that ambition and discipline, as well as family encouragement, figure in getting to and through college. Still, some mental capacity is needed to achieve a degree; and here Herrnstein and Murray tell us that favorable heredity should not be discounted. Moreover, strong links persist between additional years of schooling and scores on standardized tests. So if more people from a group finish college, that attainment will raise its average IQ.

If genetic causes can be evoked to explain mental differences between blacks and whites, then we might search for similar sources within the white group. Persons of Russian ancestry, who happen to be predominantly Jewish and hence of "Mediterranean" origin, spent much of their evolution well apart from the "Nordic" Dutch. While cultural factors obviously play a role, might not something within white gene pools lead to disparate representation in higher education? I don't know. What I find revealing, though, is that no one seems inclined to find it.

Of course, we know the reason. Undertaking such studies could pit whites against whites, which would be politically imprudent. Better, then, to focus on presumed black deficiencies, a tactic which is neither surprising nor new.

82

Embodiment and Perspective:
Can White Men Jump?

PETER HALEWOOD

Where we are positioned in society, and how we think of and live in our bodies, are questions we do not usually connect to the (both everyday and scholarly) claims we make about social and legal problems. "The body" and "knowledge" have traditionally been understood as unrelated categories. However, recent interdisciplinary work in philosophy and law emphasizes "positionality," and calls into question the abstract, disembodied quality of conventional Western theories of knowledge (epistemologies) which ground the Western conception of law. Western epistemology, its critics say, has artificially bracketed off the material particulars of experience and identity, including the spatial particularity of one's bodily experience, in determining what counts in making and defending claims about society and about law's role in maintaining or changing social order. Abstraction, universality, and reason, rather than embodied experience, govern the validity of truth claims. In turn, much contemporary critical legal theory calls into question the liberal jurisprudence which derives from conventional Western epistemology and ethics. Critics say that law's objectivity and principled determinacy have been defined so as to deny the range of experience and self-understanding common to the oppressed. For example, the range of criteria defining a valid rights-claim under liberal jurisprudence—rule governance, rationality, universalizability—are values associated (within the Western tradition) with masculinity. Femininity is associated in the same tradition with subjectivity, particularity, and the body. The immediacy and subjectivity of embodied feminine experience have been bracketed off from epistemology and in turn from liberal jurisprudence.

Consider the *epistemological* bracketing of embodiment. For example, women experience commodification when their bodies are used for commercial surrogacy; simultaneously, the uniqueness of the embodied female experience of pregnancy is denied by legal discourse governing custody disputes between surrogates and the contracting "parents." In order to comprehend the injustice of commodification (although there are some instances where it is not unjust), epistemology and jurisprudence must be able to grasp the centrality of embodiment and of the concrete experience of oppression. It is this that critiques of conventional epistemology aim to promote. I argue that the experience of commodification conditions one's epistemological standpoint. Thus embodiment and commodification constitute a distinct epistemological standpoint that law must validate. I

From "White Men Can't Jump: Critical Epistemologies, Embodiment, and the Praxis of Legal Scholarship." Reprinted by permission of the Yale Journal of Law and Feminism, Inc. from the *Yale Journal of Law and Feminism*, Vol. 7 No. 1, pp. 1–36.

suggest that the epistemological gap between the standpoints of privileged abstraction and oppressed embodiment can be partially bridged by focusing on forms of oppression and embodied experience that are common to men and women, to whites and people of color.

These critiques of disembodied epistemology have prompted a concern about how and by whom legal scholarship that focuses on subordination—for example scholarship relating to the law of gender and race equality—is produced. This is some of the most important scholarship in which legal academics engage. The critiques, and the corresponding pressure for diversity in law schools, call into question the legitimacy of scholarship concerning subordination. This scholarship is often conducted by white male legal scholars. These scholars often employ the disembodied, abstract rationality that I have mentioned. This prompts several related questions. Can a white male scholar adequately address in his scholarship forms of oppression which he does not and cannot experience?[1] Is a white male scholar situated (personally and "epistemologically," as the debate goes) so as to be able to *really* understand, unpack, and contribute constructively to scholarly debate on oppression and law?[2] Is his scholarship on oppression, with its implication of superior understanding, legitimate? *Should* he engage in scholarship on oppression? How does his white-maleness inform his scholarship? Is he likely to overlook in his scholarship ways in which law is implicated in oppression? Can he restructure his scholarship so as to ally himself with the aims of diversity and empowerment? I believe that these questions have been mischaracterized as reflecting a purely political agenda to advance the "outsider" scholarship of women and minorities by criticizing "insider" scholarship. In fact, they reflect a set of sound philosophical (that is, epistemological) propositions about the relation of scholarly knowledge to embodied experience and social reality.

I, a white and male legal academic, have encountered and reflected upon these questions in my research on problems of race, law, and gender, and while teaching feminist legal theory in several different areas of the law. I draw in part upon my experience in scholarship and teaching to illustrate some of the problems that accompany scholarship on subordination issues, and to theorize a new or modified mode of white male scholarship that goes some way toward meeting the legitimate philosophical objections raised against white male scholarship on subordination as it is currently practiced.

These objections concern the relation between overtly political legal problems (commonly sex and race discrimination), and the sex and racial identity of the legal scholar inquiring into them (commonly male and white). The debate is informed in part by recent feminist philosophical and critical race theory literature, both legal and nonlegal. Much of this literature might be characterized as postmodern because it rejects conventional objectivist models of truth and of a fixed human agency. Some of it explicitly or implicitly argues that the white male *epistemological perspective* is fixed by the elevated position of white men in the social hierarchy, a position achieved in part by having successfully privileged abstraction and disembodiment in Western rationality, epistemology, and jurisprudence. Therefore, the argument goes, the epistemological accuracy of white male scholarship on oppression is uncertain, and perhaps white men should relinquish or radically modify such scholarship. Part of this concern is that white male scholars may appropriate and profit professionally from perspectives lived and articulated by others. For the most part, white male legal scholars can safely write and say things critical of the social order that minority and female legal scholars cannot. Part of the concern is that white men simply "don't get it" on issues of subordination, and consequently cannot adequately address subordination in their scholarship.

Notes

1. Experience and embodiment are closely related, though not identical. Embodiment refers to being in the concrete world, experiencing concrete (and physical) relations with the material world, and having the theoretical perspective on reality of a thing with a body—this is the experience of embodiment as it relates to knowledge. Many white male scholars clearly have not yet acknowledged the legitimacy of questioning the relation of experience to knowledge. See, for example, Mary I. Coombs' fine article, *Non-Sexist Teaching Techniques in Substantive Law Courses*, 14 S. Ill. U. L.J. 507, 523 (1990).

Some new critical literature flags the issue of the social construction of whiteness and the possibility of deconstructing it. Whiteness codes for (largely unself-conscious) privilege, power, and expectation. [In addition to works excerpted in this book, see also T. Alexander Aleinikoff, *A Case for Race-Consciousness*, 91 Colum. L. Rev. 1060 (1991); Neil Gotanda, *A Critique of "Our Constitution is Colorblind,"* 44 Stan. L. Rev. 1 (1989); Gary Peller, *Race Consciousness*, 1990 Duke L.J. 953; L. Mun Wong, *Di(s)-secting and Dis(s)-closing "Whiteness": Two Tales About Psychology*, 4 Feminism & Psychol. 133 (1994). Ed.]

It is important to note that the relation of experience and identity has had real consequences in the academy as evidenced, for example, by the student boycott of white civil rights attorney Jack Greenberg's Civil Rights course at Harvard Law School in 1983. *See* Randall Kennedy, *Racial Critiques of Legal Academia*, 102 Harv. L. Rev. 1745, 1756–57 (1990). See also Kennedy's response to Richard Delgado's notion that white male scholars lack racial "standing" to engage in race relations law scholarship. *Id.* at 1788–89.

2. This question has been examined in the context of feminism in Men in Feminism (Alice Jardine & Paul Smith eds., 1987) (male feminist scholarship is problematic), which was answered by Engendering Men: The Question of Male Feminist Criticism (Joseph A. Boone & Michael Cadden eds., 1990) (male feminist scholarship is possible if conducted from position of empathy, e.g., from gay experience). In the race context, see Robert S. Chang, *Toward an Asian American Legal Scholarship: Critical Race Theory, Post-Structuralism, and Narrative Space*, 81 Cal. L. Rev. 1241, 1248 n.15 (1993) ("[W]hites can engage in critical race theory if they have the requisite level of empathy, an empathy that may find its source in some other type of oppression that they suffer."). A not-so-funny parody of the problem can be found in Arthur Austin, *Scoff Law School Debates Whether a Male Can Teach A Course in Feminist Jurisprudence*, 18 J. Legal Prof. 203 (1993).

83

Bell Curve Liberals:
How the Left Betrayed IQ

ADRIAN WOOLDRIDGE

Opposition to the use of IQ testing goes back as far as testing itself. Its practitioners have been accused of misusing science to justify capitalist exploitation; allowing their obsession with classification to blind them to the huge variety of human abilities; encouraging soulless teaching; and, worst of all, inflaming racial prejudices and justifying racial inequalities. To this school of thinking, *The Bell Curve* was a godsend. Charles Murray and Richard J. Herrnstein succeeded in effectively linking IQ testing firmly in people's minds with spectacularly unpopular arguments: that different racial groups have different IQ averages; that America is calcifying into rigid and impermeable castes; that the promise of American life is an illusion. The more society realizes the dream of equal opportunities, the more it breaks down into incommensurate groups, segregated not just by the accident of the environment, but by the unforgiving logic of genes.

But the history of IQ testing contains another, more enlightened tradition, one that was once the darling of liberals. It linked IQ testing with upward mobility, child-centered education, more generous treatment of the handicapped, humane welfare reform and, above all, the creation of a meritocracy. Indeed, it could be argued that it is this enlightened tradition that reflects the real essence of IQ testing, uncontaminated by local prejudices and unscientific conjectures. In ignoring this, in demonizing the purveyors of IQ, liberals have betrayed their own political and moral tradition.

This liberal incarnation of IQ testing is most articulate and influential in England, where its exponents controlled educational policymaking from the 1930s until the early 1960s. These IQ testers found their political inspiration in the meritocratic ideal, a revolt against patronage and a plea for individual justice. While attempting to wrest control of the civil service from the landed aristocracy in the mid-nineteenth century, Whig reformers such as Lord Macaulay, a historian, and Charles Trevelyan, a mandarin, argued that positions should be allocated on the basis of examinations designed to test "the candidate's powers of mind" rather than to "ascertain the extent of his metaphysical reading."

By the twentieth century, the left took up this mission. During its early years, the Labour Party saw its main role as constructing a ladder of merit, stretching from the slums to Oxbridge and regulated by objective examinations, so that the able could find their natural level. Sidney and Beatrice Webb wanted to turn Britain's educational system into a gigantic "capacity-catching machine," capable of "rescuing talented poverty from the shop or the plough" and channeling it into the national elite. H.G. Wells argued that "the prime

Originally published in *The New Republic*, February 17, 1995, at p. 22. Reprinted by permission.

essential in a progressive civilization was the establishment of a more effective selective process for the privilege of higher education." R.H. Tawney, the doyen of socialist educationalists, welcomed IQ tests for helping the huge number of talented working-class children who were overlooked in the existing system.

The psychometrists argued that IQ tests were powerful instruments of meritocratic reform, especially useful in spotting promising working-class children held back in school by poverty and providing them with a secure ladder up the social system. Far from being defenders of the status quo, the psychometrists believed in the inevitability of social mobility. The psychologist Cyril Burt calculated that, in order to ensure that people were working to their best abilities, almost one-quarter of their children would have to end up in different social classes from their parents. The really conservative theory of abilities is not hereditarianism but environmentalism: if parents can transmit all their advantages to their children, then social mobility will always be something of a freak.

Perhaps the biggest practical experiment involving IQ tests occurred in Britain after the Second World War, and the result was a huge increase in social mobility. The Second World War generated a widespread feeling that, if Britain was to justify the sacrifices of its people and survive as an economic power, it must turn into a real meritocracy. The 1944 Education Act decreed that children should be educated according to their "age, ability and aptitude." People across the political spectrum agreed that this did not mean sending all children to the same school, but rather, assigning them to schools suited to their particular talents.

Confronted with pressure to recruit children on the basis of raw ability, Britain's elite grammar schools increasingly turned to psychologists to refine their traditional examinations. By 1952 almost all local education authorities had incorporated an intelligence test into their selection exams. Even leftist critics of the tests were forced to admit that they were doing a good job. Liberal psychologists Alfred Yates and Douglas Pidgeon, for example, argued that "the examination in its best forms comes out as a highly reliable and remarkably valid instrument of prediction, considering what it is expected to do." By relying on IQ tests, the grammar schools gradually transformed themselves into thoroughly meritocratic institutions, recruiting their pupils from an ever-wider section of society (outraged contemporaries complained that the schools were being flooded with "spivs" and "smart alecks") and providing the chosen ones with a highly efficient escalator into the universities and the national elite.

Moreover, the IQ testers opposed the well-connected, muddle-headed, scientifically illiterate old fogies who dominated the establishment, and wanted to replace them with carefully selected and properly trained meritocrats. They argued that, if it was to have any chance of surviving as a serious country, Britain needed to put much more emphasis on teaching science. One of their greatest disappointments was that Conservative R.A. Butler succeeded in protecting the traditional grammar school curriculum, with its obsession with literary and classical education, from reform in the Education Act of 1944.

Unlike Murray and Herrnstein, the IQ liberals were enthusiastic about spending money on the welfare state in general, and public education in particular. They argued for raising the school-leaving age, improving teacher training, increasing the number of nursery schools, gearing instruction to the individual needs of "backward" as well as precocious learners and providing regular medical inspection for school children.

IQ testers also tended to be passionate devotees of child-centered education. Though often associated with classification and selection, the tests in fact embodied a much broader theory of aptitude development. Their earliest supporters were relentless critics of traditional pedagogy, complaining that it was designed for the convenience of adults rather than the needs of children, and arguing that teaching should be based on the unfolding abilities of children, as revealed by IQ tests.

Until the 1950s these psychologists found their most passionate supporters on the left and their bitterest opponents on the right. Labour intellectuals such as R.H. Tawney pointed to intelligence tests to prove that Britain was being disgracefully profligate with the talents of its population. T.S. Eliot argued that an educational system that sorts people according to their native capacities would disorganize society and debase education, breaking the bonds of class and tradition. Edward Welbourne, a particularly crusty Cambridge don, was even more direct: confronted with the news that a student was interested in IQ tests, he snorted, "Huh. Devices invented by Jews for the advancement of Jews."

Why were Britain's intelligence testers so much more palatable than their American colleagues? Partly because they were outsiders, marginal to Britain's snobbish social and scientific establishment. British psychologists turned to IQ tests precisely because they thought that the establishment's traditional methods of spotting talent—examination essays, Latin translations, *viva voce* examinations—were hopelessly biased in favor of the well-taught rather than the promising poor.

Britain also boasted a group of first-rate biologists, such as Lancelot Hogben, J.D. Bernal and J.B.S. Haldane, whose sympathies lay distinctly on the left. They wielded huge influence with both the scientific establishment and the popular media—Haldane, for example, was both a fellow of the Royal Society and a newspaper columnist—and they ensured that anybody who wanted to pronounce on controversial questions such as the relationship between race and intelligence had to pass the highest possible test of intellectual rigor and scientific probity. Significantly, the most bigoted British intelligence testers fled to the United States: William McDougall, a psychologist with something of a fetish for blond, blue-eyed types, left Oxford for Harvard, and Raymond Cattell, who argued, in print, that the race was being swamped by "sub-men," later followed him to the States. (Cattell lives in the United States still; a list of supporters of *The Bell Curve* in *The Wall Street Journal* included his name.)

Yet, for all their progressive sentiments, the intelligence testers fell afoul of two of the most powerful constituencies of the postwar left: the communitarians and the egalitarians. Communitarians such as Michael Young argued that the 11-plus, an IQ test taken by all of Britain's 11-year-olds, was breaking down working-class communities and churning out alienated, confused, anxiety-ridden scholarship winners. Indeed, his 1959 indictment of intelligence testing, *The Rise of Meritocracy*, foreshadows many of the central concerns of *The Bell Curve*, arguing that, as society becomes more efficient at allocating positions according to ability, the elite lose any sense of social responsibility and the poor lose any sense of self-respect.

Egalitarians argued that individual differences are the result of social circumstances rather than genetic inheritance, and that comprehensive schools would produce a much more equal society. After a long struggle between meritocrats and egalitarians for the soul of the party, Labour finally came down on the side of egalitarianism in the mid-1960s, with Labour Minister Tony Crosland declaring that he would not rest until he had destroyed "every ——ing grammar school in England. And Wales. And Northern Ireland."

Yet the Labour Party's rejection of meritocracy has hardly been a success. Communitarianism embodies a nostalgic quest for a lost world, before social mobility turned neighbors into strangers and village greens into asphalt jungles. It reflects too much of the traditional Tory complaint about people not knowing their place. Egalitarian reforms have proved strikingly counterproductive. The comprehensive schools, introduced by the Labour government in the 1960s, have replaced selection by ability with selection by neighborhood, hardly a triumph for social justice. When Conservatives tried to reintroduce selection by ability in the mid-1980s they were met with howls of protest from middle-class parents, who argued that they had paid inflated prices for their houses so that they could get their children into good schools and didn't want their children's school places commandeered by riffraff.

Policymakers on both sides of the Atlantic would do well to look again at the more enlightened tradition of intelligence testing. The more insightful on the left, led by U.S. Labor Secretary Robert Reich and the British Labour Party's new leader, Tony Blair, have realized they need to rethink ideas about the state. In a world of gigantic capital flows and globe-spanning production networks, the left has no choice but to abandon its traditional belief in picking industrial sectors or industries to support. Instead of investing in winning companies, the state should make sure it invests in winning people: ensuring that the educational system spots outstandingly promising children and allows them to make the most of their talents.

Given this agenda, the left can hardly afford to ignore IQ tests, which, for all their inadequacies, are still the best means yet devised for spotting talent wherever it occurs, in the inner cities as well as the plush housing estates, and ensuring that that talent is matched to the appropriate educational streams and job opportunities. The left, indeed, should be up in arms about *The Bell Curve*. But they should be up in arms because Murray and Herrnstein have kidnapped what ought to be one of the left's most powerful tools for opening opportunities, and have tried to turn it into an excuse for closing doors.

84

Brave New Right

MICHAEL LIND

The controversy about *The Bell Curve* is not about *The Bell Curve* only. It is about the sudden and astonishing legitimation, by the leading intellectuals and journalists of the mainstream right, of a body of racialist pseudoscience created by a small group of researchers, most of them subsidized by the hereditarian Pioneer Fund. *The Bell Curve* is a layman's introduction to this material, which had been repudiated by the responsible right for a generation.

Whatever the leaders of mainstream conservatism may claim now, in the seventies and eighties they themselves, and not merely the "politically correct" left, repudiated the kind of arguments that Herrnstein and Murray make. After the civil rights revolution, the mainstream conservative movement, though continuing to engage in covert appeals to racial resentments on the part of white Americans, was more or less successfully purged of the vestiges of pseudoscientific racism (which, it should be recalled, had been just as important as states'-rights arguments in the resistance to desegregation). By the Reagan years, the right, under the influence of neoconservatives in particular, seemed to have permanently rejected its white-supremacist past. With the zeal of recent converts, mainstream conservatives claimed to be defending the ideals of color blind sixties liberalism, of Martin Luther King, Jr., and Hubert Humphrey, against those who would betray those ideals by promulgating racial quotas and multicultural ideology. Talk of black and Hispanic racial inferiority was relegated to the far-right fringe.

During the entire period that the right was free from pseudoscientific racism, a few scholars like Arthur J. Jensen and William Shockley were nevertheless arguing that blacks as a group are intellectually inferior to whites by nature. As far back as 1971, Herrnstein set off a firestorm with his article "IQ" in *The Atlantic Monthly*. Much of the dubious research on which *The Bell Curve* rests was accumulated in the seventies and eighties. Why did Herrnstein and Murray—with Phillipe Rushton and other neo-hereditarians in their train—take conservatism by storm in 1994, rather than 1984, or 1974? Why are mainstream conservatives suddenly welcoming the revival of eugenic theory, after several decades in which they rejected anything redolent of pseudoscientific racism?

The answer has less to do with new scholarly support for hereditarianism or changes in American society as a whole than with the ongoing transformation of the American conservative movement. In a remarkably short period of time, the optimistic conservatism of the Reagan years, with its focus on the economy and foreign policy, has given way to a new "culture war" conservatism, obsessed with immigration, race, and sex. This emergent post–cold war right has less to do with the Goldwater-Reagan variety than with the older American right of radio priest Father Charles E. Coughlin and the fundamentalist minister Gerald L. K. Smith's Christian Nationalist Crusade. In its apocalyptic style as well as its apocalyptic obsessions, this new conservatism owes more to Pat Robertson and Patrick Buchanan than to William F. Buckley, Jr., and Irving Kristol. The growing importance, within the Republican Party, of the Deep South no doubt also plays a role; Goldwater's and Reagan's Sun Belt conservatism is being rewritten in Southern Gothic style.

It is not surprising that long-suppressed ideas about hereditary racial inequality are now reemerging. Their return is made easier by the crumbling of taboos that has accompanied the popular backlash against the excesses of political correctness. The nastiest elements on the right now answer any criticism with the charge that they are victims of "PC."

The most important factor behind the rehabilitation of pseudoscientific racism on the right may be the recent evolution of the debate among conservatives about race and poverty. For several years a right-wing backlash has been growing against the integrationism and environmentalism not only of liberals but also of certain prominent conservatives. A few years ago, in a perceptive article for *The American Spectator*, David Frum identified two schools of thought among conservatives about poverty in general, and black urban poverty in particular. One school, whose major spokesman was Jack Kemp, believed that poor black Americans would respond to the proper economic incentives with entrepreneurial ardor. These conservatives stressed free-market reforms such as "enterprise zones" and the subsidized sale of public housing to its tenants, reforms that might break underclass dependency on a paternalistic state. The "culturalist" school, identified with thinkers like William Bennett, was more impressed by signs of familial breakdown in the inner city and the perpetuation of a "culture of poverty." The ghetto poor could not be expected to take advantage of new economic opportunities unless their values changed first. When Frum wrote, a third school of pessimistic neo-hereditarians was not engaged in the debate; Kemp and Bennett were both environmentalists, finding the sources of black poverty elsewhere than in the inherited biological traits of poor blacks.

For all their differences, the free-marketeers and culturalists agreed that the problems of the black urban underclass could not be addressed without government activism. In effect, they had reasoned their way back to the conclusions of Daniel Patrick Moynihan in 1965 about the need to address the breakdown of the underclass black family by means of substantial social programs. The conservatives who had thought the most about race and poverty were arguing for a conservative version of Lyndon Johnson's War on Poverty. Whether it took the form of massive subsidies to public housing tenants or a national network of high-quality orphanages for the children of broken ghetto families, there would have to be government-backed social engineering on a grand scale.

It soon became clear that a conservative war on poverty would be enormously expensive. In the Bush administration, Richard Darman—vilified by the right as a big-spending country-club Republican—actually led the struggle to defeat then Housing Secretary Jack Kemp's proposals for higher spending on the urban poor. As for a national system of quality orphanages and boarding schools, that would cost billions. A call for activist government paid for by higher taxes to help the ghetto poor was not what most conservatives wanted to hear from their experts. The reaction against Kemp's "bleeding-heart, big-government" conservatism on the right was setting in even while he was still George Bush's secretary of Housing and Urban Development. The gradual isolation of Kemp within the conservative movement has probably doomed his presidential hopes. The marginalization of Kemp has been most clearly visible in *National Review*, which has criticized Kemp's views on immigration as too soft, and cast him as the defender of the black poor in a strange debate over whether there is a crime problem in America or just a "black crime" problem. The orphanage proposal has found a proponent in Speaker of the House Newt Gingrich. However, even Gingrich has not advocated increased *public* funding for orphanages and boarding schools. If he did, he would probably find himself marginalized within his own party like Kemp.

For all practical purposes, the debate among conservatives about poverty was over before the Herrnstein-Murray controversy began. Before *The Bell Curve* appeared it had become politically impossible for any conservative politician to argue for maintaining current levels of spending on the poor, much less increasing spending. The insistence of some conservatives that they merely want to redistribute responsibility between the federal government and the states and private charities is an evasion. Conservatives do not really want states to spend more in order to compensate for reduced federal spending; they want to slash public spending on poor Americans at all levels. They do not, for example, favor public job creation programs for poor people thrown off welfare. Furthermore, the claim that private charities will make up for spending cuts ignores that many private charities today receive many of their resources from government. In reality most conservatives favor absolute reductions in spending on the poor by public and private agencies at all levels; they are simply not honest enough to say so.

The conservatives agreed on the prescription—reduce or abolish spending on the poor—before they agreed on the diagnosis. The fortuitous appearance of *The Bell Curve* provided conservatives with a useful rationale for a policy of abolishing welfare that they already favored. Had there been no Herrnstein-Murray controversy, the right would still have favored abolishing welfare, but on the familiar grounds that it does not work or backfires by creating perverse incentives. Herrnstein and Murray have provided the right with a new-old argument against welfare which is even more compelling: the underclass (white as well as black) is intellectually deficient by nature, so that ambitious programs to integrate its members into the middle class are almost certainly a waste of money.

This is not the first time that elite Americans have sought to explain the problems of lower-income groups in terms of the allegedly innate biological characteristics of their members. As Dale T. Knobel writes in his study *Paddy and the Republic: Ethnicity and Nationality in Antebellum America* (Wesleyan, 1986):

> During the years immediately before [the Civil War], public officials intent upon uncovering the sources of urban poverty, crime, and disease, began to recant openly the environmental explanations of social evils accepted for decades and to adopt an "ethnologic" approach. The Massachussets [*sic*] State Board of Charities insisted that the chief cause of pauperism and public dependency was nothing less than "inherited organic imperfection, vitiated constitution, or *poor stock*," and the New York Association for Improving the Condition of the Poor concluded that "the excess of poverty and crime, also, among the Irish, as compared with the natives of other countries, is a curious fact, worthy of the study of the political economist and the ethnologist. . . ." In 1820 the Irish had only been one of several European immigrant groups regarded suspiciously because of their tutelage under authoritarian political and religious regimes. By 1860, Anglo-Americans had not only separated the Irish out from other immigrants and given them special status as an alien "race" but had also come to treat Irish character as the cause rather than the consequence of their Old World condition.

Now as then, the logic of the hereditarian argument—poverty is caused by genetic inferiority—points toward eugenics programs to discourage the allegedly inferior from reproducing and to encourage fecundity on the part of the allegedly superior. Though Herrnstein and Murray refuse to endorse eugenic measures other than restriction of immigration by persons "with low cognitive ability" and easy access for the poor to contraceptives, others undoubtedly will use their arguments to justify more intrusive eugenic engineering. Already some conservatives have suggested that welfare mothers be temporarily sterilized by Norplant as a condition of receiving relief; the logical next step would be involuntary sterilization of "feeble-minded" blacks, Hispanics, and poor whites, of the kind that was common in the United States throughout most of this century.

It remains to be seen how far the eugenic enthusiasms of the neo-hereditarian right can be taken before they collide with conservative religious convictions. In the early twentieth century, advocates of eugenic sterilization found their most committed adversary in the Catholic church. The employment of a distorted version of Darwinism in defense of the economic and racial status quo is also problematic in light of the resolute anti-Darwinism of Protestant evangelicals. In the nineteenth century the most radical American racists tended to be secular intellectuals; the biblical account of the common origin and shared opportunity for salvation of mankind prevented devout Protestant conservatives, no matter how bigoted, from treating the different races as separate species or subspecies. In what is surely one of the great ironies of our time, at the end of the twentieth century, as at the end of the nineteenth, the excesses encouraged by eugenic theory in the United States may only be checked within the American conservative movement by the dogmas of resurgent fundamentalism.

85

Race and Parentage

DOROTHY E. ROBERTS

Creating White Babies

One of the most striking features of technological efforts to provide parents with genetically related offspring is that they are used almost exclusively by affluent white people. The use of fertility clinics does not correspond to rates of infertility. Indeed, the profile of people most likely to attempt IVF [in vitro fertilization. Ed.] is precisely the opposite of those most likely to be infertile. The people in the United States most likely to be infertile are older, poorer, black, and poorly educated. Most couples who use IVF services are white, highly educated, and affluent. New reproductive technologies are popular not simply because of the value placed on the genetic tie, but because of the value placed on the *white* genetic tie.

The high cost of fertility treatment largely restricts its availability to only the affluent. The expense of these procedures, however, cannot fully explain the racial discrepancy in their use. Many black middle-class infertile couples could afford them. Besides, inability to afford a medical procedure need not preclude its use. The government could increase the availability of new reproductive technologies to the poor through public funding. It would also be possible for black women to enter into informal surrogacy arrangements with black men without demanding huge fees. Yet a stark racial disparity looms in the use of new reproductive technologies. Why? Because of a complex interplay of financial barriers, physician referrals, and cultural preferences.

The public's affection for the white babies that are produced by reproductive technologies legitimates their use. Noel Keane, the lawyer who in 1978 arranged the first public surrogacy adoption, described how this affection influenced the public's attitude toward his clients' arrangement. Although the first television appearance of the contracting parents, George and Debbie, and the surrogate mother, Sue, generated hostility, a second appearance on the *Phil Donahue Show* with two-month-old Elizabeth Anne changed the tide of public opinion. Keane explained:

> [T]his time there was only one focal point: Elizabeth Anne, blonde-haired, blue-eyed, and as real as a baby's yell. . . .
>
> The show was one of Donahue's highest-rated ever and the audience came down firmly on the side of what Debbie, Sue, and George had done to bring Elizabeth Anne into the world.[1]

From "THE GENETIC TIE," 62 U. CHI. L. REV. 209 (1995). Originally published in the *University of Chicago Law Review*. Reprinted by permission.

I suspect that a similar display of a curly haired, brown-skinned baby would not have had the same transformative effect on the viewing public.

A highly publicized lawsuit against a fertility clinic evidenced revulsion at the technological creation of black babies. A white woman claimed that the clinic mistakenly inseminated her with a black man's sperm, rather than her husband's, resulting in the birth of a black child. The mother, who was genetically related to the child, demanded monetary damages for her injury, which she explained was due to the unbearable racial taunting her daughter suffered. The real harm to the mother, however, lay in the fertility clinic's failure to deliver the most critical part of its service—a white child. The clinic's racial mix-up rendered the mother's genetic tie worthless. It is highly unlikely that the white mother would have *chosen* black features "if allowed the supermarket array of options of blond hair, blue-green eyes, and narrow upturned noses."[2] In the American market, a black child is considered an inferior product.[3]

Race and the Harm in Surrogacy

The devaluation of the black genetic tie also helps to explain the harm in surrogacy. The argument against surrogacy rests on the peculiar nature of childbearing that makes its sale immoral. Some feminists argue that surrogacy impermissibly alienates a fundamental aspect of one's personhood and treats it as a marketable commodity. Surrogacy treats women as objects rather than valuable human beings by selling their capacity to bear children for a price. The relationship between race and the genetic tie further illuminates market inalienability. It demonstrates how surrogacy both misvalues and devalues human beings. The experience of surrogate mothers is not equivalent to slavery's horrors, dehumanization, and absolute denial of self-determination. Yet our understanding of the evils inherent in marketing human beings stems in part from the reduction of enslaved blacks to their physical service to whites.

The quintessential commodification of human beings was the sale of slaves on the auction block to the highest bidder. Slaves were totally and permanently commodified. Slave women were surrogate mothers in the sense that they lacked any claim to the children whom they bore and whom they delivered to their masters. Like surrogacy, slavery forced the separation of mothers and their children when each was sold to a different master.

Perhaps the most terrifying lesson from slavery was the law's ability to sanction it. The law did more than close its eyes to slavery; the law actively promoted it. The slave auction, which provides the most powerful metaphor for surrogacy's commodification of human beings, was often a government event. The South Carolina courts, for example, "acted as the state's greatest slave auctioneering firm." "Officials and agents of the law" conducted half of the antebellum slave auctions at "sheriffs', probate, and equity court sales."[4]

The relationship between race and the genetic tie illuminates the feminist critique of surrogacy in a second way. The feminist arguments against surrogacy focus on the commodification of women's wombs. Just as critical, however, is the commodification of the genetic tie, based on a valuation of its worth.[5] Although this process devalues all women, it devalues black women in a particular way. Feminist opponents of surrogacy miss an important aspect of surrogacy when they criticize it for treating women as *fungible* commodities. A black surrogate is not exchangeable for a white one.

The Genetic Tie and Legal Parentage

The overriding assumption in cases determining a child's legal parentage is that families are created out of biological connections between individuals. Parental rights, however, are not a biological given. Rather, the law historically has interpreted the genetic tie's significance to parenthood in a way that preserves the patriarchal nuclear family. Cases concerning the parental rights of unwed fathers and sperm donors reveal that the law's central objective is to protect the integrity of families founded on heterosexual marriage, while leaving women's autonomous bonds with their children vulnerable.

Denying White Connection to Black Children

Why does the law deny some biological fathers rights to their children? Why does it discount the genetic tie between some men and their offspring? One reason is that the legal requirements for social fatherhood help to preserve the traditional patriarchal family structure. Another purpose might be to invest care of, and responsibility for, children in presumably stable husbands rather than presumably irresponsible unwed fathers. Another explanation arises from the genetic tie's role in the American system of racial slavery. The law's distinction between social and genetic fatherhood freed white men from social obligations to their black children. Since a child's legal status followed that of her mother, white men could use black women's bodies for sexual domination while preserving the racial demarcation necessary for slavery.

Uncertainty about paternity has been a universal concern throughout history. Enforcing female marital fidelity was the only way a man could know that a woman's children were his offspring. Under a racial caste system, female fidelity was doubly important: it guaranteed not only paternity but also racial purity. Since only white women could produce white children, they were responsible for maintaining the purity of the white race. The first laws against interracial fornication and marriage arose from legislators' "particular distaste that white women, who could be producing white children, were producing mulattoes."[6] The law punished with extra severity white women who gave birth to free mulatto children. These children, unlike the racially mixed children of black women, represented a corruption of the *white* race.

While the marital presumption was upheld to support white racial purity, it was discarded when white women broke the rule of racial fidelity. *Watkins and Wife v. Carlton* involved a will contest among three children of a white man, Carlton. Two of his children, Mary and Thomas, challenged their brother William's inheritance on the ground that he was a mulatto and therefore not their father's child. He argued that Carlton was legally William's father since he was married to William's mother. Rather than uphold the presumption, the Court ordered a new trial so that the jury could consider William's racial appearance and hear expert testimony about the impossibility of "the produce of the white race being other than white."[7] The Court allowed a racial exception to the marital presumption of legitimacy. A dark-skinned child born to a white woman did not benefit from the usual presumption of paternity; he was not deemed to be the son of a white husband. The absence of a genetic tie voided any legal link between a white man and a black child, just as surely as the law erased the genetic link between a white man and his black offspring.

Denying Black Connection to White Children

Race overrides not only the traditional presumption of paternity, but also the traditional presumption of maternity. Gestational surrogacy separates the biological connection between mother and child into two parts—the gestational tie and the genetic tie. In gestational surrogacy, the surrogate mother is implanted with an embryo produced by fertilizing the contracting mother's egg with the contracting father's sperm. The child therefore inherits the genes of both contracting parents and is genetically unrelated to her birth mother. Gestational surrogacy allows a radical possibility that is very convenient and very dangerous: a black woman can give birth to a white child. White men need no longer rely on white surrogates to produce their valuable white genetic inheritance.[8] This possibility reverses the traditional presumptions about a mother's biological connection to her children. It becomes imperative to legitimate the genetic tie between the (white) father and the child, rather than the biological, nongenetic tie between the (black) birth mother and the child.

Gestational surrogacy presents the possibility that white middle-class couples will use women of color to gestate their babies. Since contracting couples need not be concerned about the surrogate's genetic qualities (most importantly, her race), they may favor hiring the most economically vulnerable women in order to secure the lowest price for their services. Black surrogates would also be disadvantaged in any custody dispute: besides being less able to afford a court battle, they are unlikely to win custody of a white child. Some feminists have raised "the spectre of a caste of breeders, composed of women of color whose primary function would be to gestate the babies of wealthy white women."[9] These breeders, whose own genetic progeny would be considered worthless, might be sterilized. The vision of black women's wombs in the service of white men conjures up images from slavery. Slave women were similarly compelled to breed children who would be owned by their masters and to breastfeed their masters' white children.

Transracial Adoptions

White support for "transracial adoptions" does not fundamentally alter the rules governing claims to white and black children. All of the literature advocating the elimination of racial considerations in child placements focuses on making it easier for white parents to adopt children of color. A leading book on the subject states that "in the case of transracial adoption the children are nonwhite and the adoptive parents are white."[10] Claims about the benefits of racial assimilation are only made about advantages black children will presumably experience by living in white homes.

This bias may result partly from the disproportionate number of black children available for adoption and of white couples seeking to adopt. The thought of a black family adopting a white child, however, appears to be beyond our cultural imagination. A system that truly assigns children to adoptive parents without regard to race is unthinkable not because black children would be placed in white homes, but because white children would be given to black parents. Adoption of a black child by a white family is viewed as an improvement in the black child's social status and lifestyle and as a positive gesture of racial inclusion, while a black family's adoption of a white child would be seen as an unseemly relationship and an injury to the child. As a judge recognized forty years ago, allowing the adoption of a white child by his mother's black husband would unfairly cause the child to "lose the social status of a white man. . . ."[11] A "no-preference" adoption policy with respect to race would in effect be a regime that always prefers a white family. Although this policy would eliminate the preference for black parents in adoptions of black children, it would retain the preference for white parents in adoptions of white children. Thus, even advocates of transracial adoptions ultimately favor "a system in which white children are reserved for white families. . . ."[12]

Notes

1. Keane and Breo also revealed that the doctor who assisted in the pregnancy explained his participation in terms of eugenics: "I performed the insemination because there are enough unwanted children and children of poor genetic background in the world." NOEL P. KEANE AND DENNIS L. BREO, THE SURROGATE MOTHER 35, 36 (1981).

2. PATRICIA J. WILLIAMS, THE ALCHEMY OF RACE AND RIGHTS 186, 188 (1991).

3. A dramatic cross-cultural example is Elizabeth Bartholet's story about her efforts to get a Peruvian doctor to treat the child she adopted. ELIZABETH BARTHOLET, FAMILY BONDS: ADOPTION AND THE POLITICS OF PARENTING 88–89 (1993). Assuming the baby was of mixed Indian and Spanish heritage, the doctor suggested that Bartholet simply trade in the sick baby for another. It was only when the doctor discovered that the baby was "unusually white" that he understood Bartholet's desire to keep him. Bartholet observes, "it was overwhelmingly clear that Michael's value had been transformed in the doctor's eyes by his whiteness. Whiteness made it comprehensible that someone would want to cure and keep this child rather than discard him." Id. at 89.

4. Thomas D. Russell, South Carolina's Largest Slave Auctioneering Firm, 68 CHI.-KENT L. REV. 1241, 1241 (1993).

5. See John A. Robertson, Technology and Motherhood: Legal and Ethical Issues in Human Egg Donation, 39 CASE W. RES. L. REV. 1, 31 n.100 (1988–89) ("Eugenic considerations are unavoidable, and not inappropriate when one is seeking gametes from an unknown third party."). In his discussion of egg donation, John Robertson defends recipients' desire to "receive good genes" from women who "appear to be of good stock." Id. at 31. He advocates perfecting the technology of egg donation because it will "enhance the ability to influence the genetic makeup of offspring." Id. at 37.

6. A. Leon Higginbotham and Barbara K. Kopytoff, Racial Purity and Interracial Sex in the Law of Colonial and Antebellum Virginia, 77 GEORGETOWN L.J. 1967, 1997 (1989).

7. Watkins, 37 Va. (10 Leigh) 560, 560–62, 576–77 n.* (1840).

8. See Beverly Horsburgh, Jewish Women, Black Women: Guarding Against the Oppression of Surrogacy, 8 BERKELEY WOMEN'S L.J. 29, 39 (1993) (stating that white couples are much more likely to hire nonwhite women to be gestational surrogates than to be genetic surrogates). At least two black women in Europe have been implanted with white women's eggs in order to bear a child of their own. See Abbie Jones, Fertility doctors try to egg on donors, CHI. TRIB. § 6 at 1 (Mar. 6, 1994) (reporting that a black woman in Britain was implanted with the eggs of a white woman because there were no eggs from black women available and that a black woman in Rome underwent the procedure because she believed that "the child would have a better future if it were white").

9. Note, Parental Rights and Gestational Surrogacy: An Argument Against the Genetic Standard, 23 COLUM. HUM. RTS. L. REV. 525, 545 (1992).

10. RITA JAMES SIMON AND HOWARD ALTSTEIN, TRANSRACIAL ADOPTION 9 (John Wiley, 1977).

11. In re Adoption of a Minor, 228 F.2d 446, 447 (D.C. Cir. 1955).

12. Twila L. Perry, The Transracial Adoption Category, 21 N.Y.U. REV. L. & SOC. CHANGE 33, 104 (1993–94).

86

The Sources of *The Bell Curve*

JEFFREY ROSEN AND CHARLES LANE

By scrutinizing the footnotes and bibliography in *The Bell Curve*, readers can more easily recognize the project for what it is: a chilly synthesis of the work of disreputable race theorists and eccentric eugenicists. It would be unfair, of course, to ascribe to Murray and Herrnstein all the noxious views of their sources. Mere association with dubious thinkers does not discredit the book by itself. But even a superficial examination of the primary sources suggests that some of Murray and Herrnstein's substantive arguments rely on questionable data and hotly contested scholarship, produced by academics whose ideological biases are pronounced. To this extent, important portions of the book must be treated with skepticism.

Much of *The Bell Curve*'s data purporting to establish an inherited difference in intelligence among blacks, whites, and Asians is drawn from the work of Richard Lynn of the University of Ulster. In the acknowledgments to *The Bell Curve*, Murray and Herrnstein say they "benefited especially from the advice" of Lynn, whom they refer to elliptically as "a scholar of racial and ethnic differences." Lynn is an associate editor of, and, since 1971, a frequent contributor to, *Mankind Quarterly*, a journal of racialist anthropology, founded by the Scottish white supremacist Robert Gayre. *Mankind Quarterly* has a long history of publishing pseudoscientific accounts of black inferiority. Lynn and others have used its pages to ventilate their view that society should foster the reproduction of the genetically superior, and discourage that of the genetically inferior.

Murray and Herrnstein rely most heavily on an article that Lynn published in *Mankind Quarterly* in 1991, "Race Differences in Intelligence: A Global Perspective." In the article, Lynn reviews what he calls the "world literature on racial differences in intelligence." He notes that "the first good study of the intelligence of pure African Negroids was carried out in South Africa" in 1929, without mentioning that this study was based on an administration of the now-discredited U.S. Army Beta Test. He also asserts that the median IQ of black Africans is 70—based solely on a single test of blacks in South Africa in 1989. Murray and Herrnstein invoke this dubious figure, but they manage to confuse it: they say that the *median* black African IQ is 75.

Lynn concludes that "Mongoloids have the fastest reaction times" and the highest IQs, "followed by Caucasoids and then by Negroids." After examining what he calls "1,500 of the most important technological and scientific discoveries which have ever been made," Lynn reaches the following conclusion: "Who can doubt that the Caucasoid and the Mongoloid are the only two races that have made any significant contribution to civilization?" As Murray and Herrnstein observe in a footnote, "Lynn explains the evolution of racial

From THE BELL CURVE WARS, edited by Steven Fraser. Copyright © 1995 by Basic Books, a division of Harper-Collins Publishers, Inc. Reprinted by permission of Basic Books, a division of HarperCollins Publishers, Inc.

differences in intelligence in terms of the ancestral migrations of groups of early hominids from the relatively benign environments of Africa to the harsher and more demanding Eurasian latitudes, where they branched into the Caucasoids and Mongoloids." Similar theories, Murray and Herrnstein note without irony, "were not uncommon among anthropologists and biologists of a generation or two ago."

Murray and Herrnstein also introduce readers to the work of J. Phillipe Rushton, a Canadian psychologist. Rushton has argued that Asians are more intelligent than Caucasians, have larger brains for their body size, smaller penises, lower sex drive, are less fertile, work harder, and are more readily socialized; and Caucasians have the same relationship to blacks. In his most recent book, *Race, Evolution and Behavior,* Rushton acknowledges the assistance of Herrnstein; and Murray and Herrnstein return the compliment, devoting two pages of their own book to a defense of Rushton. Among the views that Herrnstein and Murray suggest Rushton has supported with "increasingly detailed and convincing empirical reports" is the theory that, in their words, "the average Mongoloid is toward one end of the continuum of reproductive strategies—the few offspring, high survival, and high parental investment end—the average Negroid is shifted toward the other end, and the average Caucasoid is in the middle."

In a gratuitous two-page appendix, Murray and Herrnstein go out of their way to say that "Rushton's work is not that of a crackpot or a bigot." But in an interview with *Rolling Stone,* Rushton colloquially summarized his research agenda: "Even if you take things like athletic ability or sexuality—not to reinforce stereotypes—but it's a trade-off: more brain or more penis. You can't have everything." And in a 1986 article in *Politics and Life Sciences,* Rushton suggested that Nazi Germany's military prowess was connected to the purity of its gene pool, and warned that egalitarian ideas endangered "North European civilization."

This, then, is the evolution of Murray and Herrnstein's data. The tradition which they benignly label "classicist" stretches back to the Victorian era, when Sir William Galton, the cousin of Darwin, argued that Africans were less intelligent and had slower "reaction times" than Englishmen; it extends through Charles Spearman, who argued that socially desirable traits, such as honesty and intelligence, could be measured together; and it was updated in 1969 by Arthur Jensen, who relied on Galton's hundred-year-old estimates for his conclusion that blacks were less intelligent than whites.

In addition to appropriating the data of Spearman, Jensen, Lynn and Rushton, Murray and Herrnstein faithfully duplicate the analytical structure of their arguments. It is no coincidence that Rushton's book includes the same strains of conservative multiculturalism that Murray embraced in his essay in *The New Republic* [October 31, 1994. Ed.]. Anticipating Murray's celebration of "clannish self-esteem," Rushton devotes an entire chapter of his book to a genetic explanation for ethnocentrism: "According to genetic similarity theory, people can be expected to favor their own group over others." And he speculates that "favoritism for one's own ethnic group may have arisen as an extension of enhancing family and social cohesiveness."

The Bell Curve is not an original or courageous book. It is the work of a popularizer of ideas, from the fringes of the academy, that have been repeatedly aired and repeatedly ignored. Despite the publicity that accompanied the publication of *The Bell Curve,* Murray's celebration of "clannish self-esteem" could hardly be more ineptly timed. The notion of American blacks and whites as increasingly culturally and genetically distinct "clans" seems especially implausible in an age when the healthy growth of ethnic intermarriage promises to undermine the concept of coherent racial classification entirely. It is not surprising to discover the shabbiness of the scholarly tradition on which he has staked his reputation.

87

Hearts of Darkness

JOHN B. JUDIS

One of the problems with *The Bell Curve* is that the authors continually muddy their own water with equivocation, qualification, and even contradiction. Which of these statements do Murray and Herrnstein really believe?

- "We cannot think of any legitimate argument why any encounter between individual whites and blacks need be affected by the knowledge that an aggregate ethnic difference in measured intelligence is genetic rather than environmental."
- "The assumption of genetic cognitive equality among the races has practical consequences."
- "Race is such a difficult concept to employ in the American context. What does it mean to be 'black' in America, in racial terms, when the word black (or African American) can be used for people whose ancestry is more European than African?"
- "It would be disingenuous to leave the racial issue at that. . . . Thus we will eventually comment on cognitive differences among races as they might derive from genetic differences."

Murray has further confused matters in statements and articles he has written afterwards "clarifying" the book's argument. He has insisted, for instance, that the book does not argue for a strategy of eugenics or for strengthening the rule of what they call "a cognitive elite." Yet, the book's major thrust is exactly this and the authors' attempts at equivocation and Murray's later attempts at clarification are intended largely to evade responsibility for a thesis that is morally repugnant and scientifically indefensible.

Here is their argument for eugenics. Murray and Herrnstein contend that American blacks and Latinos score on the average significantly lower on IQ tests than whites. Lower IQ contributes to greater crime, poverty, illegitimacy, welfare dependency, unemployment, and even workplace injury. And because blacks and Latinos reproduce faster than whites, their proliferation has brought down and will continue to bring down the average IQ of Americans—thereby contributing disproportionately to the country's worst social problems.

To alleviate what the authors call this "dysgenic pressure," they favor eliminating "the extensive network of cash and services for low-income women who have babies" and making "it easy for women to make good on their prior decision not to get pregnant by making available birth control mechanisms that are increasingly flexible, foolproof, inexpensive, and safe." They also recommend that we should alter our immigration policy to "serve America's interests."

Murray and Herrnstein's intent in eliminating welfare payments for the children of low-income women is not to save money or to induce self-reliance among the underclass—the usual conservative rationales—but to discourage the birth of low-IQ children. Similarly, their intent in circulating condoms is not to foster freedom of choice, but to discourage low-IQ women from reproducing. In putting limits on immigration to "serve America's interests," they are not interested in protecting American workers' jobs or preventing an overload of public facilities, but in keeping out Latinos and blacks who "are, at least in the short run, putting some downward pressure on the distribution of intelligence."

Murray has also denied that he approves of a society stratified according to intelligence, or IQ. But *The Bell Curve* is a brief for a society divided along exactly these lines. Murray deplores court rulings forbidding the use of IQ tests in hiring. He wants school funds shifted from the "disadvantaged" toward the "gifted." He wants a voucher program that will reward elite private schools. The result of these policies will be still greater segregation of society along the lines of income and of achievement in standardized tests.

Murray describes this society as the "triumph of an American ideal," but it is a perversion of the original American ideal of equality. America's Jeffersonian faith, articulated later by Andrew Jackson and Abraham Lincoln, rested on the ability of ordinary Americans to participate fully in civic and economic life. Jefferson never presumed that all Americans would be entirely equal in income, but he assumed that through the widespread dispersion of property the differences among Americans would not create the kind of invidious distinctions among classes that had ruined Europe.

Murray and Herrnstein do warn against the creation of a "custodial" state in which a cognitive elite attempts to win over and keep in check a growing underclass that reproduces itself through reproducing low IQ scores. But what seems to bother them are not the class distinctions themselves, but the "greater benefits . . . primarily in the form of services rather than cash" that the cognitive elite will bestow upon this miserable mass of misfits. They present two alternatives: a return to an earlier America of neighborhoods and communities (a worthy but probably unrealizable objective) and "dealing with demography"—in other words, discouraging the reproduction of the individuals who require the services of the custodial state. It's eugenics in the service of a racial-intellectual oligarchy.

If these unsavory political recommendations were based on some novel scientific findings, even those who abhor them might have to take them seriously. But Murray and Herrnstein's discussion on race, IQ, and dysgenics is not science. It's a combination of bigotry and of metaphysics. Their arguments are sophisticated only in the sense that they repeatedly acknowledge the obvious objections to them. But then they blithely ignore these objections. Consider:

Correlation and cause: Murray and Herrnstein acknowledge the difference between demonstrating correlation and proving causation, but consistently use the language of causation when they have merely demonstrated a correlation. They show a statistical correlation between IQ and various social maladies, but they repeatedly describe low IQ as "a factor in," "a significant determinant of," and "a strong precursor of" various social maladies. What emerges is a highly distorted picture of social dynamics. For instance, they ascribe the growing disparity in income to the growing disparity in IQ. But there are other significant factors that have *caused* (and are not merely correlated with) the growing disparity in incomes. These include the decline in unions, competition from low-wage developing countries (which disproportionately affects working-class wages), and, in the case of high CEO salaries, the particularly American identification of income and status. The only evidence that IQ scores have caused the disparity is the correlation itself.

Murray and Herrnstein's confusion of correlations with causes reaches a point of absurdity when they suggest that raising society's average IQ score will reduce crime, un-employment, and poverty. If the average IQ were to rise from 100 to 103, Murray and Herrn-stein argue, then "the poverty rate falls by 25 percent . . . high school dropouts fall by 28 percent . . . children living without their parents fall by 20 percent . . . welfare recipiency, both chronic and temporary, falls by 18 percent" and so on! This kind of crackpot utopi-anism is based upon mistaking a correlation with a cause. It's like arguing that because peo-ple with long noses happen to be more intelligent, we could produce a race of geniuses by breeding Pinocchios.

Why do erudite members of the cognitive elite make such mistakes? One reason their causal ascriptions seem plausible is that they perform a linguistic sleight of hand on the term "intelligence." While offering the predictable acknowledgment that "measures of intelli-gence . . . are a limited tool for deciding what to make of any given individual," they then identify what IQ tests measure with intelligence in the broadest sense, including thought-fulness, prudence, and wisdom. That makes it easier to attribute a causal role to low and high IQ scores. For instance, after having merely shown that individuals who score poorly on IQ tests are more likely to be unemployed, they conclude that "intelligence and its correlates—maturity, farsightedness, and personal competence—are important in keeping a person em-ployed and in the labor force." Fine—but IQ tests don't measure these qualities.

Race and genes: The authors also claim agnosticism on the question of whether genes or environment cause low IQ scores, but their analysis is heavily weighted toward genetic causes. They estimate that the genetic component of the difference in IQ between whites and blacks is between 40 and 80 percent, and accept a "middling estimate" of 60 percent, adding that "the balance of the evidence suggests that 60 percent may err on the low side." That's not likely. Indeed, much of the experimental evidence does not support an overwhelmingly genetic view of intelligence. Most scientists would agree that the difference in IQ scores be-tween two individuals brought up in apparently similar environments is attributable between 40 and 80 percent to genetic differences. But no test or experiment or finding has ever estab-lished that the difference in IQ between groups of dissimilar background and environment are due partly, slightly, or primarily to genetic factors. Of course, Murray and Herrnstein ac-knowledge "that a trait is genetically transmitted in individuals does not mean that group dif-ferences in that trait are also genetic in origin." But they then blithely assume that differ-ences in heritability between individuals can be transposed to social groups.

Why would they make such an assumption? It's probably a combination of prejudice, or what they call "underground conviction," and linguistic legerdemain. They acknowledge that neither American blacks nor Latinos represent distinct races, but are a composite of different races, nationalities, and ethnic groups. (The same is equally true of American "whites.") Yet they proceed to describe American blacks as a race and to talk about "ge-netic differences between the races." By doing this, they impute to the difference between two social groups—American whites and blacks—certain prehistoric genetic traits, making it more plausible to assert that whites are *inherently* smarter than blacks.

While offering their own dubious schemes for raising Americans' "cognitive capital," the authors naturally aver that no necessary conclusions flow from their genetic specula-tions. "We cannot think of any legitimate argument why any encounter between individ-ual whites and blacks need be affected by the knowledge that an aggregate ethnic differ-ence in measured intelligence is genetic rather than environmental." And on one level, of course, they are right. No necessary conclusions do flow from *their* speculations.

But the last four hundred years provide ample reason to believe that imputing innate inferiority to a group will affect their "encounter" with other groups. In the United States, theories of racial inferiority served as the justification for slavery and for restrictions on American immigration. In Europe, of course, these theories were a justification for Nazi genocide. If Murray's and Herrnstein's views gain currency in academic and political circles—and they have already won a warm reception among some conservatives—they will deepen the chasm already separating whites from blacks and Latinos.

Of course, the foresightful Murray and Herrnstein acknowledge that this could occur, but they maintain that it is a price we must pay for violating irrational taboos and offending "politically correct public discussion." Let's be clear, however, on what taboo is being violated. It is not some product of Stanley Fish and the academic new left, but of the great war against Nazi Germany. It's not the taboo against unflinching scientific inquiry, but against pseudoscientific racism. Of all the world's taboos, it is the one most deserving of retention.

88

Thank You, Doctors Murray and Herrnstein (Or, Who's Afraid of Critical Race Theory?)

DERRICK A. BELL

Radical assessment can encompass illustration, anecdote, allegory, and imagination, as well as analysis of doctrine and cases. I want to utilize all of these techniques to comment on a contemporary phenomenon: *The Bell Curve*. A great deal of attention and energy has been devoted to commending and condemning Charles Murray and the late Richard Herrnstein, authors of this best-selling book on racial intelligence. This book suggests great social policy significance in the fact that black people score, on average, fifteen points below whites on I.Q. tests.

This thesis has been criticized as the rehashing of views long-ago rejected by virtually all experts in the field. There is, critics maintain, no basis for a finding that intelligence is inherited and no accepted definition of the vague term "intelligence." There is, on the other hand, a depressingly strong and invariant correlation between resources and race in this country, and resources and success—including success in taking I.Q. tests. These are settled facts.

Even so, the book has enjoyed an enormous success that its critics find difficult to explain. Stephen Jay Gould, for example, writes:

> *The Bell Curve*, with its claims and supposed documentation that race and class differences are largely caused by genetic factors and are therefore essentially immutable, contains no new arguments and presents no compelling data to support its anachronistic social Darwinism, so I can only conclude its success in winning attention must reflect the depressing temper of our time— a historical moment of unprecedented ungenerosity, when a mood for slashing social programs can be powerfully abetted by an argument that beneficiaries cannot be helped, owing to inborn cognitive limits expressed as low I.Q. scores.[1]

Criticism of *The Bell Curve* has been so universal among biologists that one must wonder: Why did these two well-known men produce a book filled with rejected theories? Surely they must have known that doing so would provide pseudoscientific support for racial hostilities that always worsen during times of economic stress and anxiety. The all too easy answer is that *The Bell Curve*'s authors saw a market opportunity and took it. The book has sold over 300,000 copies and has become a major source of discussion in the media. But utilizing the conceptual and experiential tools of critical race theory, I want to suggest another possibility.

It is not difficult to imagine that the authors were aware of the generally accepted findings regarding the lack of any connection between race and intelligence. Suppose that recognizing the debilitating effects of discrimination and exclusion on African Americans, they devised an "oppression factor" and, adding it to existing data, discovered that there was indeed a discernible racial difference in intelligence measured by I.Q. tests. However, when the I.Q. data playing field was leveled via the "oppression factor," contrary to their expectations, they discovered that blacks performed fifteen points higher than whites. Quite likely, they disbelieved and thus reviewed their data several times. Each time they did so, the conclusion that they (perhaps) did not want became ever more certain. It was beyond denial. Indeed, it explained why blacks survived two centuries of the world's most destructive slavery and a century of utter subordination under segregation: Black people are simply smarter than whites.

What would they do with this information? Its release would almost certainly throw the country into turmoil. As history indicates all too well, blacks have suffered greatly as a result of discrimination often justified by the general belief in black inferiority. But history shows with equal clarity, though it is less frequently acknowledged, that indications of black success and possible black superiority result in racist outrage. Many race riots in this nation's history were sparked by white outrage over black success.[2] In the nineteenth and early twentieth centuries, blacks who were successful at business or farming were targeted by the Ku Klux Klan and other hate groups for death and destruction.[3] While protection of white womanhood is widely considered the major motivation for the thousands of blacks lynched during the latter part of the nineteenth century and the early decades of the twentieth, in fact, retaliation against blacks who dared compete successfully with white men was the real source of many, and perhaps most, of these atrocities.

A debate raged in Florida over a bill intended to compensate black victims for losses suffered more than seventy years ago, when the Klan absolutely destroyed a thriving black town called Rosewood—murdering, raping, pillaging, and finally burning all the property in sight. Denial is the usual response to even such well-documented racist rampages. State officials who opposed the measure noted that the statute of limitations had expired, and that "compensation would be 'bad for the county and bad for our state' because it would encourage similar claims."[4]

In more recent times, discrimination aimed at skilled or talented blacks is a well-understood fact of life in the black community. Journalist Ellis Cose interviewed dozens of blacks for his book, *The Rage of a Privileged Class*. They sounded a common theme:

> I have done everything I was supposed to do. I have stayed out of trouble with the law, gone to the right schools, and worked myself nearly to death. *What more do they want?* Why in God's name won't they accept me as a full human being? Why am I pigeonholed in a "Black job"? Why am I constantly treated as if I were a drug addict, a thief, or a thug? Why am I still not allowed to aspire to the same things every white person in America takes as a birthright? Why, when I most want to be seen, am I suddenly rendered invisible?[5]

In the context of law school faculties, my character Geneva Crenshaw describes an experience with which many professors of color can relate:

> When I arrived [the first black hired], the white faculty members were friendly and supportive. They smiled at me a lot and offered help and advice. When they saw how much time I spent helping minority students and how I struggled with my first writing, they seemed pleased. It

was patronizing, but the general opinion seemed to be that they had done well to hire me. They felt good about having lifted up one of the downtrodden. And they congratulated themselves for their affirmative-action policies.

   Then after I became acclimated to academic life, I began receiving invitations to publish in the top law reviews, to serve on important commissions, and to lecture at other schools. At this point, I noticed that some of my once-smiling colleagues now greeted me with frowns. For them, nothing I did was right: my articles were flashy but not deep, rhetorical rather than scholarly. Even when I published an article in a major review, my colleagues gave me little credit; after all, students had selected the piece, and what did they know anyway? My popularity with students was attributed to the likelihood that I was an easy grader. The more successful I appeared, the harsher became the collective judgment of my former friends.[6]

Richard Delgado, a well-known critical race theorist, believes the shift may be caused by "cognitive dissonance":

At first, the white professor feels good about hiring the minority. It shows how liberal the white is, and the minority is assumed to want nothing more than to scrape by in the rarefied world they both inhabit. But the minority does not just scrape by, is not eternally grateful, and indeed starts to surpass the white professor. This is disturbing; things weren't meant to go that way. The strain between former belief and current reality is reduced by reinterpreting the current reality. The minority has a fatal flaw. Pass it on.[7]

Recognizing this strong, often unconscious, white preference for black mediocrity in even the most elite professional schools, *The Bell Curve*'s authors faced a dilemma that they chose to resolve by intentionally falsifying their data, to spare blacks the reprisals and bloody retaliation they would have suffered had the real truth regarding superior test performance by blacks come out. Herrnstein and Murray may well have foreseen the serious criticism of their work, if published without their new findings, criticism that, in fact, has been heaped on them by social scientists and experts in biology. They may have feared that if they published the new data revealing the superiority of black intelligence, black people would be deemed a threat to many whites and thus placed in far greater danger than if the book served simply as a comfort to whites by repeating the oft-told tale of black inferiority.

The Bell Curve's authors must have known what every professional and skilled black has learned the hard way: that policies of affirmative action are endangered far more by the presence of blacks who are clearly competent than they are by those who are only marginally so. Because it has been difficult for many whites to acknowledge that black people are competent—even superior—at some sports, it would be impossible to gain the same acknowledgment for blacks across the board, particularly if the reluctant recognition required the admission that inferior status is the result of discrimination rather than the old racial rationales of inferior skills, lack of drive, or the unwillingness to compete. The Dodgers' official Al Campanis lost his job for saying so, but he was far from the only white person who believed that blacks lack "some of the necessities" to become managers in baseball.[8]

Finally, Herrnstein and Murray may have feared that, even if they were to convince a reluctant America of blacks' superior intelligence and ability—much of which has been smothered by racial discrimination—that reality may have opened the question for many whites as to whether they had not been similarly disadvantaged on the basis of class. Such a long-overdue revelation could well spark serious political unrest and perhaps a rebellion. Given the potential for societal mischief, the authors would almost certainly opt for conclusions that conform closely with what most people already believe. Better one more libel of blacks as an inferior people than a truth posing a greater threat that could lead to racial atrocities and class warfare. Thus, while *The Bell Curve* is condemned as a perversion of truth and a provocation for racial stereotyping, we should view it less harshly for what it is, and more sympathetically for what it might have been.

To understand the motivation for and the likely intent of racial policies in America, one need only be willing to reverse the racial composition of the major components of those policies. To see things as they really are, you must imagine them for what they might be. In this instance, the effort is intended to delegitimize the illegitimate. *The Bell Curve* captured the nation's fascination precisely because it laid out in scientific jargon what many whites believe, need desperately to believe, but dare not reveal in public or even to their private selves.

Notes

1. Stephen J. Gould, *Curveball*, NEW YORKER, Nov. 28, 1994, at 139.

2. *See generally* ANTHONY M. PLATT, THE POLITICS OF RIOT COMMISSIONS, 1917–1970 (1971).

3. *See, e.g.*, ERIC FONER, RECONSTRUCTION 425–44 (1988). "But the most 'offensive' Blacks of all seemed to be those who achieved a modicum of economic success for, as a White Mississippi farmer commented, the Klan 'do not like to see the negro go ahead.' " *Id.* at 429.

4. Larry Rohter, *Paying for Racial Attack Divides Florida Leaders*, N.Y. TIMES, Mar. 14, 1994, at A12. The Florida legislature finally passed, and the governor signed, a claims bill providing $60,000 in scholarships to compensate the Rosewood families and their survivors. *See* C. Jeanne Bassett, *House Bill 591: Florida Compensates Rosewood Victims and Their Families for a Seventy-One-Year-Old Injury*, 22 FLA. ST. U. L. REV. 503, 520 (1995).

5. ELLIS COSE, THE RAGE OF A PRIVILEGED CLASS 2 (1993).

6. DERRICK A. BELL, AND WE ARE NOT SAVED: THE ELUSIVE QUEST FOR RACIAL JUSTICE 157–58 (1987).

7. *Id.*

8. David Aldridge, *Campanis Admits Error but Maintains Innocence*, WASH. POST, July 3, 1987, at F1.

89

Dangerous Undertones of the New Nativism

DANIEL KANSTROOM

The Decline of the West

In the late summer of 1918, with the final defeat of the German empire only a few months away, the first volume of *The Decline of the West* appeared in Germany and Austria. Written by a then unknown German historian named Oswald Spengler, the book soon became a sensation with a profound impact on intellectual debate and German politics for the following two decades. Though originally conceived as a political critique of the folly and criminal and suicidal optimism of pre–First World War German foreign policy, the work grew substantially beyond that modest goal. According to Spengler, the book was begun with an assessment of both the imminence and the inevitability of the First World War, which he saw as an inevitable manifestation of the historical crisis. The basic character of *The Decline of the West,* as one leading critic has put it, is that of a "somber, murky vision of the doom of our civilization."[1] At least as interesting as Spengler's historical work is the way that work was understood by non-specialists. As one observer noted, "Never had a thick philosophical work had such a success—and in all reading circles, learned and uneducated, serious and snobbish."[2] Copies of the book were widely disseminated, including one which made its way to Oliver Wendell Holmes, Jr., who described it as "a stimulating humbug of a book."[3] The year 1919 has been called the "Spengler year" in the German-speaking world, also witnessing the formation of a small, radical, and obscure political party called the German Workers' Party, which evolved into the German Nazi Party.

Spengler was clearly not a Nazi. Indeed, he expressed a fairly consistent revulsion for many of the central tenets of Adolf Hitler's political philosophy. And yet it is more than Spengler's nationality that has caused some historians to consider him at least an inadvertent philosophical brush-clearer for the Third Reich. Part of the difficulty was that Spengler appreciated much of the message of Nazi doctrine, while expressing discomfort with certain attributes of the messengers. He had specifically opposed the National Socialists as early as 1924. His opposition, however, seems to have been as much tactical and pragmatic as principled. He found Hitler's followers to be rough and immature. Yet he had specifically lauded the Fascists of Italy for their emphasis on "results" rather than "programs and parades."[4]

Although decidedly not a racist in the biological, Hitlerian sense, Spengler was hardly a consistent anti-racist either. He had criticized the idea of a *Volk* ["people." Ed.] in *The Decline*, adopting instead a Nietzschean conception of race that was beyond blood or genetics. Race, on this view, was more akin to what others might call character. It was linked more to geography and common history than to biology. It was not manifested in bodily characteristics but in intangible essences. Thus, in *The Decline*, Spengler viewed the so-called "Jewish question" mostly as a cultural clash, in sharp contrast to Hitler's views of Semitic versus "Aryan" blood. Spengler's racial theories, however, were not entirely consistent over time. In *Man and Technics*, a small book published in 1931, for example, Spengler asserted that "the group of nations of Nordic blood" was losing control of the world. Among the reasons he gave for this was that the "colored races" had been given access to technology which, Spengler believed, they would soon turn against Nordic peoples. Despite his reservations, Spengler served as an important precursor to the Nazi regime. Hitler himself adopted much of the apocalyptic tone of *The Decline of the West*, while adding a racist component: "On [Aryans] depends the existence of this whole culture. If they perish, the beauty of this earth will sink into the grave with them."[5]

Citizenship and Deportation under National Socialism

By the time of its ascendance to state power on January 20, 1933, the German Nationalist Socialist Party had a fairly well-developed theory of immigration and citizenship. In *Mein Kampf*, Adolf Hitler wrote that the ideal, race-based "national State" should divide its inhabitants into three classes: "State citizens, State subjects, and foreigners." Birth should give no more than the status of subject, which would not include the right to vote or to hold political office. Citizenship, however, would have to be earned, and "race and nationality" would have to be "proved" as a prerequisite.[6] These qualities, as Hitler earlier had made plain, were matters of "blood," not language or upbringing.[7]

It is worth recalling that Hitler actually held U.S. immigration laws of the 1920s in rather high regard:

> There is at least one state in which feeble attempts to achieve a better arrangement are apparent . . . the United States of America, where . . . [t]hey refuse to allow immigration of elements which are bad from the health point of view, and absolutely forbid naturalization in certain defined races, and are thus making a modest start in the direction of something not unlike the conception of the national State.[8]

Thus, it seems that if Hitler is to be placed in our current debate about immigration at all it should be as an opponent of the Fourteenth Amendment and of the Civil Rights Acts of the 1960s and as a supporter of a return to the national origins quotas and racist naturalization laws that he embraced in *Mein Kampf*.

Those who support such laws should consider the full historical program of which similar laws were a part in Germany. The Nazi positions on immigration and citizenship were absolutely central to their beliefs about the idealized *Volk*-based nation-state. Changes in these laws were among the first legal steps taken by the new regime. Beyond their *Volkisch* reordering of Germany's citizenship laws, and their use of those laws to justify and develop separate classes of German citizens with sharply different rights, Nazi leaders were also strong supporters of Jewish emigration. This doctrine, like many Nazi ideas, evolved substantially over time, from encouragement of emigration, to forced deportation, and ultimately to concentration camps and extermination.

Within a very short period of time, several events demonstrated the links between early Nazi citizenship and immigration laws and the Final Solution. By 1937 it was becoming clear to the Nazi leadership that voluntary emigration was insufficient to achieve the goal of re-creating the nation-state. The Nuremberg Laws, in short, had not succeeded. Jews had been deprived of political rights by the gradation of citizenship, but they retained important civil rights, especially regarding employment and property in the private sector. Also, because German Jews had been second-class citizens in many respects since 1933, the Jewish community itself began to accept that such a situation was stable and could continue. As further laws were passed that deprived Jews of property, social benefits, and the possibility of earning a living, however, deportation measures also became increasingly harsh. The first group to feel the brunt of this policy and to be deported were those non-German Jewish residents who were formally stateless because they had never applied for German citizenship. In effect, they had now become "illegal aliens," though that specific term was not used to describe them.

In March 1938, the use of deportation became increasingly well-organized and efficient. Adolf Eichmann had been assigned the task of deporting all the Jews from Austria. His success was "spectacular." In eight months some forty-five thousand Jews left Austria. In less than eighteen months, the number of "legal" expulsions was close to one hundred and fifty thousand, roughly sixty percent of the entire Jewish population.[9]

When the Polish government announced that as of October 29, 1938, all Polish Jews residing in Germany would lose their Polish citizenship, the orderly use of deportation laws began to seem particularly cumbersome to the Nazi leaders. A group of some fifteen thousand Polish Jews were rounded up and forced by the Gestapo and the Polish government to undergo a macabre back and forth dance between Germany and Poland until the latter state finally agreed to accept them.[10] Soon the relationship between the emigration policy and the concentration camps became only too apparent. By January 30, 1939, Hitler was sufficiently confident to speak plainly: " . . . if international Jewish capitalism . . . should succeed once more in plunging the nations into war, then the result will . . . be . . . the destruction of the Jewish race in Europe."[11]

Observers of current anti-immigration rhetoric in the United States have expressed concern about much of its tone and possible direction. Undocumented immigrants are seen as doubly unpopular: Beyond their inherent "illegality," they are blamed for sapping public benefits and bankrupting state and local governments. Others have begun to worry more broadly about the apparent movement toward a smaller concentric circle of membership in which distinctions between naturalized and native-born citizens could be the next step. History tragically supports this concern. The Nazis' use of deportation to produce their ideal nation-state was abetted by their understanding of how a group of people could be progressively transformed. One starts with an over-generalized accusation and then turns it into reality.

We in the United States must be aware that we have the capacity through incremental laws to "manufacture" an underclass. Each step taken on that road may seem innocuous and even justifiable. First there is the definition of a particular group of people as "illegal aliens," with little recognition of the widely varying circumstances that lead to such a status. Some are refugees, some have overstayed visas, some are in proceedings, some have relatives here, and so forth. The epithet of illegality, however, overshadows such fine distinctions. What is worse is the widespread understanding of the racial and ethnic similarities among members of this group. Once the group is defined in such ways, as both illegal and non-white, it becomes easy to deprive "them" of the opportunity to work, to educate their children, to obtain medical care, and to have at least the minimal safety net of public benefits. Each of these legal steps is accompanied by a reasonable, ostensibly non-racist justification.

But these types of laws—whatever their fiscal or other justification—also transform the group in question into the very thing they have wrongfully been called: an uneducated, disease-bearing, criminally inclined threat to "our" people and civilization. At this point, they begin to appear even to many melting pot supporters as Jews once did to Nazis—an unassimilable group. For those of a somewhat racist disposition already, the new social reality only confirms and strengthens their views. David Duke, it should be recalled, throughout the late 1980s called for a complete end to all Third World immigration in conjunction with the racial division of the United States.[12] Even if we cannot perfectly seal our borders and fully enforce our immigration laws, we must avoid the transformation of one serious social problem into one that is potentially much worse.

Notes

1. H. Stuart Hughes, OSWALD SPENGLER: A CRITICAL ESTIMATE 7 (New York 1962).

2. Quoted from W. Wolfradt in MANFRED SCHROETER, DER STREIT UM SPENGLER: KRITIK SEINER KRITIKER 89 (Munich 1922).

3. Letter from Oliver W. Holmes to Dr. John C. H. Wu, January 27, 1925, in JUSTICE HOLMES TO DOCTOR WU: AN INTIMATE CORRESPONDENCE, 1921–1932, at 25–26 (1947).

4. Hughes, supra at 125.

5. Adolf Hitler, MEIN KAMPF 288 (Boston 1971).

6. Adolf Hitler, MEIN KAMPF 181–82 (First English Edition, Cambridge 1933).

7. "It is hardly imaginable that anyone should think that a German could be made out of, say, a Negro or a Chinaman because he has learned German and is ready to talk it for the rest of his life and to vote for some German political party; . . . nationality, or rather race, is not a matter of language, but of blood." *Id.* at 158.

8. *Id.* at 182.

9. Hannah Arendt, EICHMANN IN JERUSALEM: A REPORT ON THE BANALITY OF EVIL 44 (New York 1966 [revised edition]).

10. See generally George L. Mosse, TOWARD THE FINAL SOLUTION 210–14 Madison 1985).

11. Quoted in Mosse, supra at 213.

12. Lance Hill, *Nazi Race Doctrine in the Political Thought of David Duke,* in Douglas D. Rose, ed., THE EMERGENCE OF DAVID DUKE AND THE POLITICS OF RACE (Chapel Hill 1992).

Synopses of Other Important Works

The Decline of Intelligence in America: Seymour Itzkoff

In this 1994 book (Praeger; subtitled *A Strategy for National Renewal*), Seymour W. Itzkoff warns that America's and the West's average level of intelligence is declining generation by generation. The system of market economics, competition, and political democracy presupposes the maintenance of a form of intelligence. But this will not necessarily continue to happen. "The secret weapon and thus the secret word of national power is, of course, *natality*. Those who are born today will in twenty-five years be members of a nation's potential workforce. Their children, in turn, fifty years hence, will take that nation into the future. What happens in each nation with regard to the educability of each successive cohort will constitute the armed forces of victory or defeat in a very different kind of competition, essentially World War III" (p. 202).

The United States, then, as a matter of national strategy ought to encourage its "best" people to reproduce. Today, the brightest families have only one or two children; the others, all too many (p. 203). "The danger will be that many more individuals of potential will be excluded from the international domestic economy because we will not have produced enough of those talents in the 115–130 I.Q. range that create new ideas and enterprises. As the economy dies from the top, many more individuals of ability will find themselves displaced" (*Id.*). "Our intelligence levels are declining because more children are entering our schools from the lowest intellectual classes than from our elites. . . . It is all so simple in terms of a solution. We need to stimulate our finest to form families of the traditional sort in which children are conceived, born, raised, and educated to the highest levels for which they are capable. The helpless need to be encouraged and guided not to have children that they cannot rear and educate to functional cultural levels" (p. 204).

From the Editors: Issues and Comments

The races look different—or do they? Can you always be sure if a person with medium brown skin tone and slightly slanted eyes is Mexican, American Indian, or Euro-Asian? Have you ever made a mistake about someone's race? Children, before a certain age, do not react to race. They have to be told that race matters; before then they may be momentarily interested in differences in skin color, but no more so than differences in, say, eyebrow thickness or the shape of toenails. In this sense, are all races "constructed"—do we, that is, decide that out of the thousands of differences among individuals and populations, particular ones like skin color, hair texture, and so on matter?

Do the races exhibit *behavioral* differences, and, if so, are these physically based or the product of treatment by others and of the environment in which individuals grow up? Is this true of very basic traits, such as being "good" with numbers or words or people? Should research into race-based IQ differences be banned? Discouraged? Encouraged?

Suggested Readings

Barkan, Elazar, THE RETREAT OF SCIENTIFIC RACISM (1992).

Bendersky, Joseph W., *The Disappearance of Blonds: Immigration, Race and the Reemergence of "Thinking White,"* TELOS, Summer 1995: 135.

Delgado, Richard, et al., *Can Science Be Inopportune? Constitutional Validity of Governmental Restrictions on Race-IQ Research,* 31 UCLA L. REV. 128 (1983).

DeParle, Jason, *Daring Research or "Social Science Pornography"?* NEW YORK TIMES MAGAZINE, October 9, 1994, at 48.

Dudziak, Mary, *Oliver Wendell Holmes as a Eugenic Reformer,* 71 IOWA L. REV. 833 (1986).

Gould, Stephen Jay, THE MISMEASURE OF MAN (1981).

Keane, A. H., THE WORLD'S PEOPLE (1908).

Lombardo, Paul, *Three Generations, No Imbeciles: New Light on* Buck v. Bell, 60 NYU L. REV. 30 (1989).

Nei, Masatoshi, and Arun Roychoudhury, *Genetic Relationship and Evolution of Human Races,* 14 EVOL. BIOL. 1 (1982).

Shipman, Pat, THE EVOLUTION OF RACISM: HUMAN DIFFERENCES AND THE USE AND ABUSE OF SCIENCE (1994).

Stanton, W. R., THE LEOPARD'S SPOTS: SCIENTIFIC ATTITUDES TOWARDS RACE IN AMERICA (1960).

Stepan, Nancy, THE IDEA OF RACE IN SCIENCE (1982).

Part X

White Consciousness, White Power

Nothing is wrong—one might think—with focusing critically on one's own race and racial background and makeup. At times, however, this effort becomes distorted. The student of race decides that his or her own race is superior, or the bearer of a unique destiny. Then, all other races become irrelevant, drags, or outright threats. The rise of paramilitary "patriot" groups and others espousing white supremacy illustrate how this can happen. But what of more moderate views holding that WASPs simply are the possessors of certain admirable traits—caution, saving, law-abidingness, and so on. Is this a matter of taking pride in one's heritage—or does it verge on attitudes of supremacy and hate?

Are race-baiting messages or ones of racial supremacy to be deplored—or do they serve as useful pressure valves for feelings that, if suppressed, might emerge in even more injurious form? Do organized hate groups have a constitutional right to exist?

90

The Rise of Private Militia: A First and Second Amendment Analysis of the Right to Organize and the Right to Train

JOELLE E. POLESKY

This chapter is written in honor of my grandfather, whose perseverance in life and dedication to his family are an enduring inspiration.

Copious news coverage of Ruby Ridge,[1] Waco,[2] and the Oklahoma City bombing[3] has prompted a growing concern with the proliferation of paramilitary organizations and paramilitary activity.[4] The public's anxiety is fueled by the belief that private militia pose a threat to society. Private militia are commonly misunderstood and mischaracterized as organizations comprised solely of right-wing militants adhering to Aryan, racist ideology. Although many militia members subscribe to these views, allegiance to the far right is not a prerequisite to membership in a private militia.[5] Instead, ardent belief in the need to protect individual rights from encroachment by the federal government is the predominant attribute of these organizations.

History of the Militia

The first militias organized to prevent the rise of tyrannical government. Over time, however, the significance of the militia to free society diminished considerably, primarily because of the "emerging . . . belief that the interests of the people . . . could be protected effectively by the establishment of democratic governments, offering legal guarantees of individual rights."[6]

Militia members today believe that modern government has failed to achieve or sustain this democratic ideal. The fundamental purpose of current paramilitary organizations, therefore, corresponds with the historical justification for maintaining a militia—militia members consider their existence necessary to protect society from the federal government.[7] But what was once a viable means of supplying protection against the federal government, however, may no longer be a realistic alternative. The militia may have been an efficient means of protection when the country was small and when only a select portion of society contributed to the democratic process. Modern society simply does not

144 U. Pa. L. Rev. 1593 (1996). Copyright © 1996 The University of Pennsylvania Law Review. Reprinted by permission.

foster an environment conducive to the existence of private, armed groups protecting the citizenry.

The militia grew out of an old English custom that was adopted by the colonies, altered to conform to the American experience, and eventually incorporated into the Second Amendment. The citizens' militia developed in England to serve as an effective means of national defense and to counterbalance the strength of a professional army. The English also perceived the militia as a "critical element in their development of 'government under law' "[8] and as a means of tempering the strength of the monarchy. Although the view of the militia as a necessary force to balance the strength of the army gradually changed, such an organization continued to be a politically essential method of regulating the government. During the Enlightenment, the perception that maintaining a citizens' militia was an individual *duty* was transformed into a belief that militia membership constituted an individual *right*.

Colonial acceptance of a militia was compelled by the same concern that led to its existence in England: fear of a standing army. The colonists diverged somewhat from English custom, however, by expanding the right to bear arms to encompass both militia members and individual citizens. In time, as individual constitutions and bills of rights were formulated, a schism over this issue developed among the colonies themselves. The ensuing debate centered on whether to provide solely for a citizens' militia or whether also to provide for an individual right to bear arms.

Shortly after American independence, the need for a militia was reevaluated. The new constitutional system of checks and balances, and the provisions for individual rights, prompted Americans to question if a militia was a necessary restraint on a potentially tyrannical government. The significance of the militia waned, and its function changed considerably. In 1792, Congress enacted the first legislation regarding the militia, emphasizing the structured nature that the militia assumed.[9] The next two centuries witnessed a drastic transformation of the militia's role and general characteristics. Today, the National Guard and similar highly structured and managed military organizations are commonly considered the "militia."

Modern paramilitary organizations seek to reinvigorate the historical role and function of the militia. In addition to the legal obstacles they face, their endeavor to reinstitute a traditional militia is complicated by the sheer expanse of the United States and the diverse and disorganized nature of today's militia movement.

An Inside Look at Today's Militia

The thrust of the new grassroots movement for a state militia has its roots in the original thirteen colonies and their need to band together for the common protection of God-given Natural Rights. The government then was becoming too oppressive and tyrannical. The tolerance level was breached. Could we be witnessing history repeating itself?[10]

Members of private militia groups come from various sectors of society[11] and are spread throughout the United States. Over half the states are believed to have active militia groups and estimates of membership numbers range anywhere from 1,000 to 12,000 supporters.[12] Paramilitary organizations engage in a vast spectrum of activities and maintain a variety of structures. Although paramilitary tactics are the focus of most private militia, militia members also engage in other forms of government protest and participate in community programs. With respect to militia structure and operation, some groups prefer a clandestine approach to their activities, while others are more vocal. Possibly the only element common to the operation of paramilitary organizations is their reliance on computers as a means of communication.

Two predominant complaints about the government provide the rallying cry for private militia groups. First, the militia are infuriated by rampant "government abuse, specifically in the areas of law enforcement and taxation."[13] Belief that the government increasingly subjugates individual rights—an impression fueled by the Ruby Ridge and Waco incidents—compels militia to train ardently in anticipation of a future battle with the government. This belief leads to the militia's second fundamental complaint against government: It undermines their Second Amendment rights to bear arms and form militia.

Despite the aggressive antigovernment position promoted by today's private militia, their paramount goal is *not* to overthrow violently the government. Rather, they strive to protect the citizenry from the federal government. In essence, they aim to bring a renewed justice to the United States,[14] and, to date, in spite of "their alarmist rhetoric, most militia groups stay within the law, advancing their ideas through the usual political process[es]."[15]

Militia members assert that they will defend their ideals to the extent necessary. An examination of a sample militia oath and Militia Declaration of Independence exhibits the earnestness of militia members' convictions: "I _____ promise to defend and observe the Constitutional liberties embodied in the Bill of Rights for all American citizens by example, persuasion, and force of arms if necessary. To that end, I intend to arm myself, I voluntarily join the Free Militia, and I agree to obey its commanders. . . ."[16] A Militia Declaration of Independence provides that

> whenever any Form of Government becomes destructive of these Ends, it is the Right of the People to alter or to abolish it, and to institute new Government, laying its Foundation on such Principles, and organizing its Powers in such Form, as to them shall seem most likely to effect their Safety and Happiness.[17]

Militia members adhere to, and are motivated by, general tenets such as these. The response of private militia to perceived (or perhaps real) threats imposed by the federal government further demonstrates the interrelation of their convictions with their actions. In May 1994, a group of militia members convened in a public park, dressed in military fatigues, with war paint on their faces, and carrying guns. The meeting's purpose was to make their presence publicly known and to promote the message that they exist to protect against an increasingly tyrannical federal government.

In February 1995, an Idaho National Guard helicopter flew over the ranch of Calvin Greenup, a tax protestor. Greenup summoned twenty others, all sporting guns and planning to shoot down the helicopter in the event that it flew over his land again. Militia activists recognized that "[w]hat some call paranoia, Greenup calls patriotism. He's at the volatile fringe of a burgeoning militia movement that believes an armed citizenry is the only way to defend America from a government gone corrupt."[18]

In March 1995, the Texas militia, predicting mass arrests of militia leaders, as well as government-staged bombings that would be blamed on militia groups, called for

> militia leaders to keep weapons nearby, but not on their persons, to avoid providing a pretext for gunning them down. On the other hand, it may also be a good idea if other militiamen remain nearby, armed, with the main events in view. . . . If innocents . . . are to be killed anyway, we need to be able to protect them. . . .[19]

The existence of private militia is often viewed as destructive and anarchistic because they are founded on a fear and distrust of the federal government. They are viewed as paranoid, and many find the combination of paranoia and weapons a dangerous prospect. Militia members are, indeed, motivated by their disenchantment with the government. Nonetheless, negative portrayal of this sentiment as a virulent loathing and near obsession has often led to the creation of a self-fulfilling prophecy. People perceive militia members as fringe elements of society, and the information projected by private militia facilitates the perpetuation of this view. This perception, in turn, fosters continued fear and misunderstanding of militia objectives. The secretive nature of private militia, their training activity, and the proclamations that they will go to extreme ends to fight a tyrannical government further exacerbate the negative public image. The threat, however, if one exists at all, is certainly not imminent. Rather, it appears to be more rhetoric than reality.

Notes

1. In 1992, federal agents raided the Ruby Ridge, Idaho, residence of Randy Weaver, a white separatist. During the ensuing standoff, a United States marshal and Weaver's wife and son were killed.

2. During the 1993 siege of the Branch Davidian compound in Waco, Texas, four federal agents were killed, and 78 Branch Davidians died in the fire that destroyed the compound.

3. On April 19, 1995, a federal building in Oklahoma City was bombed, killing 168 people. The main suspects in the case are believed to be affiliated with a militia group in Michigan.

4. The words "militia" or "paramilitary organizations" should be understood to mean privately sanctioned military groups that convene to promote their views and to train with arms. They do not refer to any form of government funded, or government organized, military entity.

5. *See* Glen Justice, *Today's Militia Units Fighting Mad at U.S.*, PHILA. INQUIRER, Jan. 1, 1995, at B1, B4 ("'Some units are tied to white supremacy groups, and some are not. . . . It's not fair to paint the [entire] movement with that kind of character.'" (alteration in original)). However, the existence of racist sentiment among many militia groups cannot be discounted. Approximately one-fifth of the over 200 militia groups that exist have affiliations with neo-Nazi and white supremacist organizations.

6. William S. Fields & David T. Hardy, *The Militia and the Constitution: A Legal History*, 136 MIL. L. REV. 1, 30–31 (1992).

7. A militia field manual, under the section entitled "Principles Justifying the Arming and Organizing of a Militia," asserts that "[i]f our leaders are corrupted to the extent of imposing tyranny upon the people, then they should be forcefully overthrown and replaced by a legitimate government." MILITIA FIELD MANUAL § 1.1.4: *Principles of a Just War—Capital Punishment* (Free Militia 1994) [hereinafter FIELD MANUAL].

8. *See* Fields & Hardy, *supra* at 9.

9. For an assertion that the organized nature of the militia was not statutorily prescribed until the 1903 Dick Act, see Garry Wills, *To Keep and Bear Arms*, N.Y. REV., Sept. 21, 1995, at 62, 71.

10. Frank Isbell, *The Rebirth of the State Militia*, JUBILEE NEWS REVIEWS, Mar./Apr. 1994, at 7, 7.

11. *See* Mack Tanner, *Extreme Prejudice: How the Media Misrepresent the Militia Movement*, REASON, July 1995, at 42, 45 (reporting that he "met computer programmers, owners of small businesses, professionals, writers and artists, salaried employees, and lots of retired military officers, all well established in America's middle class" while researching the militia movement); *see also* Christopher J. Farley, *Patriot Games*, TIME, Dec. 19, 1994, at 48, 48:

In dozens of states, loosely organized paramilitary groups composed primarily of white men are signing up new members, stockpiling weapons and preparing for the worst. The groups, all privately run, tend to classify themselves as "citizen militias." They are the armed, militarized edge of a broader group of disgruntled citizenry. . . . The members . . . are usually family men and women who feel strangled by the economy, abandoned by the government and have a distrust for those in power that goes well beyond that of the typical angry voter.

12. Klanwatch, a project of the Southern Poverty Law Center in Montgomery, Alabama, publishes a bimonthly newsletter, *Klanwatch Intelligence Report*, which chronicles the findings of the Klanwatch's Militia Task Force. Several of the *Klanwatch* publications contain a comprehensive analysis and study of various militia activity throughout the United States. The June 1995 issue reports that "[a]t least 224 militias and their support groups . . . are active in 39 states." *See also* Dan Billin, *Citizen Militia Followers Invade the Mainstream*, LEBANON VALLEY [N.H.] NEWS, Aug. 31, 1994, at A1, A5 (1,000 core militia members and an additional 10,000 supporters nationwide; movement rather anarchic, with no formal structure.); Ben Macintyre, *Rambo Gets Religion*, THE TIMES (London), Dec. 10, 1994 (Magazine), at 18, 20 (Michigan Militia claims a membership of 12,000; movement has become a national phenomenon through the use of computer networks, fax, shortwave radio, home-produced video, and desk-top publishing).

13. MONTANA HUMAN RIGHTS NETWORK, A SEASON OF DISCONTENT: MILITIAS, CONSTITUTIONALISTS, AND THE FAR RIGHT IN MONTANA, January through May, 1994, at 2 (1994) (chronicling the expansion of far right organizing in early 1994 and reviewing both groups and individuals who have become active during that time).

14. One commentator suggests the antigovernment position supported by private militia is based on the Constitution:

From Michigan to Florida, the militias' claim is the same: the Constitution—guaranteeing a feeble federal government and reserving most power to the 50 states—has been abandoned. In argument with echoes of our own Euro-skepticism, militia-types fear a once proud nation is about to come under the boot of an arrogant, remote superstate.

Jonathan Freedland, *Adolf's US Army*, THE GUARDIAN, Dec. 15, 1994, at T6.

15. David Foster, *Confrontations Spread as Gun-Packing Militias Flourish in Montana*, Associated Press, Mar. 24, 1995, *available in* LEXIS, News Library, AP File (focusing on the Montana militia, particularly Calvin Greenup, a member of the Montana militia who refuses to pay federal income taxes); *see also* Tanner, *supra* at 45 (reporting a militia training leader as stating that "[w]e are not looking for an armed confrontation if we can avoid it. Every week, we pick a political issue based on what the media is reporting, and we crank out a letter on that issue which each member sends to his congressman or senator").

16. FIELD MANUAL, *supra* § 2.4.4.

17. AMERICAN JUSTICE FED'N, DECLARATION OF INDEPENDENCE 1994, at 1 (1994), also assserting that "as Free and Independent Sovereign Citizens, each has the full Power to levy War, conclude Peace, contract Alliances, establish Commerce, and to do all other Acts and Things which an Independent Sovereign may of right do." *Id.* at 3.

18. Internet Newsgroup Posting from Charles Zeps, *ALERT! MILITIAS TARGETED 24/03/95* (Mar. 24, 1995) (on file with author) (including a copy of wire report from Darby, Montana, detailing the story of Calvin Greenup).

Militia groups have also called for all militia units to convene "armed and in uniform, to . . . enforce the ultimatum. The militia will arrest Congressmen who have failed to uphold their oaths of office, who then will be tried for Treason by Citizens' Courts." Memorandum from Linda Thompson, American Justice Federation, to the Federation Membership (Apr. 21, 1994). [The memorandum does not define what the ultimatum is. Ed.]

19. Internet Newsgroup Posting from Jon Roland, Texas Militia Correspondence Committee, *Militia: Potential Threats and Security Therefor* (Mar. 3, 1995) (on file with author).

91

The Changing Faces of White Supremacy

LORETTA J. ROSS AND MARY ANN MAUNEY

White supremacy holds that the interests of people of European descent are superior to those of people who believe, act, or look differently than "normal." It perpetuates the stratification of class, race, religion, sexual orientation, and gender. It embraces Nazism, fascism, and violence. Its open manifestations are extremist hate groups; its results are political and social systems based not on the democratic ideals of majority rule, tolerance, diversity, equality, and justice, but on "white is right." White supremacists are America's deepest nightmare because they attack not only individuals and groups, but the legitimacy of our democratic process itself.

Because the percentage of whites who belong to white supremacist groups is small, many underestimate their influence. What is really significant is not the number of actual members, but the number who endorse their messages. Racists are now having a catalytic effect by tapping into the prejudices of the white majority. They are noticeably influencing public policy concerning central issues of racism, poverty, crime, reproductive rights, civil rights for gays and lesbians, the environment, immigration, and more.

White supremacy is no longer a "faction" belonging to the fringe of mainstream America. While the old Klan and new Nazis are still abhorrent to the vast majority of the American people, their sentiments have been embraced by the public when presented in a more sanitized fashion and disguised as nationalism, patriotism, and family values. The gains of the civil rights movement of the 1960s in the United States have steadily eroded over the past decade, while incidents of racism as well as anti-Semitism, homophobia, and violence against women have risen sharply.

Traditional Hate Groups

Only about 25,000 Americans are hardcore activists for the traditional white supremacist movement, a tiny fraction of the white population. They are organized into approximately 300 different organizations. No two groups are exactly alike—they range from seemingly innocuous religious sects or tax protesters to openly militant, even violent, neo-Nazi skinheads and Ku Klux Klan Klaverns. What they share in common is a desire to create a society totally dominated by whites by excluding and denying the rights of non-whites, Jews, gays and lesbians, and by subjugating women. The movement's links are global, from the pro-apartheid movement in South Africa and the neo-fascists in Germany to robed Klansmen in the deep South.

The activists are the ones on the front lines, promoting the cause, marching, recruiting, and stockpiling weapons. The number of their sympathizers is ten-fold. Hundreds of thousands of others subscribe to racist publications, attend marches and rallies, and donate money. Recorded messages crisscross the country through telephone hatelines, spewing hate-motivated speeches and propaganda while they publicize upcoming meetings and rallies. Independent racist radio and television shows air weekly on traditional airways and short-wave radio. The information superhighway is filled with computer bulletin boards and web pages that spread lies, promote conspiracies, and exploit the fears of millions.

Most white supremacists in America believe that the United States is a "Christian" nation. Because racists give themselves divine permission from God, they often fail to see that their actions are driven by hate; they claim to "just love God and the white race." If they are religious, they distort Biblical passages to justify their bigotry. A popular religion called Christian Identity provides a theological bond across organizational lines. Identity churches are ministered by charismatic leaders who promote racial intolerance and religious division. The tenets of Christian Identity assert that (1) white people are the original Lost Tribes of Israel, and therefore the "chosen" people, (2) Jews are descendants of Satan, and (3) African Americans and other people of color are beasts created by God before He created Adam. Christian Identity followers can attack and murder Jews and people of color without contradicting their religious convictions because they have been told that people of color and Jews have no souls.

Many of the distinctions between various Klan and neo-Nazi groups have dissolved. Members flow in and out because of internal squabbles and leadership battles. Leadership summit meetings and the use of common periodicals are indicators of considerable ideological cohesion. For example, Klansmen, skinheads, and neo-Nazis march together; hatelines promote various publishing houses; any number of groups, particularly skinheads, distribute National Alliance literature; and Posse Comitatus members hail the leadership of Aryan Nations. Their primary point of disagreement is whether to fight for white supremacy through violence, politics, or both.

In the 1960s, the Ku Klux Klan was the best known of the organized white supremacist organizations, with an estimated 40,000 members. By the end of the 1970s, the majority of white supremacists belonged to organizations other than the Klan. They evolved from loosely structured fraternal organizations into highly developed paramilitary groups with extensive survivalist training camps, sometimes funded by proceeds from counterfeit money and bank and armored car robberies. Since then, they have transformed themselves from a violent vanguard into a sophisticated political movement. Currently, Klan groups are on the decline, while more Hitler-inspired groups, like the National Alliance and the Aryan Nations, are growing in numbers. Swastikas and Uzis are replacing hoods and crosses.

At least 26 different Ku Klux Klan groups operate in the United States, most concentrated in the South. Still the largest, but declining in membership, is the Knights of the KKK, headquartered in Harrison, Arkansas, under the leadership of Thom Robb. Robb's Knights were the first to recruit skinheads into their ranks, and he has been quick to put promising young leaders and women into the national spotlight. It is the most Nazi-like of the Klans, maintaining strong ties to Richard Butler's Aryan Nations in Idaho. Originally founded by David Duke in the 1970s, Robb's group has moved into national Klan leadership since the dissolution of the Invisible Empire Knights of the KKK in 1993. It is typical for the 1990s' Klan to disavow violence publicly while secretly encouraging its followers to commit hate crimes under the cover of darkness. They are still known for their "Knight Riders" and the Klan calling cards used to terrorize people.

The Aryan Nations in Idaho is an umbrella organization that unites various Klan and neo-Nazi groups. Spread across the country, members attend annual celebrations of Hitler's birthday at the Idaho encampment. In 1979, founder Richard Butler convened the first Aryan Nations World Congress, attracting Klan and neo-Nazi leaders from the United States, Canada, and Europe to exchange ideas and strategies. This annual summer event has led to greater cooperation among the groups.

An example of a pro-violence religious cult is the Church of the Creator, founded in 1973. Its members are led to believe they are engaged in a racial holy war between the "pure Aryan race" and the "mud races." In 1993, members were among those arrested by the FBI when the Fourth Reich Skinheads attempted to bomb the First AME Church in Los Angeles and assassinate Rodney King. Members have also been arrested in numerous murders, violent assaults, and bank robberies. Their objective is to precipitate the race war by provoking a violent response to attacks upon Jews and people of color. While recent years have seen the influence of the Church of the Creator diminish, its believers are still active in the violent white supremacy movement.

Precursors to the current militia movement were the Posse Comitatus and Christian Patriots. More militantly anti-black and anti-Semitic than more "mainstream" militias, the members of these groups remain part of the anti-government arm of the far right. They protest taxes, social security numbers, and many of the same practices that the militias are protesting. However, their main platform is to distinguish between "14th Amendment" citizens (people of color) and "organic" citizens (white males). Their desire to return to a Constitutional government without the benefit of any Amendment after the 10th is blatant and part of an unashamedly white supremacist agenda.

The Holocaust-denial movement is the clearest expression of the anti-Semitic nature of white supremacy. Various institutions within the white supremacist movement are revising the history of Nazi Germany, insisting that the Holocaust either did not happen or was greatly exaggerated. The most sophisticated and well-financed of these groups is the Institute for Historical Review (IHR) in California. Founded by longtime racist and anti-Semite Willis Carto, the IHR offers hatred with an intellectual gloss. Although control of the IHR was wrested from founder Carto in 1994, it still remains the source of much of the anti-Semitic literature in the hate movement. Carto also founded the Liberty Lobby in the 1950s, and in 1974 began publishing *The Spotlight*, a weekly tabloid with approximately 100,000 paying subscribers. In 1984, he started the Populist Party, which ran David Duke for U.S. President in 1988.

The most violent wing of white supremacy is the growing neo-Nazi skinhead movement, of which there are about 4,000 members in the United States. A relatively new phenomenon on the United States far-right scene—the culture immigrated from Great Britain in the early '80s—their youthful appearance is rapidly changing the face of hate. Girls as well are rapidly rising into skinhead leadership.

Skinhead groups have developed their own leadership and appeal, distinct from adult Klan and neo-Nazi groups. Skinheads committed over 25 murders between 1992 and 1995 and have expanded into 40 states. Most of their victims are African Americans, Latinos, Asian-Americans, gays, lesbians, and the homeless. The typical skinhead assault begins with liquor, drugs, and hate. Rather than wait for the race war to start, they are "doing things to start the race war" according to skinheads arrested in 1994 who attempted to bomb a predominantly black housing project.

Skinheads are the "urban guerrillas" of the hate movement. More seasoned adults have abandoned open violence to sanitize their public images. Such adults recruit and encourage young people to commit crimes, just as older drug dealers use young kids to push drugs. Unfortunately, this means that hate crimes committed by juveniles are often seen as mere pranks, not the serious assaults that they really are. This tactic also frequently allows the adult leaders to escape punishment

All white supremacist groups espouse hatred for those who are not white and Christian. Their major concern is to keep their movement current, and to involve as many others as they can. Their recruiting tactics are more sophisticated than ever, and no longer involve just marching in their robes and hoods.

Recruitment into Hatred

Hate groups in the mid-1990s are refocusing their energies. They realize that they can never convince the majority of white Americans to join them. Although many whites may share their prejudices, very few will turn out with a Klan calling card or an Uzi. The new strategy is to combine old hatreds with new rhetoric and to turn subtle fears into vast conspiracies.

White supremacists cannot be dismissed as simply a few fringe fanatics. Rather, they are part of the larger problem of racism, anti-Semitism, and homophobia. Hate groups often get free publicity from tabloid talk shows eager to boost ratings. Such hosts may hypocritically hold their noses while racists advertise their toughness—and their post office box numbers—on national TV. Thus, many more people are exposed to their message and seduced by their simplistic answers to complex social problems.

White supremacists seek to reinvigorate their movement with new recruits by manipulating fear of change and difference into action. At the same time they are expanding their targets of hate, adopting homophobia and trumpeting anti-abortion, pro-family, and anti-government values in addition to their traditional racist and anti-Semitic beliefs. Broadening the issues and using conservative buzzwords attract the attention of whites who may not consider themselves racist but in their own minds are just patriotic Americans concerned about the moral decay of "their" country. Among the ranks of homophobes, anti-abortionists, racists, anti-Semites, and those who are simply afraid of a fast-changing world, white supremacists find willing allies in their struggle to control America's destiny. The growing militia mentality is one such vehicle used to expand the fear, broaden the hatred, and heighten the scapegoating techniques of recruitment into an ever-growing anti-democratic compulsion sweeping across the country.

In the 1990s, the image of organized hate is rapidly changing. No longer the exclusive domain of white men over 30, the groups are becoming younger and meaner. Many people join the movement as teenagers, including a remarkable number of young women. In the last 10 years, women have joined the racist movement in record numbers—from the White Nurses preparing for racial holy war to female skinheads producing videotapes on natural childbirth techniques. Women recruits account for nearly one-third of the membership of some hate groups. The increase in the number of women, coupled with a strategic thrust to reform the public image of hate groups, has expanded women's leadership. These new recruits do not fit the stereotypical image of wives hanging on their husbands' arms. In fact, many of them are college-educated, sophisticated, and display skills usually found among the rarest of intellectuals in the movement.

Impressionable, alienated people, both young and old, are natural recruits for this movement. They bring new energy and can be induced to act out their hatred aggressively. They can also expand the influence of the white supremacist movement—into the anti-abortion movement, into the anti-gay movement, into the English-only movement, into the militia movement—opening new avenues for the expression of old hatred.

Hatred in the 1990s

No longer able to rely on open racism as an effective recruiting tactic, white supremacists have found more socially acceptable targets for hate—lesbians and gays, immigrants, abortion providers, and the U.S. government. Hatemongers robed in clerical black are scarcely distinguishable from those hiding under white bedsheets, particularly in the eyes of their victims. "Praise God for Aids," a favorite expression of J.B. Stoner, founder of the National States' Rights Party, and "No Special Rights," the slogan promoted by various "mainstream" anti-gay groups, have the same message. Intolerance extends to fear and hatred of lesbians and gay men.

Some white supremacists, living on the United States borders, are petrified at the thought of "brown hordes swarming" into the country to take over. Their violent anti-immigrant militance has now been translated into California's Proposition 187, an "economic" issue. Hate crimes against Latinos have increased proportionately to the rhetoric of "non-racists" who want to "Save Our State."

Others are out to "save" the white race by controlling the behavior of white women and by attacking interracial couples, lesbians, and feminists. They join the anti-abortion movement, believing they can prevent white women from getting legal abortions so that the white race can carry on. Racist far-right organizations have been quick to glorify anti-abortion violence.

Still others want to save the environment for the white race. They infiltrate environmental groups, or switch sides to join the Wise Use movement. They are frantic to exploit the earth's natural resources in order to accumulate wealth before that time early in the 21st century when demographers predict that America will no longer be majority-white. The issues of "state sovereignty" are thinly veiled codes to circumvent federal environmental laws so that federal lands can belong to those who claim them for grazing rights or timber, rather than to the American people.

Conspiracy theories, anti-government outcries, and the fast-growing common law courts are the most sophisticated tactics used yet to ignore democracy. The militia movement actually grew as a result of media coverage after the Oklahoma City bombing. Dissatisfied Americans were *attracted* rather than *repelled* by the promotion of gun power over voting power. The movement has since moved further into "individualism" and "sovereignty" by denying federal and state powers, forming its own court system, and threatening government workers with charges of treason and death. White supremacy ideals heavily feed into the notions of intolerance and anti-democratic rule, through their leaders, through their rhetoric, and through their organizing and communications techniques.

Other hate groups are no longer willing to wait for the white revolution—they are ready to start the "race war" they believe is coming. They want a fast solution before "the white race is extinct." They are now leading the way as a guerrilla strike force, hoping to precipitate the purification of America of all those who are not white, straight, and Christian. Assassination plots, bomb plots, and hate crimes have been the work of those who are in the forefront of the racial battle to save America. The 1990s have seen the violent far right merge with the merely intolerant. From the fanatical to the frustrated to the patriotic, Americans are incorporating the message of white supremacists into their views. The lines between fringe and mainstream American social thought are becoming increasingly blurry.

Few Americans understand the pervasiveness of white supremacy and the importance of its ideology in America's self-definition. Thus, they are unaware of how this ideology has mutated over the years, and how it now blurs the lines between organized racists and their more mainstream counterparts in the religious right and ultra-conservative movements.

For example, recent anti-immigrant sentiments, pushed to the forefront of American politics by California voters, were once the province of white supremacists who organized their own border patrols. The issue of states' rights, used to justify slavery and segregation, is again the subject of state legislation under the guise of Tenth Amendment Resolutions or "unfunded mandates" so that federal civil rights and environmental laws can be ignored. "Scientific" reasoning for racism, provided in the form of Charles Murray's *The Bell Curve*, is just another way of saying that people of color do not deserve to be treated the same as whites. Racism is such a profound and convoluted part of our belief system that Americans don't recognize it when they hear it and don't know it when they practice it. Hate groups have not only pushed their agenda to the forefront of American politics in coded rhetoric, they make "normal" racism seem rational when compared to the overt, violent hatred they espouse.

But it's not just former Klansmen who promote the ideals of white supremacy. In the 1990s the white supremacist movement has been converging with the radical religious right, as represented by Pat Robertson, and with nationalist ultra-conservatives, as represented by Pat Buchanan. This is an alliance of religious determinists, who think that one's degree of Christianity determines one's future; economic determinists, who see themselves in a war of the "haves" against the "have-nots"; and biological determinists, for whom race is everything. Their common belief is that they are battling to save Western civilization (white Europeans) from the ungodly and the unfit (people of color, gays and lesbians, and Jews).

Though the religious right has a tremendous impact on public policy, of the three factions, the ultra-conservatives are best able to mainstream their views. They oppose the social gains of the 1960s and they share strong elements of racism and national chauvinism that can bridge their differences and speak to the frustration of middle Americans. Nativist themes favoring the rights of natural-born Americans over those of immigrants and anyone who is "different" widen their appeal.

While the Klan and other white supremacist groups are seen as being *against* all who are not white, radical conservatives like Pat Buchanan or religious leaders like Pat Robertson of the Christian Coalition prefer to advocate *for* Western civilization and Christianity. This trend continues around a series of issues: gay rights, crime and welfare reform, immigration, English Only, America First nationalism, opposition to NAFTA, and even Holocaust denial. The 1996 elections, featuring isolationist and nationalist themes and ultra-Christianity, presented an opportunity for rapprochement among all sectors of the right, allowing them to begin a backward march to power. The "No Special Rights" and "No Political Correctness" campaigns have their origins in the belief that white supremacy is right for America.

92

Hatelines: Week of Sunday, April 7, 1996

COMPILED BY THE CENTER FOR DEMOCRATIC RENEWAL

Ku Klux Klan, Templar Knights—J. D. Alder

White pride, white pride, white pride. It's great to be white! White man, fight back! First, the good news. Nigger Ron Brown and a gaggle of chief executive officers from American big business died in a beautiful plane crash. The greedy big business CEO's were in Bosnia to help *their* economy, not ours. There will be no tears shed at Klan headquarters over the well-deserved death of a bunch of greedy, scumbag internationalists and businessmen.

In other good news, that old crone, Mother Teresa . . . fell and broke her collarbone. Mother Teresa wastes her time in India fishing mud babies out of trash piles and dumpsters so she can make them grow strong enough to produce more hungry mud babies. . . . And if that wasn't enough good news, in California some real cops gave a bunch of illegal greasers something we'd all like to give them—a sound thrashing with a nightstick. Of course, the brain-dead liberals are rushing to defend the criminals and dump on the cops. Those cops showed too much restraint. They should have beat the spics into a bloody pool of grease. White man, fight back! It's us or them! Jobs for Americans, not spics! Support your local police, not criminals.

In other news, Klansmen and Klanswomen all over America will soon be celebrating the birth of the greatest white man to walk this earth. The date is April 20, and the man the Klan honors is Adolf Hitler. Mark it on your calendar. Have an Adolf Hitler birthday party in your home on April 20th. Make a swastika cake and honor the man who was the first leader of a nation to fight for white power—Adolf Hitler. Hitler was right, the swastika is the supreme symbol of white power. Wear it with pride. The niggers have their "X" and us whites have the swastika. . . .

White man, fight back. . . . It's up to us to step forward, to put our hands to the robe of the Klan, to hold high the Confederate flag and the holy swastika banner[;] . . . make history, not excuses . . .

White Aryan Resistance—Tom Metzger

April is a big month for Aryans, including Uncle Adolf's birthday on April 20th. April is recognized by many as Aryan, or white, history month . . .

[Springtime is] a time of renewal, as the sun moves back towards the northern hemisphere, giving more light and warmth to our native northland. The rebirth of the sun was celebrated by our ancient Aryan ancestors. The cross that Christians use today is the ancient Aryan cross, or sunwheel—another form of swastika . . .
[Breaks to answer questions left by callers.]

Q: How do I pursue a restaurant or any public establishment that discriminates against me just for wearing racial symbols?

A: Tom again advises callers to carry a small tape player at all times to record such encounters. He also consults callers on the procedure for filing a complaint against the establishment in question and even pursuing a case in small-claims court.

Q: Is Ralph Nader a Jew?

A: I think he is but do not have evidence at this time. I must say, however, Nader lives a very austere lifestyle and he does champion several issues . . . that are good for white working people.

Q: What's your position on the Freemen [Montana siege]?

A: Anyone who actively resists the Washington criminals must be given some of our respect. However, Freemen and militias are similar to the old Posse Comitatus of the 70s. There was a lot of smoke in those days but very little fire. It takes a lot more than a lot of big talk and running around the woods with guns. . . . Most of these people will deny up front that they are racists but . . . behind closed doors most of them talk a very racist line. What's really stupid is when they get on TV and claim they're not racist. Many of the acts of the Freemen, Sovereigns, and militias can become suicidal. You know, you don't start a war by barricading yourself on a small farm. You're supposed to have the war, and, if you have to, retreat to the small farm . . .

Q: Does WAR [the White Aryan Resistance. Ed.] have a solution to the mestizo problem? Otherwise known as the invasion from Mexico and "Points South"?

A: Encourage as much frustration as possible among the general public. It is a good issue to push as much as possible. Everyone wants to talk about it. Because even the dumbest whites know something's wrong. A pressure cooker with no escape valve must explode sooner or later. I might surprise you with the following statement, but we are 25% towards our goal [Metzger has been encouraging his followers to call right-wing radio shows and bring up such issues as immigration and race]. We have accomplished 25% of our goal. If you look around at what's being said on talk radio throughout the country. . . you'll see how far we've come in just the last very few years.

Q: Are there any good leaders in Britain?

A: British activists are under heavy legal pressure, and without a First Amendment they are limited very much in some degree . . .

Q: What if there is no upheaval or white revolution? Then what do we do?

A: Then our race is doomed in North America and eventually Europe. It is as simple as that.

The Eagle Hotline—Dan Daniels

Congratulations, you've just called the honest and best white tiger and American Patriot hotline in Florida. . . . It's the only source of truth and straight talk in Florida. If you're white and tired of the tyranny of minorities, you should ask for a membership in the NAAWP [National Association for the Advancement of White People. Daniels is a leading activist in the NAAWP]. . . . Quit talking and start walking. Fight back against black rule in America and [the] desecration of our borders by illegal aliens and Jewish rule of the dollar . . .

Black Ron Brown, wasteful Secretary of the Department of Commerce for Communist Clinton, has been killed in a plane crash in Bosnia. There were over 30 more people, military and civilian, who also died in the crash. To hear Communist Clinton gush over the loss of Brown, one would think that black Brown was God. . . . Ron Brown was under investigation for massive fraud, kickbacks, and conflict of interest. Sodders' tell us he would have gone to jail eventually. Death saved him from that and taxpayers millions of tax dollars every year. Good-bye Ron. Black or white or olive, you're no loss to America.

[Of African Americans, Daniels states] As a collective group and race they are taking America down . . .

We agree with the Freemen of Montana. That America is hopelessly corrupt. But we do not support the forgery and the stealing of funds from others that they are alleged . . . to have done. We compliment the FBI for going slow and easy.

NAAWP courtesy motor patrol[s] often roam the highways of Polk County. Elderly and female motorists who break down are given assistance by these patrols. We'll stay with you until the police or a wrecker arrives. Courtesy of the NAAWP, Polk County, Florida.

Nationalist Free Tip Hotline

Today's free tip is, "White makes Might . . . " The census bureau has recently announced . . . that if immigration and the minority birth rate stay as they are, in 50 years there will be no more America. That's right. The land will be mostly a colony of Mexico, China, and Africa. Unless reversed dramatically and quickly, you will see the collapse of your country within your lifetime. What to do? . . . Run for office, run for the Capitol. Run to power, not from power. Now, what about being a bomber? A terrorist? Bring about mayhem? . . . No, no, no! The idea of the resurrection of America is on trial, and you have to plead your case. You must plead before the American people. Your weapon is logic, and it can be solved only by a pro-majority American policy replacing a pro-minority policy. . . . Now, by this time this fall, would you like to tell how you spent your summer repairing some old fence *or* [starting] a new one against invaders of your country?! Would you like to tell how [you've] been lying in the sun at the beach *or* standing under "Old Glory" in the ranks of the resurrection?! Nationalism—your choice, your chance, your future.

93

Blue by Day and White by [K]night

ROBIN BARNES

The Klan's History—Trail of Violence

Embittered by the South's defeat during the Civil War, early Klansmen set out to keep the "niggers" in their place and to eliminate all scalawags, carpetbaggers, and other northerners who preached political and social equality for blacks. Under the banner "White Supremacy Forever," the group's activities included beatings, lynchings, torture, and mutilation, often inflicted with impunity because judges, politicians, and law-enforcement officers were fellow Klansmen or loyal sympathizers.

In 1871, during its deliberations on what has become widely known as the Ku Klux Klan Act, Congress compiled nearly six hundred pages of testimony dealing with the activities of Klansmen and the inability or unwillingness of state governments to punish their crimes. The following are excerpts of testimony from various jurisdictions:

Indiana: Of the hundreds of outrages committed upon loyal people through the agency of this Ku Klux Klan organization not one has been punished. This defect in the administration of the laws does not extend to other cases. Vigorously enough are the laws enforced against Union people. They only fail in efficiency when a man of known Union sentiments, white or black, invokes their aid.

Kansas: While murder is stalking abroad in disguise, while whippings and lynchings and banishment have been visited upon unoffending American citizens, the local administrations have been found inadequate or unwilling to apply the proper corrective. Combinations darker than the night that hides them, conspiracies, wicked as the worst of felons could devise, have gone unwhipped of justice.

Massachusetts: Now, it is an effectual denial by a State of the equal protection of the laws when any class of officers charged under the laws with their administration permanently and as a rule refuse to extend that protection.[1]

Fifty years later, not much had changed. In 1923, a group of white men, with the help of the Ku Klux Klan, burned down virtually all of Rosewood, Florida, killing dozens of people in the all-black town. No one was ever convicted of the murders, and state officials responded by simply removing the town from the map. Seventy years later, a 1993 legislative initiative to memorialize the massacre, reimburse the black families for their losses, and place the city back on the map opened as follows:

People came from all around to take part in the manhunt. They were people with a thirst for blood. The remaining survivors of Rosewood . . . are still tortured with the lingering image of a parent or grandparent being lynched or shot, of the family home being burned to the ground, of crawling through the woods in the dead of night and hiding from an armed and crazy mob: of being hated and attacked for nothing more than their color.[2]

During the civil rights movement of the 1960s, white terrorists again resorted to burning, bombing, beating, and murder in a futile effort to stop black advances. As had happened a century earlier, these offenders generally avoided arrest by Southern law-enforcement officers and almost never suffered conviction. For example, Joseph Shoemaker, a Northern white activist, was kidnapped in Tampa, Florida, where he was beaten and covered with hot tar. Seven police officers were arrested; loyal Klansmen, all were acquitted after being tried twice.[3] It was simply "not a punishable crime to kill a Negro or civil rights worker."[4] In Jonesboro, Louisiana, the Klan marched through the black section of town behind a sheriff's patrol car in the mid-1960s in mute emphasis that the Klan's effort to prevent blacks from registering to vote was backed by official sanction. A suit was filed in the federal district court of Mississippi against all sheriffs and deputies in the state, the Ku Klux Klan, the head of the Mississippi State Patrol, and the White Citizens' Council for conspiracy to commit terrorist acts.[5]

As the civil rights movement drew to an end with the passage of the Civil Rights Act of 1964 and the Voting Rights Act of 1965, Klan membership dropped to its lowest level ever. But as conservative leaders came to office announcing the need for limits upon the remedial power of civil rights legislation, enforcement of civil rights laws began to wane.[6] Against this backdrop, a new wave of anti-black militancy and polarization escalated throughout the 1980s and well into the 1990s.

Today's Militant White Supremacists

With the technological advances of the past thirty years, such as public-access television[7] and sophisticated computer networks, with military weaponry available, and with an economic base that can support national and international conventions, the purveyors of hate have broadened their scope.

Klan recruitment extends even to children. In Texas, a convicted Ku Klux Klansman was discovered teaching youngsters from an Explorer Scout Post how to fire semiautomatic weapons, decapitate enemies with a machete, and use a garrote. The group's charter application for membership in the Boy Scout Council was rejected when an investigation revealed that boys between the ages of thirteen and nineteen had gone on weekend camping trips that turned into guerrilla-warfare training expeditions. One mother recalls that her son reported a plan to "go on a mission to the Mexican border to watch for illegal alien crossings."[8]

Some groups have been stockpiling weapons stolen from military bases.[9] In 1987, a Klansman army sergeant, his brother, and a friend stole machine guns, TNT, land mines, grenades, and ammunition from Fort Campbell, Kentucky, and Fort Bragg, North Carolina.[10] And unlike many dissident political groups, militant white supremacists have gone beyond self-defense in their use of weapons. Five white supremacists calling themselves "Bruderschweigen [Silent Brotherhood] Strike Force II" were found to be in possession of assassination plans targeting federal judges, prosecutors, FBI agents, a Denver radio talk show host, television producer Norman Lear, and civil rights lawyer Morris Dees. When Dees, the director of the Southern Poverty Law Center, presented evidence of Klan violence before the Alabama legislature, three white supremacists attempted to blow up the group's building. The Klan member on trial for the crime later confessed that not only did they intend to halt Klan prosecutions by blowing up evidence, they intended to kill those participating in an upcoming civil rights march through Montgomery. Local investigators found 123 seven-ounce sticks of dynamite and eight pounds of explosives planted in the downtown sewer system; Klansmen intended to set them off when the marchers were directly overhead. According to a state bomb expert, this was enough to blow up a city block.[11]

The blueprints for militant white supremacist operations over the past ten to fifteen years have been accessible to the public and to government intelligence officers for some time. William Pierce dedicated *The Hunter* to Joseph Paul Franklin, who has not only bombed synagogues but is serving multiple life sentences for the murders of black men; Franklin also advocates the drive-by shooting of interracial couples. Pierce recently began circulating a comic book, "The Saga of White Will," about an avenging teen supremacist in a multicultural high school.[12] Pierce's novel *The Turner Diaries* provides a lurid account of a fictional underground white supremacist group preparing for war. Written to teach white-militant strategy, the book gave birth to The Order, one of the most violent white supremacist organizations in the United States. Leaders of this group orchestrated the robberies of two Seattle banks, the theft of $3.6 million from a Brinks armored truck, the attempted overthrow of the government of Dominica, the sabotage of public utilities, several bombings, and the formulation of a "hit list" of enemies for assassination. Like many of these crimes, the 1995 bombing in Oklahoma City was seemingly inspired by *The Turner Diaries*, which details how a group of revolutionaries constructed a bomb using fertilizer and diesel fuel packed in a large truck that was left in the basement parking garage of a Federal building around 9:00 A.M.—a nearly exact description of the events in Oklahoma City.

History is replete with Klan-style violence that has gone unpunished. In 1980, two Klan members were acquitted by an all-white jury after they gunned down four black women in Chattanooga, Tennessee, in a drive-by shooting. A third participant was given a nine- to twenty-month prison sentence. All-white juries have twice acquitted neo-Nazis and Klansmen of criminal charges for their roles in the shootings of five men at an anti-Klan rally in Greensboro, North Carolina. While the jury was deliberating in the second trial, six fellow neo-Nazis were charged with conspiring to set off a series of bomb explosions in Greensboro if the jurors came back with a guilty verdict. The jury hung, and the judge was forced to declare a mistrial. In July 1992, Klansman Shawn McElreath was sentenced to four years in prison for attacking a black man in Asheville, N.C.; he was paroled five months later. An all-white jury acquitted Robert Setzer and James Shook in the stabbing death of two black students in a racially charged fight at Lenoir (N.C.) High School, just days after the Christian Knights of the Ku Klux Klan marched in that city. When thirteen Klan and neo-Nazi defendants were acquitted by an all-white jury in Fort Smith, Arkansas, on charges of sedition, 150 white supremacists gathered to celebrate their release. In the late 1980s, two separate Ku Klux Klan defendants were acquitted on grounds of self-defense after killing Mexican-Americans in the town of Cedartown, Georgia, although the Klan had indulged in a "reign of terror" for more than two years that included threatening Mexican-Americans with death unless they stayed off the streets.

The terrorism that has followed publication of *The Turner Diaries* has been embraced by those closely associated with the Aryan Church of Jesus Christ Christians (ACJCC), informally known as Identity Religion. Richard Butler, founder of Aryan Nations (a related organization), purchased a twenty-acre site in northern Idaho to provide a permanent haven for the most committed Klansmen, neo-Nazis, and their sympathizers. Although Butler has settled in Hayden Lake, Idaho, law-enforcement authorities confiscated five tons of munitions from a bunker he had built in California. Identity members have murdered blacks and Jews, ambushed U.S. marshals, and conducted paramilitary training unmatched by any other hate group.[13] Newer Klan-style organizations (e.g., The Sword, the Covenant and the Arm of the Lord) subscribe to the revolutionary racist theology of Identity Religion. Some of the earliest proponents of Identity are believed to be responsible for two separate mail bombings that fatally injured the Georgia civil rights leader Robert E. Robinson and U.S. Court of Appeals Judge Robert S. Vance of Alabama.[14] The man accused of the bombings contends that they were the organization's revenge against the Eleventh Circuit judges for upholding an $800,000 judgment against the Georgia faction of the Invisible Empire and its leaders for violence against the participants in a 1987 civil rights march in Forsyth County, Georgia.[15] Richard Butler has convened the Aryan Nations World Congress and the Christian Patriot Freedom Festival at the Hayden Lake compound. Leaders in the white supremacist movements of Canada, Europe, and the United States gathered to exchange information, ideas, and strategies. According to the new rallying cry they all have one thing in common: Identity.

Identity Religion teaches racial separatism, extreme anti-Semitism, and that northern Europeans are the true descendants of the lost tribes of Israel. Butler fulminates about "Satanic Jews," "nigger wenches," and "the glory of the Third Reich," calling upon Identity members to preserve the essence of the white race as preordained by God's law. A videotape of one of his sermons features this admonition: "[Because there are] adversaries in the land, hatred is our law and revenge is your first duty."[16] Recruiting has largely focused upon white inmates of U.S. prisons, whom Identity leaders characterize as political prisoners held by ZOG, the Zionist Occupation Government. A number of prison-law cases feature white supremacists, convicted of violent crimes, seeking to import pamphlets or to conduct services and classes within the prison system in an effort to attract new recruits.

Efforts to schedule Identity Religion worship services in prison were quickly defeated in *McCabe v. Arave*,[17] which held that nothing in the First and Fourteenth Amendments required the state to tolerate them. That case concerned several prisoners in the Idaho State Correctional Facility who were members of ACJCC (Identity Religion). The warden denied them permission to conduct worship services in the prison chapel, hold group study sessions, or distribute Identity literature to white inmates, based upon his finding that ACJCC is not a recognized religion and that admitting the organization into the prison system would create serious security problems. Earlier, a black inmate's cell door had been torched to leave the outline of a cross; another black inmate had been beaten by a group of whites affiliated with Identity.[18] These incidents, coupled with reports of various problems at corrections facilities nationwide, reveal the substantial threat that Identity Religion poses within and outside of the prison system.

Notes

1. CONG. GLOBE, 41st Cong., 2d Sess., 505, 374, 334 (1871).
2. Lori Rozsa, *Massacre in a Small Town in 1923*, ATLANTA J. & CONST., Jan. 17, 1993, at M1.
3. Mary Jo Melone, *Dark Days, and Crime Paid*, ST. PETERSBURG TIMES (Florida), June 21, 1987, at 51.

4. Michael R. Belknap, *The Vindication of Burke Marshall: The Southern Legal System and the Anti–Civil Rights Violence of the 1960s*, 33 EMORY L.J. 93 (1984).

5. *See U.S. v. Price*, 383 U.S. 787 (1965) (reversing and remanding lower court opinion).

6. *See generally* NORMAN AMAKER, CIVIL RIGHTS AND THE REAGAN ADMINISTRATION (1988).

7. *See Missouri Knights of the Ku Klux Klan v. Kansas City, Mo.*, 723 F. Supp. 1347 (W.D. Mo. 1989) (upholding cause of action by KKK members seeking to enjoin cable company from deleting public-access channel on grounds that the channel had become a "public forum"); *see also U.S. Says Supremacists Targeted T.V. Shows*, N.Y. TIMES, Jan. 28, 1991, at A15.

8. *Paramilitary Actions Irk Neighbors of Texas Camp*, N.Y. TIMES, Nov. 30, 1980, at 67.

9. Hearing on Terrorism in the United States: The Nature and Extent of the Threat and Possible Legislative Responses Before Senate Comm. on Judiciary. Apr. 27, 1995.

10. *Ibid.*

11. Richard E. Meyer, *The Long Crusade: Morris Dees Has Battled the Klan for More Than a Decade; Now His Target Is Tom Metzger and the White Aryan Resistance*, L.A. TIMES, Dec. 3, 1989, at 14.

12. Bill Lambrecht, *Radical Right Has Articulate Spokesman: Author and Broadcaster Seems Highly Influential*, ST. LOUIS POST-DISPATCH, Apr. 26, 1995, at B5.

13. Joshua Hammer, *The Trail from Three Racial Slayings Leads Back to a Ring of Neo-Nazi Fanatics in Idaho*, PEOPLE, Aug. 29, 1983, at 44.

14. Michael Tackett & Mary T. Schmich, *Fourth Mail Bomb Found; Racial Motives Probed*, CHI. TRIB., Dec. 20, 1989, at 1; *A Chronology of the Mail Bombs Case*, Atlanta J. & Const., June 29, 1991, at A12.

15. *McKinney v. Southern White Knights*, No. 89–8092, slip op. (N.D. Ga. 1989), reh'g denied, F.2d 346 (1989), cert. denied 493 U.S. 957 (1990).

16. Paul Hendrickson, *Going to Extremes in Idaho*, WASH. POST, Oct. 27, 1992, at C1 (The original church was founded in 1946 by Wesley A. Swift, who with Bertrand L. Comparet developed its religious tenets: Aryans are the chosen people of God, blacks and Jews are the offspring of Satan and Eve; a race war is inevitable under the prophecy of Armageddon).

17. 626 F. Supp. 1199, 1206 (D. Idaho 1986).

18. *Id.* at 1203.

94

The Race Question and Its Solution

JAMES ARMSTRONG, JR.

The political doctrine of the equality of men is a beautiful, but self evident lie. There is no equality among people of even the same blood.

Nature delights in nothing so much as in the inequality of her products. She revels in unlikenesses, in differences, in disparities. She endows the brain of one man, or one race, with the noblest genius, while to another she gives scarcely anything at all, except a brutal instinct to satisfy the simplest of animal needs and passions. We see it in the contemplation of savage and civilized man—in the difference between the tools, the customs, the laws and the languages of a rude and those of a cultured race.

Nature is not like a plain where everything exists on a dead level of unbroken uniformity. As the surface of the earth is varied by the inequalities of mountain, hill and valley, so are mankind diversified into superior and inferior races. Racial diversity is unmistakably manifest. There are the Patagonians and the English; the Esquimaux and the French—racial extremes of physical, intellectual and moral development.

Nature stamps each product of her handiwork with an indelible mark of its value. Between the negro and the caucasian the line of demarkation is clearly and distinctly drawn. It is impossible to overlook it. It is as plain as the Mississippi dividing the States between which it flows. So, without prejudice and without abuse, it may be said the negro is vastly the inferior of the white man. As a race, he is physically, intellectually and morally lower—as much lower than the white man as the cannibal is lower than he. It is needless to point out his inequality, his inferiority, in detail; for it stands to reason that if he were the peer of the dominant race, he would also parallel it in substantial and lasting achievement. Lack of numbers is not enough to account for his inferiority.

It is not the quantity, but the quality, of a people that determines its degree of excellence. Nature gives us nothing. A race, like an individual, pays in some way for all that it gets. The white man has done the most and, therefore, has suffered the most—has felt more than all others the wear and tear, the storm and stress, of the struggle to be and to do. And within him there must be some inherent principle of superiority, the result either of his own nature or his surroundings, that gave him the start and still keeps him at the head of the long and varied procession of civilization. There is no survival except that of the fittest; no freedom except that of the wise. It is not a question of goodness and kindness, but of strength and intelligence. Character is the creature of conflict. It is born of the vigilant, the active and aggressive life. The white man must struggle, must fight, in one way or another,

From DISFRANCHISEMENT PROPOSALS AND THE KU KLUX KLAN: SOLUTIONS TO THE NEGRO PROBLEM, PART I, edited by John David Smith. Originally published in 1903, San Antonio, Texas. Reprinted by permission of Garland Publishing, Inc.

for the position he aspires to among his equals, and his inferiors will meet with the utmost resistance in their efforts to rise to his level.

But nowhere does this truly gladiatorial conflict rage so fiercely as among unlike and unequal peoples, whom the accidents of progress have thrown together in an original relation of master and slave.

The Problem

As this volume is intended to be popular and, therefore, practical, it will burden itself but little with scientific and historical research. It is assumed that the reader is fairly well acquainted with existing social and political conditions in the United States, and especially with the career of the negro since his introduction therein as a slave a few centuries ago. It may also be stated that the inferiority of the negro is not the paramount question, which is the setting forth of a plan by which he may be placed in, or rather permitted to assume, the field of his most useful endeavor.

What, then, is the race problem and in what does it consist? Under existing conditions which have prevailed in some form throughout civilization, there is a severe and unavoidable competition among all kinds of breadwinners. It varies in acuteness, according to the conditions that surround the wageworker, as illustrated in the conflicts between union and non-union labor. Capitalism, like its predecessor, monarchy, has a natural tendency to narrow the sphere of individual opportunity. It shuts out, for the most part, the small but independent speculator and promoter. The effect of this is to divide society into two classes—capitalists and laborers—of whom there is the smallest number of the former and the greatest number of the latter. In the course of time, the opportunity to make thousands, to say nothing of millions of dollars, becomes as scarce as the opportunity to find employment.

The struggle of the breadwinner is slowly intensified. Even now, the Government appreciates this, and attempts to modify it by a complete or partial exclusion of certain classes of foreigners. Such is the labor problem that is now vexing the North and the East. The race problem in the South is of exactly the same nature. It has an additional element of social danger and disaster, however, in the striving together of a servile and inferior and a proud and superior race. Our problem is thus twofold, involving, as it does, the labor question in general and the race question in particular. The double evil that we endure arises directly from a single cause—the competitive struggle for existence. In the first place, the white man is jealous of the white man, but infinitely more so of the negro.

The aggressive tendency of the white man, on the one hand, to confine the negro to strictly menial functions, at the lowest wages, and the equally aggressive tendency of the negro, on the other, to rise to higher and more remunerative employment, which he cannot do without displacing white men to the extent that he succeeds, gives rise to an irrepressible conflict between the races, which must eventuate, if things continue as they are in either the actual extermination of the negro, or in his reduction to a state but little better than that of beggary. The struggle between white men may be said to be wholly mercenary. But that between the white man and the negro is not only mercenary, but involves the passion of prejudice. Above, or perhaps below all things, he is a "Nigger," and there is no one who dares to assert that he is entitled to anything more than such humane treatment as is usually shown to animals. And his claim to this is forfeited, if he does not humbly subordinate himself to the powers that be. Attempting, as he has so often attempted, to better himself by political action, he has been constantly thwarted by every expedient of fraud and force. His ballot has been for the most part miscounted or destroyed, and growing tired at last of intimidation, bribery and deception, the people of some of the Southern States have practically disfranchised him by artful constitutional amendments.

Fine spun theorists of universal brotherhood, as well as the milder victims of Jeffersonian equality, may condemn this as much as they please, but in the end it is the right, the moral and most beneficent course to be pursued.

Prejudice as a Factor of Progress

If the negro were educated and cultured, should he be admitted to political and social equality with the white man? Assuming, as I do, that the Anglo-Saxon stands on the summit of human achievement, the question resolves itself into a consideration of how progress comes about. If it can be shown that the great exemplars of civilization, those who have taken the raw material of the universe and wrought it into a place of wondrous and beauteous abode, were developed and are still maintained by the possession of race-qualities that tend to the subduing and extermination of inferior stocks, and that it was natural and wholesome for the conquering caste to visit contempt and opprobrium upon the victim and subsequent slave, to the remotest generation, it may also be shown that any private or public act which has the effect of neutralizing the prejudice, by which alone this natural order of things is secured, is pernicious and to be repressed.

Within historic times, the Aryan race still stands, as it has always stood, at the head of the human procession. How does it come to hold that place, and having attained it, how does it keep it? Clearly, through nothing else than courage and intelligence, devoted to the subjugation and extermination of the inferior races. Out of this there comes an amalgamation or fusion of the best elements of racial life, effected almost entirely by prejudice, resulting in what we call progress. I can do no better here than produce the language of Herbert Spencer:

"Many sundry instances point to the conclusion that a society formed from nearly allied peoples, of which the conquering eventually mingles with the conquered, is relatively well fitted for progress. From their fusion results a community which is left capable of taking on new arrangements, wrought by new influences.

"Between organisms, widely unlike in kind, no progress can arise. The physiological units contributed by them respectively to form a fertilized germ cannot work together so as to produce a new organism. If the two organisms are less unlike in kind—belonging say to the same genus, but to different species, they will co-operate in making an organism that is intermediate. But this, though it will work, is imperfect in its latest evolved parts, and there results a mule incapable of propagation."

A mule, though educated and cultured, is still a mule; and since a permanently fertile breed can result only from peoples nearly allied—"hybrid societies being imperfectly organizable"—"incapable of growing into forms completely stable"—that is, they cannot contribute to the advancement of the world from the Aryan, the successful standpoint, it is proper not only to regard miscegenation as a crime, but also any attempt that tends to lift the negro to a social level with the white man as reprehensible.

To take a single instance: The dining of a representative negro by a representative white man is wholly unjustifiable, and those who, from the motives of prejudice, rather than from philosophical reasons, condemn him for such conduct, conserve, whether knowingly or unknowingly, the best interests of society and civilization. If the act began and ended with the mere consumption of a meal, it would amount to nothing. But the essence of the matter is that a representative man of the Aryan has entertained upon terms of social equality a representative man of the negro race.

A thoroughbred jackass has dined with a thoroughbred mule.

If the negroes were a tribe which it was important to conciliate concerning the safety or perpetuity of the Government of the United States, it might be excusable to wine and dine them. But since they are representative of nothing with which the world could not have easily dispensed, in so far as its success has been concerned, the dining of a big mule by a big jackass is simply an exhibition of asinine folly. The negro as a vehicle of progress and civilization, compares to the Aryan as the simple ox-cart to the compound locomotive. And though the negro, through industrial education, become greater than the fabled stithies of Vulcan, and through dining with Presidents, come at last to feed on Mount Olympus itself, he will thrive there as a lichen rather than an oak, while the Aryan, the Caucasian, the present American, is and shall ever be the Empire Express of progress and civilization.

Industrial Education

The wisest of the race have given up the salvation of the negro by the ballot. By "salvation" is meant nothing less than the lifting up of the negro, first, to a position of political, and afterward, social equality, with the white man. It can mean nothing else, for the negro has no greater love for work in itself than the white man has. If he is really progressive, therefore, he wishes power, the single object of all human endeavor.

How much power does he want? Is it possible to believe that he will at some time say—just so far will I go and no farther? Does he deny that he aspires in the long run not only to political and social equality, but even to supremacy itself? If so, he admits his inferiority and justifies the idea of the white man that he should fall in the rear of the procession of civilization. Does he assert the contrary? If he does, he makes an assertion to which every fact of history, science and philosophy is forever opposed. Having learned something of the expedient policies of the white man, the negro is beginning to hide his real motives by going out of politics and taking up industrial education.

As an independent industrial worker, he is being assisted by a lot of mistaken philanthropists who are after a spurious and pernicious sort of fame. They are the perverts of progress and the degenerates of development, who have a mania akin to that of gambling or yachting for the endowment of colleges and the setting up of universities.

Admitting that the negro is really progressive and capable of the highest possible development, can it not be seen that industrial education would afford him the leverage with which he might at last upset the world? Retaining the right of property, he can give up without loss the right of suffrage, and eventually obtain the very thing he is after—political and social supremacy, that is, if he is not incapable of the physical, intellectual and moral advancement that the ideal of industrial education presupposes?

There is also a mistaken idea on the part of many white men, who think the making alone of a skilled workman of the negro will solve the race problem. For the most part, they are those who do not come in contact with him as a breadwinner, and who do not care what becomes of their own race, so long as they themselves are comfortably situated. Such men are the sharks of their species—crass capitalists who would not only work white and black alike at starvation wages, but would coin the blood of the cradle into the sterling of their own enrichment. You cannot add to the number of skilled or unskilled workmen, under present conditions, without causing a fall in wages and a rise in dividends. The owners of factories know this, and under the guise of philanthropy, it is the single object of their efforts; and the intelligent negro, who subserves them, is doing more to hasten a conflict between the races than all the worst criminals of his own people can possibly do.

The evil that the negro criminal may from time to time inflict upon society will be forgotten with the punishment or death of the offender, but the bread that the skilled mechanic would constantly take and increasingly take from the mouth of his white competitor, would keep the fires of hatred and prejudice perpetually burning; and if by industrial education, he is to take more and more, which he must do, if it is to benefit him as it should, the blaze that now flickers will be rapidly blown into a fierce and all-consuming conflagration.

[The author goes on to discuss materialism, capitalism, the role of women, and the cause of prostitution. Ed.]

Solution of the Problem

There are just four possible solutions of the race problem. They are: Extermination, expatriation, amalgamation and subordination. The first is impractical, because it means the murder of one race by another. The second is not feasible, not only because it could not be effected without a resort to violence, but also because it is not to the interest of the white man for the negro to emigrate. The third is not to be considered at all because it would result in the degeneracy of both races, from the mingling of racial organisms, widely unlike in kind, and out of which no progress could arise. In the fourth, therefore, we must seek the solution of the problem.

The race problem consists of nothing more than the conflict of the white man and negro as breadwinners. The conflict must cease, for as long as they are competitive laborers, the problem will endure. There are but two ways in which the negro can be taken out of competition with the white man, one of which is perfectly foolish and the other thoroughly sensible. First, let the Government give every negro a pension that shall place him above the necessity of labor; second, let it industrialize him to the advantage of the dominant race.

Such industrialization should be brought around indirectly, that is the negro should be left free to choose between what to him would seem two evils—leaving the country, or remaining in it upon such terms as the white man proposed. The United States belong to the white man by the right of conquest. The white man is still in possession of the country and he has no better title to it than his ability to defend it. It is to the best interest of humanity that its government should be confided to the superior race. If it can be demonstrated that the negro is the superior race, it should be confided to him. If the equal of the white, he should have an equal share. If the inferior of the white man, he should be assigned to an inferior position.

The successful conduct of a nation consists in nothing more than the application of sound business principles upon the broadest possible scale. There has never been a government, however, that was conducted according to sound business principles. For that reason they have all become bankrupt considerably before their time. The lust of conquest has killed the most of them by overtaxing the energy of their people. Take a newspaper, for instance.

It employs both skilled and unskilled labor. The functions of the employees are both of an inferior and a superior kind. Wherein should the direction of a nation differ from the direction of a newspaper? Whether made up of one race or of different races, should not its highest functions be carried on by those who are the most qualified to do so? If composite, should not the services of each race be determined by its capacity regardless of sentimentality? Should not the management of a nation be confided to its brain and the labor to its brawn? Should it not even guard itself against the possible evil of the worst elements of the dominant race coming to the discharge of its supreme function—government—to say nothing of its being carried on by an inferior and therefore incompetent race? Are you surprised then, that the United States are fast becoming a bankrupt nation, that the most of their people are tenants and wage earners, that the Government is hopelessly in debt, that it is menaced with revolution and harassed with many and serious questions that shall overwhelm the country with ruin, unless they are solved?

What are we to do? Take the negro and other inferior races in our midst out of competition with the white man. Subordinate them to him. That labor which the white man is not ambitious to do, should be left entirely to the negro, who, in case he was not numerous enough, could be assisted by Chinese and other Asiatic immigrants. They should be placed in exactly the same relation to the white man that the wage earner is now to the capitalist. The present system of taxation could be made to redound to the especial benefit of the governing class, and as capitalism now exploits labor, the white man would then exploit the negro, with the difference of most liberal treatment of the subject class.

But even if the negro's condition were as hard as that of the coal miners of the Northern and Eastern States, and millions of other white men, women and children, whose labor scarcely keeps them from starving, would it not be better for the welfare of all concerned? There is no more reason why the white men of this country should do its manual labor than there is for the landlord to till his own farm. To emancipate the white man—that is, to take the superior and inferior races out of competition—therefore, will settle at once both the race problem and the labor problem.

The Justification

If it is right for the white man to pile up the most colossal fortunes out of the misery and death of white men—his equals—would it be wrong to do the same thing at the expense, but without the oppression, of the negro—his inferior? The existing social condition is a horrible realization of popular ignorance and political absurdity. It makes no distinction between the capable and incapable, the virtuous and the vicious, the wise and the ignorant. It does not do the best that can be done for either the negro or the white man.

Under the social condition that I propose the negro would be infinitely better off and the possibilities of the white man for development would become unlimited. The brain of the country could be given to the truly intellectual, while its brawn would be engaged in the cultivation of the material resources of a civilization that, within a few generations, would stand forth as the richest and the mightiest the world has seen. With the disappearance of poverty on all sides, crime would disappear, and unless the creation of a perfect society, that is, a society adapted in every way to the pursuit of its noblest development, is merely the dream of a visionary, immorality of all kinds would be reduced to an absolute minimum.

The success of the new system would be assured because it would be in harmony with the laws of nature. There need be no exercise of any direct authority over the modern helots. They would simply be given the choice of leaving the country, or remaining in it upon the terms of its owners—a relation between the two races that is identical with that of landlord and tenant. The negro could not reasonably ask for anything more, since it would be injurious to the white man to grant him anything more. They are forbidden by nature to mingle their bloods, upon the penalty of begetting a stock that hastens to extinction.

An inferior people cannot make a wholesome use of powers that belong solely to the superior. They must not only be taken out of competition, therefore, but they must not come into contact, either socially or politically. The sentimental notion that ignores the natural and unalterable differences among men is more foolish than that which would permit the intermingling of scrub and thoroughbred cattle. We have no more reason to believe that the negro will ever rise to the level of the white man than we have for believing the monkey will rise to the level of the negro, and the white man should as strongly and unfailingly resist social equality with the negro as the negro would oppose the same with the anthropoid apes.

Evolution is a continuous ascent. Natural conditions are variable and inequalities are everywhere inevitable. Any kind of leveling system, whether democratic or despotic, cannot but be attended with the utmost disaster to the highest interests of humanity. The inequalities must be preserved, or rather not interfered with, that the process of growth may not be arrested. It is nothing more than the organization of the white race into a mighty trust—the landlord of a national farm called the United States of America. If the negro did not wish to become the tenant, he could be permitted to leave. Overcrowded and impoverished Asia would quickly and gladly furnish all the laboring population that might be desired. It would be impossible for the negro to leave—impractical for the white man, if he could.

The only difficulty to be anticipated is the regulation of population, a difficulty which would certainly yield to a well developed science of stirpiculture. The negro would then have a chance to work out his highest destiny. If it turned out that he is possessed of the high attributes of character and intelligence, he would not be hindered in the final establishment of himself in a land of his own, if the territory were available and he had a disposition to go. A system of various and just reward for personal worth and achievement could be easily instituted among both races. The idea now is that if a man is born rich, he may live without labor, at the expense of the workers. The idea then would be that if a man was born white, he could do the same. If he was born black or yellow, he would have to work for a living.

We make some effort to recognize true merit now; it could be done infinitely better then. And in it all there is nothing impractical, nothing utopian, nothing visionary. It is simply the reduction of national right living to a science, which would be as exact as any, except, perhaps that of mathematics. It is based on the highest utility, the most refined materialism, and it is in this it finds it supremest justification.

95

The American Neo-Nazi Movement Today

ELINOR LANGER

. . .

In writing about a subject that carries with it the automatic weight of its association with Nazi Germany, I find myself . . . suspended between caution and alarm. Especially about a movement as underreported as this one, you do not write, in the first place, merely to observe "This too will pass away"; you write to sound an alert. At the same time, you know that the tests of time are different and that historians of another generation will consider the evidence and say either that it was all simply part of another "Brown Scare" in which people, as usual, lost their heads, and some their civil liberties, or that a dangerous movement was on the rise and that we failed to discern it early enough and help stamp it out. I do not know where along that spectrum the truth of the neo-Nazi movement lies. I do know that it is among us, that it is violent and mean, and that it is time to open up the subject for further investigation and discussion so that out of a broader base of information and a variety of perspectives there can possibly be fashioned a sound response.

In using the term neo-Nazi, I am referring roughly to an array of groups and individuals, including:

- Nazis: old-line groups principally descended from the American Nazi Party founded by George Lincoln Rockwell in 1959, whose members still appear in uniform, as well as other small Nazi-identified parties and groupings whose members usually do not.
- The skinheads: youth gangs in various cities with names like Youth of Hitler and the Confederate Hammerskinssome, like San Francisco's American Front, openly connected with [Tom] Metzger's WAR [White Aryan Resistance], and some not; skinheads are the fastest-growing wing of the movement today.
- The Ku Klux Klan: no longer the centralized Klan of previous eras, but three separate and rival Klan federations and innumerable splinter groups; it is a government-infiltrated and at times government-manipulated Klan, a shadow of its former self, many of whose units are, however, "Nazified" in that they cooperate freely with the Nazi groups (something that was unthinkable in the past, when the Klan's patriotism and the Nazis' Germanophilism invariably clashed) and share many of the same ideas.
- The Posse Comitatus: a decentralized, antistate and largely rural movement, which also appears as the Christian Patriots or American Freemen Association, whose adherents believe,

Research for this essay, originally published in *The Nation*, was supported, in part, by grants from the Fund for Investigative Journalism and the Dick Coldensohn Fund. Copyright © 1990 by Elinor Langer. Reprinted by permission of Georges Borchardt, Inc., for the author.

among other things, that all government should be rooted at the county level and that cooperating with any higher authority, including the I.R.S. or, indeed, even the state Department of Motor Vehicles, is wrong.

- The Christian Identity movement: an Aryan-inspired religious denomination descended from a nineteenth-century movement known as Anglo-Israelism or British Israelism, which holds that the "chosen people" of the Bible are white Anglo-Saxons, that Jews are descended from Satan and that all nonwhites are "pre-Adamic" "mud people," a lower species than whites; it is a religious movement that, as in the case of Idaho's Aryan Nations—Church of Jesus Christ, Christian (as opposed to Jesus Christ, Jew), is often indistinguishable from a political one.

The Nature of the Movement

In the phrase "neo-Nazi movement" both the terms "neo-Nazi" and "movement" require further discussion, and they have to be argued together. . . . Klanwatch Project of the Southern Poverty Law Center (S.P.L.C.) in Montgomery, Alabama . . . uses the overall heading "white supremacist" and reserves "neo-Nazi" for the groups that had their genesis with Rockwell. The term "white supremacist" is also used by another major monitoring organization, the Center for Democratic Renewal in Atlanta. The problem with this usage, it seems to me, is not that it is wrong but that it does not go far enough, retaining an old-fashioned, unduly Southern and narrowly political flavor that fails to reflect the modern racialism that comes to us directly from the Nazi era and that I think is the essential characteristic these groups share. The neo-Nazi label does have varying degrees of applicability. James Farrands, Imperial Wizard of The Invisible Empire, Knights of the Ku Klux Klan, with whom I spoke a few months ago, was indignant at being associated with neo-Nazis and at pains to assure me that "you don't have to be a Nazi to be an anti-Semite," and to find a member of the Posse Comitatus with the same revulsion would not be difficult. But for the most part these organizations have no enemies to the right. If there are those within the movement who object to their Nazi bedfellows, they do not generally make themselves heard.

More important than any differences among the groups is . . . that the individuals within them function together as a movement and know that they are one—a point on which the two monitoring organizations mentioned above, as well as the Anti-Defamation League of B'nai B'rith (A.D.L.), largely agree. Klan and Nazi units have worked together at least since their combined assault on anti-Klan demonstrators at a rally in Greensboro, North Carolina, in 1979, in which five were killed, three of them members of the Communist Workers Party. Klan/neo-Nazi joint appearances on occasions such as an annual gathering in Pulaski, Tennessee, honoring the founding of the Klan, this year also attended by Aryan Nations pastor Richard Butler, have become routine. . . . Kim Badynski, who recently relocated to the Northwest from Chicago, where his Klan faction was closely associated with various Nazi groups, is now close to pastor Butler and the Aryan Nations group in Idaho, at whose compound he has often appeared with . . . Rick Cooper, publisher of a newsletter called "National Socialist Vanguard Report" who is proud to call himself a Nazi and would probably satisfy anyone's definition. Other visitors to the Idaho compound, whose annual Aryan Nations congress has been one of the central gathering points of the movement for several years, have included skinheads, Identity Christians, Posse associates and so on. An Aryan martyrs list saluted throughout the movement would include not only Robert Mathews, founder of the violent brotherhood called "The Order," whose death in a 1984 shoot-out with the F.B.I. on Whidbey Island, Washington, is commemorated by an annual vigil, but also Gordon Kahl, a North Dakota Posse farmer convicted of tax evasion who killed two federal marshals attempting to serve a warrant for probation violation in 1983, and was himself killed in an F.B.I. shoot-out in Arkansas a few months later. The mail-order catalogues of the Christian Patriots, a Posse group, and of the National Vanguard, a West Virginia Nazi group begun by Rockwell-follower William Pierce, not only offer many selections in their specialized areas (roughly, European prehistory and myth, in the case of the Nazis; the monetary system, in the case of the Patriots) but often overlap, featuring not only such classics as Carleton Putnam's *Race and Reason* (which is still winning converts) and Henry Ford's *The International Jew* but such newer and highly influential tracts as *The Hoax of the Twentieth Century* by Arthur Butz and *Did Six Million Really Die?* by Richard Harwood. If there is a household of an adherent of any wing of the movement that does not have a copy of *The Turner Diaries*, Pierce's fantasy of the violent overthrow of the U.S. government by patriotic guerrillas, I would be surprised. . . .

The reader would undoubtedly like to know how many people are involved, a point on which the available data are unfortunately not very good. Estimates made by the three monitoring organizations mentioned above range from about 10,000 to about 20,000 members of these groups nationally, with the organizations agreeing on a rule of thumb of about ten passive supporters for every hard-core member and thus a possible total of up to 200,000 and agreeing as well that the numbers are conservative. The larger number, which by some counts includes an additional 30,000 Christian Identity followers, is also presumed to include the 100,000 or so subscribers to a Washington, D.C.–based newspaper called *The Spotlight*, published by an ideologically similar but stylistically dissimilar far-right organization, the Liberty Lobby, founded in 1957 by Willis Carto, who also founded the revisionist Institute for Historical Review and the contemporary Populist Party, as well as the 44,000 people who voted for the 1988 Populist presidential candidate, David Duke. . . .

Tom Metzger

There is a dynamism at work here that any static accounting, whether of "members" or "incidents," cannot reflect. Tom Metzger is one of the principal sources of that dynamism, as his television program makes clear.

"Hi, this is Tom Metzger, your host for *Race and Reason*, the longest-running show of its type on cable access TV, seen in approximately fifty cities across the United States, blazing a trail of real free speech, free speech for white working people for a change. *Race and Reason* is an island of free speech in a sea of managed and controlled news . . ."

The suit is brown, the shirt is blue, the tie is polka-dot, the voice is mellow and the guest tonight is "Baxter the Pagan," a skinhead leader and mainstay of the WAR organization who takes "the Pagan" from the ancient Germanic tribal religion of Odinism, of which he, like many neo-Nazis, is a follower.

"It must have been tough, a white boy in New York," Metzger begins. "How does it work?"

"I grew up in a predominantly white neighborhood," Baxter replies. "The only blacks around were in an orphanage that was very large at one time, but the race riots of the sixties took care of that, a couple of white victories here and there."

Metzger does not question this logic, but continues:

"But you gradually got out into the streets of New York?"

"Yeah. The suburbs become boring. Especially to someone with an adventurous spirit. Someone not held back by the Christian lie."

What did he find in the city? Metzger wants to know.

"Gangs," says Baxter. "Your drug gangs, your race mixers, your white gangs who don't know that they're supremists [*sic*], but they are."

They discuss the Guardian Angels, who have interposed themselves between skinheads and antiracist protesters on occasions such as the gathering known as the Aryan Woodstock, which Metzger sponsored in Napa, California, in the spring of 1989, not long before this television session took place.

"Is it true [the Angels] don't encourage white boys and white girls to work together in a group?" Metzger asks.

"It seemed that way to me," Baxter agrees. "The white girls, they talk like Puerto Rican girls, they always have black boyfriends, it seemed like in a white couple the woman would receive so much guff from the black guys about how much of a racist she is not to let their black slime between her legs, and the white guy would just be too much of a wimp to do anything about it."

What about Italians, Metzger wonders. "Did you ever go around Little Italy?"

"Oh, Mott Street, sure," says Baxter. "The Italians are very racially motivated people."

"Racially motivated," sometimes either just "racial" or "motivated," is a phrase that recurs throughout the broadcast, once in relation to Baxter's suburb ("the town I come from is still pretty racially motivated"), once in relation to Howard Beach ("the white people in New York are pretty racially motivated if not totally insane") and once in relation to the Russians, thus:

Metzger: "We get a lot of mail from young people thinking the military is going to make a man of them, but when they find this tremendous leaning over for blacks most of them want to get out as soon as they get in. What kind of defense is this mongrelized army going to give us? I mean, if the Russians really did try to invade the US . . . "

Baxter: "If the Russians really did try to invade the US, I'd probably be fighting with them."

Metzger: "That just lost us the V.F.W. vote. But when you see a Russian submarine or ship coming in, they're almost all white. You might see a Mongol . . . "

Baxter: "Or throw in an Armenian . . ."

Metzger: "But you never see a nonwhite on a Russian sub."

Baxter: "Sure, he'd be bilged before the day was up. The Russians are pretty motivated people, from what I understand."

The conversation with Baxter identifies many of Metzger's immediate enemies and highlights some of his long-range themes, "skinheads who claim they're white power but yet they'll screw a beaner chick or a half-breed gook or some epitome like that"; the conservative whites in Napa County who "technically conspired with the Marxists and lesbians and homosexuals from San Francisco" to stop the Napa concert; "cops on the front lines that are the ones giving us the most trouble . . . so aren't we really in a white civil war?"—but there are many others.

With Baxter's wife, "Monique Wolfing," head of a support group known as the Aryan Women's League, whose activities have included a clothing drive for families of fellow racialists in prison, Metzger discusses the ideal relationship between Aryan women and men, which Monique sees as neither inferiority nor superiority but as equality, "because once you have two counterparts working together you can't lose."

"Isn't there a move in this country that with the white male under attack they've given a special classification to white women and minorities to further split the white male and female up?" Metzger offers, and Monique agrees.

Another of her interests is ecology, which is likewise one of Metzger's frequent refrains. "I've noticed," he prods, "that there's an increased number of young people in the white racialist movement who are also quite interested in the ecology, protecting the animals from cruelty and things like that, and it seems to me that as we are becoming more aware of our precarious state, the white man, the white woman's, state in the world, being only about 10 percent of the population, we begin to sympathize, empathize more, with the wolves and other animals."

"Well, naturally," replies Monique. "They're in the same position we are. Why would we want something created for ourselves and yet watch nature be destroyed? We work hand in hand with nature and we should save nature along with trying to save our race." . . .

With WAR newspaper managing editor Wyatt Kaldenberg, one of a number of former leftists Metzger has recently recruited to his cause; Bob Heick, head of the San Francisco Nazi Skinhead American Front; and his son John, who on this show runs back and forth between the set and the control room, Tom relives their 1988 appearance on *The Geraldo Show* which ended in Geraldo Rivera's broken nose, observing that the network had paid for the skinheads to fly to New York City not once but twice for the program. "Sells a lot of soap for those people, eh?" Metzger chortles.

Who watches *Race and Reason* it is difficult to say. Public-access TV is neither a heavily viewed nor an effectively monitored segment of the television market, and the figure of fifty outlets that Metzger frequently uses on his broadcasts is his alone. Like many public-access programs, the show is amateurish, at times to the point of parody, and a viewer clicking through the channels would be unlikely to stop there without a reason. But if *Race and Reason* has not directly catapulted Metzger into the American living room, it has done so indirectly, for Metzger was the first to notice that by judicious use of the rules governing public access he could create, in effect, a cable network that would generate at least the appearance of national audience, . . . which in turn has generated its own reality. Thanks in large part to the controversies surrounding the introduction of *Race and Reason* into various cities, if not to the program itself, Metzger has appeared on such major television talk shows as *The Oprah Winfrey Show, Geraldo* and *Crossfire,* some of them more than once, often in the role of champion of free speech. Even when the controversial program is not his own, Metzger is apt to be called upon to defend the First Amendment. When the Kansas City, Missouri, City Council responded to the proposed airing in 1988 of a Klan-produced program called Klansas City Cable by eliminating the access channel, for instance, Metzger appeared on *Oprah* along with Klan member Dennis Mahon and A.C.L.U. attorney John Powell arguing that the program was constitutionally protected. The precise role of these appearances in increasing Metzger's following cannot be proved, but it has been noticed by the police in Portland [Oregon], for example, that when Metzger visits the city in connection with court appearances for a lawsuit (about which more later), he is recognized when he walks down the street.

"Well, I'm a Racist"

The personableness that Metzger projects, at least on his own program, appears to be a genuine aspect of his character. Raised in small-town Indiana, he carries with him the aura of a local hardware store owner with whom it would be pleasant to spend a Saturday morning chatting about tools, and he is, in fact, one of the few leaders of the neo-Nazi movement who is also a member of the work force. . . . A married man with six children, he lives in a modest house in the Latino section of Fallbrook, north of San Diego, where his neighbors, who know his beliefs, are among his customers, and his two youngest children attend public school. It is true that the material in the WAR newspaper is vicious, that on national television Metzger has more than once spontaneously revealed an ugly temper and that his message lines are filled with such hate juvenilia as the "AntiDefecation League," the "Jewnited States," "niglets" and "gooks," delivered in what I have come to think of as a Halloween, the-goblins-will-get-you-if-you-don't-watch-out kind of voice; but it is also true that his unsentimental, bad-boy matter of factness can be disarming, that he has a youthful enthusiasm that can be engaging and that a recent hour-and-a-half phone conversation revealed so little of the racist and anti-Semitic fervor on which he is staking his claim that it was almost like talking to a different person. Whether it was his sense of history, his sense of humor or his sense of himself (he was shrewd enough to ponder aloud his contrary nature and wonder, "What would I do if I became popular?") I am not sure, but by the time he excused himself to take out the garbage—he heard the trucks rumbling in the background—if anybody had asked me, "Would you want your television repaired by this man?" I might well have said, "Why not?"

The same credibility that has undoubtedly made it possible for Metzger to stay in the repair business despite his views also characterizes his political evolution, which appears to have an inner coherence that closely reflects his experience. "Once I was a conservative, once I was liberal, once I was a libertarian. I got sick of those labels, so even though I'm not too happy with labels, I finally said, Well, I'm a racist" he told a journalism class at San Diego State University in 1980. Except for the omission of the anti-Semitism that has carried over from an early Christian Identity ministry to his present atheism, the progression given in his own summary is probably correct.

Once he was a Bircher: "In the early sixties I was very depressed by the inroads of Communism. A lot of things they said made sense, so I became a Birch Society member. I believe in activism. The Birch Society took the position it was stupid to be active, you're just supposed to read books. I don't know. Maybe if you throw enough books at someone you might hit 'em, and they'll quit what they're doing." Then he became a George Wallace supporter: "When I worked for the Wallace campaign, I did not perceive myself as a racist, even though they said anybody who worked for Wallace was. I was a rebel, I've always been a rebel, and the fact of being a rebel has pushed me in the direction I've gone because when people called me a racist and I wasn't, finally I just stuck my chin out and said, well, if you want it that way, I will be, you know? And I'll be the loudest one you ever saw." Eventually he turned to the Klan, closely associating himself with the "New Klan" that emerged in the mid- 1970s around David Duke. In addition to many joint activities with Duke in California, including a Klan patrol of the Mexican border to prevent illegal immigration, he helped manage Duke's first electoral campaign, for the Louisiana Senate, in 1975. But the decisive moment in his career so far appears to have been his own "electoral period," which included three runs for office between 1978 and 1982.

Although electoral activity was part of an informal consensus among like-minded rightists nationwide, there is little doubt that Metzger believed in what he was doing. "You don't make change having fiery crosses out in cow pastures" he told the journalism class in 1980. "You make change by invading the halls of Congress and the Statehouse." In 1978 he won 11,000 votes in a nonpartisan election for San Diego County supervisor; in 1980 he won the Democratic primary in the 43d Congressional District in California with 33,000 votes against a party regular hastily recruited at the last minute to retrieve the party's honor in a foregone race against the Republican incumbent, Representative Clair Burgener, who beat Metzger by more than 250,000 votes in the general election; and in 1982 he won more than 75,000 votes in the statewide Democratic primary for nomination to the U.S. Senate. It was probably the 1980 primary that affected him most, for he won it in spite of several years of open, highly publicized and frequently violent activities as head of the California Knights of the Ku Klux Klan, and he was technically entitled to a role in the California Democratic Party, which the party decided to deny him. One moment he could boast, "I found before the primary that my parents, who were visiting from Indiana, were upset by my Klan activities and they went home in a huff; but after I won it was a whole different thing; people worship power." The next moment he was enduring a personal as well as a political rejection as he was taken from a Sacramento meeting room by a sheriff following the unanimous vote of the state Democratic Central Committee to unseat him.

"This Is WAR"

The 1980 political humiliation was not Metzger's only run-in with what he often calls "the system." In 1971, following a period of losses, he received a phone call from the I.R.S. Already angry over the Vietnam War, in which he had lost several friends, so angry, in fact, that he once collaborated with leftists in staging a mock war crimes trial, he decided to resist paying his taxes. When he recounted to me the moment, "I remember I was standing in my kitchen, and I said, 'No, I don't think I'll have you audit me this year,' and there was silence on the other end of the phone, and finally [the agent] said, 'Do you realize who this is?' and I said, 'I understand completely who this is, I'm throwing down the gauntlet and this war is going to begin,'" it had something of the feeling of a conversion. From 1971 to 1975 he was a tax protester; later, to avoid losing his home, he began paying on contract. A few years ago the I.R.S. canceled the contract and demanded immediate payment of the remaining sum, and when he came to the part of the story where he had to raise $7,000 immediately to save his house, the respect in his voice for the amount struck me, for someone who is often rumored to have received more than $1 million in stolen money from The Order, as very real.

In any case, it does not seem accidental that the words and ideas with which Metzger responded instinctively to the I.R.S. in 1971 play so big a part in his political vocabulary now. "I have a real hatred for the government, which excels any kind of displeasure I have with any racial groups. But I have to give them all the credit, because due to their actions against me they have created me," he says. When he ends his phone messages with his goblinish imprecation, "This is WAR," he is not dealing in ideological abstractions. It is "resistance to" and "war on" the government that he means.

Just what WAR is, however, is a reasonable question, for Metzger is also one of the world's great hustlers. Unlike the Klan, which requires induction, WAR is not a membership organization—"war wears no uniform, carries no card, and takes no secret oaths; [it] doesn't require you to dress up and march around on a muddy street; [it] works the modern way, with thousands of friends doing their part on the job, behind the scenes, serving their race," he proclaimed in inaugurating his Detroit phone line last winter. And with that definition, whether WAR should be called an organization at all is open to question. The television program and the newspaper both come out of the group centered around Fallbrook, and as for the message lines, though they are appearing in more and more cities, Washington, New

York, Dallas and Cleveland, to name a few, how that fact should be understood is perhaps suggested by a recent plea on the Fallbrook line for donation of another answering machine for Seattle. This is not an outfit with many resources at hand. A message line itself proves no more than the presence of a single follower willing to house the phone, and the same applies to *Race and Reason*, which, according to cable regulations in most cities, requires only a single local sponsor to be shown. If such an assessment can be comforting, however, it also can be misleading, for it appears that Metzger's appeals are hitting their targets. There are thought to be at least a thousand more skinheads now than a year ago; correspondence with Metzger has shown up in skinhead quarters as far from Fallbrook as Providence, Rhode Island; and in numerous ways, subtle and not, . . . it is obvious that his influence is growing.

Further, while the presence or absence of troops is of considerable interest to Metzger-watchers, it is not Metzger's own chief concern. A "Leninist" (his word), he sees himself as working with a "minority of dedicated people" to create a "fanatical inner structure" until the historical moment is ripe for it to be heard. He is less interested in numbers than in the ideas through which the band of fanatics understands the world. He speaks as one under intense ideological pressure, and although his royal "we think" and "we're trying" may in one sense be part of his hustle, they also seem to reflect a need to distinguish himself from the rest of the racial movement. He is against the Klan, whose members he calls "Hollywood soldiers," against ordinary conservatives, who he believes have lost important decades screaming "'Communism, Communism' while racially we went 'down the tubes,'" and he is against ordinary neo-Nazis as well. His opposition to other neo-Nazis is particularly important, for in spite of the "Aryan" in WAR, it is in his rejection of Hitler worship, which he believes has limited every American racialist since George Lincoln Rockwell, that he has taken his stand. A follower, instead, of the Nazi radical Gregor Strasser, who was executed in the Röhm purge in 1934, Metzger has taken from Strasser a combination of socialist and internationalist ideas sometimes known as the "Third Position" and, while keeping them firmly in a racialist framework, has given them a populist cast. Where other racial leaders are apt to refer to the white race in general, Metzger usually refers to the white working man, or working person (he tries to mind his feminism), and the American heroes about whom he has tried to educate his followers include Eugene Debs as well as Father Coughlin, Francis Townsend and Huey Long. Even more important than any economic ideas, which are rarely articulated, however, is Metzger's sense of belonging to an international pan-Aryan movement, which is probably the closest thing he has to a political vision. "Most of us see ourselves as simply the beginning is something time will tell." Did the Holocaust take place? "Jews gain certain advantages by promoting the Holocaust idea. It inspires tremendous financial aid for Israel. It makes organized Jewry almost immune from criticism. Whether the Holocaust is real or not, the Jews clearly have a motive for fostering the idea that it occurred." Whatever the subject, his opinions refer back to racist intellectual sources ranging from Lothrop Stoddard's *The Rising Tide of Color* and *Racial Realities of Europe,* both published in the 1920s, to *The Talmud Unmasked,* by Father Prainatis, all of which he has sold. And he has even added to the literature himself with a pamphlet called *Who Runs the Media?,* an excellent booklet, the catalogue description says, "documenting Zionist control of America's mass media, how the control was achieved, and the ramifications of this alien domination," one of his favorite themes.

His program is as consistent as his principles. A subject of constant interest has been "racial betterment." Well over a decade ago, he advocated such eugenic interventions as tax incentives for people with high IQs to have more children, and he still does. . . . His equally longstanding criticism of welfare, that it encourages those with the lowest IQs to have the most children, is also more eugenic than economic. "It's against evolution," he says. "You must understand," he has warned, "that the white people are becoming a second-class citizens' group in our own country. . . . We're losing our rights all the way across the board. White people face massive discrimination in employment opportunities, in scholarship opportunities, in promotions in industry, in college entrance examinations." On the surface, such a statement could be the platform of an illiberal but still legitimate white politician willing to trade this or swap that for a curb on the minority assistance programs that have been offered as a result of the civil rights movement, but in Duke's case its racialist roots give it a hidden meaning. . . .

The Candidate's Résumé

Whatever David Duke's personality, he has always been on the move. An activist as well as a reader, he seems to have spent the years following his Putnam epiphany searching for the correct organizational form to express his convictions: the Klan in high school; the White Youth Alliance, which he formed when he was at Louisiana State University and which became affiliated with various Rockwell-related splinter groups in college; and after graduation the Klan again, the base from which he made his initial national impact. Duke's leadership, first of the Louisiana Knights of the Ku Klux Klan and then of its national office, was important for several reasons, not least his recruitment of some powerful men, including Metzger in California, Louis Beam in Texas, Bill Wilkinson in Louisiana and Don Black in Alabama, many of whom remain central to the racial movement today. Duke also modernized the organization, welcoming women and Catholics for the first time, dressing in suits rather than robes and calling himself "National Director" instead of "Imperial Wizard." Under his auspices, the Klan conducted a military organizing drive that made itself felt at Camp Pendleton in California, at Fort Hood in Texas and in the Navy, and experienced something of a general revival as well.

In 1980, in part because of a struggle with Wilkinson, who was running the Knights of the Ku Klux Klan's Louisiana branch, Duke left to form the National Association for the Advancement of White People, which he described then, as he does now, as a "civil rights lobby for white people" and which he has used in his march into mainstream politics. That effort began in 1975, when he won about a third of the votes during an unsuccessful statewide run for the Louisiana Senate in the campaign assisted by Metzger. He ran again with similar results in 1979 but clearly did not lose the taste, and in the late 1980s he began a new electoral phase. In 1988 he ran for President in the Democratic primaries in a number of states and, when that effort collapsed, as the presidential candidate of the Populist Party, a campaign backed primarily by the party's organizational alter ego, the Liberty Lobby. In February 1989 he was elected to the Louisiana legislature from Metairie as a Republican and, although he lost a bid for the party's official nomination, he ran in Louisiana's open primary as a maverick Republican for the U.S. Senate seat held by Democrat J. Bennett Johnston.

What is important about Duke's political biography, however, is that although it is usually represented as a succession it is actually more of an accretion. On the course from his adolescent Klan membership to his present Republicanism, Duke has touched all the important bases of the racial movement in the United States and abandoned none. His relationships with former associates such as Metzger and Beam might not be what they once were, but they are not known to be broken either, and Duke's political entourage is full of familiar faces. When he announced his Democratic presidential bid in Atlanta in 1988, there cheering him on was Don Black, the Alabama Klan leader, . . . best known for his role in a neo-Nazi/Klan attempt to overthrow the government of the island of Dominica in return for land for paramilitary training camps. Black was technically Duke's successor in the national Knights of the K.K.K. and is married to Duke's former wife. Also at the announcement were Daniel Carver, then the Imperial Wizard of a different Klan organization, the Invisible Empire, and such old-line racists as Ed Fields, founder of the National States Rights Party and editor of its paper, *The Thunderbolt*, with which Duke had some connection as long ago as college.

In addition to Black, whose political life began as a Rockwell follower, Duke is also actively associated with two other men whose Nazi ties go directly back to the time of George Lincoln Rockwell: James Warner, head of an anti-Semitic church, newsletter and book publishing operation known as the New Christian Crusade Church in Metairie, Louisiana, who began as an information officer for the National Socialist White People's Party, the successor to Rockwell's American Nazi Party; and Ralph Forbes, head of a similar operation in Arkansas called the Sword of Christ Good News Ministry, who started out as the so-called commander of the American Nazi Party's western division. Warner, a longtime partner of Duke in the book business, resumed a ruptured relationship with him to assist in his legislative campaign and in January 1990 served as an elected Duke delegate to the Louisiana Republican convention. Forbes, who recently made an unexpectedly strong bid for the G.O.P. nomination for lieutenant governor of Arkansas, is publisher of a newspaper called *The Truth*, whose inaugural edition (January 1989) announced in banner type, "Good News America: There Is a White Christmas in Your Future"; sold Rockwelliana as well as many other items of neo-Nazi memorabilia, such as "Musik of the Afrika Corps"; included [in the newspaper] several pages of "satire" calling Michael Dukakis "Michael Dukikiz," presenting Willie Horton as I.R.S. commissioner and Rabbi Meir Kahane as chief justice; and featur[ed in the newspaper] a mock pledge of allegiance to ZOG (Zionist Occupation Government), presumably to illustrate the fate America so narrowly escaped. Forbes was the director of Duke's 1988 presidential campaign. So dense and long-lived are Duke's Nazi associations, in fact, that you would think the only way he could escape them would be through reincarnation. Like the fictional General Guzman in Lawrence Thornton's novel *Imagining Argentina*, Duke "sees history from the time of the Romans to the rise of Hitler as a dark age in which men and women of many nations became philosophically perverted, denying the necessity of a single-minded vision, of the purity he believes Hitler saw and embraced as fiercely as a wild-eyed prophet . . . on a windy mountaintop." Like Guzman, too, he "has met secretly in heavily guarded houses deep in the jungle, or in cafes in tiny villages where he has looked across the table at Mengele and lesser exponents of that dream which he feels more than ever was defiled by the faint of heart, the women in man's spirit," communing with his mentors, if only, in Duke's case, in his dreams.

How much Duke's present admirers understand of his vision is open to question. His campaign literature avoids obvious racialist formulations while bluntly attacking the "illegitimate welfare rate," minority set-asides, illegal immigration and affirmative action in language designed to appeal to the "middle-class, productive" American. The Louisiana Coalition Against Racism and Nazism, which follows Duke closely, believes he has been successful in detaching his past from his present, following a "dual strategy" by which "in public he promotes moderate conservatism, keyed to racial issues," while "within his activist circle, he continues a second campaign, a shadow campaign, [embodying his] long-term design, his dream of a genetically engineered super race, born into existence by a legion of white supremacists!" . . .

Portland Skinheads

At 1:30 on the morning of November 13, 1988, in a peaceful residential neighborhood in Portland, Oregon, Kenneth Mieske, Kyle Brewster and Steven Strasser, skinheads, encountered Mulageta Seraw, Wondwosen Tesfaye and Tilahun Antneh, Ethiopians; the skinheads had a bat; and Seraw, the description of whose wounds makes chilling reading, died. The contents of the skinheads' apartments, searched shortly afterward, make equally chilling reading, bats and clubs in one, the latest racial propaganda in another, a veritable library on the rise and fall of the Third Reich in the third, all used by the district attorneys to prove what, from the moment the police first arrived at the scene, hardly anyone besides other skinheads has ever doubted: that it was a racially motivated attack and not a street fight that got out of hand and brought about the death of Mulageta Seraw.

The Portland story is worth examining because both locally and nationally it marked the beginning of a new realization that when you see a bunch of black-jacketed, heavy-booted storm troopers on TV, you might not be watching a World War II film; it could be the evening news. The three skinheads are in prison—Mieske, who pleaded guilty to murder, for a minimum of twenty years; Brewster and Strasser, who pleaded guilty to manslaughter, for a minimum of ten and nine years, respectively—but the case has acquired symbolic status, and neither within the neo-Nazi movement nor among its opponents has it been forgotten. Mieske and Brewster were defendants in a multi-million-dollar civil lawsuit brought jointly by the Southern Poverty Law Center and the Anti-Defamation League on behalf of Seraw's estate, a suit that by linking the Portland skinheads to Tom Metzger, John Metzger and the WAR organization was frankly intended to put Metzger out of business. Such a result was achieved by a similar suit won by S.P.L.C. attorney Morris Dees in Alabama in 1987, which, by obtaining a $7 million settlement from the United Klans of America for a woman whose son was murdered by members of the Klan, effectively shut it down. . . .

The history of the infiltration of Portland's youth culture by Nazi ideas is difficult to document in detail, for it took place largely unnoticed by adults in a handful of clubs populated by people who were better participants than they were observers, but from conversations with a variety of onlookers, as well as from police records, newspaper accounts and other sources, at least a rudimentary outline emerges. The skinhead appearance in Portland seems, roughly speaking, to have followed a pattern established earlier in San Francisco, where, in reaction to the vaguely progressive or at least oppositional culture of punk, a group of musicians and their followers became steadily more hard-core, driving themselves through a succession of musical and personal changes until they arrived first at the style and eventually at the substance of British racist bands such as Skrewdriver, which are explicitly associated with the fascist National Front. . . .

The clearest marker for the emergence of the skinheads from the clubs to the streets is probably early 1988, when ideological links between such acts as the desecration of a synagogue and an attack on a homosexual couple led police to begin keeping records:

- "Black male victim is assaulted and called 'nigger' and 'jungle bunny' by three members of Youth of Hitler."
- "Business was burglarized and vandalized. The suspect painted Nazi Rule, White Power, Die No Name Jew, Die Nigger Lover, White Rule."
- "A note saying Niggers get out was left on a [white female's] car parked in front of her home. The WF claimed to have seen skinheads in the area and is willing to press charges. She is dating a BM [black male] and felt the note to be specific harassment."

On March 10, 1988, an event occurred that for the first time focused public attention on what was happening in the streets. HockSeng (Sam) Chin, a native of Singapore married to a white woman, was leaving a Thai restaurant in downtown Portland with his wife and child when he was set upon by three skinheads who shouted, "Go back to Hong Kong" and "Get out of our country," called his daughter a "fucking slant" and denounced his wife as a "race traitor" for being married to someone nonwhite. Portland police have had their own collisions with minorities at times, but when one of the skinheads continued his tirade even after his arrest by insisting that the United States should exclude Asian visitors and trade, it was clearly too much. "I suggested before he talked about business & trade maybe he should get an education," notes the arresting officer's report. Concern about this and other skinhead incidents, initially confined to the police, was soon widely shared. Coverage in the daily *The Oregonian* increased, and in mid-May a lengthy article in *Willamette Week* took a close look at a neo-Nazi skinhead gang called POWAR (Preservation of the White American Race). Shortly afterward members of the gang appeared live on the Sunday evening TV show *Town Hall*, a program of the ABC affiliate KATU-TV and an important local forum. . . .

Since the death of Seraw, skinhead activity in Portland has only intensified. Not only have the number of individual hate crimes attributed to skinheads and other white supremacists continued to increase but antiracist skin gangs have also emerged, encouraged in part by the San Francisco–based, leftist John Brown Anti-Klan Committee, in part by the militant Portland Coalition for Human Dignity, and confrontations are escalating. Fights between gangs of skinheads and gangs of blacks are also being reported. In recent months Tom Metzger has gained prominence, maintaining two Portland message lines where previously he had none, speaking with the press and on talk shows in connection with the lawsuit and generally keeping things moving. A good example of the underground spread of his influence occurred recently when, soon after Metzger, for reasons known only to himself, referred on his message line to *The Oregonian* as the "Oregonian," the same word appeared on a new message line run by young people who describe themselves as Christian Identity but whose language echoes Metzger's (as well as [Richard] Butler's, [Robert] Mathews's and even George Lincoln Rockwell's) in several respects. There is little doubt that whatever the outcome, with the forthcoming trial gathering national publicity, Metzger's visibility will only increase.

Attempting to account for the skinhead phenomenon nationally, some observers have arrived at the usual explanations—inadequate economic opportunity, individual pathology and broken homes—that, for Portland at least, appear to me to be insufficient. Although it is true that today's skinheads are members of the first generation that cannot expect to make more money than its parents, which undoubtedly plays a part, they are young, many still live at home, and they do not appear to worry about money much. They come from every suburb, wealthy to working-class, and from an array of families whose "functionality" or "dysfunctionality" appears to be no different from that of the people next door. As for individual pathology, even in the case of Kenneth Mieske, who wielded the bat that killed Seraw, opposing psychologists for the prosecution and defense said, respectively, "He has an interesting psychological profile which does not indicate the presence of serious psychological problems" and "I would not characterize him as showing a personality disorder," though whether that is more of a commentary on Mieske or on the psychologists is hard to say.

My own look at the Portland skinheads suggests, rather, an acute degree of painfully personal racial discomfort, which is finding its natural expression in a primitive political movement. Comparing the Portland of his youth with the Portland of today, a skinhead in his mid-20s sounded almost plaintive as he explained that "Portland isn't safe anymore and it's never going to get better; it will never be the same." Another said he didn't mind if black people went everywhere and did everything they wanted, but sometimes he and his friends just liked to be alone. Closely entwined with a sense of loss is a sense of fear. The middle-class girl driving the car in which the skinheads involved in the Seraw murder were riding was carrying a gun given to her by her father for protection. The mother of one skinhead, upon pressing her son to explain the weapons that are part of his uniform, got a desperate, "Ma, you just don't understand." Not only do Portland skinheads I talked to cite black gangs as the crucial factor in their own gang formation, but their anxiety is so free-floating that those in attendance at bail hearings for the Seraw case, including one of the passengers in the car, claim to have thought that not just the Ethiopians in the car with Seraw but even, at one point, a black observer in the courtroom, was either a Crip or a Blood. Whether the sense of intimidation felt by young whites is associated with any substantive improvements for blacks in Portland, it is not possible to say, but it is true that, like many cities, Portland has, in the lifetime of this generation, changed from an informally segregated city to an open one; that schools, parks, bus stops and malls once divided are now used by all; and that the resulting encounters between young people of different races at times and places adults rarely tread have left a wake of ill feeling that the city's predominantly liberal political establishment has been slow to acknowledge.

To what extent the skinhead movement is simply a punk version of racism elsewhere in the city and not a separable phenomenon is another question that has not been adequately discussed, but certainly the case could easily be made. Throughout the city, crimes of the sort formerly committed largely by skinheads are now frequently committed by other white supremacists as well, and while the children have been in the streets, adults have been engaged in a subtler but no less ugly struggle against the renaming of a city thoroughfare for Martin Luther King Jr. This campaign has not only resurrected the political careers of two long- term leaders of the right in Oregon, Walter and Rosalie Huss, but has brought to the city such racist leaders as Richard Barrett, head of the Mississippi-based Nationalist Movement, who before the Seraw murder usually stayed away. In these circumstances, to attribute the disturbances in Portland or any other city to Tom Metzger is like attributing the civil rights movement to outside agitators. Wherever he can find a forum, Metzger operates, but he does not create the conditions in which his words make sense. From individual white insecurity to a collective white identity; from a collective white identity to the necessity of white supremacy; and from the necessity of white supremacy to the movement for Aryan victory, with all that it implies—it is on this classic political journey from experience to ideology that Tom Metzger, among others, is attempting to lead the skinheads, but before they ever encountered him, the experience was already there.

. . .

96

Talking about Race
with America's Klansmen

RAPHAEL S. EZEKIEL

From the Reconstruction era to 1945, between 3,000 and 5,000 black Americans were killed in mob violence, much of it instigated by the Ku Klux Klan. Some victims were hanged or burned to death; often men's genitals were mutilated. Later, during the civil-rights struggles of the 1960s, reincarnations of the Klan spread terror and death, burning buses, clubbing demonstrators, and bombing homes and churches. Today we see another white racist movement, with Klansmen joined by neo-Nazis, racist skinheads, and members of intensely racist churches. Most of today's violence is perpetrated by individuals who are not formally affiliated with these organized groups—but groups such as the Klan create the climate that inspires individual terrorists.

A decade ago, I set out to gain firsthand knowledge of these militant white racist groups. This is a traveler's report, so let me tell you who I am—and why this project was particularly meaningful to me. I am a social psychologist, but I don't do experiments or surveys. I visit people on their own turf and ask questions about their lives. I am 64 years old and have spent much of my adult life in academe. But until I was 12, I lived in a Texas town of 12,000, the commercial center of an agricultural county that produced cotton, peanuts, and soybeans. Hitching posts still dotted some of the main streets—and schools, restaurants, recreational facilities, and washrooms forbade racial mixing.

I am also a Jew. My mother came to America from Russia when she was 7; my father's family were Spanish Jews who had settled in the United States decades earlier. My parents' politics blended prairie populism, Wilsonian idealism, and New Deal enthusiasm. We worshiped F.D.R. and played records by Paul Robeson; outside our home, in contrast, people spoke of "niggers" and elected race-baiting bigots. This mixed background left me with an abiding interest in race and prejudice.

For the past 10 years, 1 have watched and talked with the leaders of various Klan and neo-Nazi groups and with their followers. I have gone to their rallies, hung out at their training conferences, observed their cross burnings. I was open with the people I studied, making clear my identity as a Jew, a professor, and an opponent of racism. I also let them know that I assumed they were building lives that made sense to them. This directness opened many doors: Most people agreed to meet with me. The first half-hour usually went somewhat gingerly: after that, many people spoke more freely, although I always was viewed with some suspicion. Neither I nor the people I interviewed ever lost track of who we were.

CHRON. HIGHER ED., January 26, 1996, at A52. Originally published in the *Chronicle of Higher Education*. Reprinted by permission of the author.

This interpersonal terrain was intensely difficult for me. When I interviewed avowed anti-Semites, I had to check myself repeatedly: Was I forthcoming in how I presented myself, or was I shading and hedging to gain cooperation? Did my field notes tell the whole story—did I include emotions (the moments I felt friendship or anger) that embarrassed me? I found myself wanting to nurture some of the young neo-Nazis, then asking myself whether that was reasonable.

Private organizations that track these groups estimate that about 25,000 people now belong to hard-core white racist groups. Another 150,000 people are sympathizers who subscribe to the groups' literature and sometimes attend rallies. Approximately 450,000 more people occasionally read the groups' literature but don't maintain subscriptions. These are small numbers in a national population as large as ours. But the groups' history of violence forces us to pay attention to them. Whether racism is a major force, as it is currently, or in apparent decline, as in the late 1960s, the members and sympathizers of white racist groups keep the flame burning; they are keepers of the ideology.

The first thing one learns when one enters this world is that it is predominantly male. Only a few women came to rallies or conferences, and they were there primarily to cook and serve meals. In 10 years, I never heard a woman give a speech. I never saw a woman leader.

The groups increasingly make up a single movement. They compete with each other for membership, and their leaders speak ill of each other in private. Nevertheless, leaders of different groups spend a lot of time on the telephone with each other, and they meet and consult at rallies and conferences. Moreover, in the past two decades, the Klans (there are now at least 44 separate Klans) have taken on pretty much the same ideology as the neo-Nazi groups. Uniforms and insignia may differ, but little distinguishes the conversation of participants in any of these organizations. Everywhere you hear the same discussions of black Americans as apes, of a secret cabal of Jews that runs the country.

A peculiar theology called Christian Identity has assumed major influence in recent years. An offshoot of a 19th-century movement known as Anglo-Israelitism, it holds that God is white, and so are his people. His son, Jesus, was Aryan, not a Jew. The Israelites of the Old Testament were not related to present-day Jews; they were the first Aryans. Expelled from Canaan (Palestine), they settled Northern Europe. Today, God is calling them together in North America to enact his will. They are destined to rule the world by overcoming Satan's children, the Jews, who were born out of the union of Eve and the Serpent. Whites also are struggling against the darker races (referred to as "mud races"), who were produced by mating between human beings (that is, whites) and animals.

The first time I heard this stuff, I assumed that no one could take it seriously. But I heard pieces of it from most movement participants with whom I spoke, and I found that they really believe it. Christian Identity provides divine endorsement for white supremacy: Racist behavior is Christian love, since, as one of the Klan calling cards announces, "God is a racist."

The people whom I came to know best were members of a neo-Nazi cell in Detroit. These young men (aged 17 through 22) lived in families that had few social ties to their wider communities. For the most part, these men had lost their fathers at an early age. They had left school in the 9th or 10th grades and had little work experience and few prospects of employment. The dominant emotion that I felt in them was fear. They did not say it openly, but I came to realize that they felt that their lives were at risk.

This deep terror helped me to understand what I found so alien. Asked what they knew of Hitler's Nazis, the young men whom I interviewed referred to late-night movies. From the movies, they mainly had gained a sense that Hitler's Nazis were ruthless, unafraid to commit murder. How reassuring for deeply fearful white youths to don a swastika, stand shoulder to shoulder with comrades at rallies, shout provocative slogans. Joining with others to endure the hostile jeers of opponents who protest at neo-Nazi rallies provides a sense of reassurance: Surely one who is attacked so loudly is alive.

In contrast to the followers, I found the leaders of today's white racist movement very different: They are smart men who have risen to the top of a highly competitive vocation. They are good with words and body language, and they can act out the emotions in which their followers revel—especially righteous indignation and contempt. They draw pleasure from being able to affect a crowd. From watching and listening to them while they worked with their aides, I would say that they are utterly cynical people. Many of the leaders of racist groups are not particularly racist themselves; for them, racism is merely an organizational tool fitted to the psychic needs of potential followers.

As I look back on my research, I think that my most hopeful finding is the malleability of those who join a racist group. While joining helped many young men assuage their feelings of being at risk, it seemed to me that other groups could have filled that role just as well. I rather suspected that I could easily have led a number of these young men to an alternative outlet, were it available and were it, too, something they saw as glamorous and confrontational.

My most depressing finding was the degree to which ordinary people are perfectly happy to believe nonsense, as long as it makes them feel good. The youths I studied lacked an organized sense of reality that would let them judge whether what they were hearing was sensible or not. Education seemed more important to me than ever before.

People vulnerable to racist recruiters have little faith in democratic social processes. Little in their experience has taught them optimism or trust. The growing divide in our society between rich and poor, as the economy goes through its wrenching changes, means that more and more of the population will live in fear and distrust. This makes it even more important to understand the dynamics of alienation.

97

Antidiscrimination Law and Transparency: Barriers to Equality?

BARBARA J. FLAGG

Racial identity is not a central life experience for most white people, be-cause it does not have to be.[1] Like members of any socially dominant group, white people have the option to set aside consciousness of the characteristic that defines the dominant class—in this case, race. Thus whiteness is experienced as racelessness, and personal iden-tity is conceived in a race-neutral manner. However, race plays quite a different role in the lives of people of color in this society. It is, again as a consequence of existing social struc-tures that define and give meaning to racial identity, a central facet of life. One black fem-inist, bell hooks, describes her experience of race:

> I often begin courses which focus on African-American literature, and sometimes specifically black women writers, with a declaration by Paulo Freire which had a profound liberatory effect on my thinking: "We cannot enter the struggle as objects in order to later become subjects." This statement compels reflection on how the dominated, the oppressed, the exploited make ourselves subject. How do we create an oppositional worldview, a consciousness, an identity, a standpoint that exists not only as that struggle which also opposes dehumanization but as that movement which enables creative, expansive self-actualization? Opposition is not enough. In that vacant space after one has resisted there is still the necessity to become—to make oneself anew. Resistance is that struggle we can most easily grasp. Even the most subjected person has moments of rage and resentment so intense that they respond, they act against. There is an in-ner uprising that leads to rebellion, however short-lived. It may be only momentary but it takes place. That space within oneself where resistance is possible remains. It is different then to talk about becoming subjects. That process emerges as one comes to understand how structures of domination work in one's own life, as one develops critical thinking and critical consciousness, as one invents new, alternative habits of being, and resists from that marginal space of differ-ence inwardly defined.[2]

Thus, Keisha's employer is simply wrong in thinking that [the firm's] conformity re-quirement is race-neutral; the standard places quite a different burden on nonwhites than it does on white employees. [See Chapter 15 for Keisha's story. Ed.] Moreover, this differ-ence is not subjective, but structural. The social significance of race—the existence of a racial hierarchy—guarantees that race will intrude on the self-consciousness of nonwhites to an extent that most whites never will experience. Thus the hypothetical white candidate for promotion is unlikely to experience as race dependent the personal attributes called into question by her employer's workplace conformity rule. Even if she does experience these attributes as associated with race, they are not likely to be *for that reason* central to her self-definition. For Keisha, on the other hand, conformity is excruciatingly difficult precisely *because* it calls her *racial* identity into question.

Once one sees that race is inevitably implicated in matters of "personal choice," it becomes apparent that the assimilationist interpretation does not truly reflect a conception of race-neutral employment opportunity. Under the assimilationist interpretation, the mandate of equality is satisfied in Keisha's case because she could, in theory, conform to the employer's expectations, even though doing so necessarily would levy costs on her that are inseparably linked to her race. The pluralist conception of equal opportunity embodies a more thoroughgoing notion of race neutrality. This interpretation of equality would not hold the requirements of equal opportunity to be satisfied unless the employer at least explored ways of accommodating diverse, race-dependent means of achieving legitimate business objectives. Thus only the pluralist interpretation of equal opportunity can capture fully the vision of a workplace in which race does not matter—in Title VII's language, a workplace in which the individual is not disadvantaged "because of" race.

Of course, Title VII's vision of race neutrality is closely tied to the redistributive objective of improving the relative economic position of blacks and other racial minorities. However, redistribution is not an end in itself; it is desirable because of a history of intentional discrimination and societal deprivation.[3] Thus, to the extent that Title VII aims at redistribution at all, it does so because of a remedial objective. Here too, the pluralist interpretation of equal opportunity emerges as a clearer expression of the Act's generic goals than does the assimilationist approach.

One consequence of two centuries of discrimination and disadvantage is that whites hold a disproportionate share of business ownership and decisionmaking power within corporate structures.[4] The assimilationist conception of equal employment opportunity does not address this persistent inequality, because it deems "equal" the opportunity to compete on this existing, though white-dominated, field. The pluralist interpretation of equality is a much more effective remedial tool because it requires an employer to restructure the workplace in ways that mitigate the effects of preexisting white dominance.

In sum, the two objectives of Title VII that often are perceived to conflict in the area of race-conscious "affirmative action" converge with regard to the concept of equal employment opportunity. Both race neutrality and remedial redistribution are more completely realized by interpreting equal employment opportunity in the pluralist, rather than assimilationist, sense. It seems fair, then, to conclude that fashioning a framework for assessing liability that would effectively accommodate Keisha's claim is consistent with Title VII as written.

Notes

1. Clearly, there are some exceptions to this generalization, the most notorious of which are white supremacists. I regard them as outsiders to the mainstream of white experience.

2. BELL HOOKS, *The Politics of Radical Black Subjectivity*, in YEARNING: RACE, GENDER, AND CULTURAL POLITICS 15, 15 (1990). Keisha's Afrocentric personal style may be seen as a move toward becoming "subject" in bell hooks' sense.

3. *See* Michael J. Perry, *The Disproportionate Impact Theory of Racial Discrimination*, 125 U. Pa. L. Rev. 540, 557–58 (1977) (identifying government's remedial obligations arising from historical injustices). Redistribution as an end in itself would conflict with capitalist values. *See* Frances L. Ansley, *Stirring the Ashes: Race, Class and the Future of Civil Rights Scholarship*, 74 Cornell L. Rev. 993, 1031–35 (1989) (discussing tension between affirmative action's methods and "anti-redistributionist" ideology that is prevalent in the United States). [See this article in Chapters 54 and 98. Ed.]

4. As of 1991, 13% of white households but only 4% of black households held a financial interest in a business or profession; the median value of such assets was $10,352 for whites and $3,444 for blacks. U.S. Bureau of the Census, Statistical Abstract of the United States: 1994, at 482 (1994).

98

White Supremacy (And What We Should Do about It)

FRANCES LEE ANSLEY

Civil rights scholars have offered various analyses to explain the development of the civil rights movement, civil rights litigation, and civil rights legal doctrine. Implicit in these analyses are different ideas about the nature of racism. In asking how and why the existing system of racial dominance and subordination has survived the powerful waves of opposition and resistance that have broken upon it, scholars have necessarily confronted, directly or indirectly, the question of white supremacy's origin and why it has such staying power. According to an approach that I will call here the "race model" (and in contrast with the explanation that would flow from a "class model"), racial hierarchy is its own explanation. [See Chapter 54 for Professor Ansley's discussion of the "class model." Eds.]

In the following discussion of "white supremacy" I do not mean to allude only to the self-conscious racism of white supremacist hate groups. I refer instead to a political, economic, and cultural system in which whites overwhelmingly control power and material resources, conscious and unconscious ideas of white superiority and entitlement are widespread, and relations of white dominance and non-white subordination are daily reenacted across a broad array of institutions and social settings.

White supremacy produces material and psychological benefits for whites, while extracting a heavy material and psychological price from blacks. It assures the former greater resources, a wider range of personal choice, more power, and more self-esteem than they would have if they were forced to share the above with people of color, and deprived of the subjective sensation of superiority they enjoy as a result of the subordination of non-whites.[1] According to this "race model," this is the reason whites resist an end to white supremacy: they have a stake in the system and they will fight to defend it. The explanation, then, for the halt of the civil rights movement is the entrenched power of resistant whites who refuse to give up further privileges. Several elements of our experience suggest the power of the race model. White supremacist regimes are, in fact, not confined to any particular political economy. They can be shown to exist in non-capitalist economies, including socialist ones.

The long cycles of American race law lend strength to the supremacy-for-its-own-sake argument. Despite a sequence of dramatic changes in underlying social and economic conditions from colonial times to the present, and despite unparalleled legal upheavals, blacks as a race are still subordinate. Another piece of social experience that suggests we ought to take the race model seriously is the tendency of whites to choose race over class in their social and political allegiances. With disturbing consistency, whites, who would appear to have an identity of interest with oppressed blacks, fail to act on that purported interest, and instead identify and side with fellow whites. Time and again fragile alliances between blacks and whites fall apart when the time comes to take a stand about racism. Too often blacks experience white allies as more opportunistic than reliable.

The racism-as-tool model explains this phenomenon as the success of a ploy: the racist system has successfully instilled false consciousness in the white worker, who ends up worse off due to his own ignorance and error. Race model proponents, to the contrary, acknowledge that the bigoted white worker may in some sense be misled in his convictions, but also point to the gains all whites enjoy at the expense of blacks under a regime of racial dominance.

What are the implications of the race model of white supremacy? For one, a race model thinker would want to preserve a conscious focus on race and white supremacy as the subjects to be addressed. A focus on race in the world of political action suggests resistance to doctrines, attitudes, or coalitions that distort or distract from efforts to end white supremacy. John Calmore, for instance, advocates that blacks should even resist too easy an alliance with other people of color, that they "get off the minority bandwagon."[2] Although he acknowledges that competition for scarce resources "*unduly* sets various groups against each other," he asserts that "the plight of poor blacks is worsened as the civil rights movement has now been expanded to include others who threaten to siphon benefits. . . ."[3] If alliances built around common interests offer no long-term hope, then all alliances are suspect, but almost any alliance (including one with ruling white elites) could be justified on temporary and tactical grounds.

The race model further entails wariness of "coalitional doctrine." In this view, blacks have much to be proud of in their role as drum-majors for constitutional and social justice in America, but much to regret as well. It is ironic that black legal battles have so often been in the forefront of successful efforts to expand the creation, recognition and enforcement of individual rights, yet the majority of black people have so little to show for these gains.

One response to this pattern is to develop a doctrine that consciously takes white supremacy into account and resists "deracialization" of the legal protections and entitlements sought. Thus, black scholar Charles Lawrence notes specifically that he is "attempting to limit the merging of economic and racial discrimination . . . ."[4]

A race model analysis might lead one to look for "black law"; to stress, for example, the special claim blacks have upon the post–Civil War amendments and civil rights statutes. Such a claim is true to the history of these enactments and justified by the special harms suffered by blacks in America. Alternatively, the race model might lead one to propose new and expanded legal protections for specifically racial wrongs.

The race model also suggests that we need to understand the sources and construction of individual ideas about race—the "psychology" of racism. The race model suggests that racist beliefs are deeper than mistakes of fact, and that it is necessary to understand race at the level of individual personality. This is so not only because racism at an individual level can be seen as "pathological," but also because the power and strength of white supremacy seem to come largely from its deep roots in individual consciousness and self-concept.

Of course, no model alone yields an adequate understanding of white supremacy. For instance, the race model has problems with its vision of the future. Within our current national boundaries, blacks are a relatively small minority. Black resort to unilateral armed rebellion looks suicidal in this setting. But if all this is true, and yet coalitions are to be avoided, where does change come from, according to the race model? Some appear to have given up hope:

[T]he socio-economic deterioration of blacks will continue and will do so to the point of extermination. Any effort to reverse this *inevitable* outcome will have to take the form of violent
confrontation; to respond violently in a nation so dedicated to white supremacy over a black minority is an open invitation to extermination.

[S]tatistics make it clear that the economic road to black redemption may be a dead end. . . .
[T]he political road to black survival does not offer more promise. . . . [T]here is little reason to
place much faith in the law.

Perhaps, under these circumstances, the solemn admonition from Dylan Thomas might do
well: Do not go gentle into that good night.[5]

If blacks are an isolated and stigmatized minority and cannot ultimately trust coalitions,
then even gains achieved through massive pressure and mobilization will remain perpetually vulnerable.

A deep pessimism thus haunts the race model. (To say this is not, in itself, a meaningful "critique" of the model, of course. If it is true that while supremacy binds all whites together so that their solidarity will ultimately reassert itself in perpetuity to conquer differences among them and confirm black subordination, then American black people and
their anomalous friends *should* be pessimistic.) I will argue, however, that the pessimism
implied by a pure race model is unwarranted.

A pure race model, given United States demographics and the present national economy,
sees solid change coming only from without. Its notion of the best blacks can aim for is the
skillful use of their limited leverage and the building of formal constraints against racial
harms. Yet any strategy based on formal norms and sanctions inevitably depends on the
good will of those with the present social power to create and impose them and it would be
folly for African Americans or other minorities to place any long-term hope or faith in the
good will of those whites who are in a position to control and implement such norms and
sanctions in our society.

People of color do not have to go it alone. Many white people in our system need deep societal changes despite the undeniable benefits they gain from white supremacy. Given our
history, whites will be just as unable to achieve such change alone as minorities are. Strategic weakness for these whites does not come from lack of numbers. In order to be strong
enough to move toward change, people must be able to understand the large questions of
power and justice in their society. In this society, race is one of those important questions
of power and justice, one on a very short list of *the* most important. White people who fail
to see and understand white supremacy can and will be stopped time and again in their own
tracks. For this reason, whites and blacks needing change are in a position of mutual dependence. Bringing an end to white supremacy, and otherwise redistributing power and resources, will require the union of many kinds of people who have suffered many kinds of
harms, sometimes even at each other's hands. Nothing in history has shown either that
white supremacy will end, or that it cannot end, through such a coming together.

Notes

1. Peggy McIntosh recently has made two further interesting points. First, whites in our society
enjoy not only the subjective sensation of superiority, but also a kind of unconscious "non-sensation"
of well-being and security, all the more meaningful and valuable because those who enjoy it are
largely unaware that they "have" it while others do not. Her second point, and perhaps the more con-

testable in this context, is that whites are in some ways privileged, but in other ways profoundly damaged and retarded, by this system of "unearned advantage and conferred dominance." PEGGY McINTOSH, WHITE PRIVILEGE AND MALE PRIVILEGE: A PERSONAL ACCOUNT OF COMING TO SEE CORRESPONDENCES THROUGH WORK IN WOMEN'S STUDIES 14 (Working Paper No. 189, Wellesley College Center for Research on Women). [Reprinted as Chapter 47 of this book. Ed.]

2. John Calmore, *Exploring the Significance of Race and Class in Representing the Black Poor*, 61 OR. L. REV. 201, 217 (1982).

3. *Id.* (emphasis added). But note that Calmore later specifically approves of coalition-building. He argues that it will be safer if pursued on the basis of a well-defined, "indigestible," and self-consciously black presence. *Id.* at 219–20.

4. Charles Lawrence, *The Id, the Ego, and Equal Protection: Reckoning with Unconscious Racism*, 39 STAN. L. REV. 317, 365 note 227.

5. Derrick Bell, *A Hurdle Too High: Class-based Roadblocks to Racial Remediation*, 33 BUFFALO L. REV. 1, 25, 28 (1984). (Sidney Willhelm speaking).

99

White Superiority in America:
Its Legal Legacy, Its Economic Costs

DERRICK A. BELL

A major function of racial discrimination is to facilitate the exploitation of black labor, to deny blacks access to benefits and opportunities, and to blame all the manifestations of exclusion-bred despair on the asserted inferiority of the victims. Two other inter-connected political phenomena emanate from the widely shared belief that whites are superior to blacks. First, whites of widely varying socio-economic status employ white supremacy as a catalyst to negotiate policy differences, often through compromises that sacrifice the rights of blacks. Second, even those whites who lack wealth and power are sustained in their sense of racial superiority and more willing to accept a lesser share, by an unspoken but no less certain property right in their "whiteness." This right is recognized and upheld by courts and the society like all other property rights.

Let us look first at the compromise-catalyst role of racism in American policy-making. When the Constitution's Framers gathered in Philadelphia, it is clear that their compromises on slavery were the key that enabled Southerners and Northerners to work out their economic and political differences. The slavery compromises set a precedent under which black rights have been sacrificed throughout the nation's history to further white interests. Those compromises are the original and still definitive examples of the ongoing struggle between individual rights reform and the maintenance of the socio-economic *status quo*.

Why did the Framers do it? Surely, there is little substance in the traditional rationalizations that the slavery provisions in the Constitution were merely unfortunate concessions influenced by then prevailing beliefs that slavery was on the decline and would soon die of its own weight, or that Africans were thought a different and inferior breed of beings whose enslavement carried no moral onus. The insistence of Southern delegates on protection of their slave property was far too vigorous to suggest that the institution would soon be abandoned. And the anti-slavery statements by slaves and white abolitionists alike were too forceful to suggest that the slavery compromises were the product of men who did not know the moral ramifications of what they did.

The question of what motivated the Framers remains. In my recent book, *And We Are Not Saved*,[1] the heroine, Geneva Crenshaw, a black civil rights lawyer, gifted with extraordinary powers, is transported back to the Constitutional Convention of 1787.

There is, I know, no mention of this visit in Max Farrand's records of the Convention proceedings. James Madison's compulsive notes are silent on the event. But the omission

33 VILL. L. REV. 767 (1988). Originally published in the *Villanova Law Review*. Reprinted by permission.

of the debate that followed her sudden appearance in the locked meeting room and the protection she is provided when the delegates try to eject her is easier to explain than the still embarrassing fact that these men—some of the outstanding figures of their time—could incorporate slavery into a document committed to life, liberty, and the pursuit of happiness to all. Would the Framers have acted differently had they known the great grief their compromises on slavery would cause? Geneva's mission is to use her knowledge of the next two centuries to convince the Framers that they should not incorporate recognition and protection of slavery. Her sudden arrival at the podium was sufficiently startling to intimidate even these men. But outrage quickly overcame their shock. Ignoring Geneva's warm greeting and her announcement that she had come from 200 years in the future, some of the more vigorous delegates, outraged at the sudden appearance in their midst of a woman, and a black woman at that, charged towards her. As Geneva described the scene:

> As the delegates were almost upon me—a cylinder composed of thin vertical bars of red, white, and blue light descended swiftly and silently from the high ceiling, nicely encapsulating the podium and me.
>
> To their credit, the self-appointed eviction party neither slowed nor swerved. As each man reached and tried to pass through the transparent light shield, a loud hiss, quite like the sound electrified bug zappers make on a warm, summer evening filled the air. While not lethal, the shock the shield dealt each attacker was sufficiently strong to literally knock him to the floor, stunned and shaking.

This phenomenon evokes chaos rather than attention in the room, but finally during a lull in the bedlam, Geneva tries for the third time to be heard. "Gentlemen," she begins again, "Delegates,"—then paused and, with a slight smile, added, "fellow citizens. I have come to urge that, in your great work here, you not restrict to white men of property the sweep of Thomas Jefferson's self-evident truths. For all men (and women too) are equal and endowed by the Creator with inalienable rights, including 'Life, Liberty and the pursuit of Happiness.'"

The debate that ensues between Geneva and the Framers is vigorous, but despite her extraordinary powers, Geneva is unable to alter the already reached compromises on slavery. She tries to embarrass the Framers by pointing out the contradiction in their commitment to freedom and liberty and their embrace of slavery. They will not buy it:

> "There is no contradiction," replied a delegate. . . . "Life and liberty were generally said to be of more value, than property, . . . [but] an accurate view of the matter would nevertheless prove that property is the main object of Society."
>
> "A contradiction," another added, "would occur were we to follow the course you urge. We are not unaware of the moral issues raised by slavery, but we have no response to the [Southern delegate] who has admonished us that 'property in slaves should not be exposed to danger under a Government instituted for the protection of property.'"
>
> Government, was instituted principally for the protection of property. . . . Property is the great object of government; the great cause of war; the great means of carrying it on.[2] The security the Southerners seek is that their Negroes may not be taken from them. After all, Negroes are their wealth, their only resource.

Where, Geneva wondered, were those delegates from Northern states, many of whom abhorred slavery and had already spoken out against it in the Convention? She found her answer in the castigation she received from one of the Framers, who told her:

Woman, we would have you gone from this place. But if a record be made, it should show that the economic benefits of slavery do not accrue only to the South. Plantation states provide a market for Northern factories, and the New England shipping industry and merchants participate in the slave trade. Northern states, moreover, utilize slaves in the fields, as domestics, and even as soldiers to defend against Indian raids.

Slavery has provided the wealth that made independence possible, another delegate told her. The profits from slavery funded the Revolution. . . . The nation's economic well-being depended on the institution, and its preservation is essential if the Constitution we are drafting is to be more than a useless document.

At the most dramatic moment of the debate, a somber delegate got to his feet, and walked fearlessly right up to the shimmering light shield. Then he spoke seriously and with obvious anxiety:

This contradiction is not lost on us. Surely we know, even though we are at pains not to mention it, that we have sacrificed the freedom of your people in the belief that this involuntary forfeiture is necessary to secure the property interests of whites in a society espousing, as its basic principle, the liberty of all. Perhaps we, with the responsibility of forming a radically new government in perilous times, see more clearly than is possible for you in hindsight that the unavoidable cost of our labors will be the need to accept and live with what you call a contradiction.

Realizing that she was losing the debate, Geneva intensified her efforts. But the imprisoned delegates' signals for help had been seen and the local militia summoned. Hearing some commotion beyond the window, she turned to see a small cannon being rolled up and aimed at her. Then, in quick succession, a militiaman lighted the fuse; the delegates dived under their desks; the cannon fired; and, with an ear-splitting roar, the cannonball broke against the light shield and splintered, leaving the shield intact, but terminating both the visit and all memory of it.

The Framers felt—and likely they were right—that a government committed to the protection of property could not have come into being without the race-based slavery compromises placed in the Constitution. Without slavery, there would be no Constitution to celebrate. This is true not only because slavery provided the wealth that made independence possible, but also because it afforded an ideological basis to resolve conflict between propertied and unpropertied whites. Working-class whites did not oppose slavery when it took root in the mid-1600s. They identified on the basis of race with wealthy planters . . . even though they were and would remain economically subordinate to those able to afford slaves. But the creation of a black subclass enabled poor whites to identify with and support the policies of the upper class. And large landowners, with the safe economic advantage provided by their slaves, were willing to grant poor whites a larger role in the political process. Thus, paradoxically, slavery for blacks led to greater freedom for poor whites, at least when compared with the denial of freedom to African slaves. Slavery also provided mainly propertyless whites with a property in their whiteness.

Slavery compromises continued. The long fight for universal male suffrage was successful in several states when opponents and advocates alike reached compromises based on their generally held view that blacks should not vote. Historian Leon Litwack reports that "utilizing various political, social, economic, and pseudo-anthropological arguments, white suffragists moved to deny the vote to the Negro. From the admission of Maine in 1819 until the end of the Civil War, every new state restricted the suffrage to whites in its constitution."[3]

Chief Justice Taney's conclusion in *Dred Scott* that blacks had no rights whites were bound to respect represented a renewed effort to compromise political differences between whites by sacrificing the rights of blacks. The effort failed, less because Taney was willing to place all blacks—free as well as slave—outside the ambit of constitutional protection, than because he rashly committed the Supreme Court to one side of the fiercely contested issues of economic and political power that were propelling the nation toward the Civil War.

When the war ended, the North pushed through constitutional amendments, nominally to grant citizenship rights to former slaves, but actually to protect its victory. But within a decade, when another political crisis threatened a new civil war, black rights were again sacrificed in the Hayes-Tilden Compromise of 1877. Constitutional jurisprudence fell in line with Taney's conclusion regarding the rights of blacks *vis-à-vis* whites even as his opinion was condemned. The country moved ahead, but blacks were cast into a status that only looked positive when compared with slavery itself.

Even those whites who lack wealth and power are sustained in their sense of racial superiority, and thus rendered more willing to accept their lesser share, by an unspoken but no less certain property right in their "whiteness." In the post-Reconstruction era, the constitutional amendments initially promoted to provide rights for the newly emancipated blacks were transformed into the major legal bulwarks for corporate growth. The legal philosophy of that era espoused liberty of action untrammeled by state authority, but the only logic of the ideology—and its goal—was the exploitation of the working class, whites as well as blacks.

As to whites, consider *Lochner v. New York*,[4] where the Court refused to find that the state's police powers extended to protecting bakery employees against employers who required them to work in physically unhealthy conditions for more than 10 hours per day and 60 hours per week. Such maximum hour legislation, the Court held, would interfere with the bakers' inherent freedom of contract. In effect, the Court simply assumed in that pre-union era that employees and employers bargained from positions of equal strength. Liberty of that sort simply legitimated the sweat shops in which men, women, and children were quite literally worked to death.

For blacks, of course, we can compare *Lochner* with the decision in *Plessy v. Ferguson*,[5] decided only nine years earlier. In *Plessy*, the Court upheld the state's police power to segregate blacks in public facilities even though such segregation must, of necessity, interfere with the liberties of facilities' owners to use their property as they saw fit. Both opinions are quite similar in the Court's use of fourteenth amendment fictions: the assumed economic "liberty" of bakers in *Lochner*, and the assumed political "equality" of blacks in *Plessy*. Those assumptions required the most blatant form of hypocrisy. Both decisions protected existing property and political arrangements, while ignoring the disadvantages to the powerless caught in those relationships.

The effort to form workers' unions to combat the powerful corporate structure was undermined because of the active antipathy against blacks practiced by all but a few unions.[6] Excluded from jobs and the unions because of their color, blacks were hired as scab labor during strikes, a fact that simply increased the hostility of white workers that should have been directed toward their corporate oppressors.

The Populist movement in the latter part of the nineteenth century attempted to build a working-class party in the South strong enough to overcome the economic exploitation by the ruling classes. But when neither Populists nor the conservative Democrats were able to control the black vote, they agreed to exclude blacks entirely through state constitutional amendments, thereby leaving whites to fight out elections themselves. With blacks no longer a force at the ballot box, conservatives dropped even the semblance of opposition to "Jim Crow" provisions pushed by lower-class whites as their guarantee that the nation recognized their priority citizenship claim, based on their whiteness.

Later, Southern whites rebelled against the Supreme Court's 1954 decision declaring school segregation unconstitutional precisely because they felt the long-standing priority of their superior status to blacks had been unjustly repealed. Today, over forty years since the Court's rejection of the "separate but equal" doctrine of *Plessy v. Ferguson*,[7] the passwords that still exist for the property right in being white include "higher entrance scores," "seniority," and "neighborhood schools." Consider, too, the use of impossible to hurdle intent barriers to deny blacks remedies for racial injustices where the relief sought would either undermine white expectations and advantages gained during years of overt discrimination[8] or expose the deeply imbedded racism in a major institution, such as the criminal justice system.[9]

The continuing resistance to affirmative action plans, set-asides, and other meaningful relief for discrimination-caused harm is based in substantial part on the perception that black gains threaten priorities and preferences many whites believe they are entitled to over blacks. The law has mostly encouraged and upheld what Mr. Plessy argued in *Plessy v. Ferguson* was a property right in whiteness, while the wealthy have benefited because the masses of whites are too occupied in keeping blacks down to note the large gap between their shaky status and that of whites on top.

Blacks continue to serve as buffers between those most advantaged in the society and those whites seemingly content to live the lives of the rich and famous through the pages of the tabloids and television dramas like *Dallas, Falcon Crest,* and *Dynasty.* Caught in the vortex of this national conspiracy that is perhaps more effective because it apparently functions without master plan or even conscious thought, the wonder is not that so many blacks manifest self-destructive or non-functional behavior patterns, but that so many continue to strive and sometimes succeed, despite all.

Notes

1. Derrick Bell, And We Are Not Saved: The Elusive Quest for Racial Justice (1987).

2. See generally I The Record of the Federal Convention of 1787, at 535, 542, 593–94 (M. Farrand ed. 1911).

3. Leon Litwack, North of Slavery: The Negro in the Free States 1790–1860, at 79 (1967).

4. 198 U.S. 45 (1905) (overruled by *Ferguson v. Skrupa,* 372 U.S. 726, 730 (1963) ("[D]octrine that . . . due process authorizes courts to hold laws unconstitutional when they believe the legislature has acted unwisely [is] . . . discarded.")) .

5. 163 U.S. 537 (1896) (overruled by *Brown v. Board of Educ.,* 347 U.S. 483 (1954)("separate but equal" doctrine inapplicable to public education)).

6. See, e.g., William Gould, Black Workers in White Unions: Job Discrimination in the United States (1977); H. Hill, Black Labor and the American Legal System (1977).

7. *Brown v. Board of Education,* 347 U.S. 483 (1954).

8. *Washington v. Davis,* 426 U.S. 229 (1976).

9. McCleskey v. Kemp, 107 S. Ct. 1756 (1987).

Synopses of Other Important Works

The White Supremacist Mindset

The Fascist Mind

In a recent article ("Eternal Fascism," *New York Review of Books*, reprinted in *Utne Reader*, November/December 1995, p. 57), the novelist and cultural critic Umberto Eco offers "Fourteen Ways for Looking at a Blackshirt." These features of "Ur-Fascism, or Eternal Fascism" include: the cult of tradition; rejection of modernism; action for action's sake; the equating of disagreement with treason; fear of difference; appeal to a frustrated middle class; the notion of a new world order; a sense of humiliation at the wealth and force of enemies; the conviction that life is permanent warfare; contempt for the weak; emphasis on heroism; transference of will to power to sexual matters; populism and disdain for parliamentary government; and Newspeak—corruption of language.

Eco warns:

> Ur-Fascism is still around us, sometimes in plainclothes. It would be so much easier for us if there appeared on the world scene somebody saying, "I want to reopen Auschwitz, I want the Blackshirts to parade again in the Italian squares." Life is not that simple. Ur-Fascism can come back under the most innocent of disguises. Our duty is to uncover it and to point our finger at any of its new instances. . . . Freedom and liberation are an unending task (pp. 57, 59).

How to Speak in Code

In his book *There's No Such Thing as Free Speech, and It's a Good Thing, Too* (Oxford University Press, 1994), Stanley Fish writes of how latter-day bigots have learned to wrap themselves in the American flag, quote Martin Luther King, and appeal to principles of merit.

> Code words are all around us these days. When a politician declares that we have to stop catering to special interests and pay attention to the middle class, you know who the special interests are and you know that the color of the middle class—symbolically, if not empirically—is white. And when another politician attacks welfare mothers who breed children in order to claim larger benefits, you know that the real message is composed of two racial stereotypes: (1) the sexually-promiscuous black . . . , and (2) the lazy and shiftless negro made familiar to so many Americans by the comedian Stepin Fetchit (p. 90).

Fish goes on to detail how such speaking in code enables the speaker to play upon cultural prejudices against blacks, foreigners, and the poor while appearing to take the high road. "The favorite strategy is to find a word or concept that seems invulnerable to challenge—law, equality, merit, neutrality—and then to give it a definition that generates the desired outcome. David Duke has it down pat" (p. 91). And so, he shows, does his favorite rival, Dinesh D'Souza, who according to Fish uses innuendo and selective quotation to make it appear that it is African-Americans who are the aggressors, imposing on long-suffering, innocent whites and dragging down our universities at the same time.

"No Longer a War of Words"

First published in 1978 under a pseudonym, William Pierce's *Turner Diaries* is undergoing a new vogue. The novel details a frightening scenario in which the United States is caught up in a race war between slovenly blacks and heroic whites. Interviewed by Mike Wallace on *CBS 60 Minutes* (May 19, 1996), Pierce responded to queries as follows:

WALLACE: We are now in a process of . . . self-destruction in the United States?
PIERCE: In a process of disintegration. . . . And it's not just me—not just me and people around me who—who feel this. There's a general feeling of this throughout the society, a—a feeling that things are coming apart, a feeling that the center cannot hold. . . .
WALLACE: The central message of his novel . . . is that the United States is being ruined by blacks, Hispanics, Jews—just about everyone but those he calls his people, Aryan whites. . . .
PIERCE: Race mixing is—is one of the things which is causing the breakdown of American society, and the alienation of the people generally.
WALLACE: You refer often . . . to blacks as rapists, thugs, dumb, cannibals. . . .
PIERCE: I was envisioning the breakdown of society as a culmination of the trends that I could see in the 1970s.

A passage from *The Turner Diaries* (National Vanguard, 2d ed. 1980) follows:

September 16, 1991. Today it finally began! After all these years of talking—and nothing but talking—we have finally taken our first action. We are at war with the System, and it is no longer a war of words. . . .
. . . I'll never forget that terrible day: November 8, 1989. They knocked on my door at five in the morning. I was completely unsuspecting as I got up to see who it was.
I opened the door, and four Negroes came pushing in to the apartment before I could stop them. One was carrying a baseball bat, and two had long kitchen knives thrust into their belts. The one with the bat shoved me back into a corner and stood guard . . . while the other three began ransacking my apartment (p. 1).

Chapters describe the bombing of an FBI building (p. 32) employing homemade explosives, a flood of Mexican immigrants surging across the border (p. 33), the government's enactment of a law taking away the guns of white resisters (e.g., pp. 1, 34), and roving bands of blacks clashing with embattled white militia who operate in secrecy to protect Western civilization.

Resurgence of the Ku Klux Klan

In *Behind the Mask of Chivalry: The Making of the Second Ku Klux Klan* (Oxford University Press, 1994), Nancy MacLean highlights the way in which populist sentiment and the politics of class provide much of the momentum for the latest resurgence of this far-right organization.

Tapping the fears of worried workers about displacement, slipping behind, and loss of control, Klan leaders appeal to blue-collar men who distrust government and sense that blacks and other un-American elements are getting ahead at their expense. She explains the group's ideology in the following passage:

> Klan leaders prided themselves on their fidelity to the vision of the founding fathers. On the one hand, they exalted the old liberal tradition of possessive individualism. That property was the basis of freedom was the grounding assumption of the Klan's political theory. . . . "The function of the government . . . is to protect individuals in their right of person and right of property." The great merit of the United States Constitution was that it had "established individual property rights more securely" than any other form of government, guarding against the twin dangers of "feudalism" and "all forms of socialism or communism" (p. 79).

Hate Online

Computer technology is a leading means by which right-wing extremist groups organize, recruit new members, and stay in touch with each other. An article by Peter Stills, "Dark Contagion: Bigotry and Violence Online" (*PC/Computing*, December 1989) explains how this is done. Stills discusses neo-Nazi and skinhead boards, describes the role of the right-wing activist Tom Metzger, and quotes a number of typical listings, such as:

- If we'd destroy the Jews, there wouldn't be any need for sand niggers [Arabs] to take hostages.
- We should just wipe out the entire region with tactical nukes and show them what America can really do (p. 146).

The article explains how new users learn about the boards, earn passwords, and gain access to higher and higher levels of security. It details how many skinhead boards that once operated publicly have gone underground, using unlisted numbers or changing them periodically to keep out hostile or curious interlopers (p. 147). It shows how extremist groups have used electronic boards to coordinate activities including murder and bomb making.

Recent Postings from a right-wing hate group, culled by the editors from the Internet:

- Fuck 'em. What have they done for the preservation and advancement of the White race? They let our schools be mongrelized with Niggers. . . . They let our once fair cities get turned into Nigger, Spic, Gook, Raghead, Faggot, etc., infested cesspools. They were provided with the greatest country in the world . . . and the old bastards just squandered the damn thing away.
- We frequently hear that the Negroes are "so many years behind the White man," as though it is only a matter of time before he catches up to us. This is a flagrant error. The Negro has been developing along his own lines, while the White man developed along his, just as the higher apes have also evolved, but along a separate path. . . .
- There are pictures of White people on the walls of Western European caves which are as much as 25,000 years old. All of the evidence available . . . indicates a long separation of the principal races of man.
- It is time that we started using their laws against them. The best way to do this is in the area of religion. Laws that they enact for their religions must also apply to ours. . . .
- If they say that a child may wear a religious symbol such as a cross or a Star of David to school, then they cannot bar our children from wearing our holiest symbol, the Sacred Swastika.
- Aggression works! Passive, Mr. Nice Guy stuff only lets people walk on you. Getting in peoples' faces, like the queers do, is aggressive. Flooding the street with literature is aggressive. Shouting people down like the "Reds" do is aggressive and it works. Because of Jewish aggression, they control the White upper-classes. It pays to be pushy.

From the Editors: Issues and Comments

Is there anything wrong with being proud of your race? Where does that cross over into supremacist thought and extremism? Is it better to ignore, or take no note of, one's own ethnicity in order to avoid the excesses of Aryan or other forms of supremacy? Is it wrong to be proud of one's country? To want to limit the number of immigrants who come here? What if your policy is to encourage ones from Northern Europe and discourage the rest? Can America absorb ten thousand new immigrants from, say, Sweden, more easily than it can the same number from Ethiopia? Is there such a thing as WASP culture? Does it include saving, hard work, self-denial, and moderation in sex? If so, what is wrong with that? Germany has banned neo-Nazi groups; should the United States do likewise? Throughout history, the black community has received poor police protection and sometimes outright mistreatment at the hands of the police. Should African-Americans, then, arm themselves as private militias have done?

Suggested Readings

Chalmers, David M., Hooded Americanism: The History of the Ku Klux Klan (Franklyn Watts, 1980).

Coates, James, Armed and Dangerous: The Rise of the Survivalist Right (Noonday Press, 1987).

Corcoran, James, Bitter Harvest—Gordon Kahl and the Posse Comitatus: Murder in the Heartland (Viking, 1990).

Flynn, Kevin, and Gary Gerhardt, The Silent Brotherhood: Inside America's Racist Underground (Free Press, 1989).

Higginbotham, Leon, and Barbara Kopytoff, *Racial Purity and Interracial Sex in the Law of Colonial and Antebellum Virginia*, 77 Geo. L.J. 1967 (1989).

Mintz, Frank P., The Liberty Lobby and the American Right (Greenwood 1985).

Pierce, William, The Turner Diaries (1978).

Raspail, Jean, The Camp of the Saints (1973).

Singular, Stephen, Talked to Death: The Murder of Alan Berg and the Rise of the Neo-Nazis (Berkeley, 1989).

Wade, Wyn Craig, The Fiery Cross: The Ku Klux Klan in America (Simon & Schuster, 1987).

Part XI

What Then Shall We Do?
A Role for Whites

Whites may—and should—study race, including their own. That is the whole premise of this book. But suppose a white person wants to do more—wants to be an agent for change, wants to challenge and blast the systems of racial privilege and exclusion that bring so much misery to all those on the other side of the color line? What can a white person do? Is there a role for him or her in improving the fortunes of people of color? One author dyed his skin black and traveled in the South, acquiring a sense of empathy for the plight of black people. [See Chapter 70. Ed.] Another urges that whites take on the radical role of race traitor, under the banner "Treason to Whiteness Is Loyalty to Humanity." Others urge that whites reflect carefully on their own privilege and begin the difficult process of giving it up, or that they study their own "dysconscious racism" with a view toward unlearning the systems and habits of racial treatment that condition so much of our inner and outer lives. One author urges white people to give up being white and to destroy the idea of the white race. Would this be suicide?

100

Treason to Whiteness Is Loyalty to Humanity

AN INTERVIEW WITH NOEL IGNATIEV OF
RACE TRAITOR MAGAZINE

What is a race traitor anyway?

A traitor to the white race is someone who is nominally classified as white, but who defies the rules of whiteness so flagrantly as to jeopardize his or her ability to draw upon the privileges of the white skin.

"Race" has meant various things in history. We use the term to mean a group that includes all social classes, in a situation where the most degraded member of a dominant group is exalted over any member of a subordinate group. That formation was first successfully established in the 17th century. By then there already existed a trade across the Atlantic in laborers. Traders from both Europe and Africa sold their countrymen and were not held back because they were of the same color as those they sold. Slavery was a matter of economics. At the time it was the most efficient way of guaranteeing a labor force—provided it could be enforced.

As Theodore Allen points out in *Invention of the White Race,* the white race meant not only that no European-Americans were slaves, but also that all European-Americans, even laborers, were by definition enforcers of slavery. In the Chesapeake Bay Colony (Virginia and Maryland), people from Africa and people from Europe worked together in the tobacco fields. They mated with each other, ran away and rebelled together, at first. At the end of the 1600s, people of African descent, even those who were free, lost certain rights they had had before and that even the poorest and most downtrodden person of European descent continued to enjoy. In return for these privileges, European-Americans of all classes came to be part of the apparatus that maintained Afro-Americans in chattel slavery (and themselves in unfreedom). That was the birth of "race," as we use the term.

What do you mean when you say that race is a social construction?

We mean that it is the result of social distinctions. Many black people have European ancestors, and plenty of so-called whites have African or American Indian ancestors. No biologist has ever been able to provide a satisfactory definition of race—that is, a definition that includes all the members of a given "race" and excludes all others. Attempts to do so lead to absurdities: mothers and children of different races, or the phenomenon that a white woman can give birth to a black child, but a black woman can never give birth to a white

From *¡The Blast!* (June/July 1994). Reprinted by permission.

child. The only possible conclusion is that people are members of different races because they are assigned to them. Of course, differences exist between individuals, and the natives of West Africa in general had darker skin and so forth than the natives of the British Isles, but groups are formed by social distinctions, not nature.

Can you provide an example of a people suddenly becoming "white"?

The Irish are as clear an example as any. In Ireland, under the Protestant Ascendancy, Catholic Irish were the victims of discrimination identical to what we in America call racial, and were even referred to as a "race." Karl Marx, writing from England, reported that the average English worker looked down on the Irish the way poor whites in the American South looked upon Afro-Americans. Yet over here the Irish became "whites," by gaining the right to vote while free Negroes were losing it, by supporting the Democratic Party (the party of the slaveholders), and by preventing free Afro-Americans from competing with them for jobs. The overcoming of anti-Irish prejudice meant that the Irish were admitted to the privileges of whiteness.

What do you mean by the "new abolitionism"?

We believe that so long as the white race exists, all movements against what is called "racism" will fail. Therefore, our aim is to abolish the white race.

How does your position on race and whiteness differ from the standard political stance of anti-racism?

Racism is a pretty vague term. It has come to mean little more than a tendency to dislike people for the color of their skin. Most anti-racists, even while they oppose discrimination, believe that racial status is fixed and eternal. We hold that without social distinctions, "race" is a fiction. The only race is the human race.

Even if a person declares him/herself a "race traitor," to the vast majority of people in this society, he/she is still white and therefore allowed all the privileges of the "white club." Is it possible to abolish the white race, ironically, only as white people?

The white race does not like to relinquish a single member, so that even those who step out of it in one situation find it virtually impossible not to rejoin it later, if only because of the assumptions of others—unless, like John Brown, they have the good fortune to be hanged before that happens. So-called whites have special responsibilities to abolition that only they can fulfill. Only they can dissolve the white race from within, by rejecting the poisoned bait of white-skin privileges. If that is what you mean by abolishing the white race "as whites," then we have no quarrel.

What is the relationship between capitalism and racism?

Capital itself is color-blind, and the capitalist system, as such, recognizes nothing but atomized individuals acting independently in the market. There are places in the world where it exists without race. In this country race is central to the system of social control:

It leads some workers to settle for being "white" when they could, with some effort, be free.

Is there such a thing as a "white culture"?

No. There is Italian culture, and Polish, Irish, Yiddish, German, and Appalachian culture: There is youth culture and drug culture and queer culture; but there is no "white" culture—unless you mean Wonder Bread and television game shows. Whiteness is nothing but an expression of race privilege. It has been said that the typical "white" American male spends his childhood as an Indian, his adolescence as an Afro-American, and only becomes white when he reaches the age of legal responsibility.

In an autobiographical essay, Joel Gilbert says that most of his whiteness has washed away and that he has "plenty of black inside." How is it possible for a white person to have "plenty of black" inside? How is it possible for whites to wash away their whiteness? Should a black person accept a white person's claim to have "a lot of black inside"?

Politically, whiteness is the willingness to seek a comfortable place within the system of race privilege. Blackness means total, implacable, and relentless opposition to that system. To the extent so-called whites oppose the race line, repudiate their own race privileges, and jeopardize their own standing in the white race, they can be said to have washed away their whiteness and taken in some blackness. Probably a black person should not accept a white person's claim to have done that, but should watch how that person acts.

A common theme in Race Traitor *is that of whites "crossing over" into black culture, or what you have called "black assimilation." A lot of the examples you cite of people "refusing to be white" involve white people—especially youth—imitating black cultural forms. The line between "crossing over" into black culture and ripping off black culture is a mighty fine one; where do you draw it? Is there a necessary connection between "crossover" and the abandonment of whiteness? What makes white "crossover" in the '90s different from white youths and big businesses "crossing over" and ripping off black music in the '40s and '50s?*

In culture, the line between rip-off and respect is the willingness to pay the dues, if necessary to forgo the social advantages of being white, in order to achieve genuineness of expression. There is no necessary connection between cultural assimilation and rejection of whiteness: The crowds at professional basketball games prove that; and on the other hand, immigrants to this country may speak no English and have no interest in American culture and still refuse to take part in the oppression of black people. But for many, the rejection of whiteness seems to entail some engagement with Afro-American culture, because that is the first cultural expression of resistance they encounter, and it speaks powerfully to them. You are right to point out that whites have been ripping off Afro-American culture for years. Fundamentally, the crossover of the '90s may not be different from that of the past, although it may make a difference that the process of social dissolution is now more advanced. By itself, crossover represents a potential for race treason, not the actuality.

How does wanting to abolish racial classifications avoid doing away with cultural differences, which is what most liberal attempts to "confront racism" do?

For us, black and white are political categories, separate from, although not unrelated to, culture. One of the effects of white supremacy is that it represses the cultures of Afro-Americans and other peoples of color. If that repression were removed, who knows how they would flourish. Moreover, American culture is, as Albert Murray has pointed out, incontestably mulatto. Without race prejudice, Americans might discover that culturally they are all Afro-American, as well as Native American, and so forth.

Abolition also brings up issues of identity. People of color, in struggling against oppression, often turn toward their precolonial cultures and earlier examples of resistance to find an identity that can inspire them today. What can a so-called white person turn to after abandoning whiteness? Does s/he seek inspiration in prewhite cultures such as Judaism, Celtic or Germanic tribes, in ethnic identities such as Irish, Italian-American, etc.? In committing treason against the white race, must we seek these "intermediate" identities, abandon all identities in favor of a universal humanism, or something else?

I don't know. So far as I am concerned, there is nothing wrong with people seeking out the Celtic or Germanic tribes, or ethnicity, or anything else that can provide them with a vital alternative to whiteness, although I have my doubts about how real these are or can be made to be for modern Americans, and the last time somebody built a mass movement around Germanic tribal myths it led to big trouble. We might do better to promote models of amalgamation. The Seminole Indians, as I understand it, were composed of the remnants of several native groups who had earlier been dispersed, plus a number of runaway slaves, plus some deserters from the army. They came together and fought three wars against the U.S. government. They were never really defeated. The Seminole tribe might be a model that could inspire people. Time will tell.

In being a race traitor, to whom do you announce your treason—fellow so-called whites? Is it ever appropriate to tell a person of color that you have abandoned your whiteness?

I would never say that, although I might say I was working on it.

What kinds of relations with people of color are implied when one becomes a race traitor? How does a race traitor act politically with people of color?

Relations must be based on solidarity. People of color have a wealth of experience with white supremacy from which others can learn, but the fight against white supremacy is not something to engage in as a favor to anyone. All people who wish to be free have an equal stake—yes, an equal stake—in overturning the system of white supremacy. I'm reminded of the old IWW [Industrial Workers of the World, the "Wobblies"] slogan, "An injury to one is an injury to all." Decades of distortion have reduced the message of those words to the idea that you should oppose injustice against others today because if you don't it will come your way tomorrow. We believe in the original intent of the slogan. The Bible offers the same instruction: "Remember them that are in bonds as bound with them."

Race Traitor does an excellent job of providing examples of individuals rejecting their whiteness and joining the human race, but there is little there of collective resistance. Where is the collective political strategy in a politics of abolition? How do we, collectively, abolish the white race?

For the white race to be effective, it must be unanimous, or nearly so. The reason is that if the cops and the courts and so forth couldn't be sure that every person who looked white was loyal to the system, then what would be the point of extending race privileges to whites? And if they stopped extending race privileges, what would happen to the white race? Our strategy seeks to bring together a determined minority, willing to defy white rules so flagrantly they make it impossible to pretend that all those who look white are loyal to the system of racial oppression.

We wish we could cite more examples of collective resistance. The whites who joined the rebellions in Los Angeles and elsewhere were a good example. The Attica prison rebellion was another. The initiative by Love and Rage to launch a campaign culminating in a day of action against immigration controls and anti-immigrant violence was a good project, but unfortunately it never got off the ground. Collective struggle is crucial, but at some point every white person has to choose, like Huck Finn, between being white and striking out for freedom.

In some articles you literally break the world down into a matter of black and white. Have you ever been accused of ignoring the struggles and perspectives of nonblack people of color, and how do you respond to this charge?

Yes, I have been. I think that the line between black and white determines race in this country, and all groups get defined in relation to that line. Don't forget, I am using black and white as political, not cultural, categories. I do not mean to neglect the real and independent histories of people of color who are not of African descent. But in some cases the talk about "people of color" obscures the essence of racial oppression. Chinese are people of color and in the past they suffered fierce oppression in this country, and still suffer the effects of prejudice, but would anyone argue that Chinese in America today constitute an oppressed race? They have been defined as an ethnic group, indeed the "model minority," as shown by the high rate of social mobility among them, the high proportion of marriages with European-Americans, and the presence among them of a substantial number of capitalists who function outside of a segregated market—all in contrast to the situation of Afro-Americans. Of course they might become an oppressed race again. Or they might choose to identify as black in the struggle against white power, as many of the so-called coloureds of South Africa have done.

It seems from your journal and from thinking about your ideas that abolishing the white race would bring about widespread, radical changes in other aspects of social life. Is race treason necessarily revolutionary in that it threatens not only white supremacy but class rule as well?

It would be good if people could forget that they are white and pursue their interests as workers, or women, or whatever else moves them. The problem is that American society does not allow anyone to forget, but injects race into every political controversy. For those in power, the privileges granted whites are a small price to pay for the stability of an unjust social system. While not all forms of injustice can be collapsed into whiteness, undermining white race solidarity opens the door to fundamental social change in other areas. For so-called whites, treason to the white race is the most subversive act I can imagine.

101

How to Be a Race Traitor: Six Ways to Fight Being White

NOEL IGNATIEV

- Identify with the racially oppressed; violate the rules of whiteness in ways that can have a social impact.
- Answer an anti-black slur with, "Oh, you probably said that because you think I'm white. That's a mistake people often make because I look white." Reply "Me, too" to charges that "people on welfare don't want to work, they just want to stay home and have babies."
- Oppose tracking in the schools, oppose all mechanisms that favor whites in the job market, and oppose the police and courts, which define black people as a criminal class.
- Do not merely oppose these things but seek to disrupt their normal functioning.
- The color line is not the work of the relatively small number of hard-core"racists"; target not them but the mainstream institutions that reproduce it.
- Finally, do not reject in advance any means of attaining the goal of abolishing the white race; indeed, the willingness to go beyond socially acceptable limits of protest is a dividing line between "good whites" and traitors to the white race.

102

Rodrigo's Eleventh Chronicle: Empathy and False Empathy

RICHARD DELGADO

In Which Rodrigo Offers a Solution to the False-Empathy Dilemma, and Suggests Two Roles for White Reformers and Fellow Travelers

We picked out our desserts, which the waiter quickly brought, Rodrigo's a creamy French-Vietnamese pastry of some sort, mine a tangy lemon sorbet. After eating for a few minutes in tacitly agreed-to silence, I looked up at Rodrigo.

"I hope that my real dessert will be that you tell me what your solution is to the predicament in which we find ourselves. Reformers and minorities get little if any genuine empathy in courts, or indeed anywhere, and can count on no one but themselves to climb out of poverty and despair. Life's road is hard going. Can't we find confederates? If we can't look to our liberal friends, to whom can we turn?"

"Empathy would work in a just world, one in which everyone's experience and social histories were roughly the same, unmarked by radical inequality. In such a world, we would have things to trade. There would be reasons for needing to get to know others, for understanding what they feel and need. But we don't live in such a world."

"And since we don't," I said, "what should we do? We can't give up, can't just sit around bemoaning our plight or plotting revolution. There must be a strategy, a set of procedures for operating in an imperfect world."

"I do have a plan," Rodrigo said, drawing a deep breath. "It contains three provisions. It's all based on the idea that false empathy is worse than none at all, worse than indifference. It makes you over-confident, so that you can easily harm the intended beneficiary. You are apt to be paternalistic, thinking you know what the other really wants or needs. You can easily substitute your own goal for hers. You visualize what you would want if you were she, when your experiences are radically different, and your needs, too. You can end up thinking that race is no different from class, that blacks are just whites who happen not to have any money right now. You can think that middle-class blacks or ones with professional degrees have it made, need no solicitude or protection, when their situation is in some respects worse than that of the black who lives in an all-black, working-class neighborhood."

"Your solution, Rodrigo, your solution," I urged.

"Oh—as I mentioned, I think the solution lies in three parts. The first is essentially to

84 CAL. L. REV. 61 (1996). Originally published in the *California Law Review*. Reprinted by permission.

give up on the very idea of empathy as any sort of primary tool for our advancement. We must realize that persons of radically different background and race cannot be made vicariously to identify with us to any significant extent. Their help, if any, is likely to be misguided, paternalistic, mistaken, and unhelpful. This is especially so if they are lawyers and other court officers. Legal empathy is even rarer and less trustworthy than other kinds. Law carves up your story, serves it up to an uncomprehending judge, atomizes your claim, and sparks real resistance when it tries to do something—as it does every century or so."

"And then what?"

"The next step—after abandoning hope in liberal empathy and cross-race, cross-class identification—is to urge one of two strategies that I think *will* work. Would you like to hear them?

"Yes, yes," I said impatiently.

"The first role for white folks who would like to be helpful is what Noel Ignatiev and John Garvey call the race traitor.[1] Have you heard of the idea?"

I strained to remember. "I think I have. Don't they have a magazine by that title?"

"Yes," Rodrigo replied. "I brought you a copy. It's in that envelope back in your office. But I see you know about it already. Just when I think I have an idea or approach that will surprise you, it turns out you know about it already. It's kind of discouraging talking with you, Professor."

"Stop the flattery. You're miles ahead of me in most respects. I just have a little more experience than you. Tell me how you see the race traitor idea applying to our empathy dilemma."

"White people who want to help can become traitors to the white race. As Ignatiev and Garvey put it, 'Treason to whiteness is loyalty to humanity.'[2] For example, if a white person is in a group of whites and one of them tells a racist joke or story, the white can look up in surprise and say: 'Oh, you must have told that story in front of me because you assumed I am white. I'm not. I'm black. I may look white, but my ancestry is black. And let me tell you why I found that story offensive.' "[3]

"In other words," I said, "they identify with blacks radically and completely, not by imagining how they would feel if they were black, but by identifying themselves with blacks when other whites ask for their help in reinforcing white supremacy."

"Yes," Rodrigo continued. "And that includes rejecting white privilege, so far as a white-looking person is capable of doing that. In dozens of encounters in life, one takes on the role of being, acting, and speaking out as though one were a black—that is, one of us."

"I'm not sure how that is possible," I said. "Could you give me an example?"

"Ignatiev and Garvey themselves give many. Whiteness is a social construct, basically a readiness to accept many privileges that come to you if you look and act a certain way. If you refuse to be white you begin the process of destabilizing this construction that society relies on to preserve the current system of racial subordination. So, suppose a neatly dressed white person, who happens to be a race traitor, is pulled over by a police officer and then let go with a warning. The person ought to question the officer, 'Would you have done this if I had been black?' "

"So whites ought to reject racial privilege and challenge manifestations of racism that they observe."

"Yes. And if enough people do this, the system will collapse, because whites will never be sure which other whites are confederates—are loyal to the white race in the sense of accepting unearned privilege and conspiring tacitly to keep blacks down. The race traitor not only opposes racism but seeks to disrupt its normal functioning, and does so from within. Therein lies the concept's power. The color line is not the work of a few racist individuals but of a system of institutions and practices. Race traitors challenge each of these at every turn: tracking in public schools; location of public housing on the other side of the tracks; so-called meritocratic criteria that firms and institutions rely on unthinkingly, even though they exclude blacks and women. They put their lives on the line."[4]

"So the idea is to show total solidarity with us and our cause."

"Yes, even though this means risking one's job and friendships with whites. If the police and courts could not be sure that every person who looks white is loyal to the system, that system would fall.[5] For then, what would be the point of extending privileges based on race? Whites would reject loyalty to their own race, rejoin the human race, and the idea of the white race would fall of its own weight."

"A radical proposal, Rodrigo," I said. "I'm not sure many of our white friends would adopt it."

"It does entail a radical commitment," Rodrigo conceded. "But, as I mentioned, if only a small proportion of whites did, it would seriously jeopardize the system of white-over-black hegemony that has reigned in this country for over four hundred years. And the form of identification it would generate would be real. As we were discussing earlier, empathy is not particularly reliable. One learns only from his or her own experience, not that of others. The race traitor role allows people to begin to acquire that experience."

"Could a progressive lawyer be a race traitor? Is this a solution to law's confining role?" I asked.

"I'd like to think so," Rodrigo replied. "But I'm skeptical, for all the reasons we just mentioned. Law is structurally biased against empathy. Of course nothing prevents a lawyer from being a race traitor outside his or her work in a law office, nor from using law strategically, from time to time, to advocate the race traitor objective."

"Very interesting, Rodrigo, and it just might work, even if not for lawyers. But I think you said you had a second plan."

"My second plan sounds almost like the opposite of the first, but as you'll see it's not. It would envision whites working with whites to lift the yokes of oppression that burden both them and us. I wonder, Professor, if you heard the closing speech by the famous white radical at the recent Critical Legal Studies conference."

"I did. It was spellbinding, delivered with great panache. He held the entire room, even without a microphone."

"And I'm sure you recall what he said. He described his own upbringing as a member of the ruling class, as he put it—prep school, Harvard, antiwar rebellions, SDS. He was a creature of the sixties, and when he grew up turned to CLS for inspiration and support."

"He not only turned to Critical Legal Studies, he helped develop it," I interjected. "He was a founding father, helping the new movement carve out such notions as indeterminacy and the theory that law is essentially politics."

"And do you remember what he said, Professor, about his own engagement with racial identity groups?"

"I do. He said he had sided with Black Power and the Panthers, although as a more or less distant cheerleader and fellow traveler. He said quite candidly that he thought he had little role beyond that, and that as a member of the white privileged class he could not do much more, that there is a sort of built-in limitation. Consequently he turned to institutional politics, the politics of daily life, teaching elite law students how to survive in the corporate world and subvert their own offices and institutions. That and deconstructing legal doctrine."

"What's wrong with that?" I asked, my voice rising slightly. "I was there when he said it, and thought at the time that he was being commendably honest. What else could someone like him have done in life?"

"I don't want to seem harsh," Rodrigo said quietly. "He's a famous figure, one from whom all of us have learned much."

"But you feel there is more he could have done?"

"Yes. I keep thinking that someone with his charisma and prodigious talent could have done more. All it would have taken would have been a slight shift—a few degrees this way, rather than that."

"And that shift is . . . ," I cajoled.

"I think our famous friend should have devoted himself, at least in part, to working with his own race, that is, with disaffected working-class whites. He could have supplied them with the analyses and leadership that they needed, and at a crucial time. Working-class, blue-collar whites, ethnic whites, and poor Southern whites today are arrayed against minorities. They have turned against us with a vengeance. They are the 'angry white men' who helped bring about the Republican revolution that is setting back the cause of social and racial justice, challenging affirmative action, and demanding the end of welfare to the poor and desperate."

"You are saying that if the famous white radical, and people like him, had stopped flirting with radical chic social movements like the Panthers back in the sixties and gone to preach to their own blue-collar brothers and sisters, we would not be in the fix we are in today?"

"Yes. They might have listened to him. Lower-class whites are not our natural enemies. Quite the contrary. But they think they are. Elite whites neatly use them to deflect attention from their own crass materialism, manipulation, and profits—from the way they maintain unsafe workplaces for the workers; pay bare subsistence wages; phase out factories at the drop of a hat, creating real destitution; and send jobs overseas if it suits their interest, all at the expense of workers."

"So you are saying fancy Crits in elite positions at the top schools aided the Republican revolution and the terrible turn things have taken for our people and for the poor?"

"I am," Rodrigo replied with conviction. "They took the easy way out. Instead of taking their campaign to the factories and lower-class tenement districts, they listened to the Panthers, shivered a little, and went and wrote elegant law review articles about the structure of Western legal thought, mostly for each other's benefit. They abandoned their own people. Empathy—the shallow, chic kind—is always more attractive than *responsibility*, which is hard work."

"Is it too late?" I asked.

"It's never too late. Look at what Ralph Nader is doing. He's writing for workers in dangerous factories, consumers who buy unsafe products. He communicates effectively. He has a fancy law degree, yet he addresses his message to those who unfortunately have been led to think we are the cause of their economic pain. He's trying to redirect their attention upward, to the corporate elite that is oppressing us all, much as Martin Luther King was preparing to do toward the end of his life, just before he was assassinated. Robert Kennedy, too. Workers and middle-class whites listen to Nader—some of them, at least. There's no reason he should be working at this alone."

"Nader also spoke at the conference you mentioned. He scolded the Crits for devoting their lives to figuring out how many angels can dance on the head of a pin."

"I missed that session," Rodrigo said. "But I heard it was great. I'm hoping it's on tape. I'd like to see it sometime."

"I think they were taping it," I said. "Maybe your library can get it."

"I'll see when I get home," Rodrigo said. "But, speaking of home, Professor, I think I'd better be moving along soon. Thanks for the company. As usual, you're a great sounding board."

"You've helped me as well. I'd often wondered why empathy for our people, our causes, and for the poor seems to be sharply declining. You've helped me figure out why, and what we might do about it."

Notes

1. *See* 3 RACE TRAITOR (Spring 1994); 4 RACE TRAITOR (Winter 1995).

2. *See, e.g.,* RACE TRAITOR, *supra* (front covers).

3. *See Treason to Whiteness Is Loyalty to Humanity,* reprinted as Chapter 100 of this book; *see also* Edward H. Peeples, *Richmond Journal: Thirty Years in Black and White,* 3 RACE TRAITOR 34, 45 (Spring 1994) (describing author's act of "racial sedition" in denying he was white, when confronted by a store clerk who insisted that he could not intend to buy the "colored newspaper").

4. *Treason, supra,* (describing "six ways to fight being white"); *see also* John Garvey, *Family Matters,* 4 RACE TRAITOR 23, 26–30 (Winter 1995) (describing opposition to school "gifted program" structured to favor white children).

5. *Treason, supra* ("Our strategy seeks to bring together a determined minority, willing to defy white rules so flagrantly they make it impossible to pretend that all those who look white are loyal to the system of racial oppression."); *see When Does the Unreasonable Act Make Sense?,* 3 RACE TRAITOR 108 (Spring 1994) (editorial).

103

Obscuring the Importance of Race: The Implications of Making Comparisons between Racism and Sexism (or Other Isms)

TRINA GRILLO AND STEPHANIE M. WILDMAN

While this chapter was being written, Trina Grillo, who is of Afro-Cuban and Italian descent, was diagnosed as having Hodgkin's disease [a form of cancer]. In talking about this experience she said that "cancer has become the first filter through which I see the world. It used to be race, but now it is cancer. My neighbor just became pregnant, and all I could think was 'How could she get pregnant? What if she gets cancer?'"

Stephanie Wildman, who is Jewish and white, heard this remark and thought, "I understand how she feels; I worry about getting cancer too. I probably worry about it more than most people, because I am such a worrier." But Stephanie's worry is not the same as Trina's. Someone with cancer can think of nothing else. She cannot watch the World Series without wondering which players have had cancer or who in the players' families might have cancer. Having this worldview with cancer as a filter is different from just thinking or even worrying often about cancer. The worrier has the privilege of forgetting the worry sometimes, even much of the time. The worry can be turned off. The cancer patient does not have the privilege of truly forgetting about her cancer; even when it is not in the forefront of her thoughts, it remains in the background, coloring her world.

This dialogue about cancer illustrates a principal problem with comparing one's situation to another's. The "analogizer" often believes that her situation is the same as another's. Nothing in the comparison process challenges this belief, and the analogizer may think she understands the other's situation in its fullness. The analogy makes the analogizer forget the difference and allows her to stay focused on her own situation without grappling with the other person's reality. Yet analogies are necessary tools to teach and explain, so that we can better understand each other's experiences and realities. We have no other way to understand each other's lives, except by making analogies to events in our own experience. Thus, the use of analogies provides both the key to greater comprehension and the danger of false understanding.

Racism/White Supremacy as Social Ill

Like cancer, racism/white supremacy is a societal illness. To people of color, who are the victims of racism/white supremacy, race is a filter through which they see the world. Whites do not look at the world through this filter of racial awareness, even though they also constitute a race. This privilege to ignore their race gives whites a societal advantage distinct from any received from the existence of discriminatory racism. We use the term "racism/white supremacy" to emphasize the link between discriminatory racism and the privilege held by whites to ignore their own race.

Author bell hooks describes her realization of this connection: "The word racism ceased to be the term which best expressed for me exploitation of black people and other people of color in this society and . . . I began to understand that the most useful term was white supremacy."[1] hooks writes that liberal whites do not see themselves as prejudiced or interested in domination through coercion, and do not acknowledge the ways they contribute to and benefit from the system of white privilege. For these reasons, "white supremacy" is an important term, descriptive of American social reality. We link the term "racism" to "white supremacy" as a reminder that the perpetuation of white supremacy is racist.

This chapter originated when the authors noticed that several identifiable phenomena occurred without fail in any predominantly white racially mixed group whenever sex discrimination was analogized (implicitly or explicitly) to race discrimination. Repeatedly, at the annual meeting of the Association of American Law Schools (AALS), at meetings of feminist legal scholars, in classes on sex discrimination and the law, and in law school women's caucus meetings, the pattern was the same. In each setting, although the analogy was made for the purpose of illumination, to explain sexism and sex discrimination, another unintended result ensued—the perpetuation of racism/white supremacy.

When a speaker compared sexism and racism, the significance of race was marginalized and obscured, and the different role that race plays in the lives of people of color and whites was overlooked. The concerns of whites became the focus of discussion, even when the conversation had supposedly centered on race discrimination. Essentialist presumptions came to the fore: it would be assumed, for example, that "women" referred to white women and "blacks" meant African American men.[2] Finally, people with little experience in thinking about racism/white supremacy, but who had a hard-won understanding of the allegedly analogous oppression (sexism or some other ism), assumed that they comprehended the experience of people of color and thus had standing to speak on their behalf.

We began to question why this pattern persisted. We concluded that these phenomena have much to do with the dangers inherent in what had previously seemed to us to be a creative and solidarity-producing process—analogizing sex discrimination to race discrimination. These dangers were obscured by the promise that to discuss and compare oppressions might lead to coalition building and understanding. On an individual psychological level, we empathize with and understand others by comparing their situations with some aspects of our own. Thus, analogies deepen our consciousness and permit us to progress in our thinking. Analogies are an important, perhaps indispensable, tool in individual moral reasoning.

How the Sex/Race Analogy Perpetuates
Patterns of Racial Domination

Comparing sexism to racism perpetuates patterns of racial domination by minimizing the impact of racism, rendering it an insignificant phenomenon—one of a laundry list of isms or oppressions that society must suffer. Consider three recognizable patterns: (1) the taking back of center stage from people of color, even in discussions of racism, so that white issues remain or become central in the dialogue; (2) the fostering of essentialism, so that women and people of color are implicitly viewed as belonging to mutually exclusive categories, rendering women of color invisible; and (3) the appropriation of pain or the denial of its existence that results when whites who have compared other oppressions to race discrimination believe they understand the experience of racism.

Taking Back the Center

White supremacy creates in whites the expectation that issues of concern to them will be central in every discourse. Analogies serve to perpetuate this expectation of centrality. The center stage problem occurs because dominant group members are already accustomed to being center stage. They have been treated that way by society; it feels natural, comfortable, and in the order of things.

The harms of discrimination include not only the easily identified disadvantages of the victims (such as exclusion from housing and jobs) and the stigma imposed by the dominant culture, but also the advantages given to those who are not its victims. The white, male, heterosexual societal norm is privileged in such a way that its privilege is rendered invisible.

Because whiteness is the norm, it is easy to forget that it is not the only perspective. Thus, members of dominant groups assume that their perceptions are the pertinent perceptions, that their problems are the ones that need to be addressed, and that in discourse they should be the speaker rather than the listener. Part of being a member of a privileged group is being the center and the subject of all inquiry in which people of color or other nonprivileged groups are the objects. So strong is this expectation of holding center stage that even when a time and place are specifically designated for members of a nonprivileged group to be central, members of the dominant group will often attempt to take back the pivotal focus. They are stealing the center—usually with a complete lack of self-consciousness.

This phenomenon occurred at the annual meeting of Law and Society, where three scholars, all people of color, were invited to speak to the plenary session about how universities might become truly multicultural. Even before the dialogue began, the views of many members of the organization were apparent by their presence or absence at the session. The audience included nearly every person of color who was attending the rneeting, yet many whites chose not to attend. When people who are not regarded as entitled to the center move into it, however briefly, they are viewed as usurpers. One reaction of the group temporarily deprived of the center is to make sure that nothing remains for the perceived usurpers to be in the center of. Thus, the whites who did not attend the plenary session, but who would have attended had there been more traditional (i.e., white) speakers, did so in part because they were exercising their privilege not to think in terms of race, and in part because they resented the "out groups" having the center.

Another tactic used by the dominant group is to steal back the center, using guerrilla tactics where necessary. For example, during a talk devoted to the integration of multicultural materials into the core curriculum, a white man got up from the front row and walked noisily to the rear of the room. He then paced the room in a distracting fashion and finally returned to his seat. During the question period he was the first to rise, leaping to his feet to ask a lengthy, rambling question about how multicultural materials could be added to university curricula without disturbing the "canon"—the exact subject of the talk he had just, apparently, not listened to. The speaker answered politely and explained how he had assigned a Navajo creation myth to accompany St. Augustine, which highlighted some similarities between Augustine's thought and pre-Christian belief systems and resulted in each reading enriching the other. He refrained, however, from calling attention to the questioner's rude behavior during the meeting, to his asking the already-answered question, or to his presumption that the material the questioner saw as most relevant to his own life was central and "canonized," while all other reading was peripheral and, hence, dispensable.

Analogies offer protection for the traditional center. At another gathering of law professors, issues of racism, sexism, and homophobia were the focus for the first time in the organization's history. Again at this session, far fewer white males were present than would ordinarily attend the organization's plenary session. After moving presentations by an African American woman, a Latino man, and a gay white man, who each opened their hearts on these subjects, a question and dialogue period began. The first speaker to rise was a white woman, who, after saying that she did not mean to change the topic, said that she wanted to discuss another sort of oppression—that of law professors in the less elite schools. As professors from what is perceived by some as a less-than-elite school, we agree that the topic is important, and it would have interested us at another time. But this questioner had succeeded in depriving the other issues of time devoted (after much struggle) specifically to them, and turned the spotlight once again onto her own concerns. She did this, we believe, not out of malice, but because she too had become a victim of analogical thinking.

The problem of taking back the center exists apart from the issue of analogies; it will be with us as long as any group expects, and is led to expect, to be constantly the center of attention. But the use of analogies exacerbates this problem, for once an analogy is taken to heart, it seems to the center-stealer that she is *not* stealing the center, but rather continuing the discussion on the same topic, and one that she knows well. So when the format of the program implicitly analogized gender and sexual preference to race, the center-stealer was encouraged to think, "Why not go further to another perceived oppression?" When socially subordinated groups are lumped together, oppression begins to look like a uniform problem, and one may neglect the varying and complex contexts of the different groups being addressed. If oppression is all the same, then we are all equally able to discuss each oppression, and there is no felt need for us to listen to and learn from other socially subordinated groups.

Fostering Essentialism

Which leads to our next point: Essentialism is implicit in analogies between sex and race. Angela Harris explains gender essentialism as "[t]he notion that there is a monolithic 'women's experience' that can be described independent of other facets of experience like race, class, and sexual orientation." She continues: "A corollary to gender essentialism is 'racial essentialism'—the belief that there is a monolithic 'Black Experience,' or 'Chicano Experience'."[3]

To analogize gender to race, one must assume that each is a distinct category, the impact of which can be neatly separated, one from the other. The essentialist critique shows that this division is not possible. Whenever it is attempted, the experience of women of color, who are at the intersection of these categories and cannot divide themselves to compare their own experiences, is rendered invisible. Analogizing sex discrimination to race discrimination makes it seem that all the women are white and all the men are African American. "Moreover, feminist essentialism represents not just an insult to black women, but a broken promise—the promise to listen to women's stories, the promise of feminist method."[4]

The Appropriation of Pain or the Rejection of Its Existence

Many whites think that people of color are obsessed with race and find it hard to understand the emotional and intellectual energy that people of color devote to the subject. But white supremacy privileges whiteness as the normative model. Being the norm allows whites to ignore race, even though they have one, except when they perceive race (usually someone else's) as intruding upon their lives.[5]

Whites need to reject this privilege and recognize and speak about their role in the racial hierarchy. Yet whites cannot speak validly for people of color, but only about their own experiences as whites. Comparing other oppressions to race gives whites a false sense that they fully understand the experience of people of color. Sometimes the profession of understanding by members of a privileged group may even be a guise for a rejection of the existence of the pain of the unprivileged. For people of color, listening to whites who profess to represent the experience of racism feels like an appropriation of the pain of living in a world of racism/white supremacy. The privileging of some groups in society over others is a fact of contemporary American life. It is identifiable in the ordering of societal power between whites and people of color; men and women; heterosexuals and gays and lesbians; and able-bodied and physically challenged people. This societal ordering is clear to children as early as kindergarten.[6]

Judy Scales-Trent has written about her own experience as an African American woman, of "being black and looking white," a woman who thereby inhabits both sides of the privilege dichotomy. As one who was used to being on the unprivileged side of the race dichotomy in some aspects of her life, she discusses how the privilege of being able-bodied allowed her to ignore the pain of an unprivileged woman in a wheelchair, humiliated in seeking access to a meeting place. She realized that her role as the privileged one in that pairing likened her to whites in the racial pairing. The analogy helped her see the role of privilege and how it affects us, presenting another example of how comparisons are useful for promoting understanding. But this insight did not lead her to assume that she could speak for those who are physically challenged; rather, she realized that she needed to listen more carefully.[7]

Not all people who learn about others' oppressions through analogy are blessed with an increased commitment to listening. White people who grasp an analogy between an oppression they have suffered and race discrimination may think they understand the phenomenon of racism/white supremacy in all its aspects. They may believe that their opinions and judgments about race are as cogent as those of victims of racism. In this circumstance, something approximating a lack of standing to speak exists, because the insight gained by personal experience cannot easily be duplicated—certainly not without careful study of the oppression under scrutiny. The power of comparisons undermines this lack of standing, because by emphasizing similarity and obscuring difference it permits the speaker implicitly to demonstrate authority about both forms of oppression. If we are members of the privileged halves of the social pairs, then what we say about the dichotomy will be listened to by the dominant culture. Thus, when we employ analogies to teach and to show oppression, we should be careful that in borrowing the acknowledged and clear oppression we do not neutralize it, or make it appear interchangeable with the oppression under discussion.

The use of analogies by whites allows them to focus on their own experience and avoid working on understanding racism/white supremacy. Even whites who wish to end discrimination want people of color to teach them about race and are often unwilling to use their personal resources to explore this dangerous subject. As bell hooks writes:

> In talking about race and gender recently, the question most often asked by white women has to do with white women's response to black women or women of color insisting that they are not willing to teach them about their racism—to show the way. They want to know: What should a white person do who is attempting to resist racism? It is problematic to assert that black people and other people of color who are sincerely committed to struggling against white supremacy should be unwilling to help or teach white people.[8]

She says that many people of color have responded with an unwillingness to teach whites about combating racism/white supremacy because it often seems that white people are asking people of color to do all the work. She concludes that "[i]t is our collective responsibility as people of color and as white people who are committed to ending white supremacy to help one another."[9]

hooks encourages people of color to continue to struggle with whites about racism. To whites, the need for such encouragement may seem surprising, because many whites might ask, "How can we work on racism by ourselves, without people of color?" Listening to the reality of people of color *is* very important for learning about the oppression of racism/white supremacy. But whites need to examine their (our) own role in benefiting from that social construct. When white women analogize sexism to racism to emphasize the disadvantages society imposes on women, they (we) must also remember the privileging granted to whites by that same society.

Trying to educate whites about race is a great risk for people of color. They risk not only that whites will not care and will prefer to perpetuate the status quo, but also that even caring whites will not hear or understand the pain of racism. Talking about racism/white supremacy is painful for whites as well, but in a different way. Whites must confront their role as oppressors, or at least as beneficiaries of the racial oppression of others, in a race-based hierarchy. The pain of oppression must be communicated to the dominant group if there is to be any understanding of racism/white supremacy.

Toward Using Analogies Ethically

Given the problems that analogies create and perpetuate, should we ever use them? Analogies can be helpful. They are part of legal discourse, as well as common conversation. Consciousness-raising may be the beginning of knowledge. Starting with ourselves is important, and analogies may enable us to understand the oppression of another in a way we could not without making the comparison. It is important for whites to talk about white supremacy—rather than leaving all the work for people of color—and without drawing false inferences of similarities from analogies. Questions remain regarding whether we can make analogies to race, particularly in legal argument, without reinforcing racism/white supremacy. There are no simple answers to this thorny problem. We will have to continue to struggle with it, and accept that our progress will be slow and tentative.

Epilogue

The Sunday before Yom Kippur, I (Stephanie) go with my parents to my children's Sunday school for the closing service. The rabbi is explaining to the children the meaning of Yom Kippur, the holiest Jewish day, the Day of Atonement. "It is the day," he explains, "when we think of how we could have been better and reconsider what we did that wasn't wonderful."

He tells a story of two men who came to the rabbi before Yom Kippur. The first man said he felt very guilty and unclean and could never be cleansed, because he had once raised a stick and hurt someone. The second man said he could not think of anything very terrible he had done and that he felt pretty good. The rabbi told the first man to go to the field and bring back the largest rock he could find. He told the second man to fill his pockets with pebbles and bring them back to the synagogue, too. The first man found a boulder and with much difficulty carried it to the rabbi. The second man filled his pockets with pebbles, brought them to the rabbi, and emptied his pockets. Pebbles scattered everywhere. Then the rabbi said to the first man, "Now you must carry the rock back and put it back where you found it." To the second man he said, "And you too must gather up all the pebbles and return them to where you found them."

"But how can I do that? That is impossible," said the second man. The rabbi telling the story says that the pebbles are like all the things you have done for which you should wish forgiveness—you have not noticed them, nor kept track. And so the rabbi reminds the children that they should consider when they had ever done things that they should not have done.

He then asks them what looks different in the synagogue. The covering of the dais had been changed to white, which he explains is for purity and cleanliness. He asks the children to stand to see the special Torah covers, also white to symbolize atonement and cleanliness.

My mother leans over to me at this point and says, "Can you imagine how someone black feels, hearing a story like this?"

Although no one in the temple was intending to be racist/white supremacist, the conversation privileged whiteness in a society that is already racist/white supremacist. Is that racism the large rock, the boulder? It must seem truly that large and intractable to people of color. It seems like a boulder to me, when I think consciously about it. Yet it seems that as whites we treat our own racism like so many little pebbles; part of our privilege is that it may seem unimportant to us. So many times we are racist, privileging whiteness, and do not even realize it, and so cannot acknowledge it or atone for it, or even attempt to change our behavior. We, like the second man, say we are not racist, because it is our wish not to be. But wishing cannot make it so. The sooner we can see the boulder *and* the pebbles, the sooner we can try to remove them.

Notes

1. bell hooks, *overcoming white supremacy: a comment,* in TALKING BACK: THINKING FEMINIST, THINKING BLACK 112 (1989).

2. Essentialist thinking reduces a complex being to one "essential characteristic." See ELIZABETH SPELMAN, INESSENTIAL WOMAN: PROBLEMS OF EXCLUSION IN FEMINIST THOUGHT (1988); Kimberlè Crenshaw, *Demarginalizing the Intersection of Race and Sex: A Black Feminist Critique of Antidiscrimination Doctrine, Feminist Theory and Antiracist Politics,* 1989 U. CHI. LEGAL F. 139; Angela Harris, *Race and Essentialism in Feminist Legal Theory,* 42 STAN. L. REV. 581 (1990).

3. Harris, *supra* at 588.

4. *Id.* at 601.

5. Angela Harris writes, "In this society, it is only white people who have the luxury of 'having no color'; only white people have been able to imagine that sexism and racism are separate experiences." *Id.* at 604. Harris describes a meeting of women law professors who were asked to pick out two or three words to describe who they were. Harris reports that none of the white women mentioned race; all the women of color did. *Id.*

6. *See* FRANCES E. KENDALL, DIVERSITY IN THE CLASSROOM: A MULTICULTURAL APPROACH TO THE EDUCATION OF YOUNG CHILDREN 19–21 (1983) (describing the development of racial awareness and racial attitudes in young children). Although the prevalent view would state that children are "oblivious to differences in color or culture" (*id.* at 19), children's racial awareness and their positive and negative feelings about race appear by age three or four. *Id.* at 20.

7. JUDY SCALES-TRENT, NOTES OF A WHITE BLACK WOMAN (1995).

8. hooks, *supra* at 117.

9. *Id.* at 118.

104

White Men Can Jump: But Must Try a Little Harder

PETER HALEWOOD

I hope to demonstrate that progressive, committed, white male law teachers should engage in scholarship investigating the relation of law to social and political subordination, provided that they do so in ways that respond to feminist and minority critiques, and provided that in doing so they do not preempt or displace scholars who are white women or people of color. I think that while specific forms of subordinated experience are not at hand to white male scholars on which to base their scholarship, nonetheless one usually has some fragment of such experience from which to build bridges to other groups' experiences of subordination. Furthermore, I think that the perspective of subordinated groups is likewise inherently partial—the experiences of white women, for example, do not mirror those of women of color. Consequently, the best scholars can hope for is to work together and to combine perspectives, each contributing to an improved picture of the social whole. . . .

By "epistemology," I mean the theory of knowledge one applies in making scholarly or philosophical claims about the nature of reality, whether legal, social, or political reality, or an amalgam of these. I am concerned specifically with the claims one makes about law's relation to oppression. Conventional Western epistemology has posited an objectivist or representational relationship between the knower and reality; reality, it was claimed, could be mapped objectively onto our consciousness. Knowledge properly conceived must be abstract and perspectiveless; the knower must be a disembodied knower. From post-structuralist and linguistic critiques of conventional epistemology in the 1960s and 1970s have emerged new, postmodern or pragmatic feminist and critical race theory critiques of epistemology. These reject the objectivist, representational aspects of epistemology and posit in their place an embodied, contextualized, and experiential theory of knowledge. Knowledge is narrative. Perspectivelessness is now seen as an ideological move;[1] knowledge properly conceived is (and can only be) concrete and perspectival. Our knowledge of oppression is augmented by including the perspective of embodiment and the subjective narratives of the oppressed. . . .

It seems to me that if white male academics accept the feminist and critical race theory epistemological argument, they can learn about the perspectives of the oppressed from the oppressed themselves—the white male's privileged role in the formation of oppressed perspectives can be acknowledged—and in turn apply these perspectives on oppression to their scholarship in ways which improve its accuracy and usefulness.[2]

From "WHITE MEN CAN'T JUMP: CRITICAL EPISTEMOLOGIES, EMBODIMENT, AND THE PRAXIS OF LEGAL SCHOLARSHIP." Reprinted by permission of the Yale Journal of Law & Feminism, Inc. from the *Yale Journal of Law and Feminism*, Vol. 7 No. 1, pp. 1–36.

This claim should not be mistaken for a defense of existing white male legal scholarship on oppression. And while it may seem like the same point about well-intentioned liberal scholarship made another way, I think it differs in crucial ways from an argument about intention. Many progressive men seem to think that the entire matter is answered by attitude or intention: that once they have adopted a feminist or anti-racist "stance" and proceed with good intention, then their analysis—corrective and objective—simply flows from their intentions. Such an argument is fundamentally flawed, both as an analytic point of departure and as a basis for conducting scholarship. I think that a very different approach must be taken. Adopting a "bottom-up" rather than the conventional "top-down" epistemological analysis means that white male scholars must engage in scholarship on oppression by "looking to the bottom"[3]—learning, by careful and respectful study, a perspective on the particular form of subordination one wishes to study from those who actually live that perspective rather than attempting to master it in the abstract. This means adopting a whole new theory of the relation of experience to knowledge, and rejecting the notion of "authoritative" interpretation. It means rejecting conventional models of mastery and expertise for something more partial. Above all it means restructuring one's understanding of objectivity, recognizing both the partiality of one's own perspective and the authenticity of the plurality of perspectives "from below." This transformation entails adopting a different view of one's scholarly role; one should strive to become less the prevailing neutral expert (Kingsfield) or master theoretician (Kennedy)[4] than an interpretivist, promoting the exploration of *someone else's* (duly attributed) perspective and insights in one's scholarship. Of course the progressive white male legal scholar may also serve the purpose of "lending" legitimacy to subordinated perspectives where systemic racism and sexism otherwise might deny that legitimacy.

[See also Chapter 31 for the author's thoughts on surrogate motherhood when the contracting couple is white and the birth mother black. Ed.]

Notes

1. *See, e.g.,* Gary Peller, *Race Consciousness,* 1990 Duke L.J. 758, 806; Catharine A. MacKinnon, *Feminism, Marxism, Method and the State: An Agenda for Theory,* 7 Signs 515, 534–38 (1982); Mari J. Matsuda, *Pragmatism Modified and the False Consciousness Problem,* 63 S. Cal. L. Rev. 1763, 1763–73 (1990).

2. Such a process is suggested by the title of a recent article, Derrick Bell & Erin Edmonds, *Students as Teachers, Teachers as Learners,* 91 Mich. L. Rev. 2025 (1993).

3. Mari J. Matsuda, *Looking to the Bottom: Critical Legal Studies and Reparations,* 22 Harv. C.R.–C.L. L. Rev. 323, 324 (1987).

[T]hose who have experienced discrimination speak with a special voice to which we should listen. *Looking to the bottom*—adopting the perspective of those who have seen and felt the falsity of the liberal promise—can assist critical scholars in the task of fathoming the phenomenology of law and defining the elements of justice.

Id. (emphasis added).

4. Catherine W. Hantzis, *Kingsfield and Kennedy: Reappraising the Male Models of Law School Teaching,* 38 J. Legal Educ. 155 (1988).

105

"Was Blind, but Now I See": White Race Consciousness and the Requirement of Discriminatory Intent

BARBARA J. FLAGG

The most striking characteristic of whites' consciousness of whiteness is that most of the time we don't have any. I call this the *transparency* phenomenon: the tendency of whites not to think about whiteness, or about norms, behaviors, experiences, or perspectives that are white-specific. Transparency often is the mechanism through which white decisionmakers who disavow white supremacy impose white norms on blacks. [See also Chapters 15, 35, and 97. Ed.] Transparency operates to require black assimilation even when pluralism is the articulated goal; it affords substantial advantages to whites over blacks even when decisionmakers intend to effect substantive racial justice.

Reconceptualizing white race consciousness means doing the hard work of developing a positive white racial identity, one neither founded on the implicit acceptance of white racial domination nor productive of distributive effects that systematically advantage whites. This work can be highly beneficial. According to psychologist Janet Helms, a leading author on racial identity theory, the development of a healthy white racial identity requires the individual to overcome those aspects of racism—whether individual, institutional, or cultural—that have become a part of that person's identity, and in addition to "accept his or her own whiteness, the cultural implications of being white, and define a view of Self as a racial being that does not depend on the perceived superiority of one racial group over another."[1] One step in that process is the deconstruction of transparency in white decisionmaking. We can work to make explicit the unacknowledged whiteness of facially neutral criteria of decision, adopting strategies that counteract the influence of unrecognized white norms. These approaches permit white decisionmakers to incorporate pluralist means of achieving our aims, and thus to contribute to the dismantling of white supremacy. Making nonobvious white norms explicit, and thus exposing their contingency, can begin to define for white people a coequal role in a racially diverse society.[2]

In constitutional law, facially race-neutral criteria of decision that carry a racially disproportionate impact violate the Equal Protection Clause only if adopted with a racially discriminatory intent. This rule provides an excellent vehicle for reconsidering white race consciousness, because it perfectly reflects the prevailing white ideology of colorblindness and the concomitant failure of whites to scrutinize the whiteness of facially neutral norms.[3] In addition, the discriminatory intent rule is the existing doctrinal means of regulating fa-

91 Mich. L. Rev. 953 (1993). Originally published in the *Michigan Law Review*. Reprinted by permission.

cially neutral government decisionmaking. When government imposes transparently white norms it participates actively in the maintenance of white supremacy, a stance I understand the Fourteenth Amendment to prohibit. We need, therefore, to reevaluate the existing discriminatory intent rule and to consider a revised approach to disparate impact cases that implements the insights gained from that reassessment.

The imposition of transparently white norms is a unique form of unconscious discrimination, one that cannot be assimilated to the notion of irrationalism that is central to the liberal ideology of racism. While racial stereotyping can be condemned as the failure accurately to perceive the individual for who he really is, and bias as the inability to exclude subjective misconceptions or hostilities, or both, from one's decisionmaking processes, transparency exemplifies the structural aspect of white supremacy. Beyond the individual forms of racism that stereotyping, bias, and hostility represent lie the vast terrains of institutional racism—the maintenance of institutions that systematically advantage whites—and cultural racism—the usually unstated assumption that white culture is superior to all others. Because the liberal gravitates toward abstract individualism and its predicates, she generally fails to recognize or to address the more pervasive harms that institutional and cultural white supremacy inflict. The exercise of focusing exclusively on the transparency phenomenon as an example of structural racism, then, has transformative potential for the white liberal, both on the personal level and as a springboard for reflection on what it means for government genuinely to provide the equal protection of the laws.

White people tend to view intent as an essential element of racial harm; nonwhites do not. The white perspective can be, and frequently is, expressed succinctly and without any apparent perceived need for justification: "[W]ithout concern about past and present intent, racially discriminatory effects of legislation would be quite innocent."[4] For black people, however, the fact of racial oppression exists largely independent of the motives or intentions of its perpetrators. Whites' level of confidence in race neutrality is much greater than nonwhites'; a skeptic (nonwhite, more likely than not) would not adopt a rule that presumes the neutrality of criteria of decision absent the specific intent to do racial harm. Finally, retaining the intent requirement in the face of its demonstrated failure to effectuate substantive racial justice reveals a complacency concerning, or even a commitment to, the racial status quo that can only be enjoyed by those who are its beneficiaries—by white people.

A raised white consciousness of race would produce a very different rule in disparate impact cases. In particular, white people who take seriously the transparency phenomenon, and who want to foster racial justice, will look for ways to diffuse transparency's effects and to relativize previously unrecognized white norms. Existing doctrinal tools are adequate, in large measure, to accomplish these goals, if they are tailored to correct the evil of transparency.

Notes

1. Janet E. Helms, *Toward a Model of White Racial Identity Development*, in Black and White Racial Identity 49 (Janet E. Helms ed., 1990).

2. Becoming self-consciously white can be a painful process, because whiteness situates us as heirs of a legacy of exploitation and domination of nonwhites, a history upon which most would likely pre-

fer not to dwell. At the same time, however, increasing our awareness of whiteness presents an opportunity to reconceive the egalitarian ideals by which we often say we are defined. Just as whiteness renders us privileged and powerful, it equally positions us as able substantially to reconstruct the meaning of race in our society.

3. Most fundamentally, the requirement of discriminatory intent embodies a colorblindness perspective insofar as it views all, and only, decisions that overtly or covertly take race into account as constitutionally impermissible, but rejects the view that unequal outcomes ought to be equally constitutionally suspect.

Of course, the Supreme Court's current affirmative action doctrine, which mandates strict scrutiny of all race-specific government decisionmaking, is also an expression of the colorblindness principle. *See City of Richmond v. J. A. Croson Co.*, 488 U.S. 469, 493 (1989) (plurality opinion); 488 U.S. at 520–21 (Scalia, J., concurring).

4. Robert W. Bennett, *"Mere" Rationality in Constitutional Law: Judicial Review and Democratic Theory*, 67 Cal. L. Rev. 1049, 1076 (1979).

106

White Women, Race Matters:
The Social Construction of Whiteness

RUTH FRANKENBERG

Fundamentally a relational category, whiteness *does* have content inasmuch as it generates norms, ways of understanding history, ways of thinking about self and other, and even ways of thinking about the notion of culture itself. We need to look more closely at the content of the normative and attempt to analyze both its history and its consequences. One step in this direction is antiracist writers' increasing use of the terms Euro-American or European American alongside African American, Asian American, Native American, Latino, and Chicano. Using "European American" to describe white Americans has the advantage that it parallels and in a sense semantically equates communities of a range of geographical origins in relation to the United States. By the same token, however, this gesture "deracializes" and thus falsely equalizes communities who are, in terms of current reality, unequally positioned in the racial order. "European American," when it replaces "white," rather than being used alongside it, evades much of the racial dominance of European Americans at the present historical moment.

If the cultural dominance of whiteness were complete and unquestioned, it would perhaps go entirely unnamed. However, there are constantly struggles over the inclusion and exclusion of specific groups of people as well as over white domination, whether it is structural, institutional, or cultural. In times of perceived threat, the normative group may well attempt to reassert its normativity by asserting elements of its cultural practice more explicitly and exclusively. For example, although the social movements for racial equality that have continued from the 1960s to the present have generated only relatively modest steps toward social change, various forms of backlash in response to them by individuals and groups have sought to assert earlier forms of cultural and racial normativity. These have included campaigns for "English only" laws in states where public institutions *already* conduct business only in English, controversies over educational curricula, and the resurgence of white supremacist political movements.

At this time in U.S. history, whiteness as a marked identity is explicitly articulated mainly in terms of the "white pride" of the far right. In a sense, this produces a discursive bind for that small subgroup of white women and men concerned to engage in antiracist work: if whiteness is emptied of any content other than that which is associated with racism or capitalism, this leaves progressive whites apparently without a genealogy. This is partly a further effect of racist classification that notes or "marks" the race of nonwhite people but not whites.

To my mind, there is no immediate solution to this problem. Purely linguistic solutions cannot be effected in a political vacuum. To call Americans of European descent "white" in any celebratory fashion is almost inevitably today a white supremacist act, an act of backlash. In fact, only when white activists and cultural workers name themselves racially in the context of antiracist work does naming oneself as "white" begin to have a different kind of meaning.

Much work remains to be done in actually making visible and undermining white culture's ties to domination. This is perhaps a more urgent priority than looking for the "good" aspects of white people's heritage. Satisfying our desire for a "nonugly" white tradition requires, as much as anything, the creation of a different political reality, a different balance of power, or, at the very least, an active white antiracist movement that could generate a countercultural trajectory and identity.

In contrast with the white supremacisms of the far right, my continuing to use "white culture" and "white cultural practice" as descriptors of the things white people do or the ways white people understand themselves should not, of course, be taken as suggesting that any practice or activity engaged in by white people is "white" in an inherent or timeless sense. Rather, as with all human activity, current cultural practices of white people in the United States must be viewed as contingent, historically produced, and transformable through collective and individual human endeavor. Nor can we view "white culture" or "white cultural practice" as a uniform terrain, such that one might expect all white people to identify in similar ways with the same set of core beliefs, practices, and symbols. The borders of white *identity* have proven malleable over time. The same is, I suggest, true of white culture: through processes of syncretism and appropriation, a range of practices, symbols, and icons have been drawn from elsewhere into the cultural practice of white people.

Nor is white culture produced and reproduced in a vacuum. Whiteness is inflected by nationhood, such that whiteness and Americanness are profoundly shaped by one another. Thus British "whiteness" and U.S. "whiteness" are both similar to and different from one another, those differences and similarities being traceable to historical, social, and political processes. Similarly, whiteness, masculinity, and femininity are coproducers of one another, in ways that are, in their turn, crosscut by class and by the histories of racism and colonialism.

Given the complex, fragmented character of white cultural practice, one might ask why, then, it is necessary or productive to continue to use the term "white cultural practice" at all. There are several reasons. First, if the alternative is to continue to view whiteness and white people as "noncultural" or "cultureless," one result is continuing to view dominant practices within a dualistic framework, such that practices *not* identifiable as originating from a "bounded" group might be variously viewed as normative, correct, modern, or universal, rather than as (in my view, more correctly) local and specifiable, but dominant.[1] Second, "culture" designates a subjective sense of identity and belonging as much as it designates activity or practice. Viewing whiteness as "no culture" has the same double-edged effect on the question of identity as it has on that of practice: white individuals at times view themselves as "empty," yet at other times as the center or norm (the *real* Americans). Naming whiteness and white people in this sense helps dislodge the claims of both to rightful dominance.

Third, however, whiteness is indeed linked to dominance. Given culture as a "field articulating the life-world of subjects . . . and the structures created by human activity,"[2] it is by and large the cultural practices of *white* people (though not all white people, and certainly to varying degrees) by means of which individuals in societies structured in racial dominance are asked to engage with the institutions of those societies. Thus, to cite two examples, corporate culture and that of academia are culturally marked in ways that are (contingently) white as well as (also contingently) gendered and, so to speak, "classed." The workshops offered to train non-U.S.-born engineers in the sporting metaphors that oil the wheels of many U.S. workplaces and the support groups for students of color and "reentry women" throughout academia testify to the negative effects that unmarked (white, American, male) cultural practices have on those who do not, automatically, participate in them. Here again, naming whiteness as a cultural terrain is a vital aspect of questioning and delimiting its authority.

From the standpoints of those it marginalizes or places in "boundage," the dualistic discourse on culture is exposed as simultaneously unreal and violent. From the standpoint of the normative-residual space, however, "boundage" at times appears fascinating or enticing, a desirable space in which to live. Besides the work of critically analyzing that normative-residual space that I am calling "white cultural practice," white Americans may also want to learn more about the histories that lie behind that normativity, the multiple currents that came together to make the normative space that white Americans now inhabit, and the processes of assimilation, loss, and forgetting that took place along the way. In doing this, care must be taken not to confuse the traces of *past* subordination with the *present* subordination of other communities and their cultural practices. Engagements with "white ethnic" heritage that either romanticize the past or evade race privilege in the present continue to "deculturalize" and therefore "normalize" dominant cultural practice. Explorations both of dominant practices and of the incorporations and exclusions that produce the dominant may, I believe, enable us to engage in antiracist work from a more complex standpoint and to enter into more radical, transformative relationships with white racial and cultural identities.

Notes

1. Trinh T. Minh-Ha, "Difference: A Special Third World Women Issue," Discourse 8, Special Issue: "She, the Inappropriate/d Other," Fall/Winter 1986–87.

2. Paul Gilroy, There Ain't No Black in the Union Jack, London: Hutchinson, 1987, 17.

107

Resisting Racisms, Eliminating Exclusions: South Africa and the United States

DAVID THEO GOLDBERG

Resistance to racisms consists in vigorously contending and disputing exclusionary values, norms, institutions, and practices, as well as assertively articulating open-ended specifications and means for an incorporative politics. Where racisms are openly and volubly expressed, it is likely a matter of time before a more or less organized resistance by its objects, often in alliance with other antiracists, will arise in response; witness the emergence of resistance to slavery in the United States, to the destruction of indigenous people on all continents, to the [Nazis and their allies in Europe and to] *apartheid* in South Africa, to David Duke in Louisiana, to Jean-Marie Le Pen in France, to Gottfried Küssel and the neo-Nazi right in Germany and Austria, or to Vladimir Zhirinovsky, the extreme nationalist, in Russia. Resistance in such cases will neither be inevitable nor fully effective. Much depends on the vehemence of the racist expression (the 'Final Solution' is perhaps the limit case), its explicit or covert nature, the resources committed to sustaining the expression and to combatting it, as well as the sorts of technologies available on either side. Where racist exclusions are silent rather than silenced, insinuated without being explicated, institutionally pervasive and publicly taken for granted, any response is apt to be taken as so much paranoia, hypersensitivity, or lack of a sense of humor.

Those declaring themselves against racism may be reluctant to change because of resistance to change in general . . . or because of the perceived costs to themselves . . . or they may not recognize changing forms of racist exclusion as what they take themselves to be against. The less effort it requires of persons to express their disapprobation of racism, the more likely they will do so: signing a petition, attending a rock concert, voting against a racist candidate in an election.

Ultimately, resisting racist exclusions in the wide array of their manifestations is akin to a guerrilla war. It will involve, and often unpopularly, hit-and-run sorts of skirmishes against specific targets, identified practices, and their rhetoric of rationalization; against prejudices and institutional rules; and against pregnant silences and unforeseen outbursts. It is a guerrilla war that is often ceaseless, though there may be the equivalent of cease-fires. In this war, positional strategies and tactics of maneuver need to be as fluid as the content of the racialized discursive formation and exclusionary expressions they oppose. In these bat-

From RACIST CULTURE: PHILOSOPHY AND THE POLITICS OF MEANING (Blackwell 1993). Reprinted by permission of Blackwell Publishers.

tles, resistance may be more or less global or local. One may recognize the broad identities across all racist expressions however and wherever they manifest and the importance of standing against them, or one may immerse oneself in a particular struggle in a local community. Residents of the United States, for example, may protest *apartheid* in South Africa or they may organize to resist racist police brutality or the use of discriminatory profiles in their local precinct. German antiracists may simply join in a rally protesting the reemergence of neo-Nazism or they may engage in promoting transformation of existing community structures through incorporation of (im)migrants. And South Africans may merely protest (past) *apartheid* or they may engage in vigorously transforming the microstructures of long-standing racist institutions like universities in that country.

Resisting racisms requires also that we be sensitive to the distinction between cruelty and coercion. The harms of racialized coercion are often ignored, overshadowed by racist cruelty. Conservative liberal analysts often presume, on the basis that institutional cruelty of a racist kind has been outlawed, that the repugnant forms of racist expression are no longer. . . . But we must also confront racially motivated or effected coercion taking the form of perpetuated impoverishment, social dismissal, maintenance of artificial and contrived differences, or institutional exclusivity, for the coerced by definition have little if any recourse.

Generally, both global and local struggles are committed to dissolving racist expression. . . . This will necessitate transforming those sociomaterial conditions, in particular the political and legal economies, that promote, sustain, and extend racist exclusions and expression. It will also require undermining the conceptual conditions and apparatus, the deep grammar, in terms of which the discourse is expressed. And it will entail taking apart the mechanisms by which social subjects come to identify themselves racially and discriminate against those deemed racially other.

Responding to discriminatory employment practices on the part of employment agencies, for example, presents a range of possibilities. Where an agency engages in discriminatory practices, a formal investigation could be required. The more widespread the practice, the stronger the need for an industrywide investigation. This might entail unannounced testing and auditing. Where discrimination is found, censure, fines, and license evaluation would be in order: the more severe the (pattern of) violation, the stronger need be the response of legal enforcement.

Antiracist means may include confrontation, persuasion, punishment for racist expressions, or sometimes imaginatively rewarding anti- or even nonracist expression and racialized interaction. Where a verbal racist expression or depiction—an epithet, joke, or story, for example—can be shown to be not just offensive but harmful, as it will be in a racially charged atmosphere or where the objects of the expression are group members who have long suffered more or less extreme forms of racialized exclusion, a range of personal and social alternatives seems available. Individually, all those witness to the expression should (be encouraged to) register their very vocal rejection of it, even at considerable personal risk. The response may be immediate, through letters to the local press (even if they are rejected), contributions to antiracist organizations in kind or cash, and so on. The point is to put those expressing themselves in racist fashion as well as those responsible for licensing racist expressions on the defensive. Socially, such expressions may be discouraged through disincentives, or alternatives may be encouraged through incentives. The more extreme and likely the harm, the more pressing becomes the case for some sort of formal restriction and penalty. . . .

An institution like a university in the United States or South Africa likewise has a range of options in responding to racist expressions. . . . Racist arguments or arguments to racist conclusions by students, staff, or faculty should be vigorously challenged. . . . Where it can be shown that the argument underpins a position of exclusionary power on the part of an administrator, instructor, or student in position of responsibility, more serious consideration should be given to curtailment of that power and, where the exclusions are especially egregious, possibly to dismissal. Where there is some doubt about individual intent, and perhaps about consequences, a caution or warning may suffice. Between counterargument and dismissal, widespread options are available, especially where a more or less vicious expression is made in the absence of argument: salary freezes or cuts, lack of promotion or other awards, denial of research resources, private or public censure.

The distinction generally at issue here is between the university as the site of a vigorous and open exchange of ideas, . . . and unargued expression that extends exclusion or harm, on the other. The point is not to 'legislate civility' but to prevent the conditions for perpetuating harmful exclusion. I am unmoved by the claim, popularized by Dinesh D'Souza in his diatribe against what has popularly come to be called 'political correctness,' that a new regime of ideological terror has improperly restricted what university instructors can safely say in classrooms. D'Souza's anecdotal data, always partially described anyway, strike me almost invariably as cases of instructor insensitivity. In my classes on justice and ethics at an engineering school in the Northeast and at a large state-funded institution in the Southwest, the generally conservative student bodies have always had full license to argue back against criticisms of their popular claims concerning reverse discrimination (this, after all, is the age of the Reagan revolution). In this atmosphere, political as much as academic charges of political correctness taste like sour grapes. All D'Souza has revealed is that teaching is tough now that some can no longer be racist or sexist with impunity.

We should not, however, ignore or deny cases like those described to me by a colleague: A student charges racism of an instructor for using the word 'niggardly' in class, while another demands that a reproduction of a Klimt nude hanging in her instructor's office be removed because it is sexist. In both cases, the university administrator appealed to should engage not in placating the student conceived as consumer but in the practice for which the university in good part exists, namely, instruction. Charges of racism and sexism can be mistaken. . . . The first student might be advised to consult an etymological dictionary to reveal the roots of the two words at issue have nothing in common, the second student to read up about art, perhaps to consult a good reader on censorship and pornography, or even to pursue a reading course in these issues with the instructor who stands accused. Is it too much to think that *both* might benefit from the exchange? . . .

A black South African friend heading a university department in Cape Town was interested in moving his family into a house in an area defined as 'white' by the then still-to-be-repealed Group Areas Act. This act nevertheless made provision for servants to live on the premises of their employers. My friend made an arrangement with the institution for which he worked, a government university as all in South Africa are, to purchase the house and lease it to him. The act was repealed without his formally having to test the argument in the South African courts. Tactics of resistance employed by plantation slaves offer further examples of the dangers inherent in standing inside racist categories: Slow work and malingering undermined the plantation economy but reinforced the stereotype of laziness; slave destruction of property fueled the stereotype of incompetence; self-mutilation increased labor costs but steeled the stereotype of barbarianism. Rap songs about ghetto violence, gangs, and cop killing empower the (un)censored rage of racially marginalized youth as they reinforce status quo stereotypes of a vulgar and undisciplined underclass. Black-only dormitories or student clubs, necessitated as forms of redress or promotion of long denied autonomy, may fuel the countercharge of reverse discrimination and segregation. . . .

In the absence of available opportunities, preferential treatment programs for college admissions or job hiring and promotion seem a modest means, one among many necessary not simply to integration but to advancing an incorporative politics. Such programs have served to draw those voices into academic and professional positions that have tended to be silenced by their exclusion, voices that have mostly proved resistant to mainstream appropriation. Perhaps this is why the programs have become so controversial in the United States. We should take care not to generalize any local experience, either to assume that the failure of a racial preference program elsewhere raises doubts about such programs locally or to encourage the assumption of locally successful programs in those societies where conditions may be quite different. Suggestions have been made recently, for instance, concerning their adoption in South Africa. This seems inadequate for a number of reasons. First, a majority government in South Africa is naturally leading to appointment of its supporters in civil jobs, and appointments are overwhelmingly of black persons. Second, some positions are desperately needed—rural doctors, for example—and preferential policies will do little to meet the need. Third, emphasis on preferential treatment programs in the private or public sectors presupposes the status quo, namely, continued economic and political control by whites, and this hardly seems acceptable, though continued white economic domination may yet be the outcome of ongoing political negotiation. In general, the acceptability, if not the necessity, of preferential treatment programs will depend upon the sociohistorical conditions present in a society at a specific conjuncture. . . .

The basic shortcoming of preferential policies, then, is not that they are divisive, as Dinesh D'Souza and Stephen Carter would argue. They are only as divisive as powerful people want and direct them to be. The fundamental difficulty is deeper. In a social order that is deeply racialized, any policy that invokes race as a sign, a mark of, rather than as grounds for, preferential treatment, even where justified, is likely *to be used* to exacerbate racial tensions and divides, to magnify whatever racially characterized tensions and ambivalences there are. . . . Public policies that are racially characterized, that have a racial component, will hardly escape the political push and pull. Where race bashing gets votes in the name of fairness, watch out. . . . It is undeniable that the major beneficiaries of racial preferences in the United States have been the sons and daughters of the black middle class. They were especially well-placed to take advantage of the programs offered. However, the plight of the racially marginalized has been simultaneously erased. The message: If you cannot get a [leg] up with discriminatory programs, there's nothing we can do for you. William Julius Wilson notwithstanding, universal poverty- or need-based programs have been historically ineffectual in getting to the needs of the racially marginalized. This simply underlines the call to go further in implementing the effective grounds of equivalent opportunities for all. . . .

Assume that over his lifetime and in the absence of preferential treatment programs, the average white educated male may in principle be capable of competing for approximately seventy-five jobs. From these, the person may receive, say, three actual offers for jobs for which he in fact competes. A black person, equally qualified and without the benefit of preferential treatment programs and in the sort of racially charged world we have been used to, may effectively compete, say, for twenty-five positions and be lucky to land one. These ratios seem fair, given the recent findings in Washington, D.C., and Chicago that black job-seekers will find it three times as difficult to get job interviews and employment offers as a more or less identically qualified white person. With preferential treatment programs in place, it seems reasonable to assume, for the sake of argument, that the black candidate's competitive pool will be stretched by about half and the white candidate's reduced by about the same quantity the black person's is increased. The black candidate will now have a crack at something like forty positions, the white candidate close to sixty. Both can expect something like two offers. The difference between the number of positions each can expect to compete for is reflective of the fact that there will be more competitors in the nonpreferential category, and so the greater number of competitive possibilities will more or less equalize the competitive chances of whites. The playing field has thus been relatively leveled, and the white candidate can hardly claim to be wronged. . . .

Antiracism, accordingly, has to be an all-or-nothing commitment, a renewable undertaking to resist all racisms' expressions, to strike at their conditions of emergence and existence, to promote 'the internal decomposition of the community created by racism.' It presupposes nothing short of assuming power: the power of the racialized, of the racially excluded and marginalized, to articulate for themselves and to represent for others who they are and what they want, where they come from, how they see themselves incorporated into the body politic, and how they see the social body reflecting them. Consequently, if freedom is to ring true for all, antiracism must be committed to dissolving in theories and in practice both the institutions of exclusionary power and the powers of exclusionary institutions. These commitments face the future rather than the past.

108

Dysconscious Racism:
The Cultural Politics of Critiquing
Ideology and Identity

JOYCE E. KING

One goal of my course, when I was Associate Professor of Teacher Education at Santa Clara University, was to sharpen the ability of students to think critically about educational purposes and practice in relation to social justice and to their own identities as teachers. The course thus illuminates a range of ideological interests which become the focus of students' critical analysis, evaluation, and choice. For instance, a recurring theme is that of the social purposes of schooling. This is a key concept about which many students report they have never thought seriously. Course readings, lectures, discussions, and other activities are organized to provide an alternative context of meaning within which students can critically analyze the social purposes of schooling. The range of ideological perspectives considered includes alternative explanations of poverty and joblessness, competing viewpoints regarding the significance of cultural differences, and discussions of education as a remedy for societal inequity. Students consider the meaning of social justice and examine ways that education might be transformed to promote a more equitable social order. Moreover, they are expected to choose and declare the social changes they themselves want to bring about as teachers.

The course also introduces students to the critical perspective that education is not neutral; it can serve various political and cultural interests including social control, socialization, assimilation, domination, or liberation. Both impartial, purportedly factual information as well as openly partisan views about existing social realities such as deindustrialization, hunger and homelessness, tracking, the "hidden" curriculum, and teacher expectations allow students to examine connections between macrosocial and microsocial issues. Analysis of and reflection on their own knowledge and experience involves students in critiquing ideologies, examining the influences on their thinking and identities, and considering the kind of teachers they want to become. I also encourage my students to take a stance against mainstream views and practices that dominate in schools and other university courses. Through such intellectual and emotional growth opportunities, students in my course re-experience and re-evaluate the partial and socially constructed nature of their own knowledge and identities.

White students sometimes find such critical, liberatory approaches threatening to their self-concepts and identities. I believe this is because most students from economically privileged, culturally homogeneous backgrounds are generally unaware of their intellectual biases and monocultural encapsulation. While my students may feel threatened by diversity, what they often express is guilt and hostility. Students who have lived for the most part in relatively privileged cultural isolation can only consider becoming liberatory, social-reconstructionist educators if they have both an adequate understanding of how society works and opportunities to think about the need for fundamental social change. The critical perspective of the social order offered in my course challenges students' worldviews. Precisely because what my students know and believe is so limited, it is necessary to address both their knowledge (that is, their intellectual understanding of social inequity) and what they believe about diversity.

109

What Should White Women Do?

MARTHA R. MAHONEY

Focusing solely on the sexual exploitation of women hides both racist oppression and the strength, struggles, and multiple interests of women of color. The experience of being a woman of color cannot be understood in any way that sees only what is done to women generally. White people will think racially as whites without thinking "about race," because we tend to equate "race" with "non-white." We will not understand that we are thinking racially when we are not thinking about people of color. This aspect of our experience as white women will shape what we do, but it will be very difficult for us to see.

So if we are building theory out of the practice of women, white women need to reckon with the ways in which some of our practice will not be addressed in our theory because it is not visible to us. This problem cannot be answered by arguing that women really are oppressed as women. Rather, if we want liberation as women, we need to explore the experience and needs of *all* women. We will need to hear accounts of women's experience in which whiteness itself may become visible in ways we find uncomfortable.[1] The meaning of whiteness will therefore need to be examined and challenged.

A white woman lives the tension between ongoing oppression and the attempt to effectuate her life as if inside a bubble of dominant culture. To most of us, the bubble is transparent. The culture we live in makes the specificity of our lives invisible to us. White interactions go on whether or not we intend to subordinate another person or to interact with consciousness of race. They are part of the meanings in the culture in which we live, and they are part of how we react to things emotionally, but since they are "normal" they are as invisible as air. Feeling unlike an agent in one's life, noticing *only* the ways in which one is not powerful, may be a vision of the self which depends on the transparency of the ways in which one is privileged. The dominant mentality is protected by this invisibility, which allows it to inflict pain deliberately or unawares. For those defined outside this bubble of culture, it is not invisible at all.

If the point of feminist endeavor is to undertake the transformation of society and achieve the liberation of women, then it matters a great deal how we undertake this transformative work. Transformative work, which is part of consciousness-raising and is the point of feminist struggle, entails listening respectfully to those who can see what we cannot. It includes consciousness-raising of our own to try to undo the invisibility of whiteness. This work also requires understanding and paying close attention to women as social actors.

From "WHITENESS AND WOMEN, IN PRACTICE AND THEORY," 5 YALE J. L. AND FEMINISM 217 (1993). Originally published in the *Yale Journal of Law and Feminism*. Reprinted by permission.

Marilyn Frye describes a feminist organization in which white women were criticized for their racism by women of color.[2] The white women decided (after consultation with women of color) to hold meetings of white women to work on this issue. Shortly there-after, they were strongly criticized by a black woman for thinking they could understand it alone and for unilaterally deciding to exclude the women of color. Frye found this an intolerable double-bind—white women were racist if they didn't act, and racist if they did—and felt the criticism was "crazy." But this sense of "craziness" made her suspicious, because she knew how she herself had often seemed "crazy" to people who could not see the profound structure of sexism with which she was concerned. She responded by trying to listen differently and by trying to understand the ways in which her decisionmaking reflected a white privilege to define the terms and scope of white action against racism.

I agree with the many feminists who assert the necessity of feminist struggle against all oppression. We can conclude that feminism must be concerned with struggle against racism, and that white feminists need an active agenda against racism (including white privilege), by recognizing that "women" will not be free until "women of color" experience freedom. We could reach the same conclusion by believing that racism is so deeply entwined and so profoundly implicated in all structures of gender oppression that it has harmed white women even as it has brought us privilege in many ways, so that we will never find freedom until we help transform all of these power relationships. Either way, white women need to work actively against white privilege.

I also agree that feminism needs theory built out of the diverse experience and needs of women. How white women act will have a great deal to do with achieving the development of pluralist feminist theory. It matters how we talk with each other, and, especially, it matters how we listen. This does not mean that everything any person of color ever says must be taken by white women as objective truth, but that it be recognized as a truth, and as truth to the respected person from whom we hear it. Paying close attention to positioned truths is fundamental to progressive change.

Notes

1. Maria Lugones, *On the Logic of Pluralist Feminism, in* FEMINIST ETHICS 35 (Claudia Card ed., 1991).

2. MARILYN FRYE, THE POLITICS OF REALITY: ESSAYS IN FEMINIST THEORY 111–12 (1983).

110

Confronting Racelessness

ELEANOR MARIE BROWN

Kendall Thomas coined the phrase "we are raced"[1] as a race-conscious challenge to the abstract notions of citizen and state as they are conceptualized in liberal legalism. Thomas insists that our received notions of rights and duties in law are rife with racial implications. This is particularly the case given the highly charged racial context within which notions of rights and duties were developed, who they were meant to exclude, and our societal struggle to make the law "color-blind." In this context, abstract notions of citizen, government, rights, and duties do not begin to account for the relationship between people of color and their government, people of color and their fellow white citizens, and people of color among themselves, either as traced out in history or in contemporary times. Critical race theorists insist that the world is not as de-raced as the law, historically formed by members of the majority race, would have it seem.

We must learn to resist the sentiment that we can somehow rid ourselves of this "race thing." Such theorizing does damage to our perceptions of social relations, as it attempts to bracket off race in formulating theories of how notions of citizen, law, and the state are constructed. We retard the educational project by failing to come to terms with the enormity of race and how it subsumes us. We standardize race without recognizing that we do it, interfering with our own efforts to fight racial subjugation. Social science tells us this is the case. "Race becomes 'common sense'—a way of comprehending, explaining and acting in the world."[2]

We need a formulation of race that takes account of white people's realities. It seems to me that the very fact that we confront a "raceless" paradigm, where people are unaware of how race affects their everyday lives, forces us to incorporate this "racelessness" into our theorizing. To some extent this has been done; a fundamental goal of critical race theory has been to expose the ostensibly race-neutral "masks and other disguises"[3] that perpetuate racial oppression. The problem is that in attempting to strip away masks, we have written as though contemporary whites operate no differently than the dominative racists of the past. We can acknowledge that whites may indeed believe that their agendas are race-neutral and not merely a pretext for maintaining subordination. The point of the phrase "unconscious racism" is that it is *unconscious*.

Critical race theory does often acknowledge the unconsciousness of white actions; an important goal is to expose to the law how this unconsciousness leads to acute and nasty realities in the lives of people of color. Yet, theory has yet to ask itself the much more difficult question—that is, how to communicate with people who really believe that tools that maintain racial subordination are race-neutral, people who were raised in paradigms of meritocracy and objectivity and who steadfastly maintain that the law is color-blind. We need to move beyond a simple recognition of the way we have been socialized to think we are "raceless" to incorporate the implications of that realization.

Any formula that would move beyond the present impasse would have to account for this reality. Such a formulation would recognize that even as we are indeed raced, we are necessarily raced to varying extents. Whether or not we realize we are raced necessarily implicates the extent to which we are raced. As people of color, we have no choice but to be raced. Others have the choice to operate in a paradigm of racelessness, for their racial features constitute society's norms. The white subjects of the social science experiments differ from the critical race theorists in their fundamentally different sense of the importance of race in this world.

Some of us are raced, others of us are de-raced, and there is a continuum in between. The ambivalent whites who struggle with conflicting allegiances of how to conceptualize blacks seem to be arrayed at various points along this continuum. We should approach each instance of an individual's contact with the law and include the voices of white participants. Then we should theorize about how that individual's perceptions vary depending on race. We should write narratives that incorporate different people's realities.

Indeed, as starkly foreign as critical premises seem to traditional civil rights scholars, the movement is fundamentally a plea to be let in, to consider some distinct perspectives. *Let us in, perhaps on our own terms, but nevertheless let us in.* The paucity of communication undermines the very object of critical race theory, which is to bring distinctly different voices into legal analysis. Critical race theory must be careful to apply its own critique of the dominant paradigm to itself. Critical race theorists too write from a position of subjectivity, as we are on a mission to expose a pretense of objectivity. White attitudes are central to our enterprise not only because of what we as people of color perceive them to be, but also because of what whites perceive their own attitudes to be. As we argue that our realities have been left out of their stories, do we not then have some responsibility to make sure their realities are not left out of ours?

In the absence of this incorporation of the perspectives of white participants in critical race narratives, it will seem as though we are attacking yesterday's shadows. Our colleagues do not see themselves in the critical race narratives, just as we do not see ourselves in much of their scholarship. Unless there is progress, we can be sure that mainstream civil rights scholars will continue to operate within the paradigm of race neutrality, while those who recognize the significance of race will continue to talk past them.

The biblical metaphor beckons us forward. Scholarly interaction requires us to move beyond the Tower of Babel. We must strive to forge communicative understanding, a shared discourse in which marginalized voices are not only aired but heard.

Notes

1. Telephone Interview with Kendall Thomas, Professor of Law, Columbia University (Apr. 14, 1994).

2. MICHAEL OMI & HOWARD WINANT, RACIAL FORMATION IN THE UNITED STATES: FROM THE 1960s TO THE 1990s, 60 (1994).

3. Leslie Espinoza, *Masks and Other Disguises,* 103 HARV. L. REV. 1878 (1990).

111

A Civil Rights Agenda for the Year 2000: Confessions of an Identity Politician

FRANCES LEE ANSLEY

I am not an African-American, and I will not be speaking from the perspective of the African-American community, although I am firmly convinced that my own well-being is intimately bound up with the well-being of that community. I am a European-American, a female, someone who has counted myself a part of legal and social struggles for justice—for people of color, for women of all races, and for individuals from all races and both genders whose economic resources consist only of their increasingly uncertain ability to sell their labor to others. I have less to say to and about the African-American community than to and about the white community.

As we near the end of the millennium we seem to find ourselves at a "crossroads" in civil rights theory and practice. For members of many communities of color there is a crisis in quality of life, in education, in unemployment, and too often a crisis in survival itself—all this despite the many successes and breakthroughs of the civil rights decade of the sixties. Why might this be so? First, in far too many cases, the "victory" of formal equality is yet to come. I believe it is crucial, especially for "us white people," to realize just how much racial bigotry and unequal treatment is still with us.

Such a realization is something we will have to work at, because in the absence of special effort most of us whites simply don't have equal access to adequate information on this score. We can, of course, seek such information out, through reading and study and movie-going and cross-race conversations and through engaging in efforts to change things.

Sometimes, through some association with people of color, we stumble onto information about persistent racist beliefs and disparate treatment. I find myself remembering particular incidents. One is the racism my brother-in-law found among teachers at the local high school in the district where he and his family live. This racism never came to his attention when his two older boys, who are white, were attending the school. It became all too evident, however, in his dealings with the school when his third, mixed-race child came along.

One of my white students, who had been an undergraduate at Ole Miss, recalled inviting an African-American friend down from Nashville for the weekend. He left the friend at home for a couple of hours one afternoon while he went out, returning to find his friend shaken and enraged. Apparently the friend had made the mistake of stepping out of the apartment, where he was accosted and questioned exhaustively by security guards who simply couldn't

The complete text of this article appeared originally at 59 TENN. L. REV. 593 (1992); this edited version appears by permission of the author and the Tennessee Law Review Association, Inc. The article is based on a speech given in February 1992 at West Virginia University as part of the Franklin D. Cleckley Civil Rights Symposium.

believe he might "belong" in that apartment complex. My student's friend was angry but not surprised, whereas the student, a young white man, had learned a brand new lesson.

I had a similar opportunity myself last summer when I made a trip to the United States–Mexico border with a group of women factory workers from Tennessee. We were visiting the border area to see what is happening in the industrial zones where so many United States companies are moving. Our group was mostly Anglo, but one member of the delegation was a black woman, and during part of our trip we traveled with a Latino man who served as our translator. When we stopped at the border the whites in our group watched in amazement as the Latino man was taken off by U.S. border guards to be interrogated alone at length, the black woman was questioned extensively and with evident hostility and distrust about her country of origin, and the rest of us were waved through without a hitch. Had we been traveling without these special "tour guides," my guess is our impression of the border would have been quite different.

We white people thus may have to work at obtaining information and perspectives that others are in a position to experience on a daily basis, but I should not overstate the case. We probably have access to some information on this score that people of color often don't have: we hear the language of other whites who feel they can "speak freely" in our presence. One of my students told me of the comment he heard in his fraternity: "A black can rush this fraternity; there's not really anything we can do about that, but there will never be a black pledge as long as there is a breath in my body." Another told me of his aunt, a member of management in a Fortune 500 company, in which capacity she supervises a number of black employees. She refers to them as "niggers" when she is home, though she must be more self-conscious about her language on the job. I remember the child in my Girl Scout troop whose father told her she will not go to a college in a big city, because too many black people would be there. I recall the file clerk at a former job who was surprised I didn't know it was good luck for a white person to rub the head of a young black child.

These and similar attitudes result in hundreds of thousands of human decisions every day, such as decisions not to hire. For example, a recent study paired teams of identically qualified black and white job seekers to try their luck in two urban job markets. White applicants were three times as likely to get the jobs.[1] Such attitudes result in other decisions as well: not to rent an apartment, not to grant mortgages in a certain neighborhood, not to promote, not to make eye contact, not to mentor, not to challenge, not to befriend. . . . These hundreds of thousands of decisions help to weave a social fabric where the pattern of racial disparity is still being laid down, row by row, day by day, generation by generation.

One reason, then, why the great victory of formal equality with whites has not "worked" very well for African-Americans is that these strong attitudes and decisional patterns persist. However, they exist not as vestiges or remnants or deviant exceptions but as part of the experience of daily life for vast numbers of people.

But the problem is more complicated than simple persistent bigotry and disparate treatment. I believe that both the underlying state of the economy and the underlying state of the law in this country are such that even if true formal equality were achieved tomorrow, the great bulk of African-Americans would still be in a perilous condition, and the civil rights movement would still find itself in crisis.

Regarding the economy, suffice it to say that the group of the very wealthy is growing, the group of the poor and near-poor is growing, and what used to be the great group in the middle (typified by the blue-collar jobs in industry which were such an important ladder for black non-professional families) is shrinking with alarming speed. We are a deindustrializing society whose relative economic strength is in decline. Our government policy has been seemingly harnessed to the task of widening the gap between rich and poor, with massive social resources being shifted from those at the bottom of the social pyramid to those at the top.

As for the state of the underlying law, we have a system of property rights and legal entitlements that results in most people enjoying less security against economic disaster than in any other advanced industrialized country. The increased pressure for the United States to compete in the global economy will do nothing but exacerbate these tendencies. If you are black and are not among that top 20% of all Americans who are on the escalator going up, but instead you are part of the bottom 80% that is losing ground, then even true formal equality would yield only the opportunity for you to stand around with a lot of other people on a glass floor and pray it didn't break. Formal equality would not help you to solve your most basic problems.

What I am saying is two-fold. First, we have won formal equality in principle but continue to learn how hard it is to achieve in practice. Second, we are forced to see that formal equality, even if it were honored in practice, would mean little in a society that is in deep economic trouble and that has thus far chosen to guarantee its citizens only the barest of substantive entitlements. Faced with this dilemma, what should we do?

One answer that has emerged from the civil rights movement is what I will call "identity politics." This phrase has been applied to forms of political discourse that stress how important it is for subordinated groups of people to mobilize themselves around their own group identity. The recent history of reform movements in the United States contains a strong dose of identity politics. The civil rights movement itself, the women's movement, the gay and lesbian movement, and the movement for disability rights are all examples of identity politics at work.

Identity politics boasts some very good features: the proud identification and transmission of a group's culture can help to celebrate properly the achievements and sacrifices of subordinated people, to preserve cultural memory, and to create environments conducive to human flourishing. Participation in a movement that stresses one's bonds with others who share that identity can promote the self-esteem of group members and help them articulate powerfully their concerns and experiences to the larger community. Organizations built around identity politics can create spaces where subordinated people experience a kind of validation, growth, and healthy challenge that may be available to them in no other company and in no other environment.

Further, both history and present observation show only too clearly that certain categories of identity are drastically significant for the distribution of power and resources (and the distribution of powerlessness and pain) in our society. Holding up the lens of race or gender to our world reveals startling patterns that should be noticed and studied. A strategy based on mobilizing members of those groups around visions revealed by those "identity lenses" would seem to have much merit.

Racial subordination has been such a linchpin of our social system for so long and has been built into our lives in so many destructive ways that I believe nothing but a color-conscious movement and jurisprudence stands a chance of successfully analyzing or opposing that subordination. That color-conscious movement may find itself entering into much-needed coalitions, but it will and should also find itself insisting that its coalition partners fairly encounter and respond to the tough issues, the history, and the insights afforded by the identity politics of race.

Dangers lurk in identity politics, however. Whenever identity is an issue, defining membership in the identity group unavoidably becomes an important task. People engaged in identity politics may find themselves spending a lot of intellectual and emotional energy on questions of who is "in" and who is "out." Policing the boundaries can sap people's energy and tax their relationships with others, requiring a kind of "defense budget" for "identity security" that may not be the best use of precious resources. Consider also the problem of categories. Like all such constructs, the categories of contemporary United States identity politics can distort our vision and the way we think. One of the main distortions is that identity politics creates difficulties in coping with people who fall into two categories at once, like people who are both black and female. Of course, a moment's thought will reveal that *all* human beings fall into two (and more!) categories at once. Therefore, at least in some ways, identity politics must create difficulty in coping with each and every one of us.

I want to draw your attention to two problems with the way identity politics handles multiple categories. First, it tends to treat the different "identities" a person has as somehow separable from all their other possible identities and also from some generic humanness we all have in common. This is the kind of thinking that leads to questions like, "Which is more important to you, that you are black, or that you are a woman?" I sometimes think of this as my File Drawer Problem. I have one drawer in my filing cabinet labeled "WOMEN" and another labeled "RACE." This makes a certain amount of sense, but I run into all kinds of problems when I file things. Where should I put information relating to the problems of Latinas in South Texas, for instance? Should I create a Latina file for my WOMEN drawer or file the information in the Latino file in my RACE drawer? If, for example, I put the Latinas in my WOMEN drawer, that leaves me with a Latino file in the RACE drawer. What am I supposed to put there? If I put in it anything that relates to Latinos that is not explicitly related to women, am I not giving basic humanity to the men while reserving some special, different-from-plain-old-Latin status for women?

Those of us trying to think about, reason about, and act on these matters of identity need to be aware of the distortions of categorization that may occur when we try to build a civil rights vision based on identity politics. We do violence to people's multipleness and complexity. We blind ourselves to cases that do not fit our categories and that are obscured when we look at a situation with only one lens.

A second and related problem with categories of identity is the strong tendency for each category to carry within itself an unstated norm, and for that norm to reinforce and mirror some of the very inequities that the civil rights movement set out to overcome. For example, at one point in the development of the feminist movement white feminists launched a campaign against rape. The idea was to tell the story of sexual violence from a woman's point of view, to redefine the law of rape in a way that was mindful of women's welfare. However, we white feminists left three things out of our early accounts of rape:

- We did little investigation, and spoke very little, of the long and special history of sexual abuse of black women at the hands of white men. This is an important part of the history and dynamics of rape, and the early white feminist account was impoverished by its relative absence.
- Neither did we explore the racist use of the rape charge against black men as an instrument of racist terror during long stretches of our national history: a practice in which white women were often complicit, and a setting in which those women could hardly be described as the victims of a prosecutorial process biased against conviction.
- We also ignored the sexual abuse of black women at the hands of black men, therefore miss-

ing entirely an additional burden and constraint often borne by black rape victims seeking security and redress. These victims often experience deep ambivalence about invoking law enforcement authority against a black man because of what they know about racial politics and about the police.

In other words, white women confidently spoke of "We women." Upon closer examination, however, the "we" of those initial analyses was not really "we women," it was "we white women." The unstated norm hidden in the term "woman" was in that case "white." Black women's experiences were left out of this account, and the account itself suffered from a parochialism that weakened it for everyone. Fortunately, black feminists have provoked an extremely productive reassessment of this issue, at least in many quarters of the women's movement.

Another example of an unstated norm occurred in a class I teach on race and gender matters. One day I had asked the class to compare the events that led to passage of the Fifteenth Amendment with those leading to passage of the Nineteenth Amendment. At one point an African-American male student said something like, "Women have not had to endure the sheer inhumanity that went along with race discrimination and that we blacks have had to bear." The implication of that remark is either that all "women" are white (otherwise some of them too would have had to endure race discrimination) or that all blacks are men (otherwise it would be nonsensical to say that "women" as a group can be neatly separated from "we blacks.") The result of this unconscious train of assumptions is the erasure of black women from the mental picture. This way of conceptualizing the problem leads both white women and black men to assume their black sisters away. Black women find a home in neither file drawer.

In addition to the problem with boundaries, and in addition to the difficulty in accounting for the multiple identities which people actually do have, the turn to identity politics as a solution to the civil rights crisis can set different groups against each other—groups who ought to be making common cause. It can divide the large group of people whose interests lie in serious change into warring factions resentful and distrustful of each other, worried that any attempt to empathize with the situation of another may threaten the sense of their own identity they have worked so hard to build.

The structure of civil rights law has promoted identity politics in ways that sometimes have been very positive, but at other times have produced real problems in the achievement of meaningful social change. Our civil rights law is centrally built around the notion of membership in a victim group—what we call a "protected group" in Title VII doctrine and a "suspect class" in Fourteenth Amendment lingo. To have a cause of action under much of our civil rights law, one must assert a cognizable "identity," and beyond these special categories of recognized victimhood if one is deemed to have no grievance.

I first began to appreciate this situation as a limit and a contradiction in the area of employment law. When I had just begun to work for legal services years ago, a worker came in for an interview one day. This worker was convinced by her own astute reading of the signs that she was about to be fired. Her supervisor (a female) had begun criticizing her publicly in ways that seemed both unwarranted and calculated to make her lose her temper. I felt she was right to be concerned about losing her job.

The difficulty, however, lay in trying to explain to her about The Law. She believed that the law would protect her against all arbitrary actions by her employer. I had to explain that in the absence of a collective or individual contract to the contrary, her employer could fire her for "good cause, bad cause, or no cause at all." Actually an employer could fire her for good cause, bad cause, or no cause at all, except: an employer could not fire her because she was black. There was one particular type of bad cause that the law had put off limits. I also explained that an employer could not fire her because she was a woman or refused to grant sexual favors.

The trouble was that the experiences of this black woman didn't really fit a race discrimination or sex discrimination mold. We could have perhaps made out a case, but she didn't believe her experiences resulted from race or gender animus. She felt they were individually and personally motivated, arbitrary, and unfair. She felt she should have some recourse and basic job security, and she could not fathom why the law would protect her from one type of arbitrary treatment and not from the others.

Many arbitrary irrational classifications based on race and sex still remain. Even if those were eradicated, plenty of arbitrariness would be left. How do we explain who gets born to a college professor and who to a coal miner? Who is born to a family lucky enough to have a miner at work and who to a single mother struggling to stretch a welfare check? Who is born to a Charleston chemical company executive and who to someone in McDowell County hoping for a job in one of Appalachia's new industries: perhaps burying garbage shipped in from New Jersey or guarding prisoners shipped in from Washington, D.C.? These inequities remain untouched by American anti-discrimination law.

I am not blaming the persistence of these non-racial, non-sexual inequities on the selfishness of identity politicians, although those who complain that race and gender issues are the provenance of "special interest groups" or those who oppose affirmative action sometimes seem to suggest as much. Quite the contrary. For example, people of color frequently have litigated to expand the law beyond the suspect-classification, identity-politics branch of equal protection and to strengthen the other, "non-identity" branch of Fourteenth Amendment equality, which is rooted in fundamental rights. Likewise they have lobbied repeatedly for legislation that would benefit more whites than blacks, such as increases in AFDC benefits, food stamps, and the like. Far too often they have enjoyed far too few allies in these endeavors.

If we are searching for causes of "non-racial" problems that beset disadvantaged groups in America, we might ironically conclude that the stubborn racism of large segments of the white electorate has been the most crucial one, a racism that has prevented those segments from making common cause with people of color. This deep racial divide has been a major reason why the United States lags astoundingly behind other industrialized countries in basic indices of human welfare, such as infant mortality, universal availability of health care, employment security, and adequate education. So I do not blame us identity politicians for these other kinds of inequities. But I do want to exhort us to action. Identity politicians, and I include myself in that category, must see beyond the lens of their own group identification.

One approach would not require the discarding or transcending of one's own identity, but rather the deepening of it. Here is my proposal: all of "us identity politicians" should consciously consider the political needs of those members of our group who are least privileged. We should conceive of our problems and design our reform strategies with their needs and perspectives firmly in mind.

In other words, a woman like me (a self-identified feminist, white, employed, presently-abled, American, heterosexual, and in a two-parent, two-wage-earner family) needs to investigate the points of view of women who are, for instance, black, brown, poor, alien, ill, single, lesbian, third-world, battered, unemployed, or all of the above. Viewing women's problems from those perspectives, I believe, will complicate matters, but it will often suggest fruitful answers to strategic questions. Seen from this vantage point, for instance, the goal of helping my sister attorneys crash the glass ceilings at their law firms seems less compelling than universal health insurance, free day care centers, battered women's shelters, and family leave, not to mention development of a responsible industrial policy that aims at sustainable growth both in the United States and for our neighbors in the South.

Certain groups of women have less access to resources, fewer ways to make themselves heard or felt by others, more chances of being marginalized as deviant from a presumed norm, and more likelihood of suffering material deprivations. It is these women I am suggesting "we feminists" should place at the center in our visions and strategies. This suggestion that identity politicians should privilege the least privileged among them also suggests coalitions beyond the original identity circle and therefore an expansion beyond the particular identity group in which the project began and in which it remains rooted.

I invite you to think about your own identity and about the categories of belonging and exclusion that have helped to define you. I invite you to think about those who share some aspects of your identity but not others, and to think especially about those "at the bottom" of whatever category you have chosen for your focus or "at the bottom" of whatever efforts and institutions in which you find yourself engaged. How might the world look from their perspective?

Notes

1. *See* Julia Lawlor & Jeffrey Potts, *Job Hunt: Blacks Face More Bias*, USA TODAY, May 15, 1991, at 1A.

112

What We Believe

THE EDITORS OF *RACE TRAITOR* MAGAZINE

The white race is a historically constructed social formation. It consists of all those who partake of the privileges of the white skin in this society. Its most wretched members share a status higher, in certain respects, than that of the most exalted persons excluded from it, in return for which they give their support to a system that degrades them.

The key to solving the social problems of our age is to abolish the white race, which means no more and no less than abolishing the privileges of the white skin. Until that task is accomplished, even partial reform will prove elusive, because white influence permeates every issue, domestic and foreign, in U.S. society.

The existence of the white race depends on the willingness of those assigned to it to place their racial interests above class, gender, or any other interests they hold. The defection of enough of its members to make it unreliable as a predictor of behavior will lead to its collapse.

Race Traitor aims to serve as an intellectual center for those seeking to abolish the white race. It will encourage dissent from the conformity that maintains it and popularize examples of defection from its ranks, analyze the forces that hold it together and those that promise to tear it apart. Part of its task will be to promote debate among abolitionists. When possible, it will support practical measures, guided by the principle Treason to Whiteness Is Loyalty to Humanity.

The editors publish things in *Race Traitor* because they think that publishing them will help build a community of readers. Editorial opinions are expressed in editorials and unsigned replies to letters.

What We Believe, RACE TRAITOR. Reprinted by permission of the editors.

113

Segregation, Whiteness, and Transformation

MARTHA R. MAHONEY

Transforming the Social Construction of Whiteness and Blackness:
The Case of Residential Housing

Transformative work against segregation and racial oppression must directly confront racism and the social construction of race. Whiteness and blackness are not merely mirror images of each other. "White" does not only mean "opposite of Other" but also stands for the dominant, transparent norm that defines what attributes of race should be counted, how to count them, and who (as in white employers or mortgage bankers) gets to do the counting. Therefore, destabilizing "Other"-ness doesn't entirely destabilize the dominance of whiteness. Even though race has no natural reality or truth, it has great social force. More work is required, therefore, to undo the many forms of harm that have been part of the construction of race in America, including the perpetuation of residential segregation and the impoverishment of black individuals and communities.

Because whiteness is a transparent and dominant norm, part of the transformative project necessarily includes exposing white privilege to white people. From outside the cultural circle of whiteness, white retention of privilege looks willful. Some protection of privilege is indeed a conscious preference for whites and against people of color, a conscious protection of assets and access in society. At other times, a preference for whiteness reflects a preference for the qualities that have been attached to whiteness. For example, consider those employers who artlessly and bluntly interpret race, class, and status in describing their hiring preferences. Because maintaining white consciousness requires not-seeing whiteness and not-seeing race, in many situations white privilege will also reproduce itself unconsciously and through a formal attachment to colorblindness. As Barbara Flagg has pointed out, positioned white decision-making that protects and perpetuates white privilege usually lacks the sort of "intent" to discriminate that law often requires before being willing to remedy subordination.[1]

Transformative work on whiteness therefore requires attacking its power as a dominant norm, while seeking points of potential for change in the social construction of whiteness. *Necessary steps toward change include attacking the power of whiteness as an invisible, dominant social norm; participating in the project (necessarily repeated) that reiterates the existence of subordination and privilege by revealing the ongoing reproduction of white privilege and power; disputing the legal and social preference for colorblind approaches*

143 U. Pa. L. Rev. 1659 (1996). Copyright © 1995 The University of Pennsylvania Law Review. Reprinted by permssion.

that reproduce color and power evasion, protect privilege, and deny cultural autonomy; and seeking points of unity and transformative potential.

In the context of residential segregation, antidiscrimination law is part of the attack on whiteness as a dominant norm. Whiteness has been constructed by excluding blacks, by defining white areas as superior, and by allocating to white areas the resources that reinforce privilege. Housing discrimination perpetuates segregation. It reflects the social construction of race—blacks as undesirable residents for white areas, whites as desirable residents for those areas—and perpetuates the processes that concentrate black poverty and continue to reproduce race and racism in America. A straightforward attack on housing discrimination is therefore vital to break down walls of exclusion and begin the process of including people of color into formerly all-white or mostly white areas. Fighting housing discrimination is an important part of transforming whiteness in America. Although antidiscrimination law is necessary, however, it is inadequate to effectively undo the processes of selective investment and disinvestment that are part of the social construction of whiteness and blackness. Further measures will also be necessary to reveal white privilege and to deprive privilege of its apparently natural quality.

Because the social construction of race is not symmetrical, and because blackness is not simply the mirror image of whiteness, the effects of deconcentrating segregated housing are different for blacks than for whites. For whites, the concentration of blacks somewhere other than white neighborhoods is what allows whiteness to remain both exclusive (that is, physically populated mostly by white persons) and a dominant norm (unnoticed except when threatened). Breaking down the walls of exclusion helps break down white dominance as well as making white spaces less white. Residence in white neighborhoods obviously has some advantages for those black individuals who find that it detaches some of the social construction of blackness (including identification with "inner-city" or "unemployable") for some of the privileges of whiteness ("suburban" and, often, "employable"). However, moving blacks toward white areas fails to address some important transformative issues. Part of contesting the social construction of blackness includes defending the strengths and potential of black people and neighborhoods. Racial concentration and the effects of deconcentration are therefore different for white areas than for black areas.

Another way to attack both privilege and subordination in the social construction of race is to identify potential points of unity and mutual interest by examining the relationship between employment and residence. Employment and residence are linked in the reproduction of white privilege and power, but there are important differences between them. White working-class interests in both residential and workplace settings run at least in part counter to the perpetuation of white privilege—even though complex and partial shared interests against oppression are seldom discussed today in either context.

Part of the problem with finding shared interests against racism lies in prevailing American concepts of "class." Legal and social analysts most commonly use the term "class" to refer to socioeconomic status, rather than to describe a role in a system of production. Status-oriented accounts of white privilege, including concepts of group status and of a "property right in whiteness," are based on the concept of class as socioeconomic status. When class is understood to refer to labor, to a set of shared interests in a system of production, shared interests immediately appear that have the potential to help whites understand the need for antiracist unity with people of color.

The "property right in whiteness" is a metaphor that captures much of the systematic quality of the retention of white privilege in law and in society. But whiteness is also dynamic, continually in the process of formation, in transition for better or for worse. Therefore, it is also important to identify the ways in which many social structures operate to make the "property right in whiteness" not merely some form of additional status but a social premium that has formed the "consolation prize" for low income and lack of other substantive rights for working-class whites in America. It is the lack of those "other" substantive rights that creates further possibilities for educating whites about the costs of racism.

In the workplace, white interest in solidarity can provide the basis for finding transformative potential and shared interests against racism. Because middle-class and elite whites treat racism as a fixed artifact and then locate this artifact in the white working class, racism tends to be seen as evidence against the possibility for labor solidarity. It is true that "race"—meaning racism, or the unwillingness of whites to see their futures as interdependent with blacks and other people of color—has weakened the labor movement in America.[2] At various times, however, labor solidarity has also proved to be a mobilizing force against white privilege. Therefore, a view of whiteness as historically located and subject to change would emphasize instead the way shared interests through labor solidarity could help to work against racism.

Outside the workplace, low-income white residents of urban communities have been harmed in some ways by the social construction of race, even as it has protected them in other ways. In recent decades, racism masked economic decline in the United States. White privilege protected relatively greater access to jobs and housing by perpetuating exclusion. The racialized discourses of our time have, however, disguised long-term economic trends disfavoring all working-class people. The transition to high rates of permanent unemployment and from an industrial to a service economy have serious consequences for American labor. But these trends were racialized based on their impact on black communities. The development of an underclass, the feminization of poverty, and related phenomena were treated as racial and considered as characteristics of black inner-city communities, when in fact they are part of the nationwide transitions in work opportunity that now grip white working people as well as blacks.

An examination of Massey and Denton's statistics on segregation shows how protecting white privilege works to white material advantage in some ways while disguising white low-income interest in structural economic change. When black poverty occurs at a higher rate than white poverty, lower-income whites profit by the diminished exposure to the problems of poverty that come from concentrating black poverty.[3] Segregation significantly reduces the extent to which low-income whites must live with the effects of poverty, whether or not income segregation or racial segregation are factors in residential patterns. Therefore, the "property right in whiteness" is not merely psychological, but a material advantage in living in communities less impacted by the effects of poverty. As Massey and Denton explain, this structure shifts the effects of poverty to hypersegregated black communities and thereby intensifies the negative effects of segregation for blacks.

This form of white privilege, however, depends on acceptance of a background regime in which the economy continues to deteriorate and labor continues to be an ever-weaker social and political force. If class only means status, then it is difficult to find a shared interest in bettering conditions for all. But if blacks and whites share interests in developing jobs, improving working conditions, and improving salaries for low-income workers, then whites might be better off abandoning attachment to white race privilege and working with blacks to accomplish this goal.[4]

Downplaying race in support of social programs for low-income people cannot solve these problems of class interest. In America, social and economic programs do not exist outside the process of the construction of race. Programs like public housing, Medicaid, welfare, and food stamps have become publicly "raced" and endowed with a racial character (marked as non-white) in white perception and in much political discourse, even though whites are at least a plurality of the beneficiaries. Programs such as aid to agribusiness and bailouts for large corporations are officially treated as if they are "non-raced" when in actuality they are "white-raced." Social programs covertly coded white include Social Security, because as enacted it thoroughly excluded so many African-Americans.[5] The social construction of race is capable of overtaking nonracial programs, stigmatizing them as "assistance" and treating them as "racial" whenever any significant proportion of benefits is provided to people of color.

Class-conscious work must be anti-racist, not race-blind, to address the construction of race. Whites, especially white working-class men, are being told by political figures like Jesse Helms, Patrick Buchanan, and David Duke that they are suffering from illegitimate "preferences" for all women and all people of color. The anti-affirmative-action rhetoric of our time perpetuates the dominant norm of whiteness by treating the current distribution of power and access as natural and just. This rhetoric also makes the structural economic problems of working-class whites invisible by blaming people of color for the downturn in white working-class earning power.

Heightened racism and lowered class consciousness are both part of the conservatizing effect of residential segregation on working white Americans. Achieving home ownership—more open to working-class whites than to blacks—helped white American workers achieve "middle-class" status. The social processes that opened home ownership to whites and not blacks—and equated whiteness with positive social qualities like employability, comfort, and security—also consolidated racial attitudes that institutionalized urban/suburban divisions that in turn make shared work on job development difficult. Whites need to see how white privilege has hurt, as well as helped, the interests of many white people. The challenge is to identify the ways in which we can help show this point.

Notes

1. Barbara J. Flagg, *"Was Blind, But Now I See": White Race Consciousness and the Requirement of Discriminatory Intent*, 91 MICH. L. REV. 953, 988 (1993). *See generally* Barbara J. Flagg, *Fashioning a Title VII Remedy for Transparently White Decisionmaking*, 104 YALE L.J. (1995). [Reprinted as Chapters 15 and 97 of this book. Ed.]

2. *See generally* Karl Klare, *The Quest for Industrial Democracy and the Struggle Against Racism: Perspectives from Labor Law and Civil Rights Law*, 61 OR. L. REV. 157, 158 (1982).

3. DOUGLAS S. MASSEY & NANCY A. DENTON, AMERICAN APARTHEID: SEGREGATION AND THE MAKING OF THE UNDERCLASS 30–54 (1993) (discovering that in a hypothetical simulation, whites isolated from black poverty are able to insulate themselves from the social problems associated with income deprivation).

4. *See, e.g.,* DERRICK BELL, AND WE ARE NOT SAVED: THE ELUSIVE QUEST FOR RACIAL JUSTICE 245–58 (1987) (demonstrating the advantages of cooperation).

5. *See* Joel F. Handler, *"Constructing the Political Spectacle": Interpretation of Entitlements, Legalization, and Obligations in Social Welfare History*, 56 BROOK. L. REV. 899, 917 (1990) (arguing that the elimination of domestic and agricultural workers from coverage under the Social Security Act ensured "planter control over African-Americans," and noting that "the vast majority of elderly African-Americans were almost completely excluded" from Social Security insurance).

114

White Out

ROGER WILKINS

I live on a street in Washington, D.C., where the Speaker of the House, senators, congressmen, and a couple of Supreme Court justices also live. A few blocks away are two large public-housing projects. The Safeway where we all shop may be the most racially and economically integrated supermarket in America. Public servants with big titles shop alongside people who buy their staples with food stamps. And a couple of times a year there are street murders a half-mile away.

Since the late fifties, when I was a welfare caseworker in poor black precincts in Cleveland, my heart has never left the inner city. I've lived elsewhere and have had varied jobs in the ensuing thirty-five years, but the problems I wrestled with in Cleveland have remained at the core of my concerns. Twenty-five years ago, I was the Justice Department official President Lyndon Johnson most often relied on to respond to urban riots. Fifteen years ago, I was writing an urban-affairs column for the *New York Times*. I lived in Greenwich Village, and, when I wanted to get the feeling of black poverty back into my veins before I began writing, I would have to ride the A train to Harlem and then suppress the feeling that I was a voyeur before getting down to work.

I live where I do now because I hated being a voyeur among the most vulnerable of my fellow citizens, and also because I want my daughter Elizabeth, who is nine, to grow up in a truly integrated neighborhood. I want poor black people to be not just in our heads, but in our lives. I want us to see them whole, not as statistics and not as the stereotypes presented by our culture, but as neighbors. Whites spend a lot of time spinning fantasies about black people—especially the poorest of us. I want my poor neighbors to define themselves directly to me, unmediated.

The night before I sat down to write these words, I left a neighborhood restaurant with my daughter and one of her closest friends, a little girl named Mercy. Mercy is white, the daughter of good people and close friends of my wife and me. They are at the far end of the political pole from us: they were Reagan political appointees. But our friendship, which grew from our children's friendship, is deep and real. As the children and I were walking from the restaurant toward Mercy's house we ran into a poor black woman with a child. She told me she was homeless and that the father of her child had disappeared. She had worked as long as family members could care for her child, but, when this support collapsed, she had to leave her job. She ended up in shelters and on the streets. The child, still in a stroller and not yet talking, was, in fact, black and beautiful.

The young mother was distraught, clearly under great stress. In our neighborhood, there's not much likelihood that she would find a man with whom to form a family. There are some single black men, but the ones I know live in a homeless shelter and the most enterprising try to eke out a few dollars by wiping off our autos at the car wash. Some are quite intelligent, but none has been able to catch on. As one said to me as he was scouring my wheels one night: "The world don't seem to have no more use for me."

If drastic change does not occur, that doleful predicament may someday claim the child I saw in the stroller that night. With a distressed mother without income or a supportive extended family, the child is apt to be exposed at an early age to some of the hardest streets in our town. By the time she is fifteen, it is entirely possible that those streets, filled with poverty and with peers who have had no more chance in our America than she, will have claimed her. And so it goes.

The industrial manufacturing jobs that have been points of entry into the mainstream of the economy for unskilled southern blacks—just as they had been for wave after wave of unskilled European immigrants in earlier decades—are disappearing from this country. Dr. William Spriggs, an economist with the Economic Policy Institute in Washington, D.C., reports that the United States lost two million such jobs between 1979 and 1990. Those losses hit blacks with devastating effect. After the Los Angeles riots, Dr. Mel Oliver, an urban sociologist at UCLA, calculated that seventy thousand such jobs disappeared from Watts and South Central L.A. between 1978 and 1983. It has been estimated that the black male unemployment rate in the latter community was around 40 percent at the time that the riots occurred.

Even worse, Dr. Spriggs reports, at no time since 1979 has the black *adult* male unemployment rate been *under 10 percent*. During that period it has gone as high as 18.1 and has averaged 12.9 percent. Discouraged workers and those in jail are not included in these calculations. Much more likely to be part of the statistics are the men I see wearing worn clothing and standing on inner-city streets during working hours. In personal conversations, such men often reveal spirits loaded with weariness and despair, but occasionally they also reveal the most unlikely and poignant expressions of human hope. When glimpsed from a moving car, however, the men may appear to be shiftless or worse, the ambulatory components of yet one more shoddy and dangerous urban street scene.

For the past five years, I've been teaching at George Mason University. To get to work, I drive out to Fairfax County, Virginia, one of the nation's wealthiest suburbs. It is quiet and leafy there, and even modest neighborhoods seem safe and clean. Driving through, I feel as if I am stepping back into the fifties.

I'm not an expert on the white suburban mind, and obviously all suburbanites don't think alike. But judging from what my white students tell me about their own views and those of their parents, and from what I glean from some of my colleagues, many suburban racial attitudes have actually rolled back to something like the fifties. In those innocent days, before desegregation had really been tried, before the New Frontier and the Great Society, many of us blacks had lovely, naïve hopes for integration. We thought that it would work. We thought that desegregation would permit people to learn from and about each other and that whites would be willing to do that in order to bring personal beliefs into line with our professed national ideals. We thought that prejudice was an individual thing and that relatively few whites were virulently afflicted. We thought that the leadership classes in this country were far better than the racist few and that they would make an effort to lead their fellow whites to richer understandings. We hadn't considered the nature of racism very much.

In our naïveté, we believed that the power to segregate was the greatest power that had been wielded against us. It turned out that our expectations were quite wrong. The great-est power turned out to be what it had always been: the power to define reality where blacks are concerned and to manage perceptions and therefore arrange politics and culture to re-inforce those definitions. When we were segregated, we hadn't considered the nation's long history of racial subordination. From the dark and cramped box of segregation, the rest of the country out there looked bright and shiny. We thought the only thing it lacked was us. We didn't understand then how normal a part of national life racism had become.

August of this year marked the 373rd anniversary of the arrival—at Jamestown, Vir-ginia—of the first Africans on the North American continent. For 246 of those years, we had slavery. For a hundred years after that, many states had some form of legalized racial subordination and in the other states this oppression was rigidly enforced by the culture. For only 27 of those 373 years have we had something other than slavery or legal and cul-tural racial subordination. The habits of racism that built up over those centuries are tena-cious; they haven't died. The most powerful habit is that of defining blacks for the conve-nience and profit of whites.

One eighteenth-century white American undertook to define us in a fairly scientific way. He wrote [in *Notes on the State of Virginia*, Query XIV. Ed.]:

> The first difference that strikes us is that of color. . . . And is this difference of no importance?
> Is it not the foundation of a greater or less share of beauty in the two races? Are not the fine
> mixtures of red and white, the expressions of every passion by greater or less suffusions of color
> in the one, preferable to that eternal monotony, which reigns in the countenances, that im-
> movable veil of black which covers all the emotions of the other race? Add to these, flowing hair,
> a more elegant symmetry of form, their own judgment in favor of the whites, declared by their
> preference of them, as uniformly as is the preference of the Oran-ootan for the black woman
> over those of his own species. . . .
>   I . . . advance it therefore as a suspicion only, that the blacks, whether originally a distinct
> race . . . are inferior to the whites in the endowments both of body and mind. . . . This unfor-
> tunate difference of color, and perhaps of faculty, is a powerful obstacle to the emancipation of
> these people. . . .

This effort to define blacks as lesser beings was assayed by a man who *owned* at least a hun-dred human beings at the time. At another [earlier. Ed.] time, for another audience, the au-thor of this definition of blacks—Thomas Jefferson—wrote the most famous line in the Amer-ican heritage: "We hold these truths to be self-evident; that all men are created equal. . . ."

The practices of defining blacks and manipulating the culture around uncomfortable facts are as ancient as our republic and remain deeply embedded in the nation's soul. My students tell me that blacks and whites still do not mix very much in suburban high schools and that there is precious little encouragement for them to do so. Although one or two white stu-dents have reported that their parents have inculcated them with a sense of racial decency, most indicate that their parents have been neutral at best, or hostile in the main. One stu-dent said that, when he watched football at home, his father would invariably become im-patient with offensive huddles and would say: "I don't see why they always take so long. They've only got three plays: nigger go right, nigger go left, nigger go up the middle."

Another student reported that she had followed some advice I had given her. "I was morally courageous in a small everyday thing, just like you suggested," she told me. "At the dinner table the other day, I said, 'Grandpa, it ruins my appetite when you talk about niggers all the time when we're eating.' " These attitudes aren't peculiar to Fairfax County.

An enormous array of scholarly and journalistic evidence sustains the proposition that my students' lives reflect something deep and wrong in the country. The National Opinion Research Center at the University of Chicago reported last year that whites generally believe that blacks are less patriotic, more violent, and lazier than themselves. A number of students have given me a clear sense that situations like that of the young woman I encountered on the street that night have been taken into consideration in their families—and harshly judged. The problem is not economics, it is sex, some of my students have been told, one reporting that her mother had refused to believe the unemployment figures I had presented in class. "She is convinced that the problem is illegitimate babies," the student said.

"People are always going to act like people," I responded. When sex and economics clash, sex will win every time. People will not refrain from having sex simply because they have no economic opportunities. If they do have real economic opportunities, they're more apt to be careful to protect their future. And, with jobs, they're more apt to be good parents. "We both know," I concluded, "that good income doesn't guarantee that people will be good parents, but lack of income almost assuredly cripples the capacity to be a good parent."

"That makes sense to me," the student said. "But my mom will never believe it."

Contemporary American racial thought has been sculpted to suit the suburbs. In the current conventional analysis, history doesn't count. For example, *Newsweek*, in an issue published after the L.A. riots, dismissed the burden of racial history in an effort to "rethink" race. Yet it is impossible to understand the problem without facing the very hard facts of our racial history. By the time the Civil War ended slavery, the idea of black inferiority had become engrained in U.S. culture and whites had amassed generations of advantage in the accumulation of education, wealth, and the practices of husbanding the best opportunities for themselves and for European immigrants. As Andrew Hacker observes in his brutally honest analysis, *Two Nations: Black and White, Separate, Hostile, and Unequal*, whites had by then also made a large psychic investment in being superior to blacks.

Newsweek linked its analysis to its assertion that people who insist on looking to history believe that "poverty will not disappear until all barriers to opportunity are removed." The magazine said that such a view was "plainly undercut by the fact that about 40 percent of all African-American families can now be classified as middle class or upwardly mobile working class." This denial of history is not rational. The fortunes of talented Americans like Toni Morrison and Michael Jordan or lucky Americans like my own family or politically connected Americans have nothing to do with the life chances of others who are not so talented or lucky or connected and who are more damaged by racism than the rest of us. By denigrating the importance of history, by throwing in wrong and irrelevant assertions about remedies, *Newsweek* lightens the responsibilities of the power holders in this society. Such denials shift the burden from the nation as a whole onto the shoulders of poor black individuals, like the young woman we encountered on our way home from the restaurant.

With the suburbs now casting more presidential votes than the cities, politics 1992 were sculpted for suburbanites. Blacks were written almost entirely out of the national political equation. Bill Clinton's use of the rap singer Sister Souljah to humiliate Rev. Jesse Jackson was a striking example. Souljah had been quoted in the *Washington Post* in mid-May to the effect that it might be a good idea to have a week devoted to the killing of white people. A month later she was a participant on a panel at a conference convened by Jackson and the National Rainbow Coalition. Speaking at the meeting, Clinton used the Rainbow plat-form to condemn the rapper's remarks—and, by inference, Jackson's invitation to her. Had Clinton been genuinely concerned about Souljah's words, why did he wait a whole month to make his point? Clinton waited until he had Jackson in his sights—and then struck with-out warning.

The facts were different from what Clinton suggested. In the wake of the L.A. riots, black leaders had been urged to engage angry youth and to try to induce them to behave more responsibly. That is exactly what Jesse Jackson did in the coalition meeting. He did not pro-vide Sister Souljah a platform to repeat her views; rather, Jackson risked his popularity with the young by confronting the rapper. "Anger is fine as long as you harness it and turn it into energy inside the system. Cynicism and anger are destructive. They don't get you any-where," Jackson said to Souljah.

Jackson did a good thing. Clinton defined what Jackson had done as a bad thing. The press bought Clinton's definition and sold it as virtue, portraying Clinton as a brave man full of moral courage for "standing up" to Jackson. Clinton's polls went up, while many pundits continued to define Jackson as a pariah. The truth is that Clinton was cynical and Jackson behaved with moral courage. Clinton is white, and so, by and large, is the press. In the de-fine game, whites win most of the time.

In winning these kinds of skirmishes, though, whites are as apt to lose their country. This nation is not just made up of suburbs and white people. Looking at America from the out-side at the time of the L.A. riots, a Japanese observer offered the view that our country had made no place for poor blacks. During the riots, the *Washington Post* published census data revealing that last year forty thousand teenagers—20 percent of the sixteen- to nineteen-year-olds in L.A.—were both out of school and out of work. They represent a substantial portion of L.A.'s future, as do youngsters in similar situations all over the country.

In an earlier day, U.S. capital roamed Africa and then Europe in search of cheap labor to bring here for jobs to be done at American work stations. Now U.S. capital roams the world in search of pools of cheap labor into which formerly American work stations can be in-troduced. Great numbers of jobs left the country before the unions began large campaigns to staunch the hemorrhaging. In this major economic shift, black male workers were like the canaries that were sent into the mines to test for gas. But since the victims were black, nobody much noticed the damage. When people did begin to notice, whites began using their power to define black people in ways that made an honest confrontation of deep so-cietal problems almost impossible.

Spokespersons for the White House argue that it has created millions of new jobs. But the administration tried to bury census data that revealed that, between 1980 and 1990, the percentage of the work force laboring full time for a wage insufficient to lift a family of four out of poverty increased from 12.1 to 18 percent. Thus, even if the young woman I encountered that night last summer could find a new job and find adequate and safe child care, she probably would still remain in poverty. Like Clinton, many scholars and journal-ists have made an industry of looking past the defects of society in order to feast upon the defects of poor black people. The same government that abolished the CETA program, which provided some poor people with jobs and job training, began to raise "welfare re-form" to a high place on the national agenda in the 1970s and 1980s. Scholars such as Charles Murray and Lawrence Mead established national reputations based on their theo-ries about how to improve poor blacks.

Even when the issue of jobs is put squarely on the front burner, the subject is introduced upside down. As *Newsweek* tells it, the problem is how to wean poor black people off welfare. Writer Mickey Kaus repeats the by now familiar story of whites and middle-class blacks leaving the inner city, and adds, "Without jobs and role models, those left in the ghettos *drifted out of the labor market*" (italics mine).

A better way to say it would have been to observe that the labor market had collapsed under these people and that none now obsessed with bad black behavior and welfare reform had lifted a finger to pull them back into the economy. There is no room in the Kaus analysis for an examination of national policies that call a 5 percent unemployment rate "normal" and that accept deindustrialization. Nor is there room for studies—such as a recent one by the Urban Poverty and Family Structure Project at the University of Chicago—that indicate that immigrants are preferred by employers over blacks for low-skill jobs.

It wasn't supposed to be this way, thirty-eight years after the decision in *Brown v. Board of Education* and twenty-eight years after the passage of the Civil Rights Act of 1964. We blacks and whites were supposed to be a lot closer together than we are. When I was thirty, I thought that friendships with whites would have become fairly commonplace by this point. But now that I am sixty, I can see reasons for deep pessimism. The tenacity of white fantasies about blacks is chief among them. For me and for other black people, there is nothing to do but to stay the course. That means fighting to get decent jobs for poor blacks, fighting for support for poor families and for good education for black children. I don't contend that full employment would sop up all the problems of the inner city. But until we try a full-employment program and provide good education for our children, we'll never figure out what needs to be addressed by different kinds of social programs.

What can I say to decent white people? I think the best answer is what so many whites invariably preach to us—self-help. In a moment of deep weariness, Thurgood Marshall once said to the great black psychologist Kenneth Clark, "I'm so tired of trying to save white folks' souls." Thurgood said that about forty years ago.

We can't save white folks' souls. Only they can do that. The best have to save the rest—but to succeed, they have to work at it every day. They can start as my student started, at the dinner table. Parents need to work on their children, to weed out all the racism that is so normal in our society. They have to work to get their school boards to teach students the truth about American history, not to nurture black self-esteem or white guilt, but to give our children a rich and true understanding of our nation. And they have to re-teach themselves that the "government" is our common enterprise, set up to undertake large efforts that we believe are in the best interest of us all.

From the Editors: Issues and Comments

Do whites have any role to play in liberation movements for blacks, Puerto Ricans, and other nonwhite groups? Or is their most appropriate role working among their own people, raising consciousness and preaching racial tolerance? If a white wants to be helpful to blacks, should he or she first come to terms with his or her own whiteness—and, if so, what does that mean? If you are white, should you be a "race traitor" who goes around challenging the white point of view at every opportunity? Is every white—perhaps every person in our society—an unconscious racist, as a number of our writers assert? If so, should we all give up—or try harder?

Suggested Readings

Bonnett, Alastair, RADICALISM, ANTI-RACISM AND REPRESENTATION (Routledge, 1993).

Dalton, Harlon, RACIAL HEALING (Doubleday, 1995).

Delgado, Richard, *Rodrigo's Eleventh Chronicle: Empathy and False Empathy*, 84 CAL. L. REV. 61 (1996).

Haney López, Ian F., WHITE BY LAW (New York University Press, 1995).

Harvey, John, and Noel Ignatiev, RACE TRAITOR (Routledge, 1996).

Ignatiev, Noel, *How to Be a Race Traitor: Six Ways to Fight Being White*, UTNE READER, November/December 1994, at 85.

Katz, Judith, WHITE AWARENESS: HANDBOOK FOR ANTI-RACISM TRAINING (University of Oklahoma Press, 1978).

Kevel, Paul, UPROOTING RACISM: HOW WHITE PEOPLE CAN WORK FOR RACIAL JUSTICE (New Society Publishers, 1996).

King, Joyce E., "On Race and Education: A Response," in THIRTEEN QUESTIONS: REFRAMING EDUCATION'S CONVERSATIONS, 2d ed. (J. Kincheloe & S. R. Steinberg, eds.), 1995.

Lind, Michael, THE NEXT AMERICAN NATION: THE NEW NATIONALISM AND THE FOURTH AMERICAN REVOLUTION (Free Press, 1995).

Raybon, Patricia, MY FIRST WHITE FRIEND (1996).

Segrest, Mab, MEMOIR OF A RACE TRAITOR (South End Press, 1994).

About the Contributors

Linda L. Ammons teaches law at Cleveland-Marshall Law School, where she gives classes on administrative law, women and the law, and legislation. She is the co-author of Defending Battered Women in Criminal Cases.

Frances Lee Ansley, professor of law at the University of Tennessee, is a leading writer on discrimination, economic justice, and resistance.

James Armstrong, Jr., was a nineteenth-century Southern writer.

Robin Barnes, professor of law at the University of Connecticut, is the author of leading articles on civil rights, critical race theory, and white supremacy.

James R. Barrett is a labor historian at the University of Illinois.

Derrick A. Bell, professor of law at New York University Law School, is cofounder of the legal school known as critical race theory and author of more than a hundred law review articles, books, and chapters in books.

Laurel Johnson Black writes about pedagogy and literary composition.

Richard Brookhiser is editor of National Review and author of numerous articles, monographs, and books on American politics and society.

Eleanor Marie Brown is a graduate of Yale Law School currently doing graduate work at Oxford University.

James Campbell is a senior research officer at the Institute for Advanced Social Research at the University of the Witwatersrand, Johannesburg, South Africa, and is the author of Songs of Zion: A History of the African Methodist Episcopal Church in the United States and South Africa.

Mary Cappello writes about literature and culture.

W. J. Cash, whose 1940 classic, The Mind of the South, has never been out of print, was a journalist at the Charlotte (N.C.) News.

The Center for Democratic Renewal is a nonprofit research clearinghouse for information on white supremacist hate groups and hate crimes in the United States. Founded in 1979 as the National Anti-Klan Network, CDR monitors the ways that hate groups infringe on the civil and human rights of American citizens and helps communities constructively respond to bigoted violence.

Martha Chamallas, professor of law at the University of Pittsburgh, teaches courses in constitutional law, employment discrimination, sexuality and the law, and feminist legal thought.

Kathleen Neal Cleaver, a feminist theorist of black power, is professor of law at Emory University School of Law.

PHILIP J. COOK is a professor of public policy at Duke University.

JEROME MCCRISTAL CULP, JR., is professor of law at Duke University, where he teaches and writes in the areas of civil rights, critical thought, and law and economics.

DOUG DANIELS teaches at the University of Regina.

ADRIENNE D. DAVIS is professor of law at American University Law School and writes on critical race theory and feminism.

RICHARD DELGADO serves as the Charles Inglis Thomson Professor of Law at the University of Colorado, where he teaches and writes in the areas of critical race theory, hate speech, and law and narrative.

DAVISON M. DOUGLAS is professor of law at William and Mary School of Law, where he teaches courses in American legal history, constitutional law, and employment law.

DINESH D'SOUZA is a fellow at the American Enterprise Institute and author of several books on American universities and race, including ILLIBERAL EDUCATION (1993) and THE END OF RACISM (1995).

ANNA EVERETT teaches film studies at the University of Colorado.

RAPHAEL S. EZEKIEL is a senior research scientist with the Public Health Practices Initiative at Harvard University's School of Public Health.

DANIEL A. FARBER is the Henry J. Fletcher Professor of Law at the University of Minnesota, where he teaches and writes in the areas of constitutional law, environmental law, jurisprudence, and critical theory.

JOE R. FEAGIN teaches at the University of Florida and is the author of many highly acclaimed books on race and racism.

BARBARA J. FLAGG is professor of law at Washington University, where she teaches courses on feminist jurisprudence, sex discrimination, and critical race theory. She is a leading writer on whiteness and racism.

ERIC FONER is De Witt Clinton Professor of History at Columbia University and the author of widely acclaimed books on black history.

ROBERT H. FRANK is professor of economics at Cornell University.

KATHERINE M. FRANKE teaches law at the University of Arizona, specializing in civil rights, disability law, and feminist jurisprudence.

RUTH FRANKENBERG writes in the areas of feminism, women's studies, and cultural studies and is associate professor of American studies at the University of California at Davis.

GEORGE M. FREDRICKSON, author of numerous articles and books on race and history, teaches in the Department of History at Stanford University.

CHARLES A. GALLAGHER teaches in the sociology department at Colorado College.

NATHAN GLAZER is professor of education and sociology, emeritus, at Harvard University and the author of highly acclaimed works on American society, politics, and immigration.

DAVID THEO GOLDBERG is professor of justice studies at Arizona State University.

JAMES W. GORDON teaches law at Western New England College and is an expert on civil rights and American legal history.

JOHN R. GRAHAM is president of Graham Communications, Quincy, Massachusetts.

JOHN HOWARD GRIFFIN was a Texas journalist whose highly acclaimed book, BLACK LIKE ME, sold more than ten million copies and was translated into fourteen languages.

TRINA GRILLO, the late professor of law at the University of San Francisco, taught and wrote in the areas of constitutional law, critical theory, and alternative dispute resolution.

BONNIE KAE GROVER, lecturer, Department of Ethnic Studies, University of Colorado, is the author of several articles in the legal literature dealing with civil rights and critical theory.

ANDREW HACKER, author of TWO NATIONS: BLACK AND WHITE, SEPARATE, HOSTILE, AND UNEQUAL (1992) and many other articles and books on U.S. culture and politics, teaches at the City University of New York, Queens.

PETER HALEWOOD, a professor of law at the Albany Law School, is a J.S.D. candidate at Columbia University School of Law and holder of various fellowships in Canada and the United States.

ROBERT L. HAYMAN, JR., professor of law at Widener University School of Law, teaches and writes in the areas of constitutional law, civil rights, and postmodern jurisprudence. With Nancy Levit, he edited JURISPRUDENCE: CONTEMPORARY READINGS, PROBLEMS, AND NARRATIVES (West, 1995).

TRACY HIGGINS is a 1990 graduate of Harvard Law School, where she was an associate of and assistant to Derrick Bell.

REGINALD HORSMAN is professor of history at the University of Wisconsin, Milwaukee.

HERBERT HOVENKAMP, professor of law at Duke University, teaches and writes in the areas of antitrust, legal history, and property.

NOEL IGNATIEV is editor of *Race Traitor* magazine and the author of books and articles on race, whiteness, and reconstruction.

D. MARVIN JONES, professor of law at the University of Miami, has contributed prolifically to leading law reviews on issues of race and social construction.

JACQUELINE JONES teaches American history at Brandeis University and is the author of THE DISPOSSESSED: AMERICA'S UNDERCLASSES FROM THE CIVIL WAR TO THE PRESENT.

JOHN B. JUDIS is a senior editor at the *New Republic*.

JEROME KAGAN, professor of psychology at Harvard University, is a pioneer in child development research.

DANIEL KANSTROOM is professor of law at Boston College.

KENNETH L. KARST, professor of law at the University of California at Los Angeles Law School, is an expert on equality and civil rights, Latin America, and constitutional law.

JOYCE E. KING is associate vice chancellor for academic affairs and diversity programs at the University of New Orleans.

JORGE KLOR DE ALVA is the Class of 1940 Professor of Comparative Ethnic Studies and Anthropology at the University of California at Berkeley. The author of numerous books, he is currently editing THE NORTON ANTHOLOGY OF INDIGENOUS MESOAMERICAN LITERATURE.

CHARLES LANE is a senior editor at the *New Republic*.

ELINOR LANGER is the author of JOSEPHINE HERBST: THE STORY SHE COULD NEVER TELL and is at work on a book about skinheads and neo-Nazis.

NANCY LEVIT, professor of law, University of Missouri, Kansas City, writes about feminism, civil rights, and narrative theory and is co-editor of JURISPRUDENCE: CONTEMPORARY READINGS, PROBLEMS, AND NARRATIVES (West, 1995).

MICHAEL LIND is a former senior editor at the *New Republic* and is the author of UP FROM CONSERVATISM.

PEGGY MCINTOSH writes in the areas of women's studies, education, and racism. She is Codirector, National S.E.E.D. (Seeking Educational Equity and Diversity) Project on Inclusive Curriculum at the Wellesley College Center for Women.

CATHARINE A. MACKINNON, professor of law at the University of Michigan, originated the legal claim for sexual harassment and is currently representing Bosnian women survivors of genocidal rape. She is the author of many articles and books, including FEMINISM UNMODIFIED.

MARTHA R. MAHONEY, professor of law at the University of Miami, teaches and writes in the areas of civil rights, property, and socially responsible law practice.

JERALD N. MARRS, an Armed Forces veteran, is a law student at the University of Colorado.

GEORGE A. MARTINEZ writes in the areas of jurisprudence and legal interpretation and teaches at the Southern Methodist University School of Law.

MARY ANN MAUNEY is Research Director for the Center for Democratic Renewal.

CHERRÍE MORAGA is a feminist and activist, and author of LOVING IN THE WAR YEARS, as well as other novels, poems, and plays.

TONI MORRISON, recipient of the 1993 Nobel Prize for literature, is author of numerous books, including THE BLUEST EYE and BELOVED.

DANIEL PATRICK MOYNIHAN is a United States senator from New York who has influenced national policy in several areas, including poverty, welfare, and race.

JAMES OAKES is the author of SLAVERY AND FREEDOM: AN INTERPRETATION OF THE OLD SOUTH. He teaches in the Department of History, Northwestern University.

TOD OLSON is a writer for *Scholastic Update*.

JUAN F. PEREA is professor of law at the University of Florida and the author of leading law review articles on Latinos and American history. IMMIGRANTS OUT! his anthology documenting the neo-nativist upsurge, was published by New York University Press in 1996.

ADRIAN PIPER, a writer and artist, has exhibited widely in the United States and the United Kingdom.

JOELLE E. POLESKY, a recent graduate of the University of Pennsylvania Law School, is currently clerking for Judge Roderick R. McKelvie, District of Delaware.

DOROTHY E. ROBERTS, professor of law at Rutgers University, is the author of leading articles on race and reproductive rights.

DAVID ROEDIGER is professor of labor history at the University of Minnesota and author of leading books and articles on whiteness and the history of race.

JEFFREY ROSEN is the legal affairs editor for the *New Republic*.

LORETTA J. ROSS writes for the *Progressive* on the American far right.

THOMAS ROSS, professor of law at the University of Pittsburgh, writes and teaches in the areas of civil rights, constitutional law, poverty, and legal rhetoric.

MARGARET M. RUSSELL, professor of law and associate dean at the Santa Clara University School of Law, teaches and writes in the areas of employment discrimination law, civil rights, and constitutional law.

KAREN BRODKIN SACKS is professor of anthropology at the University of California at Los Angeles.

JUDY SCALES-TRENT, professor of law at the State University of New York, Buffalo, teaches and writes in the areas of employment discrimination, law and literature, and women and the law.

PETER M. SHANE is dean and professor of law at the University of Pittsburgh.

SUZANNA SHERRY serves as the Earl R. Larson Professor at the University of Minnesota, where she teaches and writes in the areas of feminist jurisprudence, constitutional law and theory, federal courts, and civil rights.

EARL SHORRIS is a contributing editor of *Harper's* and the author of ten books, including LATINOS: A BIOGRAPHY OF THE PEOPLE.

JEAN STEFANCIC, research associate in law at the University of Colorado, is the author of numerous books and articles on civil rights and critical theory, including NO MERCY: HOW CONSERVATIVE THINK TANKS AND FOUNDATIONS CHANGED AMERICA'S SOCIAL AGENDA (Temple University Press, 1996).

SUNG-HEE SUH, a 1990 graduate of Harvard Law School, was an associate of and assistant to Derrick Bell.

CALVIN TRILLIN, sometime poet, is an essayist for the *Nation* and the *New Yorker*. Among his numerous books on American culture is ENOUGH IS ENOUGH (AND OTHER RULES OF LIFE).

EMILY FIELD VAN TASSEL is professor of law at Widener University School of Law, where she teaches and writes in the areas of American legal history, contracts, gender and the law, and civil rights.

CORNEL WEST is professor of Afro-American studies and philosophy of religion at Harvard University. He is the author of RACE MATTERS, among other books.

STEPHANIE M. WILDMAN, professor of law at the University of San Francisco, is the author of numerous articles and books on feminist theory and white privilege, including PRIVILEGE REVEALED (New York University Press, 1996).

ROGER WILKINS is a columnist, writer, and civil rights leader.

GREGORY H. WILLIAMS is dean of Ohio State University School of Law. He is an expert on police conduct, search and seizure, and criminal law.

CHRISTOPHER WILLS writes on evolution and genetics. His latest book is THE RUNAWAY BRAIN: THE EVOLUTION OF HUMAN UNIQUENESS.

ADRIAN WOOLDRIDGE is a member of the editorial staff of the *Economist*.

LUTHER WRIGHT, JR., is a recent graduate of Vanderbilt Law School.

DANIEL ZALEWSKI is a writer for *Lingua Franca* magazine.

Index

aborigines, Australian, 56

abstraction, black. *See* black abstraction

academics, of working-class background, 381–86, 387–94

Affectionately Yours (film), 268

affirmative action, 10, 24–26, 27–31, 32 n. 8, 185, 395–401, 488–89; for whites, 310–13. *See also* quotas

African Americans. *See* blacks

Africans, perceptions about, 59–64, 146–48, 181–82

Against Exceptionalism (Rick Halpern and Jonathan Morris, eds.), 402

Alchemy of Race and Rights, The (Patricia Williams), 284

Alien and Sedition Acts of 1798, 374

Allen, Theodore, 190, 607

Allport, Gordon, 41

American Indians. *See* Native Americans

Americanization. *See* assimilation

American Protective Association, 351

American race, 143–44, 403

Ammons, Linda L., 276

analogizing, 619–25

Andersen, Margaret, 295

Anglo-Saxonism, 140–44, 287, 324, 350–52, 369, 396, 568–69. *See also* WASP (White Anglo Saxon Protestant)

Ansley, Frances Lee, 214, 327, 592, 646

anthropology, and race, 203–5

anthropometrics, 201

anti-Catholicism, 350–52, 364, 373

anti-Communism, 396

anti-immigrant sentiments. *See* nativism

anti-miscegenation rules, 155–56, 187

anti-Semitism, 351–52, 364, 395–401, 414–17, 538–41, 554, 564. *See also* Jews

apes, 61–62, 149

Appiah, Anthony, 255

Armstrong, James, Jr., 566

Arrogance of Race, The (George Fredrickson), 38–45, 190, 266

Aryan Church of Jesus Christ Christian, 563–64, 574

Aryan Nations, 553–54, 563, 574

Aryan race and Aryans, 53–54, 63, 139–42, 539, 547, 568, 580

Asian Americans: attitudes toward, 174–75; and higher education, 414–17; as immigrants, 395

assimilation, 352, 365, 366, 368–77, 402–5, 410–11

Association of American Law Schools (AALS), 620

Association of White Male Peace Officers, 6

Attaway, William, 354, 355

aversive racism. *See* racism: aversive

Baby M case, 196, 197–98

Bailyn, Bernard, 82

Baldwin, James, 285–86, 356

Barnes, Robin, 561

Barrett, James R., 402

Bartlett, Roscoe G., 99

Barton, Josef, 404

Battle at Elderbush Gulch, The (film), 174

Beckley, Pendleton, 207–8

Behind the Mask of Chivalry (Nancy MacLean), 602–3

Bell, Derrick A., 106, 438–42, 534, 596

Bell Curve, The (Richard Herrnstein and Charles Murray): controversy about, 179–85, 510–11, 515–18, 519–22, 528–29, 530–33, 534–37, 557

Bell Curve Wars, The (Steven Fraser, ed.), 179, 510, 519, 528, 530

Bennett, William, 520

Berea College, 199–200

Berea College v. Kentucky, 199–201, 206

Berger, Vada, 109

Beverly Hills Cop (film), 269

Beyond the Melting Pot (Nathan Glazer and Daniel Patrick Moynihan), 368–77

biological determinism, 151, 179–85, 201

Birth of a Nation, The (film), 172, 267–68

Black, Laurel Johnson, 387

black abstraction, 89–96, 263–65

Black Image in the White Mind, The (George Fredrickson), 190

Black Like Me (John Howard Griffin), 432–37

Black Like Me (film), 271

blackness: attitudes toward, 60–61, 188, 259; images of, 255–56; and inferiority, 286–88; social construction of, 484–92, 654–57. *See also* darkness

blacks: as Anglos, 486–92; attitudes toward, 112–15, 147, 159, 170–73, 355–56, 432–37; and disease, 259, 285; and G.I. bill, 310–13; inferiority of, 146–51, 179–85, 186; and Latino/as, 482–92; perceptions about, 70–71, 72, 73–74, 256, 285 black/white paradigm, 231–37, 482–92

Blassingame, John, 39

Blood on the Forge (William Attaway), 354–56

Blue Chips (film), 284

Blumer, Herbert, 41, 43

bohunk. *See* hunky

boss, 159, 376

Bowen, Revonda, 499–500

Bradley, Justice, 91–92

Breathitt, James, 200–202, 204

Brigham, Carl Campbell, 511

Broken Arrow (film), 174

Brookhiser, Richard, 16, 360

Brookshire, Stanford, 118, 120–21

Brown, Eleanor Marie, 112, 644

Brown, Justice, 92–94

Brown, Sterling, 30–31

Brown, William Wells, 171

brown hordes, 556

Brown v. Board of Education, 94–96, 101, 117–23, 239, 240, 241, 243, 328

Bruderschweigen Strike Force, 562

Bryce, James, 207

Buchanan, Pat, 557

Buchanan, Robert, 206–8

Buckingham, James S., 42

Burt, Cyril, 516

Butler, Richard, 553, 563–64, 574

Calhoun, John C., 260

Calmore, John, 593

Campanis, Al, 536

Campbell, James, 145

capitalism, 348–52, 608–9

Cappello, Mary, 381

Captivity and Restoration (Mary Rowlandson), 173

Carto, Willis, 554, 575

Cash, W. J., 339

Cassagne, Verna, 467–69

Castanon, Lisa, 108

Cattell, Raymond, 517

Cedartown (Georgia), terrorism in, 563

center, 621–22

Center for Democratic Renewal, 552, 558, 574

Chamallas, Martha, 493

Charlotte (North Carolina), and desegregation, 117–23

Charlotte-Mecklenburg School Board, 121–23

Chavez, Linda, 98

Chesnutt, Charles, 172

Chester, Mitchell, 109

Chevalier, Stuart, 207–8

Chicanas, 471–74. *See also* Latino/as

Children's Defense Fund, 129

children's stories, and race consciousness, 287–88

Childress, Alice, 307

Chin, HockSeng (Sam), 584

Chinese, rights of, 235–37

chosen people, 140, 141

Christian Identity, 553, 574, 575, 587

Christianity, 144, 146, 153, 155; and innocence, 27, 255–56

Christian Patriot Freedom Festival, 564

Christian Patriots, 554, 573

Church of the Creator, 554

City of Richmond v. J.A. Croson Co., 66, 441

Civil Rights Cases, 91–92

Claiborne, William, 261

Clansman, The (Thomas Dixon), 171–72

class, and race, 161, 327–28, 339–47, 355–56, 395–401, 402–5, 407–11, 473–74, 482–92, 655–57

Cleaver, Kathleen Neal, 157

cognitive dissonance, 536

college education, value of, 311, 378–80

colorblind remedies, failure of, 85–87. *See also* race-neutral decisionmaking

color imagery, 286–88. *See also* blackness; darkness; whiteness

color line, 243–46, 357–59, 458–66, 493–98

Color Line, The (William Benjamin Smith), 207

Combahee River Collective, 298

comparisons, danger of making. *See* analogizing

conservative movement, and eugenics theory, 519–22

Constitution, slavery compromises in, 214–17, 596–98

Cook, Philip J., 378

Cose, Ellis, 535

courts: and blacks, 227–30, 231–37, 320–22, 467–69, 599–600; and Chinese, 235–37; and Mexicans, 210–12

Crenshaw, Geneva, 438–43, 596–98

Crenshaw, Kimberlè, 277, 286, 317

Crenshaw, Rodrigo, 614–18

crime, 66–75

critical race theory, 644–45

Croker, Richard, 373, 375–76

Culp, Jerome McCristal, Jr., 227, 438

cultural identity, 407–11, 485–92

cultural minorities. *See* ethnic groups

cultural pluralism, 368–72

Curtin, Philip, 39–40, 57, 58–59

dago, 405

Daniels, Doug, 51

darkness: and American literature, 79–84; as a metaphor, 60–61, 66–75, 80–84, 255–56, 263–64, 286–88. *See also* blackness

Darwin, Charles, 201, 204. *See also* evolution

Davenport, Charles Benedict, 13, 397

Davis, Adrienne D., 231, 314, 317, 323

Davis, David Brion, 39, 60

Davis, John W., 95

Decline of Intelligence in America, The (Seymour Itzkoff), 542

Decline of the West, The (Oswald Spengler), 538–39

Dees, Morris, 562–63, 583

Degler, Carl, 40, 145

Delgado, Richard, 98, 170, 614; and cognitive dissonance, 536

desegregation law, 117–23, 239–43

Disfranchisement Proposals and the Ku Klux Klan (John David Smith, ed.), 566

Dixon, Thomas, 171

Dr. Doolittle, 287

dominant gaze, and race, 267–72

Do the Right Thing (film), 271–72

Douglas, Davison M., 117

Douglass, Frederick, 171; and Irish music, 355

Dovidio, John, 113

Dred Scott v. Sandford, 89–91, 214, 264

Driving Miss Daisy (film), 269

D'Souza, Dinesh, 55, 100

Du Bois, W. E. B., 157

Duke, David, 541, 553, 575, 578, 581–83

Dunbar, William, 82–84

Dyer, Richard, 287

dysconscious racism, 128–32, 640–41

Eagle Hotline, 560

eastern Europeans. *See* southern and eastern Europeans

Eco, Umberto, 601

Edelman, Marian Wright, 129

Edgerton, Robert, 56

Elkins, Stanley, 38

Elliott, E. N., 154

empathy, 265; and James Baldwin, 356; and false empathy, 614–18, 619–25; and Justice John Marshall Harlan, 444–56; as a solution to racial problems, 614–15

employment discrimination. *See* Title VII

Employment Division v. Smith, 101

End of Racism, The (Dinesh D'Souza), 55–65

England: class structure of, 147–48; and values of colonialism, 349–50. *See also* Anglo-Saxonism

English language, 261; and immigrants, 352, 381, 385–86, 398; and working-class people, 388–89, 391–94

English Protestants, and immigration, 348–49

environmentalism, 57–59, 60, 62, 63, 146, 149, 150, 186, 202

epistemological barriers to cross-racial empathy, 198. *See also* white males: epistemological perspective

equality, forms of, 202–3

essentialism, 622–23, 650

"Eternal Fascism" (Umberto Eco), 601

ethnic groups, 368–72, 407–11; identity of white, declining, 7–8, 610; and whiteness, 52

eugenics, 397; and race, 519–22, 530–33, 539. *See also* pseudoscientific theories of race

European attitudes toward nonwhite cultures, 55–64

European civilization, development of, 55, 58–59

European racism, 62–64

Evans, Marnie, 297

Everett, Anna, 280

evolution, and intelligence, 202, 204

exclusion, 632–34, 635–39; of Asians, 174, 396; of Jews, 395–401; of Mexican Americans, 210–12; of non-WASPs, 365–66

Explorer Scouts, 562

Ezekiel, Raphael S., 133, 586

false empathy. *See* empathy

Fanon, Frantz, 255

Farber, Daniel A., 414

Farrands, James, 574

fascism, 601

Fatal Shore, The (Richard Hughes), 56

Feagin, Joe R., 278, 348

Federal Housing Authority (FHA), 273–74, 312

Federal Slum Clearance and Urban Renewal Program, 321

Fehrenbacher, Don, 216

Fields, Barbara J., 146

Fields, Karen, 295

Fields, Mamie, 295

film, and race, 267–72, 280–84

Fish, Stanley, 601

Fitzhugh, George, 153–54

Flagg, Barbara J., 85, 220, 589, 629

flea markets, 387–88, 394

Foner, Eric, 24

Ford, Henry, and Anglocentric values, 352

Founding Fathers, racial views of, 134, 183, 258–59, 596–98

Framers. *See* Founding Fathers

Francis, Samuel, 6

Frank, Robert H., 378

Franke, Katherine M., 467

Frankenberg, Ruth, 330–31, 632

Franklin, Benjamin, 16, 20, 258–59

Franklin, Joseph Paul, 563

Fredrickson, George, 38, 190, 266

free white labor. *See* working-class whites

Frye, Marilyn, 314, 643

Gaertner, Samuel, 113

Gallagher, Charles A., 6

Galton, William, 529

Galton Society, 397

Garrison, William J., 182

Garvey, John, 615

Gayre, Robert, 528

genetic tie, 186–88, 523–27

Genovese, Eugene, 39

German immigrants, 361, 369–70

G.I. bill, 310–13

Glasgow, Yvette, 107

Glazer, Nathan, 368

Gobineau, Joseph Arthur de, 62–64, 140, 256

Goddard, Henry, 511

Goetz, Bernhard, 71–73

Goldberg, David Theo, 635

Gordon, James W., 444

Gotanda, Neil, 321–22

Gould, Benjamin A., 207

Gould, Stephen Jay, 534

Graham, John R., 3

Grant, Madison, 365, 396

Great Chain of Being, 148

Greek immigrants, 403–5

Green v. County School Board, 240–41

Greensboro (North Carolina), and desegregation, 117–18, 120

Gregory v. Baugh, 165–66

Griffin, John Howard, 271, 432

Griffith, D. W., 267

Grillo, Trina, 323, 619

Grover, Bonnie Kae, 34

growing up white, reflections on, 34–35, 36–37

güera, 471–74

guinea, 403, 404

Hacker, Andrew, 510, 661

Hakluyt, Richard, journeys of, 55

Haldane, J. B. S., 517

Halewood, Peter, 195, 512, 627

Ham, curse of, 255–56

Hammond, James Henry, 154–55, 182

Handlin, Mary, 145

Handlin, Oscar, 145

Haney López, Ian F., 248, 321, 420

Harlan, James, 444–56

Harlan, Justice John Marshall, 92, 444–56

Harlan, Robert, 444–56

Harlem Renaissance, 172

Harris, Angela, 622–23

Harris, Cheryl, 46

hate groups, 552–57, 573–85; computer bulletin boards of, 558–60, 603. *See also* Aryan Nations; Ku Klux Klan; neo-Nazis; skinheads

Hawkins, Reginald, 122–23

Hayman, Robert L., Jr., 239

Head of Christ (painting), 253

Hearst, William Randolph, 175

Helms, Janet, 629

helping behavior, studies of, 113–14

Hernández, Berta, 324

Hernandez v. State, 211

herrenvolk republicanism, 160

Herrnstein, Richard. See *Bell Curve, The*

Higginbotham, A. Leon, Jr., 190

Higgins, Tracy, 106, 107

higher education, 378–80; and working-class students, 381–86, 387–94

Hill, Anita, 4

Hill, Pamela, 276, 278

Himes, Chester, 354

Hitler, Adolf, 538–39

Hoffman, Frederick L., 204–5

Hollywood Shuffle (film), 268

Holmes, Oliver Wendell, Jr., 538

Holocaust-denial movement, 554

Home Owners Loan Corporation (HOLC), 273–74

hooks, bell, 318, 589, 620, 624

Horsman, Reginald, 139

House Made of Dawn (N. Scott Momaday), 174

Hovenkamp, Herbert, 199

Hudgins v. Wrights, 165, 232–37

Hughes, Robert, 56

human geography. *See* environmentalism

Hume, David, 62, 256

hunky, 354, 355, 402, 403–4

Hunt, Sanford B., 201, 203–4

Hunter, The (William Pierce), 563

hydra, 317

hypodescent. *See* miscegenation

Icons of American Protestantism (David Morgan), 253

identity politics, 648–52; of whites, increasing, 9–10

identity religion. *See* Aryan Church of Jesus Christ Christian; Christian Identity

Ignatiev, Noel, 420, 607, 613, 615

Illiberal Education (Dinesh D'Souza), 100

images: of Asian Americans, 174–75; of blackness, 81, 255–56, 263, 286, 287; of blacks, 38–44, 171–73; of Jesus, 253–54; of Mexican Americans, 175–76; of Native Americans, 173–74; of nonwhites, 55–64; of white heroes, 191; of whiteness, 79–80, 263, 287–88, 625. *See also* dominant gaze, and race; stereotypes

immigrants: attitudes toward, 348–52, 360–66, 395–401, 402–5, 407–10, 414–17; inbetween identity of, 403–5

Immigrants Out! (Juan Perea, ed.), 348, 538

immigration policy of United States, and Adolf Hitler, 539

Immigration Restriction League, 351

immigration to the United States, 348–52, 360–66, 395–401

imposition, 98–105

inbetween identity, 403–5

Independent School District v. Salvatierra, 211

Indians. *See* Native Americans

Inequality of Human Races, The (Joseph Arthur De Gobineau), 62–63

Inland Steel Co. v. Barcelona, 210

innocence, white. *See* white innocence

In re Camille, 210

In re Rodriguez, 210

In re Young, 210

Institute for Historical Review, 554, 575

intelligence and IQ, 507–9, 510–11, 519–22, 528–29, 530–33, 542. *See also* pseudoscientific theories of race

intelligence testing, 179–85, 397, 507–9; in England, 515–18; and the oppression factor, 534–37

intent requirement in civil rights law, 223–24, 600, 630

interest groups, 370–72

interracial marriage, 499–500. *See also* miscegenation

intersectionality, 195, 198, 318, 649

In the Matter of Color (A. Leon Higginbotham, Jr.), 190

Invention of the White Race, The (Theodore Allen), 190, 607

in vitro fertilization, 523

IQ. *See* intelligence testing

Irish Catholics, and nativism, 350, 521

Irish immigrants, 362–64; in New York City, 372–77; perceptions about, 160–61, 190, 191

Iron Cages (Ronald Takaki), 285

Isaacs, Harold R., 287

Italian Catholics, and nativism, 351

Italian immigrants, 361–62, 381–86, 402–5

Itzkoff, Seymour W., 542

Ivy League, 378–80, 382

Jackson, Andrew, 259

Jay, John, 258, 373

Jefferson, Thomas, 150, 183–84, 214, 259, 261

Jeffries, Leonard, 12

Jensen, Arthur J., 519, 529

Jesus, image of, 253–54

Jews: and higher education, 311–12, 397–401, 414–17; as illegal aliens in Europe, 538–41; and nativism, 351–52, 396–401; and whiteness, 395–401

Jim Crow, 171, 180–81

Jones, Charles, 120

Jones, D. Marvin, 66, 255

Jones, Jacqueline, 179

Jordan, Winthrop, 40, 60, 145, 187, 277

Judis, John B., 530

Kagan, Jerome, 507

Kanstroom, Daniel, 538

Kant, Immanuel, 62

Karabel, Jerome, 398

Karst, Kenneth L., 407

Keller, John, 311

Kemp, Jack, 520–21

Kerner Commission on Civil Disorders, 274

Keyes v. School District No. 1, 241–42

Killers of the Dream (Lillian Smith), 295

King, Joyce E., 128, 640

King, Martin Luther, Jr., 24, 134

King, Richard, 14

King, Rodney, 68–71

Klanwatch, 574. *See also* Southern Poverty Law Center

Kleugel, James, 114

Klor de Alva, Jorge, 482

Knobel, Dale T., 521

Kovel, Joel, 349

Ku Klux Klan, 133, 164, 171, 351, 553–54, 558, 561–64, 573, 581–83, 586–88, 602–3

Lamarck, Jean-Baptiste, 205

Lane, Charles, 528

Langer, Elinor, 573

language: and code words, 601; and oppression, 314–18

Latino/as, 323–26; and blacks, 482–92; social construction of, 487–92. *See also* Mexican Americans

Law and Society annual meeting, 621–22

law, role of in construction of race and racial categories, 195, 198, 199–201, 206–8, 210–12, 214–16, 223–24, 227–30, 232–37, 239–43, 320–22, 475–81

Lawrence, Charles, 28–29, 30

Lear, Norman, 562

Lee, Spike, 271

legal scholarship, and race, 227–30

Lemon Swamp (Karen and Mamie Fields), 295

lesbianism, 381, 472–74

Levit, Nancy, 239

Lhermitte, Leon, 253

Liberty Lobby, 554, 575

Life on the Color Line (Gregory Williams), 357–59, 458–66; review of, 493–98

Like One of the Family (Alice Childress), 307

Lincoln, Abraham, and race, 66

Lind, Michael, 519

Linfield, Michael, 110

Ling Sing, 235

Lipset, Seymour Martin, 41

Lochner v. New York, 599

Lodge, Henry Cabot, 396

Loguidice, Joseph, 402

Lorde, Audre, 277

Los Angeles Police Department, 68–71

Loving v. Virginia, 186, 264

Lowell, A. Lawrence, 397
Lynn, Richard, 528–29

MacKinnon, Catharine A., 300
MacLean, Nancy, 602
Mahoney, Martha R., 273, 305, 330, 642, 654
Malcolm X, and the word "nigger," 354
Malone, Paul, 125–26
Malone, Philip, 125–26
Manichean allegory, 72
manifest destiny, and race, 139–44, 171
Mankind Quarterly, 528
Marrs, Jerald N., 36
Marshall, Justice Thurgood, 95–96, 214, 227–29, 265
Martineau, Harriet, 154
Martinez, George A., 210
master-slave relationship, 152–56
Mauney, Mary Ann, 552
McCabe v. Arave, 564
McCleskey v. Kemp, 229–30
McConahay, John, 113
McDougall, William, 517
McIntosh, Peggy, 291, 306, 316–17, 325, 331
McPherson, Ardith, 227–29
McQueen, Butterfly, 268
Mecklenburg Organization on Political Affairs, 122
Mein Kampf (Adolf Hitler), 539
melanin, and racial superiority, 12–15
melting pot, 352, 368–77. See also assimilation
merit: cognitive dissonance about, 536; critique of, 414–17
meritocracy, 515–18
mestizaje, 259
Metzger, Tom, 559, 575–81, 583–85
Mexican Americans: as aliens, 260; attitudes toward, 175–76; and census categories, 211; perceptions about, 212, 259–61; race of, 210–12. See also Latino/a(s)
Mezzrow, Mezz, 355
Michael Jackson pill, 438–43
militia, 547–50
Milliken v. Bradley, 107, 242, 243
Million Man March, 467, 469
Milner, David, 287
Mind of the South, The (W. J. Cash), 339–47
Minnich, Elizabeth, 292–93
minstrel shows, 159–60
miscegenation, 155–56, 160, 264, 425–31, 444–56, 476–78. See also interracial marriage; mixed race people; racial classification
mixed race people, 357–59, 425–31, 444–56, 458–66, 467–69, 471–74, 475–81, 493–98, 499–500
model minorities, 414–17
mongrelization, 395
Montoya, Margaret, 326

Moraga, Cherríe, 471
Morgan, David, 253, 254
Morgan, Lewis Henry, 204
Morrison, Toni, 79, 231; and the word "nigger," 354, 355
Morton, Samuel George, 201, 203
Moynihan, Daniel Patrick, 368, 520
mulattoes, 166–67, 188, 201, 204–5, 207–8, 358, 444, 451
Muller v. Oregon, 199, 200, 207
Mulvey, Laura, 268
Muncie (Indiana), black life in, 458–66
Murray, Charles. See Bell Curve, The

NAACP, 119, 121, 172, 206, 328
Narrative of Arthur Gordon Pym, The (Edgar Allan Poe), 79–80
National Association for the Advancement of Colored People (NAACP). See NAACP
National Association for the Advancement of White People (NAAWP), 581
Nationalist Free Tip Hotline, 560
National Research Council, 112
National States' Rights Party, 556
National Vanguard, 575
Native Americans: attitudes toward, 173–74; perceptions about, 190, 259
nativism, 395–401, 557; and Nazi doctrine, 538–41; origins of, 348–52
Nazis and Nazism, 538–41, 588
neo-Nazis, 133, 573–85, 586–88. See also skinheads
nigger(s), 354–56, 458–66, 487–88, 567
Nightmare before Christmas, The (film), 281–82
nonwhite cultures, European attitudes toward, 55–64
Notes of a White Black Woman (Judy Scales-Trent), 475–81
Notes on the State of Virginia (Thomas Jefferson), 150, 183–84, 660
Nott, Josiah, 183
Nunez, Rene, 324

Oakes, James, 145
O'Connor, Justice Sandra, 66
Oklahoma City bombing, 556
Olson, Tod, 499
Omi, Michael, 501
"On Being 'White' and Other Lies" (James Baldwin), 285–86, 356
one-drop rule. See miscegenation
On the Origin of Species (Charles Darwin), 201
Order, The, 563, 574
Out of This Furnace (Josef Barton), 404

Paddy and the Republic (Dale T. Knobel), 521
pain, appropriation of, 623–24

partus sequitar ventrem, 187
Pasadena City Board of Education v. Spangler, 242–43
passing for black, 432–37
passing for white, 166–67, 320, 425–31, 438–43, 467–69, 497–98
Passing of the Great Race, The (Madison Grant), 365, 396
Patria (film), 175
People v. Hall, 235–37
Perea, Juan F., 258
Perfect Woman, The (film), 281–82
Petracca, John, 381, 385–86
Pettigrew, Thomas, 277
philology, nineteenth-century, 141
Phipps, Susie Guillory, 320, 427, 501
Pierce, William, 563, 575, 602
Pioneer Fund, 519
Piper, Adrian, 425, 502
Player, The (film), 282–83
Playing in the Dark (Toni Morrison), 79–84
Plessy v. Ferguson, 92–94, 101, 106, 110, 166, 172, 239–40, 264, 445, 599–600
Plunkitt, George Washington, 377
Podair, Simon, 286
Poe, Edgar Allen, 79
Polesky, Joelle E., 547
poor whites, in southern United States, 339–47, 598
pornography, and women's oppression, 302
Posse Comitatus, 554, 573
Powell, Cathy, 307
Powell, Justice Lewis, 229
privilege: and language, 314–18; of white women, 300–303, 306–7. *See also* white privilege; white males, privilege of
Privilege Revealed (Stephanie M. Wildman et al.), 314, 619
property interest in whiteness, 46, 106–11, 188, 599–60, 655–57
Proposition 187 (California), 556
Protocols of the Elders of Zion, The, 415
pseudoscientific theories of race, 143, 171, 183, 186–87, 396, 507–9, 510–11, 517, 519–22, 528–29, 530–33, 534–37, 538–41

Quillin, Frank U., 208
quotas, hiring, for whites, 24–26

Raab, Earl, 41
race, 438–43, 475–76; and class, 161, 327–28, 339–47, 355–56, 395–401, 402–5, 407–11, 473–74, 482–92, 655–57; and the Constitution, 214–18; and geography, 478–81; and legal education, 214–18; and legal scholarship, 227–30; as a mask, 67–68; social construction of, 67, 187, 210–12, 243–44, 273–75, 305–9, 607–8; and surrogacy, 524

Race and Manifest Destiny (Reginald Horsman), 139–44
Race and Reason (Carleton Putnam), 575–81
race consciousness of whites. *See* transparency phenomenon
racelessness, possibility of, 644–45
race mixing, 199–208. *See also* miscegenation
race-neutral decisionmaking, 221–24, 227–30, 589–90, 629–30, 644–45. *See also* colorblind remedies, failure of
race traitor, 607–12, 613, 615
Race Traitor magazine, 607–12, 613, 653
race war, 602
racial attitudes: in early U.S., 158; in nineteenth-century U.S., 171
racial classification, 148–49, 164–67, 187–88, 320–22, 476–78, 493–98, 500, 501–2, 610. *See also* miscegenation
racial covenants, 273–75
racial formation, 349–50, 404, 467–69, 501–2, 644–45; of blacks, 232–35; of Chinese, 235–37; of Mexican Americans, 210–12; of Native Americans, 232–35; of whites, 6–10, 231–37, 258–59, 330–32
Racial Formation in the United States (Michael Omi and Howard Winant), 501
racial fraud, 125–27
racial hoax, 73–74
racial imagery. *See* stereotypes
racialism, nineteenth-century, 142–43
racialization. *See* racial formation
racism, 115, 145–51, 176–77, 306–9, 438–43, 635–39; aversive, 113–14; combating, 646–52, 658–63; dysconscious, 128–32, 640–41; and Gobineau, 62–64; persistence of, 245–46; and *Plessy*, 93–94; and privilege, 291–99; in South Africa, 635–39; unconscious, 29–31
Racist Mind, The (Raphael S. Ezekiel), 133–34
Radin, Margaret, 195
Rage of a Privileged Class, The (Ellis Cose), 535
Rankin v. McPherson, 227–79
Really the Blues (Mezz Mezzrow), 355
Reconstruction, 91–92
redlining, 273–75
Red scare, 396
Reed, Adolph, 328
Regents of the University of California v. Bakke, 107, 109
religious right, 557
residential segregation, 654–57; in Louisville (Kentucky), 206–8, in suburbia, 273–75
resistance, as antiracist strategy, 607–12, 613, 614–18, 635–39, 642–43, 653
reverse discrimination. *See* affirmative action; quotas, hiring, for whites; victimization of whites
Reynolds, William Bradford, 214–15

rhetoric: expansionist, 139–44; of freedom, 143; of
    imposition, 98–105; of Supreme Court opinions,
    89–96; of white innocence, 264
Rice, Thomas D., 171
Rich, Adrienne, 295
Richards, Eric, 110
Ricoeur, Paul, 27
rights of dependency, 152–56
Rise and Fall of the White Republic, The (Alexander
    Saxton), 191
Rise of the Meritocracy, The (Michael Young), 517
Roane, Judge, 232–34
Robb, Thom, 553
Roberts, Dorothy E., 186, 523
Robertson, Pat, 557
Roediger, David R., 191, 334, 354, 402; and *The
    Wages of Whiteness*, 157–61
Rolling Stones, 277
Roosevelt, Theodore, 366, 396
Rosaldo, Renato, 331
Rosen, Jeffrey, 528
Rosewood (Florida), 535, 561
Ross, Loretta J., 552
Ross, Thomas, 27, 89, 263
Rowlandson, Mary, 173
Rush, Benjamin, 150, 259, 285
Rushton, J. Phillipe, 519, 529
Russell, Margaret M., 267
Russell, William Howard, 42

Sacks, Karen Brodkin, 310, 395
Sage, Rufus B., 260
St. Mary's Honor Ctr. v. Hicks, 441
Sallman, Warner, 253–54
Sambo (stereotype), 38–44
Sanchez, Jose Maria, 260
Sanger, Margaret, 364
S.A.T., 378–79
Saxton, Alexander, 191
Scales-Trent, Judy, 475, 623
Scalia, Justice Antonin, 227–29
Scenes from the Class Struggle in Beverly Hills
    (film), 283–84
Scholastic Aptitude Test, 378–79
Schultz, Marge, 314
Scotch Irish immigrants, 361
Second Amendment (right to bear arms), 547–50
segregation, 94–96, 150, 180; in Kentucky, 199–201,
    206–8
Seguin, Juan, 261
separate but equal doctrine, 166
Seraw, Mulgeta, 583–85
Serbo-Croatian immigrants, 405
Shades of Pale (David Roediger), 354–56
Shakespearean images of nonwhites, 28, 60, 173, 263

Shaler, Nathaniel Southgate, 205
Shane, Peter M., 493
Shannon, Alexander Harvey, 207–8
Shaw v. Reno, 441
Sherry, Suzanna, 414
Shockley, William, 519
Shorris, Earl, 482
Simpson, Nicole Brown, 276
skin color, 146–47, 150; and language, 286–88; and
    melanin, 12–15
skinheads, 554–55, 573, 583–85, 603
skinwalkers, 478–81
slavery, 215–16, 446–47; benefits of, 181–83; in
    colonial U.S., 190–91; compromises in the
    Constitution, 596–98; justifications for, 38–44,
    59–64, 344–47; maintaining, 148–49; and
    miscegenation, 477–78; of Native Americans,
    232–35; origins of, 147–48; and racial classification,
    187; and rights, 152–56
slaves, white images of, 38–44, 82, 152–56, 158,
    164–66, 171, 182–83
Slavic. *See* southern and eastern Europeans
Smith, Al, 363, 372
"Sleepy-Time Stories," 287
Smith, Eliot, 114
Smith, Lillian, 295
social construction of race. *See* race: social
    construction of; racial formation
social construction of whiteness. *See* whiteness: social
    construction of; racial formation: of whites
social science data about race, 199–208
Soul Man (film), 269–72
South, mind of the, 339–47, 566–72
South Africa, racism in,104, 635–39
southern and eastern Europeans, and nativism,
    351–52, 354–56, 360, 395, 403
Southern Poverty Law Center, 583. *See also*
    Klanwatch
Spengler, Oswald, 538–39
Spotlight, The, 554, 575
Stanhope, Samuel, 150
Star-Spangled Banner, The, 158
State v. Treadway, 166
Statue of Liberty, 365
Steele, Shelby, 100
Stefancic, Jean, 98, 170
stereotypes, 170–77; of Asian Americans, 174–75; of
    blacks, 30–31, 38–44, 170–73, 276–78; in film,
    267–72; of Mexican Americans, 175–76; of Native
    Americans, 173–74
Stills, Peter, 603
Stoner, J. B., 556
Storey, Moorfield, 206–7
Stowe, Harriet Beecher, 171
Stuart, Carol, 73–74

Stuart, Charles, 73–74
students: attitudes of, about race, 7–10, 51–54, 106–11, 128–32, 216–18, 231, 640–41
suburbia, housing for whites in, 273–75
Suh, Sung-Hee, 106
Sunseri, Cyril, 467–69
Sunseri v. Cassagne, 467–69
Supreme Court. *See* courts
surrogate motherhood, 195–98, 523–27
Swann v. Charlotte-Mecklenburg Board of Education, 241, 243
Sword, the Covenant and the Arm of the Lord, The, 564
Symbolism of Evil, The (Paul Ricoeur), 27

Takaki, Ronald, 285
taking back the center, 621–22
Tammany Hall, 372–77
Tanaka Memorial, 415
Taney, Chief Justice, 89–91
Tawney, R. H., 516–17
There's No Such Thing as Free Speech, and It's a Good Thing, Too (Stanley Fish), 601
Thind, Bhaget Singh, 397
This Bridge Called My Back (Cherríe Moraga and Gloria Anzaldua, eds.), 471
This Fine Place So Far from Home (C. L. Barney Dews and Carolyn Leste Law), 381–86, 387–94
Thomas, Clarence, 4, 467, 469
Thomas, Kendall, 644
Thompson, E. P., 42–43
Tillich, Paul, 254
Title VII, and racial discrimination, 85–87, 590
Tocqueville, Alexis de, 57–58
Tourgee, Albion, 172
Towards the Abolition of Whiteness (David Roediger), 191
Townsend, Robert, 268
transparency phenomenon, 85–87, 220–24, 589–90, 629–30
transracial adoptions, 526–27
Trevelyan, Charles, 515
Trevor, John B., 360
Trillin, Calvin, 33
Tucker, Judge, 232–34
Turner Diaries, The (William Pierce), 563, 602
Tweed, William March, 372
Two Nations (Andrew Hacker), 661
Types of Mankind (Josiah Nott), 183
Tyson, Edward, 61

Uncle Tom, 171
unconscious racism. *See* racism: unconscious
United Way, 3
University of Regina (Canada), 51

upward mobility, 354–56, 360–66, 368–77, 378–80, 381–86, 387–94, 395–401, 402–5, 407–11, 414–17, 515–18
U.S. Census Bureau, 211
U.S. Office of Management and Budget (OMB), and race of Mexicans, 211

Van Tassel, Emily Field, 152
veterans' benefits. *See* G.I. bill
victimization of whites, 9–10, 28–31, 72
Voyagers to the West (Bernard Bailyn), 82–84

Wages of Whiteness, The (David Roediger), 157–61, 334
Walker, James J., 372
Walker, Mary, 320
Wallace, Mike, 602
Warley, William, 206–8
Washington v. Davis, 107, 223
Washington Legal Foundation, 214
WASP (White Anglo Saxon Protestant), 16–23, 360–66, 369. *See also* Anglo-Saxonism
Watermelon Man (film), 271
Waters, Maxine, 99
Watkins and Wife v. Carlton, 525
Way of the WASP, The (Richard Brookhiser), 16–23, 360–66
Webb, Beatrice, 515
Webb, Sidney, 515
Webb, Walter Prescott, 212, 260
Weber, David, 212, 259, 260
Wells, H. G., 515–16
West, Cornel, 115, 482
Where Do We Go From Here? (Martin Luther King, Jr.), 24, 134
White Aryan Resistance, 559, 579–81
White by Law (Ian F. Haney López), 278
White Citizens' Council, 562
white ethnics, 7–8, 191. *See also names of various ethnic groups*
Whitehead, Mary Beth, 196–98
white innocence, 27–31, 72, 73–74, 89–96, 255–56, 263–64
white males, 609; demise of, 3–5, 6; epistemological perspective, 196–97, 512–13, 627–28; privilege of, 291–92, 297, 300–303, 310–13
white man's burden, 171
"White Man's Guilt" (James Baldwin), 356
whiteness, 34–35, 36–37, 248, 625, 629–34; and American literature, 79–84; and European immigrants, 348–52, 354–56; and Greeks, 404; and the Irish, 420, 608; and Italians, 402–5; and Jews, 395–401; legal construction of, 467–69; and Mexican Americans, 210–12; as property, 46, 106–11; social construction of, 157–61, 212,

285–86, 305–9, 330–32, 350, 354–56, 400–401, 402–5, 420, 654–57; in suburbia, 273–75; and superiority, 287; transparency of, 85–87, 220–24, 589–90, 629–30, 644–45

White Over Black (Winthrop Jordan), review of, 145–51

white privilege, 210, 273–75, 291–99, 306–9, 315–18, 323–26, 331–32, 611, 619–25, 654–57. *See also* white males: privilege of; white women, and privilege

white race, 653; perceptions about, 51–54, 160, 220–24, 260–61, 286

White Racism (Barry Schwartz and Robert Disch, eds.), 286

white supremacy, 561–64, 619–25, 629–30; class model analysis of, 327–28; cost of, 596–600; nineteenth-century, 157–61; race model analysis of, 592–94; twentieth-century, 350–52, 552–57, 558–60, 561–64, 566–72, 573–85, 586–88. *See also* European racism

white women, and privilege, 300–303, 305–9, 632–34, 642–43

whites: attitudes toward blacks, 112–15, 658–63; genetic distinctions among, 510–11; racial purity of, 165, 167, 186–88, 205, 425–31, 476–78, 525; rationale for slavery, 149; self-interest of, 117–23

Whites' Beliefs about Blacks' Opportunity (James Kleugel and Eliot Smith), 114

Wildman, Stephanie M., 314, 323, 619
Wilkins, Roger, 658
Willhelm, Sidney, 328
Williams, Gregory Howard, 357, 458, 493–98
Williams, Patricia, 284
Wills, Christopher, 12
Wilson, James Q., 408
Winant, Howard, 501
Winner-Take-All Society, The (Philip J. Cook and Robert H. Frank), 379
Wise Use movement, 556
Wolfing, Monique, 576–77
women, status of, 300–303
women of color, 301–3, 642–43
Wooldridge, Adrian, 515
working-class whites, 157–61, 191, 381–86, 387–94, 402–5, 598, 617–18
Wright, Luther, Jr., 125, 164, 320
Wright, Wilhelmina, 106
Wright v. Council of Emporia, 241
Wygant v. Jackson Board of Education, 107

Yerkes, Robert, 397
Yom Kippur, 625
Young, Michael, 517

Zalewski, Daniel, 253
Zionist Occupation Government, 564